*For Larry, Liz and David and their children
that they may appreciate the richness of their Louisiana heritage*

ABOUT THE EDITOR

Vaughan Burdin Baker is Professor of History and Humanities and Head of the Department of History and Geography at the University of Louisiana at Lafayette. She earned the Ph.D. in Modern European History from the University of Southwestern Louisiana in 1975 and pursued post-doctoral studies at St. David's College of the University of Wales. She directed the Women in Louisiana Division of the Center for Louisiana Studies from 1977 to 1983 and served as Director of the University of Louisiana at Lafayette's Interdisciplinary Humanities Program from 1985 to 1991. Her books include *Louisiana Gothic: Recollections of the 1930s,* with Glenn R. Conrad and *Louisiana Tapestry: Ethnicity in St. Landry Parish*, with Jean T. Kreamer. Her articles on Louisiana's social and cultural heritage have appeared in *Louisiana History* and *Louisiana Cultural Vistas.* Baker was awarded the L. Kemper Williams Prize for the Best Manuscript in Louisiana History in 1989. She served as President of the Louisiana Historical Association in 2000.

ACKNOWLEDGEMENTS

Glenn Conrad awakened me long ago to the rich potential of Louisiana history and invited me into this project; my first debt is therefore to him. Glenn's peerless knowledge of the literature on Louisiana subjects and his generous sharing of it helped me immeasurably to navigate what at times seemed to be a very wide ocean. My association with him and with Carl Brasseaux in the Center for Louisiana Studies has been a defining experience in my academic life for over two decades. Their guidance to sources, examination of ideas in both formal and informal arenas and willingness to consult shaped both my appreciation and my understanding of the many dimensions of Louisiana's cultural and social heritage. I greatly appreciated Regina LaBiche's always cheerful and gracious assistance in preparing manuscript materials and I owe warm thanks particularly to Nathaniel Weston for his efficiency in finding and copying possible selections and his enthusiasm in suggesting appropriate alternatives. As friends and colleagues, each of them enhanced the multi-faceted satisfactions of working on this volume. Most importantly, I can only acknowledge most profoundly my husband, Amos Simpson, for his unfailing support in this and in all of my scholarly endeavors. Any deficiencies in the final product, of course, are fully my own responsibility.

The Louisiana Purchase Bicentennial Series in Louisiana History

Glenn R. Conrad, General Editor

VOLUME I
THE FRENCH EXPERIENCE IN LOUISIANA

VOLUME II
THE SPANISH PRESENCE IN LOUISIANA, 1763 - 1803

VOLUME III
THE LOUISIANA PURCHASE
AND ITS AFTERMATH, 1800 - 1830

VOLUME IX
LOUISIANA SINCE THE LONGS
1960 TO CENTURY'S END

VOLUME X
A REFUGE FOR ALL AGES:
IMMIGRATION IN LOUISIANA HISTORY

VOLUME XI
THE AFRICAN AMERICAN EXPERIENCE IN LOUISIANA
PART A: FROM AFRICA TO THE CIVIL WAR

VOLUME XIII
AN UNCOMMON EXPERIENCE:
LAW AND JUDICIAL INSTITUTIONS
IN LOUISIANA, 1803 - 2003

VOLUME XV
VISIONS AND REVISIONS
PERSPECTIVES ON
LOUISIANA SOCIETY AND CULTURE

VOLUME XVI
AGRICULTURE AND
ECONOMIC DEVELOPMENT
IN LOUISIANA

VOLUME XVIII
EDUCATION IN
LOUISIANA

The Louisiana Purchase Bicentennial Series
in
Louisiana History

VOLUME XV

VISIONS AND REVISIONS
PERSPECTIVES ON
LOUISIANA SOCIETY AND CULTURE

EDITED BY

VAUGHAN BURDIN BAKER

CENTER FOR LOUISIANA STUDIES
UNIVERSITY OF LOUISIANA
AT LAFAYETTE

2000

Library of Congress Catalog Number: 96-84494
ISBN Number: 1-887366-36-9

Copyright 2000
University of Louisiana at Lafayette
Lafayette, Louisiana

Published by The Center for Louisiana Studies
P.O. Box 40831
University of Louisiana at Lafayette
Lafayette, LA 70504-0831

CONTENTS

Editor's Dedication v

About the Editor vi

Acknowledgements vi

About the Series xi

Introduction to Volume 1

PART I   RACE AND CLASS IN LOUISIANA

The New American Racial Order 9
    by Caryn Cossé Bell

The Emergence of Classes in the Antebellum Period 28
    by Carl A. Brasseaux

The Americanization of French Louisiana 45
    by Lewis William Newton

Class and Race Strife 64
    by Roger W. Shugg

Race and the Working Class: The Black Worker and His Image, 1880-1890 90
    by David Paul Bennetts

"Lost Boundaries": Racial Passing and Poverty in Segregated New Orleans 125
    by Arthé A. Anthony

Racial Repression in World War Two: The New Iberia Incident 142
    by Adam Fairclough

PART II   ON THE FRINGE: WOMEN AND CHILDREN IN LOUISIANA

Cherchez les Femmes: Some Glimpses of Women in
    Early Eighteenth-Century Louisiana 160
    by Vaughan B. Baker

The Ursuline School in New Orleans, 1727-1771 175
    by Joan Marie Aycock

Le Mari est Seigneur: Marital Laws Governing Women in French Louisiana 189
    by Vaughan B. Baker, Amos Simpson, and Mathé Allain

Family and Kinship: Development on Three Louisiana Plantations..........................198
   by Ann Patton Malone

Child Welfare and Public Relief in the Antebellum Era..221
   by Robert E. Moran

Sally Muller, the White Slave 227
   by Carol Wilson

Introduction to *Madaline*..243
   by Dell Upton

Guidebooks to Sin: The Blue Books of Storyville 279
   by Pamela D. Arceneaux

Parlors, Politics, and Privilege: Clubwomen and the Failure of Woman Suffrage
   in Lafayette, Louisiana, 1897-1922..285
   by Barbara Smith Corrales

The Gift House: Jean M. Gordon and the Making of the Milne Home, 1904-1931.....299
   by Rebecca Carrasco

PART III LIFE IN LOUISIANA

The Moral Climate of French Colonial Louisiana, 1699-1763 311
   by Carl A. Brasseaux

The Plantation of the Company of the Indies...324
   by Samuel Wilson, Jr.

New Orleans Society..349
   by Marcel Giraud

The Material Culture of the Attakapas District in the First Two
   Decades of the Nineteenth Century..373
   by Glenn R. Conrad

Virginians in the Teche Country: John D. Wilkins and the Louisiana
   Beginnings..386
   by Glenn R. Conrad

Family and Society...400
   by Craig A. Bauer

The Wettest Dry City in America..426
   by Louis Vyhnanek

The Human Dimension of the Flood of 1927..457
    by Carl A. Brasseaux

Cultural Conflict and the 1928 Presidential Campaign in Louisiana........................506
    by Steven D. Zink

PART IV LOUISIANIANS AT WORK

The Business Community, 1803-1815 526
    by John D. Clark

Workhouses and Vagrancy in Nineteenth Century New Orleans...............................543
    by Nathaniel P. Weston

Free Men of Color as Tomb Builders in the Nineteenth Century.............................554
    by Patricia Brady

Louisiana Labor in the First Half of the Twentieth Century....................................564
    by Thomas A. Becnel

Getting Places in a Hurry: The Development of Aviation in Long-Era
    South Louisiana..578
    by John A. Heitmann

Late Plantation Days, 1930-1959 593
    by Michael G. Wade

PART V LOUISIANIANS AT LEISURE

A Window on Slave Culture: Dances at Congo Square in New Orleans, 1800-1862 ...632
    by Gary A. Donaldson

A Community and Its Team: The Evangeline League's Lafayette
    White Sox, 1934-1942..643
    by Doug Taylor

The Presence of the Past in the Cajun Country Mardi Gras....................................659
    by Carl Lindahl

PART VI JUSTICE AND INJUSTICE IN THE LOUISIANA EXPERIENCE

Two Utopian Socialist Plans for Emancipation in Antebellum Louisiana..................669
    by Carl J. Guarneri

Keeping Law and Order in New Orleans Under General Butler, 1862.......................684
    by Joy J. Jackson

Black Policemen in New Orleans During Reconstruction 697
    by Dennis C. Rousey

Justice Delayed: *Appoline Patout* v. *the United States*, 1864-1918 715
    by Michael G. Wade

Louisiana and the Child Offender 731
    by Robert E. Moran

Organized Crime in Louisiana History: Myth and Reality 750
    by Michael L. Kurtz

Lynching and Criminal Justice in South Louisiana, 1878-1930 767
    by Michael J. Pfeifer

Index 783

ABOUT THE SERIES

It was in the spring of 1992 that first thought was given to the matter of how best the Center for Louisiana Studies might commemorate the bicentennial of the Louisiana Purchase in 2003. For the next few months the Center's staff and members of its Advisory Council intermittently discussed the possible project, but no consensus was forthcoming. Perhaps the reason being that the Purchase looms so monumentally in United States history there are seemingly few memorials of proper proportion to commemorate the event's bicentennial.

Nevertheless, as time passed the outlines of a project began to take shape. To properly mark the occasion the Center for Louisiana Studies should produce a lasting tribute not only to the people who crafted the Louisiana Purchase but also to the people who, during the last two hundred years, have had a role in transforming that vast wilderness into the heartland of America. But the Center's focus is not mid-America for all practical purposes, it is Louisiana, the state that took its name from the Purchase territory. Therefore, the Center's project would concentrate on a Purchase bicentennial memorial that embraced the full range of Louisiana history.

There was another reason for this decision. In March of 1999 the Gulf Coast and the Mississippi Valley would mark the tercentennial of the founding of the French colony of Louisiana and the beginning of the region's historical era. Thus, if the Center's endeavor for the Purchase bicentennial was to be a history of Louisiana, then it should tell not only about the American experience in the area but also the Native American, French, Spanish, African, British and other influences that helped to lay the foundations for the present-day state.

Questions arose: Will the Center's Purchase bicentennial memorial be yet another history of Louisiana? If so, should it be another survey or should it be a more detailed account? Who would write this account of our times and those of our forebears? What interpretation would emerge from such a monograph? Who was expert enough to incorporate a harmonious blend of the political, economic, and social ingredients of our society?

Another year slipped by while we pondered these and other questions concerning the Center's memorial to the Purchase bicentennial and the tercentennial of the founding of the colony. After more discussion, there began to emerge a collective concept that was at once imaginative, exciting, and, above all, challenging. As a fitting memorial for the Louisiana Purchase bicentennial, the Center would organize and direct the publication of a major historical series. Marking the anniversaries, however, should not be the only reason for such an endeavor.

As discussion of the nature of the series evolved, it became obvious that there was an overriding reason for it. The series, to be known as the LOUISIANA PURCHASE BICENTENNIAL SERIES IN LOUISIANA HISTORY, would be a fine sampling of twentieth-century scholarship, particularly the scholarship of the last half of the century which embraced new methodologies leading to broader interpretations of the state's history. Here, in a multi-volume series the student of Louisiana history would be exposed to a wide range of scholarship reflecting multiple interpretations of historical events.

Thus, the decision was made; the Series would bring together in one place the very best articles, essays, and book parts that have been published about Louisiana in the twentieth century, particularly the latter half of the century. Its focus would be to inform scholars, teachers, students, and laypersons on far-ranging topics of Louisiana history drawn from a great reservoir of scholarship found in media ranging from scholarly to popular to obscure.

Most important to the development of such a series, however, was the person or persons who would select the "very best" to incorporate into the Series. The answer came quickly, only widely recognized experts, acting as volume editors, would determine from the broad spectrum of sources those essays which reflect the best in research, writing, and interpretation on topics in Louisiana history.

Initially, twenty broad topics of Louisiana history were identified, and the Center plans to publish these twenty volumes between 1995 and 2003. There may be additional volumes, if they are warranted. It should be noted, however, proper presentation of some topics in Louisiana history cannot be confined to a single book; hence, some volumes may incorporate several parts in order to present the full spectrum of scholarship on the subject. Finally, the volumes will not be published in sequential order, although Volume I, *The French Experience in Louisiana* was the first to appear. Each volume will be announced upon publication.

THE LOUISIANA PURCHASE BICENTENNIAL SERIES IN LOUISIANA HISTORY presents a great source of information for anyone interested in the history of the colony and the state. It stands as an appropriate memorial to the men and women who shaped the colony and state down to the dawn of the twenty-first century.

Glenn R. Conrad, General Editor

INTRODUCTION

Research and writing on Louisiana's past has undergone a sharp change since the 1970s: from a prevailing emphasis on "history as past politics" to a view of the past that embraces richer dimensions. Changes in the scholarship both in and on Louisiana have reflected, as have many of the historical currents sweeping the state, shifts in the national experience in the post-World War II era. While an advocacy of social history or "history from below" has origins in the first decades of the twentieth century and its practice in Louisiana scholarship is not entirely new as this volume will demonstrate, historical research in Louisiana until the challenges of the 1960s buttressed a predominant "drum-and-trumpet" approach to exploring the past. Interpretations resting on the activities of dead male historical actors, almost all white, and the visions of largely white and largely male historical analysts held the field. A denigration of the significance of local and state topics enforced through the judgments of program chairs of historical conferences and journal editors throughout the country further discouraged the application of new methodologies and new interpretations in Louisiana historical endeavors. A widely expressed belief existed that only amateur historians, mostly women and genealogists with antiquarian interests, addressed narrow subjects of local and state history and that professional historians, with their superior training and superior understanding, cast wider nets of inquiry.

Newer generations of historians since the 1960s have effectively expanded the scope of Louisiana historical studies. They have embraced with enthusiasm trends in American historiography that encourage the analysis of topics once considered unworthy and the use of source materials formerly unimagined or ignored. Political history, biographical accounts of the lives of the men who shaped the state's development from its earliest exploration, and the trials of war and reconstruction have continued to hold an important place in the historical literature. These topics, however, now compete with more inclusive studies innovative not only in their new analyses of race, class, and gender but also in the methodologies applied in their inquiries. New fields and new visions, along with interpretive revisions of old topics, have consequently enriched the corpus of earlier historical work on the development over time of Louisiana's unique culture and distinctive society.

This volume in the *Louisiana Purchase Bicentennial Series in Louisiana History* focuses attention on aspects of Louisiana's social and cultural development and on the changing nature of the discourse in Louisiana historiography that have taken place through the course of the twentieth century. It provides samples of both the older and the newer research on Louisiana society and culture. The challenges in compiling it were daunting. First, many of the subjects normally addressed in comprehensive social and cultural histories had volumes of their own: Charles Vincent's survey of the African American experience grew to three volumes in size, Patricia Brady's and Mathé Allain's volumes highlighted the arts, Michael Wade's thoroughly investigated education, and Warren Billings and Judith Schafer's examined legal history and judicial institutions. Other volumes covered economic history and concentrated chronological periods. Secondly, many articles that seemed natural selections were already included in other volumes; to repeat them was boring and redundant. These realizations guided my rationale and my choices and have resulted in what might seem to be glaring and obvious omissions. For example, selections from Gwendolyn Midlo Hall's and Kimberly Hanger's studies that have so enriched the discussion of Louisiana's early development from the perspectives of both race and gender are notably absent from this volume. Finally, as I completed a survey of the literature on Louisiana society and culture fundamentally dictated by a determination to provide fresh examples of Louisiana historical scholarship and a wish to demonstrate changing and more all-embracing approaches to historical inquiry, I faced exceptionally difficult choices of articles on some topics because of the many fine possibilities, and found a dearth of substantive interpretations in others.

The volume is organized in six parts. Some might have been longer, but the selections chosen for final inclusion sufficiently indicate the present status of historical opinion on the subject. Others might have been shorter but have been subjected to such searching attention that paring threatened to distort the historiographical picture. Each part aims to throw light on an aspect of Louisiana's development excluded in other volumes. The territory of the historian has greatly expanded in the last two decades with the encroachment of new and sometimes controversial theories. Historians interested in pursuing research in or on Louisiana face a multitude of theoretical and methodological possibilities. In its basic conception, the volume offers to those who are interested in learning about the experiences of ordinary and sometimes forgotten people in Louisiana a sampling of the rich variety of analyses available in the literature. To those who wish to find new opportunities for research, it provides a suggestion of the gaps in the literature inviting attention.

Part I offers a selection of articles ranging from early analyses of race and class that have become classics in the literature to end-of-the-twentieth-century interpretations shaped by postmodern theory and concerns. It begins with Caryn Cossé Bell's 1997 study of changing patterns of racial order in Louisiana. Bell discusses a three-tiered racial structure in Louisiana that differentiated between free and slave blacks and differed sharply from Anglo-American patterns confining all persons of color to an inferior caste. Focusing her study in New Orleans, Bell shows that the social and economic status of a flourishing intermediate class of free persons of color eroded in the nineteenth century under the steady imposition of a more typically Southern and American racial order that reduced all persons of color to a debased status. She argues that Louisiana's and particularly New Orleans' liberal religious tradition delayed the imposition of a sharply defined two-tiered racial hierarchy until after 1830. Carl Brasseaux examines developing patterns of minority class stratification in Louisiana's Acadian population. The state's French-speaking, Catholic Acadians have until recently been commonly viewed from a myopic perspective and understood as a homogeneous, classless, isolated, linguistically separated population clinging to anachronistic ways of life and resisting cultural assimilation. Brasseaux shows that acceptance of American mainstream materialist values led to the transformation of the Acadian population into a highly diversified society in the nineteenth-century.

Lewis William Newton's 1929 exploration of the Americanization of French Louisiana and Roger Shugg's 1939 study of white farmers and laborers in the nineteenth century represent examples of classic studies that have strongly influenced historical understanding of the state's social structures. Newton discusses the relationship between Francophone and Anglophone populations and the degree of political accord that by the middle of the nineteenth century had replaced earlier conflict. He shows that division had diminished if not disappeared as the French population increasingly understood and accepted American political and cultural institutions. By the time of the Civil War, he says, political and economic assimilation was almost complete although Louisiana's formerly dominant Creole population retained a distinct but diminished silhouette, resisting full absorption into American cultural ways. Newton's early analysis and Brasseaux's more recent one strengthen an understanding of the development of Louisiana's emerging identity. Roger Shugg shows that nineteenth and earlier twentieth-century interpretations of post-Civil War Reconstruction fail to understand the complexities of race and class in Louisiana. In his dissection of the dynamics of the power struggle between blacks and whites, Shugg like Newton both anticipated and influenced recent theoretical approaches to Louisiana's past. He shows that no race, class, or party was free of prejudice and ambition in the struggle for power during Reconstruction. Newton and Shugg's pioneering social analyses have remained strong in the face of contemporary approaches to understanding class and race dynamics in Louisiana.

Issues of race and class permeate any historical analysis of Louisiana's social development. David Paul Bennetts notes that by the 1880s blacks represented one-third of the New Orleans working class population. No city in America had more black residents in the last decades of the nineteenth century; the city had far more skilled black laborers than any other city in the nation as well. Blacks were vital to urban economic life and not unaware of their importance. Many had a proud heritage as free artisans. Bennetts shows that the relationship between blacks and whites in the 1880s was both complex and ill defined, influenced by racial philosophies and economic exigencies. Black workingmen struggled as the century closed to define their role in an economy where opportunities for advancement were limited but viable choices and alternatives remained. Arthé Anthony adds gender concerns to the literary mix in concentrating on racial boundaries with an emphasis on black working women. Resting a perceptive analysis on oral histories of Creole women born between 1885 and 1905, Anthony draws attention to a subject formerly shrouded in secrecy: racial passing. The women Anthony interviewed experienced both racial and sexual discrimination in the decades following Reconstruction when increased racial violence, segregation, economic exploitation, and denial of citizenship rights intensified. They accepted the risks of passing as white rather than suffering the conditions of living as black in Louisiana's black-or-white society. Racial passing was a last resort strategy in response to pervasive racial oppression, but many of the women interviewed, after passing for white, ultimately chose to be black. Anthony's use of oral interviews to gather information on subjects undocumented with traditional source materials casts valuable light on the dynamics of class and gender in New Orleans in the last decades of the nineteenth century and the first two decades of the twentieth.

Adam Fairclough closes Part I with an examination of an incident of violent racial repression in New Iberia in May 1944. His account demonstrates the furious determination of whites to maintain a racist *status quo* through the first half of the twentieth century. The incident reveals, however, that the first tremors of the Civil Rights movement began in Louisiana even before the end of the Second World War as well as details the formidable degree of resistance to challenges to white supremacy. Fairclough's discussion appropriately suggests that further probing studies of the shifting shapes of power in Louisiana promise to reward richly our understanding of race and gender relationships in a state where a unique cultural heritage has often skewed national patterns.

Part II centers attention on the experience of women and children in Louisiana. Gender studies have not attained a highly visible presence in Louisiana despite the legitimacy they have gained in national arenas. Research on Louisiana women has suffered from problems in locating and utilizing appropriate source materials and from a sexist relegation of research concerning women and family to a second-class status, perhaps a lingering reflection of Southern patriarchal conservatism. Fertile opportunities for gender-focused historical research in Louisiana history remain in every period of the state's development. The selections in Part II provide a sampling of early and more recent work directing attention to women and reveal the scarcity of studies of any aspect of childhood as a viable subject of historical inquiry in Louisiana historiography. My 1990 article on women in the beginning years of the French colonial period, based on research funded by the National Endowment for the Humanities, was an early reconnaissance of information on the subject. When it was written, information on women in the French period was largely buried in monographs and almost illegible documents, some only in French. After preliminary forays into the documentary material and a consequent recognition of how rich the possibilities for new gender-focused research Louisiana's past remained, I issued a call for further careful studies on women's diverse experiences under the state's changing administrations, stressing the importance of women in instilling the unconscious cultural assumptions that shaped the emergence of Louisiana's multi-ethnically influenced identity. In an article on New Orleans' eighteenth-century Ursuline school for girls, Joan Marie Aycock highlights the importance of women's religious orders in building educational institutions in Louisiana's early settlement years. Her discussion of the Ursulines underscores their significance in establishing opportunities for girls in the rough atmosphere of the early Louisiana colony. While a few other studies of the contributions of women's religious orders to the development of the state in later periods exist, glaring gaps beg attention.

Mathé Allain, Amos Simpson, and I joined efforts to understand the impact on women's lives of French customary law as it was applied in the early colonial period. Our analysis of the provisions of the *Coutume de Paris* revealed that women in Louisiana governed by a French legal regime subjected to an Enlightenment rationale enjoyed economic protections that allowed at least a shifting basis of female autonomy. While misogynist in its fundamental assumptions of male superiority and subjecting married women completely to the power of their husbands, French law in the eighteenth century nevertheless rested on premises of natural law and of female worth and dignity and preserved rights and property protections aimed at strengthening social stability. French legal codes consequently shaped a colonial experience for women in Louisiana that differed from their experience in Anglo-American cultural areas. French law afforded important benefits to unmarried women, widows, women operating businesses (public merchants) and underage children of both sexes enjoying forced heirship. Anne Patton Malone utilized legal documents of another kind in her analysis of succession records and inventories to reveal marriage, family, and kinship patterns in the slave population in the antebellum period. She provides telling detail and concrete examples demonstrating the pressures of slavery on black women and kinship networks.

Robert E Moran's article calls attention to early efforts to develop child welfare programs and public relief in the period before the Civil War. He notes the state's weakness in providing adequate facilities and protections for white children, and its complete neglect of blacks. Indeed, he shows that although black slave children faced restricted freedom and sometimes severe hardship, free black orphans had less security and even more dismal lives. Benevolent efforts to provide institutions to care for destitute free black children were frustrated by state-legislated impediments and a common belief that poverty and dependency were personal evils stemming from gambling, drunkenness and indolence.

Introduction

In scrutinizing the lives of ordinary people rather than privileged elites, social historians often expose the darker aspects of a society's past experience. Carol Wilson traces the misfortunes of an orphaned German immigrant enslaved in antebellum New Orleans and demonstrates that even in Louisiana's racist hierarchy, a white skin offered no guarantee of security. Sally Muller's gripping story as a white slave demonstrates that ideas about slavery and race were scarcely as clear as is commonly believed. Ultimately freed after a Supreme Court appellate decision, Sally's story underscores that the antebellum system of racial designation was not only unrealistic, but also threatening to individuals of every color.

In drawing from the nineteenth-century shadows Madaline Edwards, a penniless, middle-aged woman struggling for existence on the social fringes of New Orleans' respectable white society, Dell Upton shows the devastating consequences of widely accepted aspects of nineteenth-century social and moral values. Madaline Edwards' two failed marriages and her dependent status as the kept mistress of a married businessman marked her as a social outcast. Upton sympathetically details Madaline's talents and strengths in her efforts to define a place for herself in a world that offered little to women without the protection of husbands or fathers. Pamela D. Arceneaux goes even deeper into society's margins. She used the clandestinely circulated guidebooks to Storyville, New Orleans' turn-of-the-twentieth-century red-light district, the first legally designated and most notorious district of brothels and houses of prostitution in the United States, to cast poignant light on an otherwise dimly illuminated aspect of women's lives. Storyville's "Blue Books," marketing guidebooks of hedonism, reveal a seldom-glimpsed aspect of the American discourse on vice before the First World War.

Barbara Smith Corrales shifts attention from the frustrations of women's lives on the economic and social margins of Louisiana society to the restrictive effects of the Southern patriarchal milieu on middle-class white women. She studies clubwomen in rural and small-town Louisiana and their rejection of woman suffrage out of a misguided attempt to preserve a perceived position of racial privilege. In contrast to their aggressive activism for social reform, the failure of middle-class white women to champion the cause of votes for women suggests a deeply rooted cultural predisposition to patriarchy. Rebecca Carrasco, on the other hand, details Jean Gordon's dedicated advocacy of children and society's rejects. With her sister Kate, Louisiana's most effective champion of woman suffrage and women's rights, Jean Gordon overcame formidable social and economic obstacles to establish the Milne Home for mentally retarded girls.

Part III offers insight into aspects of daily life in Louisiana from early settlement to the twentieth century. Taken together, these quite diverse analyses underscore the impact of the state's unique environment and cultural heritage. Carl Brasseaux opens the section with an article demonstrating the early origins of Louisiana's fabled hedonism. He discusses the consistently unsuccessful efforts of French Catholic clergy to regulate morality and nurture religious fervor from 1699 to 1763, the period of French rule. Louisiana's frontier environment afforded colonists greater freedom from moral constraints than was possible in more settled areas of New France or in the mother country. Church and secular officials alike decried the gambling, public drunkenness, and sexual promiscuity that were commonplace in the Louisiana territory. Sam Wilson, Jr., traces the development of the plantation of the Company of the Indies, describing in detail the physical structures located in present-day Algiers, across the river from the center of the early New Orleans. The plantation's principal function was to receive the African slaves brought in for sale to French colonists. Wilson's descriptions of plantation buildings give a clear visual understanding of the material conditions of life for both blacks and whites in the French colony.

Marcel Giraud's description of life in French colonial New Orleans is a notable example of early historical analyses that remain classic. A pioneering student of life in Louisiana during the French regime, Giraud's path-breaking volumes trace the growing stabilization of the colony in the first decades of its settlement. Giraud describes New Orleans society in the 1720s—a population that included Canadian *voyageurs* and hunters, blacksmiths, bakers, coopers, masons, carpenters, tailors, and locksmiths. Skilled craftsmen represented one of every eight city residents in a total population of 800. Far ahead of the historiography of his time, Giraud included data on the lives of the women who went to a colony where poverty and destitution were the common lot. Glenn Conrad looks at daily life in the state's rural areas in the first decades of the nineteenth century. He attacks commonly held misconceptions of southwest Louisiana's Acadian population as homogeneously primitive and poor. Analyzing slave, land, and estate records, he shows that prosperity was instead the norm in the Attakapas region. In a second article, Conrad turns our attention to Anglo-American settlers in rural Louisiana with a detailed case study of a transplanted Virginian whose family prospered through the opportunities in Louisiana's Teche country. Craig Bauer provides another perspective on Anglo-American family life in looking at Duncan Kenner's experiences as a prominent antebellum sugar plantation aristocrat. Bauer argues that the flood of Americans into Louisiana after 1803 affected every aspect of political, cultural, and social practice, adding a capitalistic flavor to the good life in Louisiana. He describes American pastimes and entertainments that developed social clubs, fostered education and literacy, fueled gambling and horseracing, and gave rise to thriving theatre and opera traditions in New Orleans.

These articles show that the hedonistic reputation of New Orleans in particular and Louisiana in general derives from deeply rooted values and attitudes affecting all of the state's diverse population. Louis Vyhnanek confirms the impression with an examination of prohibition in New Orleans, arguing that it was an effort doomed to failure. He shows that the Crescent City was the "wettest" in America during the 1920s and that attempts to enforce the Volstead Act were a losing battle because the vast majority of New Orleans' citizens disapproved government attempts to legislate morality.

In a discussion of the disastrous 1927 flood, Carl Brasseaux reminds us, however, that the state's hard-playing citizens frequently faced extreme challenges in an environment that despite twentieth-century technological advances can be hostile and unpredictable. Inundating thousands of miles of farmland in seven states, the flood was described by contemporary journalists as America's greatest peacetime disaster; its destruction remained a defining experience in the lives of Louisianians of every class and background. Brasseaux details the poignant human dimensions of the cataclysm, underscoring the enduring resilience of a population in an environment that has from its colonial beginnings been subject to nature's unpredictable punishment.

Steven Zink closes Part III's survey of life in Louisiana with an examination of the 1928 presidential campaign. His discussion ranges beyond traditional political accounts in emphasizing the enduring impact on political behavior of the basic cultural divisions that have shaped Louisiana responses into the twentieth century. Zink notes the striking predominance in Louisiana in the 1928 election of a traditional Democratic vote and shows that Protestant-Catholic issues, racial tensions, and rural-urban resentments shaped electoral allegiances in a state where elections turned on such culturally divisive matters as prohibition, parochial schools, the influence of the Ku Klux Klan, and machine politics in New Orleans.

Introduction

Parts IV and V cast light on Louisianians at work and at leisure. John Clark examines business elites in the years following the Louisiana Purchase. He focuses attention on the new forms of capitalist enterprise in a unique urban environment. New Orleans' river and port and its solidly entrenched Creole establishment shaped and controlled its economic development. His detailed analysis of businesses and businessmen demonstrates the degree to which relatively few individuals dominated corporate enterprise in the city until after 1813 when an expansive economy opened a new era and new business strata emerged.

Nathaniel Weston, on the other hand, uncovers a glimpse of the out-of-work population in his study of workhouses in New Orleans in the nineteenth century. Focusing on attempts through the penal system to control vagrancy by establishing workhouses, institutions of both incarceration and moral improvement, he shows that the workhouses ultimately failed in their efforts at rehabilitation and remained predominantly places of incarceration. They nevertheless stimulated new concepts of public responsibility and are notable in illustrating largely ignored aspects of urban problems in Louisiana.

Thomas Becnel's study of agricultural workers in the early twentieth century further enriches the picture of the work experience in Louisiana. He shows that in the rural areas organized labor posed little threat to the political or economic establishment, and that the labor movement lacked strong political allies or a unified voice, enjoying only limited success by mid-century. John Heitman's article on the emergence of new technological and business enterprises reveals the state leadership's ambivalent attitudes toward modern industrialization and a seldom-viewed aspect of Huey Long's legacy in Louisiana. Heitman focuses on the aviation industry, the most dynamic new technology of Long's time. Long embraced technocratic ideas, believing that technology would create wealth, but, despite his support, the aviation industry in Louisiana failed to sustain developmental momentum, in part because of the reluctance of the state's educational and research institutions to respond to technological challenge.

Michael G. Wade throws his spotlight on a mid-twentieth century sugar plantation and its difficulties in meeting the challenges of modernization. Depression, growing governmental regulation, and changing technologies forced difficult decisions in M. A. Patout and Son, Ltd., a family business in rural Louisiana. Wade demonstrates that while family, church, the store, and other community institutions provided continuity and cohesion, financial exigencies led to an increasingly corporate reality.

Turning to Louisianians at play, Gary A. Donaldson probes elusive aspects of African American slave culture in a study of slave dances and celebrations in New Orleans' Congo Square where slave families gathered on Sundays for cultural, economic, and religious interactions. Festivities at Congo Square served as a focal point for the expression of a distinct African-rooted sub-culture within the framework of a dominant white culture. Its importance in both reflecting and preserving Africa's cultural heritage cannot be overestimated.

Doug Taylor looks at small-town popular sports institutions in his account of the Lafayette White Sox between 1934 and 1942. As a focal point for social contact for local residents, the team's ballpark provided not only entertainment but also important community dialogue, playing a significant role in defining community identity. The team's ultimate decline in the 1950s mirrored nationwide trends as minor league baseball collapsed everywhere under the impact of new opportunities for entertainment provided through advances in transportation and communication technologies.

Carl Lindahl also scrutinizes popular leisure expressions in his discussion of the Cajun Country Mardi Gras, an altogether different ritual from the more widely known urban pre-Lenten celebrations. Applying the insight of a folklorist and concepts derived from anthropological and linguistic theory, Lindahl shows that an analysis of such a deeply rooted community ritual uncovers essential structural and symbolic aspects of the society. He concluded that the Cajun Mardi Gras serves as an important community-binding exercise in giving, providing memories for the old, stories for the young, and food for the town.

Carl Guarneri opens Part VI's survey of justice and injustice with a discussion of Louisiana's little-known participation in the nineteenth-century Utopian socialist movement that linked Europe and America. He examines the emancipation plans of American disciples of the French Utopian Charles Fourier and concludes that even Utopian ideals were insufficiently capable of attracting Louisiana Fourierists and combating the force of political, economic and social pressures on slaveholders. Joy Jackson casts another light on antebellum responses to attempts to regulate Louisiana society in her account of New Orleanians' rebellion against General Ben Butler's martial law during the Union army's 1862 occupation of the city. Determined citizen resistance to Butler's harsh and controversial actions in the first year of occupation placed a heavy burden on law enforcement officials and overshadowed local recognition of his positive improvements in levees, canals, streets, and the war economy.

Michael Wade introduces gender issues into questions pertaining to the state's multifaceted nineteenth-century judicial experience. He investigates the post-civil war damage claims of French-born St. Mary Parish plantation mistress Appoline Patout. Basing his account on the under-utilized records of the French-American Claims Commission, Wade shows that Appoline Patout's persistent search for justice never achieved satisfactory resolution. Robert E. Moran, focusing on penal institutions for child offenders, shows that despite recurring efforts at reform through the nineteenth century, conditions for criminals of all ages remained dismal. Delinquent, dependent and neglected juveniles both male and female were confined in inadequately financed reformatories with few effective programs of rehabilitation. Juvenile courts in Louisiana were among the most poorly equipped, poorly organized, and poorly staffed in the nation. Michael Kurtz concludes the section's summary survey of the literature on crime and punishment in Louisiana with an article addressing the persistent myth of the Mafia's control of the state. He attacks popular conceptions that Italian crime syndicates have operated freely in Louisiana since the nineteenth century, showing that anti-Italian xenophobia through the first three decades of the twentieth century perpetuated beliefs of pervasive organized Italian crime syndicates. After 1936 with the development of an extensive state slot machine empire that broadened into one of the nation's largest illegal gambling operations, clear evidence of established criminal organizations appears.

In summary, the volume demonstrates that Louisiana historians have enthusiastically applied a rich variety of methods and interpretations in studying the social and cultural dimensions of the state's past The health of historical studies in Louisiana is indicative of the vitality of historiographical discourse and practice among scholars interested in exploring Louisiana's multifaceted and multicultural experience for the light it casts on the human journey through time and space. Louisiana's social history is distinguished by the visions and revisions of talented scholars who have applied powerful interpretive approaches with thoughtfulness and expertise. Rather than replacing older subjects and interests, social history's validation of once-excluded topics and methods continues to expand our understanding of our Louisiana heritage.

PART I

RACE AND CLASS IN LOUISIANA

THE NEW AMERICAN RACIAL ORDER*

Caryn Cossé Bell

As the pattern of a dual racial order spread through the South during the opening decades of the nineteenth century, a three-tiered caste system set New Orleans apart. The city's unusual racial pattern contrasted sharply with an Anglo-American order that attempted to confine all persons of color—both slave and free—to a separate and inferior caste. In Creole New Orleans, an intermediate class of free people of color had gained a measure of social acceptance under Latin European influences. Until the 1830s, the city's liberal religious culture helped to delay the imposition of a sharply defined, two-tiered racial hierarchy.

Louisiana's Catholic Church never achieved the institutional strength to impose a strict code of morality upon masters and slaves. Still, Catholicism exerted a considerable influence on race relations. Under the French colonial regime, the church's efforts to incorporate free blacks and slaves into the religious life of the community contributed to a state of racial flux. After the Spanish takeover, the church's integrative policies acquired new momentum and produced an important alliance between black New Orleanians and the Spanish clergy.

In the 1770s, under instructions from metropolitan authorities, Spanish Capuchins began demanding adherence to provisions of the Spanish slave code that prohibited miscegenation, banned labor on Sundays, regularized slave marriages, and required the religious instruction of slaves. Opposed to interference in the master-slave relationship, white Creole planters withdrew from active participation in the church and generally refused to comply with statutes designed to protect their slaves' spirituality and religious obligations. Free blacks and slaves, perceiving the Spanish clergy as a useful ally, filled the resulting vacuum by taking the place of whites as godparents for unbaptized African and Creole slaves. The church reciprocated with its legally sanctioned policy of religious

---

*First published as chapter 3 in Caryn Cossé Bell, *Romanticism, Social Protest and Reform* (Baton Rouge: Louisiana State University Press, © 1997), 64-88. Reprinted with the kind permission of the author and publisher.

protectionism. In an incident in 1784, the Capuchin friars clashed openly with Spanish officials over the treatment of one of their slaves.[1]

In June, Bishop Cirilo threatened to report the *alcalde* (provincial magistrate) Francisco Maria de Reggio to the Crown for his treatment of Batista, a slave of the Capuchin household. Earlier in the month, Spanish troops captured sixty *cimarrones* (runaway slaves) led by the daring San Malo. In the ensuing inquiry, San Malo testified that he, Batista, and two of their companions were captured in May by a group of Americans. The *cimarrones* freed themselves, except for Batista, and murdered the three men, a woman, and a boy. San Malo described Batista's role: "You, Batista, you could do nothing because the English (Americans) distrusting you more than anyone else tied your hands more carefully than the others."[2]

The *alcalde* sentenced Batista to receive one hundred lashes at the foot of the gallows where San Malo and three of his followers were to be hanged. The Capuchin priests criticized the hastily convened legal proceedings and argued that Batista had been denied due process of law. When the bishop threatened to lay the matter before the Crown, the *alcalde* retorted that he would be pleased to give an account of the incident to the king. Testimony revealed that Batista had been illegally hired out to work two miles from the Capuchin residence. Nevertheless, in an act of defiance, the priests refused to accompany the accused men to the scaffold. They protested to the *alcalde*'s emissary that "their hearts could not endure to see an innocent creature, 'a child of their very house,' suffer unjustly." On the day of the public executions, Reggio delayed the hangings in an attempt to persuade a priest to accompany the *cimarrones* to the gallows. Father Antonio de Sedella, the vicar of St. Louis Church, confronted Spanish authorities and refused Reggio's request, declaring that the condemned men had already been shriven and that "anyone could help them to die."[3]

When Bishop Cirilo, Sedella, and their supporters appeared on the gallery of the church residence on the Plaza de Armas (Jackson Square) to witness the executions, they cried out against the injustice of the punishment. Reggio described Cirilo's violent public attack when the sentence was passed, declaring that the bishop behaved in a way "not at all becoming to his elevated and respectable character."[4]

During the 1780s, Cirilo continued his campaign to ensure the humane treatment and spiritual well-being of the slaves. He complained repeatedly to his superiors of the extent to which planters neglected their slaves' spiritual welfare. In June, 1791, a fellow Capuchin, Father Joaquin de Portillo, criticized Governor Esteban Miró in an incident involving the illegal burial of a four-year-old slave girl. A black woman with "more religion than many whites," Portillo pointed out, had informed him of the unlawful interment of the child in the private garden of Monsieur Segui. The woman had also offered to pay for a burial in consecrated ground. Although many slaveholders reaped the benefits of slave labor, Portillo charged, they refused to provide their slaves with a Christian burial; the governor ignored such abuses, though he was well aware of the problem. Stung by Portillo's accusation, Miró demanded that Segui exhume the child's body, provide for the cost of a Christian burial, and pay a fine of ten *pesos*.[5]

In July, Portillo encountered slaves working near St. Louis Cathedral on a holy day of obligation. When the priest ordered the slaves to stop, they replied that their master would simply make them work elsewhere. Infuriated, Portillo notified Miró. The governor halted the work and warned that such violations of church law would be severely punished. In January, 1792, Governor Carondelet upheld Miró's threat and affirmed his intention to ensure humane treatment of the slaves. Determined to counteract planter power and dissipate the threat of slave rebellion, Carondelet enforced provisions of the Spanish slave code that prohibited excessive brutality and permitted slaves to file complaints against their masters.[6]

The transfer of Louisiana to the United States in 1803 revolutionized church/state relations. Governmental support for religious policies designed to ensure the slave's moral and physical well-being ended. Nonetheless, the new schismatic head of the Catholic Church, Antonio de Sedella, continued the Spanish Church's protectionist and assimilationist policies and maintained the loyalty of black New Orleanians.

Sedella, the friar who had confronted Spanish officials over the treatment of the Capuchin slave, was first appointed pastor of St. Louis Parish Church in 1787. Wearing open sandals and a long, brown-hooded robe tied with a thick cord at the waist, the enigmatic clerical leader purported to shun the temporal affairs of the church in observance of his Franciscan vow of poverty. After the Louisiana Purchase, the Spanish Crown granted him a pension and invited him to return to Spain. Though he decided to remain in New Orleans, Sedella retained close ties to his superiors in Spain and supplied the Spanish government with intelligence reports.[7]

In the absence of an officially recognized ecclesiastical authority after 1800, a contest for the St. Louis pastorate ensued. In 1805, Sedella was at the center of the controversy. In March, the religious schism resulted in a public confrontation in the cathedral, in which hundreds of Catholics assembled to elect a parish priest. The congregation proclaimed Sedella their pastor and also chose a lay committee of trustees or *marguilliers* (church wardens) to handle cathedral affairs. Sedella's supporters justified their novel selection process on the grounds that the church belonged to the people and not to autocratic ecclesiastics. The Marquis de Casa Calvo, a former Spanish governor and supporter of Sedella, sanctioned the action by transferring all church properties to the newly chosen committee of *marguilliers*.

In September, a papal bull placed the church and the Diocese of Louisiana under the jurisdiction of the bishop of Baltimore. Ignoring the decree, the lay committee retained control of St. Louis Cathedral and reserved the authority to appoint their own pastors. They based their independence from Rome on French precedents. During the Revolution, the Civil Constitution of the Clergy adopted by the Constituent Assembly in July, 1790, asserted the French nation's independence from Rome and provided for the popular election of the clergy.

Historically, the mendicant nature of Franciscan missions required the establishment of church proprietorships. Lay trustees managed church finances and properties, while the friars devoted their energies to the spiritual and corporal welfare of the congregation. Still, the "election" of Sedella and the church wardens represented a highly irregular break with church practice. The system of church *marguilliers* underwent a unique transformation in the 1805 schism.[8]

The popularity of Sedella and earlier Capuchin friars with native Louisianians stemmed in large measure from their willingness to adapt to prevailing conditions. Under the French and Spanish regimes, the Catholic Church tolerated practices that had contributed to instability and revolution in France. Near the time of the Louisiana Purchase, the French traveler C. C. Robin described the extraordinary liberality of Sedella and his fellow Capuchins: "Religion in this colony is all in form; there is no longer any of the spirit in it. . . . In the city they are well satisfied with the Capuchins who perform the functions of the parish priests. They leave the conscience free. In no other country in the world is tolerance more extended. Women, negroes, and officers in the governor's suite are almost the only ones who go to church."[9]

After 1803, priests assigned to New Orleans complained bitterly to their American superiors of Jansenist religious practices. Despite their outcries, Sedella condoned the unorthodox religious movement. Jansenism, a dissident and amorphous revival movement in Catholic France, flourished in eighteenth-century Louisiana. Though the French monarchy and Catholic Church leaders made sporadic attempts to suppress the fractious religious movement, Jansenism remained a potent influence in Catholic Louisiana. During the years of Sedella's curacy, Jansenists enjoyed free expression of their religious beliefs; the movement remained influential among the city's French-speaking Catholics into the twentieth century.

Sedella exercised the same spirit of tolerance toward freemasons. Condemned, like Jansenism, by the papacy, freemasonry flourished in New Orleans. During the early decades of the nineteenth century, Sedella welcomed members of the masonic fraternity into the Catholic fold and accorded them all of the church sacraments. He allowed them to display their masonic regalia in the cathedral and insisted that Catholic priests accompany coffins adorned with masonic symbols to the cemetery. In memorial services for Napoleon Bonaparte in December, 1821, Sedella invited the renowned masonic orator Judge J. F. Canonge to deliver the commemorative address.[10]

As may be surmised from his treatment of Jansenists and freemasons, Sedella exercised a remarkable degree of tolerance toward other religious denominations. During the early decades of the 1800s, his broadmindedness promoted an exceptional spirit of religious ecumenism. Not long after her arrival in the city in May, 1818, the Catholic nun Philippine Duchesne described events on the Sabbath thus: "Protestants stop preaching on Sundays to hear the holy Pastor, who preaches in English. They love him as much as the Catholics do." Only the year before, Sedella had allowed a Protestant minister to address a large Catholic congregation assembled in the cathedral.[11]

The Spanish curé's unorthodox notions of religious tolerance revolutionized the city's Catholic Church. His acceptance of democratizing influences identified with revolutionary France strengthened the city's liberal Latin European religious culture. Under Sedella, the church itself served as a transmitter of liberal social practices and radical French ideas during the early decades of the nineteenth century. His actions delayed the emergence of conservative proslavery forces within the Catholic Church in New Orleans.

Sedella's unconventional practices carried over into his dealings with black Catholics. Disregarding church doctrine and criticism by American Church authorities, he administered sacraments to slave and free black concubines and their illegitimate children. Newly appointed diocesan priests complained bitterly of having to perform baptisms, marriages, and burials for concubines, prostitutes, divorcées, and freemasons. In 1826, such practices prompted one of Sedella's rivals to describe the city as a "new Babylon," the "sewer of all vice and refuge of all that is worst on earth."[12]

Reminiscent of the Spanish mission's complaints in 1772, Sedella's rivals also criticized living arrangements within the Catholic rectory. Sedella's new contender for control of St. Louis Cathedral in 1815, Louis DuBourg, the recently assigned bishop of New Orleans, informed his superiors in Rome of the excessive influence within the rectory of Sedella's mulatto housekeeper. Some of his informants, DuBourg wrote, believed that a liaison existed between the two. As evidence of such a relationship, Sedella's critics pointed to the young boy who assisted the priest during Mass and performed other duties around the church. Owing to the boy's physical resemblance to the priest and conditions within the church residence, some observers believed Sedella was the child's father.[13]

In all likelihood, the American Church authority also frowned upon Sedella's involvement in two highly controversial court cases brought by slaves. In 1819, Sedella testified in favor of Marie, a slave, and her son by a white man, Erasmus R. Avart. Avart provided for the emancipation of Marie and the boy in his will. Avart's heirs, however, contested the document on the grounds that Marie's lover, "consumed with passion" for the slave woman, was of unsound mind. In spite of the testimony of Sedella and others that Avart was in complete possession of his mental faculties, Marie and her son remained enslaved.[14]

In 1820, Sedella again testified, in behalf of Rose, a freedwoman, and her young child. Although Rose's former master, who was her father, had signed emancipation papers in Cuba in 1805, he reclaimed the free woman of color and her child after their arrival in New Orleans. Sedella baptized Rose a free person and espoused her cause. In this instance, the court decided in favor of the woman and her offspring.[15]

In opposing orthodox Catholicism and advocating the rights of free blacks and slaves, the Spanish priest maintained the loyalty of the city's free black population. Near the time of Sedella's "election" to the St. Louis pastorate in 1805, Governor Claiborne noted the friar's "great influence with the People of Colour." As their status deteriorated under the American regime, Afro-Creole Catholics recalled the spirit of tolerance fostered by

Sedella. Their special rapport with "Père Antoine" remained a powerful source of spiritual inspiration.[16]

When Sedella executed his will in December, 1828, he provided that a sum of five hundred dollars be divided among his *filleule et filleuls* (female and male godchildren) without distinction of color. His death the following year brought the city to a standstill. Edward Livingston adjourned the First District Court with a eulogy. "His holiness and virtues," the city leader declared, "entitled him to canonization." There was not one reason, Livingston continued, "why he should not be received as a saint in heaven" for he had "led the life of one on earth."[17]

Businesses, theaters, newspapers, and city government suspended operations on the day of the funeral. Together with a "vast number of gentlemen of all denominations" and nearly all the city's public officials, a large contingent of freemasons attended the funeral services. Masonic leaders, recalling Sedella's devotion to masonry's founding principles, urged lodge members to attend the services. They reminded their fellow masons that Sedella had "never refused to accompany to their abode the mortal remains of our Brethren."[18]

Thousands of candles flickered in St. Louis Cathedral, where the deceased Sedella "seemed like a saint, rapt in holy meditation." Long lines of mourners of "all ages, sexes and colors flocked to pay their last tribute of respect to him, whom, when alive, they regarded as their guide, their father and friend."[19]

For many years after Sedella's death, St. Louis Cathedral's large, racially mixed congregations attested to the persistence of Latin European racial patterns. Many startled visitors to the city described the diversity of the church's communicants. In 1838, Harriet Martineau wrote that the cathedral was a place where "the European gladly visits, as the only one in the United States where all men meet together as brethren. . . . Within the edifice there is no separation." According to Martineau, all knelt together from the "fair Scotchwoman or German to the jet-black pure African." During the sermon the sight of the "multitude of anxious faces, thus various in tint and expression, turned upwards towards the pulpit, afforded one of these few spectacles which are apt to haunt the whole future life of the observer like a dream."[20]

In 1833, the British visitor Thomas Hamilton offered a similar observation:

> Both Catholic and Protestant agree in the tenet that all men are equal in the sight of God, but the former alone gives practical exemplification of his creed. In a Catholic Church. . . the slave and master, kneel before the same altar in temporary oblivion of all worldly distinctions. . . . But in Protestant churches a different rule prevails. People of colour are either excluded altogether or are mewed up in some remote corner, separated by barriers from the body of the church. . . . Can it be wondered, therefore, that the slaves in Louisiana are all Catholics; that while the congregation of the Protestant church consists of a few ladies, arranged in well-cushioned pews, the whole floor of the extensive cathedral should be crowded with worshippers of all colours and classes?[21]

On a visit to the city in 1845, Dr. Thomas L. Nichols, a Northern social reformer, noted "something very interesting in the appearance of the worshippers" in St. Louis. Never had he seen such a "mixture of conditions and colours." On the church pavement, "white children and black, with every shade between, knelt side by side" with "no distinction of rank or colour." The most zealous abolitionist, Nichols continued, "could not have desired more perfect equality." Interracial mixing continued in the cathedral throughout the nineteenth century.[22]

Practices in St. Louis Cathedral contrasted sharply with an increasingly prevalent pattern of racial segregation and exclusion in religious institutions elsewhere in the South. The persistence of the city's Latin European religious culture, together with Sedella's radical notions of religious tolerance, forestalled the emergence of a conservative proslavery orthodoxy—an orthodoxy that had engulfed most of the South by 1830.

In 1815, Abbé Henri Baptiste Grégoire, a radical republican bishop and Jansenist sympathizer in France, had forwarded abolitionist tracts to Bishop John Carroll, head of the American Catholic Church. Grégoire urged Carroll to take a stand against slavery. Grégoire's pleas notwithstanding, the South's Catholic Church leaders adopted an aggressively proslavery stance and largely ceased to minister to Southern blacks. They affirmed planter dominance by furnishing a scriptural rationale for slavery and the conservative social order.[23]

In New Orleans, although the liberality of the city's religious culture helped delay the erosion of free black status and privilege, the city's Catholic Church gradually succumbed to the forces of racial repression. Still, Sedella's unique philosophy of religious tolerance and his spirit of revolt remained potent forces. Liberal-minded, French-speaking Catholics of both races nurtured his legacy of dissent as conservative church leaders and their supporters rallied to the South's proslavery standard.

In Virginia, in the wake of the Haitian Revolution, the Gabriel Prosser plot of 1800, and a major increase in the size of the free black population, state lawmakers enacted a new body of laws designed to consolidate and safeguard the slave regime. Following Virginia's lead, other Southern states promptly implemented similar laws. While the new codes obligated slaveholders to provide for humane treatment of their bondsmen, the laws also discouraged manumission and restricted free black's association with slaves. At the same time, distrust of the free black population inspired widespread efforts to expel them from the region. In Louisiana in 1807, the territorial legislature enacted a restrictive manumission law and a statute prohibiting the entry of free black males, which followed the South's new pattern of social control.[24]

In Louisiana, severe penalties accompanied the exclusionary law. The 1807 statute levied a fine of twenty dollars a week upon free black migrants. If the offender failed either to leave the state or pay the fine within a two-week period, the statute empowered legal authorities to arrest the violator and hire out his services to cover the costs of his trial and confinement. In New Orleans only two years earlier, city officials had attempted to restrict the movement of free people of color with a residency ordinance. The 1805 regulation required free black inhabitants to present legal proof of their free status at the mayor's office in return for a residency permit. Territorial and municipal laws notwithstanding, large numbers of free blacks migrated into the region from the North and South. In New Orleans, the free black population climbed from 4,950 in 1810 to 11,562 in 1830. Lured by the prospect of economic opportunity during the decades of economic expansion following the War of 1812, the majority of free black immigrants entered Louisiana clandestinely by way of the state's extensive network of waterways.[25]

During the territorial period, measures designed to impose a stricter social regimen accompanied attempts to impede the growth of the free black population. According to territorial legislation of 1806, free blacks must never "conceive themselves equal" to whites. The law prohibited free persons of color from insulting or striking a white person under penalty of fine or imprisonment. The legislature also required free blacks bearing arms to carry freedom papers.[26]

The Louisiana Civil Code of 1808 required free persons of color to identify themselves on public documents with the initials "f.p.c.," "f.w.c.," or "f.m.c." The code prohibited marriages between free persons of color and whites. The colonial *Code Noir* had also banned marriages between whites and free people of color, but Spanish authorities were authorized to issue dispensations. In his first year as governor in 1766, Antonio de Ulloa sanctioned the marriage of a white Frenchman and a Negro woman. Under General Alejandro O'Reilly, colonial officials also acknowledged the racially mixed marriage in November, 1769, of Catiche Villeray, a free woman of color, and Jean Paillet, a white native of France. Moreover, Spanish authorities largely ignored the widespread practice of interracial concubinage for almost twenty years. Under American authority, Louisiana prohibitions against interracial marriages were carried to such an extreme that, in at least one instance, the white male partner in an interracial union was required to take an oath that Negro blood flowed in his veins.[27]

Under the Spanish regime, lenient provisions of *Las Siete Partidas* had also provided for the legitimation of mixed-blood children born in concubinage. The statutes entitled the offspring of such relationships to become legal heirs. Accordingly, the Spanish official Nicholas Vidal bequeathed "an equal portion of his estate" to his four mixed-blood children, the progeny of his illicit relationship with a free black woman.[28]

Similarly, Andres Juen, a native of France who died in 1784, provided in his will for his three illegitimate, racially mixed children. With plantations on Bayou St. John and in Mandeville, Juen bequeathed large sums of money to his son, Juan Luis, and his two daughters, Roseta and Goton, all of whom he had "fed, educated and maintained in his home, as his own family."[29]

The Louisiana Code of 1828 strictly prohibited such practices. Under Spanish law and subsequent Louisiana statutes, an illegitimate child could acquire legal status when a parent acknowledged paternity before a notary in the presence of witnesses. By contrast, according to the terms of the new law, legitimation could occur only after the subsequent marriage of the natural parents. Although an 1831 law provided for other means of legal recognition, it likewise prohibited the legitimation, under any circumstances, of a mixed-blood child. Categorized as bastards, such children could not inherit from either parent. The court concluded that the law had placed such persons "under certain disabilities and incapacities, from which it is not the province of the courts of justice to relieve them." Unmoved by a bill in 1857 to legitimize the mixed-blood children of an interracial relationship, state senator H. M. St. Paul of Orleans Parish bitterly condemned the proposed measure: "Oh! but we are told that some of them are rich—some of them are fair, scarce a characteristic of the African origin remaining. What if they Be?. . . Does it therefore follow that we are to recognize their social equality, invite them to our homes, and give our children to them in marriage? Never! Never!"[30]

After 1812, an array of state and local regulations restricted interracial contact and free black access to public accommodations. A New Orleans ordinance of June, 1816, segregated theaters and public exhibitions. The regulation prohibited whites from occupying "any of the places set apart for people of color; and the latter are likewise forbidden to occupy any of those reserved for white persons." Beginning in the 1820s, omnibus lines either excluded persons of African ancestry altogether or operated separate cars for them as a matter of company policy. During the antebellum period, free blacks and slaves were either completely excluded or assigned to separate and usually inferior facilities in places of public accommodation.[31]

During the 1820s, mounting resentment over more intimate forms of race mixing led to an attempt to halt the infamous quadroon balls. The "Mother of a Family" complained in the *Louisiana Gazette* of the behavior of free women of color. While their insolence drove white women from the walkways, she wrote, their sexual liaisons with white men threatened the racial purity of Louisiana's best families. In June, 1828, city officials bowed to public pressure with an ordinance that prohibited white men from attending "dressed or masked balls composed of men and women of color."[32]

Boom conditions in antebellum Louisiana and a corresponding demand for labor resulted in the growth of slave and free black populations (see table). By 1830, Louisiana's nonwhite majority represented 58.5 percent of the population. The state's black majority, as well as an attempted slave revolt in March, 1829, only forty miles north of New Orleans, which left an "insurrectionary spirit" in its aftermath, prompted a reassessment of the state's security system.

Early in 1830, the arrest of Robert Smith, a free black New Orleans merchant, for the possession and dissemination of an abolitionist tract added to the frenzied atmosphere. The pamphlet was David Walker's *Appeal . . . to the Colored Citizens of the World*, published in 1829; it condemned slavery and urged blacks to rise up in revolt against white tyranny. Another free black and a number of slaves were also arrested for possessing copies of the pamphlet.

The specter of black rebellion spurred lawmakers into action. The legislature launched another major campaign to restrict the growth and movement of the free black population. In addition to renewed attempts to reduce the size of the state's nonwhite majority, the legislative agenda also included plans to organize a new militia. In the movement to reform the state's security forces, state lawmakers delivered the *coup de grace* to the free black militia. When the 1834 state militia bill withdrew formal authorization from the "Battalion of Chosen Men of Color," the free black militia came to an official end.[33]

WHITES, FREE PEOPLE OF COLOR,
AND SLAVES IN NEW ORLEANS, 1769-1860
Population figures

Year	Whites		Free People of Color		Slaves		Total
1769	1,803	(57.6%)	99	(3.2%)	1,227	(39.2%)	3,129
1788	2,370	(44.6%)	823	(15.5%)	2,126	(39.9%)	5,319
1805	3,804	(43.2%)	1,566	(19.0%)	3,105	(37.8%)	8,475
1810	6,331	(36.7%)	4,950	(28.7%)	5,961	(34.6%)	17,242
1820	13,584	(49.9%)	6,237	(23.0%)	7,355	(27.1%)	27,176
1830	20,047	(43.5%)	11,562	(25.1%)	14,476	(31.4%)	46,085
1840	50,697	(60.4%)	15,072	(18.0%)	18,208	(21.6%)	83,977
1850	89,452	(76.9%)	9,905	(8.5%)	17,011	(14.6%)	116,368
1860	144,601	(85.0%)	10,939	(6.4%)	14,484	(8.5%)	170,024

Source: Adapted from Joseph Logsdon and Caryn Cossé Bell, "The Americanization of Black New Orleans, 1850-1900," in *Creole New Orleans: Race and Americanization*, ed. Arnold R. Hirsch and Joseph Logsdon (Baton Rouge, 1991), 206.

After 1830, continued evidence of discontent in Louisiana, the emergence of an increasingly militant abolitionist movement in the North, and the Nat Turner insurrection of 1831 stiffened planter resolve. The legislative enactments of 1830 contained seventeen sections designed to regulate the activities of free people of color and reaffirmed the 1807 ban on the entry of "free negroes and mulattoes." Another law required slaveholders to ensure the removal of emancipated slaves within thirty days by posting a one-thousand-dollar bond. A modification of this measure in 1831 permitted slaveholders to forego the bond payment by obtaining permission to free a slave from the parish police jury. In this measure the legislature shifted the weight of the decision-making process to planter-dominated police juries. The juries' familiarity with local conditions, it was determined, would serve to curtail the number of domestic emancipations. Under such circumstances, the number of manumissions varied greatly from parish to parish. After 1852, however, no parish police jury approved an emancipation petition; those seeking such permission redirected their appeals to the state legislature.

Free persons of color who had entered Louisiana after 1825 were ordered to leave the state within sixty days. Although the law was modified, governing authorities reserved the right to expel any free black whom they considered undesirable. Free blacks who had entered the state between 1825 and 1830 were allowed to remain only after obtaining a special license. If they left the state, however, they would not be allowed to return, even with the license.

A subsequent modification of the law the following year permitted free black residents to return to Louisiana provided they did not "go to or return from, the West India Islands" or their absence did not exceed two years. Furthermore, state lawmakers demanded that all free blacks who had entered the state between 1821 and 1825 register their names with the parish judge where they resided or in the New Orleans mayor's office, "setting forth their age, sex, color, trade, or calling, place of nativity, and the time of their arrival in the state."[34]

In 1842, when the earlier statutes forbidding the entry of free blacks were restated, Louisiana lawmakers even anticipated the entry of prospective freedmen by banning a category of slaves referred to as *statu liberi*; the term designated a slave entitled to future emancipation. Anyone found guilty of bringing such a slave into Louisiana was subject to a fine of one thousand dollars and imprisonment.[35]

Ultimately, changing labor patterns in New Orleans also limited free black social and economic mobility. Except for a city resolution of 1822 that instructed municipal managers to hire only white laborers, economic conditions favored the class of free black skilled tradesmen, retailers, and businessmen. Under the French and Spanish, free blacks and slaves had dominated the skilled professions. As the city evolved into one of the nation's largest port cities, free black artisans continued to dominate some skilled trades. By the 1850s, however, most of the city's free black workers were unskilled laborers facing intense competition from European newcomers. During the 1840s, in the wake of a large-scale movement of German and Irish immigrants into the city, free black waiters, hotel workers, peddlers, cabbies, draymen, stevedores, and steamboat roustabouts were almost completely replaced by European workers. Competition from white laborers also contributed to the erosion of the free black property base.[36]

Under colonial conditions, white men had often bequeathed land and slaves to their black mistresses and racially mixed children. Interracial relationships had formed the basis for the state's prosperous class of Creoles of color; during the late eighteenth and early nineteenth centuries, free persons of color accumulated considerable wealth and property. After the Louisiana Purchase, free blacks benefited from the boom conditions associated with westward expansion. In 1836 in New Orleans, 855 free persons of color paid taxes on $2,462,470 worth of property (almost $3,000 worth of property per owner). During the 1840s, however, the city's free black property holders suffered a major setback. The decline of Latin European racial patterns, competition from white laborers, a sustained economic depression from 1837 to 1843, and a new array of state and local law designed to limit their mobility dealt a severe blow to free black property holders in New Orleans.

By 1850, their holdings had dropped to $755,765 and in 1852, the total real estate holdings of 234 property owners had declined to $401,300 (an average of $1,715 worth of real estate per owner).[37]

By 1860, free persons of color had recouped some of their losses. In that year, 283 free black property owners possessed $724,290 worth of real estate ($2,559 per property owner). Still, during the antebellum era some militant anti-Negro factions challenged the right of free blacks even to own property. In 1795, Spanish law had affirmed that "free people of color, enjoying by law the same advantages with the other members of the nation with which they are incorporated, may not be molested in the possession of their property, injured, or ill-treated under the penalties provided by laws for the safety and security of the property of white persons." Accordingly, Spanish statutes exempted free people of color from taxation. While American law required free blacks to pay taxes, Louisiana's governing bodies generally upheld colonial precedents touching on property rights. In 1836, the Louisiana Supreme Court decided in favor of François Boisdoré and John Goulé, both free men of color, in a case involving their rights as stockholders. The directors of the Citizen's Bank of Louisiana had attempted to deprive the men of their bank stock on the grounds that the bank's corporate charter denied stock ownership, "either directly or indirectly" to "persons not being a *free white citizen* of the United States." Boisdoré and Goulé won their case on appeal. In 1859, state lawmakers devised an extreme attack on free black property rights with legislation that prohibited them from owning liquor licenses, coffeehouses, and billiard halls.[38]

Free blacks sometimes fought and sometimes evaded the increasingly sever legal restrictions that governed their lives up to the outbreak of the Civil War. In 1833, a group of armed men attacked a segregated streetcar bound for Lake Pontchartrain after the white driver refused to allow them to board. During the summer of 1843, Voltaire Vonvergne, a free man of color, led a group of his friends onto a railway car reserved for whites. When he and his associates refused to leave the coach, railway workers unfastened the car from the train. In the ensuing violent confrontation, Vonvergne fired a shot at the conductor. An angry white mob attacked and nearly beat him to death before New Orleans police arrested him for violating the state's segregation ordinances.[39]

Separate institutions created by the city's Anglo-Protestant free black community evoked a similarly harsh reaction. After the Louisiana Purchase, free blacks who migrated to New Orleans from other areas of the United States gravitated to the city's American section, the Faubourg St. Marie or Second Municipality, which stretched from Canal to DeLord Street (present-day Howard Avenue). Protestant and English-speaking, they introduced their own distinctive blend of African and North American culture into Creole New Orleans. In response to the rising tide of race discrimination, they established two historically autonomous black institutions, the African Methodist Episcopal (AME) Church and Prince Hall freemasonry.[40]

Anglo-Protestant free black leaders had founded the AME Church and Prince Hall freemasonry in the North during the revolutionary era. At the outset, they condemned slavery and demanded equal rights. Even though they assumed a much less militant demeanor in creating churches and lodges in the antebellum South, the church suffered a major setback in 1822, when South Carolina suppressed the large AME congregation in Charleston as a consequence of the Denmark Vesey conspiracy. In New Orleans, despite repeated raids and arrests, the free black church, in tandem with the Prince Hall masonic lodges, flourished as a separate black institution until the late 1850s, when city authorities forced the church to close.[41]

Although conditions worsened in the South during the 1830s, an AME organizer planned for the establishment of a church in New Orleans. Early in the 1840s, local Prince Hall freemasons established contact with a Missouri AME minister working on a steamboat shuttle from St. Louis to New Orleans. In 1844, when white leaders of St. Paul's Methodist Episcopal Church introduced segregated seating and other discriminatory measures, free black leaders withdrew from St. Paul's and established their own church under AME auspices—St. James AME Church. In 1848, the burgeoning congregation acquired legal authorization from the state legislature with an act of incorporation. The church's existence as a corporate entity, however, was short-lived.

From the outset, city officials harassed and arrested church members. In 1848, surveillance of St. James produced evidence of white participation in religious services. Suspecting the whites of seditious activities, police raided the church and arrested over fifty free blacks and slaves and four whites (three men and a woman). A city official forwarded details of the incident to the state attorney general with a recommendation for legislative action. In 1850, lawmakers adopted an enactment that revoked the church's corporate status. Nevertheless, the church and the lodges continued to grow, with overlapping leadership. Within ten years, black leaders established five AME churches and three Prince Hall masonic lodges.

During the 1850s, police continued to harass church and lodge members. The AME minister John M. Brown was arrested five times for refusing to exclude slaves from services. In 1853, in a press account of the church, a New Orleans correspondent for a Mississippi newspaper characterized St. James as one of a number of evils in the city that required a "root and branch" eradication. The writer described the "large brick church . . . which is under the control of a negro Bishop, and where services are performed by a negro minister, in direct violation of the laws of the State." The observer also warned its readers that a "Bishop Allen, of Philadelphia, occasionally visits this city to look after the fortunes of his black flock, and no doubt infuses in them a spirit of hostility to the whites."[42]

Similarly, many whites must also have viewed the unsupervised activities of the city's clandestine masonic lodges with extreme alarm. In February, 1857, police arrested about thirty free blacks and slaves gathered at the Orleans Ballroom for a masonic ceremony. A city magistrate, charging the men with unlawful assembly, fined the free blacks twenty-five dollars and ordered beatings for the slaves.[43]

Finally in 1858, mounting public concern over the increasing size and frequency of gatherings of persons of color led city officials to enact a severe new ordinance. The law prohibited assemblages of either free blacks or slaves for religious services or any other purposes, without white supervision. On the basis of the new regulation, the city immediately closed St. James and seized control of church property.

In subsequent legal proceedings, attorney J. J. Michel defended the city's action on the grounds that the assemblage of free persons of color in St. James represented a threat to the institution of slavery. Such gatherings afforded free blacks an opportunity to "excite to rebellion and crime, the slaves of the country; among whom may be found their kindred and friends." Furthermore, the boldness of St. James leaders in expanding their churches demonstrated "the encroaching disposition of these free negroes. If this course were allowed to go on, in a very few years the white population would really be unsafe from their aggressions." The Louisiana Supreme Court upheld the city attorney's views, concluding that the "African race are strangers to our Constitution, and are the subjects of special and exceptional legislation."[44]

In outlying areas of the state, free blacks suffered more violent forms of repression and persecution. The Attakapas region, with the largest concentration of free blacks outside of New Orleans, became the scene of a virtual reign of terror. One contributor to a St. Landry Parish newspaper, the Opelousas *Patriot*, characterized free persons of color as a "cancer upon society." Another St. Landry resident urged the expulsion "from among us [of] all free Negroes or people of mixed blood." The editor of the *Patriot* warned free black residents of the region to "flee the society of the white man voluntarily before you are compelled to do so by his irrevocable decrees."[45]

Finally in 1859, white militants in the Attakapas parishes organized vigilante committees and launched a violent campaign to drive free blacks and "suspicious" whites from the area. After a particularly bloody attack on a racially mixed colony near Bayou Queue de Tortue in Lafayette Parish, Governor Robert Wickliffe ordered the committees to disband. Continued forays by the marauders, however, persuaded many free black residents of southwest Louisiana to leave the region.[46]

Beginning in New Orleans in 1855, Lucien Mansion and other Afro-Creole leaders mobilized to assist the evacuees. Mansion, a wealthy black philanthropist, Romantic writer, and cigar manufacturer, contributed large sums of money to the migration movement. Louis Nelson Fouché, a highly educated Afro-Creole activist, also attempted to assist the refugees in the crisis. Fouché undertook plans for resettling the migrants in a proposed colony in Mexico.[47]

In July, 1857, Fouché entered into an agreement with the *Propriétaires-Associés de l'Habitation de la Confrérie de St. Pierre* (Proprietor-Members of the Dwelling Place of the Brotherhood of St. Peter). With the sanction of the Mexican government, Fouché and his associates planned to organize a colony, Eureka, for foreign emigrés and Mexican nationals in the state of Veracruz. The contract required Fouché to transport one hundred families of no fewer than four hundred persons by ship from New Orleans over a period of two to four years. In return for renouncing their American citizenship, the settlers would be assured of all the rights of Mexican citizens. Mexican President Ignacio Comonfort expressed confidence that the undertaking "will yield great good for the Republic."[48]

During the summer, another small group of St. Landry Parish refugees settled on the banks of the Popolopan River in the state of Veracruz. Their encouraging reports of the absence of caste distinctions and their success with corn cultivation prompted others to migrate. A number of St. Landry families, including members of the prosperous Donatto family, joined the Louisiana exiles.

In 1858, Emile Desdunes, a Haitian-educated native New Orleanian and an associate of Fouché, acted as an agent for Emperor Faustian Soulouque after the Haitian ruler invited the refugees to immigrate to Haiti. Desdunes offered the desperate evacuees free transportation to the island nation and assured them of political and social equality. In May, 1859, 150 free people of color departed New Orleans for Haiti. One newspaper report estimated that nearly two hundred free black residents left for the Caribbean island the following month from East Baton Rouge and St. Landry parishes. As a consequence of the turmoil surrounding Soulouque's overthrow and the reestablishment of the republic in 1859, a large number of emigrés returned to Louisiana by the end of the summer. Still, Haiti's new president, Fabre Geffrard, continued Soulouque's policy of encouraging emigration from Louisiana, and in early 1860, a group of eighty-one refugees from the Attakapas region left for Port-au-Prince.[49]

Some New Orleans newspapers also clamored for the expulsion of free people of color from the state. The *New Orleans Bee* (*L'Abeille*) claimed that without guidance from the "superior [white] race" free blacks would "lapse into a state of barbarism and crime." Such a class of persons, the *Bee* maintained, should be expelled since they were "dangerous companions to the slaves." The *New Orleans Daily Picayune* advocated their expulsion on the grounds that free blacks were a "debauching, drunken, insolent group whose main object was to tamper with slaves and thereby make them discontented." In 1859, the paper urged Louisiana legislators to follow the example of Mississippi, where lawmakers had enacted a measure requiring all free blacks to leave within a specified period of time.[50]

Though Louisiana did not banish free blacks from the state, laws designed to suppress the growth of the free black population reached a climax during the 1850s. An 1852 state law required emancipated slaves to leave the United States within twelve months. The master of the manumitted slave was required to provide $150 for deportation costs, and if the slave's departure was delayed beyond the twelve-month limit, the freedman was subject to reenslavement. Although the legislature modified the law in 1855 because of a flood of petitions, the new restrictions were equally stringent. Finally in 1857, slave emancipations were entirely prohibited, and two years later, the legislature admonished "free persons of African descent to choose their own masters and become slaves for life."[51]

After 1840, exclusionary measures and the campaigns of intimidation and violence produced the desired results. While the number of free blacks in New Orleans increased steadily between 1810 and 1840, the size of the population dropped significantly after that, from 15,072 in 1840, to 10,939 in 1860. During the same period, the population of free persons of color for the entire state dropped from 25,502 to 18,647.[52]

In 1856, the state supreme court boasted that "in the eye of the Louisiana law, there is (with the exception of political rights, of certain social privileges, and of the obligations of jury and militia service,) all the difference between a free man of color and a slave, that there is between a white man and a slave." A dissenting opinion, however, revealed a harsher reality. Slaves and free people of color, the opposing minority declared, made up "a single, homogenous class of beings, distinguished from all others by nature, custom and law and never confounded with citizens of the State. No white person can be a slave; no colored person can be a citizen."[53]

Latin European influences and economic and military necessities favored the perpetuation in New Orleans of an intermediate class of free persons of color during the early decades of the nineteenth century. Ultimately, however, the decline of Latin European institutions and the immigration of white European laborers eroded the social and economic status of the free black class. In Louisiana, as elsewhere in the South, segregation, anti-miscegenation laws, and the legal ostracism of racially mixed children signified the imposition of a two-category pattern of racial classification. While increasingly restrictive manumission laws and exclusionary measures curtailed the size and mobility of the free black population, the movement toward a dual racial order reduced all free persons of African ancestry to a degraded status.[54]

Relegated to a debased status, deprived of citizenship, denied free movement, and threatened with violence, free blacks evaded, resisted, or fled the rising tide of white oppression. In New Orleans, some French-speaking intellectuals chose to remain in the city. Like intellectuals in France and the Caribbean, they channeled some of their discontent into a new mode of artistic expression influenced by European models.

Notes for "The New American Racial Order"

[1]George M. Fredrickson, *White Supremacy: A Comparative Study in American and South African History* (New York, 1981), 94-99, 129-30; Laura Foner, "The Free People of Color in Louisiana and St. Domingue," *Journal of Social History*, 3 (1970): 406-7; James Thomas McGowan, "Creation of a Slave Society: Louisiana Plantations in the Eighteenth Century" (Ph. D. dissertation, University of Rochester, 1976), 50-275.

[2]Roger Baudier, *The Catholic Church in Louisiana* (New Orleans, 1939), 201-2. Father Cirilo de Barcelona replaced Father Dagobert de Longuory as pastor of St. Louis Church and the head of the Capuchin mission in Louisiana with the latter's death in 1776. In 1782, Cirilo was appointed auxiliary bishop by the Bishop of Cuba, with authority over Louisiana (Baudier, *The Catholic Church*, 187-200). Quotation from Gilbert C. Din, "*Cimarrones* and the San Malo Band in Spanish Louisiana," *Louisiana History*, 21 (1980): 256, n58.

[3]Din, "*Cimarrones*," 257; Caroline Maude Burson, *The Stewardship of Don Esteban Miró 1782-1792: A Study of Louisiana Based Largely on the Documents in New Orleans* (New Orleans, 1940), 117.

[4]Baudier, *The Catholic Church*, 202.

[5]Ibid., 205-6, 213.

[6]Ibid., 213; Gwendolyn Midlo Hall, *Africans in Colonial Louisiana: The Development of Afro-Creole Culture in the Eighteenth Century* (Baton Rouge, 1992), 323-24; Hans W. Baade, "The Law of Slavery in Spanish Louisiana, 1769-1803," in *Louisiana's Legal Heritage*, ed. Edward F. Haas (Pensacola, Fla., 1983), 52.

[7]Baudier, *The Catholic Church*, 275. For a firsthand description of Sedella, see A. Levasseur, *Lafayette en Amérique, 1824-1825, ou journal d'un voyage aux Etats-Unis*, 2 vols. (Paris, 1829), 2:232. For evidence of Sedella's intelligence activities, see "Letters of Padre Antonio de Sedella" (typescript translation), Howard-Tilton Memorial Library, Tulane University, New Orleans, 93-145.

[8]Baudier, *The Catholic Church*, 256-60, 275.

[9]James Alexander Robertson, ed., *Louisiana Under the Rule of Spain, France, and the United States, 1785-1807*, 2 vols. (Cleveland, 1911), 1:211.

[10]Baudier, *The Catholic Church*, 30, 275-339; Glen Lee Greene, *Masonry in Louisiana: A Sesquicentennial History, 1812-1962* (New York, 1962), 76; Auguste Viatte, *Histoire littéraire de l'Amérique Française des origines à 1950* (Paris, 1954), 221.

[11]Philippine Duchesne to Louis Barat, June 21, 1818, cited in Louise Callan, *Philippine Duchesne: Frontier Missionary of the Sacred Heart, 1769-1852* (Westminster, Md., 1957), 247. Callan incorrectly identifies the English-speaking pastor as Bishop Louis DuBourg. See Annabelle M. Melville, *Louis William DuBourg: Bishop of Louisiana and the Floridas, Bishop of Montauban, and Archbishop of Besançon, 1766-1833*, 2 vols. (Chicago, 1986), 2:518-19; Greene, *Masonry in Louisiana*, 75.

[12]Baudier, *The Catholic Church*, 275-79, 305.

[13]Charles Edwards O'Neill, " 'A Quarter Marked by Sundry Peculiarities': New Orleans, Lay Trustees, and Père Antoine," *Catholic Historical Review*, 76 (1990): 272.

[14]Judith K. Schafer, " 'Open and Notorious Concubinage': The Emancipation of Slave Mistresses by Will and the Supreme Court in Antebellum Louisiana," *Louisiana History*, 28 (1987): 179-82.

[15]Ibid.

[16]Claiborne to Secretary of War Henry Dearborn, October 8, 1806, in Dunbar Rowland, ed., *Official Letter Books of W.C.C. Claiborne, 1801-1816*, 6 vols. (Jackson, Miss., 1917), 4:25-26. Sedella's close ties to the Afro-Creole community are corroborated by Audrey Marie Detiege, *Henriette Delille, Free Woman of Color: Foundress of the Sisters of the Holy Family* (New Orleans, 1976), 11.

[17]Albert A. Fossier, *New Orleans: The Glamour Period, 1800-1840* (New Orleans, 1957), 334; Melville, *Louis William DuBourg*, 2:857-58.

[18]Melville, *Louis William DuBourg*, 2:858; Fossier, *New Orleans*, 331, 333.

[19] Melville, *Louis William DuBourg*, 2:857; Fossier, *New Orleans*, 332.

[20] Ira Berlin, *Slaves Without Masters: The Free Negro in the Antebellum South* (New York, 1974), 326; Harriet Martineau, *Retrospect of Western Travel*, 2 vols. (London, 1838), 1:259.

[21] Thomas Hamilton, *Men and Manners in America* (Philadelphia, 1833), 40-41.

[22] Thomas Low Nichols, *Forty Years of American Life* (1864; reprint ed., New York, 1937), 127-28.

[23] Randall M. Miller, "The Failed Mission: The Catholic Church and Black Catholics in the Old South," in *Catholics in the Old South: Essays on Church and Culture*, ed. Randall M. Miller and Jon Wakelyn (Macon, Ga., 1983), 157-70; Ruth F. Necheles, *The Abbé Grégoire, 1787-1831: The Odyssey of an Egalitarian* (Westport, Conn., 1971), 251 n39, 277.

[24] Willie Lee Rose, *Slavery and Freedom*, ed. William W. Freehling (New York, 1982), 24-27. For developments in Louisiana along the lines Rose describes, see Joe Gray Taylor, *Negro Slavery in Louisiana* (Baton Rouge, 1963), 223-24.

[25] H. E. Sterkx, *The Free Negro in Ante-Bellum Louisiana* (Rutherford, N.J., 1972), 93-164; see population table in Chapter 3.

[26] Sterkx, *The Free Negro*, 161, 240-41.

[27] Marcus Christian, "A Black History of Louisiana," Typescript, Marcus B. Christian Collection, Earl K. Long Library, University of New Orleans, n.d., chapter 16:34; Virginia R. Dominguez, *White by Definition: Social Classification in Creole Louisiana* (New Brunswick, N. J., 1986), 24-25; Mary Louise Christovich and Roulhac Toledano, "Role of Free People of Color in Tremé," chapter 16 in *Faubourg Tremé and the Bayou Road*, eds. Christovich and Toledano, *New Orleans Architecture*, 8 vols. (Gretna, La., 1980), 6:90; Annie Lee West Stahl, "The Free Negro in Ante-Bellum Louisiana," *Louisiana Historical Quarterly*, 25 (1942): 301-96.

[28] Christian, "A Black History," chapter 16:34; Christovich and Toledano, "Role of Free People of Color in Tremé," in *Faubourg Tremé*, ed. Christovich and Toledano, 6:91.

[29] Laura L. Porteous and Walter Prichard, "Index to Spanish Judicial Records of Louisiana, 71, September, 1784," *Louisiana Historical Quarterly*, 24 (1941): 1260.

[30] Sterkx, *The Free Negro*, 180, 246.

[31] Roger A. Fischer, "Racial Segregation in Ante Bellum New Orleans," *American Historical Review*, 74 (February, 1969): 931-33.

[32] (Baltimore) *Niles' Weekly Register*, November 5, 1825; Fischer, "Racial Segregation," 935.

[33] Roland C. McConnell, *Negro Troops of Antebellum Louisiana: A History of the Battalion of Free Men of Color* (Baton Rouge, 1968), 102-4; Sterkx, *The Free Negro*, 98.

[34] *Acts of the State of Louisiana*, 1830, 90; Sterkx, *The Free Negro*, 101, 121-29, 144; Schafer, "Open and Notorious Concubinage," 167; Christian, "A Black History," Chapter 6, 34-37.

[35] Stahl, "The Free Negro," 330.

[36] Sterkx, *The Free Negro*, 221; Christian, "A Black History," Chapter 3, 1; Foner, "Free People of Color," 423-27; Roger W. Shugg, *Origins of Class Struggle in Louisiana: A Social History of White Farmers and Laborers During Slavery and After, 1840-1875* (1939, reprint ed., Baton Rouge, 1968), 118-19; Robert C. Reinders, "The Free Negro in the New Orleans Economy, 1850-1860," *Louisiana History*, 6 (1965): 274-85.

[37] Loren Schweninger, "Prosperous Blacks in the South, 1790-1880," *American Historical Review*, 95 (February, 1990): 34-38; Reinders, "The Free Negro in the New Orleans Economy," 280; Richard Tansey, "Out-of-State- Free Blacks in Late Antebellum New Orleans," *Louisiana History*, 22 (1981): 384-85.

[38] Christian, "A Black History," Chapter 15:13; Reinders, "The Free Negro in the New Orleans Economy," 283; quotations from David C. Rankin, "The Tannenbaum Thesis Reconsidered: Slavery and Race Relations

in Antebellum Louisiana," *Southern Studies*, 18 (1979): 25, and *Boisdoré and Goulé, f.p.c. v. Citizen's Bank of Louisiana*, No. 2956, 9 La. Ann. 506 (1836).

[39]Fischer, "Racial Segregation," 936; Sterkx, *The Free Negro*, 245.

[40]Joseph G. Tregle, Jr., "Creoles and Americans," in *Creole New Orleans: Race and Americanization*, eds. Arnold R. Hirsch and Joseph Logsdon (Baton Rouge, 1992), 154-56; Joseph Logsdon and Caryn Cossé Bell, "The Americanization of Black New Orleans," ibid., 208.

[41]Lerone Bennett, Jr., *Before the Mayflower: A History of Black America*, rev. ed. (New York, 1986), 82-84; Donn A. Cass, *Negro Freemasonry and Segregation: An Historical Study of Prejudice Against American Negroes as Freemasons* (Chicago, 1957), 13; Loretta J. Williams, *Black Freemasonry and Middle-Class Realities* (Columbia, Mo., 1980), 12-14; Charles Spencer Smith, *A History of the A.M.E Church* (1922; reprint ed., New York, 1968), 14.

[42]Smith, *A History of the A.M.E.*, 33-36; for the act of incorporation, see 430-31. Joseph A. Thornton, "A History of St. James A.M.E. Church," in *The Jubilee Anniversary Program, St. James A.M.E. Church* (New Orleans, 1945), 18-20; Joseph A. Walkes, Jr., *The History of the Prince Hall Grand Lodge of Louisiana, 1842-1979* (N.p., 1986), 17-19; *New Orleans Daily Crescent*, October 2 and 3, 1848; *Acts of the State of Louisiana*, 1850, 179; quotations from Boston *Liberator*, September 16, 1853.

[43]*New Orleans Daily Delta*, February 22, 1857.

[44]*A.M.E. Church v. City of New Orleans*, No. 6291, 15 La. Ann. 441 (1858).

[45]Sterkx, *The Free Negro*, 111, 113, 298.

[46]Ibid., 297-301.

[47]Rodolphe Lucien Desdunes, *Our People and Our History*, trans. and ed. by Sister Dorothea Olga McCants (Baton Rouge, 1973), 65, 112-13, 133; Charles B. Roussève, *The Negro in Louisiana: Aspects of His History and His Literature* (New Orleans, 1937), 48, 66-67.

[48]*Documens relatifs à la colonie d'Eureka, dans l'état de Veracruz* (New Orleans, 1857), 11.

[49]Desdunes, *Our People*, 112-13; Sterkx, *The Free Negro*, 296-97, 302-3.

[50]*New Orleans Bee*, February 9, 1856, and *New Orleans Daily Picayune*, January 17, 1859, cited in Sterkx, *The Free Negro*, 308-309.

[51]Schafer, "Open and Notorious Concubinage," 167-68; Christian, "A Black History," Chapter 16:40.

[52]The statewide population figures for 1860 are taken from U.S. Bureau of the Census, Eighth Census, 1860, 194-96. Berlin, *Slaves Without Masters*, 136. The decline of the free black population in Louisiana was not an isolated phenomenon; in the South, the free black population dropped from 8.1 percent of the total black population in 1840, to 6.1 percent in 1860 (Fredrickson, *White Supremacy*, 86).

[53]Judith K. Schafer, "The Long Arm of the Law: Slavery and the Supreme Court in Antebellum Louisiana, 1809-1862" (Ph.D. dissertation, Tulane University, 1987), 9.

[54]Fredrickson, *White Supremacy*, 94-99; 129-30.

THE EMERGENCE OF CLASSES
IN THE ANTEBELLUM PERIOD*

Carl A. Brasseaux

Outsiders have consistently viewed the Acadians as a monolithic group of honest, but ignorant, and desperately poor fishermen and trappers, clinging tenaciously to an ancient way of life in the isolation of Louisiana's swamps and coastal marshes. Indeed, some popular and scholarly writers have suggested that Acadiana[1] has remained relatively unchanged since the time of the Acadian migration. Dudley J. LeBlanc, perhaps the most widely read of these writers, summarily dismisses the entire nineteenth century in his two classic works on the Acadians as though it didn't exist, ostensibly because nothing significant changed in Acadian society. Recent scholarship, however, suggests that this widely held view holds no merit.[2]

Indeed, it would appear that the foundation of the highly diversified Acadian society of the modern era was laid in the antebellum period. The catalyst for the sociological transformation of Louisiana Acadian society lay in its acceptance of materialism. In pre-dispersal Acadia and in the early years of Acadian settlement in Louisiana, the Acadians were not materialistic in the modern sense. These early Acadians aspired only to a comfortable existence, and, while it is true that they consistently produced small surpluses for the acquisition of iron and other commodities that they could not themselves produce, they did not labor to produce cash surpluses for the sake of possessing specific material goods, particularly the trappings of high social status. Thus, though significant economic differences existed between individuals, the poorest pre-dispersal Acadian considered himself no less worthy an individual than his wealthiest neighbor.[3]

This world view was carried to Louisiana by the 2,500 to 3,000 Acadian exiles who carved a new homeland in the Mississippi Valley between 1764 and 1803. Yet, it was during the late eighteenth century, when the exiles labored feverishly to recreate life as they had known it in Canada, that the seeds of a new society were planted. This new

---

*First published in Carl A. Brasseaux, *Acadian to Cajun: Transformation of a People, 1803-1877* (Jackson, Miss.: University Press of Mississippi, 1992), 3-19. Reprinted with the kind permission of the author and the University Press of Mississippi.

society was nurtured by the social and economic systems in which it took root. Frontier egalitarianism had been comparatively easy to maintain in Acadia, where slavery was unknown and where indentured servitude was a distant and unpleasant memory. In lower Louisiana, however, Negro slavery was a well established institution at the time of the Acadian migrations, and, while most of the exiles demonstrated little interest in the peculiar institution, their children and grandchildren exhibited no such apathy. Beginning in the 1780s, significant numbers of Acadians began to acquire slaves, first as wetnurses and later as field hands. By 1810, a majority of the Acadians residing in the alluvial lands along the Mississippi River and bayous Teche and Lafourche owned slaves.[4]

Automatically elevated in social status through the acquisition of their human chattel, these Acadian slaveholders soon aspired to the rarified social position of Creole planters, an ascent necessitating adoption of the materialistic values and lifestyle of their slaveholding neighbors. (Creole society, like its Acadian counterpart, was not monolithic, and upwardly mobile Acadians wished to emulate only those Creoles of higher social status than their own.) The Creole planters, descendants of European settlers in Louisiana, generally sought to recreate in Louisiana a romanticized vision of feudalistic France, with themselves as the New World aristocracy. Inspired by the French nobility's belief that a person was only as rich or powerful as he appeared to be, ambitious Creoles mimicked the Old World aristocracy, and sustained their social pretensions by building grand homes, and by purchasing carriages, fine furnishings, and domestics.[5]

Upwardly mobile Acadians who aspired to the planter caste embraced their wealthy neighbors' proclivity for conspicuous consumption; this, in turn, increased their need for money, which ultimately meant expansion of both their real property holdings and their slave labor force. Many other Acadians, however, rejected this materialistic mentality and sought to perpetuate their traditional life style in the relative isolation of the lower Lafourche Basin and in the vast prairies of southwestern Louisiana. Between these polar extremes lay a majority of the descendants of the Acadian exiles—the Acadians—who found themselves torn increasingly between the self-sufficiency of the past and the materialism of the present.

The fragmentation of the once extremely cohesive Acadian community appears to have taken place between 1790 and 1810, when second and third generation Acadians embraced both slavery and the plantation system. Slavery had been anathema to many of the original Acadian immigrants, for the refugees from the Middle Atlantic colonies— particularly Maryland—had often worked shoulder to shoulder with blacks during their long residence in the region's tobacco-producing areas. Yet, some Acadian exiles began to acquire slaves in the late 1770s. These slaves were usually females, who were apparently used as wet nurses, for they consistently appear in households with infant children. But by the 1780s, a few Acadians along the Mississippi and the south Louisiana bayous had begun to purchase male fieldhands to assist in clearing their densely wooded *habitations*. The number of Acadian slaveholders continued to grow throughout the late eighteenth century, despite an abortive slave insurrection in the predominately Acadian Lafourche District (present-day Assumption and Lafourche parishes) in 1785 which demonstrated all too clearly the ever-present threat of violence posed by the servile population. Indeed, the Acadians' increasing dependence upon slavery persisted throughout the late 1780s and 1790s, despite the exiles' rejection of Spanish efforts to engage them in more labor-intensive staple crop production.[6]

The growing acceptance of slavery by Acadians gradually transformed their transplanted culture, particularly in the waterbottoms, where staple crop production slowly began to take root. Though Acadian slaveholders still constituted a minority of the total Acadian population in the early 1800s, a majority of the Acadians residing along the Mississippi River and Bayou Teche owned human chattel by 1810. A significant majority of these Acadian slaveowners produced large surpluses of cotton for sale to the New Orleans commercial establishment.[7]

The rapid development of the emerging plantation system in Acadian settlement areas was temporarily arrested by the British blockade of Louisiana during the War of 1812, the resulting local economic depression, and a simultaneous army worm invasion, which virtually destroyed the cotton industry along the lower Mississippi River, near New Orleans, and along Bayou Teche. These setbacks, however, proved only temporary. Sugar production in Louisiana surged dramatically in the mid-1820s, as die-hard South Louisiana cotton planters turned to sugar as a result of repeated crop failures due to the "rot." By 1830, plantations were flourishing in most of the original, eighteenth-century Acadian settlement sites.

The rejuvination of the recently depressed economies in the Acadian parishes resulted directly from the introduction of sugar cultivation. The 1828 crop in particular provided an impetus for economic regeneration. Impressed by the substantial profit margin which the sugar industry then afforded planters, a small number of Acadian farmers began to cultivate sugar in the mid-1820s. The Pierre A. Delegos report on sugar production indicates that, in 1829, ninety-two Acadian farmers—constituting approximately .5 percent of the state's Acadian heads of households—produced sugar commercially. Among these pioneer Acadian sugar growers, fifty-six farmers produced at least twelve hogsheads (1,000 lbs.) of sugar in the river parishes (St. James, Ascension, Iberville, and West Baton Rouge), while fifteen Acadian households manufactured an average of fourteen hogsheads in Assumption and Lafourche parishes. West of the Atchafalaya River, thirteen St. Martin and Lafayette parish Acadians boasted a median output of 31.6 hogsheads per farm.[8]

From these modest beginnings, the Acadian sugar growers quickly emerged as a significant force in the Louisiana sugar industry. By 1849, 295 Acadian sugar growers were scattered widely among South Louisiana's parishes: West Baton Rouge, 29; East Baton Rouge, 1; Iberville, 62; Ascension, 23; St. James, 17; Assumption, 59; Lafourche, 23; Terrebonne, 7; St. Mary, 12; St. Martin, 38; Lafayette, 23; St. Landry, 6; Vermilion, 3; Calcasieu, 1. The uneven geographic distribution of sugar growers

The Emergence of Classes in the Antebellum Period

matched their varying degrees of commitment to the industry. Along the Mississippi, for example, Acadian participation in the sugar industry was confined to a small circle of wealthy planters in St. James and Ascension parishes. The wealth generated by the industry attracted more and more Acadian farmers to sugar. Literally hundreds of Acadian farmers in neighboring Iberville and West Baton Rouge parishes—at least 650 and 262 respectively—became sugar growers by 1850. Meanwhile, the number of Acadian sugar growers in Assumption and Lafourche parishes tripled between 1829 and 1850.[9]

The marked increase in Acadian participation in the sugar industry coincided with a significant rise in sugar production levels on individual farms and plantations. In 1829, for example, only five Acadian sugar planters produced 100 hogsheads or more of sugar in the river parishes, while none of their Vermilion, Teche, and Lafourche Valley counterparts could claim this distinction. In fact, only two of the fifteen Lafourche area sugar growers produced more than twenty-five hogsheads, their largest output being forty-two hogsheads. The tentative nature of the Acadian sugar industry changed rapidly in the 1830s and 1840s. Capital investment in the industry rose dramatically during these decades as production levels increased.[10] The growing Acadian commitment to the sugar industry produced a corresponding rise in local sugar production. Sugar production in the Acadian parishes rose from 2,820 hogsheads in 1829 to 16,590 hogsheads in 1850; profit margins increased proportionally as cane growers began to employ the economies of scale.[11]

The significant profits generated by sugar in the late antebellum period served as the catalyst for the socio-economic transformation of Acadian society in the mid-nineteenth century. This transformation is perhaps best reflected in the sudden and dramatic growth of the number of slaves on Acadian plantations. In 1810, only one Acadian owned more than fifty slaves; by 1860 forty-nine met this criterion, the minimum required for classification as a large slaveholder according to Karl Joseph Menn. (See Appendix A) Scores of additional Acadians also counted themselves among the region's planter aristocracy by the Civil War, having acquired at least $10,000 in real estate and more than twenty slaves. Yet, the wealthy remained a relatively small segment of the total Acadian population. With the exception of Iberville Parish, where planters resided in slightly over thirty percent of all Acadian households, planters constituted between eight and fifteen percent of all Acadian households in the parishes along the Mississippi River. Planters formed a significantly smaller segment of the Acadian population along bayous Lafourche and Terrebonne—5.4, 2, and 1 percent respectively in Assumption, Lafourche, and Terrebonne parishes. Planters were equally rare west of the Atchafalaya River, except in St. Martin Parish, where they were found in 20 percent of all Acadian households. Along bayous Teche and Vermilion, for example, planters constituted 8, 3 and 2 percent respectively of the Acadian households in St. Mary, Lafayette, and St. Landry parishes.[12]

Less affluent, but aspiring to the lofty socio-economic heights attained by the members of the planter caste, prosperous farmers constituted the more numerous antebellum Acadian upper middle class. The decennial federal census reports of the late antebellum period indicate that a large plurality of the sugar growers along the Mississippi River as well as bayous Lafourche and Teche were either farmers with small slaveholdings or planters of moderate means. The 1860 census, for example, indicates that 34 percent of all Acadian sugar growers in Ascension, Assumption, Iberville, and West Baton Rouge parishes failed to meet the financial criteria used in this study for identification of the planter class—ownership of at least $10,000 in real estate and twenty slaves. But even the Acadian planters, however, were only moderately wealthy by Southern standards, with 48 percent of all Acadian planters owning between $10,000 and $20,000 in real estate. Acadian sugar planters, particularly those along the river, consistently owned less than 30 percent of the total property holdings in their respective parishes. For example, in Iberville Parish, where sugar planters owned 80 percent of all real wealth, and 60 percent of all personal property, Acadian sugar planters owned 14 and 11.7 percent of each category respectively. Moreover, in Ascension Parish, where sugar planters possessed 91 percent of all wealth, Acadian sugar planters owned 28 percent of all real property and 19 percent of all personal wealth. In Assumption and Lafayette parishes, Acadian sugar growers owned 12.5 and 19.4 percent of all local property respectively.[13]

Though the economic gap between the small planter and the typical farmer was frequently small, the groups were separated by an ever-widening cultural gap. Having risen to the upper economic class either through their own, or, more commonly, through their parents' labors, Acadian sugar planters rapidly assumed the culture of their new economic class and its attendant social caste. *Nouveau-riche* Acadians bent upon divesting themselves of their cultural baggage initially looked to the local Creole elite for role models. By the late antebellum period, however, Acadian planters had begun to remake themselves in the image of South Louisiana's new economic kingpins—Anglo-Americans transplanted from the Eastern Seaboard. Thus, in the early nineteenth century, Acadian planters' homes, furnishings, and cultivated tastes for liquors were often slavish imitations of their Creole counterparts, particularly along the Mississippi River. In addition, many Acadian planters on both sides of the Atchafalaya—especially those with political aspirations—had begun to publicly identify themselves as Creoles, having come to consider the term "Acadian," or rather "Cajun"—its nineteenth-century incarnation, as degrading. Then, quickly responding to the emergence of new economic pacesetters later in the antebellum period, the Acadian elite followed their new Anglo-American role models to popular Gulf Coast watering holes, began raising Kentucky thoroughbreds, and built elegant Greek Revival homes resembling those introduced by the Anglos.[14]

Perhaps even more indicative of their cultural transformation are the numerous, late antebellum business ventures initiated by Acadian planters. Many Acadian planters diversified their business interests, in emulation of the Anglo-American transplants, organizing sugar-refining corporations—some with capital in excess of $100,000—and taking active roles in the organization of banks, steam navigation companies, and railroads.[15]

To maintain the lifestyle expected of their caste, antebellum Acadian planters demanded ever-increasing output from their agricultural operations. The resulting surplus in disposable income was employed not only for conspicuous consumption, but also to pay the tuition for their sons, who were sent to the finest schools in the Midwest, along the East Coast, and in New England, and their daughters, who were sent to in-state Catholic finishing schools. Upon completion of their educational careers, these Acadian scholars frequently applied their talents to management of their fathers' plantations, or to the legal, medical, and educational professions, the latter group forming the nucleus of an Acadian bourgeoisie, centered in the local parish seats.[16]

Like the planter class, the Acadian bourgeoisie was confined geographically to the fertile waterbottom parishes bordering the Mississippi River and bayous Lafourche, Teche, and Vermilion. Though the managerial, medical, educational, and legal professions were the exclusive domain of the well-born, many other trades were manned by Acadian artisans from the lower economic strata. The 1860 census lists no fewer than seventeen categories of Acadian tradesmen in Lafourche Parish. Particularly prominent among the craftsmen who constituted 20.8 percent of Lafourche's Acadian work force were carpenters, brick masons, and coopers, the latter being an indispensable segment of the local sugar economy. By 1860, these trades had become so institutionalized that Acadian artisans' households—particularly those of brick masons and carpenters—frequently included resident apprentices.[17]

The emergence of an Acadian bourgeoisie and planter class was one facet of the changing economic order in the antebellum Acadian parishes. In the late eighteenth century, Louisiana's Acadians had constituted a remarkably homogeneous group. But by 1860, wealth was concentrated in increasing amounts within the planter class and bourgeoisie. In Assumption Parish in 1860, for example, the planter class, which constituted only 5.4 percent of the Acadian households, controlled 54 percent of the total Acadian real and personal (i.e., movable) property holdings. In the river parishes, the planter caste was an even greater economic force; 15.85 percent of all Acadian households there owned 77 percent of all Acadian-owned real property and 71.88 percent of all Acadian moveable property.[18]

The trend toward concentration of wealth among the planter class in the sugar bowl parishes was not confined to the Acadian community. This point is best exemplified by the 1860 census of Ascension Parish, which reveals that although Acadian, Creole, and Anglo-American sugar planters possessed over 91 percent of all personal property within the region, Acadians owned only 19 percent of this total, and only 28 percent of the parish's real estate. Moreover, though Acadians were clearly wealthier than their Creole neighbors, who controlled only 12.9 percent of all local real estate and 10.5 percent of all local moveable property, their property holdings were dwarfed by those of the neophite Anglo-American planters. That the Americans were the real economic kingpins in Ascension Parish is revealed by the fact that only nineteen Anglo-American households possessed 50.3 percent of all local real estate and 62 percent of the area's personal wealth.[19]

The rapid accumulation of wealth by the local elite, however, did not smother the more tradition-bound Acadian yeomanry. Living in the shadow of the planter aristocracy, many Acadians maintained the mores of their late colonial-era forebears, continuing to produce small agricultural surpluses with the assistance of their sons and two or three slaves. In 1860, nearly 60 percent of Louisiana's Acadian population, a majority of whom were small farmers, resided on sugar plantations east of the Atchafalaya River.[20]

This is not to say that the coexisting cultures were entirely compatible. American sugar planters generally viewed the Acadian small farmers and the far less numerous *petits-habitants* (subsistence farmers possessing no slaves), as nuisances who "demoralized" their slaves. Not only did the small farmers' comfortable existence persuade blacks "that it was not necessary for men to work so hard as they themselves were obliged to," but the Acadians frequently hired slaves to do odd jobs, paying them with "luxuries" which their masters did not wish them to have. Planters—particularly American planters—were thus quite anxious to buy out their less affluent neighbors at prices "two to three" times their properties' actual value.[21]

Contrary to the findings of popular and scholarly writers of the late 1970s, however, the pressures did not result in a massive, involuntary exodus of Acadians from their second homeland, the so-called "Second Expulsion." The *petits habitants* were generally not intimidated by the planters' expropriation efforts and most remained on their farms, except in the river parishes. Most Acadians abhorred indebtedness and many river parish debtors—probably unlucky gamblers—found the planters' generous offers all too appealling. Other Acadian farmers lacked either the means or the willingness to comply with the flurry of police jury ordinances enacted after "the great flood of 1828" mandating the construction and maintenance of levees and public roads on waterfront properties and thus gladly accepted the planters' offers. Moreover, several Acadian families, whose eighteenth-century efforts to join relatives at Attakapas and Opelousas had been thwarted by restrictive Spanish settlement policies, sold their property at the first opportunity under the American regime and moved to the prairie parishes west of the Atchafalaya. Additional settlers, burdened with large families, sought unoccupied lands along the lower Lafourche and in Terrebonne Parish, for acquisition of riverfront property at the now-inflated prices with their modest financial resources was difficult, if not impossible.[22]

Louisiana's forced heirship laws, which required equitable division of estates among all children, made further land division impractical on many small landholdings by the 1830s. As early as 1807, 87 percent of all Acadian river-parish landholdings included less than 7 arpents frontage on the Mississippi River, while 55 percent encompassed 4 arpents or less. The typical migrant Acadian family in Terrebonne Parish, moreover, contained seven persons. Thus, with five or more heirs in the average family, young Acadian migrants from the river parishes faced the bleak prospect of inheriting a small portion of the family farm, which had already been reduced to one or two arpents in width. Finally, some *petits habitants* were undoubtedly dissatisfied with the changes wrought in their community by the emergence of the plantation system and sought relocation in more isolated regions, where more traditional Acadian values still held sway.[23]

The displaced Acadians followed two migratory patterns: Residents of the river parishes found new homes in the Lower Lafourche Valley and, to a far lesser extent, in St. Landry Parish, while settlers from the Upper Lafourche Valley established themselves in northern Terrebonne Parish, the Pierre Part region of Assumption Parish, and along Bayou Black in western Terrebonne and southeastern St. Mary parishes. The extent of these migrations is best reflected in the 1830 census of Terrebonne Parish, which indicates that 44 percent of Terrebonne's Acadian community were residents of either Assumption Parish or the river parishes in 1810. The Acadian influx continued after 1830, though on a much smaller scale. Nevertheless, immigration, coupled with the established settlers' propensity for large families, contributed to the Terrebonne Acadian community's remarkable growth rate—452 percent—between 1830 and 1860, a rate 1.65 times greater than that of Louisiana's Acadian population as a whole.[24]

Not all river Acadians were displaced by the emerging plantation system. On the contrary, a plurality of the male Acadian residents of the eastern sugar parishes were yeoman farmers. In 1860, for example, Acadian yeoman farmers, who produced small agricultural surpluses, usually with the aid of a handful of slaves, constituted 34 percent of all Assumption Parish Acadian men whose occupations were identified in the federal census reports. They also formed 41 percent of the Acadian work force in Ascension Parish, 47 percent of the St. James Acadian work force, 38 percent of the Lafourche Acadian work force, and 34 percent of the Terrebonne Acadian work force. Unlike the Acadian planters, who engaged in extensive, staple-crop production, the yeoman farmer tilled four to twenty acres—depending upon the size of the family and the number of sons in the family labor pool—and produced small quantities of cotton, sugar, peas, beans, sweet potatoes, and corn. Each of these products, with the exception of corn (which in Ascension Parish was produced in quantity for sale to planters), was grown strictly for home consumption. The diet of bayou Acadians—indeed Acadians throuhgout antebellum Louisiana—was little different from that of poor whites throughout the antebellum South. Similarly, small numbers of horses, milk cattle, hogs and work oxen provided meat, milk, leather, and transportation.[25]

Through such diversified agriculture, the typical small farm was essentially self-sufficient. Nevertheless, the presence of waterborne peddlers offering items such as calico and iron cookware apparently created the demand for manufactured goods which could not be duplicated at home, and many Acadian freeholders in the Upper Lafourche Valley supplemented their income by working as day laborers on sugar plantations, cutting cane for $1.25 per day. In Ascension, Assumption, Lafourche, and Terrebonne parishes, the number of Acadian laborers rivalled that of the freeholders: Ascension, 19.5 percent; Assumption, 27 percent; Lafourche, 28 percent; and Terrebonne, 49 percent.[26]

Acadian day laborers were far more common in Terrebonne Parish, where the standard of living was much lower than in the upper Lafourche area and in the river parishes. Fifty-one percent of Terrebonne's Acadian residents—primarily displaced river parish residents and their children, who in 1860 constituted 44 percent of the local Acadian population—owned no real estate in 1860. Most of these landless immigrants, 49 percent of all gainfully employed Terrebonne Acadians in 1860, worked as day laborers, apparently to acquire funds for land purchases and perhaps for home and land rental charges.[27]

The lot of Terrebonne's freeholders was little better than that of their landless neighbors. Families were consistently larger in Terrebonne than in other South Louisiana parishes. The typical, mature Acadian family in antebellum Terrebonne Parish was composed of eight to twelve individuals, although the median family size in 1860 was reduced by bachelors, newlyweds, and aged couples, and thus included only 7.10 persons. Median family sizes for other Acadian parishes, based on the 1860 census are as follows: Assumption, 5.53; Ascension, 5.04; Lafourche, 5.00; Iberville, 5.15; West Baton Rouge, 4.44; St. James, 5.62; St. Mary, 5.20; St. Martin, 5.69; Lafayette, 4.97; St. Landry, 3.49; Vermilion, 3.49; Calcasieu, 5.32. Yet the terrain of the Bayou Terrebonne country militated against the traditional means of supporting large numbers of dependents. For example, Acadian settlers who congregated along the low-lying banks of Bayous Terrebonne, Little Terrebonne, Black, Little Caillou, Caillou, Du Large, and Blue were able to clear only eleven percent (an average of 13.35 acres) of their natural levee landholdings, only twenty-eight percent as much property as their counterparts in Lafourche Parish. The Terrebonne Acadians thus raised only a few head of livestock, grew small quantities of corn and sweet potatoes, and adopted rice, a crop better suited to the swamp environment. In fact, by 1850, rice cultivation was so well established that Acadian yeomen individually produced small surpluses, probably for sale to local Anglo-American and Creole sugar planters. However, as the Terrebonne Parish Acadians could devote less land to herding than their Lafourche Valley neighbors, they were more dependent upon hunting as a means of augmenting their protein supply.[28]

The Terrebonne Acadians as well as their swampland cousins in the Pierre Part region of Assumption Parish did not completely sever their ties to the land. Indeed, even the residents of the ribbons of dry land along the eastern fringe of the Atchafalaya Basin were generally subsistence farmers, occasionally producing small cotton surpluses. But none of the Pierre Part residents engaged in swamp-oriented pursuits, such as cypress lumbering, fishing, and moss gathering. In 1860, only two Acadians east of the Atchafalaya were designated as "hunter-fowlers", while only one, an Iberville Parish resident, was listed as a "swamper". This swamper, however, owned $10,000 in real estate and $1,000 in personal property.[29]

Subregional, socio-economic differences among swamp, bayou, and river Acadians also characterized the Acadian population west of the Atchafalaya River. As in the east, staple crop production served as a catalyst, transforming the once classless society into a highly stratified agrarian community. At the pinacle of the new socio-economic order were sugar planters who abandoned cotton production in the 1820s for small-scale sugar cultivation. In 1829, six Lafayette Parish and fourteen St. Martin Parish Acadian sugar growers produced an average of 29.8 hogsheads. Though the number of sugar growers was initially small, and, concomitantly, production levels were low at the outset, the Acadian sugar industry grew gradually during the 1830s and 1840s. In 1850, though sugar growers constituted only 6.6 percent of the Acadian households listed in the federal agricultural census of predominately prairie Lafayette Parish, 27 percent of St. Martin Parish's Acadian farms produced sugar—an increase of 15 percent over the 1829 level. Production levels also increased. Median individual sugar production in Lafayette Parish more than doubled between 1829 and 1850, rising from 29.8 to 72.48 hogsheads per farm.[30]

Residents of Lafayette and St. Martin parishes dominated the Acadian sugar industry west of the Atchafalaya River, but small numbers of Acadian farmers cultivated sugar cane in St. Landry and St. Mary parishes. Despite the ravages of the army worm in the mid-1840s, which prompted many Anglo-American and Creole cotton farmers to adopt sugar cultivation, only three Acadian farmers in St. Landry Parish switched to this labor-intensive agricultural industry by 1850. St. Mary Parish's small Acadian community, on the other hand, engaged in sugar production, particularly in the extreme northwestern portion of the parish, where several transplanted St. Martin Parish residents congregated. In 1850, six of St. Mary's twelve Acadian farmers produced an average of 77.33 hogsheads of sugar.[31]

The scarcity of Acadian sugar growers on the upper and lower Teche vividly reflects the concentration of the Acadian sugar industry in the central Teche Valley, particularly in the areas surrounding present-day Cecilia and Loreauville. Although restricted to a small geographic area, saddled by modest production levels, and confined to a small percentage of the western Acadian population, the western Acadian sugar growers played an important role in the economic development of the southwestern parishes. Led by such influential men as Alexandre Mouton, pioneer sugar growers amassed small fortunes in the 1830s and 1840s.[32]

Many of the Acadian small farmers in the upper Teche and Vermilion valleys adopted staple crop production in imitation of the sugar planters, growing increased quantities of cotton which was not only better suited to prairie soils, but which required a small labor supply. Nevertheless, commercial cotton production demanded increased dependence upon slave labor, and Acadian slaveholdings in the western cotton belt—eastern Vermilion Parish; southeastern St. Landry Parish; the Breaux Bridge, Grande Pointe, Anse Charpentier, and Petit Anse areas of St. Martin Parish; and Lafayette Parish—grew more commonplace and progressively larger. By 1850, 61.2 percent of St. Landry's Acadian farms produced an average of 9.95 bales of cotton, while 50 percent of St. Martin Parish's Acadian farms, particularly those in the Breaux Bridge and Parks areas, produced cotton commercially, harvesting an average of 6.82 bales annually. Finally, in Lafayette Parish, on the other hand, 55.4 percent of all Acadian farms engaged in commercial cotton production.[33]

Lafayette Parish was the hub of the cotton belt's emerging commercial agricultural system. In 1860, 75 percent of the region's large slaveholders were of Acadian parentage. Slaveholding was prevalent in all segments of local Acadian society. In 1850, 61 percent of the area's Acadian farmers engaged in the production of staple crops, particularly cotton and sugar, while, in 1860, 83 percent of all Acadian households possessed black slaves.[34]

Lafayette Parish was at an agricultural crossroads, located on the fringes of the Central Louisiana cotton belt, the South Louisiana sugar bowl, and the Southwest Louisiana cattle country. Plantations thus reflected the mingling of the region's diverse economic pursuits. In 1850, for example, the Alexandre Guidry plantation produced 113 hogsheads of sugar, 4,520 barrels of molasses, 15 bales of cotton, 240 bushels of sweet potatoes, and nearly 1,300 head of livestock. With the exception of sugar and molasses, this pattern of production was maintained, on a smaller scale, on small slaveholders' farms, which constituted the backbone of the Acadian cotton belt economy. This stability permitted large and small Lafayette Parish farmers to experiment with new staple crops during the last decade of the antebellum period. Rice was the most successful of these experimental crops, with local rice production increasing from less than one ton in 1850 to nearly 380,000 pounds in 1860, the third highest total in the state.[35]

Rice was grown on the prairies west of Lafayette Parish, but only as "providence rice" sown haphazardly in low areas and watered only by rainfall. The benign neglect exhibited by these rice growers pervaded all aspects of agriculture in the Acadian prairies. Commercial agriculture and the slaveholdings which it necessitated consequently were practically unknown on the southwestern prairies. Unlike the fertile Lafayette, St. Martin, and southern St. Landry Parish waterbottoms, the prairies possessed thick sod and a very shallow clay pan which militated against agriculture, particularly with the wooden implements traditionally used by the prairie Acadians. It is hardly surprising, therefore, that the overwhelming majority of prairie Acadians depended upon cattle production for their livelihood.

The ease with which cattle could be raised on the open prairies as well as the availability of unclaimed land had drawn Acadians away from the region's principal water courses since the 1770s. The influx of Acadians into the remote areas west of Bayou Vermilion and north of Bayou Queue Tortue, however, remained small until the late antebellum period, when hundreds of non-slaveholders migrated to western Vermilion, St. Landry, and Calcasieu parishes.

As in the river parishes, the exodus of small farmers was apparently prompted by the emergence of the local plantation system, progressively shrinking family landholdings through forced heirship, and the availability of cheap government lands in the southwestern prairie area. The Acadian migration to the unsettled prairie is clearly reflected in the 1830 census of St. Landry Parish, in which Lafayette and St. Martin Parish immigrants constituted 28 percent of all parochial households. In the remote areas of present-day Acadia Parish, such as the Mermentau River Valley, however, immigrants constituted an overwhelming majority—73 percent—of the region's Acadian households.[36]

The transplanted bayou Acadians soon developed a life style far different from that of their erstwhile eastern neighbors, a mode of living much more compatible with their ancestor's non-materialistic values. The Acadians frequently squatted on government lands, particularly along the narrow gullies punctuating the treeless plains. In 1860, for example, 49 percent of all Acadian households in St. Landry Parish owned no real estate. The prairie Acadians perpetuated the self-reliant spirit of their Acadian forebears, engaging in subsistence agriculture and ranching without the assistance of slaves. The 1860 slave census, for instance, indicates that the slaveholding percentages among the Acadian communities of Calcasieu and Vermilion parishes were 16 and 22 percent respectively. Thus relying upon the family labor pool, prairie Acadians cultivated eight to ten acres of corn—the staple of the antebellum Acadian diet—and only one acre of providence rice. These crops were grown on real estate holdings which in Vermilion and Calcasieu parishes averaged only $529.67 in value. In St. Landry Parish, Acadians cultivated only one or two acres of cotton for home consumption. Finally, the typical prairie farmer raised twenty-five to one hundred cattle and twenty to forty hogs.[37]

Although the prairie dwellers retained the subsistence agricultural practices of their non-materialistic forebears, many western Acadians paradoxically became commercial livestock producers during the antebellum period, apparently in order to acquire land. The increasing emphasis upon livestock production was prompted by the rapid proliferation of herds with only minimal management on the verdant prairies as well as consistently high beef prices which, as early as 1811, ranged from $15 to $20 per head at New Orleans. Attracted by such favorable market conditions, some Acadian cattlemen regularly drove their herds to Crescent City[38] markets, using the same trails blazed by their ancestors. Proceeds of these sales were invested in cheap government lands, and, over the years, these acquisitions were consolidated into large *vacheries* (ranches). By 1850, St. Landry, Vermilion and Calcasieu parishes boasted twenty 500-acre ranches and one *vacherie* containing 5,000 acres.[39]

The growth of the Acadian *vacheries*, a barometer of the region's growing prosperity, accurately reflects the corresponding increase in livestock production. In 1850, fully one-fourth of Calcasieu Parish's Acadian ranches contained over 500 head of beef cattle. Moreover, thirteen southwestern Louisiana *vacheries*—seven of which were in Calcasieu Parish—contained over 1,000 beeves. Cattle, however, were the not the only measure of wealth on the Acadian prairies. Small, sturdy Creole ponies abounded on the grasslands; in fact, of the 233 Acadian households enumerated in the 1850 agricultural census of southwestern Louisiana, only two lacked horses. Moreover, 31 percent of the aforementioned residences contained at least twenty horses, and 11 percent, most of them in Calcasieu Parish, boasted at least fifty mounts.[40]

Despite the evident prosperity and increasing concentration of wealth among the emerging Acadian cattle barons, life changed very little on the prairie frontier. Unlike their counterparts in the cotton and sugar belts, wealthy ranchers did not engage in conspicuous consumption. On the contrary, the typical rancher lived in a two-or-three room cypress and *bousillage*[41] house which differed only in its proportions from its more modest, one-room predecessor which remained in use among the less affluent prairie cattlemen. Ranchers' homes were sparsely furnished with cypress furniture, a striking contrast to the elegantly appointed homes of the Acadian planter class. Unlike the planter class, the *nouveau riche* ranchers generally shared their poor neighbors' disdain for formal education, preferring instead training in agriculture and the domestic arts for their numerous progeny.[42]

The cattle barons' life style was little different from that of their employees. Indeed, the 1860 census indicates that a significant minority of prairie Acadians, most of whom were small landholders, worked as day-laborers, probably herdsmen and drovers employed by the large ranches. In Calcasieu and Vermilion parishes, adult laborers constituted 33.5 and 22.5 percent respectively of all gainfully employed Acadian adults. These laborers evidently sought temporary employment to finance the acquisition of locally plentiful public lands or to expand existing herds, for fully 80 percent of the Vermilion Parish laborers owned real estate and cattle. The laborers' median property holdings[43] furthermore constituted only 20.5 percent of the parochial average.[44]

The emerging social stratification on the Acadian prairies typifies the regional socio-economic and cultural differences which emerged in Louisiana's Acadian community in the antebellum period. Originally composed of an economically homogeneous group of subsistence farmers and ranchers, Acadian society was transformed by changing economic conditions, particularly the rise of staple crop production in the waterbottom areas and the adoption of commercial agriculture by many local Acadian farmers. Rapid accumulation of wealth and slaves between 1830 and 1860 by these commercial farmers, particularly by the sugar growers, resulted in rigid social stratification.

Notes for "The Emergence of Classes in the Antebellum Period"

[1] Dudley LeBlanc, *The Acadian Miracle* (Lafayette, La., 1966); and Dudley LeBlanc, *The True Story of the Acadians* (Lafayette, La., 1932). On the body of mythology clouding Acadian history, see Glenn R. Conrad, "The Acadians: Myths and Realities," in Glenn R. Conrad, ed., *The Cajuns: Essays on Their History and Culture* (Lafayette, La., 1978), 1-20. On the changing view of the nineteenth-century Acadians in recent historiography, see, among others, Vaughan B. Baker, "The Acadians in Antebellum Louisiana: A Study in Acculturation," in Conrad, ed., *The Cajuns*, 115-28; Carl A. Brasseaux, "The Founding of New Acadia: Reconstruction and Transformation of Acadian Society in Louisiana" (thése de doctorat, 3e siécle, Université de Paris, 1982), vol. 2; James H. Dormon, *The People Called Cajuns: An Introduction to an Ethnohistory* (Lafayette, La., 1983), passim; and Lawrence E. Estaville, Jr., "Changeless Cajuns: Nineteenth-Century Reality or Myth?," *Louisiana History*, 28 (1987): 117-40.

[2] Carl A. Brasseaux, *The Founding of New Acadia: The Beginnings of Acadian Life in Louisiana, 1765-1803* (Baton Rouge, 1987), 3, 16, 124, 131, 132, 188.
    The Acadian world view was due in part to the failure of the French colonists to duplicate in the New World the feudalistic trappings of the Old. See William J. Eccles, *France in America* (New York, 1972); William J. Eccles, *The Canadian Frontier, 1534-1760* (Albuquerque, N.M., 1969); and R. C. Harris, *The Seigneurial System in Early Canada* (Madison, Wis., 1966).

[3] Brasseaux, *New Acadia*, 188-97.

[4] Mathé Allain, *Not Worth a Straw: French Colonial Policy and the Early Years of Louisiana* (Lafayette, La., 1988), 70-88; Lilian Creté, *Daily Life in Louisiana, 1815-1830*, trans. by Patrick Gregory (Baton Rouge, 1981), 68-77, 88-91, 96-116; Sidney Louis Villeré, *Jacques Philippe Villeré: First Native-Born Governor of Louisiana, 1816-1820* (New Orleans, La., 1981).

[5] Brasseaux, *New Acadia*, 35-54, 188-97.

[6] Ibid., 128, 196-97; Walter Prichard, Fred B. Kniffen, and Clair A. Brown, eds., "Southern Louisiana and Southern Alabama in 1819: The Journal of James Leander Cathcart," *Louisiana Historical Quarterly*, 28 (1945): 823-24; Joseph Landry Estate, February 1809, Probate Records, St. Landry Parish Courthouse, Opelousas, Louisiana; hereinafter cited as St. Landry Probate Records; Anaclet Cormier Estate, January 27, 1810, St. Landry Probate Records; Elizabeth Godin Estate, July 5, 1810, Ascension Parish Original Acts, Book J, 195; Pierre-Louis Berquin-Duvallon, *Vue de la colonie du Mississipi, ou des provinces de Louisiane et Floride occidentale, en l'année 1802* (Paris, 1803),118.

[7] Jehu Wilkinson, "Judge Jehu Wilkinson's Reminiscences," *Attakapas Gazette*, 11 (1976): 141; J. Carlyle Sitterson, *Sugar Country: The Cane Industry in the South* (Lexington, Ky., 1953), 100-150. Louisiana's sugar output increased again significantly in the early 1830s, when the plantation system emerged in the Acadian river parishes. Mark Schmitz, *Economic Analysis of Antebellum Sugar Plantations in Louisiana* (New York, 1977), 15; André LeBlanc, "The Parish of Assumption," *DeBow's Review*, 9 (1850): 289; Pierre A. Delegos, *Statement of the Sugar Made in 1828 and 1829* (New Orleans, 1829, copy on deposit at The Historic New Orleans Collection.

[8] In this chapter, the term "sugar grower" signifies anyone engaged in sugar cultivation. Delegos, *Statement*; P. A. Champomier, *Statement of the Sugar Crop Made in Louisiana, 1849-1859* (New Orleans, 1860), 1849, 9-50.

[9] Delegos, *Statement*.

[10] Ibid.; Fifth decennial census of the United States, 1830, Iberville Parish; hereafter cited as 1830 census, with parish name; Seventh decennial census of the United States, 1850, agricultural schedules, Iberville Parish; hereafter cited as 1850 Agricultural Census, with parish names; 1850 Agricultural Census, West Baton Rouge, Lafourche, Assumption, Terrebonne, St. Mary, St. Martin, Lafayette, St. Landry, Vermilion, and Calcasieu parishes; Sitterson, *Sugar Country*, 100-150.

[11] Delegos, *Statement*; 1850 Agricultural Census, West Baton Rouge, Iberville, Asccension, St. James, Assumption, Lafourche, Terrebonne, St. Mary, St. Martin, Lafayette, St. Landry, Vermilion, and Calcasieu parishes; 1810 Census, West Baton Rouge, Iberville, Ascension, Assumption, St. James, Lafourche, St. Martin, and St. Landry parishes; Eighth decennial census of the United States, 1860, Population Schedules, West Baton Rouge, Iberville, Ascension, St. James, Assumption, Lafourche, Terrebonne, St. Mary, St. Martin, Lafayette, St. Landry, Vermilion, and Calcasieu parishes; hereafter cited as 1860 Census, with parish names.

[12] 1860 census, West Baton Rouge, Iberville, Ascension, St. James, Assumption, Lafourche, Terrebonne, St. Mary, St. Martin, Lafayette, St. Landry, Vermilion, and Calcasieu parishes.

[13] For an excellent study of this phenomenon, see Vaughan B. Baker, "The Acadian in Antebellum Louisiana: A Study of Acculturation" in Conrad, ed., *The Cajuns*, pp. 115-28. See also, Joseph G. Tregle, Jr., "Early New Orleans Society: A Reappraisal," *Journal of Southern History*, 18 (1952): 20-36; W. H. Sparks, *The Memories of Fifty Years: Containing Brief Biographical Notices of Distinguished Americans and Anecdotes of Remarkable Men; Interspersed with Scenes and Events Occurring During a Long Life Chiefly Spent in the Southwest*, 4th ed. (Macon, Ga., 1882), 380-81; *Houma Ceres*, August 16, 23, 30, 1856; *Opelousas Courier*, August 7, 1858; *New Orleans Daily Picayune*, August 14, 15, 16, 1856; Leonard V. Huber, *Creole Collage: Reflections on the Colorful Customs of Latter-Day New Orleans Creoles* (Lafayette, La., 1980); Zelia Rousseau Mouton to Alexandre Mouton, January 12, 1830, Mouton Papers, Collection 40, folio 1-i, Southwestern Archives, University of Southwestern Louisiana, Lafayette, Louisiana; hereafter cited as Mouton Papers, with folio numbers; Desirée Martin, *Les veillées d'une soeur ou le destin d'un brin de mousse* (New Orleans, 1877), 12-14; George F. Reinecke, trans. and ed., "Early Louisiana French Life and Folklore: From the Anonymous Breaux Manuscript, as Edited by Professor Jay K. Ditchy," *Louisiana Folklore Miscellany*, 2 (1966): 7; hereafter cited as *Breaux Manuscript*.

[14] Amos Webb to Alexandre Mouton, May 17, 1834, Mouton Papers, Box 1, folio 1-s; Sidney A. Marchand, *The Flight of a Century (1800-1900) in Ascension Parish, Louisiana* (Donaldsonville, La., 1936), 103; Alexander Mouton (grandson of the governor) Memoirs, Lucile Meredith Griffin Papers, Collection 26, Tablet 1, p. 7, Southwestern Archives, University of Southwestern Louisiana.

[15] Newspaper advertisement quoted in Marchand, *The Flight of a Century*, p. 58; William Henry Perrin, *Southwest Louisiana Biographical and Historical*, 2 parts (1891; reprint ed., Baton Rouge, 1971), Pt. 2:15, 62, 68, 94, 95, 99, 121, 158, 166, 206, 209, 210, 211, 228-230, 242, 244, 246, 315, 320; *Goodspeed's History of Southeast Missouri . . .* (1888; reprint ed., Cape Girardeau, Mo., 1964), 419-20; Harry Lewis Griffin, *Attakapas Country: A History of Lafayette Parish* (1959; reprint ed., Gretna, La., 1974), 44; *Biographical and Historical Memoirs of Louisiana*, 2 vols. (1892; reprint ed., Baton Rouge, 1975), 2:418; "A Condensed Autobiography of Louis Hebert" (photostatic copy in the author's possession); Napoleonville *Pioneer of Assumption*, November 24, 1877.

[16] In 1860, for example, Assumption Parish's work force boasted thirty-three carpenters, five apprentice carpenters, seven masons, and four apprentice masons. 1860 Census, Assumption Parish.

[17] 1860 Census, West Baton Rouge, Iberville, Ascension, and St. James parishes.

[18] The composite wealth of the Ascension planter caste was 91 percent of the Acadian total. 1860 Census, Ascension Parish.
    Though individual amounts varied, the pattern of property ownership exhibited in Ascension Parish appears also in West Baton Rouge, Iberville, St. James, and Assumption parishes. In Iberville Parish, for example, planters owned 49.8 percent of all real wealth and 56 percent of all personal property in the parish. Acadian, Creole, and American planters possessed the following, respective percentages of the local wealth: 12, 10, and 30. 1860 Census, Iberville Parish.

[19] 1860 Census, Population Schedules, West Baton Rouge, Iberville, Ascension, St. James, Assumption, Lafourche, Terrebonne, St. Mary, St. Martin, Lafayette, St. Landry, Vermilion, and Calcasieu parishes.

[20] Frederick Law Olmsted, *A Journey in the Seaboard Slave States, in the Years 1853-1854, with Remarks on Their Economy*, 2 vols. (1860; reprint ed., New York, 1904), 2:332-33; G. W. Pierce, "Terrebonne," *DeBow's Review*, 11 (1851): 606.

[21] William F. Rushton, *The Cajuns: From Acadia to Louisiana* (Ne York, 1979), 89; Dormon, *The People Called Cajuns*, 27. For a refutation of the Rushton findings, see Glenn R. Conrad, comp., *The Land Records of the Attakapas*, Volume 1, *Land Grants, Claims and Confirmations in the Attakapas District, 1764-1826* (Lafayette, La., 1990), ix-xxxviii.

[22] Sparks, *Memories*, pp. 375-377; LeBlanc, "Assumption," 292.
    With regard to the early nineteenth-century movement of Acadians from the river to other areas of South Louisiana, see, for example, Petition to Unzaga, March 2, 1772, Archivo General de Indias, Seville, Spain, Papeles Procedents de Cuba, legajo 189A, folio 358; *American State Papers*, 2:263; Donald J. Hebert, comp., *Southwest Louisiana Records*, 35 vols. (Cecilia/Eunice, La., 1974-1990), vol. 1.
    1810 Census, West Baton Rouge, Iberville, Ascension, St. James, and Lafourche parishes. 1830 Census, St. James, Ascension, Assumption, Lafourche, and Terrebonne parishes. 1860 Census, St. James, Ascension, Assumption, Lafourche, Terrebonne, and St. Mary parishes. Franklin *Planter's Banner*, September 24, 1847;

The Emergence of Classes in the Antebellum Period 43

Sparks, *Memories*, 379; Charles Lyell, *A Second Visit to the United States of North America*, 2 vols. (New York, 1849), 2:112.

[23] Examination of the 1840 and 1860 census reports for Terrebonne Parish indicates that 17 percent of all Acadian heads of households in 1860 resided in other parishes, particularly Lafourche Parish, twenty years earlier. See also "Death of Joseph Adrien LeBlanc," *Thibodaux Minerva*, February 9, 1856.

[24] Statistics for West Baton Rouge and Iberville parishes are unavailable, for census takers failed to differentiate between yeoman farmers and planters. 1860 Census, Ascension, Assumption, Lafourche, St. James, and Terrebonne parishes; Seventh decennial census of the United States, 1850 census, agricultural schedules, West Baton Rouge, Iberville, Ascension, Assumption, Lafourche, and Terrebonne parishes. Sam Bowers Hilliard, *Hog Meat and Hoecake: Food Supply in the Old South, 1840-1860* (Carbondale, Ill., 1972), 38-53.

[25] Sparks, *Memories*, 375; Pierce, "Terrebonne," 606; 1860 census, West Baton Rouge, Iberville, Ascension, assumption, St. James, Lafourche, and Terrebonne parishes.

[26] Henry Marie Brackenridge, *Views of Louisiana, Together with a Journal of a Voyage Up the Mississippi River in 1811, 1814* (1818; reprint ed., Chicago, 1962), 173; Berquin-Duvallon, *Vue de la colonie espagnole*, 51; Pierce, "Terrebonne," 603-6; Sparks, *Memories*, 373-78.

[27] Pierce, "Terrebonne," 601; 1850 census, agricultural schedules, Lafourche and Terrebonne parishes. In Lafourche Parish, the typical Acadian landholder cleared 47.63 acres--46 percent of his property. Sparks, *Memories*, 374; Pierce, "Terrebonne," 606.

[28] Malcolm Comeaux, *Atchafalaya Swamp Life: Settlement and Folk Occupations* (Baton Rouge, 1972), 14.
Swamp Acadians did shift from agriculture to hunting, fishing, lumbering and other non-agrarian pursuits, but only in the postbellum period, when severe floods inundated Acadian farmland along the eastern fringe of the Atchafalaya Basin, compelling the small farmers to seek their livelihood in the swamps. Ibid., 13-21.

[29] See "Judge Jehu Wilkinson's Reminiscenses," 141; Delegos, *Statement*.
Lafayette Parish's Acadian sugar growers constituted only 2 percent of the local acadian community. Delegos, *Statement*; 1830 census; 1850 census, agricultural schedules, Lafayette and St. Martin parishes.

[30] *Opelousas Gazette*, August 31, 1844.
In 1860, there were 333 Acadian residents in St. Mary Parish, most of whom were found in the Jeanerette area. 1860 census, St. Mary Parish.

[31] Seventy-five percent of St. Martin Parish's Acadian sugar growers resided at Grande Pointe (present-day Cecilia) and Fausse Pointe (present-day Loreauville). 1850 agricultural census, St. Martin Parish.
By 1860, the typical Acadian sugar planter in Lafayette Parish owned $31,023 in real property and $65,102 in personal wealth. 1860 census, Lafayette Parish; 1850 agricultural census, St. Martin, Lafayette, and St. Landry parishes.

[32] 1860 census, Lafayette Parish; 1850 agricultural census, St. Martin, Lafayette, and St. Landry parishes.

[33] Karl Joseph Menn, comp., *Large Slaveholders of Louisiana* (New Orleans, 1964), 260-61; 1860 census, Lafayette Parish; 1860 census, slave schedules, Lafayette Parish.
For detailed studies of slavery in antebellum Lafayette Parish, consult Vaughan B. Baker, "Patterns of Acadian Slave Ownership in Lafayette, Louisiana," *Attakapas Gazette*, 9 (1974): 144-48; and Richard McGimsey, "Police and Slave Patrol Regulations, 1823-1857," *Attakapas Gazette*, 10 (1975): 146-52; 1850 Census, agricultural schedules.

[34] 1850 census, agricultural schedules, Lafayette Parish; Carl A. Brasseaux, "Prosperity and the Free Population of Lafayette Parish, 1850-1860," *Attakapas Gazette*, 12 (1977): 105-6.

[35] 1830 census, St. Landry and St. Martin parishes; 1810 census, St. Landry and St. Martin parishes.

[36] Brackenridge, *Views*, 171; Frederick Law Olmsted, *A Journey Through Texas*, 2 vols., 2nd ed. (New York, 1904), 2:395; Emily Caroline Douglas Autobiography, 105-7, Department of Archives, Louisiana State University, Baton Rouge, Louisiana; 1860 census, Vermilion and Calcasieu parishes; 1850 census, agricultural schedules, Calcasieu, Vermilion, and St. Landry parishes.

[37] New Orleans.

[38] Brackenridge, *Views*, 171; Olmsted, *A Journey Through Texas*, 2:393; Glenn R. Conrad, comp., *New Iberia: Essays on the Town and Its People* (Lafayette, La., 1979), 59-60; *Planter's Banner*, March 11, 1849; Opelousas *Gazette*, November 18, 1843; 1850 census, agricultural schedules, Calcasieu, Vermilion and St. Landry parishes.

[39] Median livestock production among Calcasieu's Acadian ranches totalled 589 cattle. 1850 census, agricultural schedules, Calcasieu parish.

Frederick Law Olmsted described Creole ponies as being "descended from Norman and Arabian blood, and more valuable than the Spanish stock from Texas, being more intelligent, less vicious, better formed, but so small as to be suitable only for the saddle." In the mid-1850s, Creole ponies were valued at "twenty to sixty dollars." Olmsted, *A Journey Through Texas*, 2:393.

[40] *Bousillage* is an insulating material composed of mud and Spanish moss and, occasionally, horse hair. The mixture had many of the same insulating properties as adobe, used in the American Southwest. It was used as an infill material in external walls.

[41] Olmsted, *A Journey Through Texas*, 2:393-95, 402-3; Sylvére Thibodeau Estate, September 23, 1850, No. 1221, St. Landry Parish Probates; R. Warren Robison, "Louisiana Acadian Domestic Architecture," 64-68; and Carl A. Brasseaux, "Acadian Education: From Cultural Isolation to Mainstream America," in Conrad, ed., *The Cajuns*, 212-14.

[42] $161 in real estate, $423 in personal [movable] property.

[43] $535 in real estate and $2,303 in personal property.

THE AMERICANIZATION OF FRENCH LOUISIANA*

Lewis William Newton

It appeared to one observer of the early fifties that the rapidity and thoroughness with which the Americans were effacing the Creole civilization was much greater than that with which the Romans transformed the peoples who submitted to their arms, and that this betokened a power in American institutions and manners which nothing could resist.[1] The American advance is to a degree evidenced in the changing map of the state. Before the census of 1830 there had been but two new western or northwestern counties created since statehood; between 1830 and 1840 there were six others formed; and by 1846 at least seven additional ones had been carved from the newer section.[2] But it was not alone from the immigration from other states of the Union that the Creoles were threatened with inundation. Of Louisiana's total white population of 255,491 in 1850, 60,641 were born in other states of the Union, but this was exceeded by the foreign born, there being of this kind 67,308 whites.[3] Not greatly different were the returns for 1860, which gave a total of 295,247 free persons in the state, of whom 80,953 were born in other states, as compared with the free foreign born of 80,975. The percentage of Louisiana's foreign born was exceeded by only four other states in 1860—California, New York, Wisconsin, and Minnesota.[4]

If has been indicated in an earlier chapter of this study that in the forties there was beginning to be manifested a considerable degree of political accord between the old and the new populations. This was due, no doubt, to a better understanding among the French element of the nature and conduct of American government and their more general acquaintance with the English language, as well as to a greater willingness on the Anglo-American side to conciliate a group whose influence was no longer in the majority and whose ratio was constantly diminishing. Far from being eradicted, jealousies between the

---

*First appeared as chapter 8 in Lewis William Newton, "The Americanization of French Louisiana: A Study of Process of Adjustment Between the French and Anglo-American Populations of Louisiana, 1803-1860" (Ph. D. dissertation, University of Chicago, 1929), 192-226.

two continued to linger, but they were not so openly displayed as heretofore nor were they often marshalled in campaigns, in voting, or in public discussions.[5]

Nothing was so clearly indicative of the passing of French influence as the constitutional convention of 1844-1845. As the Anglo-American population of the state had increased, opposition to the Constitution of 1812 had risen. Dissatisfaction over the apportionment of representation in the state legislature was strong in the West Florida parishes, in New Orleans, and in the newer western and northwestern parts of the state. The doctrine of manhood suffrage had been carried far in the thirties throughout all parts of the Union, and it was particularly appealing to the small farming class of western and northwestern Louisiana as well as to the propertyless men of New Orleans. Consequently, the convention which assembled in Jackson in the summer of 1844 had three general purposes: 1. The extension of the suffrage. 2. The reapportionment of representation. 3. The reform of the judicial system.[6] The program was therefore chiefly an Anglo-American one.

There is notable evidence of the dwindling of French influence in the roster of members of the convention. Of the seventy-five names printed in the *Daily Picayune*,[7] twenty-one appear to have been French or Spanish descendants, one of whom was born in Santo Domingo, two in France, one, G. S. Guion, in Natchez, and the others in Louisiana. Two of these, Bernard Marigny, the only member of the convention who had sat in the convention of 1812, and Pierre Soulé, born in south France under the First Consul, exiled during the Restoration, and a resident of New Orleans thereafter,[8] were conspicuous defenders of the French element in the convention. With a note of regret Marigny remarked on the change in thirty-three years, since now out of seventy-seven members of this body, there are but twenty-one of French origin;"[9] and Soulé cried out with more oratorical fervor as he plead for greater senatorial representation for the district of New Orleans:

> When we cast our eyes about us we must admit that we are but strangers in this land of Louisiana. In looking around this Convention, the painful reflection is forced upon us that out of seventy-seven members, there are only eighteen coming from that population that once had the property and every thing, that were possessors of this vast territory. They have yielded to the iron rule of time, and all that they ask of this new and unconquered population that have covered the land, is to be heard. They do not ask it as an act of generosity, but they ask it as an act of justice. Will you listen to their demands? That is the question.[10]

A sense of propriety was not wanting in the selection for the presidency of the convention of General James Walker, native of Louisiana, with an Englishman for a father and a French Creole for a mother.[11]

Of the other fifty-four members listed by the *Daily Picayune*, forty were natives of other states of the Union, distributed as follows: six from South Carolina, five each from Virginia, North Carolina, and Tennessee, four each from Kentucky and Mississippi, three from Maryland, two each from Pennsylvania and Georgia, and one each from

Massachusetts, New York, Ohio, and Missouri. One was a native of Germany, and only thirteen were natives of Louisiana.

The interplay of nationalistic interests disclosed itself from time to time during the discussions and proceedings of the convention. Both French and English were spoken on the floor of the convention, about half the members being acquainted with both languages,[12] The clash of national jealousies flashed out in the consideration of three fundamental problems. The first was personal, and involved the relative rights and privileges to be accorded to the natives of Louisiana, the permanent immigrants from other states of the Union, the "birds of passage" or temporary residents, who were quite numerous, and the naturalized citizens. The second was sectional, and had to do with the balancing of power between the old French section of the state and the newer American portion, or between New Orleans and the country, which was sometimes merely a city against country contest and sometimes representative of the old against the new. The third was nationalistic, and involved the struggle for the preservation of old judicial forms, the perpetuation of the use of the French language in the legislature and in public documents, and generally the maintenance of the identity of the French population.

Though the convention had first assembled in Jackson, it adjourned from that place on the August 22, 1844, to reassemble in New Orleans on January 14, 1845.[13] It was here, in his native city, that Bernard Marigny fought the great battle both for his own population and for the naturalized citizens. He did not favor elections in June or July[14] when probably one hundred thousand "birds of passage" were in the state to exert an influence; Mr. [Christian] Roselius of New Orleans did not wish the elections in September, as a month when many native inhabitants of the state not yet baptized in yellow fever would be away while Mr. [Isaac T.] Preston, a former South Carolinian, was for inerpreting the length of residence for citizenship very liberally and was willing to give all encouragement to immigration, since it was the immigrants from other states and even "those birds of passage" who had contributed so greatly to the energy, talent, industry, wealth, and general prosperity of the state.[15] It was finally agreed that the time of elections should be the first Monday in November.[16]

On the various propositions to require four years of residence in the state and four years of citizenship of the United States for representatives to the legislature, two years of residence and of citizenship for voters, and that the governor should be a natural born citizen of the United States, there was much discussion. Some viewed these measures as unduly restrictive of immigration, some believed them necessary as a protection against temporary residents, but Mr. Marigny took them as a text for extensive discourses on the services to the state of naturalized citizens, and urged that the time of residence in the first cases be not made to run from and after naturalization and that a naturalized citizen be made eligible for the governorship. Opposing such long residence requirements, Mr. Downs of Ouachita stated there were already restrictions in Louisiana, such as the parish courts and the civil law, which tended to cause immigrants to crowd upon the Arkansas-Louisiana line "as thick as bees," who even cultivated land in Louisiana, "but they kept themselves out of her jurisdiction."[17] Marigny at different times pointed out of the honor shed upon the state by such naturalized citizens as Alexander Porter, Mazureau, Pitot, Boré, Nicholas Girod, Judge Dominick Hall, Sauvé, Derbigny, Poydras, and Don Andre de Almonaster. Against what seemed to him to be the odious attempts to restrict the rights of such as these, he exclaimed: "If ever there was a time in my life, Mr. President, that I regretted my inability to speak English fluently, it is now."[18] Marigny was ably supported in his plea by his colleagues Soulé,[19] and Eustis,[20] but his greatest antagonist was John Grymes, the distinguished lawyer of New Orleans.[21] Finally, the problems that gave rise to these debates were arranged by compromises: representatives should have been citizens of the United States for three years, residents of Louisiana for three years and of the parish for one year previous to election; suffrage should be limited to citizens of two years, residents of Louisiana two years and of the parish one year; and the requirement of nativism for the governor was struck out by a vote of 41 to 27, but no minister of any religious sect was eligible to the governorship.[22]

Sectional issues intruded themselves upon almost every occasion of debate. The country members had an irrepressible fear that New Orleans would come to engulf the political influence of the balance of the state and to control its destinies; indeed, if it had not already done so. In that light they viewed the move to transfer the convention from Jackson to New Orleans, the tenacity with which that city held to the seat of government and tried to prevent a constitutional provision for its removal, the efforts of some to set the time of elections when the city would be most populous, the motion to distribute representation in the legislature on the basis of white population, which would be more favorable to the city than to the country, and the final struggle to secure an equitable apportionment on the basis of population actually adopted in the constitution.[23] It was largely in vain that the eleven members from Orleans County, supported by others from the nearby Creole counties, combatted the Anglo-American western and northwestern delegates. When the aim was to extend suffrage to propertyless men, it little availed to show how the city alone paid half the taxes and had half the wealth of the state, while by the addition of the "sugar bowl" the proportion would run to more than two-thirds of these.[24] In voicing the attitude of his Creole constituents against the rising west, Wadsworth of Plaquemines exclaimed: "Parishes that have doubled themselves in wealth and population since 1812, are denied representation for pine-woods and sand banks. You might as well represent the deserts of Arabia. We are the wealth, the producing sources, and yet we are to have no power in the State!"[25] But the newer sections were to win. The capital was to be moved by 1847 to a point no nearer than sixty miles to New Orleans, and not to be further removed except by consent of four-fifths of the legislature; representatives were to be based on the number of electors, every parish to have at least one, but no new parish to be created of less than six hundred and twenty-five square miles; and New Orleans was limited perpetually to not more than one-eighth of the membership of the senate.

The Americanization of French Louisiana

There was something pathetic in the spirit of men like Soulé and Marigny as they watched the old order crumbling around them. They saw the parish court system, described by Eustis as "this nine-office power," that had existed since 1805 swept away to give place to the justice and district courts and the other regular American judicial arrangement.[26] It was conceded none too readily that the constitution and laws were to be promulgated in both French and English, and Marigny had no little difficulty in securing the provision to require the clerk of each house to have an acquaintance with both languages so that a member might use the language of his choice in debate. Pleading for an additional translating clerk to turn the constitution into French, Soulé remarked that

> He could not anticipate that the demand presented would be yielded as a favor to that portion of the population whose maternal language was French. They stood on an equal footing. They demanded no favors. They asked for justice alone, and that was all that could be awarded with propriety . . . all this debate . . . was surely not intended to deprive a large portion of the population of the State of the means of making themselves acquainted with the Constitution. . . . For himself and those whose maternal language was French, they were ready to yield up the vanity of speaking in the language most familiar to them, and to address the Convention in English; but what they insisted upon was this, that all the proceedings, all that was said and done should be published as well in French as in English, for the information of their common constituents.[27]

Again, in pleading for the allotment of senators by municipalities, rather than to the city in general, he exclaimed:

> The first and third municipalities are occupied by a scattered population; they are the remnants of those that once alone occupied all the extensive territories of the State. They have yielded to the new population that have overflowed the land, and whose activity and energy have raised the State to so high a degree of prosperity. But in ceding, they are still there, and as American citizens, they have a right to be heard and consulted. Will this house turn a reluctant ear to their demand through me, that they have the privilege conserved to them of being represented by those they may choose to delegate?[28]

At another time proud Marigny, often speaking in defense of the loyalty of both Creole and naturalized French, exclaimed with bitter regret:

> The Anglo-Saxon race have invaded every thing. They have supremacy in both houses of the legislature. . . . The hostility to the French language is stimulated by the design to abrogate our civil system of law. . . . I know that the Anglo-Saxon race are the most numerous and therefore the strongest. We are yet to learn whether they will abuse the possession of numerical force to overwhelm the Franco-American population. . . . We could have become Americans without you, for we have the moral and political virtues that characterize the true republican, and it depended alone upon ourselves to restrain you from any superiority. Beware of abusing the power which we have supinely suffered to pass from our hands to yours.[29]

And as if to assuage the poignancy of the French feeling, men like Mr. Ratliff of West Feliciana were heard to exclaim at one time:

> The day has gone by when there is any danger growing out of a difference in population, to guard against. We have become a united people.[30]

And at another:

> Why should we indulge in petty jealousies and idle apprehensions? Is it probable that the legislature will ever be composed of strangers to our institutions, of persons having no vote or interest in our community? We have only to look at the principal and most of the subordinate offices of our State, to be convinced that there is a natural feeling of preference in favor of the native population. There is no need of fostering it by unworthy appeals. The highest offices of the State are in the hands of creoles of the State. The Speaker of the House, the president of the Senate, the governor of the State, the treasurer of the State are all creoles. The two gentlemen whose names have been mentioned, as probable candidates for governor, are both creoles. Has any one complained? No, the American population from the other States, and the naturalized population, are well satisfied that it should be so.[31]

The entire opposition of fifteen votes to the final adoption of the constitution in the convention came from Orleans County and adjoining counties,[32] but in the popular referendum the constitution went over in the state by a majority of 12,173 in favor to 1,245 against it.[33] The first legislature under the constitution decided upon the removal of the capital to Baton Rouge after January 1, 1849.[34] For a while both French and English were spoken in the senate, but in the house this practice seems to have disappeared by 1846.[35] In 1853 a bitter controversy arose in the house over the mere proposition to dismiss the two enrolling clerks who did not understand French or to employ others who did.[36] And in 1858 a bill passed the house by unanimous vote providing that no document or other matter should be printed in French except such as was directed by the 129th article of the constitution.[37]

While Slidell was building his great political fortune upon the buoyant democracy of the west and northwest parts of the state, together with the aid of political methods in whose use few even of the Anglo-Americans were adept,[38] it was yet an asset to Soulé and less distinguished office seekers to be able to address the French in their native tongue while intermingling with them at their barbecues or other public gatherings.[39] By 1857 it was thought by the *Daily Crescent*[40] to be a "novel proposition" and "altogether anti-Democratic to talk about a 'question of races' in connection with politics," though it had just discovered in the French side of the *Courier* a presentation of a candidate as a Creole. In addition to those of French nativity who had represented Louisiana in Congress, the *Crescent* named Bouligny, Gayarré, and Mouton as Creoles who had gone to the Senate, and Aristide Landry, Alcée Labranche, B. G. Thibodaux, Emile LaSère, Louis St. Martin, and George Eustis, Jr., as of that group who had served in the House. In the thirty-four years of statehood from 1812 to 1846 governors of the French element had served for eighteen years and those of the Anglo-American for sixteen, but from 1846 to 1860 only one of French name, Paul O. Hébert, served in that office, and for only three years.[41]

Let us say that a decade or more before the Civil War political and economic assimilation between the French and Anglo-Americans in Louisiana was almost complete, and that afterwards political and economic blocs in that state were to be formed on other bases. To a certain degree, also, there had come about a social interfusion. But where racial differences were reenforced by contrary languages, laws, habits, and religion it is not to be expected that full cultural assimilation had taken place in a little more than a half of a century. It is to a consideration of some of the forces which affected this cultural amalgamation that attention is now directed.

By some it might be expected that an investigation would disclose that public education in Louisiana was much retarded because of the predominance there of the Catholic religion. That does not seem to have been the case. When the United States acquired the territory its civilization was raw, which it is believed that the foregoing study will show was due to other causes than religion. It was reported to Jefferson that not more than half the inhabitants could read and write,[42] Major Stoddard declared that a person in the country who could read and write was considered as something of a prodigy,[43] and Sparks related that it was the practice to inquire of any new grand jury who among them could write in order that he might be made foreman.[44] Governor Claiborne repeatedly recommended measures for the encouragement of education, believing it to be the best means of eradicating national antipathies,[45] but aside from the difficulty of conducting schools in both languages, of raising funds, and of a certain inertia among the Creole population, he was met by the same indifference to the benefits of public education that then prevailed among people of other states.

By the thirties several colleges had been established, some of which were receiving annual appropriations from the state, and a statute had been in existence since 1811 providing for an annual state subsidy to one school in each county.[46] Whether private religious, or state-supported, these institutions usually taught both French and English, were attended by pupils of both populations, and the Catholic colleges do not seem to have exerted pressure to proselyte the Protestant students who entered their halls.[47] It was said by an Anglo-American paper[48] that the inaugural message of Governor Derbigny, of the French party, 1828, was strong for education, much stronger than the two preceding messages of Governor Johnson. In 1842 the second municipality of New Orleans instituted the first real public free school with an attendance of 260 pupils, which by 1846 had grown to 1,936.[49] About the same time the first municipality established a similar school for its complex elements.[50] The report of the state treasurer at the close of 1844 showed that the expenditures by the state for public education in the period 1812-1844 had amounted to $1,710,559.40.[51] After the Constitution of 1845 had made provision for the establishment of a public school system,[52] an act was passed in 1848 establishing such a system and appropriated $550,000 for its maintenance during the next year.[53] The principal argument which seems to have retarded this legislation was that of the impossibility of the success of a general and public common school system in such a scattered population of such diversity of languages and interests.[54] It was in this crucible of weakly supported colleges and a public school system which had perhaps been too "hastily cobbled up, to comply with the Constitutional provision,"[55] where the French and English languages were about on a parity before the Civil War, that an important element of the youth of both populations learned much of one another and to a degree wore off their mutual antipathies.

In so far as they contributed to the dissemination of general information, especially of the political or economic kind, the newspapers of Louisiana were an aid to assimilation, but in so far as they were printed in both French and English they tended to perpetuate the distinction of language. It has been noted that the *Moniteur de la Louisiane* was the first to make its appearance, in 1794. A semi-weekly, with never an extensive circulation,[56] and that almost wholly among the French population, it took no part in the politics of the United States and was chosen by Governor Claiborne as the vehicle for the publication of the laws in French. The *Louisiana Gazette*, semi-weekly, in the beginning printed only in English, an avowed Federalist paper, indulged at times in criticism of Claiborne's administration. The *Orleans Gazette*, a daily, and both the *Louisiana Courier* and the *Telegraph*, tri-weeklies, were each printed in both French and English. Enjoying the most extended circulation, the *Courier* survived all the others of these early journals, and under the editorship of [J. B. S.] Thierry and [Joseph Charles] St. Romes was a force in upholding the rights of the Creole population, but was for the most part a supporter of the established government.[57] Besides other temporary journals, *L'Ami des Lois*, or the *Friend of the People* [sic], printed in both French and English, made its appearance just before the close of the territorial period.

Ephemeral journals sprang up from time to time, and in 1827 there were said to be in the state some fifteen or sixteen newspapers, seven of which were in the country.[58] However, within the next five years James Stuart reported: "*Ten* newspapers were published in Louisiana in 1810, and now *only nine* are published. Louisiana is the only state in which the number of newspapers has decreased in the last twenty years. . . .[59] In 1836 *The Bee*, in analyzing the newspaper reading habits of the thirty thousand whites in New Orleans, remarked that "we may suppose that not 1 in 8 persons are subscribers to newspapers—probably not 1 in 10. Many of these 3,000 take two or more of our journals—of which there are still 4 morning and 2 evening. . . . *The Bee* has about two-thirds that number; the *Bulletin* has more than one-half."[60] Three years later Buckingham pronounced *The Bee* the largest daily in New Orleans if not in the world. *The Bee*, the *Louisianian*, the *Louisiana Advertiser*, and the *Courier* were all printed in both French and English in the French quarter, the *Courier* being "the most moderate, gentlemanly, and fair," and read chiefly by Creoles. The American quarter had five dailies, all in English: the *Commercial Bulletin*, the *True American*, which was no honor to its name, the *Picayune*, the *Times*, and the *Sun*, the last three of which were classed as small papers with nothing much in them but puffs and jokes.[61] By 1847 the first municipality, or

French quarter, was reported to have only one newspaper, the third none, and the second ten dailies.[62] The New Orleans *Crescent* and the New Orleans *Delta* were the other important papers to appear before 1860. Commenting upon the rivalry for the office of printer for the constitutional convention of 1852, the *Delta* spoke of it as a "brisk contest between the representatives of Old Fogyism, the Bee, and young America, the Crescent." The caucus of the convention decided 39 to 26 in favor of the *Crescent*. "And thus Young America triumphed, and great was the flow of champagne!"[63]

Though something has been said in an earlier chapter concerning the more local influences of the theater in New Orleans, it is necessary here to consider that institution as a cultural influence upon the population of the state. For the attendance at the New Orleans theaters was not limited to the people of the city, but, in fact, extended to those of the entire southwest. The first theatrical performances were wholly in French, and not until the close of 1817 is it recorded that an American company was struggling to maintain itself at the theater on St. Philip's Street. With much insistence the *Louisiana Gazette* recounted the financial losses of the company and urged better support, adding: "On the encouragement now afforded, will, perhaps, depend the existence of an American Theatre, in this city, for many years to come."[64]

After the building of the great Orleans Theater in the French quarter and of Caldwell's American Theater in Faubourg St. Mary, there were performances of high excellence and rivalry of great piquancy. James Stuart pronounced the renditions at the French theater by Parisian performers as especially good, and though the admission to the boxes and pit was then two dollars the house was filled to excess.[65] During the season 1833-1834 the *Louisiana Advertiser* and the *Mercantile Advertiser* engaged in a heated controversy with the *Louisiana Courier* over what was believed to be the hostility of the last of these journals toward the American Theater and its performers. The *Courier* denied the charge of hostility, but thought itself free to criticise such a "lame" production as that of the "Beggar's Opera", the "money-making managers, a company with the same sickening grimaces and gestures every night, many of the members of which seldom deeming it of importance to learn their parts, an orchestra that cannot play a national air correctly, and nightly disturbances in the house that forbid the presence of ladies."[66] In the middle thirties Tyrone Power found the French theater "an exceedingly well appointed, handsome place, with a company very superir to the American one, and having its pieces altogether better mounted." It was not only chiefly the resort of Creole families, but also of many "American ladies of the best class."[67]

Some comments in the *Weekly Picayune* of 1833 and 1839 are vividly descriptive of the status of the New Orleans theater of that time. "This season," ran an excerpt from the first of these, "if those who are fond of impressive harmony do not have their fill, it will be the fault of none but themselves. The theatre in Orleans street will assemble all that is fine in genius and talent—the orchestra will be perfect—the *artistes* numerous, and the charms complete."[68] After attending the performance of Rossini's *Barber of Seville* at Orleans Theater on the opening night, the writer commented upon the large and fashionable audience, adding: "The Creoles are devoted to their theatre, and instead of dividing patronage among opposing interests, they apply their united energy to the support of one." This was the only way they could employ the best actors from Europe and keep them for a year. He was gratified, too, with the "entire courtesy and easy politeness visible in every part of the house, and extended by every individual to his neighbor," the "silence observed during the performance, and the propriety of the plaudits," no actor ever being improperly interrupted.[69] Later he rejoiced at the probability of the reestablishment of the Italian opera, since New Orleans was "the central point for all nations," and the proportion of those coming there with a love for music was about ten to three. "The Frenchman, the German, the Neapolitan and the Spaniard," he continued, "form two-thirds of our population, and the two last named nations, would, in the person of the lowest laborer, give their last dollar to the characters of their native airs."[70]

But the American editors of the *Picayune* were forced to admit the superiority of their French neighbors over themselves in a refined taste for music. This was particularly impressed upon one of their staff after witnessing a performance at the St. Charles Theater. The first piece was but "some little trifling chickabiddy song," which was vigorously encored from the pit. During the overture, "There was a general hitching about, bustle, talking, and a feeling of uneasiness and inattention." Thereupon an old Frenchman in the audience finally exclaimed:

> Sacre! I 'ave nevaire see one people like dese Americaines. He 'ave no—no wat you call him, gusto for de bon music. He come to de theatre, and wen de grand overture is play superb, magnifique, he no make de applause—he no say noting. Dam, he made de row—he chaw away on apple and chestnut, and every ting, like pig, and make such disturbance, dat he keep every one from de enjoyment. Why he no do so all de time? Wen dat gal come on de stage, and begin for sing 'one petite baby catch some sleep', aha! dat is de music for him—den he clap his hand and make de grand encore all for disturb me now? Oh! mon Dieu! mon dieu! dis is too much for one man to carry.[71]

And so the French Theater continued its sway till after the Civil War. Lyell pronounced its orchestra the best in America, its audience quiet and orderly, and, like many another, went into raptures over the beautiful and handsome Creole women, who "were attired in Parisian fashion, not over dressed, usually not so thin as the generality of American women; their luxuriant hair tastefully arranged, fastened with ornamental pins, and adorned simply with a colored ribbon or a single flower."[72] Ampère, too, praised this opera as better than that at New York, and was struck with "the charming types of half Parisians, half Creoles," especially in the boxes.[73] It was amid such music lovers that Jenny Lind, on her visit in 1851, could sing to crowded houses, at first drawn almost wholly from the American portion of the city, but later also from the French quarter and the surrounding country as far as Mobile.[74]

To this brief treatment of the three chief vehicles for intellectual and artistic influence in Louisiana—the school, the press, and the theater—a little must be added concerning the church as it represented or affected the relations between the two chief populations of the state. It may be stated at the outset, however, that no attempt will be made here to compare the relative merits as civilizing agencies of the Catholic church, to which almost all of the French population adhered, and of the Protestant church, to which most of the Anglo-Americans professed allegiance. Nor will it be attempted to separate the traits and habits of the one or of the other group that might seem to have grown from its particular religion. If the greater levity and indulgence in amusement among the French population on the Sabbath was attributed by some of their American neighbors to their Catholic religion, it could be answered that this was a result not of religion but of national or European influence. The Catholic churches were usually filled during the Sunday morning services, but the afternoons and evenings were spent in such gayety as shocked the more puritanical among the Americans. On the other hand, there were few of the strictly puritanical kind among the early American settlers of Louisiana. The hard circumstances of western life together with the fact of sparse settlements, especially before the thirties or forties, had contributed to lessen the dependence of the people of that region upon the institutional church and to make them more inclined to follow the bent of their economic or social interests without respect to religious consideration. Consequently, when settlers migrated from the western states to Louisiana, or through that alembic from the states farther east, they were so totally lacking or else so easy-going in religious attitudes as not only not to become offended with the practice of Catholicism but even, if it suited their interests, to fall in with it. Even as those who maintained their Protestant faith came slowly into contact with the Catholic majority, each tended to tolerate the other if agreeable to their mutual economic interests. It was for these reasons, no doubt, that so little evidence of religious animosities between the two populations appears before 1860.

From the beginning of American domination until about 1824 there ran a schism in the Catholic organization in Louisiana which illustrates the difficulty of breaking the roots which enmeshed that organization in a foreign attachment and of adapting it to the soil of the United States. When Bishop Peñalver, whose seat had been at New Orleans, departed for Havana in 1803, he left Reverend Patrick Walsh as administrator in Louisiana. But the authority of the latter was disputed by Father Antonio Sedella, parish priest of New Orleans, whose claim to independence was recognized by a sufficient majority in the city as to enable him for nearly two decades to hold complete control of St. Louis Cathedral. Many of the Spanish clergy departed with the Spanish authorities, and with them went also all the ladies of the Ursuline Convent save six choir nuns and two lay sisters. Father Walsh tried in vain to detach the people from Sedella's authority by withdrawing from him the faculties of the church and by establishing the Convent of the Ursulines as the only place for the administration of the sacraments and the celebration of divine offices.[75]

In September, 1805, Louisiana was placed under the jurisdiction of Bishop Carroll of Baltimore, and the following year he appointed as vicar-general for the diocese of New Orleans Reverend John Olivier, formerly chaplain of the Ursuline nuns. Having left copies of the papers of his appointment with Governor Claiborne, Olivier wrote to Sedella in order to secure recognition of his authority in New Orleans, but in a letter of the 25th of February, 1807, Sedella openly refused to recognize Olivier's authority. Aged, sickly, and impotent in the exercise of his offic, Olivier permitted all the parish churches to suffer from want of attention until his resignation in 1810. Meanwhile, Governor Claiborne and Secretary Madison had chosen to regard the quarrel between the Catholic oficers as a factious one within the church, with which the government need have no concern, until it began to appear that Sedella was intriguing to secure recognition of his authority by Napoleon. When it was learned that Sedella was the intimate friend of the Spanish Casa Calvo and that he and a Mr. Castillon had furnished a Mr. Castanedo with four thousand dollars to obtain from Napoleon an immediate nomination of Sedella to the bishopric of New Orleans, Claiborne called upon Castillon to furnish him a copy of the correspondence which had arisen between Mr. Portalis, the Miniser of Worship in France, and himself over the late schism among the Catholics of the city, promising that no use would be made of it to Castillon's injury.[76] Secretary Madison also wrote Bishop Carroll denouncing such an attempt at foreign interposition, which he promised would "be made by our minister a topic of such observation, as without overcharging the wrong, may be calculated to prevent repetitions." He believed that many of the inhabitants of New Orleans had fallen in with this intrigue not through "any deep or insiduous designs," but rather through flattery of the Sedella party and the natural tenderness of France towards a people once a part of the French nation.[77]

On the 29th of December, 1810, Reverend Mr. Sibourd arrived in New Orleans from France, having been appointed by Bishop Carroll to succeed Olivier. He endeavored to collect the English-speaking Catholics at the Ursuline chapel, but at first found few who cared to profit by his ministry.[78] Two years later Du Bourg was appointed administrator-apostolic of the diocese of Louisiana and the two Floridas. Having secured at first a sort of recognition from Sedella, though he would not attempt to say mass in the cathedral, he at length aroused such excitement by an attempt to suspend Sedella from office that he was forced to flee to the parish of Acadia. However, being more in favor with General Jackson than the foreign-intriguing Sedella, Du Bourg had the honor to return to New Orleans and conduct a great public service of thanksgiving in St. Louis Cathedral for the Hero of New Orleans. Leaving Sibourd to contest authority with Sedella, Du Bourg sailed for Rome, where in September, 1815, he was consecrated bishop of New Orleans. But on his return, the cathedral still being against him, he decided to make St. Louis the center of administration. In the meantime, Sedella had thought of applying to Congress to incorporate the trustees of the cathedral in his favor.[79] To exalt St. Louis over New Orleans as a seat of the bishopric was something to alarm the citizens of the latter place, and by 1820 they were imploring Du Bourg, who before had feared to risk his life among them, to come to the cathedral and say mass. He was greeted with joy when he presided over the Christmas mass of that year, and the schism was at last practically healed. In 1824 he transferred his seat premanently to New Orleans.[80]

The growth of Protestantism in Louisiana was slow. Governor Claiborne took pains to assure the people of their freedom of religion in order to prevent the break-down of religious worship of any kind.[81] Until the spring of 1805 not one step had been taken toward the introduction of a Protestant minister into New Orleans, but in May and June of that year meetings of the Protestants of the city took steps which led to the incorporation of a congregation of Protestants of the County of Orleans with an Episcopal pastor who should receive a salary of two thousand dollars a year. When the vote was taken upon the election of a clergyman, forty-five favored an Episcopalian, seven a Presbyterian, and one a Methodist.[82] Yet three years later, though there were enough Americans in the city to form a respectable congregation, not a Protestant church had been built and there was little encouragement given to a Presbyterian preacher who had recently moved in.[83]

When Schermerhorn and Mills, Presbyterian missionaries sent out under the patronage of the Massachusetts Missionary Society and the Missionary Society of Connecticut, visited New Orleans in 1812 with the object of forming a Bible society, they found all religious life in Louisiana at a low ebb. There were perhaps fifteen of the Catholic clergy in the state, five or six of whom resided in New Orleans. Presbyterian missionaries had visited the city the winter before, and there was at that time a Baptist and a Methodist missionary in New Orleans, but, for lack of encouragement, the former departed with Schermerhorn and Mills and the latter was preparing to leave soon. Not one Protestant church existed in the state, unless the one about to be established by the Baptists at Opelousas be counted. The Methodists had an itinerant preacher upon the Red River and the Washita. A Presbyterian church might be established with a prospect of success, and a French missionary might do some good, but otherwise missionaries would be of little value until the people should learn the English language. They found the Catholic authorities willing to cooperate in the distribution of Bibles,[84] and on the return of Mills in 1815 not only did Sedella take an active part in the circulation of the New Testament, but so absolutely clamorous were the inhabitants for the three thousand copies printed in French that as many as fifty were said to be calling for one at the same time.[85]

On the 27th of July, 1815, the corner stone of the first Protestant church in New Orleans was laid[86]—of the Episcopal demonination. In the early part of 1818 the legislature incorporated the Presbyterian Church of New Orleans, "a second Protestant Church for this growing city."[87] A year later Latrobe found the Presbyterian clergyman, Mr. Learned, and the Episcopalian, Mr. Hull, devoting their principal energies against the pretended profanation of the Sabbath, and he believed that in time the American majority would enable them to make that day as "gloomy and ennuyant, as elsewhere among us."[88] At present, however, though the Americans were inclined to sneer at the French manners and morals, they were much too busy in their mad rush to make money to give much heed to religious observance.[89] When Timothy Flint descended the Mississippi in 1823, he did not see "a single Protestant house of worship" from Baton Rouge to New Orleans, but Catholic spires were seen at intervals of six or seven miles. At that time there were an Episcopal and a Presbyterian church in the French quarter of the city and a Presbyterian one in Faubourg St. Mary.[90]

By the beginning of the thirties the laxity of Sunday observance in New Orleans seems to have gripped the Americans quite as strongly as the French. Apparently in 1831 for the first time the American Theater gave Sunday evening performances, when the house was "thronged."[91] James Stuart observed that there were "fewer churches here in relation to the population than in any other of the American cities," that the general tendency was towards Sunday amusements, and that neither the one Presbyterian church, now become Unitarian, nor the one Episcopal church was well attended.[92] Contradicting the general charges that the Catholic clergy who countenanced such laxity were themselves immoral, the Reverend Theodore Clapp, Congregationalist minister in New Orleans in 1832, pays them a high tribute for their "unflagging zeal, and ardent, persevering industry," and especially for their spirit of self-sacrifice when they to a man remained in the city during the cholera epidemic of that year, while the Protestant clergy departed with the exception of himself and another who was confined to his bed with consumption.[93]

A fairly correct idea of the relative strength of Catholics and Protestants in the state may be obtained from a review of several contemporary estimates. Ingraham about 1832 judged that New Orleans had fifteen or sixteen thousand Catholic whites and nearly six thousand Protestant, that there were nearly seven hundred Protestant and about sixty-five hundred Catholic communicants, and that there were ten Protestant churches, presided over by seven or eight clergymen, and six Catholic chapels and churches, with twenty-five regularly officiating priests.[94] In 1833, Tanner accounted for sixteen Baptist churches in the state, with twelve ministers and two hundred and seventy-eight communicants, two Episcopalian ministers, and about twenty parishes most of which were provided with priests.[95] Buckingham, about the close of the decade, gave a similar estimate of the Catholic clergy, and stated that there were in Louisiana fourteen Baptist ministers with about one thousand communicants, twelve Methodist ministers with about two thousand members, five Presbyterian clergymen with about three hundred communicants, and three Episcopalian ministers with not more than two hundred members. In New Orleans were four Protestant churches—the Episcopal church on Canal Street, the Presbyterian church on Lafayette Square, built in 1834, the Methodist Episcopal church on Poydras Street, erected in 1836, and the Congregational church, oldest of all, built as a Presbyterian church in 1819.[96]

Understanding as one does the anti-Catholic, as well as the anti-foreign, principles of the Native American party, it is not surprising that during the forties and fifties, when this political association was remarkably aggressive and when the new American majority was particularly overweening in Louisiana, the discord between Protestants and Catholics should have reached its highest point before the Civil War. Yet, even during this period, the Catholicism of the Creoles seems to have softened the antipathies of the Protestants which were in fact directed primarily toward the Irish and German Catholics. Exception was taken in the lay press to anti-Protestant insinuations appearing in the *Catholic Messenger*, which was described as the official paper of the archbishop of New Orleans,[97] and in the *Southern Standard*, another Catholic paper in the city,[98] political candidates bandied the religious question on the hustings,[99] and a writer in one of the journals of 1855, in enumerating the characteristics of that year listed this: "Effervescence of religious intolerance having reached its highest degree of intensity."[100]

Neither at the beginning nor at the close of the Civil War was the Creole effaced from his native land. He was outnumbered, his power was broken, in his political and economic relations he was trimmed to the American pattern, his tongue was forced more and more toward English phrases, and is blood tended little by little to lose its purity through intermarriage. But there remained of him still a distinct, if somewhat diminished, silhouette; a personality that scorned full absorption into Americanism; a lover of music, of French opera, and of blossoming gardens; a dreamy laggard on the road to progress; when blessed with a plantation, living like an old seigneur, when all but a human derelict in the Acadian community, eking out a scant subsistence and a foe to change; and at all times gayer and perhaps even kinder than his neighbor, the Anglo-American.

Notes for "The Americanization of French Louisiana"

[1] J. J. Ampère, *Promenade en Amérique—États-Unis-Cuba-Méxique*, 2 vols. (Paris, 1860).

[2] *Fifth Census or Enumeration of the Inhabitants of the United States*, 1830 (Washington, 1832), 104-7; *The Sixth Census of the United States, 1840* (Washington, 1853), 258-62; H. N. Burrough's *Map of Louisiana*, 1846.

[3] *The Seventh Census of the United States, 1850* (Washington, 1853), 474.

[4] *The Eighth Census of the United States, 1860* (Washington, 1864), 194-96.

[5] This statement of Pierce Butler, in his *Judah P. Benjamin* (Philadelphia, 1907), 65, could yet describe the feeling existing about 1842: "The French Creole might be a Democrat, or he might be a Whig, but in the eyes of his English neighbor he was always a Frenchman, constitutionally opposed to development and progress."

[6] Statement of Mr. Preston, *Debates in the Louisiana Convention of 1844-1845* (New Orleans, 1845), 190.

[7] September 1, 4-8, 8, 13, 1844.

[8] Alfred Mercier, *Biographie de Pierre Soulé, Sénateur à Washington* (Parish, 1848), 1-28; J. W. Cruzat, "Biographical and Genealogical Notes concerning the Family of Philippe de Mandeville Ecuyer Sieur de Marigny, 1709-1810," in *Publication of Louisiana Historical Society*, 5 (1911): 42-53.

[9] *Debates in the Convention*, 866.

[10] Ibid., 639. Soulé does not seem to have included himself and the two others of foreign birth in his reckoning.

[11] *Daily Picayune*, September 1, 1844.

[12] According to Mr. Lewis, *Debates in the Convention*, 835.

[13] *Debates in the Convention*, 1845, 1-19.

[14] The up-country trade began to move toward New Orleans with the spring rains and reached its peak in May, June, and July.

[15] *Debates in the Convention*, 19-23.

[16] The constitution, ibid., 951-60.

[17] *Debates in the Convention*, 61.

[18] Ibid., 62, 226-32, 322-23.

[19] Ibid., 178.

[20] *Debates in the Convention*, 94.

[21] Ibid., 70, 105, 210ff. Mr. Grymes (page 70) uttered this view on immigration which was characteristic of a later period: "The United States is the property of her citizens, who have a perfect right to enjoy exclusively the liberties and privileges belonging to her institutions—the heritage bought by the blood of their ancestors. They have fostered and protected those institutions, which are our own. If we choose to call others to participate, well and good."

[22] Ibid., 263, 951-60.

[23] *Debates in the Convention*, 23-24, 34-38, 94, 118, 143-55, 308-12, 325-33, 337-61, 390, 397, 462, 537-42.

[24] Ibid., 153, 326-27, 338.

[25] Ibid., 550.

[26] *Debates in the Convention*, 693ff., 697ff., 796.

[27] *Debates in the Convention*, 90.

[28] Ibid., 605.

[29] Ibid., 866.

[30] *Debates in the Convention*, 60.

[31] Ibid., 87.

[32] Ibid., 941.

[33] *New Orleans Weekly Delta*, December 1, 1845.

[34] Niles's *Weekly Register*, 70 (March 21, 1846): 36.

[35] Sir Charles Lyell, *A Second Visit to the United States of North America*, 2 vols. (New York, 1849), 99, found English used exclusively in the house, but both languages were used in the senate.

[36] *Official Report of the House of Representatives of the State of Louisiana* (New Orleans, 1853), 8-9.

[37] *New Orleans Daily Crescent*, February 1, 1858.

[38] Mary Lilla McLure, "The Election of 1860 in Louisiana," in *Louisiana Historical Quarterly*, 9 (1926): 609-10.

[39] As did Declouet, *Daily Picayune*, September 7, 1849; and Preaux, *Daily Delta*, October 7, 1852.

[40]November 2, 1857.

[41]J. G. de Baroncelli-Javons, *Une Colonie Française en Louisiane* (New Orleans, 1909), 97.

[42]"An account of Louisiana, being an abstract of Documents in the office of the Departments of State and Treasury" (Philadelphia, 1803), pamphlet, 38.

[43]Major Amos Stoddard, *Sketches, Historical and Descriptive of Louisiana* (Philadelphia, 1812), 308.

[44]W. H. Sparks, *The Memories of Fifty Years* (Philadelphia, 1870), 377.

[45]W. C. C. Claiborne, *Official Letter Books of W. C. C. Claiborne*, ed. by Dunbar Rowland, 6 vols. (Jackson, Miss., 1917), 1:346; 3:277; 4:293.

[46]An act passed, 1805, for the establishment of the University of New Orleans—*Louisiana Gazette*, June 25, 1805. An act of March 17, 1810, appropriated $20,000 for the establishment of a college—*Moniteur*, March 21, 1810. In 1811 the legislature appropriated $39,000 to establish a college in the territory and a school in each parish, appropriating $3,000 annually to the support of the former and $500 a year to each of the latter; in 1819 the support to each parish school was increased to $600, and in 1821 to $800, a year; and an appropriation of $5,000 annually was later made to the college at Jackson—Niles's *Weekly Register*, 31 (Jan. 6, 1827): 304. Few parishes had taken advantage of the state appropriation before 1823—Timothy Flint, *The History and Geography of the Mississippi Valley*, 2 vols., 3rd ed. (Cincinnati and Boston, 1833), 323-324. In the late thirties, the following colleges were receiving state aid: College of Louisiana, at Jackson in E. Feliciana; Jefferson College, in St. James Parish; Franklin College, at Opelousas; and Centre and Primary Schools at New Orleans—J. S. Buckingham, *The Slave States of America*, 2. vols. (London and Paris, 1842), 1:361.

[47]Joseph Holt Ingraham, *The Southwest by a Yankee*, 2 vols. (New York, 1833), 1:169, 194. He estimated that about one-third the pupils in all the schools were Americans, the others French. Both languages were spoken fluently.

[48]*Baton Rouge Gazette*, December 27, 1828.

[49]Nile's *Weekly Register*, April 5, 1845, 68, 68; *Daily Delta*, December 16, 1846.

[50]*De Bow's Review*, 1851, 11:96, gives the report of the superintendent of schools of the first municipality: 2,256 scholastics registered, of whom the mother tongue of 979 was French, of 909 English, of 308 German, of 43 Spanish, of 16 Italian, and of 1 Polish. 1,163 were born in Louisiana, 306 in other states of the Union, 269 in France, 227 in Germany, 167 in Ireland, 69 in England and Scotland, 16 in Italy, 11 in Spain, and others in various countries.

[51]*Debates in the Convention* (1845), 295.

[52]Ibid., 951-960.

[53]Nile's *Weekly Register*, 75 (January 10, 1849): 32.

[54]*Weekly Delta*, April 20, 1846.

[55]*The Weekly Comet* (Baton Rouge), December 9, 1855.

[56]C. C. Robin, *Voyages dans l'interieur de la Louisiane, de la Floride Occidentale, et dans les Isles de la Martinique et de Saint-Dominique, pendant les années 1802-1806*, 2 vols. (Paris, 1807), 2:385, says that in 1804 it had not over eighty subscribers.

[57]Claiborne to Robert Smith, November 18, 1809, *Official Letter Books*, 5:13-17, gives an appraisement of newspapers then existing.

[58]*Baton Rouge Gazette*, March 31, 1827.

[59]James Stuart, *Three Years in North America*, 2 vols. (Edinburgh, 1833), 2:245-46.

[60]*The Bee*, February 24, 1836.

[61] Buckingham, *The Slave States of America*, 1:370-81.

[62] Niles's *Weekly Register*, 72 (July 2, 1847): 280.

[63] *New Orleans Weekly Delta*, July 11, 1852.

[64] *Louisiana Gazette*, March 10, 1818; also various issues from December 9, 1817, to March 21, 1818, inclusive.

[65] Stuart, *Three Years*, 2:236-37.

[66] *Louisiana Courier*, May 22, 1833; January 23, 28, 29, February 8, 1834.

[67] Tyrone Power, *Impressions of America: During the Years 1833, 1834, and 1835*, 2 vols. (Philadephia, 1836), 2:113.

[68] *Weekly Picayune*, November 5, 1838.

[69] Ibid., November 12, 1838.

[70] Ibid., December 17, 1838.

[71] *Weekly Picayune*, January 7, 1839.

[72] Lyell, *A Second Visit*, 2:93.

[73] Ampère, *Promenade en Amérique*, 2:133.

[74] C. C. Rosenberg, *Jenny Lind in America* (New York 1851), 150-51.

[75] John G. Shea, *History of the Catholic Church in the United States*, 4 vols. (Chicago and New York, 1886-1892), 2:585, 587, 588.

[76] Claiborne to Castillon, December 29, 1806, *Official Letter Books*, 4:72.

[77] Shea, *History of the Catholic Church*, 2:589-95; Thomas O'Gorman, *A History of the Roman Catholic Church in the United States*, 3rd ed. (New York, 1900), 290-91.

[78] Shea, *History of the Catholic Church*, 2:641.

[80] The material in his paragraph is from Shea, *History of the Catholic Church*, 2:671, 673; 3:356-74; O'Gorman, *History of the Roman Catholic*, 293-94, 329-31; *Records of the American Catholic Historical Society of Philadelphia*, 19 (1908-1909): 188, 196-97, 200.

[81] *Official Letter Books*, 2:12, 71-75, 82-83.

[82] *Louisiana Gazette*, April 20; May 28 and 31; June 4, 11, 14, 18; August 22, 1805.

[83] Christian Schultz, *Travels on an Inland Voyage, 1807-1808*, 2 vols. (New York, 1810), 2:193.

[84] John F. Schermerhorn and Samuel J. Mills, *A Correct View of that part of the United States which lies West of the Alleghany Mountains, with regard to Religion and Morales* (Hartford, Conn., 1814).

[85] *Louisiana Gazette*, April 27, 1815; *American Catholic Historical Researches*, 19:123-24.

[86] *Louisiana Gazette*, August 1, 1815.

[87] Ibid., February 5, 1818.

[88] Benjamin Henry Latrobe, *The Journal of Latrobe, 1796-1820* (New York, 1905), 175-76.

[89] Ibid., 169.

[90] Timothy Flint, *Recollections of the Last Ten Years, passed in Occasonal Residences and Journeying in the Valley of the Mississippi* (Boston, 1826), 300, 303-4.

[91] Niles's *Weekly Register*, 41 (1811): 378, quoting from the *Free Press*.

[92] Stuart, *Three Years in North America*, 2:239-40.

[93] Theodore Clapp, *Autobiographical Sketches and Recollections, During a Thirty-five Years' Residence in New Orleans* (Boston, 1857), 231-32.

[94] Ingraham, *Southwest by a Yankee*, 1:187.

[95] H. S. Tanner, *View of the Valley of the Mississippi, or the Emigrant's and Traveller's Guide to the West* (Philadelphia, 1834), 325, 327, 329.

[96] Buckingham, *Slave States of America*, 1:309, 327-29.

[97] *Weekly Delta*, February 6, 1853.

[98] *Baton Rouge Weekly Comet*, June 24 and July 5, 1855.

[99] Ibid., August 5 and 12; October 21, 1855.

[100] Ibid., August 5, 1855.

CLASS AND RACE STRIFE*

Roger W. Shugg

Thy kingdom is divided among the Yankees and Abolitionists!
—J. B. BROMLEY[1]

My sympathies are with the white man and not with the negro. My hand is against the African, and I am for pushing him off the soil of this country.
—W. T. STOCKER[2]

I am in favor, first, of the poor whites, secondly, of the middle classes, ad lastly of the rich.
—R. KING CUTLER[3]

The reconstruction of Louisiana[4] prolonged the civil war between North and South and precipitated within the state first a social revolution and then a counterrevolution. Each phase was marked by a new constitution which changed, directly or indirectly, the dispensation of power. White labor altered the government with the charter of 1864; black labor, with that of 1868; and the counterrevolution which restored white supremacy was signified by the Constitution of 1879. The long struggle was a political contest between white and colored people for the exclusive right to rule. This has been the traditional theme of historians of reconstruction. But it should not be forgotten that at first neither race was solidly united against the other, nor were the spoils of office their only concern. Political turmoil obscured but did not conceal the deeper social and economic problems of the period. There was the bitter racial question, whether whites or blacks should gain social ascendancy,[5] and the closely related economic question of which class, whatever its color, should own the soil and manage the commerce of Louisiana. Carpetbaggers fought planters and merchants for the possession of rich natural resources and the control of black and white labor. The carpetbaggers were defeated because they

---

*First published as Chapter 7 in Roger W. Shugg, *Origins of Class Struggle in Louisiana: A Social History of White Farmers and Laborers during Slavery and After, 1840-1875* (Baton Rouge: Louisiana State University Press, 1939), 196-233.

turned from economic to political exploitation, preyed upon whites more than blacks, and arrayed all classes of the former race against the latter. The final triumph of planters and merchants, with the essential support of white farmers and laborers, was a counterrevolution which crushed the bewildered and abortive attempts, first of white, and then of black, labor, to rule the state and mold society in their own images.

The revolution began with the establishment of a government under Northern auspices. On Lincoln's initiative,[6] and with the supervision of the Federal army,[7] a civil administration was set up for the territory redeemed from the Confederates. This area embraced nineteen parishes and over half the prewar population.[8] To elect two congressmen from New Orleans in 1862, scarcely three thousand voters had taken the oath of allegiance to the Union.[9] But more than ten thousand citizens, exceeding one-tenth of the prewar electorate, cast ballots for state officials in 1864; and three-fifths of this number elected delegates to a constitutional convention.[10]

Two leading parties disputed the main issues of the day. The Free State party contended that Louisiana had committed political suicide by secession and must be created anew through the repudiation of secession and the abolition of slavery. Opposed to them were so-called Conservatives, who agreed that secession should be repealed, but desired to retain the Constitution of 1852 and slavery.[11] Both parties were loyal to the Union. Even their divergent views as to the status of the Negro were not wholly irreconcilable, for the Conservatives were willing to accept compensated emancipation. The fundamental issue between them was whether Louisiana should be restored to the control of planters and merchants under the old constitution, or put in the hands of a majority of loyal white people under a new organic law.[12]

The latter view was championed by the Free State party, and it triumphed at the polls not only through the favor of General Banks and the Federal army, but also by virtue of its revolutionary appeal to New Orleans labor. Naturalized immigrants and native mechanics who voted for Douglas in 1860 and opposed secession, had always been loyal to the Union and inclined to economic radicalism. In 1863, with the inauguration of political reconstruction,[13] they organized the Working Men's Union League. Its platform called for the abolition of slavery, the removal of every Negro from Louisiana by colonization, and the admission of all white men to suffrage without restrictions as to residence.[14] These objects had been secretly cherished by immigrant laborers before secession.

Now their Free State candidate for the governorship was Michael Hahn, a prewar immigrant born in Bavaria, whose bitter hostility to the old slaveholding regime attracted a large following. He attacked the Constitution of 1852 as "more calculated to protect and benefit the slaveholder than . . . other classes," and condemned its representation of slaves as unjust "to the small planters and farmers, the adventurous frontiersmen, the honest mechanics." Previous legislators, in his opinion, had "confined themselves almost exclusively to legislating for the protection of the interests of slavery."[15] A new constitution was necessary to abolish not only slavery but also "the power of the aristocracy," and to give "the poor man that which he has never had—an equal voice in the State."[16]

Hahn's speeches articulated the class interest of labor in New Orleans and exposed the reactionary danger of pleas by the Conservatives for political *laissez faire* and restoration of the old order.[17] Other candidates on the Hahn ticket excited radical jealousy by attributing to extremists, who composed a third faction, secret designs for Negro suffrage.[18] These adroit tactics contributed to the victory of the party.[19] Numerous if not preponderant among their supporters at the polls was labor.[20] In the Free State torchlight parade on the eve of election marched the Workingmen's Association, the German Union, the Mechanics' Association, the Workingmen of Louisiana, and the Crescent City Butcher's Association.[21]

Labor was even more prominent in the Constitutional Convention of 1864. According to a workingmen's petition, it was "the only liberty-loving constitutional body, composed purely of the laboring class, that has ever convened in the State of Louisiana."[22] Not all the members, of course, were laborers. But among those whose occupations may be ascertained were two steamboatmen, a few clerks, a tailor, decorator, fireman, and several mechanics and laborers.[23] All the delegates were mildly class-conscious, and the class to which they were most devoted was labor.[24] "It is the poor laboring men who have worked on the canals and streets, and added millions of dollars to the wealth of the city, [that] deserve the consideration of the Convention," remarked one delegate, and his words struck the keynote of the gathering.[25]

The Convention of 1864 was called by General Banks, with Lincoln's approval,[26] chiefly to abolish slavery.[27] It was a revolutionary body, sitting "in a time of revolution," and representing not "a majority of the people..., but... the entire loyalty of the State."[28] In determining the basis of representation, Banks followed suggestions of the Free State party, and counted only the white instead of all the people.[29] This was done in order to deprive slaveholding planters of their former influence over legislation and to give New Orleans a voice proportionate to its numbers.[30] Colored people could neither vote nor be represented,[31] for the delegates were chosen by a white electorate.[32] Sixty-three came from New Orleans, but only thirty-five from the country, because the larger part of the state was still held by Confederates.[33] Over half the votes were cast in New Orleans,[34] which proved that the convention was to be largely a city affair.[35]

For this and other reasons the convention has been subjected to severe criticism by Ficklen. He thought it "in no sense a representative body."[36] But it represented more citizens than the Confederate legislature of western Louisiana, which was meeting without elections at Shreveport.[37] Almost as many people in New Orleans participated in the choice of convention delegates as in some prewar polls, and many more laborers voted now that Know-Nothings no longer intimidated them. But it was impossible for any legislative body to represent the majority in a state divided by civil war.

The Convention of 1864 has also been characterized as an assembly of Northern unionists, men of Banks' party, and not Louisianians.[38] The proportion of delegates who were recent immigrants from the North, and natives of New Orleans, cannot be ascertained. But the fact that all had to take the "iron-clad" oath of loyalty to the Union does not necessarily mean that any considerable number were from the North.[39] There were many unionists among the laborers of New Orleans before secession, and they were doubtless ready to show their true colors when Federal troops protected them.[40] Two members of the convention may serve as examples. One was taunted as the "member from New York": born there, he lived in Louisiana twenty-seven years, left before secession, and returned with Butler's army to supervise public works.[41] Another delegate, who protested that he represented "the poor white people, to which class I have the honor to belong," lived in New Orleans twenty-six years and always voted for Democrats, but was apparently anxious to assist in restoring Louisiana to the Union.[42]

Ficklen also criticized the convention because it was so extravagant. He believed that it cost over $100,000.[43] As a matter of fact, it ran up the amazing bill of $364,000.[44] There was no excuse for this enormous waste of public money by a body in which neither carpetbaggers nor corrupt Negroes were present. If one seeks an explanation, however, it may be found partly in the "get-rich-quick" fever which afflicted wartime New Orleans, and partly in the blunders and peculations of the delegates.[45]

The members of the convention were too unaccustomed to politics to be well tutored in the management of public affairs. Among them sat no representatives of the old slaveholding regime, although there were some of conservative temper. The most distinguished delegate was Christian Roselius, a brilliant lawyer and erstwhile opponent of secession, who resigned his seat when colleagues voted to subscribe twice to the ironclad oath.[46] His withdrawal left the convention in the hands of a new order of men with little or no experience in public life. Debates revealed their liberal intentions but not the education of gentility. They came from a social class which had never before been important in Louisiana politics. The fact that they occupied seats of power was of even greater revolutionary significance than the new organic law which they complied.[47]

The Constitution of 1864, contrary to Ficklen, was not simply, "a revised and amended copy of the constitution of 1852,"[48] but an extraordinary document which contained reforms and innovations of greater social import. It remedied the chief grievances of which farmers and laborers complained before secession. The franchise was extended to all white men who had lived in Louisiana one year;[49] and the basis of representation in both chambers of the legislature was changed from total population to the qualified electorate, without any restriction on the number of seats to which New Orleans might be entitled.[50] The agrarian measures of the Constitution of 1845 were partially revived by forbidding the legislature to charter banks or create corporations by special act.[51] Internal improvements, on the other hand, were encouraged by continuing the provisions of the Constitution of 1852.[52]

But the convention was not content to reform the old order. Its innovations were revolutionary. It abolished slavery,[53] inaugurated progressive income taxation,[54] opened the public schools to every child, black or white, between the ages of six and eighteen,[55] and established a nine-hour day and minimum wage of two dollars for all laborers engaged in public works.[56] The debate on these provisions revealed a startling change in the political temper of Louisiana.

There was no objection to the abolition of slavery,[57] for even the most reluctant delegate conceded it to be inevitable. But a stormy debate arose over the demand of a dozen conservatives that slaveholders be compensated for emancipating their property. The leader of this group, Edmund Abell, spoke for three days like a ghost from the dead, reciting the arguments which had once justified slavery and invoking the constitutional precedents which had protected it. He was himself no longer a slaveholder, but ardently defended the vested rights of others. Human bondage was approved by the fathers of the Republic and supported by the Constitution, he declared. It was superior to other systems of labor, and essential to keep the black from ruinous competition with the white. If slavery must be abolished, however, it was unjust to rob "the widow and orphan" of their property. A convention that represented only ten thousand voters, few of whom held slaves, had no right to liberate the slave without compensating his master.

Some delegates jumped to the unwarranted conclusion that Abell was upholding rebellion, which was commonly assumed to be synonymous with slavery, and would have shouted him down. But the majority insisted that he be allowed a freedom of speech never before permitted in Louisiana on the question of slavery. Patient, courteously extending his time, they listened to him extolling Negro bondage with pleas that ranged from the Bible, through the Constitution, to considerations of human nature and political economy.[58] Delegates sat dumfounded, astonished by the unreality of his harangue.

Then one after another rose to denounce in turn compensated emancipation, slavery, and rebellion. They excoriated all planters and the old order of society. The slaveholder had destroyed his property by rebellion, they said, and deserved to suffer expropriation. He had no vested rights because the majority of people had never owned Negroes, and the majority alone could determine what was right. To remunerate slaveholders would necessitate taxing for their benefit the free laborers of New Orleans. The poor had lost more than the planters in this civil war. Why not indemnify them for their lives, their farms, their savings? The demand for compensated emancipation was but a ruse to maintain human bondage, to perpetuate the power and increase the wealth of planters who had ruled Louisiana too long. "The emancipation of the African," concluded a delegate from Rapides, "will prove to be . . . the true liberation and emancipation of the poor white laboring classes of the South." So their representatives in the Convention of 1864 voted to abolish slavery immediately and without compensation.[59] They did not heed Abell's warning that because of this reform "a system of peonage would be established, all inducement for white labor over-ridden, and the safety of the State menaced."[60]

These delegates lived too close to the Negro to have any desire to make him politically their equal.[61] They showed the race prejudice characteristic of poor whites rather than the sympathies of racial abolitionists. If more farmers had been present, their aversion to the Negro would doubtless have become articulate.[62] When colored people

Class and Race Strife

were attacked, however, some delegates rose to their defense. "Drive the negro population from the State," said one, "and you would. . . remove from it the labor-power that made Louisiana before the rebellion. . . a State of planters and merchant princes."[63] But without debate the convention refused to accord colored labor the right to vote.[64] General Banks and Governor Hahn exerted pressure on enough delegates to authorize the legislature, if it so desired, to enfranchise "such persons" as might be deemed fit because of military service, taxation, or education.[65] Except for taxation, these qualifications for colored suffrage had been originally suggested by President Lincoln.[66] When they were presented to the convention, one delegate shouted, "that's a nigger resolution."[67] He was a man from New Orleans by the name of Sullivan, who had once been a poor white laborer; and like others, his prejudice against the Negro was not confined to suffrage.

"I will never tax white men to educate negro children," he declared, when a committee recommended separate colored schools to be supported from public funds.[68] Even conservatives like Abell took this stand, for Louisiana slaveholders had prohibited by law teaching a Negro to read or write.[69] Yet General Banks had already established schools for freedmen in New Orleans, and their education seemed as inevitable as abolition. The convention refused, therefore, to keep learning a white monopoly.[70] A long debate raged over the question of who should pay for colored schools, and it was at first resolved to make each race foot its own bill.[71] But friends of the freedman continued to work in committee, traded votes, and finally reached a compromise whereby taxation was left to the legislature with a guarantee of free public instruction for all children, both colored and white.[72] It was to prove the beginning of Negro education in Louisiana.

Perhaps nothing revealed more clearly the degree to which white labor dominated the Convention on 1864 than its establishment of minimum wages and hours. A petition for a nine-hour day had been circulated among the mechanics and artisans of New Orleans.[73] It was presented to the convention and entered in the journal, where one may read the names of nearly fifteen hundred laborers who had signed it.[74] Their appeal was stilted but earnest: "The past recurs to our vivid memory, when the capitalist could demand and exact from us ten to twelve hours a day devoted to toil, physical or mental, as the case required; that they frequently reserved for the white that which was detrimental to the black. Therefore, your petitioners most respectfully ask of you, your incorporation of some act into the organic law of the State in token of our recognition, by which we may be relieved of the burden we have heretofore borne, that of working to suit the convenience of men who acquired wealth and position to the injury and oppression of us."[75]

This petition was referred to a committee of delegates who were workingmen themselves. Their favorable report was evidence that a social revolution was incipient in Louisiana. Labor was "the most afflicted portion of our race," in the opinion of the committee, and "most likely to be kept down in the cesspool of poverty, simply by the antagonism between labor and capital." The workingman received small pay and endured long seasons of unemployment, but he had to buy his daily bread in small quantities, at high retail prices, with the addition of interest whenever he relied on credit. A multitude of middlemen were said "to produce nothing, . . . serve as speculative go-betweens," and burden labor with extortionate prices. "This popular speculating, this fashionable subsisting upon the labor of the mechanics and workingmen, is becoming well nigh intolerable." It would appear at first glance that these sentiments expressed nothing but hostility to merchants for wartime profiteering. But there was more. "The homage that capital requires of labor is beginning to be insupportable and detestable." Hence, "some efficient plan must soon be instituted to . . . emancipate [the poor man] from the mountainous interests and antagonisms that now oppress and keep him in bondage to poverty."[76]

The practical relief proposed by the committee called for maximum hours and minimum wages on public enterprises. A provision that work of this nature be restricted to nine hours a day was passed with little debate.[77] It scarcely needed to be said, as one delegate charged, that this measure was designed to win approval of the new constitution. It was significant that labor could only be satisfied by this kind of social legislation. The scheme for minimum wages, which was frankly admitted to be a "laborers' bill," was sponsored by a former steamboatman, Benjamin Orr. The bill was carried, with reduced rates which were made permissive rather than mandatory, by trading votes with those delegates who also desired to establish a wage schedule for the city police.[78] The legislature was authorized to fix the remuneration of all labor engaged in state or municipal enterprises, provided that minimum daily wages should not be less than $3.50 for foremen and cartmen, $3.00 for mechanics, and $2.00 for laborers.[79]

The debate showed that advocates of this law were on the defensive. They argued that it was not class legislation, because the general public rather than any group would eventually pay for these wages as it did for the tariff. The opposition complained that the measure would violate freedom of contract, interfere with the law of supply and demand, destroy the incentive of the poor to work, reduce all to the same level, and "take from the laborer his right to dictate his own terms." The bill was demagogic: nothing but a bid for votes.[80] Each of these objections was to be repeated against all social legislation proposed in the future, but this was the first time they were heard in Louisiana. "I do not ask you to make these men rich," replied the sponsor of the bill, "but to give them enough to eat, drink and wear."[81] As a result of his plea, instead of receiving fifty cents a day, laborers on public works could henceforth expect at least two dollars.

This novel concern for labor showed which way the political winds were blowing in Louisiana as the Civil War drew to a close. The workingmen of New Orleans, backbone of the Free State party, made their first stride toward a more democratic social order in 1864. But it was to be their last step for almost a generation.

The new constitution won the approval of President Lincoln, who pushed its ratification; and it was accepted by the people who lived within Federal lines.[82] But they were too small a minority of the white population, and divided into too many factions, to give life to this law. Typical of the cross-purposes at which unionists worked in Louisiana was Denison, collector of the port and local promoter of the presidential ambitions of the secretary of the treasury, Salmon P. Chase.[83] Although Dension approved the constitution, he cordially disliked its military sponsor, General Banks, and called his "whole civil reorganization in Louisiana . . . a cheat and a swindle."[84] In Congress the reconstructed government of the state found but little support, since Lincoln's policy was under fire by Wade, Davis, and the radicals.

Because the new constitution had failed to enfranchise the Negro, it was buried in a Senate filibuster led by Sumner.[85] In vain Lincoln pleaded in the last speech he was ever to make: "Concede that the new government of Louisiana is only to what it should be as the egg is to the fowl, we shall sooner have the fowl by hatching the egg than by smashing it."[86] But there was no agreement at Washington or New Orleans as to what species of egg was desirable. Lincoln wished states to be quickly restored to the Union with a full measure of home rule; the radical Republicans looked upon the South as conquered territory to be retrieved on a conqueror's terms, which would deprive rebel leaders of suffrage but extend it to their former slaves. The Free State party of New Orleans sought a local government responsive to the majority of loyal white people; the demobilized Confederates, an administration which would restore Louisiana to its antebellum condition, except that peonage would replace slavery.[87]

It was almost inevitable that Confederates should resume control of Louisiana, when they returned from the battlefield, because they were preponderant in numbers and influence. They had not been disfranchised by the Free State legislature;[88] and none but Confederate officeholders and the wealthiest planters were excluded from citizenship by President Johnson's proclamation of amnesty.[89] The voting strength of the soldiers was immediately enlisted by Governor Wells, a unionist planter who was moved to reconcile the veterans by a shrewd calculation that they held the balance of power in his re-election.[90] Old Democrats campaigned through the country on a platform hostile to Negro suffrage and Northern radicalism,[91] and persuaded the majority of farmers to vote for white supremacy and home rule.[92] They swept the polls and gained possession of the legislature.[93] So spectacular a triumph crushed the opposition, which was only a remnant of the Free State party, unpopular because it lacked Confederate leadership and laid no claim to compensation for emancipated slaves.[94] Thus the Democracy recaptured Louisiana by a peaceful counterrevolution at the ballot box.

But the old order was not to remain. There followed in swift succession the events at New Orleans and Washington that brought in the Federal army, ousted the Democrats from power, filled their places with radical Republicans of both races, and inaugurated the second phase of social revolution by a grant of civil and political rights to the freedmen.[95]

This train of events was unwittingly set in motion by the Democrats. In order to discipline colored labor and make it profitable, the planters who sat in the legislature and on parish police juries enacted vagrancy and apprenticeship laws that horrified the North.[96] To radical Republicans it seemed as if the stalwart Confederates were determined to restore human bondage and cheat the country of the fruits of war.[97] It is true, of course, that the new black code was milder than the old laws of slavery, and not as harsh in Louisiana as in some other states.[98] It recognized no proprietary rights on the part of white men to own and exchange those who were colored; but it did provide for their management and employment as something less than free men. It reduced the Negro to a condition which lay between peonage and serfdom. He was to be forever a field hand, and to owe his services to all white planters rather than to individual masters.

The Louisiana black code abridged the freedom of agricultural labor, limited its mobility, and added legal compulsion to the incentives to work which naturally arose from economic necessity. Negroes could not organize unions, nor strike, for whoever was found guilty of "tampering" with them—a word and an idea associated with slavery— to interrupt or improve their employment, was subject to fine and imprisonment. Planters could not create a free market for labor nor raise the level of its wages by competition, since they were required to give certificates to workers whom they discharged, and to hire none but those who showed evidence of having fulfilled their previous contracts. A supply of compulsory labor was assured for the plantations. Agricultural workers were obliged to undertake service for the year within the first ten days of January, and to include in these agreements all members of their families. Each worker was "free" to choose an employer, but some employer he must find, and once a contract was made with him the worker could not quit without forfeiting all wages. The laborer's hire was a prior lien on whatever he raised, and not over half the produce was to be removed from the fields until his charges had been met; to facilitate crop-sharing, which was clearly anticipated, half the wages could be withheld until completion of the annual indenture. Uniform hours of work, ten in summer and nine in winter, were set for all plantations. To enforce discipline and diminish the costs of inefficiency, labor was subject to so many fines that even the best could hardly avoid a few.[99] Except for damages to tools, livestock and crops, however, half of the fines were to be pooled in a bonus fund which would be distributed at harvest as a dividend.

These arrangements for resuming operation of the plantations were nominally quite different from the worst realities of slavery. There were even ingenious devices for putting labor under the trusteeship of justices of the peace, who would witness the signing of indentures, enforce them on both employer and employee, hear complaints from either party, and arbitrate their disputes.[100] But such elaborate safeguards of the Negro's rights could hardly be effective, much less equitable, when planters were justices of the peace. Freedmen who were so bold and intelligent as to appeal to them would be confronted by their employer or his friends in the guise of the state.

As a result of these laws, observed Carl Schurz, "the blacks at large belong to the whites at large."[101] Schurz did not exaggerate the Negro's predicament in spite of his radical predilections and sympathy for the race. It was hard to understand how the freedman could escape serfdom in any circumstances so long as he owned almost no land.[102] The difficulties of his situation were apparent to the South. "Negroes must remain in the worst possible condition of slavery so long as the whites own the land, and that they would soon regain and monopolize, if it were all given to the negroes tomorrow."[103] If the Negro was to depend on the white race for his livelihood, thought Northern and colored radicals, it was essential that he should be politically free to vote, in order to assert his rights and improve his future. The necessity of colored suffrage was argued at length by two revolutionary newspapers, the *New Orleans Tribune*[104] and *St. Landry Progress*,[105] which were published in French and English by educated Negroes.[106] A copy of the New Orleans paper was sent to every member of Congress, and radical Republicans were inspired to denounce the policies of President Johnson and Southern Democrats.[107]

The agitation of these local newspapers for colored suffrage and civil rights showed that radical Reconstruction was not introduced into Louisiana entirely from the outside. Rather was it advocated with equal zeal from within the state by an active minority of free colored people, who had enjoyed liberty even in the days of slavery when their industry accumulated property worth in the aggregate several millions of dollars.[108] They sought to push the social revolution begun by war to an agrarian conclusion in behalf of the masses of their race who had been slaves, to protect their own status, and to admit to power the majority of both races. "The planters are no longer needed in the character of masses"; with this belief they challenged the old order. "Our basis for labor must now be put on a democratic footing. There is no more room, in the organization of our society, for an oligarchy of slaveholders, or [even of] property holders."[109] If the suffrage should remain in practice exclusively white, "we may expect and prepare also for mobs of white against colored laborers, and white . . . against colored mechanics."[110]

But the attempt of some irresponsible white radicals to transfer the franchise from Confederate veterans to freedmen provoked the famous riot of 1866 in New Orleans.[111] It came about in this way. About forty former members of the Convention of 1864 summoned it to meet again by virtue of an ambiguous resolution which had been enacted by this body for its continuation.[112] The purpose of the radicals in renewing its life was to enfranchise the Negro,[113] and probably to drive the Democrats from power. They were embarked on a desperate *coup d'état*,[114] but with the knowledge and apparent support of such influential Republicans in Congress as Thaddeus Stevens, Boutwell, and Conkling, who as members of the radical Reconstruction Committee were seeking to undermine President Johnson and to undo his settlement of the South.[115]

The significance of the rump convention lay in the reaction of national opinion to the bloodshed with which it opened. A colored procession, which stopped to cheer the assembly, ended in a race riot. About thirty-four Negroes were killed, and over two hundred were wounded. A leading radical, Dr. A. P. Dostie, who was animated by a fanatical ambition to subdue rebels and elevate slaves, was among the four white men who lost their lives, only one of whom was sympathetic to the South.[116] On the other side, so to speak, only ten policemen were wounded, and no one was arrested or punished.[117] Thus it was reported that a massacre had been plotted and perpetrated in cold blood by the New Orleans Democracy, and this was the verdict of the congressional radicals who investigated the affair.[118] No historian has endorsed their judgment except

Du Bois,[119] and it is impossible to untangle the confused and partisan testimony in the case.[120] Violence had always been common in New Orleans, and was inevitable when racial antagonism became fierce.[121] Whatever the true explanation of the riot, it was widely believed outside the South that a white mob had murdered Negroes, with the connivance of government, in order to intimidate a radical convention which proposed to enfranchise the race to which the dead belonged.

A fearful conviction that the South was restoring slavery, however groundless in fact, spread through the North. The black codes indicated that the Negro was not wholly free; the New Orleans massacre appeared to demonstrate that the lives of Republicans were in jeopardy. These conditions were thought by radicals to be a natural result of the amnesty and home rule which President Johnson had granted the South. Whether congressional leaders were sincere in converting Northern voters to this view, or simply intent on Johnson's defeat and the establishment of Republican supremacy, the events in Louisiana made good propaganda for their plans of coercion.

Nothing was more needed to discredit the Lincoln-Johnson policy in the eyes of the North, and to put the South at the mercy of men in Congress like Sumner and Stevens, but the rejection of the Fourteenth Amendment. This was done in Louisiana by unanimous vote of the aristocrats who controlled the legislature,[122] for they were resolved to invite repression rather than to disfranchise themselves.[123] There followed, as night the day, military reconstruction. Surely no period or policy in American history has earned a less appropriate name; it was not to be one of reconstruction, but of destruction and depression, of partisan dictatorship by corrupt political machines which exploited both races in the name of one.[124]

There will always be speculation over the causes of this calamitous state of affairs. Perhaps what doomed to failure the peaceable reconstruction undertaken by Lincoln and Johnson, at least in Louisiana, was the traditional identification of class with race, a heritage of slavery, so that men were not united by their common economic interests, but divided despite them by color. Racial animosity was always stronger than class consciousness;[125] and white people who differed over secession and war were quickly rallied to oppose the Negro, as slave or freedman. Only a minority of the laboring population, entirely white and urban, had found its voice in 1864; its strength wasted away, instead of being recruited by demobilized Confederates, because those who were poor and white were also divided by the enmity born of civil war. The patriotic restoration to office of conservative Democrats introduced the black code as an economic settlement along racial lines. Local leadership was provided by the old planters and merchants and Confederate officers, who had the confidence of all whites in the face of colored suffrage, and there were none to dispute their power but Northern adventurers and native radicals, who were supported by the Republican chiefs in Congress and the colored masses.[126] The necessities of national politics, especially of Republican supremacy and industrial growth, were to cast the die of local affairs. Since the rule of Southern

Class and Race Strife

Democrats was not to be tolerated by the victorious North, the radicals were bound to have their spell of power over Louisiana.

Military reconstruction reduced all the former states of the Confederacy except Tennessee to the status of conquered territory, which could regain their sovereignty only by obedience to the dictates of Congress, enlargement of the suffrage to include Negroes, and ratification of the Fourteenth Amendment.[127] To fulfill these conditions in Louisiana, a constituent assembly was elected by all "loyal" men on a war basis, for loyalty was interpreted by General Sheridan as barring Confederate veterans and Democratic officeholders from the polls.[128] A contemporary newspaper estimated that half the white citizens were disfranchised.[129] Whatever the number who were disqualified, and it must have been large, the registration was heavily colored.[130] No one was surprised that radicals elected to the Convention of 1868 all but two of their candidates.[131]

The local Republicans who thus won control of Louisiana had organized their party in 1865. Thomas Durant, an old Douglas Democrat, presided at its first convention. Henry Clay Warmoth, a poor, white lawyer of Southern ancestry who was more a scalawag than a carpetbagger, became its moving spirit. His program from the start was one of radical reconstruction; he promoted it unofficially on the floor of Congress,[132] and came into power when this body made it law. The original party membership was composed of free men of color, emigrants from the North, demobilized Federal soldiers, and native unionists. Northerners were always influential but never in the majority; as late as 1874 there were only about seven thousand voters who confessed to having been born Yankees.[133] The strength of the party at the polls rested with the colored masses.[134] To carry the Convention of 1868, over fifty thousand freedmen were organized in a Republican Loyal League.[135]

With the elevation of this race from slavery to free suffrage, the revolution entered its second stage: black labor was ostensibly in a position to control the state. It might be supposed that the Negro would rule the Republican party, not only by the sheer weight of his numerical preponderance, but also because he was led by educated mulattoes such as Oscar Dunn and P. B. S. Pinchback, a type which was the peculiar product of antebellum racial relations in Louisiana. That this was not to be the case became apparent early in the Convention of 1868. The delegates elected to this assembly had been drawn equally from both races by agreement of the party of chiefs in order to avoid conflicts of color.[136] The important committee to draft a constitution was nevertheless composed of five white and four colored members, who divided by race and submitted different reports. The document which finally emerged from the convention was the product of many compromises, but followed essentially the recommendations of the white majority.[137] The Negroes suffered another loss when their gubernatorial candidate was defeated by Warmoth on a ballot polled according to color; their nominee was then satisfied with the lieutenant-governorship.[138] The colored delegates sustained additional defeats when they lost their fight for agrarian legislation,[139] and against drastic disfranchisement of their former masters.[140] Henceforth, the Negroes who had been "Pure Radicals" failed to take the lead in shaping the policy of their party. In vain they had boasted "we have more than the ballot: we compose a majority in the State, and with the help of our Radical white friends . . . the colored masses are the masters of the field."[141] White Republicans led by Warmoth, Casey, Carter, Kellogg, and Packard became the masters of reconstruction and ruled the state with the support of colored officeholders and voters, and the protection of Federal troops.

The Constitution of 1868 nevertheless gave the Negro many nominal advantages, several of which actually worked to his disadvantage. Although he had but recently emerged from a servile condition of enforced ignorance, and was on the whole illiterate, he was granted the right to vote and to hold any office in the state.[142] These dubious privileges only made him the tool of others until he became intelligent enough to have a will and understanding of his own.[143] For the convention it was enough to open all public schools to freedmen,[144] though five delegates warned their colleagues that to mix the races in this way and to waive all color discrimination would be to wreck the educational system.[145]

No less disastrous for the immediate future of the Negro was the convention's unqualified declaration of social equality,[146] which aroused greater resentment among white people than colored suffrage. It was adopted largely by colored votes at the insistence of Pinchback.[147] The abolition of civil and social discrimination was difficult to challenge in theory and as a principle of abstract right.[148] But the traditions and temper of popular white opinion made all questions relating to the freedmen a race problem, not one of philosophical doctrine or politics. It was widely believed, even by sensible people, that if the Negro could ride with them in streetcars and sit next to their children at school, there would be nothing to prevent miscegenation.[149] The colored press replied that these apprehensions were unjustified, and that Democrats deliberately inflamed them in order to regain political control. Social equality meant nothing more to the intelligent Negro than the right of any man, whatever his color, to come and go in public places, and to pursue his own happiness, provided he did not infringe the equal right of another. There was no thought of racial intermarriage, even among the uneducated, but only of the admission of freedmen to civil society so that they might be free to walk the streets, frequent public institutions, attend schools, and appear in courts of law like other citizens.[150] But white members of the convention who were sympathetic to the aspirations of colored people protested that there was no use in making laws so far advanced of public opinion.[151] Such doctrines were especially offensive to white farmers and laborers, who saw no good in the Constitution of 1868.

This document was hailed by colored radicals as "the deathblow of the slave oligarchy in Louisiana."[152] Their optimism was justified in so far as the old leaders of the state, the planters and merchants, were temporarily disfranchised and their ballots handed over to those who had formerly been their slaves. The power to make laws was ostensibly reposed with a colored majority, for seats in both houses were allotted according to total population.[153] This revival of the 1852 basis of representation was bitterly resented by

Class and Race Strife

white people, because the colored were no longer merely counted but actually allowed to vote and represent themselves. Although the black belt possessed no more legislative seats than before the war,[154] the majority of Negroes in this region, and not a minority of white planters, were now in a position to control legislation. This obliteration of the color line which had previously determined who should constitute a majority in the state led to a fierce struggle between blacks and whites. Peace was to be restored only with the triumph of white supremacy in 1877.

For nine years previous to this date, however, Louisiana was in the grip of carpetbag government. Its political structure, based on the Constitution of 1868, was strong because it centralized "imperial power in the governor's hands."[155] The degree to which he controlled the state became extraordinary as one law after another augmented his overlordship. It is notable that the only opposition to him within the government arose from the Custom House, because he did not administer Federal patronage.[156] In the state he was supreme. He was able to appoint and remove local registrars of voters, tax collectors, and assessors, besides the board of public works and metropolitan police officers for New Orleans; he could name special constables with power to make summary arrests everywhere, and fill all vacancies of office, even in parish police juries.[157] If a hostile judge should be elected to any court, the legislature would gerrymander his district, as in New Orleans, and create a new one, to which the governor forthwith appointed a friendly judge.[158] Elections "were a farce," since "the governor appointed the registrars, and through them returned his friends to the legislature."[159] The registration never tallied with tax or census figures, and in some places embraced more Negroes than were alive. It was easy for corrupt voters to repeat and stuff the ballot box since a citizen could use any poll in his parish or—in New Orleans—in his ward.[160] Whatever the actual vote, a central returning board, composed of a Republican majority confirmed by the Senate, could change the results to suit its own rules of political arithmetic.[161]

This gubernatorial despotism was the antithesis of democratic government. It gave one man, at first H. C. Warmoth and then W. P. Kellogg, the control of elections, courts, and taxation; and by his leadership of the Republican party, he dominated the legislature and the making of laws. The governor was generally supported in the face of local opposition by President Grant, who maintained a "Federal protectorate" over Louisiana with national troops.[162] The state was policed for a decade by soldiers whose mission was to preserve law and order, especially at elections, but the law was whatever a corrupt legislature ratified, elections were determined by fraudulent returns, and the overseer of Louisiana was the governor.

There were nevertheless said to be permanent benefits which accrued from misrule of this type, especially in South Carolina and Mississippi, but they were overlooked until one historian called attention to them in 1910.[163] He claimed that during this period the South achieved democratic government, free public schools, and important social legislation.[164] If these reforms were introduced in other states,[165] Louisiana was conspicuous for their absence. Government became nominally democratic by the

Constitution of 1868, as we have seen, but in practice it proved to be despotic. The free public schools which had been established in 1844, and were now open to both races, suffered almost complete collapse because of racial prejudice, fraud, and inefficiency.[166] Of effective social legislation, there was none. When Nordhoff examined the statutes enacted during reconstruction, he "met with dozens of petty swindles," and reached the conclusion that "a more amusing and preposterous exhibition of wholesale legislative plundering it would be difficult to imagine."[167]

Anyone who goes through the sessional laws of this period will confirm Nordhoff's opinion. The overwhelming bulk of the legislation divided itself into two categories, political and economic, which had the single aim of maintaining in power Republican politicians and rewarding their friends. Whether it was the creation of a new parish like Grant, for exploitation by carpetbaggers as notorious as the Twitchells, or the issue of railway, land, and improvement bonds, the telltale mark of fraud was upon each law. There would be no point in a tedious explanation of these corrupt statutes,[168] especially when the truth of their unsavory negotiation, shrouded in discreet mystery from the start, has been forever lost.

It is more important to realize that no race, class, or party could lay a virtuous claim to clean hands. In each case the majority were honest, of course, if only because they were powerless or indifferent. But politicians bribed legislators for party and parish favors, and businessmen and corporations bribed the politicians for economic privileges.[169] There was some truth in Governor Warmoth's speech to the bankers who were lobbying to protect and advance their interests. "I tell you," he said, "these much-abused members of the Louisiana legislature are at all events as good as the people they represent. Why, damn it, everybody is demoralizing down here. Corruption is the fashion."[170] In these circumstances even the honorable businessman had to resort to bribery to avoid political reprisals and to pay off legislative blackmail, and prices were high because corruption was rampant. But it should be remembered, as Du Bois observed, that colored men obtained only a small share of the graft, which was designated in legislative accounts as "sundries and incidentals," while white men took the lion's share of state bonds, warrants, charters, and land.[171]

Carpetbag rule was eventually caught in two dilemmas, and its failure to solve them provoked violent opposition which led ultimately to its downfall. First was the fact that its electoral majorities consisted of colored votes: without support of the Negro at the polls, radicals could not obtain office; but to rely on the ballots of one race, and that the weaker, was to unite the other and stronger race in implacable hostility; and the Negro would prove to be unreliable in the face of such enemies, because whatever his political allegiance, his economic necessities bound him to the white planter.

Second was the no less important fact that the carpetbag government fed on corruption; since radicals lacked the confidence of business or white citizens, and depended on the protection of the Federal army for their precarious tenure of power, they could not draw their party funds and individual prerequisites from the economic development of the state. So they turned to political exploitation and feathered their nests directly from the public revenue, which raised taxes higher without increasing receipts, further depressed trade and agriculture, and completed the process of alienating the white electorate. Each dilemma was inescapable; the first was of racial and social character, the second, racial and economic; together they issued in the race strife, apparently more social than economic, which finally put an end to carpetbag rule.

Oppressive taxation was largely responsible for bringing men of property and influence into violent collision with the radicals. The rate for the state jumped from 37 1/2 cents on $100 in 1866 to $2.15 in 1871.[172] Notwithstanding these increased levies, the debt rose from about eleven millions after the war to over fifty millions in 1875. There was also a rapid rise in the local rates for most parishes. In Natchitoches, for example, where $13,475 had been sufficient revenue in 1860, the sum of $82,207 was not enough in 1873 to cover local expenses and peculations.[173] These heavy fiscal demands were made of a people who had not recovered from the losses of war before they were further depressed by the Panic of 1873. The consequences for New Orleans were disastrous. Here the value of residential property was cut in half, and the sheriff made more than 47,000 seizures for taxes from 1871 through 1873.[174] The situation was no better in the country.[175] It was especially hard for "small farmers," according to Nordhoff, because they were "forced to pay the heavy taxes, while in many cases their rich neighbors resist[ed]."[176] The fiscal crisis had become acute by 1872.

It was truly said that "office-holders grow rich, while the people are impoverished." With "capital . . . flying from the State, [and] commerce . . . decreasing,"[177] resistance to confiscatory taxation spread far and wide. A league was formed in New Orleans and the rural parishes to refuse all payments, and merchants and planters were foremost in this rebellion.[178] Some fifty-five lawyers in New Orleans offered to defend tax suits without charge.[179] The movement coincided with the first vigorous and united election campaign by the whites against carpetbag rule in 1872. It can hardly be doubted that the resistance to taxation inspired a relentless struggle for home rule.[180] The "same old crew of political buzzards and insatiable jackals who have robbed and plundered us to the verge of bankruptcy, and paralyzed all industry in the State,"[181] could not be borne for long if agriculture and trade were to survive.

While it was chiefly the propertied citizens who rebelled against the oppressive taxation of reconstruction, the poor and white were stirred no less by pride of race and hatred of any Negro who attempted to rule them. Where parish officials happened to be colored, as in Natchitoches or St. Landry, murders and riots were frequent.[182] It was an unpleasant sight for a poor, white farmer to watch a poor Negro grow prosperous in public office, and galling him to pay the taxes which were too often the source of his prosperity.[183] The colored men who were corrupt, ignorant, dissolute, and bold, though a very small minority, earned for their race the distrust and contempt of the white man.

In the rural parishes of the hard-working, farmers sometimes lost their patience and carried out with violence or intimidation the desperate threats uttered by propertied men or abusive newspapers.[184] It was the poor, white men, to judge by the comparative poverty of such a large proportion of the people after the war,[185] who made up the forces which struggled under McEnery, Ogden, and Nicholls to restore Democratic home rule. They figured in the savage race riots at Colfax in 1873, and Coushatta in 1874,[186] marched among the five thousand citizens who participated in the New Orleans uprising of September 14, 1874,[187] and filled the ranks of the White League.

It is impossible to estimate the strength or to exaggerate the importance of an organization like the White League. When the *New Orleans Bulletin* put its enrollment at fourteen thousand men, "organized and armed," a North Louisiana paper claimed that there were at least ten thousand men who belonged to it in that region alone.[188] The support of newspapers in every part of the state indicated how widespread and strong the movement was.[189] Its temper was desperate, and grew especially bitter in 1874. Two years before, President Grant had robbed the McEnery-Warmoth coalition of their apparent electoral victory and placed Governor Kellogg in power with national troops.[190] The Louisiana Democrats, encouraged by national party successes in the lower house of Congress, were resolved to throw off the yoke of carpetbag rule. "*We intend to succeed by intimidation*," not with guns but with a virtuous cause, declared the New Orleans *Times*.[191] But the *Shreveport Times* gave voice to the force which lay behind this peaceable profession: "If a single gun is fired between the whites and blacks in this and surrounding parishes, *every carpet-bagger and scalawag that can be caught will in twelve hours therefrom be dangling from a limb.*"[192]

The local political parties, Democratic or "people's" and Republican, had divided the races and set them against one another.[193] Economic coercion of the Negro on the plantations, to change his allegiance or persuade him to be neutral, was approved and widely practiced.[194] Thus the stage was set for the overthrow of carpetbag government and the restoration of white supremacy.[195] All that was needed was a change in the national government, the succession of Hayes to the presidency, to withdraw Federal soldiers in 1877, for they were the last mainstay of carpetbag rule.

"To use a modern phrase," remarks a recent historian, "government under Radical Republican rule in the South had become a kind of 'racket.' "[196] Charles Nordhoff, an intelligent observer who was the less prejudiced because he had been brought up to hate slavery and sympathize with the Negro, entered an eloquent judgment on conditions in Louisiana which has not been altered by research. A "small band of white men," he wrote in 1875, "have for more than six years monopolized all political power and preferment in the State. They have laid, collected and spent (and largely misspent) all the taxes, local taxes as well as State; they have not only made all the laws, but they have arbitrarily changed them, and have miserably failed to enforce any which were for the people's good; they have openly and scandalously corrupted the colored men whom they have brought into political life; they have used unjust laws to perpetuate and extend their own power; and they have practiced all the basest arts of ballot-stuffing, false registration, and repeating, at election after election."[197] It was gang rule, the kind of government to which

American cities were accustomed, but which had never seized a state with such flagrant impunity and ease until the destruction of reconstruction was visited upon Louisiana by misguided national politics and politicians.

There was no genuine relief to be anticipated for many years. After the withdrawal of Federal troops in 1877, white Democrats assumed power, but their "legislation . . . disappointed the people."[198] In the following year almost half the merchants of New Orleans rose in opposition.[199] "The Democratic party," testified a conservative lawyer who had fought for the overthrow of radical Republicanism, "had fallen into the hands of men who were using it. . . to their own ends for a few profitable local offices, and so arranging the election machinery as to deprive the people of a fair expression of the popular will."[200]

The habits of reconstruction politics were not easily broken; its vices lingered on; and special privileges of an economic and political character, notably the Louisiana Lottery, continued to corrupt the government. Nordhoff had predicted that after Federal interference ceased and white supremacy had been assured, the Democratic party would split into two factions, "and each will try, with the help of the negroes, to beat the other."[201] This was to be the nemesis of Populism in the nineties. It would then appear to all men that the evils of reconstruction were not peculiar to carpetbag government or to any race, but were rather of the nature of economic and social conditions.

Notes for "Class and Race Strife"

[1]*Debates in the Convention for the Revision and Amendment of the Constitution* (New Orleans, 1864), 181; hereafter cited as *La. Const. Conv. Debs., 1864*.

[2]Ibid. Stocker, as one might guess, was the most violent Negrophobe in the convention. He had been one of the seven Co-operationist delegates to the Convention of 1861 who refused to sign the ordinance of secession. *La. Const. Conv. Debs., 1864*, 166.

[3]Ibid., 510. Cutler was a New Orleans lawyer who had lived in Louisiana over twenty years. Ibid., 554; *Gardner's New Orleans Directory for 1866, s.v.*

[4]It is not our intention to repeat the familiar story of reconstruction. The political history of this period in Louisiana has been exhaustively described by J. R. Ficklen, *History of Reconstruction in Louisiana (through 1868)* (Baltimore, 1910), and Ella Lonn, *Reconstruction in Louisiana after 1868* (New York, 1918). It only remains for us to analyze the part played by white farmers and laborers. The permanent and far-reaching changes in education, religious organization, and other social institutions will be treated later for the light they throw on Populism, with which they appear to be more closely connected than with reconstruction.

[5]Ficklen, *History of Reconstruction*, 179.

[6]Lincoln to Banks, August 5, 1863, quoted in *New Orleans Times*, May 7, 1865. To Louisiana the President applied his "ten per cent plan" for restoring seceded states to the Union. See James D. Richardson, comp., *Messages and Papers of the Presidents, 1789-1897*, 10 vols. (Washington, 1899), 6:214, and *New Orleans Era*, January 1, 1864.

[7]*New Orleans Era*, February 17, 1864.

[8]Auditor of Public Accounts, *Annual Reports, 1864*, 94. At that time the following parishes had been restored to the Union: Ascension, Assumption, Avoyelles, Carroll, Concordia, East Baton Rouge, Iberville, Jefferson,

Lafourche, Madison, Orleans, Plaquemines, St. Bernard, St. John the Baptist, St. Charles, St. Mary, St. Martin, St. James, Terrebonne, and Tensas.

[9] Ficklen, *History of Reconstruction*, 42.

[10] Ibid., 62, 68.

[11] Ibid., 46-47.

[12] Ibid., 45-68.

[13] Ficklen, *History of Reconstruction*, chapter 3.

[14] *Era*, May 12, 1863. The abolition of residence qualifications appealed to both naturalized foreigners and Northern immigrants.

[15] *Speech of Hon. Michael Hahn before the Union Association of New Orleans*, November 14, 1863, 8-10.

[16] *Era*, February 18, 1864.

[17] Ibid., February 5, 1864.

[18] Ibid., February 21, 1864. The Flanders faction denied this charge. *Times*, February 14, 1864.

[19] The vote was 6,171 for Hahn (Free State), 2,959 for Fellows (Conservative), and 2,225 for Flanders. See Ficklen, *History of Reconstruction*, 62.

[20] Ibid., chapter 3, neglects this aspect of the campaign, and treats the Free State party as General Banks' administration machine.

[21] *Era*, February 20, 1864. These were not simply banners carried in the parade, but large and active organizations.

[22] *La. Const. Conv. Debs., 1864*, 418.

[23] Ibid., 4-5, 395, 554, 577. *Gardner's New Orleans Directory, 1866.*

[24] See above, n3.

[25] *La. Const. Conv. Debs., 1864*, 360.

[26] See above, n6.

[27] *La. Const. Conv. Debs., 1864*, 300.

[28] Ibid., 160, 298, 300.

[29] *Era*, March 9, 1864. An electoral basis would have been adopted if there had been any registration lists for the country parishes.

[30] Banks later admitted that his action was inspired by these motives, which he held in common with the Free State party. See the Louisiana Election Case, *38 Cong., 2 sess., H. R. Rpts.*, no. 13, 19.

[31] *La. Const. Conv. Debs., 1864*, 247.

[32] Each delegate was supposed to represent 2,384 white people. *Era*, March 9, 1864.

[33] The country was entitled to eighty-seven delegates, but only parts of the following parishes held elections: Ascension, Avoyelles, Concordia, East and West Baton Rouge, East Feliciana, Iberville, Jefferson, Lafourche, Madison, Plaquemines, Rapides, St. Bernard, St. James, St. John, St. Mary, and Terrebonne. Ibid., 4-5.

Class and Race Strife

[34] Ibid., 408.

[35] Even the adoption of a quorum of seventy-six, which would also have been the number had every parish sent delegates, did not prevent the city from nearly forming a quorum by itself.

[36] Ficklen, *History of Reconstruction*, 69.

[37] Ibid., 65.

[38] Ibid., 69.

[39] *La. Const. Conv. Debs., 1864*, 12-14.

[40] Butler had declared that only the poor in New Orleans were loyal to the United States. Ibid., 360.

[41] Ibid., 554.

[42] Ibid., 395.

[43] Ficklen, *History of Reconstruction*, 76-77.

[44] Auditor of Public Accounts, *Annual Reports, 1864*, 30, 40. Figures reduced above to round thousands; hereafter cited as *Rpt. Audit. Pub. Accts., 1864*.

[45] Analysis of the expenses shows that some of the delegates were personally corrupt. For a session of four months, each member received about $1,130, or a little less than ten dollars a day. This was customary remuneration. A scandalous contingent expense was the sum of nearly $10,000 for liquors and cigars. Half the entire cost of the convention, or $156,000, was for printing the journal and debates, a common source of rebates, commissions, and graft in the later years of reconstruction. But see *Senate Debates, 1864-65*, 24-25, 26-29, 79-82; hereafter cited as *La. Sen. Debs., 1864-65*.

[46] *La. Const. Conv. Debs., 1864*, 12, 14, 18-20.

[47] Ficklen, *History of Reconstruction*, chapter 4.

[48] Ibid., 79.

[49] *Constitution of the State of Louisiana, 1864*, Art. 14; hereafter cited as *Const. 1864*.

[50] Ibid., Arts. 11, 23.

[51] Ibid., Art. 121.

[52] Ibid., Arts. 112-14.

[53] Ibid., Art. 1.

[54] Ibid., Art. 124.

[55] Ibid., Art. 141. It should be observed that while this provision extended the age limit of educable children, it did not adopt discriminatory taxes for the support of Negro schools.

[56] Ibid., Arts. 134-35. Ficklen shows himself typical of many political historians of reconstruction in that he does not even mention these extraordinary articles.

[57] Carried by a final vote of 72-13, with the minority standing for eventual, compensated emancipation. See *La. Const. Conv. Debs., 1864*, 224.

[58] Ibid., 140-44, 148-56, 165-67, 184-88, 192-94, 196.

[59] Ibid., 167-69, 170-72, 176-79, 184, 189-90. To placate the minority, Congress was asked to reward *loyal* slaveholders. Ibid., 313-14.

[60] Ibid., 98.

[61] *Era*, March 16, 1864.

[62] *La. Const. Conv. Debs., 1864*.

[63] Ibid., 216.

[64] Ibid., 211. The vote was 55-26.

[65] Ibid., 450; *Const. 1864*, Art. 15; Ficklen, *History of Reconstruction*, 71.

[66] Letter to Governor Hahn, quoted by Ficklen, *History of Reconstruction*, 63.

[67] *La. Const. Conv. Debs., 1864*, 450.

[68] Ibid., 474-76.

[69] Ibid., 493-94.

[70] Ibid., 475-76. The vote was 44-33.

[71] Ibid., 523. The vote was 50-19.

[72] Ibid., 601. The vote was 53-27. This seems the only possible conclusion after comparing the roll calls. Ibid., 496-99.

[73] Ibid., 450.

[74] Ibid., 418-24.

[75] Ibid., 418.

[76] Ibid., 430.

[77] Ibid., 451. The vote was 56-25.

[78] Ibid., 312, 362, 431-32, 439, 594-95. The vote was 67-10, but compulsion was defeated 42-40.

[79] Ibid., 640.

[80] Ibid., 434-39, 361-63. "Show me the man who advocates the rights of poor men," grumbled conservatives, "and I will show you a man holding a fat position in the city government. A man who, if he had to pay workmen for services out of his own pocket, would sing an entirely different song."

[81] Ibid., 362.

[82] Ficklen, *History of Reconstruction*, 80-81. The vote in twenty parishes was, 6,836-1,566, with New Orleans casting five-eighths of the total ballots.

[83] "Diary and Correspondence of Salmon P. Chase," *American History Association Report, 1902*, 2:297-458. Unlike Ficklen, who relies heavily on these letters, I do not find Denison a trustworthy observer. He was a zealous but obsequious agent of Chase, and reported affairs to the end that the interests of himself and his employer might be advanced. He was an ardent admirer of General Butler and never saw any good in the work of his successor, General Banks, whom he suspected of being a Seward man. His prejudice against Banks and Hahn, as well as against the social character of the Convention of 1864, leads us to discount much of what Denison wrote.

[84] Ibid., 445.

[85] James F. Rhodes, *History of the United States from the Compromise of 1850*, 7 vols (New York, 1893-1906), 5:53-55.

Class and Race Strife

[86] Quoted by Ficklen, *History of Reconstruction*, 82.

[87] Ibid., ch 6.

[88] *Louisiana House Debates, 1865* in State Law Library and Howard Memorial Library, 394. The vote was 46-15.

[89] Richardson, *Messages and Papers of the Presidents*, 6:310-12.

[90] Ficklen, *History of Reconstruction*, 104-5.

[91] See their platform, *Appleton's Annual Cyclopedia, 1861-75*, vols. 1-15 (New York, 1861-75), *1865*, 512.

[92] *Picayune*, July 2; *Times*, October 3, 1865.

[93] *Journals of the Senate, 1864-65*. [State Law Library], 25-27; hereafter cited as *La. Sen. .J, 1865*.

[94] Ficklen, *History of Reconstruction*, 111.

[95] Ibid., chapters 6-11.

[96] *Louisiana [Extra] Session Laws, 1865*, enacted by the General Assembly, 3 ff; hereafter cited as *La. [Extra] Sess. Laws, 1865*. The severest laws were enacted by the police juries, not the legislature. See W. L. Fleming, *Documentary History of Reconstruction*, 2 vols (Cleveland, 1906), 1:279-81.

[97] James G. Blaine, *Twenty Years of Congress: from Lincoln to Garfield, with a review of the events which led to the political revolution of 1860*, 2 vols. (Norwich, Conn., 1884-86), 2:101-2.

[98] For a judicial explanation of the conditions in the South which led to the adoption of these black codes, and their similarity to previous legislation for free people of color, see J. S. Randall, *The Civil War and Reconstruction* (Boston, 1937), 724-30.

[99] For sickness, the daily wage was lost; for idleness or refusal to work, a fine double this amount was levied, with wages to be calculated at twenty-five cents an hour and two dollars a day. Each occasion of "disobedience," which included swearing, fighting, neglect of duty, and absence without leave, was to cost a laborer one dollar. Theft was to be reimbursed double the value of whatever was stolen.

[100] *La. [Extra] Sess. Laws, 1865*, Acts nos. 10, 11, 16, 20, 58.

[101] *Report on Condition of the South, 1865*, by Carl Schurz, *Sen. Docs.*, 39 Cong., 1 sess., I, no. 2, 24.

[102] *New Orleans Tribune*, March 1, 1865.

[103] *De Bow's Review*, 3 (April-May, 1867), 354. *New Orleans Picayune*, October 25, 1867.

[104] *New Orleans Tribune*, January 17, February 22, 1865.

[105] *Le Progrès de St. Landry*, July 27, 1867, published at Opelousas by Michel Vidal.

[106] The editors of the *Tribune* were refugees from San Domingo. One of them, Dr. J. T. Roudanez, was a physician of some affluence. The principal editor, Paul Trevigne, was the son of a soldier in the War of 1812, and spoke several languages. W. E. B. Du Bois, *Black Reconstruction in America* (New York, 1935), 456.

[107] *Congressional Globe, 1840-73* (Washington, 1841-73), 39 Cong., 1 sess., 39.

[108] *Tribune*, March 31, 1865.

[109] Ibid., March 1, 1865.

[110] Ibid., May 31, 1865.

[111] *Report of the Select Committee on the New Orleans Riots* [1866], *H. R. Rpts.*, 39 Cong., 2 sess., no. 16, *passim*; hereafter cited as *Report on the New Orleans Riots*. This investigation lacked all semblance of judicial procedure and was conducted chiefly to obtain evidence that would justify radical military reconstruction. The report is consequently unsatisfactory, despite the searching questions of the minority member from Pennsylvania. See the analysis by F. P. Burns, "White Supremacy in the South," *Louisiana Historical Quarterly*, 18 (1935): 592-94, 603-5.

[112] *Report on the New Orleans Riots*, 46-47, 60.

[113] Burns, 597.

[114] *Report on the New Orleans Riots*, 439-40.

[115] Ibid., 40-41, 50, 54-57. Judge Howell and the other leaders conferred with Conkling, Stevens, *et al.* Gideon Wells believed that "the New Orleans riots had their origin with the Radical members of Congress . . . [and were] part of a *deliberate conspiracy* . . . to secure . . . Radical ascendancy." Quoted by Burns, 605.

[116] Burns, 614-16.

[117] *Report on the New Orleans Riots*, 12-16.

[118] Ibid., 16-20.

[119] Ficklen, *History of Reconstruction*, 174-75; Du Bois, 464-65.

[120] Mayor Monroe, who was determined to disperse the convention, employed as marshals some notorious thugs, not unlike the police who committed similar outrages against Irish immigrants during his administration before the war. *Report on the New Orleans Riots*, 139-40, 142-47, 441; Monroe to General Baird, 494, 499.

[121] According to Ficklen, *History of Reconstruction*, 175, it was largely caused by "the natural exasperation felt by the white people of New Orleans when it was found that a handful of men proposed, with the assistance of the Federal government, to establish negro supremacy in their midst by putting the heel of the ex-slave on the neck of his former master." Burns, 614.

[122] *Times*, February 1, 10, 1867.

[123] Ibid., February 8, March 17, 1867. See also W. A. Russ, Jr., "Disfranchisement in Louisiana (1862-70)," *Louisiana Historical Quarterly*, 18 (1935): 572-73.

[124] Charles Nordhoff, *The Cotton States in the Spring and Summer of 1875* (New York, 1876), 43. Nordhoff wrote the best contemporary analysis of this political pathology.

[125] A furtive example of racial rapprochement occurred in the election of delegates to the Convention of 1868. A candidate from Terrebonne, who was actually a poor Creole, was said to belong "to that class which. . . negroes used to designate as 'low white trash'"; and his colleague was a carpenter who had always been a free man of color. Houma *Civic Guard*, September 21, quoted in *Commercial Bulletin, 1866-67*, September 23, 1867. Ibid., September 2, 1867, for a report from East Feliciana.

[126] Russ, "Disfranchisement in Louisiana," 570.

[127] The three reconstruction acts of 1867 which made this policy law are to be found in *U. S. Statutes at Large*, 14:428, 15:2, 14.

[128] Fleming, *Documentary History of Reconstruction*, 1:433-35.

[129] *Times*, April 21, 1867.

[130] Lonn, *Reconstruction in Louisiana after 1868*, 5.

[131] Ficklen, *History of Reconstruction*, 193. With the colored registration alone amounting to 82,907, there were 75,083 votes cast in favor of holding the convention.

Class and Race Strife

[132]Henry Clay Warmoth, *War, Politics, and Reconstruction; Stormy Days in Louisiana* (New York, 1930), 43-45.

[133]*Reports of the State Registrar of Voters, 1874*, Table 2.

[134]Nordhoff, *The Cotton States*, 41.

[135]*Republican*, November 17, 1867.

[136]Ficklen, 1:433-35.

[137]Du Bois, *Black Reconstruction*, 468.

[138]Warmoth, *War, Politics, and Reconstruction*, 54-55. The vote was close, 45-43. A mulatto, Oscar Dunn, honest and intelligent, was nominated for lieutenant governor.

[139]See below, chapter 8.

[140]Russ, "Disfranchisement in Louisiana," 575-76. Pinchback declared himself opposed to this measure. Article 99, because he believed "that two-thirds of the colored men of this State do not desire disfranchisement to such a great extent."

[141]*New Orleans Tribune*, October 30, 1867.

[142]*Constitution of the State of Louisiana, 1868*, Articles 2, 98; hereafter cited as *Const. 1868*.

[143]See Richard Taylor's illuminating report of his conversation with Charles Sumner on this subject for a revelation of the *non sequitur* in radical thought, *Destruction and Reconstruction* (New York, 1879), 245.

[144]Unfortunately for both races the convention rejected a proposal, 56-8, to restrict suffrage after 1872 to the literate. *Official Journal of the Proceedings of the Convention for Framing a Constitution for the State of Louisiana* (New Orleans, 1867-68), 175; hereafter cited as *Const. Conv. J., 1868*.

[145]Ibid., 200-201.

[146]*Const. 1868*, Article 13.

[147]*Const. Conv. J., 1868*, 242-43. It was passed, 58-16, and opened public places to both races. Ficklen, *History of Reconstruction*, 198.

[148]Ibid., 291-92.

[149]*New Orleans Tribune*, April 14; *New Orleans Times*, May 6, 1867.

[150]*Le Progrès de St. Landry*, September 12, 1868.

[151]*Const. Conv. J., 1868*, 275-77.

[152]*St. Landry Progress*, April 11, 1868.

[153]*Const. 1868*, Arts. 21, 30.

[154]*United States Census, 1860, Preliminary Report of the Eighth Census*, under the direction of J. C. Kennedy, *Sen. Docs.*, 37 Cong., 2 sess. (Washington, 1862), 262; *Const. 1868*, Art. 22.

[155]*Report on Affairs in Louisiana* [1872], *H. R. Reports.*, 42 Cong., 2 sess., 4, no. 92, p. 21, minority rpt.; hereafter cited as *Rpt. on Affairs in Louisiana* [1872].

[156]Lonn, *Reconstruction in Louisiana after 1868*, chapter 4, 73 *ff*.

[157]Nordhoff, *The Cotton States*, 44.

[158] Ibid., 46-47.

[159] See above, *n*. 157.

[160] Nordhoff, *The Cotton States*, 65.

[161] Ibid.

[162] Ibid., 68.

[163] W. E. B. Du Bois, "Reconstruction and Its Benefits," *American Historical Review*, 15 (July, 1910): 781-99.

[164] Ibid., 795-96.

[165] See also F. B. Simkins and R. H. Woody, *South Carolina during Reconstruction* (Chapel Hill, N. C., 1932), which is a pioneer work on this and other questions.

[166] *Superintendent of Public Education, Annual Reports, 1850-61, 1869-77,* 1872 passim; 1877, passim; hereafter cited as *Rpt. State Supt. Pub. Educ.*

[167] Nordhoff, *The Cotton States,* 60-62.

[168] Ibid.

[169] "The legislative corruption involves both parties. Among the principal movers in legislative jobs were wealthy, influential, and highly respectable democrats." *Rpt. on Affairs in Louisiana* [1872], page 37, separate dissent by H. B. Smith. See Warmoth's testimony on Democratic votes for four railway subsidies, ibid., 38-39.

[170] *Report of the Select Committee on Condition of the South* [1875],*H. R. Rpts.*, 43 Cong., 2 sess., 5, no. 261, pt. 3, 973; hereafter cited as *Rpt. on Condition of the South* [1875].

[171] Du Bois, "Reconstruction and Its Benefits," 792.

[172] *Rpt. on Condition of the South* [1875], 974.

[173] Nordhoff, *The Cotton States*, 54.

[174] Ibid., 62-63.

[175] *Affairs in Louisiana* [1873], *H. R. Docs.*, 42 Cong., 3 sess., 7, no. 91, chap 8; hereafter cited as *Affairs in Louisiana* [1873].

[176] Nordhoff, *The Cotton States*, 59.

[177] *Affairs in Louisiana* [1873], 21, 29, testimony of J. B. Eustis.

[178] *Rpt. on Condition of the South* [1875], 965.

[179] Ibid., 963.

[180] *Natchitoches Vindicator*, quoted in ibid., 921-27.

[181] *Alexandria Caucasian*, quoted in ibid., 767.

[182] This state of affairs continued, even without colored officials to incite them, to 1878. See the partisan but revealing *Report into Alleged Frauds and Violence in the Elections of 1878, etc.*, 45 Cong., 3 sess. [1879], *Sen. Rpts.*, 4, no 855, pt. i; for Caddo, 3-110, 589-93; Natchitoches, 115-66, 484-558; Tensas, 169-354, 453-83; Concordia, 355-78; St. Mary, 381-96; Pt. Coupee, 411-29.

[183] Interview with H. L. Brian, May 2, 1933.

[184] The *Shreveport Times*, under the vehement editorship of Leonard, set the tone for the country press in the northern parishes.

[185] H. O. Lestage, Jr., "The White League in Louisiana and Its Participation in Reconstruction Riots," *Louisiana Historical Quarterly*, 18 (1935): chapters 8, 9.

[186] See Lestage, "The White League in Louisiana," 619-93.

[187] *Commercial Bulletin*, September 13, 14; *Picayune*, September 14; *Times*, September 14, 1874; quoted in *Rpt on Condition of the South* [1875], 798-807, 814-34.

[188] *Minden Democrat*, August 29, 1874, quoted in ibid., 792.

[189] See citations from nine newspapers in ibid., 764-68, 770-72.

[190] Randall, *The Civil War and Reconstruction*, 869.

[191] August 5, 1874, quoted in *Rpt. on Condition of the South* [1875], 765.

[192] July 29, 1874, quoted in ibid.

[193] See the Baton Rouge platform of the white coalition "opposed to the Kellogg usurpation," in *Picayune*, August 26, 1874, quoted in ibid., 908-9. The Republican chairman, Packard, told Nordhoff, *The Cotton States*, 41, that only about five thousand whites voted this party's ticket by 1874.

[194] *Shreveport Times*, October 14, 1874.

[195] Randall, *The Civil War and Reconstruction*.

[196] Ibid., 852.

[197] Nordhoff, *The Cotton States*, 43.

[198] *Rpt. into Alleged Frauds and Violence in the Elections of 1878*, 446.

[199] Ibid., 435.

[200] Ibid., 433, testimony of Clement L. Walker.

[201] Nordhoff, *The Cotton States*, 42.

RACE AND THE WORKING CLASS: THE BLACK WORKER AND HIS IMAGE, 1880-1890*

David Paul Bennetts

Leaders of the nineteenth century labor movement and historians who have since studied that movement recognized that the working class in the South was unlike that of any other section of the country. While the differences were exaggerated and the similarities often overlooked, the working class of the South was indeed unique; and though it was not always openly admitted, the main reason for that uniqueness was the presence of the black worker. The northward migration of the American Negro was largely a twentieth-century movement, and the "problem" of the black worker during the Gilded Age was a Southern "problem." As one historian has written, "It remained for the New South to find what Reconstruction had failed to find: the measure of the emancipated slave's freedom and a definition of free labor, both black and white; for the white worker's place in the New Order would be virtually conditioned by the place assigned the free black worker."[1]

No city in the nation had more black residents during the Gilded Age than New Orleans. By the end of the nineteenth century, the Crescent City claimed more than 77,000 permanent black residents and during certain seasons that number increased significantly.[2] While blacks were always a minority in the city, never much more than one-fourth of the population, they contributed at least one-third of the working class population. Furthermore, New Orleans had far more skilled black workers than any other city in the nation and black workers were crucial to the cotton trade. Thus, white employers and workers could scarcely ignore the importance of the Negro to the economic life of the city. They, like their counterparts elsewhere, struggled to define their own position in light of this fact. The decisions were not theirs to make alone, however. Blacks were not unaware of their own importance nor did they view lightly the precedents which were being established. Many of the black workers had a proud heritage as free

---

*First appeared as chapter 4 in David Paul Bennetts, "Black and White Workers, New Orleans, 1880-1900" (Ph. D. dissertation, University of Illinois at Urbana-Champagne, 1972), 137-89.

black artisans and were not willing to stand idly by while white society assigned them to the bottom rung of the economic ladder.

The relationship between white and black workers in New Orleans was both complex and ill-defined throughout the Gilded Age. It was dependent on many factors in addition to how white and black workingmen felt about each other. The attitudes of employers were obviously important, and they were influenced by the racial philosophies of the period as well as by economic exigencies. Black leaders—employers, clergymen, union heads, editors and educators—played an important role. In fact, at least in New Orleans, the black worker was a member not only of the city's working class but of a rather rigidly stratified black society as well. His status in one group was not unrelated to his position in the other. The Negroes' existence as workingmen was certainly not isolated from their existence as social and political beings. All of these factors, and many others, bore heavily on the relationship between black and white workers in the city. Finally, it must be understood that the Gilded Age was a period of transition for both the workers and the city. Since this was true not only in terms of class, but race as well, the black workers were especially vulnerable. At times, workers in New Orleans were forced to decide which should take precedence—their loyalty to an economic class or to the white race. Their choice was not always the same.

When Frederick Law Olmsted visited New Orleans before the Civil War he reported "a most revolting sight"—Irish laborers waiting on Negro masons.[3] While the sight may have been just as revolting to native New Orleanians and was surely distasteful to the Irish, it was not an unaccustomed sight. In fact, the available information suggests that black workers, free and slave, were not only numerous but were recognized as being equally or more skilled than white workers in several trades.[4] This was especially true in the building trades. In 1850 the director of the census counted 355 carpenters and 325 masons who were free Negro men. In addition, there were free black painters, ship's carpenters and building mechanics.[5] These figures, of course, did not include the slaves who were active in the building trades and many others. Several structures in the city, including the impressive Wesley Methodist Episcopal Church, were built entirely by slave labor, even to the making of the bricks.[6] While statistics are not available for the slave population, among free Negro men the ratio of skilled to unskilled was considerably higher than among Irish and German immigrants, and there is no doubt that they were a dominant force in certain skilled trades.[7]

Despite their obvious contributions as skilled craftsmen, most of the free blacks in New Orleans, numbering 10,000 in the 1850s, were unskilled laborers. They were widely employed on the docks and as steamboat hands and, of course, as domestic help. Three-fifths of the city's free Negroes were women, and they were more likely to be unskilled than the men. The women were generally employed as domestics or worked in their homes as washerwomen and seamstresses.[8] Whether skilled or unskilled, blacks were subject to changing labor patterns during the fifteen year period which preceded the Civil War. New Orleans labor was not affected by the flow of immigrant workers into the

TABLE 1
Selected Occupations of Free Negro Males, 1850[9]

Occupation	Number	Mulattoes
Carpenters	355	299
Masons	325	213
Cigar Makers	16	143
Shoe Makers	92	76
Mechanics	52	46
Painters	28	24
Coopers	43	26
Tailors	82	79
Barbers	41	35
Blacksmiths	15	11
Butchers	18	17
Laborers	179	178

country to the extent that labor in the North was. Still, black workers felt the impact more than any others. Most of the immigrants were German or Irish and they worked cheaply—considerably cheaper than slave labor. The result was that European labor tended to replace black labor, free and slave, in many occupations formerly dominated by Negroes. By the 1850s free Negroes had been largely replaced by the Irish and Germans as domestic servants, waiters, and hotel workers. Cabs and drays were taken over by whites, and the St. Charles hotel, which once employed free Negroes, had an almost all Irish staff by the time of the war. Even the docks and steamboats became Irish preserves during the decade before the war, and the free Negro peddlers were replaced by Germans.[10]

Several crafts all but excluded Negroes, especially free Negroes, during the antebellum period. Few blacks engaged in printing, baking, sailmaking, glazing, lithography, engraving or piloting. In addition, blacks seldom worked as screwmen or as yardmen in the cotton presses. By the 1850s, slave labor was too valuable to be used digging ditches, building levees or driving drays. Jobs which would soon become 'nigger jobs' were known as 'Irish jobs' when the guns erupted at Fort Sumter.[11] It is interesting to note that the free black population of New Orleans declined in numbers during the fifteen years before the Civil War.[12]

Though whites displaced blacks in many occupations, the displacement was seldom complete. The immigrants worked side by side with Negroes at certain jobs, and the black artisans maintained their hold on some of the trades, especially the building trades. Nor was the displacement permanent. Emancipation forced thousands of former slaves, skilled and unskilled, into competition with free blacks and white workers. By 1880, a casual observer might have felt that the labor pattern had gone full circle and jobs were distributed among the races as they had been prior to the influx of immigrants. Black workers had regained control, or at least reappeared, in several occupational areas. They were again evident in the hotels and as domestic servants. By the end of Reconstruction, Negroes once more predominated among the teamsters and roustabouts and were even found working as screwmen and in the yards of the cotton presses. Beneath the surface, however, matters had changed considerably. Without the political and economic support of his master, the former slave found it difficult to compete. Much of the training received by the skilled blacks as slaves was inferior and they were not prepared to compete with free labor, white or black. The master had generally arranged for the hiring of his slaves or had at least backed them in their efforts, and after emancipation many employers turned away from black workers. The master had also arranged for the training or apprenticeship of his slaves. The freedmen found it far more difficult to learn a trade without his master's influence and backing. Finally, some slave artisans simply renounced their trades as badges of their servitude.[13] For these reasons, and several others to be discussed later, black artisans steadily lost ground in several trades after emancipation.

Other notable signs of change appeared. Blacks were "winning" back the "Irish jobs" they had lost prior to the war. Unskilled freedmen and former rural artisans who were unable to find comparable positions in the city now worked for less than the immigrants or immigrant children. While ditch digging may have been too menial a chore for a valuable slave, it was not recognized as such for a penniless and oppressed freedman. Though the black population of the city had decreased between 1820 and 1860 (From one out of two residents to only one in seven), the proportion of Negroes in the population climbed steadily after the war. By 1880, blacks comprised more than one-fourth of the population.[14] The unskilled laborers who were black, lacking political and economic power and faced with the hostility of a white society no longer dominated by the planter class, were forced to accept the least prestigious and lowest paying jobs. Increasingly, the former "free men of color" found themselves grouped, economically and socially, with the freedmen.

It remained to be seen how workers, black and white, would react to the changing situation. One thing was certain. The slave regime had left a legacy of distrust which would inevitably affect working-class relations in the city. White workers had been frustrated by unfair competition from slaves in the antebellum period. Many free blacks had lost their jobs to immigrants and some immigrants had been forced to work as laborers for skilled Negro artisans. Both groups feared the entrance of rural freedmen into the city labor market.

Meanwhile, employers had to choose between profit and white supremacy—both significant philosophies of the New South. As a logical proposition employers tended to hire workers on the basis of their merit regardless of race. When market and social forces allowed it, this was a rational decision for any businessman. But "rational decisions" were dangerous when they challenged white supremacy or gave jobs to blacks while white workers were unemployed. Some employers preferred not to disturb the social customs of the "Old South." Others boldly ignored their critics and bought their labor at the cheapest market. Most attempted to use racial hostility to discipline the class antagonism of the New South whenever possible. The situation was not promising for black-white labor solidarity.

Black society in New Orleans was as rigidly stratified as white society, perhaps more so, and black workers were just as conscious of job status as white workers. Thus, while black workers were not always treated on a basis of equality with white workers having comparable skills, neither did they ignore class differences based on job status within their own community. The term "Negro worker" reveals very little about the status, compensation, treatment or work of a particular black wage-earner. Throughout the Gilded Age, Negroes were found in virtually every job category in the city. In fact, the 1890 census report on occupations reported Negro males working at every occupation listed, and Negro females were missing only from the lists of bookkeepers, accountants, stenographers and typists.[15] Ten years later Negro males were active in every reported occupation with the exception of architects, designers, draftsmen and telegraph and telephone operators. Black women were still not employed as stenographers or typists and had lost their few positions as textile mill operatives; but they were employed in every other job category and had at least broken through as bookkeepers and accountants.[16] Black workers, thus, were spread across the entire job spectrum and often shared more in common with their white co-workers than other members of their own race.

New Orleans had at least its share of black professionals considering the limited opportunities available to Negroes in the professional fields. Clergymen were, of course, the most evident. Blacks had over one-half of the churches in the city by the 1880s, and the 1890 census reported 104 Negro clergymen active in New Orleans.[17] By the end of the century the number had increased to 126.[18] With about one-fourth of the population, New Orleans blacks had 41 percent of the clergymen in 1890. In addition, there were eighteen physicians and surgeons, eight lawyers, ninety-seven female professors and teachers and thirty-four government officials. The 1900 census was more extensive and showed eleven dentists, three journalists, forty-three male teachers and professors in colleges, twenty-one undertakers and several teachers of music. While the number of female teachers and professors and male physicians increased, there was a decrease in the number of lawyers (8 to 7) and government officials (34 to 21).[19] Throughout the period there were several black bankers, brokers, and businessmen.

Most of these professionals and businessmen were accorded high status in the black community, as were their white counterparts in the white community. But these people were not legitimate members of the working class. Nor was upper class status limited to these few. To a greater extent than in the white community black wage earners might be accorded high status within their own racial group. During the Gilded Age, upper-class, or at least upper middle class, status was accorded to a group that ranged from headwaiters, porters and butlers, through screwmen, barbers, carpenters and postal employees. The prestige enjoyed by a worker was dependent on a number of factors. The domestic servant class, which was gradually passing from upper class status, inherited their standing from antebellum days. Black screwmen mirrored the status accorded to white screwmen long before there were any Negroes active in the trade. Headwaiters, stevedores, and foremen supervised other workers, almost always other Negroes, and thus commanded a certain amount of respect, though white sources frequently insisted that blacks did not like to work under other blacks.[20] Skilled artisans were often granted high status as much because of their former status as free men of color as because of their skills. As will be demonstrated, several other factors—degree of blackness, Creole heritage, union strength, relationship with white workers, and contribution to the city's economy—determined the status of a given worker or class of workers.[21]

When compared with the white community, high status in the black community was given more readily to members of the working class. It was also true that several high status positions for blacks were not recognized as such by the white community when occupied by white workers. The most obvious examples can be found in the domestic and personal services occupations. A white barber did not enjoy the same status in his community as a black barber did in his. The reason is perhaps obvious. With so many prestige positions closed, or almost closed, to them, blacks selected their elite from what was available. A black screwman had climbed about as high as a Negro could reasonably expect to get on the New Orleans docks in 1890, but a capable and ambitious white man could realistically strive for a position as a stevedore or ship's agent. The white screwman was certainly respected by his fellow dock workers and even by other citizens, but not to the same extent as the black screwman. While never admitting that prejudice restricted black opportunities—there were other means of "explaining" the failure of blacks to achieve beyond a certain level—white society expected more from its own workers if they hoped to be labeled a success. Finally, it should be noted that white society used a different set of criteria in evaluating black workers than that employed by the black community itself. The degree of blackness, for example, was of some importance in determining status, but the two communities often adopted different points of view on the relationship between color and status.[22]

As already noted, New Orleans blacks were employed in virtually every occupation offered by the city during the Gilded Age. Not surprisingly, however, their strength was much more apparent in certain areas of employment than in others. Keeping in mind what has been said above, it is worthwhile to examine the distribution of black workers within the Crescent City labor force. Prior to World War I, the great cities of the North were conspicuous for the scarcity of black artisans employed within their boundaries. Such was not the case in the South where most of the Negro craftsmen of the country lived. In 1890, more than 18,000 of the 22,318 black carpenters in the United States lived in the South. Two-thirds of the Negro painters and more than 70 percent of the bricklayers were employed in Southern states during that same year. The situation was much the same for the other skilled trades.[23] Several skilled trades in the South were actually dominated by blacks, the best examples being the plasterers, cement finishers, and bricklayers. The employment of black artisans in Southern cities, which was where most of the Southern white artisans were located, varied depending upon location and demand. In the border cities, blacks were prominent in brickmaking and iron and steel making. In the more typically Southern cities, like Atlanta, Charleston, Memphis and Nashville, carpenters and masons were the most conspicuous.[24]

No city in the country had more skilled black workers than New Orleans. Of the sixteen cities in the nation providing employment for more than four hundred skilled blacks in 1890, New Orleans ranked eighth in the percentage of skilled blacks in its black labor force. Yet, the Crescent City easily outdistanced her nearest rival in the total number of skilled Negroes employed.[25] Furthermore, New Orleans showed more variety than the other cities in the type of work pursued by skilled blacks. Of the twenty-four skilled job categories listed in W. E. B. DuBois' study of the Negro artisan, New Orleans led all other cities in the number of blacks employed in eight of these fields. No other city topped more than four categories. New Orleans ranked second or third in six additional areas.[26]

As was true during the antebellum period, skilled blacks were especially prominent in the New Orleans building trades. In 1900, approximately 22 percent of the carpenters, 19 percent of the painters, glaziers, and varnishers, 76 percent of the masons, 79 percent of the pasterers, and 68 percent of the roofers and slaters were Negroes. Taken as a group, these skilled blacks totaled 1,764 workmen.[27] These figures far exceeded the national average; and with the exception of the painters and carpenters, they exceeded the average for the Southern states. In the case of the two exceptions, New Orleans compared favorably with the rest of the South.[28] In addition, blacks made significant contributions in related areas as hod-carriers, stone and marble cutters, paper hangers, and saw mill employees.[29] Not surprisingly, a majority of the most imposing structures in New Orleans during the Gilded Age were built by black workers, including the new Cotton Exchange in 1881 and the stone library at segregated Tulane University.[30]

While the city's building trades provided the best examples of the importance of skilled black labor, Negro craftsmen and mechanics were active in several other trades as well.[31] In most cases their strength was in those fields which had formerly been controlled by slaves or free men of color. In others blacks were employed and trained because, even though they were skilled jobs, white workers were not attracted to them. The plasterers provide an excellent example of how blacks maintained control of a trade. The high proportion of Negro plasterers was, to a large extent, attributable to the ability of black laborers and plaster tenders to become "graduated artisans." The plastering trade was made relatively unpleasant by the dust and the necessity of standing in uncomfortable

TABLE 2
Skilled Negroes in New Orleans, 1900[32]

Selected Occupations	Aggregate	Negroes
Bakers	947	107
Barbers	904	238
Blacksmiths	768	141
Boot-Shoe Makers	1,147	253
Butchers	701	62
Cabinetmakers	247	30
Carpenters & Joiners	2,753	598
Coopers	883	311
Harness-Saddle Makers	198	3
Marble-Stone Cutters	91	14
Masons	684	518
Painters, glaziers & varnishers	1,261	227
Paper Hangers	111	14
Plasterers	323	255
Roofers & Slaters	242	166
Tailors	438	40
Tinware Makers	380	37
Upholsterers	219	92
Wheelwrights	122	6

positions for long periods while applying plaster to walls and ceilings.[33] Until well into the twentieth century, when they were once again attracted by high wages, Southern whites were content to leave this kind of work to Negroes. In 1890 blacks controlled 68 percent of the trade and by 1900 they had increased this to 79 percent.[34]

Obviously, blacks employed in trades which they dominated or at least contributed to significantly enjoyed certain advantages not shared by black workers in other fields. White employers were forced to hire them; white labor was forced to cooperate with them and they controlled the apprenticeship programs. Generally, labor presented its most united front in those trades controlled or shared equally by blacks.[35] Shortly after the Civil War, for example, the white bricklayers in New Orleans went out on strike demanding higher wages. They ignored the black bricklayers and the strike failed. After that, white and black bricklayers began to cooperate and had one of the most successful histories of racial harmony found anywhere in the South during the Gilded Age.[36] For apparent reasons, it was important for blacks to at least maintain their share of a given trade. While difficult, if not impossible, it was also advantageous for them to increase their strength in those areas where they were numerically weak. The extent to which they were able to do this would determine, in large part, their ability to compete with white artisans and receive equal treatment from white employers.

When W. E. B. DuBois was compiling statistics and collecting information on the Negro artisan at the turn of the century, he concluded that the Gilded Age had been a period of change for the skilled black worker. For many years after the Civil War, Negroes became less and less important as artisans than before the conflict. In some communities, he discovered, this retrogression continued through the Gilded Age and into the twentieth century. In others, blacks were able to halt the decline and by 1900 were either holding their own or enhancing their position in the skilled trades. Based on the opinions of those who reported local conditions to DuBois, black artisans were gaining ground in Birmingham, Washington, Atlanta, Pittsburgh, Charleston, Richmond, Houston, and "slowly" in Chicago. They were reported as losing ground in Baltimore, St. Louis, Raleigh, Charlotte, Cincinnati, Memphis, and Dallas. The black artisans of New York, Boston, Philadelphia, Savannah, and Augusta were "holding their own."[37] Others, such as Booker T. Washington, were convinced that Negroes had neglected the skills acquired under slavery and lost what had been practically a monopoly of the skilled labor in the South at the close of the Civil War.[38] Later investigations concentrated more on the different trades than on different communities. They argued that blacks continued to lose ground after Reconstruction in blacksmithing, carpentry, and painting in the South despite small increases in the nation. It seems, however, that they more than held their own in the "trowel trades"—bricklaying, plastering, and cement finishing.[39] The losses were partially attributable to migration northward, but more importantly to the failure of black craftsmen to obtain a proportionate share of the increased employment opportunities.

The reports DuBois received from New Orleans were contradictory. One reporter claimed there was no way of telling the number of Negro artisans in the city or their share of the work. Another insisted that they were increasing both in number and efficiency. One investigator said black artisans were "either gaining or at least not losing," though he admitted that the competition from white mechanics was increasing.[40] In view of the confusion and the importance of the matter, a comparison of the census reports on occupations for 1890 and 1900 is both revealing and necessary.[41] As shown by Table 5, black artisans were losing ground, relatively, in four occupations—barbering, baking, tailoring, and boot and shoe making. During the ten year period between 1890 and 1900, blacks made significant gains as butchers, cabinetmakers, upholsterers, coopers, stone-cutters, masons, and plasterers. Changes of less than 2 percent took place in five additional fields. In three areas there was an absolute decrease in the number of blacks employed—boot and shoe makers, carpenters and joiners, and tailors—but the number of white shoemakers and tailors also decreased. Since they contributed one-fourth of the total population of the city, blacks controlled at least a proportionate share of the positions in 1890 in five out of thirteen occupational areas. By 1900 blacks controlled

TABLE 3
Black Artisans in New Orleans, 1890 and 1900 Compared[42]

Occupation	Number of Black Workers 1890	1900	Percent of Total 1890	1900
Barbers	200	238	30	26
Bakers	107	107	14	11
Blacksmiths-Wheelwrights	116	147*	15	16
Boot-Shoe Makers	366	253	25	22
Butchers	48	62	6	9
Cabinet Makers and Upholsterers	92	122	20	26
Carpenters and Joiners	603	598	22	22
Coopers	235	311	28	35
Marble-Stone Cutters & Masons	495	532**	65	79
Painters, glaziers & varnishers	200	227	17	18
Plasterers	239	255	58	79
Tailors	59	40	10	9
Tinners and Tineward Makers	36	37	9	10

*All but six were blacksmiths. **All but fourteen were masons.

less than their share in boot and shoe making but had gained an equitable position as upholsterers and cabinetmakers. Finally, if all of the occupations listed in Table 5 are considered together, the percentage of black artisans increased by about 1 percent during the ten-year period. Still, the figure stood at only 24 percent of the total skilled work force in 1900.

What all of this seems to suggest is that the black artisan, who apparently lost ground in the years immediately following the war, had at least halted the decline during the Gilded Age. Slightly more than one out of every four residents was of Negro descent and slightly less than one out of every four artisans was black. Not surprisingly, they made their greatest advance in those occupations which they had dominated for years—the trowel trades. It is interesting to note, considering the increased racial tensions of the 1880s, that blacks decreased in importance most significantly as barbers, the most intimate of the occupations listed. Generally, however, the black artisan was "holding his own" in New Orleans and was represented in proportion to his numbers in the total population.[43]

While the city's black artisans were struggling to hold their own during the Gilded Age, white workers were almost being driven off the docks. While exact figures are not available, it has been estimated that at the close of Reconstruction about 30 percent of the more than ten thousand dockworkers were Negroes. Conservative estimates put the figure at 50 percent by 1900, and the proportion of Negroes steadily increased until there were very few white workers left. Not until the 1930s did the whites begin to regain some of their positions on the docks.[44] Severe physical strain, risk, intermittency of employment, and the "shape-up" hiring system were all aspects of dockwork which made for a high overall undesirability and tended to reduce the number of white workers. With employment opportunities limited in several other spheres, blacks were attracted to the docks. Of course more workers, black and white, were always available than needed. In several cases, the jobs were segregated with certain types of work being done exclusively by one race or the other. The coal wheelers, for example, were all Negroes, but the pumpers, with few exceptions, were white.[45] The black and white longshoremen, the largest groups, were about equal in strength for most of the period.

Because the work was classified as "skilled" and because they were the aristocracy of the port, the racial composition of the screwmen merits special attention. Prior to the Civil War, the screwmen were an entirely white group with no Negro permitted to stow cotton in New Orleans. But as the prestige of their job increased and their self-image was enhanced, many of the white screwmen shied away from the heavy work which accompanied their more skilled activities. They hired black assistants and employed Negro longshoremen to help them heave the screws. As a result, a number of Negroes became "initiated into the mysteries of the craft."[46] These black screwmen formed their own organization, and because they threatened to take jobs from white screwmen and could act as strikebreakers, the white screwmen initiated a work-sharing agreement. Thus, blacks had successfully integrated—perhaps more accurately, infiltrated—the strongest of all local crafts. By 1895 there were as many, if not more, black screwmen as white on the docks of the Crescent City.[47]

For most of the period 1880-1900, black and white workers were nearly equal in numbers on the docks, and it was there that they worked in perhaps the closest proximity, competed for the same jobs, had the same employers and belonged to some of the same labor organizations. It was there that the working class experiments in racial harmony were most severely tested, and the reactions of the workers and employers were closely watched by the rest of the community. As will be shown, the degree of racial harmony evident on the docks at any given time was subject to several pressures. Racial harmony varied with the availability of jobs, shifts in the racial composition of the workers, and the outcome of struggles between employers and workers. Despite numerous examples of cooperation, there was a steady undercurrent of racial tension which occasionally erupted into violent race riots.

Closely related to the longshoremen, screwmen and other dock workers were the roustabouts and sailors, teamsters, and cotton press employees. In these occupations, as on the docks, black workers were numerous. Almost without exception, the roustabouts were Negroes; and while several observers suggested that they should be replaced with whites, this never happened. The roustabout's world was a black world and few whites apparently cared to invade it. Fewer Negroes were found employed as sailors, and black pilots were rare indeed. The 1890 census reported that 1,298 New Orleans residents were employed as boatmen, canalmen, pilots and sailors and 458 were black. Ten years later there were 371 Negro boatmen and sailors or about 31 percent of the total.[48] More than half of the teamsters, draymen, and hackmen in the city were blacks and most of the Negro teamsters were employed handling cotton. Teamsters, on the other hand, were largely employed by the railroads, warehouses, and individual merchants. By 1900 there were more than 1,500 Negro drivers and they represented 51 percent of the total for New Orleans.[49] Both blacks and whites were employed by the cotton presses in almost equal numbers, though several jobs were closed to Negro workers. Generally, these "closed jobs" were those which involved a certain amount of responsibility and integrity, characteristics which the white community was convinced the black worker lacked. Negroes might be employed as weighers' assistants or scale hands, but not as weighers or reweighers.[50] Still, the black workers were well represented in the cotton presses. When the teamsters, roustabouts, and press employees are considered along with the dockworkers, the importance of the black worker to the commerce of the port becomes apparent.

While New Orleans Negroes held their own in the skilled trades and enhanced their already powerful presence on the docks and in the cotton trades, they were not largely employed in the city's manufacturing establishments. They were especially excluded from those positions which could be labeled skilled or semi-skilled. According to the census tables, there were only seventeen black iron and steel workers out of 373 in 1890. While the number of such workers increased to 438 by 1900, only five of them were Negroes. In 1890 there were 1,918 people employed in the city as textile mill operatives, machinists, ship and boat builders, and saw and planning mill employees, but fewer than 250 were Negroes and 110 of those were employed in the saw mills. Blacks had an even smaller share of this type of work ten years later.[51] Granted, blacks were employed extensively by the clothing industry and in several of the processing plants such as the cotton seed mills. But the former were largely women who worked in their homes and the latter were generally unskilled yard hands. Only in the tobacco and cigar factories were blacks largely employed as operatives.[52]

By the end of the century it was clear that New Orleans blacks had not received the training nor been offered the type of jobs which would have allowed them to share in whatever economic opportunities the industry of the New South offered. In 1900 there were 769 machinists and nine were Negroes; there were 225 male cotton mill operatives and twenty were Negroes, and only 145 of 1,369 stationary engineers and firemen were black, most of them firemen.[53] Furthermore, when manufacturing moved out of the small shop and into the factory, blacks frequently lost their jobs because they were not trained to operate the machinery or because white women were hired. This was no doubt one of the reasons for the decline in the number of Negro tobacco workers. Between 1890 and 1900, the number of female operatives increased by almost two hundred while the number of men employed dropped by more than three hundred. More than half of the male operatives were Negroes in 1900, but only thirty-seven black women were found among the 534 female operatives. This was eight less than in 1890.[54] Negro males in this field increasingly found themselves employed as warehousemen or common laborers though they had at one time been skilled or semi-skilled workers.[55]

The textile industry almost completely excluded black workers. The Southern textile industry was largely a post-Civil War development and during its early growth "it served almost as a crusade to rehabilitate the South and to provide work for the poverty-stricken poor whites."[56] In New Orleans it served as a crusade to assist women who were forced to earn a living. In 1890, 444 female operatives were employed by the city's mills and this figure included seven Negroes. Ten years later there was not a single black woman listed among the 558 operatives. The few black males employed—eighty-eight in 1890 and twenty in 1900—held menial jobs as janitors, warehousemen, and outside laborers.[57] There is some evidence to suggest that blacks employed in other industries received similar jobs and many of them were children.[58] Black workers were not largely employed at skilled positions in New Orleans industry. In this, New Orleans was like the rest of the South.[59]

As the river trade of New Orleans decreased in importance during the last two decades of the nineteenth century, the railroads took up the slack. In addition to the obvious commercial importance of the railroads, they provided needed jobs for the working class. Between 1890 and 1900, the number of men employed by the railroads in New Orleans almost doubled. Yet, like New Orleans industry, the railroads did not benefit black workers to the degree that was true for white labor. It was not that the railroads did not hire blacks. In fact, Negroes in New Orleans had more than their share of the jobs provided by the railroads and they held 32 percent of the positions in 1900.[60] Again, however, they performed only the most menial chores. It was almost unthinkable that Negroes would be hired for such high status jobs as conductor or engineer, and they seldom were. Generally only whites were employed as signalmen, telegraphers, towermen, agents, dispatchers, building mechanics, and section-gang foremen. Thus, in the clerical, freighthandling, and station employee groups, blacks were employed only in common labor and service occupations. Negroes were employed as trainmen, firemen, and brakemen, but these jobs were hot and dirty and, in the case of the brakemen, dangerous. Until they improved with technological advances and became stepping stones to better positions, these jobs did not attract white applicants. Blacks were, of course, largely employed as track laborers and yard workers, but only infrequently as foremen for these crews.[61] It is worth noting that most railroad unions, including Eugene Debs' American Railway Union, barred Negroes from membership by constitutional provision.

The railroads and the factories of New Orleans were not unique in their treatment of the black workers. In fact, despite the existence of the black carpenters, plasterers, bricklayers and screwmen, and the claims of the longshoremen and others that they were skilled workers, most New Orleans blacks were unskilled laborers. They vastly outnumbered white workers in the menial jobs. While one of four citizens was black, more than half of those who listed their occupation simply as "laborer" were Negroes. This category did not include the dockworkers, factory workers, or railroad employees mentioned above, yet it encompassed more than eleven thousand black workers in 1900. A majority of the hostlers, porters, levee laborers, customs-house laborers and even the ragmen were Negroes.[62] Of course blacks were far more numerous than whites as servants, waiters, and stewards, despite complaints that the Negro domestics were no longer the faithful, industrious servants of the past.[63] In 1900 there were 8,653 Negro servants, waiters, and stewards in the city. Sixty percent of the janitors and sextons were black.[64] The list could, of course, be extended. Thus we should not overemphasize the fact that New Orleans had more skilled blacks than any other city in the nation.[65]

Some mention has already been made of several occupations which, for a variety of reasons, were almost completely dominated by whites. In addition to specific trades such as the machinists, harness makers and saddlers, plumbers, electricians, and gas and steam fitters, there were entire areas of economic activity in which New Orleans Negroes played little or no role. The "white collar" jobs, which perhaps not legitimately within the scope of this paper, suggest the limitations placed on Negroes in the city. Not only were the collars white, but the faces usually were as well. If we consider salesmen, saleswomen, insurance agents, real estate agents, bookkeepers, clerks, accountants, copyists, stenographers, and typists as a single economic group, we find that only 2 percent of all such positions were filled by Negroes.[66] Since these jobs employed close to 14,000 people in New Orleans in 1900, the exclusion of blacks represented a serious limitation on their employment opportunities.

It is somewhat ironic that the city's newspapers never tired of expounding on the opportunities available for black residents of the Crescent City. The entire publishing business was dominated by whites. Less than 6 percent of the journalists, printers, pressmen, engravers, copy boys, lithographers, and bookbinders were Negroes.[67] Were it not for the Negro newspapers in the city, even fewer blacks would have been employed in these areas. The Southern locals of the International Typographical Union, and New Orleans had one of the strongest, barred Negroes from membership. They argued that there were few blacks trained in the printing trades and their stance, thus, was inconsequential. But it was not only a lack of the necessary skills that kept Negroes out of the business. Apparently only eight blacks out of a total of 120 newspaper carriers had the "skills" necessary to perform that job. There were as many black printers, proportionately, as there were black carriers in 1900.[68] The white monopoly of jobs in communications was further demonstrated by the fact that 98 percent of the jobs as telegraph and telephone linemen and operators were held by whites. There were no Negro operators.[69]

Perhaps the most interesting of all the white-dominated job areas was the street railway. In 1890, the street railway companies employed 357 men. Four of them were

Negroes. By 1900, there were 850 employees collecting their pay from the streetcar lines. Four blacks, quite possibly the same four, were employed.[70] The few blacks who were hired worked in the stables. This situation becomes all the more interesting when the nature of the job is considered. For most of the period the cars were mule driven, and the number of Negro teamsters and hackmen shatters any notions that blacks could not handle a team of mules. Even when the lines began to convert to the electric trolley, the black drivers in the city were no worse off for the change than the white drivers who had to be instructed by experienced hands brought in from the North. No black men were trained to drive the new electric trolley cars. Furthermore, the job of streetcar driver had many of the characteristics normally associated with "nigger jobs." It was long, hard work with poor compensation. The rules on some of the roads were little short of tyrannical.[71] Yet, the job of driver had certain characteristics which demanded, at least in Gilded Age New Orleans, that it be filled by a white man. The driver was also the conductor and, therefore, handled the money. Thus the job carried a certain amount of responsibility. In addition, the driver had to be a public relations man. He had to keep his customers happy, act as a referee and win the confidence of the riders. Few felt a black man could do this under any circumstances, but the streetcar situation was made more trying by the fact that nine of every ten riders were white and many were women. White citizens rode in streetcars with Negroes as a matter of convenience, but no one believed they would tolerate black drivers. So the streetcars of New Orleans, one of the last forms of public conveyance in the South to be segregated, was always driven by white men.[72]

The hiring procedure of the streetcar lines shut-out most Negroes even if other factors had not prevented their being hired. A man seeking a job needed two letters of recommendation and twenty-five dollars for a uniform. He was graded on personal appearance, had to pass both an oral exam on the company rules and an on-the-job competency test, had to be able to read and write and a native of the city.[73] It is difficult to imagine anyone who was able to meet these requirements being satisfied with the position, and it is certainly possible that white applicants were not forced to meet them. It is also possible that this technique was used in other areas where black workers were not wanted, though such sophistication and subtlety were probably not generally necessary. One thing is certain; blacks were aware of the discriminatory practices of the streetcar lines, and they demonstrated their disapproval on several occasions.[74]

Because it was the largest city in the South, a leading port and the site of several United States government offices as well as a mint, New Orleans offered numerous government jobs. In addition to government officials, there were many jobs of lesser importance. Blacks filled several of these positions in the mint, customs office, courthouses, and post office. All of the bailiffs in the United States Courts were Negroes and there were a few black mailmen.[75] Thirteen percent of the women employed in the United States Mint were also black.[76] A local newspaper claimed in 1881 that there was an "army" of black employees at work in the federal offices of the city. A rival paper, however, challenged this statement: "The great army of employees spoken of by the *Observer*, are seven or eight assistant janitors, whose salaries until recently were twenty-five dollars per month, and a few dozen pig iron and sale weighers who work periodically averaging two or three days per week, such work as few white men aspire to."[77] Only an occasional political favorite rose above the position of janitor, porter, or laborer in the federal offices and even fewer in the state and city buildings. As will be shown, they had difficulty being accepted on the police force and even more difficulty staying on it.

Despite the obstacles in their path, some black men did manage to climb out of the mass of the laboring people while still maintaining close contact with the workers. There were, in other words, black foremen, bosses, and employers. The non-locomotive engineers employed in the city were, by the very nature of their work, bosses of a sort. They exercised direct authority over several others because of their skill and because work in a cotton press, seed mill, or sugar refinery centered on the operation of its boilers and engines. The usual situation was a white engineer assisted by a Negro fireman and black helpers, but there was an occasional black engineer.[78] On even rarer occasions, black engineers supervised white assistants.[79]

The census takers uncovered six Negro foremen or overseers in 1900.[80] While the figure is probably low, depending on the definition of a foreman, it demonstrates the extent to which it was felt necessary to place white foremen in charge of black workers. Yet, there was some black foremen in the mills and supervising black crews repairing the streets and levees.[81] It need scarcely be mentioned that black foremen supervised black workers; and when there were black and white laborers employed and Negroes were hired as foremen, there were also white foremen.[82] Not surprisingly, black foremen were most common in those skilled trades dominated by Negroes. The *Daily Picayune* reported that the black bricklayers, for example, generally worked "under foremen of their own race."[83] The same newspaper had earlier reported an incident involving Negro laborers at work on the asphalt pavement. There was a black foreman and, according to the reporter, the crew did not like taking orders from him. Trouble was generally avoided by keeping a white superintendent on hand, but he was absent when the reporter visited the scene.[84]

Black foremen were undoubtedly subject to the same stresses as white foremen and in a given situation were probably just as successful. Much depended on the type of work being done, the workers employed, and the abilities of individual foremen. The bricklayers, obviously, did not resent taking orders from a highly skilled black foreman, but the street workers would probably have resented someone selected at random to be "foreman-of-the-day" and lacking the skill for the job. White newspapers tended to emphasize the trouble encountered by black foremen while Negro-operated papers pointed to the many highly successful experiments with black bosses.[85] Black or white, the life of those in authority tended to be difficult at times. On one such occasion, a group of black laborers finished unloading a barge and lined-up to receive their pay. One worker accused the Negro paymaster of cheating him and demanded more money. The paymaster refused and was struck by the worker, whereupon the paymaster drew a knife and charged his antagonist. In an effort to defend himself, the worked picked up a rock and aimed it at his opponent. He hit the paymaster but the rebound struck the white timekeeper. He, in turn, drew a revolver and started firing indiscriminately. By this time, the friends of both parties had taken sides with their favorites and sparked a full scale brawl. The victors were never determined since the police arrived and the crowd scattered, but a black paymaster and a white timekeeper had momentarily regretted their promotions.[86] These incidents were common to both races, and foremen, paymasters, and timekeepers were favorite targets. Whether the result of deficiencies in the workers' mathematics or the paymasters' integrity, they enlivened many a daily tabloid.

Foremen, of course, were seldom responsible for hiring or major decision making, but New Orleans did have a limited number of black citizens who were involved in these processes. Negro contractors competed for several contracts and one such individual reported in December, 1888, that he had completed $35,000 worth of state levee work using white and black laborers.[87] Most of the black contractors and subcontractors, however, were in the construction business. Again, they were not numerous in the "Negro trades," especially bricklaying. C. F. Ladd, a Negro contractor, was one of the most active house builders in the city and a avid promoter of the building and loan association concept among black residents.[88] In July, 1887, Joseph St. Auge, a Negro subcontractor, had his men employed in the construction of five four story buildings on Canal Street, the rebuilding of an "immense" drug store destroyed by fire, and the building of the Commercial Cotton Press.[89] The most prominent of the black builders, however, was Henry H. Hill. "No better evidence of the success of our people in mechanical work can be found than in the career of Mr. Henry H. Hill, the boss bricklayer," applauded the editor of the Negro weekly in 1887.[90] In the spring of that year, Hill's men were at work doing the brickwork on the construction of the largest oil mill in the world, a large three-story bakery and several houses. He was employing between eighty and one hundred bricklayers.[91]

"If we had more men like Mr. Hill," an observer prophesied, "our people would be better off."[92] While the statement may have been based on a shallow understanding of why there were not more Mr. Hills, there was more than an element of truth in it. In addition to their value as a morale booster and argumentative weapon for those who insisted that blacks could and did succeed, these men controlled jobs. When St. Auge, the subcontractor mentioned earlier, was erecting the buildings on Canal Street, he employed twenty-two artisans and laborers. Only one of them was white. Furthermore, St. Auge probably owed something to the advantages of black capitalism as well. The Mercier Brothers, the proprietors of the stores he was contracted to build, were Negroes.[93]

Unfortunately, there were not enough black men in job-controlling positions to guarantee equality of treatment. Throughout the nation, the 1880s witnessed a remarkable development of Negro business which was closely related to the gradual urbanization of the American blacks.[94] New Orleans had its black bankers, merchants, builders, and other businessmen. Some were worth hundreds of thousands of dollars. Thomy Lafon, a merchant, moneylender, and real estate dealer, left an estate valued at half a million when he died in the 1880s.[95] Most black "businessmen," however, were of the artisan-entrepreneur variety. Many of them were quite successful. A local daily noted a black shoemaker who was so "swamped with business" that he was unable to get his shoes repaired by the promised dates. His prosperity proved a curse as he was assaulted and severely beaten by a white customer whose shoes were not ready when he called for them.[96] These artisan-entrepreneurs were not, however, large scale employers, and their numbers were steadily decreasing. Most black workers depended on white employers. Furthermore, black employers did not invariably prefer nor favor black workers.

Statistics tell us a great deal about the role of black workers in Gilded Age New Orleans. We know what they did and did not do for a living. We know that most economic activities employed both blacks and whites, though several job categories were largely or completely dominated by one race or the other. But these facts leave a large part of the story untold. If blacks and whites worked together, did they have similar duties? If there was discrimination, was it passed down from the employer or was it the result of animosities between the workers. Finally, and perhaps most importantly, did blacks and whites working at the same job really work *together* or did they merely tolerate a situation they found distasteful? Was there a undercurrent of hostility which occasionally erupted and served to widen the gap between the races, or did sharing a job erase many of the old prejudices? These are questions vitally important to an understanding of the role played by race in the history of the city's working-class. While many will be answered in later chapters, some surface observations here will help set the stage and complete the general picture painted by the statistics.

Much of the job discrimination in New Orleans did not take the form of exclusion from a particular activity but rather resulted in blacks being assigned the least desirable and, thus, the worst paying jobs. Several examples of this have already been given, the most apparent being in industry and on the railroads. Even in the United States Mint, an employer somewhat removed from local influences and pressures, not a single black man held a position above that of a common laborer.[97] Even when blacks and whites worked for the same employer at the same job, there might be occupational segregation. In 1882, Hernsheim's Tobacco Manufactory employed females of both races. Hernsheim boasted that no factory in the country had better conveniences for labor or was more concerned with employee welfare. He was careful to point out that the "white females are separated from the colored, and they have separate entrance, exits, and dressing rooms.[98]

In other areas job differentiation was more symbolic than actual. While white and black screwmen did the same work for the same wage, at least until 1894, they usually did not work on the same vessels. If they did, however, the white screwmen insisted upon working the side of the ship next to the wharf and blacks were forced to work the side away from the wharf. The longshoremen had similar arrangements. This apparently was the price the Negroes paid for being accepted as co-workers, and while it worked no actual hardship, it maintained the facade of white superiority and racial separation. It also was an indication of the absence of real labor solidarity, and black workers occasionally objected to the practice. In 1887, the black longshoremen pushed through an agreement that stevedores not only hire an equal number of blacks, but that they also be distributed equally inside and outside the vessel.[99] Not all black workers were strong enough to demand this sort of treatment.

With the possible exception of an outright refusal to hire blacks, the most blatant forms of discrimination were found in those areas where blacks did not receive equal pay for equal work. It is difficult, if not impossible, to determine how widespread this practice may have been. Workers who were classified as second- or third-class men, for example, were paid less than first-class men; but there is usually no way to determine how many of the former were blacks nor whether the classification was justified. The District Assembly of the Knights of Labor campaigned for equal pay and treatment for women in New Orleans but never mentioned black workers in this regard.[100] Either the issue was cautiously avoided, not an unusual stance for a Southern assembly, or blacks generally received equal pay and no issue existed. The city's press was emphatic in its claims that black workers were treated equally in New Orleans, especially the skilled workers. "While the white people here have energetically opposed the Africanization of their State Government," a local editor noted, "they have never made the slightest discrimination against the negro as a laborer or artisan."[101] Later, the same writer was even more explicit: ". . . the real truth of the matter, and that from the colored workmen themselves, that in all departments of skilled labor—in the city of New Orleans at least—they receive the same wages as the whites for the same sort of service. . . . The negro mechanics cannot, if they would, work for less rates than are paid to white men of like skill, as they would incur the hostility of the white workmen."[102]

When New Orleans editors boasted that the problem of balancing social inequality with labor equality had been thoroughly solved in their city, they were generally careful to draw their examples from the building trades and make their comparisons with Northern cities. When the issue was argued on these terms, New Orleans Negroes tended to agree with their fellow citizens. The editor of the Negro journal *The Weekly Pelican* was convinced that the hiring of men was a business transaction, and the "wide awake businessmen" would hire the most capable workers available, "be they black or white."[103] DuBois' informants also insisted that Negro artisans received equal pay in the Crescent City.[104] Again, a familiar pattern is apparent. If blacks dominated a trade or at least formed a sizable minority, it was virtually impossible to discriminate against them. Of all the black building trades artisans in the city, only the carpenters were paid less than their white counterparts, and only 22 percent of the carpenters were black. There were enough black screwmen and longshoremen to make it imperative that white workers support their demands for equal pay. In fact, the white workers insisted on equal pay. If they did not, those "wide-awake businessmen" would hire the cheapest labor, and either white wages would be forced down or white workers would lose their jobs.[105] As for the unorganized and unskilled laborers, the matter of equal wages was largely academic.

White men forced to accept "nigger jobs" were a minority and no doubt received the same low wages as paid their black co-workers. These white workers may have found some comfort in the doctrines of white supremacy, but they found none in their pay envelopes. As far as their employers were concerned, they had crossed the "color line" going the wrong way.

Undoubtedly there were cases of wage discrimination in Gilded Age New Orleans which defy documentation. Teachers, though their membership in the working class might be questioned, provide assurance that, if practical for employer and white employee, there was no hesitancy in applying a double standard. In 1888-1889, a white male teacher in New Orleans received an average of fifty dollars a month and a white female averaged forty dollars. Their black colleagues received thirty-five and thirty dollars respectively.[106] We can only guess at the plight of skilled or semi-skilled blacks who were a distinct minority in their trades. When a Louisiana congressman (not from New Orleans) argued in 1886 that Negroes were entitled to equal pay for equal work, the conservative press was convinced he belonged in a "strait-jacket."[107] There is no evidence to suggest that employers would have been criticized by white New Orleanians for using a double wage standard.

Yet, without slighting the many exceptions, it can be said that black workers in New Orleans received wages which, in most cases, were equal to those received by whites doing similar work. Equality of wages was not the greatest issue before the black workers during the Gilded Age. It was not unequal pay but unequal opportunities that stymied the black worker. The fact that an employer may have paid a Negro machinist on a parity with white machinists was of little importance since blacks were not being trained as machinists. The dozen or so Negro stonecutters in the city received equal pay, but there was only one marble works willing to employ them.[108] The public would not accept black streetcar drivers, and white railroad engineers kept black firemen from learning the trade and entering the brotherhoods. Civil service jobs promised equal wages, but few blacks ever took the examinations because they rarely passed them.[109] Until blacks won equal opportunities, equal pay was not a relevant issue for most New Orleans Negroes.[110]

It has been noted that there were several occupations largely monopolized by either black or white workers. There were, in addition, various techniques of separation employed on certain jobs and in many industries which employed both races. Yet, in many cases, blacks and whites worked side by side at the same jobs, and in most of the segregated positions some contact between the races was inevitable. It is worthwhile to inquire whether this contract was accepted, openly opposed, or simply tolerated by white workers. In the 1880s there were surprisingly few instances where white workers actually refused to labor alongside Negroes. In 1881, the white employees of the Dominion Warehouse attempted to draw the color line and refused to work in the same gangs with blacks. Only the timely arrival of the police prevented a disturbance. Still, it was reported that "the brethren were soon working peacefully together."[111] Incidents such as this were scarce and were generally short-lived. It was too inconvenient for employers to segregate these workers; and since they were unskilled, white employees who caused trouble could be easily replaced.

Trouble between black and white workers most frequently resulted when one side accused the other of violating the work-sharing agreements which were in operation throughout the city. A typical confrontation erupted at the Union Oil Mills in 1889. The white employees initiated a work stoppage and demanded that the manager discharge all of the Negro employees. In the past, they charged, the mills had operated on an unwritten agreement that the work would be divided equally between the races; but the number of blacks employed unloading cotton seed from the freight cars had been gradually increased until they outnumbered the whites. The white workers, "joined by some drunken hoodlums," attacked and stoned the black employees and the manager was forced to halt operations in the mill. As often happened in a situation such as this, the white workers vented their hostility on the black community. Negroes were indiscriminately assaulted on the streets and their homes bombarded with stones and bricks. Only the threat to call out state troops prevented further violence.[112]

The crisis at the Union Oil Mills and others like it provide several insights into the on-the-job relationships between black and white workers. Obviously, there was a strong undercurrent of racial distrust which, when it erupted into open violence, threatened the entire black community. Labor disputes, thus, always contained the potential for igniting race riots. White workers seldom broke the work-sharing agreements because these agreements usually benefited them. With more blacks than whites seeking unskilled positions, a fifty-fifty job sharing agreement provided white workers with more than their share of the jobs. There was no evidence to suggest that white workers were being discharged and replaced by Negroes at the Union Oil Mills nor that white applicants were being passed over by the manager. The white workers were merely protecting the agreement and seeking to halt a trend which they no doubt feared would make them a minority in a "nigger job." They probably did not expect to be able to force the dismissal of all the black workers. Finally, it should be emphasized that these agreements usually worked, and black employees honored them even though they were not receiving a fair share of the jobs. They were only too familiar with what would happen if the agreements were violated.

Not infrequently, black and white workers stood together in protecting their jobs and their agreements from a common foe—the outside laborer. The outburst at the Union Oil Mills took place at a time when the mills were operating at full capacity. During this season, outside workers from the rural parishes swelled the population of New Orleans and surrounding communities. Since these rural workers were largely black, the Negroes vastly outnumbered the whites and job competition was aggravated by racial hostilities. Fortunately, the tension created during these periods seldom resulted in violence and the rural workers left when the mills began to reduce operations. Occasionally, however, the outside hands would attempt to keep their jobs or would seek employment in the mills during the slack season. Trouble was almost inevitable. In December, 1881, nine former plantation hands, all Negroes, secured employment at the Planters' Oil Works in Algiers. Their presence was resented by the resident employees and within a month violence resulted. Three of the new hands were assaulted by a gang of old workers. In defense, one of them drew a revolver and fired—killing a sixteen-year-old boy, an innocent bystander. Two hundred employees and friends followed the police to the home of the new men to guarantee their arrest. The attackers and most of the police escort were Negroes.[113] Black residents were not usually willing to jeopardize their security nor their relationship with their white co-workers for the benefit of outside laborers. Labor violence did not always pit white against black.[114]

Far more numerous than the large scale confrontation was the fracas involving a few individuals. Not surprisingly, the trouble frequently had racial overtones. In October, 1886, a Negro blacksmith was shot and killed by a white blacksmith. Both men were employed at the same shop, but the Negro had been given the most steady employment. It was not the irregular work that bothered the white employee and led to the confrontation, but rather the fact that he was unemployed when a black man was working.[115] Toleration disintegrated and hostilities surfaced when unemployment became a factor in working class race relations. These incidents in the 1880s were forerunners of things to come in the 1890s.[116] There were other difficulties of this nature, and death or severe injury was all too often the result. Thus, two white levee workers left their black co-worker with a skull fracture and two broken arms after they accused him of stealing tools and hit him with a skiff of oars.[117] On another occasion, a white dry dock laborer was shot by a Honduran after the former had insulted the latter's Negro wife.[118] The fact that workers in New Orleans, and most everyone else, seem to have carried guns and knives as a matter of course made minor arguments a serious affair.[119]

While there can be little doubt that blacks working in close proximity to whites constituted a potentially explosive situation and that many of the incidents which took place were probably never reported, the run-ins must be viewed in their proper perspective. Many of the hassles involving black and white workers were not the result of race hatred. A teamster's wagon sideswipes a longshoreman and a fight results. If the men are armed, it may result in death or injury. In a situation such as this, race was not the source of the trouble, though the affair might become more serious if the teamster were black and the longshoreman white.[120] It should also be noted that difficulties involving members of the same race were just as common as interracial disputes and could be just as violent. There is even some evidence to suggest that during strikes blacks were left to discourage black strikebreakers and white strikers handled their own race's scabs. Of course, a fight between black and white workers attracted more attention than the other brawl which occurred almost daily. Racial implications were attached to incidents which had none. In March, 1890, for example, two black teamsters became involved in an argument with two white boss draymen over the payment of twenty-five cents wages. Both white men were wounded by pistol shots. The incident was unfortunate, though not uncommon, but it scarcely deserved the headline it received in the *Daily Picayune*: "Cowardly Attempt to Assassinate Two White Men."[121] Whatever the source of the trouble, these violent confrontations did little to improve race relations in the city, though they seldom seriously divided black and white labor. As will be shown, these encounters became more frequent in the 1890s and received press coverage they did not deserve. Even then, however, they were the *result* of a breakdown in working class race relations and not the *impetus* for it. As for the 1880s, black and white workers may not have enjoyed working together, but the degree of toleration was remarkable.[122]

As was true for the slave, the free black worker in New Orleans was forced into a stereotyped role. White Southerners could scarcely deny the importance of the black worker or the reality of his existence. They thus faced the task of assigning him a "proper role" commensurate with the goals of the New South and the racial attitudes of the Old South. A whole set of myths, rationalizations, and half-truths were expounded by editors, employers, white workers, and even some Negro spokesmen. At times they were directed to a Northern audience and were designed to demonstrate that no one understood the abilities and the limitations of the black man better than the Southern white. At other times, employers defended their hiring practices, unions defended their restrictive clauses, and white workers soothed wounded egos. Frequently the statements made about black workers in the city ignored obvious realities, and contradictions are not difficult to find. There is no way of telling how complete the acceptance of the many statements may have been. In some cases it is difficult to imagine their being accepted at all— evidence to the contrary was too apparent. Yet, the stereotyped image of the black worker which was being created in New Orleans and elsewhere during the Gilded Age eventually gained wide acceptance. Even Samuel Gompers gave it his seal of approval by 1900, and many New Orleanians were more willing to agree with him then than would have been true twenty years earlier.[123] Thus, an understanding of the image of the black worker, however erroneous, must be coupled with the statistical realities if the events of the Gilded Age are to be accurately interpreted.

Most observers agreed, or at least conveyed the impression that they agreed, that blacks were physically and mentally equipped to handle certain jobs while being totally unfit to handle others. These abilities, or lack of them, were racial characteristics; and no one openly admitted that there was any correlation between skills and environment, training and opportunities. "The hand skill capacity of the race is fairly good," a white editor cautiously admitted in 1889, "and in all work that is based on a regular system of routine the negro is able to make good attainments."[124] In this way, the editor accounted for the number of black bricklayers in the city. He felt compelled, however, to qualify his statement:

> When, however, judgement, discretion, calculation and the management of unexpected conditions come in for consideration, the negro displays his inferiority. He can learn to do well routine carpentry, but as a skilled joiner he is not a success. He can work around and with machinery, but he should not have the care of it for he is

> efficient in the capacity for regulating it, while his habitual improvidence prompts him to neglect what requires constant and systematic attention. . . . There are many good routine blacksmiths and shoemakers, but they work as they have learned, with no talent for originality. . . .[125]

Lacking judgment, discretion, and learning and management abilities, blacks could not be employed as engineers, machinists, highly skilled artisans or foremen. The few who succeeded in these positions were, it was argued, exceptions to the general rule. Convinced that blacks were ill-equipped for these positions, white observers completed the stereotype by noting that Negroes did very well at jobs requiring muscle and endurance. It was even suggested that blacks were happiest when doing this type of work. A woman who had often observed black laborers at work in the 1890s recalled years later that they were always laughing and singing and doing "monkeyshines to delight the watchers."[126] It was comfortable transition from "contented" field slave to "contented" free laborer. Comfortable, at least, for everyone but the black workers.

The myth of the black worker involved much more than a simple definition of abilities. One of the most persistent notions was that black workers were more easily managed than their white counterparts. Employers and other spokesmen of the New South frequently advertised the docility and tractability of black labor. The editor of the *Daily Picayune* felt that this fact gave the South an advantage not enjoyed by the North or the West. "The negroes are tractable and peaceable. They do not strike at every opportunity, thereby losing their wages for the fancied gains of pressure. They are not incendiaries. . . . They do not indulge in vaporing sentiment about the enmity of labor and capital. . . . They are," he assured his readers, "naturally the friends of the employer. . . ." He concluded that the South would only have itself to blame if it did not properly manage such a labor supply.[127] Despite evidence to the contrary, especially prior to 1894, spokesmen for the New South persisted in this belief. For a variety of reasons, none of which had anything to do with inherent racial characteristics, black workers increasingly conformed to this mold; but this was because they received little assistance in their attempts to resist the "place" assigned them by the New South Advocates. White New Orleanians were not surprised when Northern employers began to import Negro strikebreakers in the 1890s. Though there was little in the experience of the Crescent City to justify this position, the use of black strikebreakers fit the image that had been created.[128]

In addition to being physically strong, mentally weak and docile, the stereotyped black worker was immoral, or, at least, had less admirable character traits than his white co-workers. They spent their wages in "drinking, gambling, dissipation and vice."[129] He failed, as one observer claimed, to recognize "the sanctity of the moral and social obligations that rest on him."[130] This was, of course, the same black worker labeled dependable, peaceable, and tractable. Depending on the situation, the proper image could be called forth to justify a particular action or proposal. When black workers expressed dissatisfaction, paraded the levee in protest or went on strike, they were subject to criticism more vehement than that directed at white workers. Thus, pressure was exerted on black labor to conform to the image created for them. It is ironic that even though the spokesmen for the New South claimed that black labor was a sectional advantage, the remedy for black labor unrest was to replace the discontented black workers with white employees. Thus, when the black roustabouts demanded higher wages in 1880, a local river editor decided that one thousand good white men on the levee would settle the affair. "Then the foolish and avaricious roustabout will see the folly of his ways," he proclaimed.[131] A month later he jubilantly reported that the "high-priced darkey" was being replaced by "sensible white men."[132] His optimism had no basis in fact, but it was typical of the reaction to labor troubles involving black workers. Similarly, when the black waiters at the St. Charles Hotel struck for higher wages, they were replaced by white girls. The *Daily Picayune* reported that the girls were "infinitely more polite, attentive and painstaking than their predecessors," and "the amount of common sense with which they are endowed is so far superior to the Negroes' that no comparison is possible."[133] Yet, despite the availability and "superiority" of white girls, the other hotels did not change the sex and color of their waiters.[134] Black waiters were inferior only when they ceased to be docile.[135]

Obviously, the image of the black worker was a collection of contradictions, half-truths and racist clichés. Enough evidence could be found in Gilded Age New Orleans to refute every aspect of the image, and even those who subscribed to the myth were, at times, made painfully aware of its weak foundation in facts. Yet, the image survived in 1880s and gained new adherents during the next decade. It survived because, in some way, it gave comfort to almost everyone. Employers saw black workers as a source of cheap, tractable labor which could be used to transform the dreams of the New South into reality. If employers could win the loyalty of black workers, those workers could provide a wedge to divide labor in times of crisis. Even if black workers were loyal to a united labor front, the image of the docile, pro-employers, anti-union black created a distrust which employers could use to their advantage.[136] The black worker became the scapegoat for strike failures, wage cuts, unemployment and most of the other frustrations common to the early labor movement. While it had nothing to do with his failure to "outgrow the influences of slavery," as one authority suggested, the black worker did, on occasion, find advantage in siding with his employer.[137] A capitalistic ally was better than no ally at all. Finally, it should also be noted that the image provided ammunition for the South and, of course, New Orleans in its continuing debate with Northern critics. The "loyalty" of the black worker was an indication of his contentment. Where in New Orleans, it was asked, do the Negroes suffer as the black workers of the North suffer? Indeed, where in New Orleans did the black workers suffer as the "shirt-making and needle-women of New York and other large cities suffer?"[138] If the New Orleans black practiced loyalty, frugality, and temperance, he need never lack food, clothing or shelter.[139] Thus did the Southern spokesman defend their handling of the free black laborer.

The image of the black worker described above was never completely accepted by everyone in New Orleans. Various groups adopted parts of the stereotype while rejecting those elements which did not conform to their needs. Part of the value of the image was its flexibility. Acceptance of the image was dependent upon several conditions such as job competition, degree of labor unrest and racial hostility and, certainly, individual inclinations. Among white workers, acceptance was far more complete in the 1890s than it had been during the preceding decade. In his memoirs, Terence Powderly repeated a warning he had issued several times before:

> It is not the negro alone who stands ostracized in the South by the remnant of the Bourbon element, which still exists to protest against the progress of the Southern States. The white man who works is held in no higher esteem than the black man, and his ignorance is taken advantage of when he is patted on the back and told that he 'is better than the negro.'[140]

Undoubtedly, many poor whites in New Orleans failed to see the self-destructive potential of their own racial prejudices. Others, afraid that they would be dislodged from their position on next-to-the last rung of the status ladder, chose to sacrifice economic progress in favor of the psychological comfort they received from the myth of the black worker's inferiority. Even employers who preferred black workers were often able to placate white labor by suggesting that the work was unfit for white men.[141]

As events to be described later will demonstrate, it would be incorrect to suggest that no white workers heeded Powderly's warning. Several had, in fact, come to the same conclusion on their own as a result of their experiences in New Orleans. At a meeting of New Orleans mechanics in 1884, a white ship's carpenter revealed his anxieties to a racially mixed audience. Employers, he noted, had been playing the blacks against the whites and the whites against the blacks "until both classes had been ground down so low that the best workmen had been driven away." If different results were desired, he advised contractors to hire the best men of whatever race and pay them equal wages. If the bosses refused, organization and cooperation was the only alternative.[142] This worker's awareness of the situation was significant and not unusual. Others had made similar statements, and his proposal had been put into action years before by the workers in the cotton trades. Even the *Daily Picayune*, in one of its unguarded moments, admitted that "negro labor is growing to be the standard by which all other labor will be measured."[143] Faced with this prospect and aware of the disadvantages of division, many white workers refused to accept the stereotyped image of the black worker or, if they accepted it, worked to change or surmount that image. They may have harbored a hatred for their black co-workers, but they refused to be "patted on the back" and reminded of their superiority while employers took advantage of them.[144]

The black workers in the city were, of course, in a precarious position. Negro leaders in the community frequently advised them to accept, in part and for a time, the image created for them. They were counseled to "husband their resources," "Let politics alone," "quit the street corners" and strive to excel in those jobs open to them. It was even suggested that blacks were, indeed, better adapted to certain work than white men and that this situation could be used to advantage.[145] It was hoped, somewhat naively, that if blacks proved themselves capable workers they would receive equal treatment and new opportunities. This approach implied an acceptance of the image of the black worker because it related the Negroes' position to a failure to achieve. It was, as well, an approach designed to influence employers. If black workers demonstrated their ability and loyalty to their employers, they would be protected by those employers.

Certain black leaders blamed the Negroes' lack of education for his failure to get high status jobs. An excerpt from a graduation speech given by the president of Straight University in 1880 is revealing:

> When I walk along the levees and see the vessels freighted with fleecy cotton, and see the colored men in the capacity of roustabouts and common laborers, I desire to see them so interested in education as to make them owners of some of this staple; . . . to see some of those vessels . . . owned and managed by colored men. When I ride upon the steam cars and see colored men acting in the capacity of firemen, etc., I long to see the day when education will cause them to command the throttle. . . . Yes, let them be engineers as well as firemen.[146]

Like Booker T. Washington some years later, several black leaders in New Orleans, especially clergymen and educators, were convinced that industrial schools would halt and reverse the economic demise of the Negro. But there were more serious obstacles preventing a Negro from becoming an engineer, and by 1900 it was reported that the industrial programs for New Orleans blacks had yielded no significant results.[147]

In one other way, New Orleans Negroes adopted an argument frequently used by white defenders of the Southern labor system. Not surprisingly, New Orleans blacks were proud of the accomplishments of their artisans and mechanics. Much of this pride was the result of the comparisons made between Northern blacks and those of the Crescent City. James Levis, an Exposition Commissioner for the 1884 Colored Peoples' Exhibit, noted that blacks in the North had been excluded from mechanical and manufacturing pursuits by the employer class and the unions. "When I told people up North," he added, "that great numbers of the colored people of the South are skilled mechanics and artisans, they were surprised; and when I assured them that every brick in such extensive monuments as the Pickwick Club House, and others . . . , was laid by colored masons, they could scarcely believe me."[148] While understandable, this type of pride bordered on complacency and tended to accent the positive while ignoring the negative.

From the examples given it is clear that certain black leaders accepted certain aspects of the stereotyped image of the black worker. They counseled loyalty to employers, accepted the contention that blacks were, by nature, better able to perform certain functions than others and stressed the success and contentment of the black worker in New Orleans. Certainly their reasoning was often different from the white spokesmen.[149] If

Race and the Working Class

black men were ill-equipped to be engineers, it was an educational deficiency and not a mental deficiency. Still the image remained essentially intact. But what of the black workers themselves? Only infrequently did black workers comment directly on this issue in such a way that their comments have survived in newspapers or other sources. Occasionally the editors of Negro newspapers presented what they believed to be black labor's point of view, and in a few instances black unions published "cards to the public" explaining their position on a given issue. But it was the actions of black workers which most frequently and explicitly demonstrated their self-image.[150] Black workers organized, threatened employers, assaulted "scabs" and participated in strikes, both with white workers and by themselves. If they believed themselves docile and tractable, they did not generally act accordingly. Black workers resisted any attempt, by employers or white workers, to label them inferior or second-class workmen. There is no evidence to suggest that blacks acted as strikebreakers any more frequently than whites. On several occasions black workers were the first to organize in a given occupation and on several others they initiated strikes and continued them when white workers hesitated or capitulated. What all of this suggests, especially considering their positions, is that black workers were either unaware of how they were expected to act or refused to conform to the image.

The role of the black worker in Gilded Age New Orleans almost defies definition. It was, as in so many other areas, a period of transition for the Southern black. Not only was the nature of their citizenship being debated and a new racial system being devised, but blacks were also largely workingmen and had much at stake in the struggles between capital and labor which typified the last two decades of the century. And, of course, the New South advocates had their plans for the most effective use of the black labor supply. From the black point of view, there were both encouraging and discouraging signs. Granted, an image of the black worker was being formed and his opportunities for self-improvement and economic advancement were already severely limited in 1880. Yet, C. Vann Woodward's comments on race relations in general are valid for the black New Orleans worker as well: "There were still real choices to be made, and alternatives to the course eventually pursued with such single-minded unanimity and unquestioning conformity were still available."[151]

Notes for "Race and the Working Class: The Black Worker and His Image, 1880-1890"

[1] C. Vann Woodward, *Origins of the New South, 1877-1913* (Baton Rouge, 1951), 205.

[2] Department of Commerce, United States Bureau of the Census, Samuel L. Rogers, Director, *Negro Population, 1790-1915* (Washington, 1918), 782.

[3] Frederick Law Olmsted, *A Journey in the Seaboard Slave States, With Remarks on Their Economy* (New York, 1856), 587.

[4] Charles T. Rousseve, *The Negro in Louisiana, Aspects of His History and His Literature* (New Orleans, 1937), 33.

[5] Department of Commerce, *Negro Population, 1790-1915*, 511.

[6] Rousseve, *The Negro in Louisiana*, 33.

[7] Robert C. Reinders, "The Free Negro in the New Orleans Economy, 1850-1860," *Louisiana History*, 6 (1965): 274.

[8] Ibid.

[9] Department of Commerce, *Negro Population, 1790-1915*, 511.

[10] Ibid., 276-77; Arthur Raymond Pearce, "The Rise and Decline of Labor in New Orleans" (M. A. Thesis, Tulane University, 1938), 14-16.

[11] Ibid., 16; Reinders, "The Free Negro in the New Orleans Economy," 277.

[12] An excellent summary of the antebellum interaction between slave labor, free black labor, and free white labor can be found in Sterling D. Spero and Abram L. Harris, *The Black Worker: The Negro and the Labor Movement*, Atheneum edition (New York, 1968), 1st ed. 1931, Chapter 1; see also Richard C. Wade, *Slavery in the Cities, the South 1820-1860*, (New York, 1964), especially 243-52, 258-59, 261-63, 273-78; and Robert C. Reinders, "Slavery in New Orleans in the Decade Before the Civil War," *Mid-America*, 44 (1962), passim.

[13] These post-Civil War developments, of course, were not unique to New Orleans. See Rousseve, *The Negro in Louisiana*, 135-36; Spero and Harris, *The Black Worker*, 14-15; Lorenzo J. Green and Carter G. Woodson, *The Negro Wage Earner* (Washington, D. C., 1930), 34-35.

[14] Department of Commerce, *Negro Population, 1790-1915*, 782.

[15] *Eleventh Census of the United States, 1890*, I, Pt. 2 (Washington, 1897), 702-3. There were, however, 160 black males working as bookkeepers and clerks.

[16] *Twelfth Census of the United States Taken in 1900*, "Special Reports: Occupations at the Twelfth Census" (Washington, 1904), 630-35. Hereinafter cited as *Twelfth Census, Occupations*.

[17] *Eleventh Census of the United States, 1890*, I, Pt. 2:702-3; Dorothy Rose Eagleson, "Some Aspects of the Social Life of the New Orleans Negro in the 1880s" (M. A. thesis, Tulane University, 1961), 5-7.

[18] *Twelfth Census, Occupations*, 630.

[19] *Eleventh Census of the United States, 1890*, I, Pt. 2:702-3; *Twelfth Census, Occupations*, 630-635.

[20] Examples of this, as well as evidence which seems to refute the validity of this claim, will be given below.

[21] For a brief discussion of class status in the black communities of the larger cities, see August Meier, *Negro Thought in America, 1880-1915: Racial Ideologies in the Age of Booker T. Washington* (Ann Arbor, 1963), 151.

[22] This fact will become clear in the discussions which follow in this chapter and others; but let it suffice for now to suggest that a light complexion was an advantage for a Negro in certain situations but a disadvantage in others. Employers frequently looked upon a light skinned Negro as a potential trouble-maker.

[23] Herbert R. Northrup, *Organized Labor and the Negro* (New York, 1944), 18; Spero and Harris, *The Black Worker*, 159.

[24] W. E. B. DuBois, ed., *The Negro Artisan: Report of a Social Study Made Under the Direction of Atlanta University* (Atlanta, 1902), 89.

[25] Ibid., 90. The nearest rival in this case was Charleston, South Carolina, while that same city led in the percentage of skilled blacks in the black labor force (7.63). The corresponding figure for New Orleans in 1890 was 4.97.

[26] Ibid.; *Eleventh Census of the United States, 1890*, I, Pt. 2:702.

[27] *Twelfth Census, Occupations*, 632.

[28] Spero and Harris, *The Black Worker*, 159; Northrup, *Organized Labor and the Negro*, 18; DuBois, *The Negro Artisan*, 89-90.

[29] *Eleventh Census of the United States, 1890*, I, Pt. 2:702; *Twelfth Census, Occupations*, 632.

[30] DuBois, *The Negro Artisan*, 127-28; *New Orleans Daily Picayune*, September 14, 1881.

[31] See Table 4.

[32] *Twelfth Census, Occupations*, 632.

[33] Northrup, *Organized Labor and the Negro*, 42.

[34] *Eleventh Census of the United States, 1890*, I, Pt. 2:702; *Twelfth Census, Occupations*, 632.

[35] This was true throughout the South. See, for example, Northrup, *Organized Labor and the Negro*, 39, 233; and Ray Marshall, "The Negro in Southern Unions," *The Negro and the American Labor Movement*, Julius Jacobsen, ed. (New York, 1968), 134. See also Ray Marshall, *The Negro and Organized Labor* (New York, 1965). That it was also true in New Orleans will be made apparent by events described in later chapters.

[36] Marshall, "The Negro in Southern Unions," 134.

[37] In many cases the losses were relative and not absolute. There were more black artisans but their share of the work was less. DuBois, *The Negro Artisan*, 150-51.

[38] See, for example, Meier, *Negro Thought in America, 1880-1915*, 103-4.

[39] See, for example, Northrup, *Organized Labor and the Negro*, 18, 20-21; and Spero and Harris, *The Black Worker*, 159.

[40] DuBois, *The Negro Artisan*, 150-51, 127.

[41] See Table 5.

[42] *Eleventh Census of the United States, 1890*, I, Pt. 2:702; *Twelfth Census, Occupations*, 632. The 1890 census included Indians, Japanese, and Chinese citizens under the general heading of Colored. This fact, however, does not affect the percentages given in the table and in no category did it result in more than one addition.

[43] It should be apparent, of course, that "holding his own" in numbers did not necessarily imply equal treatment, a fair share of the jobs, nor sound relations with white workers. These are matters which will receive attention later, in this chapter and others.

[44] Willaim Ivy Hair, *Bourbonism and Agrarian Protest: Louisiana Politics, 1877-1900* (Baton Rouge, 1969), 175; Northrup, *Organized Labor and the Negro*, 149. Spero and Harris suggested that New Orleans dock labor had been largely black since the Civil War, but other evdience denies the accuracy of this claim. Spero and Harris, *The Black Worker*, 185.

[45] *Daily Picayune*, January 15, 1884.

[46]Spero and Harris, *The Black Worker*, 185-86. See also Marshall, "The Negro in Southern Unions," 133.

[47]Northrup, *Organized Labor and the Negro*, 149; Spero and Harris, *The Black Worker*, 185-86; Marshall, "The Negro in Southern Unions," 133; Roger Wallace Shugg, "The New Orleans General Strike of 1892," *Louisiana Historical Quarterly*, 21 (1938): 548; and Covington Hall, "Labor Struggles in the Deep South," undated manuscript in the Manuscript Division of the Howard-Tilton Memorial Library, Tulane University, New Orleans, Louisiana. Though the manuscript is undated, Hall claims personal involvement in the events of late nineteenth-century New Orleans. The *Daily Picayune* under date March 5, 1899, contains a letter from Hall to the editor.

[48]*Eleventh Census of the United States, 1890*, I, Pt. 2:702; *Twelfth Census, Occupations*, 632.

[49]*Twelfth Census, Occupations*, 632.

[50]For descriptions of these jobs, see Chapter 2 of David Paul Bennetts, "Black and White Workers, New Orleans, 1880-1900" (Ph. D. dissertation, University of Illinois at Urbana-Champaign, 1972).

[51]*Eleventh Census of the United States, 1890*, I, Pt. 2:702; *Twelfth Census, Occupations*, 632.

[52]*Eleventh Census of the United States, 1890*, I, Pt. 2:702; *Twelfth Census, Occupations*, 632. In 1890 there were 575 Negro men and women employed as tobacco and cigar factory operatives. This was 42 percent of all those so employed. In 1900 the figures were 439 and 36 percent.

[53]*Twelfth Census, Occupations*, 632.

[54]*Eleventh Census of the United States, 1890*, I, Pt. 2:702; *Twelfth Census, Occupations*, 634.

[55]The *Daily Picayune*, January 20, 1890, reported the suicide of a mulatto cigarmaker who was unable to find employment in his trade and was working in the warehouse of a tobacco factory at the time of his death. The first report of the Bureau of Statistics of Labor of Louisiana, based on statistics for the year 1900, provided information on three tobacco factories in the state—probably in New Orleans. One employed 30 percent blacks, another 1 percent and the third employed no Negroes. *First Annual Report of the Bureau of Statistics of Labor for the State of Louisiana: 1901* (Baton Rouge, 1902), 149.

[56]Northrup, *Organized Labor and the Negro*, 119.

[57]*Eleventh Census of the United States, 1890*, I, Pt. 2:702; *Twelfth Census, Occupations*, 632, 634; *Daily Picayune*, February 7, 1894, and August 7, 1896.

[58]See, for example, *Daily Picayune*, May 25, 1880, February 20, 1894 and August 7, 1896.

[59]DuBois uncovered only 2,213 skilled Negro laborers employed in industry in thirteen Southern states. Louisiana had 23 firms in nine industries, out of forty investigated by DuBois, employing 114 skilled black workers. DuBois, *The Negro Artisan*, 181-82.

[60]*Twelfth Census, Occupations*, 632.

[61]Northrup, *Organized Labor and the Negro*, 82, 92; Marshall, "The Negro in Southern Unions," 135-36; *Daily Picayune*, May 1, 1880.

[62]*Eleventh Census of the United States, 1890*, I, Pt. 2, 703; *Census, Occupations*, 632; *Daily Picayune*, November 9, 1879, May 6, 1880, April 27, 1880, and October 16, 1886.

[63]The editor of the *Daily Picayune* complained that they had "become yearly more indolent and unreliable." *Daily Picayune*, September 22, 1889. By the 1890s there was a great demand for white domestics and newspaper inquiries were specifying 'white domestics only.' *Daily Picayune*, November 13, 1892.

[64]*Twelfth Census, Occupations*, 632, 634.

[65]Paul Worthman's compilation of selected occupations in Birmingham, Alabama, shows that in 1900 nearly half of the city's workers were black and more than three-fourths of the unspecified laborers were Negroes. In New Orleans the corresponding figures were about one-third and one-half. Paul B. Worthman, "Black Workers and Labor Unions in Birmingham, Alabama, 1897-1904," *Black Labor in America*, Milton Canton,

Race and the Working Class

ed. (Westport, 1969), 70. Worthman's study is one of the few local studies with which developments in New Orleans can be compared.

[66] *Eleventh Census of the United States, 1890,* I, Pt. 2:702; *Twelfth Census, Occupations,* 632, 634.

[67] Ibid., I, Pt. 2:702; Ibid., 632.

[68] *Twelfth Census, Occupation,* 632; Marshall, "The Negro in Southern Unions," 133.

[69] *Twelfth Census, Occupations,* 632.

[70] Ibid.; *Eleventh Census of the United States, 1890,* I, Pt. 2:702.

[71] *Daily Picayune,* October 20, 1883; see also the discussion in Chapter 2.

[72] The issue of segregated streetcars will be discussed later.

[73] *Daily Picayune,* November 8, 1896.

[74] See Chapter 5.

[75] *Weekly Louisianian,* August 27, 1881.

[76] *Daily Picayune,* March 30, 1884.

[77] *Weekly Louisianian,* August 27, 1881.

[78] See, for example, *Daily Picayune,* January 13, 1884.

[79] Ibid., December 28, 1888.

[80] *Twelfth Census, Occupations,* 632.

[81] *Daily Picayune,* March 1, 1889, June 25, 1885; *Weekly Pelican,* February 16, 1885.

[82] See, for example, the case reported in *Times-Democrat,* December 30, 1888.

[83] *Daily Picayune,* March 1, 1889.

[84] Ibid., June 25, 1885.

[85] See, for example, ibid., and *Weekly Pelican,* February 16, 1889.

[86] *Daily Picayune,* April 27, 1880.

[87] *Times-Democrat,* December 30, 1888.

[88] *Daily Picayune,* April 27, 1880.

[89] *Weekly Pelican,* July 9, 1887.

[90] Ibid., June 11, 1887.

[91] Ibid., May 7, June 11, 1887.

[92] Ibid., June 11, 1887.

[93] Ibid., July 9, 1887.

[94] Meir, *Negro Thought in America, 1880-1915,* 139.

[95] Ibid., 140.

[96] *Daily Picayune*, January 27, 1889.

[97] *Weekly Louisianian*, July 16, 1881. The relegating of Negroes to low-prestige, low-paying jobs was, of course, a paractice not restricted to New Orleans; see John A. Garraty, *The New Commonwealth, 1877-1890* (New York, 1968), 131.

[98] *Daily Picayune*, August 18, 1882. By 1900, the tobacco industry in the South had developed a rigid occupational segregation pattern which was imitated in several other areas of manufacturing. See Northrup, *Organized Labor and the Negro*, 103.

[99] Spero and Harris, *The Black Worker*, 191; *Daily Picayune*, September 14, 1887.

[100] See, for example, *Daily Picayune*, March 26, 1886.

[101] Ibid., October 5, 1886.

[102] Ibid., October 24, 1886.

[103] *Weekly Pelican*, March 26, 1887.

[104] DuBois, *The Negro Artisan*, 127-128.

[105] As will be shown, this was exactly what happened when labor solidarity disintegrated in the 1890s.

[106] John P. Dyer, "Education in New Orleans," *The Past as Prelude: New Orleans, 1718-1968*, ed. Hodding Carter (New Orleans, 1968), 133.

[107] Hair, *Bourbonism and Agrarian Protest*, 192-193.

[108] *Weekly Pelican*, May 28, 1887.

[109] Ibid., July 16, 1887.

[110] It should be noted that black workers in New Orleans, like their white co-workers, were better paid than most Negroes elsewhere in the South and certainly in rural Louisiana. See, for example, *Weekly Pelican*, August 3, 1889, which contains the results of a survey taken by the *Chattanooga Tradesman*. Despite the limitations, there were more opportunities for black workers, especially skilled workers, in New Orleans than elsewhere in the state. The statistics already given for New Orleans can be compared with state statistics found in DuBois, *The Negro Artisan*, 127.

[111] *Weekly Louisianian*, January 15, 1881.

[112] *Daily Picayune*, June 3, 1889.

[113] Ibid., January 8, 1882.

[114] See, for example, ibid., July 30, 1889, and August 13, 1889.

[115] Ibid., October 26, 1886.

[116] See also ibid., October 17, 1884.

[117] Ibid., April 10, 1880.

[118] Ibid., February 22, 1880.

[119] See, for example, ibid., November 30, 1879, May 31, 1881, and January 6, 1884; *Weekly Louisianian*, January 22, 1881.

[120] See, for example, *Weekly Louisianian*, December 3, 1881.

[121] *Daily Picayune*, March 9, 1890.

Race and the Working Class

[122] The changes of the 1890s will be discussed in a later chapter.

[123] It will become apparent to the reader that the myth of the black worker drew heavily on attitudes common to the antebellum period. The basic tenets of white supremacy had not changed, but they had to be restructured to accommodate the free black worker.

[124] *Daily Picayune*, July 22, 1889.

[125] Ibid.

[126] Marion S. Oneal, "Growing Up in New Orleans—Memories of the 1890s," *Louisiana History*, 5 (1964): 82.

[127] *Daily Picayune*, June 23, 1881. According to the Worthman study, Birmingham industrialists had a similar impression of black workers. Worthman, "Black Workers and Labor Unions in Birmingham, Alabama," 74.

[128] See, for example, *Daily Picayune*, July 27, 1893.

[129] Ibid., June 30, 1883.

[130] Ibid., March 23, 1895.

[131] Ibid., October 15, 1880.

[132] Ibid., November 24, 1880.

[133] Ibid., October 16, October 23, 1880.

[134] Ibid., October 31, 1880.

[135] On this point, see also ibid., June 30, 1883.

[136] Several examples of this will be given in later chapers, but see ibid., September 3, 1881. See also the reactions of merchants, politicians, and others to labor unrest and the role of black workers in *The Daily Item*, October 31, 1894.

[137] This explanation of the tractability of the black worker given in *Daily Picayune*, March 23, 1895.

[138] Ibid., February 28, 1880.

[139] Ibid.

[140] Terence V. Powderly, *Thirty Years of Labor: 1859-1889*, revised and corrected edition, of original 1889 edition, published in 1890, reprinted by Augustus M. Kelley, Publishers (New York, 1967), 352.

[141] See, for example, *Daily Picayune*, October 17, 1884.

[142] Ibid., March 17, 1884.

[143] Ibid., March 23, 1895.

[144] Again, the 1880s provide the best examples of racial cooperation. The depression and the increasd racial hostilities of the 1890s brought about a more complete acceptance among white workers of the image of the black worker. In cases where reason had triumphed in the 1880s, emotion and race hatred triumphed in he 1890s.

[145] See, for example, the meeting of Negro workers described in the *Daily Picayune*, October 23, 1882.

[146] *Weekly Louisianian*, June 5, 1880.

[147] Meier, *Negro Thought in America*, 103-4; DuBois, *The Negro Artisan*, 33-35, 69, 127.

[148] *Daily Picayune*, November 19, 1884.

[149]Thus, Negro editors sometimes took an anti-union stance because they felt that when labor and capital collided, it was the black workers who suffered the most. See, for example, *Weekly Louisianian*, September 10, 1881.

[150]These "actions" are detailed and evaluated in David Paul Bennetts, "Black and White Workers, New Orleans, 1880-1900" (Ph. D. dissertation, University of Illinois at Urbana-Champagne, 1972). Reference will be made to the editorials and "cards" as well.

[151]C. Vann Woodward, *The Strange Career of Jim Crow*, second revised ed. (1955; New York, 1966), 44. The Woodward revisionists have argued that Woodward put too much faith in the possibility for solutions more favorable to blacks. There is some justification for this criticism and one of the most interesting and effective arguments is Lawrence J. Friedman, *The White Savage: Racial Fantasies in the Post-Bellum South* (Englewood Cliffs, N.J., 1970). But a fatalistic approach, at least in the case of New Orleans labor, answers few questions and requires that one ignore too many sincere attempts, whatever the motivation, at cooperation, discussion, and rational solutions.

"LOST BOUNDARIES": RACIAL PASSING AND POVERTY IN SEGREGATED NEW ORLEANS*

Arthé A. Anthony

> On sunny summer Sunday afternoons in Harlem
> when the air is one interminable ball game
> and grandma cannot get her gospel hymns
> from the Saints of God in Christ
> on account of the Dodgers on the radio,
> on sunny Sunday afternoons
> when the kids look all new
> and far too clean to stay that way,
> and Harlem has its
> washed-and-ironed-and-cleaned-best out,
> the ones who've crossed the line
> to live downtown
> miss you,
> Harlem of the bitter dream,
> since their dream has
> come true.
> —Langston Hughes, 1951

Racial passing is a well-known theme in pre-World War II African-American literature.[1] Adrian Piper's recent essay, "Passing for White, Passing for Black," is an example of continued interest in the topic.[2] In addition, "passing" is used in cultural studies as a metaphor for masking the real—and most often marginalized—self.[3] This article examines racial passing, with an emphasis on the lives of black Creole women, in relation to the economic impact of racial repression and segregation on black life in New Orleans.[4] My conclusions are drawn, in large part, from an analysis of thirty extensive oral history interviews that I conducted with eighteen women and twelve men born between 1885 and 1905, and living in downtown New Orleans in 1977.[5] Each of the men and women that I interviewed thought of themselves as "Creole," and participated in the familial and social networks of the city's black Creole community.[6]

Their occupations and educations were representative of the choices then available in New Orleans. All of them worked, although the kind of work that they did changed over

---

*First published in *Louisiana History*, 36 (1995): 291-312. Reprinted with the kind permission of the author and the Louisiana Historical Association.

the life cycle; they were primarily cigar makers, seamstresses, skilled craftsmen in the building trades, postal carriers, printers, and school teachers. A few of them attended the city's private high schools and normal schools, an accomplishment that has to be understood within the context of the limited availability of an education—private or public—for African Americans at the turn of the century.[7] Many others were forced to terminate their educations, in more than one instance as early as the third grade, to begin working, whereas others finished apprenticeships.[8] Their personal lives were equally varied as reflected in the extended, nuclear and augmented households in which they lived, and their individual experiences with parenting, divorce and remarriage, as well as widowhood and desertion. Most, but not all of them, were Catholics.[9] Despite their individual differences, as a group the Creoles of color that I interviewed shared first-hand experiences with hard work and racial discrimination. The women—a group that has been overlooked in New Orleans historiography—experienced both racial and sexual discrimination.[10]

Each of the men and women I interviewed offered insightful interpretations of the worlds in which they lived. They were all very familiar with the myriad practices of racial passing; although they were not all light-skinned, they all knew of individuals—often a parent, spouse or friend—who had passed. More important than examples of the intricate mechanics of passing were their observations about the reasons individuals did so. Lillian Gelbart Simonet, for example, born in 1904, identified a relationship between passing for white and poverty when she remarked:

> There are whole families of these people in New Orleans, (who are not necessarily Creoles), who have just been absorbed and gone to various parts of the country and they're white. Sometimes you just can't blame them because they have had a hard time. Creole people, with all of the airs, had a hard time to get along [because] they [the young women] would not be domestics. Some were fortunate enough to get work at El Trelles, a cigar factory . . . and Wallace Marine had a cigar factory . . . they weren't prepared to do any kind of work that required any kind of education at all because half of them hadn't finished high school.[11]

The observations of Mrs. Simonet, a retired public school teacher, call attention to the limited opportunities available to the majority of black Creoles who were poor and uneducated, unlike herself.

In the larger scheme of twentieth-century American race categorization, individuals were either black or white. Individual whites may have had preferences for light-skinned or dark-skinned African Americans in their employ.[12] But overall the ethnic and cultural nuances and phenotypical differences that were critical to the intraracial dynamics of the black community were disregarded by whites in the segregated economy of New Orleans in the 1900s-1920s. Many Creoles of Color consequently were willing to accept the risks of passing for white rather than suffer the deteriorating material and social conditions endured by persons living and working as "colored."[13]

The instability of both their civil and economic status was not a new phenomenon despite their history of freedom and their colonial and antebellum privileges, often described as those of a third racial class.[14] The historical basis of those privileges recently has been questioned by Thomas N. Ingersoll. He concludes that between 1718 and 1812 planters used "the powers of the local, state, and federal governments against free blacks to degrade them and limit their numbers, [to ensure] the system of racial supremacy that allowed them to exploit blacks."[15] Their social position eroded further between 1830 and the Civil War.[16] However, as Loren Schweninger argues a distinction has to be made between the changes in their civil status and their wealth because "during the 1840s and 1850s, the economic standing of the group remained strong."[17]

If during the Civil War Louisiana's free people of color were generally anxious about their future Schweninger makes it clear that they had every reason to be: In the postbellum era their status, as evidenced by their property ownership, deteriorated. His study includes black Creoles in New Orleans and demonstrates that they were equally affected by the changes brought by the war. For example, he notes that "a close study of Creoles of color in the Fourth, Fifth, and Sixth wards, the heart of the free mulatto community, reveals a marked decline." Only a few individuals survived the war with their wealth intact; moreover, a substantial percentage of those he studied, including well established skilled craftsmen, either "experienced losses" or "lost everything."[18]

The decades that followed Reconstruction have been described as "the nadir" of African American life in the United States because of the increased racial violence, segregation, economic exploitation, and denial of citizenship rights which occurred. The black Creole community of New Orleans was also affected by these circumscriptions. In response, black New Orleanians, including Creoles, utilized a variety of forms of social protest against the growing virulence of Jim Crow, including the courts, strikes, and interracial union collaboration.[19] A far less public strategy of resistance against the crises of racial repression was the practice of racial passing. This was a well-known consequence of the economics of "race prejudice" as observed by Dr. William L. Bulkley when he addressed the National Negro Conference in 1909. He included racial passing as an indictment against race prejudice because it forced "across the line thousands of mixed-blood."[20]

The oral histories of black Creoles born at the turn of the century indicated that racial passing was a last resort strategy employed by individuals in response to the pervasive racial repression that shaped occupational patterns in the early decades of the century.[21] This cohort was born between 1885 and 1905, a period in which intertwined local and national events significantly curtailed the economic opportunities available to members of this group as they matured.[22] Their childhoods were shaped in part by white supremacy as evidenced by the codification of segregation and the pervasiveness of racial violence. For example, this era was marked nationally by the 1896 U. S. Supreme Court decision of *Plessy v. Ferguson* and the local "Robert Charles Riot of 1900," as well as the anti-labor conflicts that culminated in the city's strikes of the 1880s and 1890s.[23] Concurrently, the

Crescent City struggle to regain some of its antebellum economic prosperity against the backdrop of the depression of 1893-1897 and the panic of 1907.

The city's attempts to diversify its economy included such changes as the growing importance of the "men's ready-to-wear clothing industry [which] became important by 1900, employing a large number of pieceworkers . . . Another industry of significance was the manufacture of cigars and other tobacco products."[24] Cigar making and the ready-to-wear clothing industry were major sources of jobs for Creoles of color, including Creole women. However, overall African Americans were marginal as exploited workers in a segregated economy. Eugenia Lacarra, who not only worked as a cigar maker but was the daughter and granddaughter of cigar makers, recalled the impact of segregation on the ability of African Americans to make a living:

> I stop to think sometimes, and I wonder how the poor colored people got along. You couldn't work in the department stores, the men couldn't drive a bus, you couldn't work for the telephone company, you couldn't work for the Public Service, so if you didn't do menial labor, or housework, or learn to be a cigar maker, or you weren't lucky enough to get an education to teach, well, you were in very bad luck because then these people had nothing to do. You see, they didn't give the poor colored people jobs.

Specific occupations and job sites were defined by race. Black cigar makers, for example, could work in the city at Marine's, a factory promoted by Mrs. Lacarra's father, but owned by "two Jews." Those jobs, however shortlived, were welcomed because in the early decades of the century virtually all of the major cigar manufacturers—which were white-owned—had "whites only" employment policies, or unsatisfactory segregated working conditions for African Americans. Consequently, according to Mrs. Lacarra, in order to find work some black Creoles passed for white while they worked as cigar makers at certain "whites only" companies as well as in a number of other occupations throughout the city.[25]

Many of the black Creoles that I spoke with also described more aggressive forms of resistance against the inequities of segregation. For instance, Marguerite "Mag" Puryear (1902-92) recalled that she and her older sister felt desperate when Marine's cigar factory closed in the early 1920s: "We were desperate and we went to Hernsheim [a white-owned cigar manufacturing company]. Hernsheim gave us a job, but we weren't with the white girls, we were downstairs. We soon got tired of that.[26] El Trelles was a new factory owned by Spanish people . . . We felt that the girls working there were making good money so several of us decided to go there. We went there, and an old Spanish fella came out and he said that he didn't have colored girls. I told him that we could understand that but that we could make cigars as good as any of the girls that he did have—if he would give us a chance. He told us that he would consider it." Mag and her sister were convincing, as she explained: "I shall always remember it was the day that my niece was born [early 1920s] . . . I got the letter telling me to come with the two other girls that had been with me. We went and got the job and it was paying so much more. So we went up and up [in promotions] and had the best jobs. And he put us with the white girls, and we sat even with the white girls. There was no segregation at Trelles."[27]

Male cigar makers had additional options such as trying their luck with one of the very small independent factories known as "buckeyes." Mrs. Lacarra described how they operated: "different people had a little factory in their kitchen or they would make cigars out in a room somewhere, out in the back yard, or in the shade. They used to call them buckeyes, but they didn't pay too much. Most of the men who had those worked for themselves. They made their own and they sold them, but those were little places."[28] Some of the men, particularly the fathers and grandfathers of Mrs. Lacarra's generation, were forced to leave the city to look for work in other American cities including Tampa or Chicago, or outside of the country in Montreal, Canada, or Havana, Cuba. These men had to leave, according to James M. Montoya, Sr. (1891-1989), "to work when work was slack." He further explained that they traveled because "when there was no work here you went that far to survive."[29]

Although economics were a major motivation for passing, black Creoles confronted the inconsistencies and ironies of white Louisianians' relentless efforts at racial categorization, what Piper refers to as "the offensive and irrational instrument of racism," long before they looked for work.[30] For instance, race affected such fundamental institutions of personal and public life as education and religion.[31] Participation in the blessed sacraments was, for example, segregated as Montoya recalled about passing for white when he made his First Communion:

> I made my First Communion when I was going to Straight when I was about thirteen or fourteen years old [in 1904 or 1905] . . . I went to catechism at St. Louis Cathedral because my father didn't want me to go to Sacred Heart Church, which was a block or two from us, because he said there was too much discrimination there. I had an aunt living in St. Louis Cathedral's parish and I went there as [i.e., passed as] white. My father said that if I had to follow behind the white boys to make communion that I'd never make it. He wanted me to make First Communion like everybody else.[32]

During my interview with Everette (1901-80) and Alice Simon Chevalier (1905-81) they recalled an experience at the uptown Mother of Perpetual Help Church which further exemplifies the pervasiveness, and irrationality, of racial classification. According to Alice: "We were standing up in the back [of the church]. The usher came and he took Everette in the front [white section] and left me standing in the back." Everette—in an effort to explain why they were separated—interjected, "he [the white usher] could see that she was a nigger, you understand."[33] Much to their dismay, Everette was mistaken for white that evening unlike his wife whose facial features were more clearly negroid.

The recollection of that incident reminded Alice of numerous additional examples of mistaken racial identities, as well as planned decisions to cross-over: "We've had friends that have lived one life and died another. Not long ago [1970-71] a friend of mine died.

She and her husband worked as white, but they lived in a colored neighborhood. When she died she was laid out in a white funeral parlor. She always wanted to be white, and she looked white—she was fair and she had blue eyes. And her husband worked as white. When she died he laid her out in a white funeral parlor. Everette and I were the only niggers at the wake. That hasn't been any more than about six or seven years ago."[34]

My interview with the Chevaliers was also instructive about the dynamics of race, class, and gender and the world of work in New Orleans in the 1910s and '20s, the years in which my interviewees grew to maturity. The Chevaliers' adolescence and young adulthood are examples of the many working-class Americans of their generation, because they "were poor and we had to work."[35] Everette's father was a barber with a shop "at his house [on St. Ann Street] in the front room," and his mother "used to wash and iron for white people," an occupation well known to black women in this period. Therefore, it is not surprising that Everette went to work as a delivery boy when he was sixteen years old in 1917 at the St. Louis Drug Company.[36] He was forced to work because his parents' collective wages in the service sector were inadequate to support the family. This was not unusual, for Alice Kessler-Harris has noted "the inability of families of unskilled [white] male workers to exist without several wage earners."[37] Moreover, in addition to being "poor" Everette and his black contemporaries had to contend with the impact of racial discrimination on the types of jobs that were available. For instance, from the drug company he went to work lining barrels at a cooper shop where both whites and blacks were employed. When I asked him how his employers could determine his racial identity—given his light-complexion—he replied, "When I went there I didn't go as white. When I got the job they asked me what I was." It is clear that when we talked he understood the profundity of that decision. He knew, for example, that as a young man he could have changed his racial identity for better work and, in turn, wages if he had passed for white. However, he chose to not pass because of the importance of his family ties—"because of my relations. I lived with my ma and them."

Although Alice Simon Chevalier was unable to pass for white her experiences illustrate the points made earlier by Mrs. Simonet about the economic conditions that those who passed for white sought to escape. For example, Alice was the youngest of seven children and one of six daughters born to Richard (1870-1908) and Anecia Paltron Simon (1871-1964). Alice's father, a cooper, died when she was three years old in 1908. In addition to her mother, who sewed piecework, everyone in the family consequently went to work as soon as they were able. Alice, for instance, began working at fourteen years of age in 1919 for $3.00 a week in the "mangle room," catching sheets and pillow cases to fold them when they came out of the "mangle," a pressing machine, of the Dixie Laundry on Tulane and Basin streets. When asked about the amount of hours she worked a week, she replied "for as long as they wanted." Her experiences with poverty and the familial obligation to work are very similar to those of white "working-class daughters" discussed by Leslie Woodcock Tentler. However, her low wages are indicative of the limited choices of young black girls. Tentler, for instance, describes laundry workers in

New York City as desperate married white women who averaged $6.16 per week in 1913, twice as much as what Alice remembered making six years later.[38]

Like many of the young and poor girls employed in cities in the late 1910s at places like the Dixie Laundry, Alice was not only underpaid but underage for employment. Therefore, when the inspectors "would come around to find if you were working under age," she recalled, "we used to go hide in the toilet." She subsequently worked for two or three years in the cigar factory promoted by Wallace C. Marine, Mrs. Lacarra's father, making $9.00 or $10.00 a week—an amount she considered a fortune compared to her laundry wages. Over fifty years later she also remembered that the working conditions at Marine's constituted a significant improvement because "it wasn't as hot as the laundry." After she left Marine's establishment, she worked for nearly twenty-five years at the Trelles cigar factory. At any point, particularly in her youth, Alice might have chosen to "cross-over" for less arduous work and the possibilities of upward mobility if passing for white had been a viable option for her.[39] She rationalized the decision of others to pass in the following manner: "In those days if you were kind of fair you didn't want to be a nigger. That's a bad word to use, but that's the word they used in those days. You would go pass for white and try to get a job as white; you'd work as white. Now [1977] you don't have to do that."

Alice Chevalier worked virtually all of her life although married black Creole women were not supposed to work at all. As Mrs. Justine Frank Marcard, who married at sixteen in 1920, put it: "The women were supposed to marry; men felt that a lady's place was in the house." Mrs. Marcard recalled that she began working as a mere child—although it is also important to note that she also described her childhood as "very happy." She left school after the third grade

> because we were a very poor family; I used to go out and make little day's work for the people in my neighborhood—the white folks I'm talking about. When I was about fourteen I went and worked in a factory . . . When I was about fifteen my husband began coming around my house with some of my brothers, and we met then. We had our courtship and I married when I was sixteen years old.[40]

Women like Justine Frank Marcard and Alice Simon Chevalier were forced to work as children and adolescents because of the deaths or inadequate wages of their fathers. In addition, despite the turn-of-the-twentieth-century ideal of the middle-class housewife, these women continued to work once they were married because of their husbands' insufficient wages.[41] The middle-class ideal was so pervasive among women (as well as many husbands), that many wives felt compelled to rationalize, and thereby diminish, the value of the work that they did after marriage. For example, when I asked Mrs. Marcard if she worked after her marriage, she replied, "I never worked after I got married." When I commented that a mutual friend had told me that she used to "write lottery," she elaborated: "I had a shop in my house. The people would come and they would play [i.e., buy numbers] lottery with me. I would write it down on a sheet, whatever they wanted to play. I'd count up my sheets, tally it, and I'd get so much money and I'd have to turn in so much to the boss. I would take my amount out and I would bring the rest to the place where they had the drawing."[42] Lottery sellers, praline and *calas* (rice-flour pastry) vendors, seamstresses, pieceworkers, and laundresses who worked at home represent the various forms of work available to poor, married, black women. The women who worked for cash at home—"inside"—not only complemented ideal notions of womanhood but performed several jobs simultaneously: they were paid workers, housewives, and most often also mothers.

A significant number of the women that I talked with, and virtually all of their mothers, worked "inside." This was also true of the mothers and wives of the men that I interviewed. For example, when I asked Mr. Montoya if his mother worked he answered emphatically, "Never. She worked in the home when the family got large. I am from a family of twelve . . . when work [for my father] was scarce my mother would sew. She would also make *calas* and we [the children] would sell the *calas* in order to buy bread to eat. That's the only work she did—in the house. She never went outside one day to work." The economic problems generated by twelve children and his father's frequent unemployment were compounded by his father's numerous bouts with malaria. His mother consequently "did everything to try and make money. She had a little store in the front room, and she used to send us out with baskets of soap and needles, and things like that. But she never worked outside." Montoya also proudly explained that his wife "never" worked. He nevertheless explained that she was a dressmaker, "but she never worked outside, and my mother never worked outside a day."[43]

As a result of their families' poverty Creole boys were also forced to begin working at an early age as indicated by the experiences of James Montoya and Everette Chevalier. Their experiences were representative of the hardships of many others of their generation. As a child, Montoya, (who was ten years older than Everette), began working as a street peddler. He formally went to work at about fourteen years of age because he was obligated, like Alice, Everette, and Justine, to help support the family. He remembered making $2.50 a week around 1905, but he also recalled how difficult it was to make even that much money because jobs were scarce in the city's Jim Crow economy. He thus felt compelled to work as white:

> The first [printing] shop I worked in was the only place where they hired Negroes at that time and I went there as a Negro. I got into an altercation with the foreman so I had to quit. . . . Then I turned around and I got a job as a white boy . . . at one of the biggest [printing] companies in the city. I stayed with them for a few years . . . It was against my grain to work as white. I didn't like to, and when I did it was because I had to—it was an economic necessity. I had gone to another place that hired Negroes but they offered me a salary that was the same thing that I had gotten for doing less.

But "passing," he explained,

was not easy, it was hard. You'd be around there and the whites would be talking about Negroes and you'd have to take it. Once I had been seen at night . . . and was later asked what was I doing with all those niggers. I told them that it was none of their damn business who I was with. They never asked me that anymore, but I didn't like it.[44]

Although it is impossible to determine either the frequency of passing or the number of its varied manifestations, the two most prevalent forms have been described as part-time, or discontinuous passing—such as passing for white at work—and continuous passing or "crossing-over" the racial divide into a new life with a new racial identity.[45] That many members of their community passed full-time or part-time was common knowledge among black Creoles born at the turn of the twentieth century. But passing was not a frivolous matter because it demanded tolerance for racism, as Montoya acknowledged, as well as the fear of discovery and betrayal, pressures imposed by maintaining a double life. In the early 1920s, Mrs. Evelina Laserna enrolled for a short time in a commercial school for whites because she thought she would learn more than at Guillaume's, the only commercial school for blacks in the city. She stopped attending the white school, however, "because it made me nervous." "I couldn't stand it especially because the girls wanted to visit and I just couldn't take that."[46]

One of Mrs. Laserna's contemporaries, Judith Wolf Aymard, also attended Guillaume's commercial school in the early 1920s. Black women, however, found it difficult to secure a secretarial job even with professional training. When Aymard discovered that the city's black-owned companies were not hiring in 1923, her guardian expressed concern that she would lose her skills. Consequently, she was encouraged to seek employment as white despite her disdain for doing so. Her guardian helped her look for jobs advertised in the Sunday newspaper: "She had cut some ads out of the paper and gave me my car fare, but I'd go anywhere but near the place. . . . I'd come back with some tale, that they had somebody. She began to get suspicious because she knew that I never did want to work on the 'outside'."[47] Clearly outwitted, Mrs. Aymard responded to an advertisement for young ladies to address envelopes. She recalled going to the Maison Blanche building and being a part of a group of applicants, all of whom were white—or so she assumed—except herself, and being asked to give a sample of her writing. However, much to her relief she learned that the positions had been filled. "I was so happy that I could go home and tell her that," she remembered. But before she could leave, her name was called:

> 'Now, who is Miss Judith Wolf?' I don't know where the speech came from, but in a very faint voice I said, 'I am.' When he asked that I remain I nearly died because the first thing I thought he was going to ask me was 'why are you here?' I was scared unto death, but he dismissed the others and put me to work.

Foiled by excellent penmanship, Aymard was disheartened by what in her estimation was a decidedly mixed fortune: she finally had a job, but it required that she pass for white.

However, upon her return home that evening she learned that her fortune had quickly changed for the better. She recalled: "When I got home the [black-owned] Louisiana Insurance Company had sent for me—you talk about thanking the Lord." She was relieved to find employment in a black company because despite the lower wages such a placement offered her the freedom to be herself—despite her appearance she saw herself as a member of the black community.[48]

Piper's recent essay, "Passing for White, Passing for Black," draws on her family's experiences with passing to analyze the meanings of racial categorization in the United States. She comments,

> Although both of my parents had watched many of their relatives disappear permanently into the white community, passing for white was un-thinkable within the branches of my father's and mother's families to which I belonged. That would have been a really, authentically shameful thing to do.[49]

By contrast, Dr. Bulkley, born a slave, interpreted racial passing as a consequence of "race prejudice." In 1909 he identified passing as one of the five major economic consequences of race prejudice, as he explained:

> In the fourth place, we do not get the full economic credit due to us, because of the loss of a host of mixed-bloods who cross the line. Even in the South this occasionally happens. Sometimes the whites know it and wink at it. . . . There is scarcely a [colored] man who could not tell of some friend or relative who has crossed the line North or South, now prominent in business, professors in institutions of learning, married into good society, and rearing families that have no dreams of the depth that their parents have escaped. We could tell the story, if we would—but who would be the knave to disturb their peace?[50]

The stories of crossing the line, although I have not focused on them, are poignant because they are about individuals who were willing to "lose their boundaries"—evidence of the tragic legacy of slavery and the deep-seated nature of racism in our society.

Most often the discussion of passing, full or part-time, focuses on members of the African-American middle class; it is rare that attention is paid to members of the black working class. Perhaps this is because, much like the history of migration, the individuals who were most able to cross racial lines to assume a new identity had the resources to do so which included money and skills.[51] The challenges of any type of passing were similar to both the obstacles faced by black migrants prior to desegregation, and the even earlier experiences of runaway slaves: It was, for example, probably much easier for men to find work, even if the disguise required underemployment, and to move outside or even within their home town or region. By contrast, a woman alone was hampered by the extremely limited options for making a living—even as white—as a respectable woman unless she had an education. The complexities when couples—although not uncommon—and entire families tried to pass can only be imagined.[52]

Although the history of racial passing does not evoke the clear-cut ethical responses that we have to slavery it is an important part of the larger story of racism and racial repression in this country. The frequency of passing is further evidence of the fraudulence of race as a meaningful construct for other than divisive exploitation. The experiences of the black Creole men and women that I have focused on are examples of the extreme risks African Americans born at the turn of the century often felt forced to take to circumvent a poverty that was socially engineered by white supremacists who wanted to preserve decent paying jobs for whites. Therefore, to read the history of "passing" as a tragic mulatto story of self-hatred, or as evidence of a "devil may care," Caribbean-style multiracial identity in South Louisiana is to misread the history of American race relations.[53]

By way of conclusion it seems appropriate to try to identify—or at least speculate about—the variables that might apply to those black Creoles born at the turn of the century who were able to pass but ultimately chose to be black. For example, despite the deteriorating effect of the Civil War on the wealth of many of the black Creole elite the community continued to pride itself on the integrity of their ethnic distinctiveness which included a history of freedom and Catholicism. Their pride was reenforced by endogamous marriages and patterns of association reflected in the membership of unions and organizations such as benevolent societies.[54] In addition, during the decades in which these men and women were young, many black Creoles continued to benefit from their skills in such crafts as bricklaying and plastering. These skills enabled many black Creoles to own their often modest homes, concentrated in the downtown wards, despite their working class status.[55] In addition, the city's residential segregation was less severe than was common throughout other Southern cities. And in contrast to the overwhelming majority of blacks who were rural agricultural workers or recent arrivals in Southern cities, black Creoles in New Orleans had experienced the relative anonymity of urban life for many generations. Taken together, the black Creole community had much to offer its members despite the racism, general poverty, and hard work. Perhaps it is for these reasons that this generation of Creoles were generally unlikely to participate in the first "great migration" to Northern cities.

What is clear is that not all African Americans, including Creoles, who could pass for white did so. Perhaps Everette Chevalier's (1901-1980) explanation of why he did not take advantage of his appearance to pass for white is instructive; he explained that he did not pass "because of my relations. I lived with my ma and them." I think that Uncle Everette, or *Paran* as we also called him, simply did not want to lose his most cherished boundaries.[56] Perhaps he understood, unlike James Weldon Johnson's 1912 anonymous narrator, that the real risk in crossing-over was the possibility of regretting that he had "chosen the lesser part, that I have sold my birthright for a mess of pottage."[57]

Although a great deal is known about the politics, economics, and violence of segregation and discrimination, historians have documented painfully little about how daily life—or to paraphrase Mrs. Laserna, what people could and could not take—was shaped by race and racism for non-agricultural black Southern workers.[58] Therefore, the experiences of Mr. and Mrs. Chevalier, Mrs. Lacarra, Mr. Montoya, Mrs. Puryear, and the others are significant because they augment our understanding of segregation's impact on blacks in general and on one ethnic community in particular. Moreover, to bring attention to the experiences of heretofore neglected women is critical for an understanding of the dynamics of gender, as well as class, within New Orleans's black Creole community.

Notes for "Lost Boundaries: Racial Passing and Poverty in Segregated New Orleans"

[1] Central texts include Charles W. Chesnutt, *The Marrow of Tradition* (Boston, 1901), James Weldon Johnson, *The Autobiography of an Ex-Coloured Man* (Boston, 1912), Jessie Redmon Fauset, *Plum Bun: A Novel Without a Moral* (London, 1928), and Nella Larsen, *Passing* (New York, 1929). Passing was also of interest, albeit for different reasons, to European American and European writers; see, e.g., Joachim Warmbold, "If Only She Didn't Have Negro Blood in her Veins: The Concept of *Métissage* in German Colonial Literature," *Journal of Black Studies,* 23 (1992): 200-209, A. L. Nielsen, "Mark Twain's *Pudd'nhead Wilson* and the Novel of the Tragic Mulatto," *Greyfriar: Siena Studies in Literature,* 26 (1985): 14-30; Daniel Aaron, "The Inky Curse: Miscegenation in the white American literary imagination," *Social Science Information,* 22 (1983): 169-90, and James Kinney, "The Rhetoric of Racism: Thomas Dixon and the 'Damned Black Beast'," *American Literary Realism,* 15 (1982): 145-54.

[2] *Transition,* 58 (1992): 4-32. See also, for example, G. Reginald Daniels, "Passers and Pluralists: Subverting the Racial Divide," in *Racially Mixed People in America,* ed. Maria P. P. Root (Newbury Park, Calif., 1992), F. James Davis, *Who is Black? One Nation's Definition* (University Park, Pa., 1991), Paul R. Spickard, *Mixed Blood: Intermarriage and Ethnic Identity in Twentieth-Century America* (Madison, 1989), and Virginia R. Dominguez, *White By Definition: Social Classification in Creole Louisiana* (New Brunswick, N.J., 1986).

[3] See, e.g., Lauren Berlant, "National Brand/National Body: *Imitation of Life*,". in *Comparative America Identities*, ed. Hortense J. Spillers (New York, 1991), 110-40; and bell hooks, *Black Looks: Race and Representation* (Boston, 1992). Valerie Smith has applied the term to the subtext of films in which black working class characters attempt to transcend their class background to "pass" for middle class. Paper delivered at the Symposium on Critical Issues in African American Life and Thought, University of California, Irvine, October 27, 1992. Also of note is the popularity of the films *Paris is Burning* and *The Crying Game*, pop singer Ru Paul, and the comic persona of Dame Edna.

[4] Twenty-seven of these interviews were taped and transcribed, and are in the author's possession. Additional interviews are as cited. The names of most of the interviewees have been changed. Note that throughout the essay the terms black Creole, Creole of color and Creole are used interchangeably unless otherwise indicated. "Creole" is the term used within this community which does not mean that individuals do not also see themselves as Negro or black.

[5] Sources on the value of oral history include Sherna Berger Gluck and Daphne Patai, eds., *Women's Words: The Feminist Practice of Oral History* (New York, 1991) and Paul R. Thompson, *The Voice of the Past: Oral History* (Oxford, 1978).

[6] There are differences between New Orleanian Creole of color identity and Creole identity in rural and small town southern Louisiana. For a discussion of colored Creole identity in New Orleans see, for example, author, "The Negro Creole Community in New Orleans, 1880-1920s: An Oral History" (Ph. D. dissertation, University of California, Irvine, 1978); James H. Dormon refers to "prairie Creoles" in "Louisiana's 'Creoles of Color': Ethnicity, Marginality, and Identity," *Social Science Quarterly,* 73 (1992): 615-26. The term

"Creole" is also used by blacks outside of southern Louisiana, see for example, D. C. La Foy, "A Historical Review of Three Gulf Coast Creole Communities," *Gulf Coast Historical Review,* 3 (1899): 6-19; and William S. Coker, "Tom Moreno: A Pensacola Creole," *Florida Historical Quarterly,* 67 (1989): 329-39. In addition, Carole Ione describes a South Carolinian black Creole family history in *Pride of Family: Four Generations of American Women of Color* (New York, 1991). For a discussion of white Creoles see, for example, Joseph G. Tregle, Jr., "Creoles and Americans," in Arnold R. Hirsch and Joseph Logsdon, eds., *Creole New Orleans: Race and Americanization* (Baton Rouge, 1992), 131-85.

[7]Donald E. DeVore and Joseph Logsdon, *Crescent City Schools: Public Education in New Orleans, 1841-1991* (Lafayette, La., 1991), discuss the opening of Southern University's elementary and secondary departments in 1881, 94. They also note that after Southern left New Orleans and moved to Baton Rouge in 1913-14, McDonough 35, the high school for Negroes, did not open until 1917. Of equal significance was the New Orleans school board's elimination of "the three bridge grades . . . between elementary and high school" in 1900, 189.

[8]Straight University, established by the American Missionary Association in 1869, was the most important high school and normal school, and later college, for this generation. See Joe M. Richardson, "The American Missionary Association and Black Education in Louisiana, 1862-1878," in *Louisiana's Black Heritage* (New Orleans, 1979), 157-62. For a discussion of Straight, Leland and New Orleans universities—all established by Protestant organizations—see John W. Blassingame, *Black New Orleans, 1860-1880* (Chicago, 1976), 124-30; and DeVore and Logsdon, *Crescent City Schools.* The other private schools that were important to this group of Creoles included St. Mary's Academy for Young Ladies of Color, established in 1880 by the Sisters of the Holy Family, and Medard Nelson's school. Small private schools of uneven quality that taught primarily Catholic catechism in preparation for First Holy Communion were common.

[9]Arthé Anthony, "Catholicism, Race and New Orleanian Creole of Color Identity" (Paper delivered at the American Anthropological Association annual conference, San Francisco, December 1992).

[10]Discussions that emphasize the experiences of New Orleanian black women in the late nineteenth and twentieth centuries are rare. Examples include Violet Harrington Bryan's discussion of Alice Dunbar-Nelson in *The Myth of New Orleans in Literature: Dialogues of Race and Gender* (Knoxville, 1993), 62-78, Doris Dorcas Carter, "Refusing to Relinquish the Struggle: The Social Role of the Black Woman in Louisiana History," in Robert R. MacDonald et al., eds., *Louisiana's Black Heritage* (New Orleans, 1979), 163-89. Vaughan B. Baker's critique of traditional historical methodology for its limited ability to examine the lives of women is worth noting, "*Cherchez les Femmes*: Some Glimpses of Women in Early Eighteenth-Century Louisiana," *Louisiana History,* 31 (1990): 21-37. The problems that she brings attention to are magnified exponentially when the complexities of not only gender but race and class are under consideration.

[11]Lillian Gelbart Simonet, interview with author, New Orleans, Louisiana, February 14, 1977.

[12]For example, advertisements in newspapers for the hiring of light-skinned girls continued to appear in the city's want-ads into the 1960s.

[13]Passing for white was not a uniquely colored Creole phenomenon as is made clear by the attention given to the topic in African American literature. Slave narratives, e.g., the story of William and Ellen Craft, also made reference to this strategy. Racial passing has also been discussed by historians and social scientists, e.g., Caroline Day Bond, *A Study of Some Negro-White Families* (1932; reprint, Westport, Ct. 1970), Ira Berlin, *Slaves Without Masters: The Free Negro In the Antebellum South* (New York, 1976), 160-64, and Blassingame, *Black New Orleans,* 201-2. For a more personal account see Kathryn L. Morgan, *Children of Strangers: The Stories of a Black Family* (Philadelphia, 1980), 25, 78-85.

[14]See, for example, H. E. Sterkx, *The Free Negro in Ante-bellum Louisiana* (Rutherford, N.J., 1972), 160-99, and David C. Rankin, "The Politics of Caste: Free Colored Leadership in New Orleans During the Civil War," in *Louisiana's Black Heritage,* 107-46, and Laura Foner, "The Free People of Color in Louisiana and St.

Domingue: A Comparative Portrait of Two Three-Caste Slave Societies," *Journal of Social History,* 3 (1970): 406-30. The most recent scholarship is represented by Gwendolyn Midlo Hall, *Africans in Colonial Louisiana* (Baton Rouge, 1992) and Kimberly S. Hanger, "Avenues to Freedom Open to New Orleans' Black Population, 1776-1779," *Louisiana History,* 31 (1990): 237-64.

[15]Thomas N. Ingersoll, "Free Blacks in a Slave Society: New Orleans, 1718-1812," *William and Mary Quarterly,* 48 (1992): 200.

[16]Sterkx, *The Free Negro in Ante-Bellum Louisiana*, especially chs. 4 and 7, and Logsdon, "Americans and Creoles in New Orleans: The Origins of Black Citizenship in the United States," *Amerikastudien/American Studies* (West Germany) 34 (1989): 187-202.

[17]Loren Schweninger, "Antebellum Free Persons of Color in Postbellum Louisiana," *Louisiana History,* 30 (1989): 358; Loren Schweninger, *Black Property Owners in the South, 1790-1915* (Urbana, 1990), 112-21.

[18]Schweninger, "Antebellum Free Persons of Color," 357, and Schweninger, *Black Property Owners*, 190-96. What we don't know is how many women and men chose to pass for white, and whether or not they remained in the area, in response to not only economic loses but racial repression. See Blassingame, *Black New Orleans,* 201-2. Stories abound regarding passing including a version of Leander Perez's ancestry which asserts that his father was an Afro-Cuban whose birth records conveniently turned to ashes in a mysterious fire.

[19]Eric Arnesen offers a concise overview of these events in *Waterfront Workers of New Orleans: Race, Class and Politics, 1863-1923* (New York, 1991), 181-89. See also, Otto H. Olsen, *The Thin Disguise: Turning Point in Negro History, Plessy v. Ferguson* (New York, 1967); and Charles A. Lofgren, *The Plessy Case: A Legal-Historical Interpretation* (New York, 1987).

[20]Dr. William L. Bulkley, "Race Prejudice as Viewed from an Economic Standpoint," in Philip S. Foner, ed., *The Voice of Black America,* 2 vols. (New York, 1975), 2:64. Rodolphe L. Desdunes also refers to passing for white as a controversial strategy for enjoying "the rights and privileges accorded this standing," Rodolphe L. Desdunes, *Our People and Our History,* trans. and ed. Dorothea Olga McCants (Baton Rouge, 1973), 62.

[21]William H. Harris, *The Harder We Run: Black Workers Since the Civil War* (New York, 1982).

[22]For a discussion of the male leaders of previous generations see, for example, Joseph Logsdon and Caryn Cossé Bell, "The Americanization of Black New Orleans 1850-1900," in Hirsch and Logsdon, eds., *Creole New Orleans*, 201-61.

[23]For a discussion of the extremes of racial violence in Louisiana see for example Gilles Vandal, "The Policy of Violence in Caddo Parish, 1865-1884," *Louisiana History,* 32 (1992): 159-82, William Ivy Hair, *Carnival of Fury: Robert Charles and the New Orleans Race Riot of 1900* (Baton Rouge, 1976), and Joy J. Jackson, *New Orleans in the Gilded Age: Political and Urban Progress, 1880-1896* (Baton Rouge, 1969), 19-21 and 226-31.

[24]Jackson, *New Orleans in the Gilded Age,* 221-22.

[25]Interview with Eugenia Marine Lacarra by the author, New Orleans, Louisiana, December 9, 1977. The ownership of the company changed over the decades. For example, in 1900 the company was listed as a branch of the Havana-American Co., and in 1930 Hernsheim Cigar was located at 508 Iberville Street, *Soards'*, Louisiana Division, New Orleans Public Library.

[26]Interviews with former cigar makers suggest that some black Creoles had passed while working for Hernsheim's. Construction on the new S. Hernsheim & Bros. cigar factory, at Magazine and Julia streets, began in February 1882, *Daily States*, February 14, 1882.

[27] Marguerite Puryear, interview with the author, New Orleans, Louisiana, February 17, 1977. She recalled going to work at Trelles the same year her niece, who lives in Los Angeles, was born. According to her recollections this dates the closure of Marine's as 1921. However, Soards'—a helpful but flawed source—has the Marine Cigar Inc. last listed in 1924. M. Trelles & Co., which moved several times in the early 1920s, is listed at 600 Tchoupitoulas Street in 1921-24, and in 1925 at 701-715 So. Peters Street where it remained into the 1940s, *Soards'* and *Polk's* New Orleans Directories 1920-42, Louisiana Division, New Orleans Public Library.

[28] Lacarra interview.

[29] James M. Montoya, Sr., interview with author, New Orleans, Louisiana, March 15, 1977. Mr. Montoya noted that his father worked for Hernsheim's, and he also worked in Tampa and Chicago. Mrs. Lacarra remembered that her father worked in Montreal, which is where her brother was born.

[30] Piper, "Passing for White, Passing for Black," 30.

[31] Dolores Egger Labbé discusses the 1895 establishment of St. Katherine's as a "black" church despite the protests of many for whom it was designed, see *Jim Crow Comes to Church: The Establishment of Segregated Catholic Parishes in South Louisiana* (Lafayette, La., 1971), 49-56. Although the church was intended for black parishioners it was also attended by white nurses and doctors who worked at Charity Hospital, interview with Eugenia Lacarra. Stephen J. Ochs examines the fitful history of black priests and the church's views about race in *Desegregating the Altar: The Josephites and the Struggle for Black Priests, 1871-1960* (Baton Rouge, 1990).

[32] Montoya interview.

[33] Part of the irony of their experience was that it was acceptable for a man who was believed to be white to be in the company of a colored woman. Alice Simon and Everette Chevalier, interview with the author, February 21, 1977, New Orleans, Louisiana.

[34] Ibid.

[35] Chevalier interview, and Gary Nash et al., *The American People: Creating a Nation and a Society* (New York 1986), 699-705.

[36] Chevalier interview. The St. Louis Drug Company, according to *Soards'*, was at 841 N. Rampart Street in 1917. His parents work experiences, particularly the fact that his mother worked, are similar to those of other urban African-American families in this period. See, for example, Mary White Ovington on "The Black Woman as Breadwinner," in Nancy F. Cott, ed., *The Root of Bitterness*, (Boston, 1986), 343-47, and William H. Harris, *The Harder We Run*, 23-24 and 36-37.

[37] Alice Kessler-Harris, *Women Have Always Worked: A Historical Overview* (Old Westbury, N.Y., 1981), 71, and Melvyn Dubofsky, *Industrialism and the American Worker, 1865-1920* (Arlington Heights, Ill., 1985), 27.

[38] According to *Soards'* Dixie Laundry was at 1126 Tulane Avenue in 1919. Alice Woodcock Tentler, *Wage-Earning Women: Industrial Work and Family Life in the United States, 1900-1930* (New York, 1979), ch. 4 and 146-47. Regarding the hours Alice worked: in 1908 state regulation prohibited women from working more than a "10-hour day or 60-hour week . . . in any mill, factory, mine, packing house, manufacturing establishment, workshop, laundry, millinery or dressmaking store or mercantile establishment." In 1930 the maximum hours of employment for women were reduced to a nine-hour day and a fifty-four-hour week. Florence P. Smith, United States Department of Labor and Women's Bureau, *Chronological Development of Labor Legislation for Women in the United States*. Bulletin of the Women's Bureau, No. 66-II (Washington, D.C., 1932), 46-7.

[39] When she retired from M. Trelles & Co. she worked part-time in a school cafeteria. Her experience was representative of urban working class African-American women, and in contrast to the work histories of white working class wives given that a relative minority of them worked prior to World War II, see Tentler, *Wage-Earning Women*, ch. 6; and Harris, *The Harder We Run*, 22-4.

[40] Justine Frank Marcard, interview with the author, New Orleans, Louisiana, February 15, 1977.

[41] Their experiences, and those of their mothers, were similar to those of other black women in that historically a larger percentage of married black than married white women worked. See, for example, Nancy Woloch, *Women and the American Experience* (New York, 1984), 225-30.

[42] Marcard interview. According to Joy J. Jackson the legal Louisiana Lottery was terminated on January 1, 1894, and continued to operate illegally via Honduras until 1907, *New Orleans in the Gilded Age*, 134-5. However, the experiences of my informants suggest that an illegal lottery lasted much longer than 1907.

[43] Montoya interview.

[44] Ibid.

[45] Daniels, "Passers and Pluralists: Subverting the Racial Divide," in *Racially Mixed People*, 92-4 and Domínguez, *White by Definition*, 200-204. Some individuals also passed on very isolated occasions such as attending a movie, shopping, or sitting in the front of the screen on public transportation.

[46] Evelina Laserna, interview with the author, New Orleans, Louisiana, March 2, 1977. According to Judith Wolf Aymard the school was located in the Pythian Temple building; tuition was $5.00 a month in the early 1920s, interview with the author, New Orleans, Louisiana, December 12, 1977.

[47] In this context "outside" is in reference to passing for white, i.e., posing as someone "outside of the race."

[48] Aymard interview.

[49] Piper, "Passing for White, Passing for Black," 10.

[50] Bulkley, "Race Prejudice as Viewed from an Economic Standpoint," 67.

[51] For a discussion of the "great migration" of blacks in relation to migration theory see Carole Marks, *Farewell—We're Good and Gone: The Great Black Migration* (Bloomington, 1989).

[52] I am familiar with many examples of wives and husbands who changed identities and remained in New Orleans, as well as cases of individuals who left Louisiana. For historical examples of passing consider the experiences of Ellen Craft and her husband; she was disguised as an invalid white male while he posed as the invalid's colored servant, in Arna Bontemps, comp., *Running a Thousand Miles for Freedom, or the Escape of William and Ellen Craft from Slavery* (Boston, 1969). There is the other well known example of Harriet Jacobs who felt compelled to hide in an attic for seven years because she could not bear to leave her children behind in order to runaway, Linda Brent, *Incidents in the Life of a Slave Girl* (1861; reprint, New York, 1973).

[53] This does not mean to suggest that Creoles of another generation have not preferred to see themselves as other than black. However, Creoles born at the turn-of-the-century were born into a black and white world. For interpretations of Creole of color identity as flexible and multiracial see Domínguez, *White by Definition* and Daniel, "Passers and Pluralists," in *Racially Mixed People in America*. For a view of marginality as "the major determinant of the Creole ethnic experience," see Dormon, "Louisiana's 'Creoles of Color'."

[54] Anthony, "The Negro Creole Community in New Orleans, 1880-1920s."

[55] Jerry Wilcox and Anthony V. Margavio, "Occupational Representation by Race, Ethnicity, and Residence in Turn-of-the-Century New Orleans," *Social Science Journal,* 24 (1987): 1-16.

[56] Arthur Flannigan-St. Aubin, an expert on Francophone literature, has pointed out that *paran* is an appropriate Creole spelling for the French *parrain*, meaning godfather. Everette acquired this name because he had been *paran* to many.

[57] Johnson, *The Autobiography of an Ex-Coloured Man,* 211.

[58] Experiences with segregation and the frequency of passing are stories well known in black families. For example, while writing this essay friends have shared countless anecdotes, e.g., of the aunt who worked in a Chicago department store in 1921, the cousin who worked as a librarian at Stanford University in the 1940s, and more recently the cousin who assumed an East Indian identity as she travelled from Indianapolis to Oakland in 1980.

RACIAL REPRESSION IN WORLD WAR TWO: THE NEW IBERIA INCIDENT*

Adam Fairclough

During the week of May 15, 1944, a dozen blacks, including the leaders of the local NAACP, were expelled from the town of New Iberia. Four of them suffered beatings, one so severe that the victim died soon afterward. The incident vividly illustrated the determination of many Louisiana whites to defend the racial status quo and the fury with which they sometimes reacted to wartime black militancy. It also exposed the inability or unwillingness of the federal government to protect the civil rights of black Southerners. Despite affidavits from the victims, protests from the national office of the NAACP, and an extensive FBI investigation, the Department of Justice failed to secure the indictment and prosecution of the perpetrators. The events that occurred in New Iberia serve as a reminder that the first stirrings of the modern civil-rights movement began long before the Montgomery bus boycott, during the tense, turbulent days of the Second World War. They remind us, too, of the perils that faced the obscure and all-but-forgotten pioneers of the NAACP in Louisiana.

The Second World War placed every facet of the South's racial system under pressure. Mobilization uprooted millions from homes and farms, herding them to factories, shipyards, and military bases. In the teeming cities, whites and blacks crowded together in a physical proximity unknown since slavery. The transience and turmoil of war ruptured traditional relationships, and the apparent certainties of the color line gave way to challenge, doubt, resentment, and fear. Beneath the blare of patriotism and propaganda, racial tensions simmered and sometimes exploded, in outbursts of violence ranging from barroom fisticuffs to full-fledged riots. And in this tinderbox atmosphere, rumor and speculation magnified anxieties: whites feared an insurrection; blacks anticipated a wave of postwar lynchings.[1]

---

*First published in *Louisiana History*, 32 (1991): 183-207. Reprinted with the kind permission of the author and the Louisiana Historical Association.

The war years saw a generation of blacks begin to slough off the humility and resignation with which black Southerners had formerly accepted their lot. As the conflict raged blacks clamored for fair employment, agitated for the ballot, insisted on better public facilities, denounced segregation, and protested vociferously against police brutality. The new militancy was infectious. The mere fact of being at war seemed to encourage a devil-may-care attitude that easily translated into racial assertiveness. "People were in a belligerent mood," remembered Ernest Wright, one of the most outspoken black leaders of the period. When once they would have swallowed their pride, accepting insult and injury, many blacks now stood their ground. Soldiers clashed with the military authorities; civilians argued with bus drivers and policemen; shipyard workers walked off the job. Blacks were speaking and acting in a way not seen since Reconstruction.[2]

Some white politicians, asserting that black militancy endangered the segregated foundations of Southern society, deliberately sought to arouse white fears. In his 1942 campaign for the U. S. Senate, E. A. Stephens warned of "social equality" being "forced down the throats of white people," and alleged that "colored organizations are sitting around midnight candles" plotting the overthrow of white supremacy. Although Stephens lost, this kind of rhetoric prompted Senator Allen Ellender to underline his segregationist credentials so as to avoid being outflanked. Congressman F. Edward Hébert of New Orleans played a similar tune, denouncing a plan to convert the Senator Hotel into a seamen's hostel as a "diabolical scheme" to "equalize the negroes and the whites" and promote "a permanent mixture of the races." Even liberal whites stressed that segregation was sacrosanct.[3]

The prospect of blacks voting also filled whites with grave misgivings. In 1940 the Southern Negro Youth Congress, which met in New Orleans that year, launched a "Right to Vote" campaign, flooding the South with pamphlets urging blacks to register. A few months later a group of black Creoles sought the blessing of state senator Joseph Cawthorn, a prominent Longite, for the creation of a "colored Democratic party." Gubernatorial candidates Earl Long and Sam Jones each accused the other of supporting black voting; both vehemently denied the charge. In 1941, however, the prospect of blacks gaining the ballot increased when the U. S. Supreme Court ruled that the Democratic primary was an integral part of Louisiana's election machinery; this made it, by implication, subject to the ban on racial discrimination contained in the Fourteenth and Fifteenth amendments.[4]

As the NAACP prepared to challenge the "white primary" in various Southern states, blacks in Louisiana stepped up their agitation for the ballot. In New Orleans, Ernest J. Wright, a CIO organizer and SNYC vice president, founded the People's Defense League, which soon became, in the FBI's estimation, "the most powerful black organization in New Orleans," thanks to Wright's militant leadership. The city's most influential black Baptist, the Reverend A. L. Davis, joined forces with Wright, and the two men addressed right-to-vote rallies in Shakespeare Park under the auspices of the Louisiana Association for the Progress of Negro Citizens. In 1942 a few blacks in New Orleans attempted to vote in the Democratic primary: most, including Wright, were turned away. The following year the NAACP laid plans to file suit against Louisiana's registration laws. In April 1944, word finally came from Washington that the Supreme Court had struck down the white-only primary. Hailing the decision as "the Negro's Second Emancipation," black organizations prepared for a statewide campaign of voter registration and political mobilization.[5]

Blacks also moved against white supremacy on the economic front. Determined to share in the prosperity of war, they sought jobs in the burgeoning defense industries and pressed for admittance to wartime training programs. Pressure from Northern blacks, in the form of A. Philip Randolph's March on Washington Movement, induced President Roosevelt to establish a federal Fair Employment Practices Committee. Even black teachers, traditionally the most docile of groups, developed signs of assertiveness: by 1944 teachers in Orleans, Jefferson, and Iberville parishes had filed suit in federal court to challenge salary discrimination. Under the leadership of J. K. Haynes, the Louisiana Colored Teachers Association worked even more closely with the NAACP, which was itself establishing new branches, expanding its membership, and organizing on a statewide basis.[6]

Outside New Orleans, particularly in the cotton and sugar parishes, white planters saw their traditional supply of cheap black labor in jeopardy. Attempts by the Louisiana Farmers Union to organize sharecroppers and farm laborers had already provoked threats, beatings, arrests, and near-lynchings. The Farm Security Administration, which helped set up black tenants as independent farmers, also incurred the enmity of planters. In Natchitoches Parish, threats and political pressure caused the FSA to withdrew its black officials from the area in 1942. The following year, in Caldwell Parish, a black FSA official was slain. Now the war threatened to drive up agricultural wages by luring blacks to the cities and drafting large numbers into the armed services. The *Louisiana Weekly* alleged that blacks in Alexandria were being "picked up off the streets" and forcibly dispatched to the cane and cotton fields. In 1943 the Department of Agriculture forbade farm workers to leave their home counties unless a "labor surplus" had been officially declared. By 1944 sugar planters were employing 4,600 German prisoners-of-war—labor that had the added benefit of causing black workers to worry about being displaced. "As a result," one planter reported, "the negroes are working better and are staying on the job throughout the week."[7]

The events that occurred in New Iberia in the spring of 1944 portrayed, in microcosm, the racial tensions that gripped Louisiana during the Second World War. They also provide a fascinating case study of the first, fumbling attempts by the federal government to protect the civil rights of black Southerners.

Blacks in New Iberia organized a branch of the NAACP in the summer of 1943, apparently unaware of the white hostility they were arousing. In August, several prominent whites received invitations to attend a mass meeting to mark the installation of the new branch officers. But city and parish officials had no intention of sanctioning the activities of the NAACP, and they asked a Roman Catholic priest, the pastor of a black parish, to discreetly warn the blacks that they would gain nothing by pushing for their rights too assertively. Shortly after the mass meeting, the branch officers were summoned before Sheriff Gilbert Ozenne and another white official, who sternly warned that the NAACP activists would be "personally held responsible for anything that may happen in New Iberia." In December Sheriff Ozenne confided to an FBI agent that the NAACP was stockpiling ammunition; the agent dismissed this allegation as fantastic. Nevertheless, the newly elected sheriff, a former highway patrolman, began to gird himself for an armed confrontation.[8]

In March 1944, seemingly oblivious to the mounting tension, the NAACP held a rally addressed by Ernest Wright, who stressed the vital urgency of obtaining the ballot. At a mass meeting on April 28, hard on the heels of the Texas primary decision, branch president J. Leo Hardy declared that the United States had the first honest Supreme Court and the first honest president since Abraham Lincoln. As the audiences echoed their approval with "Amens," Hardy decried the fact that white children rode to school while black children had to walk; and that white neighborhoods boasted paved roads and sidewalks while the streets fronting black homes comprised dirt and mud. Now was the time, he concluded, for blacks to secure the same rights as white people, including the ballot.[9]

It was the NAACP's demand for a welding school, however, that prompted white leaders to rid New Iberia of the emerging militant leadership in one fell swoop. Why did this issue prove so contentious and occasion such drastic action?

Industrial training had assumed great importance for blacks, symbolizing their determination to break down the employment discrimination that confined them to menial and agricultural jobs. But although the docks and shipyards were crying out for skilled labor, management and unions colluded to exclude blacks and recruit untrained whites. In New Orleans, for example, welding jobs were controlled by the white-only Brotherhood of Boilermakers, Iron Shipbuilders and Helpers of America. Operating through the powerful Metal Trades Council, the AFL unions kept black welders, carpenters, and other skilled tradesmen out of the giant Delta shipyard. Blacks made some limited gains elsewhere: a survey of 175 firms in New Orleans revealed that by June 1943 twenty-seven had dropped their color bar, and nineteen others now employed blacks in previously white-only jobs. The shipyards, however, were still drastically understaffed because of their refusal to recruit skilled black labor.[10]

Faced with a national manpower shortage, the federal government funded an industrial training program, but each state retained tight control over the money. In New Orleans, for example, the parish school board offered courses to blacks in printing, shoe repairing, and motor mechanics, but it refused to run courses in welding. State and local officials believed that industrial training would draw blacks away from the agricultural areas and place them in direct competition with white workers. And the consequences of the latter were explosive. In May 1943, under pressure from the FEPC, the Alabama Dry Dock

Company in Mobile placed twelve newly upgraded black welders alongside white workers. The white work force erupted in violence, and federal troops had to quell the outbreak. The following month white shipyard workers rioted in Beaumont, Texas. In the Delta shipyard in New Orleans, blacks organized a mass walkout after two of their number suffered beatings. Despite such conflicts, the FEPC stepped up pressure on the Southern states to train and upgrade black workers. According to historian Merl Reed, "To many Southern whites the committee was no less feared and hated than the enemy overseas."[11]

In 1941 the State Department of Education set up a welding school in New Iberia for whites; when blacks asked for similar opportunities they were rebuffed. Faced with a complaint from a local black that had been forwarded by the federal government, Lloyd G. Porter, the superintendent of schools for Iberia Parish called in a group of hand-picked blacks and, in the company of the sheriff, confronted them with the complaint. The blacks nervously assured Porter that they knew nothing about the offending letter; one pointed out that it could not have been written by the black complainant, Lawrence Viltz, because he was barely literate. Despite the presence of an FEPC official, the blacks denied any desire for a welding school, suggesting that "some white trash" had probably sent the complaint "in an attempt to cause friction between the whites and the blacks."[12]

Viltz pressed his complaint, however, and the newly organized NAACP branch backed him up. On March 6, 1944, a field examiner from the FEPC, Virgil Williams, visited New Iberia to resolve the dispute; he left with the understanding that the school board would establish a welding school for blacks, with the State Department of Education providing the equipment and Gulf Public Service Co. furnishing the power. Porter undertook to operate the school on two six-hour shifts, five days a week. Hardy gave him a list of over one hundred prospective trainees.

When the welding school opened on May 7, however, it operated one shift only, and at 8 p.m., two hours after the first class began, Porter told the instructor to finish the class at 10 p.m. because white residents were complaining about the noise of the machinery. The following day the school began operating a daytime shift that ended at 7 p.m., causing several trainees to drop out. The NAACP sent a deputation to ask that the welding class be moved to a black neighborhood, but Porter, allowing only one of them into his office, pointed out that the black school had no electric power and that he had no money to run in cables. Hardy asked the FEPC, which was closely monitoring the progress of the welding school, to intercede again, alleging that the school's current location on the edge of a white neighborhood was a deliberate attempt to deter blacks.[13]

Precise responsibility for the ensuing expulsions is difficult to establish, but the sequence of events is reasonably clear. On the afternoon of Monday, May 15, two sheriff's deputies picked up Hardy at the welding school. Within minutes, Hardy found himself standing in the sheriff's office, facing Sheriff Ozenne and Superintendent Porter. According to the account written by Hardy a few days later—the only evidence directly linking Ozenne and Porter to the expulsions—the sheriff began to browbeat him. Did Hardy know who was talking to him? Did he realize that his letters to Porter (one of which had demanded "an immediate answer") were insulting? Terrified, Hardy became obsequious. He apologized and punctuated every sentence with "yassuhs."[14]

Then Porter spoke. Hardy would not be writing any more letters to the FEPC, the War Manpower Commission or any other "outsiders." He, Porter, would run the welding school as he saw fit—not even the president of the United States could make him do otherwise—and he would close the school down if he chose to. Hardy's repeated "yassuhs" seemed merely to infuriate Porter. "You yellow son of a bitch," he shouted. "You are saying 'yes sir,' but deep down in your heart you would cut my throat." Hardy was the very one organizing the blacks to overthrow the whites. He had in mind to kill Hardy, and if he weren't too old he would do it with his own hands. With Porter's assent, Ozenne gave Hardy until ten the next morning to get out of town.

Unable to complete his arrangements for leaving, Hardy lingered in New Iberia throughout the next day, despite warnings from friends not to spend the night in his home or stay with any of his relatives. At about eight in the evening he was chatting with friends outside Uncle Tom's Saloon at French and Robertson streets when a black sedan carrying four deputy sheriffs drew up. The men ordered Hardy into the car and took him to the sheriff's office. After threatening to kill him, one of the deputies asked Hardy where he wanted to go. When Hardy suggested that they take him by his house, the deputy retorted, "Hell, no. Do you want to go east or west?" Ozenne then proceeded to curse, pommel and kick Hardy while two deputies held his arms. After half an hour in a cell, he was bundled into a car and driven out of town; a deputy in the back seat grabbed hold of his necktie and punched him in the face. Dumped in the road, he was ordered to walk fast, not look back, and never return. The deputies drove behind him for a time, one of them firing a parting shot. When he reached the hamlet of Burke, Hardy phoned Dr. Howard Scoggins, a New Iberia physician and druggist, for help. Scoggins found Hardy standing by the roadside about five miles from town, bleeding from the nose and mouth. After applying first aid, he took his injured friend to Lafayette. The following day, the doctor drove back to Lafayette with clean clothes. Hardy took an overnight train to Monroe, two hundred miles distant.[15]

But the expulsions had only just started. On the evening of Wednesday, May 17, Walker and two other deputies picked up, in turn, Dr. Ima A. Pierson, a dentist; Dr. Luins H. Williams, a physician; and Herman Joseph Faulk, a teacher. Like Hardy, they were driven out of town and dumped by the roadside. All suffered beatings of varying severity: Pierson and Williams were pistol-whipped; Faulk was "clubbed over the right eye, knocked to the ground, and stomped in the face." Faulk left a particularly vivid account of his ordeal. Before letting him loose, one deputy held him against the hood of the Plymouth sedan while Walker slapped his face and berated him. "You are a damn smart nigger, eh? . . . Nigger, you mean to tell me that you and your wife work for Mr. Porter, knowing he doesn't like that damn organization you niggers got, and you wouldn't quit it? . . . You are one of those niggers going around telling other niggers they will be voting soon. We are going to beat the hell out of you for the first ballot you cast."[16]

News of the expulsions spread through New Iberia's black community like electricity. Others who had been involved in the NAACP's welding school campaign also fled. Octave Lilly, Jr., an insurance salesman, saw Pierson in Lafayette and, after seeing his bandaged head and hearing his tale, decided to leave New Iberia one step ahead of the sheriff's deputies. Franzella Volter, a schoolteacher and NAACP branch secretary, also left town on May 17; so did Dr. E. L. Dorsey, who owned a clinic, an insurance company, and a funeral home. When a black barber saw Williams being taken away, he went to warn Dr. Scoggins, who barricaded himself in his house that night and drove to Lafayette on the morning of May 18. Roy Palmer, the black welding instructor, also took flight.[17]

In New Orleans, A. P. Tureaud, one of the two black lawyers in the state, tried to piece together the facts for the NAACP's national office. "All attempts to talk with the people of New Iberia have failed," he informed Thurgood Marshall, the NAACP's top attorney. "I called a Catholic priest there and he said he could not discuss the matter over the phone." According to the *Louisiana Weekly*, the black schools closed early and an unofficial curfew kept blacks off the streets after dark. Blacks were paralyzed by fear. While the New Orleans papers hushed up the affair, Tureaud and the national officers of the NAACP pressed the Justice Department to prosecute the culprits. As Tureaud told Marshall, "These pecks down in Louisiana fear no government agency as they do the Department of Justice." Victor Rotnem, head of the Justice Department's Civil Rights Section, passed on Tureaud's information to the Criminal Division. Malcolm Ross, chairman of the FEPC, also demanded action. On May 25, Assistant Attorney General Tom Clark authorized the FBI to enter the case. Five days later, FBI Director J. Edgar Hoover ordered the New Orleans office to conduct a "preliminary investigation" within three weeks, including interviews with the victims "if possible." Special Agent in Charge A. P. Kitchin assigned two "G-men" to the case.[18]

Even before the FBI formally entered the case, one of its agents in New Orleans had heard about the affair during a social event. A white woman from New Iberia told him that a vigilante committee had been organized, and several black leaders had been given thirty days to leave town. Local blacks, she added, had been instructed by the NAACP not to work for white people. Shortly afterwards, visiting the town, Agent Dill learned from a member of the Sheriff's Department that some deputies had employed "strong methods against some of the local negroes" because "the negroes were becoming very sassy and [they] had to keep them in order." The Sheriff's Department had also planned a raid on black bars and nightclubs to confiscate "razors, knives, guns and other weapons," but the crackdown had been cancelled because Sheriff Ozenne decided that local blacks were sufficiently intimidated already. Ozenne and other white officials had talked to the blacks "and apparently scared them plenty;" further repression might cause the blacks to " 'fold up or leave town' and would not leave any colored help for the merchants and planters." All this information, of course, was strictly off-the-record.[19]

When Agent Dill finally interviewed Ozenne on June 10, he found him in a belligerent mood, armed to the teeth, but clearly nervous about possible retaliation. The sheriff complained that blacks were insubordinate and alleged that Deputy Sheriff Gus Walker recently had his telephone go dead when a black cut through the line. But his men were prepared "for anything that might happen," Ozenne boasted, and he showed Dill his gun vault. The agent noted two Thompson machine guns, six shot guns, five rifles, and quantities of tear gas—a veritable arsenal. "It seems about time that several blacks resist arrest," said Ozenne ominously. "Then they will quieten down for a while." When asked about the expulsions, however, he claimed that no such incidents had taken place. Sitting beside the sheriff was Lloyd Porter, superintendent of schools, a revolver strapped to his waist. Ozenne asked Porter if he needed more ammunition.[20]

On June 20, Special Agent in Charge A. P. Kitchin forwarded a thirty-one-page report, the result of a six-day inquiry by two agents. The FBI had failed to identify the men responsible for the expulsions, but one informant, a Catholic priest, admitted that local gossip singled out two particular sheriff's deputies. One of them was Gus Walker, whose nicknames "Rough House Walker" and "Killer Walker" testified to his unsavory reputation. However the only black witness interviewed in New Iberia, the barber who witnessed Dr. Williams's abduction, had been unable or unwilling to name any of the whites involved.[21]

The NAACP accused the Justice Department of dawdling. In late July Thurgood Marshall and Leslie Perry, chief of the NAACP's Washington Bureau, met Victor Rotnem of the Civil Rights Section. Why had the government failed to make a case against Gus Walker, they asked, when all the victims had positively identified him? And why had the FBI visited New Iberia without interviewing possible black witnesses?[22]

Genuinely sympathetic, and concerned that publicity surrounding the case might lose black votes in the presidential election, Assistant Attorney General Clark asked for a full investigation, which was completed by September 7. Anxious to secure a prosecution, Clark prodded the Bureau to follow up all leads that might clearly identify who carried out the expulsions; he also asked that "discreet efforts" be made to ascertain whether the deputies wee acting under Ozenne's orders. Hoover impressed upon his agents that "the Criminal Division has expressed great interest in this case" and that they should report within two weeks—but for some inexplicable reason, these new instructions were mistakenly sent to the FBI office in Jackson, Mississippi, and did not reach New Orleans until October 9. Despite the delay, the New Orleans office moved slowly, not reporting until December 8. In the meantime, Leo Hardy visited Washington to relate his experience to Victor Rotnem, a meeting that apparently helped convince the Justice Department to present the case to a federal grand jury. The Department's renewed interest prompted Hoover to press New Orleans to follow up some further leads; another report followed on December 28. On January 16, 1945, however, when U. S. attorney Herbert W. Christenberry presented the evidence to a federal grand jury in New Orleans, the government's case collapsed when the jurors refused to return any indictments.[23]

The New Iberia expulsions, contained a multitude of meanings. They exposed, most obviously, the apparent impotence of the federal government when it came to prosecuting civil-rights violations in the South. Since the creation of the Civil Rights Section in 1939 the Justice Department had certainly become more sensitive to the maltreatment of Southern blacks. In 1940 it brought the first federal prosecution for police brutality; two years later it broke new ground by intervening in a lynching case. By 1944, however, it had yet to secure the conviction of a single lyncher, and only three police-brutality cases had resulted in guilty verdicts. White jurors were loathe to indict and even more reluctant to convict whites accused of violence against blacks, especially when the accused included law-enforcement officers. Moreover, the Reconstruction statutes under which such prosecutions were brought had been so weakened by the federal courts that they had atrophied through lack of use. Reviving them proved to be an uphill struggle. As Victor Rotnem admitted in 1945, "unusually exceptional elements must be present if we are to have a successful case in the field."[24]

The Justice Department's dependence on the FBI posed another difficulty: the Bureau's performance in the New Iberia investigation typified its palpable lack of enthusiasm for civil-rights cases. Hoover disliked civil-rights cases because, in part, they were difficult to prosecute and too many failures marred the Bureau's public image. In addition, police-brutality probes endangered the FBI's close relations with local law-enforcement agencies, jeopardizing its investigations in other areas. It has to be admitted that the FBI's reluctance to take on civil-rights cases reflected, more generally, the low status of the black in the Roosevelt administration's hierarchy of political concerns. But it also stemmed from the political conservatism that suffused the FBI and the thinly veiled racism that could be found in Bureau personnel from top to bottom. The main activities of the New Orleans office in the field of race relations were the monitoring of "foreign inspired agitation among negroes," the investigation of black and leftist organizations for "Communist influence," and the surveillance of such alleged "Communists" as Ernest Wright. It pursued the New Iberia investigation only because of continual prodding from the Justice Department.[25]

To be sure, FBI agents faced problems in gathering evidence about the expulsions. Although many whites in New Iberia admitted that the black leaders had been run out of town, none would sign a statement confessing direct knowledge of the affair. Blacks were loathe to testify for an entirely different reason: fear. A man who witnessed Hardy's abduction refused to name the deputies "because if he did he would be found dead in a gutter somewhere." Two other witnesses were similarly reticent. Eventually, in the relative safety of the Federal Building in New Orleans, one of the frightened blacks named the three deputy sheriffs who had accosted Hardy. The FBI found three other witnesses who identified one or more of the deputies from photographs. Gus Walker was recognized by at least three people. In the context of the Southern courts, however, the federal case was flimsy. All the government witnesses were blacks, and only one of them, Hardy, could link Ozenne and Porter to the expulsions. One deputy admitted to being present during Hardy's questioning on May 15, but when pressed further he became "vague and evasive." Against the government was arrayed virtually the entire white community of Iberia Parish, including its men of wealth, status, and political influence.[26]

The FBI's dismissive attitude toward the case did nothing to enhance the credibility of the black witnesses. The FBI reports exhibited a veneer of impartiality. They scrupulously included contradictory opinions and made extensive use of the word "alleged." But the investigating agents shared the view of their white informants that Hardy and the others had violated the unwritten rules of the racial caste system and were thus the authors of their own misfortune. Leo Hardy, they wrote, had been employed as a card dealer and bartender at Uncle Tom's Saloon before being fired "because of his constant trouble making and impudence." As president of the NAACP he had been "endeavoring to incite trouble." Octave Lilly had a "chip on his shoulder" and was considered a "trouble maker." Herman Faulk had been a "constant source of trouble" as a schoolteacher. Scoggins was "hot-headed" and "bitter about the racial situation." Williams had become "very arrogant." Dorsey was "flashy and showy" and wore a "perpetual grin on his face" that might be interpreted as a "grin of arrogance." Pierson had been "increasingly more arrogant just prior to his leaving New Iberia." Scoggins, Williams, and Dorsey had "somewhat shady" reputations. The local agents placed little credence on the victim's testimony. Summarizing the case on October 4, the Bureau argued that Hardy and others "may have suffered mishandling at the hands of law enforcement officials," but the evidence "failed to substantiate" that they had been beaten and "run out of town." And the allegations against Porter and Ozenne depended on the word of Hardy alone, whom Agent Dill described to Tureaud as "a bad character . . . a gambler and a trouble maker."[27]

Still, the evidence bias of the FBI reports provides valuable insights into white attitudes. For local whites, the welding-school controversy symbolized a growing challenge to the traditional pattern of race relations that carried profound social, economic, political, and sexual implications. They detected racial threats all about them: in black demands for the vote, for skilled training, and for industrial jobs; in the shift in black leadership from docile teachers and preachers to independent businessmen and professionals; above all, in the assertive demeanor of ordinary blacks. Again and again, whites used the words "arrogant" and "sassy" in complaining of black behavior; they were unnerved and felt physically threatened by blacks who failed to display the traditional signs of deference and humility. "The negro [welding] students would crowd up on the sidewalk," complained one resident, "and then when some of the women in the neighborhood tried to pass, they would not move." The Catholic pastor cited a similar incident: black children had ganged up on a white child, shoving him off the sidewalk and beating him. Alert to every gesture and nuance, whites sometimes attributed insult and insubordination to the most innocent of actions. Dr. Luins Williams, for example, caused a major scandal when he began entering the public-health clinic by the front door, hanging his coat and hat on the "white" rack, and even, on one occasion, allowing the tail of his coat to brush the shoulder of a female clerk.[28]

Significantly, a number of prominent whites cast the issue in economic terms. Iberia Parish was primarily agricultural, the mayor pointed out, and its sugar plantations and salt mines required black labor. He could not understand, therefore, how New Iberia "could profit by having a welding school," especially when sugar was such a critical war material. The state director of War Production Training made the same point, adding that the shipyards in Morgan City refused to hire black welders anyway. The white welders intended to preserve that ban, and they had vigorously objected the opening of the New Iberia training school. In light of the recent race riots in Mobile and Beaumont, the sensitivity of the state authorities to a possible racial conflagration should not be underestimated.[29]

Who ordered the expulsions? That Walker and the other deputies acted under orders from Sheriff Ozenne seems hard to dispute. Ultimate responsibility for the episode, however, is more difficult to pinpoint. Only the testimony of Leo Hardy directly implicated Lloyd Porter, the superintendent of schools, and the involvement of other "higher ups" is largely a matter of speculation. The Catholic priest interviewed by the FBI in June doubted that Ozenne would have instigated the expulsions by himself "inasmuch as the Sheriff is an ignorant man who had apparently been put into office by one Paulin Duag [sic], a wealthy oil man." The priest also testified to the longstanding concern of the city fathers, including the mayor and the city attorney, about the activities of the NAACP. There may even have been collusion in the expulsions by state officials. Lloyd Porter had travelled to Baton Rouge in early May to attend the inauguration of Governor James H. Davis and Lieutenant Governor J. Emile Verret and may well have discussed the welding-school problem. Certainly, officials in the departments of Education and Public Health were aware of the mounting white concern in New Iberia that the NAACP leaders needed restraining.[30]

The evidence—admittedly circumstantial—points to a carefully planned operation, approved by local bigwigs and acquiesced in by state officials, to rid New Iberia of selected black activists. This was not the indiscriminate violence of a mob. On the contrary: the people who ordered the expulsions wished to avoid the kind of mob action that might cause blacks to flee the area, accentuating the labor shortage. Ozenne's deputies knew who they were looking for and expelled the victims with cool, clinical efficiency. The mayor boasted that not a single black family had left New Iberia apart from those involved in the incident. Whites also congratulated themselves that the departure of the town's black doctors had not led to any increase in black ill-health. (Actually, some of those who fled had not been on Ozenne's hit-list at all, and, despite their denials, white leaders did feel concern about the absence of black doctors. Shortly after the expulsions one of the remaining NAACP officers, a druggist, journeyed to Lafayette to persuade one of the fugitive doctors to return to New Iberia, having been assured of Ozenne's protection.) Nevertheless, the expulsions achieved their desired end: the "troublemakers" left town but there was no general black exodus.[31]

How did New Iberia's blacks feel about the expulsions? Surprisingly, some of the FBI's black informants agreed with local whites that the NAACP leaders—particularly Hardy, Faulk, Lilly, and Scoggins—were irresponsible "hot-heads" who only had themselves to blame. They had tried to take the situation into their own hands, thereby provoking white anger. Several blacks were at pains to disassociate themselves from the NAACP. One explained that he had only joined "because he was afraid if he did not join the blacks of that community would attack him." Two others claimed to have resigned from the NAACP after Hardy became president because, as one of them put it, "he saw trouble brewing." It had been folly to "agitate the racial situation," he added, when "relations between the whites and blacks in the town had always been the very best." Some praised Lloyd Porter's efforts to improve black schools, and accused Faulk of spreading discontent among teachers at the colored high school in an attempt to undermine and possibly oust Principal A. B. Simon.[32]

But there was another side to the picture. Some blacks spoke up for the victims and refused to supply the FBI agents with derogatory information. The expulsions were outrageous, said one. "He had never heard of any trouble in which any of these people had been involved." All the doctors "had very good reputations," a member of the NAACP insisted, and their leaving had been a great loss. Faulk, he complained had been "brutalized." The testimony of the one black druggist who remained in New Iberia is particularly illuminating. This man, who had been active in the NAACP, admitted that many blacks had criticized him for journeying to Lafayette and persuading one of the doctors there to set up practice in New Iberia. The absence of black doctors, they argued, would keep the memory of the expulsions alive and highlight the need for federal intervention. Indeed, some told him he ought to leave town too in order to show solidarity with his race.[33]

Which set of reactions most accurately expressed the feelings of local blacks can only be surmised. However, it is easy to detect an anti-NAACP bias in the FBI reports. The agents seized upon any criticism of Hardy and the other activists, however minor, in order to bolster their thesis that the victims had caused the expulsions through their own provocative behavior. Some blacks undoubtedly said the words attributed to them and needed little prompting to denounce the NAACP leaders. Two informants were old men in their seventies who exhibited the diffidence and deference characteristic of many of their age. Other black informants—Principal Simon is an obvious example—were beholden to the white authorities and dare not, even if they wished to, side with the NAACP. However, the frequency of words like "arrogant" and "hot-headed" leads to a suspicion that the FBI men put words into the mouths of their black informants or, at the very least, sometimes distorted or exaggerated what they were told. NAACP lawyer A. P. Tureaud may well have described Scoggins as "hot-headed" and stated that "the white people and the blacks had gotten along well in New Iberia," but it is unlikely that he would have agreed with the way his words were interpreted. And while some blacks seemed only too ready to denigrate the NAACP leaders, others treated the FBI agents with suspicion and parried their questions. It seems safe to conclude that while many blacks were wary of the NAACP, many more were shocked and angered by the expulsions.[34]

The *Louisiana Weekly* speculated that many whites privately disapproved of the expulsions, but there is little evidence to support this view. Of course, a degree of caution is needed when generalizing about white racial attitudes, particularly on the basis of FBI reports. For one thing, the investigating agents spoke mainly to officials; the attitudes of these middle- and upper-class informants were not necessarily representative of the white community as a whole. When the agents interviewed white residents in the vicinity of the welding school, for example, most stated that the black trainees had not bothered them in any way. Secondly, the FBI tended to be dismissive of dissenting white opinions. One nurse at the public-health clinic flatly disbelieved the claim that Dr. Williams had exhibited rudeness to the female clerks; she acquitted the doctor of arrogance and praised his "gentlemanly manner." But the FBI men did not place much credence in this woman when they were told she was a patrician type well-known for her heterodox opinions. Finally, fear may have silenced whites who disapproved of the expulsions. One white, reinterviewed in late 1944, claimed that Ozenne had abused and threatened him over the telephone. The frightened informant—possibly the Catholic priest—begged to be left alone "because he could be liquidated by the Sheriff's office without too much difficulty."[35]

Nevertheless, few whites apparently regretted the expulsions. According to one white informant, the town's "most substantial citizens" all agreed that "the job done by the sheriff was a job expertly done"—adding, with a smile, "We do not have any bad negroes here any more." (FBI reports never quoted the word "nigger.") Another informant, "one of the most outstanding citizens in town," deplored the "Gestapo methods" of the sheriff's department but described the expulsions as the "best thing that could have happened." The blacks "were beginning to get the upper hand," he explained. "The fact that these negroes were run out of town quieted the black situation down for a while at least." Even the Catholic priest, pastor of a black parish, shared this sentiment. The blacks had been increasingly arrogant, he told the FBI. His own parishioners had petitioned him to exclude the few whites who attended the church. Of course, the priest descried Ozenne's "Gestapo tactics." But he thought it just as well that the "trouble makers" had left town. Ozenne certainly paid no political penalty for his actions: a few weeks later the Louisiana Sheriff's Association elected him to the post of vice president—recognition, some believed, for his expulsion of the NAACP leaders.

At the same time, paradoxically, whites boasted about their community's friendly race relations. They pointed out that in New Iberia, as in other parts of southern Louisiana, whites and blacks had traditionally mingled together in a degree of physical proximity rare elsewhere. Blacks in New Iberia and the surrounding sugar belt were treated exceptionally well, claimed the mayor. The planters looked after their blacks when they were sick, pensioned them off in old age, and attended their funerals when they died. Only intervention by outsiders, whites agreed, had disturbed the friendly atmosphere. Several blamed "all of this trouble" on black newspapers imported from New Orleans. The mayor claimed that blacks had been "sent into New Iberia for the purpose of organizing and agitating the black situation." If they were not Northerners, he stated, they had been "sent in by northerners." Leo Hardy, a native of New Iberia, was the obvious exception to the "outside agitators" thesis. Whites agreed, however, that Hardy was a born troublemaker. He would "never do anything that he was told to do without an argument," complained the white owner of Uncle Tom's Saloon; worse, he "tried to agitate the colored people who came into the bar and tell them how they should have equal social rights with the white persons." Another informant suggested that the NAACP had deliberately picked on New Iberia thinking the town's "excellent racial relations" would enabled to gain a foothold. In another parish, claimed one informant, the blacks would have been run out of town long ago.[36]

Yet brutal as the expulsions were, the perpetrators exercised a degree of circumspection that would have been unusual fifty or even twenty years earlier, when lynching had been commonplace. Between 1900 and 1919 these atrocities claimed at least 148 victims in Louisiana alone. After the "red summer" of 1919, however, lynchings declined throughout the South: during the 1920s, they claimed fourteen victims in Louisiana. The death toll rose again during the early 1930s, but thereafter fell sharply. By the 1940s, writes historian Howard Smead, "ritualized public executions were a thing of the past," with lynchers becoming "considerably more surreptitious."[37]

Many factors contributed to lynching's decline. Although Congress failed to legislate against the evil, the NAACP's campaign for a federal anti-lynching law exposed each successive incident to the horrified gaze of the nation. Within the South, organizations like the Commission on Interracial Cooperation and the Association of Southern Women Against Lynching worked quietly but doggedly to turn public opinion against the practice. True, the slayers of blacks could still evade punishment, but they no longer enjoyed public approbation. And with the creation of the Civil Rights Section in 1939, lynching communities faced the certainty of a federal investigation as well as damning nationwide publicity. By the Second World War state governments were exerting pressure on local politicos to prevent lynchings. When Clinton Clark, an organizer for the Louisiana Farmers Union, was detained in Natchitoches jail in 1940, State Attorney General Eugene Stanley sternly instructed the district attorney to keep the prisoner alive. "We've got to be careful," he pointed out. "The State is on the spot. [We] can't afford that kind of thing with the federal government like it is. Remember now, no lynching!" For whatever reason, Ozenne and his henchmen stopped short of murder.[38]

It was, to be sure, a sad comment on the state of race relations that progress had to be measured in such terms; to call this "restraint" would be to dignify brutality. Nevertheless, wartime predictions that peace would bring a wave of lynchings and race riots like that of 1919 proved inaccurate. Not that such fears were groundless: in 1946 five blacks fell victim to lynch mobs: four in Monroe, Georgia, and one in Minden, Louisiana. All were cruelly tortured. But these outrages aroused such national concern—persuading President Truman to appoint a Committee on Civil Rights—that a potential "red summer" was averted. By the 1950s lynching had virtually disappeared. The Minden lynching turned out to be Louisiana's last, although one intended victim, Edward Honeycutt, avoided death in 1949 only by diving in the Atchafalaya River and escaping his would-be lynchers. The following year "persons unknown" beat Alvin Jones as he accompanied prospective black voters to the St. Landry Parish Courthouse in Opelousas. Jones died several months later.[39]

But if the New Iberia incident illuminated a wider pattern whereby whites were increasingly wary about employing violence against blacks, it also furnished a measure of the formidable white resistance to racial equality. The Second World War did not lead to the decisive breakthrough against white supremacy that blacks in Louisiana and elsewhere hoped for. The defense of segregation did not depend primarily upon violence and brute force: it rested on political power, economic strength, and legal stratagems—and was no less effective for that. The foundations of segregation remained intact as Louisiana's white leaders, in concert with their fellow Southerners, voted to abolish the FEPC, helped to wreck President Truman's civil-rights program, attempted to suppress the NAACP, and proceeded to stymie school desegregation.

In New Iberia itself, race relations remained frozen for a decade and more. In August 1948 six blacks attempted to register to vote only to be turned away. Gus Baronne, the leader of the group and NAACP branch president, left town after receiving threatening telephone calls. The NAACP lingered on, but when the state of Louisiana obtained an injunction against the Association in 1956, the ailing branch finally expired. It did not revive until 1964 when, with the civil-rights movement at its zenith, Dr. James H. Henderson, a black dentist who hailed from North Carolina, recruited two hundred members and secured a new charter from the national office. Under Henderson's leadership, the New Iberia branch established itself as one of the strongest and most effective in Louisiana. At Henderson's right-hand was Franzella Volter, the branch secretary, who twenty years earlier had fled New Iberia after the beating of J. Leo Hardy.[40]

Notes for "Racial Repression in World War Two: The New Iberia Incident"

[1] Charles S. Johnson, *To Stem This Tide: A Survey of Racial Tension Areas in the United States* (Boston, 1943), 106-7; Howard N. Odum, *Race and Rumors of Race: Challenge to American Crisis* (Chapel Hill, 1943), passim; Richard Polenberg, *War and Society: The United States, 1941-1945* (Philadelphia, 1972), 99-100; Neil A. Wynn, *The Afro-American and the Second World War* (New York, 1976), 72; James A. Burran, "Urban Racial Violence in the South During World War II," in Walter J. Fraser, Jr., and Winfred B. Moore, eds., *From the Old South to the New: Essays on the Transitional South* (Westport, 1981), 167-77. One of the first riots of the war occurred in Alexandria, on January 13, 1942, when black soldiers clashed with white M.P.'s and civilian policemen; see the New Orleans *Louisiana Weekly*, January 17, 24, 1942.

[2] Ernest J. Wright, interviewed by Giles A. Hubert, July 1959, p. 5, box 2, folder 11, Hubert Papers, Amistad Research Center, Tulane University; hereafter cited as ARC; Richard Dalfiume, "The 'Forgotten Years' of the Negro Revolution," in Bernard Sternsher, ed., *The Negro in Depression and War: Prelude to Revolution* (Chicago, 1969), 298-311; Harvard Sitkoff, "Racial Militancy and Interracial Violence in the Second World War," *Journal of American History*, 58 (1971): 661-681.

[3] Johnson, *To Stem This Tide*, 65; *Louisiana Weekly*, September 5, 1942; Statement of F. Edward Hebert, n.d., box 15, folder 3, A. P. Tureaud Papers, ARC.

[4] C. Alvin Hughes, "We Demand Our Rights: The Southern Negro Youth Congress, 1937-1949," *Phylon*, 48 (1987): 46; Ernest Bayard, Sr., to State Senator Joseph Cawthorn, November 16, 1940, box 18, folder 20; "Long Raises the Race Question," campaign flyer, 1940, box 18, folder 11, both in Tureaud papers, ARC; Robert K. Carr, *Federal Protection of Civil Rights: Quest for a Sword* (1947; reprint ed., Ithaca, 1964), 85-94; The *United States* v. *Classic* case arose out of election irregularities on the part of the anti-Long "reform" faction in Louisiana.

[5] Keith Weldon Medley, "Ernest Wright: 'People's Champion,' " *Southern Exposure*, 12 (1984): 53-54; FBI report, "People's Defense League," September 11, 1943, 100-232896-1; Johnson, *To Stem This Tide*, 66; *Louisiana Weekly*, February 6, 1943; May 20, 1944; A. P. Tureaud to James Nabrit, December 12, 1943, box 56, folder 7, Tureaud Papers, ARC; Carr, *Federal Protection of Civil Rights*, 94-97. Edward Hall, president of the St. John the Baptist Parish branch of the NAACP, filed suit against T. J. Nagel, the registrar of voters, on July 27, 1945.

[6] Raphael Cassimere, Jr., "Equalizing Teachers' Pay in Louisiana," *Integrated Education* (1977): 3-8; Barbara A. Worthy, "The Travail and Triumph of a Southern Black Civil Rights Lawyer: The Legal Career of Alexander Pierre Tureaud" (Ph. D. dissertation, Tulane University, 1984), 37-50. The NAACP organized a state conference of branches in early 1943. An attempt in 1920 to form a statewide organization had failed. See Paul Ted McCulley, "Black Protest in Louisiana, 1898-1928" (M. A. thesis, Louisiana State University, 1970), 130.

[7] George A. Dreyfous and M. Swearingen, "Report to the Executive Committee of the LLPCR on Investigations in West Feliciana Parish," [August 1937], box 2, folder 19; Clinton Clark, Affidavit, August 21, 1940; Margery Dallet, "The Case of Clinton Clark," August 7, 1940, both in box 3, folder 19, all in Harold N. Lee Papers, Rare Books and Manuscripts Section, Howard-Tilton Memorial Library, Tulane University; Johnson, *To Stem This Tide*, 24-25; *Louisiana Weekly*, October 10, 1942; Anthony P. Dunbar, *Against the Grain: Southern Radicals and Prophets, 1929-1959* (Charlottesville, 1981), 200-201; Thomas A. Becnel, *Labor, Church, and the Sugar Establishment: Louisiana, 1887-1976* (Baton Rouge, 1980), 84-86. Southern political pressure contributed to the decision to begin liquidating the FSA's resettlement programs in 1944. The FSA itself was abolished in 1946.

[8] FBI, "Unknown Subjects: Eviction of Negro Civil Rights Leaders, New Iberia, Louisiana, May 17, 1944," June 20, 1944, 44-999-6; hereafter cited as FBI Report. The FBI's file on the New Iberia incident, released to this writer under the Freedom of Information Act, presents serious problems of interpretation. The material as originally released contained so many excisions, and so many pages were withheld in their entirety, that it was practically useless as historical evidence. However, upon appeal to the Justice Department, which declared the subject to be of "significant historical interest," the FBI released an additional eighty pages of documents. The file has now been released in something like its original form, but with the names of the FBI's informants excised. It is therefore difficult to identify the sources of the FBI's information. Nevertheless, they can generally be identified according to sex, race, occupation, and so on, and it is sometimes possible to identify individuals. The identification of informants, however, involves a certain amount of guesswork.

[9] *Louisiana Weekly*, March 18, June 3, 1944; FBI Report, September 7, 1944, 44-999-10.

[10]Merl E. Reed, "The FEPC, the Black Worker, and the Southern Shipyards," *South Atlantic Quarterly*, 74 (1975): 446-53; Warren M. Banner and J. Harvey Kerns, "Review of the Economic and Cultural Problems of New Orleans . . . as They Relate to Conditions in the Negro Population," 1950, 28-36, Hubert Papers, ARC.

[11]Mary L. Muller, "The New Orleans Parish School Board and Negro Education, 1940-1960" (M. A. thesis, Louisiana State University in New Orleans, 1975), 10; Burran, "Urban Racial Violence in the South," 169-170; *Louisiana Weekly*, February 19, 1944; Reed, "The FEPC," 451-55.

[12]FBI Reports, June 20, 1944, 44-999-6; September 7, 1944, 44-999-10.

[13]L. Virgil Williams to Lloyd G. Porter, April 14; J. Leo Hardy to Leonard M. Brin, April 22, May 11, 1944, all in FBI Reports, September 21, 1944, 44-999-13, pp. 2-9; June 20, 1944, 44-999-6, p. 26.

[14]Hardy's account of his expulsion is taken from Hardy to Leonard M. Brin, May [18], 1944; affidavit of Octave Lilly, Jr., May 19, 1944, both in box 34, folder 5, Tureaud Papers; Hardy, affidavit, June 14, 1944, in FBI Report, June 20, 1944, pp. 29-32, "Why Negroes Are Angry," *New Republic*, September 25, 1944, 360.

[15]Affidavit of Howard C. Scoggins, May 31, 1944, in box 34, folder 5, Tureaud Papers, ARC.

[16]Affidavits of Luins H. Williams, May 20, 1944; Ima P. Pierson, May 20, 1944; Herman Joseph Faulk, May 27, 1944, all in box 34, folder 5, Tureaud Papers, ARC; testimony of Negro barber, in FBI Report, June 20, 1944, p. 27; *Louisiana Weekly*, May 27, June 3, 1944. The deputies posed at first as FBI men.

[17]Affidavits of Lilly and Scoggins; A. P. Tureaud to Rachel B. Noel, June 15, 1944, box 34, folder 6, Tureaud Papers, *Louisiana Weekly*, June 10, 1944.

[18]Tureaud to Thurgood Marshall, May 19, October 11, 1944; February 1, 1945; Tureaud to Victor Rotnem, May 19, 20, 27; Tureaud to Tom C. Clark, June 7, 1944; all in box 34, folders 5, 6, 21, Tureaud Papers; *Louisiana Weekly*, June 3, 1944; Tom C. Clark to J. Edgar Hoover, May 25, 1944, 44-999-1; Hoover to Clark, May 29, 1944, 44-1006-1; Hoover to SAC, New Orleans, May 30, 1944, 44-999-2.

[19]FBI Report, June 20, 1944, p. 4.

[20]Ibid., June 20, 1944, pp. 4-5.

[21]Ibid., June 20, 1944, pp. 27-31.

[22]Thurgood Marshall to Victor Rotnem, July 5, 1944; Francis Biddle to Walter White, July 10, 1944; Leslie Perry to Tureaud, July 27, 1944; Tureaud to Perry, July 31, 1944, all in box 34, folder 6, Tureaud Papers, ARC.

[23]Clark to Hoover, June 24, 1944, 44-1001-3; September 21, 1944, 44-999-13, 14; December 8, 1944, 44-999-31; J. C. Strickland, memorandum for Mr. Ladd, September 20, 1944, 44-999-9; Hoover to Tom C. Clark, September 25, 1944, 44-999-11; Hoover to SAC, Jackson, September 26, 1944, 44-999-12; SAC, Washington, "Foreign Inspired Agitation Among the American Negroes in the Washington Field Division," October 10, 1944, 100-135-168, pp. 8-9; Hoover to SAC, New Orleans, December 13, 1944, 44-999-32; FBI Report, February 10, 1945, 44-999-35; Hoover to Clark, February 16, 1945, 44-999-35.

[24]Carr, *Federal Protection of Civil Rights*, 41-45, 106-14, 134-41, 152-71; Dominic J. Capeci, Jr., "The Lynching of Cleo Wright: Federal Protection of Constitutional Rights During World War II," *Journal of American History*, 72 (1986): 689-884.

[25]Carr, *Federal Protection of Civil Rights*, 152-53; Hoover to Attorney General, September 24, 1946, reprinted in United States Commission on Civil Rights, *1961, United Commission on Civil Rights*, Book 5, *Justice* (Washington, D. C., [1961]), 213-15.

[26]FBI Report, December 8, 1944, 44-999-27, p. 9; December 28, 1944, 44-999-33, p. 1-2.

[27]FBI Report, September 7, 1944, 44-999-10, pp. 1-3, 16, 27; September 21, 1944, 44-999-13, pp. 1, 11; J. C. Strickland to Mr. Ladd, October 4, 1944, 44-999-18; Tureaud to Marshall, October 24, 1944, box 34, folder 21, Tureaud Papers, ARC.

[28]FBI Report, June 20, 1944, p. 29; September 7, 1944, 15-17, 32.

[29] Ibid., June 20, 1944, p. 26; September 7, 1944, pp. 13-14, 18.

[30] Ibid., June 20, 1944, pp. 25-28; Leo Hardy to Leonard M. Brin, May 8, 1944, in ibid., September 27, 1944, pp. 7-8; September 7, 1944, pp. 12-13.

[31] Ibid., September 7, 1944, pp. 18, 27-28, 30-31; September 21, 1944, pp. 13-14; Elizabeth Wilson and Ward B. Melody, "4 Negroes Clubbed, Driven from Louisiana Town," *PM* Magazine, June 17, 1944, 1. Scoggins, it seems, also received an invitation to resume his practice, but he preferred to stay in New Orleans. "I can't return," he told the magazine *PM*. "I don't trust the New Iberia kind of white democracy." Roy Palmer, the welding school instructor, was another fugitive whom Ozenne had now, apparently, intended to expel. When Palmer phoned Lloyd Porter from Baton Rouge, the school's superintendent told him to return to New Iberia.

[32] FBI Report, September 7, 1944, pp. 4, 10-11, 19-20, 29; September 21, 1944, pp. 10-11, 15.

[33] Ibid., September 7, 1944, pp. 22, 25-28; September 21, 194, pp. 13-14; December 28, 1944, pp. 1-2.

[34] An insurance company official refused to divulge the personnel records of Octave Lilly, Jr. Lilly's former supervisor greeted the FBI men with a hatchet and "kept the hatchet in his hand during the entire interview" because "he just wanted to be on the safe side."

[35] *Louisiana Weekly*, June 17, 1944; FBI Report, September 7, 1944, pp. 16-17; December 8, 1944, pp. 3-4.

[36] FBI Report, September 7, 1944, pp. 2, 13-18, 26; September 21, 1944, pp. 14-15; June 20, 1944, pp. 28-29; December 8, 1944, pp. 4-5, 11. Ozenne remained sheriff of Iberia parish until his death in 1951. Stuart O. Landry, ed., *Louisiana Almanac and Fact Book, 1953-1954* (New Orleans, 1953).

[37] Robert L. Zangrando, *The NAACP Crusade Against Lynching, 1909-1950* (Philadelphia, 1980), 6-7; McCulley, "Black Protest in Louisiana," 75, 110-11; Howard Smead, *Blood Justice: The Lynching of Mack Charles Parker* (New York, 1986), xi.

[38] George B. Tindall, *The Emergence of the New South, 1913-1945* (Baton Rouge, 1967), 550; Zangrando, *The NAACP Crusade Against Lynching*, 102-5; Jacquelyn Dowd Hall, *Revolt Against Chivalry: Jesse Daniel Ames and the Women's Against Lynching* (New York, 1979), 226-36; Margery Dallet, "Cast of Clinton Clark," August 17, 1940, box 3, folder 19, Harold N. Lee Papers, Special Collections, Howard-Tilton Memorial Library, Tulane University.

[39] *Louisiana Weekly*, August 24, September 9, October 26, 1946; June 10, 1950; *New Orleans Times-Picayune*, March 7-8, 1949; *Baton Rouge Morning Advocate*, June 7, 1950; Walter F. White, *A Man Called White* (London, 1949), 322-31; William C. Berman, *The Politics of Civil Rights in the Truman Administration* (Columbus, 1970), 47-52; Zangrando, *The NAACP Crusade Against Lynching*, 175-181. The FBI investigated the beating of Jones but failed to identify the attackers; in 1952 the Department of Justice dropped the case. (FBI documents declassified at this writer's request.)

[40] *Louisiana Weekly*, August 7, 1948; Dr. James H. Henderson, interviewed by Adam Fairclough, August 28, 1987.

PART II

ON THE FRINGE:
WOMEN AND CHILDREN IN LOUISIANA

CHERCHEZ LES FEMMES:
SOME GLIMPSES OF WOMEN IN
EARLY EIGHTEENTH-CENTURY LOUISIANA*

Vaughan B. Baker

Despite a growing literature on the varied aspects of French Louisiana, many lacunae remain. Perhaps the largest void in the scholarly exploration of Louisiana in the French period concerns women. Although an abundance of documentation exists to study such questions as the woman's experience in eighteenth-century Louisiana, the role of women in Creole and Cajun cultures and the influence of women in developing and preserving Louisiana's cultural patterns, little attention has been paid to these and other important topics that would provide a better understanding of French Louisiana.[1]

The problem of producing a more balanced picture of Louisiana's cultural legacy is fundamentally methodological. The historical record of French Louisiana has been firmly established in a methodology focused on leading statesmen, or major, often cataclysmic events (such as the Acadian *dérangement*), supplemented perhaps with descriptions of Creole society. This model of Louisiana's French heritage has remained largely unchallenged because new methodologies have been slow to penetrate the small cadre of researchers interested in reshaping the orthodox view of Louisiana history. The orthodoxy, in short, has perpetuated itself as a canon resistant to modification. So long as research remains fixed in the conventional patterns, however, the picture of Louisiana's legacy will remain incomplete.

French anthropologist Claude Lévi-Strauss, with his structural approach to studying early and primitive societies, has argued that in order to understand a society we must see the cultural patterns as part of overall structures. Culture, he argues, is the product of both conscious and unconscious models, or rules of behavior. An analysis of a society's models or behavioral regulations is necessary before any part of that society can be decoded or understood.[2] In attempting to delineate unconscious rules of behavior, the role

---

*First published in *Louisiana History*, 31 (1990): 21-37. Reprinted here with the kind permission of the author and the Louisiana Historical Association.

of women cannot be ignored, as women in their various nurturing roles, both in childhood and in later life, bear much of the responsibility for instilling unconscious patterns of behavior. The task of analyzing social and cultural models, however, is complicated by the fact that people usually have conscious models, "folk grammars," for their behavior, which are often taken to be the totality of their culture. This has been particularly true in Louisiana research, where the popular cultural mythology has greatly strengthened the folk grammars.[3] In studying the French legacy in Louisiana, Lévi-Strauss's arguments must be considered. "Folk grammars" of Louisiana French culture continue to be taken as totalities. The unconscious cultural models of behavior in Louisiana society cannot be fully understood until it is understood how women fit into the overall cultural structures.

In looking at "French culture in Louisiana," one must first ask, "what French culture?" Louisiana's French legacy is diverse, with a number of varieties of ethnic French contributions, and with homogeneous cultural patterns changing over time. No one can speak of "women" without specifying, or focusing on, the many groups of women who populated Louisiana. Indian, French, African, German, Acadian, and Spanish women came to Louisiana; single women, married women, young girls, old women, free women, slave women—the list lengthens with every glance at the documents. This article presents glimpses of some of the women who came to Louisiana in the early eighteenth century. The intent is to challenge the prevailing methodological orthodoxy and to open new avenues of investigation in the scholarly examination of Louisiana's French legacy. It offers only a sampling of the rich material available for more indepth studies of such questions as: what was life like, in all its reality, for women in French Louisiana? What role did women—all the many women who came—play in establishing and building the colony, and in creating the cultural synthesis that today distinguishes Louisiana? What institutions shaped their behavior and their experience?

Women were involved in the Louisiana experience from its beginnings. The first French women came to Louisiana with the explorer La Salle, four ships of colonists leaving La Rochelle in 1684.[4] By January 1687, the colonists numbered only twenty or twenty-one, seven of them women, and dire hardship in Louisiana continued to decimate their ranks. The surviving accounts tell grimly of women and children being forced to participate in hunting if they wished to eat, of diminishing supplies, with little lead for the remaining powder, sometimes requiring that one musket ball be used, found, and reused repeatedly. All of La Salle's colonists finally died but for a few who survived among the Indian tribes in the coastal wilderness.[5]

The land La Salle explored and which Iberville and Bienville later successfully colonized was no tropical paradise, despite the idyllic descriptions circulated after 1720 by the Company of the Indies.[6] La Mothe Cadillac, who replaced Bienville as governor of Louisiana in 1710 and lived in the barely established colony until 1712, described it to Minister of Marine Jérôme de Pontchartrain in 1713 as "an unhealthy country, without bread, without wine, without meat and without clothes."[7] Sudden, fierce hurricanes, heavy floods, drowning winter and spring rains, cold comparable to northern France in the winter, alternating with sharp fluctuations to summer-like warmth and unrelenting, sweltering, humid heat in the summer and fall made the climate extremely difficult for the emigrants from France and Canada who attempted to populate Louisiana's marshy coasts and mosquito-infested interior. Relatively few individuals pioneered the occupation of lower Louisiana, the southern portion of the vast territory stretching from Canada to the Gulf Coast, but women are mentioned in the earliest records. The initial settlement at Fort Maurepas near present-day Biloxi had a population of about eighty men, approximately eighteen of them soldiers, the rest Canadians, freebooters from St. Domingue, and a few artisans and cabin boys.[8] The men who came to the rough settlements in a hostile environment, again according to Cadillac, were "a heap of the dregs of Canada, jailbirds without subordination for religion and for government, addicted to vice, principally with the Indian women whom they prefer to French women."[9]

Not that many French women were there at first, but they soon came in numbers. The initial occupation of Louisiana, begun by Pierre Le Moyne, sieur d'Iberville, between 1698 and 1702, was slow and difficult and the early colony was predominantly male (neither the 1699 census nor the 1700 census of the Biloxi colony list any women).[10] Women began arriving in the colony, however, as early as 1704. Twenty-three women accompanied by two families were sent to Louisiana on the *Pélican,* departing from the port of La Rochelle. We know very little about them, but they were undoubtedly sent in response to the often-repeated requests of the colonial leaders in Louisiana.[11] The census of 1706 lists eighty-five *habitants,* with women and children forming 78 percent of the total population; thirty women and thirty-seven children were listed. Nicolas de La Salle, who reported the census, estimated, however, that between 1706 and 1708 nine children died, with few new births to replace them.[12]

The colonial leadership constantly pleaded that more women be sent to the colony, utilizing the argument that women and families provided stability. "If you find an opportunity to send girls here," Governor Périer wrote the directors of the Company of the Indies in 1727, "do not fail to do so. There are also many workmen who will settle down if they find it possible to get married." Families should be granted passage, he argued, as "the more respectable [families] there are here, the more we shall live in peace and harmony."[13]

The creation of John Law's Company of the West in 1717 further illustrates the multiple roles women played in the colony's development. The three major shareholders in the Company of the West were Law himself, François-Marie Farges, *fournisseur* of the French army, and Catherine Barré, madame de Chaumont, the wife of Antoine Chaumont, honorary secretary of the king. Her investment was 850,000 *livres*[14] and her concession near Pascagoula gave her a vital place in the Company's activities, although her disinterest in managing her investment is clear. In 1726 the manager of her concession complained to the council of the Company of the West that he had heard nothing from her in three years. He wished to give up the concession and sell her slaves to pay her debts.

Cherchez les Femmes

In 1727 the council begged the directors for news of her and directions of what she wished done. She appointed a power of attorney, and remained disengaged.[15] Madame de Chaumont does, however, stand as a strong example that the development of the Louisiana colony involved women at many levels.

Eventually, women came in larger and larger numbers. The ship lists give a clear record of women's contributions to the settlement effort. Although it is true that some were deported, many others came voluntarily. Some were indentured (though fewer than in the English colonies); some were sent, like the celebrated casket girls, as *épouseuses*, intended to marry and civilize the rough woodsmen and populate the wilderness.[16] (See Appendix I) Between 1717 and 1721 several thousand immigrants arrived; one estimate counts 7,020, of whom 1,215 were women and 502 children. The actual numbers seem to be far fewer, although numerous enough to warrant admiration for the courage of those who ventured so bravely into the unknown, some with infants, occasionally with servants, sometimes with skilled trades, more often without. Surviving documents list thirty ships leaving the ports of La Rochelle and Lorient with a total of 514 women. Of these, ninety-six are listed as "sent from Paris on the order of the king,"[17] but by far the largest majority travelled to concessions with their husbands and children, and occasionally their servants. Among the passengers are listed two free black women.[18] Few of the ship lists give occupations of the passengers, but those that do provide interesting insights. For example, in August 1720, twenty-eight women and ten children embarked from Lorient with 176 women on the ship *La Loire*, for the concession of St. Catherine, a concession of the Company of the West. The women's occupations were listed: one tailoress, one knitter, two dressmakers, three bakers, one cook, two laundresses, two linen drapers, one *ravaudeuse* (a mender of old clothes, who certainly would be busily occupied in the Louisiana colony) two "laborers" and three "protégés."[19] (See Appendix II) The clamor for women and families continued unabated throughout the early years of settlement.

Surely they all came—at least those who came voluntarily—with high hopes and a sense of opportunity. Nearly all were unprepared for the life awaiting them in Louisiana. Charles Legac, one of the local directors of the Company of the West, a bureaucrat vitally interested in statistics and detail, recounts a common experience of a settlement group. Charles Scourion de La Houssaye and Hector Scourion de Vienne, gentlemen from Normandy, brought a party of seventy-seven, eleven members of their own households and sixty-six colonists. Both were accompanied by their wives, Marthe Daumois and Marianne de Bertier. Legac considered all of them "unsuitable as colonists." Although twenty-two masters and craftsmen were included in the party, none seemed fit for the rigors to be faced in Louisiana, and all possessed only half the supplies necessary to survive. After consuming "great quantities" of supplies on the journey and suffering misunderstandings among the leaders over the question of authority, they separated into two groups, dividing the remaining supplies. Each group then split again, and the settlement for which the directors had held great hope, failed. The Scourions, with their families, stopped in Natchez. The other half of the group became stranded only sixty miles from Mobile, drifting aimlessly. Most died, and those who survived became *engagés* in order to subsist. Of the leaders, a third died, others returned to France, the rest did what they could "to extricate themselves from the whole affair."[20] Since eighteenth-century French law required that women live where their husbands lived,[21] one cannot help but wonder how willingly these women followed their husbands to death and hardship on the swampy Louisiana frontier.

The conventional eighteenth-century attitude toward women is revealed in the letter written by one Chassin, a colonist who obtained a twenty-arpent concession on the Mississippi. "I intend to put a half-dozen negroes on it next year while waiting for more," he wrote, "You see, Sir, that the only thing that I now lack in order to make a strong establishment in Louisiana is a certain article of furniture that one often repents having got and which I shall do without like the others until . . . the Company sends us girls who have at least some appearance of virtue. If by chance there should be some girl with whom you are acquainted who would be willing to make this journey for love of me, I should be very much obliged to her and I should certainly do my best to give her evidence of my gratitude for it." He closed by stating that had his sister come, she would have looked after him as much as he should have looked after her, but he feared that his hopes for her joining him had gone up in smoke. His letter, equating a wife with an article of furniture and slaves, and rather less desirable than his sister, nevertheless indicates that even self-reliant colonial adventurers believed women indispensable to the establishment of enduring settlements.[22]

Survival, physical and economic (and the latter often determined the former), was the first task of those women who endured the trans-Atlantic voyage and arrived in Louisiana. In the early years they faced recurring shortages of food, Indian attack, and death from childbirth if not from disease and want. In the Natchez massacre which took place on November 28, 1729, thirty-five women and fifty-six children died, along with 144 men. Among them were four pregnant women, whose stomachs were ripped open and their infants killed. Not all the Natchez women died—some were carried off by the Indians. When Sieur Le Sueur and a band of Choctaw allies pursued the rampaging Natchez they recovered fifty women and children.[23]

Despite reports of massacre and hardship, women continued to come. Some even came alone. In 1720 on the *Charente*, Madame de Larme and her mother arrived; so did three widows, one with two young children.[24] Those who survived the hardest years often did find happier opportunities than perhaps awaited them at home. "Mademoiselle Marguerite did well . . . ," says one gossipy letter. "She certainly married better than could have been expected."[25] Once married, the frightening mortality rate that prevailed in the colony could work to a woman's advantage, if it did not include her first. The Louisiana law, established in the colony in 1712, provided economic protections for women which allowed them considerable control over inherited property. It also guaranteed an inheritance when their husbands died.[26] Women who managed to survive their husbands could, even if they married a second time, enjoy a degree of economic independence. The records of the early colony are consequently full of economic transactions involving women.

The salient features of the law in French Louisiana, particularly after the colony finally rooted and stabilized, had a profound impact on the lives of women. The charter of transfer of the colony to Antoine Crozat in 1712 established the legal code of Paris or the *Coutume de Paris* as the fundamental law of the Louisiana territory. The *Coutume de Paris* stipulated a matrimonial property regime that established between spouses a "community of movables and acquets." All prenuptial immovable property owned by either spouse and all property acquired during marriage came into community ownership at the celebration of the marriage. The wife could thus inherit separate property owned by her husband before marriage as well as half of any property they acquired together.[27]

The law regulated marriage to white women's advantage in many ways, despite the fact that it subjected them to the husband's complete domination during the marriage. The power of the husband over wife and children prevailed but was not unrestricted. In the frontier society of Louisiana, conditions which shortened the lives of men and of marriages called into play the more positive aspects of the law. The precarious nature of life on the frontier interacted with the provisions of the law to create many a widow who if not merry was at least rich.

The *Coutume de Paris* forbade the husband to sell, exchange, partition, or indebt either his wife's personal legacy or her separate property without her consent. Nor could he acquire full rights to her property, as English law allowed him to do. Even a thoroughly besotted wife could not sign away her property by gift—the law strictly regulated donations between husband and wife, allowing them only when they were mutual. And at death, the husband's freedom to dispose of property was sharply curtailed. Half the community belonged to his wife; forced inheritance further disposed of his share to his children.[28]

A glance at eighteenth-century census records turns up widow after widow who gained not only property but also a new husband, attracted as much perhaps by her prosperity as by her charm. Moreover, in a second marriage the husband did not enjoy marital power (the French phrase is "*la puissance du mari*") over his wife's property. The property she brought into a marriage from an earlier union was hers by inalienable right. The ownership of her separate property gave her a measure of independence which she could use to manipulate her husband and probably often did. Thus in the eighteenth century we find the Widow Beaulieu, a large landowner with her husband DeMouy managing thirty-six arpents "belonging to the Widow . . . whom he has married." Similarly, Mr. Bimont lived on ten arpents belonging to his wife, the Widow Richaume, Mr. Marcilly farmed eighteen arpents belonging to his wife the Widow Trépagnier. All in all, in one small area of the German Coast there are listed a total of ten men working land acquired by marriage to propertied widows.[29] In 1737, after her husband's death, Françoise Michel, widow of Louis Jouaneaulx, moved to collect over 30,331 *livres* from a couple named

Faucon who had owed the sum to her husband since 1714. The records do not tell if she shared the wealth with a new husband or kept her financially secure independence, or if she did, in fact, manage to collect the debt.[30]

Some widows were less fortunate. In 1765 Louise Pailleau, the widow of Bernard Petit, declared that her husband left her practically penniless with two children, one seven years old, the other an infant. The Petits had sold their plantation but she could not pay the community debts with the proceeds of the sale. Listing her possessions, she claimed only one eight-year-old Negro boy named Laurens, a cypress table, three old chairs, two old wood chests without locks, four earthenware dishes, some other kitchen crockery, a bed and a mattress, and an old shotgun. Her experience shows that for many women, whatever protections frontier life and law might provide were not enough.[31]

Eighteenth-century women often suffered unhappy, even desperate, marriages and had few ways of escaping them. The law recognized very few grounds for separation. If a husband refused to furnish his wife "the necessities of life," if he openly admitted heresy, or if he treated her with extreme cruelty, she could be granted a separation, but a strong case had to be made. In July 1727 Marie Magdelaine Mangnon de La Tour appeared before the Superior Council petitioning for separation from her husband, named St. Malo. She told of his cruelty and petty tyranny and requested a "board allowance," the colonial version of alimony. In August St. Malo appeared before the Superior Council and promised that he would "behave becomingly and . . . avoid disgrace." With no further guarantees, the court ordered Marie Magdelaine to return to him and, adding insult to injury, made her pay half the court costs.[32]

In February 1728, Louise Jousset La Loire, the wife of New Orleans surgeon Pierre de Manadé, fled her husband's "violent cruelty" and sought refuge in the Ursuline Convent. Moving to recover from him her marriage portion, she also applied for a board allowance. De Manadé, whose credit was seized, protested vigorously and condemned the Ursulines for harboring his wife but finally consented to a separation of property. In a most unusual arrangement, he refused to consent to a separation of "bed and board." The documents remain teasingly silent on how the unhappy De Mañadé marriage finally worked out.[33]

The law also allowed women, even married women, to act independently if they acted as "public merchants."[34] Many documents offer glimpses of women engaged in commercial activities. In 1723, for example, the Widow Belsaguy furnished the directors of the Company of the Indies "sixty barrels of tar or pitch . . . in a very bad condition . . . they all leak and in addition to that they were all very small." Mme Belsaguy was clearly having serious business problems. Her cooper wished to leave her, and she owed the Company one hundred barrels of pitch by the end of the month. She petitioned the directors for four Negroes, promising to teach them the trade and declaring that "in three years she will make them perfect." The Company agreed, feeling that it was not a bad bargain since Mme Belsaguy would be responsible for the price of the blacks if one died before the end of the three years.[35]

In another report in 1723, a woman called only "the Big Flemish woman" sold to the wife of a New Orleans coppersmith a five-pound loaf of blackbread for fifteen *livres*, an exorbitant rate of three *livres* per pound. She was brought to court and charged with usury. Reputedly a notorious usurer who had previously sold brandy and other items for several times their normal price, she claimed innocence. After a night in prison, she finally broke down, saying it was the baker's fault. The court ordered her to return thirteen *livres* to the woman who had bought the bread and then fined her five hundred *livres*, the fine to be spent buying food for patients with venereal disease.[36]

The problem of venereal disease suggested by this document is revealing of another aspect of the colonial experience. Debt, poverty, disease, and want reduced many of the emigrants, both male and female, to extremes. Writing to the directors of the Company of the Indies in 1725, the Council of Louisiana noted "There are several women detained in Louisiana for the debts of their husbands. They are libertines who will always be a burden to the colony and who will not pay the Company at all."[37]

The documentation that exists for the colonial period tends to give us a distorted view of the women of the time, as much of it concerns women only when they are in difficulty or for some reason come to the attention of the authorities. There are occasional references to such women as Mme de Graveline who was devoted to religion and instructed her servants in it, apparently to her husband's pride and satisfaction, and Mme de Mandeville, "the ornament of Mobile society."[38] Eighteenth-century misogyny, however, appears frequently in the correspondence. Diron Dartaguiette, commandant at Mobile, wrote of the laziness of the colonists, especially the women, who were "ruined by luxury," slothful by nature, with tastes for Spanish trade goods.[39] It is difficult to see what luxuries might have so spoiled them.

Some women did rebel against the colonial administrators. A midwife in 1713 complained vociferously when 50 percent of her pay was deducted after she refused to do laundry or serve the soldiers. She had been hired, she said, only to midwife. Care of the sick was contrary to her profession, she insisted, and most of the soldiers were infected with scurvy. If she nursed them, she ran the risk of infecting the women and children for whom she was professionally responsible. Despite her admirably assertive arguments, Bienville reduced her salary anyway.[40] Her rebellion reminds us of the dangers and difficulties of bearing children despite the stringent conditions of life in the colony, as do the birth records from the period which quietly attest the courage of countless women. These records deserve careful analysis. As only one example, in New Orleans, seventy infants were baptized in 1728. Interestingly, 40 percent were female births.[41]

The misery of the early settlements in lower Louisiana is repeatedly a matter of report. Bienville, writing in October 1719, stated, "misery reigns always in Louisiana." Decrying the lack of human and material resources to carry supplies to the settlers, he noted that there were only two carpenters in the colony. "All is in disorder and misery," he repeated.[42]

Labor, both male and female, remained one of the colony's most pressing needs. Indian and African slaves met some of the demand. Iberville wrote in 1701 that the French colonial leaders should accept prisoners from their Indian allies in order to enslave them. The men could be sent to the islands, but the women should be kept, as they would "augment" the colony.[43] Their use was clear, as one emigrant revealed when he wrote, "a few days after my arrival I bought an Indian female slave . . . in order to have a person who could dress our victuals."[44] French-Indian alliances did not work as well as administrators had hoped, however, and marriages or concubinage with Indian women came to be seen as a detriment to colonial progress.[45]

As early as 1712 colonial leaders were requesting African slaves[46] and black women became a part of the Louisiana experience in the earliest stages of its development. We can as yet only glimpse the experiences of black women in early Louisiana. In 1723, for example, we find six black women working in agricultural situations and taking care of the animals, and four others serving in the hospital.[47] Black families were in demand for labor on the concessions. French administrators recognized the slave family, as they did European families, as a major source of stability in the colony. From the early 1730s they enforced Article 43 of the Black Code.[48] It protected slave families from being sold separately when they belonged to the same master. There were few free black women in early Louisiana—only 20 in 1763. A total of two hundred mulattos in the 1730s suggests that interracial sex was more of a problem with the Indians than with Africans until later in the colony's development.[49] This is another question deserving of closer examination. Documenting the private lives and experiences of the many still-nameless women of eighteenth-century Louisiana will present a persistent challenge to researchers for some time to come. Where black women are concerned, the task has scarcely begun.

Finally, religious women made vital contributions to the Louisiana enterprise. The Company of the Indies contracted with the Ursulines to establish a school in New Orleans. These courageous women pioneered education in Louisiana, but also played major roles in the religious and social development of the colony. They began the first free day school in America, holding classes for Indian and black children as well as whites. They sheltered the city's orphans and housed and chaperoned the *épouseuses* until they chose husbands.[50]

We should not at this point draw too many conclusions about women in the colonial period. It is tempting, though. Even a scouting expedition through the documents shows that the women of French Louisiana were energetic, imaginative, dynamic, courageous, and more assertive than is usually supposed. Their lives were as varied in experience as it is possible to imagine. Long and dangerous sea voyages, snakes and alligators to compete with for place, Indian attack, business ventures, no certainty of security, and an almost certain insecurity faced most of the first women who lived in what is now Louisiana. In surveying women in eighteenth-century Louisiana, only glancing mention has been made of black women, Indian women, religious women who arrived after 1765, and the German women who were among the earliest setters in the colony.

Ultimately, Louisiana's culture developed out of the blended efforts of all these women who peopled Louisiana. If we cannot yet analyze with full credibility the objective data about their lives, we can at least recognize their contributions to the structures of everyday life and to the Louisiana legacy.

APPENDIX I

*List of Women and the Two Families
Who Must Go to Louisiana*
First:
Françoise Marieanne de Boisrenaud
Jeanne Catherine de Beranhard
Jeanne Elizabeth Le Pinteux
Marie Noël du Mesnil
Gabrielle Savaret
Geneviève Burel
Margueritte Burel
Marie Thérèse Brochon
Angélique Brouyn
Marie Driard
Marguerite Tavernier
Elisabeth Deshays
Catherine Christophle
Catherine Tournant (did not go)
Marie Philipe
Louise Marguerite Housseau
Marie Madeleine Ouanet
Marie Dufresne
Marguerite Guichard
Renée Gilbert
Louise Françoise Lefevre
Gabrielle Borret
Marie Jeanne Masbe, Chaperon
Families
Estienne Burel
Marguerite Rousseau, wife of Burel
Louis Burel, son
Laurent Closquinet, husband of the midwife
Catherine de Moutois, midwife
Henry Savarit
Total of thirty persons.

Sieur Bégon, intendant of the Navy at the port of Rochefort, is ordered to embark the individuals on the present list on His Majesty's vessel Le Pelican, commanded by Sieur du Coudroy, captain of artillery who must travel to Havana.

Done at Fontainebleau, October 3, 1704.[51]

APPENDIX II

*Etat des passagers embarqués sur "La Loire"
pour la concession de Sainte-Catherine
Depart: L'Orient. August 20, 1720.*[52]

Roll of Women

Jeanne de Broise, tailoress
Germaine Vessaille, knitter
Margueritte Roussel, dressmaker
Anne Coudrey, protégé
Jeanne Le Darce
Marie Cardinal, baker
Anne Conaud, protégé
Marie Delarue, dressmaker
Perrine Negrette, cook
Vincente Corley, baker
Yvonne Marie Lereg, laundress
Marie Doley, baker
Marie Duval, protégé
Françoise Chatrenay, worker
Marie Freval, laundress
Marie Doré, linen draper
Perinne Grapalière, worker
Marie Julie, lainée
Marie Julie, la cadette
Guillemette Masson, mender of old clothes
Anne Le Fevre, linen draper

Louise Tabibot, young girl
Jullienne Tabibot, young child
Renote Gourniel de Vannes
René Doré
Nicolas Duregard

Total: 214 passengers: 176 male, 28 women and 10 children.

Cherchez les Femmes

Notes for "*Cherchez les Femmes*: Some Glimpses of Women in Early Eighteenth-Century Louisiana"

Research for this paper was funded in part by a grant from the National Endowment for the Humanities. A shorter version of this paper was presented at the First International Colloquium on the French in the United States at Paul Valéry University, Montpellier, France, January 4-6, 1989. I also wish to give special credit to my research assistant Isabel Deutsch for her diligence and dedication in reading eighteenth-century French handwritten documents.

[1] For examples of traditional studies, see John Francis McDermott, ed., *Frenchmen and French Ways in the Mississippi Valley* (Urbana, Ill., 1974); Joseph Wallace, *The History of Illinois and Louisiana under the French Rule* (Cincinnati, 1893); and Sheila Sturdivant, "Rich Man, Poor Man, Beggar Man, Thief: Frenchmen Exiled to Louisiana, 1717 to 1721" (M.A. thesis, University of Southwestern Louisiana, 1971). Investigations into the role and functioning of French women in Louisiana in any period are sparse. Among the few studies available, see Vaughan B. Baker, "*Les Louisianaises:* A Reconnaissance;" Mathé Allain, "*Manon Lescaut et Ses Consoeurs:* Women in the Early French Period, 1700-1731," in James J. Cooke, ed., *Proceedings of the Fifth Meeting of the French Colonial Historical Society, March 29-April 1, 1979* (Lanham, Md., 1980), 6-26; Vaughan B. Baker et al., "*Le Mari Est Seigneur:* Women and the Law in French Colonial Louisiana," in Edward F. Haas and Robert Macdonald, eds., *Louisiana's Legal Heritage* (Pensacola, Fla., 1983). For a survey of the documentary sources available for studying women in Louisiana, see Vaughan B. Baker, "Women in Louisiana History," in Light Townsend Cummins and Glen Jeansonne, eds., *A Guide to the History of Louisiana* (Westport, Ct., 1982).

[2] Harold W. Sheffler, "Structuralism in Anthropology," in Jacques Ehrman, ed., *Structuralism* (Garden City, N.Y., 1970), 58-59.

[3] A few exceptions to the conventional methodology in Louisiana historical studies can be noted. Mathé Allain has admirably incorporated information on women in her *"Not Worth a Straw": French Colonial Policy and the Early Years of Louisiana* (Lafayette, La., 1988). Few similar discussions can be found in the French period although some noteworthy exemplary studies have been completed in later periods. Ann Patton Malone's model article, "Searching for the Family and Household Structure of Rural Louisiana Slaves, 1810-1864," *Louisiana History*, 28 (1987): 357-73, has applied new techniques to the analysis of slave families; Judith K. Schafer has undertaken a model study of concubinage and inheritance through the early nineteenth-century Louisiana Supreme Court records in "'Open and Notorious Concubinage': The Emancipation of Slave Mistresses by Will and the Supreme Court in Antebellum Louisiana," *Louisiana History*, 28 (1987): 165-82. Gary Mills comes closest to revising the established approaches in research in *The Forgotten People: Cane River's Creoles of Color* (Baton Rouge, 1977). He has utilized courthouse records and oral sources to study the descendants of Marie Thérèse Metoyer, a mulatto slave of the Natchitoches Post. The remaining sparse literature on women in Louisiana chiefly concerns Anglo women in the nineteenth and twentieth centuries.

[4] Marcel Giraud, *Histoire de la Louisiane française*, 5 vols. (Paris, 1953-1974; Baton Rouge, 1991), 1:6ff; A. Baillardel and A. Prioult, *Le Chevalier de Pradel: Vie d'un colon français en Louisiane au XVIIIe siècle* (Paris, 1928), 8.

[5] "Relation de voyage du Sieur de La Salle par le Sieur Joustel, July 24, 1684, to November 10, 1684 to November 10, 1688," #1, France. Archives Nationales, Archives des Colonies (hereafter AC), Cartes et Plans, #1-I, volume 57, pp. 178, 261.

[6] See, for example, "Mémoire instructif des profits et avantages des interressez dans la Compagnie des Indes et de Mississippy (1720)," in the Rosemond E. and Emile Kuntz Collection, Tulane University Manuscript Collection.

[7]Cadillac to Pontchartrain, October 26, 1713, in Dunbar Rowland and A. G. Sanders, trans. and eds., *Mississippi Provincial Archives, 1729-1740: French Dominion,* 3 vols. (Jackson, Miss., 1927-1932), 2:169; hereafter cited as *MPA.*

[8]See Giraud, *Histoire,* 1:58.

[9]Cadillac to Pontchartrain, October 26, 1713, *MPA,* 2:167. The problem of populating the colony is a recurrent theme in the early correspondence. See Baker, "Les Louisianaises," 8-9; and Allain, "Manon Lescaut," 18-19.

[10]Charles R. Maduell, Jr., comp. and trans., *The Census Tables for the French Colony of Louisiana from 1699 Through 1732* (Baltimore, 1972), 1-7.

[11]For the 1704 colonists, see "Liste des filles et des deux familles qui doivent passer en Louisiane, October 3, 1704." AC, Series B (royal instructions), volume 25, folios 9-10; see Appendix II. For a discussion of the appeals for women and the *Pélican* girls, see Allain, "*Not Worth a Straw,*" 83-86.

[12]"Census of Families and Habitants of Louisiana Taken August 1, 1706, by Nicolas de La Salle," in Maduell, *Census Tables,* 10.

[13]Dartaguiette to Pontchartrain, February 26, 1708. AC, C 13a, 2:237-38; *MPA,* 2:540-41.

[14]See Paul Harsin, "La Création de la Compagnie d'Occident," *Revue d'Histoire Economique et Sociale,* (1956), 7-41; and Marcel Giraud, "La Compagnie d'Occident, 1717-1718," *Revue Historique,* 226 (1961): 23.

[15]Council of Louisiana to Directors of the Company of the Indies, August 28, 1725, *MPA,* 2:499; Périer and La Chaise to Directors of the Company, November 2, 1727, *MPA,* 2:557; Périer and La Chaise to Directors, November 3, 1728, *MPA,* 2:600; Jay Higginbotham, "The Chaumont Concession: A French Plantation on the Pascagoula," *Journal of Mississippi History,* 36 (1974): 358ff, details the story of the concession. Forty-two passengers embarked from L'Orient for the Chaumont concession on August 13, 1720. Among them were Jeanne Tremant, wife of Jean Philippe Brousse, 26 years old; Guillemette Percha, wife of Jacques Cidar, 30 years old with an infant; Catherine Barot, wife of Jean Batiste Bequet, 23 years old; four unmarried girls, aged from 18 to 22. "Rolles des hommes et femmes embarquez et a emberquer dans la Gironde pour la colonie de M. de Chaumont pour la Louisiane." AC, Series G1 (Civil Lists), volume 464.

[16]Allain, "Manon Lescaut," 20-21; Baker, "Les Louisianaises," 9; Walter H. Blumenthal's *Brides from Bridewell: Female Felons Sent to Colonial America* (Rutland, Vt., 1962), is a weak, superficial examination of the deportees.

[17]"Noms des passagers et filles destinez pour passer à la Louisianne, embarquez sur la frégatte la Mutine . . . 1719." AC, F5b, 37:n.p.

[18]Marie, free Negress, servant of Madame and Monsieur Pellerin, embarked November 15, 1718, on the *Comte de Toulouse.* "Rolle des passagers embarquez sur le vaisseau le Comte de Toulouz commandé par Monsieur le Chevalier de Grieu, pour aller a la Louisianne." AC, G1, 464:n.p.; Marie, free Negress, listed in a party of concessionaires on the *Marie,* left La Rochelle on May 25, 1718. "Rolle des concessionnaires passagers qui passent sur le vaisseau la Marie. . . ." AC, F5b, 37:n.p.

[19]"Rolles des ouvriers de la Compagnie de Ste-Catherine embarques sur la flutte de la Compagnie des Indes, La Loire." AC, G1, 464:n.p.

[20]Charles LeGac, "Mémoire d'après les voyages sur la Louisiane," B.I., Ancien Fonds, 487:508, Tulane University Manuscript Collection. Glenn R. Conrad, trans. and ed., *Immigration and War, 1718-1721: From the Memoir of Charles LeGac* (Lafayette, La., 1970), 10, 11. The ill-fated members of the De La Houssaye party are listed on the May 23, 1718, "Rolle des concessionnaires et passagers qui doivent passer sur le vaisseau la Duchesse de Noailles. . . ." AC, F5b, 37:n.p.

[21]Baker et al., "*Le Mari Est Seigneur,*" 12.

[22]Chassin to Bobé, July 1, 1722, *MPA*, 2:278-79.

[23]Dartaguiette to Maurepas, February 9, 1730, *MPA*, 1:57-58, 122-26.

[24]"List of Private Passengers and German Families Embarked on the *Charente* Commanded by M. Mirambault, Bound for Louisiana," in Glenn R. Conrad, *The First Families of Louisiana*, 2 vols. (Baton Rouge, 1970), 1:24-28.

[25]Devin to Pauger, August 29, 1724. AC, C 13a, 8:204.

[26]Robert Joseph Pothier, *Traité de la Communauté* (Paris, 1819), Vol. 2. The eighteenth-century French jurist Pothier was the most important influence on Louisiana community-property laws.

[27]For a detailed discussion of the provisions of the *Coutume de Paris* and its eighteenth-century philosophy of law, see Baker, et al., "*Le Mari Est Seigneur.*"

[28]The Louisiana French laws (and, in fact, the eighteenth-century French law in general) aimed to protect the institution of the family. Illicit relationships and their progeny, and they were numerous in the colony, did not enjoy the sanctions of the inheritance laws. For a discussion of the problems that plagued women into the nineteenth century because of the rigid family codes of the law, see Schafer, "Open and Notorious Concubinage."

[29]Conrad, *First Families*, 2:49-56.

[30]Heloise H. Cruzat, comp., "Records of the Superior Council of Louisiana, April 9, 1737," in *Louisiana Historical Quarterly*, 9 (1926): 121; hereafter cited *LHQ*.

[31]Succession of Bernard Petit, Known as La Grenade, January 10, 1765, #8876 (75047), Superior Council Records of Louisiana, Louisiana State Museum Archives.

[32]"Records of the Superior Council, July 31, 1727," *LHQ*, 4 (1921): 224.

[33]"Records of the Superior Council, February 15, 1728," Ibid., 243, 247, 248.

[34]A woman was considered a public merchant if she sold merchandise separate from her husband's. Pothier, *Traité de la Puissance du Mari*, 7:9.

[35]La Chaise to the Directors, September 6, 1723, *MPA*, 2:352; October 18, 1723, *MPA*, 2:384; Superior Council of Louisiana to the General Directors of the Company of the Indies, February 27, 1725, *MPA*, 2:403.

[36]La Chaise to the Directors, "Official Report and Ordinance Against a Woman Called 'The Big Flemish Woman,'" September 6, 1723, *MPA*, 2:355. This woman is possibly "Anne, the *force femme* of Louis of Flanders," who departed La Rochelle on *Le Philippe*, January 26, 1719. "Rolle des passagers embarques sur le vaisseau le Philippe de la Compagnie d'Occident . . . [January 26, 1719]." AC, F5b, 37:n.p.

[37]Council of Louisiana to Directors, August 28, 1725, *MPA*, 2:502.

[38]Devin to Pauger, August 29, 1724. AC, C 13a, 8:204vo.

[39]Dartaguiette's memoir, May 12, 1712. AC, C 13a, 8:803-9.

[40]Cadillac to Pontchartrain, October 26, 1713, *MPA*, 2:170.

[41]Conrad, *First Families,* 2:114-15.

[42]Bienville letter, October 28, 1719. AC, C 13a, 5:208-21.

[43]Iberville's memoir, 1701. AC, Cartes et Plans, vol. 67, #14.

[44]Quoted in V. Alton Moody, "Slavery on Louisiana Sugar Plantations," *LHQ*, 7 (1924): 204-5.

[45]Allain, "Manon Lescaut," 19.

[46]"Necessité de nègres en Louisiane pour aider les habitants," in Tiras de Gourville to Pontchartrain, June 1712. AC, C 13a, 2:737-41.

[47]Etat des nègres, négresses et negrillons pour le service de la Compagnie en Louisiane, August 26, 1723. AC, B 43:31a.

[48]Daniel H. Usner, "From African Captivity to American Slavery: The Introduction of Black Laborers to Colonial Louisiana," *Louisiana History*, 20 (1979): 25-48. For the regulations of the *Code Noir*, see Carl A. Brasseaux, "The Administration of Slave Regulations in French Louisiana, 1724-1766," *Louisiana History*, 21 (1980): 139-58. See also James T. McGowan, "Creation of a Slave Society: Louisiana Plantations in the Eighteenth Century" (Ph. D. dissertation, University of Rochester, 1976).

[49]McGowan, "Creation of a Slave Society," 176.

[50]Heloise Hulse Cruzat, "The Ursulines of Louisiana," *LHQ*, 2 (1919): 6-23. The superior of the religious who journeyed to New Orleans in 1727 wrote an account of the voyage and of the arrival and establishment of the order in New Orleans. Marion Ware, ed., "An Adventurous Voyage to French Colonial Louisiana: The Narrative of Mother Tranchepain, 1727," *Louisiana History,* 1 (1960): 212-29.

[51]AC, B 25:9-10.

[52]AC, G1, 464:n.p.

THE URSULINE SCHOOL IN NEW ORLEANS, 1727-1771*

Joan Marie Aycock

On April 24, 1728, Sister Marie Madeleine Hachard, a newly arrived Ursuline novice, described New Orleans as "a very pretty city, well constructed and regularly built." Along the wide streets were white-washed, paneled houses that gave a bright and cheerful appearance to the city.[1]

As bright and cheerful as New Orleans appeared, the city faced major problems not apparent to the casual observer. Foremost among these was the need for permanent, industrious settlers. Without schools, however, it was difficult to attract families who would have a stabilizing influence on the young colonial settlement. The original plans for New Orleans made no provision for such a school.[2]

Colonial Louisiana's first recorded teacher was Françoise de Boisrenaud who arrived on the *Pelican* in 1704. Before her departure in 1718 because of poor health, she provided a rudimentary education to some of the colony's young girls and gave religious instruction to Indian slave girls. Mademoiselle Boisrenaud presumably conducted classes in her home.[3]

The first formal Louisiana school was opened by Father Raphaël de Luxembourg, Capuchin superior. As early as 1723, Father Raphaël had approached the Company of the Indies for help in founding a school for boys. He felt that the establishment of such an educational institution was the duty of the Company and a matter that was inextricably connected with the Company's obligation to establish the Catholic religion in the colony. The Company, however, refused support for a school.[4]

On September 15, 1725, Father Raphaël wrote to France that he had opened a "little school" of about nine students near St. Louis Church. The early teachers were Brother

---

*First published in Glenn R. Conrad, ed., *Cross, Crozier and Crucible: A Volume Celebrating the Bicentennial of a Catholic Diocese in Louisiana* (New Orleans, La.: Archdiocese of New Orleans in Cooperation with the Center for Louisiana Studies, 1993), 203-18. Reprinted with the kind permission of the author and the publisher.

Saint-Julien, Father Cyrille de Rochefort, and Pierre Fleurtel, the parish choirmaster. This tuition-free school included a basic literary track and a more advanced Latin-liberal arts curriculum. The priest embarked with enthusiasm on the endeavor, convinced that "there is nothing upon which the establishment of a colony more essentially depends than upon the education of the young."[5]

The same year that he opened the boys' school, Father Raphaël proposed that a second school be established in the city for Native Americans. Several young Indian boys would be trained here in Christian living and doctrine and return to their tribes as catechists and missionaries. One young Natchez brave was already under instruction in New Orleans. This imaginative evangelization plan and school were not implemented.[6]

Father Raphaël's school was short-lived. On May 18, 1728, the priest wrote that enrollment was still low, due in part to the colonists' indifference. The majority "are satisfied to have them [their children] taught to read and write and regard all the rest as useless." The school was still functioning as late as 1731, though it lacked a solid financial base. The school was discontinued later in the decade, although the exact date of its closing is not known.[7]

By 1726 there was still no school for girls in the colony. Wealthy parents could afford to send their sons to France to be educated. Mothers, however, were far less willing to send their daughters abroad because of the dangers encountered during travel.[8]

As early as 1723 Louisiana colonial officials had been asking continuously and unsuccessfully for Brothers of Charity, Grey Nuns, or Hospital Sisters to staff more efficiently the royal military hospital at New Orleans. When Father Nicolas-Ignace de Beaubois, S.J., returned to France from Louisiana in 1725, he persuaded French officials to extend this invitation to the Ursulines "in imitation of Canada" and include the education of young girls in the mission's work.[9]

The order that was invited to come to Louisiana had been founded by Saint Angela Merici (1474-1540). Angela formed the Company of St. Ursula in Brescia, Italy, in 1535 to assist her with the catechetical instruction of young girls. Angela's era, like modern times, was a time of religious, moral, social, and political upheaval. Angela believed that society could be revitalized only through the home, and that the most effective means of safeguarding and strengthening the Christian home was the education of young girls, who, as wives and mothers, would become the mainstays of family life. Although the original company took no formal vows, the members followed a rule that included the promises of virginity, poverty and obedience. In 1544 the first papal approval was given to Angela's small company of women, and in 1612 the rule of St. Augustine was adopted and the Ursulines became the first officially approved teaching order of Catholic nuns.[10]

The Ursulines spread throughout Europe, especially in France, where there was an Ursuline monastery as early as 1596. In 1639 the Ursulines from France established at Quebec their first North American monastery, the oldest institution of learning for women in North America. By 1700 in France alone there were about 9,000 Ursulines in 350 monasteries.[11]

Father Ignace de Beaubois successfully approached the Ursulines concerning the Louisiana mission. On September 13, 1726, the formal contract between the Ursulines and the directors of the Company of the Indies was signed; five days later, the king approved the contract by royal warrant.

The Company of the Indies agreed to subsidize only six religious, including the superior; any additional nuns had to be supported by the Ursulines themselves. Although their primary apostolate in Europe and Canada was education, the Ursulines agreed to assume the care of the military hospital in New Orleans as soon as they reached Louisiana. (Articles 1-5)

The Company agreed to subsidize only one religious to teach at the proposed New Orleans school; a second religious could assist at the school or hospital as necessity demanded. (Article 6)

The only other article that mentioned the education of girls stated, "When the religious can do so conveniently, they will take, if they judge proper, girl boarders at the rate the Superioress will have regulated. . . ." Hospital nuns, however, could not be assigned to the school. (Article 24)[12]

Father de Beaubois recruited the core of the Louisiana mission at the Ursuline convent in Rouen: Mother St-Augustin Tranchepain (superior of the new mission), and Sisters St-Jean l'Evangéliste Judde and Angélique Boulanger. Other members of the original band included Sisters Ste-Thérèse Salaon (Plöermel); St-Michel Marion (Plöermel); Ste-Marie Yviquel (Vannes); St-François Xavier Mahieu (Havre); St-Joseph Cavalier (Elbeuf); Ste-Marthe Dain (Hennebont); Marie-Madeleine Hachard, novice; Claude Massy, postulant; and Anne Frances, postulant. In all, twelve women embarked for Louisiana on February 22, 1727.[13]

Sister Marie-Madeleine Hachard has left a detailed and entertaining record of the ordeals of the five-and-a-half-month voyage to the New World, not the least of which were terrible seasickness, encounters with pirates, severe storms, cramped quarters, and an introduction to Louisiana mosquitos which "sting without mercy."[14]

Angela Merici had gathered around her women to share her ministry of evangelizing and educating young girls. As followers of Angela, the Ursulines were primarily educators. The French nuns who first left for Louisiana followed in this same tradition, although they accepted the challenge of staffing the military hospital as well as organizing a school for girls.

The Convent-School Buildings

The first weary band of Ursulines saw New Orleans early on the morning of August 6, 1727; the remaining sisters arrived the following day.[15] After a warm greeting from Father de Beaubois and many of his friends, the nuns proceeded to their "temporary" home–the large, two-story Kolly House at the corner of Bienville and Chartres streets.

These quarters served as their first monastery and school in Louisiana. Because of numerous construction delays, they remained at the Kolly House for seven years.[16]

The Kolly House was too small to house boarders or to accommodate day students. The nuns immediately had a small house built nearby to provide for both the boarders and day students.[17]

The Ursulines' permanent convent adjoining the military hospital, originally planned for completion in 1728, was not ready for occupancy until 1734. The half-timber construction, located slightly closer to the river than their subsequent convent, included three stories and provided room for the sisters, day students, and boarders. On July 17, 1734, the solemn procession of clergy, government officials, soldiers, nuns, children, and citizens proceeded from the Kolly House to the new convent.[18]

The new convent included a dining room for boarders, a small office, the nuns' refectory, and the community recreation room on the first floor; two infirmaries, a dormitory, and fifteen small rooms on the second floor; and sleeping areas for the boarders and orphans on the third floor. The nuns were chagrined to find that their new home lacked a bakery, laundry, sacristy, storeroom, and classrooms for day students. Former hospital space had to be converted into a classroom for day students, a storehouse, and laundry.[19]

By 1745 this convent's wooden frame, exposed so long to the elements during construction, had already begun to deteriorate. Plans were drawn up for a new convent. Like the first building, the nuns' new home experienced interminable bureaucratic and construction delays. It was not until 1752 or 1753 that they were able to occupy the second convent and transfer there the school. The nuns remained in this convent, the oldest building in the Mississippi Valley, until 1824 when they moved to a new convent downriver.[20]

The Ursuline Community

Nine professed religious, one novice, and two postulants formed the original Ursuline community that landed in New Orleans in 1727. During the next forty-four years, twenty-four additional women formed part of that community at one time or another.

Sisters Ste-Marthe Dain and St-Michel Marion, unable to endure colonial life, returned to France within three months. Religious life was not to be for the two postulants, Anne Frances and Claude Massy; the former returned to France in 1729; the latter left the community the same year. Within six years, the community was further reduced by the deaths of four sisters: St.-François Xavier Mahieu (1728); St-Jean l'Evangéliste Judde (1731), Ste-Thérèse Salaon (1733), and Mother St-Augustin Tranchepain, the superior (1733). By 1733 only four of the original band of twelve nuns remained at New Orleans. Sister St-Stanislaus Hachard had completed her novitiate and pronounced her first vows on March 15, 1729, the first such ceremony in Louisiana.[21]

The first group of additional nuns did not arrive until March 16, 1732: Sisters St-Pierre Bernard (Caen), St-Andre Melotte (Caen), and François Xavier Hébert (Bayeux). At Mother St-Augustin's death in 1733, Sister St- André Melotte was chosen as the new superior.[22]

Seven nuns–four from the original band and three 1732 arrivals–participated in the celebrations held in honor of the move from the Kolly House to the new convent in 1734. Madeleine Hachard wrote her father: "We are not too many, and I assure you that we are all occupied from morning until night. We have not a moment to ourselves; the time taken to write this is taken from my night's rest."[23]

Additional nuns continued to arrive periodically to assist the local community in its many-facetted mission: Sister Ste-Radegonde de St-Marc in 1736; Sister St-Madeleine de Jésus (Marguerite) Bigeaud de Belair, Sister St-Louis de Gonzague, and Sister de Sacré-Coeur (Elizabeth) Bigeaud de Belair in 1742. Nine additional sisters arrived between 1745 and 1755: Sisters St-Jacque Landelle, St-Joseph de la Motte, and St-François Regis (1751), St-Etienne (1753), Marie des Anges Quemenor, and Ste-Reine Lestang (1754), Ste-Thérèse de Jésus de Beaumont, St-Gabriel Cormoray, and St-Ignace du Liepure (1755). Of the nine, Sisters St-Joseph and Ste-Reine returned to France.[24]

The expectations and the conditions of the contract with the Company of the Indies were great; the number of religious was small. Article 25 of the original contract, however, prohibited the nuns from receiving young women from the colony into religious life without the permission of the Company's council. Young women were needed as wives and mothers for the settlers; any replacements at the convent had to come from France. The first young women born in this country who were allowed to enter religious life were Marie Turpin of Illinois in 1749, Marthe Delatre in 1757, and Charlotte de Mouy, a native of Louisiana and a pupil of Sister St-Stanislaus Hachard, in 1766. Other sisters who entered between 1765 and 1770 were Ste- Angele Caue (a young Creole woman), Ste-Monique Le Blanc, and Marie Joseph Broul (Acadia, Canada).[25]

Death continued to deplete the ranks of the few laborers in the Louisiana vineyard. In 1742 Sister St-Joseph Cavalier died; in 1747 St-André Melotte; in 1752 Ste-Thérèse de Jésus de Belair; in 1755 St-Francis de Paule; in 1760 St-Stanislaus Hachard; in 1761 Ste-Marthe Turpin; in 1762 St-François Xavier Hébert; in 1763 St-Pierre Bernard and St-Marie Yviquil; in 1764 Ste- Thérèse de Jésus de Beaumont and Ste-Radegonde. Sister Angélique Boulanger, the last of the original band, died on June 29, 1766.[26]

The Ursuline School

The Ursulines began their work of education immediately after their arrival in the city. This educational effort was aided by the lumbering French bureaucracy which dragged out the permanent convent's construction for seven years. The Kolly House was located at the opposite end of the town from the military hospital; the nuns' rule of cloister did not allow them to appear in public, much less parade from one end of the town to another each day. They could not work in the hospital until their new convent was ready; their zealous efforts, therefore, were channeled into the school.

Within a short time, the nuns had more than thirty applicants for their boarding school. After the small house near their residence was completed, the first boarding students were accepted on November 17, 1727. Several days later classes for day students were begun. The nuns also started afternoon classes for black and Indian girls.[27]

Soon afterwards, Father de Beaubois brought to the convent a young orphan girl, "serving in a house where she did not have a very good example." Although not included in their contract for the colony, the nuns agreed to care for the girl. Several other orphan girls were also taken in, thus adding an orphanage component to their educational work.[28]

A letter from Mother St-Augustin to Abbé Gilles Raguet dated April 20, 1728, gives a good idea of how the work of the nuns progressed during the first year:

> We have at last the happiness of having a large number of boarders and day pupils with whose education the parents appear satisfied, and they hope it will produce in a few years great benefits for the colony where religion is little known and still less practiced. Besides we have a special class for the Negresses and Indians. . . We have also been charged with the care of the orphans to provide them with a suitable education which will put them in a position to earn a living according to their condition. We have so far only three in our house but we are expecting others. I assure you, sir, that it gives great joy to my heart, and animates me more and more to undertake all for love of Him who has done us this great favor of using us to make Him known and loved in a place where He is so neglected and so forgotten.[29]

In another letter, Sister Stanislaus wrote that the convent had eight boarders, a large number of day pupils, and a large number of black and Indian girls who came daily for instruction. Before the nuns' arrival, young girls in the colony had married at the age of twelve "without even knowing how many gods there are." Now all received religious instruction before marriage. Some of the young boarders from nearby plantations "had never heard of God." The nuns found these young women "docile and ardently desirous of being instructed."[30]

The convent school became the refuge for the innocent young survivors of the November, 1729, massacre at the Natchez Post. The young girls who were rescued from the Indians by the French retaliatory force were placed with the nuns. Father Mathurin Le Petit, S.J., wrote:

> The little girls whom none of the colonists wished to adopt have increased the interesting group of orphans whom the nuns are bringing up. The great number of these children serves but to augment their charity and their attentions. They have been formed into a separate class of which two teachers are in charge.[31]

Although the exact number of young Natchez survivors who were placed at the convent is not known, the nuns were caring for forty-nine orphans in 1731. The

Ursuline School

Company of the Indies agreed to provide 150 *livres* for each orphan's care, but little progress was made on the much needed new convent.[32]

When the Louisiana colony was retroceded to the king in 1731, the government considered withholding the subsidy for the orphans at the convent. When local officials pointed out the long-term folly (and expense) of such a policy, the king partially relented and agreed to provide funds for thirty of the forty-nine orphans. Local officials, however, were ordered to see that the orphans were well educated and quickly married.[33] Roger Baudier calculated that the nuns were paid the equivalent of $1.25 per week in French coinage, approximately six cents a day, for each orphan.[34] Baudier also noted additional ministeries that the nuns undertook, namely accepting and caring for wayward girls and battered wives.[35]

The move to the completed convent in 1734 had a two-fold effect on the Ursuline School. First, the new convent provided ample room for boarders, although the nuns had to find additional space for a classroom for day students. Secondly, the nuns could now begin their ministry at the royal hospital–a ministry which reduced the staff available for teaching.

The 1752 or 1753 move to the new, smaller monastery raised new difficulties for the school. The new building contained no chapel and no room for boarders. Apparently, a separate building was utilized.[36]

Only scattered school records survive from the French period, providing the names of some students and their tuition. There are, however, lists of names of students and adults who were members of the Sodality of the Children of Mary. The following were established as officers of the adult Sodality: Widow Carriere; Widow Marie Rivard, née [B/D]riard; Madame Bourbon; Madame Thomelain; Widow Fonder; Madame Chavan; Madame Banville; Madame Anne Caron, née Monie; Madame Vendôme; Madame Marie Sautier, née Lepron; Madame Fabre; Madame Jeanne Antoinette Rivard, née De Villemont; Madame Mathurine Aufrère, née Guillemotte; and Madame Marie Anne Brantan, née Hubler.[37]

The general atmosphere of the school, however, can be constructed from the detailed administrative and pedagogical guide that the Ursulines used for their New Orleans school.

Ursuline Educational Philosophy and Pedagogy

The Ursuline nuns responded generously to any challenge with which they were presented, but it was the educational challenge that awaited them in the colony for which they were best prepared. They were trained educators. They brought with them a copy of the 1705 edition of the *Règlemens des Religieuses Ursulines de la Congrégation de Paris*, in the Ursuline academies in America referred to as the *Règlements*, the equivalent of the *Ratio Studiorum* of the Jesuits.[38] It contained detailed rules and methods for administering a school and teaching individual subjects such as reading, spelling, writing, and catechism, as well as training young girls in manual work and in the social graces.

The Ursulines of New Orleans applied and adapted the rules and methods of the *Règlements* to the needs of the various groups of young girls they were teaching in the colony: boarders, orphans, day pupils, Indians and slaves.

The traditional method of Ursuline education has been defined as collective family education. The religious are to act as spiritual mothers; their students are the children of God. St. Angela said to her daughters:

> I beg you to take care of all of your daughters, having each and every one engraved on your mind and heart, not only their names but also their situation and character and every detail about them. . . Look at human mothers; even if they had a thousand sons and daughters they would have them all firmly fixed in their hearts. . . With still more reason, spiritual mothers can and should do this.[39]

Angela also told her daughters that they could become positive forces in the formation of these young women only in so far as they established between themselves the bonds of charity and unity.

The *Règlements* placed a mistress general in charge of each school (boarding and day). Each class was assigned to a class mistress who was responsible for supervising instructions, as well as order and discipline. Serious offenses became the responsibility of the mistress general. All corrections had to be administered with a calm, serene spirit.

> Whatever the fault of the pupil, the correction must be given without brusqueness, hurtful words, and as much as possible without apparent emotion; never the less [sic] one must not confound passion with a grave and severe tone. Let the pupil ever feel that a teacher punishes only with great regret and through duty. The teacher should defer the correction if the child is too ill disposed to receive it well, but in such a fashion that neither she nor the class doubt that the punishment is only delayed, so that the child may know that this delay is given in order to give her time for reflection.[40]

The *Règlements* specified that there should be conferences between teachers and teachers, and between teachers and supervisors. Class preparation was also required.[41]

Students were grouped according to age. The number of girls in each class was determined by the level. The larger groups were broken down into smaller groups when there was need for individual drilling in a particular subject.[42]

The *Règlements* also gave specific directives for teaching each major subject. Arithmetic began with learning the Arabic figures and the Roman numerals; the children were then taught to count to one thousand. They were taught to add and subtract using *jetons*—small, round, flat pieces of ivory or metal. When the basic concepts were mastered, the children were taught to apply them to life situations, much the same as they are taught today. Among the school supplies listed, there is no mention of pencils but only pens, paper, and penknives, so all of their "figuring" must have been done with pen.[43]

Reading was taught from handwriting books. The teacher spelled out five or six lines, and then read about a page or so, pronouncing well, and observing the pauses and accents, while at the same time, all the class followed in their own books and read in a low tone, word for word, with the teacher. Following this each child was called upon to read the passage by herself. In France the morning classes were conducted in French, while the afternoon classes were taught in Latin. In New Orleans the morning classes were taught in French, and the afternoon classes were taught in English so the child read in French in the morning and English in the afternoon classes.[44]

Writing was taught at the long tables in the dining room, so that the children could have as much space as they needed. Here again pens were used with small pieces of linen or taffeta near to wipe them. Students were to sit up straight and hold their pens with three fingers. Writing class lasted an hour. Beginners were given help for six weeks, after which time they were expected to be able to practice on their own. When a student had mastered the letters, the teacher advised the class mistress that she was ready to learn orthography. The more advanced writers were chosen to write the class notices on the saints' days.[45]

Spelling was taught to eight or ten children at a time; every child did not have spelling every day. Two or three lines were dictated to a student and then corrected for spelling errors. The misspelled words were studied and then the passage was read again. The lesson was not changed until the passage was written without a mistake.[46]

Religion was taught at 3 p.m. The students worked in pairs memorizing the assigned texts. At 5:15 p.m. the students were questioned on what they had studied. Stress was placed upon the importance of understanding what they had memorized. If a student could not explain a matter, the teacher retaught it.[47]

While many of those who boarded did so because of the distance of the school from their homes, most girls boarded at the convent because their parents wanted them to have the additional training in domestic science and character development provided to boarders by the nuns. There was, therefore, a specific set of rules and procedures in the *Règlements* governing the training of boarders.[48]

The young ladies were taught how to manage a household. Whenever there were a few free moments, the girls reached for their sewing. They were taught to make and mend their own clothes. Sometimes they were read to as they sewed. As their ability increased, they were taught tapestry work, embroidery, and lace work. They took turns folding clothes, ironing, and setting and clearing the table. They were taught to make their beds and keep their personal belongings in order.[49]

Instruction in social skills appropriate to young ladies was also an important part of Ursuline education. It was the nuns' responsibility to train the students in table etiquette and courtesy. They were to see that the girls developed poise in speech and manner without affectation, displayed a serene and pleasing face, and spoke in a soft and moderate voice. The girls were corrected for improper speech.[50]

The boarders were allowed to visit with parents and friends in the parlor, and on special occasions were allowed to go home. Thursdays and Sundays are spoken of as free days, in the early years. The girls were limited in vacation periods, because the nuns felt it distracted them from their work.[51]

To help with teaching duties in the day school, the nuns chose those students who excelled in intelligence, moral character, and school spirit to help with drilling their fellow students in reading, writing, arithmetic, and catechism. These young teachers' aides, known as *dixainières*, were held in high esteem by the other students.[52]

The mistress general, whom today we would call the principal, held an assembly once a year to read to the students the regulations regarding their conduct in school and the program of Christian duties which they were expected to carry out in their own homes. For example, they were not allowed to copy each other's work or eat in the classroom. There was to be no rudeness, laziness, or neglect.[53]

The dominant tone for class instruction was thoroughness. No lesson was completed until it was mastered. Promotion depended on mastery of the material rather than a set period of time spent in class.[54]

While there were no textbooks for class instruction as we know them, the *Règlements* refer often to books. One of the responsibilities of the *dixainières*, the teachers' aides, was to distribute and collect books each day, as the students were not allowed to take any books home.[55]

The nuns had brought books with them from France. The Ursuline Convent in New Orleans still houses a remarkable library from these early days. It is a real inspiration to open a book and find the signature of Sister Angélique, one of the founders. Some of the other books still housed in the archives are *Catechismes ou Abrégés de la Doctrine Chrétienne* (1708), *Abrégé des Antiquités Romaines* (1729), *Emblèmes ou Devises Chrétiennes ouvrage mêlé de Prose et de Vers et Enrichi de Figures* (1717). It is interesting to note that any book not having the approval of the king was condemned.[56]

The nuns used emulation and awards as a positive approach to encourage their young charges in their efforts at becoming intelligent, caring young women.[57]

An integral part of the training in these schools was to educate young Christians to that life-expression of Christianity known as the liturgy or official prayer of the Church. The prayer periods in the school at 2:15 p.m. and 6:45 p.m. were devoted mainly to the recitation of vespers or of matins. On feast days the girls could attend the Solemn Office, which the nuns chanted on these days. The Ursuline Museum still preserves the large missal used at all three convents.[58]

The first communion ceremony as we know it today originated with the Paris Ursulines of the Rue St-Jacques to counteract some of the false values in the French court of the day.

> To understand aright the mind of the Ursulines, one must remember that at the time of this *Règlements* of theirs, at the time of the establishment of this ceremonial, ceremony was the very breath of French society, and the nuns, dealing with future

members of that society, strove simply to teach their young pupils the reverse of the false values prevailing at the French court, and ruining an intelligent and infatuated people. For during those days, in the palace chapel at Versailles, the brocaded and perfumed ladies, Catholics all, knelt, by court custom, not so much facing the altar on which they believed the Real Presence to be, as turning with their faces towards the rear gallery where sat King Louis XIV, enthroned. The protest of the Ursulines was perhaps embodied in this little ceremony at the monastery. They trained the young daughters of the court sycophants as best they could, not indeed to depreciate ceremony, provided right authority were its center, but to value all human dignity only proportionately with the Divine. The least little girl who had received her God into her heart, ranked above all, as 'the queen in vesture of gold.'[59]

The directives in the *Règlements* called for making the day on which first communion was received a very special one indeed. The first communicants "are to dress in white linen, with a coif of white taffeta, and a cincture of the same. They wear white veils." They sat at a table apart with the mistress general in the dining room, and they had the privilege of leading the grace at table.[60]

The first and second class liturgical feasts of the Church were days of special celebration that included general recreations and a table covered with tasty treats.[61]

In the Ursuline academies in France there was no required uniform; however, there were certain restrictions: the young ladies must have their necks covered, and they must not be "frizzed or powdered." We do not know if these restrictions applied in the New Orleans school, but apparently uniforms were not worn in the early days, as no mention is made of them until after 1828.[62]

One of the great blessings handed down from St. Angela to her daughters was a freedom to change when there was a need, and upon good advice. Even though the directions contained in the *Règlements* were very explicit, the teachers were free to innovate if they found that it would be for the best of the students. Tradition and progress have ever been the watchwords of Ursuline education.[63]

Although the Spanish first occupied Louisiana in 1766 and again in 1769, Spanish ecclesiastical rule did not begin here until the arrival of the first Spanish Capuchins in 1771. The final years of the French period were a time of uncertainty for the Ursuline community as there were no Ursuline monasteries in Spain at that time. In 1770 the nuns were relieved of their responsibility at the royal hospital; once again education became their primary ministry. Their school has continued without interruption, up to the present day.[64]

Sister Jane Frances Heaney, drawing on her scholarly study of the early Louisiana Ursuline community, summarized best the atmosphere that Louisiana's pioneer teachers created in their small New Orleans school:

> From the writings of Mother St. Augustin and Sister St. Stanislaus we know that the first teachers of the oldest school for girls in the Mississippi Valley were equipped with religious zeal, physical courage, mental alertness, executive ability,

and a sense of humor: admirable qualities upon which to build an educational institution. They were women of keen observation and common sense. In their letters, the food and how to cook it, the trees, the flowers, the mosquitoes, the customs of the inhabitants were described, compared, and contrasted with an acuteness that any teacher might emulate. Their training was not strictly in accord with twentieth century demands, but it was comprehensive, resourceful, and effective. The preparation for the teaching of Christian doctrine required the most study. This, however, was so linked up with the religious life of the teachers that the essence of their best teaching was the product of their individual lives.[65]

Notes for "The Ursuline School in New Orleans, 1727-1771"

[1] Myldred Masson Costa, trans., *The Letters of Marie Madeleine Hachard, 1727-1728* (New Orleans, 1974), 54.

[2] Samuel Wilson, Jr., *The Capuchin School in New Orleans, 1725, The First Louisiana School* (New Orleans, 1961), 14, citing Father Raphaël's September 15, 1725, letter to Abbé Gilles-Bernard Raguet, ecclesiastical director of the Company of the Indies.

[3] Marcel Giraud, *Histoire de la Louisiane Française,* 5 vols. (Paris and Baton Rouge, 1953-1991), 1:143, 166; 2:22; 3:342.

[4] Claude L. Vogel, O.M. Cap., *The Capuchins in French Louisiana, 1722-1766* (Washington, D.C., 1928), 69, 73.

[5] Wilson, *The Capuchin School,* 11-14.

[6] Charles E. Nolan, *St. Mary's of Natchez: The History of a Southern Catholic Congregation,* 2 vols. (Natchez, 1992), 1:7.

[7] Wilson, *The Capuchin School,* 20-27.

[8] [Austin Carroll,] *Ursulines in Louisiana, 1727-1824* (New Orleans, 1886), 5.

[9] Jane Frances Heaney, "A Century of Pioneering: A History of the Ursuline Nuns of New Orleans, 1727-1827" (Ph.D. dissertation St. Louis University, 1949), 28-34.

[10] Ibid., 1-11; *Catholic Encyclopedia,* s.vv. "Angela Merici, Saint," and "Ursulines"; *New Catholic Encyclopedia,* s.vv. "Merici, Angela St." and "Ursulines."

[11] Heaney, "A Century of Pioneering," 15-24; *Catholic Encyclopedia,* s.vv. "Ursulines" and "Ursulines of Quebec"; *New Catholic Encyclopedia,* s.v. "Ursulines."

[12] Heaney, "A Century of Pioneering," 34-44; Therese Wolfe, O.S.U., *The Ursulines in New Orleans and Our Lady of Prompt Succor, 1727-1925* (New Orleans, 1925), 167-72.

[13] Ursuline Private Archives, obituary notices giving the dates of entrance, profession, death and age at death, 6-7.

[14] Heaney, "A Century of Pioneering," 55-63; Costa, trans., *Letters of Marie-Madeleine Hachard,* 25-47.

[15] The familiar painting by DePoincy of the arrival of the Ursulines portrays all of the nuns arriving in the city simultaneously.

[16] Heaney, "A Century of Pioneering," 63-67; Samuel Wilson, Jr., "An Architectural History of the Royal Hospital and the Ursuline Convent of New Orleans," *Louisiana Historical Quarterly,* 29 (1946): 568-69; Heloise Hulse Cruzat, "The Ursulines of Louisiana," *Louisiana Historical Quarterly,* 2 (1919): 10-11.

[17] Heaney, "A Century of Pioneering," 67.

[18] Ibid., 70-74; Wilson, "Architectural History," 16-37.

[19] Wilson, "Architectural History," 37-38; Heaney, "A Century of Pioneering," 124.

[20] Wilson, "Architectural History," 46-55.

[21] Heaney, "A Century of Pioneering," 83, 93-94, 118-21; Cruzat, "The Ursulines of Louisiana," 8, 11-12.

[22] Personnel Records, Ursuline Convent Archives, New Orleans; hereafter UCANO, 8.

[23] Wolfe, *Ursulines in New Orleans*, 232.

[24] Personnel Records, UCANO, #4, 9-13.

[25] Wolfe, *Ursulines in New Orleans*, 39-42, 172-73; Cruzat, "The Ursulines of Louisiana," 16-17; Heaney, "A Century of Pioneering," 37, 162-67, 170, 172.

[26] Cruzat, "The Ursulines of Louisiana," 8, 17-18; Personnel Records, UCANO, 9-11.

[27] Heaney, "A Century of Pioneering," 67-68.

[28] Ibid., 68.

[29] Mother Augustin Tranchepain to Abbé Gilles Bernard Raguet, New Orleans, April 20, 1728. Archives Nationals, Paris. Transcript in Library of Congress. Copy in UCANO.

[30] Heaney, "A Century of Pioneering," 69-70.

[31] Cruzat, "The Ursulines of Louisiana," 12.

[32] Heaney, "A Century of Pioneering," 105.

[33] Ibid., 108, 113-14.

[34] Roger Baudier, address given to the Ursuline Academy Co-operative Club in 1942. Copy in UCANO.

[35] Roger Baudier, *Through Portals of the Past: The Story of the Old Ursuline Convent of New Orleans* (New Orleans, 1955), 9.

[36] Heaney, "A Century of Pioneering," 159-60.

[37] UCANO, "Premier Registre de la Congrégation des Dames Enfants de Marie Le 28 mai 1730-août 15, 1744." Bound Volume 10 x 15. 285 pp., of which 24 were used. From the account of the establishment of the Sodality. First and maiden names reconstructed from Earl C. Woods and Charles E. Nolan, eds., *Sacramental Records of the Roman Catholic Church of the Archdiocese of New Orleans*, 7 vols. (New Orleans, 1987-1992), 1 (1718-1750): 6, 33, 41, 223, 235.

[38] Marie de St-Jean Martin, *Ursuline Method of Education* (New Jersey, 1946), 57.

[39] Saint Angela Merici, *Rule, Counsels, Testament* (Rome, 1985), 95-96. (Early Italian text with modern translation).

[40] *Règlements des Religieuses Ursulines de la Congrégation de Paris* (Paris, 1705). Copy of the original in UCANO: Part I, Chap. II, Art. 7.

[41] M. Monica, *Angela Merici and Her Teaching Idea, 1474-1540* (New York, 1927), 370.

[42] Monica, *Angela Merici*, 367.

[43] Ibid., 382-83.

[44] Ibid., 381-82.

[45] Ibid., 379.

[46] Ibid., 380-81.

[47] Ibid., 385.

[48] *Règlemens des Religieuses Ursulines;* Book I.

[49] Monica, *Angela Merici,* 384.

[50] Martin, *Ursuline Method of Education*, 78.

[51] Monica, *Angela Merici*, 364; Heaney, "A Century of Pioneering," 127.

[52] Monica, *Angela Merici*, 364.

[53] Ibid., 368.

[54] Heaney, "A Century of Pioneering," 128.

[55] Monica, *Angela Merici*, 366.

[56] (Books in Ursuline Library)

[57] Monica, *Angela Merici*, 369.

[58] Ibid.

[59] Ibid., 389-90.

[60] Ibid., 389.

[61] Ibid., 376-77.

[62] Ibid., 372.

[63] Ibid., 378.

[64] Heaney, "A Century of Pioneering," 181-87.

[65] Ibid., 128-29.

LE MARI EST SEIGNEUR: MARITAL LAWS GOVERNING WOMEN IN FRENCH LOUISIANA*

Vaughan Baker, Amos Simpson, and Mathé Allain

Domestic law is a primary facet of the legal system in any human society. In pre-industrial and early modern societies, the laws governing domestic relationships, along with the laws of inheritance, were the aspects of law that most closely touched the individual member of the community. Regulating the family unit, the foundation of the social structure, these laws generally reflected the most fundamental premises of the social order.

Although the contemporary community property regime has received considerable recent attention and its origins have been the subject of debate by legal historians,[1] few scholars have examined the theoretical bases of the laws governing women and marriage in French colonial Louisiana for understandings concerning the social and economic role of women in early Louisiana society. Such an examination clarifies the role of women in the Louisiana colony and points to important new directions for research into the economic activities of women in the eighteenth century. This essay therefore explores the theory of the marital laws governing women in French colonial Louisiana.

Civil government began in Louisiana in 1712 when Louis XIV ceded the colony to Antoine Crozat. The charter of transfer established the *Coutume de Paris* and the edicts of the king as the fundamental law of Louisiana. Examination of the marital laws governing women must, then, begin with an understanding of the legal status of women according to the provisions of the *Coutume de Paris*.[2]

The fundamental theory of the marital laws contained in the *Coutume de Paris* contradicts modern assumptions concerning the misogynist attitudes of the pre-modern period. While it is true that under the *Coutume de Paris* married women were relegated to an inferior legal status and severely restricted in their rights and prerogatives, the law provided women with economic protections which allowed them an extraordinary measure

---

*First published in Edward F. Haas and Robert R. Macdonald, eds., *Louisiana's Legal Heritage* (Pensacola, Fla.: Published for the Louisiana State Museum by the Perdido Bay Press, 1983), 7-18. Reprinted here with the kind permission of the authors and the publisher.

of economic security and, theoretically at least, accorded them personal dignity and social value. Women's inferior legal status in the French marital regime was a conclusion rationally derived from the most fundamental premises of the ancient customary law and the eighteenth-century worldview. Assumptions governing the role and status of women were rooted in a firmly entrenched hierarchical ideology given new impetus in the seventeenth and eighteenth centuries. In an age which believed strongly in a natural order governed by natural law, every member of society had a place in the orderly scheme of the universe. As the hierarchical conception approached its zenith, symbolically represented in the figure of *"Le Roi Soleil,"* women were assigned a rank in what appeared to be a divinely ordained and firmly fixed natural order of society. That position was below the rank of the male.

Eustache Nicolas Pigeau,[3] Professor of Law at the University of Paris and an influential legal commentator of the eighteenth century, served as spokesman for the age when he explained that Providence had gifted men and women differently, endowing men with greater strength. Since the two spouses formed a community which required government, one had to have superior authority. Although women had been given virtues which adorned their sex, their strengths were less conducive to good government than were the male's. The "weakness and feebleness" of the woman made her less able to administer and protect the conjugal community. The *puissance maritale* of the husband was, consequently, necessary to the security of the family and the society. Pigeau stated the theory quite succinctly, ". . . the authority confided to the husband must be considered established in favor of the wife and the conjugal society even as the duties and obedience toward the political power are established to enable the state to fulfill the goal of its institution. They are in favor of the people and not in favor of those who govern."[4]

In the Customary Law of Paris the power of the husband over the wife and the parents over the children prevailed. Resting on fundamental concepts established in the customary laws of the Germanic peoples, the provisions of the law aimed to preserve stability in family institutions and the preservation of family property. Thus preference was given to a system of incontrovertible protection of inheritance, and therefore to the male descendants.[5]

Concerning women, the fundamental premise of the *Coutume de Paris* was "the married woman is under the power of husband." *"Le Mari est Seigneur,"* said Article 225 —"the husband is lord."[6] This *puissance du mari* extended to her person and her property. The wife's obligation consisted of dependence and submission, not simple respect, to such extent that married women could perform no valid legal act without the husband's consent, unless she acted as a *marchande publique*, or public merchant, in which case she had independent legal rights. The duty of wifely submission was repeatedly reiterated in legal commentaries. That marital power, stated Robert Joseph Pothier, the most celebrated jurist of the eighteenth century, was based in natural law; the wife owed her husband "all the obligations which are due a superior and his authority extended to her person and possessions."[7]

The wife's duty of submission was not, however, rooted in "the weakness of her reason." Married women who needed their husband's authorization were not rationally inferior to single girls and widows, who did not need legal authorization. But in a society where the concept of descending authority was basic, broad marital powers were a logical extension of the contemporary hierarchical premise.

Despite the eighteenth-century obsession with reason, the justification of the theory of the *puissance marital* seemed, at times, to confound logic. Thus, the husband retained his authority even if he went mad. "When the husband falls into a demented state," Pothier commented, "that state being an infirmity which overcomes him without his fault, it must not deprive him of any of his rights, and, consequently, of the right of power which he has over his wife; it alone must not prevent his exercising [his martial authority]."[8] A minor husband had authority over his wife, even if she had attained majority, and separated women were still subject in many ways to the authorization of their husbands. Even if the husband's whereabouts were unknown, the wife could not act legally without authorization, requiring instead a judge's approval. Only if the husband was believed dead could she so act, having then attained the independent status of a widow.[9]

Pothier, reflecting the philosophy of his time and of the legal theorists who preceded him, saw civilized society as a social contract where marriage, "the most excellent and most ancient of all contracts," functioned as the most essential contractual obligation.[10] It was, however, a contract between equals. As such, it imposed mutual obligations on husband and wife. The reciprocal nature of obligations in the areas ruled by French Customary Law limited the husband's marital power. In southern France, where Roman Law prevailed, the husband's power was virtually unbounded; in Pothier's words, "It resembled the power that masters have over their slaves."[11] In contrast, French Customary Law precisely defined the duties of both wife and husband, emphasizing the mutual nature of marital obligations. The wife's place and dignity were protected; in the fundamental theory of contractual organization she yielded sovereignty in the interest of social security, but retained her rights and her responsibilities.

The husband's obligations fell into two major areas. First, the law forbade him to abuse the power that nature and the law itself had given him over his wife and required him to protect and defend her as far as he was able against "insults and injuries and persecutions."[12] Secondly, he had to administer his wife's share of the conjugal property, conserving and augmenting it, in order to insure the economic support he owed her. He was strictly prohibited from frustrating her rightful claims to her share of the community property. The husband was required to love his wife—a term interpreted differently then than it is now—to furnish her with all that was necessary for life to the best of his ability and according to his station, and to bear responsibility for her faults, correcting them in reasonable ways. The law further required that he "have for her a reasonable indulgence, without, however, encouraging her bad habits." Finally, he was obligated to be faithful to her, giving himself to her whenever she demanded it, and abstaining from sexual intercourse with any other woman.[13] Perhaps no provision of eighteenth-century law more clearly revealed the gap between theory and practice than this one.

The community of acquets and gains was a common right in almost all areas of French Customary Law, and a salient aspect of the *Coutume de Paris*. Article 220 of the *Coutume* stated, "Men and women joined together by marriage are common in immovable goods and in the assets acquired during the said marriage."[14] The community began the day of the nuptial benediction; once established, it was immutable and could be neither renounced nor modified by either party. It could, however, be modified or indeed disavowed by mutual contract between afinanced individuals prior to marriage.[15]

The community of goods included antenuptial movables although it did not include immovable property that either party acquired before marriage.[16] Nor did it include property given as gift by marriage contract. Unless renounced by written contract, personal debts fell into the community; the husband as head was held responsible for his wife's debts, even those incurred before marriage, following the ancient adage, "who espouses a woman espouses her debts." The wife, however, was legally responsible for only half her husband's debts.[17] The community remained in existence until the death (natural or civil) of one of the spouses, or until a judicial separation *de corps ou de biens* (of body or of goods). On the dissolution of the community by death of the husband, the wife could accept its continuation or repudiate it, thereby renouncing its debts. The husband did not have the right to renounce the community.[18]

The husband was *seul seigneur* of the community and the goods of which it was composed. As head of the community, he had sole rights of administration with extensive powers of control. Although the law ordered that he administer the property for the good of the conjugal society, legal commentators insisted that his power over the community property was so unrestricted that he could squander it as he pleased without being accountable. A reflection of the growing strength of bourgeois values and bourgeois claims to absolute property rights, Pothier stated of the husband's power of administration, "He can degrade the inheritance, break the moveables, kill through his brutality the horses and other animals belonging to the community without being accountable to his wife for any of these things."[19] The law forbade him, however, to sell, exchange, partition or indebt his wife's personal legacy without her consent. Nor could he contract or obligate her separate property without her consent.[20] Moreover, he could not acquire full rights to her property by marital gift. The law strictly regulated donations between husband and wife, allowing them only when they were mutual gifts. Wives were consequently protected from undue pressure from husbands to bestow by gift their own separate property. At his death, the husband's freedoms to dispose of the community property were sharply curtailed. If there were no children, he could dispose of only half the community property in his will; the other half belonged to his wife. Were there children, his patrimony was divided between his offspring and his widow. His was, then, in essence a usufruct responsibility.[21]

For her part, the wife was obliged to love her husband, submit to him and obey him in everything that was not contrary to God's law. She should work with all her might for the good of the household. She was required to gain her husband's good favor "by her mildness and her pleasing ways," and if, even doing all in her power, she could not please him, she could only oppose her patience to his bad manners and even his bad treatment. As he did her, she owed him physical satisfaction whenever he demanded it, and utter fidelity.[22] Her obligations to the community property were simply defined: she must not interfere in the administration which the law entrusted to her husband; she could, however, dispose of her share of the community goods and her own separate property by will, even should she predecease him.[23]

The *puissance maritale* and the wife's duty of submission required her to live wherever the husband chose. Jean Baptiste Denisart stated that obligation most succinctly: "The woman must live and reside with her husband. It is an obligation imposed on her by natural law and civil law.[24] She could under no circumstance refuse to follow him unless he left the kingdom. As a significant reflection of developing values, French jurists asserted that women owed more to *la patrie* than to their husbands and were not, therefore, obliged to abjure the homeland even if their husbands did. If, however, the wife left the husband's domicile by choice, he could sue her and force her to return. Moreover, he could sue anyone who gave her refuge, even her parents.[25]

From the husband's right to determine domicile, Pothier, with magnificent eighteenth-century logic, concluded that polyandry, but not polygamy, violated natural law. "It is the essence of marriage," he said, "that the wife be subject to her husband and obey him, and follow him wherever he elects to live; but a woman with two husbands at the same time could not obey both when they gave her contrary orders. She could not follow both when they wanted to live in different places. Polyandry is therefore contrary to the nature of marriage and to natural law."[26]

Family stability also dictated that the husband's adultery should be treated differently from that of the wife. His adultery was not legal ground for separation. Hers was, being "more contrary to the good order of civil society since it tends to despoil families and to put possession in the hands of adulterous children who are strangers."[27] Although the wife convicted of adultery lost all her dower rights, her matrimonial privileges, even her *dot*, and could be secluded in a convent for two years, her husband could not punish her with death, as he could under Spanish law. Adultery was considered a private and not a public matter; as Denisart said, it troubled "the order of the household where it is committed rather than the public order."[28]

The law unsurprisingly recognized few grounds for separation; given the fundamental premise that marriage was an indissoluble union essential for a stable society, what is remarkable is that any existed at all. A wife could ask for separation on several grounds: if her husband refused to furnish her the necessities of life; if he falsely accused her of a capital crime; if he openly professed heresy; or if he treated her with extreme cruelty. No illness on the part of the husband, however contagious, provided valid grounds, not even venereal disease, despite the fact that the wife might have strong suspicions that he had "acquired it by his debauchery."[29]

Women could, and did, sue for separation on grounds of ill treatment. In dealing with such a claim, of course, judges had to consider carefully the circumstances because a husband's difficult behavior could and even should be viewed by his wife "as coming on God's order, as a cross sent for the expiation of her sins." Only if the ill treatment threatened "her life, her sanity or her tranquility to such a degree that cohabitation became intolerable," could separation be justified.[30]

In the instance of a woman's second marriage the new husband enjoyed full marital powers over his wife's person, but not over her property. Although the married woman could not "give, alienate, dispose or otherwise contract without the authority of her husband," the property that she brought into the marriage from an earlier union was nevertheless hers by inalienable right.[31] The ownership of separate property gave her a modicum of independence which she could use to manipulate her husband, and undoubtedly frequently did. The protection of women's property rights and the responsibility of the husband for the wife's antenuptial debts meant that the written, legally recorded marriage contract assumed exceptional importance.

Female property rights were not limited to a claim to half of the community property. The *Coutume de Paris,* like most of French Customary Law, prescribed dower rights. The *douaire*, separate from the *dot* which her parents provided her on marriage, was the property claim granted a woman from her husband's personal property for her upkeep and subsistence should she survive him. It gave widows the means of living honorably, according to the station of their dead husbands. As it was an obligatory share of his property, the *douaire* could not be regarded as a donation, which the husband could make of his own volition.[32] It had been originally the price of the bride's virginity; the *Coutume de Normandie* stated bluntly, "The wife earns her dower in bed," and the *Coutume de Paris* said the *douaire* was made by the husband "*in pretium deflorata virginitatis*" (as a price for her deflowered virginity).[33] A case that Pothier cited involved a young Louisiana widow, eleven years and nine months old. Hoping to regain her dower, her deceased husband's heirs challenged the validity of the marriage on the grounds that she was under age. They lost. The young widow proved she was pregnant, the marriage was judged valid, and she was entitled to enjoy her dower and other matrimonial conventions.[34]

According to the *Coutume de Paris* the wife became eligible for a dower as soon as she received the marital blessing, even should her husband fall dead at the door of the church.[35] There were two kinds of dower rights defined by law: the "Conventional," which the contracting parties could themselves negotiate; and the "Customary," which was prescribed. The *Coutume de Paris* defined the customary dower as half the inheritance the husband held the day of the marriage and half of what he might inherit from his parents or other ascendants during the marriage. Lengthy tomes have been written on the *douaire;* its provisions were precisely fixed for second and even third marriages.[36] Its importance underscored the degree to which women were economically protected in French Customary Law.

The economic protections guaranteed women in the *Coutume de Paris* assured, both in France and in the colonies, a shifting basis of female autonomy. Although women were expressly excluded from holding public office, they could wield considerable economic influence. Single women (although few colonial women retained that status for long) could remain legally and financially independent. Widowed women obtained both legal and financial independence and were, like single women, able to administer their property unrestrained by male authority. Even if they remarried, their separate property remained their own and allowed them a considerable psychological measure of freedom from a husband's domination if the woman chose to exercise it. Even married women, while juridically subjected to the *puissance maritale,* could act independently in business (as a *marchande publique)* and retained legal protections which assured them a greater measure of economic security than women of other nationalities enjoyed. The *Coutume de Paris* sanctioned above all the preservation of the patrimony and the preservation of the social order.

The precarious nature of life in eighteenth-century Louisiana meant that the provisions of the law interacted with the exigencies of frontier life to create a society distinct from the mother country and from the English and Spanish colonies. Only a close scrutiny of the surviving records will yield a valid picture of women's experience in the Louisiana colony. Undoubtedly, in a frontier wilderness, the theory which declared the husband *seul seigneur* had less force than a more highly structured, less dangerous milieu. Such a scrutiny will undoubtedly reveal quite a different picture of the economic participation and social influences of women in the colony than has heretofore been portrayed in the Louisiana historical literature.

Notes for "*Le Mari est Seigneur*: Marital Laws Governing Women in French Louisiana"

---

[1] See, for example, Rodolfo Batiza, "The Louisiana Civil Code of 1808: Its Actual Sources and Present Relevance," *Tulane Law Review*, 46 (1971): 4-165; and Robert A. Pascal, "Sources of the Digest of 1808: A Reply to Professor Batiza," *Tulane Law Review*, 46 (1972): 603-27. See also "Community Property: Symposium on Equal Rights," *Tulane Law Review*, 48 (1974): 560-617.

[2] Henry Plauché Dart, "The Legal Institutions of Louisiana: French Period," *Louisiana Historical Quarterly*, 2 (1919): 72-103.

[3] Eustache-Nicolas Pigeau, born at Mont-Leveque near Senlis in 1750, became Professor of Civil and Criminal Procedure at the University of Paris in 1814. The son of simple artisans, Pigeau began the study of law in his early teens as a clerk in the office of *procureur*. From the age of seventeen he laid the foundations for his classic work, *Practicien du Châtelet de Paris et de toutes les jurisdictions ordinaires du royaume,* published in Paris in 1773, reprinted in 1779-1787 with numerous additions as *La Procédure du Châtelet de Paris et de*

toutes les juridictions ordinaires du royaume. Pigeau was the first to study methodically the precedents of practice at the Châtelet de Paris, the most important court of justice in the kingdom next to the *Parlement*. He served as an *avocat* of the *Parlement de Paris* from 1774. Conservative and fiercely dedicated to order in society, he deplored the excesses of the French Revolution and assisted in drafting the Napoleonic Code. He died on December 22, 1818. *Société de Gens de Lettres et de Savants, Biographie Universelle Ancienne et Moderne,* 33 (Paris, 1832): 307-8.

[4]Eustache-Nicolas Pigeau, *La Procédure Civile de Châtelet de Paris et de toutes les juridictions ordinaires du royaume, démontrée par principes et mise en action par des formules,* 2 (Paris, 1787): 175-76.

[5]According to Tacitus, Germanic women enjoyed extensive legal, social and frequently military equality with their men, even accompanying them in battle and in the hunt. "The wife . . . is warned . . . that she comes to share hard work and peril; that her fate will be the same as his in peace and in battle, her risks the same." Tacitus, *Germania,* M. Hutton, trans., *Tacitus in Five Volumes,* 1 (Cambridge, Mass., 1970): 159. Other sources, however, indicate a considerably more inferior status for women among Germanic tribes. Lombard and Saxon law, for example, viewed women as perpetual minors under male guardianship. Male permission was necessary in any transfer of property. Paradoxically, Roman law, intrinsically harsh in its provisions concerning women, liberalized the laws of some Teutonic tribes. Visigothic law, after exposure to Roman law, allowed joint administration by husband and wife of either's separate property, considered gains acquired after marriage community property, permitted the wife control of the family property and the inheritance of minor children if the husband died, and dictated equal inheritance rights for boys and girls. Frances and Joseph Gies, *Women in the Middle Ages* (New York, 1978), 15-18.

[6]M. Charles Giraud, *Précis de L'ancien Droit coutumier français* (Paris, 1852), 15; Claude de Ferrière, *Nouveau commentaire sur la Coutume de la Prévôté et Vicomté de Paris* (Paris, 1719), 30; Robert Joseph Pothier, *Traité de la Communauté* (Paris, 1819), Part 2, Art. 1, no., 471, par. 259.

[7]Giraud, *L'Ancien Droit,* 15-16; Pothier, ibid., Part 1, Art. 1, no. 1; *Traité des Personnes et des Choses,* Part 1, Title 6, Sec. 1, 128, Vol. 9 in Robert Joseph Pothier, *Oeuvres de Pothier,* 10 vols. (Paris, 1845-1848); M. Argou, *Institution au Droit Français* (Paris, 1771), 201.

[8]Pothier, *Traité de la Puissance de Mari,* Part 1, Art. 1, sec. 1, Par. 3; Part 1, Art. 1. sec. 2, par. 23-28, pp. 10-12.

[9]Ibid., Part 1, Art. 1, See. 2, pp. 7-12.

[10]Pothier, *Traité de Contract du Mariage,* Vol. 6, Part 1, p. 337; Pigeau, *Procédure Civile,* 236. Jean-Louis Flandrin points out that the family as an institution was seen as a civil or public society and that kinship relationships served as a model for all social and political structures. The king's authority and the father's authority were closely identified. *Families in Former Times: Kingship, Household and Sexuality in Early Modern France* (Cambridge, 1979), 1-8.

[11]Pothier, *Traité des Personnes et des Choses, Oeuvres Complets,* Vol. 9, Part 1, Art. 4, See. 2, no. 129.

[12]Pigeau, *Procédure Civile,* 175.

[13]Pothier, *Traité du Contrat du Mariage,* 7:176; Pigeau, *Procédure Civile,* 176.

[14]Ferrière, *Commentaire sur la Coutume de Paris,* Art. 220, p. 5. Except in the *Coutumes* of Normandy and Riems, the community of goods established between spouses was a common right in all areas of the customary law. Giraud, *L'Ancien Droit,* 61; Denis Le Brun, *Traité de la communauté entre mari et femme avec un Traité des communautéz ou sociétz tacites* (Paris, 1754), 41-50.

[15]Ibid., 3-5.

[16]"Movables" included debts, rents, and all obligations as well as those goods commonly considered moveable such as furniture, domestic animals, etc. Ferrière, *Commentaire sur la Coutume de Paris,* 6; Le Brun, *Traité de la Communauté entre mari et femme,* 57-59.

[17]Article 221, *Coutume de Paris,* in La Ferrière, ibid., 9; Giraud, *L'Ancien Droit Français,* 63-64. The obligations of the community for antenuptial debts and the right to modify the community property system by pre-marriage agreement meant that marriage contracts assumed major importance. Standard form for marriage contracts in pre-revolutionary France included a clause disclaiming antenuptial debts. Virtually all

marriage contracts examined in Paris in the eighteenth century contained this disclaimer. In practice, therefore, the matrimonial regimes of eighteenth-century France were more frequently determined by marriage contract than by the precise stipulations of the community property laws. See Hans W. Baade, "Marriage Contracts in French and Spanish Louisiana: A Study in 'Notarial' Jurisprudence," *Tulane Law Review*, 53 (1978), 15-18. Claude Ferrière stated that the marriage contract was "the most important transaction made between individuals." Ferrière, *Commentaire de la Coutume de Paris*, 13. The marriage contract could not, however, stipulate that a woman could alienate her separate property without the consent of her husband nor could the husband renounce the *puissance maritale*. Denisart stated that "this would be contrary to the dependence of the wife on the husband," contrary to the welfare of the conjugal community, and contrary to "good manners." Jean Baptist Denisart, *Collection de décisions nouvelles et de notions relatives à la jurisprudence* (Paris, 1788), 708.

[18]Giraud, *L'Ancien Droit Français*, 65; Ferrière, *Commentaire sur la Coutume de Paris*, 62, Art. 237.

[19]Pothier, *Traité de la Communauté*, Part 2, Art. 1, Sec. 470, p. 259.

[20]Ferrière, *Commentaire sur la Coutume de Paris*, Art. 226, p. 33; Art. 228, p. 37; Pothier, *Traité de la Communauté*, Part 2, Art. 1, sec. 261; Giraud, *L'Ancien Droit Français*, 64.

[21]Pothier, *Traité de la Communauté*, 7:261; Ferrière, *Commentaire sur la Coutume de Paris*, 54.

[22]Pothier, *Traité du Contrat de Mariage*, 6:175; 7:235.

[23]Pigeau, *Procédure Civile*, 176; Ferrière, *Commentaire sur la Coutume de Paris*, Art. 228, pp. 24-25.

[24]Denisart, *Decisions Nouvelles*, 543.

[25]Pothier, *Traité de la Puissance du Mari*, Part 1, Art. 1, par. 1, pp. 1-2; *Traité du Contrat de Mariage*, 6:175.

[26]Pothier, *Traité du Contrat de Mariage*, Vol. 6:43.

[27]Ibid., 7:238.

[28]Denisart, *Decisions Nouvelles*, 266; Jean-François Fournel, *Traité de l'adultère, considéré dans l'ordre judiciare* (Paris, 1778), 10-12.

[29]Pothier, *Traité du Contrat de Mariage*, 7:237; Giraud, *L'Ancien Droit Français*, 16-18.

[30]Pothier, *Traité de Personnes et des Choses*, Part 1, Title 6, Sec. 2, no. 132, pp. 236-37; Pigeau, *Procédure Civile*, 238.

[31]Pothier, *Traité de la Puissance du Mari*, Part 1, Art. 1, par. 2, p. 2.

[32]Pothier, *Traité du Douaire*, 318-24.

[33]Ferrière, *Commentaire sur la Coutume de Paris*, Art. 237, pp. 114-15.

[34]Pothier, *Traité du Douaire*, 39-40.

[35]*Coutume de Paris*, Art. 248, in Ferrière, *Commentaire sur la Coutume de Paris*, Giraud, *L'Ancien Droit Français*, 70.

[36]*Coutume de Paris*, Art. 237, in Ferrière, *Commentaire sur la Coutume de Paris*, 114. Roman law did not recognize dower rights, which were unguaranteed as well in the areas of southern France where the influence of Roman law prevailed. The tradition of the *douaire* derived from Germanic tribal custom and was limited to the regions regulated by customary law.

FAMILY AND KINSHIP DEVELOPMENT ON THREE LOUISIANA PLANTATIONS*

Ann Patton Malone

A progressive trend toward family and kinship development is apparent in the household analysis of Oakland, Petite Anse, and Tiger Island slaves, from the foundation of their permanent slave force to their last full inventory before emancipation. Once more, the vulnerability of slave domestic organization is revealed. In both migration communities the trauma of separation from prior family and kin networks was overcome with difficulty. After two decades during which slaves built new family and kindred ties at [Walter] Brashear's home plantations, the start-up of Tiger Island with transferred and newly purchased slaves set back family and kinship development there and exacted a cost in social stability. At Oakland, estate divisions dispersed family and kinship groups twice. Kinship developed fairly naturally only at Petite Anse, and it was there that family and kinship networks were most pervasive in 1860.

Each slave community's persistence in forming family units (an inclination that grew stronger as the years passed) demonstrates its high regard for family and kinship. The great value that slaves placed on family and kin was recognized, if not always respected, by their owners. This is particularly apparent at Oakland and Petite Anse, where the owners made concerted efforts to keep family groups intact and, through purchases, to maintain a viable marriage pool. Even at Tiger Island, the owners' forwarding of messages between the Kentucky migrants and their relations in Bardstown and Lexington shows that they recognized the intensity and durability of the ties between separated slave kin.

Oakland Many of the early workers at Oakland married and quickly began families, but that bright beginning was dimmed by Nathaniel Evans's death and estate partition in 1822. Some kinsmen were separated, and other entire families were removed from the plantation and area (such as Peter, Rhoda, and their children, who left no kin behind at

---

*From *Sweet Chariot: Slave Family and Household Structure in Nineteenth-Century Louisiana* by Ann Patton Malone. Copyright © 1992 by the University of North Carolina Press. Used by permission of the publisher.

Family and Kinship

Oakland).[1] As they sought to rebuild their fractured workforce, Sarah and John N. Evans bought many young, unattached slaves in the 1830s and 1840s, and this contingent produced most of the families that were present in 1857.[2] By 1850, Oakland's slave community was as strong and stable as it would ever be. Family formation and kinship development would have been extremely intricate by 1860 if it had not been disrupted by the estate division following the death of Sarah Evans in 1851.[3] This division again separated Oakland slaves from a bevy of relatives. The division hit the oldest kin groups hardest; most of the new families had been bought by John Evans, and they were directly affected only if they had intermarried with Sarah Evans's slaves.[4]

As in 1822, the ordeal was greatest for the slaves inherited by the DeHart's, who were transferred to the ill-fated Orange Grove Plantation in St. Mary Parish, where they would have little or no opportunity to interact with their friends and families in West Feliciana.[5] The transfer to the Attakapas must have been particularly difficult for the family of Henry and Charity, who were members of one of the earliest and largest kinship groups of Oakland. Charity had been a child among Nathaniel Evans's early workers, the daughter of Nancy and Jerry, whom Evans had owned since 1809. Charity's father, Jerry, was twenty in 1814 and already married to seventeen-year-old Nancy. They had at that time an infant daughter, Phoebe, who died early. Two more daughters were born by 1817—Charity and Ellen. Both lived to marry and have their own families at Oakland. Jerry died in the 1830s, but Nancy lived to raise two orphan girls, Susannah and Kitty.[6]

Jerry's widow, Nancy, her four daughters, and their families were greatly affected by the 1852 estate division. One daughter, Charity, her husband, and their children were drawn by the DeHarts. Nancy and two of her other daughters, Kitty (adopted) and Ellen (along with Ellen's children) were drawn by John Evans and remained at Oakland. The remaining daughter, Susannah (adopted), and her husband and children were drawn by Francis Evans. John Evans soon traded the mother, Nancy, and the youngest adopted daughter, Kitty, to the DeHart heirs in exchange for several slaves who were married to his workers.[7] It is not known whether he was also accommodating the wishes of Nancy, Charity, and Kitty, who might have wanted to stay together even if they all had to leave Oakland. In any case, Nancy moved away from Oakland at the age of fifty-four, leaving in West Feliciana two daughters, several grandchildren, and a lifetime's accumulation of friends and memories. At Orange Grove, however, she would be with her daughter Charity, her son-in-law Henry, her adopted daughter Kitty, and nine grandchildren.

With the departure of Charity, Henry, and their children, Oakland lost a vital branch of two old and respected kinship lines. Charity's husband, Henry, was the offspring of original Oakland slaves, Jacob and Hannah, who had, in addition to Henry, at least one daughter and four other sons.[8] Surviving members of Henry's family remained in West Feliciana, the property of the two Evans brothers. Henry and Charity's marriage had been very productive. By 1851, they had nine healthy children ranging in age from six months to eighteen years, the youngest named Jacob, for Henry's long-deceased father. Family and kin obviously meant a great deal to the couple, for they named two more of their children for grandparents: Little Nancy and Little Jerry, for Charity's parents.

Even at Orange Grove, Charity and Henry's family was not impervious to further separations. The appraised value of their large family unit was $3,675 in 1851, far more than the value of the other single family units inherited by the DeHarts. To effect an equal distribution, Henry and Charity's immediate family was further divided among the four DeHarts. Henry and Charity formed a lot with their four children under the age of ten, as required by Louisiana law. They and fourteen-year-old Charles Henry were allotted to Louisa DeHart. Sarah DeHart drew two other sons—Albert and Jerry—as well as their grandmother Nancy and aunt Kitty. The remaining children (Willis and Joice) were drawn by Dr. John DeHart. The legal separation on paper did not necessarily involve physical separation; they were all initially sent to Orange Grove. But Sarah DeHart married a Mississippi planter shortly thereafter, and it is not known whether she took her slaves with her.[9] The transfer of Henry and Charity, their children, Charity's mother, and her younger sister separated parents from grown children and grandchildren and divided siblings, as well as a host of aunts, uncles, and cousins from both Charity's and Henry's lines.

It is true that Henry and Charity's family was not thrust in the midst of utter strangers because Orange Grove was originally peopled with Oakland slaves. Henry and Charity might have dimly remembered some Orange Grove slaves with whom they had played as children at Oakland. And Nancy would have been well acquainted with Peter, Rhoda, Harry, and Liddy with whom she and Jerry had picked cotton as high-spirited teenagers. But only Harry and Liddy were still at Orange Grove in 1852 to greet their old friends from Oakland. They had six daughters and six grandchildren on the plantation, although their firstborn, Manuel, was among those executed in 1841 for the murder of Captain DeHart. Nancy's close friends Peter and Rhoda were dead or sold, for an 1854 listing shows not a single member of their family left on the plantation. Two of the sons, Carlos and Booker, were among those executed; what happened to the others is not known. Maria—the mother of Billy, the alleged ringleader in the murder of DeHart—never remarried after the sale of her husband, but she eventually had two more daughters by an unknown father. By 1854 she headed her own household, which included two grandchildren, at Orange Grove. She, too, would have been there to help ease the adjustment of Nancy, Charity, and Henry, although her own experience in St. Mary could hardly have encouraged them.[10]

Nancy's other daughter, Ellen, and her sizable family remained at Oakland, but Susannah, her husband, and two children were sent to Francis Evans's plantation.[11] For Susannah, separated from her sisters and mother and the children from their maternal grandmother, her closest kin at her new home, except for her husband and children, was her brother-in-law's mother, Hannah. Of Hannah's once large family, only Henry—now at Orange Grove—and her youngest daughter, Retty, remained. Retty, twenty-six, was also at Francis Evans's place, as was Hannah's four-year-old grand-daughter and namesake, Little Retty.[12]

Another example of family and kin separated by Sarah Evans's estate division was Gunny and Vicy, who, with their nineteen-year-old son Washington, were inherited by Francis Evans and removed from Oakland. Both were part of Oakland's earliest labor force. Vicy had her daughter Mima at the age of seventeen, but she remained unmarried for about ten years. By 1834, she and Gunny had married and were parents of two-year-old Washington. By the 1840s, Vicy's daughter Mima had married a new purchase, John Briton, and had started her own family with a daughter named Vicy after her grandmother. They would eventually have many more children. Mima, her husband, and children would remain at Oakland after the estate division, whereas her mother and stepfather became the property of Francis Evans and were transferred to his estate, which was, fortunately, close enough to Oakland to allow for occasional visits.[13]

There are only a few of the Oakland family and kinship groups that were disrupted by estate divisions. Scarcely a family was not affected. Kinship was so advanced among the older Oakland residents by 1851 that it would have been difficult to make a division that did not sever parents from adult children and grandchildren or separate adult siblings and their families from each other. Although separation of kinsmen beyond the standard nuclear family was perhaps less traumatic than separation of spouses or parents and minor children, it was nevertheless extremely painful. Owners often commented upon the sadness of parents whose nearly grown children were sold or transferred.

The Oakland community continued to be family based, but another generation would pass before kinship would be as extensive as before. Most of the families present at the last inventory in 1857 were headed by individuals who had been purchased by John Evans in the 1830s and 1850s as part of the rebuilding process after his father's demise. The new purchases intermarried extensively; only a few married offspring of the original laborers. By 1857 they were in their late thirties or forties and had large and growing families that would soon reach marriageable ages. Among these couples were John Briton and Mima, Peter Barlow and Ailsy, Jim and Jane West, and Peter Murphy and Susan. Thanks to Evans's timely purchases, kinship would soon flourish anew at Oakland. But for the slaves at Oakland belonging to the original kin groups whose relations were dispersed between three holdings, this was little consolation.

Petite Anse Some of the laborers brought to Petite Anse from New Jersey and New York by William Stone and John Marsh founded major kinship groups with lines extending until 1860, but these generally resulted from unions with nonmigration slaves. The strongest kinship groups present in the last recorded inventory were produced by slaves brought into the labor force during the 1820s and 1830s. Therefore, even when estate divisions did not result in the exodus of many slaves, the kinship networks of the earliest generation appear to have been less vigorous than those produced by later unions.

Peter was one of the few New Jersey slaves to found a lasting kinship line on Petite Anse. He was bought as a boy of eleven or twelve in 1818 and appeared as a twenty-year-old solitaire on the 1826 inventory. In 1827 he married nineteen-year-old Milly, who had been purchased the year before from a New Orleans slave dealer. By 1836 they had five children: John, Mary Ann, Jerry, Margaret, and Peter, Jr.[14]

In 1854 Peter and Milly had been married for about twenty-seven years. Their household consisted of Mary Ann, Jerry, Margaret, and Peter, Jr., as well as three additional children born since the previous inventory: Henrietta, Dave, and Jane. In addition to their own children, Peter and Milly's household also contained a two-year-old grandchild, Catherine, the daughter of Mary Ann, who was unmarried.[15]

Peter and Milly still appear as a married couple on the 1860 inventory. Most of their children, including some with spouses, are listed directly after them, although they were appraised separately. Whether these grown children and their families lived with their parents cannot be determined because no cabin lists have survived. But it is certain that they were considered part of a kinship group headed by Peter and Milly and formed part of their multiple family household. Old Pete (as he was now called) and Milly headed a large clan, which included single daughters Margaret, Jane, and Mary Ann along with Mary Ann's two children; Henrietta and her husband, Allen, and their two sons; and Dave and Peter, Jr. Another son, Jerry (along with his wife and children), appears elsewhere on the inventory, as part of the multiple family household of his wife's parents, Gus and Arena.[16]

Peter is a prime example of a migration slave who intermarried with a new purchase, had a long marriage, and promulgated a major kinship group on the island. By 1860 three generations of his line were present on Petite Anse, many of whom formed a portion of his large, sprawling household.

In many ways, however, Peter is exceptional. The most enduring family and kin groups at Petite Anse emanated from slaves bought in Louisiana. For example, Sylvia was the progenitor of one family still present on the island in 1860. She had been bought from a New Orleans trader on April 20, 1826, when she was twenty-two and pregnant.[17] In 1836 she was the still unmarried head of a household that contained her two sons, John Congo and George (also called Roy), and two daughters, Effy and Mary Ann. By 1839, she had married Edmund, ten years younger than she, who had been bought between 1836 and 1838.[18] Edmund and Sylvia had no known children together. She had died by 1854, as had her daughter Mary Ann. Her sons, John Congo and Roy, were still at Petite Anse, as solitaires. Effy was either in New Iberia or was mistakenly left off the 1854 inventory, for she reappears on the 1860 list as the young wife of a former widower. Roy also appears on the 1860 inventory as the husband of the sixteen-year-old daughter of John and Maria Houston. John Congo is not listed on the 1860 inventory, but he had not died, for he alone among Sylvia's descendants was listed among the freedmen having a credit account with Petite Anse owners in 1867.[19]

Family and Kinship

Sawney [McCall] was another purchase from the 1820s who founded a major kinship group on Petite Anse. He was bought by Stone and Marsh at the estate sale of Jesse McCall in St. Martin Parish, December 23, 1824.[20] Portions of Petite Anse Plantation were purchased by Stone and Marsh from McCall, and Sawney may have been born on the island. If so, he was the only known member of the early slave force with previous ties to the plantation. Sawney married Maria about 1833 or 1834, possibly earlier. In 1836 they had a daughter, Betsy Ann, and another daughter, Sarah, was born by 1839. In 1854 Sawney and Maria's household consisted of themselves, Betsy Ann and Sarah, now in their upper teens, and two-year-old Lucy. An additional daughter, Fanny, was born in 1860. By that year Betsy had married Gus and Arena's son Bob and had produced a grandchild for Sawney and Maria. The eldest daughter, Sarah, was married to John and Maria Houston's son Tom, and they had a four-year-old daughter, Rosana.

Along with Cane and Gus, Sawney was one of the acknowledged leaders of the Petite Anse slave community. He and many of his progeny continued to work on Petite Anse after emancipation.[21]

The most extensive kinship group on the island in 1860 was formed by one of the few families that had been purchased as a group in the 1820s, Augustus or Gus, his wife, Arena, and their nine-month-old daughter Fanny, bought together in Adams County, Mississippi, on May 19, 1827.[22] In 1836, Gus, the plantation's blacksmith, lived with Arena and their sons Foster, Bob, and Little Gus. The eldest daughter had died by 1839, but another daughter, Celia, had been born. By 1854 Gus and Arena, both in their forties, had six children, including three grown sons and three daughters. In addition to Celia, the daughters were Rachel and Lavenia, both born since the previous inventory. The family proliferated, and in 1860 it consisted of Gus, Arena, their youngest daughters, Rachel and Lavenia, and their son Gus, now twenty-two. Listed consecutively and forming part of a solid kinship grouping were Foster, Bob, and Celia, along with their spouses and children. With their parents' households, these young families formed part of a large multiple family household unit.[23]

One of the most unusual families emanating from the 1820s purchases was that of Harriet. Described in her bill of sale as an eighteen-year-old mulatto, Harriet was bought by William Stone from a Charles County, Maryland, planter on November 17, 1823.[24] She served as a maid or cook for the Marsh family for the remainder of her life.

Harriet and "her children," Ben, Lizzie, and John Henry, are all mentioned in a family record of house servants at Petite Anse.[25] Ben was Harriet's very light-skinned son by an unnamed local white man. He was born after 1826 but before 1836, for he appears on the latter inventory with his mother, Harriet, although his age is not stated.[26] Northern-born Marsh disapproved of both concubinage and the casual sexual freedom that many Louisiana white men took with attractive slave women; therefore, I do not believe that Ben was an illegitimate offspring of the Marsh family. Marsh may not have known who Ben's father was, but he did have unusual compassion for the "neither black nor white" children of his slave community, and he took a special interest in the boy. Ben was kept in New Iberia most of his youth and was trained as a house servant. Eventually, Marsh freed him. For that reason, Ben usually does not appear on subsequent inventories with his mother, although they kept in close contact.[27]

In 1839 Harriet was enumerated in a household consisting of herself, her slave husband, William, and a one-year-old daughter Elizabeth, whom they called Lizzie.[28] Lizzie was the only one of Harriet's children who had a slave father. William died in the early 1840s, and Harriet eventually bore another son by a white man whom Marsh identified only as "Hoyt." That child, John Henry, may have been reared in Harriet's home during his early years, but he, like his half-brother Ben, was not enumerated with the other slaves because he was marked for eventual manumission.[29] The 1854 inventory of Petite Anse slaves mentions only Harriet and her daughter Lizzie, omitting both boys. Trained as her mother's helper, Lizzie would eventually replace Harriet as the cook at Petite Anse. Harriet was no longer listed on the 1860 Petite Anse inventory, but Lizzie was, along with her husband, Butler, and their two-year-old daughter Cora.[30]

Harriet's two mulatto sons were of constant concern to Marsh and his family. In 1856, John Marsh signed a document manumitting John Henry, stating that "Hoyt," John Henry's "reputed father," had paid for his son's freedom by the "building of a sailboat for me called Little Red." Hoyt apparently had some occasional business dealings with Marsh, perhaps on short-term contracts as a carpenter or overseer. In a letter of 1845 George Marsh had written his father about plantation matters and incidentally mentioned that "Hoyt is in N Orleans." In the 1856 manumission document, Marsh stated that the "boy John Henry is now in the charge of my son George Marsh." But two days before, Marsh had written George to tell him that Casimere Pinta "informed me this morning that he had got a good place for John Henry to get his schooling. . . in the city [New Orleans]." Marsh was obviously willing to undertake the cost of tuition and boarding for the boy, but John Henry—if he ever did attend school in New Orleans—returned to Petite Anse. His name was among those in the freedmen account records for the plantation in 1866-67.[31]

Harriet's oldest son, Ben, married Georgianna, the young daughter of Maria Houston, by 1850. In 1853 Georgianna lived with her two small children in the household of her mother and stepfather, but Ben was in Rahway Township, New Jersey, with his old master, John Marsh, who was attempting to find occupational training and a degree of acceptance for the young man. In a letter of May 16, 1853, Margaret Marsh Henshaw wrote her father in New Jersey, asking him to "tell Ben that his Mother [Harriet] is now with me [in New Iberia] on a visit of pleasure, she is well and sends her love to him. Lizzy [Ben's half-sister] is confined to her bed with measles. His baby [with Georgianna] is well and the very image of him—I sincerely hope that Ben is ere this put to a trade, he will never be worth one cent until he is made to work and earn a living." A month later Marsh wrote back that he had been unsuccessful in placing Ben in New Jersey. "Ben is now in sight mowing. . . . I shall probably send him back . . . as he cannot be placed here at a trade with comfort to himself as he is neither white nor black and would become the butt of the other apprentices."[32]

Ben returned to Petite Anse and was emancipated by the same 1856 document that freed John Henry. In that document Marsh provided that Ben, his "servant boy," would become free on April 1, 1859. Marsh informed his heirs in that same record that Ben had agreed to pay fifteen dollars per month in the three-year interval before his emancipation became effective. It appears that in the interim Ben was allowed to hire out his own time or was paid wages by the family.[33] During the three-year period, Ben was to be supervised by William Robertson, the husband of Marsh's daughter Eliza.

Ben's emancipation was effective in 1859 so he is not listed as a slave on the 1860 inventory. But his wife, Georgianna, appears, along with their five children, including an infant son who was named Ben for his father.[34] Both Ben and Georgianna remained family servants for many years.[35] Despite John Marsh's efforts in their behalf, Ben and John Henry were not able to make lives for themselves off the plantation. Since a stigma against mulattoes should not have prevented their assimilation in to at least some respectable trades in New Orleans, one might suspect that family ties were equally important in drawing Ben and John Henry back to Petite Anse.

Harriet's daughter Lizzie was strong-willed and independent, causing frequent clashes with the overseer, but she was a family favorite. During her mother's temporary absence in 1854, Lizzie was left in charge of the house servants at Petite Anse, although she was only seventeen.[36] Daniel Avery, the attorney husband of Sarah Marsh, wrote of problems with Lizzie at Petite Anse in a letter to his wife in Baton Rouge: "'Jim' [the overseer] yesterday told me for the first time that during my absence he had much trouble with 'Lizzy' who was either at the Millers or had my household full of his Negroes, & that was the way the fowls were stolen & my Bridle missing & unless some steady woman was placed to stay with him & Lizzie sent away he would not stay after I left, as he could not control her."[37] Despite the overseer's low opinion of Lizzie, she matured unto a very responsible woman. She married William Butler, and both are mentioned in the Avery papers as esteemed family servants of long duration.[38]

During the 1830s Marsh expanded his Petite Anse slave force and replaced deceased members, buying as many females as males. There were only two children under age eleven among his 1826 contingent, and he was sensitive to the value of a labor force that could reproduce itself. One woman Marsh bought about 1833 is noteworthy in two respects. She became the progenitor of a large family of Petite Anse slaves, and she left an informative account of her journey from Norfolk, Virginia, to New Orleans as a newly purchased slave. The woman was Maria, generally referred to as Big Maria before her marriage to John Houston to distinguish her from several other Marias on Petite Anse. Big Maria was part of a group of slaves purchased by Marsh from the cargo of the *Ajax*, a coastal slavetrading vessel.[39] She often related the story of her voyage to Louisiana, and it was transcribed by an Avery family member when Maria was in her seventies. She and her fellow slaves sailed from Norfolk to New Orleans aboard the *Ajax* on a journey that she said took two months. Before her sale, Maria and her brother Thornton were owned by Henry Phillips of Fredericksburg, Virginia. Her brother remained on Phillip's farm, but Maria was sold to a trader, separated from her only kin, and crowded aboard a ship bound for the lower South. On the long, painful voyage from Norfolk to New Orleans, "when the wind failed," Captain Bangs would "call out the fiddler," making the women dance "to start the breeze," according to Maria. When revenue officers came aboard the ship to check credentials, a frightened young Maria believed them to be pirates. And as the ship finally neared the crowded port of New Orleans, she saw a massive "poplar grove," mistaking the masts of sailing vessels docked at the port for the familiar slender, silvered trunks of poplar trees of her home. Maria's story may have been embellished by time, but it indicates that her transportation to Louisiana as slave cargo was both a terrifying and adventuresome experience for a naive eighteen-year-old girl who had probably never been off her master's farm.[40]

The 1836 Petite Anse inventory listed Maria as a single parent, heading a household that included her children Francis, Perry, and Evelina or Vina.[41] Vina was Maria's daughter by a William Hudson, a white man. At Vina's birth in 1835, John Marsh had agreed to emancipate the child when she reached the age of twenty-one, according to the terms of a bargain struck with Hudson, her "reputed father," who paid him $100.[42] Until she reached that age, Marsh put Vina in charge of his grandson John Marsh Henshaw. Vina remained with the Henshaws in New Iberia and does not appear on subsequent Petite Anse inventories with her mother, Maria. As Marsh had promised William Hudson, Vina was emancipated in 1856.

Maria was still single in 1839. Her household included Francis, Tom (the same person as Perry), and an infant daughter Georgianna. By 1844 she had married John Houston, who had been purchased at a public auction in New Orleans in 1837 and was single before his marriage to Maria. Houston, a highly skilled brick mason, was among the most valuable of Petite Anse's slaves.

By 1854 Maria's family and household were drastically altered. Both Maria and her husband were in their forties. They headed a fourteen-member multiple family grouping. Francis and Tom, now young adults, remained part of their stepfather's and mother's household, as did Georgianna and her two small children fathered by Ben, Marsh's mulatto servant. Maria had borne another daughter, Maria, Jr., shortly after the 1839 inventory. John Houston was the likely father, although they were not yet married. In 1854, Maria, Jr., now fourteen, had a newborn infant by an unknown father. Both resided in the household of John and Maria. The exact year of John and Maria's marriage is not known, but Maria's last five children, all enumerated on the 1854 inventory, were John's.[43]

In 1860, the multiple family household headed by John and Maria Houston had increased to eighteen members and included four nuclear families. John and Maria and their five younger children formed one family. Maria's son Tom, his wife, and their daughter formed a second. John and Maria's oldest daughter, Helen, and her husband, Roy, formed the third. The last of the multiple family components was formed by

Maria's daughter Georgianna, the wife of Ben, now manumitted, and their five children. Maria, Jr., was now regarded as a twenty-one-old solitaire because she had apparently lost the baby (named Vena after Maria, Jr.'s, sister) born to her in 1854. She no longer resided with John and Maria.⁴⁴

Some members of John and Maria Houston's family remained associated with the plantation for half a century. In the 1866-67 accounts listing freedmen appear the names of John and Maria Houston, their son William Houston, and their daughters Rebecca and Matilda, the latter having married one of the sons of Peter and Milly Stephens.⁴⁵ Georgianna and her husband, Ben Keller, remained Avery family servants. Maria, Jr., also remained a house servant after emancipation and eventually married Aaron from a nearby plantation. Of the family, at least Maria Houston was still alive and with the Avery family in 1883.⁴⁶

Petite Anse's owners purchased other slaves in the 1830s, but one that had particular impact on the subsequent development of the slave community was a group bought by Marsh at an estate sale in Pointe Coupée Parish in 1838.⁴⁷ Among them was John Pierre, his wife, Aime, and their daughter Clemence. John Pierre had died by 1854, but Aime (now Americanized to Amy), headed a household that included Clemence and her two children Emile, two, and an infant, Rosana.⁴⁸ In 1860, Amy lived as a solitaire. Clemence was married to Gus and Arena's son Foster, and in their household lived Emile, her child before marriage, and three additional children, one of whom was named Foster for his father.⁴⁹ Among the same group of slaves bought at the Pointe Coupée estate sale was Fannie, forty-nine, and her fifteen-year-old daughter Mary Ann. Both were house servants, and Margaret Marsh Henshaw took Mary Ann as her particular charge. A lively girl who soon attracted many suitors, Mary Ann often proved to be a challenge for her mistress. Margaret Henshaw's siblings made amused comments on her apparent difficulties in dealing with Mary Ann and her admirers. In a June 1845 letter George Marsh told his sister Margaret that "Mary Ann has become quite a bug—has already had three proposals and receives a *killing* . . . glance from every passing *Buck*." Also in 1845, Sarah Avery asked her brother George on Petite Anse, "How does Mary Ann flourish. I hope you will keep a strict watch over her on Margarets account for she has had too much trouble with her to lose her now entirely." She further commented that Mary Ann was "naturally bad enough. I never saw anyone but Margaret that could begin to find her in her sly capers."⁵⁰

By 1854 Mary Ann was living in the household of her mother, Fanny, with a five-year-old son George. Sadly, by 1860 the once sprightly Mary Ann was permanently bedridden, unmarried, and still the mother of only one son.⁵¹

The major kinship groups of the Petite Anse slave community in the 1854-60 period were formed from the slaves present before 1840—mainly those just discussed in detail. But throughout the decades of the 1840s and 1850s Marsh and his sons-in-law continued to buy young slaves, some of whom married into the old kinship groups by 1860. Because of a staggering death rate, the owners were not able to sustain a healthy rate of increase, and the work force reproduced itself only in the first generation. Largely through the constant infusion of young purchases of both genders, however, the owners provided nonrelated potential mates for the children of the early slave residents as well as vigorous young workers for the sugar operation.

Tiger Island Many of Tiger Island's slaves were severed from prior kinship connections twice—by the migration from Kentucky to Louisiana and by the start-up of an additional plantation in the late 1830s and early 1840s. Despite these and other disruptive actions taken by the Brashears, the Tiger Island slave community continually sought to attain a society defined by family and kinship. In their quest, the slaves overcame many obstacles, beginning with those connected with the migration process. The Walter Brashear family repeated a common pattern among slaveholders relocating in the lower South. Planters and farmers migrating to the fertile and inexpensive lands of the Southwest usually brought with them only the younger and more choice slaves, later fleshing out their work forces through purchases and trades, replacing the migration slaves who failed to acclimate and died early or those that could not adapt to the new work expectations. The old slave community was almost always dissolved by the migration. The generation of slaves who were severed from their birthplaces and most of their kin (certainly parents, grandparents, aunts, uncles, and cousins, and often siblings, spouses and older children as well) suffered protracted periods of grief and homesickness. Although they understood it was unlikely, migration slaves nevertheless cherished hopes of going back to Kentucky, Virginia, Maryland, Georgia, or the Carolinas to see the old home place once more and to be reunited with lost kinsmen and childhood friends.[52] Migrating white families endured similar periods of displacement and adjustment, but the planter class was often able to maintain ties with its former home and distant relatives through correspondence and occasional visits.

For migration slaves, the pain of separation subsided very slowly, as families and then communities began to form. By the second or third generation at the new plantation, kin networks were usually sufficiently developed to provide a web of security and stability around individual members of the community. Individuals born in an advanced-stage slave society surrounded by kin often had little understanding of the utter desolation experienced by migration slaves or individuals sold away from their communities. Walter Brashear's slaves went through this painful, migration-spawned pattern of destruction and reconstruction, first described by Herbert Gutman in his seminal work on the black family.[53]

Brashear's early slave force in Louisiana had great difficulty adjusting to the loss of their prior community. Their discontent was often reflected in a reluctance to form lasting relationships and in messages or inquiries sent back home through the correspondence of their owners. Only the more privileged migration slaves had this opportunity, but the messages movingly demonstrate their longing for loved ones in Kentucky. Walter Brashear's wife included the following message from Belle Isle slaves in a letter to her daughter in Lexington, Kentucky: "In your next letter tell Rachel how her relations come." She added, "Poor little Hannah says ask Miss Caroline if she sees Daddy to give my love to him." Another letter mentioned that a migration slave begged for word of his brothers. Brashear family members frequently traveled back and forth between Lexington, Kentucky, and their holdings in Louisiana, and they usually cooperated in forwarding the slaves' messages to their Kentucky kin and relating responses. In 1827, for example, Walter Brashear, visiting in Kentucky, instructed his wife in Louisiana to "tell Lowny his family is all well and his friends very glad to hear he is in good health."[54]

A more detailed look at some of Brashear's migration slaves reveals some of their difficulties in adjustment and their high regard for family and kin remaining in Kentucky. Most of the young male solitaires whom Brashear brought to Louisiana from Kentucky did not marry and disappeared from the record after 1831. Among these were several slaves from Margaret Barr Brashear's inheritance, including Andrew and Peter, as well as some Walter Brashear owned in his own right, such as Lowny.[55] The deaths of a few are documented in the records of the 1830s, but it is unlikely that so many died after having survived acclimatization, and some must have been sold.

Another Kentucky slave who never married was Brooks. Only thirteen or fourteen years old at the time of the removal, he was one of those slaves who seemed genuinely devoted to his master and his master's family.[56] Brooks was particularly fond of Walter Brashear, Jr., who died at school in Kentucky. Both of the young men loved Belle Isle and its sleek, free-ranging cattle. In 1830 Brooks sent a message to Walter, Jr., via a letter from Rebecca Brashear. It expresses the affection he held for his young master, but—more significant—it demonstrates a persistent awareness of kinship even among slaves who had been separated from their families as children.

> Brooks wishes me to write you that he has been very ill for the last twelve months but is now getting well. He wishes you to see his brother and say to him that he almost thinks of him as a stranger as it has been almost eight years and he has never written to him to let him know where and how his brothers or sisters are. . . . He should have acted differently had their situations been reversed.
>
> He says when you [were] here you requested him to look after your cattle which he has done faithfully and now he can have the pleasure to let you know they increase very fast and all look well. He requests me to say to you that he *adores* you and intends one day or other to be your devoted slave.

Brooks died in a cholera outbreak in 1849, along with several other young men.[57]

Another of the young male solitaires from Kentucky was Eli, the brickmaker whom Brashear sent ahead to construct Belle Isle's house and outbuildings. He, too, never married or fathered any known children, although he lived into the 1850s.[58]

An additional slave artisan who did not marry in Louisiana was Sight. He was part of the Barr inheritance and was employed both at Belle Isle (while Brashear still operated it in partnership with the Barr brothers) and at the home of David and Emily Barr Todd in Franklin (Emily was Margaret Brashears' sister). He could not adjust to his new surroundings. Todd wrote relatives in Kentucky that "Old Sight is here & expressing a wish to go back to Kentucky—indulgence to him will not answer a good purpose—he has drank hard this winter and spring."[59] Sight drops off all Brashear and Todd records shortly thereafter, so perhaps he was sent back to Kentucky.

Isaac and Fanny Henderson were a married couple in their thirties when they removed to Louisiana with the Brashears. Fanny died by 1831, but Isaac Henderson remained part of Walter Brashear's slave community until he, too, died, about a decade after his wife. The couple remained childless in Louisiana.[60]

A young mother, Rachel, was also among the Kentucky migrants, along with her two small children. She and her children first appear as Walter Brashear's slaves on a Kentucky mortgage document of September 1814. Rachel is listed below Bill, thirty-two, who might have been her husband, and they were all identified as part of Margaret Barr Brashear's inheritance from her father.[61] Bill remained in Kentucky. One of Rachel's children died during the migration or shortly thereafter, but a daughter, Ellen, lived with her mother at Belle Isle.

Rachel's parents, Ben and Sabina, were slaves of the affluent Barr family. In an 1822 letter to her daughter in Lexington, Margaret Barr Brashear asked her to "give Rachel's love to Ben and Sabina [and] tell them she is well."[62]

Between her arrival in Louisiana in 1822 and her death in 1830 after a long illness, Rachel gave birth to several additional children—Elisha, Carillo, and a girl, Sabina, named for her Kentucky grandmother. A Brashear daughter announced the birth in a letter to her sister in Lexington with the comment that baby Sabina was "as white as Ellen," the infant's older half-sister.[63] The baby grew into a beautiful woman and was bought by a white man for his concubine in 1849, along with her own small child. In 1850 Frances Brashear Lawrence wrote that "Sabina has gone to Gibbons Point and taken up her avende. I wonder if she lives in the same house with him, or if he has put her up in a house there?"[64]

The father of Rachel's Louisiana-born children (Elisha, Carillo, and Sabina) is not known, but it might have been Carillo, who appears as a twenty-five-year-old solitaire on an 1825 list.[65] He is not in the 1831 records, and Rachel had died in 1830. Her orphaned younger children were reared by her close friend, possible relative, and fellow Kentucky migrant, Milly.

Rachel's oldest known child, Ellen, moved to Louisiana at the age of eight or nine. Like her mother, she had been part of Margaret Brashear's inheritance.[66] Also like her mother and younger sister Sabina, Ellen appeared to be white. She spent most of her life as a slave at Belle Isle. But in the start-up phase of Tiger Island, she was among the young slaves transferred. She was present on the island in 1833, in a household with two young boys, Ben (named for his grandfather in Kentucky), five, and Patrick, two.[67] Patrick might have been the son of Hannah Jones, who accompanied young Frances Brashear to school in 1830s, leaving her children on the plantation in the care of friends or relatives.

Family and Kinship

Ben was Ellen's son with another migration slave, Franklin, to whom she was married for several years. Franklin had a wife or sweetheart named Milly in Kentucky (not to be confused with the Milly who raised Rachel's orphans in Louisiana). Some affection lingered, for he attempted to contact Milly in 1832, provoking Margaret Brashear to write her daughter in Lexington, "I do not know who wrote Franklin's letter to Milly—as he has taken our Ellen to wife. I think it was not worth his while to have written to her at all, but he is a great rake at any rate."[68]

The marriage between Ellen and Franklin did not last, but whether because of divorce or Franklin's death is not known. In any case, Ellen appears on an 1848 Golden Farm inventory as the single mother of sons Elias, nine, and Patrick, one. Her older son Ben was on his own, and the earlier Patrick had probably been emancipated, as will be related in the story of his presumed mother, Hannah. Ellen apparently named her baby son Patrick after the boy she had kept for several years. By 1848, Ellen had three daughters—Josephine, seven, Caroline, four, and Susan, three—in addition to Elias and Patrick. These children were fathered by a Brashear slave, Billy Brown, but he and Ellen did not share a household as a married couple.[69]

Ellen had become very sick by late 1849. Despite efforts by Frances Brashear Lawrence to heal Ellen's chronically diseased leg by taking her to a hot springs in Arkansas, she died in 1850.[70] Ellen's daughters Caroline and Josephine were among the valued servants whom Walter Brashear bequeathed by name to family members in his will. They were still alive at the outbreak of the Civil War, as was Elias, who appeared on a Golden Farm inventory in 1861.[71]

As was the case with many of the Kentucky women, Milly—another migrant—did not marry in Louisiana. She did, however, found a major kinship line on Tiger Island. She was listed as age thirty on the Tiger Island list of 1833, already the mother of five children between the ages of twelve and two: Maria, Jenny (named for her mother in Kentucky), Ann, Sandis, and Horace. She was also rearing Rachel's children, Sabina, Elisha, and Carillo. Nine years later, Milly's biological children also included Esther, nine, and Leven, five.[72]

Milly died between 1843 and 1847, but her surviving children remained at Tiger Island and proliferated. By late 1842 the eldest, Maria, was married to the strong-willed Jim Roy and had two children by him (Coleman and Delphy). Jenny, the second of Milly's daughters, was married to Ed Davis in 1842 and had a small daughter, Laura. Ann disappeared from the lists and probably died, and Milly's adopted children had been transferred to Bayou Boeuf Plantation.

By 1857, Milly's children had formed solid alliances and were fostering a new generation of Tiger Island slaves. Esther had married Henry Todd and had a small daughter. Sandis had married and had six children, ranging in age from one to fifteen. Maria had remarried, to Henry Brient. Jenny, like her younger sister Esther, had married an older man who was her mother's contemporary, Ed Davis. In addition to Laura, they had four children. And Laura, whom Jenny had borne at the age of fourteen, was married to Alfred and had her own infant (Joe), born when she was fifteen. Joe's birth marked the fourth generation of Milly's line to be born on Tiger Island. By 1860, the deceased Milly's blood descendants on the island numbered at least twenty-eight, including four great-grandchildren. Including her adopted children, grandchildren, and great-grandchildren, her descendants numbered thirty-five.[73]

As far as can be determined, Hannah also remained a single parent in Louisiana. She was the personal maid of Walter Brashear's daughter Frances for many years. When she was little more than a child, Hannah had accompanied her mother (also named Hannah) and five siblings to Brashear's Belle Isle plantation, leaving her father behind in Kentucky. It was young Hannah who in 1822 had sent the poignant message to "ask Miss Caroline if she sees Daddy to give my love to him."[74]

While barely in her teens, young Hannah gave birth to a daughter, Clarissa, and, four years later, to a son, Sinclair. Both children probably had the same father, but he was not named. No more children appear with Hannah on plantation or court documents for eleven years. Nevertheless, she did have another child, Patrick, born about 1830, who is never listed with her in the inventories. His existence is documented in the will of Robert R. Barr, the brother of Margaret Barr Brashear. Barr was an early partner in Brashear's sugar undertakings and a frequent visitor to the plantation.[75] Barr was almost certainly Hannah's lover and the father of Patrick. Barr wrote his will in 1832, while at Belle Isle. Part of it reads, "It is my will that Walter Brashear or his family shall inherit no part of my estate as legal heirs until Hannah Jones and her son Patrick are emancipated & sent to Kentucky and $2,000 paid to trustees for their support and the education of Patrick Jones."[76] Barr died within four years, but Hannah was not emancipated as he had willed. It is possible, though I have been unable to confirm it, that Patrick was emancipated and sent back to Kentucky to the Barr plantation. It appears that Patrick was placed in the care of Ellen between 1832 and Barr's estate settlement in 1836 or 1837 and was thereafter manumitted.

Robert Barr's wishes for Hannah were never carried out by Walter Brashear. Brashear's daughter Frances did apparently sympathize with her deceased uncle's attempt to force Brashear to manumit Hannah and her son. Hannah lived in Lexington for much of the mid- and late 1830s, serving as Frances's personal maid while she was at school. Perhaps after 1836 Patrick was there also. Frances pressed her father to free Hannah and allow her to remain in Kentucky. In response to one of Frances's inquiries, Brashear tersely replied in 1838 that "Hannah Jones cannot be freed in Kentucky as there exists a law of the state which prevents her returning to it. The object can be attained here under certain forms prescribed by the laws of Louisiana." He did not offer to pursue the matter, but he did add that "Hannah's children are quite well and growing finely."[77]

Hannah was back in Louisiana by 1841. Perhaps recognizing that she would probably die a slave, she either resumed a former union or began a new one and gave birth to five additional children in rapid succession: Edward, William, Alice, Mary, and Sophia. By 1848 she was also a grandmother. Her eldest child, Clarissa, now twenty-

Family and Kinship 213

two and a single head of household, had two children of her own—Cornelius, two, and an unnamed infant.[78]

Hannah and many of her younger children died before 1860, but among the slaves who remained with the Brashears after most had fled to the Federal forces were the older children, Sinclair and Clarissa. Clarissa, still single, was listed with her own large family, including Cornelius, Isaac, Daphne, Becky, Thomas, and Lewis.[79] The older children and their offspring had become permanent members of the Tiger Island slave force.

Yet another migration slave who remained single in Louisiana was Queny, although she headed another family that lasted for at least thirty years. Queny had two children who accompanied her in the 1822 Kentucky migration—Henry Todd and Matilda, both of them teenagers. On an 1825 list of Belle Isle slaves, they were on their own and Queny was described as thirty-three and single, although a son Augustus would have been born by then. She was on Tiger Island in 1833, listed with her son Augustus and daughters Flora and Courtney.[80]

Queny was not a permanent resident of Tiger Island. Like others of the original Kentucky slaves, she spent most of her life at the Belle Isle and Golden Farm home plantations with the old master, Walter Brashear. She lived at least through 1861 and was listed, at the age of seventy, as part of Walter Brashear's estate, along with her daughter Flora, her son Augustus, and a bevy of grandchildren.[81] Queny's daughter Courtney lived only to early adulthood, but her daughter Rachel was a Brashear family favorite, bequeathed by Brashear to one of his granddaughters. One of Flora's daughters, Fanny, was likewise left to a Brashear grandchild. Augustus never married. Flora married a Golden Farm slave, Oliver, by 1845, and in 1860 they had at least seven children. Oliver and Flora were among the slaves for whom Henry and Frances Lawrence provided land at the end of the war.[82]

Unlike Hannah and Queny, who stayed on Tiger Island only temporarily, Queny's daughter Matilda remained on the island from 1833 until the slave community was dissolved in 1860-61, the unmarried head of a large and vigorous clan. Matilda bore children from at least 1824 through 1857. Her first five children, as listed in 1842, were Corilla, Anne, Rhody, Annette, and Allen. By 1850 she had, in addition, Quincy, Mina, Webster, and Stuart—the youngest only two years old. She was also rearing a twelve-year-old orphan, Primus, the son of the deceased Maria. Corilla, Anne, and Annette had died or were transferred by 1850. Rhoda married Aaron Smith, a Tiger Island man who was her mother's contemporary. He had been purchased with seventeen other men and four women in a single lot in 1830.[83] Rhoda and Aaron had a lasting marriage despite a fourteen-to-eighteen-year age difference, and by 1860 they had five children, ranging in age from three to sixteen. The same inventory shows Matilda at the age of fifty the formidable head of a household of six children, ranging in age from seven to seventeen.[84]

Henry Todd, the eldest son of Queny and the only male adult to appear on the 1833 mortgage list for Tiger Island, resided on the plantation for the remainder of his life as a slave. He, too, had been brought to Louisiana from Kentucky in the early 1820s, as an adolescent. He was still unattached in 1842, but as he neared the age of fifty, he married Esther, the seventeen-year-old daughter of Milly, who had been one of his co-workers on the island in 1833. By 1860 they had two small daughters.[85]

The six adults constituting the first known generation of Tiger Island slaves have already been discussed; they were Hannah, Queny, her adult children Henry Todd and Matilda, Milly, and Ellen. They were the first Tiger Island slaves with ties to the Kentucky slave community although other Kentucky slaves on Belle Isle or Golden Farm were occasionally transferred to Tiger Island. Five of the six were women, and all had small children. All but one of the children had been born in Louisiana, presumably at Belle Isle, suggesting that new alliances were formed in Louisiana, although none of the women had married the fathers of their Louisiana offspring.

Cut off from their prior familial antecedents, the fourteen families of the 1842 Tiger Island inventory had provided the basis for a supportive kinship system by 1860. By 1842, many of the migration slaves were no longer at Tiger Island, but their progeny continued to increase, and several new kinship groups were formed.

The most vigorous lines, however, resulted from alliances begun by newcomers. One of these families was formed by Jerry and Maria Key. Maria's origins cannot be determined from existing records, but Jerry was part of a lot of young men between the ages of fourteen and twenty-six who were purchased in 1830.[86] Jerry, at the time of his purchase, married Maria, daughter of Belle Isle slaves originally from Kentucky. Jerry and Maria had a young family on Tiger Island in 1842, and by 1860 they had eight known children and eleven known grandchildren, or nineteen direct descendants.[87] All of the surviving children produced by the long marriage between Jerry and Maria Key themselves married and formed standard nuclear families at young ages.

A second family of 1842 consisted of Jim Roy and Maria. Roy's origins are unknown; he was probably purchased in the early 1820s. He was sold by the mid-1840s. Maria was a daughter of Milly, a Kentucky slave and one of Tiger Island's first settlers. Jim and Maria had two known children and a grandchild by 1860, although by that time she had remarried.

A third family from 1842, that of single parent Mary Brien, had produced four known children and one known grandchild by 1860. A fourth family was that of Daniel Atter and Eliza, who had six known children and two known grandchildren in the 1860 community, although Daniel Atter died about the time of his last child's birth. A fifth family, that of Henry and Eliza Cox, included seven known children and two grandchildren by 1860. The sixth couple, Bob Willis and Betsy, had produced six known children but no grandchildren by 1860. In the seventh family, single mother Scilla had given birth to ten known children and by 1860 had ten grandchildren as well. The eighth family was also headed by a single mother, Matilda, who had ten known children and five grandchildren by 1860. The ninth family was headed by Ed and Jenny Davis, who included among their progeny by 1860 three natural children, two adopted children, and four grandchildren. Although

Family and Kinship

she and two of her daughters did not survive until 1860, Lucinda contributed four known children to the Tiger Island kinship; likewise, Maria did not survive, but her son Primus continued her line. The twelfth family was begun by Becky, another old Kentucky slave, who had at least three children and five grandchildren on the island in 1860. As observed earlier, Milly had borne seven known children and raised three adopted children. Along with various natural and adopted children and great-grandchildren, she had thirty-five descendants who lived at least part of the 1842-60 period on Tiger Island. The fourteenth 1842 family consisted of Violetta and her children. She died early, and two of her five children were adopted by Ed and Jenny Davis, the female child eventually having two children of her own.

In all, the fourteen 1842 families had by 1860 produced at least 145 blood descendants, most of whom still survived on Tiger Island. Every known match was made without indulging in consanguinity, but the families headed by Scilla and Jerry Key intermarried heavily. Finding nonkin to marry would have become an extremely acute problem by the time the grandchildren and great-grandchildren of the 1842 community had reached sexual maturity. They would be to a large extent a generation of cousins. Fortunately, emancipation intervened, freeing the young slaves to seek mates off the plantation.

The records of Oakland, Petite Anse, and Tiger Island have allowed the backward tracing of the families that contributed to the kinship networks of the last recorded community. The naming of children after parents and especially grandparents—both those present and in Kentucky—demonstrates affection and a respect for familial continuity and kin identification. Household composition reveals that slaves in the three communities often ministered to the needs of family members, orphaned kin, and nonrelated, dependent children who might be considered fictive kin in the framework of existing households. The role of kinship beyond that contained in individual households and families was probably equally supportive to that of individual families in providing slaves with continuity, stability, and even limited economic assistance, but it is much more difficult to document and measure. Social historian Robert Wheaton has warned that "the emphasis which household censuses put on co-residence tempts one to ignore the kinship system as it extends beyond the household." He points out that because households leave a "clearer historical and, particularly, legal record," the connections between the household structures and the larger kinship systems of which they are part are often obscured. He warns that "we can understand household structure only within the larger context of the kinship system."[88]

Notes for "Family and Kinship Development on Three Louisiana Plantations"

[1] Inventory, October 23, 1819, "Estate of Nathaniel Evans"; Mortgage, April 3, 1822, regarding the "Estate of Nathaniel Evans," Probate file 32, St. Francisville, La., West Feliciana Parish Probate Records.

[2] List of Taxable Property, 1834-41, Sarah B. Evans and John N. Evans, Plantation Record Book 37, St. Francisville, La., West Feliciana Parish Historical Society Library and Archives, Evans Papers. Hereafter cited Evans Papers.

[3] See "Last Will and Testament," Sarah Bloomfield Spencer Evans, October 1, 1851, Probate Drawer 31 and recorded in Inventories, Vol. F:597-99, 607; Inventory and Appraisement, April 14, 1851, "Estate of Sarah B. Evans," all in West Feliciana Parish Probate Records.

[4] John Briton (John Evans's slave) married Mima (Sarah Evans's slave); Big George (John Evans's slave) wed Barbara (Sarah Evans's slave); Robin (John Evans's slave) married Patsy (Sarah Evans's slave); Jem Gillum (Sarah Evans's slave) married Mary (John Evans's slave); and Squire (John Evans's slave) married Ellen (Sarah Evans's slave). Several of these matches produced large families. Family reconstitutions were done by the author from Evans Papers, Louisiana State University and West Feliciana Parish Historical Society.

[5] "Memoranda, Property Received by Heirs of Mrs. C. L. DeHart from the Estate of Mrs. S. B. Evans, 1852"; "Partition of Estate of S. B. Evans, January 30, 1852—Personal Property" in box 7, folders 47 and 48, Evans Papers.

[6] Rolls, 1811, 1814, 1817, Plantation Record Book 36, ibid.

[7] The family for which J. N. Evans traded was that headed by his slave Bob. It consisted of Bob's wife, Louisa, and their three children, Emma, Louis, and Patience. Evans made at least one more trade. On one memo, and "X" is scribbled in pencil with the notation "swapped for Kitty." Apparently he traded Kitty (who would remain with her adopted mother, Nancy) for an old Oakland slave, Alex, who was drawn by the DeHarts and had orphaned grandchildren at Oakland.

[8] Roll, 1811, 1811 Work Record, Plantation Record Book 36, Evans Papers; Inventory, October 23, 1819, "Estate of Nathaniel Evans."

[9] "Property of Heirs of Mrs. C. DeHart from the Estate of Mrs. S. B. Evans," January 30, 1852, box 7, folder 48, Evans Papers.

[10] Estate Partition, December 5, 1854, in "Estate of Cornelia L. Evans on Petition of Heirs of Margaret E. DeHart, deceased," Conveyance, Vol. J:459-65, St. Mary Parish Probate Records.

[11] Inventory, April 14, 1851, "Estate of Sarah B. Evans." Both Susannah and her husband, Ben Hill, appeared as unmarried on an 1846 Blanket List of Sarah B. Evans's Negroes, November, Plantation Record Book 37. Ben was bought about 1845. Susannah [Susanne] was born to an unnamed mother at Oakland in 1830. See "List of S. B. E's Negroes, August, 1834," Plantation Record Book 37, Evans Papers.

[12] Roll, 1811, Roll, 1814, Plantation Record Book 36, Evans Papers; Inventory, October 23, 1819, "Estate of Nathaniel Evans"; Inventory, April 14, 1851, "Estate of Sarah B. Evans."

[13] Inventory, April 14, 1851, "Estate of Sarah B. Evans"; Roll, 1814, Roll, 1817; Quarter Bill, 1817, Plantation Record Book 36. The 1834 roll contained a notation that Mima had a daughter Vicy (born 1843), and all subsequent inventories of Mima's family mention Vicy. See "List of S. B. E's Negroes, August 1834," Plantation Record Book 37, Evans Papers; Inventory, April 14, 1851, "Estate of Sarah B. Evans."

[14] Consent form for slave Peter, October 21, 1818, New Jersey, folder 2, Avery Papers (this consent form did not state the country); Inventory, March 4, 1836; "Estate of Euphemia Craig Marsh"; Bill of Sale, April 23, 1826, for slave Milly, Samuel Woolfolk [New Orleans] to William Stone and John Marsh, St. Mary, folder 3, Avery Papers.

[15] Conveyance, April 19, 1854, A. B. Henshaw to Daniel Avery.

[16] Inventory, February 20, 1860, "Estate of George Marsh."

Family and Kinship 217

[17] Bill of Sale, April 26, 1826, for Sylvia, Samuel M. Woolfolk [New Orleans] to William Stone and John C. Marsh, folder 3, Chapel Hill, N.C., Avery Family Papers; Inventory, March 4, 1836, "Estate of Euphemia Craig Marsh."

[18] Conveyance, January 1, 1839, John C. Marsh to George Marsh.

[19] Conveyance, April 19, 1854, A. B. Henshaw to Daniel Avery; Inventory, February 20, 1860, "Estate of George Marsh"; Plantation Account Book, Vol. 4, Avery Papers.

[20] Bill of Sale for Sawney, Estate of Jesse McCall, deceased, December 23, 1824, to William Stone and John C. Marsh, Register Vol. A:344-45, St. Martinville, La., St. Martin Parish Probate Records.

[21] Among those with freedmen accounts were Sawney McCall (the surname of his first master), Lucy Stephens (Sawney's daughter, who married Peter Stephens, Jr.), Betsy Ann McCall, and Fanny McCall (Plantation Account Book, 4:20-21, 25, 66, 68, Avery Papers).

[22] Bill of Sale, April 19, 1827, for slaves Augustus, Arena, and Fanny, Austin Woolfolk and Ira Bowman, Adams County, Mississippi, to John C. Marsh and the heirs of William Stone, New Iberia, Louisiana, folder 3, ibid.

[23] Inventory, March 4, 1836, "Estate of Euphemia Craig Marsh"; Conveyance, January 1, 1839, John C. Marsh to George Marsh; Conveyance, April 19, 1854, A. B. Henshaw to Daniel Avery; Inventory, February 20, 1860, "Estate of George Marsh."

[24] Bill of Sale, November 17, 1823, for slave Harriet, a "mulatto girl," Raphael Semmes, Charles County, Maryland, to William Stone, Louisiana, folder 3, Avery Papers.

[25] "Servants at Petite Anse Homes" in "Ledger and Anecdotes about Family Servants," Vol. 6, ibid.

[26] Inventory, March 4, 1836, "Estate of Euphemia Craig Marsh."

[27] An 1840 list of slaves on the reverse of a letter shows eighty-two slaves and is divided into two groups, apparently those residing on the two Marsh properties. Ben, Vina, and John Henry are listed together and appear to be at New Iberia (John C. Marsh, Baltimore, to George Avery, New Iberia, August 4, 1840, folder 5, Avery Papers).

[28] Conveyance, January 1, 1839, John C. Marsh to George Marsh.

[29] "Oleographic Statement," May 5, 1856, and John C. Marsh to George Marsh, May 8, 1856, folder 6, Avery Papers.

[30] Conveyance, April 19, 1854, A. B. Henshaw to Daniel Avery; Inventory, February 20, 1860, "Estate of George Marsh."

[31] "Oleographic Statement," May 5, 1856; George Marsh, Petite Anse Isle, to John Marsh, August 25, 1845, and John C. Marsh, New Iberia, to George Marsh, Petite Anse Island, May 8, 1856, folder 6, Avery Papers; Plantation Account Book, 4:63, ibid.

[32] Margaret Marsh Henshaw, New Iberia, Louisiana, to John C. Marsh, Rahway, New Jersey, May 16, 1853, and John C. Marsh, Rahway, New Jersey, to Margaret Henshaw, New Iberia, Louisiana, June 21, 1853, folder 6, ibid.

[33] "Oleographic Statement," May 5, 1856.

[34] Inventory, February 20, 1860, "Estate of George Marsh."

[35] "Ledger and Anecdotes about Family Servants."

[36] Harriet is inventoried at Petite Anse but made frequent trips to New Iberia with her mistress. See Margaret Henshaw, New Iberia, to John C. Marsh, Rahway, New Jersey, May 16, 1853.

[37] D. D. Avery, New Iberia, to Sarah Avery, East Baton Rouge, May 20, 1854, folder 6, Avery Papers.

[38]"Ledger and Anecdotes about Family Servants."

[39]U. B. Phillips mentions the brig *Ajax* as one of the ships that "consigned numerous parcels [of slaves] to various New Orleans correspondents." He found ship manifests regarding the *Ajax* and other slave carriers in the Library of Congress collection of ship manifests from the internal trade (*American Negro Slavery,* 196).
[40]"Recollects by Aunt Maria Houston," in " Ledger and Anecdotes about Family Servants."

[41]Inventory, March 4, 1836, "Estate of Euphemia Craig Marsh."

[42]John C. Marsh, New Iberia, to George Marsh, Petite Anse Island, May 5, 1856. John C. Marsh states his wishes regarding eventual emancipation of certain slaves, including Vina, in this letter and the accompanying "oleographic statement," both in folder 6, Avery Papers.

[43]Conveyance, April 19, 1854, A. B. Henshaw to Daniel Avery; Bill of Sale for John Houston, Bien and Cohen of New Orleans to John C. Marsh of New Iberia, February 8, 1837, folder 4, Avery Papers. Houston's value as a skilled slave is noted in Conveyance, John C. Marsh to George Marsh, January 1, 1839.

[44]Inventory, February 20, 1860, "Estate of George Marsh." The child, a light mulatto with a white father, might not have been inventoried, as had been the case of other children for whom emancipation was planned, or she may have been sent to New Iberia to be reared. This child is specifically mentioned in George Marsh's will: "I further desire and request that Mr. Avery's interest in the mulatto girl called Vena (the daughter of yellow Maria and born July 9, 1854) be purchased by my estate, and that my God Daughter Sarah Avery shall take charge of the said Vena after she arrives at the age of eight or ten. . . The said Vena to remain with her until she is twenty-one years old and then to be set free" (Will, George Marsh, July 15, 1858, Succession 1042). Yellow Maria is Little Maria. The baby was named Vena (or Vina) after her sister.

[45]Plantation Account Book, 4:11-15, Avery Papers.

[46]"Ledger and Anecdotes about Family Servants."

[47]Conveyance, January 1, 1839, John C. Marsh to George Marsh.

[48]Conveyance, April 19, 1854, A. B. Henshaw to Daniel Avery.

[49]Inventory, February 20, 1860, "Estate of George Marsh."

[50]George Marsh, Petite Anse, to John Craig Marsh, New York City, June 14, 1845, and Sarah Marsh Avery, Baton Rouge, to George Marsh, New Iberia, August 3, 1845, folder 5, Avery Papers.

[51]Conveyance, April 19, 1854, A. B. Henshaw to Daniel Avery; Inventory, February 20, 1860, "Estate of George Marsh."

[52]Frederick Law Olmsted, *The Slave States*, Harvey Wish, ed. (New York, 1959), 121; David Todd, Franklin, Louisiana, to Thomas T. Barr, Lexington, Kentucky, May 6, 1822; Margaret Brashear, Belle Isle, Louisiana, to Caroline Brashear, Lexington, Kentucky, November 16, 1822; Walter Brashear, Lexington, Kentucky, to Margaret Brashear, Belle Isle, August 9, 1827, folders 2 and 3, Brashear Papers, Southern Historical Collection.

[53]Gutman, *Black Family*, 129.

[54]Margaret Brashear, Belle Isle, Louisiana, to Caroline Brashear, Lexington, Kentucky, November 16, 1822; Rebecca T. Brashear, Belle Isle, Louisiana, to Walter Brashear, Jr., Bardstown, Kentucky, January 18, 1830; Walter Brashear, Lexington, Kentucky, to Margaret Brashear, Belle Isle, Louisiana, August 9, 1827, folders 2 and 3, Brashear Papers, Southern Historical Collection.

[55]Mortgage of Slaves, June 14, 1824, Walter Brashear, Louisiana, to Robert R. Barr, Fayette, Kentucky, Deed Book V:33-35, Fayette County, Kentucky, Conveyance Records.

[56]Brooks's age was given as sixteen in 1825 (Mortgage of Land and Slaves, Walter and Margaret Brashear to Bank of Louisiana, July 13, 1825, Mortgage Vol. A-B:54-55, St. Mary Parish Mortgage Records; Mortgage of Slaves, June 14, 1824, Walter Brashear to Robert R. Barr).

Family and Kinship

[57]Rebecca T. Brashear, Belle Isle, Louisiana, to Walter Brashear, Jr., Bardstown, Kentucky, January 18, 1830, and Frances Brashear Lawrence, Belle Isle, to Henry E. Lawrence, New Orleans, February 10, 1849, folders 3 and 15, Brashear Papers, Southern Historical Collection.

[58]Mortgage, Walter Brashear to W. W. Montgomery, April 15, 1833, Mortgage Vol. B-5:212-14, St. Mary Parish Mortgage Records; Fanny [Frances] Lawrence, to Henry E. Lawrence, January 1850, folder 17, Brashear Papers, Southern Historical Collection.

[59]David Todd, Franklin, Louisiana, to Thomas T. Barr, Lexington, Kentucky, May 6, 1822, folder 2, Brashear Papers, Southern Historical Collection.

[60]Mortgage, Walter Brashear to W. W. Montgomery, April 15, 1833; Conveyance of Land and Slaves, Walter Brashear to Henry E. Lawrence, April 11, 1848, Conveyance, Vol. G:203-4, St. Mary Parish Conveyance Records; Mortgage of Slaves, Walter Brashear to James Darrack, Fayette County, Kentucky, September 20, 1814, Deed Book L:218-20, Fayette County, Kentucky, Mortgage Records.

[61]Mortgage of Slaves, Brashear to Darrack, September 20, 1814.

[62]By 1830 Rachel was gravely ill. Rebecca Brashear wrote her brother, "It is probable she will never recover" (Margaret Brashear, Belle Isle, to Caroline Brashear, Lexington, Kentucky, November 16, 1822, Rebecca T. Brashear, Belle Isle, Franklin, Louisiana, to Walter Brashear, Jr., Bardstown, Kentucky, January 18, 1830, folders 2 and 3, Brashear Papers, Southern Historical Collection).

[63]Mary Eliza Brashear, St. Mary Parish, to Caroline Brashear, Lexington, Kentucky, February 19, 1823, folder 2, ibid.

[64]Conveyance of Land and Slaves (Golden Farm), Henry E. Lawrence to Walter Brashear, March 27, 1848, Conveyance Vol. G:203-4; Fanny Lawrence to Henry E. Lawrence, January 1850, folder 17, Brashear Papers, Southern Historical Collection.

[65]Mortgage, Walter and Margaret Brashear to Bank of Louisiana, July 13, 1825, Mortgage Vol. A-B:54-55, St. Mary Parish Mortgage Records.

[66]Mortgage, Walter Brashear to Robert R. Barr and Thomas T. Barr, June 14, 1824, Deed Book V:33-35, Fayette County, Kentucky, Mortgage Records.

[67]Mortgage (Tiger Island), June 1, 1833, Walter Brashear and Wife to New Orleans Canal and Banking Company; Mortgage (Tiger Island) November 19, 1842, Robert Brashear et al. to Walter Brashear.

[68]Margaret Brashear, Belle Isle, to Frances Emily Brashear, Lexington, Kentucky, April 14, 1832, folder 5, Brashear Papers, Southern Historical Collection.

[69]Inventory (Golden Farm), March 28, 1848, with Conveyance, Henry E. Lawrence to Walter Brashear.

[70]Fanny E. Lawrence to Henry E. Lawrence, January 1850, folder 17, Brashear Papers, Southern Historical Collection; Will, Walter Brashear, September 17, 1860.

[71]Inventory of Golden Farm Slaves, January 4, 1861, contained in "Lease of Land and Slaves," Mrs. Frances Lawrence, St. Mary Parish, to Robert D. Hockley, Nelson County, Kentucky, Conveyance Vol. O:217-21 (original lease dated July 13, 1860), St. Mary Parish Conveyance Records.

[72]Mortgage (Tiger Island), June 1, 1833, Walter Brashear and Wife to New Orleans Canal and Banking Company; Mortgage (Tiger Island), November 19, 1842, Robert Brashear et al. to Walter Brashear.

[73]Inventory and Partition, May 28, 1860, "Estates of T. T. and Robert Brashear."

[74]Margaret Brashear, Belle Isle, to Caroline Brashear, Lexington, Kentucky, November 16, 1822.

[75]Will of Robert R. Barr of Fayette County, Kentucky, but written at Belle Isle, Louisiana, October 14, 1831, Will Book M:315-16, Fayette County, Kentucky, Probate Records. Barr lived with the Brashears for long periods at a time during the 1820s and early 1830s.

[76] Robert R. Barr died about February 20, 1836, legally "without issue." His heirs were his three surviving sisters and the children of Walter Brashear (Estate of Robert R. Barr, Succession 203, April 6, 1837, in Sanders, comp., *Selected Annotated Abstracts of St. Mary Parish, Louisiana, Court Records*, 3:78).

[77] Walter Brashear, Golden Farm, to Frances Brashear, Lexington, Kentucky, September 16, 1838, folder 7, Brashear Papers, Southern Historical Collection.

[78] Inventory (Golden Farm), April 11, 1848, Conveyance, Henry E. Lawrence to Walter Brashear.

[79] Inventory and Partition, May 28, 1860, "Estates of T. T. and Robert Brashear."

[80] Mortgage (Belle Isle), July 13, 1825, Walter and Margaret Brashear to the Bank of Louisiana; Mortgage (Tiger Island), June 1, 1833, Walter Brashear and Wife to New Orleans Canal and Banking Company.

[81] Inventory (Golden Farm), January 4, 1861, in "Lease between Frances Lawrence and Robert D. Hockley"; Will, Walter Brashear, September 17, 1860.

[82] Lease, February 15, 1866, Henry E. Lawrence to Oliver Richardson et al., Brashear Papers, Morgan City Library and Archives.

[83] Bill of Sale, April 12, 1830, for a lot of seventeen slaves, M. Payne of Bedford County, Tennessee, to Walter Brashear and Robert Barr, co-partners, Belle Isle, Mortgage Vol. B-5:69, St. Mary Parish Mortgage Records.

[84] Inventory and Partition, May 28, 1860, "Estates of T. T. and Robert Brashear."

[85] Ibid.

[86] Bill of Sale, April 12, 1830, M. Payne, Bedford County, Tennessee, to Walter Brashear and Robert Barr, co-partners, Belle Isle, Louisiana.

[87] Mortgage (Tiger Island), November 28, 1842, Robert Brashear et al. to Walter Brashear; Inventory and Partition, May 28, 1860, "Estates of T. T. and Robert Brashear." The information in the following two paragraphs is from the same sources.

[88] Robert Wheaton, "Family and Kinship in Western Europe: The Problem of the Joint Family Household," *Journal of Interdisciplinary History*, 5 (1975): 606-8.

CHILD WELFARE AND PUBLIC RELIEF IN THE ANTEBELLUM ERA*

Robert E. Moran

Throughout the nineteenth century, poverty and dependency were regarded as personal evils accredited to gambling, drunkenness, and individual indolence. Men were not generally regarded as being victims of an economic or social system over which they had little or no control. The family, the church, and private philanthropy would take care of the misfortunate. Only the sick, at least in New Orleans, would be cared for through public funds. The Louisiana code of 1825 stated that children were bound to support their parents and other relatives in need.[1]

Edward Livingston the principal author of Louisiana's civil code, proposed to the legislature in 1822 that the state appropriate funds to provide work for the unemployed on work-relief projects. He argued that it was cheaper for the state to support a plan to give the unemployed work than to continue supporting able-bodied persons by private charity.[2] His suggestion unfortunately went unheeded for nearly a century; thus, Louisiana continued throughout much of the nineteenth century the policy of earmarking small amounts to New Orleans charities. The state, however, refused, during the same period, to accept the concept of outdoor relief as a regular governmental function.

Just as it was the responsibility of parents to care for children and for children to care for aged parents, by law the master was obliged to care for the disabled slave. The Black Code of 1806 stated that every master was to provide for his sick or aged slaves and to procure for his sick slaves "all kinds of temporal and spiritual assistance which their situation require." Moreover, the law required that whenever an old and disabled slave was offered for sale, he should only be sold along with one of his children who would care for him. Frederick Law Olmsted, the nineteenth-century traveller, tells of reading a news account of an old Negro slave who was found lying dead in the woods. At the coroner's inquest it was found that the seventy-year-old Negro was too old to work and so "they

---

*First published as chapter 1 in Robert E. Moran, *One Hundred Years of Child Welfare in Louisiana* (Lafayette, La.: Center for Louisiana Studies, 1980), 1-5. Reprinted with the kind permission of the author and the University of Louisiana at Lafayette.

drove him forth into the woods to die." On the other hand, Olmsted also relates how a New Orleanian owned but one slave, an old woman he bought purely out of compassion. The man reportedly supported the slave for several years without receiving the smallest amount of work in return.[3] Between these two extremes of callousness and compassion lay the middle ground, perhaps best described by Kenneth Stampp. According to Stampp, very few aged "aunties" and "uncles" spent their declining years as pensioners living leisurely and comfortably at their master's expense, even though cost of supporting these few was negligible. Most slaves over sixty, though largely unproductive, did enough work to pay for their own support.[4]

In 1855 Louisiana adopted an act which made it illegal for a slaveowner to evade his responsibilities to an aged slave by emancipating him. The slave might be emancipated, but his master was required to post a $1,000 bond for the slave, a requirement designed to guard against the slave's becoming a public charge should he be emancipated with permission to remain in the state.[5]

Along with the care of the aged, the law provided that the master's responsibility included the sick and the pregnant. When it was discovered that a slave woman was pregnant, she was placed with others like her and assigned only to light duties. Unprincipled or overzealous overseers would occasionally overwork pregnant women, but generally speaking, progressive planters took pride in their care of mothers and their infants. When the mothers were able to return to work, they were again assigned to light jobs and permitted to visit the "nurse house" to attend their infants at least three times each day. Olmsted relates that when he visited a certain Louisiana plantation he saw several Negro women en route to the nursery to suckle their children—the overseer's bell having rung to summon them from work for that purpose. The plantation owner explained that he allotted the women two hours at noon to be with their children and one hour prior to the end of the working day.[6] The law also provided that children under the age of puberty were not to be sold separately from their mothers, except the child of a slave incarcerated for life. A child born to a life termer became the property of the state and when ten years of age was sold for cash, the proceeds going to the free school fund of the state.[7] Very few funds must have been collected from this source because in 1857 only two women were in the penitentiary, with no report of either being pregnant. While the slave lacked freedom, he did have social security of a sort. Outside of charity hospitals, state and local governments made little provision for the destitute. In 1857, the Legislative Committee on Charitable Institutions considered Charity Hospital at New Orleans, the insane asylum at Jackson, and the Institution for the Deaf, Dumb, and Blind at Baton Rouge as being the only agencies provided by the state for persons in need. The dependent child was placed in an orphanage located in New Orleans and the vagrant was placed in jail. The Charity Hospital of New Orleans often served as an almshouse and home for the aged, but there were some local citizens who opposed the principle of a "charity hospital which they felt treated lazy foreigners at the expense of hard working Americans."[8]

As previously stated, Louisiana prior to 1900 made little attempt to provide public relief for its dependent population, including its children. Until the 1870s the state appropriated small amounts of money to various private agencies, but depended chiefly upon philanthropical and private funds for the maintenance of social welfare institutions. A committee representing the state legislature occasionally visited the various private and public agencies which received money from the state, but the committee had little or no power to demand financial reports or provide guidelines for the management of these agencies.

One of the first institutions for destitute children in America was established in New Orleans in 1727 by the Ursuline nuns under the leadership of Mother Marie Tranchepain de St. Augustin. Here, for nearly a century, the nuns, despite scant means and public apathy, ministered to the sick, reared orphans, and educated white, black, and Indian girls. For some unknown reason, the orphanage attracted the attention of the city fathers in 1824. The city council received a report which stated that the orphan girls in the asylum were not treated properly and suggested that the orphans be withdrawn and placed in another institution. After an investigation, the girls were removed from Ursuline Convent to the recently built Poydras Asylum, on the condition that the mayor pay the directors of Poydras Asylum $1,600 for twenty-four girls and that they be taught French and English as well as the tenets of their respective religions.[9]

In 1816 Julien Poydras, poet, statesman, and philanthropist, donated a large lot and house for the purpose of establishing an asylum for orphaned girls. When the legislature in 1817 incorporated the Female Orphan Society or the Poydras Asylum, it established the first of a long list of Catholic, Protestant, and Jewish institutions caring for orphans and widows which received some state aid. In the act of incorporation the state promised to pay $2,000 for the benefit of the agency which opened the same year with fourteen orphans.[10] Ten years later, in 1827, it enrolled nearly ninety girls, including those from the old Ursuline Convent. The Poydras Male Orphan Asylum, also endowed by Julien Poydras, was established as the result of an appeal by the mayor and a group of women to help care for twenty orphan children brought into port by a plague-stricken immigrant ship.

Another philanthropist, Alexandre Milne, provided for two asylums in his will of 1838. Lengthy and costly litigation slowed the opening of the asylums, and caused the boys' asylum to close soon after it opened. It reopened in 1854 with a $5,000 donation from Judah Touro, the Jewish philanthropist.

The population of New Orleans, residents of a semitropical port city, were frequently victims of yellow fever or cholera epidemics. Between 1796 and 1850 New Orleans experienced some twenty serious outbreaks of yellow fever. The 1850s, however, would mark the climax of the scourge, especially the years 1853 and 1858. Then, during the second half of the century, the incidence of yellow fever diminished until the disease disappeared from the United States in 1905.[11] Nevertheless, following each epidemic of the preceding century, the problems of the destitute were intensified and new asylums had to be organized for their care.

One such agency was the Protestant Society for the Relief of Destitute Orphan Boys which was organized at a meeting held in 1824 in the Presbyterian church. An act of the legislature in 1825 incorporated the Society and authorized the state treasurer to donate $2,000 to the institution on behalf of the state of Louisiana.[12] Despite difficulties, the Protestant Society survived the epidemic of 1832, and, during the next two years, received 319 orphans, of whom 48 died, 65 were apprenticed, and 119 were taken in by friends, leaving 87 in the asylum.[13] Until 1841 the contributions from the community sustained the institution, but it was without permanent endowment. When fire destroyed the dormitory, library, and schoolhouse, the orphanage appealed to the public for assistance. John McDonogh, an eccentric but rich old bachelor, who died in 1850, bequeathed a large amount of money and property to the free schools of Baltimore and New Orleans, including $100,000 to the Society which enabled it to rebuild. Until 1900 it was supported chiefly by income derived from rentals of its own property.

In 1853, the year of the worst yellow-fever epidemic, the disease took the lives of 8,130 men, women, and children. A group to emerge from this disaster was the Howard Association, businessmen concerned with the plight of the destitute. With funds contributed by well-wishers throughout the country, the Howards established three orphan asylums, one of which was the Protestant Orphans' Home. This institution received its financial support from the Howard Association which placed there 56 of the 241 children left to its care. Each child brought a dower of $100, and the Association donated an additional $2,000, making $7,600 in all. The other 185 children were placed in other asylums established by the Association. The Howards not only founded new orphanages but also gave money to the old ones and otherwise helped the needy.[14]

Also in 1853, the Joint Committee on Charitable Institutions of the Louisiana Legislature suggested that appropriations be given to four private institutions: the Orphan Boys' Asylum with 118 boys, Poydras Female Orphan Asylum with 124 girls, the Female Orphan Asylum with 360 girls, and the St. Mary's Orphan Boys' Asylum with 226 boys. The committee recommended that $1,000 be given Poydras Asylum if it received a financial statement concerning the disposition of these state funds. The committee suggested withholding funds from all institutions which did not provide the state with a financial statement. The committee's recommendation went unheeded by both legislators and institutions, and whereas the committee recommended $1,000 for Poydras Asylum, the legislature actually appropriated $1,500 for the orphanage.[15]

The plague, to say the least, aggravated an appalling situation. Homes, such as the Female Orphan Asylum, which normally cared for about forty girls, found themselves with as many as three hundred on any one day. The inconveniences and suffering experienced by these children are hardly imaginable. The Joint Committee Report of 1857 stated that the terrible scourge of 1853 had filled to capacity the orphanages of the state and caused an increase in their number. The narrowness of the committee members' views can be seen in their suggestion that the state foster those institutions which had for their primary object the elevation of the morals and cultivation of the minds of the orphan children of the state. The number of institutions recommended for state aid was increased to nine, but no aid was given to the Milne Asylum since it had an endowment. The committee recommended the establishment of a board of visitation whose duty would be to supervise the institutions of the state "in common with the immediate supervisors of the institutions."[16] This suggestion was to go unheeded for nearly fifty years. Other institutions for children established before the Civil War included the Protestant Orphan Home of Baton Rouge, founded in 1847, and the Jewish Orphans' Home of New Orleans, founded in 1856.

If the state neglected to provide adequate facilities for white children, it completely ignored the plight of the free Negroes. There was no problem of dependent children among slaves since every child had an owner and he could find a "mother" in his quarters. Children were often separated from their parents through sale, although on numerous occasions the slave mother and her children were advertised for sale as a group so that they might remain together. On the other hand, the free Negro orphan had no such guaranteed security. Like his Creole counterpart, he had to be cared for by friends or relatives until such time as he could care for himself.

There was, therefore, a need in the antebellum era for an institution to care for destitute Negro children. Madame Bernard Couvent, a widowed free woman of color living in New Orleans, recognized this need and in her will bequeathed some property to promote education among her people. Additional funds were gathered by other wealthy free Negroes who then organized the Société Catholique pour l'Instruction des Orphelins dans l'Indigence. Funds were tied up in court for a number of years, preventing the school from officially opening until 1848. In 1852 Armand Lanusse became its first principle and had on his staff some of the leading Negro intellectuals of New Orleans. The Institution Catholique des Orphelins Indigents was not recommended for state aid until after the Civil War. At that time the Joint Committee reported that there were about 280 children in the school, all of whom were descendants of the original free colored population of New Orleans. One half of those paid a monthly fee; the remainder paid nothing.[17]

In 1855 the legislature placed an impediment in the way of Negroes who would have liked to organize for benevolent purposes. It specifically excluded free persons of color from an act which permitted six persons to incorporate for religious, scientific, literary, or charitable reasons.[18] Nevertheless, as John Hope Franklin indicates, free Negroes held fraternal and benevolent organizations in high esteem, and, even though these societies were illegal in Louisiana, they persisted right up to the eve of the Civil War.[19]

Notes for "Child Welfare and Public Relief in the Antebellum Era"

[1] Article 229 of the Louisiana Civil Code of 1825.

[2] Charles Havens Hunt, *The Life of Edward Livingston* (New York, 1864), 267.

[3] Frederick Law Olmsted, *Journey in the Seaboard Slave States* (New York, 1861), 623, 710.

[4] Kenneth M. Stampp, *The Peculiar Institution: Slavery in the Ante-Bellum South* (New York, 1956), 318.

[5] *Louisiana Acts of 1855*, No. 308, Section 72.

[6] Olmsted, *Journey in the Seaboard Slave States*, 657.

[7] *Louisiana Acts of 1848*, No. 4, ex. sess.

[8] Robert C. Reinders, *End of An Era* (New Orleans, 1964), 91.

[9] Edwin A. Davis, *The Story of Louisiana* (New Orleans, 1960), 92; Albert E. Fossier, *New Orleans, the Glamour Period, 1800-1840* (Natchez, Miss., 1957), 247.

[10] *A General Digest of the Acts of the Legislature of Louisiana Passed from the Year 1804 to 1827* (New Orleans, 1828), 2:260.

[11] John Duffy, *Sword of Pestilence* (Baton Rouge, 1966), 7. See also Jo Ann Carrigan, "The Saffron Scourge: A History of Yellow Fever in Louisiana, 1796-1905" (Ph.D. dissertation, Louisiana State University, 1961), passim.

[12] *A General Digest*, 2:165, 167.

[13] Fossier, *New Orleans, the Glamour Period*, 252.

[14] *Report of the Howard Association* (New Orleans, 1853), 23, 27.

[15] *Report of the Joint Committee on Charitable Institutions, Documents of the Louisiana Legislature* (New Orleans, 1853).

[16] *Special Report of the Legislative Committee on Charitable Institutions*, Documents of the Louisiana Legislature (New Orleans, 1857), 3.

[17] *Report of the Committee on Charitable Institutions*, Documents of the Louisiana Legislature (New Orleans, 1867), 6.

[18] *Louisiana Acts of 1855*, No. 132, p. 185.

[19] John Hope Franklin, *From Slavery to Freedom* (New York, 1962), 223.

SALLY MULLER, THE WHITE SLAVE*

Carol Wilson

> A white skin is no security whatsoever. I should no more dare to send white children out to play alone, especially at night . . . than I should dare send them into a forest of tigers and hyenas.
>
> (Parker Pillsbury to William Lloyd Garrison, 1853)[1]

One day in the spring of 1843, Mrs. Karl Rouff, a German immigrant, went into a cafe on Levee Street in New Orleans. The slave who served her looked familiar, and eventually Madame Karl, as she was known, realized that the woman was one of her compatriots, Salome Muller. The two had last seen each other more than two decades earlier when both arrived in the city with several hundred other Germans. Muller's mother and infant brother had not survived the voyage, and her father and older brother died soon after arrival. Salome and her sister Dorothea, both under age six, had never been seen or heard from again.[2]

Madame Karl questioned the slave, who displayed no recollection of her previous life. She explained that she was the property of Louis Belmonti, owner of the cafe. Madame Karl then took Muller to the home of Eve and Francis Schuber, who had traveled on the same voyage. Mrs. Schuber was Muller's cousin and godmother. The Schubers also positively identified her as the missing girl, Salome, known as Sally. With their help, she sued in court for her freedom, first losing, then winning on appeal to the Louisiana State Supreme Court.[3]

Muller's story was known to nineteenth-century Louisianans. In 1889, popular author George Washington Cable published *Strange True Stories of Louisiana*. It contained a piece entitled "Salome Muller, The White Slave," about a German girl who came to Louisiana as a child with her family, and after being orphaned, found herself enslaved. Later, as an adult, she successfully sued in court to regain her freedom. The same year, a German scholar at Tulane University, J. Hanno Deiler, also published an

---

*First published in *Louisiana History*, 40 (1999): 133-53. Reprinted with the kind permission of the author and the Louisiana Historical Association.

account of the Muller case, in a pamphlet on the history of Germans in Louisiana.[4] But since then, the fascinating case has fallen into obscurity.

How could a white person become enslaved in the antebellum United States, in a society that clearly equated slave status with black skin? How could a German immigrant be mistaken for an African American? Although certainly not common, Muller's experience was not unique.[5] The enslavement of a white person reveals that American ideas about slavery and race were not nearly as clear cut as many whites believed.

In 1817, the Mullers left their home in the town of Langensoultzbach, Wurtemburg, part of a large migration of southern Germans during the aftermath of the Napoleonic Wars,[6] when a reactionary government had instituted press censorship and harrassment of intellectuals. Probably more important for the masses, however, was the local economic crisis. Wurtemberg, like other nearby states, had a large population to support on land poorly suited to agriculture. In 1817, the region experienced one of the most devastating famines in its history. That year alone, over sixteen thousand people left Wurtemberg.[7]

The Mullers paid full passage to Philadelphia, planning to move west of the city into the farm country inhabited by many of their countrymen. Though some of their Wurtemberg neighbors were farmers, members of the Muller family were skilled artisans. Sally's father Daniel was a shoemaker, his brother Henry a lockmaker. Still, they had been negatively affected by the poor agricultural economy, and in April, they set out with a large party of friends and relatives for Amsterdam.[8]

Arriving in August, laden with all their worldly possessions, they were sent to Den Helder, the deep-water port on the North Sea. Here they remained, along with nearly nine hundred other anxious passengers aboard the *Rudolph,* a huge Russian ship, and several smaller ships for three to four months. Winter was growing near, food supplies were dwindling, and eventually the passengers discovered that they had been swindled. The agent to whom they had paid their passage to the United States had absconded with their money.[9]

This put the Mullers, like their relatives and neighbors, in a precarious position. While not completely impoverished, they had spent their savings booking passage to the United States, traveling to Amsterdam, and buying provisions for the journey. Now those provisions were nearly exhausted. Some of the emigrants resorted to begging in the streets. Eventually the Dutch government intervened on their behalf and arranged for three ships to take them to the United States. They sailed in December 1817.[10]

But the worst was not yet behind the Mullers. Incredibly, the unfortunate travelers faced further hardship. First, they were informed that their destination was no longer Philadelphia, but rather New Orleans, over a thousand miles farther south.[11] A more different location would have been hard to imagine. New Orleans in 1818 was less than two decades in American hands, and seemed in many ways still a European outpost. Residents spoke French, street signs were in French or Spanish, and even the legal system, as Sally Muller was to discover years later, bore the stamp of the Roman civil code, rather than English common law. Philadelphia, a large, sophisticated, prosperous port, had served previously as the nation's capital and still carried its distinctive Quaker influence. New Orleans was a backwater by contrast, but it had become a boom town whose population had doubled in the decade after American aquisition. This population was diverse; particularly surprising to European arrivals was the large number of black and mixed-race residents. Situated in a swamp, the city was unhealthy in the extreme. Immigrant guidebooks warned travelers away from the city during the yellow-fever season, extending from May to October.[12]

But the change in destination hardly constituted the worst of the immigrants' problems. The voyage itself was nightmarish. While about nine hundred persons had departed Holland, only about three hundred arrived alive in New Orleans on March 6, 1818. The journey to a new life brought death instead for many passengers, including Dorothea Muller, Sally's mother, and her infant child, named Daniel after his father. Like others who had died, they were buried at sea. The cause of these two deaths as well as the other passengers' is not fully known, but starvation clearly played a part. Most of the food supplies had been used up while the ill-starred passengers waited at Den Helder. Those who were already ill or weakened, as Dorothea Muller likely was, having given birth prior to the journey, were particularly vulnerable.[13]

At least the arriving Germans were not alone. Since the early eighteenth century, Louisiana had attracted German immigrants. In antebellum New Orleans, they congregated in Lafayette, a suburb (absorbed by the expanding metropolis, Lafayette became the Fourth Municipality in 1852), and in the Faubourg Marigny (the city's Third Municipality). By 1839, the German community had its own German-language newspaper, and in 1847, a German Society had organized to help immigrants.[14] But this was of little help to the Muller family.

The surviving Mullers—father Daniel, and his three young children, Jacob, Dorothea, and Sally—prepared to start new lives in what for them was a new world. But still trouble plagued them. Although the Dutch government had paid full passage for the Mullers and their compatriots, who had already paid passage once, at least one captain tried to get more. Claiming that the immigrants were responsible for paying their way, Captain Grandsteever of the *Juffer Johanna* arranged to sell some of the Germans into indentured servitude through advertisements in a local newspaper.[15]

Although more commonly associated with early colonial settlement of the eastern seaboard states, indentured servitude was still a source of labor in the nineteenth-century United States. The abolition of the international slave trade in 1808 had heightened interest in alternative methods of acquiring workers. The region of Germany from which the Mullers hailed, ravaged by war and famine, was a particular target of ship owners and their agents. Those too poor to pay passage across the Atlantic could obtain transportation by selling their labor, usually for three to eight years. At the end of their terms, they were to be "redeemed," hence the term commonly applied to them, redemptioners.[16] The system was abusive enough, however, to incite public outrage and several states passed laws to regulate it, as Louisiana did immediately after the case of the Mullers and their compatriots attracted journalistic attention.[17]

Such action came too late, though, to help the Mullers. Despite protests by the immigrants and their defenders in New Orleans, and even a court inquiry which should have shown clearly that they were being swindled yet again, some of the unluckier passengers among them found themselves indentured, the Muller family included. Less than a month after their first sight of America at the Balize, the Mullers were journeying upriver to either the Attakapas region, the south-central portion of the state known for cattle-raising, or nearby Opelousas, their services apparently having been purchased by a farmer.[18]

Impossible though it seems, even further tragedy awaited the Mullers. On the trip, Daniel Muller died. Reports identify the cause of his death variously as drowning, fever, or apoplexy. His young son Jacob fell overboard and drowned. Accidents were not uncommon for boat travelers at this time. According to historian Donald J. Millet, "Rivers and bayous deviled boat captains by the existence of snags, log jams, and fallen and overhanging trees that were a constant menace to navigation."[19] What became of the two little orphaned girls was not known. Numerous friends and relatives searched for them, but they vanished without a trace, until Madame Karl's shocking discovery of Sally a quarter-century later.[20]

How did Sally, age four when she was orphaned, become a slave? The answer is not known, for at the time of her disappearance while en route westward she disappears from the historical record as well. She reappears four years later, listed on a deed of sale from slave trader Anthony Williams of Mobile, Alabama, to John Fitz Miller of New Orleans.[21] Exactly how she came into Williams' possession is not clear, but it is possible to surmise. A young child, orphaned, speaking no English, indentured to a farmer in an isolated rural area of the state, was easily exploited. Who would protect her rights? The kidnapping of free black children into slavery was not uncommon; apparently it could happen to whites as well.[22]

Sally Muller spent most of her life in Louisiana as the slave of John Fitz Miller. From 1822 to 1838, Muller worked for Miller and his widowed mother, Sarah Canby.[23] (As the slave of John Miller, Sally was known as Sally Miller, but for reasons of clarity, this writer has chosen to refer to her by her original name of Muller.)

John Fitz Miller was one of New Orleans's prominent citizens. A wealthy businessman, he started out in the lumber trade, establishing a sawmill in the city. As he prospered, Miller expanded his enterprises, adding a second sawmill, a sugar mill, and a rum distillery. He also acquired a good deal of land in the Attakapas region. Like Sally, he was not a native of New Orleans; ironically, he came from Philadelphia, the city she and her family had been trying to reach. Never married, Miller lived with his mother in the Crescent City and later at several residences across the state, including one at New Iberia, and one on what is today called Jefferson Island, where Miller helped found a resort and thoroughbred racetrack.[24]

Sally worked as a house servant, and if accounts of Miller's friends are to be believed, she, like his and his mother's other slaves, was not particularly ill-treated. During her time at Miller's she gave birth to three children, the first, Lafayette, born in 1825. In 1838, Miller sold Muller to Louis Belmonti, who ran a cafe in the Faubourg Marigny, close to Miller's New Orleans mill and residence. She had been working six years for her new owner when she filed her lawsuit.[25]

After being discovered by her long-lost German friends, Sally Muller sued Louis Belmonti and John Fitz Miller in District Court on the grounds that she was a free, white woman and had been illegally held in slavery.[26] Her case was argued by a team of lawyers including Christian Roselius. Considered one of the most brilliant attorneys in Louisiana's history, Roselius, at the time of the trial, had just finished serving as the state's attorney general. He was later a delegate to two state constitutional conventions and was professor and dean of the University of Louisiana (now Tulane University) Law School. But he, like his client, had humble origins. Born in Bremen, Germany, in 1803, Roselius had come to New Orleans in 1819 as a redemptioner.[27]

His almost equally well-known opponent, John R. Grymes, served as Miller's attorney. A former state legislator, Grymes was best known for having defended successfully the Lafitte brothers against charges of piracy. Grymes also had a connection with German redemptioners. He, with his partner Edward Livingston (who later became famous as the coauthor of the state's heralded civil code), had acted as counsel for the 1818 immigrants in their unsuccessful lawsuit against the ship's Captain Grandsteever. Grymes' feelings regarding this apparent conflict of interest are not known. His inexpert handling of the Germans' original case contributed directly to Sally's enslavement; now, a quarter of a century later, Grymes was fighting to perpetuate that enslavement.[28]

Muller's suit was based on several legal points. Most prominent was the testimony of witnesses who had known her as a child and could identify her and attest to her resemblance to the Muller family. Several German immigrants who had journeyed to this country with the Mullers in 1818 remembered the little girl and either noted the plaintiff's strong resemblance to the family, or recognized her more specifically as Sally Muller. These witnesses included both relatives and non-relatives. Among the former were her cousin and godmother, Eve Schuber, and Schuber's husband, Francis, a butcher who had been ship's steward on the voyage. Sally's cousin, Daniel Muller, who had also come over at the same time, traveled from his home in Wilkinson County, Mississippi, to identify her. These witnesses were adamant in their statements, Daniel Muller saying he had no doubt that she was the lost girl, and Eve Schuber claiming that she could recognize the plaintiff as her missing cousin "out of a hundred thousand people."[29]

The existence of birthmarks on the plaintiff's body provided even stronger evidence that she was in fact Sally Muller. A number of the German witnesses, especially women who had cared for the little girl after her mother died on board ship, recalled the young Sally as having two birthmarks. Described as similar in appearance to coffee beans, she had one on the inside of each thigh. Two prominent New Orleans doctors, Armand

Mercier and Warren Stone, examined the plaintiff, and attested to the fact that she did indeed possess such marks and that she had been born with them.[30]

Also supporting the plaintiff's case was the testimony of three witnesses who recalled hearing her speak, soon after arriving at Miller's home in New Orleans, with a German accent. One of these, a Madame Poigneau, who described herself as a Creole who spoke no English, stated that the plaintiff "always spoke German."[31]

Although she was too young to remember the details herself, her petition asserted that John F. Miller had purchased the indentures of the Muller family and took Sally to the Attakapas region, where he made a slave of her.[32]

In his defense John Miller claimed the plaintiff was not Sally Muller, but rather a "mulatress slave" known either as Bridgett or Mary Bridgett whom he had acquired through legal means in 1822; he denied any knowledge of her prior to that time. Defense witnesses made assertions as to Miller's and his mother's good character and rebutted the prosecution's statements.[33]

Several witnesses attested to the plaintiff's appearance being in accord with that of a non-white person. People who had known her when she worked for Miller assumed that she was of mixed race, "colored," or a "quadroon." One added that he had seen slaves whiter than she.[34] Clearly these people were not shocked by the existence of slaves who physically looked to be white. It was apparently not a unique experience.

Those who knew her when she worked at Miller's home and mill in New Orleans all claimed that she had no German accent. Emile Johns, a Polish musician who had arrived in the city in 1819, said that he would have known if there had been a "dutch girl" at Miller's. Another witness, German-born Joachim Kohn, also stated that she had no German accent.[35]

Rosalie Labarre, a midwife and neighbor of Miller's, said that she had been present at the birth of the plaintiff's first child and denied seeing any birthmarks on her body.[36]

Against the plaintiff's claim that she had been in Miller's possession since 1818, Miller produced the bill of sale which showed that he had purchased her in New Orleans from Anthony Williams, slave trader of Mobile, in 1822. In fact, Williams had left Muller with Miller to be sold by him, and had been given only one hundred dollars advance on the potential sale. Why had Williams been willing to part with her so cheaply? There is no indication that he ever returned or contacted Miller to collect the full sale price or even to see if she had been sold. Efforts to find him during the trial were unsuccessful. Cable suggests that Muller was so white-looking as to be a liability on the slave market. Unable to sell her easily, Williams was apparently willing to have her taken off his hands for a small amount.[37]

Miller's attorneys also argued that the plaintiff was too old to be Sally Muller, who according to witnesses, was about four years old when she arrived in this country in 1818. That would have made her only eight or nine years old when she became Miller's slave in 1822. His witnesses put her age, based on appearance, closer to twelve or thirteen at the time. She gave birth to her first child around the time of General Marie Joseph Paul

Yves Roch Gilbert Motier, marquis de Lafayette's visit to New Orleans in April, 1825. This testimony, however, was not consistent. Witnesses variously stated the child was born in 1823, '24, and '25. One witness claimed that the child, named for Lafayette, was already eight or nine by 1824.[38]

A verdict was issued in favor of the defendants Miller and Belmonti. Judge A. M. Buchanan provided several reasons why Muller had lost her case. First, he noted that the age of the plaintiff and the age of the lost German girl (the "real" Sally Muller) did not coincide. The plaintiff had given birth to a child in 1825 when Sally Muller would have been ten years old. Secondly, he argued that the defense witnesses were more credible than those of the plaintiff. Virtually all of Muller's witnesses were German immigrants who had known her only as a child. Thirdly, according to the defense witnesses, as far back as 1822, when Miller acquired her, Muller had no trace of a German accent or appearance. Lastly, the plaintiff had not established a link between Miller and Muller: it was obviously not John Miller who had purchased the Muller family as redemptioners in 1818. All the evidence pointed to her not coming into his possession until 1822. Judge Buchanan concluded by suggesting that if her supporters were still convinced that the plaintiff was really Sally Muller, they could purchase her, adding that "they would doubtless find [the defendant] well disposed to part on reasonable terms, with a slave from whom he can scarcely expect any service, after what has passed."[39]

Was this last statement an indication that the judge entertained some doubt about Muller's status? On each point where the plaintiff's and defense witnesses disagreed, Buchanan sided with the defense. Yet his final comment hardly encouraged the retention of Sally Muller in slavery. Perhaps he suspected her true identity but found it difficult to publically side with a slave against a powerful white businessman.

Rather than follow the judge's advice, Muller appealed her case to the State Supreme Court, arguing that the decision ran contrary to the evidence presented and that since the first trial new evidence supporting her claim had been uncovered.[40]

In the appeal, one of her attorneys, Wheelock S. Upton asked if his client was not the real Salome Muller, then who was?[41] Since the case had attracted much attention in the press, he argued, surely the long-lost German girl would have heard of it. She was alleged to have been sent to Attakapas, where John Miller happened to own a large plantation; why didn't he produce the real German woman? There was no one, Upton noted, other than the plaintiff, who claimed to be Sally Muller.[42]

Upton reiterated the powerful physical evidence in his client's favor. Numerous friends and relatives, including the midwife present at Sally Muller's birth and others who had cared for her intimately as a child, not only testified that the plaintiff bore a strong resemblance to other members of the Muller family, they positively affirmed that she *was* Sally. Her birthmarks, verified by two physicians, provided even further proof.[43]

Public opinion was in her favor, too, Upton argued, noting that Judge Buchanan had dismissed this as mere sympathy. It is interesting that her lawyer said that he had drawn attention to her public support not to evoke an outpouring of public sympathy, "but to show that she must be white." Physical appearance aside, he claimed that quadroons were different in character from whites, quadroons being, in his opinion, "idle, reckless, and extravagant." Surely, he contended, such a person could not fool white people into supporting her. Therefore, the plaintiff must be white.[44]

The newfound evidence involved the question of Sally's age and the possibility that both Miller and Belmonti had been aware that they were enslaving a white woman. On the subject of her age, Muller's attorney raised two points. One included testimony which reconciled the plaintiff's age with Sally Muller's. The German girl's birth certificate, obtained from Alsace, confirmed that she had been born on July 10, 1813, thus making her nearly four years old when she arrived at New Orleans, as most of her witnesses agreed. Added to this was the testimony of a Madame Bertrand, who had been absent from court during the first trial because of illness. She said that she had been present at the birth of Lafayette, the plaintiff's first child, in 1827 or '28. In addition, N. W. Wheeler, who had testified at the first trial that the child had been born in 1824 or '25, now recalled that it had in fact been 1827 or '28. Sally Muller would have been fourteen or fifteen, old enough to have a child, in 1827 or '28.[45]

The plaintiff's lawyers also noted that Miller's own records contradicted his witnesses' claims that the plaintiff had borne a child in 1824 or '25. In the 1838 bill of sale for the plaintiff which Miller gave to Belmonti, her age is given as 22. That would place her birth date in 1816, making it highly unlikely that she had borne a child in 1827 or '28, at age 8 or 9. Lafayette's bill of sale from Miller to his mother Sarah Canby lists the boy's age as five in 1834, placing the date of his birth in 1829, five years later than Miller's witnesses. Thus, Miller had been allowed to contradict his own evidence in the first trial. All of this new evidence supported the plaintiff's claims that she was Sally Muller, born in 1813. She certainly could have borne her first child in 1829 at age sixteen.[46]

On the second issue, new testimony was added to corroborate that of Eve Schuber, Muller's godmother, who had overheard Belmonti say "that he was informed by Miller that the plaintiff could not be held in slavery—that she was white." Peter Curren, a pilot at the Balize, said that within the last year he and Belmonti had had numerous conversations about the court case. Belmonti said that he had known something like this would happen. A few weeks after he bought Muller, he told Curren, Belmonti had quarreled with her and had gone to Miller's to rescind the sale. Miller revealed that Muller "was in fact a white woman and was only to be held as a slave by kindness and coaxing." According to Curren, Belmonti was so angry that he wanted to shoot Miller.[47]

In summing up the Supreme Court opinion, Judge Henry Adams Bullard first addressed the issue of the plaintiff's physical appearance. He noted that since the case of *Adelle* v. *Beauregard* (1810), persons of mixed racial background were presumed free, the burden of proof thus falling on the person claiming the plaintiff as a slave.

The proof with regards to Muller's complexion, Bullard wrote, was strong. Not only was there no evidence of her having African parentage, a point crucial to proving slave status, the judges were impressed by the testimony of one of the defense witnesses, John

Lawson Lewis, who described Muller as being "as white as most persons."[48] Lewis was a general of the state militia who won election as sheriff of Orleans Parish in 1845. He later served as the city's mayor from 1854-56.[49] The judges appear not to have examined the plaintiff's appearance themselves.

A reporter for the *New Orleans Daily Picayune* noted Muller's olive complexion and added that "when young [she] must have been pretty good-looking." The *New Orleans Tropic* gave a more detailed description: "though somewhat of a brunette, and her parents were both of a dark complexion, her long, straight, black hair, hazel eyes, and Roman nose and thin lips strongly proclaim her origin." The newspaper noted that Muller's time spent working outdoors in the sun obviously darkened her skin, but concluded that "no one, it seems to us, can have doubts that she is a white woman."[50]

In addition, the court noted the testimony of numerous relatives and acquaintances who either recognized the plaintiff as Sally Muller or saw the family resemblance. The birthmarks that witnesses recalled seeing on the German child were confirmed by medical examination of the plaintiff's body. The defense counsel had claimed that the German witnesses were not persuasive, but the court noted that they had nothing to gain by falsely claiming to recognize the plaintiff.

Bullard addressed the issue raised by the defendants that under the Spanish law (support for which still lingered in Louisiana's legal system), when the master in a freedom suit produced title to the slave, the burden of proof then fell upon the plaintiff. But in this case, the court argued, the slave trader, Anthony Williams, authorized the sale of a child "apparently white" at a time when the law forbade the sale of any slave child from its mother.

Therefore, the judges concluded that the only relevant question was whether Sally Muller had been born free. Bullard wrote that "if there be in truth two persons, about the same age, bearing a strong resemblance to the Millers [Mullers] and the plaintiff is not the real lost child . . . *it is certainly one of the most extraordinary things in history.*" This time, the five sitting judges agreed with the plaintiff. The Supreme Court declared Sally Muller a free white woman and ordered her released from slavery.[51]

A party was held in Lafayette to celebrate Muller's victory, according to newspaper accounts, "with music and dancing, a sumptuous feast and an abundance of rich wines, and they enjoyed themselves until a late hour. More than two hundred ladies were present—the rich, the beautiful, the accomplished representatives of the best portion of our German resident population." Muller's attorney, Wheelock S. Upton, gave a speech in her honor:

> When we consider her sex, her station, and her means, and contrast them with the wealth, and the power, and the influence of those who contended against her, it is indeed a matter of gratulation [*sic*] and joy that her success was triumphant. Truth, however might it may be in its simplicity, has not always prevailed against the machinations of the wicked and the arts of the fraudulent.[52]

Another newspaper found significance in the ballroom's decor: "The room was well adorned with the emblems of American liberty, and *that* 'Star-Spangled Banner' which has so long floated o'er *our* 'land of the free and home of the brave,' was the principal decoration of the room where this happy reunion took place."[53]

But Sally Muller's story did not end with this happy reunion. After losing his case in the Supreme Court, John Fitz Miller retaliated against his former slave, suing her for fraud. In a suit begun in 1848, Miller claimed to have discovered the *real* Sally Muller, along with her sister Dorothea, living in Moorehouse Township, in the northern part of the state. Miller also produced the indenture agreements of the Muller family from 1818, showing them bound to Thomas Grayson, a Boeuf Prairie farmer. Miller introduced a parade of several dozen witnesses, including Dorothea Muller (but not the woman he claimed was really Sally, who had died by the time of the 1848 trial).[54]

This time District Court Judge A. M. Buchanan sided against John Miller, writing simply that the allegations of his petition had not been proven. Miller appealed to the supreme court, which upheld the district court's decision.[55] In his opinion, Judge Pierre Rost gave three reasons for the dismissal. First, he noted that no suit to annul a judgment of the supreme court (referring to the previous decision in which Muller was declared free) could be maintained by a lower court. Secondly, Miller had not refunded Belmonti the money he paid for Muller. Therefore, Miller "had no interest in contesting the former decree and therefore, no capacity to do so." Louis Belmonti, who had effectively lost the seven hundred dollars he had paid for the slave, might have had a reason for challenging the earlier decision, but John Miller did not.[56] Even if Muller had still been in Miller's possession, her restoration to bondage was extremely unlikely. The Louisiana Supreme Court tended to follow the dictum that once a slave had been declared free, that freedom could not be revoked.[57]

In fact, Miller did have an interest in seeing the case overturned, but it was not financial. In his petition to the court, he claimed that the trial had resulted in the "throwing upon himself and upon his aged mother, in the minds of many, who do not know them, the suspicion of having been parties to an act which, had they really committed it, would have justly made them objects of scorn and reproach to the community." The case had received much publicity, especially in New Orleans, a city with an unusually large number of newspapers. According to William Turner, John Miller's former business partner, it "had been the town talk for some months."[58]

This publicity had even prompted Miller, during the course of the first trial, to defend himself in the press. In a statement printed by the *Daily Picayune,* he related the circumstances of Sally Muller's life as he had heard them reported, and those of his slave Bridget, a different person altogether. He emphasized that until his former slave had brought her lawsuit, he had "never heard of any claim of freedom being made by her." Nor did he believe her to be anything other than a mulatto. Miller reminded readers that he had been a respectable resident of New Orleans for thirty-six years and stated that anyone who knew him could not possibly believe him guilty of the crime with which he was charged.[59]

That crime was a serious one indeed. Miller and his mother stood accused of one of the worst offenses in American society, knowingly holding a white woman in bondage. Miller had been bested publicly by a woman, a former slave, his obvious social inferior. He had been humiliated. It was this final point that the supreme court addressed. The best they could do for his reputation was to note that "we have carefully perused the new evidence discovered by him [Miller]; that it stands in the record unimpeached, and is in direct conflict with that adduced by the defendant in the former suit to prove her birth and condition. If it can be true that the defendant is of German extraction, we consider the plaintiff as exonerated of all knowledge of that fact."[60]

Was Sally Muller, the former slave, truly the lost German girl? It seems more likely than not. The testimony of so many witnesses who knew her only as a child, yet recognized her a quarter century later is powerful. As the Supreme Court justices noted, Muller's witnesses had nothing to gain by pretending to recognize her if they really did not. There is no indication that they held abolitionist leanings. The Germans probably would not have settled permanently in Louisiana had they been strongly opposed to the institution of slavery.

The birthmarks provide even stronger physical evidence that the plaintiff was Sally Muller. Two doctors agreed that the woman they examined had been born with marks identical to those recalled on the body of the lost girl by numerous people. Muller's attorney raised a good point when he asked in his appeal to the Supreme Court, if this woman was not Sally Muller, the lost German girl, then who was?

If Sally Miller the slave was also Sally Muller the German immigrant, then how could a white person have been enslaved under a social and legal system that considered slavery predicated on race? In the first Supreme Court appeal, Judge Bullard explained that under Louisiana law, as defined in the case *Adelle* v. *Beauregard* (1810), a person of color was presumed free. In the slaveholding states, Bullard asserted, the burden of proof was upon the person claiming another as his or her slave. Citing the argument from *Adelle,* he wrote,

> Persons of color may have descended from Indians on both sides, from a white parent, or mulatto parents in possession of their freedom. Considering how much probability there is in favor of the liberty of these persons, they ought not to be deprived of it upon new presumptions, most especially as the right of holding them in slavery, if it exists, is in most instances, capable of being satisfactorily proven.

This presumption of freedom was especially applicable to a person already in possession of freedom. Ownership, especially when supported by written title, was considered evidence, but not conclusive proof, of slave status.[61]

One clarification must be made. The judge's use of the term "person of color" had a connotation more specific than the modern usage. Today it is frequently used to describe any person not of wholly European extraction; the terms "black" and "person of color" are sometimes used interchangeably. In antebellum Louisiana, however, the term was used more specifically to distinguish people of mixed racial ancestry from blacks or Africans. People of color or mulattos were presumed to be free unless proven otherwise, but blacks were not.[62]

In other Southern states, slaves suing for their freedom needed a guardian, a free person, to initiate the suit on their behalf. According to historian Judith Schafer, "The ability of a slave to sue for freedom directly was unique to Louisiana." This right derived from the Spanish code of law under which slaves gained the ability to purchase their freedom (coartacion.) In order to make such transactions, slaves were granted standing in court. Although coartacion did not survive, the ability to sue directly for freedom did. This was the only instance in which slaves had legal standing. Throughout the antebellum period, the State Supreme Court usually ruled favorably in freedom suits.[63]

In cases where slaves claimed freedom based on white ancestry, the plaintiff's physical appearance could be a persuasive argument regardless of legal doctrine. But appearance was not an absolute, rather it was interpreted through the lens of an individual's beliefs about the nature of race. The evidence of Gen. John Lawson Lewis provides an illustration. Lewis, the witness who so impressed the supreme court (probably because of his social position; other witnesses made statements similar to his but were not noted), although a witness for Miller, actually helped Sally Muller gain her freedom. He described Muller's physical appearance as being "as white as most persons" and added that he had seen other slaves as "bright" as she. Although he had once thought she had a somewhat "colored" appearance, upon reflection, he concluded that it was merely because he only saw her in the company of other slaves and *assumed* her to be a slave, and therefore, black.[64]

This was a candid observation for a white man in antebellum Louisiana, and one which highlights the issue here. Once a person was enslaved by another, he or she was presumed to be a slave, and therefore, of African ancestry. When the person being claimed was a child, an orphan from a foreign country, and the claimant a wealthy prominent citizen, the chances of her status being challenged were reduced even further.[65]

The circumstances by which this white child was transformed into a slave are not known. What happened to Sally Muller during the years between 1818, when she disappeared with her sister en route to Attakapas, and 1822, when she reappeared in the possession of the trader Anthony Williams and was sold to John Fitz Miller, is still unclear.

Did the abundance of people of mixed race throughout the South, especially in Louisiana, where they were openly recognized, open the door for white enslavement? If only "full-blooded" Africans and their descendants were eligible for slavery, a white person held in bondage would have been instantly noticed. Why, then, did whites cling to a system of racial designation that was not only unrealistic, but which even created a threat for them?

Some whites found white slavery easy to ignore because they did not feel themselves in jeopardy. All whites were not vulnerable to the same degree. Those who created and perpetuated the system—those who made the laws, interpreted them in court, influenced the public through their control of the press and setting of behavioral standards, the Southern planter elite—had little to fear from the dangers of white slavery. Upper and middle-class Northerners, by the same token, likely found the threat of enslavement personally remote.

Those who were wealthy, powerful, literate, and well-known in their communities were extremely unlikely to find themselves at the mercy of the capricious system of racial definition. The poor—urban and rural, immigrants, prisoners, and children, especially orphans—even when white had much more to fear. Youth, illiteracy, poverty, unfamiliarity with American life, and the legal presumption of slave status of those claimed as slaves, could all work against the white person unfortunate enough to become enslaved.

Southern whites accepted the discrepancy between reality and perception because it allowed them, at least those in power, to determine an individual's status. As philosopher Adrian Piper has written, one thing that makes a person black is the perception of others that he or she is black.[66] Sally Muller, then, was transformed into a black person because John Miller said she was, then turned back into a white because the Louisiana Supreme Court decided otherwise.

Notes for "Sally Muller, the White Slave"

[1] Parker Pillsbury to William Lloyd Garrison, *National Anti-Slavery Standard,* November 12, 1853.

[2] *Sally Miller v. Louis Belmonti and John Miller (called in warranty)*, First District Court of Louisiana, July 24, 1844, Docket #23,041, Supreme Court of Louisiana Collection, Earl K. Long Library, University of New Orleans (hereafter referred to as *Miller v. Belmonti* 1844.)

[3] *Miller v. Belmonti* 1844; *Sally Miller v. Louis Belmonti and John Miller (called in warranty)*, Supreme Court of Louisiana, July 16, 1845, Docket #5623, Supreme Court of Louisiana Collection, Earl K. Long Library, University of New Orleans (hereafter referred to as *Miller v. Belmonti* 1845.)

[4] George Washington Cable, *Strange True Stories of Louisiana* (New York, 1889). The chapter on the Sally Muller case was also published in the magazine *Century,* 38 (1889): 56-69. J. Hanno Deiler, "The System of Redemption in the State of Louisiana" *Louisiana Historical Quarterly,* 12 (1929): 426-47, trans. Louis Voss. William Wells Brown, the first African American novelist, also referred to the case in his novel *Clotel; or The President's Daughter* in William L. Andrews, ed., *Three Classic African-American Novels* (New York, 1990).

[5] For other cases, see Carol Wilson and Calvin D. Wilson, "White Slavery: An American Paradox" *Slavery and Abolition,* 19 (1998): 1-28.

[6] *Miller v. Belmonti* 1844.

[7] Carl Wittke, *We Who Built America: The Saga of the Immigrant* (New York, 1939), 188-89; John F. Nau, *The German People of New Orleans, 1850-1900* (1954; reprint ed., Leiden, 1958), 2-3; Walter D. Kamphoefner et al., eds., *News From the Land of Freedom: German Immigrants Write Home,* trans., Susan Carter Vogel (Ithaca, N.Y., 1988), 2; LaVern J. Rippley, *The German-Americans* (Boston, 1976), 40.

[8] *Miller v. Belmonti* 1844.

[9] Ibid.

[10] Ibid.

[11] Ibid.

[12] Virginia R. Dominguez, *White By Definition: Social Classification in Creole Louisiana* (New Brunswick, N.J., 1986), 112; Paul Wilhelm, Duke of Wurttemberg, *Travels in North America, 1822-24* (Norman, Okla., 1973), 32-34; Anita M. Mallinckrodt, *From Knights to Pioneers: One German Family in Westphalia and Missouri* (Carbondale, Ill., 1994), 119; Joseph Logsdon, "Immigration Through the Port of New Orleans," in M. Mark Stolarik, ed. *Forgotten Doors: The Other Ports of Entry to the United States* (Philadelphia, 1988), 107-13.

[13] *Miller v. Belmonti* 1844.

[14] Joan B. Garvey and Mary Lou Widmer, *Beautiful Crescent: A History of New Orleans* (New Orleans, 1988), 80, 86; John S. Kendall, "The Foreign Language Press of New Orleans" *Louisiana Historical Quarterly,* 12 (1929): 363; Don H. Tolzmann, ed. *Louisiana's German Heritage: Louis Voss' Introductory History* (1927; reprint ed., Bowie, Md., 1994), 76.

[15] *Miller v. Belmonti* 1844; *Louisiana Gazette,* March 5-11, 1818. There is some confusion over the captain's name. Cable refers to the ship's captain as Grandsteiner, the *Gazette* as Krahnstover. I have relied on the handwritten court documents, which identify him as Grandsteever, as the most direct source.

[16] Frederick M. Spletstoser, "Back Door to the Land of Plenty: New Orleans as an Immigrant Port," 2 vols. (Ph. D. dissertation, Louisiana State University, 1978), 1:25; Albert B. Faust, *The German Element in the United States,* 2 vols. (1909; reprint ed., New York, 1969), 1:66, 68-69, 72.

[17] *Louisiana Gazette,* March 14, 1818; *Niles' National Register,* April 11, 1818; Henry A. Bullard and Thomas Curry, *A New Digest of the Statutes of the State of Louisiana* (New Orleans, 1842), 1:692-95; Howard B. Furer, ed., *The Germans in America, 1607-1970* (Dobbs Ferry, N. Y., 1973), 22.

[18] *Miller v. Belmonti* 1844; Attakapas was the term given to the region encompassing the parishes of St. Mary, Lafayette, Vermilion, St. Martin, and Iberia. The Opelousas region included present-day St. Landry, Evangeline, Acadia, Jefferson Davis, Allen, Cameron, Calcasieu, and Beauregard parishes. Carl Brasseaux et al., *Creoles of Color in the Bayou Country* (Jackson, Miss., 1994), 5.

[19] Donald J. Millet, "The Saga of Water Transportation into Southwest Louisiana to 1900," *Louisiana History,* 15 (1974): 342.

[20] *Miller v. Belmonti* 1844.

[21] Ibid.

[22] Carol Wilson, *Freedom at Risk: The Kidnapping of Free Blacks in America, 1780-1865* (Lexington, Ky., 1994).

[23] *Miller v. Belmonti* 1844.

[24] Glenn R. Conrad, *New Iberia: Essays on the Town and Its People,* 2nd ed. (Lafayette, La., 1986), 67, 361-26.

[25] *Miller v. Belmonti* 1844.

[26] Muller, a slave, was able to sue directly because of a statute unique to Louisiana which gave slaves legal standing in freedom suits. *Digest of 1808,* Title VI, Chapter 3:30; *Civil Code of 1825,* Article 177, p. 28, in Judith Kelleher Schafer, *Slavery, the Civil Law and the Supreme Court of Louisiana* (Baton Rouge, 1994), 220.

[27] Glenn R. Conrad, ed., *A Dictionary of Louisiana Biography* (New Orleans, 1988), 2:696-97; Tolzmann, *Louisiana's German Heritage,* 63-64.

[28] Conrad, ed., *Dictionary of Louisiana Biography,* 1:363; *Miller v. Belmonti* 1844.

[29] *Miller v. Belmonti* 1844.

[30] Ibid.

[31] Ibid.

[32] Ibid.

[33] Ibid.

[34] Ibid.

[35] Ibid; Conrad, ed., *Dictionary of Louisiana Biography*, 1:436.

[36] *Miller v. Belmonti* 1844.

[37] Ibid.; Cable, *Strange True Stories*, 176-77.

[38] *Miller v. Belmonti* 1844.

[39] Ibid.

[40] *Miller v. Belmonti* 1845. The Supreme Court normally did not consider new evidence, but freedom suits were an exception. The precedent was established in *Marie Louise v. Marot* (1835), in which Chief Justice George Mathews wrote that the Court was obliged to do everything possible to establish a plaintiff's claim of freedom, including the consideration of new evidence. Schafer, *Slavery, the Civil Law and the Supreme Court of Louisiana*, 270.

[41] According to Cable, Roselius and Francis Upton argued her case before the Supreme Court; the latter's brother, Wheelock Upton, filed the original appeal. Cable, *Strange True Stories*, 171-72, 186, 187.

[42] *Miller v. Belmonti* 1845.

[43] Ibid.

[44] Ibid.

[45] Ibid.

[46] Ibid.

[47] Ibid.

[48] Ibid.

[49] Conrad, ed., *Dictionary of Louisiana Biography*, 1:511.

[50] *New Orleans Daily Picayune*, May 25, 1844; *New Orleans Tropic*, quoted in *Anti-Slavery Bugle*, July 25, 1845.

[51] *Miller v. Belmonti* 1845; *Miller v. Belmonti* 11, *Robinson's Reports* 339.

[52] *New Orleans Tropic*, quoted in *National Anti-Slavery Standard*, July 21, 1845.

[53] *New Orleans Jeffersonian Republican*, June 24, 1845.

[54] *John F. Miller v. Sally Miller*, Fifth District Court of Louisiana, May 17, 1848, Docket #24,454, Supreme Court of Louisiana Collection, Earl K. Long Library, University of New Orleans (hereafter referred to as *Miller v. Miller* 1848.)

[55] Ibid.

[56]*John F. Miller v. Sally Miller*, Supreme Court of Louisiana, May 21, 1849, Docket #1114, Supreme Court of Louisiana Collection, Earl K. Long Library, University of New Orleans (hereafter referred to as *Miller v. Miller* 1849); *Miller v. Miller* 4; *Louisiana Annual*, 354.

[57]Schafer, *Slavery, the Civil Law and the Supreme Court of Louisiana*, 275-76.

[58]*Miller v. Belmonti* 1844.

[59]*Daily Picayune,* May 31, 1844.

[60]Ibid.

[61]*Miller v. Belmonti* 1845; *Miller v. Belmonti,* 11 Rob 339. See also *Adelle v. Beauregard,* I Mart. La. 183, Fall 1810.

[62]Ibid.

[63]Schafer, *Slavery, the Civil Law and the Supreme Court of Louisiana,* 220-21.

[64]*Miller v. Belmonti* 1845.

[65]For other cases of white enslavement, see Wilson and Wilson, "White Slavery: An American Paradox."

[66]Adrian Piper, "Passing for White, Passing for Black," in Elaine K. Ginsburg, ed., *Passing and the Fictions of Identity* (Durham, 1996), 234-36.

INTRODUCTION TO *MADALINE**

Dell Upton

For most of her short life Madaline Selima Cage Elliott Edwards was a woman on her own and on the move. Between her marriage in 1831 and her death less than a quarter of a century later, she lived in Tennessee, Mississippi, Alabama, Louisiana, and California. As the penniless veteran of two failed marriages and the mistress of a married man, she was denied a recognized place in a society that made none for women without money and without the protection of husbands, fathers, or brothers. As a woman fascinated by words, she understandably turned to books and writing to help construct, reveal, and sometimes conceal a self.

In Madaline Edwards's diaries and letters, we read of the social being, the woman struggling to earn a living and to find fulfillment in a love affair on the social and urban fringes of New Orleans. In all her writings she worked to construct a tale that would make sense of her experience, give it a moral, redeem it. As she shaped the story of her life, Edwards tried on a variety of identities that might define a place for her, if not in the world's mind then at least in her own. She described ill-starred efforts to play her roles as daughter, niece, wife, mother, and schoolteacher acceptably. She earned a modest but erratic living as a teacher of painting and gained satisfaction and some repute, if no money, as an author. At times she fantasized about other callings, as astronomer, missionary, and even soldier, occupations that fascinated her or that she thought suited her temperament but that she believed were closed to her.[1]

The intersection of Madaline Edwards's daily life and imaginative life in her writings elicits from modern readers the "interest," or empathy for recognizable fellow beings, that nineteenth-century critics attributed to the best novels. In her work we detect a common

---

*First published as the Introduction in Dell Upton, *Madaline: Love and Survival in Antebellum New Orleans* (Athens and London: University of Georgia Press, 1996), 1-47. Reprinted with the kind permission of the author.

human dilemma, that of an ordinary person caught between "should" and "is," between the demands of society and the exigencies of personal circumstances. Edwards lived her life within social and moral structures that in many instances she painfully acknowledged to be appropriate and even just. Yet her "situation," as she called it, constantly demonstrated their limitations. When she was caught between contradictory dicta or trapped by those that seemed unfair, she questioned assumptions that most of her contemporaries accepted without thought. Edwards challenged the constraints of received moral and social precepts and of middle-class notions of gender and gentility by evoking other, equally common, precepts derived from Enlightenment religion and nineteenth-century popular literature.[2]

Edwards's predicament is less surprising than her detailed, explicit firsthand commentary on it, which offers a rare personal assessment of the life of a nineteenth-century woman at odds with her society. For that reason, Edwards is of interest not only to general readers but also scholars who wish to understand the relationship between social structures and the people who live them. In recent years many anthropologists, archaeologists, sociologists, and geographers have turned back to the personal, recognizing that the grand structures of society are frameworks within which particular lives are conducted. These scholars seek to void accounts of structures so overarching that they stultify individual action as well as romantic interpretations of personal action that ignore the defining role of social context. In his work on the Pacific Islands, for example, the anthropologist Marshall Sahlins depicts the networks of social rules, beliefs, and values—the ought-tos of our existence, the setting within which we frame our expectations of our lives and surroundings—but he also shows that these structures are placed at risk every time people act. Structure is tested in action, stretched, warped, and sometimes broken and cast aside.[3]

Sahlins calls the process of testing and modifying structure "history." Oddly, though, historians have been less openly interested in the problem of personal agency in a social context. Whey they have considered individual actions, they have traditionally examined the actions of great men (and, less often, of women) relatively divorced from social structure. Since the 1960s historians have democratized the field, opening it up to include ordinary men and women like Madaline Edwards. Yet they have tended to speak more of entire social groups and grand patterns, leaving no room for the good and bad human choices that nineteenth-century critics thought created "interest" in a good story and that attracted readers to older great-man history.[4]

For historians, then, Edwards's writings are valuable for their explicit juxtaposition of structure and individual action. She analyzed her own actions in the light of her social milieu, weighing the claims of self and society carefully. At the same time, her work was often self-consciously literary—not great literature, certainly, but a revealing effort to pour daily life into the molds of popular culture. In this respect, it illuminates the meaning of reading to ordinary people, a problem that has fascinated literary scholars in recent years.

Introduction to Madaline

A Choice and Its Consequences

Madaline Edwards wrote these diaries, letters, poems, and essays as a young woman aged twenty-six to thirty years old. By her own description, she was then five feet seven inches tall, weighed about 145 pounds, and was "well proportioned so I'm told." She had a high forehead and "large and full green eye[s]." "I sometimes paint but not my face," she added.[5]

Edwards had already lived a life that would have been eventful for someone twice her age. Clues to her history are scattered throughout her writings and to the extent that her words can be confirmed by other documents, there is no reason to suspect that she misrepresented or distorted biographical facts, although her interpretations of them varied from time to time. The story she told was a strikingly familiar one, of a powerful but unforgiving family, of parents unable to control their own lives, and of a daughter similarly unable to establish a satisfying life or personal relationships.

Selima Madaline Cage (she would later reverse her first and middle names— was born on December 28, 1816, in Sumner County, Tennessee, to Lofton Cage (born 1783) and Naomi (or Nabury) Gillespie Cage. She was the third child, after a brother who died as a young adult when Madaline was thirteen years old and a beloved sister, Eliza, who is mentioned frequently in Madaline's writings. A younger brother, Albert, and a younger sister, Fanny, played much smaller roles in her life.[6]

Madaline's family were leaders of the Sumner County community where she grew up. Her paternal grandfather was William Cage, a Virginia native and a major in the American Revolution. An early colonist in Tennessee, he settled at Cage's Bend on the Cumberland River before 1791. Major Cage was an active politician who had been the treasurer of the state of Franklin (the predecessor of the present state of Tennessee) and a county magistrate. After serving as county sheriff, Cage passed the office on to two of his sons in succession. One, William Cage, Jr., probably the uncle who raised Madaline, was a merchant and land speculator in partnership with James Winchester. Together they founded the town of Cairo, where they were the principal merchants and owners of the first steamboat based in the town.[7]

As the daughter of one of Sumner County's leading families, Madaline was a privileged child. She attended the female academy and the dancing academy at Gallatin, the county seat. For much of her childhood she lived with her uncle at the "ancestral homestead" (which was not much more than twenty-five years old when she was born), her grandfather's house adjacent to the family burying ground at Cage's Bend. There the child Madaline "loved (for I was a tomboy) to go in the fields and ride home in the carts loaded with the grain of the field and throw up the fodder and hays, but more than all the other joys dearest to me was the one of taking my book and steal[ing] away from all my companions. Her uncle's well-stocked library whetted this appetite for reading. As a young woman she was "daily accustomed to hear the violin and flute together and was ever in motion to dance."[8]

In her essays Edwards reminisces about rural beauties, beloved relatives, and the joys of the old homeplace. Yet these scenes of childhood idylls and of the genteel upbringing of a young woman destined for a comfortable life owe as much to the clichés of popular literature as to her own experience. They contrast sharply with the specifics of Cage family life that she reported.

Although she was descended from local gentry, Madaline Edwards was the child of a broken marriage, separated from her siblings and left to Cage family care soon after she started school. She rarely saw her parents until she was an adult. As late as 1844 Madaline had not met her brother Albert, who was then twenty-four years old. The separation from her immediate family was a bitter one that remained with her throughout her life. "I have never known a Mother yet I am her child and it is natural to drop a tear to her memory." By this time her parents were divorced, and her father had remarried and moved to Mobile.[9]

The entire extended Cage family were to Edwards's mind a hard-bitten, judgmental lot who held highly restrictive notions of a young woman's path. Despite Madaline's love of books, her uncle pulled her out of school before she was fourteen years old, "having given me the rudiments of an english education." After she had moved to New Orleans, the Cages pursued her, mostly to torment her, as she saw it. They could muster little tolerance or understanding for their female relative's misfortunes, owing in part to their strict Methodist views. After an early misadventure, or the appearance of one, her uncle, she said, "ruined me upon a charge of which I was as clear as my angel babe before Gods throne." One day in 1845 Madaline encountered "an uncle and five cousins who are not my friends . . . they deem me pollution."[10]

Raised in such a family, can it be any surprise that an unhappy, defiant, but confused Madaline chose to marry a few days after her fourteenth birthday? She wed Dempsey Elliott on January 2, 1831, which she later called "the most unfortunate day of my life." In her autobiographical "Tale of Real Life," Edwards claimed that pity for her hapless suitor had overridden a powerful, instinctive sense of impending disaster. She noted defensively that "as I had no Father, Mother or brother to please in this union I did not conceive that the world had a right to judge," but the opposite may have been true. Nine years after the couple married and three years after they separated, Madaline's husband, Dempsey Elliott, and her father, Lofton Cage, were next-door neighbors and business associates in Mobile. This simple fact, gleaned from the United State Census for 1840, makes one wonder how long husband and father had known each other, and whether the girl had been pressured to marry a parental friend.[11]

Soon after the wedding, Dempsey and Madaline moved to the small college town of Clinton, Mississippi, just outside Jackson. According to the "Tale of Real Life," Madaline missed her friends and soon regretted her marriage to an untutored man who was ill equipped either to support his wife or to introduce the intellectually ambitious young woman to the town's lettered society. Three children—an unnamed boy, Mary Jane, and William—were born and died in Clinton during the five or six years of the couple's

Mississippi sojourn. The two oldest children died within a few days of each other, probably during an epidemic of scarlet fever, a disease from which their mother also suffered. The couple then moved to New Orleans, where a fourth child, Isabella, was born.[12]

Around 1837 Madaline and Dempsey Elliott separated. In her "Tale," Edwards described her former husband as "a steady, industrious, and honourable man," "kind and devoted," a man who loved his infant daughter and who reluctantly left their home at his wife's insistence. She forced him to leave because he had lost heart and refused to work to support his family, but she promised reconciliation if he changed his attitude, Edwards wrote. In other essays, however, she implied that he had been unfaithful or that she was simply tired of him. "I had often thought of a separation and wished for it," she admitted, "but the fear of the opinion of the world that makes and keeps so many in misery" had stopped her, so that she had "lived my best years with a bad choice doomed to bear the penalty of my said choice unpitied but not unblamed.[13]

At the age of twenty, Edwards now faced the problem of supporting herself. She had begun to sell her paintings before she and Dempsey separated. Now she supplemented that income by teaching at the New Orleans Female Orphan Asylum. Teaching was a recurrent occupation throughout her residence in New Orleans, but this stint was short-lived. Soon after she began work, she resigned to care for the mortally ill Isabella, who died when she was about nineteen months old.

The story of Edwards's life in Clinton and New Orleans until she met her lover Charles William Bradbury is undocumented except in the "Tale." She moved back to her uncle's house in Tennessee during this period, where she took up with another "E," probably the Edwards from whom she took her preferred surname. She returned with him to New Orleans. Again Madaline knew the bargain was a bad one, brought on by her own circumstances and by her sense of pity for a man. Again an inner voice warned her against an impending mistake but was unable to dissuade her from making it. "Wants too numerous to relate sometime after again brought me under the necessity of giving my hand to one that I must have loved better than I did the former although had I been left free to choose would not have been my choice. And here again my benevolence caused my misery." Since she had returned to her uncle's house to live, these wants were financial. Instead, the stern regime of the Cages was probably too much for a woman already branded as a failure for having left her marriage, and she could not stand to remain there.

I have found no evidence that Edwards ever formally divorced Dempsey Elliot. Although some recent historians argue that divorce was easier to obtain in the antebellum South than is sometimes supposed, others note the reluctance of some southern courts to grant women divorces even under the most extreme abuse. In either case, it is unlikely that one would have been available to a woman in Madaline's straitened circumstances. Yet she married the otherwise unidentified and unknown Edwards and nursed him through yellow fever, then pursued him to Red River (the region around Alexandria, Louisiana) and Alabama after she found out that he too was already married. All we know of the end of this relationship is dramatically related in the "Tale of Real Life."[14]

During the years between her separation from Dempsey Elliott and her encounter with Charles Bradbury in New Orleans, Madaline Edwards circulated among her family, staying at her uncle's house in Tennessee, her sister Eliza Coleman's house in Jackson, Mississippi, and her father's house in Mobile, Alabama, before returning to New Orleans in 1842 or 1843.[15] These years were evidently eventful ones, and Madaline did more than languish in her relatives' homes. This must have been the time when she knew F. G., "the young man who brought me to my ruin when he was assuming the garb of friend in Vicksburg." We know nothing more of the incident. We know little more about the way that Edwards and Bradbury met. Neither party ever described the encounter, but the words of both suggest that the circumstances were less than genteel. When Bradbury first met Edwards, he admitted, he was sexually attracted to her: "It was the *Animal* that first prompted me to seek an interview with you, for then I was as ignorant, as the child unborn, of your identity." He learned she was a deeply religious woman who imagined herself unworthy to attend worship services or even to pray. Put simply, he then seduced her by taking her to church. Here the Edwards letters and diaries published in this book take over the story.[16]

An Available Woman?

Madaline Edwards's gender was the defining circumstance of her life. The differences between women's and men's powers, possibilities, and responsibilities, the disparate standards to which men and women were held in her era, in her city, and in her social world, governed her daily life, shaped her understanding of her past, and colored her assessment of her future. Because she had no acceptable relationship with a man, Madaline Edwards was on her own. Although she often fantasized about living entirely alone, that was impossible. Because she was a woman on her own, she could not support herself and was forced to rely on the assistance of men. Edwards's male partners and acquaintances were exempt from the moral censure and inability to make a living that her gender inflicted on her.

When Madaline Edwards decided to rectify her first, poor choice of a mate, she became a woman on her own. Everything else followed from that action, which, first and finally, "ruined" her. "Were moral laws so constructed that a fallen female might reinstate herself by any penance that life could endure however severe how gladly would I embrace it," she wrote, but she knew that "this cannot be." Unable to make a respectable alliance, she was faced with the prospect of living with her uncle or her father or of allying herself with men who would not scruple at her "fallen" character, such as the bigamous Edwards or the philandering Bradbury.[17]

Nineteenth-century America had little room for women not under the protection of father, husbands, or brothers. Legally, single women enjoyed the same rights as men to own property and earn money, and some women were able to make substantial livings on their own. Such careers, however, were unusual, and they contradicted customary notions of female public passivity. It required great force of character or great economic need for a woman to act publicly on her own. In the South this was particularly true. As Elizabeth Fox-Genovese has noted, both single women and opportunities for them were rarer there than elsewhere in the United States.[18]

Edwards's opportunities to support herself were limited by her status as a woman with a broken marriage. She tried all the avenues available to respectable females: she taught painting and sold her own works, she took in needlework, and she taught children. These were suitable occupations for women, it was sometimes argued, because they accorded with women's physiological makeup, as refined but relatively weak beings who bore and nurtured children.[19] Painting, sewing, and teaching evoked customary elements of women's education and women's domestic duties. Furthermore, they allowed women to work privately. Edwards did needlework at her own home and at her clients' residences and gave painting lessons and taught school in her own home as well. Even teaching in a school, as she did at the Female Orphan Asylum and later at the Marshall School, was not really "public work," since teachers worked in a controlled setting where they met only children and where they were supervised by a male school board and a male principal. These men saw to it that teachers did not stray from the moral paths laid out for women.[20]

Yet as nineteenth-century observers as well as modern historians have pointed out, it was nearly impossible for women to earn an adequate living by this respectable means. Work was difficult for Edwards to come by, and when she did find it she often had trouble getting paid. More than once she complained that "all my debtors seem not to pity me in the least for I can not get a dime."[21]

Edwards sewing accounts show that even in the best of circumstances she could not make enough to subsist. Long hours of hard sewing in December 1844 brought in $14.50 for the month. In January and February 1845 she made $16.50 a month, but only $8.20 in March. Her best month was July, when she made $19.50, but then she broke her arm. The next month she needed $72.00 from Bradbury to help her get by.[22] During her brief career as a public-school teacher, she made $35.00 a month.

There were demands on this income. Just as gendered limits constrained what she might do to earn money, so class and racial limits controlled what she might do for herself. After a shortage of food, she complained most often about lacking money to pay a laundress. When she thought she was pregnant, Bradbury hired a slave, Maria, to help her. Edwards had to feed and clothe the young girl and was sometimes unable to do so. The situation might have been worse. Her mortgage required an eight-hundred-dollar payment in one year, which would clearly have been impossible had Bradbury, who held the note, forced her to pay. Renting the same house, according to the award a New Orleans district court made to her in 1853, would have cost her twenty-eight dollars per month.[23]

Alone, without the assistance of a family and without an independent fortune or income, Edwards and women like her depended on male assistance. Frequently, Edwards's diary entries record gifts of food, money, and clothing from Bradbury. Many of her other male friends extended occasional assistance. She received gifts of money and goods from her admirers Mr. Scott and Mr. Sayre, from Bradbury's brother James, and from the brothers' friend Henry J. Budington.

During the years of her liaison with Charles Bradbury, Madaline Edwards never forgot her economic dependence, which was a recurrent source of tension between the lovers as his fortunes rose and fell. In one of her first surviving letters, she asked for a loan but acknowledged "that you have lately had to spend much money and that times are dull in your business and that it will look to you as though I intend to make a practice of this, but it shall be the last time." A year later she "took a good cry" after one of Bradbury's visits, "for I felt bad and have not a cent to spend and he did not offer me any and I could not ask."[24]

Edwards was probably correct in believing that Bradbury's financial problems finally ended their affair. Although the relationship had been strained for years as a result of her desperation and his own fear of discovery, he did not break it off until after she lost her teaching position in 1847 and seemed unable to find any other way to support herself.

Bradbury's exasperation was obvious. After Edwards was fired, he wrote that "determined to propose to you to muster your little means together, and with the aid of one or two friends, commence a small retail establishment by which I then believed, and do still believe, that you could make a support, and perhaps realise a handsome little living for old age. But this scheme did not seem to meet favor in your mind. I was then prompted to make the other proposition, which you have now rejected."[25]

Bradbury was irritated by Edwards's apparent refusal of genuine offers of assistance. She thought he was searching for an excuse to cut her off. He had accused her of infidelity, she said, when his real problem was that she had become a financial burden. In a clear-eyed assessment notably different from her earlier praise of his unfailing generosity, she observed that "I have ever noticed one thing. If men neglect their wives, that is extend to them no pecuniary assistance, or, if men do not treat their mistresses as they had once been able to do," they cover their embarrassment by accusing the women of faithlessness, as Bradbury had done. His real reason, she had no doubt, was "that you no longer extended to me the means of living."[26]

It was a revealing exchange. In Bradbury's eyes, Edwards's only bond to him was money. In hers, emotional attachment was paramount, for despite her financial need, she turned down several suitors to remain with him. Now she was desperate, her arm broken and badly healed and her job lost, and she felt victimized by his charges. She believed that she had made good-faith efforts to free herself from his largess and would have tried harder had she known his predicament: "Have I called on you for means? Have I ever grumbled. No, often have I wanted a dime so much that I would resolve to ask you, but my heart or pride would fail me, and I would eat stale bread and sometimes none until I could get a trifle for my sewing."[27]

The conflict touched on undercurrents that ran powerfully, if not always visibly, through many aspects of Edwards's life, for economic dependence had metaphorical and social as well as monetary dimensions in antebellum New Orleans. Many of her social relationships incorporated an element of exchange or transaction that, in the nineteenth-century gendered context, evoked prostitution. There is no evidence that Edwards turned to prostitution at any time in her life, yet it was a subtext for her self-conception and a specter that could easily be raised against her. The letters and diaries are full of allusions to it. Throughout her affair with Charles Bradbury, arguments often provoked words that made Edwards's heart ache: "Before he left one little question caused me intense pain." On other occasions, her Bradbury "laid his first charge against me" or "began some jesting words which I feared was half in earnest, which with my gloomy feelings ended in tears." A visit from her suitor Mr. Sayre provoked "an evening of misery for me" when Charley found him there. "He did not intend to wound me but an unguarded word did it all." The contexts of these remarks imply that Bradbury had accused her of prostitution. Eventually he was more direct, charging her with "mercenary" behavior. After she was fired from the public schools, Edwards turned the charge around, warning Bradbury that her circumstances "left [her] no hope but that of abandoning [her] self to a life that [she] detested."[28]

Prostitution was more than an insult or a threat to the numerous, usually unnamed, casual male visitors who found their way to Edwards's house. Common male beliefs about the relationships between men, women, and money allowed them to assume her availability. The attentions of these men were always unwanted and usually hurtful. Some taunted her openly. "Slandered and abused by one too low to notice" one day, on another she was "accosted by a stranger on my return [from church] who mortified my feelings much in offering language though chaste he did." Even friends took advantage of her vulnerability, as happened the day she took a walk with Sayre, "to avoid an insult." These men required repeated demonstrations of "firmness" to discourage them.[29]

Ironically, Madaline Edwards's unsuitability for respectable marriage made her world overwhelmingly masculine. The diaries are filled with references to her male friends and even suitors. Bradbury's male friends and relatives were often found at her house as well. At times when tensions between Edwards and Bradbury relaxed, these social occasions took on a friendly, appealing tone, as Edwards and her men friends chatted, joked, read aloud, combed one another's hair, and took walks. Such lighthearted gatherings permitted a male-female sociability that was more informal than that found in polite society. At the same time they depended on the less appealing asymmetry of gender roles that colored all of Edwards's existence. The money nexus as well as the loneliness occasioned by her social stigma encouraged her to open her home to these men even when she preferred to be alone. The power of their money gave them a freedom to associate with women like her, whom they believed to be beneath them, while they remained unstained in their own minds.

Although the evidence is sparse, apparently the men who enjoyed themselves at Edwards's house were mostly business and professional men, mostly young, not wealthy but no longer junior clerks either, and mostly single. They tended to work in the "American district" downtown and to dabble in real-estate speculation at the developing upriver edge of the city where they resided. For example, the New York-born Henry J. Budington (ca. 1814-76), the "Bud" or "Henry Josephus" of the diaries, was "employed in commerce" in 1840. He may have been between marriages at the time Edwards wrote, for according to census records one woman between twenty and thirty years of age lived in his household in 1840, yet in 1850 his wife, Margaret, was only twenty-four years old. In the mid 1840s Budington owned three lots in the city, but by 1850 he had accumulated real-estate holdings worth ten thousand dollars.[30]

Charles Bradbury's brother James (ca. 1816-71) lived alternately in New Orleans and Terrebonne Parish and was a physician later in his life. Like Budington, he owned some New Orleans real estate, although his dealings are difficult to separate from his brother's, since the two regularly bought and sold land for and to each other.[31]

Edwards's most prominent acquaintance, and the one with whom she had the most casual connection, was the exception to this pattern. Dr. John Leonard Riddell (1807-65) owned the house next door to hers. A well-known scientist, professor of chemistry at the Medical College of Louisiana, public lecturer, physician, melter and refiner at the United States Mint, and New Orleans postmaster by appointment of his friends John Tyler and William Henry Harrison, Riddell was an active real-estate speculator. He owned nearly thirty parcels in all parts of the city during the mid-1840s. Two of them were assessed at fourteen thousand dollars in 1843. Riddell described himself in 1846 as "moderately independent. If living at the north, I should consider myself rich with my present means."[32]

Like his brother and his friend Henry Budington, Charles Bradbury was an aspiring businessman who believed a prosperous future lay before him. Bradbury was perhaps a year older than Edwards, having been born in central New York on May 9, 1815 or 1816. His parents immigrated to the Ohio River Valley in 1821, where his older brother Cornelius had already established himself in 1819. During Charley's young manhood, Cornelius, then the effective head of the family, was a flour merchant in Cincinnati. Other siblings lived nearby in Madison, Indiana, where one of them ran a flour mill and a sawmill. Young Charles Bradbury moved to New Orleans in 1835.[33]

In his new home, Bradbury set out to make his fortune, following Cornelius's advice to find placement in "one of the first houses . . . with steady & active employment, giving entire satisfaction to your employers." He wrote to James Waller Breedlove, president of the Atchafalaya Railroad and Bank, and obtained a job there.[34]

After leaving the bank, Bradbury worked for the Royal Insurance Company, whose offices were on Camp Street in downtown New Orleans. In 1840 he bought a house at

Introduction to Madaline

the corner of Bacchus (Baronne) and Erato streets, then on the edge of the city, and lived there for the rest of his life. Bradbury had already begun to buy real estate, a common nineteenth-century route to an independent existence and retirement from active business. During the time he knew Madaline Edwards, Bradbury owned as many as six parcels, including his own house and hers. Yet he was constantly mortgaging and redeeming the properties to raise cash, perhaps to finance business projects of his own, for he never achieved the fortune he sought. Instead, his lifelong pattern was to set up badly capitalized, short-lived manufacturing businesses, then to return to insurance clerking when they failed. During the 1850s, for example, he purchased an interest in the patent for a new cottonseed-oil manufacturing process, but two factories failed. After another period of clerking and a brief stint in the Confederate Army, he tried cottonseed-oil manufacturing again and apparently failed once more. When Bradbury died, his estate consisted of only his house.[35]

Bradbury's double character as sexual adventurer and pedantic moralist is evident in Edwards's writings. His own papers show that he became expert at using women to his advantage early in life. When he left Cincinnati, Bradbury left behind a brokenhearted sweetheart, Helen Hart, who wrote to him in a semiliterate version of the same pleading tone that characterized many of Edwards's writings. On the steamboat trip downriver, he made the acquaintance of a Mrs. Ellis, and through her fell in with the young women on the boat. "Several evenings I sat out upon the guards & plaid the flute for the ladies and they sang while I plaid."[36]

Bradbury's interest in women was long-standing, wide-ranging, and rarely as innocent as on the steamboat journey. While Charles wrote letters full of pious moralizing to his older brother Cornelius, the ones he exchanged with his brother Marcus were much racier. "I do not know how my old dulcena M.F.P. comes on more than [what] Beck Wilson said," wrote Marcus to Charley. "She joined the Methodist Church lately and intends to reform her old ways some or Make it a cloke to cover her hypocracy and cockollogy as her mother does before her for she is so full of it it must come out."[37]

In Louisiana, Charley sought his fortune in business, but also by another time-honored means: he courted a well-to-do young widow, Mary Ann Taylor Hamilton, whom he married in the Reverend Theodore Clapp's First Congregational Church on February 12, 1837. When he learned of Charley's plans, Cornelius was enraged, believing, probably with justice, that his younger brother aimed to take advantage of a woman's vulnerability to enrich himself. Cornelius sent a blistering letter that characterized his brother in terms that seem appropriate to his behavior a decade later as well:

> You say on 25 Mar. that she is a young Girl, O.B. [a Mr. O'Brien] says, she is a Widow—with 2 Children. . . . I am really astonished, not however at your folly & madness, but that a woman having the reputation of common sense should so far forget her self & dignity, as for one moment to have sanctioned any advances from You, (a lad in your teens) which could be construed by you as meeting with her

> approval or sanction. A widow to[o], said to be rich[,] true, but what signifies that to you, I know that with you, that is the moving string, the ground attraction. What signifies her fortune to you, do you suppose that her money is to be at your controul? No Sir if she has any, she will understand your motive & your rations in the article you will find very soon meted out to you. Suppose she dies, where is her fortune? Not at your Controul I guarantee—and where is our gentleman then? A Widower—a poor Gentleman—a poor Widower—out of business, out of funds—out of employment—out of habits of business & out upon the World[.] I am truly sorry, that I have an occasion to talk so lightly of the good sense & prudence of any worthy woman, as far as one moment to suppose she could be found so destitute of all these qualities [in] risking herself with you, at this Period of your lifetime[.] With yourself your doings & actions, I have some early impressions, & well know that an opportunity is only wanted, to do just so foolish a thing. . . . Marry and your fate is seal'd. You never rise in the World if at this time & under the circumstances. There is time for all things. Think of this.[38]

Cornelius was not offended that Charley planned to enrich himself by marrying but thought he was too young to do it well. He had not established a secure financial base for himself, so he was dependent on his wife's money. Consequently he had exposed himself to her whims. Cornelius passed along his wife Sarah's observation "that she had [not] thought you among all the Bradburys were one who would be willing to place your dependence for daily supper upon a woman—who would at every application for the needful pettishly enquire what you wanted of it & be constantly throwing it up into your face, that she had no desire to support you &c &c." Cornelius thus placed in a woman's mouth a critical statement of the relationship between men, women, and money: whoever controlled the money controlled the relationship, and it ought to be the man who did so. To place oneself at a woman's mercy was to risk one's whole future. On the other hand, to have one's own money was to be able to chart one's own course and others'. It was a lesson young Charley learned well.[39]

Charley Bradbury's friends repeatedly tried to tell Madaline Edwards that he was an adventurer, but she would not hear it. During Bradbury's extended trip north in the summer of 1844, Henry Budington, Edwards wrote, "talked of my beloved C. . . . He asked me if I would be jealous if I knew he was kissing some other woman." Just before Bradbury's return, Budington tried again, telling her "a great deal I wished not to hear." Edwards's suitor Mr. Sayre also had uncomplimentary things to say about his rival's conduct. Bradbury himself may have revealed something in December 1844, when "we had some unusual conversation and although I felt very unhappy at some of his confessions yet I stifled my emotions for once and did not let him see my pain."[40]

As evidence of one man's failings, Bradbury's behavior was unremarkable. It is more meaningful when we place it within the larger patterns of male sociability and extramarital male-female relationships that we glimpse in Edwards's writings. The Edwards-Bradbury affair opens a new window on sexuality in a city that had long been renowned for its "immorality."

Introduction to Madaline

Men in antebellum New Orleans enjoyed a range of possibilities for sexual relationships with women outside marriage. Brothels were common, and for a time in the 1850s prostitutes were licensed. Nor was New Orleans a stranger to the kinds of furtive, ephemeral, exploitative sexual connections between white men and their slaves that occurred throughout the South. Among the city's elite white society, particularly among the Creoles, extramarital alliances between white men and free black or mixed-race women were relatively common and relatively open, even though they were illegal. In some instances, these relationships were stable and long-lasting, families in every sense but the legal one.[41]

Jean Boze, a French émigré, commented on several such households formed among the acquaintances of his patron and correspondent Henri de Ste. Gême, who had fathered several mixed-race children himself. According to Boze, some wealthy Creoles had two or even three separate households. In 1831, for example, Boze mentioned a M. Sauvinet, who was building a house in the Faubourg Marigny for his second mistress, a native of Saint Domingue, and their two minor children. Sauvinet's first lover, Lize Thuet, remained in the house he had built for her. The next year Boze reported the death of Barthélemy Macarty, who had formed two families in addition to his legal white family "du premier lit." Macarty left money to have his sons by his first mistress, Luce, educated in the North. When Luce was middle-aged, Macarty had started a third family with her daughter Cécé, to whom, it was rumored, he bequeathed $130,000. In the process, he disinherited his white family. Although such bequests were usually successfully challenged by white heirs, the relationships that prompted them necessitated no loss of respectability in white Creole eyes. When sugar planter Pierre Caselar died, he left many "enfans naturels de couleur" but was nevertheless "keenly mourned by society on account of his widely recognized probity and his humanitarian acts."[42]

The stable, open relationships of the Creole polygamists and the fleeting intercourse of brothel patrons and slave-owing rapists violated the public morality of New Orleans's American residents and the political platform of the business community. Since the second decade of the nineteenth century, for example, business leaders had pushed ordinances against bawds and bawdy houses through the city council, and they made the suppression of prostitution a part of their 1852 campaign to reunite the city, which ethnic animosities had caused to be divided into three semi-independent "municipalities" in 1837. Yet the life in and around Madaline Edwards's house reveals a fourth scenario of illicit male-female relationships among New Orleans's Americans, who were no more upright, but only more secretive, than their Creole neighbors.[43]

The purchase of Madaline Edwards's house, a joint project of Charles Bradbury, his brother James, and their friend Henry Budington, is emblematic of the labored secretiveness that extramarital affairs required in respectable American circles. Budington bought the property from John Craig and Joseph Stanley on November 2, 1843, for eight hundred dollars. A month later he sold it for nine hundred dollars to Jim, "now absent," with Charley acting as his attorney. Jim in turn conveyed the house to Charley, and

Charley mortgaged it to Madaline for eight hundred dollars plus a two-hundred-dollar down payment. The entire series of transactions was an elaborate blind to disguise Charley's purchase of the house for his lover, but the arrangement was advantageous to James Bradbury and Henry Budington as well. Edwards's house was just six blocks down Bacchus Street from Charley's and served as their boys' club, a male refuge where they gathered to socialize. In addition, Budington used Edwards's home to meet a woman named Adelle, who eventually broke off the affair and returned his presents, but not before she had borne their child at Edwards's house.[44]

In many respects Madaline Edwards's and Charles Bradbury's affair was as much a joint project of the three male friends as the house purchase. To be sure, Henry Budington and James Bradbury were true friends of Edwards. They spent many evenings in her company, reading and talking. They helped her when her lover was away, and they tried to protect her from his worst behavior. Not only did they warn her against relying too much on Charles, but when Edwards sued him to overturn the foreclosure on her mortgage, James testified against his brother. Mostly, though, their help was directed toward facilitating and concealing the relationship on Charles's behalf.

Edwards's own affair with Charles Bradbury and that between Henry Budington and Adelle were only two of several such liaisons, and possible liaisons, within Edwards's circle: John Leonard Riddell, a casual acquaintance, was the lover of Ann Hennefin during these years. He had two sons by Hennefin, and the birth and baptism of one of them, "christened by his mother John William Riddell," were among the rare personal events to intrude in his lengthy scientific diaries. Riddell never named Hennefin in his diaries or alluded to her in any other context. In fact, in 1846, on the tenth anniversary of his first marriage, he wrote that "my wife lived three years and a half to the day. Six years and a half therefore have I been a widower. Thus advances time. I doubt not it might have been better, if I had married again in the mean time." Six months later, on December 1, he wed Angelica Eugenia Brown. Both wives and their children were buried in the Riddell family tomb in the Girod Street Cemetery, but not Ann Hennefin or her sons.[45]

While the affairs of Bradbury, Budington, and Riddell were concealed from respectable notice, they were obviously well known among the confederates. By virtue of her "situation," Edwards was one of these confederates, privy to this knowledge, but she was also an object of it, an available woman prey to men on the make. On one notable occasion, she "had some very unwelcome visitors," one of whom "took the pains to tell me . . . my character was lost and I could make it no worse by doing as would persuade me." It was an encounter that drove home the duplicitous nature of such relationships in the city's anglophone society, for while this visitor tried to seduce her, Edwards noted without further explanation, "that very mans wife was in a great measure the cause of my ruin."[46]

Edwards's encounter with James Waller Breedlove, which precipitated the final break with Charley, illustrates the nexus of money, power, and gender in her life. The Virginia-born Breedlove (ca. 1790-1867) was a longtime friend of Andrew Jackson and a conspicuous figure in New Orleans politics and business life. In addition to serving as the president of the Atchafalaya Railroad and Bank, he was a commission merchant and had been Mexican consul, collector of the Port of New Orleans, and first president of the New Orleans Temperance Society. When he entered Edwards's life, he was still a prominent public figure but had fallen on hard times. A credit agent reported in 1847 that he had "small means" and in 1848 added that he "had some difficulty in settling his [accounts] wh[ich] were deficient."[47]

Charles Bradbury may have introduced Breedlove, his first New Orleans employer, to Edwards in November 1845. Once again she found herself caught between the public and private morality of New Orleans's American community. Breedlove's wife, Maria Ellen Winchester, became Madaline's friend and defender; she was almost certainly the subject of the poems of November 17 and November 20 addressed "to Mary." They were followed by the diary notation "There is a benevolent lady who had learned that I am M and has taken it into her head she can elevate me to the standing her kind wishes alone dictate and I am in torture about the unpleasant feelings it may create on her husbands part."[48]

Edwards was right to be apprehensive. Maria's husband had begun to make visits of his own. "JB was here this evening and I do not wonder if he will make his visits fewer for he so often leaves me in tears," she wrote the day after her comment on Maria's friendship. He was there again a few days later. The next November he was still pressing his attentions on her, "determined by his visits to carry out the worlds suspicion though I remain innocent." Madaline complained to Charley, "I will no longer keep you ignorant that he is pressing a certain point."[49]

By that time Edwards was Breedlove's employee, for he was a member of the Second Municipality School Board and had been appointed to the board's new Committee on Teachers just as Edwards was bring hired to teach at the Marshall School, in October 1846. The pressure intensified. "I told him today that I would rather he would dismiss me from the School than to hold me under obligations I could not fulfill," she wrote in November.[50]

In January 1847 the school board turned its attention to Edwards. A committee was appointed "to investigate the rumors in relation to Mrs Edwards. . . as well as to her conduct as a lady; as to her treatment of the Scholars." Twelve days later the board dismissed her. The Edwards-Bradbury letters reveal that the board had examined her relationship with Breedlove, not Bradbury. Yet Edwards believed that Breedlove had sabotaged her, and she "curse[d] ten fold the circumstances that led him to damn instead of befriending me." If he betrayed her, Breedlove did it remarkably coolly and duplicitously. He was the only board member to vote against dismissing her, and he was one of three (out of twelve) to vote against paying her only one month's salary for the three she had worked. Six years later Breedlove testified on Edwards's behalf in her lawsuit against Bradbury.[51]

More likely, Charley was the informer. Two people told Edwards that he "had you put out of the schools in order to make you feel your dependance." Bradbury denied it vehemently: such an action would have made him "too base even to be called a man." However, he had "fears of Breedlove," whom he suspected of trying to win Edwards's affections away from him. This would have injured Bradbury's male pride more than his heart, since he had lost interest in her by this time. Charley had secured Madaline's position by lobbying Joseph A. Maybin, another school board member. Since Maybin introduced the resolutions calling for her dismissal and for docking her pay, Bradbury may have decided to thwart Breedlove's plans by intervening with Maybin again.[52]

Edwards's misfortune did not deter Breedlove or Bradbury. After she was fired, the banker offered to buy her a slave and to take care of all her needs, "if I would say he might visit me occasionally." Bradbury pretended that the school board's charges against her were true and used them as a pretext to break off the relationship. Thus Edwards was caught between the amorous rivalries of a patron and his protégé trapped by the demands of a suitor who was also an employer. She could only "curse the day I ever entered that school or saw B[reedlove]."[53]

A Lover's Ethic

Madaline Edwards understood the matrix of men, women, and money in nineteenth-century New Orleans, and she recognized the double standard by which men and women were judged, but she drew different conclusions from her knowledge than most of her male acquaintances did. They believed she was an available woman. She thought of herself as a woman who had made mistakes but whose moral trajectory was upward toward respectability, even though she acknowledged that others might never see her that way.

True, money forced Edwards to rely on Bradbury, and this colored her feelings for him. One July night in 1844, when her lover was far away to the north, "I dreamed twice of seeing my dear Charley. One time I thought he filled by lap with gold, which did not make me half so glad as the sight of him." Financial need forced her to endure and to excuse many more slights than she might otherwise have done. Still, she genuinely loved him, and in her view they were moving toward a morally if not a socially legitimate relationship. This is the only way to understand the astonishing testaments she left in her diary and writing book when she thought she might die in childbirth. Edwards took it for granted that if she died Bradbury would acknowledge their child as his own, raise it, and teach it about its mother. These assumptions spoke less of naïveté than of the intensity of her desire for a stable, lifelong bond. She believed that their love had been sealed when Bradbury placed "a plain gold ring" on her finger one day in 1844 and she vowed to wear it for the rest of her life. Edwards's faith in the future and rightness of the alliance allowed her to reject determined, eligible suitors, most notably the otherwise unidentified R.P. Although she obviously returned R.P.'s affection, when he said "serious things" to her she ruefully turned him down, despite Bradbury's own advice to accept the proposal.[54]

Edwards's interpretation of her actions marked the moral distance she had traveled from the teenage girl who married out of anger and pity. The young wife who developed the courage to part with an indolent husband was still horrified to find that her second partner was already married. The mature Edwards entered the affair with the married Bradbury with her eyes open, goaded as always by her precarious situation, yet she still felt a need to define an ethical basis for the relationship. She could do so because, occasionally and dimly, the older, less naive Madaline glimpsed the cracks and ill-fitting joints of the moral structure she was expected to inhabit. She acknowledged the sanctity of Bradbury's marriage, the primacy of his responsibility to his wife, and Mary Ann Bradbury's moral superiority to herself. From one point of view, she admitted that Charley's actions might be construed as "acting a faithless part by [his] wife." but she preferred to describe her own relationship with him as a charitable one. She was helpless and ignorant; he was a man acting on "the noble wish of your heart to raise the oppressed and deserted being who once shone as fair as the dear one by your side."[55]

Against the obligations of marriage, however, Edwards set the claims of love. "My love is deeper than hers," she wrote in the same letter. The power of her love sanctioned condescension toward Mary Ann Bradbury and toward wives in General. "Doubtless [Mary Ann] loves you with all the force of her nature," she told Bradbury, but it could not be as intense as her own love for him. On occasion Edwards even gave him flowers to take to his sick wife, a gesture that was kind, that recognized his marital bond, but that was also a kind of covert jibe directed at an unsuspecting spouse.[56]

Desperately wanting Bradbury without feeling free to disparage his marriage, Edwards imagined a kind of polygamy, represented by the plain gold ring and exposed in her vivid dreams. In one dream she found herself at the Bradbury's table: "His wife seemed much pleased with me and I did not feel unjust towards her." In another she, not Mary Ann, found herself embracing Charley at the Last Judgment. "Mrs B passed by us in that position but did not seem the least displeased." Yet she also dreamed, presciently, that her lover had "resolved to act paltroon no longer" and had abandoned her.[57]

Most often, Edwards's condescension and fantasy succumbed to jealousy and bitterness. Chance encounters with the Bradburys always brought a "mind . . . full of torture" or "a flash of bitter feeling": "I strive against it yet I am human." She vented her anger in a long essay on husbands and wives that blamed marital troubles on women's self-absorption and their inability to subordinate their trivial whims to their husbands' serious worries.[58]

Madaline Edwards salved her conscience by cloaking herself in conventional gender stereotypes. Men were to be strong but courtly; women were naturally weak and yielding. Just as Charley was concerned to portray himself in a manly light, so Madaline expected men to act in that manner. In the autobiographical "Tale of Real Life" she dismissed both her husbands as "womanish," meaning, respectively, evasive and timid. In the same story, she attributed her downfall in part to her pity for the two men. By being womanish, they were unworthy of her regard, but as a woman she could not help pitying them. At the same time, she possessed a powerful inner voice—an intuition—that warned against these and other disasters, but she was too womanish to resist them.

In depicting herself in this way, Edwards echoed the argument made in a pamphlet given to her by her suitor Mr. Sayre. In *Woman Physiologically Considered,* the phrenologist Alexander Walker argued that women's "sensibility and observing faculties are great; [their] reasoning faculties are small." Women are naturally intuitive. They could grasp any situation instantly, but lacking powers of reason or strength, they were unable to analyze the situations they understood intuitively or to act on their intuitions. "Extreme sensibility is the great characteristic of her mental system, but it is at the same time the very basis of all instinctive action. Feebleness equally characterizes her locomotive system." The instinctive sensibilities of women impelled them, among other things, to a great capacity for pity, and it also made them feel emotions deeply and helplessly that men might not even notice.[59]

Although couched in the jargon of phrenology, Walker's arguments recapitulated common nineteenth-century view of women's capacities. There is no evidence that his pamphlet was a direct inspiration for Edwards's self-portrayal. Of the many books that she mentioned in her diary, this is one of the few that she simply noted without any comment on its contents or even an indication of whether she had read it, so the gift may say more about Sayre's attitudes than her own. Still, it suited Edwards to adopt this common caricature of women's abilities from time to time. She bowed to Bradbury's manly wisdom, for "he had strove so hard to lead my mind to higher aims, as he may term it." In return, he gladly played the pedant. One January evening in 1845 "we agreed to adopt another mode to improve our minds. I made a grammatical error and he reproved me for it."[60]

In short, Edwards took advantage of the inconsistencies in conventional gender roles to shape an individualized moral universe for herself. Her ethical sphere, like her contemporaries', emphasized lifelong male-female relationships, but it gave primacy to love and charity over legal ties. It acknowledged some traditional claims for men's strength and women's weakness, then used them to reverse the double standard, offering more moral leeway to women than to men. None of the elements of this morality were novel, but Edwards's synthesis of them was idiosyncratic.[61]

A Woman's Creed

The theme of judgment permeated Edwards's writings. She thought that she was constantly being judged. Her personal morality provided a platform from which she assessed her own failings and a set of ground rules for acknowledging responsibility for her actions and accepting judgment. Edwards developed a strong sense of who had a right to judge her (and an equally strong conviction that she had no right to condemn or judge others). She rejected "the stern decrees of society" when they were applied by hypocrites. She declined to be judged by her family, by "some dashing ladies" too frivolous to take seriously, or by people who had no claims on her. So she obtained a restraining order against a Mrs. R.'s "language," which had caused "a good cry." In a tougher mood, she "had quite a farce" with someone who saw Charley leave her house and wished that "persons who accidently become acquainted with me would let me act as I please."[62]

On the same principles, Edwards freely submitted her actions and her character to be judged by her friends and acquaintances, particularly by men, and most of all by Bradbury. She "told Mrs W my position" and was relieved that they remained friends. She was delighted that Mr. H. "is highly pleased that I am to be a mother. Approves and encourages my love for the father though unknown to him." She was grateful to be "forgiven" for her way of life by her cousin Jack, and she dreamed of "full forgiveness" from a younger brother she had never met.[63]

Nevertheless, Edwards understandably sought ways to mitigate judgment. Her pose as a woman too weak to avoid choices she knew were wrong or to resist temptation and coercion by stronger men or unfair social structures was a strategy for doing so.

The essays "Woman" and "Man," written in response to a pair of sermons preached by Theodore Clapp in April and May 1844, vividly capture the ambivalence of Edwards's moral position. Clapp's sermons were based on familiar nineteenth-century conventions of morality and gender, of passive women and active men, spiritual females and worldly males. Edwards listened to the sermon "Woman" skeptically. She admitted her own errors as usual and accepted her exclusion from the role of "angelic wife or mother," and indeed from social reconciliation of any sort. But she objected to Clapp's notion that "women create their own sorrows" (a jibe that Bradbury repeated at the end of their relationship), arguing instead that others had "dug the grave" of her happiness. As a woman, she was prey to the bad-intentioned, but she had also been rescued by the good-intentioned. Although rejected by polite society, Edwards argued that she had been redeemed by God and Charles Bradbury. Consequently, she did not hear Clapp's sermon as a condemnation of her own ways: she had owned and transcended her sins. Instead, it was a warning to the "[un]reflecting and prosperous part of my sex" who might unthinkingly fall into the errors that had ruined her.[64]

Edwards's reaction to the sermon on men was much more emotional. When the pastor denounced men who seduced women, she burst into tears in church as she recalled her own seduction. She fixed her eyes on Charley, who was sitting across the church with Mary Ann, and she desperately hoped that he would not take Clapp's words so to heart that he would abandon her. But then Edwards returned to her moral confidence. She had erred, she knew, but there was no reason for her to hear these things. She believed that God wanted her to be happy and that his purpose was not served by reminders of things she could not change.[65]

As Edwards's essays suggest, her sense of the hypocrisy and imbalance of power inherent in nineteenth-century gender relations mitigated her guilt and at times encouraged a moral condescension similar to the emotional condescension she sometimes expressed toward Mary Ann Bradbury. She took great comfort in the belief that she had transcended her errors: respectable people needed the preacher's warnings more than she did.

If judgment was one great theme of her writing, another was redemption. Men were the cause of Edwards's downfall, and they were the agents of redemption. At times she seemed to have difficulty distinguishing Christ, Charles Bradbury, and her pastor, Theodore Clapp, for she wrote of all three using language steeped in Christian metaphors of grace and unmerited salvation. Sometimes Charley was an evangelist, sometimes a savior. He had "spoke[n] words that acted like magic upon me. He said I had a heart too good for such a life. He said I could yet be a better and happier woman. He pointed to me a minister whose blest admonitions and promises would tranquilize my wounded spirit, and by his kind and eloquent reasoning induced me to hope I was not lost." Charley was her "adored preserver," sent by God to save her, but his "friendship is not based upon my virtue and moral goodness." Edwards admired Clapp as greatly as she did Bradbury, for the same reason: he offered her hope. "God alone knows how I venerate and bless that man." Trapped in a world controlled by men, she turned to men to save her.[66]

Edwards was attracted to Theodore Clapp by his forceful and kindly personality and perhaps because he, too, fit uneasily into the confines of conventional belief. A Massachusetts-born clergyman, Clapp (1792-1866) had come to New Orleans in 1822 to replace the popular pastor of the First Presbyterian Church, Sylvester Larned, who had died of yellow fever. He quickly established himself as an equally popular preacher, but during the first decade of his service his theology drifted toward antitrinitarian principles. He was tried for heresy and expelled from the Presbyterian ministry in 1833. A group of theological traditionalists, including Edwards's school board persecutor Joseph Maybin, withdrew to form a new Presbyterian congregation. Clapp carried on in the old building, and his church flourished owing to his vivid preaching, his energetic ecumenicism in a polyglot city, and the patronage of the wealthy merchant-philanthropist Judah Touro, who paid off the building's mortgage.[67]

At Clapp's church Madaline Edwards found a pastor and a congregation that welcomed outsiders. Because the church set aside an entire gallery for those from outside New Orleans and from other city churches, it was known as the Strangers' Church. The minister's impassioned preaching, which so engrossed Edwards, was compelling enough that it attracted even those who rejected his doctrine. The diarist Luther Tower frequently attended Clapp's services, even though he dismissed the sermons as "original without head or tail discourses" or "strange." Yet Edwards thought that to hear other preachers after Theodore Clapp was "like drinking slops after the richest wines."[68]

Clapp's popularity owed as much to his social ministry as to his public performances. He was famous for his steadfast presence in the city during its many yellow fever and cholera epidemics, when most other clergymen fled. He also preached religious ecumenism in an era when Protestants had little tolerance for other beliefs. Clapp praised his Jewish patron, Judah Touro, as a man who better exemplified Christian charity than most of his Christian neighbors, and he wrote at length about the salutary moral leadership of the Roman Catholic Church. On the most volatile social issue—slavery—he modified his opinions to suit the cherished principles of New Orleans's white leaders.[69]

Parson Clapp was "eminently a social man," according to the historian of his church, and more than anything he "enjoyed the society of his fellowmen, young and old, always ready to interest himself in their pleasures and troubles, their occupations and undertakings, touching elbows with the people in the labors and commonplaces of their daily lives." He assisted supplicants in finding homes for children and jobs and even made small loans to them. "His counsel reached the flotsam of a great city." memoirist Eliza Ripley recalled. Madaline Edwards was among this mass of humanity. After nearly two years of listening to him from the pews, she finally met him. "Though our conversation was short and my feelings so overcam[e] me yet I found him the same kind and dear being that he is in the pulpit. I told him many of my errors but he said all was not lost to one who wished to return." Later Clapp offered advice to Edwards on obtaining a new job after she was dismissed from the schools, and on the disposal of her house when she moved to California.[70]

The preacher's personal ministry was a comfort to Edwards, but his teaching was more important to her, for it helped her to define her own moral universe. It is easy to understand why his doctrine appealed to her. In the winter of 1833-34, during the time he was expelled from the Presbyterian clergy for antitrinitarianism, Clapp came to question the doctrines of original sin and eternal damnation. He concluded that there was no such thing as absolute or eternal evil, and thus no such thing as eternal punishment. They were inconsistent with the nature of God's justice as he understood it. Good was to be found in the most degraded people, a point that Edwards took personally. Original sin and predestination implied a capricious God and removed free will from humanity, for if people could do nothing but evil, how could they be responsible? This was a familiar Arminian argument that Edwards embraced enthusiastically. Like Clapp, she believed that people were responsible for their own sins. However, they sometimes made errors for excusable reasons, such as ignorance or diminished capacity (which was sometimes the product of "inferior phrenological developments," according to Clapp). Though these errors were still sins, their seriousness was mitigated. Sin demanded punishment, but it would take place in this life. Clapp denied the existence of hell, arguing that sinners create their own hell on earth. After death, God's free grace would save everyone.[71]

Edwards sought happiness in the wonders of divine creation and the glimpses they offered of future bliss, for the minister insisted not only on personal responsibility but also on the autonomy of personal judgment. Hearing a Clapp sermon on mercy, she "gloried in the emphasis he placed on 'I *will not* be cheated out of my opinion.'" She avidly devoured religious books, mostly rationalist treatises on natural religion derived from the Enlightenment tradition, which served her in the way that devotional tracts did orthodox Christians. She read them over and over, extracting lessons for her life.[72]

Edwards explored deist writers such as Constantin-François Volney, whose *Law of Nature* she read twice and to whom she steered a friend, "a catholic of the old irish school," but her two favorite authors in 1844 and 1845 were Thomas Dick and George Combe. Dick was an astronomer who, "connected with Mr. Clapp's preaching has unfolded to my mind a new world and induce[d] me to hope though lost in this world yet there is another home for me." He aimed "to illustrate the harmony which subsists between the system of nature and the system of revelation." It was a point that Edwards made repeatedly in her essays on nature and religion: glimpses of the heavens "increased my conception of the Deity," she said. Echoing the natural theologians of the seventeenth and eighteenth centuries, she wrote that "the right study of nature is of itself sufficient to lead the heart to God," although "it needs the bible to support and confirm the conceptions it may have formed." Still, if it were necessary to choose between the Bible and nature, only the latter was indispensable.[73]

Combe was a moral philosopher who claimed the rationalist heritage of the Scottish Common Sense philosophers Francis Hutcheson, Adam Smith, Thomas Reid, Dugald Stewart, and Thomas Brown, which he elaborated "with the aid of the new lights afforded by Phrenology." He argued that God had made the world in such a way that it was capable of being understood by human powers. Thus "the divine Spirit, revealed in Scripture as a power influencing the human mind," acted through natural laws. "Nature is religion," and "a knowledge of the natural laws is destined to exercise a vast influence in rendering men capable of appreciating and practicing Christianity."[74]

Madaline Edwards's devotional reading convinced her that God might be discovered through scientific knowledge: the more one knew of the natural world, the more one approached divinity. In Combe's work she read that "knowledge is truly power; and it is highly important to human beings to become acquainted with the constitution and relations of every object around them." Her pursuit of knowledge turned her against both orthodox theology and popular religious beliefs. "I never could comprehend how three persons could exist in one and be separate, yet one and the same," she wrote of the Trinity. She rejected the popular notion of heaven, "a golden City paved with jewels in which God sits enthroned while it is the duty and only employment of his angels to bow down before him and sing his praises with golden harps," preferring instead to imagine a realm of eternal rest and spiritual peace "where the A b C we have learned of God and his attributes will go on to higher and higher grades." In the afterlife the knowledge we accumulate on earth will vastly expand, as will our capacity to understand and the portion of creation with which we are familiar, she was convinced." "In a future world we will commence just where we leave off in this, and . . . the more intellect and knowledge we imbibe in this world the more our happiness is increased even here and we are fitted for a higher state of bliss in that far off home to which we are approaching."[75]

Edwards's religious inquiries had unexpected consequences: they tended to undercut the sense of helplessness that her "situation" and her relationship with Bradbury promoted, as well as the feminine passivity that she often affected. Edwards's religious convictions buttressed her personal moral universe, leaving room for an independence of mind and an intellectual adventurousness that was at odds with conventional views of women's capacity. Even as she acted a stereotypically feminine role, Edwards educated herself to exercise her own judgment. As a counterbalance to the rhetoric of the female sinner rescued by charitable men, she found a theology that offered redemption to a woman on her own.

Madaline Edwards's independence of mind and her curiosity led her through a wide range of reading as she explored issues that were male provinces and that were often declared to be beyond women's understanding. To each she brought the critical moral sense and intellectual independence that had been shaped by her life experience.

In 1844, for example, a presidential election and a heated debate over Texas annexation drew her attention to politics. In some respects, her political views were colored by what historian Suzanne Lebsock has called the "personalism" of women's concerns. She leaned toward Whig politics because Bradbury was a Whig. She supported the annexation of Texas because Bradbury owned land there and because a beloved cousin, John Coffee Hays, was a founder of the Texas Rangers. Yet her politics were more than simple affirmations of her menfolks' vested interests. She followed political issues carefully, reading tracts, speeches, and treaties and expressing points of view that were often at odds with those of her friends and with the politics of the parties she preferred. Edwards's political opinions and her right to them were accepted by her male friends, who argued with her and teased her about them. She bet her physician Dr. James Ritchie, a Democrat, that Texas would be annexed, while Henry Budington brought her Democratic newspapers "for he knows I am a whig."[76]

Throughout the 1844 presidential campaign, Edwards supported Henry Clay, and she was disappointed when he lost the election. Yet she rejected Clay's opposition to Texas annexation. Instead, she read and applauded Democratic politician Robert J. Walker's widely distributed and enormously influential pamphlet, which advocated annexation as a way to end slavery in the United States. Walker also argued that unless the United States took Texas, New Orleans might fall under British domination, a view that found wide support in the Crescent City. In addition to supporting the Democratic Party's position on annexation, Edwards was attracted to the politics of the new Native American Party and eventually published her poems and essays in New Orleans's nativist newspaper.[77]

Edwards's personal experience gave her moral and emotional insight into important political issues even when she did not discuss them in the explicit political language of her day. She never enunciated her views on slavery or race, for example, but they were on her mind (and Bradbury's, who once "nodded and dreamed he was in England hearing a discourse on slavery"). Edwards lived in a slave holding society, and most of her male acquaintances owned slaves, including Bradbury, Budington, Riddell, her father, and her estranged husband, Dempsey Elliott. Her revered pastor Theodore Clapp arrived in New Orleans as an abolitionist but ultimately became an ardent defender of slavery. Edwards was happy to employ slaves when she could. In one of her first surviving letters, she mentioned a desire to buy one, and she was gratified when Charley hired a slave girl, Maria, to assist her. Yet some of her favorite authors opposed slavery on practical or moral grounds. Not only did Walker's pamphlet on Texas advocate the end of slavery (or it claimed to), but Combe's *Constitution of Man,* which Madaline read at least three times, contained a violent attack on slavery in the United States as "a heinous moral transgression."[78]

Most likely Edwards took the personalist course of "unsteady complicity" that Lebsock has described. She did not oppose her slaveowning friends and relatives on principle, but her moral sense and her own sad experience promoted a predilection to view free and enslaved blacks sympathetically. She recognized African Americans as kindred spirits, at least in the sense that she thought they were usually unfairly judged. A striking passage in her testament asked Bradbury to teach their child "that it should never utter a word of detraction against the poorest African and where it was compelled to do so or remain silent, to always choose the latter." These passages hint that Edwards understood the oppressive nature of slavery and was uncomfortable with it. Her empathy allowed her to relate to the few blacks she encountered as human beings. She was sad to lose Maria's company when the girl's term was up, and she ran charitable errands for a poor black woman. This act of kindness stands out in a society that most often denied poor free people of color much assistance and instead treated them as quasicriminals.[79]

Edwards understood that even in a so-called free society the benefits of freedom were denied to many by their circumstances. Metaphors connecting her own situation with that of all sorts of trapped beings, from caged birds to convicts and slaves, pervade her poems and essays. A diary entry and essay on the celebrations of July 4, 1844, developed this theme at greatest length. She had always celebrated the American republic in the abstract, Edwards wrote, but "I felt that though I was included among the free-born Americans never had a 4th of July dawned on me as free and independent until this morning." Before then "I was more than a slave in bondage, for I was a slave to the worst of misfortunes and a football for the heartless. Now I am free and surely no liberated convict feels the contrast more forcibly."[80]

An Imagined Life

Madaline Edwards's insights never led her to an outwardly radical politics. Instead they turned her inward to a personal morality that often transcended the pieties of her upbringing and her era and gave her room to make a life and a self. This is what I mean when I write of the tension between structure and action.

In truth, Edwards fashioned several different selves in life and in words. They were linked by her determination to take charge—however helpless she liked to think herself— to shape the ways others perceived her, and to guide her own fortunes as much as possible.

Self-education—building the knowledge that she believed drew the individual closer to God—was central to Edwards's self-creation. Like many educated women of her era, she had been a voracious reader in her childhood. In the prevailing nineteenth-century view, reading was an appropriate pastime for women until they married. Then their hearts and minds were supposed to turn to their husbands and families. This expectation frustrated many antebellum women writers. Edwards confronted it as soon as she was married, when, according to her autobiographical "Tale of Real Life," her husband's limitations thwarted her own intellectual development. During the twelve years between her marriage and the beginning of her affair with Bradbury, her reading may have been sacrificed to the turmoil of births, deaths, and marital difficulty. By the time of the first letter to Charley, though, she had taken advantage of her single status and particularly of her isolation from urban life to return wholeheartedly to her studies.[81]

Madaline Edwards was an active and critical reader, careful to distinguish her own views even from those of her favorite writers. As a reader and a writer, she was intellectually engaged, a conscious, even if self-deprecating, participant in the public world of culture. She identified with the community of women authors, and when Bradbury remarked that no one could believe that a woman had written her published works, she found it "very strange when such abler pens are daily used by females too. But so it is," she added, perhaps surprised by "Dear C's" obtuseness.[82]

Partly by her own choice and partly as a consequence of Charley's attempt to "model" her, Madaline cast her literary net widely. As with so many of her contemporaries, novels were the centerpiece of her reading. In the mid 1840s the European domestic novelists Sarah Stickney Ellis and Frederika Bremer were her favorites, but passing references show that she was familiar with Lydia Sigourney, Felicia Hemans, Hans Christian Andersen, and Washington Irving.[83]

In 1844 and 1845 about half the books Edwards read were novels. She gave nearly as much time to theological and scientific works such as Combe's and Dick's and to political tracts during the 1844 election season. She read the ancient Jewish historian Flavius Josephus, Milton's *Paradise Lost,* and Alexander Pope's poems, and she read part of the New Testament every day.

Whatever Edwards's momentary interests, Lord Byron was the center of her literary consciousness. She quoted him frequently (with enough minor errors to indicate that she wrote from memory) and alluded to him even more often. To her mind, the poet's literary value was often lost to sight, even by "our dear minister" Theodore Clapp, through the public's obsession with his "immoral" personal life. Edwards devoted an entire essay to defending Byron's morals from unjust condemnation and his poetry from oblivion. Her view of the poet was consistent with her religious convictions, particularly with her belief that one might transcend previous sins and achieve a kind of moral peace in the face of society's disdain. Edwards recognized the connection with her own life and identified deeply with Byron. She pointed out the providential resemblance between the circumstances of her own marriage and his and, more to the point, the similarity of their temperaments: "There is so much congeniality between his melancholy and my own that I never tire of poring over some of his productions," she wrote. For Madaline Edwards, the juxtaposition of Byron's life and the literary greatness inspired confidence in her own writing.[84]

Left to her own spiritual and moral resources, Edwards had "to make a friend of my pen, to commune with for I have had no one else." She was a writer before Bradbury gave her a diary and a notebook, but his gift was an excuse to devote herself even more energetically to her literary calling. Edward tried to write every day, and she took it upon herself to submit poems and essays to the *Native American*. More than that, she used writing as an indispensable tool for analyzing her identity. In her powerful personal essays and poems, "the pen was called into requisition to unfold my sad tale."[85]

Although we respond easily to the intense emotion of Edwards's writing, to the strength of her voice, and to the simple facts of her life, it is obvious that her work is neither a naive nor an unfiltered record of experience (if any writing ever is). She created a character, "Mad," who presented her author as she wished to be seen, within the constraints of certain assumptions about writing and about her readers.

Edwards's literary works presumed the ever-present Charles Bradbury as her principal audience. He encouraged her to write, and he read and commented on her work. She wanted him to return to it after her death, to remind him of her existence and of her love for him. The diaries, essays, and poems depicted the gendered relationship of dominance and subordination that Charley clearly expected the couple to play out. They were her ultimate act of submission to his judgment and made the case for the good heart that lay behind her failings: "I know when these come up before you that no force of imagination could convey to you what I feel, but all I ask is your charity for my many faults."[86]

Occasionally, Edwards imagined that others would read her private words after her death, but these readers were only of passing interest to her. She did want outsiders to read and like her published writings, but even there Charley's approbation meant the most to her. Since all her readers' expectations were as gender-bound as Bradbury's, gender conventions colored her publications. Like many women writers, Edwards took for granted the male point of view as normative, as her dismissive comments on silly, conventional "females" show. She conceived literary authority as dominantly male and deferred to it, submitting her "scribbling in Prose and Poetry" for publication assuming that it would be rejected. She was grateful when the editor of the *Native American* gave her "free use of the paper." But while she sought to distance herself from other women, Edwards stuck close to the mainstream of women's occasional writing in her poems and essays, flirting with male correspondents, composing religious meditations and nature sketches, and in general playing the female.[87]

In both public and private writings, then, Edwards felt constrained to cast her view in gendered terms acceptable to herself and to her readers. This is not to say that she was insincere, but that she never conceived her writing as pure self-revelation. Instead, it was

Introduction to Madaline

self-justification and self-defense, and most of all self-definition. In the end her ambivalence about being judged guided her hand. By concealing herself, she could deflect unwanted judgment; by revealing a carefully constructed persona, she invited judgment on her own terms. She was at once deferential and elusive, a conventional woman because her unconventionality was concealed.[88]

Edwards's many names are an important key to the layering of fragmentary identities that was her most important strategy for concealment. Many nineteenth-century women writers cloaked their ambivalence about exposure and the contradictions of going public to support private values behind a curtain of anonymity. As Mary Kelley has noted, "the woman surfaced as a published writer, but she surfaced in disguise. The writer was a woman, but the published work was not ascribed to her. These women had not stepped beyond the bounds of their homes; only their works had, and anonymously at that." This reticence was an element of Edwards's work. Her use of the initial M in her publications nodded to propriety, particularly since many of her writings bantered playfully with pseudonymous male counterparts, such as "Coelebs," with whom she exchanged humorous poems about marriage and courtship. Edwards's anonymity had another dimension. Whereas Kelley's novelists were afraid their publications would taint their private purity, Edwards was afraid that her private notoriety would taint her public innocence, that readers would discover that the flirtatious M was the tainted Madaline, even though she could not help alluding to her faults on occasion.[89]

Edwards's name play began long before she had published a word. Selima Madaline Cage added the surname Elliott after her first marriage and probably acquired the name Edwards from her bigamous second husband. By the time she began her diary in 1844, she had reversed her first and middle names and called herself Madaline S. Edwards, the name she preferred for the rest of her life. She may have continued to be known to her friends and acquaintances in New Orleans as Mrs. Elliott, though.[90] In her legal battles with Charles Bradbury in 1849 and 1853, she was Mrs. S. M. Cage, widow of Dempsey Elliott. She signed her personal letters Mad and her published writings M. When she died in San Francisco the *Wide West* reported that she was "well known as the Madeline of the New Orleans *Delta* and *Picayune*."[91] Although the information was probably supplied by her cousin John Coffee Hays, the report misspelled her name and attributed her writing to the wrong newspapers.

Had she known of them, those errors might have pleased Edwards, for they added more layers of uncertainty to her identity. The difficulties that others had in getting her names right were emblematic of her opacity and even invisibility to her neighbors, but also of her success in concealing herself. In choosing and changing her names, she shaped the self she wished to be. No one else could discover anything that she wished hidden. To a newspaper poet, W.A.P., she wrote,

> The truth I boast will not allow;
> That you should undeceived be
> You have not seen M I avow
> Some one has April-fooled thee.[92]

Edwards's reading, particularly her reading of fiction, provided the models for her self-concealment and her self-revelation, which were carefully and consciously literary. The literary transformation of experience is clearest in her autobiographical story "A Tale of Real Life." To mid-nineteenth-century readers, a tale was a narrated story with a relatively simple plot. In her tale, Edwards chose the very common narrative device of a conversation between a main character, Justine, and her long-lost friend Sarah K.[93]

In its combination of revelation and concealment, "A Tale of Real Life" is aptly titled. It is real, and it is a tale. It is Edwards's true story, an account of the things that happened to her, but, more important, also of her strategies for survival. Yet she never allows us to be comfortable in what we are reading. This is a "tale," a fictional type, but "a tale founded on facts": "The only fiction I shall borrow is that the conversation never will take place that I shall here represent, but those parts that shall be called up as having passed between myself and friend in happier days are true." That is, the central event of the story—the conversation—is a fiction, but its substance is real. Sarah's name is real, but her presence is imaginary. The "Tale" is Edwards's story, but she chooses to take the pseudonym Justine. The sites of the episodes and the names of the players are disguised with initials, and the events are reduced to their emotional essences. We learn of events only as much as is necessary to set the stage for emotional drama. Justine is a woman whose being is reduced to emotive states and whose actions and motivations, as we are given to understand them, consequently arise from raw emotion. There is no need to describe her meeting with the Bradbury figure because only his effect on her emotional well-being is relevant to the tale. Yet Edwards writes that the tale "will easily be perceived to contain a few of the incidents of my own life." The "Tale" is inscribed in the writing book, intended for Charley, though with the added thought that later generations might see it. Nevertheless, "what inducement there was to write it is alone known to myself." Having said this, Edwards immediately revealed the inducement: she wrote her "Tale" in the hope that "one far away"—Bradbury—and "one dear object"—her unborn child—might read it, and she wrote as well to occupy her mind and to make her grateful "to my God and my dear C" when he had gone north and seemed to have forgotten her.[94]

The playful elision of fact and fantasy conceals more significant reversals, for the meanings of "A Tale of Real Life" depend on our understanding of the conventions of several genres of mid-nineteenth-century fiction. Edwards made her way in literature by exploiting the peculiarities and contradictions of novelistic convention, as in real life she exploited the vagaries of social convention.

As a straightforward narrative of early happiness transformed into adult sorrow through misguided choices, culminating in rescue, the "Tale" falls into the genre that literary historian Nina Baym has labeled a moral fable, a plot type that "arranges events in an order that displays the ineluctable operations of a principle; although settings may be real, they are rather implied than represented. Action and character are schematized according to the principle being illustrated." In addition, the "Tale," like many of Edwards's other discussions of her life, evoked those early nineteenth-century novels that historians refer to as seduction novels: a helpless female is betrayed by men, gives in to her sexual passion, and is punished by death or, in Justine's case, social death. By eliding aspects of her own background in the "Tale"—her family's power, her privileged upbringing—Edwards could cast herself in the role of the poor, orphaned heroine, thrown by misfortune to the world's mercy, or mercilessness. Alliance with the wrong man had "ruined" her, alliance with the right one—the unnamed Bradbury—rescued her. She was restored to a kind of happiness, but one that was sadder, wiser, and more knowing than the innocent happiness of her childhood. Justine was no longer Eve: she had become Mary Magdalene.[95]

Justine is a woman out of control, completely dominated by her passions, in need of a male rescuer. Our understanding of Edwards's message, however, is transformed when we call to mind a third mid-nineteenth-century narrative formula that lurks behind the "Tale" and that surfaces more visibly in Edwards's other writings. In the so-called domestic novel, a heroine overcomes her misfortunes by developing her inner strengths: "Helped occasionally by people in her community, the heroine also called on God for strength as she mustered her own internal resources."[96] Justine is an antitype of this heroine. Her helplessness resonates with an unexpected twist on the literary stereotypes of gender that Edwards employs. Yes, Justine falls because she is weak and passive, but her weakness and passivity are manifested in an interesting way: most of her wrong moves are made in performance of her womanly role. Whenever she listens to the voices of her family, her friends, her society, she comes to grief. She rejects a man who would have been a good husband because she has unrealistically romantic views of love. To marry the man she is expected to would be disastrous, she knows. Nevertheless, she marries one who fills socially accepted criteria of eligibility, and she does so out of pity, an emotion that nineteenth-century writers like Alexander Walker thought natural to women. Similarly, Justine's union with her second husband springs from pity for his misfortunes and a charitable desire to nurse him through a dangerous illness. Her socially poisonous separation from her first husband is prompted by a mother's desire to protect her child's welfare. On the surface, then, all her choices are the right ones. Her fatal weakness is to follow others' standards, rather than the promptings of her own best judgment. Had she been more attentive to her inner voice, she would have been a happier woman, but in acceding to the norms of her society, she finds herself transgressing its most sacred standards of women's behavior. Thus the "Tale," cast as a seduction novel, is really a kind of anti-domestic novel: the woman without inner strength and self-reliance comes to grief. Doing right did her wrong.

Because Madaline Edwards wrote her personal history partly for her own benefit, and partly for Charles Bradbury's, the domestic and seduction models are held in unresolved tension in her telling. Justine is a type of the "Mad" we encounter in the diaries, in some of the letters to Bradbury, and in the early essays, the Mad who was present whenever Charley appeared on the page. But there was a second Mad who was very different, whose lineage can be traced to the domestic novel. This was the Mad who inhabited many of the contemplative essays and the religious writing, where Edwards presented herself as a person who, through dint of self-discipline and study, had rescued herself morally, one who no longer needed the sermonizers' warnings as happier but less aware women did.

In fact, Madaline Edwards enacted her life in ways that were closer to those of the domestic novel's heroine than the seduction novel's victim. Although the tone of many of her writings is despairing and occasionally self-pitying, her actions were those of a woman not afraid to take decisive action. To free herself of the burden of Dempsey Elliott, to break off the marriage at a time when, legally, even violence was not always seen as a sufficient cause for divorce, must have taken great courage in a twenty-year-old woman. So her immigration to California, during which she was alone as usual and with few economic resources, and her return from California to press her lawsuit against Bradbury were beyond the physical and spiritual resources of most women—or men—in the nineteenth century.

Linking these defining incidents was a life of less dramatic but equally determined action. The account in the "Tale of Real Life" of nursing Mr. Edwards, when Madaline had "to sew for my very life for the means to keep him alive," is of a piece with her reports of daily life in the diary. For over a year she struggled through a long false pregnancy that masked a serious illness. Through the entire time of the diaries, she was ill with headaches and fevers for several days of every month. She also suffered a bout of malaria and a horrifying experience with a broken arm that never set or healed properly because her treatment was left until after her male companion's was completed. Despite these setbacks, Edwards refused to become an invalid. She worked diligently to support herself and walked all over the city on business. She negotiated her boundary dispute with Dr. Riddell and took legal action in two separate instance in 1844 and 1845, one time to press an unexplained lawsuit, and on another occasion to obtain a restraining order to "stop the slander of Mrs R."[97]

Literary historian Felicity Nussbaum has argued that "it is the spaces between the cultural constructions of the female and the articulation of individual selves and their lived experience, between cultural assignments of gender and the individual's translation of them into text, that a discussion of women's autobiographical writing can be helpful."[98] Nussbaum's words recall the structure-action tension with which this essay began. The contrast between Madaline Edwards's conduct of her life and her presentation of it are remarkable. The structures of antebellum social thought, particularly those of gender and religion offered Edwards multiple frameworks for interpreting her experience, but they were inadequate as means for projecting action. Justine's history in "A Tale of Real Life" is an extended moral fable of the dilemma of a woman on her own in antebellum New Orleans. To follow the dictates of society was to invite disaster, but to contravene them offered the same unhappy fate. Edwards's history is different in a small but important way. However difficult her life, she relished her right to make choices. Her strength of mind led her to thread a personal history through the cracks and disjunctures of social practice and moral rules. Convention caused her anguish, but it could not control her. Unlike Justine or Mad, Madaline S. Edwards was able to shape her own destiny by changing her life and by reimagining it in her writings.

Notes for "Introduction to *Madaline*"

[1] Madaline Selima Edwards, Writing Book 1 (hereinafter WB1): 30, 53*; Writing Book 2 (hereinafter WB2): 87* (References to Madaline Selima Edwards's (hereinafter MSE) writings not included in this volume are marked with an asterisk.

[2] Nina Baym, *Novels, Readers, and Reviewers: Responses to Fiction in Antebellum America* (Ithaca, N.Y.: Cornell University Press, 1984), 72-76, 80-81.

[3] Marshall Sahlins, *Historical Myths and Mythical Realities: Structure in the Early History of the Sandwich Islands Kingdom* (Ann Arbor: University of Michigan Press, 1981), 67-72; idem, *Islands of History* (Chicago: University of Chicago Press, 1985), 136-56. Social scientists sometimes use the terms *structure* and *agency* to denote the dichotomy of context and human action, and refer to the entire reciprocal process of structure guiding agency and agency reshaping structure as *structuration*. See Anthony Giddens, "Time, Space and Regionalisation," in *Social Relations and Spatial Structures*, ed. Derek Gregorys and John Urry (London: Macmillan, 1985), 265-95; and idem *A Contemporary Critique of Mistorical Materialism*, vol. 1 (Berkeley: University of California Press, 1981), 26-29. For an archaeologist's view of agency, see Ian Hodder, *Reading the Past: Current Approaches to Interpretation in Archaeology*, 2d ed. (Cambridge: Cambridge University Press, 1991), 156-66.

[4] On the expansion of historians' social vision, see Lawrence W. Levine, "Clio, Canons, and Culture," *Journal of American History*, 80 (1993): 849-67.

[5] WB2: 92. On her weight, see MSE to Charles W. Bradbury (hereinafter CWB), Nov. 15, 1846.

[6] Biographical details of MSE's life before 1843 were pieced together from her own writings, as well as from Jeannette Tillotson Acklen, comp., *Tennessee Records: Tombstone Inscriptions and Manuscripts Historical and Biographical* Nashville, 1933), 98, 137-38, 428; Jay Guy Cisco, *Historic Sumner County, Tennessee, with Genealogies of the Bledsoe, Cage, and Douglass Families, and Genealogical notes of Other Sumner County Families* (1909; Nashville, 1971), 191-95; Silas Emmett Lucas, Jr., ed., *Marriages from Early Tennessee Newspapers, 1794-1851* (Easley, S.C., 1978), 69; Silas Emmett Lucas, Jr., and Ella Lee Sheffield, eds., *35,000 Tennessee Marriage Records and Bonds, 1783-1870*, 3 vols. (Easley, S.C., 1981), 1:275, 413; Joyce Martin Murray, *Sumner County, Tennessee, Deed Abstracts, 1793-1805* (Wolfe City, Tenn., 1988); and Edythe Rucker Whitley, comp., *Marriages of Sumner County, Tennessee, 1787-1838* (Baltimore, 1981), 10. MSE's older brother is not included in Cisco's sketch Cage genealogy, but MSE wrote explicitly that in her fourteenth year "I was called to the death bed of a brother who had just attained the age of manhood" (Cisco, *Historic Sumner County*, 195; "Music," WB2: 86*). MSE was known as Selima at least until she was married, and she changed her surname several times. For clarity, she will be referred to as Madaline Edwards throughout the Introduction.

[7] In addition to the sources cited in the previous note, see Walter T. Durham, *The Great Leap Westward: A History of Sumner County, Tennessee, from Its Beginnings to 1805* (Gallatin, Tenn., 1972), 37-38, 94, 108, 111.

[8] WB1: 96*; WB2: 32*; WB1: 9*; "Music," WB2: 86*.

[9] MSE Diary, 1844 (hereinafter D44), Aug. 8, WB2: 1; D44: March 13.

[10] WB1:67; MSE to CWB, Apr. 9, 1847; MSE Diary, 1845 (hereinafter D45): February 9.

[11] D44: Jan. 2; WB1: 141; United States Census, Mobile County, Alabama, 1840, microfilm, p. 143, Mississippi Division of Archives and History (hereinafter MDAH), Jackson, Miss.

[12] WB1: 137. Mississippi kept no vital records until the twentieth century, so there is no way to establish exact birth or death dates for any of the children.

[13] All quotations in this and the following paragraphs derive from "A Tale of Real Life."

[14] On divorce, see Jan Turner Censer, "'Smiling Through Her Tears': Ante-Bellum Southern Women and Divorce," *American Journal of Legal History*, 25 (1981): 24-47; Suzanne Lebsock, *The Free Women of Petersburg: Status and Culture in a Southern Town, 1784-1860* (New York, 1984), 68-72; and Victoria E. Bynum, *Unruly Women: The Politics of Social and Sexual Control in the Old South* (Chapel Hill, N.C., 1992): 63-76.

[15] Recall that Dempsey Elliott had lived next door in 1840. MSE never mentioned this, or him, in connection with her visits to Mobile.

[16] D45: May 5; CWB to MSE, Mar. 9, 1847. See also WB1: 3.

[17] WB1: 126.

[18] Cathy N. Davidson, *Revolution and the Word: The Rise of the Novel in America* (New York: Oxford University Press, 1986), 117-22; Bynum, *Unruly Women*, 44; Jane H. Pease and William H. Pease, *Ladies, Women, and Wenches: Choice and Constraint in Antebellum Charleston and Boston* (Chapel Hill, N.C., 1990), 10-11; Michael Grossberg, *Governing the Hearth: Law and the Family in Nineteenth-Century America* (New York, 1984), 34, 145; Lebsock, *Free Women of Petersburg*, 112; Elizabeth Fox-Genovese, *Within the Plantation Household: Black and White Women of the Old South* (Chapel Hill, N.C., 1988), 256.

[19] This was the argument of "Walker on Women," a book that MSE read: Alexander Walker, *Woman Physiologically Considered, as to Mind, Morals, Marriage, Matrimonial Slavery, Infidelity and Divorce* (New York, 1843), 25-26.

[20] Lebsock, *Free Women of Petersburg*, 97-98; Christine Stansell, *City of Women: Sex and Class in New York, 1780-1860* (Urbana, Ill., 1987), 11-18. The school district's rule 2 of 1843 "stated that teachers were to hold their stations at the pleasure of the Board of Directors; and superior qualifications in reference to moral character, literary attainments, industry, and practical skills were required for their appointment and continuace in office" (Alma Hobbs Peterson, "The Administration of Public Schools in New Orleans, 1841-1861 (Ph.D. dissertation, Louisiana State University, 1964, pp. 54, 62).

[21] Lebsock, *Free Women of Petersburg*, 22-27; Stansell, *City of Women*, 11-18, 71-73, 111-12; D45: July 31.

[22] Accounts of income and expenses in the back of D45; Peterson, "Administration of Public Schools," 70.

[23] Orleans Parish, First District Court records (hereinafter cited as OPDC), 1846-54, in New Orleans Public Library (hereinafter cited as NOPL).

[24] MSE to CWB, Oct. 9, 1843; D44: Nov.4.

[25] CWB to MSE, Mar. 9, 1847. The "other proposition" was never specified.

[26] MSE to CWB, Apr. 9, 1847.

[27] Ibid.

[28] D44: June 10; D45: Mar. 18, Jan. 6; D44: May 18; CWB to MSE, Mar. 9, 1847.

[29] D44: Nov. 25; D45: Feb. 2; D44: Aug 18, May 30.

[30] United States Census for New Orleans, 1840, p. 129, MDAH; United States Census for New Orleans, 1850, p. 268, NOPL; *New Orleans Daily Picayune* (hereinafter *DP*), Feb. 9, 1876, 4:5; Louisiana State Museum, Cemetery Inscription File (hereinafter LSM/CF), Girod Street Cemetery: New Orleans Notarial Archives (hereinafter NONA); Orleans Parish, Conveyance Books (hereinafter OPCB), 34:53, 35:124, 427, New Orleans City Hall; city directories.

[31] Charles W. Bradbury Papers, University of North Carolina at Chapel Hill (hereinafter cited as BP); NOCB 29:659; *New Orleans Commercial Bulletin*, Nov. 13, 1871, 1:1.

[32] Karlem Riess, *John Leonard Riddell, Scientist-Inventor; Melter and Refiner of the New Orleans Mint, 1839-1848; Postmaster of New Orleans, 1859-1862* (New Orleans, 1977); Glenn R. Conrad, ed., *A Dictionary of Louisiana Biography* (New Orleans, 1988), 659, hereinafter cited as *DLB*.

[33] CWB's obituary suggested that he was born in 1815, but a letter from his brother, discussed below, implied that he was born no earlier than 1816. I have assembled CWB's biography from the following sources: BP; Andrew B. Booth, comp., *Records of Louisiana Confederate Soldiers and Louisiana Confederate Commands*, 3 vols. 1902; Spartanburg S.C.: Reprint Co., 1984), 2:80; Harvey Hall, *The Cincinnati Directory for 1825* (Cincinnati, 1825); C. S. Williams, *Williams' Cincinnati Director, City Guide and Business Mirror; or, Cincinnati in 1856* (Cincinnati, 1856); New Orleans city directories; United States Census for New Orleans, 1860, NOPL (Bradbury's only appearance in the United States Census, although he lived in the same house for thirty-nine years).

[34] Cornelius S. Bradbury, Cincinnati, to CWB, New Orleans, Feb. 24, 1836; James W. Breedlove to CWB, June 6, 1838, and Nov. 9, 1838, all in BP. All the Bradbury family letters cited are in BP.

[35] NOCB, vols. 28-45; BP; city directories; Orleans Parish, Louisiana, Second District Court, Succession Records, 1846-80, no. 42088, microfilm, NOPL. Sources reporting to the credit agency R. G. Dun and Company wrote in 1854 that "it is not known that he has any means" and dismissed the prospective partners of his second cottonseed-oil factory as men of even less consequence, Louisiana 11:269, R. G. Dun and Company Collection, Baker Library, Graduate School of Business Administration, Harvard University.

[36] CWB, New Orleans, to Mrs. Sarah Bradbury, Cincinnati, Nov. 7, 1835.

[37] Marcus J. C. Bradbury, Madison, Ind., to CWB, New Orleans, Feb. 15, 1836.

[38] Cornelius S. Bradbury, Cincinnati, to CWB, New Orleans, May 15, 1836. See also First Congregational Church, New Orleans, Marriage Records, 1834-47, microfilm LN60, 1:77, NOPL. Mary Ann Bradbury had two children, but they are not mentioned in CWB's or MSE's surviving writings. There is some evidence that CWB expected his wife to die young and to leave him her money. A letter from Mary Ann to CWB implies that she was a chronic invalid, and MSE raised the possibility of her early death several times. Mary Ann was still alive when the 1860 census was taken, although she disappeared from the records after that. There is no New Orleans death certificate for her, and when CWB died on June 22, 1880, he left no surviving wife. Death Certificates, Orleans Parish, 76:1061 (June 22, 1880), NOPL.

[39] Cornelius S. Bradbury, Cincinnati, to CWB, New Orleans, May 15, 1836.

[40] D44:June 25, Oct. 2, Dec. 26, Dec. 9.

[41] Henry J. Leovy, *The Laws and General Ordinances of the City of New Orleans*, rev. ed. (New Orleans, 1857), 376; Mary P. Ryan, *Women in Public: Between Banners and Ballots, 1825-1880* (Baltimore, 1990), 107-8; Judith K. Schafter, "'Open and Notorious Concubinage': The Emancipation of Slave Mistresses by Will and the Supreme Court in Antebellum Louisiana," *Louisiana History*, 28 (1987): 165-82. Although the term *Creole* has acquired racial connotations in twentieth-century Louisiana, in nineteenth-century Louisiana usage it meant only "a native of," as in "creole de Saint-Domingue" or creole de la Louisiane," but it implied a French speaker. Similarly, "American" strictly meant someone from the United States north and east of Louisiana, but it implied an English speaker.

[42] Boze, "Nouvelles Diverses," Sept. 26, 1839, Mar. 25, 1831, Apr. 27, 1832, May 31, 1832; "Suite au bulletin," Mar. 28, 1836, all in Henri de Ste. Gême Papers, The Historic New Orleans Collection (hereinafter cited as HNOC), Schafer, "'Open and Nororious Concubinage.'" According to Boze, Macarty o"n'a pas meme lainé un picaillon a Ces Enfans naturels du premier lit" ("Nouvelles Diverses," May 31, 1832).

[43] Petition to Mayor Nicholas Girod, Mar. 17, 1817, John Minor and Bonnie Matthews Wisdom Collection, Tulane Library (hereinafter cited as TUL); *Ordinances Ordained and Established by the Mayor & City Council of the City of New Orleans* (New Orleans: J. C. de St. Romes, 1817), 6; *Journal de la Première Municipalité* (New Orleans, n.d.), 1, Favrot Collection, TUL; Leovy, *Laws and General ordinances*, 142; Ryan, *Women in Public*, 107-9.

[44] Craig and Stanley to Budington, Nov. 2, 1843, NOCB B12:394; Budington to J. A. Bradbury, Dec. 27, 1843, BP; OPDC, case 8573; D44: Dec. 28; D45: Mar. 6, Mar. 21, Mar. 24 (the birth), Mar. 29, Apr. 2, Apr.3, Apr. 5.

[45] Riess, *John Leonard Riddell*, 29, 39, 51; *DLB*, 659; Riddell, vol. 17 (Dec. 2, 1844, May 26, 1845), vol. 18 (June 18, 1846 [quote], May 17, 1847); LSM/CF, Girod Street Cemetery.

[46] D45: May 21.

[47] Albert E. Fossier, *New Orleans, the Glamor Period, 1800-1840: A History of the Conflicts of Nationalities, Languages, Religions, Morals, Cultures, Laws, Politics, and Economics During the Formative Period of New Orleans* (New Orleans, 1957), 391; LSM/CF, Girod Street Cemetery; *DLB*, 108; Dun and Company Collection, Louisiana 9:90.

[48] *DLB*, 108; WB2: 76; D45: Nov. 25. M was MSE's newspaper pen name. Also: "Mrs B[reedlove] and judge C called on me today. If I should live to see this twelve months I wonder if they will be my friends" (D45: No. 29).

[49] D45: Nov. 26; MSE to CWB, Nov. 15, 1846.

[50] Orleans Parish, School Board, Second Municipality, Minutes, June 3, 1843-Sept. 4, 1847, University of New Orleans Library, 235 (hereinafter cited at OPSB). The Second Municipality included that part of the city upriver from Canal Street. New Orleans's free public school system had been established in 1841. The Marshall School, a boys grammar school, was on St. Mary Street between Girod and Julia streets. *Cohen's New Orleans Directory . . . for 1853* (New Orleans, 1852), 315.

[51] OPSB, 256-57; MSE to CWB, Apr. 9, 1847.

[52] CWB to MSE, Mar. 9, 1847; MSE to CWB, Apr. 9, 1847; OPSB, 256-57.

[53] MSE to CWB, Apr. 9, 1847.

[54] D44: July 8, May 27; D45: Mar. 21.

[55] MSE to CWB, ca. Sepot. 1843.

[56] Ibid., MSE to CWB, Oct. 12, 1843. A reference to one gift of flowers can be found in D45: Jan. 28.

[57] D44: July 27, Oct. 22, Aug. 3.

[58] D45: Mar. 31, June 16; "Domestic Happiness," WB2: 10-17.

[59] D44: Apr. 17; Walker, *Woman Physiologically Considered,* 3-11. Walker's point was also made by Sarah Stickney Ellis, whose *Poetry of Life* was a favorite book of MSE's. "From the peculiar nature and tendency of woman's character, love and grief may be said to constitute the chief elements of her existence." But Ellis believed that "she is preserved from the overwhelming influence of grief, so frequently recurring, by the reaction of her own buoyant and vivacious spirit, by the fertility of her imagination in multiplying means of happiness, and by her facility in adapting her self to place and time . . . , happily for woman, her internal resources are such as to raise her at least to a level with man in the scale of happiness." Sarah Stickney [Ellis], *The Poetry of Life* (Philadelphia, 1835), 2:46-47.

[60] "Departure," WB1: 57*; D45: January 31.

[61] This paragraph benefited from an observation of Zeynep Kezer's.

[62] MSE to CWb, ca. Sept. 1843; D45: Jan. 10, July 17, July 22, June 25.

[63] D45:Apr. 11; D44: Aug. 15; MSE to CWB, Apr. 25, 1847; D44: August 8.

[64] "Woman," WB1: 41-45.

[65] "Man," WB1: 50-52.

[66] WB1: 3, 2, 41; WB1: 6.

[67] My account of Clapp's career is based on Theodore Clapp, *Autobiographical Sketches and Recollections, During a Thirty-five Years' Reisdence in New Orleans* (Boston, 1857); *Cohen's New Orleans Directory . . . for*

Introduction to Madaline 277

1854 (New Orleans, 1853), vii-viii; J. R. Hutchinson, *Reminiscences, Sketches, and Addresses Selected from My Papers During a Ministry of Forty-five Years in Mississippi, Louisiana, and Texas* (Houston, 1874), 169; Eliza Ripley, *Social Life in Old New Orleans: Being Recollections of My Girlhood* (New York, 1912), 120-24; John Duffy, ed., *Parson Clapp of the Strangers' Church in New Orleans* (Baton Rouge, 1957); Timothy F. Reilly, "Parson Clapp of New Orleans: Antebellum Social Critic, Religious Radical, and Member of the Establishment," *Louisiana History,* 16 (1975): 167-91; idem, "Religious Leaders and Social Criticism in New Orleans" (Ph.D. Dissertation, University of Missouri, 1972), 106-39; John F. C. Waldo, *Historical Sketch of the First Unitarian Church of New Orleans, La.* (New Orleans, 1907); and Samuel Wilson, Jr., *The First Presbyterian Church of New Orleans: Its Buildings and Its Ministers* (New Orleans, 1988), 13-17. The church building where MSE worshiped stood on St. Charles Avenue near Gravier Street. It was built in 1819 and burned in 1851.

[68] Clapp, *Autobiographical Sketches,* 251; Ripley, *Social Life,* 120-21; Tower, Apr. 27, 1845, May 4, 1845; D45: Apr. 6. Tower's first comment referred to a sermon that MSE thought was "most edifying."

[69] Reilly, "Religious Leaders," 108, 124-32; idem, "Parson Clapp," 170, 183-86.

[70] Waldo, *Historical Sketch,* 8; Ripley, *Social Life,* 124; D45: Dec. 9.

[71] Clapp, *Autobiographical Sketches,* 168-73; Theodore Clapp, *Theological Views, Comprising the Substance of Teachings During a Ministry of Thirty-five Years, in New Orleans* (Boston, 1859), 205. My summary of Clapp's theology is based on these passages and on *Autobiographical Sketches,* 268-69; 290, 412, 415; and *Theological Views,* 176-77, 187, 192, 195-96, 202-5, 210-11, 272, 286-87, 296-303.

[72] D45: Feb. 23.

[73] Constantin-François Volney, *The Law of Nature; or, principles of morality, deduced from the Physical Constitution of Mankind and the Universe* (Pittsfield, Mass., 1807); D44: Aug 30, Sept. 18; "Dr. Dick," WB1: 47*; Thomas Dick, *The Christian Philosopher* (1824), quoted in *Encyclopedia Britannica,* 20th century ed. (1902), s.v. "Dick, Thomas"; D44: Aug. 28; "Nature is Religion," WB1: 106*. Clapp also described astronomy as a testimony of divine purposes (*Theological Views,* 185).

[74] George Combe, *The Constitution of Man Considered in Relation to External Objects* (New York, 1844), x, 307.

[75] Ibid., 7; WB1: 5; "To J.A.B.," WB2: 70*; WB1:24-25*.

[76] Lebsock, *Free Women of Petersburg,* 112-45; D45: Mar. 7; D44: Apr. 30, Mar. 26.

[77] D44: May 6; [Robert J. Walker], *Letter of Mr. Walker, of Mississippi, Relative to the Annexation of Texas: In Reply to the Call of the People of Carroll County, Kentucky, to Communicate his Views on That Subject* (Washington D. C., 1844); Frederick Merk and Lois Bannister Merk, *Fruits of Propaganda in the Tyler Administration* (Cambridge, Mass., 1971), 23-27, 98-101, 123-28.

[78] D44: June 3; Combe, Constitution of Man, 237-38.

[79] Lebsock, *Free Women of Petersburg,* 101-3, 141; WB2: 3; D44: June 3. An obvious exception to MSE's kindly view of African Americans is an incident of 1844; she found a black man trying to get into her yard, frightened him off, then tried to obtain a pistol in case he should return (44: July 10, 12, 13).

[80] "July 4th," WB1: 73-74.

[81] Kelley, *Private Woman, Public Stage,* 40-43, 57.

[82] D45: Mar. 22.

[83] MSE to CWB, Nov. 10, 1843.

[84] "Byron," WB2:79-80; "Tale of Real Life." WB1: 141-42.

[85] MSE to CWB. November 10, 1843.

[86] WB1: 29.

[87] D44: Oct. 5. On women writers and the authoritative male point of view, see Mary Jean Corbett, *Representing Femininity: Middle-Class Subjectivity in Victorian and Edwardian Women's Autobiographies* (New York, 1992), 90-91.

[88] On the avoidance of self-exposure in nineteenth-century women's autobiography, see Corbett, *Representing Femininity*, 92-98.

[89] Kelley, *Private Women, Public Stage*, 125-28 (quote on 127).

[90] In an 1846 list of letters at the New Orleans Post Office, there is one for a woman named M. S. Eliott (*DP*, Jan. 2, 1846, 1:4).

[91] Obituary, *Wide West*, August 27, 1854.

[92] "Answer to W.A.P," WB2: 108.

[93] Nina Baym, *Woman's Fiction: A Guide to Novels by and about Women in America, 1820-1870*, second ed. (Ubana, 1993), 33-34.

[94] WB1: 137, 161.

[95] Baym, *Novels, Readers*, 65; Felicity A. Nussbaum, "Eighteenth Century Women's Autobiographical Commonplaces," in *The Priave Self: Theory and Practice of Women's Autobiographical Writings*, ed. Shari Benstock (Chapel Hill, 1988), 150; Beth Maclay Doriani, "Black Womanhood in Nineteenth-Century America: Subversion and Self-Construction in Two Women's Autobiographies," *American Quarterly*, 43 (1991): 204; Baym, *Woman's Fiction*, 35-36.

[96] Doriani, "Black Womanhood, 204-5.

[97] WB1: 149; D45; July 17.

[98] Nussbaum, "Commonplaces," 149.

GUIDEBOOKS TO SIN:
THE BLUE BOOKS OF STORYVILLE*

Pamela D. Arceneaux

New Orleans's Storyville was one of the first legally designated red-light districts in the history of the United States. Other cities had their tenderloin areas, but only New Orleans attempted to regulate the activities of "lewd and abandoned" women by consigning them to a prescribed section by an ordinance of the city council.[1] This ordinance, prepared and sponsored by Alderman Sidney Story, hence "Storyville," was passed on January 29, 1897. For roughly twenty years Storyville was, in the day's parlance, "red hot' and reigned supreme as the most notorious tenderloin district in North America. The federal government forced Storyville to close in 1917 when open prostitution was prohibited within five miles of any United States military installation.

Storyville was not in the French Quarter as many erroneously believe, although prostitution existed there before and after the establishment of "the District." Rather, Storyville encompassed the area from the downtown side of Iberville Street to the uptown side of St. Louis Street and from the lake side of Basin Street to the river side of Robertson Street. It was also the only such district to advertise itself in its own press with any degree of regularity.

Guidebooks to the houses and their "jolly good fellows," a Victorian euphemism for easy women or prostitutes, were published in Storyville for a time and made available to visitors as they left the train at the Southern Depot at Basin and Canal streets. Also distributed at bars, at barber shops, and by newsboys, these guides were appreciated by sports exploring New Orleans's playground of vice who knew the value of the adage, "You can't tell your players without a program."

The various "programs" to Storyville's gaudy palaces are most often known by the collective title "Blue Books." The "blue" of the title refers, however, more to subject matter than the color of the covers which was not always blue. The term "tenderloin

---

*First published in *Louisiana History*, 28 (1987): 397-405. Reprinted with the kind permission of the author and the Louisiana Historical Association.

400" was used on some, indicating that those listed were the creme of the demimonde.[2] Prostitutes working in cheap one- or two-room "cribs" were not included. New Orleans was not the only city to have a special directory of its tenderloin. In 1889, several years prior to Storyville's formation, Chicago sports consulted *The Sporting and Club House Directory, Chicago: Containing a Full and Complete List of All Strictly First Class Clubs and Sporting Houses*.[3] New Orleans, however, appears to have offered these directories on a more regular basis than any other city with a sizable red-light district.

Assigning a date to individual Blue Book issues is a deductive process, as only a few have a date printed on them. According to Al Rose in *Storyville, New Orleans: Being an Authentic, Illustrated Account of the Notorious Red-Light District*, a *Green Book*, or *Gentlemen's Guide to New Orleans* is mentioned in a pre-Storyville 1895 issue of the newspaper *The Mascot*.[4] No copies of this *Green Book* have been found. The earliest extant guidebook to Storyville appeared in 1900; on its cover it shows a picture of a lady holding a fan with the words "Blue Book" above and "Tenderloin 400" below. Although thousands of copies of various issues were published, few editions are identified. Rose gives the most likely dates of edition as 1900, 1902/03, 1906, 1908, 1912, with a final printing of the last edition in 1915.[5] He identifies editions by changes in the cover, but other Blue Books have appeared with different covers which are not illustrated in his book. Some Blue Books are marked as numbered editions. The first so marked is identified in the text as the "Sixth Edition," but is undated. The first numbered and dated Blue Book is the "Seventh Edition" (1906). A Blue Book with the words "Blue Book" in Old English type and "1907" on its cover is marked "Eighth Edition" inside. A Blue Book with a red cover and a squared swag design is identified inside as the "Ninth Edition," but is undated. The "Tenth Edition," also undated, has a double row of *fleurs de lis* running the length of its cover. Other Blue Books, whether before or after these identified editions, are not dated or marked as specific editions.

The Blue Books were published by Billy Struve, a former police reporter for the New Orleans *Daily Item* who identified himself as "Billy News" in opening pages of the little guidebooks. Struve had his office on the second floor of Lulu White's saloon, which was on the comer of Basin and Bienville streets and next door to her famous den of sin, Mahogany Hall. This saloon building was built in 1908.[6] Perhaps Blue Books were published in Anderson's Annex prior to this location as Struve was also the manager of Tom Anderson's Annex Cafe on the comer of Basin and Iberville streets. This cafe featured "private dining rooms for the fair sex," and "all the latest musical selections nightly, rendered by a typical Southern darky orchestra."[7] Tom Anderson was the "Mayor of Storyville," proprietor of several cafes and chop houses, member of the state legislature, and paramour of such well-known madams as Josie Arlington and Gertrude Dix whom he eventually married.

Blue Books published prior to 1908 could have been published by *The Sunday Sun*, a New Orleans newspaper devoted to the doings of its "scarlet society." The typography of the newspaper and the Blue Books is very similar. By the time Storyville was

The Blue Books of Storyville

established, *The Mascot*, another underground newspaper, had ceased publication, but perhaps its hardware was used to produce these guidebooks.[8]

The Blue Books are roughly the same size (5 1/2" x 4 1/4" or slightly smaller), are usually printed in red and black ink on coated paper, and the pages are unnumbered. The Preface and "A Word to the Wise" first greet the reader, explaining the purpose of the book and the boundaries of the district. A later edition has this to say under the motto, "Honi Soit Qui Mal y Pense":[9]

> This Directory and Guide of the Sporting District has been before the people on many occasions, and has proven its authority as to what is doing in the 'Queer Zone.' Anyone who knows to-day from yesterday will say that the Blue Book is the right book for the right people.[10]

Under the heading, "Why New Orleans Should Have This Directory" were these reasons:

> Because it is the only district of its kind in the States set aside for the fast women by law.
> Because it puts the stranger on a proper and safe path as to where he may go and be free from 'Hold-ups,' and other games usually practiced upon the stranger.
> It regulates the women so that they may live in one district to themselves instead of being scattered over the city and filling our thoroughfares with street walkers.
> It also gives the names of women entertainers employed in the Dance Halls and Cabarets in the District.[11]

Some of the reasons given appear to be justification for the red-light district itself, rather than the directory. Readers were further informed that the book contained facts and not dreams from a "hop-joint" (opium den), and that the book must not be mailed probably because of postal regulations.

Listings of women follow, arranged either alphabetically by last name or sometimes by street address. The madams appear in capital letters or boldface print and everyone is identified as either "w," white, "c," colored, or "oct.," octoroon. Jewish prostitutes are designated with a "J," and an asterisk indicates Frenchwomen in the Blue Book marked "Seventh Edition" inside and dated 1906 on its cover.

The advertisements for the various brothels are among the most entertaining aspects of the Blue Books. Mostly couched in rather coy terms, these ads seem tame now. Vulgar or explicit descriptions of the women or of the activities offered at each house are never employed. The words "whore" or "prostitute" do not appear.[12] Instead, the magnificence of the house, the array of charming, well-bred, and pretty entertainers, and the devotion to providing visitors with a good time is repeated again and again. Throughout the several issues of the Blue Books, these advertisements and their peculiar, often ungrammatical phrasing remain much the same. Here are a few examples:

> Miss Margaret Miller 337 N. Basin Street
> While but a late resident of the Tenderloin District, she has gained more friends than the oldest in the business. Margaret is known as the 'idol' of society and club boys, and needs but little introduction, as she is known by the elite from New York to California for her wit and loveliness. 'Margaret' is very winsome, and appeals to everyone, as she is clever and beautiful. Her mansion is handsomely furnished, everything being the best that money could procure. Aside from the grandeur of her establishment, she has a score of beautiful women, who, with their charming landlady, form a group that eannot [sic] be forgotten. Phone 466 MAIN[13]
>
> Miss Como Lines 1565 Iberville Street
> Miss Lines is one woman among the fair sex who is regarded as an all-round jolly good fellow. Nothing is too good for 'Como,' and she regards the word 'Fun' as it should be, and not as a moneymaking word. She is a good fellow to all who come in contact with her. Miss Lines also has the distinction of keeping one of the quietest and most elaborately furnished establishments in the city, where an array of beautiful women and good times reign supreme. A visit will teach more than pen can describe. Bessie also has an array of beautiful girls, who are everlastingly on the alert for a good time, so Phone 1919 MAIN[14]
>
> Miss Bertha Golden 1504 Iberville Street
> Bertha has always been a head-liner among those who keep first-class Octoroons. She also has the distinction of being the only classical Singer and Salome dancer in the Southern States. She has had offers after offers to leave her present vocation and take to the stage, but her vast business has kept her among her friends. Any person out for fun among a lot of pretty Octoroon damsels, here is the place to have it. For rag-time singing and clever dancing, and fun generally, Bertha stands in a class all alone. Remember the Number Phone 1535 MAIN[15]

Some are more succinct:

> Miss Grace Simpson 223 N. Basin
> House full of pretty and clever women Phone 788 MAIN[16]

In addition to these ads probably purchased by the madams, many of the Blue Books contain photographs of interiors of the more elegant bagnios. The rooms are crammed with furniture and bric-a-brac in the Victorian taste and are often designed around a theme—the Japanese den, the Turkish den, the Vienna parlor, the American parlor. Other products, services, and events are also advertised. There are ads for whisky, champagne, beer, bottled water, cigars, restaurants, candy, jewelers, drug stores, venereal disease "cures" under the guise of patent medicines, and glassware and crockery. One lawyer advertised in several issues, along with a piano tuner and a bath house.[17] Notices for the "French Balls" held during carnival season may indicate that the Blue Books were issued in anticipation of increased business from visitors during that time.

Other Storyville guides were produced, and a bibliography published in 1936 by "Semper Idem" attempted to list them all.[18] Two tiny booklets (2 3/4" x 2 1/8"), *The Lid* and *Hell-0*, nearly alike in size and format, contain single-line listings of telephone numbers, madams, and addresses. There are ads for Tom Anderson's various enterprises, and one is asked not to "misconstrue the name" of the second item and "read it backwards." They date from about 1904. Another small booklet (4 1/2" x 3"), the *Sporting Guide,* has a red cover and several ruled pages for notes, followed by bordello ads similar to those found in the Blue Books. *The Red Book* (5 1/2" x 3 3/4") appeared in 1901 and says, "Give them a call, boys, You'll get treated right."[19] It contains a picture of Lulu White which really is not the famous "Queen of the Octoroons" but one of her girls. Miss White issued her own advertising booklet (4 3/4" x 3") which featured a picture of her New Mahogany Hall on its tan cover and individual portraits of her "guests" within. The picture of Lulu in her own booklet is not her either, but is another of her girls. It appears that a couple of girls posed more than once using different names and captions.

After 1917 when Storyville officially closed, prostitutes scattered to every district of the city, but concentrated in the French Quarter, Julia Street, Tulane Avenue, and North Rampart Street.[20] Prostitution again became a clandestine activity which did not lend itself to advertising, even in such a specialized medium as the Blue Books. Despite the great numbers of these books which were widely distributed during Storyville's heyday, they are considered collector's items now. The Historic New Orleans Collection has several issues of the Blue Books and other tenderloin guides, many of which were once part of the vast collection of Americana amassed by bibliophile Thomas Winthrop Streeter.

Notes for "Guidebooks to Sin: The Blue Books of Storyville"

[1] In 1903, Shreveport followed suit with a city ordinance which confined its bawds to an area known as St. Paul's bottoms.

[2] "The Four Hundred" was a term coined by lawyer and social leader Samuel Ward McAllister in 1888 to indicate the elite of American society.

[3] Ruth Rosen, *The Lost Sisterhood: Prostitution in America, 1900-1918* (Baltimore, 1982), 81, 194.

[4] Al Rose, *Storyville, New Orleans: Being an Authentic Account of the Notorious Red Light District* (University, Ala., 1974), 136.

[5] Ibid., 136, 142, 145, 146.

[6] Ibid., 42.

[7] Blue Book, The Historic New Orleans Collection, 77-2346-RL, n. p.; hereafter cited as Blue Book, with accession number.

[8] Rose Interview, May 20, 1986.

[9] Translation: "Evil to Him Who Evil Thinks."

[10] Blue Book, 77-2346-RL, n.p.

[11] Ibid., n.p.

[12] A "facsimile" Blue Book has recently appeared which contains some of the typical advertisements for the madams which compare with advertisements to be found in other authentic Blue Book issues. Other extremely graphic descriptions, however, appear in this "facsimile" interspersed with the more familiar advertisements. The "facsimile" is marked "Ninth Edition," but the pages of salacious blurbs are not to be found in an authentic "Ninth Edition." Also, the typography is markedly different from that of other Blue Books examined.

[13] Blue Book, 86-165-RL, n.p.

[14] Ibid., 1969.19.7, n.p.

[15] Ibid., 77-370-RL, n.p.

[16] Ibid., 1969.19.8, n.p.

[17] Ibid., 77-2346-RL, n.p.

[18] "Semper Idem" (Always the Same) was perhaps the pen name of Charles Heartman of *Heartman's Historical Series*. The Blue Books pictured and described in his book appear to be the same ones which are now housed at The Historic New Orleans Collection.

[19] *The Red Book*, The Historic New Orleans Collection, 1969.19.5, n.p.

[20] Rose, *Storyville, New Orleans*, 170.

PARLORS, POLITICS, AND PRIVILEGE: CLUBWOMEN AND THE FAILURE OF WOMAN SUFFRAGE IN LAFAYETTE, LOUISIANA, 1897-1922[*]

Barbara Smith Corrales

The unprecedented growth of women's clubs throughout the late 1800s and early 1900s provided an important impetus for the Progressive reform movement that swept through the nation at the turn of the twentieth century. The role of women's organizations was initially less significant in patriarchal Southern communities that severely restricted public expression by women, but, over time, Southern women's clubs effectively loosened social restraints, permitting a broader application of the feminine gender's "natural traits" (nursing, nurturing, and moral guidance).[1] Women utilized this new freedom to promote reforms, eventually including woman suffrage.

In the South, this metamorphosis occurred at least a generation after Northern women's clubs had redirected their focuses.[2] Most of Louisiana's women's clubs also lagged behind their Northern counterparts. The women's clubs of Lafayette, Louisiana, however, constituted a notable exception, for although they embraced many Progressive-era reforms, they rejected woman suffrage in a misguided attempt to preserve their privileged social position.

Women's clubs in Louisiana's larger cities, but most notably in New Orleans, generally emulated the increasingly militant women's groups in other Southern urban centers.[3] The impact of the women's movement on rural and small-town Louisiana, however, has remained largely a matter of speculation. In Lafayette, woman suffrage was never an important topic of public debate, though the parish had a white female population of over 9,000 by 1914.[4] Some limited discussion of women's rights occurred in Lafayette when the editor of the *Lafayette Daily Advertiser* endorsed a state

---

[*]First published in *Louisiana History*, 38 (1997): 453-71. Reprinted with the kind permission of the author and the Louisiana Historical Association.

constitutional amendment giving women the legal right to serve on various boards for educational or charitable purposes.[5] Lafayette women had acted as "school trustees" since 1906, although their responsibilities are unclear,[6] and it appears that these trustees performed their duties well enough to merit the paper's support. Yet, by all accounts, even this modest endorsement of women's political rights by the Lafayette newspaper ran counter to prevailing local attitudes.

Despite the paper's stated determination to "always be open to a fair and full discussion of all legitimate public questions . . . [of] public interest,"[7] the *Daily Advertiser*'s editor generally chose to ignore the increasingly volatile local issue of women's political rights.

It is clear, however, that on at least two earlier occasions, Mrs. Laura Lake Meehan, a leading figure in the New Orleans suffrage movement, spoke to Lafayette audiences on woman suffrage.[8] Although her address in February 1913 was described as "exceedingly interesting," the audience, when urged to "discuss the subject pro or con" after Meehan's presentation, could not be "induced to respond."[9] An effort was made to organize a suffrage organization when Meehan visited Lafayette again at Mrs. John (Marie) Keith's invitation in June 1913. Though the *Daily Advertiser* made no mention of the local response to Meehan's visit, the results appear to have been disappointing for proponents of woman suffrage. Following a debate on woman suffrage at the time of Meehan's second visit, members of the Alethian Club, who were also prominent in Woman's Club affairs,[10] agreed to vote on the question of whether or not females *would* eventually get the vote, not if they *should* be enfranchised.[11] Even then, they indicated their opinions only by secret ballot. The Lafayette newspaper reported "9 votes cast for the affirmative and 7 for the negative"—hardly a resounding endorsement of woman suffrage.[12]

On September 28, 1914, the *Daily Advertiser* reported an upcoming Woman's Suffrage Club meeting at the home of Marie Keith.[13] The meeting's announcement lay nestled unobtrusively alongside other social club news. Mrs. Keith, president of the Woman's Suffrage Club and a member of the Civic League of Lafayette, was also active in the State Federation of Woman's Clubs.[14] It is unclear if she had organized the Woman's Suffrage Club earlier or if this was the group's inaugural meeting.

The next day, the newspaper noted that the suffrage group had met and discussed "important matters . . . but no conclusions could be reached." The group would "meet again Thursday to complete business."[15] Conclusions reached at Thursday's meeting, if indeed any were reached, apparently did not merit journalistic mention.

On October 5, 1914, the *Daily Advertiser* featured a front-page appeal, signed by Marie Keith, who invited all citizens of Lafayette to a suffrage rally scheduled for the following Friday, which had been designated Ladies' Day at the local fairgrounds. Anticipating that featured speaker, Jean Gordon, a well-known state suffrage organizer, would attract a large turnout, Mrs. Keith boasted that the rally "promises a great successful awakening of the women to the responsibilities of citizenship for which every good woman must necessarily prepare herself."[16] To encourage attendance by women who were ambivalent about woman suffrage, the Lafayette suffragist promoted woman suffrage as being beneficial to "the study of shaping the course that will show the way to lower the cost of living and other vocational branches so near to home and fireside."

It is noteworthy that Mrs. Keith failed to mention either the personal or political benefits of women's enfranchisement. Cloaking her call for suffrage support in terms of citizenship, household concerns, and "better ideals" belies a prevailing conservatism which necessitated down-playing the primary purpose of the suffrage movement, women's right to vote.[17]

The *Daily Advertiser* reported nothing about the public response to, participation in, or demonstrations of support for suffrage at the rally. The newspaper also issued no report on Gordon's speech.

Evidently woman suffrage on a local level was not sufficiently important to merit more than occasional mention in the *Daily Advertiser*'s pages, and the debate on whether women should have equal suffrage held at commencement exercises of the Southwest Louisiana Industrial Institute (S.L.I.I.) (present-day University of Southwestern Louisiana) perhaps was considered newsworthy[18] only because suffrage advocates lost the debate. Not coincidentally, the judges of the debate had wives prominent in Lafayette's women's clubs in the late nineteenth century. The judges' opinions, according to available evidence, accurately reflected those of their wives. Woman suffrage was evidently not a viable option for most, if not all, of the local elite.

From 1890 to 1921, Lafayette's clubwomen of all faiths (including numerous Jews), consistently refused to take a public stand for woman suffrage in any form. Extant records suggest that no Woman's Club members attended Marie Keith's suffrage rally. It is indeed noteworthy that Keith never belonged to this organization.[19]

Mrs. Crow Girard, a member of the elite Woman's Club of Lafayette, articulated the prevailing attitude of Lafayette's clubwomen when she publicly announced the local group's secession from all suffrage organizations in an effort to disassociate itself from the question of women's rights. On May 25, 1920, taking a position anathema to that of the National Federation of Woman's Clubs, of which she was an active member, Mrs. Girard said, "We are not mixing in the suffrage question whatever. We have our personal opinion on suffrage. The Federation is not mixing in the suffrage struggle whatever."[20] Mrs. Girard was simply making public what had been for years an entrenched position for Lafayette clubwomen. The Federation, unlike Mrs. Girard, encouraged all of its member-clubs to agitate for enfranchisement. In Lafayette, however, women's clubs chose instead to limit activity to civic improvement and social reform work, foregoing entirely a proactive political role.

This is not to say that Lafayette clubwomen were unaware of women's gains. In March 1909, Mrs. F. E. Davis, speaking before a State Federation of Woman's Clubs convention in Lafayette, proclaimed that "it is a woman's age, blossoming with opportunities, grander than one has ever dreamed of in past centuries."[21] Despite Mrs. Davis' rosy prediction, little had changed in the Hub City ten years later. When leading

New Orleans suffrage proponent Kate Gordon spoke in Lafayette, the paper noted only that she would speak on "the white plague" in her capacity as vice-president of the Louisiana Anti-Tuberculosis League.[22] Her activism for woman suffrage was not mentioned.[23] The paper reported nothing more about her lecture.

In her public acknowledgment of "blossoming" possibilities for women, Mrs. Davis overlooked enfranchisement as a desirable opportunity. This active Lafayette clubwoman enthusiastically participated in many worthwhile reform projects, but she deliberately emphasized woman's familial duties, as did other local clubwomen.[24] Why did these women choose to remain aloof from the suffrage movement? The motivations for this conscious decision are complex and varied.

The reluctance of Lafayette's clubwomen to agitate for woman suffrage was due in part to ideological polarization among the state suffrage rank and file. State and regional disagreement over which amendment merited suffragist support divided the Louisiana woman suffrage organization. The actions of Kate Gordon made matters worse.

Although many in the National American Woman Suffrage Association (NAWSA) preferred a federal mandate, the organization would have accepted a state suffrage amendment, if necessary. Kate Gordon, preoccupied with maintaining white supremacy, adamantly refused a federal measure. Her often acrimonious criticism of a federal amendment negated any gains made in Louisiana by the suffrage movement, and in the South as well.[25] Gordon actively worked with federal amendment opponents and effectively paralyzed the woman suffrage movement throughout the region.[26]

Although admittedly a contributory factor, organizational divisiveness alone did not prevent Lafayette's clubwomen from advocating suffrage. The influence of other factors is seen most clearly in the composition and activities of the Woman's Club of Lafayette, the town's preeminent woman's club.

Originally organized in 1897 as the Ladies' Five O'Clock Tea Club, and still active in 1997, the Woman's Club of Lafayette was formed before the Hub City installed its first electric lamp.[27] Charter members included spouses of wealthy entrepreneurs, bankers, doctors, lawyers, and politicians. They were local aristocrats and they ruled the town. According to Quintilla Morgan Anders, a founding member, the Woman's Club of Lafayette formed because of the "stagnation of a woman's life."[28] Clearly this signified pervasive boredom and abundant leisure time. Club work provided a satisfactory diversion for many of these affluent women.

As with most women's clubs throughout the nation, the first avowed purpose of the Lafayette Woman's Club was self-improvement.[29] Also, like Northern groups, the club's focus later shifted to civic and municipal improvement projects. Over the years, however, the group's agenda remained consistently limited to non-political projects, although club members, acting through the Ladies' Aid Auxiliary Campaign Committee, did aggressively police the polls when a bond issue for school improvement appeared on a ballot.[30] Mrs. Anna Margaret Denbo, Woman's Club historian, noted many years later that "Women at this time did not have the privilege of the vote. The old idea still prevailed that the woman's place was in the home, let the men do the outside work, consequently we had opposition to fight—sometimes quite unpleasant." Nevertheless, she continued, "All the members went out to contact the men not in favor of the tax." Of her own participation she said, "From the time the polls were opened until they closed, I stood firmly at my post of duty—that was on the Northeast corner of the courthouse yard."[31]

The ladies worked at the behest of Mayor Charles O. Mouton.[32] The mayor publicly acknowledged the women's significant political influence when he noted that "if the bond issue is supported by the ladies, it is bound to succeed."[33] One wonders, then, if women had this much political acumen and publicly acknowledged power, why was it not focused on advancing women's rights? Mayor Mouton's wife was a prominent member of the Woman's Club, the Ladies' Auxiliary Campaign Committee, and other women's groups.[34] Mrs. Mouton and her cohorts could very likely have convinced local men to vote in favor of any issue, including woman suffrage, had they considered it desirable, as they did on other occasions.[35] And, in a period when a growing middle class struggled to emulate their social "betters," clubwomen could have swayed local women of all classes.

At the same meeting, former Lafayette mayor C. D. Caffery recognized the ladies' work in securing the establishment of S.L.I.I.[36] Caffery joined Mayor Mouton in calling on gentlemen present to "assist the ladies in any way that they could be of service."[37] Caffery's wife, like Mayor Mouton's spouse, was prominent in several women's organizations, including the Lafayette Woman's Club.[38] Clearly these women could be effective when it suited their purpose.

Clubwomen's enthusiastic public support of the bond issue was manifested in their participation in a promotional parade. Local clubwomen were thus not averse to public activism. The success of the S.L.I.I. campaign combined with the success of the bond issue amply demonstrated the clubwomen's powers of persuasion. Lafayette's male leaders obviously appreciated the women's abilities. One can only speculate why these clubwomen, having full understanding of their collective political strength, so assiduously avoided the suffrage issue. Was it unacceptable for aristocratic Lafayette women to work publicly for the betterment of women of all classes? If this were true, then why was it acceptable for these women to aggressively police the courthouse when voters cast their ballots? Was this not also a public political exercise? Such actions were not the actions of women "delicate and dainty of habit and personal character" who lived a "sheltered existence."[39] Unfortunately, available records of the Woman's Club offer little insight into clubwomen's personal thoughts on the matter.

The Woman's Club's minutes for the period after 1897 document the group's movement toward a public-service orientation, but there was never any recorded discussion at club gatherings about enfranchisement. Club members nevertheless did subscribe to a suffrage publication; hence, they were unquestionably aware of suffrage agitation elsewhere in the nation.[40] Karen Blair, Anne Firor Scott, Carmen Lindig, and other leading authorities on women's history describe the evolving role of Southern clubwomen who moved from the pedestal to the parlor, to public activism for woman suffrage in the wake of the Civil War.[41] But in Lafayette, members of women's clubs rarely moved in any direction that did not buttress their position as Southern "ladies" who dispensed largesse from various elite parlors, while ministering to the needs of a favored few. Countless social gatherings and innumerable meetings among these Southern "ladies" were a conduit for charitable work.[42]

Lafayette clubwomen in this period personify the Southern "ideal of ladydom" and "domestic feminism." This was a time when Southerners virtually deified womanhood as part of a determined effort to preserve the image of the "lost cause."[43] Southern "ladies" typically remained aloof from politics. Many women progressively abandoned pedestal and parlor, but Lafayette's clubwomen, with very few exceptions, chose to remain in a position of exclusivity and privilege for many years after the Nineteenth Amendment became the law of the land. Some *never* left their pedestals. In a time when domestics and field hands were black and subservient, this was a choice in complete accordance with the clubwoman's chosen role of gracious Southern "lady" in a dominant white society. Racial prejudice most definitely played a large role in the failure of woman suffrage in Lafayette.[44]

Because most white voters were alienated by the suffrage movement's Northern origins and historical ties to abolitionism, the struggle for women's enfranchisement was indeed difficult in the South. The movement was further hampered because "female suffrage" was a generic term that included all women, regardless of color. Many Southerners feared that whites would lose political power if black women gained the vote. The Nineteenth Amendment was consequently a "lost cause" in Louisiana, particularly in Lafayette, despite the best efforts of state and national suffrage activists to sway state and local leaders.

When Louisiana lawmakers confronted the issue of suffrage ratification, the *Daily Advertiser* was not optimistic, despite Governor John Parker's earlier pledge of support.[45] Popular resistance to suffrage seemed insurmountable in Louisiana and particularly in Lafayette Parish. By June 1920, the National Women's Party, which had fought valiantly, sometimes violently, for woman suffrage, lost all hope of favorable state action.[46]

Throughout the debate over ratification of both federal and state suffrage amendments, Lafayette's women's clubs consistently refused to become publicly involved. Mrs. Girard merely acknowledged a long-standing tradition in 1920 when she spoke to the Legislation Committee of a Louisiana Women's Federated Clubs Convention. Reports published in the local paper throughout much of 1920 made it clear that, despite the national preoccupation with woman suffrage, Lafayette's leaders were clearly more concerned with local matters, such as the federal census results, than with obtaining equal political rights for women.[47] Yet, municipal leaders considered Lafayette a Progressive community, despite local rejection of woman suffrage.[48]

The suffrage amendment did not fail in Lafayette and Louisiana simply because of apathy. Local politics and an entrenched power structure played an equally destructive role in the amendment's rejection. A large measure of responsibility lies with the area's state legislators.

As in other Southern states, there was a major problem inherent in Louisiana's suffrage struggle: State legislators, as a group, refused to enact any extension of enfranchisement in an attempt to maintain a "solid South."[49] Indeed, legislators used all possible means to sabotage the state's march toward woman suffrage. As late as 1920, Lieut. Gov. Ruffin G. Pleasant publicly urged rejection of the Federal amendment.[50] State representatives A. M. Martin and P. A. Landry of Lafayette Parish were both absent when the House of Representatives voted on the Anthony amendment on June 15, 1920, but Representative L. A. Moresi of Iberia Parish, Lafayette Parish's neighbor to the south, gave his reasons for voting against the measure. He said, among other things, that "If the Nineteenth Amendment was finally adopted, it will mean race war and sex war." He voted against it, he said, "to preserve white supremacy."[51] Were Lafayette-area legislators really afraid of "race war and sex war" as Moresi's statement indicates? If not, what prompted such determined, outspoken opposition?

One possibility is that many male leaders may have seen women's enfranchisement as a serious threat not only to Southern white supremacy, but to Southern white-male power and social control. Concern over loss of white-male authority was a significant factor in the failure of woman suffrage to find a modicum of support in Louisiana's patriarchal society, as Moresi's statement suggests.[52] Thus, if maintaining the existing white-male power structure was truly the primary concern of all white authority figures, local results of the November 1918 election are not surprising. Although a preliminary count showed that Lafayette voters were almost evenly split on the suffrage amendment,[53] the measure was overwhelmingly defeated in the final vote tally.[54] It is difficult to determine, however, whether woman suffrage's resounding local defeat was the product of intense opposition or paralyzing indifference.

In the first primary, held the previous month to select a replacement for recently deceased United States Senator Robert F. Broussard, 1,144 of the more than 3,500 eligible local voters cast ballots.[55] In the second primary, to which ballot the state suffrage amendment was a last-minute addition, however, only 448 votes were cast either for or against the suffrage amendment.

Most eligible voters were clearly indifferent about woman suffrage, and they simply ignored the amendment on the ballot. This allowed the amendment's most vocal opponents to carry the election. The casual tone of Mrs. Harold Demanade's public comment on the state amendment's failure further reinforces this supposition: "On the fifth of November woman suffrage . . . seems to have been lost. Bad men for bad reasons voted against. Good men for seemingly good reasons, mistaken chivalry for the most part, voted against."[56]

Mrs. Demanade may have believed in mistaken chivalry, but she and her sister clubwomen clearly did nothing to convince male voters of women's right to the franchise. Instead of "policing the polls" in the November 1918 election as they did in the earlier school bond election, Lafayette's clubwomen allowed a small number of male voters to speak for all local women.

What really motivated the men of Louisiana to reject the amendment? Was it simply mean-spiritedness, or was it a misdirected sense of chivalry, as Mrs. Demanade suggested? Could it possibly have been something few men may have acknowledged even if asked?

Like most Southern legislators, white Louisianians keenly suffered from feelings of personal insecurity after the Civil War. Loss of power and control in the wake of devastating defeat during Union occupation and subsequent Radical Reconstruction had curtailed former slaveowners' power over freedmen. Some men in positions of power viewed dominance over women as the last social stronghold of Southern white men.

This attitude is seen most clearly in an open letter from Harry Gamble, chairman of future Gov. John Parker's campaign committee, to U. S. Senator Joseph Ransdell.[57] The letter stated Gamble's belief that "one may possess a thing whose main value to him consists in his right to keep another's hands away from it. He keeps it principally because he fears what another may do with it." He further stated that "a thing which is a weak shield in my hands might easily become a crushing weapon in the hands of a giant."[58] Cloaked in terms of a state's rights and a state amendment, Gamble's bald description of how women could later be disfranchised at the whim of state legislators should they so desire, indicates a fear of all women's voting power, not just former female slaves. As Parker's campaign manager, Gamble surely published this letter with Parker's support. Harry Gamble did not stand alone in his position. Fear of losing this last vestige of power was a factor in Louisiana legislators' rejection of woman suffrage. Even a presidential appeal could not sway them.[59] Governor Parker, who failed to honor his promise to suffragists, may have shared this motivation, as did Senator J. R. Domengeaux of Lafayette.[60]

Domengeaux, local businessman and former postmaster, contributed to the failure of the suffrage amendment on the local level. Domengeaux served as president of the Men's Anti-Woman Suffrage League, organized by state legislators allied against female suffrage in any form.[61] Senator Domengeaux retired from office before his term expired to become, for the second time, postmaster of the Lafayette Post Office.[62] His appointment suggests approval of his anti-suffrage stand by town leaders of both sexes.

Domengeaux's anti-suffragist activities went largely unchallenged in Lafayette because of the absence of local chapters of the NAWSA, the Southern States Woman Suffrage Conference (SSWSC), or any other organized pro-suffrage group. The contents of an open letter to the women of Lafayette, written by state amendment supporter Dr. E. L. Stephens, president of the Southwestern Louisiana Industrial Institute (present-day University of Southwestern Louisiana), and published in the *Daily Advertiser* two weeks before the November 1918 election, laments the absence of a locally organized, pro-suffrage organization.

> I wish to convey to our Lafayette women that it is up to them to boost this amendment locally if they wish to have men vote for it in this parish. And I hereby notify any and all of them that the advertising matter, posters, etc., sent me by their State campaign headquarters is at my office, and that I will turn it over to any of them at any time.
>
> I mean by this—not only that my time and attention are imperatively demanded by other matters—but that *it would be manifestly absurd for me to conduct a local campaign for votes for women, when not a woman in the town or parish, so far as I know, is ready or willing to make an effort in that direction.*[63] [emphasis added.]

Despite the indifference of local clubwomen and the best efforts of Domengeaux and opponents of woman suffrage, the Nineteenth Amendment became law when Tennessee became the thirty-sixth state to ratify the measure on August 18, 1920.[64] Ironically, Domengeaux's appointment as postmaster became public knowledge the same day the registrar of voters in Lafayette Parish reported that most of Lafayette Parish's approximately 250 newly registered voters were male.[65] That the local paper even questioned the registrar about the sex of new voters indicates that, even in Lafayette's apathetic environment, women's voting rights could not be completely ignored. The predominance of males among newly registered voters, however, again demonstrates continuing and pervasive antipathy among local clubwomen, who only wished to preserve their social status and increasingly outdated Victorian ideals.[66]

The enactment of the Nineteenth Amendment into federal law in August 1920, consequently made little immediate impact upon this community.[67] Lafayette clubwomen belatedly organized a local branch of the National Women's Party, the group that had so militantly supported woman suffrage, only after passage of the Nineteenth Amendment,[68] but they would not organize a League of Women Voters until 1945.[69]

It is thus hardly surprising that few women took advantage of their newly won rights, despite the fact that the *Daily Advertiser* urged area politicians to "give some thought to the new conditions . . . [because] times do change . . . [and] ladies are now on the brink of becoming political factors."[70] The newspaper obviously anticipated a large female turnout for registration. Such was not the case.

By September 25, 1920, the registrar counted only eighty newly registered women, and he noted that most of these female voters resided in the parish seat.[71] Very few rural women registered. The registrar attributed this to the fact that the "ladies were more interested in local elections than national campaigns and would register more rapidly for that than now."[72] By October 1, 1920, only 211 women had registered at the Lafayette Parish Courthouse.[73] By February 1, 1921, the names of only fifteen more women had been entered into the registration books, but only three of these registered as Democrats.[74] Numbers were somewhat better in January 1922, however, when nearly 20 percent of newly registered voters were female.[75] Though few in number, nearly every registered Lafayette woman voter cast a ballot in the next election.[76]

The marginal interest of Lafayette clubwomen in women's political rights contrasts sharply with their great enthusiasm for civic improvement projects. Lafayette clubwomen tirelessly worked for, and achieved, remarkable goals, but long after woman suffrage was ratified, they felt it necessary to emphasize "women's work" over women's rights. When contrasted with their shamelessly aggressive public activism for social reform measures, the failure of these clubwomen to work for woman suffrage can be seen only as a conscious policy decision. They focused instead on parlor politics, good citizenship, and "social housekeeping" to the detriment of woman suffrage.[77] Woman suffrage guaranteed equality of rights on one level, but it also threatened the political influence that elite clubwomen had been able to wield through their social connections. The actions of clubwomen in Lafayette in the Progressive period strongly suggest that, for these women at least, patriarchy was preferable to political equality.

Notes for "Parlors, Politics, and Privilege: Clubwomen and the Failure of Woman Suffrage in Lafayette, Louisiana, 1897-1922"

[1] Karen J. Blair, *The Clubwoman as Feminist: True Womanhood Redefined, 1868-1914* (New York, 1980), 4. According to Blair, the term "Domestic Feminism" originated with Daniel Scott Smith who coined the term to describe the practices of nineteenth-century women using accepted "womanly" traits to justify the restriction of sexual activity with their husbands (limiting sex meant better care for other children because it prevented pregnancy). Later, the term was politicized and extended to encompass all the virtues associated with being a "lady." Smith wrote, "By invoking their supposed natural talents, women took the ideology of the home with them. Domestic Feminism resulted when women redefined the ideal lady."

[2] Mary Martha Thomas, "The Ideology of the Alabama Woman Suffrage Movement, 1890-1920," in Virginia Bernhard et al., eds., *Southern Women: Histories and Identities* (Columbia, Mo., 1992), 109.

[3] New Orleans was home to the Portia Club, founded in 1892 by Caroline Merrick, pioneer women's rights activist, and the ERA Club, founded in 1896 by Kate and Jean Gordon, outspoken suffragists. The two clubs eventually joined forces to work for woman suffrage statewide. In 1896 the National American Woman Suffrage Association held its convention in New Orleans and in 1898 Kate Gordon, in the forefront of the suffrage movement in Louisiana, made history by organizing the New Orleans Women's Sewerage and Drainage League to force the passage of a water and drainage bond issue. For more information on Gordon's role, see B. H. Gilley, "Kate Gordon and Louisiana Woman Suffrage," *Louisiana History*, 24 (1983): 289-306.

[4] *Abstract of the Thirteenth Census of the United States, 1910.*

[5] *Lafayette Daily Advertiser*, October 27, 1914. The editor of the *Daily Advertiser* believed women should be allowed to serve on these boards because "these causes particularly appeal to women . . . because of their home experience."

[6] Ibid., July 11, 1906. Women were appointed to serve as "school trustees," presumably by an all-male school board.

[7] *Daily Advertiser*, June 6, 1903. As the new owner and editor of the paper, W. A. LeRosen said the paper was "politically Democratic but not partisan . . . but articles and communications of a personal nature and not calculated to subserve the public interest in a wide, measure will be excluded from its columns."

[8] Ibid., February 11, 1913; June 13, 1913.

[9] Ibid., February 11, 1913.

[10] The Woman's Club of Lafayette was the preeminent woman's club in the city. Members were consistently spouses of Lafayette's business and political leaders.

[11] Mrs. Kelly took the affirmative position in the debate, Mrs. R. C. Voorhies, the negative. *Daily Advertiser,* July 1, 1913.

[12] Ibid.

[13] Ibid., September 28, 1914.

[14] *Daily Advertiser*, October 30, 1914. The newspaper reported Mrs. Keith's participation in the district meeting of the State Federation of Woman's Clubs. John, Marie Keith's husband, was an official and secretary-treasurer of Consumer's Cold Storage and Cannery Co. Ltd., of Lafayette.

[15] Ibid., September 29, 1914.

[16] Ibid., October 5, 1914. Mrs. Keith also said, "We hope to have a large attendance of men and women at our suffrage rally and get together a movement for better ideals, cooperation and uplifting and extend a cordial invitation to you and all to help the 'movement.'"

[17] Mrs. Keith took the radical step of using her maiden name in the open invitation to the rally.

[18] *Daily Advertiser*, May 23, 1903. The judges of the debate, Mayor C. D. Caffery and Mr. F. V. Mouton, "decided against" (woman suffrage) but gave a medal to Miss Bell, "her debate being judged the best."

[19] The Woman's Club records contain a membership list going back to the club's first meeting in 1897. Marie Keith's name does not appear on the club's official record.

[20] *Daily Advertiser*, May 25, 1920. The paper observed that "Mrs. Crow Girard, reporting for the legislation committee of the women's Federated clubs, reports a successful week lobbying for the minimum wage bill and . . . library commission." Mrs. Girard said, "Our efforts at Baton rouge [sic] are confined to these bills. . . ."

[21] Ibid., March 28, 1909. Mrs. Davis, a prominent member of several women's groups, spoke to forty members at the tenth annual convention of the State Federation of Woman's Clubs.

[22] Ibid., October 2, 1919. The paper noted only that "[Miss Gordon's] subject will deal with the importance of the work."

[23] Kate Gordon worked diligently for woman suffrage through a state mandate. Although from New Orleans, her work was nationally recognized.

[24] The *Daily Advertiser*, September 25, 1920, reports that Mrs. Davis, as a member of the Alethian Club, spoke on the club's topic of the year for 1920, the influence of women in the home.

[25] Gordon's refusal to consider the effect of her actions is examined through the work of several historians, but most clearly by Elna C. Green in "The Rest of the Story: Kate Gordon and the Opposition to the Nineteenth Amendment in the South," *Louisiana History,* 33 (1992): 171-89.

[26] There is an abundance of material on Kate Gordon and her sister, Jean. All demonstrates Kate Gordon's role in the defeat of the suffrage amendment in Louisiana because of her adamant stand against a federal amendment. She firmly believed this would destroy white supremacy in the South. So determined was Gordon to prevent a federal amendment, she formed and headed a rival suffrage group, the Southern States Woman Suffrage Conference (SSWSC), in November, 1913. On this subject, see Kenneth R. Johnson, "Kate Gordon and the Woman-Suffrage Movement in the South," *Journal of Southern History,* 38 (1972): 365-92. Also, B. H. Gilley provides additional insight into Kate Gordon's motivation in "Kate Gordon and Louisiana Woman Suffrage," 289-306.

[27] The first electric street light was installed outside the First National Bank building on January 8, 1898, at eleven o'clock on a Saturday morning, according to the *Daily Advertiser* of that date. The Woman's Club organized in May, 1897.

[28] This quote is from papers in the Quintilla Morgan Anders Collection, #106; in Dupré Library at the University of Southwestern Louisian, Lafayette, part of her original manuscript for *History of Institutions and Organizations in Lafayette, La.* (Lafayette, La., 1951).

[29] Ibid. Also, see *Daily Advertiser*, May 1, 1897.

[30] *Daily Advertiser*, May 16, 1906. The bond issue passed by 107 votes. The paper noted on page one that "all day long, supporters of the bond issue worked zealously. Ladies and school girls in relief squads spent the day on the court house square and did valiant service."

[31] Original manuscript of the *History of Institutions and Organizations in Lafayette, Louisiana*, 218, Quintilla Morgan Anders papers. Copies of Mrs. Denbo's personal record of this incident are in the Woman's Club records as well. See Collection #79, Dupré Library Archives, University of Southwestern Louisiana, Lafayette, Louisiana.

[32] *Daily Advertiser*, May 2, 1906. After inviting all ladies to join in the effort to pass the bond issue, Mayor Mouton stated, "No class dare oppose a cause recommended, endorsed and fostered by the ladies.

[33] Ibid.

[34] The pages of the *Daily Advertiser* testify to Mrs. Caffery's club activities.

[35] For instance, Mrs. Harold Demanade, president of the Civic League, planned a campaign to enlist 500 paying members at ten cents each to clean up the city. *Daily Advertiser,* May 23, 1919. Also, throughout most of 1918 these women worked devotedly for the Red Cross and for collecting pledges for War Savings Stamps. The *Daily Advertiser* of June 22, 1918, reports that the women collected "a record $9,652.07 in six days." Also, in this period they convinced fourteen people (thirteen men and one woman) to enroll in the Limit Club which required a donation of $1,000.00 for purchase of War Savings Stamps.

[36] *Daily Advertiser*, May 2, 1906. The Industrial School, Southwestern Louisiana Industrial Institute (S.L.I.I.), was established by the Louisiana Legislature in 1898, but classes did not begin until September 18, 1901. In 1960 the Institute became today's University of Southwestern Louisiana. Caffery was mayor of Lafayette at the time the school was established.

[37] Ibid. Also, see the *Lafayette Gazette*, May 5, 1906.

[38] The Minutes Book of the Woman's Club lists all members' names since 1897. Mrs. Caffery's name is among them. See the Woman's Club of Lafayette records.

[39] Mary Jo Buhle and Paul Buhle, *The Concise History of Woman Suffrage* (Urbana, 1978), 44.

[40] The Minutes Book of the Woman's Club of Lafayette clearly indicates the extent (and limits) of club evolution to Progressive reform projects. Page 190 of the Woman's Club Minutes Book does indicate correspondence with Kate Gordon, president of the ERA Club in New Orleans, an important suffrage organization. Members of the Woman's Club agreed to subscribe to *Progress*, the ERA publication. See the Woman's Club Records. The Quintilla Morgan Anders papers provide much information about the Woman's Club and its work.

[41] See, Blair's *The Clubwoman as Feminist*, Carmen Lindig's *The Path from the Parlor: Louisiana Women 1879-1920* (Lafayette, La., 1986), and (among her many excellent works on the subject) Anne Firor Scott's *The Southern Lady: From Pedestal to Politics 1830-1930* (Chicago, 1970).

[42] The social life of elite clubwomen fills the pages of the *Daily Advertiser* throughout the period, but the same pattern is evident for decades thereafter.

[43] Blair, *Clubwoman,* 117. As Blair notes on page 119, the failure of clubwomen (such as those in Lafayette) to "challenge the concept of ladydom or the myth of woman's instinctive domestic and moral traits" precluded any overt suffragist activity. In the case of Lafayette clubwomen, this position was consciously chosen and deliberately maintained.

[44] Kate O'Bryan Conrad papers, Collection 74, Box 2, Folder 2-b, Dupré Library Archives at the University of Southwestern Louisiana, Lafayette, La. Although unacceptable today, public expressions of ingrained racist ideas were the norm in the area during this period. For example, on page one of Abbeville, Louisiana's *The Independent High School News*, March 5, 1906, describes the black man as a "square headed and flat nosed beast," black women as "negro wenches," Booker T. Washington as an "audacious negro," and further states that, "we do not propose to place ourselves on an equality with the beasts who were once our slaves." Another article on page two concludes with this description of the negro: "Be he created by a God or be he created by a devil, he was created to be a beast to the full extent of the word." This view of blacks still prevailed during the suffrage struggle. It still survives to varying degrees in many areas of Louisiana today.

[45]*Daily Advertiser*, April 24, 1920. The newspaper reported that "Governor John Parker is pledged to suffrage—has publicly stumped for it."

[46]Ibid., June 4, 1920. The National Women's Party was an extremely militant group, and their militancy was denounced by NAWSA. In a report from the National Women's Party headquarters, suffragists expressed loss of hope of Louisiana becoming the 36th state to ratify the Nineteenth Amendment, deciding to focus on Vermont instead.

[47]Ibid., May 26, 1920. The paper reported that a Federal Census population figure of 7,855 was a "grave injustice." The newly organized Lafayette Chamber of Commerce was called upon to act in the matter. The disputed number proved to be a major topic of discussion among Lafayette's leading citizens for much of the remaining year.

[48]Ibid., February 3, 1921. In an editorial entitled "Progressive Work," the Woman's Council of Lafayette was congratulated for focusing its attention on community service and for not "taking up the time of the Constitutional Convention."

[49]*Daily Advertiser*, November 1, 1920. When inviting voters to Moss Music Hall to await returns after the November 5 presidential election, the paper said all voters were welcome. "If you are a Democrat in Louisiana or a Republican in the U.S., come on anyway."

[50]Ibid., May 13, 1920. The lieutenant governor urged both houses of the legislature to reject the federal measure.

[51]*Official Journal of the House of Representatives*, 240. Interestingly, Jules Dreyfous, Iberia Parish's second State Representative, was in favor of the Nineteenth Amendment, but accepted defeat and voted against it. In explaining his vote against the amendment, Dreyfous said, "There is as much courage, patriotism, love of country and its institutions to accept the verdict of the majority, than to taste the sweet, exhilarating fruit of victory." He ended with the hope that "women shall come into their own." Despite his stated position in support of woman suffrage, Dreyfous' explanation for voting as he did is doubtful, if not an outright attempt to garner favor from both camps.

[52]Margaret Ripley Wolfe, in *Daughters of Canaan: A Saga of Southern Women* (Lexington, 1995), discusses patriarchy and paternalism as Southern social structures, and the obvious constraints this placed on women. Lafayette clearly exhibited an exceedingly patriarchal social pattern.

[53]*Daily Advertiser*, November 7, 1918. A preliminary count of the local vote on the Haas-Powell State suffrage amendment showed 79 votes for and 68 votes against.

[54]Ibid. Tucked away on the fifth page of the paper, the official count shows a 165 to 283 loss for the amendment, almost two to one against.

[55]The January 11, 1908, edition of the *Lafayette Gazette* notes that "The voting strength of Lafayette parish is between 3,000 and 3,500 judging by the number and amounts of poll taxes paid." Of these poll taxes, "about 500 . . . are paid by negroes, which will reduce the number of votes to be polled at the [up]coming primary."

[56]*Daily Advertiser*, November 9, 1919. Mrs. Demanade's husband was a director of the First National Bank in Lafayette, and Mrs. Demanade was active in several women's clubs.

[57]Gamble further reveals to Ransdell his feelings about women when he states that "Manifestly, under (states authority) large classes of undesirable women might be excluded. That is Senator if there is any class of women which might, by reckless persons be said to be undesirable. Not, of course, by you and me, Senator, since, alas, in these parlous days we would not commit ourselves on so perilous a matter." Gamble's real position (and surely the position of his boss, Louisiana's next governor, John Parker, becomes clear when he writes, "Once a guarantee is in the Federal Constitution it will never come out. In the state Constitution it could come out." Since it was socially acceptable to publicly insult all Blacks, both men and women, Gamble was evidently afraid to anger white women. See Collection 144, Robert F. Broussard papers, Series 3, film 069, folder 121-26.

[58]Ibid.

[59]*Daily Advertiser*, June 6, 1918.

[60]Ibid., April 24, 1920. Although Gov. John Parker had publicly supported suffrage, Lt. Governor Hewitt Bouanchard was opposed (to the federal amendment), as were "several leading figures in both houses."

Unless he had deliberately lied earlier, Parker clearly changed his position. Harry Gamble could not have publicly stated his position as he did to Senator Ransdell without Parker's prior approval. Thus, Gamble's views can be considered Parker's as well. See note 48 above.

[61] Green, "The Rest of the Story," 179. E.L Simmons of Breaux Bridge, a small community near Lafayette, was vice-president of the league which was a member of the National Association Opposed to Woman Suffrage.

[62] *Daily Advertiser*, January 3, 1922.

[63] *Daily Advertiser*, October 23, 1918. The state suffrage amendment would appear on the November 1918 ballot. It is interesting that Woman's Club records reveal that Dr. Stephens' wife was not a member.

[64] Ibid., August 18, 1920. The *Daily Advertiser* noted that "women will vote in the (upcoming November) presidential election unless the amendment is blocked in the courts or a reconsideration changes the result." On the previous July 8, the Louisiana General Assembly had rejected the bill by a vote of 53-46.

[65] Ibid., January 13, 1922. No numbers were given by the registrar to indicate the male/female ratio of new voters. The election was to decide whether the city should lease the local light and water plant. The registrar stated his expectation that women would begin registering in the near future and the office would be open for thirty days more to facilitate registration. The failure of local women to register indicates a lack of interest. It also shows that the registrar had been mistaken earlier when he stated that women's lack of interest in registering was because the first election after suffrage became law was a presidential one and women were more interested in local elections. Evidently such was not the case. See ibid., September 25, 1920.

[66] It is most intriguing that John and Marie Keith left Lafayette on November 21, 1918, just two weeks after Lafayette rejected the state amendment. They left for Texas because "Mr. Keith is interested in a banking business." One can easily interpret the move as a reaction to ostracism by the local gentry in response to Marie's unpalatable stand for woman suffrage.

[67] *Daily Advertiser*, August 26, 1920. Reports of the Nineteenth Amendment becoming law were printed alongside notice of an Elks Club spaghetti supper, the fifth anniversary party for Mrs. A.C. Mouton and children, and Mrs. Tolson's bridge party.

[68] Ibid., January 31, 1922. Mrs. A.B. Denbo headed the local branch of the Louisiana National Woman's Party and Mrs. Earl Barnett was appointed vice-chairman. The organization formed after a meeting at the Elk's home called by local clubwomen. Speakers from Baton Rouge and Shreveport were present and discussed state laws which were "discriminatory against women."

[69] The League of Women Voters records, 1945-66, Collection 124, Dupré Library, University of Southwestern Louisiana, Lafayette, Louisiana.

[70] *Daily Advertiser*, August 19, 1920.

[71] See note 65. The *Daily Advertiser* reported that "the clerk gave as a reason for the city women registering faster [than rural women] that the law provided that the registering clerk was required to spend a day in each ward but that the [suffrage] law was passed at such a late date that it was impossible for this to be done at this time."

[72] Ibid. The coming election was a presidential election.

[73] *Daily Advertiser*, October 1, 1920.

[74] *Daily Advertiser*, February 1, 1921. There were 563 newly registered voters in January.

[75] Ibid., January 30, 1922. The Registrar reported that of the 773 who had registered during the month, about 150 were women.

[76] Ibid., February 5, 1921.

[77] Nancy Woloch, *Women and the American Experience* (New York, 1984), 299. Woloch contends that by the end of the nineteenth century, the clubwoman had "become a social housekeeper, an active participant in civic affairs." This phrase describes Lafayette clubwomen perfectly.

THE GIFT HOUSE: JEAN M. GORDON AND THE MAKING OF THE MILNE HOME, 1904-1931*

Rebecca Carrasco

The historical literature on New Orleans women has largely overlooked the "child saving work" of Jean Margaret Gordon.[1] In four decades of service to local society, this social worker, civic leader, and reformer aided and defended child laborers and grappled with educational problems, the plight of orphans, and the exploitation of mentally retarded persons. Gordon's dedicated advocacy for oppressed and helpless groups, as well as her interest and participation in the American eugenics movement, led her to establish the first "home-school" for feebleminded girls in New Orleans.[2]

Jean Gordon was the daughter of Margaret Galiece and George Hume Gordon. Her father was a Scottish educator who emigrated from Edinburgh to New Orleans, where Jean was born on May 27, 1867. Reared in comfort in New Orleans' Garden District, she was educated locally at Jackson and Peabody Normal Schools. Early in her life, Gordon sought to help those who could not help themselves. Along with Eleanor McMain, she organized the first New Orleans day-nursery at the Kingsley House, and with her elder sister Kate Gordon she established a tuberculosis hospital in the Gentilly section of New Orleans.

Gordon began her beneficent career in 1888 with the Charity Organization Society, which later became the Family Service Bureau. She soon observed that many of those who sought charity, when asked why they were jobless, would reply: "I have lost my speed." She learned that invariably they had been factory laborers as children, and she concluded that their break-down in early youth had been due to this child labor. For this reason, she became interested in the new but growing child-labor movement.[3]

With the help of her sister Kate, and their famous suffrage Equal Rights Association (ERA) club, she began a child-labor movement concerned with the Southern states.[4] She attracted favorable attention, which prompted the new governor of Louisiana, Newton C.

---

*First published in *Louisiana History*, 34 (1993): 309-26. Reprinted with the kind permission of the author and the Louisiana Historical Association.

Blanchard, to appoint her in 1904 as the president of the board of directors of the New Orleans Milne Asylum for Destitute Orphan Girls. In 1907, Governor Blanchard appointed her as Louisiana's first woman factory inspector. In this capacity, she soon denounced the state's existing child-labor bill as unenforceable and set about getting a better one adopted. She examined the child-labor laws of various states, selected their best features, and then went repeatedly to the legislature to lobby for legislation known as the Jean Gordon Child Labor Bill. As Kate Gordon later said, "when Jean was convinced that a thing was right it did not matter what it cost her, she would brave public opinion, no matter how unpopular in its behalf." After two years, the legislature passed the bill regulating the employment of children, young persons, and women. Kate Gordon wrote, in 1932, that "under its enforcement by Jean, New Orleans has the national credit of the best child labor enforcement in the United States."[5]

During her tenure as factory inspector, Gordon noticed the reading and comprehension difficulties of many children seeking work certificates.[6] She also came into contact with a class of women known as "repeaters"–young girls who drifted from one factory to another, unable to keep permanent positions, and who finally took refuge in prostitution.[7] Gordon later discovered that this pattern of social maladjustment was often attributed to the girls' feeblemindedness.

At one of the Southern Child Labor Conferences, Gordon heard Dr. Hastings Hart of the Russell Sage Foundation urge women "to make the passing of laws for the sterilization of feebleminded girls and women their top priority."[8] Such adherents of the eugenics movement supposed that the "unfit"–those classified as insane, feebleminded, criminals, and paupers–were characterized by inferior abilities and inclinations, their poverty or other deficiency being seen as a consequence of their innate failings. The eugenists believed that the government should control the reproduction of unfit citizens. Gordon went on to study the situation and became firmly convinced that the community would benefit enormously if the feebleminded female could be segregated, cared for, and prevented from propagating and spreading disease.[9] Thus, in Gordon's case, Hart's appeal to eugenic themes–the menace of feeblemindedness and the utility of sterilization–struck home.[10]

As Gordon battled for passage of the Child Labor Bill, she simultaneously immersed herself in her duties as president of the Milne Asylum for Destitute Orphan Girls. Funds for separate asylums for orphaned boys and girls had been established by Alexander Milne, a wealthy landowner.[11] At his death in 1837, he left the city of New Orleans more than one million dollars, stipulating that it was to be used mainly for the benefit of two existing asylums and two new asylums which would bear his name.[12] For decades after Milne's death, nothing was done to effect Milne's wishes until Norman Walker, editor of the *New Orleans Times-Democrat*, initiated inquiries.[13]

Walker investigated the Milne trust and found only a few bonds belonging to the Boys' Asylum. When Gordon's board began functioning, sixty-five years after the 1839 act of incorporation, the money turned over to them was found to consist of "the incredibly ridiculous sum of sixty-seven cents." The other assets were 295 acres of land between Bayou St. John and the hamlet Milneburg on Lake Ponchartrain, near the modern-day University of New Orleans. The land was largely swamp, with a railroad track running through it, and some of the land had already been sold to pay taxes. On this inadequate foundation the board was to build an asylum to carry out Alexander Milne's bequest.[14]

The two boards organized without delay and conferences were held during the years 1905-1907 to discuss a possible merger of the two institutions, so that a facility for orphan boys and girls could be constructed on the "cottage system," providing the children both a home environment and a vocational education.[15] Gordon believed such an institution would be most economical and provide "the more modern doctrine of education for the two sexes."[16] Norman Walker, as president of the board of directors for the Boys' Asylum, in his biennial report to the governor agreed with Gordon that the best approach involved "bringing up our youth on the farms and enabling them to support themselves."[17]

Unlike Gordon, some of the women members entertained doubts about the propriety of merging the two boards.[18] Felix Dreyfous of the Boys' Asylum argued against merging the two funds, but thought it sensible for the two boards to work together, and even to build one institution. This, he believed, was in keeping with Milne's will.[19] Indecision on this matter continued, however, and the plan for merging the boards and establishing a single asylum for both boys and girls was eventually abandoned.[20]

On Thursday, December 17, 1908, the two boards assembled again, this time to hear Reverend J. P. Dysart, superintendent of the Wisconsin Society for the Placing Out of Dependent Children, which had sparked a movement to relieve pressure on asylums by placing as many orphan children as possible in adoptive families. Gordon also argued against establishing more asylums, for nearly two dozen institutions already existed in New Orleans. She thought that the Milne money could best be used by building a cottage-system industrial farm, while attempting to encourage adoption. She felt that the children would be given the best preparation for life by a system of industrial farms and schools that would permit them, despite their limited abilities, to learn a trade. Gordon wanted to assure care and attention for these orphaned children, while at the same time treating them as much as possible in the way that ordinary children, with homes and families, were treated. In short, she wanted to put less emphasis on charity and more on education.[21]

Gordon hoped that another year would not have to elapse before her board would take the initiative in this new direction and show the "community what an injustice is done the dependent child when he or she is herded with hundreds of other little personalities, all expected to conform to certain rules and regulations, with no recognition of the different effects of heredity and early environment of each child."[22] Gordon regarded heredity as more significant than environment in the creation of the feebleminded, but she felt that Louisiana's asylum system was the principal cause of the pauperism in New Orleans, because it failed to prepare children to deal with the problems of city life. She warned that "we who know these things become *particeps criminis* if we do not try to bring about a change."[23]

In addressing the board in January 1910, concerning the previous year's efforts, Gordon contrasted the care of dependent children in Louisiana unfavorably with the standard set by other states which, she felt, realized that "the greatest asset any state has is her children, dependent as well as independent." She requested, and received, the support of all the orphan asylums in promoting a bill providing institutions with the authority to determine to whom the child would be discharged upon reaching legal maturity. Her concern was to protect those children placed in institutions by parents or relatives who later sought to retrieve them when the children were old enough to work in factories. Under prevailing conditions, institutions had been obliged to comply with existing laws granting automatic custody to next of kin. Advocates for this measure felt a sense of accomplishment when the bill was introduced by Rev. James O'Connor and successfully passed.[24]

The board attempted to operate a provisional home, where children could receive care until the asylum's swampland site could be drained and the necessary cottages built. A house and a superintendent, Charlotte Elliott, were selected, but the Milne Board for Destitute Boys refused to cooperate, and again plans had to be abandoned.[25]

During these years, the Milne board gradually built up its funds by selling its land until it was no longer dependant upon funding from the Boys' Asylum.[26] But the question of how to carry out Alexander Milne's wishes was still unanswered and the board held regular meetings for consideration of this matter.

In 1912, Gordon attended the Southern Sociological Congress in Nashville and met Dr. Alexander Johnson, secretary of the National Conference of Charities and Correction since 1904.[27] She heard his address on "The Menace of the Feeble-Minded," and also heard, a second time, Hart's plea concerning feebleminded girls. Public care for the feebleminded was at that time nonexistent in Louisiana.[28] The only active public institutions in the South, according to Johnson, were in Maryland, Missouri, Oklahoma and Kentucky.[29] Gordon decided, as Johnson later recorded, that Louisiana must "do its part for the mental defectives."[30]

Johnson gave nineteen lectures to various groups in New Orleans.[31] The following year, he was appointed field secretary for the Committee on Provision for the Feebleminded, established by the Extension Department of the Institution for the Feebleminded at Vineland, New Jersey. This committee was the first national body to promote improvement of state laws and funding for the feebleminded.[32] The committee also helped establish mandatory medical examinations in public schools, for early detection of mental retardation.

In 1914, the Milne board's attention was drawn to emergeing national interest in mental retardation sparked by Dr. A. S. Hill's advocacy of institutional programs.[33] The board first sought legal advice regarding possible diversion of Milne funds originally

The Gift House

earmarked for orphan girls to the feebleminded. After studying the legislative acts of 1839, the board's legal counsel, Solomon Wolff, determined that the board could spend the funds as it saw fit, as long as it remained within the limits of its charter.[34]

In 1916, Gordon attended two conventions to obtain information about persons classified as feebleminded. The first, in Indianapolis, focused on the best ways of handling mentally retarded patients. Six months later, she visited a home for feebleminded patients in Vineland, New Jersey.[35] A month later, the board asked Alexander Johnson for his opinion regarding requirements for care of the feebleminded.[36] He responded that with their land and their accumulated funds they could count upon a successful start, but he could not commit any assistance.

In 1917, the American Red Cross charged Johnson with responsibility for the Southern states, headquartered at New Orleans. The Red Cross directed Johnson to encourage the establishment of institutions for the feebleminded and, in particular, to cooperate with the Milne board.[37] But the board was unable to exploit this opportunity for cooperative development because of renewed financial problems. High building costs during the First World War forced the board to set the project aside again.

In June 1919, Gordon leased a farm in Kenner, Louisiana, for fifty dollars a month.[38] The Milne board invited Johnson to attend its July meeting, but he was unable to go to New Orleans until August.[39] In a letter to Gordon, Johnson wrote of his dream for their home-school, a dream he had entertained for twenty years. He wanted "to see the Milne home develop into the best kind of home-school for boys and girls who will spend six or eight or ten years of their life within its sheltering arms," and to see agricultural and industrial colonies for adult males and females.[40] Work in the school, he said, would be "especially educational and only secondarily productive; while in the colony all the work will be especially productive and only incidentally educational."[41]

In a more practical vein, Johnson suggested that the proposed facility accommodate some twenty mildly retarded girls, ten to fourteen years old.[42] The estimated expenses were $450 a month.[43] He returned to New Orleans on August 18, 1919, and the home was opened with one patient and a motto: "Happiness comes first, all else will follow."[44]

Despite the unexpected loss of its first director, the home enjoyed notable early success. In March, 1920, poor health forced Johnson to resign,[45] but his daughter, Enid Johnson, completed the year as director. Yet, the home already had twenty-five girls, who were supported by a $5,000 annual state subsidy and private contributions. The home would soon outgrow its Kenner facility.[46]

Throughout the year, Gordon energetically attempted to draw the general public's attention to the problem of feeblemindedness, sending out nearly two hundred letters on the subject. The board urged social workers and nurses to report all cases of feeblemindedness.[47]

In the fall of 1921, the board decided to purchase from Dr. S. F. Mioton property at 1913 Gentilly Road—Milne Home's present site. However, the move from Kenner was not made until April of the following year. Two empty houses, known as the Derby

Houses, which were owned by the Anti-Tuberculosis League, a group founded earlier by Kate Gordon, stood on the Gentilly Road property. The Gordon sisters were able to rent the two houses for a brief period, but soon the Anti-Tuberculosis League needed them, thus highlighting the need for permanent dormitory.[48] Gordon obtained the Kenner dormitory after informing Charles Weinberger, manager of the Kenner property, that the board had spent over $2,000 on the building, and thus believed that it was entitled to the structure.[49] She persuaded a housewrecker to contribute half-a-dozen expert workers to dismantle the building and borrowed thirty-one trucks to transport the materials. "Gordon secured so many donations of bricks, lumber, and other materials that the completed dormitory became known as the 'Gift House' in honor of the contributions."[50] The Gift House was dedicated on February 24, 1923, and Gordon received, for the second time, the Times-Picayune Loving Cup, an annual award given for distinguished contribution to the betterment of the city.[51]

Gordon then assumed the office of superintendent. She hoped that Milne would become "the social center for the city for those men and women who were interested in civic betterment."[52] She also believed that Milne would have educational value for its local and out-of-town visitors.[53] Gordon wanted the community to know that the Milne Home was providing care for its children as well as any out-of-state institution.

During these years, Gordon also worked in cooperation with the Orleans Parish School Board to bring to Milne feebleminded children, who were not allowed into the public schools.[54] In return, the School Board provided teachers who taught singing, chair-caning and weaving, and helped to enlarge the Milne schoolroom. Gordon was convinced that the institution did not need psychologists or psychiatrists, but rather "someone able to make these attendants make those that are capable of so doing do the work of this institution."[55] Much of the Milne Home's work was in fact done by the children. According to Gordon, this active life and a well-balanced diet were responsible for "the remarkable health of the inmates."[56] She observed, for example, that, as a result of their agricultural work, the girls were no longer "being dazed with narcotics in order to make them sleep, they now sleep the natural refreshing sleep which follows after a day of normal work."[57] In fact, when the secretary of the British Eugenics Association in London, Mrs. C. B. S. Hodson, visited Milne, Jean Gordon heard a flattering report on the opinions the visitor had gathered during her trip from Boston to California. "It was said everywhere that she was recommended to go to New Orleans to see some very remarkable outdoor work which women were being trained to do."[58]

Gordon felt a duty to raise public consciousness regarding "the menace of the feebleminded," and she encouraged ongoing public discussion of the issue.[59] She travelled to eugenic conventions to hear, and also to give, lectures on the subject she viewed as the nation's most pressing problem. The minutes of one board meeting report that she called feeblemindedness "the biggest question today," that, if left unchecked would mean "the destruction of our civilization, for no nation rises higher than the intelligence of its people." The late war, she continued, showed that "fifty-five percent of our army did not have an intelligence higher than that of a boy seven years old."[60] Indeed, in 1919, army draft authorities estimated that almost half of the white Americans, and nearly nine-tenths of the African-Americans, had a mental age of twelve or under.[61]

But not everyone agreed with Gordon. An early critic of intelligence tests was J. E. Wallace Wallin, a psychologist who believed that "the army results were a *reductio ad absurdum* of the assumption that all persons below the mental age of twelve were under suspicion of feeblemindedness." It was obvious, he thought, that all these millions of useful citizens could hardly be feebleminded, despite the fact that their mental-test scores would have classed them as morons.[62] The scientific controversy over IQ testing that began at that point has continued to the present day.[63] But the army figures became a rallying point for American eugenists who anticipated doom and lamented a decline in the nation's intelligence resulting from the mixture of races and social classes.[64]

Gordon energetically supported the American eugenic creed, which advanced a two-part plan to promote racial betterment: "negative eugenics" preventing the reproduction of those regarded as unfit, and "positive eugenics" encouraging the reproduction of those considered fit.[65] For instance, during a trip to Chicago, Judge Harry Olson, chief justice of the Chicago Municipal Courts, urged Gordon and other women associated with institutions like Milne to "take up the fight for race betterment."[66] Gordon noted that everyone she spoke to seemed to agree that America had doomed itself through "the mongrelization of the race."[67] Kate Gordon, in a letter to Laura Clay, wrote with similar distaste of the "influx of latin immigrants now flooding the ports of entry in the south and who have no race antagonisms" and warned that "if something is not done we will be as mongrelized as Cuba."[68]

Many individuals in the movement, like Jean and Kate Gordon, believed in the existence of racial stereotypes, accepted the myth that certain races possess a monopoly of desirable or undesirable traits, and thought racially determined differences were hereditary, and hence resistant to change. Jean Gordon, consequently, stressed the importance of "heredity versus environment."[69] Despite the confident assertions made by eugenists about their Anglo-Saxon superiority, there also existed a great deal of anxiety among "old stock" Americans who belittled ethnic minorities they feared might become majorities. Gordon, like others, worried that, "Europe having unloaded her mentally and physically unfit upon our shores, our democratic institutions are threatened."[70]

In order to combat these "hereditarily unfit" groups, Jean Gordon came to support the idea of sterilization. She believed that "as women we have to preach the sacredness and right of birth control," to prohibit the physically and mentally defective from marrying, and to allow appropriate institutions to intervene medically to "prevent conception."[71] In 1926, and again in 1929, she fought hard to get the Louisiana legislature to enact a bill that would grant to superintendents of institutions for the insane and feebleminded the authority to have sterilization operations performed upon inmates.[72]

Gordon considered birth control by such means humanitarian and economical for the state. She contended that there were in Louisiana at least 8,000 feebleminded and that at least half of these "should be in institutions right now, for as long as they are at large they are reproducing their feebleminded kind."[73] The cost of raising these women's progeny to maturity, she estimated, conservatively, at $4,000 per child. The Gordon sisters believed that Milne's operation protected society from the burden of additional illegitimate children. Kate Gordon suggested that had the women at Milne been at large they would have had 600 children.[74] Gordon thought that if laws were to be passed to provide "mothers' pensions," laws should also be passed preventing mothers from "continuing to bring helpless babies into the world."[75]

To her disappointment, the sterilization bill again failed in the legislature in 1929, partly because of opposition from religious groups. Gordon remained convinced that her approach was sound. She was certain that "far from interfering with the will of God on sex questions, we are doing His work when through the knowledge he has sent us, we try to stamp out of His world the unfit, and there are only two ways to do this, through segregation and birth control." However, the tenor of social opinion about these questions was already beginning to change.

In May, 1929, Gordon attended a convention in Atlanta of the National Association for the Study of the Feebleminded. She returned "convinced that sterilization must be accomplished by women–while all the superintendents are heartily in favor of the measure, I find they are not as keen on the question of the feebleminded woman bearing children as are the women." Many of the doctors, she found, thought that it would "not do to rid the world altogether of feeblemindedness because there arises the question who will do the hard, dirty work of the world." At the convention, she heard arguments for "stabilizing" feebleminded women and placing them in industry, but these struck her as impractical. "When we know how little stabilization we have among the population who are not classified feebleminded, it interested me to hear of stabilizing these feebleminded women." The social workers, she felt, "run their institutions very well but are not going to worry over the future of the race."[76]

After the Second World War, the caricature of eugenist ideas embodied in Nazi social programs rendered these ideas almost impossible to discuss for a number of years. But Jean Gordon did not live to see, or participate in, these late twentieth-century developments. She presented her twenty-sixth annual report on January 5, 1931, "with much pleasure and pride."[77] Her pleasure and pride were justified in an institution that, in an earlier address to the board, she had called "unlike any Home with which any of us have ever been connected." It was, she said, "a Home, a training school, a farm, a dairy, with all domestic activities thrown in. I know of no institution in New Orleans where all these activities are attempted."[78]

On February 24, 1931, Jean Gordon died, leaving behind her "child"–the Gift House. Kate Gordon assumed her sister's responsibilities as director of the Milne Home and president of its board. She used the occasion of the annual report for 1932 to review the decades of struggle and sacrifice on her sister's part.[79] A year and a half after her sister's death, Kate Gordon also died, on August 24, 1932, and the Gordon era at Milne came to an end. The sterilization bill the sisters had fought so hard for failed again to pass in 1932. Six decades later, the Milne Home continues to operate and hold its girls within its sheltering and confining arms.[80]

Notes for "The Gift House: Jean M. Gordon and the Making of the Milne Home, 1904-1931"

[1] See Kathryn W. Kemp, "Jean and Kate Gordon: New Orleans Social Reformers, 1898-1933," *Louisiana History*, 24 (1983): 389-401; and Carmen Lindig, *The Path from the Parlor: Louisiana Women, 1879-1920* (Lafayette, La., 1986).

[2] Jean Gordon also founded the Society for the Prevention of Cruelty to Animals and was president of the ERA Club and Women's State Suffrage Association. See "Minister Lauds Charity Work of Gordon Sisters: Tribute to Founders of Institution Praised by the Rev. Girelius," New Orleans *Times-Picayune*, May 22, 1938; *Week Calendar Unitarian Church*, September 18, 1932. Gordon Material, 1932-1939, Collection 674, Box 5 of 5, Folder 6, Jacob D. Dresner Papers, in the Manuscript and Archives Division, Tulane University, New Orleans, Louisiana.

[3] Letter from Kate M. Gordon to Mrs. R. B. Knott, January 16, 1932, Box 1, Milne Home Papers, The Milne Home, New Orleans. Mrs. Knott in a previous letter had asked Kate to write in detail about her sister's life. See also Isabelle Dubroca, *Good Neighbor Eleanor McMain of Kingsley House* (New Orleans, 1955), 50-52 and 60-65; Glenn R. Conrad, ed., *A Dictionary of Louisiana Biography*, 2 vols. (New Orleans, 1988), 1:351.

[4] For additional information on Jean and Kate's suffrage work with the ERA Club, see: B. H. Gilley, "Kate Gordon and Louisiana Woman Suffrage," *Louisiana History*, 24 (1983): 289-306; Kenneth R. Johnson, "Kate Gordon and the Woman-Suffrage Movement in the South," *The Journal of Southern History*, 38 (1972): 365-92; Glenn R. Conrad, ed., *A Dictionary of Louisiana Biography* (New Orleans, 1988), 351; Elna C. Green, "The Rest of the Story: Kate Gordon and the Opposition to the Nineteenth Amendment in the South," *Louisiana History*, 33 (1992): 171-89. Jean Gordon was president of the Southern Child Labor Association.

[5] Letter from Kate M. Gordon to Mrs. R. B. Knott, January 16, 1932, Box 1, Milne Home Papers, Milne Home, New Orleans.

[6] Ibid.

[7] See Al Rose, *Storyville, New Orleans: Being an Authentic, Illustrated Account of the Notorious Red-Light District* (Tuscaloosa, Ala., 1974), 64.

[8] Mrs. Harry McCall, "History of Money Left by Alexander Milne." This typescript was assembled by an anonymous compiler from research–the original sources in some cases being inaccurate–gathered by Mrs. McCall before her death in 1963. It is included in the Milne Papers.

[9] Ibid.

[10] Letter from Kate M. Gordon to Mrs. R. B. Knott, January 16, 1932, Milne Papers. For more information on those American eugenists who advocated sterilization, see Philip R. Reilly's *The Surgical Solution: A History of Involuntary Sterilization in the United States* (Baltimore, 1991).

[11] Milneburg, Louisiana, was named after him.

[12] The Milne Home for Destitute Orphan Girls, Minutes of Meetings of the Board of Directresses, Meeting of January 6, 1929, Milne Papers. Milne also left $110,000 for the establishment of a free school in his homeland, Fochabers–near Aberdeen, Scotland.

[13] Mrs. Harry McCall Papers, Milne Home, New Orleans.

[14] Ibid.

[15] Minutes of Meetings of the Board of Directresses, Special Meeting including Board of Directors of the Milne Home for Destitute Orphan Boys, February 2, 1907, Milne Papers.

[16] Minutes of Meetings of the Board of Directresses, Annual Report for 1905, dated January 1, 1906, Milne Papers.

[17] *Times-Democrat,* January, 1906. Taken from a message from Governor Blanchard to the General Assembly.

[18] Meeting of the Board of Directresses, May 23, 1906, Milne Papers.

[19] Special Meeting of the Board of Directors and Directresses of the Milne Home of Destitute Orphaned Boys and Girls, February 2, 1907, Milne Papers.

[20] Mrs. Harry McCall Papers, Milne Home, New Orleans.

[21] *The Times-Democrat*, December 18, 1908; an editorial.

[22] The Milne Home for Destitute Orphan Girls, Minutes of the Meeting of the Board of Directresses, Annual Report for 1908, dated January, 1909. "The proposition to rent a cottage and start a home experiment plan was made by Miss Gordon, with the suggestion that Mrs. David Zable be secured as matron." This plan failed because of inadequate funds and indecision by both boards.

[23] Ibid.

[24] The Milne Home for Destitute Orphan Girls, Minutes of the Meeting of the Board of Directresses, Annual Report for 1909, dated January 3, 1910.

[25] The Milne Home for Destitute Orphan Girls, Minutes of the Meeting of the Board of Directresses, Annual Report for 1910, dated January 1, 1911. Miss Elliott, while in Boston, had investigated the methods used in placing out children. She was "sent by the Board to study the system used there."

[26] See the Annual Reports of 1908, 1909, and 1910.

[27] Reilly, *The Surgical Solution,* 44.

[28] Mrs. Harry McCall Papers, Milne Home, New Orleans. It was not until 1921 that a state institution was opened. The Milne Home was thus a pioneer institution in the state for the severely mentally handicapped.

[29] Alexander Johnson, *Adventures in Social Welfare* (Fort Wayne, Ind., 1923), 399.

[30] Ibid., 402.

[31] Ibid. Johnson discusses Jean Gordon and the places he gave his lectures.

[32] Mrs. Harry McCall Papers, Milne Home, New Orleans.

[33] Ibid.

[34] Ibid. See also the Minutes of August 9, 1916; and a letter from Solomon Wolff to Jean Gordon, dated February 7, 1917, Milne Papers.

[35] Milne Home, Minutes of Meeting of the Board of Directresses, April 12 and October 20, 1916. For more about the Vineland home, see Edgar A. Doll, ed., *Twenty-five Years: A Memorial Volume in Commemoration of the Twenty-Fifth Anniversary of the Vineland Laboratory, 1906-1931* (Vineland, N.J., 1932).

[36] Milne Home, Minutes of Meeting of the Board of Directresses, November 8, 1916.

[37] Mrs. Harry McCall Papers, Milne Home, New Orleans. Also, see the Board Minutes of January 2, 1916: "Dr. Johnson had generously accepted a salary at a figure of one half what he had been earning."

[38] Ibid. See also the Minutes of June 15 and July 3, 1919. The farm had been previously occupied by the American Protective League, an organization concerned with reclaiming prostitutes. See Jean Gordon, Annual Report for 1909.

[39] Ibid. See also the Minutes of July 3, July 9, and July 28, 1919.

[40] Letter from Alexander Johnson to Jean Gordon, July 31, 1919, Box 1, Milne Home Papers, Milne Home, New Orleans. He tells her that "the little home school" is but a "tiny seed out of which I hope to see grow a large work. . . ."

[41] Ibid. He says also that "the work will be planned so as to meet the capabilities of the different colonists."

The Gift House

[42] According to Goddard, "idiots" had a mental age of two or below, "imbeciles" a mental age between three and seven, and "morons" a mental age between eight and twelve. See Daniel J. Kevles, *In the Name of Eugenics: Genetics and the Uses of Human Heredity* (Berkeley, 1986), 78.

[43] Mrs. Harry McCall Papers. See also the Minutes of March 26, 1917, and July 28, 1919.

[44] Ibid. They also used the Vineland slogan, "Devoted to the care, training, and happiness of those whose minds have not developed normally."

[45] Ibid. See also the Minutes of the Annual Meeting for 1920, dated January 3, 1921. In Johnson's *Adventures in Social Welfare*, he discusses his directorship of the Milne Home and his leaving due to "a breakdown in health."

[46] Ibid. See also the Annual Report for 1922, dated January 2, 1923.

[47] Milne Home, Minutes of Meeting of the Board of Directresses, Annual Report for 1920, dated January 3, 1921. Also, Johnson wrote a series of four articles on the problem of feeblemindedness that were sent to all the leading newspapers. Gordon believed that feeblemindedness was the root of SVC (sex versus civilization). This theory argued that "civilization declines when problem-makers increase at a greater rate than problem-solvers." For further information, see David Smith, *Minds Made Feeble* (Rockville, Md., 1985), 179-80.

[48] Mrs. Harry McCall Papers. See also the Annual Report for 1922, dated January 2, 1923.

[49] From the Annual Report for 1922, dated January 2, 1923.

[50] Ibid. Also, see the Annual Report for 1922, dated January 2, 1923, where Gordon thanks the companies that helped, by numerous donations, to finish the construction of the Gift House.

[51] Minutes of Meeting of the Board of Directresses, Annual Report for 1923, dated January 7, 1924, Milne Papers. Gordon had received her first Times-Picayune Loving Cup in 1921, "for her work on behalf of unfortunate girls." See Mary Gehman and Nancy Ries, *Women and New Orleans* (New Orleans, 1985), 115. (Unfortunately, the information about Gordon given in this book is sketchy.)

[52] Ibid. See also the Annual Report for 1922.

[53] Milne Home, Minutes of Meeting of the Board of Directresses, July 1925.

[54] Milne Home, Minutes of Meeting of the Board of Directresses, January 7, 1924. Also: Ethel Hutson Papers, Collection 14, Tulane University, Manuscript and Archives Division, New Orleans, where there is an article from the *Times-Democrat*, dated October 29 (no year is given), entitled "Board Hopes for Outside Help for Tubercular and Feeble-Minded Scholars." But in 1929, when Jean wanted to share expenses in building a school to accommodate the increasing numbers of feebleminded students, the School Board refused assistance.

[55] Milne Home, Minutes of Meeting of the Board of Directresses, June 1, 1925.

[56] Milne Home, Minutes of Meeting of the Board of Directresses for the Annual Report for 1926, dated January 1927.

[57] Milne Home, Minutes of Meeting of the Board of Directresses for the Annual Report for 1923, dated January 7, 1924.

[58] Milne Home, Minutes of Meeting of the Board of Directresses for the Annual Report for 1929, dated January 6, 1930.

[59] Milne Home, Minutes of Meeting of the Board of Directresses, Annual Report for 1922, dated January 2, 1923. See also Stanley P. Davies (Executive Secretary for the Committee on Mental Higiene, New York State Charities Aid Association), *Social Control of the Feebleminded: A Study of Social Programs and Attitudes in Relation to the Problems of Mental Deficiency* (New York, 1923), 134; and Henry Herbert Goddard (director of the Research Laboratory of the Training School at Vineland, New Jersey), *Feeblemindedness: Its Causes and Consequences* (New York, 1914), 1-20.

[60] Ibid. Also, see Davies' book, *Social Control of the Mentally Deficient* (New York, 1930), 14-26, for a good discussion of the history of feeblemindedness.

[61] Mark Haller, *Eugenics: Hereditarian Attitudes in American Thought* (New Brunswick, 1963), 114.

[62] Ibid., 113-14.

[63] See also Kevles, *In the Name of Eugenics,* especially 269-90; N. J. Block and Gerald Dworkin, eds., *The IQ Controversy* (New York, 1976); Brian Evans and Bernard Waites, *IQ and Mental Testing: An Unnatural Science and its Social History* (London, 1981); and Carl N. Degler, *In Search of Human Nature: The Decline and Revival of Darwinism in American Social Thought* (Oxford, 1991).

[64] See Stephen Jay Gould, *The Mismeasure of Man* (New York, 1981), 196.

[65] For the history of eugenics, see Mark H. Haller, *Eugenics: Hereditarian Attitudes in American Thought* (New Brunswick, 1963), and Kenneth M. Ludmerer, *Genetics and American Society: A Historical Appraisal* (Baltimore, 1972), in addition to the works cited above.

[66] Minutes of Meeting of the Board of Directresses, November, 1924, Milne Home.

[67] Ibid. And see John Higham, *Strangers in the Land: Patterns of American Nativism, 1860-1925* (New Brunswick, 1955).

[68] Letter from Kate Gordon to Laura Clay, March 30, 1907, Box One, Folder Two, Collection 700, Laura Clay Papers, Tulane University, Manuscript and Archives Division, New Orleans, Louisiana.

[69] Milne Home, Minutes of Meeting of the Board of Directresses, November 1924.

[70] Milne Home Papers, Box 1, miscellaneous thoughts by Jean Gordon, undated typescript.

[71] Milne Home, Milne Papers.

[72] Milne Home, Minutes of Meeting of the Board of Directresses, July 13, 1926 (a report for June 13th). The Milne Papers also contain Gordon's original thoughts about the menace of feeblemindedness and the value of the Milne home.

[73] Milne Home Papers, Box 1, miscellaneous thoughts by Jean Gordon, undated typescript.

[74] Milne Home, Minutes of Meeting of the Board of Directresses for the Annual Report for 1924, dated January 5, 1925.

[75] Milne Home, Milne Papers.

[76] Milne Home, Minutes, Report for April, dated May 21, 1929. Gordon adds: "Our friend, Dr. Walter Otis, was there speaking against sterilization every time I spoke of it. The burden of his opposition is that due to the auto-sterilization of the rich, where will the race come from if we sterilize the unfit. One of the doctors asked him if he thought it a wise plan to have the race carried along from the feebleminded if as he claimed the rich and prominent were limiting their offspring, and he said better so than to have the race wiped out! The utter contempt of the other doctors was marked. He did not seem to have anyone with him and took his meals alone."

[77] Milne Home, Minutes of Meeting of Board of Directresses for the Annual Report for 1930, dated January 5, 1931.

[78] Milne Home, Minutes of Meeting of the Board of Directresses for the Annual Report for 1925, dated January 1926.

[79] Kate Gordon, Annual Report for 1931, dated January 1932.

[80] I am grateful to Mrs. Dot Holbrook, superintendent of the Milne Home; to Dr. Wilbur E. Meneray, of Tulane University Library's Manuscript and Archives Division; and to Dr. Michael Clark and Dr. Jerah Johnson, of the University of New Orleans' Department of History. Without their generosity, assistance and guidance, this project would not have been possible. I would also like to thank Edward Johnson for advice about revision, and for originally drawing my attention to Kate Gordon; it was in the course of researching Kate's life that I became aware of her sister's importance.

PART III

LIFE IN LOUISIANA

THE MORAL CLIMATE OF FRENCH COLONIAL LOUISIANA, 1699-1763*

Carl A. Brasseaux

In the growing body of historical literature on French Louisiana, works examining the role of the Catholic Church have focused almost exclusively upon the constant feuding between rival religious orders, the interaction between the colony's bureaucrats and clerics, or the activities of missionaries to the region's indigenous population.[1] Conspicuously absent from these ecclesiastical studies is any detailed discussion of the priests' efforts to regulate morality and to nurture religious fervor within their respective parishes. Indeed, in light of contemporary royal and ecclesiastical directives, such parochial responsibilities should have ranked among the colonial clerics' principal sacerdotal concerns,[2] but parishioners and parochial affairs are seldom mentioned in ecclesiastical correspondence of the French period.

This sin of omission stems directly from the fact that, throughout the period of French rule in Louisiana (1699-1763), Catholic missionaries were consistently unsuccessful in their efforts to dictate the colony's moral values. Indeed, clerics repeatedly lamented that their European- and Canadian-born parishioners had little regard for their religious message, and even less respect for the dignity traditionally accorded their station in France.[3] Because of the impotence of the traditional arbiters of morality, the moral tone of French Louisiana was initially determined by Canadian immigrants who constituted the backbone of early colonial society. These settlers brought to Louisiana a social and cultural heritage markedly different from that of their French confreres. These differences stemmed in part from the frontier environment of New France, which afforded colonists far greater personal freedom than was accorded their counterparts in the mother country, and partly from their intimate association with Indians. In the seventeenth century, Canadians were in almost constant contact with Native Americans, and, as William J. Eccles has noted, it is thus "hardly surprising that the Canadians early adopted much of the Indian way of life and became imbued with some of their characteristics."[4]

---

*First published in *Louisiana History*, 27 (1986): 27-41. Reprinted here with the kind permission of the author and the Louisiana Historical Association.

The result was a socio-cultural metamorphosis of New France society. Many young Canadians of the late seventeenth century preferred the life of fur traders in the wilderness, "where their parents, the *curés*, and the [government] officials could not govern them," to the *habitant*'s mundane and ordered existence. The wilderness, however, offered other liberties unavailable in church-dominated New France. According to Jesuit missionaries, when not engaged in fur trading, which actually occupied only a small portion of their time, hundreds of *voyageurs* annually devoted the bulk of their energies to travelling, "drinking, gambling and lechery." Indeed, quick to exploit the Indians' relative promiscuity, these adventurers—many of whom were married to white *Canadiennes*—reportedly employed Indian women instead of men on trading expeditions because of their willingness to work for lower wages, to perform menial tasks, and to gratify the Canadians' less utilitarian needs.[5]

The example of the uninhibited traders effectively undermined the efforts of Catholic missionaries to impose upon the natives the asceticism of Counter-Reformation Catholicism. Though outraged, the beleaguered priests found themselves unable to curb effectively the excesses of the Christian renegades. In the wilderness areas of the Mississippi Valley frequented by these adventurers at the dawn of the eighteenth century, missionaries lacked all but moral authority over the *coureurs des bois*, who had abandoned their own moral code for the Indians' relatively permissive mores, and, when they attempted to use this authority to guide the wayward Catholics, priests found their admonitions to reform held little persuasive power. In fact, not only did these Canadians openly live "in debauchery" with women of friendly tribes, but they also raided indiscriminately villages to "obtain slave concubines."[6] Some *coureurs des bois* also worked to discredit the missionaries in the eyes of their potential Indian converts,[7] thereby extinguishing the religious threat to the frontiersmen's way of life.[8]

The example of the *coureurs des bois* was not lost upon the early Louisiana colonists, with whom they were in frequent contact. Indeed, the young Canadians deposited at Biloxi by Iberville in 1699-1700 quickly emulated their role models when thrust into the frontier setting of the French Gulf Coast. Father Paul du Ru, writing in March 1700, complained that the Biloxi Canadians, who grudgingly attended his services, were "boisterous" and disrupted Mass.[9] Such sacrilegious demonstrations soon paled by comparison to subsequent improprieties as the French elements of the colonial population were seduced by the promiscuous moral climate established by the Canadians. Canadians and their French confreres exhibited what was, in the opinion of many Louisiana clerics and administrators, an unhealthy interest in Indian women. The soldiers' preoccupation with *les sauvagesses*, however, could hardly have been surprising to anyone, as Biloxi was a backwater military outpost populated primarily by bachelors from 1699 until 1704, when twenty-two French girls were dispatched to Louisiana at the insistence of colonial officials.[10] This influx failed to satisfy the garrison's need for women, and those soldiers fortunate enough to find French brides soon had cause to regret their decision, for their mates often proved not only homely, but also prone to constant nagging about frontier conditions. Leery of the consequences of domesticity, many members of the garrison remained bachelors, and these men—officers and enlisted men alike—seized upon any opportunity to visit friendly Indian villages.[11]

Trappers, who appeared at intervals in Biloxi and, after 1702, in Mobile, quickly exploited the soldiers' continuing demand for female companionship by establishing a black-market trade in *sauvagesses* seized in the interior and sold to members of the garrison as slaves.[12] By 1710, the acquisition of female slaves had become so pervasive, and the sexual exploitation of the Indian women so flagrant that Commandant Jean-Baptiste Le Moyne de Bienville and *Commissaire* Nicolas de La Salle, who could agree on nothing else, both insisted that the colonial ministry send French women as brides for the garrison's numerous bachelors.[13] But no ministerial action was immediately forthcoming, and the abuse continued.

When twelve girls, entrusted to the care of Mme Antoine de La Mothe Cadillac finally reached Louisiana aboard the *Baron de La Fauche* in 1712—the first of several projected shipments of *des jeunes filles de bonnes familles*—Louisiana officials anticipated the establishment of a more stable society, in which familial responsibilities would force *les colons* to settle down and become productive citizens.[14] Such was not to be the case, however. The prospective brides were not only unattractive, but they had also acquired a rather dubious reputation upon landing, as rumors of their seduction by the ship's officers and passengers circulated throughout Mobile. Only three are reported to have found husbands.[15] This incident, and the waning economic fortunes of colonial proprietor Antoine Crozat prevented the continued immigration of French women into the predominantly male settlement.

Frontier values thus continued to prevail in the tiny Louisiana colony, much to the chagrin of the provincial clergy. Venting his frustration in a lengthy memoir to the colonial ministry, Father Henry de La Vente, the pastor at Old Mobile, noted in 1713 or 1714 that

> the principal source of the public and habitual lack of religion in which they have languished for so long is not being able to . . . , or not wanting to bind oneself to any woman through a legitimate marriage. They prefer to maintain scandalous concubinages with young Indian women, driven by their proclivity for the extremes of licentiousness. They have bought them under the pretext of keeping them as servants, but actually to seduce them, as they in fact have done.[16]

Pregnancies frequently resulted from these illicit unions, and, according to one observer, many parents strangled their half-breed infants, apparently to avoid detection by the civil authorities, who frowned upon miscegenation.[17]

The problem of Indian concubinage was soon overshadowed by the influx of several hundred French criminals brought to Louisiana by forced immigration between 1717 and 1720. The most conspicuous of the approximately 1,300 deportees were 160 prostitutes and 96 teenaged *débauchées* from Paris's La Salpétrière house of correction for women; by 1721, this group had come to constitute 21 percent of the colony's female population.[18]

Though some of these women found husbands in the colony and settled down to productive lives, becoming, in the process, the matriarchs of prominent Louisiana "first families," many of these *débauchées* reverted to their only means of gainful employment to support themselves in the colony.[19] Prostitution was nothing new to Louisiana, but it had been confined to isolated cases, such as a Frenchwoman on Dauphin Island who, Cadillac noted in 1716, "sells herself to all comers, the Indians just like the whites."[20] The impact of the former inmates from the *maison de force*, however, was felt throughout lower Louisiana. Indeed, soon after their arrival, the problem of Indian concubinage vanishes from administrative correspondence, and never again would it create a moral controversy in the colony, despite the dramatic growth of Louisiana's garrison after 1717.[21]

This is not to say that Indian concubinage became a mere memory. To the contrary, enslaved concubines remained a fixture at such frontier posts as Fort Tombecbé and Natchitoches. Nor was interracial concubinage confined to isolated military garrisons. Louisiana's experiment with Indian slavery had proved largely unsuccessful by 1720, prompting the colony's proprietary government to seek a new labor source. In the more rapidly developing areas of the colony where Frenchmen displaced the local Indian population, particularly the emerging plantation area immediately above and below New Orleans, African slaves, whose arrival coincided with that of the white deportees, supplanted their native American counterparts. The pattern of exploitation of African women in the agrarian settlements paralleled closely that of Indian women by frontier garrisons, and, by 1763, the colony contained a significant and rapidly growing mulatto population.[22] These abuses, however, were rarely reported, because the agrarian and military posts were generally commanded by bachelors who often shared the guilt of their subordinates.[23]

Far more conspicuous were the public displays of debauchery in the capital and major posts. Scandals were so widespread and so disruptive that Louisiana officials, at the insistence of clerics, attempted unsuccessfully to establish a *maison de force* (house of detention) at New Orleans.[24] Public promiscuity was symptomatic of the instability of the many loveless marriages of convenience forged in the colony. Broken marriages were unknown in Louisiana prior to 1719, but in the 1720s and 1730s they became commonplace, despite the efforts of some priests to settle amicably domestic quarrels.[25] In suits for separation, promiscuity, dissoluteness,[26] and physical abuse figured prominently as legal grievances.[27] When plaintiffs were able to substantiate their charges, which was generally the case, the colonial judiciary consistently approved requests for the separation of bed and board, and the ease with which these suits could be prosecuted and won by disgruntled spouses further undermined the social institution upon which Louisiana's continued development hinged.

The flurry of suits to dissolve marriages in the colony is an accurate barometer of the lax moral climate in frontier Louisiana society. In the austere religious climate of late seventeenth- and early eighteenth-century France, Frenchmen of the lower social orders—from which the vast majority of Louisiana's colonists were drawn—were compelled to attend Mass on Sunday, to conform to the prevailing standards of church decorum, and to pay homage to the local priest. Indeed, French historian Pierre Goubert notes in his landmark work, *La Vie quotidienne des paysans français au XVIIe siècle*, that

> attendance at mass, as well as repose [on Sunday] were entirely obligatory, particularly at the height of the reformation of Catholicism at the end of the [seventeenth century]. Woe to him who thought himself exempt: He risked being denounced from the pulpit and on occasion being prosecuted by the local magistrate .... (p. 201)

The very existence of such enforcement machinery, of course, suggests moderate religious apathy among the common Frenchmen, and the criminal background of thousands of forced emigrants to the Mississippi Valley, reveals an even stronger disregard for the precepts of the Church. When transported to an area in which the clergy maintained only a shadowy presence, these transplanted French Catholics felt free to exhibit their formerly suppressed feelings toward the Church. Indeed, Louisiana immigrants quickly discovered that traditional moral constraints (particularly peer pressure and the threat of arrest by self-righteous officials) did not exist on the Franco-American frontier, and many French men and women consequently practiced only selective adherence to traditional, or "official" morality. It is thus hardly surprising that common law and bigamous unions were widespread, even among the social elite.[28] Chevalier de Louboey, commandant at Mobile, was officially reprimanded for "*du scandale qu'il donne au public par son mauvais commerce avec la dame Garnier* ...."[29] Mme Baudin, wife of the government storekeeper at Balise, created a scandal by her extramarital affairs "with several officers" at the post.[30] Charles D'Arensbourg, commandant at Côte des Allemands publicly maintained a concubine despite the opposition of the Church.[31]

As in the case of D'Arensbourg, the admonitions of the clergy were generally ignored. The Church's lack of influence in early Louisiana stemmed from a combination of factors. First, the Catholic mission was chronically understaffed. Second, the very modest administrative stature of the vicars general, who constituted the leading religious officials in Louisiana until the 1790s, effectively limited the amount of influence that the Church could exert on local civil functionaries. Third, the moral fiber of the priests themselves was often suspect, as seen in the child sired by Father St. Cosme and Father Beaubois's attempts to seduce Gov. Etienne Périer's pretty French-born *domestique* while administering the sacrament of confession.[32] Moreover, Louisiana's vicar general acknowledged, in 1725, that many priests sent to Louisiana had been "interdicted in their [respective French] dioceses and had fled to Louisiana to avoid punishment for their disorderly lives."[33] The clerics' serious character flaws tended to diminish the Church's moral authority in the eyes of the colonists. Fourth, throughout the period of French colonization, the clergy was far more concerned with its creature comforts, material possessions, and political prestige than with its spiritual mission.[34] Priests rarely ventured from the security of their *presbytères* and thus Catholics in all but the most densely populated posts lacked religious services. Finally, the Louisiana missionaries generally viewed their assignment to Louisiana as a most distasteful form of exile and, soured by their personal frustrations, these clerics developed abrasive personalities which alienated many of their parishioners.

Most colonists consequently were at least apathetic, if not openly hostile, toward the clergy. In the first decades of Louisiana's existence, clerics encountered a remarkable lack of enthusiasm among the colonists for church construction. Churches at old Mobile, Dauphin Island, and New Orleans were either not completed or delayed because of popular apathy.[35] No church was built in New Orleans, for example, until nine years after the post's establishment.[36] During the interim, however, numerous cabarets and billiard halls had been erected, and they flourished to such an extent that the bulk of the town's population assembled at these establishments instead of the church services held in makeshift quarters.[37] Nor would attendance improve after construction of St. Louis Church. Commenting upon the situation, Mother Tranchepain noted in 1728 that, in the colony, "religion is little known and practiced even less."[38]

It was difficult for the priests to exercise any moral authority when the churches were empty. Ecclesiastical sources indicate that only half of the Catholics living in proximity to the colonial churches actually made their Easter duties, and extant documents also imply that a far smaller number of parishioners attended Sunday services.[39] Indeed, Father Raphaël complained in 1725 that there was practically "no difference between the holy days of obligation and Sundays and work days, between Lent and Carnival, [between] the Easter season and the rest of the year."[40] This situation would persist throughout the French period. The numerous military and economic crises faced by the colony in succeeding years should have constrained many Louisiana Catholics to seek solace in religion, particularly in the chaotic war years of the 1750s and 1760s; yet, after 1725, church attendance declined steadily. This is not to suggest, however, that Catholics were remiss in observing the sacraments deemed necessary by their faith for salvation. Baptismal and marriage registers particularly are replete with entries in all French colonial-era parishes along the Gulf Coast. Yet, the fact remains that between 1699 and 1763, the Church failed to attract a majority of parishioners within commuting distance of chapels to compulsory weekly services.

Many of those who attended Church services were hardly more pious than those who frequented the taverns on Sundays. Attorney General François Fleuriau, his wife, and the wife of Superior Council member Perry ran afoul of the clergy for laughing and creating a disturbance in church. After repeated warnings from the church warden and himself, Father Hyacinthe, the officiating priest, ordered Fleuriau and his companions to leave church. The women refused to leave; other members of the congregation rose to denounce the priest; and Fleuriau "arose in anger and commanded the Father to shut up and continue the Mass, upbraiding him loudly in church for what he styled affectation."[41] In another episode, the officers of the colonial garrison, who had been relegated to the choir loft by the rental of pews by the New Orleans pastor, demanded that pews be provided their wives in the front of church, as befitted their status. When the priest refused, the officers "chased him into the church and pursued him even into the very sanctuary, raising a scandalous tumult in these sacred precincts. . . ."[42] Intimidated by their effrontery, the pastor conceded one pew, but the officers, still dissatisfied, moved the lectern from its customary side of the altar to the opposite end of the sanctuary just before Mass over the next several weeks to torment their nemesis.[43]

The clergy was hardly content with this state of affairs, but they lacked the administrative machinery to alter the situation. The colony's secular leaders, moreover, were not always sympathetic to the wishes of Church officials, who often were less than diplomatic. Father La Vente created a sensation in Old Mobile by refusing to permit Bienville, the acting colonial commander, to serve as a child's godparent because of his alleged misconduct with a recently arrived Frenchwoman;[44] the missionary then submitted to the humiliated commandant his proposals for dealing with the problem of Indian concubines. It is hardly necessary to note that La Vente's plan was never implemented.[45] Even Cadillac, Bienville's moralistic successor, appears to have been alienated by the colonial clergy, and though he paid lip service to the church's ideals, he made no genuine effort to alter the colony's lax moral climate. Finally, Father Raphaël de Luxembourg, the zealous Capuchin superior in the 1720s, attempted to browbeat members of the colonial council into promulgating regulations designed to curb the excesses of the secular population.[46] Raphaël's efforts met with a singular lack of success until his appeals to France created a demand for change from the directors of Louisiana's proprietary company.[47] As a consequence, in 1725 and 1727, the Superior Council, Louisiana's chief judicial and quasi-legislative body, adopted ordinances prohibiting talking in church during Mass, gambling and drinking in cabarets during divine services, and requiring pregnant women to file an official declaration regarding their condition with the nearest judicial officer.[48] These ordinances merely succeeded in placating the irrepressible Father Raphaël, but, because of their lax enforcement, did nothing to resolve the colony's festering moral issues. In fact, despite the moralistic image projected by Governor Périer in the late 1720s, the colonial government did not attempt to reform local society until after Louisiana's retrocession to the Crown in 1731.[49]

Pursuant to the wishes of the colonial ministry, Bienville, who assumed command of Louisiana for the third time in 1732, and *Commissaire-ordonnateur* Edme Salmon launched an official crusade in 1733 to rehabilitate the colonial population.[50] Chevalier de Louboey was officially reprimanded for his scandalous affair with Mme Garnier.[51] Then Salmon, who observed that the common Louisianian was a drunkard and gambler "who spent on Sunday all of the money he had earned during the week," pushed through the Superior Council measures banning all forms of gambling and prohibiting the sale of liquor at the times of divine services.[52] Though these ordinances, like their predecessors, were subject to lax enforcement, the show of resolve on the part of the Crown, and particularly the disciplinary action taken against Louboey, forced the general population to exercise greater discretion in their indiscretions.

This is not to suggest that Louisiana's moral climate changed substantially after 1733. While it is true that conservative agricultural communities based on traditional European morals emerged in Mobile and on the German Coast and other river settlements near the colonial capital (though even here scandals were not unknown among prominent French families), frontier morality continued to flourish throughout French Louisiana. The numerous marriages to legitimize children of townspeople, the many suits for separation, and scores of administrative reports indicate that sexual promiscuity continued unabated, though less conspicuously.[53] Soldiers dispatched to the frontier openly engaged in debauchery with Indian women and, less frequently, with white women in isolated posts. French military agents among the Southeastern Indians were notorious for "raping" Indian women, and, indeed, the Vaudreuil Papers strongly suggest that the deterioration of Franco-Choctaw relations stemmed directly from soldiers' sexual crimes. According to Chief Tatoulimataha (Red Shoe's brother) the anti-French activities of his sibling in the mid-1740s were precipitated by broken French promises and the provocative behavior of Gallic "chiefs [officers] and other Frenchmen . . . who behaved badly towards them [Choctaw chiefs] and their wives."[54]

The sexual exploits of French military personnel in the field were apparently matched by those of the soldiers in the New Orleans garrison. Despite the government's moralistic policies, royal physicians were compelled to open a hospital at New Orleans for victims of venereal diseases in the late 1730s.[55] This institution closed apparently by 1740; however, it was resuscitated in 1756 as other venereal strains were introduced into Louisiana by new recruits in 1751-1752, and by virtue of the soldiers' *libertinage* they spread to epidemic proportions.[56]

The recruits of the early 1750s created other problems in Louisiana. Gambling, for example, had been a problem of long standing in the colony. As early as 1723, the Superior Council had banned all games of chance involving sums in excess of 100 *livres*.[57] Additional regulations were promulgated in 1725, and gambling was prohibited altogether in 1733 and again in 1744.[58] As the repeated issuance of these regulations indicates, gambling was never driven entirely from the colony; indeed, by the early 1750s, gaming tables were publicly displayed in New Orleans. But gambling was not considered a major problem until after 1753.[59] By 1753, small fortunes were being won and lost at faro tables in New Orleans. Responding to public complaints Governor Louis Billouart de Kerlérec made a concerted effort to close the "gambling dens" located "in all parts of the city," but, because the gamblers, including many prominent military officers, "never play[ed] two consecutive nights in the same place" and because of vocal public opposition, he was unsuccessful. He therefore attempted, but failed, to beat them at their own game by opening a government-run casino at New Orleans during the carnival season.[60]

In addition to patronizing the illicit New Orleans gambling dens, the French recruits of the 1750s—primarily "professional deserters" arrested in France and exiled to Louisiana—were so given to "unrestrained debaucheries of liquor and women" that Governor Kerlérec, writing during the Seven Years' War, considered his garrison "more dangerous to the colony than the enemy itself."[61] The many *libertins* in the garrison obtained their liquor and apparently prostitutes from a large, ostensibly unemployed class of *gens sans avoue* in New Orleans.[62] Composed of the aging male forced immigrants of the 1720s, these individuals operated for decades unlicensed "cabarets" in "the rear of the City."[63] Usually working under cover of darkness, these black market distributors of wine and *guildive* also plied their trade among Indians and slaves, who often stole articles from townspeople to barter for liquor.[64] When the garrison was withdrawn from Louisiana in 1763, the latter groups became the dealers' principal market, and the shift in emphasis produced an unprecedented rash of burglaries in New Orleans.[65] Reacting to the problem in typical fashion, the Superior Council adopted an ordinance summarily banishing the culprits, but, as usual, no effort was made to enforce the decree.[66]

The fact that the forced immigrants of the 1720s would figure so prominently in the last major moral controversy of the French period clearly reflects the persistence of the permissive moral climate established at the dawn of Louisiana colonization. Embracing the moral code forged in the wilderness by *coureurs des bois,* Louisiana's independent, anticlerical, and hedonistic pioneers effectively resisted the limited moralizing influence of the Catholic clergy while creating a frontier society that reflected their newly acquired values. Their influence is seen most clearly in the rapid conversion of French immigrants to their way of life. Moreover, contrary to popular belief, these *libertines* and the less conspicuous male deportees had a lasting impact on colonial Louisiana. Indeed, the influx of hundreds of forced emigrants into Louisiana under the Law regime momentarily inundated the colony with persons of dubious moral fiber, and their presence in the colony seriously retarded the moderating influences that demographic growth and the concomitant expansion of governmental and religious authority would normally have had in the area. Indeed, the evidence suggests that this sociological maturation made significant strides only in the densely populated farming belt immediately above and below New Orleans and perhaps in Mobile, but, even in those areas, the emergence of a local mulatto population indicates that the population's sedate appearance was only superficial. In the other areas of the colony, including the capital, the colonists were only somewhat less discreet.

The pervasive colonial permissiveness was sustained by the limited influence and worldliness of the Catholic clergy. Rival orders feuded constantly over territorial rights and local ecclesiastical preeminence. Moreover, clerics rarely ventured from their *presbytères,* and, by the 1760s, they were devoting, according to their Spanish successors, an inordinate amount of time and energy to the administration of their large landed estates. Finally, the priests' lack of diplomacy in promoting their designs usually only succeeded in alienating their few genuine adherents. It is thus hardly surprising that the number of New Orleans Catholics attending Sunday Mass fell from less than 50 percent in the mid-1720s to under 25 percent at the end of French rule.[67] The percentage of Catholics attending Church services on holy days of obligation was even smaller.

In the absence of moral constraints normally provided by the Catholic Church and reinforced by weekly homilies, a frontier morality developed as successive waves of

Canadian and French soldiers and settlers deviated at will from traditional values. Irreligion was often manifested in criminality. Gambling, public drunkenness, and sexual promiscuity were commonplace in the colonial capital and all of the frontier posts in lower Louisiana and would remain so for decades after the departure of the colony's French garrison in 1763. The persistence of these problems reflects the pervasiveness of the region's frontier values among the civilian population. Thus, in terms of morality, Louisiana in 1763 differed little from the turbulent colony of 1723. Writing in 1764, Jean-Jacques-Blaise D'Abbadie, the last governor of French Louisiana, echoed the thoughts of his predecessors in noting that every effort must be made "to reestablish the good order entirely absent in the conduct and in the morals of the residents of this colony. . . ."[68]

Notes for "The Moral Climate of French Colonial Louisiana, 1699-1763"

[1] Jean Delanglez, *The French Jesuits in Lower Louisiana, 1700-1763* (New Orleans, 1935); Claude L. Vogel, *The Capuchins in French Louisiana, 1722-1766* (Washington, D.C., 1928); Charles Edwards O'Neill, *Church and State in French Colonial Louisiana: Policy and Politics to 1732* (New Haven, Ct., 1966); Roger Baudier, *The Catholic Church in Louisiana* (New Orleans, 1939); Henry C. Semple, *The Ursulines in New Orleans and Our Lady of Prompt Succor: A Record of Two Centuries, 1727-1925* (New York, 1925).

[2] Memoir on the French in Louisiana (1713 or 1714). France. Archives Nationales, Archives des Colonies, Subseries C 13A (Louisiane: Correspondance générale) (hereafter AC, C 13a), volume 3, folios 389vo-395; Capuchin Fathers to the Company of the Indies, August 16, 1724. AC, C 13a, 8:418vo-419; Fr. Raphaël to Abbé Raguet, May 18, 1726. AC, 3 13a, 10:44; Royal memoir to Cadillac, December 20, 1712. France. Archives Nationales, Archives des Colonies, Series B (hereafter AC, B), volume 34, folio 141; Regulations by the commissioners for the administration of Louisiana by a council of the Company of the Indies, September 5, 1721. AC, B 43:311.

[3] Memoir on the conduct of the French in Louisiana (1713 or 1714). AC, C 13a, 3:389vo-406; Capuchin Fathers to the Company of the Indies, Aug. 16, 1724. AC, C 13a, 8:418-419vo; Fr. Raphaël to Abbé Raguet, May 15, 1725. AC, C 13a, 8:399-419; Mother Tranchepain to Abbé Raguet, April 20, 1728. AC, C 13a, 11:274.

[4] William J. Eccles, *The Canadian Frontier* (New York, 1969), 89-90.

[5] Ibid., 90. The *coureurs des bois*, or *voyageurs* as they were sometimes called, annually constituted a large portion of the young male element in New France: by 1700, 500 men of a total population of 15,000. Ibid., 90-91.

[6] Jay Higginbotham, *Old Mobile: Fort Louis de la Louisiane, 1702-1711* (Mobile, Ala., 1977), 283, 423; Dunbar Rowland and Albert Godfrey Sanders, trans. and eds., *Mississippi Provincial Archives* (hereafter *MPA*), 3 vols. (Jackson, Miss., 1927-1932), 2:218-19; O'Neill, *Church and State*, 82, 86.

[7] O'Neill, *Church and State*, 82; La Salle to the Minister, May 12, 1709. AC, C 13a, 2:399vo.

[8] O'Neill, *Church and State*, 27; Marcel Giraud, *A History of French Louisiana*, Vol. 1, *The Reign of Louis XIV, 1698-1715*, trans. by Joseph C. Lambert (Baton Rouge, 1974): 346-48.

[9] Ruth Lapham Butler, trans. and ed., *Journal of Paul du Ru (February 1-May 8, 1700): Missionary Priest to Louisiana* (Chicago, 1934), 37.

[10] Charles R. Maduell, Jr., comp., *The Census Tables for the French Colony of Louisiana, From 1699 through 1732* (Baltimore, 1972), 8; Higginbotham, *Old Mobile*, 161-86.

[11]*MPA*, 2:38, 40-41, 49, 55, 60.

[12]Between 1704 and 1708, the number of Indian slaves at Old Mobile increased from 11 to 80. By 1726, there were 226 Indian slaves in Louisiana. Grady Kilman, "Slavery and Forced Labor in Colonial Louisiana, 1699-1803" (MA thesis, University of Southwestern Louisiana, 1972), 29-30.

[13]Bienville to Minister, October 12, 1708. AC, C 13a, 2:177; La Salle to Minister, May 12, 1709. AC, C 13a, 2:395.

[14]Minister to Cadillac, December 18, 1712. AC, B 34:141; Minister to Cadillac, December 20, 1712. AC, B 34:157; *MPA*, 2:57, 72.

[15]*MPA*, 2:184-85.

[16]Memoir on the conduct of the French in Louisiana, (1713 or 1714). AC, C 13a, 3:390vo.

[17]Ibid.; *MPA*, 2:58, 206-8, 218-19.

[18]Sheila T. Sturdivant, "Rich Man, Poor Man, Beggar Man, Thief: Frenchmen Exiled to Louisiana, 1717 to 1721" (M.A. thesis, University of Southwestern Louisiana, 1971), 50-51; Glenn R. Conrad, trans. and ed., *Immigration and War, Louisiana, 1718-1721: From the Memoir of Charles Le Gac* (Lafayette, La., 1970), 58.

[19]Conrad, trans. and ed., *Immigration and War*, 58, 62, 64; Emile Lauvrière, *Histoire de la Louisiane française, 1673-1939* (Baton Rouge, 1940), 215-16; John Duffy, ed., *The Rudolf Matas History of Medicine in Louisiana*, 2 vols. (Baton Rouge, 1958), 1:24.
   For a partial list of the *femmes de force* who did not marry, see the 1726 census of New Orleans in Jay K. Ditchy, trans., "Early Census Tables of Louisiana," *Louisiana Historical Quarterly*, 13 (1930): 218, (hereafter *LHQ*).
   For a case study of one of the *femmes de force* who married and became the matriarch of a "first family," see Mathé Allain, trans. and ed., "Anne-Françoise Rolland: An Early Settler," *Attakapas Gazette*, 15 (1980): 188-91.

[20]Cadillac to minister, January 5, 1716. AC, C 13a, 4:532vo.

[21]The colonial garrison grew from 70 soldiers in 1709 to approximately 500 in 1726. *MPA*, 3:137, 496.

[22]In May 1726, Fr. Raphaël noted that "the number of those who maintain young Indian women or negresses to satisfy their intemperance . . . remain enough to scandalize the church and to require an effective remedy." Fr. Raphaël to Abbé Raguet, May 19, 1726. AC, C 13A, 10:46vo.
   There were 187 mulattoes in Louisiana in 1763. Jacqueline K. Voorhies, comp., *Some Late Eighteenth-Century Louisianians: Census Records of the Colony, 1758-1796* (Lafayette, La., 1973), 103.

[23]Fr. Raphaël to Abbé Raguet, November 15, 1728. AC, C 13a, 8:406-406vo; Gary B. Mills and Elizabeth Shown Mills, "Louise Marguerite: St. Denis' *Other* Daughter," *Southern Studies*, 16 (1970): 321-28.

[24]Périer and La Chaise to the Company of the Indies, November 3, 1728. AC, C 13a, 11:122; Minister to Bienville and Salmon, September 2, 1732. AC, B 57:810.

[25]"Records of the Superior Council," *LHQ*, 15 (1931): 93, 572; 16 (1933): 143, 333; 21 (1938): 888-92; *MPA*, 2:462, 520.

[26]See, for example, "Records of the Superior Council," *LHQ*, 21:889.

[27]See ibid., 14 (1931): 93, 456, 572, 582; 16 (1933): 143, 333, 711, 713; *Madeleine de Mangon de la Tour* v. *Jean Antoine Malo*, July 31, 1727, Louisiana Historical Center, Louisiana State Museum, PR, 27/160.

[28]Fr. Raphaël to Abbé Raguert, May 18, 1726. AC, C 13a, 10:46-46vo.

[29]Minister to Bienville, October 14, 1732. AC, B 57:858vo.

[30]Salmon to the minister, December 15, 1737. AC, C 13a, 22:207-8.

[31]Fr. Raphaël to Abbé Raguet, May 15, 1725. AC, C 13a, 8:406-6vo.

[32] Périer to Abbé Raguet, November 15, 1728. AC, C 13a, 11:238; Account of the Grand Soleil of the Natchez, son of Fr. St. Cosme, missionary, 1728. BN, MSS. fr., n.a., 2550:115.

[33] Fr. Raphaël to Abbé Raguet, May 15, 1725. AC, C 13a, 8:402.

[34] O'Neill, Church and State, 71; Higginbotham, Old Mobile, 247, 248, 257; Baudier, Catholic Church, 185-86. O'Neill's Church and State provides the best overview of the religious orders' political feuding.

[35] Higginbotham, Old Mobile, 249-58; Hubert to the Council, June 2, 1717. AC, C 13a, 4:49; Baudier, Catholic Church, 56, 73-77, 81, 91.

[36] Baudier, Catholic Church, 56.

[37] Ibid., 56, 73, 91; Henry Plauché Dart, ed., "Cabarets of New Orleans in the French Colonial Period," LHQ, 19 (1936): 577-81.

[38] Mother Tranchepain to Abbé Raguet, April 20, 1728. AC, C 13a, 11:274.

[39] Fr. Raphaël to Abbé Raguet, May 15, 1725. AC, C 13a, 8:402vo; Fr. Raphaël to Abbé Raguet, May 18, 1726. AC, C 13a, 10:44, O'Neill, Church and State, 114.

[40] Fr. Raphaël to Abbé Raguet, May 15, 1725. AC, C 13a, 8:402.

[41] Baudier, Catholic Church, 92-93.

[42] Ibid., 92.

[43] Ibid.; Fr. Raphaël to Abbé Raguet, May 15, 1725. AC, C 13a, 8:399-406.

[44] O'Neill, Church and State, 56.

[45] Ibid., 72.

[46] Ibid., ch. 6; Baudier, Catholic Church, 97-100.

[47] Fr. Raphaël to Abbé Raguet, May 15, 1725. AC, C 13a, 8:399-406; Fr. Raphaël to Abbé Raguet, May 18, 1726. AC, C 13a, 10:44.

[48] Decree of the Superior Council prohibiting talking in church during divine services, November 7, 1725. AC, A 23:65; Decree of the Superior Council requiring pregnant women to make a declaration regarding such pregnancy to the chief judicial official of the post, July 29, 1727. AC, A 23:86; Decree of the Superior Council prohibiting drinking and gambling during divine services, April 11, 1725. AC, A 23:58.

[49] O'Neill, Church and State, 186; Fr. Raphaël to Abbé Raguet, April 18, 1727. AC, C 13a, 10:321.

[50] Royal memoir to serve as instruction to Bienville as governor of Louisiana, September 2, 1732. AC, B 57:706.

[51] Minister to Louboey, September 2, 1732. AC, B 57:824vo.

[52] Ordinance prohibiting all forms of gambling, March 26, 1733. AC, A 23:111; Ordinance prohibiting the selling of wine in any quantity on holy days of obligation or during divine services, March 26, 1733. AC, A 23:111.

[53] For marriages to legitimize children born at Mobile in the late 1730s and early 1740s, see the Mobile Marriage Register, volume 1, folios 19a-3, 19b, 19b-1, 30b-2, Diocese of Mobile.
    For other examples of promiscuity, see "Records of the Superior Council," LHQ, 5 (1922): 266; 13 (1930): 663, 680; 14 (1931): 93, 456, 572, 582; 21 (1938): 888-92; Salmon to Minister, March 6, 1733. AC, C 13a, 17:76vo-77; Salmon to Minister, March 9, 1733. AC, C 13a, 17:224; Diron to Minister, April 29, 1735. AC, C 13a, 20:269vo; Salmon to Minister, December 15, 1737. AC, C 13a, 22:207-8; Vaudreuil to Minister, April 25, 1747. AC, C 13a, 31:56; Michel to Minister, July 20, 1751. AC, C 13a, 35:328; D'Abbadie to Minister, June 7, 1764. AC, C 13a, 44:50-58; Carl A. Brasseaux, trans. and ed., A Comparative View of

French Louisiana, 1699 and 1762; The Journals of Pierre Le Moyne d'Iberville and Jean-Jacques-Blaise d'Abbadie (Lafayette, La., 1979), 131.

[54]Diron to the Minister, April 29, 1735. AC, C 13a, 20:267; Michel to the Minister, July 20, 1751. AC, C 13A, 35:328, Patricia Galloway, "Louisiana Post Letters: The Missing Evidence for Indian Diplomacy," *Louisiana History*, 22 (1981): 35, 37-39.

[55]Minister to Salmon, September 16, 1737. AC, B 65:520. See also "Records of the Superior Council," *LHQ*, 5 (1722): 111.

[56]Kerlérec and Dauberville to Minister, April 8, 1756. AC, C 13a, 39:133, Kerlérec to Minister, October 20, 1757. AC, C 13a, 39:273.

[57]Decree of the Superior Council to serve as instructions for the colony, April 29, 1723. AC, C 13a, 7:99-100.

[58]Ordinance prohibiting all forms of gambling, March 26, 1733. AC, A 23:111; Ordinance prohibiting gambling in Louisiana, November 4, 1744. AN, AD 7:2a.

[59]Kerlérec to Minister, December 18, 1754. AC, C 13a, 38:120-22.

[60]Ibid.

[61]Kerlérec to Minister, October 20, 1757. AC, C 13a, 39:273.

[62]Michel to Minister, January 18, 1752. AC, C 13a, 36:227vo.

[63]Ibid.; Dart, ed., "Cabarets," 580-81.

[64]Michel to Minister, July 20, 1751. AC, C 13a, 35:328.

[65]See Brasseaux, trans. and ed., *Comparative View*, 119-20.

[66]Dart, ed., "Cabarets," 580-81.

[67]Baudier, *Catholic Church*, 230.

[68]D'Abbadie to Minister, June 7, 1764. AC, C 13a, 44:50-50vo.

THE PLANTATION OF THE COMPANY OF THE INDIES*

Samuel Wilson, Jr.

Much of the land around the site which he selected for New Orleans in 1718 was claimed by the city's founder, Jean-Baptiste Le Moyne de Bienville for his own use. Included in the vast acreage was the greater part of the land located across the river from the city in what is now known as Algiers. It was part of this land that the Company of the Indies asked him to cede to it in order to establish a plantation for itself.[1]

Meanwhile, however, Adrien de Pauger, one of the king's engineers and engineer-in-chief of Louisiana after the death of Pierre Le Blond de la Tour in 1723, had claimed this land and had begun to clear it and to erect a house for himself. Writing to the Company from Fort Louis of Biloxi on May 25, 1722, Pauger added a postscript:

> Dare I again, Gentlemen, to ask you the grace of granting me the land opposite New Orleans, marked in my name on the plan of the course of the river, where I have nine or ten arpents cleared in order to have a plantation begun, which has cost me near a thousand livres before M. de Bienville had claimed this land for himself, not being set there because he himself thought it very inundated, and as his plantation named Bel Air, which is a league below could, without that, be extended four leagues square. Besides, the nine or ten [arpents] which are conceded to him adjoining New Orleans had made me in no ways doubt that he was envious of that which I beseech you to have granted to me.[2]

The map to which Pauger refers is probably the undated one entitled "Particular Map of the St. Louis River, ten leagues above and below New Orleans, where are marked the plantations and the lands conceded to several individuals in the Mississippi." This map shows the land claimed by Pauger located almost opposite the center of the city and between the plantations and lands of Bienville and Pailloux de Barbezan. The land of

---

*First published in *Louisiana History*, 31 (1990): 161-92. Reprinted with the kind permission of the Louisiana Historical Association.

The Plantation of the Company of the Indies 325

Pailloux was subsequently acquired by Governor Etienne Périer, and some years later was occupied by the plantation of the chevalier Jean de Pradel.

When it appeared that the land which Pauger claimed was about to be granted to the Company of the Indies, he appealed to the Superior Council in order to have himself maintained in the possession of his plantation, addressing a petition to the governing body of the colony on February 3, 1724:

> To the Gentlemen of the Superior Council of Louisiana
> M. de Pauger very humbly represents to you Gentlemen that for three years he has been in possession of an unoccupied terrain on the other side of the water opposite New Orleans, where he has built a house and cleared eight arpents or thereabout, of the terrain in front in condition for yielding a passable crop; that in order to support this enterprise he had bought a negro for whom he refused, last year, eighteen hundred livres, which several individuals offered him, which negro (*pièce d'Inde*) is since dead from the strain of having worked on the said terrain; had put a German family there during one year to which he had made heavy advances, as also to five or six workmen whom he had maintained during more than fifteen months, fed with French bread, brandy and meat, hoping after this peaceful possession to increase this plantation and to put it on a good footing. He has been surprised to learn today that Monsieur de Bienville wishes to evict him from it in order to cede it to the Company, which, knowing him to be in possession of 4 leagues frontage of terrain here and there along the River, asked him for some portion of it for itself, which Monsieur de Bienville could easily do without figuring to cede to himself this, particularly, which according to law could not belong to him.
>
> The reasons of M. Pauger are:
>
> First, He possessed it for nearly three years without any trouble or judiciary demand which might have given a blow to his possession.
>
> Second, He has built, cleared, made the expenditure of more than 2500# on the place and lost a negro (*pièce d'Inde*) worth 1800#.
>
> Third, His triennial peaceful possession and pursuit of a clearing and successive cultivation without interruption gives him an incontestable character of property according to the laws made for seized waste and uncultivated lands.
>
> Considering this, Gentlemen, and in view of all these just reasons, may it please you to order that my said Sr. de Pauger shall be maintained and kept in the possession and property of the said plantation and do justice.
> At New Orleans this 3rd February 1724.
>
> de Pauger
>
> Let it be communicated to Monsieur de Bienville for furnishing his response to it.
> At New Orleans, the 3rd February, 1724.
> Bruslé   Fazende   Perry[3]

This was the opening of one of the important lawsuits of the early days of New Orleans. Although the Superior Council on February 9, 1724, confirmed Bienville's ownership of the land, Pauger was to be paid for the improvements which he had already established on the land. The appraisal was set at 1,000 *livres*, but this sum had not yet been paid at the time of Pauger's death in 1726.

In spite of the protracted litigation over the final settlement of the claim, the Company of the Indies began the operation of its plantation on Pauger's former lands. The principal function of this plantation was to provide a place to receive the African slaves brought in by the company for sale to the French colonists and for use in its various construction projects, in the preparation of lumber, and in limited farming operations to produce food for their own maintenance. In his report on the census of Louisiana dated November 24, 1721, Dartaguiette Diron, inspector general of troops, added the following remarks on the subject of Negroes:

> It is absolutely necessary to send many negroes to the Colony. They are more suited than the whites for the working of the land, and so the towns of America have only been established by negro slaves. Louisiana will never do well if a sufficient quantity of them is not sent. They do wonderfully in the climate and there is no other constraint than that of clothing them in winter; the expense of it is modest.[4]

A few months before, regulations concerning the sale of Negroes in Louisiana were adopted in Paris:

> Ordinance of Our Lords, the Commissioners of the Council appointed by the King for the Administration of the Company of the Indies.
> In favor of the Inhabitants of the colony of Louisiana
> On the 2 September, 1721
> ....
> Article First
> The negroes will be sold to the Inhabitants at the price of six hundred sixty livres, *pièce d'Inde,* conforming to that which has been previously ordered by the Company, for the payment of which they will make their notes payable in three years in equal parts from the day of delivery, in tobacco or in rice according to what shall be ordered by the Directors in conformity to the quality of the lands of the Inhabitants.[5]

Negroes were already on the plantation by September 18, 1724, and many more were expected so that the Superior Council on that date resolved that it was "advisable to provide early for the subsistence of the said negroes, and of those that we have both at the Balize and on the plantation, the provisions of the Company's plantation not being sufficient."[6] Later that same year, on November 15, Pauger was directed to make a survey of all the plantations below New Orleans in order to confirm the titles, starting down one side and "coming upstream on the other side of the river as far as that of the Company which is opposite New Orleans."[7]

With the increased number of Negroes on the plantation, it was necessary that another overseer be appointed. On April 7, 1725, therefore:

The Plantation of the Company of the Indies

> M. Fazende explains to the Council that since the works to be done on the plantation of the Company are becoming more considerable every day both with reference to the clearing and cultivation of the land and the building of a barn and cabins for negroes that it is advisable to build, so that a single foreman of the negroes cannot be sufficient and cannot keep his eye at the same time on all the negroes and negresses who are under his command. That is why it would be well to have on the said plantation an overseer well acquainted both with the cultivation of the land and with the other work in order that everything may move along in an orderly manner and for the good administration of the said plantation. . . .
>
> On the statement above of M. Fazende on this the seventh of April, 1725, the Council has decided to appoint Sieur Neboul as administrator and overseer of the said plantation with the salary of six hundred livres per year and a ration and a half, on the good evidence of his capacity and correctness that has been given to the Council.[8]

The Company received all the Negroes destined for the colony and sold them to the settlers. Thus it was usually only the rejected ones who were left to operate the plantation. In spite of this, however, the Council reported on May 20, 1725, that it "hoped for a fairly good harvest this year."[9] Cattle were also kept and disposed of in a similar manner on the plantation, cows from Biloxi belonging to the Company being brought here and other cows and sheep being sold. The census of January 1, 1726, lists on the plantation of the Company opposite New Orleans a commander named Perrie, a hired man, twenty-five negro slaves, fourteen horned cattle, and sixty arpents of cleared land."[10] On March 17, 1726, there were "fourteen cows, one heifer and one bull on the Company's plantation. Many of them have died and there are several that have become wild at Biloxi."[11]

> When Perier became governor in 1726, he brought with him . . . 'three Englishmen whom he found at the Cape who are three tobacco growers and who understand it wonderfully. There is one from Carolina whom we have put on the Company's plantation and who expects to grow good tobacco there. We shall send one to the Natchez and the other to the Choupitoulas to show them the way to grow it. They do not yet have any fixed wages. We shall regulate them for them according to their work. We expect to send you some good tobacco from your plantation at the end of the year. The man from Carolina has promised to grow us some seed. They have found that [tobacco] of this country perfectly good and the soil very well adapted to the cultivation of this plant.'[12]

Périer also asked that more Negroes be sent who could be traded with the Spaniards in order to attract their commerce. These would be put on the plantation, clearing ground and growing provisions until sold.

With Périer's arrival, the plantation improved greatly. At that time, Le Page, Louisiana historian and architect, had had a plantation at Natchez since 1718. He sailed from La Rochelle and arrived at Dauphin Island on August 25, 1718, came to New Orleans just after its founding by Jean-Baptiste Le Moyne de Bienville, spent a brief period on Bayou St. John, and finally established himself at Natchez. He obtained a small concession and, according to the census of January 1723, owned two Indian slaves and one Negro slave. The January 1726 census shows Le Page, concessionaire, with two Negro slaves, three Indian slaves, and five arpents of cleared land. Later in 1726, he gave up his Natchez concession and returned to New Orleans. When he left Natchez, "two children belonging to M. Le Page Du Prat" were left at the Concession of the White Earth (Terre Blanche), the Dasfeld concession of which the architect Ignace François Broutin was the director.[13] These children, perhaps children of his slaves, were among those killed in the Natchez Massacre on November 28, 1729. Le Page makes no mention of these children in his account of the massacre in his published history.

Le Page intended to return to France, but he was induced by Governor Périer to remain in the colony and become the manager of the Company's plantation. On August 24, 1726, Périer had obtained a grant from the Company of the Indies of a ten-arpent plantation across the river from New Orleans, and on October 21, following, had acquired the former ten-arpent plantation of Pailloux de Barbezan adjacent to the Company's plantation below and his own above. Périer, as the adjoining property owner, was naturally interested in having the neighboring plantation well managed and improved.

The census of 1731 lists the Plantation of the Company of the Indies under the name of the Sieur Le Page, and lists also 2 hired men, 201 Negroes or Negresses, 20 Negro children, 2 guns, and no horses, cattle, or sheep. Le Page considered himself well qualified to run the Company's plantation and experienced in the management of Negroes. In his history of Louisiana, which he published in France in 1758, he included these remarks:

Manner of Governing the Negroes

Prudence demands that your negroes be lodged at a sufficient distance so as not to be inconvenient, however, near enough to perceive what happens among them. When I say that they must not be put so near that they can inconvenience you, I mean by the stench which is natural to some nations of negroes, such as the Congos, the Angolas, the Aradas, and other. This is why it is appropriate that there be a bath in their camp, of boards sunk in the ground a foot or a foot and a half so that there might never be more than this depth of water, for fear of the children drowning. Besides it is necessary that there be some edges so that the smallest ones cannot get in. It is necessary to have a pool above and beyond the camp for serving to maintain the water and to keep fish.

This camp of the negroes ought to be closed with palisades with a gate locked with a key. The cabins ought to be isolated, because of fire and arranged in a line, as much for propriety as for facility in knowing the cabins of each negro; but in order to be less inconvenienced by their natural odor, it is necessary to take the precaution of putting this camp to the north of your house, or toward the northeast, because the winds which blow from those sides are never as hot as the others & since it is only when they are hot that they exhale an insupportable odor.

What I just told you about the odor of negroes who smell bad ought to make you take care not to come near them at work except from the windward side, not to let your children approach them, which besides the bad air, could never teach them anything good, neither for morals, nor for education, nor for language.

Those who smell the worst are those who are the least black.[14]

The above remarks were probably based on Le Page's experience on his own plantation at Natchez, as well as from what he learned as manager for the Company. His account of his return to New Orleans in 1726 and his description of his work there is particularly interesting, and contains the most complete known account of the plantation:

> The same year [1726] a strong desire possessed me to quit the post of the Natchez where I had lived for eight years. I took this resolution in spite of the attachment that I had for this Establishment. I communicated my thought to a friend who approved it, & who wished to do the same. We sold our possessions & we descended to New Orleans which had quite changed in appearance, since it was entirely built. I found M. de la Chaise, commissary General, who recognized me, having searched for medicinal plants for him, which were sent to France by order of the Company. I counted on returning to Europe with my friend who was recrossing; but M. Périer, Governor, and M. de la Chaise pressed me so strongly that I accepted the administration of the Plantation of the Company, which a short time after became the Plantation of the King.
>
> This Plantation looked like a half-cleared forest; the cabins of the negroes were spaced here and there. These negroes had several small pirogues which they used for crossing the river to go to rob all the inhabitants on the other side, which was that of the city. Every Sunday at least four hundred negroes were found on the Plantation, including two hundred fifty who belonged to it. I had the land cleared & cultivated. I had the pirogues of the negroes broken to pieces & forbid them ever to have any more. I agreed with the other inhabitants on what we had to do to prevent these assemblies of negroes, which could only end in damage to the Colony, & I succeeded in abolishing them.
>
> I built a camp for the negroes of the Plantation. It was composed of a square in the center, & of three wide streets where I disposed their cabins, between which I left a suitable space. I surrounded this camp with strong palisades. I left only one gate which was the only place where they could come out. Besides on the outside of this gate I had two cabins built, one of which was for the white commander, & the other for locking up the sick ones & having them dressed. A young negro who followed the Surgeon slept & lived in this latter cabin, to the end of being within reach for bloodletting or for putting a first dressing if the case was pressing. I learned several years after this negro was one of the good surgeons of the colony. . . .
>
> During low water I had a small port dug out opposite my house which could contain a vessel & the pirogues of the Plantation, so that I no longer feared the trees which the river carried in its overflows. Things were thus in order and I found myself more conveniently [situated] & more satisfied.[15]

Le Page, being an architect and engineer, was probably responsible for many of the buildings which were constructed on the plantation during the period of his administration. From his statements regarding the Negro camp, it would seem that he was certainly the one who designed it. This camp was the subject of one of a series of drawings by the architect Alexandre DeBatz showing the plantation buildings, one of which is entitled "Plan of the Negro camp with their cabins constructed on the plantation of the Company, of post in the ground roofed with bark. Surveyed and drawn on the spot the 9 January 1732." This camp was perhaps begun in 1727.

There were no drawings of the individual cabins nor of the cabin of the commander, nor was the small building to the right of the entrance identified as being a hospital, as mentioned by Le Page. However, Périer and La Chaise, in writing to the Company on July 31, 1728, said:

> We are at present having a hospital for the negroes built on the plantation of the Company in order to keep them in it when they arrive sick, and we intend to put a surgeon in it who will remain there as long as there are any patients. We ask you to send us for that place the remedies mentioned in the memorandum enclosed herewith.[16]

This hospital, where Le Page had had M. Baldy named as surgeon major, was the subject of another in the series of DeBatz drawings, which were undoubtedly measured drawings and not plans for proposed buildings. The drawings were likely intended to show the buildings that reverted to the king when the Company of the Indies gave up its operation of the colony in 1731. The hospital was typical of the smaller buildings of half-timber construction erected by the first French in Louisiana and by their descendants for generations. Two rooms, each divided by a line of posts, were separated by a passageway clear through the building. The peculiarly spaced posts in the rooms may have formed a partition with a door, from which the filling had been removed, the posts being left for structural reasons. This building seems to have been erected on a brick foundation, the filling between the posts of the framework probably being a mixture of mud and Spanish moss known as *bousillage*, still found in many old buildings in Louisiana today. The steep roof with its steeper hips was probably roofed with cypress bark. While the drawing is not detailed sufficiently to indicate sash in the windows, it is almost certain that the doors and windows were closed by batten shutters. This hospital, together with the cabins of the camp, which were no doubt of a similar general appearance, must have formed a very picturesque group of plantation outbuildings.

The boundaries of the plantation are described by Sieur Jean-Pierre Lassus, who surveyed the property in 1727:

> Survey of the plantation of the Company of the Indies
> made by the Sieur Lassus.
>
> February 8, 1728
>
> I, undersigned surveyor of the Province of Louisiana, certify to those to whom it shall pertain that the first day of October, one thousand seven hundred twenty-seven, I expressly transported myself with the Sieur [Lassus de] Marcilly, also a surveyor,

onto the plantation of the Company of the Indies opposite New Orleans in order to there measure the eighteen arpents of frontage which is reserved for it. We have begun at the boundary of Monsieur Perier, Commandant General, continuing on the line which forms an angle of 50 degrees with that of the river bank, and finishing the eighteen running arpents on the limit of Monsieur de Bienville. We have there had planted a boundary mark of cypress wood and two pieces following to form the south line which is the common limit of the Company and of Monsieur de Bienville up to the twenty-five arpents in depth, at the end of which we found the meeting or incidence of the common limit of the Company and of Monsieur Perier, the eighth of the same month.

The same day, the first of October, we transported ourselves in order to plant the boundary mark of the Company common with Monsieur Perier, and two other pieces of cypress wood to form the S.E. line which we have also measured up to twenty-four arpents of depth where we made several crosses on some trees which are found at the point of the said meeting of the two limits, the third of the same month in the presence of the Sieurs Joseph and Amelin, both managers.

Messrs. Perier and de Noyan, this latter acting for Monsieur de Bienville, after having been witnesses to their boundary marks on the said river are agreed that they would take the line of the SSE reciprocally as a limit, which is precisely half of the angle of 45 degrees formed by the meeting of the two lines mentioned in the present proces verbal, which could not be more inclined in order to spare the terrain of the Company which equally forms a triangle and a circle segment made by the sinuosity of the point as may be seen on the plan.

Messrs. Perier, de la Chaise, de Noyan, and Broutin who are themselves transported onto the said terrain are agreed together to what is specified in the present [act] which I will verify everywhere where need may be.

[signed] Lassus Perier
de la Chaise de Noyan[17]

This survey, and others by Lassus, is accompanied by a map of all of Bienville's lands, showing the precise location of the various plantations mentioned in Lassus's survey.

The year before he made this survey, Lassus had apparently visited the Company's plantation and used it as the vantage point for his large drawing of the colonial city, which he entitled *Vue et Perspective de la Nouvelle Orléans, 1726*. This remarkable view, now in the Archives Nationales in Paris, shows in the foreground the Negroes of the Company's plantation engaged in clearing the land, felling and burning trees, and even driving off or killing a large alligator on the edge of the river.

Governor Perier attempted to grow tobacco on his adjacent plantation, but continual rains for forty days almost completely ruined a hundred thousand feet of it in 1728. On August 14 of that year he wrote:

In spite of the loss of the greater part of our tobacco I expect by the provisional estimate that I have made of it that we shall have more than two hundred thousand pounds of it to send to France this year, and if all the inhabitants were equipped with mills to hull rice, we should be in a position to make a large return, the year having been very favorable for them on account of the heavy rains that we have had. We are having work done at present on a pestle-mill [*moulin à pilon*] to hull the rice but one that can be of service only so long as the river is high.[18]

This rice mill was also located on the Company's plantation and was of construction similar to that of the hospital—that is, of heavy timber frame, probably filled in with *bousillage*. DeBatz included a drawing of it in his survey of the plantation buildings, this one being dated January 14, 1732, certified by Broutin, engineer of the king, on January 15.

The principal room of the mill was quite large and high, with a stairway leading to an attic above. On one side was a lean-to containing the miller's rooms. The millwheel was located in an attached building built over a canal into which water from the river was allowed to flow when the river was high. The room containing the millwheel, to the right of the mill, was built at a higher level, alongside. Its roof was of a lesser pitch. DeBatz made several drawings of this mill, which are in the French archives.

Another building on the plantation, which probably stood quite near the mill, was a large warehouse for the storage for rice. It was of two stories, with a hatch in the center of the upper floor for hoisting the rice. A large, arched central doorway permitted carts to be driven inside by means of a ramp. The lower floor was elevated several feet above the ground, apparently on brick foundations. The windows were like those of the hospital and the mill, those of the lower floor having segmental heads and those of the second floor being square. The proportions between the floor heights—a high lower floor and a very low upper story—seem to have been characteristic of the half-timbered buildings being erected in New Orleans at that time, such as the first Ursuline Convent (1727-1734), for which DeBatz was one of the architects.

The last building included in DeBatz's survey is the manager's building, the house in which Le Page undoubtedly lived. It is quite similar in design and proportion to the rice warehouse, having a high first floor and a low second. The plan of this house is particularly interesting, and characteristically French. The entrance in the vestibule was under the stairway and opposite the entrance to the main living room. The stairway, which had carefully spaced windows, had a closed string like the stairways of the old Ursuline Convent and the Girod House in New Orleans today. The living room had a large French fireplace with a narrow chimney breast above. An unusual feature was the inclusion of the kitchen in the main body of the house. Other rooms on the ground floor were for offices and storage. The upper floor, containing the bedrooms, was similar in plan to the lower. Almost all the partitions were structural. This house, like the rice warehouse, had a low-pitched roof. For this reason, it is not likely that bark or shingles were used as on the hospital. Instead, curved tiles were probably used, as they were on the first Ursuline Convent, which was under construction at the same time.

During this period, 1729 through 1731, Pierre Baron was engineer of the king, having succeeded Ignace François Broutin. The similarity in the design and detail of these

The Plantation of the Company of the Indies

buildings and the first Ursuline Convent and Baron's observatory on Dumaine Street would certainly seem to indicate that they were all the work of the same man. Whether this was Baron or DeBatz, both of whose names appear on the cornerstone of the first Ursuline Convent, is impossible to tell. Le Page himself undoubtedly had some part in the design. Like the convent, the timber framework and the *bousillage* infill of the plantation buildings may have been left exposed, which led to their rapid deterioration.

The date at which the warehouse and the manager's building were built does not appear in the records, but they were probably done at about the same time as the observatory, which was erected in 1730. The drawings, which are signed by DeBatz and Broutin were, of course, made after their completion, and were done at the time the colony was returned by the Company to the king in 1731. Baron was dismissed at that time and returned to France, as reported in Perier's letter of November 25, 1731.[19]

Shortly before the DeBatz drawings of the plantation buildings were done, an inventory of the plantation was made on November 2, 1731. It included "all the buildings, merchandise, provisions and tools, Negroes and cattle in charge of the Sr. Le Page." The plantation was said to contain "eighteen and two-thirds arpents of front on the river by 25 4/5 running to the South [and] 18 2/3 running to the South East . . . containing in area around 250 arpents, of which quantity there is one hundred fifty arpents cleared and under cultivation." It was valued at 4,000 *livres*. The buildings were described and valued as follows:

Buildings

The Building in which is the pestle mill of 70 ft. of length by 30 of width Estimated with another intermediate building on the sluice of the said mill, a lean-to, also intermediate, and the Mills, according to the specification in the state that it is in at present 19,971.13
The hospital, a Building of 30 Ft. of Length by 20—Estimated here........ 5,367.""
The Warehouse, 100 Ft. of Length by 30 of Width with an upper story Estimated According to the Specification in the state that it is in at................12,489.6.8
The House of the Manager of 40 ft. of Length by 20 of width Estimated according to the Specification at..5,197.7"
One Cabin of Stakes in the Ground of 24 ft. by 15 serving as a kitchen with an old Brick oven Estimated..170.""
One Cabin in which there is a Brick forge of 20 ft. by 15 [feet]...................80.""
One ditto of 20 by ditto serving as lodging to the blacksmith
One ditto for kitchen at the Hospital of the negroes. ....80.""
Thirty two ditto of 20 by 12 in a yard Surrounded by Palisades, Together   2,240.""
Two ditto at the gate and outside the said yard with brick chimney, and entrance gate of the camp..420.""
One ditto of 24 by 15 Serving as Stable and garden close and cattle pen.   <u>260.""</u>
                                                                                                                50,255.6"[20]

There followed a list of tools for the plantation, tools for the mill, tools for the forge, and a list of the Negroes by name, trade, and value.

In the same year, 1731, a plan of New Orleans was drawn by a man by the name of L'Herbours, which also shows the bank of the river opposite the city. Here he shows the land "cleared by the Company," with several buildings indicated, including a square palisaded enclosure, probably the camp for the Negro slaves. On the upriver side of the Company's land is shown the land "cleared by Mr. Perier."[21]

It was not long after that the plantation, now known as the Plantation of the King, was reduced in importance as an economy move. Le Page gives an interesting account of the last days of this notable plantation, the reduction of which closed his career in Louisiana.

> In 1734 M. Perier, Governor of Louisiana, was relieved by M. de Bienville, & the Plantation of the King was reduced as an economy in the intelligent manner of the one who advised the affair. A flatterer who wished to pay court to the Cardinal de Fleuri told this Minister that this plantation cost His Majesty ten thousand livres every year, & that he could be saved this sum. But this giver of counsels kept from telling His Eminence that this plantation, for these ten thousand livres, saved at least fifty [thousand].
>
> My post was reduced; I was also. Messrs. Perier and de Salmon engaged me to remain some months more on the plantation in order to manage the interests of the King in the sale which I made of the negroes, the price of which I knew better than anyone else. My superiors did what they could to excite me to remain, representing to me that in a short time there would certainly be some post vacated which would suit me at least as much as the one I had just exercised. Even M. de Bienville on his arrival, & when he had learned that I wished to return to France counselled me to remain for reasons which it would seem ought to have flattered me. But prudence spoke to me in a quite different tone. I replied, in spite of fine propositions, that my real interests determined me to make this decision in spite of myself. Then no promises were capable of retaining me there any longer. . . . We set sail the tenth of May 1734 . . . and arrived at the roadstead of Chaidbois before La Rochelle the twenty-fifth of June following, which made forty-five days crossing from Louisiana to France.[22]

In his *Histoire de la Louisiane*, Le Page describes how, while serving as manager of the plantation, he thwarted a plot among the slaves to revolt and seize New Orleans from the French. He reports having overheard a group of eight of them discussing the conspiracy secretly and managed to arrest them all without creating a disturbance in the camp. They were confined in the town prison, on the site of the present Cabildo, where they were tortured into confessing the plot, tried, convicted, and condemned. The one woman involved was hanged and the seven men were put to death on the rack.

No reference to this plot has been found in other colonial records, but there are two other references relating to Le Page in the records now in the Louisiana Historical Center of the Louisiana State Museum. In one case, dated May 18, 1729, Philippe François

Vellard, a carpenter, complained that Le Page had falsely accused him of theft. The other document is a power of attorney, granted by Le Page, "being on the point of crossing to France," to Honnorée Jean Breusle, dated April 27, 1734, less than two weeks before his departure on May 10. In this document, Le Page's full name is given as Jean-Ba[p]tiste Michel Le Page. This seems to be the same Le Page who wrote the *Histoire,* and whose name is generally given as Antoine Simon Le Page Du Pratz.

The king's plantation was not disposed of, and its buildings were still standing, though perhaps unused, on September 3, 1735, when Bienville and Salmon wrote that, the powder magazine being found entirely rotted, "we came to the decision of removing the powder, which we have had put in a warehouse on the plantation which the King had [obtained] from the Company on the other side of the river, where several minor repairs were made to a fence of stakes in the ground, and where M. de Bienville has established a guard of eleven men with an officer."[23]

By the following February, a new powder magazine had been built in the town and the powder removed from the plantation. It was soon after discovered that the plantation buildings were rapidly deteriorating, and on June 20, 1736, Bienville and Salmon wrote again:

> We see by a sad experience that all the buildings constructed in the time of the Company are falling in ruin, and that there is not one of them that is not in need of very urgent repairs, as much those which are in the town as those which are on the plantation which the King bought from the Company on the other side of the river. As this detail would be long completing, M. de Villers, who has seen them, will be able to render to Your Highness an exact account when the repairs will be entirely finished.[24]

These repairs preserved the king's buildings for a number of years, but by 1749 they were all in worse condition than ever. On August 3 of that year, Governor Pierre Rigaud de Vaudreuil and the Intendant Honoré Michel de Rouvillère reported on the general decay of the buildings throughout the colony, including those on the plantation, now known as the king's domain:

> All the buildings on the King's Domain opposite the city would be already down if they were not shored up in every direction. It is dangerous as the first windstorm will carry them off.... While awaiting your orders, we will still be obliged to have work done on the most pressing which cannot support any delay.[25]

A few days later, the king's engineer, Bernard Deverges, completed plans and specifications for a new house for the plantation manager to replace the one that had housed Le Page in the 1730s. These specifications are dated August 24, 1749, and the contract for its construction was signed with Joseph Dubreuil on August 27, for a house "built in masonry of 40 feet of length by 20 of width, outside dimensions in order to lodge the guardian-manager on the land of the Domain of His Majesty on the other side of the river, opposite New Orleans."[26] The completion of the work was reported by Deverges in his annual report of December 31, 1750.

The use to which the domain was being put is not entirely clear, but it was evidently quite different from its original use. It was no longer a plantation, but a sort of receiving station and storage place, and for this purpose Michel had another building erected, writing on September 29, 1750:

> I have likewise had built, as I have had the honor to send you word by my preceding [letters], a large shed of a hundred six feet of length on the Domain of the King opposite the city. This edifice, which is absolutely necessary for keeping the provisions, will be useful when disembarking new troops to form a hospital or a barracks building according to the need.[27]

On May 29, 1751, Michel reported that "the warehouses that I have had built for the King here [in New Orleans] and on His Domain are very well built and I can answer for this work."[28] This building was all of brick, and every precaution was taken to avoid the defects which had caused the decay of the earlier buildings. In the same letter, Michel wrote:

> That [decay] is because it was not foreseen that in a country as humid as this one, brick and mortar would conserve a dampness which would rot the joists and beams encased in it. The expedient which we have found and which we are using will be to dry them well in the fire and even to burn the ends and to have them covered with sheet lead before enclosing them in the walls. That is one of the first causes of the little durability of the King's buildings, which will not happen any more since we know the remedy for it. But there is place for believing also that there was not enough attention paid in the past to have good materials used. The brick was almost always badly made; and the mortar was never worth anything for lack of lime which was too sparingly used—and the little that was used was mixed, for lack of sand, with a rich and sandy earth which had little body with this lime. I have attended to this inconvenience since I have been here, and in order not to be obliged to send word about it every day as has been done formerly, I have preferred that it should cost the King more lime, and that the mortar be good, fat and solid.[29]

This warehouse was the last major building erected on the king's domain, although when Vincent de Rochemore became intendant, he proposed that a new powder magazine be erected there. He believed the one in town was too small and constituted a danger by its proximity, fearing that it might be struck by lightning. Instead of erecting a new building, however, the warehouse built by Michel became a powder magazine, and Rochemore established a poultry yard for his own use on part of the domain. This work was done and paid for in 1758 and 1759.[30]

In 1760, while France and England were still at war and the fortification of New Orleans was being undertaken, Rochemore found it necessary to rebuild the Negro cabins on the king's plantation, as was reported in the investigation of the conduct of Rochemore and Kerlérec conducted in Paris in 1764. Among the items listed in this reports was:

> 6th. The cabins of the King's negroes.
> A part of those which were still standing, falling in ruin through oldness, the Sr. de Rochemore ordered the construction of 20 to 25 new ones. One named Dubuelet was charged with this enterprise, and on 30 March 1760, a contract was made before the Notary of the Marine. The obligations of this contractor and the price of each cabin are explained in this contract.[31]

A few years later, in 1763, Louisiana was ceded by France to Spain and the king's plantation became the property of the king of Spain. On July 25, 1767, a general inventory and estimate of all the properties being transferred from France to Spain was begun by Denis Nicolas Foucault for France and Jean Joseph de Loyola for Spain.[32] Among the properties included in this detailed inventory was the king's plantation. Its boundaries were described as established in the survey of Lassus. The upper limit, which was then the plantation of the Sr. Pailloux, was now that of the late Sr. Pradel, and the lower limit, formerly Bienville's own land, was the property of the Widow Renault.

The new manager's house described in the inventory was quite different from the curious, medieval sort of house it was in 1732. It was a typical, small Louisiana plantation house of two large square rooms with a fireplace in each, backed up to each other on the partition wall. It had galleries on all four sides, a fairly steep roof, and dormer windows in the attic. The differences between this 1749 house and the earlier one illustrated in the DeBatz drawing of 1732 are significant in the development of Louisiana plantation architecture, for they illustrate the evolution of a regional style required by the exigencies of the climate. The frequent rains and strong sun made the addition of galleries a necessity if the soft brick masonry and timber framing of the walls were to be preserved, the doors and windows enabled to be left open for maximum ventilation, and the outside stairway protected. The kitchen of the new house was in an outbuilding of "posts in the ground, enclosed and roofed with stakes and with a masonry chimney."[33]

The masonry warehouse was also described in the inventory, but the old rice warehouse had evidently disappeared. The old pestle mill was still standing, in part, being described as a "shed with a lean-to at each end, under which shed is set up a pestle-mill; the whole done of posts in the ground and roofed with shingles."[34] There were also the numerous cabins which had been rebuilt by Rochemore in 1760. The total value of the plantation buildings was given at 57,219 *livres,* 17 *sols,* 7 *deniers.*

This inventory was made "in consequence of the orders that M. Charles Philippe Aubry, commandant for His Most Christian Majesty in Louisiana, has received to remit the said colony to Señor Don Antonio de Ulloa, sent by His Catholic Majesty to take possession of it."[35] After Ulloa was expelled from the colony in the Rebellion of 1768, Alexandro O'Reilly was sent to succeed him, to suppress the revolt, punish the revolutionists, and establish Spanish authority. O'Reilly was not satisfied with the inventory that had been made in 1767, considering the appraisals of the properties excessively high, and on September 27, 1769, ordered a new inventory and appraisal. With this new inventory were twelve plans "of all buildings belonging to His Most Christian Majesty in New Orleans and its environs."[36] Plan No. 11 was the "Plan of the Warehouse on the other side of the river." By then, O'Reilly had disposed of most of the land of the king's plantation, and a note on Plan No. 11 states:

> Note
> That this Plantation and its land were sold to Don Luis Beaurepos so they are omitted from the Plan.
> The warehouse [magazine] that is on this land belongs to His Majesty with all the land extending from its front to the margin of the river and twenty toises on the perpendicular of its other three sides, to the end that in the future it shall not have in its vicinity any combustible materials that might set it on fire.

A third inventory of these same properties in the archives of the Ursuline Convent is entitled:

> Inventory of the Public properties in New Orleans dated August 4, 1797, for comparison with a similar inventory made by Gov. Alexandro O'Reilly when he took possession of the colony.

This inventory was made by a royal order of Charles IV of Spain, dated March 28, 1794, and contains the following item:

> 11. Magazine and plantation on the other side of the river. The former is being used to keep Powder and the plantation has been sold to Don Luis Beaurepos. The lot that remains for the said magazine is fifty-seven toises, four feet [346 feet] front to the river and forty-five toises [270 feet] in depth.

This inventory in the Ursuline archives is accompanied by crudely drawn copies of the drawings included with O'Reilly's inventory, and was apparently made in support of the nuns' claim to some of the lands of the convent, the royal hospital, and the barracks.

With the sale to Beaurepos, the king's plantation passed into private ownership, except for a small, triangular lot in the upper corner where the powder magazine was located. The transfer of the plantation was made by O'Reilly to Beaurepos on February 3, 1770, who a few months later, on December 12, 1770, sold it to Jacques Rixner. On October 31, 1777, Rixner sold it to Pierre Burgand, whose will on February 6, 1786, left it to his nephew, Martial Lebeuf. Barthélemy Duverje bought it from Lebeuf on August 9, 1805, for $18,000, and a few days later, on August 14, 1805, sold the upper four arpents to Toussaint Mossy.[37]

The Plantation of the Company of the Indies

Pierre Clément de Laussat, who had been sent by Napoleon to Louisiana to receive the colony from Spain and who transferred it to the United States on December 20, 1803, in his memoirs described his visit to the powder magazine on May 21, 1803. He wrote:

> On the other side of the river, opposite the port, is situated the *Powder Magazine*. If it should blow up it would occasion great devastation to the town. The Baron de Carondelet had it built on what was formerly called the *Plantation of the King*. It appeared to have been quite neglected.[38]

Duverje built a fine plantation house with brick columns on the ground floor and rather heavy, round ones on pedestals on the upper story. The engraved map of the city from a survey by Jacques Tanesse in 1815, published in 1817, shows the Duverje house with its surrounding galleries and formally arranged outbuildings, gardens, and orchards. It also shows, in the upriver corner, a double row of fourteen barracks buildings near the powder magazine. A large group of buildings, gardens, and orchards is also shown on the adjacent Mossy plantation. The triangular upper corner of this property adjacent to the powder magazine is marked "property of the city."

Soon after the death of Barthélémy Duverje in 1820, his widow, Alix Bienvenu, decided to dispose of the plantation and inserted the following advertisement in the *Louisiana Courier* for January 29, 1821:

> FOR SALE
>
> MRS. WIDOW DUVERJE offers for sale, by lots, squares, and tracts, agreeably to the plan deposited at Mr. Hughes Lavergne notary's office, No. 76, Chartres street, made out by Mr. C. N. Bouchon, surveyor general of the state, the plantation of the late Barthélémy Duverjé, situate opposite the city of New Orleans.
>
> That property is too well known to need any particular description. It will only be observed that the communications with the city have lately been much facilitated by the establishment of a steam ferry which has just been put into operation, and that said property, the sale of which shall be made agreeable to the above mentioned plan, presents a fair opportunity to speculate, and has on it the three following buildings, to wit:
>
> 1st. A fine two story dwelling house, built of bricks with pillars and a gallery all round, measuring 72 feet in length on 52 in width, consisting of 12 apartments besides eight closets. In the yard are 4 pavilions and the negro huts all built of brick.
>
> 2d. Another house, built of bricks, between posts, measuring 60 feet in length on 30 in width.
>
> 3d. Finally, a brick yard, measuring about two superficial arpents, containing a kiln, sheds, and all the other requisites to begin working immediately.
>
> The houses and buildings above mentioned are new and well made, and shall if required be bartered for brick houses well situated in the city of New Orleans, or for slaves.

On March 4, 1826, Madame Duverje purchased and extensively remodeled the old house of Dr. Joseph Montegut, now 731 Royal Street.[39] She died in 1838.

The plan for the subdivision of the plantation, drawn by State Surveyor General C. N. Bouchon in 1821, was oriented so that the plantation house was in the exact center of one of the squares. The house faced Villeré Street (since renamed Morgan), between Seguin and Barthélémi (since renamed Bermuda), and Delaronde in the rear. The plan of the Duverje subdivision, as shown on the Charles F. Zimpel plan of 1834, is probably based on the original Bouchon plan of 1821. The streets were named for family members or neighbors of the Bienvenu plantation on the site of the Battle of New Orleans. The widow Duverje was a daughter of Antoine Bienvenu. The street on the west side nearest the river was called Church Street, probably intended for a church site. The next street parallel to it terminated at the old Spanish powder magazine. All of Church Street and most of Powder Street, as well as the site of the old magazine, have since been swallowed up by the river. The powder magazine partially collapsed in 1826 and a contract for a new one five miles below the city, designed by Joseph Pilié, was awarded to G. G. Holdship, builder, on February 25, 1836.[40]

In 1833 the remaining four arpents of the old plantation of the Company of the Indies, which had been sold in 1805 by Duverje to Toussaint Mossy, were subdivided and sold at auction. On February 26, 1833, Mossy inserted the following in the *Courier:*

TO-MORROW
BY F DUTILLET

PLANTATION MOSSY, in Lots at public auction.—The subscriber begs leave to notify the public, that having been repeatedly solicited for years past, to divide and lay off into Town Lots, (by persons desirous of purchasing and establishing themselves there,) his beautiful, and in point of situation, unique, country seat, (believing that the time has now arrived when the public interest requires that it should be done,) has in consequence, formed a plan thereof, assisted by Joseph Pilié, Esq., city surveyor, on a grand and extensive scale, and will offer it for sale in Lots, at public auction, at Hewlett's coffee house, on Wednesday the 27th day of February, instant, at 12 o'clock, on a credit of one, two and three years, with notes, satisfactorily endorsed, and mortgage on the property until final payment. To my fellow citizens generally, nothing further than the above notification would be necessary, but for the information of the great number of strangers now among us, I will add that this estate now laid off into town lots, is situated on the right bank of the river Mississippi, immediately in front of the city of New Orleans, (covering its point from opposite the lower market house, up to the custom house,) that its site is not equalled in beauty by any other in the neighborhood of New Orleans, and that it possesses many and great advantages. The city and harbor of New Orleans, laying in front of it, (the whole of which is taken in by the eye at a single glance,) with the river, and adjacent suburbs on either hand, makes the view from it magnificent and delightful. Its harbor is excellent, and in point of security for vessels, greatly superior to that of New Orleans, as it is defended by its banks and position, from the most dangerous winds; and possesses a bold shore with water of sufficient depth for vessels of the largest class; ships, in consequence, can heave down, or load and

The Plantation of the Company of the Indies 341

unload their cargoes there with great facility; and the time is not distant when in its magazines and store houses, will be deposited a great part of the productions of our vast interior. From the situation of this town it must rapidly increase, lying, as it does, between the two towns of Macdonogh on one side, and Duverges on the other, with the streets and avenues of which town, the streets and avenues of this, are made to intersect and correspond. Nothing is wanted to give an immediate and great value to property on the opposite side of the river to New Orleans, and to induce persons in easy circumstances to reside there with their families in preference to residing on the city side, but two steam ferry boats, which constantly ply between the two banks, (which boats are now about to be established.) Were those boats now running, let me ask, would any man of common sense, any mechanic, carter, drayman, or laborer, whose business lay in the city, purchase property or reside in the suburbs of Lafayette or Livaudais, (requiring a walk through the mud or hot sun, of three miles to reach their house, and three miles back to return,) when they might cross the river and be at home in five minutes time—certainly no, not one. Even now with the common boats used as a ferry, the river is crossed in six or eight minutes, (it being nineteen hundred feet only in width,) so that a person living on the other side of the river, may leave Mr. Hewlett's coffee house, and be at home in eight or ten minutes with all ease. In point of health, (the yellow fever never having been on that side of the river,) and the elevation of the land is not exceeded by any on the river. As these lots will be sold without reserve, for such prices as shall be offered, it is but seldom that such opportunities for good investments occur. The plan, which is one offering great advantages, will be exhibited at the Exchange in a few days.

Also, after the sale of the lots, a gang of 40 SLAVES, belonging to me, will be sold at a credit of one and two years.

feb 26 TOUSSAINT MOSSY

Pilié's plan for the Mossy plantation subdivision was tied into and became an integral part of the plan of McDonoghville, immediately upriver from it. The streets of Duverjeville were at a sharp angle to McDonogh's, which were laid out parallel and perpendicular to the river, while the earlier subdivision streets were laid out in relation to the Duverje house. These streets were originally intended to extend to the rear point of the plantation, but these back lots were apparently not sold, and eventually the area beyond what is now Opelousas Street was integrated into the McDonoghville-Mossy street pattern. The entire west bank area, which was annexed to New Orleans in 1870, had become known as Algiers before 1849.

The splendid Duverje mansion, one of the finest early Louisiana plantation houses, became a city police station and courthouse in 1869, and was destroyed in the great Algiers fire in October 1895.[41]

The present Algiers courthouse on the same site was erected in 1896, designed by City Engineer Linus Brown and Alonzo Bell. John McNally was the contractor. The site of the French colonial Plantation of the Company of the Indies is now absorbed in the thriving community of Algiers.

APPENDIX A
Foucault Inventory, 1767

Extract from "A General Inventory and Estimation of All the Artillery, Arms, Munitions, Effects, Warehouses, Hospitals, Vessels, Etc., Belonging to His Very Christian Majesty, in the Colony of Louisiana." [Made by Foucault on remitting the colony to Spain, dated July 25, 1767.] AC, C 13a, 46:131.

THE BUILDINGS OF THE PLANTATION OF THE KING ON THE RIGHT BANK OF THE RIVER OPPOSITE NEW ORLEANS

These buildings are situated on a terrain of 18 arpents of frontage to the river deriving from the Comp[an]y of the Indies, forming a scalene triangle, whose joint upper limit with the plantation of the late Sr. Pradel is of 24 arpents in length running in depth to the S, and its joint lower limit with the plantation of Mme Widow Renault of 25 arpents in length running in depth to the SE, according the *procès verbal* of survey of the Sr. La Suze, under the date of October 1, 1727, signed by Messrs. Perier, Commandant-General; Delachaise, Director of the Company; and de Noyant, acting for Monsr. de Bienville.

The Building of Masonry

serving as lodging for the manager of 40 ft. in length by 20 feet in width with galleries of 7 ft. in width on the two fronts and of 10 ft. on the two gable ends.

Excavation of Earth

The digging for the trenches of the foundations of the exterior walls as well as of the partitions, of the sub-base of the walls of the galleries, of the gable ends, of the double chimney and of the enveloping walls of its chimneys, as well as of the ramps of the two entrance stairs to the front galleries...23.0.0

Gross Masonry

The gross masonry which composes the building . . . from which it is considered proper to deduct 500 *livres* for minor repairs to be made to this said masonry as well as to the masonry that which is going to be mentioned here below..............................5,384.3.4

*Masonry Between Colombage
of 4 inches in thickness*

The filling in masonry between the framing of the partition to which the double chimney is backed, and that between the framing of the walls that form the revetment of the closets under the gallery...236.11.10

The Plantation of the Company of the Indies 343

Chimney Masonry

The double chimney measured from top to bottom..227.17.3

Pavement in Brick Flatwise

The brick paving of the hearths of the two chimneys...................................... 26.11.3

Framing

The wood employed in the construction of this building 2,924.18.0

Roofing

This building is roofed with shingles on laths which is so old that mention is made of it only as a memorandum... Memorandum

Carpentry

The upper and lower floors of the main building as well as of the galleries and various partitions ... of various types of carpentry ... in consideration of their service
.... 1,203.10.10

The seven doors with their casings and frames and the fifteen shutters for the windows as well as for the dormers ... in consideration of their service...................... 231.0.0

Iron for Heavy Duty

The heavy iron employed in this building consists of sixty-eight hinges of two branches, four chimney girths and two bars for the recess 380.16.0

Hardware

The hardware for the doors, shutters, dormers, etc., consists of thirty-eight pairs of plate hinges, seven locks, fourteen spring bolts, large as well as small, seven thumb latches, fifteen hooks, fifteen handles, and sixteen foot bolts..<u>444.10.0</u>
11,082.18.6

THE KITCHEN FOR THE USAGE OF THIS BUILDING

This building is thirty ft. in length by fourteen ft. in width, of posts in the ground, enclosed and roofed with stakes, with a masonry chimney and a lean-to affixed to the said kitchen also made of posts in the ground, enclosed and roofed with stakes, with a masonry oven and its roof of stakes, estimated in a bloc.. 375.0.0

THE MASONRY WAREHOUSE

of one hundred four feet ten inches in length, by thirty feet six inches in width.

Excavation of Earth

The digging of trenches for the foundations 91.13.4

Gross Masonry

All the gross masonry that composes this building, including a mass that was made after its construction, in order to place there a trough or mortar destined for the work of refining defective powders—from which it is deemed proper to deduct six hundred livres for the minor repairs to make to this masonry as well as to that of the chimneys which is going to be treated hereafter.. 17,234.11.8

Chimney Masonry

The masonry for the two chimneys as well as for the ten dormers.................. 1,025.18.4

Framing

The wood employed in the construction of this building 9,677.14.0

Roofing

This building is roofed with shingles nailed on a board surface instead of laths—in consideration of its oldness...1,832.13.4

Lead-work

The valleys of the ten dormers are lined with lead 250.0.0

Carpentry

The flooring downstairs on the ground floor is made of boards two inches in thickness planed on one side and tongued and grooved—in consideration of its service..... 1,620.19.5

The flooring of the garret and the revetment of the tambour at the top of the staircase of the said garret 1,274.17.6

The three doors on the front as well as of the partition, the upper part of the imposts (transoms) of two of these doors, and the twenty-two shutters of the ground floor windows as well as of the dormers—in consideration of their oldness 169.17.6

Iron for Heavy Duty

The iron for heavy duty employed in this said building consists of forty-eight spikes for the ventilators under the flooring of the ground floor, of four corner irons at the four angles of the building, of two anchors for the partition-walls, of sixteen tie-rods for the small beams, of twenty-four other tie-rods for the sleepers of the entablature, of two anchors in double "S" for the flues of the two chimneys, of sixty hinges of two branches on the doors and windows, of four girths and two bars for the recesses of the two chimneys..3,193.9.0

Hardware

The hardware employed in this building consists of fifty-three pairs of plate hinges, three pairs of butt hinges, two strikers in masonry, eight spring bolts, four thumb latches, with handle, three locks, two round bolts, forty-four hooks, forty-four handles, forty-four supports, twenty stirrups, and three swivel ring bolts...................................... 714.5.0

CABINS PROVIDED FOR THE NEGROES AND OTHER DEPENDENT PARTS OF THE SAID PLANTATION

A shed with a lean-to at each end; under which shed is set up a pestle mill; the whole done of posts in the ground and roofed with shingles....................................1,800.0.0

A cabin of twenty-eight feet in length by sixteen in width enclosed and roofed with stakes... 100.0.0

Another cabin of thirty feet in length by eighteen feet in width enclosed with stakes and roofed with clapboards... 500.0.0

Another lean-to cabin roofed and enclosed like the preceding 80.0.0

Twenty-one negro cabins of twenty-four feet in length each by thirteen feet in width enclosed and roofed with stakes 5,250.0.0

The enclosures of upright stakes constituting the yards, garden, and other dependencies of this plantation (not including the enclosures or fences of its limits)—in consideration of their oldness... 910.0.0

In those enclosures are found four communication gates in their frames with their hardware—in view of their bad condition.. 36.0.0

57,219*l*.17*s*.7*d*

Total for the Buildings of the Plantation of the King

Fifty-seven thousand two hundred nineteen livres, seventeen sols, seven deniers.

APPENDIX B
Vinache Inventory, 1804
AC, C 13a, 53:155

18th February 1804

*Estimate of the large powder magazine situated
on the left bank of the river opposite the city of New Orleans*

This magazine of 210 feet of length by 18 of height is divided by two partitions of masonry in its interior; its width is of 32 feet. The general survey of the masonry of this building has given to the total the quantity of 37 toises cubed and 204 feet. The bad state of this masonry, which can only be regarded as susceptible of being demolished, has made it estimate 180# the toise cube, which makes in silver of France..........................4,050

A guardhouse and a kitchen, dependents of the powder magazine, the whole in very bad state has given to the survey 3 toises cubed estimated in total...............................200#

Hardware

All the hardware of this magazine consists in bulk iron, locks, shutter furnishings, bolts, hinges, and it has been estimated at..565

Framing and Carpentry

The framing and carpentry estimated (after the compared actual prices of wood and workmanship) for all the buildings designated above, the whole evaluated at the price of 3,155.2

Joseph Vinache
Battalion Chief of Engineers

Laussat

Notes for "The Plantation of the Company of the Indies"

[1] "Sidelights on Louisiana History," *Louisiana Historical Quarterly*, 1 (1917): 140.

[2] Archives Nationales, Paris, France, Archives des Colonies, Series C 13a (General Correspondence of Louisiana), volume 6, folio 346; hereafter cited as AC, C 13a, with volume and folio numbers.

[3] Ibid., 8:65; "Sidelights on Louisiana History," 139.

[4] Louisiane—Recensements, 41, Louisiana State Museum, Louisiana Historical Center, New Orleans, Louisiana; Archives Nationales, Paris, France, Archives des Colonies, Series G1 (Civilian lists), volume 464, non-paginated; hereafter cited as AC, G1, with volume and folio numbers.

[5] Kuntz Collection, Howard-Tilton Memorial Library, Tulane University, New Orleans, Louisiana.

[6] AC, C 13a, 8:127.

[7] Ibid, 146.

[8] Ibid., 9:82.

[9] Ibid., 140.

[10] Recensements, 180.

[11] Ibid., 177.

[12] AC, C 13a, 10:169.

[13] "Sidelights on Louisiana History," 130; Recensements, 351.

[14] Le Page du Pratz, *Histoire de la Louisiane*, 3 vols. (Paris, 1758), 1:340.

[15] Ibid., 3:226.

[16] AC, C 13a, 11:51.

[17] Concessions, p. 24, Louisiana Historical Center.

[18] AC, C 13a, 11:9.

[19] Ibid., 13:3.

[20] Ibid., 24:784.

[21] Estampes, Bibliothèque Nationale, Paris, France.

[22] Le Page du Pratz, *Histoire*, 3:397.

[23] AC, C 13a, 20:116.

[24] Ibid., 21:62.

[25] Ibid., 34:28.

[26] Miscellaneous Louisiana Manuscripts, fol. 914, Library of Congress, Washington, D.C.

[27] AC, C 13a, 34:347.

[28] Ibid., 35:266.

[29] Ibid.

[30] Miscellaneous Louisiana Manuscripts, fols. 1341-1357.

[31] AC, C 13a, 44:181.

[32] Ibid., 46:131.

[33] Ibid.

[34] The DeBatz drawings are illustrated in Samuel Wilson, Jr., "Louisiana Drawings by Alexandre DeBatz," *Journal of the Society of Architectural Historians,* 22 (1963): 75-89.

[35] AC, C 13a, 46:131.

[36] Kuntz Collection.

[37] Lafcadio Hearn et al., *Historical Sketch Book and Guide to New Orleans* (New York, 1885), 287; Acts of Narcisse Broutin, August 9, 1805, Vol. 10, No. 594, New Orleans Notarial Archives; hereafter cited as N.O.N.A.

[38] Pierre Clément de Laussat, *Mémoires sur ma vie à mon fils* (Paris, 1851), 41; Pierre Clément de Laussat, *Memoirs of My Life to My Son during the Years 1803 and After . . . ,* ed. by Robert Bush, trans. by Agnes Josephine Pastwa (Baton Rouge, 1978).

[39] Acts of H. Lavergne, March 4, 1826, N.O.N.A.

[40] New Orleans *Louisiana Courier,* June 14, 1826; Acts of Felix de Armas, February 26, 1836, Vol. 47, No. 69, N.O.N.A.

[41] *New Orleans Daily Picayune,* week of March 16, 1869; Acts of A. Hero, Jr., September 13, 1870, Vol. 11, No. 3210, N.O.N.A.

NEW ORLEANS SOCIETY*

Marcel Giraud

New Orleans was a town under construction, in which administrative buildings were still few and the overall visual monotony was broken only by some gardens "for show," laid out near the parade ground, and in the first row of blocks.[1] Yet a new society already was being formed here, despite all the hazards entailed by life in a settlement hemmed in so closely by the natural environment.

It was a society whose diverse origins reflected the still-recent period of John Law and his concept of the colony. Some persons, come from all parts of France, remained in Louisiana from that period; those who possessed particular manual skills strove to profit by them in the new capital where they had just settled. They were joined by artisans who had come from France on their own initiative. Together, these groups formed a nucleus of small craftsmen, without much capital, who provided as well as they could for the needs of the nascent town and the elementary demands of its population. Other newcomers took jobs as servants to families of a certain status or, perhaps, in some cases, in the administrative or hospital services. The census of January 1726 records, in a population of 600, about fifty servants or hired persons and nearly sixty craftsmen doing the sort of work usual in any growing town: blacksmiths, bakers, carpenters, joiners, tailors, locksmiths. It is not possible to discover what proportion of these servants and artisans had previously been members of the staffs of the concessions. Ordinary day laborers and workmen capable of manual tasks but having no particular skill were not very numerous, as Madeleine Hachard noted as soon as she arrived.[2] On the other hand, as was to be expected in this colony and in accordance with the possibilities it offered, there were about a score of *voyageurs* and hunters. The *voyageurs*, specialists in navigating the river, were often from Canada, though some were sons of families exiled in Law's time. They moved constantly up and down the river, taking supplies to the remoter posts. The hunters spent the winter months in the region where the buffalo grazed, beyond the

---

*Excerpt first published in chapter 6 of Marcel Giraud, *A History of French Louisiana, Vol. 5: The Company of the Indies, 1723-1731* (Baton Rouge: Louisiana State University Press, © 1987), 256-85.

Arkansas River and especially around the Saint François (Saint Francis) river, and in the spring brought down from there the salted or smoked meat of these animals to be sold freely in New Orleans.[3]

The scene changed little between 1726 and 1727, except that the number of craftsmen increased markedly. The census of July 1727 mentions 106 of them in a population of 800, distributed among the crafts mentioned above. Particularly noticeable was a sharp increase in the number of skilled building workers, owing to the growing number of construction jobs in the public and private domains. There were twenty carpenters in 1727 as against ten in 1726, and eleven joiners instead of five. A squarer had appeared, to see to the shaping of the building timbers, and there were also "nail makers," to serve the growing demand for nails in the frame houses, where the beams and half-timber crosses hitherto had been merely tied to the sole of the building.[4]

It is difficult, however, to establish where these new craftsmen had come from, especially as not many of the ones listed in 1726 reappeared in the list for the following year; further, the passenger lists of ships going to Louisiana at that time make no mention of craftsmen for the colony.[5] Was this increase the effect of apprenticeships already instituted in New Orleans or of the retreat to the town of the concessions' last indentured servants, who increasingly were being replaced in agricultural work by black labor?

Certainly, beginning in 1727 and continuing until 1730, the Company of the Indies revived the articles of engagement current in Law's time and proceeded to recruit a relatively large number of men in the ports of La Rochelle, Lorient, and Saint-Malo. At La Rochelle some were hired through Captain Jean Béranger, who had long experience of sailing to and from Louisiana, but most were hired by Henry Edme, "correspondent of the Company of the Indies and of Louisiana." At Lorient the hiring was done by the commandant of the port, Pierre de Fayet. At Saint-Malo it was the royal notaries of the town who drew up the contracts of engagement, which concerned mainly men from Saint Servan, recruited by an agent of whom little is known, one Etienne La Vallée, a master shipbuilder who himself may have gone to Louisiana. Several of these contracts are indexed also in the records of the notary Girard at La Rochelle.[6]

The yearly wages offered by the Company usually ranged from 300 to 400 *livres*, payable in the currency of the country, for a period of three or four years. The hired man was to be fed according to "the usual workman's ration" and might enjoy extra benefits if he could make himself especially useful, for instance by teaching a skill to a black.[7] But the rate fell to 150 *livres* a year in the case of a mere pit sawyer. The Company managed in this way to send to Louisiana forty-nine indentured servants, most of whom were coopers, caulkers, or carpenters, with a few masons and brickmakers.[8]

In principle, all these men served the Company, which had engaged them and which paid them. In fact, this work force also served the common interests of the colony as a whole. The coopers' task made possible an increase in the packing and shipment of tobacco, which was good both for the Company and for the producers. The caulkers worked primarily for the Company, which owned the somewhat larger vessels that sailed on the river and along the coast, but they also served the numerous private owners of smaller boats, thereby increasing the inhabitants' opportunities for moving supplies and for travel. The masons and carpenters were intended by the Company, first and foremost, to help with the building work that its engineers were doing in New Orleans and at the Balise. In 1728, however, when it made redundant a large number of the carpenterrs, joiners, and pit sawyers it employed (so as to leave the contractors free to choose their own workmen), the Company thereby increased the number of skilled men available to the public. Sometimes its contracts even gave permission for a hired man to free-lance as he pleased in the hours or days when he was not working for the Company.[9]

This group of about fifty craftsmen, together with those already in the colony, would have helped the settlers even more if many of those hired had not been alarmed at the prospect of long residence in so badly reputed a country. The poverty in which most of them had lived in France had been the principal motive for their contracting to serve in Louisiana, and several already were thinking of nothing so much as how to get out of their obligations—even before they reached the Mississippi. This was the case with Jean Lescot, one of the two specialists in the storing of tobacco: having arrived in Louisiana in the *Dromadaire* in 1731, he left in the same ship, despite the advances he had been paid by the Company before quitting France. Departing with him in the *Dromadaire* were four of the seven indentured servants who had arrived in the same year in the *Gironde*.[10] True, the Company had just abandoned responsibility for Louisiana; this also may have had something to do with the large number of persons who left in the *Saint André*, several of them being indentured servants who probably were worried at the prospect of no longer receiving their wages.

Moreover, for many people, Louisiana was still a country to which convicted criminals were transported. In fact, although the practice of transportation had not ceased altogether, it was now confined to isolated cases: a few commutations of sentences for desertion into service for life in the colony; some fairly numerous instances, especially in 1729, of exile for cheaters of the tobacco monopoly; and also one nobleman, a certain chevalier de Conflans de Brienne, the reason for whose punishment is unknown but whose identity it was sought to conceal under the name of Champlain. But all these sentences remained merely theoretical, owing to the Company's hostility to the principle of transportation. Its directors general in Paris urged the king not to transport anyone to Louisiana, because of the harm this could do. They even reminded him that transportation had been abolished in 1720 and that its principal disadvantage lay in exposing the colony to the danger of desertions, as in the case of an advocate named Blanchard's son, who was arrested as he was on the point of crossing into Spanish territory.[11]

In reality, the cheaters of the tobacco monopoly never left Lorient, and the chevalier de Conflans remained in the citadel of Port-Louis.[12] At most there were the embarkations of two tobacco-monopoly cheaters (at the time, a Lyons merchant was still asking that his son be sent to Louisiana as punishment for misbehavior).[13] Also in 1730, a temporary exile figured in the *Baleine*'s passenger list, but under the guise of a prominent person. In 1731 an illegal salt maker became the last person transported to Louisiana before the retrocession. Nevertheless, taken together with the transportations of earlier years, the number of which cannot be precisely estimated, these few cases gave the population the impression that there were still too many of them, burdening the town with "idle and unskilled persons," and the Council proposed to get them out of New Orleans by exiling them to places in the interior, as many people advised.[14]

Perhaps this stigma at least partly explains why there was no immigration, in the strict sense, into Louisiana in the last years of the Company of the Indies, apart from individual engagements contracted for by the Company or arranged by a few settlers during visits to France—for example, the four sabot makers recruited in Bas-Limousin by Jean de Pradel and an inhabitant of New Orleans with a view to introducing into the colony a trade, still unknown there in 1730, that could provide strong footwear for the nearly always barefooted slaves, whose feet soon went bad. Here and there an edge-tool maker, a carpenter's mate, or a tailor took passage to Louisiana without any contract and at his own expense, in the hope of finding employment. Also, a few craftsmen were in the personal service of officers or settlers.[15] But these passages, few and far between, brought no substantial contribution to the colony.

More interesting was the Company's attempt to launch a policy of settlement by granting special facilities to women who wished to go to Louisiana and make their homes there, as well as to indentured servants accompanied by their wives and children, the family being conveyed free and fed at the Company's expense during the voyage. The Company had no objection to paying a gratuity to a workman's daughter going out to Louisiana if she agreed to stay and get married there. It even assembled trousseaux for the two daughters of an inhabitant who was going to settle in the colony. The Company thus revived the already time-honored procedure of the "casket girls," who were given the money they needed to buy their trousseaux, and also paid an allowance until they married. On this basis, nineteen girls set out in the *Loire* in 1724, each equipped with a trousseau that the Company had enabled her to buy, and with the Company's promise to support her until marriage.[16]

Sometimes a woman would come to the office of the Company's representative in La Rochelle and express the wish to settle in the colony. The agent would agree at once, giving her the 200 *livres* she needed to assemble her trousseau, along with 15 *sols* per day to meet her living expenses before she embarked; he also would promise, in a deed authenticated by a notary, to maintain her during the voyage and until she was settled. This happened, for example to Marie-Louise Mariette, aged nearly 16, from Trèves, the daughter of a surgeon and medical officer in Saillant's regiment. She applied to go to "the new town of Orleans" in Louisiana in order to "work to the best of her ability and settle down there."[17] She set out in April 1728, along with three other women (one of them a widow, accompanied by her daughter) for whom Henry Edme had promised the same conditions; she married in the colony about six months later.[18]

The passenger lists often recorded the departure of widows alone or with close female relatives, all receiving the usual sum of 200 *livres* paid by the Company for the cost of a trousseau. A few women traveled on their own and at their own expense or relied on the Company's promise to pay them the usual wage of an indentured servant, 400 *livres* a year, until they married.[19] Through these forms of encouragement that the Company offered for the creation of new houholds, together with its readiness to convey free of charge wives who wished to join their husbands who were serving in the colony as workmen or soldiers, it would have been possible, had the experiment been continued longer, gradually to renew the population of New Orleans without resorting to the questionable system of compulsory transportation of girls—which system [Etienne] Périer nevertheless advised should be reintroduced.[20]

The women who went to Louisiana found themselves in a country where poverty was the keynote and where remarkably high prices corresponded to a general shortage of goods. As soon as he arrived in the colony, Périer was astonished by this state of penury. He noted in particular the extreme scarcity of coal, which was essential for the smithies, and the lack of salt, which resulted in excessive prices being charged, even as much as 60 *livres* a pound. Everything needed for the creation of normal conditions of life was in short supply, beginning with clothing: articles of everyday usage, cloth, fabric, shirts, ribbons, footwear, wigs—everything was scarce, expensive, and of poor quality. The Council considered, not without reason, that the colony was treated as the outlet for trash that merchants in France wanted to dispose of for a good price.[21] Prices did indeed reach extreme levels. A pair of stockings in bad repair, for example, worth six *sols* in France, sold for six *livres* in New Orleans. Broadly speaking, prices were three or four times as high in Louisiana as in France, and it is understandable why the Council spoke in its correspondence of the need to help good people who were in want.[22]

Lighting also presented a serious problem in New Orleans. There were practically no candles in the colony, and the candles that were sent from France usually arrived either broken or melted as a result of the heat. [Jacques de] La Chaise advised that tallow be sent instead. This material could have been used to make candles during the winter months, and it was especially needed for lighting and handling of brigantines after nightfall. In 1724 candles were still so scarce that they usually arrived in passengers' personal baggage, and the Council sometimes was obliged to appeal to passing Spaniards in order to supply the colony with its needs.[23] Candles alone enabled the guardhouse to be lighted and deserters pursued by night, and they were indispensable for landing goods from ships at the Balise, which sometimes was practical only at night, owing to the tide. In 1727, with consignments from the Illinois country and an increase in the number of pigs, the situation improved slightly. In spite of everything, candles continued to be a scarce commodity, since the natural wax from wild plants had not been exploited sufficiently to provide the material required.[24]

Destitution prevailed in many other spheres, too. Some may seem of minor importance, but they counted for much in so unprovided a country. The scarcity of nails, already mentioned, was a great obstacle to the construction of houses, especially since the nails that arrived from France were usually brittle and poorly shaped, so that twice as many were needed as should have been. As soon as the meager stock of nails was exhausted, makeshift methods had to be employed, beams being tied as best one could to the base that supported them. Paper also was in short supply. Especially troublesome was the inadequate availability of ropes of every kind, these being essential both for the ships and for dragging trees out of the cypress groves.[25]

Glass could be used only in a few buildings, such as the house of direction, since the colony had to wait till 1728 for the first consignments of this material, together with the first diamond for cutting it.[26] Before that, glass usually was substituted for by transparent fabric that was itself hard to obtain. Madeleine Hachard expressed pleasure, when she arrived, at the transparency of the platilla used in place of window glass in the Ursulines' house, not realizing that most of the inhabitants, the majority of whom were poor, used more common pieces of fabric, often not transparent at all, which formed the only protection for their windows. Penury was marked in every aspect of life. Horses and cattle were becoming more numerous but there was no harness for either, and no leather suitable for making it. In 1729 there was still no saddler in the colony, nor even a specialist in farriery. All that was to be had was some sets of harness, gone rotten, left from the first years of immigration when there had been no use for them, and with these the settlers had to make do.[27]

As for the town's food supply, for a long time it was as poverty-stricken as everything else, and there could be actual famine when consignments from the home country failed to arrive. The year 1723, which followed several years of shortage, was especially hard. Only a small quantity of foodstuffs and beverages arrived from France, and war with the Natchez Indians, which had erupted the previous fall, had held up the arrival of "wild food," especially corn. These circumstances resulted in a kind of famine to which La Chaise and Raphaël testified. The arrival at the beginning of 1724 of the *Chameau,* laden with food and commodities, saved the situation for the moment. But the floods that occurred that spring prevented sowing of the land between New Orleans and the Natchez country, and they were followed by six weeks of uninterrupted rain. The famine thus caused was made still worse by the arrival in the first months of 1724 of the slave ships *Expédition* and *Courrier de Bourbon,* bringing additional mouths to feed. The situation seemed so bad that the councilors instituted a systematic visitation of barns and storehouses to discover whether there remained some reserves of foodstuffs that might prevent an excessive increase in the prices of rice and corn—which took place anyway, despite all their efforts.[28]

These were two of the colony's most difficult years. Improvement came only in 1725. Three ships arrived from France in quick succession, the year's harvests were comparatively good (largely owing to the levees with which the inhabitants had protected their fields), and the growing herds of cattle furnished a plentiful supply of meat, competing with the salt buffalo brought down in the spring from the hunting grounds.

New Orleans Society

Nevertheless, the two years that followed were still uncertain, even though the local produce—rice, corn, beans, sweet potatoes, pumpkins—could now make up to some extent for the inadequacy of imports, especially as corn was being eaten more than before, along with bread made of a mixture of rice and flour, consumed by those who lived on the Company's rations.[29]

Not until 1728 did the food situation become stabilized. Périer was then able to inform the Company that no shortage of meat had been experienced during the summer, whereas, normally, few animals were slaughtered during the hottest months, owing to the risk of decomposition. In 1730 Périer considered that the colony was in a position to feed its inhabitants and the soldiers stationed there out of its own resources, because the blacks had begun to develop the land, because the irrigation works increasingly ensured the rice harvests even in periods of drought, and because butchers' meat was beginning to be widely available in summer—though only if one had something to offer in exchange, what was most appreciated being brandy, because of its invigorating power.[30]

Even if not independent as regards food supply, the colony did have produce of its own that furnished precious aid to its economy: bear grease came in through the Natchitoches post and served as cooking oil, lard, and butter in place of butter and olive oil, which could not be kept in summer in the Company's storehouses; rice and corn could be used instead of wheat flour when properly hulled or ground (mills were now widespread, so less slave labor was needed for these tasks); vegetables were abundant; and fish was to be had in great quantity in Lake Pontchartrain. The country could not do without France altogether, as the food from home was considered indispensable, especially the flour and wine that in many cases constituted the workmen's wages. There was, indeed, the resource provided by the wheat flour of the Illinois country. But access to that depended on freedom of navigation on the Mississippi, and the Natchez revolt that began in 1729 showed the brittleness of this link. Thus, Périer in 1732 expressed the hope that the Crown would not cease altogether to send foodstuffs from France to Louisiana, since otherwise the country would remain vulnerable so long as peace was not completely restored along the river.[31]

And yet, despite deficiencies, the supply of locally grown produce to New Orleans was gradually organized in the years before the Natchez uprising. A beginning had been made in conveying to town the produce of the habitations spread out along the river, especially those of the Germans, whose fields, tilled by hard-working and orderly people, contributed an abundance of vegetables of very kind, as well as maintaining sizable numbers of pigs and poultry. These habitations were twenty-five miles upstream from New Orleans, however, and access to the town entailed a long voyage by pirogue through the confused mass of timber borne down by the river. In 1724, despite the distance, pirogues laden with vegetables created a rudimentary market on the levee, at the point where the vessels landed. The entire population, reinforced by soldiers and sailors, went to meet them and, in an episode typical of frontier society, seized the produce and carried it off by force, cheating the Germans of the profit of their protracted labors. The Conseil

Supérieur had to intervene to stop this practice. It forbade the popoulation to board the vessels, ordering them to wait until the producers had set out their goods on the parade ground before making the purchases they needed. To prevent any disorder, this operation was placed under supervision of the Council's registrar, aided by a guard of soldiers. This was the first market in New Orleans, and it seems to have continued for some time on the spot assigned to it by the Council, although it may have moved closer to the river in 1725: the Council noted that it was held "at the edge of the water." Possibly, also, retail trade began to be carried on in private houses, where the goods sold may not have been solely those supplied by the German market gardeners. In any case, in 1728 Périer and La Chaise reserved a site for the market "in the front part of the town." Behind the market they planned to establish butchers' shops, against the day when cattle would be available in sufficient numbers to be sold at retail. This project, however, seems not to have been implemented by the time the Company gave up the colony.[32]

The women who arrived from France intending to make their homes in this remote province must have felt bitter disappointment at first. The shortage of goods, the housing conditions, the food situation, and the country itself—especially its climate—all must have seemed repellent to them. The marriages they made often failed to improve their living conditions, for they were placed in the midst of an all-round poverty. If a woman married a craftsman, whatever his wages, which might be as much as seven or eight *francs* a day, it still was difficult for him to attain a comfortable situation, owing to the high prices of food and other goods: a dozen eggs cost forty-five or fifty *sols*, a jug of milk, *"mi-mesure de France,"* cost fourteen *sols*. "Very few people," said Perry, "are in a position to give to charity." [Edme] Salmon added that poverty affected the workmen especially, as they spent what they earned without trying to save anything.[33]

The only exceptions were the few craftsmen, [Michel] Seringue and others, who excelled in their specialities and could take on the responsibility of a contract to perform a piece of work. But the cost of living left even them few resources: the scarcity of money, the depreciation of the notes that served in its place, and the necessity of resorting to the black market in order to procure the most essential goods were all factors that weighed heavily on everyone's budget, The Company, which failed to supply its storehouses adequately, above all made the mistake of keeping up indefinitely too high a price level for the fabrics it wanted to sell to the Spaniards—which, failing to find a buyer, deteriorated with the passage of time. The Company haggled over the shipment of fabrics for current use, stockings, and footwear, while refusing to bring down to an accessible level the prices of the Carcassonne cloth and Brittany linen with which its warehouses were glutted. Hence, Périer's criticism of their action in forbidding the cultivation of hemp, which would have provided cheap textiles instead of expensive imported materials.[34]

The position of clerical officials was not much better than that of craftsmen. Only the holders of high appointments (secretary to the Council, senior bookkeeper, cashier general, etc.) drew annual incomes that were comparatively satisfactory, varying from

2,000 to 3,000 *livres*. Such salaries were confined to a minority. The majority, whose wages ranged fromn 410 to 1,200 *livres*, were no better off than the military people. All complained of the burden of rent, which they considered too great for their means, and they compensated for this by curtailing as much as possible the time they gave to their work. This attitude was congruent with the careless habits that began to spread among these people who had been transplanted into a debilitating climate to which many of them could not adapt. Yet there were not a few clerks and bookkeepers who agreed to go and work in Louisiana. They swelled the petty administrative staff attached to the Councils, but most were persons of little competence, whose wages remained very low.[35]

Alongside the poorly paid clerical categories and the modest craftsmen, a large number of humble people lacked any trade and were without wages, some of them recently arrived from France, the rest being survivors from the first years of the occupation or from the great wave of immigration under Law's System. For these people, the only way out of their poverty was to operate on the black market or (a rather widespread practice) to sell at a profit the vouchers for goods that the Council issued to them. There was also small-scale retail trade, carried on from persons' homes, especially after 1728, when local beef, pork, and milk began to be less scarce.[36] But this situation created an atmosphere of speculation and fraud at the expense of the public or the Company: speculation that resulted in profiteering price increases, made easier by the inadequate supply of the goods of prime necessity that everyone wanted; fraud committed with others drawn by the Council on the Company's storehouses and, still more, with the official weights and measures, duly standardized by the Company, for which retailers and even the hospital's baker substituted false ones, giving rise to lawsuits, house searches, court cases, fines, and confiscations.[37]

The most widespread and perhaps the most flourishing of these little businesses that operated more or less illegally were the drink shops, as Salmon noted when he arrived. In principle, what they sold was the local beer, brewed from corn or, more rarey, from wild hops. Living in New Orleans were a master brewer and a master hop-worker, who both may have served in the brewery belonging to the Dreux brothers. But wine was still the people's favorite drink, along with brandy, both of which were considered essential when one was ill, but which soon became a source of drunkenness. In the taverns, owing to the Company's monopoly, drinks were sold illegally.[38] Games of chance of every kind quickly made their appearance in these places, followed by the usual excesses, with players frequently losing all they possessed, which led to many brawls and the creation of an atmosphere of general delinquency. To all this was added a looseness of morals rooted in part in the transportations of previous years.[39]

The conditions under which the town had begun to be inhabited, the transportation of numerous women convicts from the Salpêtrière penitentiary, and the promiscuity that resulted from this had favored the growth of prostitution. The denunciations of disordered morals uttered by the religious may seem to be expressed in extreme terms, especially those emanating from Father Raphaël: the Capuchin superior even brought about vigorous intervention with the rulers of the colony by the bishop of Quebec, who called upon them to put an end to the practice of concubinage, which Attorney General [François] Fleuriau dared not condemn publicly.[40] But there is evidence that cannot be denied, especially the strong denunciation by the Conseil Supérieur in 1725, emphasizing "the need to purge the colony" of "many evil-living women who are utterly lost." There is also the testimony of Périer and Salmon that, without the help given by the Company and the Ursulines, girls who were orphans and without resources could have no alternative but to sink into vice. Moreover, the community of soldiers and sailors, especially the crews of the Company's ships that put in at New Orleans, clearly provided a milieu in which prostitution could flourish.[41]

The Company reacted to these disorders and to the difficult conditions under which most of the population lived with measures appropriate to specific problems. It set out precise regulations, which were translated into repeated decrees by the Council, issued under royal authority. For instance, the Council forbade the taverns to sell any drink or permit any games of chance during the religious ceremonies on Sundays or in the evening after the offical time of retreat. It also provided for fixing the prices of foodstuffs, when it considered that they had risen too high; persons who disobeyed this decree were subject to fines, which went to the hospital funds. In most cases the population managed to dodge the regulations because the Council lacked sufficient staff to enforce them. Also, many persons opened drink shops for only a few days—enough time to sell off some small quantity of alcohol they secretly had obtained, but not long enough for the authorities to track them down. Consequently, the regulations often remained ineffective.[42]

It was Périer who attacked all these disorders with the greatest resolution. His correspondence denounced even more boldly than Father Raphaël's the evils that he thought had infected the colony's society. "Idleness and vice," he said, "prevail here more than in any other country in the world." He attacked the abuse of alcohol, especially of brandy, rejecting the excuses about the climate or illness. His special target, however, was prostitution, which he thought too widespread. With a view to ending it, he applied a policy directly contrary to the one followed until then. La Chaise and the members of the Council had always advocated the expulsion of prostitutes, as of all useless persons, from New Orleans.[43] Instead, Périer ordered the leaders of the inland posts to send *to* him their "worst of most scandalous individuals," and he did not shrink from inflicting corporal punishment on these offenders, having the most persistent prostitutes flogged by the soldiers.[44] He also asked the Company, with La Chaise's approval, to authorize him to build a jail, to be situated next to the hospital and the future convent of the Ursulines. Meanwhile, on the site provisionally allotted for their present convent, at the top of the enclosure reserved for the nuns, he established a "reformatory room," which proved to be adequate and made the proposed jail unnecessary.[45]

In exerting authority, the Company and its representatives did not fail to aid the poorest elements in the population. It is even surprising to note how frequently the Company took steps to help its clerks and other employees, as well as the humbler settlers, by means of pay increases and gratuities or, if the exigencies of the service were involved, indemnities.[46] These were, of course, only palliatives; they could do no more than modestly improve the circumstances of those whose appeals reached the Council. Nevertheless, as opposed to the parsimonious spirit in which the Company managed the country in general and the care it took to confine the economy within the strict limits of its monopoly, these meansures constituted the outline of a policy of public assistance that affected a fairly large number of persons.

In 1724 and 1725 the Company urged the members of the Conseil Supérieur to see to the relief of "worthy people in need" and give support to workers who wanted to settle down, and the Council took a number of measures conforming to this directive. It gave a Company employee's widow who had two small children an allowance of thirty-six pounds of flour per month; it advanced 200 *livres*, repayable when the harvest was in, to an inhabitant whose land had been ravaged by floods and by blackbirds; it provided food for a widowed sailor with a small child. In addition, as an item in the hospital's budget, the Company allocated a sum for meeting the needs of poor patients that greatly exceeded the amount that the Crown was to grant, at first, for this purpose.[47]

Following instructions from the directors general in Paris, assistance was given in particularly numerous instances to orphan children. When the Ursulines arrived, however, such assistance was restricted to a food ration for the orphans, a mere allowance of bread made of wheat mixed with rice. This was certainly not much, but it was enough to induce poor families to take in and care for abandoned children whose rations would increase their own supply of food. The situation improved only after intervention by the nuns and, to a large extent, by Father [Ignace] de Beaubois.[48]

Amid this general poverty, the Company's representatives of course had the highest status. Inevitably, the most respected families were those of La Chaise and Périer. La Chaise's family received particular attention because his numerous children form an additional factor in his position: nearly all of them settled in the colony, and people accused him of aiming, through his family, to make himself sole master of Louisiana. Only one of his sons returned to France.[49] All the others married in the colony, and all his daughters found well-to-do husbands there. His eldest son, Jacques, helped him manage the storehouses and later worked at the Natchitoches post; he founded a family in the country and remained there till the end of the Crown's administration.[50]

One of La Chaise's daughters married a sublieutenant on the *Duc de Noailles*, Bisotton de Saint Martin, son of a former investigating commissioner at the Paris Châtelet; another married Dr. L. Prat; a third became the wife of Jean de Pradel, son of the lieutenant general of the see of Uzerches in Limousin and himself a captain of infantry in the Louisiana troops. Bisotton de Saint Martin gained much from his marriage, being made secretary to the Council, from which job La Chaise had caused Chavannes to be dismissed. Subsequently Saint Martin was a storekeeper, and after that he busied himself with a "habitation," for which the Company advanced him a work force of twenty blacks. Finally, after La Chaise's death, he succeeded Cullo de Crémont in charge of Mobile. But the finest catch was the one made by La Chaise's fourth daughter, Félicité, who married in 1732 the son of Joseph Villars Dubreuil, the rich settler in the Tchopitoulas country. This was possibly the first case of a marriage based on a fortune acquired in the colony, with the bride bearing the honorific title of daughter of "the former Crown commissioner and director general of the colony."[51]

Périer also advanced the career of his son-in-law, a young ensign in expectation of promotion, Chambellan Graton, who distinguished himself during the Natchez events and served with success in the engineer corps.[52]

Though ranking a little below the heads of the colony, the members of the Conseil Supérieur et de Régie also had a share in forming the new society in Louisiana. After their attempt to leave and go back to France, Fleuriau and [Jacques] Fazende married, as also did [Antoine] Bruslé, into closely related families: that of a woman named Desmorières and that of the storekeeper of New Orleans, Henry Le Blanc, who had recently died. The councilors thus entered a circle of persons already deeply attached to the colony, and they also became linked to one another by the bonds of kinship among their wives. The later marriage (in 1726) of the surgeon Alexandre Vielle with Le Blanc's daughter strengthened this alignment.[53] Indeed, what was interesting in all these marriages was their reinforcement of the society that was alowly coming into existence in the colony. The men were uniting themselves with families that were determined not to abandon the colony, as Le Blanc's daughters had proved by leaving France, where they had been brought up, to return to Louisiana and marry there.[54]

In this same period, the phenomenon of the formation of a new society was expanded still further by unions between families only recently arrived and families even older than Le Blanc's, families going back to the first years of the French occupation. Confined at first to the little settlement of Mobile, these older families increasingly moved to the new capital or its outskirts, and marriages became frequent between them and the more recently immigrated families. One of the oldest was the family of Gabrielle Savary, with her four children from three successive marriages. She continued to be known by the name of her first husband, a soldier called Jean-Baptiste Saucier or Saussier, a Canadian who came to Louisiana with Iberville and died in 1716. Having several times received advances from the Company of the Indies, which wanted to keep her in the colony for the sake of her children, she followed the profession of midwife, at the same time carrying on some commercial activity, and managed to bring up her children, one of whom, François Saussier, became an engineer, with the help of the Capuchins.[55]

Along with this family, those of Geneviève Burel and Claude Trépagnier, of François Trudeau, of the Carrière brothers, and of the Chauvin brothers formed the original foundation of Creole society. It was above all through marriages into this circle by recently arrived Frenchmen that Creole society began to take shape and grow as the town itself grew. For example, Lassus de Marcilly married Geneviève Burel, widow of Claude Trépagnier; Huot de Vaubercy, captain of the *Dromadaire,* and the apothecary François

Damaron married Burel's two daughters; and the cashier Etienne Dalcourt and Lieutenant Guérin de La Boulay married two of her direct descendants.[56]

Marriages already were taking place fairly often between descendants of the newcomers and direct descendants of older colonial families. The daughter of the concession holder Mirbaise de Villemont, who had arrived in Law's time and came from Poitiers, married the son of Antoine Rivard, one of the first to clear the land along Bayou Saint Jean. The daughter of Bachemin Corbin, who came to the colony only in 1727, married the son of the former notary Jean-Baptiste Raguet, who had been present when Mobile began.[57] Furthermore—and this fact is particularly revealing of the intermixing that was taking place more and more in the colony—two daughters of Faucon-Dumanoir (the manager from Saint-Malo of the Sainte-Catherine concession in the Natchez country who had such protracted disputes with Kolly and his associates) married in 1730 Bienville's nephews, the chevaliers de Noyan and de Chavoy, who were their uncle's representatives and agents at New Orleans. These two men's antecedents ensured the rapid integration of their wives into local society, especially since Dumanoir was called upon to act as the Company's agent in Louisiana and to take possession of the concession he had formerly managed.[58] At the same time as it took shape, Creole society was diversified by the increasing addition to its ranks of German settlers who married into it. The most striking case of this was the marriage in 1740 of the son of Joseph Chauvin de Léry to Louise d'Arensbourg, the daughter of Frédéric d'Arensbourg.[59]

The first signs of affluence now were appearing in this developing society. They were most noticeable in the few families that dominated the colony's political and administrative life, who added to the emoluments of their functions the income from the more or less extensive lands that most of them owned along the Mississippi. These lands had been granted to them without payment and were not yet subject to any obligations; Périer had not applied the tax of five *livres* for each black that the Company had requested, and the work force was not paid, since it consisted of slaves. Besides these families, of whom La Chaise's was the outstanding example, there were those that emerged from marriages that brought or promised affluence, as in the case of La Chaise's daughter marrying the well-known settler in the Tchopitoulas country or Bienville's nephews marrying into Dumanoir's family.

Above all, however, and contrasting with an incalculable number of humble inhabitants who lived wretchedly by the river bank, there were some families who engaged exclusively in work on the land who already had succeeded admirably in their undertakings. Some of these families were of French origin, like that of Villars Dubreuil, others from Canada, like that of the Chauvin brothers. The most fortunate lived in the rich Tchopitoulas sector, which, as Father Raphaël wrote, was "truly well provided." There, affluence prevailed and was apparent. The local families maintained a surgeon to attend to their personal needs and those of their numerous slaves, giving him board and 1,200 *livres* a year, and also a cook, whose wages were 600 *livres*. These expenses came easily to persons most of whom enjoyed an annual income of 40,000 *livres*.[60]

Alongside the civil authority, whose prestige was essentially due to the fact that the Company ruled the colony for the time being, the military authority—with the commandant general as sole exception—owed the respect it enjoyed in the town to the role that had been assigned to it: not only to defend the country, but also to maintain law and order in New Orleans. For the military alone possessed a prison that could be used either for offenders against army discipline or for delinquents of any kind, a circumstance that sometimes gave rise to incidents with members of the civilian government.

The four companies—all that were assigned in 1730 for the defense of Louisiana—generally were commanded by simple men who had no brilliant titles of nobility to display. Jean de Pradel could, if need be, make something of his ancestry, but he was only a younger son and so could not inherit the family title, which went to the eldest. It was the same with Henry de Louboey, a younger son of a Béarn family. Along with him, Joachim de Gauvry, the son of the receiver of tithes in the bishopric of La Rochelle, was one of the oldest officers in the colony, where he had served since 1716 after already having had a long military career in France. Gauvry had integrated himself into the life of Louisiana, dividing his time between his habitation on Bayou Saint Jean and duties with his company. Captain Dartaguiette, brother of Dartaguiette Diron who had played so active a role in the colony's beginnings and who was still very influential with the Company of the Indies, had inherited none of the family titles that his eldest brother so cleverly had increased through speculations in Law's time. Renaul d'Hauterive, son of a road surveyor of Tours, was reckoned to be "meritorious" and "well conducted," but made a very humble marriage in the colony. He was not of noble origin.[61]

The authenticity of the titles of nobility claimed among the lieutenants, sub-lieutenants, and ensigns is not to be accepted without a pinch of salt. Lieutenant Petit de Livilliers, who adopted the title of his father, the seigneur of Livilliers in Picardy, might perhaps justifiably call himself "Esquire," but one must be more hesitant in the case of the ensign Jean Maret or with Guérin de La Boulay. In fact, there were only two really authentic noblemen, apart from the younger sons of Pradel and Louboey. One was the *major* François de Marigny de Mandeville, Esquire, seigneur of Hautmeslin. When commanding the Mobile post in 1723, he sought to succeed Captain Louis Poncereau de Richebourg as commandant of New Orleans, but obtained satisfaction only in 1727.[62] He was then made the Company's proxy for defending its interests against Kolly and his associates. He failed in this mission and died the following year without having done anything worth mention. His widow later married Broutin. His post was taken over by Henry de Louboey, who held it from 1730 to 1732 and then became, on the comte de Gramont's recommendation, *lieutenant de roy* at New Orleans.[63]

But it was above all the baron de Cresnay who dominated this circle of officers, by virtue of a nobility of some distinction. He belonged to the family of Poilvilain de Cresnay in the viscounty of Avranches. He had served for a long time, though not brilliantly, during the War of the Spanish Succession, after which he gave up military life and returned to his estate to lead the life of country gentleman until the day came when, through the backing of the duc d'Orléans, he was promoted to the post of commandant general of troops in Louisiana, with the rank of lieutenant colonel of infantry. This honorific title was accompanied, moreover, by some special commercial facilities that the Company left him quite free to exploit in the colony.[64]

Baron de Cresnay had no qualifications for performing these new functions or for undertaking a military operation during the then current war against the Natchez, with whom he had never had the slightest contact. There was no justification whatsoever for creating such a command. He had the opportunity to display a certain courage, but he easily let himself be duped in his dealings with groups of the Natchez, whose way of thinking was unfamiliar to him even without the tricks that they were capable of employhing against him. In 1731 his command was abolished, and he was offered as compensation the post of *lieutenant de roy* at Mobile, in place of Diron, who had temporarily given it up at the retrocession.[65] In the following year, however, he went back to France on the pretext that he could not stand the climate in the colony: this added a note of ridicule to the failure of his brief colonial career, which was not redeemed by his appointment to Cayenne.[66]

It was regrettable that the nobility had no representative more distinguished than Mandeville or Cresnay, and that titles of nobility were so rare in the companies in New Orleans. Such titles were, indeed, no guarantee of military efficiency. But in this little community where quarrels over precedence were so frequent and so bitter, and in which anyone who held, even provisionally, a public office of some kind always looked for the slightest evidence of noble origin in order to enhance his surname—like Joseph Lassus tacking on the name of his village of Marcilly—a noble title could have been a source of prestige for an officer who had only his modest pay as captain of infantry, and it might have done something to improve his situation.

For these men, many of whom performed their duties conscientiously, led hard lives. First there was the problem of the climate. The officers often proved unable to adapt themselves to it and soon fell victims to the colony's usual sicknesses. This happened to Pradel and to Renaul d'Hauterive, although both managed (at the cost of frequent and painful crises) to pursue their careers and also to find wives in Louisiana. Then there was the fact that, in this colony where the cost of living was so high, the pay was extremely meager. Captains received only 90 *livres* a month, lieutenants and sublieutenants 60 and 50 *livres*. The pay of a captain on the retired list did not exceed 600 *livres* a year, as was the case with Gauvry, who lost rank owing to the reductions in numbers carried out by the Company. He did not recover his captaincy on the active list until Pauger intervened on his behalf in 1726, pointing out that he had a big family to maintain.[67]

During the Company's first years, under the old *régie*, the officers managed to overcome their difficulties, more or less, by obtaining from the storehouse advances of goods that they either used themselves or sold at a profit. When La Chaise arrived, he recognized that an officer with only his pay of 90 *livres*, which, supplemented by a small allowance for food, provided him with no more than 1,245 *livres* a year, was in no position either to pay rent or to feed himself. Consequently, he agreed that the officers should be allowed to take some goods from the storehouse and sell them. But he had not allowed for the amount of debt already contracted in this way by some officers. He demonstrated to the Conseil de Régie that many of them were living in houses that they had been able to build thanks to advances from the Company's previous agents, and that there could be no question of providing new facilities for those who were looking for somewhere to live.[68]

The Company ordered that the officers must pay their debts, but did not insist on immediate repayment in full. It decided to keep back one-fifth of the total amount of officers' pay until everything had been repaid. The proportion held back was not great, but it worsened still further the material condition of the officers and made them very angry with La Chaise, who had compiled the record of their debts. They all shared the general belief that he had systematically increased the prices of the goods involved, so as to favor the Company's interests. [Pierre Dugué de] Boisbriant supported their view and opposed the principle of docking pay. He accused La Chaise of responsibility for the economizing measures applied by the Company, especially those that were most detrimental to the military, such as the cut in the number of soldiers and the reductions in the presents given to the Indians—a move that was to lead to serious complications in France's relations with some tribes.[69]

Whether the proposed retentions of pay were put into effect in the years that followed is unknown, since the scales of pay in the payrolls were not altered until the retrocession. The system of advances was not completely abolished but was restricted, in principle, to officers who offered guarantees of repayment. And while several officers were cashiered at La Chaise's request for having failed to repay any part of what they owed, only one cashiering was stubbornly maintained, apparently through personal ill will on La Chaise's part: that of Captain César de Blanc, who soon was reduced to extreme poverty.[70]

It was in any case obvious that no officer could survive, even though exercising the greatest frugality, unless he could profit, over and above his pay, from some small-scale commercial activity: perhaps the sale, at more or less profiteering prices, of some articles of prime necessity, in accordance with the general practice; or else a larger-scale selling of the goods that some officers obtained permission to bring in from France. This was done by Pradel, which caused Bienville to record the view that he was "more interested in trade than in service."[71]

The exploitation of a habitation beside the river could be another way of turning a profit, but it was necessary to have a work force big enough to cultivate the land, and few officers were in a position to acquire any blacks. Gauvry managed to develop his habitation beside the bayou road without the help of slaves, but only through his exceptional qualities of hard work and endurance. That was a rare case, however, and when Pauger got him restored to his rank in 1726, Gauvry succeeded in having some blacks delivered to him to furnish needed help. Lieutenant Petit de Livilliers seems to have made more rapid progress on his land, possibly owing to greater means at his disposal or to the facilities Bienville provided for him because he came from Canada. These enterprises, moreover, could be only small-scale affairs, with slave households of no more than eight or ten and with a poor yield, because the exigencies of the service, such as the frequent duty of an officer to be somewhere else, were incompatible with the interests of a big estate.[72]

Lacking as they did any great resources and being without brilliant titles of nobility, these officers were often reduced to marrying women without dowries. Yet their weddings were frequently stylish occasions, owing to the quality and number of those who attended. Even for Gauvry, who was of modest origin, the commandant Périer and the commissioner La Chaise figured among the first witnesses, followed by the military personages of the garrison. Boisbriant or Périer, [Jean] Pérault or La Chaise, Fleuriau or Noyan were always present at officers' weddings and signed their names as witnesses. When Broutin married Madeleine Lemaire in 1729, he did not have Périer as one of his witnesses, because this was the period when Baron had completely supplanted him in the commandant's favor. But La Chaise's family were there in great number, together with Fleuriau and the *major* Louboey.[73]

Unfortunately, except perhaps for Pradel's marriage to the daughter of La Chaise, to whom her father had certainly given a dowry, the marriages contracted by the officers often failed to improve the husband's situation.[74] Périer wrote about this to Maurepas in 1732. Most of the officers, he said, married women who brought them nothing. Indeed, he asked for help for the officers' wives who had been left widows, requesting pensions for them becuse the loss of their husband's pay had plunged them into poverty. The most striking case was that of Lieutenant La Boulay, who died shortly after marrying a lady named Trudeau, leaving her and her four children with no means of existence beyond what she could expect from her parents.[75]

A factor that made the troops in Louisiana rather unusual was the inclusion in their companies, beginning in 1716, of a growing number of cadets. One of the first of them to serve in the colony was Joseph Boissy, the son of a Saintonge gentleman, and after him the numbers gradually increased. The year 1719 alone saw the arrival of thirty-four cadets, mostly commoners, and they continued to come, in groups of different sizes, all through the following years. They came from different backgrounds, and were not required to present proof of any title of nobility. None of them carried any official document categorizing him as a cadet, and this remained the case until Bienville returned to Louisiana.[76] The reason was that the "cadets" were simply young men who wanted to follow a military career and were undergoing an elementary apprenticeship to their trade by serving as private soldiers, without receiving any higher pay.

After doing so, they had to wait many years without promotion before obtaining the rank of ensign in a subordinate capacity. One named La Vergne, for example, the son of a counselor at the Châtelet, spent six years in the colony as a mere cadet, returned to

France in 1725, and later achieved nothing more than the basic rank of ensign. Charles Demoüy, son of a receiver of taxes at Melun who had lost money through Law's "System," arrived in 1728 and also spent six years in Louisiana without gaining promotion. All of these men performed the soldier's usual tasks, doing guard duty and drilling on the parade ground, for the same pay as a private soldier, which was nine *livres* and twelve *sols* a month. Among them there were a few young gentlemen, subject to the same obligations as the rest, such as Des Tuilettes de Vauparis, the son of a former lieutenant of infantry, who served in Gauvry's company from 1729; Denis Bodin de Sainte-Marie, a cadet from 1724; and Laurent Du Coderc, who arrived in 1729 and was doubtless a brother of the lieutenant who was killed fighting the Yazoo in that year.[77]

In 1724 the Company of the Indies began to appeal to the soldiers of Plantin's company, which it originally had formed to defend the port of Lorient, to volunteer for Louisiana. It was following this appeal that some cadets of repute, detached from this company, began to arrive in the colony. Thus, among the passengers who disembarked from the *Baleine* in 1728 were Populus de Saint-Protais, only nineteen years old, son of a captain of grenadiers in Louvigny's regiment, and Claude Joseph Favrot, born at Versailles in 1708, son of a brigadier in the king's armies, Pierre Joseph Favrot.[78] The younger Favrot already possessed seven years' seniority as a cadet in Bassigny's regiment, in which he had begun his military career. Known as the chevalier de Favrot and backed by the duchesse de Mazarin, he served with distinction in the Natchez war. A few years later he married a local Creole, born on Dauphin Island, Louise Elisabeth Bruslé. That was the origin of a family that was to play a major role in the settlement of Louisiana and many of whose descendants, in a collateral line, still live there.[79]

Favrot and Saint-Protais seem to have enjoyed the benefit of some serious recommendations when they left France, which no doubt explains why they set out for Louisiana with a sergeant's pay, sixteen *livres* ten *sols* a month, rather than that of a mere private soldier, which was the lot of most cadets. They also were allowed to take their meals in the galley while on the voyage; soldiers, including cadets, normally had to subsist on rations. When they arrived at New Orleans, however, they were subject to the same duties as the rest. Favrot was listed among the ordinary sentries posted in the town, in Captain Dartaguiette's company, and serving under his orders. The cadet Du Coderc, who arrived in 1729, also from Plantin's company, was classified and paid as a private soldier serving under Gauvry. The fact that this Du Coderc was the son of a mere *major de place* of a fortified city perhaps accounts for the difference between his pay and Favrot's.[80]

It was indeed rare for a cadet to enjoy such advantages as Favrot possessed. Most of them had no means beyond their meager pay, and Périer endeavored in 1732 to draw the minister's attention to their poor prospects. He suggested appointing them to the inland posts as supernumerary ensigns in a subordinate capacity, so as to accustom them to using the native languages, knowledge of which would enable them to attain high ranks;

otherwise, paid as they were and confined to garrison life, they could influence the troops only by setting an example of discipline and good conduct. . . .[81]

Notes for "New Orleans Society"

Abbreviations

AC	Archives des Colonies (Archives Nationales, Paris)*
AE	Archives Etrangères (Archives du Ministère des Affaires Etrangères, Quai d'Orsay, Paris)
AG	Archives de la Guerre (Château de Vincennes, Vincennes)
AM	Archives de la Marine (Archives Nationales, Paris, and Château de Vincennes)*
AN	Archives Nationales
AN, MC	Archives Nationales, Minutier Central (Notarial Files)
Arsenal	Archives de la Bastille (Bibliothèque de l'Arsenal, Paris)
BN	Bibliothèque Nationale, Paris
BN, FF	Manuscripts, Fonds Français, in the Bibliothèque Nationale
DFC	Dépôt des Fortifications des Colonies (Archives Nationales, France d'Outre Mer, Paris)
Lorient	Archives of the Port of Lorient
LSHM	Louisiana State Historical Museum, New Orleans
Sem.	Archives du Séminaire Laval, Quebec

*All letters in the series AC, C 11A, C 13A, C 13B, and AM, B 3 and B 4, when given without indication of destination, are to Jérôme Phélypeaux de Maurepas, the minister of marine. Those in AC, B, and AM, B 2, unless otherwise indicated, emanate *from* Maurepas.

[1]AC, DFC, Map 89B, Gonichon (Dec. 1731).

[2]AC, G 1 464, Census of New Orleans (Jan. 1726); Marie-Madeleine Hachard, *Relation du voyage des Ursulines de Rouen à la Nouv. Orléans* (reprint ed., Paris, 1872), 1:28.

[3]Le Page du Pratz, *Histoire de la Louisiane,* 1:319; *Lettres édifiantes,* 6:392-94, Letter from Fauther Du Poisson; AC, B 43, f. 453-54, Ordinance of Sept. 6, 1724.

[4]AC, G 1 464, General census of the inhabitants (and) Negroes . . . of New Orleans who were there on July 1, 1727; LSHM, *Mémoire* on the works carried out by Rasteau, master roofer, Nov. 13, 1730; Summons of M. Rossard by a building contractor, April 10, 1731.

[5]AC, FS 5B 49, nos. 72, 74, 75, Passengers on the *Dromadaire,* the *Saône,* and the *Baleine.*

[6]Lorient, 1 P 74, f. 9-16, 19-20, 24v-25, 34-39, 45-46, 47, 51v-54v, 56v-58, 61-62, 71v-78; 1 P 307, bundle 75, doc. 101; 2 P 24-I, no. 18.

[7]Lorient, 1 P 74, f. 10-11, 15v-16. The mason Jean Revers was promised 100 livres "for every Negro he will instruct to the Company's advantage."

[8]Lorient, 1 P 74, f. 12-13; AC, F 5B 49, nos. 82, 83, 85, 88, 89, 90, 93, Lists of passengers in various ships.

[9]AC, B 43, f. 828-29. General list of expenditure for 1729; Lorient 1 P 74, f 72v-73, Hiring of Gabriel Pen and François Malejac, June 28, 1730.

[10]Lorient, 1 P 74, f 77v-78. Hiring of J. Lescot at Tonneins, Aug. 22, 1730; 2 P 24-II, no 3, Passengers in the *Dromadaire* (in both directions).

[11]AC, G1 464 (General correspondence), *Mémoire* on various affairs concerning private persons (Blanchard case), 1732; C 13A 9, f. 267v-68, Proceedings, No. 21, 1725; C 2 22, f. 63-64, The directors of the Company to Maurepas, March 31, 1729. The name Champlain seems to have been a false one designed to conceal the identity of S. de Conflans de Brienne: B 53, f. 20v-21, To M. de Fayet, March 3, 1721; f. 465, To Périer, March 22, 1729; Order by the king, March 3, 1729; B 55 f. 588, To Périer and Salmon, May 22, 1731; B 54, f. 38, To M. Robert, May 7, 1730.

[12] AC, F 5B 49, nos. 71, 83, 82, 89, Passengers in the *Loire*, the *Aurore*, the *Baleine*, and the *Alexandre* (roll of which mentions that S. de Champlain remains at Port-Louis); B 55 f. 633v-34, 635v, 636, Order for deportation to Louisiana, May 1731.

[13] AC, F 5B, nos. 88, 87, Passengers in the *Baleine*, the *Durance;* AM, B 3 335, f. 134, Petition to Maurepas from Jacques Allier, merchant of Lyon (1729).

[14] AC, F 5B, nos. 88, 85, Passengers in the *Baleine*, the *Dromadaire;* C 13A 7, f. 21, La Chaise, Sept. 6, 1729; C 13A 9, f. 241, 249, Letters from the Council, Aug. 28, 1726, March 17, 1726; C 13A 13, f. 170v, *Mémoire* by St-Denis, Nov. 30, 1731; LSHM, Sept. 2, 1724, Action by the deputy attorney general.

[15] Jean de Pradel, *Recueils des lettres du chevalier de Pradel* (Paris, 1928), 80, 87, 100; AC, C 13A 10, f. 200, Périer, April 30, 1727; F 5B 49, nos. 91, 92, Passengers in the *Prince de Conty* (May 1730), the *Vénus* (Feb. 1730).

[16] Lorient, 1 P 74, f. 62v, Hiring of a carpenter, with payment of an indemnity for his wife, Dec. 30, 1729; AC, F 5B 49, nos. 83, 90, Passengers in the *Aurore*, the *Gironde*, 1730; F 5B 49, nos 84, 71, Passengers in the *Prince de Conty*, 1728, the *Loire*, 1724. Among the passengers in the *Aurore* was a stave splitter accorded indemnity for his daughter if she married and settled in Louisiana.

[17] Lorient, 1 P 74, Dec. 23, 1727 (or Girard bundle and Girod register at La Rochelle, Dec. 23, 1727); AC, F 5B 49, no 82, Passengers in the *Baleine*, 1728.

[18] Lorient, 1 P 74, Hirings on Jan. 1 and 2, 1728; AC, F 5B 49, no. 82, Passengers in the *Baleine*, 1728.

[19] See AC, F 5B 49, no. 90, n71. Passengers in the *Gironde* and the *Loire*, for the case of the widow Desmorières (sister of the former storekeeper at New Orleans), who left with her six nieces in the *Loire* in 1724. See F 5B 49, no. 87, Passengers in the *Durance*, and Parish register, New Orleans, May 25, 1727, Nov. 7, 1729, for the case of Mlle Lerocq du Havre, whose sister was already married in New Orleans and who herself married, soon after her arrival, a brother of the Canadian Jacques Larchevêque.

[20] AC, F 5B 49, nos. 82, 83, 89, 90, 91, Lists of passengers in various ships; C 13 A 10, f. 176-176v, Périer, April 22, 1727.

[21] AC, C 13A 7 f. 23, 20v, La Chaise, Sept. 6, 1723; C 13A 8, f. 407-407v, Raphaël, May 26, 1725; C 13A 9, f. 250v, Extract from the Council's letters, March 17, 1726; C 13A 10, f. 192-192v. Périer and La Chaise, Nov. 2, 1727.

[22] AC, C 13A 8, f. 407v, Raphaël, May 26, 1725; C 13A 9, f. 70, Conseil Supérieur, Feb. 27, 1725.

[23] AC, C 13A 7, f. 39v-40, La Chaise, Sept. 6, 1723; C 13A 8, f. 101v-102, 384v-385, Proceedings March 6, 1724, Sept. 15, 1725.

[24] AC, C 13A 8, f. 101v-102, Proceedings, March 6, 1724; C 9B 9, f. 6-d, 7-a, Cirou and Girard (Saint Domingue), Oct. 18, 1727; C 13C 1, f. 385v, On the state of this colony; *Lettres édifiantes,* 7:95, Father Vivier, Nov. 17, 1750; AC, C 13C 4, f. 95v-96, *Mémoire* of the information obtained by S. Béranger from Louisiana (1722?).

[25] AC, C 13A 11, f. 60, 334v-35, Périer and La Chaise, July 31, 1728, March 25, 1729; f. 346v, Proceedings of the directors' meeting, June 3, 1729; f. 364-364v, Périer and La Chaise, Aug. 26, 1729.

[26] AC C 13A 8, f. 116-21, List of expenditure on the works (1723-24); C 13A 10, f. 197v, Périer and La Chaise, Nov. 2, 1727; C 13A 8, f. 106-106v, 108, Proceedings, May 31, June 20, 1724; f. 116-21, Expenditure on the works.

[27] AC, C 13A 8, f. 346v-47, Proceedings, Aug. 7, 1725; C 13A 11, f. 64v, Périer and La Chaise, Aug. 18, 1728; f. 144v, 364, Périer, Nov. 3, 1728, Aug. 26, 1729.

[28] Marcel Giraud, *Histoire de la Louisiane française,* 4 vols. (Paris, 1953-74), 4:289-98; C 13A 9, f. 57-57v, The Conseil Supérieur to the directors, Feb. 27, 1725; C 13A 8, f. 11v, Pauger, Jan. 3, 1724; AM, B 3 287, f. 252-252v, Du Parc (Port-Louis), Sept. 10, 1723; C 13A 9, f. 57v-59, Conseil Supérieur, Feb. 27, 1725.

[29] AC, C 13A 9, f. 251v-52, Letter from the Conseil Supérieur, April 4, 1728; C 13A 10, f. 198, Périer and La Chaise, Nov. 2, 1727; f. 245-53, Boisbriant, Jan. 12, 1727; LSHM, April 17, 1726, On the lack of flour at the Company's bakery.

[30] AC, C 13A 11, f. 11, Périer, Aujg. 14, 1728; f. 28-28v, 117v, Périer and La Chaise, April 1728, Nov. 1, 1728; C 13A 12, f. 140-140v, La Chaise, Aug. 10, 1729; f. 310v, Périer to Maurepas, Aug. 1, 1730; C 13C 1, f. 115, *Mémoire* for the establishment of Louisiana.

[31] AC, G 1 465, List of the infantry companies, Banès, May 1724 (Natchitoches); AN, T 66(1/2), doc. 26, Kolly to Deucher, Aug. 15, 1728; Ac, C 13A 8, f. 377-377v, Proceedings, Sept. 5, 1725; C 13A 9, f. 261v, 246v-47, Proceedings, Oct. 29, 1725, March 17, 1726; Hachard, *Rélation du voyage*, 2:6-7; AC, DFC, 12, *Mémoire* on the present condition.

[32] AC, G 1 464, Census of the community in the German village, Hoffen (1724), with commentaries attached; A 23, f. 49-49v, Decision of the Conseil Supérieur, Nov. 20, 1724; f. 59v, Decision of the Council, July 19, 1725; C 13A 11, f. 146v, Périer, Nov. 3, 1728.

[33] AC, C 13A 7, f. 16v, La Chaise, Sept. 6, 1723; C 13A 8, f. 412, Raphaël, Sept. 15, 1725; Hachard, *Rélation du voyage*, 1:25; Ac, C 13A 8, f. 162v, Proceedings, Dec. 23, 1724; C 13A, 13, f. 121v, Salmon, Dec. 8, 1731.

[34] AC, C 13A 10, f. 192-192v, Périer, April 20, 1727.

[35] AC, B 43, f. 647-48, General list of expenditure, 1726; F 5B 49, nos. 71, 72, 74, 75, 82, 87, Lists of passengers in various ships.

[36] AC, C 13A 9, f. 82, Proceedings, March 20, 1725; G 1 465, List of the infantry companies, Banès, 1724 (New Orleans); A 23 f. 59c-60, Decisions of the Council, July 19, 24, 1725; C 13A 11, f. 11, Périer, Aug. 14, 1728.

[37] AC, A 23, f. 59v, 60, 64, Decisions of the Council, July 19, 24, Oct. 11, 1725; LSHM, July 18, 1725; Search by Jacques de La Chaise; Sept. 11, 1726, Search following complaint by the nurses.

[38] AC, C 13A 14, f. 30, Périer and Salmon, Dec. 5, 1732; LSHM, Dec. 4, 1724, May 20, 1723, Brewers of beer, Hachard, *Rélation du voyage*, 2:6; AC, C 13A 11, f. 362, Périer and La Chaise, Aug. 26, 1729; C 13A 8, f. 260-260v, Pauger, Oct. 14, 1725; C 13A 14, f. 10-10v, Périer and Salmon, Mar. 19, 1737.

[39] AC, A 23, f. 38v-39, Decision of the Conseil Supérieur, April 29, 1723; C 13A, 7, f. 105v-106, Decision of the Conseil Supérieur, May 13, 1723; C 13A 8, f. 161-161v, Proceedings, Dec. 22, 1724; LSHM, June 25, 1725, Case of ruin through gambling.

[40] AC, C 13A 8, f. 418v-419v, Raphaël, Oct. 12, 1725; f. 422-23, Bishop of Quebec to Raphaël, July 4, 1725; *Lettres édifiantes*, 6:392-93, Father Du Poisson, Oct. 3, 1727.

[41] AC, C 13A 8 f. 161-161v, Proceedings, Dec. 22, 1724; C 13A 9, f. 135v, Private letter from La Chaise, April 26, 1725; f. 241, 249, Letters from the Council, Aug 28, 1725, March 19, 1726; AC, C 13A 14, f. 8-8v, Périer and Salmon, Mar. 29, 1732; C 13A 7, f. 21v, La Chaise, Sept. 6, 1723; DFC, 12, *Mémoire* on the present condition, with commentary by Périer.

[42] AC, A 23, f. 38v, 39, 58v, 79v-80, 84-84v, 111-12, 114v, Decisions and regulations of the Conseil Supérieur, April 29, May 13, 1723, April 11, 1725, Oct. 5, 1726, March 29, 1727, March 26, 1733.

[43] AC, C 13A 12, f. 333v, 393v, Périer, Aug. 1, March 18, 1730; C 2 23, f. 188v-89, Périer, Aug. 1, 1730; C 13A 7, f. 21v, La Chaise, Sept. 6, 1723; LSHM, Sept. 2, 1724, Report by the deputy attorney general.

[44] AC, C 13A 9, f. 71, Decisions of the Conseil Supérieur, Feb. 27, 1725; C 13A 11, f. 12v, Périer, Aug. 14, 1728; C 2 23, f. 188-89, Périer, Aug. 1, 1730; Hachard, *Rélation du voyage*, 1:63, 2:9-10.

[45] AC, C 13A 11, f. 145-145v, Périer and La Chaise, Nov. 23, 1728; C 13A 14, f. 8-8v, Périer and Salmon, Jan. 18, 1732; Hachard, *Rélation du voyage*, 1:67-68.

[46] AC, C 13A 8, f. 128v-130v, 134, 145v-46, 197, 373v, 374b-75, Proceedings, Sept. 20, 27, Nov. 20, 1724, Dec. 15, 1726, Aug. 30, Sept. 2, 1725.

[47] AC, C13A 9, f. 70, Conseil Supérieur, Feb. 27, 1725; C 13A 8, f. 137, 182v, Proceedings, Oct. 6, 1724, Feb. 3, 1725; C 13A 13, f. 121-22, Salmon, Dec. 8, 1731.

[48] AC, C 13A 8, f. 180, Proceedings, Feb. 1, 1725; C 13A 11, f. 145, Périer and La Chaise, April 3, 1728; Parish register, New Orleans, Sept 9, 1720, Marriage of Marguerite Salos.

[49] AC, F 5B 49, no 67, Passengers in the *Chameau*, 1723; Lorient, 1 P 22, no. 11, 2 P. 21-II, no. 9, Passengers in the *Galatée*, the *Baleine;* C 13A 8, f. 330-330v, Proceedings of the Conseil de Régie; f. 345, Proceedings, July 28, 1725; G 1 464, no. 73, Passengers in the *Gironde*, 1724; AM, B 3 309, f. 214v, Renault (Port-Louis), May 20, 1726.

[50] LSHM, Sept. 2, 1729, Report on the searches by Jacques de La Chaise; Feb. 12, 1759, Jacques de La Chaise, keeper of the royal storehouses; July 4, 1760, (La Chaise) Councilor in the Conseil Supérieur; Jan. 19, 1762, Marriage of his son; AC D 2E 10, List of employees, 1793 (La Chaise at Natchitoches).

[51] Parish register, New Orleans, Feb. 28, may 9, 1729, May 22, 1730; AC, C 13A 12, f. 281, Raphaël, April 27, 1729; AC, B 43, f. 883, Order for delivery, Paris, Sept. 26, 1729; D 2D 10, Replacment of clerical officers, Sept. 1, 1737; Parish register, New Orleans, Jan. 12, 1732.

[52] AC, D 2C 51, f. 90v, List of active officers.

[53] AC, C 13A 9, f. 14-14v, The Council to the directors of the Company, Jan 20, 1725; F 5B 49, no. 71, Pasengers in the *Loire*, 1724; Parish register, New Orleans, June 25, 1726.

[54] AC, D 2C 51, f. 30v, List of infantry officers, 1721 (Le Blanc shown in 1719); B 43, f. 460, Disposition of the infantry companies in Louisiana, 1724; f. 497, Leave without pay for Le Blanc, to recover his health, 1724.

[55] AC, F 3 241, f. 148, Extract from an inventory made in Louisiana on Aug. 22, 1717; C 13A 10, f. 176v, Périer and La Chaise, April 22, 1727; LSHM, Aug. 9, 1736, Recognizance by Henry Saussier, AC, G 1 464, Census of New Orleans, 1726 (rue St-Pierre); Census of July 1727 (rue Royale); Parish register, Mobile, Feb. 25, 1719, Oct. 18, 1721, Baptisms of Gabrielle Savary's children. See also John Francis McDermott, *Frenchmen and French Ways in the Mississippi Valley* (Urbana, Ill., 1968), 199ff. (François Saucier).

[56] Giraud, *Histoire,* 3 and 4, passim; Parish register, New Orleans, May 12, 1725, May 8, 1731, May 30, 1723, Aug. 5, 1726.

[57] Giraud, *Histoire,* 4:243-44; Parish register, New Orleans, Feb. 20, 1730, May 4, 1728.

[58] AC, D 2C 50, f. 13, List of officers maintained in Louisiana, April 1730 (Re-establishment of Noyan in his rank as captain); D 2C 51. 105v, Marginally noted list of 1734 (the chevalier de Noyan-Payen); f. 191, Service record of the chevalier de Noyan; D 2C 59, f. 10 (Service record of the chevalier Chavoye); D 2C 222 (Lafillard, *Colonies*), Summaries of the family's service records. See La Chesnay Desbois, *Dictionnaire de la noblesse,* 11:231. Dumanoir's three daughters (Jeanne, Marie, and Charlotte) came to Louisiana with their mother in the storeship *Gironde* in 1730; SF 5B 49, no. 90.

[59] Parish register, New Orleans, Jan. 15, 1724, Jan. 15, Nov. 19, 1725; AC, D 2C 51, f. 117-18, April 17, 17343, Request by Bienville for a pension for d'Arensbourg from the property of the Protestants, owing to his edifying behavior since adjuring Protestantism; LSHM, Marriage contract (Léry-d'Arenbourg) of May 22, 1740.

[60] AC, C 13A 8, f.403, 412, Raphaël to Abbé Raguet, May 15, Sept. 15, 1725.

[61] Giraud, *Histoire,* 4:32, 34-35, 52, 112-14; *Le Mercure,* July 1729, p. 1658, May 1730, p. 1040; Giraud, *Histoire,* 3:214-15, 4:113; AC, D 2C 51, f. 83, 88v, Lists of the detached naval companies and their officers, with marginal notes, March 1730, Dec. 1731; f. 106, 177, List, with recommendations, of the officers in Louisiana (1734); D 2C 50, f. 20v, Recommendations by Périer concerning Renauld d'Hautrive; LSHM, 30/224, Oct. 11, 1730, Appeal by the Company against Renauld's wife.

[62] Parish register, New Orleans, Jan. 14, Aug. 5, 1726, June 26, 1730; Parish register, Mobile, Feb. 28, 1722; AC, C 13A 7, f. 39, La Chaise, Sept. 6, 1723; B 43, f. 268, The Company to Mandeville at Mobile; f. 687, Request for post of *major* at New Orleans; f. 738-39, Commission for Mandeville; G 1 465, Proxy to F. de Mandeville.

[63] AC, C 13A 11, F. 22-a, Périer, Nov. 12, 1728; A 22, f. 110v-111v, Commission as *major* for Louboey, April 23, 1730; B 43, f. 870-71, 901-902, Commission and presentation to the king of S. de Louboey, April 1730; D 2C 50, f. 16, Promotion of Louboey in 1732; AG, XB 17, Service records of officers of the regiment of Navarre; AC, B 55, f. 590v, The minister to the chevalier de Louboey, May 22, 1731.

[64] AC, D 2C 50, f. 12, Replacement of military officers, 1731; B 43, f. 904-908, Presentation to the king of S. de Poivilain, baron de Cresnay, April 6, 1730. (The spelling "Cresnay" is taken from the notaries' minutes.)

[65] AC, DFC, 41, f. 7-10, 11, Account of what happened at the Natchez fort, by Lieutenant Juzan; C 13A 14, f. 38, Périer and Salmon, May 12, 1732; C 13A 13, f.268, List of the officers whom the king has decided to establish in Louisiana; B 55, f. 31 (The minister) to Cresnay, May 22, 1731; f. 363-363v, to Lamirande, July 17, 1731; f. 590-a-590v, to Cresnay, to Dartaguiette Diron, May 22, 1731.

[66] AC, D 2C 50, f. 27, Replacement of military officers, aug. 17, 1732; F 3 24, f. 292-94. The deeds relative to the Poilvilain family do not mention the baron de Cresnay (AN, MC, 116-226, 109-489, 89-399).

[67] AC, D 2C, 50, f. 20v, Recommendations by Périer concerning Renault; D 2C 51, F. 88-88V, List of active officers who are to command the eight infantry companies, Mar. 6, 1730; f. 106, List with recommendations, of the officers (appraisal of Renault d'Hauterive); B 43, f. 52-53, List of what has to be paid for the infantry companies, 1721; f. 568-71, List of active supernumerary officers, 1725; f. 612, Commission for S. de Gauvrit; f. 641ff., General list of expenditure; 1727; f. 736, Warrant to give permission for S. Gauvrit to wear the cross, 1727; C 13A 9, f. 376, Pauger, April 3, 1726.

[68] AC, C 13A, 7, f. 22v, La Chaise, Sept 6, 1723; B 43, f. 641ff., General list of expenditure, 1727; C 13A 8, f. 149-51, 333-35, Proceedings, Nov. 17, 1724, July 18, 1725; C 13A, f. 111-23, Proceedings of May 1726.

[69] AC, C 13A 9, f. 126v, Proceedings, April 23, 1725, with marginal notes by the Company; C 13A 8, f. 248, *Mémoire* of M. de Boisbriant (1726); C 13A 9, f. 95v-97v, Proceedings, April 17, 1725.

[70] AC, C 13A 8, f. 148-51, Proceedings, Nov. 17, 1724; f. 246v, *Mémoire* for M. de Boisbriant (1726); B 43, f.554, Orders for cashiering of M. d'Arensbourg; f. 556, of S. Coustillas; f. 740, of S. du Puy Planchard (1725-27); D 2C 51, f. 81, Review of the garrison of New Orleans, 1731; f. 102-102v, *Mémoire* by Bienville on De Blanc, May 18, 1733; D 2C 50, f. 58v (Recommendation concerning De Blanc, 1759).

[71] AC, D 2C 51,f. 116, Bienville (to the minister), April 17, 1734.

[72] AC, C 13A 9, f. 376-376v, Pauger, April 3, 1726; C 13A 8, f. 148-51, Proceedings, Nov. 17, 1724; D 2C 51, f. 88v (Favorable marginal note by Périer, 1730); G 1 464, Census of July 1, 1727, Habitations on the left, going upriver.

[73] AC, D 2C 51, f. 105v (marginal notes); Parish register, New Orleans, Aug. 5, 1727; LSHM, 30/224, Oct 11, 1730, Death of the cashier Duval; Parish register, New Orleans, Aug. 5, Jan. 14, 1726.

[74] For example, none of the following marriages seems to have brought the husband any additional resources: that of Charles Petit de Livilliers with the sister of Verteuil, the administrator of the former Paris-Duverney concession; that of the ensign Jean Maret with the sister of the brigantine captain Esnoul de Livaudais; or even that of Broutin with François de Mandeville's widow, Madeleine Lemaire, about whose personal finances we have no precise information. Parish register, New Orleans, Jan 14, 1726, June 26, 1730, Sept. 26, 1729.

[75] AC, C 13A 14, f. 8v-9.

[76] AC, D 2C 51, f. 112, Cadets serving without letters (Marginally noted list of officers, Bienville, April 25, 1734); F 5B 57, nos. 8, 11, 13, 15, 18, Lists of passengers in various ships; G 1 464-C, nos 7, 17, 19, Lists of passengers in various ships; D 2C 51, f. 112-112v, 117, Cadets serving without letters (1734).

[77] AC, D 2C 50, f. 22v, 63v, Military officers in Louisiana; D 2C 51, f. 112-112v, Cadets serving without letters; C 13A 14, f. 15-15v, Périer and Salmon, Mar. 28, 1732; D 2C 51, f. 81, Review of the garrison of New Orleans, 1731; G 1 465, f. 40, Bienville and Salmon to Maurepas, 1734 (refers to the cadets whom it is appropriate to send among the Indians in order to learn their language); D 2C 51, f. 72-72v, cadet (Du Coderc) embarked as a private soldier on the *Alexandre* in 1729; f. 81 (Du Coderc sentry at New Orleans in 1731).

[78]Giraud, *Histoire,* 4:44-45; AC, D 2C 51, f. 62-63, List of cadets and soldiers detached from Plantin's company and embarked on the *Baleine* for Louisiana, April 20, 1728; F 5B 49, no. 82, Passengers in the *Basleine;* D 2C 51, f. 110v, Records of subordinate ensigns; LSHM, June 19, 1758, Marriage Contract of Louis de Populus de St-Protais.

[79]AC, D 2C 51, f. 62-63, 105-109, Marginally noted list of troops, April 1734 (f. 109, List of active ensigns); D 2C 50, f. 24v, Recommendation by the duchesse de Mazarin; C 13A 13, f 75, Périer, Dec. 10, 1731; LSHM, Marriage contract of Sept. 30, 1735.

[80]AC, D 2C 51, f. 109, Active ensigns, 1734; f. 62, Conditions provided for Favrot and St-Portais (contrast these with the conditions provided for Laurent du Coderc [D2C 51, f. 72]); F 5B 49, no. 82, Conditions during the voyage for Favrot and St-Protais; D 2C 51, f 81-82 (companies of Gauvrit and Dartaguiette); f. 110 (marginal note on Du Coderc, 1734).

[81]AC, C13A 14, f. 15-16, Périer and Salmon, Mar. 28, 1732.

THE MATERIAL CULTURE OF THE ATTAKAPAS DISTRICT IN THE FIRST TWO DECADES OF THE NINETEENTH CENTURY*

Glenn R. Conrad

Until I undertook detailed research into day-to-day life in the Attakapas District of Louisiana[1] in the early nineteenth century, I had come to that point in my academic career where I was willing to accept (largely as a result of sparce scholarship on the subject but strong oral tradition) the view that Attakapas at the beginning of the American period, less than fifty years after the area was truly opened to European settlement,[2] was a frontier region, largely isolated from the mainstream of life along the Mississippi River and in New Orleans. I tended to accept the popular and sometimes scholarly view, largely put forward in the 1950s and 60s, that everyday life in Attakapas, especially for the many Acadian settlers, in the late eighteenth and early nineteenth centuries had been primitive but pastoral and protective of ancient customs. One hundred years after its publication, *Evangeline* was still influencing many conceptions of early Attakapas, including my own. By the 1970s, however, with the coming of the French renaissance in Louisiana, the civil rights movement in America, and the separatist movement in Quebec, the earlier legends born of the *grand dérangement* and the romancing of Longfellow's *Evangeline*, were incorporated into a new body of literature which saddled these older pastoral visions of the Acadian past with a stark economic interpretation with attention-getting consequences. It was now stated that the economic conditions of the early American settlers of Louisiana, namely their poverty and its social consequences, were owing to the avarice of other ethnic groups who settled in Louisiana, particularly the French Creoles and the Anglo-Americans. According to this interpretation, beginning with the Louisiana Purchase, Acadians were systematically pushed off their good, wealth-producing lands by the legal and financial manipulations of the Creoles and Anglos, but particularly by the

---

*First published in the *Attakapas Gazette*, 27 (1992): 15-25. Reprinted with the kind permission of the author and the Attakapas Historical Association.

sugar interests among those two ethnic groups. The consequences for the Acadians, according to this interpretation, were comparable to a second *grand dérangement*. They were now exiled to Louisiana's swamplands and marshlands where, only by their wits did they keep body and soul together. Scorned by other ethnic groups, denied access to the riches of Louisiana, antebellum and post-Civil War Acadians were only, at best, second-class citizens. From these dreary accounts of the Acadian lifestyle during the group's first century and a half in Louisiana was born the heroic legends of how these depressed people survived in order to come into their own in the latter half of the twentieth century.[3]

Indeed, it was only when I began to question these interpretations and the related theses of oral tradition that I undertook this study of life, particularly Acadian life, in Attakapas in the years between the Louisiana Purchase and the Civil War. It did not seem reasonable to me that in a land as rich as Louisiana everyone, including the Acadians, should not, after the initial period of pioneer adjustments, begin to produce surplus wealth which would ameloriate the pioneer lifestyle so typical of the American frontier. Why, I repeatedly asked myself, was it necessary for Acadians, particularly beginning with the second generation, to live in a world of such deprivation where the only clothing they possessed were garments made of cotton that they had grown, picked, carded, spun, and weaved? Why did they always have to go barefooted, or, at best, succeeded in producing only some primitive footware which harkened back to serfdom in Europe? Frontier men and women elsewhere in America were wearing shoes and boots, why not the Acadians? Didn't the Acadians develop a long tradition of wearing shoes and boots in Acadia? Furthermore, why did legend and the 1970s interpretations insist that Acadians were usually ekeing out a subsistence existence on small farms when one of the cheapest commodities in Attakapas was land.[4] Were the Acadians driven off their lands by greedy Creoles and Anglos? Was the legend that Acadians seldom owned slaves based in fact? Was Attakapas such a backwater of civilization that no one had yet dared to bring the products of early nineteenth-century technology into the area so that settlers and their immediate descendants had to be self-sufficient? Was it that entrepreneurs saw the poverty of the people, especially the Acadians, and wrote off investment in Attakapas as a waste of time and money? Questions such as these bothered me sufficiently so that by 1987 I began this research into Attakapas lifestyles in the antebellum era. The results to date have been astounding and form the bases of the Attakapas Land Record Series.

The analysis of land and slave proprietorship between 1804 and 1818, which I presented in Volume II, Part 1, of the Land Records Series[5] clearly indicates that social classes quickly developed among Attakapas Acadians. It also confirms that some of the wealthiest people of Attakapas were Acadians; more importantly, however, it shows that there was a strong middle class developing among Acadians. Now, an analysis of estates for the same period, 1804-1818, indicates much the same, but the successions tell us a great deal more about the lifestyle of the people of Attakapas than do the conveyance records. In order to put that larger picture of day-to-day life in better focus, I compiled from estate inventories and/or sales a partial list of objects found in the homes of

Attakapas residents and stores of Attakapas merchants between 1804 and 1818.[6] Without doubt, it is the material culture aspect of the estates which casts new light on life in the Attakapas in the early nineteenth century. At first glance at the region's material culture, there were, of course, certain objects found in practically every home: beds, chairs, tables, armoires, dishes, and various utensils. Outside the house, the same was true: there were plows, harrows, carts and wagons, hand tools of all kinds, the ubiqutous caleche, tubs, buckets, grindstones, etc. This investigation, however, turned up objects which I would have never expected to find had I adhered to the vision of legend or the interpretations of the 1970s. As a result of page-by-page research of conveyance and succession records, I now have a more realistic view of life in Attakapas in the early nineteenth century, a view that is far more compatable with frontier life, or near-frontier life, as it was elsewhere in early nineteenth-century America.

House Construction

After going through the succession inventories, there is no escaping the clear message that early nineteenth-century residents of Attakapas were frugal people, whether they had to be or not, and perhaps this is characteristic of pioneers. Certainly, there is nothing that one could point to as being ostentatious, and this is true not only for wealthy individuals like Martin Duralde and Amand Broussard but also for the larger group of middle-class people.

The homes of Attakapas residents, based on evidence at hand, seem to have been nothing more than was absolutely necessary for everyday family life. Amand Broussard's house, for example, appraised at $600 in the boom year of 1818.[7] Most houses were of frame construction, wood being the most readily available building resource. Cypress was used inside and out, bousillage was commonplace in house construction. Houses seldom had more than five rooms, although it is difficult to determine what was a "room" and what was a glorified closet.[8] Because so much of nineteenth-century living was out-of-doors, for example, eating, visiting, and working on house porches, the need for rooms was confined in most instances to the basic requirements for sleeping and protection from the elements. While many houses were fitted with solid wood window blinds and solid wooden doors ranging from crude construction to carpenter finished,[9] many houses had sashes fitted with glass lights and doors which incorporated some glass. Panelled doors were available for Attakapas residents. Darby House, near New Iberia, which dated from approximately 1816, had panelled doors on the interior and exterior. Brick houses, while uncommon, were not rare.[10] The Darby family seem to have been devotees of brick houses, building them at Baldwin and Lake Tasse.[11] Agricole Fuselier built the beautiful house now known as "Alice" during the course of the years under review.[12] There is no doubt, however, that the majority of houses were of cypress frame construction, built on cypress piers. The roof covering was almost always cypress shingles. Almost all houses had a gallery in front and back. If the house was all-cypress construction, there was no need for painting the wood for protection against insects and the elements. Thus, many Attakapas homes were unpainted, and with time the cypress exterior boards developed a soft grey patina. If bousillage was employed in construction, it was usually covered with boards or white-washed[13] for further protection against the high annual rainfall of the area. All Attakapas merchants sold slaked lime for making white-wash. Some residents, however, elected to paint their homes.[14] One individual's inventory carried three kegs of paint, blue, green, and brown. All Attakapas merchants had on hand white lead and linseed oil, two ingredients of paint.

Furnishings

The interiors of the houses were sparcely furnished as one would expect in a frugal society. Usually only what was needed and used was found in the house. Even the homes of wealthy individuals seem to have had few superfulous furnishings. Take, for example the Martin Duralde household.[15] After reviewing the community property inventory, I wonder how was it possible for this well-known, wealthy couple to entertain and accommodate the many prominent members of their family and other visitors with so few bedroom accommodations. The inventory indicates that the couple had one cherrywood double bed, two cypress double beds, and a single bed. These would hardly seem sufficient to accommodate a visit from Duralde's son-in-law, Gov. W. C. C. Claiborne and his family as well as the residents of the house. Nevertheless, the Duraldes had 20 pair of bedsheets and 19 bedspreads, but, oddly enough, only 4 mosquito bars were inventoried.

If, however, the Duraldes were planning to entertain at dinner, they were apparently well outfitted for the occasion. They had 5 tables, 2 described as being square, 4 of cherrywood, and 1 of mahogany. For these tables there were 12 chairs, two of which were armchairs. One might assume, therefore, that the Duralde dinner parties did not exceed 10 guests. This assumption is reinforced by the fact that the inventory lists 12 silver coffee spoons, despite the fact that the couple owned 18 silver place settings.

Interestingly enough, the Duralde inventory does not include anything that might be construed to be parlor furniture; however, the list does include two mirrors and a pierglass. With the exception of the one couch mentioned in Estate No. 139 and the cushioned chairs found in Estate No. 233,[16] there is no indication of "parlor" furniture in the homes of Attakapas. Mirrors, other than "shaving mirrors," are only rarely found in estate inventories between 1804 and 1818. I found only two clocks inventoried (Estate Nos. 120 and 288), but as with agricultural societies everywhere, the exact division of time may have been of little concern.[17] To my utter surprise, Augustin Broussard had a sundial. Candelabra and candlesticks are conspicuous by their absence from the majority of inventories, and only 3 vases (Estate No. 4) were listed between 1804 and 1818. Clearly, bric-a-brac was something for the future.

Furnishings which appear in the inventories are largely for bedrooms and dining rooms. As the inventories indicate, much of this furniture was "country made," meaning homemade. But the inventories strongly imply that there was furniture in Attakapas homes made by craftsmen. The woods used in local furniture-making were cypress, cherrywood, and walnut.[18] One does find, however, the occasional piece made of mahogany—an imported wood.[19] There is not to be found in these records anyone in Attakapas identified as a professional cabinetmaker. Nevertheless, the inventory of the mercantile firm of Garrigou and Abat indicates that these merchants had 7 bedsteads for sale. They also had tables and chairs for sale.[20] Someone, either locally or elsewhere, had to have made them. The best guide to the craftsmanship of furniture inventoried is its appraisal value. Similar items appraised at different prices suggest better craftsmanship for the higher value.

Kitchens, Pantries, Dining Areas

If other rooms of the house were usually sparsely furnished, kitchens, pantries, and dining areas were most substantially outfitted. In the kitchen there was usually a plethora of iron pots, but other cooking vessels are seldom mentioned. One gets the impression that the ubiquitous iron pot served in the preparation of almost everything eaten. Most household inventories for the era reveal numerous demijohns which contained most of the liquids used for drinking or for food preparation. Almost every kitchen and pantry had a great many bottles, sometimes a household would have as many as 500 bottles. Although the inventories imply that the bottles were empty (because nothing is recorded as "15 bottles of this" or "10 bottles of that"), we cannot infer that they were not used. First of all, as the merchant inventories reveal, many liquids were bulk packaged in barrels or casks. The customer would arrive at the store with empty bottles in hand to be filled by the merchant. The same was probably true of demijohns. Also, one must take into consideration that while merchant inventories usually indicate large stocks of alcoholic beverages, household inventories seldom reveal the presence of spirits. There can be little doubt that some of these bottles were used for homemade wine, beer, and cordials. At least one merchant in the area sold bottle corks.[21]

Most households had an array of dishes, platters, soup bowls, drinking glasses, cups and saucers, crockery, and the occasional candy or sugar dish. With rare exception none of these items seems to have been of sufficient quality to set it apart from the "run-of-the mill."[22] On the other hand, a surprising number of Attakapas households had silver soup ladles. While the ladles and silver place settings reflect appropriate values, everyday table knives, forks, and spoons seem to have been unusually cheap. A dozen table knives or forks sold for $1.00.

Tablecloths and napkins are frequently included in the inventories. One gets the distinct impression that if someone in early nineteenth-century Attakapas wanted to impress family or guests, it was done at the dining table. It was there that one detects a slight splurge on the part of householders. In addition to the silver place settings, the silver soup ladle, one finds, through the inventories, that there were assorted serving dishes, soup tureens, covered dishes, tumblers, cups and saucers. True there is no indication that any of the plates, bowls, cups and saucers were made of fine china, nor is there any mention of stemmed crystal wine or water glasses; nevertheless one gets the distinct impression that many Attakapas dining tables had the option of being well appointed.

Foodstuffs

The merchant inventories provide an insight to what foodstuffs were available for sale. As one might expect of the times and the place, these foodstuffs were almost always those things which were not produced locally. One does not find in these early nineteenth-century stores the fully stocked shelves of canned goods, preserved and pickled items, and boxed products found on the shelves of the general merchandise store of the late nineteenth century. Moreover, the foodstuff inventories reflect the self-sufficient condition of the local population in regard to fresh, smoked, and salted meats and fresh and dried vegetables. Only occasionally does a household estate reveal some of the edible items on hand, and these are usually potatoes, peas, corn, and rice. Although the estates fail to inventory barnyard fowl of any kind, there can be little doubt that just about everyone had chickens, ducks, and geese and perhaps other fowl such as guinea fowl and turkeys. Soup (or was it gumbo?) was obviously standard fare, judging from the number of soup bowls and tureens.[23] Corn, corn mills, and cornmeal are found in many inventories, suggesting, of course, that a considerable amount of cornbread was consumed, along with couche-couche, milk or clabber. The grease needed for frying the couche-couche must have always been nearby in one of the many lard jars inventoried. But we must not think that the early residents of Attakapas were limited to cornbread. Merchants had on hand barrels of wheat flour, which sold for about $10 per barrel.

In addition to flour, the merchants usually carried large stocks of sugar and salt. The sugar was either domestic or Havana sugar. Havana sugar was considered better because it was whiter than the domestic product. Such large amounts of sugar on hand in the stores would suggest that the residents of Attakapas were using it for something more than their coffee. Possibly some of the sugar was going into fruit preserves. After discovering the amount of sugar on hand and the easy availability of sugar, one wonders if the people of Attakapas used honey in any quantity. There is absolutely no mention of honey in the inventories surveyed.

The large inventories of salt are to be expected. Of course some was used for seasoning, but the great bulk of salt consumed was used in preserving meat and pickling other products. Salt was readily available in Attakapas from at least the very early days of the nineteenth century. By 1812, Major Jesse McCall had established a salt-evaporation works on what is presently Avery Island (then called McCall's Island). His production must have been significant because he bought a schooner to transport his salt to market.[24] Salt sold for $7 a barrel in 1810.

If salt was available for seasoning, so was pepper. Naturally, one immediately thinks of the people of Attakapas using red pepper. That was quite likely; however, if they did use red pepper, they did not buy it from the local merchant, they grew the peppers and prepared them in the household, probably using some of their many bottles on hand to store the finished product. The seasoning bought from local merchants was black pepper. This fact is somewhat surprising, for black pepper had to be imported, and one merchant's supply was appraised at $5.00 per pound.[25] This might be considered expensive, but the fact that four Attakapas merchants had black pepper on hand indicates that there was a demand for it.

In addition to flour, salt, and pepper, local merchants usually had on hand large inventories of coffee and small amounts of tea. Coffee, while not grown in Louisiana, could be easily obtained from Cuba, Haiti, or Jamaica. Tea, on the other hand, had to be imported across great distances. That fact is reflected in the price of $1.25 per lb. asked by one Attakapas merchant.[26] Coffee, on the other hand, sold for about 30¢ per lb. on average throughout the era investigated.[27] Again, however, tea was found in Attakapas because there was a demand for it, albeit small.

Spirits, Tobacco, and "Laissez les bons temps rouler."

Merchants also supplied the local demand for wine, whiskey, tafia, rum, brandy, assorted liqueurs (cordials), tobacco and snuff. Although there are many listings in the inventories under the term "wine," there were several references to "Malaga wine" and "Madeira wine." The interesting absence was any reference to "Bordeaux wine." Perhaps, however, the appraisers simply assumed that their reference to "wine" was, of course, Bordeaux wine. There is no indication whether the tafia was local or was coming from the West Indies, but there is no doubt about the entry for "Jamaican rum." There is no mention of beer in the inventories, but this may have been produced at home.[28] Wine and tafia like other spirits, came in bulk and was sold in smaller amounts to the customer who usually provided the bottles or demijohns necessary to take home this purchase. This was not the case with liqueurs, they were sold already bottled. I might add that syrup and certain oils, for example olive oil and palm oil, were sold already bottled. Only one merchant had cherry bounce in stock.[29] Tobacco was available from the merchants, but it would appear from their stocks of this item that the commodity was not used in great quantities, most of it being used for pipe smoking or chewing. Only one merchant had a small quantity of snuff on hand.[30]

If spirits and tobacco might be thought of as products used for leisure or festive times,[31] they bring to mind another matter. I was struck by the absence of musical instruments in the inventories, whether household or merchant. The only musical instruments inventoried were two violins, one found in a household inventory and one for sale by a merchant.[32] The latter violin was offered with its case for $25.00, not an extraordinary price when one considers that residents of Attakapas were buying slaves for $1,000 to $1,500 each. There is, as yet, no acceptable explanation for this dearth of musical instruments.[33]

Textiles, Wearing Apparel, and Footwear

If there was a dearth of some items in the everyday lives of the people of Attakapas, certainly that dearth was not to be found among textiles. The evidence of the quantity, variety, and quality of textiles available to the people of Attakapas in the first two decades of the nineteenth century is simply astounding. That evidence lays to rest forever the oral tradition that Attakapas cottonade persisted as the principle textile for everyday wearing apparel in early nineteenth-century Attakapas. I never expected to encounter the volume or variety of textiles such as that which turned up in Attakapas homes and stores. So astonishing was this revelation that I decided to record as much information as possible about these textiles.[34]

Oral tradition has long maintained that the people of Attakapas, especially the Acadians, grew their yellow cotton, ginned it, carded it, spun it, weaved it, and sewed it into wearing apparel. And, indeed, they did, and undoubtedly some were continuing to do so in the first two decades of the nineteenth century because the inventories do record spinning wheels and looms in the area.[35] But, if the twenty spinning wheels and eleven looms carried in the 172 inventories analyzed are any reflection of the actual number of these items in Attakapas, one has to conclude that either the persons owning spinning wheels and looms were working day and night to provide cottonade for Attakapas, or the people of Attakapas were using other textiles for wearing apparel.[36] Common sense dictates that the merchants of Attakapas would not have had on hand, throughout the era under investigation, such large supplies or varieties of textiles if there had not been a corresponding demand for them. Further evidence of the fact that the spinning wheel may have passed its heyday by the beginning of the nineteenth century is found in the large inventories of thread found in local stores. Only Garrigou and Abat, among the merchants of St. Martinville, carried homespun thread. On the other hand William Maquillé offered his customers skeins of silk thread. More about textiles in a moment.

If oral tradition has kept alive the cottonade-clad Acadian, it has also perpetuated the misconception of the barefooted Acadian. Of course, it must be understood that this oral tradition is based solidly on the misconception that the Acadians of Attakapas were universally poor and lived in a classless society. Hopefully, this investigation has dispelled both notions, certainly with regard to the early nineteenth century. I was never able to quarrel with the idea that many people chose to go barefooted at certain times of the year and in certain circumstances because this is still a common practice in the South. But to suggest, as C. C. Robin did, that the Acadians were barefooted most of the time

The Material Culture of the Attakapas District 381

and wore shores only on special occasions, seems somewhat farfetched.[37] Indeed it was, if one looks carefully at the succession inventories.

One of the first things to become obvious is the relatively large number of leather tanners, making leather widely available in Attakapas. Next, one discovers that the region had a fair number of cobblers. Indeed, the merchants stocked cobbler's supplies—nails, hammers, pincers, etc. Then, there are some household inventories that actually specify the number of shoes and boots in the household, although this is not common because often all wearing apparel, including footwear, was lumped together and given a single appraisal value. But there can be no mistaking the fact that footwear, other than that found in the cobbler's shop, was readily available to everyone in the stores of Attakapas. One discovers that ladies' shoes were not only plentiful, but ladies had a choice of leather or silk.[38] Louis Lingois' inventory indicates that he had 65 pair of ladies leather shoes on hand and 48 pair of ladies' fancy shoes. William Maquillé had on hand 26 pair of ladies' moroccan leather shoes and 3 pair of spangled silk shoes.[39] Cobblers' inventories indicate that they had mens' shoes and boots for sale. The use of shoes and boots by the people of Attakapas is also supported by the number and variety of stockings on hand in the stores for both men and women. It was utterly surprising to discover that the ladies of Attakapas had silk stockings available to them as early as the first decade of the nineteenth century.

Robin's observation that the Acadians along the Mississippi River seldom wore clean clothes is interesting.[40] There were large quantities of soap available in Attakapas and presumably on the Acadian Coast. Merchants of Attakapas had all kinds of soap available for sale, even something called "American Soap" which must have been stocked for the Anglo-American clientel. In addition, one Attakapas merchant even carried lady's perfume. There were the usual array of ribbons for the hair and a variety of combs for grooming, but one thing obviously missing from the inventories were brushes. One does not find a brush of any kind.[41] But there were earrings, necklaces, and breastpins.

Now, let us look at the textiles available in Attakapas in the early years of the nineteenth century. During the course of the fifteen years from 1804 to 1818, there are 5 merchant inventories: Joseph Melançon's in 1807; Garrigou & Abat in 1810; Maquille's General Merchandise, in 1812; Dominique Prévost's in 1813; and Louis Lingois in 1818. The inventories indicate that these stores carried the following fabrics:

Bombazet	Bontane	Book Muslin	Brabant Linen
Bretagne	Broadcloth	Calico	Cambric
Casimir	Check	Chintz	Cholet
Colette	Coutil	Crepe Cerise	Dimity (Basin)

Drap (broadcloth)	Drape de Soie	Duck	Fil d'Epreuve
Fil de Rennes	Flamed fabrics	Gingas	Gingham
Guernsey	Guinea	Gurrah	Hessian
Limbourg	Listados	Marcella	Marly
Morlaix	Muslin	Nankeen	Organdi
Osnaburg	Pagne	Pekin	Piqué
Percale	Platilla	Russian sheeting	Satin
Seersucker	Taffeta	Velure	Velvet
Vesting	Voile	Worsted Stuff[42]	

For the spinners of legends, let me report that 4 of the 5 merchant inventories indicate cotton on hand totalling 195 ells (an English textile measurement approximating 45 inches in length) or 243 yards of this material. But for weavers of fact, the merchant stocks of platilla and nankeen are astounding. Platilla is described by Florence Montgomery[43] as a well-bleached linen, first imported into America in 1693. All 5 Attakapas merchants carried large stocks of platilla as indicated by the five inventories. The total for the 5 inventories was 2,430 yards. Platilla sold for about 22¢ per ell.

Nankeen is interesting because of the Attakapas cottonade tradition. Nankeen was a cotton cloth of plain weave made from yellow cotton originally in China. In the West, nankeen was traditionally thought of as a yellow cloth. By 1750 the textile mills of Manchester, England, were turning out vast quantities of nankeen, but because the yellow cotton supply could not keep up with the English mills, the British used white cotton and dyed it the shade of yellow of nankeen. By 1790 New York and New England textile mills were turning out huge amounts of nankeen for domestic American use. These mills produced the fabric in the traditional yellow, but also in white, pale blue, and black. Montgomery notes that the fabric was extremely popular for use in making shirts, culottes, and trousers. All 5 Attakapas merchants carried large stocks of nankeen. To give some idea of the apparent popularity of this fabric, the total amount of nankeen in the 5 inventories amounted to 7,470 yards. Attakapas merchants carried the four basic colors of yellow, pale blue, white, and black. Nankeen sold for about 14¢ an ell during the entire period under investigation.

There was also something called nankeen lange, which was a heavy nankeen suitable for making cotton blankets. It sold for 50¢ per ell. Attakapas merchants apparently carried large stocks of other fabrics, including calico, cambric, dimity, gingham, linen (other than platilla), seersucker, and velvet. Garrigou and Abat, alone, had 126 ells of velvet on hand in 1810. It sold for about $1.00 per ell.

In conclusion, let me say that there is little doubt that Attakapas legends will continue to prosper, but the fact is that by the beginning of the nineteenth century a well-developed mercantile trade system between St. Martinville, New Orleans, Philadelphia and New York, and England and France had come into being. The people of Attakapas prospered during the 15 years from 1804 to 1818, as the records attest, and enjoyed, if they wanted to do so, a broad array of products which until now legend has largely succeeded in obscuring.

Notes for "The Material Culture of the Attakapas District
in the First Two Decades of the Nineteenth Century"

[1] The old Attakapas District of Louisiana are the five present-day parishes of St. Martin, St. Mary, Lafayette, Vermilion, and Iberia. The district was an administrative unit until 1811 when St. Mary Parish was established. The records consulted for Volume 2, Part 2, of the Land Records Series include those of the entire District from 1804-1811 and those of St. Martin Parish (present-day St. Martin, Lafayette, Vermilion, and part of Iberia parishes) between 1811 and 1818. The cutoff date of 1818 was chosen because in that year occurred the highwater mark of the post-War of 1812 economic boom.

[2] The first land grants in the Attakapas District were made in the early 1760s. It was not, however, until 1765, with the coming of the exiled Acadians, that the district had a recognizable European population. For more on the pioneers of Attakapas, their colonial landholdings, and the land claims they put forward to the American government, see Glenn R. Conrad, *Land Records of the Attakapas District, Vol. 1, The Attakapas Domesday Book* (Lafayette, La., 1990).

[3] For a discussion of the foregoing interpretations, see the "Introduction to the Series," ibid., ix-xxviii.

[4] So cheap during the colonial era of Attakapas, 1764-1803, that it was given away for the asking. Volume 1 of this series confirms the fact that the Acadians knew how to ask for and receive land grants.

[5] Glenn R. Conrad, *Land Records of the Attakapas District, Volume 2, Part 1, Conveyance Records of Attakapas County* (Lafayette, 1992); hereafter *Conveyance Records, 1804-1818*.

[6] See *Estates, 1804-1818*, Appendix 2. This is not, by far, a complete listing of every object found in every inventory of every estate reviewed. The repetition would have been not only boring but also overwhelming. What I have tried to do is list everyday items found in most households or in area stores two or three times for different years of the analysis to determine any fluctuation in price. I have, however, made a determined effort to list unusual items found in households or stores. Moreover, I became so amazed by the quantity and variety of textiles found in the inventory of local merchants that I listed every inventory or sale reference to textiles.

[7] See *Estates, 1804-1818*, Estate No. 288.

[8] By "glorified closets," I have in mind some of the *cabinets* that were usually a part of Attakapas houses.

[9] Only in the estate of Dr. Ramus Davis (*Estates, 1804-1818*, Estate No. 305) did I find mention of panelled doors. Perhaps the only reason for this mention was that they had not been installed and therefore were being inventoried separately from the house. It would seem likely that panelled doors had been installed in other Attakapas homes by this time. Darby House, near New Iberia, which dated from approximately 1816, had panelled doors on the interior and exterior.

[10] Many houses were installing brick chimneys by the second decade of the nineteenth century. Charles Pecot, for example, required a double brick chimney for the new house he had built in 1815. See *Conveyance Records, 1804-1818*, 213.

[11] The house at Baldwin survives to this day. The Darby House near New Iberia was destroyed by fire in February 1979. See Gertrude C. Taylor, "Last Days of Darby," *Attakapas Gazette*, 13 (1978): 103-6.

[12] See Glenn R. Conrad, "A Lady Called Alice," *Attakapas Gazette*, 13 (1978): 124-28.

[13] As Estate Nos. 126 and 305 (*Estates, 1804-1818*) attest, slaked lime was available in Attakapas.

[14] The inventory of Estate No. 305 (*Estates, 1804-1818*) lists three kegs of paint, blue, green, and brown. Charles Pecot's contract for building a house called for the house to be "painted" white (*Conveyance Records*, 213). Appendix 2 of *Estates, 1804-1818* lists white lead and linseed oil, two ingredients of paint. Also found in that appendix is an entry for copperas, which would have produced a green hue; however, copperas was usually used to make a green dye.

[15] *Estates, 1804-1818*, Estate No. 233.

[16] Ibid., Estates 139 and 233.

[17] Pocket watches fare only slightly better. For the period of 1804 to 1818 only five gold or silver pocket watches were inventoried (Estates Nos. 11, 228, 237 [2], 303). Of course, one can assume that most pocket watches simply passed down to heirs and therefore did not enter succession inventories.

[18] The term used in French is *noyer*. Black walnut trees did grow in South Louisiana, and it is possible that this wood was used in furniture-making; however, the term was also used by the early French settlers for pecan wood. The wood of the wild cherry tree is still considered by cabinetmakers to be excellent in furniture-making. Interestingly enough, nowhere in the inventories does one find furniture said to be made of oak, to say nothing of pine.

[19] The Duraldes (Estate No. 233) had a mahogany table, and Adrien Dumartrait and his wife (Estate No. 311) had a mahogany bed and armoire.

[20] *Estates, 1804-1818*, Estate No. 60.

[21] Ibid., Estate No. 126.

[22] An exception is found in Estate No. 311 where a porcelain tea service and tray are listed and appraised at $20.00.

[23] One merchant had on hand a case of vermicelli which is frequently used in soupmaking.

[24] *Conveyance Records*, 149, 183.

[25] *Estates, 1804-1818*, Estate No. 92.

[26] Ibid., Estate No. 60.

[27] Coffee was selling for 30¢ per lb. as late as the World War I years of 1917-1918. During the 1920s coffee prices fluctuated between 30¢ and 50¢ per lb., but during the 1930s depression years coffee prices ranged between 21¢ and 29¢. By 1943 the price of a pound of coffee was again 30¢, but coffee prices were then under wartime price controls. Coffee has not been that price per pound since 1945 and has not been below 50¢ per lb. since 1948. See *Historical Statistics*, Part 1:213.

[28] If there was homebrew of any kind, it does not show up in the household inventories.

[29] Dominique Prévost (Estate No. 126) was the only merchant to stock cherry bounce (2 demijohns). From my own experience, however, I would think that this delicious concoction was usually made at home from the fruit of the Louisiana wild cherry.

[30] *Estate, 1804-1818*, Estate No. 92.

The Material Culture of the Attakapas District

[31] Coffee-drinking should also be included in this category.

[32] *Estates, 1804-1818*, Estates 252 and 302.

[33] When discussing this lack of musical instruments in home or store with my colleague Barry Ancelet, he suggested that perhaps the *dance ronde* or play-party song provided a tune for dances instead of musical instruments. He also suggested that musical instruments in Attakapas at the time may have been crude devices which were not thought worthy of appraisal. C. C. Robin recorded that the Acadians living along the Mississippi River loved to dance and did so even though music was provided by only "a couple of fiddles." C. C. Robin, *Voyage to Louisiana*, trans. Stuart O. Landry, Jr. (New Orleans, 1966), 115. If the succession inventories are any indication of the number of violins in Attakapas, Robin may have been astonished. He says nothing about dancing in Attakapas.

[34] For a listing of the various textiles, laces, ribbons, shawls, etc., see *Estates, 1804-1818*, Appendix 2. For a description of the textiles found in Attakapas, see ibid., Appendix 3, Glossary of Textiles.

[35] I found it interesting that many of the spinning wheels and looms were described as "old." This designation made me wonder whether the spinning wheels and looms were still in use or were relics of the past which had made their way to the attic. Also I did not find a spinning wheel or loom listed in a merchant inventory and presumably for sale.

[36] Amand Broussard, one of the wealthiest persons in Attakapas, had three "old" spinning wheels in his home when the succession inventory was taken in February, 1818. It is somewhat difficult to imagine Mrs. Broussard sitting at the loom and weaving cottonade when the stores of St. Martinville were brimming with a broad variety of textiles. There is the suggestion, however, that slaves were sometimes spinners and weavers. It would be interesting to know whether their finished product was being used as wearing apparel for their masters or for their fellow slaves.

[37] Robin, *Voyage to Louisiana*, 115. Certainly the Acadians, when in Acadia, had worn some sort of warm, water-tight footwear. I must assume that they did so when they were in exile in the British East Coast colonies. Why, suddenly, would the Acadians virtually abandon footwear. In oral tradition they did so usually for one of two reasons, they were too poor to have shoes or because of the warm Louisiana climate. What the raconteurs have overlooked, however, in their back-to-nature vision of the Acadians is that the very same warm Louisiana climate often requires one to wear boots or shoes. For anyone familiar with the countryside, Louisiana undergrowth is notorious for its tangle of briars and brambles that not only scratch the unprotected leg but can slice the flesh like a knife. Poisonous reptiles were everywhere in the early days of Attakapas, making snakebite on the bare foot or leg a real hazard. Moreover, as adept as a person might be with an axe, there was always the potential for accident. The prudent woodchopper, it seems to me, would have protected his feet and legs with boots. At leisure around the house, or at work around the house and the barnyard, Acadians and others probably went barefooted in warm weather, especially if the ground was muddy. I quickly learned as a small boy that it was easier to wash muddy feet than it was to clean muddy shoes.

[38] When one finds so many shoes available in Attakapas, one has to wonder about the tired old story of the Cajun girls going to the dance with shoes in hand "because they did not want to wear out their shoes." Having known Louisiana in the days before there were many paved streets or roads, I wonder if the practicality of the young ladies rested more on the fact that they did not wish to arrive at the dance with muddy shoes.

[39] *Estates, 1804-1818*, Estates 92 and 302.

[40] Robin, *Voyage to Louisiana*, 115.

[41] The same can be said for brooms and mops. Although every household must have had a broom of some sort, these items seem never to have entered the inventories. Storekeepers apparently did not stock brooms and mops.

[42] For a description of these fabrics, see *Estates, 1804-1818*, Appendix 3.

[43] Florence M. Montgomery, *Textiles in America, 1650-1870* . . . (New York, 1984).

VIRGINIANS IN THE TECHE COUNTRY: JOHN D. WILKINS AND THE LOUISIANA BEGINNINGS*

Glenn R. Conrad

John Douglass Wilkins was born in Brunswick County or Greensville County, Virginia in 1780.[1] He was the son of Douglass Wilkins and Tabitha Ann Wyche.[2] The elder Wilkins was a Revolutionary War veteran, militia officer, local politician,[3] and planter. His wife was descended from the prominent Wyche family, southern Virginia Tidewater planters.[4] In addition to John, Douglass Wilkins' other children were Joseph, who married Elizabeth (Betsy) Jones, the daughter of John Jones and Elizabeth Binns,[5] Patsy, who married Sterling Peebles of Greensville County, April 20, 1788; Elizabeth, who married Dr. William Purnell of Greensville County, November 1, 1799; Tabitha Ann, who married John W. Cocke of Greensville County, August 28, 1807; and Benjamin, who married first Jane Taylor of Tennessee and secondly Sarah Overton, also of Tennessee.[6]

Very little is known about the Douglass Wilkins family before 1801. In August of that year Wilkins executed his last will and testament, a document which affords limited insight into the family's activities. From the terms of Wilkins' will, one can deduce that Tabitha Ann Wyche had brought a large dowry to her marriage. To his wife, Wilkins bequeathed "in lieu of her dower of land, all the land the east side of the Rocky Run and all the cleared land above the run." In lieu of her dower of Negroes, Wilkins bequeathed to his wife twenty-eight slaves. Finally, in lieu of her dower of the personal estate, he willed her as many animals "and household furniture as will serve her to keep House."[7]

To his son John Douglass, the elder Wilkins bequeathed his plantation in Brunswick County.[8] The will notes that Wilkins and his son had already concluded an arrangement whereby John had occupied the plantation and had acquired some of his father's slaves to operate the place. An addendum to the will states: "I desire John D. Wilkins' house to be

---

*Excerpts first published in the *Attakapas Gazette*, 17 (1982): 8-18, 58, 63-64. Reprinted with the kind permission of the author and the Attakapas Historical Association.

finished by the Negroes. . . ." Douglass Wilkins was therefore providing for his second son (as he had for the elder Joseph[9] and as he would provide for the younger Benjamin[10]) as he entered adulthood.

Because his youngest son was then but a child,[11] the senior Wilkins provided that his wife was "to have the use of Benjamin Wilkins' Negroes upon her schooling him and maintaining him till he comes of age." Following that, the administration of Benjamin's estate would pass into the hands of his elder brother, John, who would be obligated to complete Benjamin's education and provide him with animals for his plantation. That plantation was the 1,600-acre "home place" in Greensville County.

To each of his children Douglass Wilkins bequeathed movable and/or immovable property according to whether or not he had entered into a previous arrangement for entitling them to a portion of his possessions. He named his wife, William Maclin,[12] Joseph Wilkins, and John D. Wilkins to be executors of his will. Douglass Wilkins died in early 1802, for his will was probated at the May (1802) session of county court.

Little data have been uncovered concerning John D. Wilkins in the years before his marriage. Dr. Alfred Duperier (in a series of articles in the *New Iberia Enterprise* between March 18 and April 1, 1899) noted that he was a well-educated individual, having been schooled at the University of Virginia. That, however, is unlikely because the University of Virginia was not founded until 1819, the year that Wilkins was thirty-nine years old.[13]

Research has so far failed to reveal when and where John Wilkins married. It is known, however, that he married Maria Cole Claiborne, also a Virginian. The Wilkinses had four children who survived to adulthood: John Henry, born in 1810; Imogene; Mary Ann; and Richard, born May 14, 1815.[14]

As his family expanded in number, Wilkins must have prospered, for from 1811 to 1821, in a series of purchases, he added 727 acres to his plantation on Shiny Creek and purchased the "home place" in Greensville County from Benjamin.[15] Interestingly enough, John Wilkins purchased only two slaves during this decade.[16]

The era of building suddenly ended, however, in the late summer of 1825. At that time John Wilkins began to close out his extensive Virginia agricultural operations. Slightly more than four years later, he had liquidated most of his immovable property and, at age fifty, sought a new life for himself, his family, and his slaves in a rather remote region of Louisiana.

The motivation necessary to cause a nearly fifty-year-old man to quit his native land and the acquisitions of generations must have been great indeed. Many of the factors behind such a decision have already been investigated in the introduction to this series of articles. All that remains is to investigate those factors which could have attracted John Wilkins to Louisiana.

First, there was the lure of the Old Southwest, a new frontier that had been opened with the Louisiana Purchase. For many Easterners the "grass looked greener" across the Mississippi River. Second, by the 1820s sugar culture in Louisiana was well established. Tales of fortunes to be made in sugar were beginning to circulate in the older states of the Union. Many Easterners listened with rapt attention. As Sam B. Hilliard notes, "Despite obstacles [to growing sugarcane in Louisiana], profits were high, and the incentive to become a sugar planter lured thousands of settlers in . . . [Louisiana] during the early nineteenth century.[17]

But there was more than just profits in sugar cultivation. The culture required large amounts of human labor. An increasingly irksome problem for Wilkins was the ever-growing number of slaves he owned. A sugar plantation in subtropical Louisiana would certainly be able to give work to his slaves on a year-round basis. The milder climate, moreover, would allow for nearly year-round food production for the slaves.[18] Finally, in 1826, the federal government offered for sale large tracts of public land in Louisiana at a price of $1.25 per acre.[19]

Between 1825 and 1829, therefore, Wilkins sold most of his Virginia lands and began to buy, in partnership with his nephew, Henry Wyche Peebles, large tracts of public and private lands in St. Mary (later Iberia) Parish, Louisiana.[20]

The sales began when, on November 2, 1825, Wilkins and his wife sold 814 acres of the "home place" to Samuel Avent.[21] An interesting aside to emerge from this sale is mention of the fact that the sale property was bounded on one side by that belonging to Joseph Wilkins, "now deceased."[22] This sale netted $3,663.

The same day the Wilkinses sold another fifty acres of "home place" to John Ferguson for $300.[23] The remnant of "home place" was sold after John Wilkins moved to Louisiana. That transaction was handled by John G. Claiborne of Brunswick County. Claiborne held Wilkins' power of attorney.[24] On December 24, 1833, Claiborne sold the remaining 688 acres of "home place" to Ruffin E. Walton for $667.50. In view of the price, less than one dollar per acre, one can conclude that the land sold was either wooded or exhausted.[25]

Some time between 1825 and 1828 John Wilkins and Henry Peebles formed a partnership, eventually known as John D. Wilkins & Co.,[26] and, in the fall of 1828, they arrived in Louisiana to purchase public lands.[27] Proceeding to the federal land office in Opelousas, they selected land in the Isle aux Cannes area of St. Mary Parish. Their purchases began on January 25, 1829, and continued until March. By that date they had acquired 1,388 acres of undeveloped land for $1.25 per acre.[28]

Wilkins apparently made certain arrangements for the occupation and improvement of the land, which must have also included the building of a home.[29] With that done, he returned to Virginia to sell his remaining property and conclude his business affairs before beginning the Louisiana adventure. Early in the fall of 1829, John and Maria Wilkins, their children, slaves, and much of their animal stock left Virginia. They arrived in Louisiana on November 23.[30]

At present there is only Dr. Duperier's account of the Wilkinses' arrival in Louisiana. From that account it is known that they came up Bayou Teche by boat and landed at the Olivier plantation about three miles distant from the lands Wilkins and Peebles had purchased. This information, however, raises more questions—questions for which answers are not forthcoming in the present research. What type of boat did the Wilkinses arrive on? Was it a Teche steamer that the family took from New Orleans or was it a coastal schooner that perhaps Wilkins hired in Norfolk to bring his family and belongings to Louisiana?[31] Dr. Duperier tells us that the stock arrived on the same boat with the Wilkinses.

Dr. Duperier also records that Wilkins brought with him a letter of introduction to Col. Olivier from Henry Clay. Did Wilkins or Peebles know the great Kentuckian, or was it Benjamin, then living in Kentucky, who asked for a letter of introduction for his brother and nephew? Unfortunately, we are now too far removed from the event for our meager documentation to provide an answer to this question.

During 1830 the family must have settled into their new home and began the work of clearing and draining the land. The 1830 federal census indicates that there were 135 slaves on the Wilkins-Peebles lands. Since this figure is greater than the 80 slaves thought to have been brought by Wilkins, the additional slaves must have been provided by Henry Peebles.[32]

The public lands that Wilkins and Peebles acquired in 1829 were but the beginnings of a huge estate that they would come to own collectively and individually. The purchase of public lands in the Isle aux Cannes occurred in three stages after the initial acquisitions. The second round of purchases occurred in February, 1831, and February, 1832, and added 619 acres to the company's holdings.[33] The third stage of public land acquisition occurred in 1834-35. In February, 1834, the partnership bought 81 acres; on December 10 and 11, 1835, Wilkins and Peebles purchased 1,025 acres of unimproved land at Isle aux Cannes.[34] The company's final purchase of public land took place in 1836 when the partners purchased twenty parcels of land at Isle aux Cannes, totaling over 4,150 acres.[35] Thus, between January 1829 and June, 1836, the partnership had acquired over 7,000 acres of public land.[36]

Public land, however, did not constitute the only land acquisitions by Wilkins and Peebles. Between 1831 and 1845 they purchased several parcels of privately owned land, totaling 862 acres, including the residence of Nicolas Broussard.[37] Thus, the partners had acquired nearly 8,000 acres of public and private lands. Although this amount of land indicates a large holding, probably one of the largest in Louisiana, it must be recalled that most of this land was wooded and/or marshy; therefore, unfit for agricultural production without extensive improvement. Indeed, the total amount of acreage which John Wilkins had under cultivation shortly before his death (500 acres) was but a small portion of the 3,300 acres he personally owned.[38]

On April 20, 1843, Wilkins and Peebles divided some of the lands they owned at Isle aux Cannes. An amicable dividing line was established along the course of Jack's Coulee. Peebles took sole possession of some tracts of land west of the coulee; Wilkins did the same with regard to some tracts on the east side. This act of partition was recorded in New Iberia by Simon Walsh and was witnessed by John Devalcourt and John Mitcheltree.[39]

A second partition of the partnership's lands occurred immediately after the death of John Wilkins.[40] Before this division, however, the partners had sold 420 acres at Isle aux Cannes to Benjamin Wilkins.[41] Interestingly enough, this was the only sale of the company's lands before Wilkins' death in 1852.

In addition to jointly purchased lands, Wilkins and Peebles individually acquired real estate. On April 19, 1844, for example, Wilkins bought from Simon White of St. Martin Parish a parcel of land one league square near Lebanon, Texas. This tract adjoined the town about three or four miles from the San Antonio River, on both sides of Manarroy Creek in Goliad County.[42] This property and more in Victoria County was still owned by Wilkins at the time of his death.[43]

John Wilkins had come to Louisiana to engage in sugar production. Before that was possible, however, the land had to be cleared and drained. Whether he was aware before he left Virginia of the investment necessary, in labor and capital, to accomplish this is impossible to know. What is known is that the first stalk of cane was not planted for at least six years while the slaves labored to clear and drain the land. At the time he settled his first wife's estate, in 1836, Wilkins stated that he had spent $14,000 on improving the land. When this proved to be insufficient, he sold some of his slaves to David Hayes for $5,500 and plowed this money into developing the plantation. Finally, in order to buy seed cane to plant his lands, in early 1836 Wilkins mortgaged one thousand acres to the Citizens Bank of New Orleans. Thus, Wilkins' first cane crop could only have been harvested in the fall of 1836, fully seven years after he had come to Louisiana.[44]

Whether the Wilkins and Peebles partnership grew cane in the late 1830s is unknown. From the Franklin, La., newspaper, the *Planters' Banner*, and from Champomier's *Statement of the Sugar Crop. . .* , it is possible to gather production figures for the company and for Wilkins individually, but only beginning in the 1840s.[45]

The *Banner*'s compilation does not indicate production for Peebles and Wilkins individually or collectively, for the crop year 1843. For the three crop years of 1844, 1845, and 1846 Peebles and Wilkins produced 380 hogsheads (1100 lbs. per hogshead) of sugar for 1844 and 1845 and 250 hogsheads for 1846. Wilkins and son (Richard or John Henry) are listed as producing 320 hogsheads in 1844.[46] At approximately five cents per pound for sugar at the time, the partnership would have grossed nearly $21,000 for each of the 1844 and 1845 crops.[47]

Champomier's reports for the decade of the 1850s afford some insight to growing conditions each year and therefore provide reasons for the fluctuation in production. For example, Wilkins alone produced 195 hogsheads in 1849, but only 141 in 1850, and 144 in 1851. Champomier reports that cold weather was late in coming in 1849-50; that most planters were able to harvest and process their entire crop before the first frost. The harvest of 1850, however, was impaired by a cold and rainy spring followed by a drought from July to the end of the harvest season. To climax the woes of the planters the first frost made its appearance on the night of the 25th of October, although light, did great injury to all plantations in the prairies. A killing frost . . . took place on the nights of the 15th and 16th of November; and the last frost, which was as severe as any remembered in Louisiana, took place on the nights of 7th and 8th December. The ground was frozen hard, and all the cane standing was destroyed.[48]

The 1851 crop was damaged by drought. Meaningful rainfall did not occur until late September and early October, causing the cane to put forth a "luxuriant growth." Thus, there was insufficient time for the cane to mature before it was harvested with the result that it was low in sucrose. Many planters postponed harvesting to let the cane mature, but this proved to be a mistake when early cold killed the plants.[49]

As every sugar farmer, then or now, will attest, not every year is a bad year for sugar growing. Thus, all growers await the good year or years. The crop year 1852 was one of these. Wilkins' production (he had died in February 1852) jumped to 320 hogsheads. As Champomier notes in his annual report: "The season was probably the most favorable for agricultural products generally that has ever been known in Louisiana." That it was a good year for sugar production is reflected in the fact that the 1852 crop generated over 300,000 hogsheads of sugar for the first time in the history of sugar production in Louisiana.[50]

It is impossible to determine whether John D. Wilkins ever considered himself to be a successful sugar planter and therefore justified in his move from Virginia to Louisiana. Certain figures, however, speak for themselves. Of the 192 St. Mary Parish sugar producers in 1851, Wilkins ranked seventy-fifth in production, In 1852, of the 189 St. Mary Parish sugar farmers, Wilkins' production ranked thirty-second. Such statistics, although far from conclusive, would indicate that the Virginian's sugar production was increasing significantly in relation to other parish growers.[51]

John D. Wilkins: His Ideas and the End of the Louisiana Adventure

There is very little information about the day-to-day activities of the Wilkinses in Louisiana. What is known about them comes from scattered sources, civil and church records, or an occasional newspaper or magazine item. These give, however, some insight to the character and philosophy of John D. Wilkins. Dr. Duperier, for example, recounted the story of how, upon reaching Col. Olivier's plantation en route to his own, Wilkins was warned to keep a close watch on a neighbor who had a reputation for stealing livestock. Without hesitation, the Virginian, a few days later, confronted the neighbor and told him that whenever he had need of meat for his large family he could take what he needed, so long as he notified Wilkins of his intention to do so. He must not, however, steal the animals. Some time later, in the dead of night, Wilkins and his body servant were awakened by noise in the hog pens. With guns in hand they moved quietly out of the house and toward the pens where they came upon the neighbor in the act of stealing a hog. Wilkins seized and bound the man and awaited daylight to take his prisoner to Franklin, where he was subsequently jailed. Because of Wilkins' sense of justice and charity, he supported the man's family during his imprisonment.[52]

On a more serious side, Dr. Duperier, in his "Narrative," recalled that John D. Wilkins was "a man of deep thought and a natural philosopher." At some time, probably after his move to Louisiana, Wilkins became quite interested in the writings of Charles Fourier, the French utopian socialist. When, in 1843, Fourier's followers in the United States began publication of a newspaper, *The Phalanx,* Wilkins became a staunch supporter of their goals.[53]

Then, on January 5, 1844, the editors of the *Phalanx* announced that "through the liberality of a gentleman in Louisiana . . . we are enabled to send the Phalanx [*sic*] to the Senior Class of every College and University in the United States."[54] A few years later, in February 1847, the editors acknowledged receipt of a $1,000 donation from Wilkins "to be expended either in propagating the theory or the practice of the Association."[55]

Wilkins interest in utopian socialism was accompanied by a devotion to agricultural reform, in particular, and to "natural philosophy," in general. There appears to have occurred within the man a strange marriage of neo-classical and romantic intellectual currents. He obviously recognized a certain compatibility in the theories of Fourier and the theories and practices of John Taylor of Caroline.[56] Wilkins sought the "natural" solution to the problems of humanity and argued that mankind must live in harmony with nature. In 1843, the same year that he began financial contributions to the Fourierist movement, Wilkins published *Man's Artificial Institutions of Agriculture, Tested by God's Natural Institutions of Agriculture.* As Carl Guarneri has noted, the book is devoted to "practical suggestions for a more intensive and less wasteful destructive agriculture, based on the 'natural truth' of observation."[57] Wilkins recommended "such things as plenty of manure, deep ploughing, confined grazing, [and] live fences."[58]

The Louisiana planter also published a thirty-page pamphlet entitled *Practical Education, Morals, and Legislation, Tested by "Natural Truth."*[59] From every indication, ambiguous as some may be, Wilkins put into practice much of what he recommended in print. This may account for the fact that he was at least six years in preparing his farmland to receive its first crop of sugarcane.[60]

Like Taylor in Virginia, Wilkins projected his ideas of reform into the local political arena. As Dr. Duperier indicated, Wilkins ran for governor of Louisiana in 1849 "on what he called a triangular platform. His address to the people was full of reform suggestions. He pledged the salary of the office, if elected, to charitable objects."[61] The Boston *Daily Chronotype* described Wilkins' campaign for governor.[62]

On the domestic scene, the three decades spent by the Wilkins family in Louisiana were filled with the joys and sorrows of every family as it plays out its destiny. The first of the children to marry was Mary Ann. She married Hardin Burnley of Virginia. This happy event soon turned to sorrow, however, when Mary Ann died unexpectedly, probably in childbirth for her daughter, Mary Wilkins Burnley.[63]

If the loss of a daughter was not tragic enough for John Wilkins, his grief was compounded when, on September 15, 1832, Maria Claiborne, his companion in the Louisiana adventure, died.[64] No information has been forthcoming about the circumstances of Mrs. Wilkins' death. Four years later John D. Wilkins settled his first wife's estate. It is from this document that there is derived some information concerning the family. The estate was being settled at this particular time because Wilkins was preparing to mortgage 1,000 acres of land to the Citizens Bank of New Orleans. Before that was possible, however, he had to establish the rights of his wife's heirs to the community property.

Wilkins gave the value of the community property on the day of his wife's death as being $14,747. He stated, however, that 2,585 acres of the plantation were bought with funds belonging exclusively to him. Despite this, at the time of his wife's death the community had outstanding debts of $14,000—debts incurred bringing the plantation into production. Wilkins stated furthermore that following his wife's death, he was forced to sell some of his personally owned slaves for an additional $5,500 to invest in the plantation. Thus, by 1836, his wife's succession and he had incurred a total debt of $19,500 in the establishment of the plantation. Since he was responsible for the payment of this debt, he concluded that he owed nothing to his wife's heirs from her half of the community property....[65]

On December 31, 1839, John D. Wilkins remarried. His second wife was Maria Nolan (sometimes spelled Noland), a resident of New Iberia, La., but a native of Ireland. They were married by Father Beaupré of St. Peter's Church. The ceremony probably took place at the home of Mrs. David Weeks....[66]

... John D. Wilkins died on February 5, 1852.[67] The *Franklin Planters' Banner* carried a brief obituary:

> John D. Wilkins died on his plantation the 5th inst.
> He was revered by all who knew him.[68]

John Wilkins died intestate; therefore, his heirs and widow asked Jules G. Olivier, a long-time friend of the family and a St. Mary Parish attorney, to serve as administrator of the estate. Mr. Olivier's first act was to inventory and appraise Wilkins' personal property as well as the property he owned in community with his wife. This document indicates that Wilkins personally owned fifty-four slaves and had movable and immovable property valued at $47,655. The community property included 860 acres of land, eight adult and six juvenile slaves, some Texas property, and other movable and immovable property valued at $30,000.[69]

What plans the widow and heirs had for partitioning the estate, particularly the community property, will probably never be known, for on September 18, 1852, while John D. Wilkins' estate was being probated, Maria Nolan Wilkins also died intestate.

Having no known relatives, her estate was declared vacant and the court ordered that her share of the community property be sold with that of her late husband's in order that a partition might be effected among the heirs of John D. Wilkins....[70]

The sale of the Wilkins estate occurred over a period of two years following the death of John D. Wilkins and can be described as falling into two parts. The first part involved the lands which Wilkins had bought in partnership with Henry Peebles. The Wilkins share amounted to 1,934 acres. On March 17, 1853, this plantation was sold to François Optat Darby for $17,000.[71] Slaves and movable property brought another $18,854, for a total of $36,654.[72]

The second part of the sale of John Wilkins' lands occurred at an auction held on March 29, 1854. With this and movable property sold, the estates of John D. Wilkins and Maria Nolan Wilkins had generated nearly $100,000....[73]

With the legal processes completed, the heirs of John Douglass Wilkins and Maria Nolan Wilkins partitioned the estates and went their separate ways.

Notes for "Virginians in the Teche Country: John D. Wilkins and the Louisiana Beginnings"

[1] The uncertainty surrounding John D. Wilkins' place of birth stems from the fact that Brunswick County was divided by an act of October 1780 which took effect on February 1, 1781. *William and Mary Quarterly*, 1st ser., 12:31. The 1850 federal census of St. Mary Parish, Louisiana, records John Wilkins' age as 70.

[2] John Wilkins' mother's name is given in the record of his second marriage, St. Peter's Parish, New Iberia, La., Marriage Book 1; however, a published piece on Brunswick County, Va., marriages indicates that Douglass Wilkins married Tabitha Sims, the daughter of Adam Sims, on December 23, 1771. See Augusta B. Fothergill, *Marriage Records of Brunswick County, Virginia, 1730-1852* (privately printed, 1953), 128. It may be that Douglass Wilkins was married twice, first to Tabitha Sims, and second to Tabitha Wyche.

[3] Wilkins was sheriff of Brunswick County in 1778-79. Janet Gay Neale et al., *Brunswick County, Virginia, 1720-1975* (Richmond, 1975), 394. Douglas Wilkins was among those who took an active role in the creation of Greensville County in 1781. Two years later he was recorded as having forty-six slaves, the fourth largest slaveowner in the county. His plantation in Greensville County was known as "Oakland." He had another plantation in Brunswick County known as "Dry Bread Plantation." For this and additional information on Douglass Wilkins, see Douglas Summers Brown et al., *Historical and Biographical Sketches of Greensville County, Virginia, 1650-1967* (Richmond, 1966), 49, 83, 105.

[4] For additional information on the Wyche family, see the forthcoming article on that family in the *Attakapas Gazette*.

[5] For additional information on the Jones family, see "Jones of Petersburg," *William and Mary Quarterly*, 1st ser., 19:290.

[6] The names of Douglass Wilkins' children are set out in his testament, dated August 10, 1801, and recorded in Greensville County Register of Marriages, 1781-1853. Concerning Joseph's marriage and family, see footnote 22 below. Benjamin Wilkins' marriages and family will be discussed in a future segment of "Virginians in the Teche Country."

[7] Greensville County Will Book 1, p. 455.

[8] Douglass Wilkins purchased this 1,212-acre plantation from Robert Turnbull on April 15, 1795, as recorded in Brunswick County Deed Book 16:357. The property is described as being on "Shining" Creek in west-central Brunswick County. Today the stream is known as "Shiny" Creek. Interview with Mrs. J. W. Kidd, deputy clerk of Brunswick County, Lawrenceville, Va., August 28, 1981.

Virginians in the Teche Country 395

[9]On January 27, 1791, Douglass Wilkins sold to his son Joseph a tract of land comprising 1,100 acres in Greensville County. According to Brown, *Historical and Biographical Sketches,* 105, this was Oakland Plantation. Sale price was 5 pounds sterling, a token payment. For a record of the transaction, see Greensville County Deed Book 1:348. Judging from the date of this sale, one can speculate that Joseph was about ten years older than John. No birth date for Joseph or John was located in Virginia.

[10]See a later segment of this article dealing with the career of Benjamin Wilkins.

[11]According to his tombstone inscription, Benjamin Wilkins was born December 10, 1796. The tomb of Dr. Wilkins is located on his former plantation, now the property of Mr. James D. Singleton of Arnaudville, La.

[12]William Maclin, Jr., was the son of the senior Maclin who emigrated from Scotland to Brunswick County in the early eighteenth century. Julia McKinley, "Maclin Family," *William and Mary Quarterly,* 1st ser., 7:108-9. William Maclin, Jr., married Winnie Wyche on September 20, 1781. Mrs. J. O. James, "Greensville Co. Marriage Binds [sic], *Virginia Magazine of History and Biography,* 24 (1916): 307. It is quite possible that William Maclin's wife was the sister-in-law of Douglass Wilkins.

[13]No one named John D. Wilkins matriculated at the University of Virginia in the nineteenth century. Helen H. Shelton, Recorder, Registrar's Office, University of Virginia, Charlottesville, Va., to the author, August 5, 1981. Wilkins may have attended Washington College, the predecessor of present-day Washington and Lee University. That institution, however, has no record of Wilkins' attendance. Harold S. Head, University Registrar, Washington and Lee University, Lexington, Va., to the author, August 21, 1981. It was also possible for Wilkins to have attended The College of William and Mary, but a search of the College's records failed to produce any evidence in this regard. James W. Oberly, Assistant Archivist, College of William and Mary, Williamsburg, Va., to the author, September 8, 1981. A final possibility was Hampden-Sydney College. The author's inquiry about Wilkins' possible matriculation at that institution went unanswered.

[14]The Wilkins children who survived to adulthood are identified in St. Mary Parish, La., Estates 331 and 361. The 1810 federal census of Brunswick County, Va., indicates that John Henry was born that year; however, his tombstone gives the natal year as 1811. John Henry's tombstone is located on the James Singleton property. He is buried next to his uncle Benjamin. Richard Augustin Wilkins' birth date is derived from his tombstone in Live Oak Cemetery, Selma, Alabama.

[15]The largest of the purchases on Shiny Creek was for 465 acres bought from William Rivers Estate on August 23, 1813. For this conveyance, see Brunswick County Deed Book 22: 160. Wilkins' other additions to this plantation are recorded in Brunswick County Deed Book 21: 174 (Mar. 26, 1811); Book 21: 274 (Sept. 23, 1811); Book 23: 50 (Nov. 28, 1815); Book 23: 306 (Jan. 1, 1817); Book 25: 150 (June 2,1821). Wilkins' numerous purchases between 1811 and 1815 may have been for wheat production during the years of the Napoleonic wars. The 1817 and 1821 purchases may have been in response to "the burgeoning demand for cotton" in the years immediately following the War of 1812. For the effect this demand had on opening up public lands in the Old Southwest, see Paul W. Gates, "Federal Land Policies in the Southern Public Land States," *Agricultural History,* 53 (1979): 206-27.

[16]According to the 1810 federal census of Brunswick County, Va., Wilkins then owned thirty-one slaves.

[17]Sam B. Hilliard, "Site Characteristics and Spatial Stability of the Louisiana Sugarcane Industry," *Agricultural History,* 53 (1979): 256.

[18]Although he nearly tripled his land holdings between 1801 and 1821, John D. Wilkins is recorded as having bought only two slaves. His slave holdings came to him in several ways: 1) by arrangement with his father; 2) by inheritance from his father; 3) by purchase; 4) by natural increase. As noted below John Wilkins probably brought all of his slaves to Louisiana. His reason for doing so, undoubtedly, was that he could not sell them in Virginia at a profit or even a break-even price.

It should be noted here that in late August, 1981, the author visited the approximate areas of the Wilkins plantations in Brunswick and Greensville counties. These lands are today rolling, forested hills with an occasional clearing for small patches of corn or soybeans or for cattle grazing. In a conversation with Mrs. J. G. Neale, a local historian, she confirmed that by the 1820s many of the counties' plantations were "burnt out," and that the slave population had become a pressing problem for many local planters. Interview with Mrs. J. G. Neale, Lawrenceville, Va., Aug. 28, 1981.

The *Richmond Enquirer,* a leading Virginia newspaper of the day, for example, ran advertisement after advertisement offering plantations for sale in 1828 and 1829. One advertiser announced, "Pleasant Hill Plantation for sale in Mechlenburg County, owner moving west." Another advertisement advised Virginians to move to Alabama where "in many instances [slaveowners would] more than double the value of their property by purchasing good farms at low price." *Richmond Enquirer,* Oct. 14, 21, 1828.

[19] For public land sales in Louisiana, see the U. S. Tract Books for the four districts of the state.

[20] Henry Wyche Peebles was the son of Sterling Peebles and Patsy Wilkins, the sister of John D. Wilkins. According to his gravestone inscription (Rose Hill Cemetery, New Iberia, La.), Henry Peebles was born on January 1, 1795. He was therefore fifteen years the junior of his uncle John.

[21] Sale recorded in Greensville County Deed Book 6:69.

[22] Joseph Wilkins died in August or September 1816. It is his will, given on August 1, 1816, that provides information concerning the family. Joseph and his wife, Elizabeth (Betsy), the daughter of Capt. John Jones and Lucy Binns Cargill, had four children. At the time of his death, Joseph had two plantations, one in Brunswick County and one in Greensville County. He owned 40 slaves. He was growing corn, wheat, and cotton on the Greensville plantation and tobacco on the Brunswick plantation. John D. Wilkins was administrator of his brother's estate until December 1824. This apparently forged a close bond between him and his nephew Douglass, as future events would indicate. Joseph Wilkins' will is found in Greensville County Will Book 3: 7.

[23] Greensville County Deed Book 6:104.

[24] On September 12, 1829, John Wilkins "designing to remove from the state of Virginia" constituted John G. Claiborne his attorney to act in his name. Brunswick County Deed Book 28:332.

[25] Greensville County Deed Book 7:152. Judging from the purchase price paid Benjamin Wilkins in 1819 and the aggregate price received from the sale of "home place" in 1825 and 1833, John Wilkins lost over $4,600 in the sale of the place. This would clearly indicate deteriorating land values in Virginia in the 1820s, a factor that probably contributed greatly to Wilkins' emigration.

[26] The company's name is found in St. Martin Original Suit 2571, dated July 18, 1840.

[27] This information is provided in a deposition later given by John D. Wilkins. The deposition in found in St. Mary Parish Original Suit 4098. The *Richmond Enquirer* advertised in the late summer and early fall of 1828 that the *Jefferson* would sail from Norfolk for New Orleans sometime between October 1 and 15. It is possible that this was the ship that first brought Wilkins to Louisiana. *Richmond Enquirer,* Sept.-Oct., 1828.

[28] The lands are located in Township 13 South, Ranges 6 and 7 East. They were first offered for sale on the first Monday of November, 1826. For a record of these purchases, see U. S. Tract Book 10:144-46, and Book 11:39-42.

[29] In the deposition found in St. Mary Parish Original Suit 4098, Wilkins notes that he "placed there [the newly acquired lands] some of his slaves to improve the land and make it habitable."

[30] The arrival date is found in ibid.

[31] It is interesting to note, but perhaps only coincidental, that the brig *Ajax* sailed from Norfolk in October, 1829, and arrived in New Orleans "with some slaves" on November 19, four days before the recorded arrival of the Wilkinses. For the proposed sailing of the *Ajax* from Norfolk, see the *Richmond Enquirer* for late August and September, 1829. For the arrival of the *Ajax* in New Orleans, see *L'Abeille,* November 19, 1829.

[32] St. Martin and St. Mary parish records indicate that Wilkins rarely bought or sold slaves. When he did so, it was only an individual slave; therefore the 55 additional slaves were not bought after his arrival in Louisiana. The land purchased by Wilkins and Peebles was only a few feet (five to ten) above sea level and poorly drained; thus, unsuitable for sugarcane cultivation. One of the first tasks undertaken by the slaves therefore had to be the construction of a major drainage system. Key to that drainage system was a large canal conveying water into the coastal marsh. The canal became known as the Wilkins Canal and can still be found on official maps of Iberia Parish. In recent times, however, the stream has been labeled Bayou Jack (or Jack's Coulee). Originally, however, Jack's (John Wilkins' nickname) Coulee was a stream that flowed into the Wilkins Canal. A portion of this drainage system was based on some natural water courses which were cleared and deepened. One such watercourse still bears the name of the first landowner of the area: Peebles Coulee.

Virginians in the Teche Country 397

[33] For a record of these purchases, see U. S. Tract Book 10: 144, and Book 11: 40, 42. These lands adjoined those bought in 1829.

[34] These purchases are recorded in ibid.

[35] Ibid.

[36] It is unknown why the company ceased purchasing public land in 1836; however, the financial panic of the next year may have been largely responsible. Henry Peebles and John Wilkins did buy additional public land in Louisiana later on, but this they did individually.

[37] These conveyances were: from Eloy J. H. Landry, April 12, 1831, St. Mary Conveyance Book C:276 (200 acres); from John M. Singleton, Oct. 26, 1834, Book D:211-12 (20 acres); from Nicolas Broussard, Nov. 25, 1835, Book 8:76 (480 acres and residence); from Simonet Broussard, Aug. 20, 1841, Book F:83 (40 acres); from Raphael Broussard, Mar. 17, 1843, Book F:143-44 (81 acres); from Jean-Pierre Landry, Aug. 2, 1843, Book H:309 (40 acres); from Granville Laughlin, Mar. 27, 1844, Book J:319 (100 acres); from Catherine Dorsey, Feb. 14, 1845, Book J:322 (40 acres).

[38] Agricultural Census, St. Mary Parish, Louisiana, 1850. At the same time Peebles owned 8,310 acres but had only 810 under cultivation. Ibid.

[39] The division of the partnership's land is recorded in St. Mary Conveyance Book F:149. No reason has been found for this partition of some of the company's lands at this time.

[40] See St. Mary Parish Original Estate 761.

[41] The sale to Benjamin Wilkins is recorded in St. Mary Conveyance Book I:271. Benjamin was then a resident of Hinds County, Mississippi. This purchase, however, does appear to be the first step taken by him in his move to the Teche country, where he spent the remaining twenty years of his life.

[42] This sale is recorded in St. Mary Conveyance Book 14:388. In 1850 Wilkins bought seven certificates of title to one league of land square each. The certificates were issued to various individuals but all of the land was located in Jasper County in southeastern Texas. For the details of this acquisition, see St. Mary Parish Conveyance Book H: 98.

[43] See St. Mary Parish Original Estate 761.

[44] Wilkins' statements concerning his investment and losses in his Louisiana plantation are found in St. Mary Original Estates 331, 761; also in St. Mary Original Suit 4098. The land was not entirely useless, however. During these first six years Wilkins grew corn and peas to feed his slaves.

[45] The *Planters' Banner* reported on January 14, 1847, the amount of sugar produced by each St. Mary Parish planter for the 1843 to 1846 crop years. P. A. Champomier's *Statement of the Sugar Crop Made in Louisiana* (New Orleans, 1850-59) provides production statistics for each Louisiana plantation for the crop years 1849 to 1858.

[46] *Planters' Banner*, January 14, 1847.

[47] Although Wilkins and Peebles partitioned their jointly held lands in 1843, they apparently continued to have some arrangement for putting the land into production. It would appear that Peebles was, during the 1830s and most of the 1840s, an absentee landowner. Therefore, it may be assumed that the figures reported in the *Banner* and in Champomier's reports were for John D. Wilkins and Co.

[48] Champomier, *Statement of the Sugar Crop* (1850-51), 44,46.

[49] Ibid. (1851-52), 43-44.

[50] Ibid. (1852-53), vi-v.

[51] Ibid (1851-52), 31-36; (1852-53), 31-36.

[52] *New Iberia Enterprise,* March 25, 1899.

[53] Among the purposes of the *Phalanx*, as set out in the first number (October 5, 1843), was to "explain the system of universal Association or principles of a New Organization of Society, discovered by Charles Fourier"; and to "expose [the] evils and defects of . . . leading social institutions." The *Phalanx* was succeeded by *The Harbinger.*

[54] In a footnote, the editor identified the "gentleman in Louisiana" as being John D. Wilkins. He also noted that as a result of Wilkins' contribution the *Phalanx* was being sent to 103 colleges and universities. The *Phalanx,* January 5, 1844. The editor, Osborne McDaniel, was apparently so taken with Wilkins' support and generosity that he visited the planter in his south Louisiana home. For a public address given by McDaniel while in Franklin, La., see the *Franklin Planters' Banner,* May 6, 1847.

[55] *The Harbinger,* February 6, 1847. One can be certain that there were few utopian socialists in Louisiana, particularly among the planter class. Carl J. Guarneri in an article entitled "Two Utopian Socialist Plans for Emancipation in Antebellum Louisiana [*Louisiana History,* 24 (1983): 5-24] discusses, in some detail, Wilkins' attachment to the Fourierist movement.

[56] John Taylor of Caroline (1753-1824) was a Virginian, a Revolutionary War veteran, a state legislator and a United States senator. It was, however, his agricultural and political publications which brought him considerable fame. In 1813 he published what is perhaps his most famous agricultural work, *Arator.* In this, he set out the results of his practical experiments and lauded the virtues of an agrarian society. For a brief biographical sketch of Taylor, see D. Harland Hagler, "John Taylor," in *The Encyclopedia of Southern History,* eds. David C. Roller and Robert W. Twyman (Baton Rouge, 1979), 1181.

[57] Wilkins' ideas concerning conservation may have been born of his experiences on the burned-out farmland of southeastern Virginia.

[58] Carl Guarneri to Glenn Conrad, March 12, 1982. I am especially grateful for Professor Guarneri's kindness in sharing with me that portion of his research dealing with John D. Wilkins. Guarneri located a copy of Wilkins' book at the New York Public Library; however, the book does not circulate.

[59] Ibid. A copy of this book is on deposit in the rare-book collection of the library of The College of William and Mary.

[60] Wilkins' "natural" approach to agriculture may have also been responsible for his move to Louisiana where he could test his theories in virgin soil.

[61] *New Iberia Enterprise,* March 25, 1899.

[62] *Boston Daily Chronotype,* as cited in Guarneri to Conrad, March 12, 1982.

[63] Hardin Burnley was probably a native of Hanover County, Va. He and Mary Ann Wilkins may have been married before the Wilkinses left Virginia in 1829; however, there is no Burnley-Wilkins marriage record in either Brunswick or Greenville counties. The records of Hanover County for this era were destroyed during the Civil War. Clerk of Court of Hanover County, Va., to Glenn R. Conrad (telephone conversation), Sept. 22, 1981. There is no record of their marriage in St. Mary Parish, La. Through deduction from extant records, it is possible to conclude that Mary Wilkins Burnley was born in 1831 or in the spring or summer of 1832, but before September of that year. Records indicate that Mary Ann Burnley was already deceased when her mother, Maria Claiborne Wilkins died on September 15, 1832. When John D. Wilkins died in February, 1852, Mary Wilkins Burnley was still a minor. Therefore, her birth date had to be in 1831 or the spring or summer of 1832. The deduction is drawn from information provided in St. Mary Parish Original Estates 331 and 761.

[64] Maria Cole Claiborne was the daughter of John Herbert Claiborne and Mary Cole Gregory. Maria's paternal grandfather was Augustine Claiborne, the great-grandson of William Claiborne who arrived in Virginia in 1621. Augustine's brother, Nathaniel, was the grandfather of William C. C. Claiborne, Louisiana's first American governor. Thus, Maria Claiborne Wilkins and Governor Claiborne were third cousins. For more on the Claiborne family genealogy, see G. M. Claiborne, comp., *Claiborne Pedigree, A Genealogical Table of the Descendants of Secretary William Claiborne* (Lynchburg, Va., 1900); and Nathaniel Claiborne Hale, *Roots in Virginia: An Account of Captain Thomas Hale, Virginia Frontiersman* (Philadelphia, 1948). The author is grateful to Mrs. Robert Bourne, Jr., of Camden, Tenn., for supplying the Claiborne genealogy. Mrs. Bourne is a descendant of John D. and Maria Claiborne Wilkins.

[65] The matter is recorded in St. Mary Parish Original Estate 331. The reason for the instrument appears to be that Wilkins had to establish the right of the heirs, particularly those of the minor child Mary Wilkins Burnley, before he could mortgage a portion of his land. With particular regard to the rights of the Burnley minor, Wilkins noted that at the time of his daughter's marriage to Hardin Burnley, he had given the couple seven of his personally owned slaves as a wedding present. The slaves were then valued at $4,000. Ibid.

[66] Maria Nolan, at 36, was thirteen years younger than her husband. She was the daughter of Edward Nolan and Fannie Frances Griffith of Ireland. She had immigrated to the United States in 1826 under unknown circumstances. There is nothing to indicate what might have brought her to New Iberia. The marriage record is found in St. Peter's Catholic Parish, Marriage Book I: 15. Background on Maria Nolan is found in St. Mary Parish Probate Book, 1852: 232.

[67] St. Mary Parish Original Suit No. 4098.

[68] *Franklin Planters' Banner.* Extensive investigation has failed to reveal Wilkins' grave site.

[69] St. Mary Parish Original Estate No. 761. It is somewhat baffling why a man of John Wilkins' intellect would not have prepared a will. Perhaps it was the family circumstances which convinced him that by dying intestate his estate would be administered by a disinterested third party, but one acceptable to all heirs.

[70] St. Mary Parish Original Suite No. 4576. . . . Details concerning the estate of Maria Nolan Wilkins can be found in "Proceedings in the Estate of Maria Nolan, Decd. wife of John D. Wilkins," St. Mary Probate Book 1852:232-46.

[71] St. Mary Parish Original Estate No. 761.

[72] Ibid.

[73] Ibid. The land they owned in Texas was not sold until later and would be in addition to the Louisiana sales.

FAMILY AND SOCIETY*

Craig A. Bauer

Despite a wealth of historical evidence and literature on the realities of the plantation culture of the South, many inaccurate notions concerning life during the antebellum era have received wide acceptance. The mint julep and magnolia romanticism has infected much of the popular literature written on the subject of the Old South. Some of the more tenacious and damaging conceptions on the subject date back to the antebellum period when abolitionists' attacks upon the planter class presented the belief that the slaveholders did little but live off of the fruits of the back-breaking labors of their Negro workers. It is true that rich planters, like rich industrialists, had time and money for leisure activities. However, the wealth had to be made. The sugar plantation was a large and complex business which required a great deal of effort and skill by its owner to keep it functioning smoothly. The operation of an estate was a twelve-month undertaking which required sophisticated business and management skills to which Duncan Kenner and most of his planter colleagues gave much personal attention.[1]

Though most sugar planters worked hard at advancing their interest by good management, they did not usually put much effort into taking joint action with others in finding common solutions to some of the problems faced by members of their profession. A few agricultural societies were formed to promote the common interests of the sugar growers, yet they seldom accomplished much and usually just languished until they ceased to exist. The typical antebellum sugar planter was an individual who, when it came to managing his affairs, looked to himself for his needs. Similarly, most planters took a narrow approach to the pursuit of other economic activities. The majority of the region's sugar growers did not seek other financial investment opportunities.[2]

---

*First published as chapter four in Craig A. Bauer, *A Leader Among Peers: The Life and Times of Duncan Farrar Kenner* (Lafayette, La.: Center for Louisiana Studies, 1993), 70-97. Reprinted with the kind permission of the author and the University of Louisiana at Lafayette.

Family and Society 401

Duncan Kenner did not subscribe to the limited economic perspectives held by the majority of his planter colleagues. He frequently shared with others ideas on ways to improve their craft. Kenner was also among the relatively few planters who had both the capital and insight to broaden his activities to include other financial endeavors. Although he read the law for some time after he returned from his European studies, Kenner, unlike Judah P. Benjamin, the proprietor of Bellechasse Plantation in Plaquemines Parish and one of the South's leading barristers, used his legal training primarily to meet his own needs. One area, however, where Kenner invested his time and capital was in real estate speculation.[3]

Kenner's involvement in the real estate market started early in his life. With the death of his father when he was only eleven years old, Kenner inherited a considerable amount of land. From that time on in his life, Kenner was continually involved in the buying and selling of properties. Though he purchased holdings in various sections of both Mississippi and Louisiana, Kenner concentrated his real estate interests in the New Orleans area.

Although only a secondary business interest of his, Kenner's real estate investments were a major source of income for him throughout his life. At the time of his father's death, the family's finances were slowly recovering from a severe setback. Much of William Kenner's legacy to his children consisted of his extensive property holdings. Fortunately for Duncan and his siblings, at the time they acquired their holdings the area was undergoing a rapid population increase. Following the War of 1812, a constant stream of settlers from other areas of the country and from Europe landed at New Orleans. While most of these newcomers moved up the Mississippi and settled in the Mid-West, many remained in the area. By 1840 the population of Louisiana had reached 350,000, and New Orleans had become the fourth largest city in the United States, challenging New York for the title of the country's largest port. So extensive and long lasting was this period of prosperity that the five decades between the ending of the War of 1812 and the outbreak of the Civil War are referred to by historians as the golden years of New Orleans.[4]

As the Old Quarter of the city filled with the influx of new residents, many of the newcomers looked to the less populated areas to the west of the city for places to live. Settled mostly by Americans, these little communities or faubourgs expanded rapidly. Eighteenth-century sugar plantations and many small farms with modest structures were replaced with high density residential and commercial areas. The real estate boom of the city's golden years brought with it opportunities of which only a few of the area's planters took advantage. In the wheelings and dealings which accompanied the boom times, fortunes were quickly made and sometimes just as quickly lost. Among those planters who successfully speculated in the Crescent City's land boom was Duncan Kenner, who continued to buy and sell property in the city and elsewhere until the eve of the Civil War. Among his more valuable city holdings were thirteen lots and residences located in some of the community's more prestigious neighborhoods; the Three Sisters, an imposing columned structure on Canal Street; and the valuable city square bounded by the streets of Carondelet, Common, Baronne, and Gravier.[5]

Kenner also was careful to invest resources in other money-making activities. Though his investments became much more diversified after the war than they were before, nevertheless, during the antebellum period he did go beyond the common practice of many planters of investing their surplus funds almost exclusively in additional slaves and land. Primarily as a hobby, Kenner invested heavily in thoroughbred race horses. He also purchased stock in promising companies, including the Southern Pacific Railroad. Kenner also derived a modest income from the interest he charged on loans of money which he made to acquaintances. Surviving records reveal dozens of transactions over a span of years between Kenner and other individuals, often including members of his wife's family. Although most of these loans were obviously made by Kenner to his wife's relatives as an act of kindness to help them through financially difficult times, most loans earned Kenner respectable interest income which usually ranged from eight to ten percent.[6]

An important factor in helping him survive the periodic economic setbacks which afflicted the sugar economy of the region, Kenner's diverse financial holdings were somewhat extraordinary for a large-scale sugar planter. Some sugar growers did not attempt to diversify their holdings simply because they lacked the capital and time to do so; others simply were content with their life style and were averse to making any changes in the way they carried on their business. Chief among this latter group of planters were those individuals who were descendants of settlers of the region before it became American territory. Often inaccurately labeled by postbellum writers as "Creoles,"[7] these *anciennes'* outlook on life was often considerably different than that of the many newcomers who entered Louisiana following its acquisition by the United States in 1803.

The cultural differences between the *anciennes* and the newcomers were of such magnitude that they remained one of the major themes which affected the political, cultural, and social history of the region during much of the antebellum period in Louisiana. The aristocratic *anciennes* generally held themselves aloof from the Americans and built a social barrier of bitter resentment between themselves and the newcomers. Theirs was more of a seigniorial existence than that of their American neighbors. Not unlike their slave-owning counterparts in Brazil and elsewhere, the *anciennes* worked to preserve the good life and shied away from the pursuit of material gains or highly intellectual activities which might prove detrimental to their slow and pleasant rhythm of existence. They objected to the use of English as the official language of the state and many refused to learn it. Most were resentful and contemptuous of their American neighbors and looked upon those who were Protestants as being irreligious and evil.[8]

The Americans on the other hand, including Duncan Kenner and his father William, added a capitalistic flavor to their pursuit of the good life in Louisiana. Most had come to their new home with the hope of adding to their fortunes, and they aggressively pursued this objective. Architect Benjamin Henry B. Latrobe noted in his journal in early 1819 that the new American immigrants to the Crescent City were "in an eternal bustle . . . [with] their limbs, their heads, and their hearts, [moving] to that sole object, . . . buying and selling, and all the rest of the occupations of a money-making community."[9] The assertiveness of the Americans often put them at odds with the *anciennes*. The concerns of the *anciennes* over the possible loss of their way of life were dismissed by the newcomers, who accused them of being backward, ignorant, and innocent of the sophisticated ways of the modern world.[10]

So involved became the rivalry between the two groups that at times bemused visitors to the region joined in the fray. While visiting New Orleans in the 1820s, the Duke of Saxe-Weimar expressed displeasure with the American populace because they seemed only motivated "by the desire to accumulate wealth." By contrast, he considered the *anciennes* of the city to be "a warm hearted generation." Timothy Flint, who visited the city several years after the duke, observed that the *anciennes* were "mild, an amiable people with less energy and less irascibility than the emigrants from the other states." He was quick to add that they were also "generally more sober and moral than the Americans."[11]

The commercial, political, and cultural competition between the two groups in southeastern Louisiana was intense. Commercially, the *anciennes'* limited experience in the ways of finance and their narrow educational background put them at a disadvantage in their attempt to compete with the aggressiveness of the Americans. Thus, by the time young Duncan Kenner returned to America from his studies in Europe, the Americans in New Orleans had succeeded in gaining financial ascendancy over their more conservative neighbors. Politically, however, the *anciennes* held numerical superiority over the Americans for some time and were able to influence the political events of the period. While their political power remained strong in the rural sections of South Louisiana, the *anciennes* steadily lost ground in New Orleans, where the number of immigrants continued to swell throughout the antebellum era.[12]

Culturally, the *anciennes* considered themselves superior to the newcomers, they were averse to making changes, and they were content with their individualistic way of life. To limit the American influence upon their culture, the *anciennes* established broad social barriers designed to limit contact between the two cultures. Even intermarriage with the Americans was frowned upon by the old families of the state.[13]

The passage of time and the onset of the Civil War eventually reduced the tension between the two groups. However, during most of the antebellum period, the Americans and *anciennes* rarely shared common interests. Accommodations between the groups were usually made by individuals rather than by large-scale cooperation between the cultures. On occasion the more diplomatic among the young Americans of the time mastered French and some of the colloquial customs of the *anciennes* and began to court and marry their daughters.[14]

One such young American who was able to transcend the cultural barriers between the rival groups was twenty-six-year-old Duncan Kenner. With his father having been among the first Americans to establish himself in New Orleans and his mother being a member of one of the leading families of the Natchez region, Kenner was looked upon with less suspicion by the *anciennes* than many of his American peers. Kenner's father had established close business and personal ties with many of the leading *ancienne* families of the area. When William Kenner died, many of the old families assisted the Kenner children in getting established on their own. Among this group was the prominent Bringier family.

The Bringiers resided on some of the most elegant estates in the region. Emmanuel Marius Pons Bringier, the first member of the family to settle in Louisiana, had established White Hall Plantation in St. James Parish on which was situated one of the grandest homes in Louisiana. His son, Michel Doradou Bringier, owned the nearly-as-impressive Hermitage Plantation in Ascension Parish. This estate had been a wedding gift to Doradou and his bride, Elizabeth Aglaé DuBourg, from his father. With the death of his father, Doradou acquired the former's holdings at White Hall and thus became one of the most powerful planters in the region. It was during his patriarchy that the great influx of Americans into the region occurred and the rift between the two cultures developed.[15]

Despite his position as the head of one of the wealthiest and most respected of the *ancienne* families, Bringier apparently was not as suspicious of the Americans as were many of his *ancienne* neighbors. For example, of his six daughters, five married Americans and only one married a member of one of Louisiana's *ancienne* families. Marie Elizabeth Aglaé Bringier, the fourth of Doradou's daughters, married her cousin Benjamin Tureaud, a member of one of the oldest and most opulent of South Louisiana's *ancienne* families. The Tureauds resided at Tezcuco Plantation. The rest of Doradou's daughters married prominent Americans. Among these was his eldest daughter, Rosella, who married Hore Browse Trist, the brother of Nicholas P. Trist, who negotiated the Treaty of Guadalupe Hidalgo. The two brothers had been wards of Thomas Jefferson and were reared at Monticello in Virginia. Rosella and her husband lived on Bowden Plantation in Ascension Parish, and he served as the first American Collector of the Port of New Orleans. Louise Françoise Bringier, the second eldest of Bringier's daughters, married Martin Gordon, Jr., the son of Martin Gordon, Sr., one of Andrew Jackson's closest friends. Louise's husband was one of the area's leading commercial factors and served in that capacity for Duncan Kenner. The youngest Bringier girl, Anne Octavie, married Allen Thomas of the New Dalton and New Hope plantations. A lawyer, Thomas rose to the rank of brigadier general in the Confederate army during the Civil War and after the conflict was active in Democratic politics, eventually being appointed United States minister to Venezuela.[16]

Although the sons-in-law discussed above represented an impressive cross section of the elite of the American community in Louisiana, it was Doradou Bringier's other two daughters, Myrthé and Nanine, whose husbands were most in the public eye. Louise Marie Myrthé married Richard "Dick" Taylor. The Louisiana-born and only son of

President Zachary Taylor and his wife lived on Fashion Plantation in St. Charles Parish. During the war he proved himself to be a capable commander by defeating the superior Union forces of General Nathaniel P. Banks at the Battles of Sabine Crossroads, which turned back the North's ambitious Red River Campaign of 1864. Gradually rising in rank, he eventually ended up as commander of the Confederacy's Department of Alabama, Mississippi, and East Louisiana.[17]

The fourth of the Bringier children and the third eldest daughter, Anne Guillelmine, would fall in love and marry a young planter and politician named Duncan Kenner. Probably named after her great uncle and godfather, the Catholic apostolic administrator for New Orleans, Bishop Louis Guillaume Dubourg, she was known all her life as Nanine. The courtship and marriage of Duncan and Nanine personified the social changes which were gradually affecting the way the American and *ancienne* cultures learned to live together in Louisiana.[18]

Although few details of the young couple's courtship are known, it is unlikely that it followed the *ancienne* custom in Louisiana of arranged marriages. Nanine's mother had been a fourteen-year-old bride of convenience in a matrimonial alliance between her family and the Bringiers. Arranged by her uncle and her future father-in-law, she only saw her groom once before the marriage ceremony. On the other hand, it is likely that the courtship of Nanine and Duncan followed more closely the American custom of courting. They probably knew each other for some time before they became engaged. Despite the suspicions that the *anciennes* held toward the Americans, the Bringiers continually came in contact with them and probably were quite familiar with the members of the Kenner family. William Kenner and the Bringiers did business together. Furthermore, the Bringiers' city homes on the Esplanade and later on Canal Street in New Orleans brought the two families into proximity with one another. While staying at their city residences, it is likely that both families on occasion frequented some of the same social events. Likewise, it is possible that the families became close simply because their plantations were located in proximity to one another. The Bringiers had a reputation for being among the most extravagant entertainers who lived along the banks of the lower Mississippi. When they entertained, they doubtless invited their neighbors from the surrounding estates. To have done less would have been a breach of the area's custom of hospitality which included the tradition of opening one's home to any traveler, friend, or stranger, who might have been passing through the vicinity and, because of the lack of public inns, needed a place to stay for the night.[19]

Throughout the antebellum South, parents carefully supervised the social contacts that their daughters were allowed to make. While allowed to attend social events, they were constantly chaperoned. Often male suitors of eligible belles called at the girl's home in pairs so as to avoid neighborhood gossip. A single or frequent visitor to a belle's house could provoke speculation about his intentions. Unlike suitors in the North who were given the opportunity of private audiences with their sweethearts, Southern couples were not allowed to meet alone. The mother of the girl or some other family member usually was expected to be in the room with the young couple at all times. Furthermore, the New England custom of bundling (the practice of wrapping a courting couple in covers and allowing them to sleep in the same bed) was not practiced in the antebellum South and was looked upon as being odd and totally inappropriate.[20]

As a native Louisianian or "Creole," Duncan Kenner was afforded a greater degree of acceptance by the *anciennes* than some of the Americans who were just settling in the region. Having spent most of his life in Southeast Louisiana, he was familiar and comfortable with the *anciennes'* culture and also spoke fluent French. Thus when the courtship between Duncan and Nanine grew serious, her father and mother, along with the rest of the *ancienne* community, accepted the idea of marriage between the twenty-six-year-old American and his sixteen-year-old *ancienne* fiancée.[21]

Weddings were one of the most important social happenings during antebellum times in the South. Members of the planter class found such events to be of enormous interest. Friends and family members from far and near, from parents to distant cousins, were invited to attend the nuptials, which were usually elaborate ceremonies attended by large numbers of convivial guests.[22]

Except for the fact that it took place at the home of the bride's father, little is known of the details of the marriage ceremony between Duncan and his young bride; however, considering the status of the two families involved, it is probable that the wedding on June 1, 1839, followed the Southern antebellum tradition of extravagance. Among those who served as witnesses for the Catholic nuptials were the bride's parents, Duncan's older brother Minor, A. Christopher Colomb, a first cousin of the bride, and a family friend, P.W. Nicholls.[23]

Following the wedding the young couple set up housekeeping on Duncan's property in Ascension Parish, where they moved into a small dwelling while their grand home was under construction. Completed within a few years, the beautiful Ashland plantation house remained the family's home throughout most of Duncan's life. Set back from the river and backdropped with live oak, magnolia, pecan, and other trees, the large square-shaped house possessed a monumental quality. The interior of the house was nearly as impressive as the outside. It was furnished with magnificent pieces of furniture, some made by the area's leading craftsmen and others painstakingly crafted by slave artisans who lived on the estate. The house was tastefully adorned with many engravings, prints, and oil paintings. Other keepsakes from Kenner's horse-racing competitions also decorated the home's interior. As the Kenners were connoisseurs of both mind and palate, the house was also equipped with one of the most splendid private libraries in the region.[24]

The young couple adjusted well to married life at Ashland. Kenner remained busy overseeing the construction of the new house and the growing of the estate's crops, as well as with his business interests in New Orleans and a budding political career. Nanine occupied her time buying furniture for the new house and visiting her relatives who lived near Ashland. Fortunately for Nanine, her marriage to Kenner did not take her very far

Family and Society

from her family and the area in which she had grown up. Thus, during Kenner's frequent trips away from Ashland, Nanine did not have to suffer the hours of loneliness that many other antebellum wives had to endure while their husbands were away on business. Her family and their Hermitage Plantation were only a few miles and a short buggy ride downriver from her home at Ashland.

Taught from birth to devote themselves to their blood relatives, antebellum women sometimes experienced difficulties when they married and were required to shift loyalties to their husbands. This does not seem to have been a problem for Nanine for, although relationships with in-laws were crucial to family harmony in the antebellum household, the Kenners and the Bringiers apparently had no major difficulties in their relations with one another. It was not uncommon for Southerners to become embroiled in squabbles with their children and their children's spouses. Among the most common causes of such intra-family quarreling were financial matters. At times, planters openly meddled in their married children's business affairs. However, despite being involved together in several financial undertakings, these two families avoided the squabbling which often affected other antebellum families. One reason for the congenial relations between the Bringiers and Kenner was that the financial dealings between them were not one-sided. It was not just a case of well-to-do in-laws lending the struggling young couple money and giving advice on how to get started. Although Kenner borrowed a great deal of money—at least $150,000—from Nanine's father during the first few years of his marriage, surviving records from both Kenner and the Bringiers reveal that, as his prosperity increased and theirs declined, Kenner loaned members of Nanine's family amounts of money running into six figures during the final years of the antebellum period.[25]

Despite the differences which sometimes erupted among family members, closeness between children and in-laws was the rule in the South during antebellum times. Although Kenner's support of his wife's family members might have been unusually strong, support by planters of their in-laws was commonplace. As long as an individual had any blood or marriage claim, custom held that the planter possessed an obligation to support them. One such family encumbrance which cost Kenner a sizeable amount of money involved Nanine's brother Martin. The youngest of the nine Bringier children, Martin had a great fondness for drink and good times. A true example of the rich and reckless spendthrift, Martin was nevertheless jealously safeguarded by his mother. With the death of his father in 1847 and the accompanying decline of the Bringier fortune, Martin's devil-may-care ways led him to exhaust his resources, thus forcing him to turn to Kenner for assistance. Not wanting to let down a member of the family, Kenner provided him with a monthly allowance which remained his primary source of income for several years.[26]

The home of the antebellum planter in Southeast Louisiana was frequently a busy and crowded place. As a consequence of the code of hospitality which encouraged visits from relatives and friends, the plantation home was usually filled with children of both sexes, all sizes, and many colors—for it was not uncommon for the children of the slave house servants to have the run of the house. Although women in the Old South felt an obligation to have a child during their first year of marriage, the Kenners did not have their first child for nearly two years after their marriage. Named for his father, baby Duncan was born in 1841.[27]

Kenner and Nanine did not have their second child until five years after the birth of young Duncan. The birth of a child was usually a joyous occasion for the antebellum family. However, the birthday of Martha Blanche Kenner on May 2, 1846, was a day of tragic irony for the Kenners and their relatives. For on the very day that the family was blessed with the birth of a healthy young daughter, the family was devastated by the death of five-year-old Duncan. Surviving data do not reveal the cause of death of the Kenners' first-born child.[28]

The death of a child was not an uncommon event for the antebellum family. Parents were usually careful to take extreme precautions to protect the precarious health of their infants. Despite these efforts, the South was plagued with an infant mortality rate higher than the rest of the nation. A comparative survey cited by Catherine Clinton in her study of the plantation mistress found that, while the infant mortality among Northern planters was 12 percent, the rate for the Southern planter class was 14 percent. According to the same source, a comparison of 1860 mortality rates revealed that where there were 7,267 deaths of children aged zero to five years in the North, there were 17,619 deaths in the same category in the South.[29]

Fortunately for the Kenner family, the rest of the children born to Nanine and Duncan were healthy and all lived to reach maturity. A second daughter, Frances Rosella Kenner, was born at Ashland on April 23, 1849. She eventually married on her twenty-first birthday the Confederate Civil War hero Joseph Lancaster Brent.[30] The Kenner's final child was a son. George Currie Duncan Kenner was born on the Ashland estate on February 11, 1853. Named for his father's beloved brother, George later moved to Nashville, Tennessee, where he died in January, 1881, thus being the only one of Nanine's and Duncan's adult children who did not outlive their father.[31]

Despite the joy relatives felt over the survival of childbirth by both mother and child, society placed a priority on dynastic survival. Female babies sometimes suffered from the preference shown to male offspring. Historian Clinton, in her work *The Plantation Mistress*, maintains that the Southern preference for male progenies went deeper than just the belief that Southerners without sons were faced with genealogical extinction. According to Clinton, it was part of a larger ideological structure that held that men were superior and women were inferior. Not only were gender roles rigidly applied to the societal status of individuals in the Old South, they also permeated the antebellum family. For the family was not only a microcosm of Southern society as a whole, but it was also an instrument of implementation. The home, according to Clinton, served as training ground for the cultural gender roles of the era, with the preferred status of males being generated as well as reinforced by family roles. Whatever pampering a daughter might receive from her parents, she was never accorded the options that her brother was

Family and Society 409

given. Instead, she was usually given the power only to influence children in such a way as to maintain the societal status quo.[32]

Despite their close association with their husbands who were the movers and shakers of the political and social events in the antebellum South, Nanine and other aristocratic white women of the region had relatively little input into the outcome of the major events of the time. The inferior status of the antebellum female was largely the result of the romantic attitude toward women which dominated the culture of the Old South. Chivalry, as practiced during the antebellum period in the South, dictated a code of gracious manners which determined that a woman was to behave always in a highly feminine way and that it was her place to look up to the male as the protector and augur of wordly wisdom. It was her duty to marry early, stay within the sphere of the home, bear and raise numerous children, and uphold the traditions of the South, which included the defining of gender roles. With only a few exceptions, such as the famous feminists and abolitionists Sarah and Angelina Grimké of South Carolina, most women of the period accepted without public protest the status of their sex.[33]

Though theoretically placed on a pedestal by society, the majority of Southern women spent many laborious hours carrying out important responsibilities. Despite the presence of many servants, Nanine and the wives of most other planters were in charge not merely of the everyday events in the mansion but of the entire range of domestic operations across the plantation, from food and clothing to the spiritual and physical care of both their white and black families. The domain of the plantation mistress often extended from the locked pantry in the Big House to the slave hospital to the estate's slaughtering pen for livestock. Few events on the plantation escaped the attention of the mistress, unless they were crop-related, in which case they were considered the responsibility of the overseer. On occasion, she was even called upon to serve as an intermediary between slave and master, thus circumventing the authority of the overseer and making her role pivotal in the effective operation of the plantation.[34]

Most mistresses of estates the size of Ashland used house servants to mitigate the burdens associated with the rearing of their children. However, despite the presence of these slave assistants, most of the tiresome details of child care remained the responsibility of the planter's wife. Even the task of administering daily discipline to the planter's children was assigned to their mother. Southerners believed that the delinquency of a child was usually the result of negligence by the youth's mother, for only diligent efforts on the mother's part would prevent children from wandering astray.[35]

Despite such parental concern for their behavior, the life of a child on the sugar estate was a happy one. European visitors to the region sometimes took note of the Americans' indulgence of their children. A French nobleman who visited Louisiana during the antebellum period observed that the children of the region were "absolute masters of their fate [with] the authority of the parents [being] no restraint at all." One despairing plantation mistress commented that "our children are spoiled by our institution. It is very difficult to educate them; they never exert themselves in any way; they always depend on the slaves."[36]

In addition to being responsible for her children's discipline and physical well-being, the antebellum Southern female played a pivotal role in the spiritual realm of her family. Throughout the South religious affiliation varied from region to region. Episcopalianism dominated the planter class in the upper and coastal regions, whereas Catholicism prevailed in Maryland and the sugar regions of Louisiana. The major non-Anglican Protestant sects, including the Baptists, Methodists, and Presbyterians, were sprinkled across the rest of the plantation South. In Southeast Louisiana most of the *ancienne* planters were Roman Catholic, with the Methodist faith being the most common Protestant sect among the non-*ancienne* population. There were also sizable numbers of Episcopalians and Presbyterians in the region.[37]

Kenner was reared as an Episcopalian and Nanine as a Roman Catholic. However, denominational affiliation, though hotly contested by some individuals, was not emphasized by many of the planters in the sugar parishes of Louisiana. In some families and communities, individuals who belonged to one church occasionally attended services of another denomination. It was also common for individuals to switch churches. Among these was Duncan Kenner. The exact date of his conversion to Roman Catholicism is not known; however, since he and Nanine were married in a Catholic ceremony it is possible that Kenner's change of religion came early in his adulthood.[38]

The educational facilities in Louisiana had changed little in the years since Kenner's childhood. The state still lacked an effective educational system and suffered from a high rate of illiteracy. It was not until the state adopted a new constitution in 1845 that the legislature was directed to establish free schools throughout the state. Despite this and other efforts, results were mixed. There was little support among the people for public education. Most individuals gave little thought to the advantages of an education. Children were needed at home to assist their parents in working the family's farm or business. Likewise, few wealthy families availed themselves of the opportunity to place their children in the state's schools because of the belief held by most Southerners that attendance in the public primary and secondary schools carried with it the stigma of accepting charity. Most planters in rural Louisiana generally preferred to provide their children with tutors and private schooling.[39]

In spite of the existence of what at that time was considered a fairly effective public school in the town of Donaldsonville just a short distance from their plantation, Duncan and Nanine, like most members of their class, chose not to send their children to the state-supported schools. Instead, they followed the practice of hiring a tutor to educate their children. Most families of means used tutors to prepare their children for future entry into private schools located nearby, or into prestigious institutions in the East or in Europe. The services of a tutor varied in cost. Some lived in the homes of their students and were paid as little as $15.00 a month, while others, such as the teacher who worked for Kenner's uncle, William J. Minor, were paid as much as $1,500 a year. The spending

Family and Society

of such funds did not always insure a quality education for a planter's children. So disappointed was Nanine with the quality of training her children were receiving at their home in Ascension Parish that she spent most of her time during the winter months in New Orleans with her children so that they could be schooled by the "good teachers."[40]

The education received by the Kenner children was not very different from the classical curriculum followed by their father as a young student. The entire educational system of the antebellum South from the elementary level through college was based on the classical tradition. Though this was also true for education in the North, the Southern devotion to the traditional values of the classics was greater. "Gentlemen" of the Old South were expected to have a classical education. Curriculums often included studies in Greek, Latin, French, reading, writing, calculation, orthography, geography, design, and music. Female students were given courses designed to prepare them to be good wives and mothers. Subjects covered included manners, morals, modern language, piano playing, singing, drawing, painting, and fancy needlework.[41]

The tastes and habits acquired during their years of formal education were not forgotten by Southerners after that schooling was completed. Many sugar planters devoted much of their time to reading and to study. Kenner was said to have possessed at Ashland and in his New Orleans town mansion one of the finest private libraries in the state. Each day he attempted to devote several hours to literary pursuits. A person of enterprise and inquisitiveness, he read for both pleasure and business. From his readings he often acquired new ideas which he applied to his agricultural and business ventures. Kenner's love of reading was not an isolated occurrence in the Old South. For although there was widespread illiteracy among Southerners, many others read and owned considerable numbers of publications. For example, the libraries of Daniel Clark and of D. Rouquette included over 700 and 1,300 volumes respectively. The region also boasted of several community libraries such as those found in New Orleans, St. Francisville, and Alexandria.[42]

The material that the planters read varied greatly and lacked a concentration in any special area. Reading for both enjoyment and information, they exhibited broad literary interests which were indicative of the cosmopolitan nature of planter society. Though Southerners read the works of such earlier writers as William Shakespeare, John Milton, John Bunyan, Oliver Goldsmith, and Miguel de Cervantes, they preferred the works of the nineteenth-century school of romantic authors. Among the most popular of these were Lord Byron, Thomas Moore, James Fenimore Cooper, Alexandre Dumas, Southern author William Gilmore Simms, and the very popular Sir Walter Scott, whose *Ivanhoe* had great influence upon the South's romanticism. Besides their love of romantic fiction and poetry, Southerners also enjoyed many nonfictional works, including the histories of W. H. Prescott, George Bancroft, and Edward Gibbon. Theological works, scientific works, travel accounts, and gift books also were popular reading materials on the plantations. Finally, Southerners read a great deal of periodical literature, ranging from such contemporary newspapers as *Le Vigilant*, which was published in Donaldsonville just a few miles from Ashland, to the periodicals *De Bow's Review*, *Harper's Magazine*, and *The Southern Literary Messenger*. Included among Kenner's favorite reading materials was the popular horse racing periodical *Spirit of the Times*, to which he subscribed for many years both before and after the Civil War.[43]

In addition to their reading, planters, like most other Southerners, enjoyed outdoor activities. Hunting was the most popular of these activities in the sugar region of Louisiana. The area's many bayous and lakes abounded with ducks and other wildlife. Wild deer, bears, rabbits, and quail were found in great numbers in the swamps and forests of South Louisiana. Both day- and week-long hunting trips were common events during the antebellum era. Similarly, with the area's many waterways—most notably Lake Pontchartrain and the Gulf of Mexico—providing some of the most productive opportunities, fishing was a popular sport among the people of Southeast Louisiana.[44]

Such outdoor diversions were important, for they helped break the tedium which sometimes occurred during the uneventful periods on the sugar estate. Although located in an area where some of the South's wealthiest residents lived, Ashland, like most other plantations, sometimes suffered from a dull and monotonous routine. Except for the frequent visits by friends and relatives and the occasional stopover by flatboats which floated by the Kenner estate on their passage down the Mississippi River to New Orleans, life at Ashland, though sometimes adorned with luxurious trappings, was largely a solitary and simple existence.[45]

Though the Kenners knew and corresponded with their counterparts throughout the state, their actual contacts with them were mostly limited to occasional meetings when the planters and their families were visiting in New Orleans. Each area in the sugar region did, however, have its own self-contained social orbit. Within each neighborhood, including the lands bordering the Mississippi, Bayou Lafourche, Bayou Teche, and the Attakapas region of Louisiana, there were often close associations among friends and relatives. In Ascension Parish the Kenners, Bringiers, Trists, Tureauds, McCalls, Prestons, Mannings, Minors, Doyals, and Landrys, all enjoyed neighborly contacts.[46]

The rural nature of Louisiana made it difficult for a planter to find alternatives to the routine of the plantation. Though the population of the state had increased rapidly during the antebellum period, showing a 55 percent increase during the first forty years of the nineteenth century, few urban areas developed. In 1860 there were just a handful of urban communities in the state. Excluding New Orleans and its surrounding faubourgs, the only urban communities were Baton Rouge, Shreveport, Plaquemine, Donaldsonville, Homer, Alexandria, Thibodaux, and Minden. Of these, only Baton Rouge had a population in excess of 5,000, with the others having fewer than 2,500 each.[47]

Located a short distance across the river from Ashland was the town of Donaldsonville. With nearly 1500 inhabitants in 1860, the little community had limited offerings for the region's planters in the areas of culture and entertainment. Described by the British traveler William Russell in 1861 as a place of "odd, little, retiring, modest houses," the only structures of note in the town were the elegant Ascension Catholic

Family and Society 413

Church and the Ascension Parish Court House and jail. Besides being the location where Kenner usually attended church services and handled much of his legal business, the town of Donaldsonville also served as a commercial center where Kenner and the other planters of the region were able to make supplementary purchases of items needed on their estates. The town also offered the inhabitants of the region some simple diversions from their day-to-day routines. Included among the town's offerings were weekend horse races; frequent military parades, reviews, and balls sponsored by the local militia units; several restaurants; and an assortment of other merchandise outlets, including the shop of "the Parisian Rougeau" where books were bound and popular novels and nonfiction works were rented for $3.00 per year.[48]

Despite its rural location and relatively small size, the Donaldsonville community manifested a keen interest in the arts. Not only were theatrical events in New Orleans closely covered in the local press, but the town boasted of its own active theater. "Le Théâtre des Variétés" featured both locally produced productions and the works of traveling groups, with offerings in 1850 alone ranging from the internationally popular *Le Barbier de Seville* to the not-so-famous *The Wife Won a Lottery Prize*. The local newspaper, *Le Vigilant*, also did its part to preserve and promote the area's culture. By waging a tireless campaign for a national literature in French, the small town paper gave the sugar region of Southeast Louisiana an extraordinary impetus in literary production. Publishing both local, national, and international authors, the paper included in its column many different types of works including poetry, fables, ballads, short stories, novels, and novelettes which had Louisiana as a background.[49]

In addition to their frequent visits to the town of Donaldsonville, the Kenners and their planter neighbors in the river parishes also spent considerable time in New Orleans. Whether for reasons of business, shopping, schooling for the children, or the desire for the entertainment of the city, the Kenners sometimes spent weeks in the Crescent City. Though it was common practice for planters and their families to stay in one of the city's more lavish hotels while visiting New Orleans, some of the more prosperous planters, including the Kenners and the Bringiers, maintained townhouses. With extensive real estate holdings in the city, over the years Kenner used several different properties as his townhouse. However, Kenner's favorite and the one he and Nanine lived in until his death was an impressive mansion located at 257 Carondelet Street in the American sector of the city. When Kenner was away on business or remained at the plantation and Nanine and the children stayed in the city they sometimes stayed at "Melpomene," the magnificent townhouse of her parents.[50]

Regarded by many as the Paris of America, antebellum New Orleans offered its visitors a welcome relief from the tiresome routine of life on the plantation. One of the nation's leading commercial centers, the Crescent City during the period leading up to the Civil War was also considered to be one of America's cultural centers. Though the American influx during the first decades of the nineteenth century had altered the commercial character of the community, culturally the city continued to possess an air which was thoroughly French. As was the case in the Kenner household, many inhabitants of the area often used French instead English to communicate with one another at home and while visiting others. Besides the continued widespread use of the language, the French influence permeated many of the means of entertainment and relaxation in the city. Like few other places in the nation at the time, in New Orleans there existed a passionate love of the good life.[51]

The theater was one of the main forms of entertainment in New Orleans. It was enjoyed by both residents and visitors. With tickets usually costing between $1.00 and $1.50, the theater was popular entertainment for the common people of the city as well as for the more affluent residents. Of the city's theaters, the American generally offered performances for the lower classes. The upper classes usually attended either the Théâtre d'Orléans, where the works were usually performed in French, or the lavish St. Charles Theater, with its four tiers of boxes, magnificent chandelier, and finely appointed private rooms, where the offerings were in English. Among the more successful productions performed in the city during this period were the plays *King Lear*, *Richard the Third*, *Regulus*, *Marie Stewart*, and *William Tell*. The classic works of Corneille, Racine, and Voltaire were particularly popular with the patrons of the Théâtre d'Orléans.[52]

The opera was also a very popular entertainment for both the rich and poor. The city boasted of one of the oldest resident opera companies in the country. However, despite its popularity among city dwellers, seemingly Kenner was not attracted to the opera. As a leading member of the prestigious Boston Club, he is listed in the organization's records as having donated money to several fund-raising drives for needy causes, but his name is conspicuously absent from the list of contributors to the French Opera House.[53]

Along with the Pelican and Pickwick clubs, the Boston Club was one of the leading gentlemen's clubs in New Orleans. Active even today, the club is the oldest social club in the Crescent City. Founded by a group of affluent gentlemen for the purpose of playing the card game of "Boston," membership in the club was restricted, normally taking years of being on a waiting list before an individual could obtain entry into the club. Usually restricted to approximately 150, the membership consisted of men who could not only mix a good drink or play a good hand of cards but also were the moving forces behind the political and commercial destinies of the state. Among its more prominent members were the so-called "big four" of antebellum Louisiana politics—Judah Benjamin, John Slidell, Pierre Soulé, and Randall Hunt.[54]

Despite its social trappings and political status, the Boston Club remained largely a place of relaxation and gambling. At times quite large sums were bet at the club's gaming tables. Playing a card game similar to poker known as "brag," John R. Grymes was said to have lost many thousands of dollars. However, the distinction of perhaps the largest loss at a single sitting of cardplaying at the club during the antebellum years belongs to Duncan Kenner. It was reported by a club member that in just one sitting of "Boston" Kenner lost $20,000, and this was said not to have been an unusually large sum for him to lose! A person who loved to gamble, Kenner spent large sums of money to support his gambling habits, which involved both card playing and horse racing. An individual of lesser resources could hardly have supported such an extravagant hobby.[55]

New Orleans also offered planters and their families many fine shops which catered to the tastes of the wealthy with the latest styles and products from the North and from Europe. Families were also able to enjoy the city's fine restaurants and public squares. Another popular entertainment was a visit to the various circuses which frequented the city in the winter months because of its mild climate.[56]

The residents and visitors to the city also enjoyed celebrating national and religious holidays. Among the most important celebrations were the anniversary of the Battle of New Orleans, Washington's Birthday, and the Fourth of July. These occasions were observed with a great deal of patriotic fervor with parades by the local militia units, fireworks, and special religious services. Like today, the most significant of the religious holidays observed by the city's inhabitants was Christmas. A day primarily reserved for religious observance, it was not celebrated except by the children who received a visit from Papa Noël. Adults exchanged gifts a week later on New Years, which was celebrated as a day of gaiety and rejoicing.[57]

The most famous of New Orleans's pastimes was its annual Mardi Gras. During the antebellum period this pre-Lenten event gradually evolved from being observed with balls to the form for which it has become so widely known today with parades and street parties. An event celebrated by all segments of the community, Mardi Gras soon became a major social event eagerly participated in by members of the community's upper class—including Duncan Kenner, whose participation is noted in the court journal of Rex, the king of carnival.[58]

Private balls and dinner parties were also favorite pastimes of the social elite in Louisiana. Just as popular on the plantation as they were when the family stayed at their townhome in the city, these events of formal entertainment were usually extravagant and grand. Because of the Southern tradition of hospitality, the planter and his family often had guests for meals. By contrast, the ball was special; it was usually an infrequent celebration, often seasonal in nature, in which the host planter used the opportunity to showcase his wealth and liberality.[59]

Like most individuals who enjoyed the social status that they held, the Kenners from time to time held their share of elaborate and fanciful balls. Little is known of the details of these special events; however, it is unlikely that they varied much from those described by the writer Louise Butler when she wrote of the typical planter ball as having

> beautiful women, gorgeous costumes in real lace, real silk or hand embroidered lavishness, jewels, plumes, made the scene . . . delightsome music filled the air. Then the staircase was garlanded in roses all the way up its three-storied extent, vases on mantels and brackets filled with flowers. . . . About midnight supper was announced and the hostess led the way to the dining room. Of the menu, the cold meats, salads, salamis, galantines quaking in jellied seclusion, . . . were served from side tables leaving the huge expanse of carved oak, be-silvered, be-linened and be-

laced, for flowers trailing from the tall silver epergne in the center . . . fruits, cakes in pyramids or layers . . . , iced and ornamented; custards, pies, jellies, creams, Charlotte Russes of home-concocted sponge cake spread with raspberry jam encircling a veritable Mont Blanc of whipped cream dotted with cherry stars; towers of nougat or caramel, sorbets and ice creams served in little baskets woven of candied orange peel and topped with sugared rose leaves or violets.

Various wines in cut glass decanters, each with its name carved in silver grapeleaf suspended from its neck, champagne frappeed, were deftly poured by the waiters into gold traced or Bohemian glasses.

Illuminating the whole were wax candles in crystal or bronze chandeliers, and, on the table, in silver or delicate Dresden candelabra.

More dancing followed supper and just at dawn when the guests were leaving . . . a plate of hot gumbo, a cup of black coffee and enchanting memories sustained them on the long drive to their abodes.[60]

In addition to their extravagant social events and their frequent visits to the city, the Kenners and most other successful planters also varied their life style with occasional travel. Though Kenner himself made frequent trips for business and political reasons, the other members of the family also were able to travel. Among the family's most common destinations were the homes of Duncan's relatives in Natchez. Like many other sugar planters, they also enjoyed vacationing with the Bringiers in Newport, Rhode Island, and at the popular White Sulphur Springs in Virginia where there were comfortable accommodations in a large hotel and numerous cottages. However, since these resorts were so far from home and required such an effort to get the family there, most planters preferred to vacation at the various resort cities along the Mississippi Gulf Coast. Because of the poor health conditions which usually prevailed in subtropical New Orleans during the summer months and because of the lack of intensive planting activity at this time on the area's plantations, most of the region's well-to-do families chose the summer months to visit the coast where the gulf breeze and the high ground and pine forest offered a welcome change from the uncomfortable conditions found back home. With the humidity of summer beginning to settle on New Orleans, Martin Gordon, Kenner's factor and brother-in-law, wrote in early June 1855 to his friend Benjamin Tureaud, who was vacationing at Bay St. Louis: "Doctor Campbell and his gang take their departure today for the Bay of St. Louis; On Friday next, Kenner and his troupe will go over; You will soon have a devil of a Crowd at the Bay." Gordon ended his letter with the comment, "I wish to God I could leave the City," a sigh of regret and envy probably voiced by many an individual whom circumstances required to remain in the city through the summer months.[61]

Though the numerous diversions listed above amused large segments of the populations of antebellum Louisiana, it was also during this period that interest developed in organized sporting events. Clubs were started to help finance and encourage many different types of sporting activities. Interest in these activities grew quickly. In the space of roughly five decades, organized sports rose from a relatively insignificant place in the region's leisure habits to a leading role. By the end of the century sporting events had become the major source of amusement in New Orleans, a city renowned for its variety of entertainments and pleasures.[62]

The earliest organized sporting activity to take hold in the area was that of thoroughbred horse racing. The sport in America traced its roots to the colonial period in New York and the Southern colonies. However, with the rise of strong anti-gambling feelings in these areas during the latter decades of the eighteenth century, enthusiasm for the sport declined sharply along the East Coast. Just as the interest in turf sports began to wane in the East, it began to increase in the lower South. Many prosperous planters in the latter region, like Kenner, were either migrants or the sons of migrants from the East where horseracing was an established pastime of the gentry. Hence, as they accumulated wealth, they also adopted some of the trappings that they had associated with the well-to-do from their past experiences.[63]

Corresponding to the rapid expansion and success of the sugar and cotton interests in the lower South, the popularity of horse racing soared markedly during the 1830s and 1840s. During this period, local and out-of-town turfmen founded three jockey clubs and several racetracks in the New Orleans area alone. These included the Louisiana Course, located slightly to the southeast of the city; the Eclipse Course, near present-day Audubon Park; and the area's leading track, the Metairie Course, which was located on the Metairie Ridge in Jefferson Parish. During most of the antebellum period, racing in the New Orleans area was supported primarily by the region's well-to-do citizens. Although Sunday scrub races often attracted large crowds, most regular meetings catered to the affluent and were scheduled on weekday afternoons; this effectively limited the attendance of most working-class citizens. Furthermore, seating arrangements separated the various spectators at the races. Women, who came by invitation, occupied the ladies' stand, jockey club members and their guests the members' stand, and everyone else the public stand. The admission price of one dollar, the figure charged at most tracks, also discouraged working-class attendance, for that sum represented a day's wage or more for many of the region's laborers.[64]

Though patronized primarily by individuals of high social ranking, the sport was not universally popular among persons of that class. Despite their love of good times, most of the *anciennes* preferred the pleasures of masked balls, concerts, the theater, and games of chance and seldom shared the Anglo-American love for the turf. One such American who, despite close ties to the *anciennes* community, loved the sport of horse racing nearly as much as his prized plantation was Duncan Kenner.[65]

Kenner's enthusiasm for the sport came to him naturally. As a migrant from Virginia, where the sport was extremely popular for some time, it is probable that William Kenner introduced his sons to horse racing. Though the connection between William Kenner and his eastern relatives is unclear, it is known that many of the Kenners who resided in Virginia loved and participated in horse racing, especially Captain Rodham Kenner, a Revolutionary War hero who was considered one of the greatest racers of the colonial period. Furthermore, Duncan's older brother Minor was among the earliest individuals in Louisiana to promote horse racing as a sport. Along with several other leading citizens, including John Slidell—the individual who helped train Duncan in the law—Minor was among the first to become a member of the New Orleans Jockey Club in 1837.[66]

Having been interested in racing from his youth, Duncan, while continuing his education in Europe in the 1830s, studied the sport as it existed in England and on the Continent. When he returned to Louisiana he concentrated his efforts on his Ashland estate. There he indulged his taste and started to build a stable of the finest horses he could find. Not just content with the locally available stock of horses, Kenner looked to both the Eastern Seaboard and Europe for prized animals to improve his own stables. Because the subtropical climate of southern Louisiana did not promote proper growth in racing horses, Kenner and other planters of the region with racing stables seldom bred their animals in the Deep South itself. Instead, they bred their mares with Northern sires and foaled them in Virginia, Carolina, Kentucky, or Tennessee.[67]

At Ashland Kenner constructed a full-size racetrack and employed a full-time trainer to run his stables. George Washington Graves, a long-time companion, was the individual who assisted him the most in building a successful racing stable. Originally from Virginia, Graves' friendship with Kenner extended back to the time when Duncan and his brother George had lived together and shared ownership of Ashland. It was also during that period, before Duncan's marriage to Nanine, that Kenner acquired his first racehorses. From that time on Graves remained employed as Kenner's trainer. So close was the relationship between the two that Kenner constructed for Graves a small one-story cottage just to the rear of the Great House. The trainer was also afforded the privilege of taking both his breakfast and dinner with the family at the main house, and his supper was brought out to him at his residence. The Kenner children looked upon him almost as a member of the family. As soon as he was heard moving in the morning they would run out to meet him. They also loved to sit and talk with him for hours as he sat in one of two large-bottom armchairs which stood on each side of his front door. When the children were not in the chairs listening to his stories, Kenner and Graves often would sit and leisurely discuss their horses.[68]

Few individuals were as successful as Kenner at being a breeder, and racer of thoroughbred horses. From the time he became interested in horse racing until many years later when he retired from active participation in the sport, Kenner continually worked toward improving the sport. One example of his successful efforts to improve the quality of racing in the South was Kenner's use of professional jockeys. Through much of the antebellum period, little regard was accorded jockeys, many of whom were slaves. Most turfmen of the period placed their confidence in their horses, believing that well-qualified riders contributed little to a race's outcome. Kenner, on the other hand, gave nearly as much attention to the training of his young Negro riders as he did to his steeds. The success of his efforts was demonstrated when one visitor to the estate wrote about the jockeys: "These little fellows sat their horses so well, one might have thought till the

Family and Society 419

turn in the course displayed their black faces and grinning mouths, he was looking at a set of . . . young gentlemen out training."[69] Only a few jockeys ever became widely known for their riding ability. Among these was one of Kenner's slaves, Abe Hawkins. Known familiarly just as "Abe," during his career he rode many of the antebellum South's champion mounts. Another of Kenner's riders was Henry Hammond. A light-skinned mulatto slave who had originally come from Virginia, Hammond's work with Kenner's horses so impressed his owner that when he grew too heavy for racing he was made the family's coachman and eventually became the favorite slave of the Kenners and was able to advance to the favored slave roles of family cook and butler.[70]

Kenner was not alone in his efforts to improve the caliber of antebellum horse racing in Louisiana. Joining with Kenner to spearhead the effort were three other planters—Thomas Jefferson Wells, whose brother James Madison Wells would become a Reconstruction governor of the state; Adam L. Bingaman, a Mississippian; and William J. Minor. The single-minded devotion and intense competitiveness of these four enthusiasts did more to improve the quality of the Southern thoroughbred than the efforts of any others in the Deep South. They gained little financially, for, when compared to current standards, the purses which they won were not very large. Raised primarily by entry fees and contributions from local hotels, social clubs, and newspapers, the money won in competition mostly went for the payment of salaries for trainers, transportation costs, stabling fees, and other miscellaneous expenses.[71]

If it was not for pecuniary gain, why then did business-wise individuals such as Kenner spend so much of their personal fortunes and dedicate so much of their energy to the sport of thoroughbred racing? The answer was that the sport by its expensive nature and tradition was identified with the upper classes of Europe and colonial America. It was a badge of aristocracy which relatively few of the South's many planters had the money and expertise to excel in. Those who did were truly in a class by themselves, admired by their peers and by the many popular spectators of the sport. Added to this avidity for recognition was the Southerner's sense of individualism, which, according to historian W. J. Cash, was "far too much concerned with bald, immediate, unsupported assertion of the ego . . . placed too great stress on the inviolability of personal whim, and . . . was full of the chip-on-shoulder swagger and brag of a boy." This attitude was translated into the satisfaction which flowed to Kenner and his fellow racers when one of their favorite thoroughbreds demolished the opposition on the turf.[72]

The grandiloquence which colored the gentlemanly racing competition of the antebellum period was demonstrated in the sometimes heated rivalry between Kenner and Thomas Jefferson Wells. The most famous incident in the competition between these two leading racers occurred at the fashionable Metairie racecourse sometime before the war. After one of Kenner's horses had beaten one of Wells' animals, Wells loudly proclaimed that if he and not his jockey had ridden his steed the race would have been won. Hearing the boast, Kenner impetuously challenged Wells to enter the same two horses in a $1,000 sweepstakes with the two planters themselves as the jockeys. Not only did Wells eagerly accept the proposition but an Englishman known as Mr. Holland requested and was given permission to ride his horse in the race and to add another $1,000 to the stake.[73]

On the day of the race dozens of friends of each of the three riders gathered to witness the event. Racing during the antebellum period differed from the modern sport in several ways. Rather than the single dash of today, most races consisted of heats at distances of one to four miles each. This practice was designed to test an animal's endurance as well as its speed. Since the usual practice was for a winning horse to have to capture two or three heats, depending on the distance, some contests required as many as eight heats for a winner to be named. As was the case with Kenner and Wells, most wagers were made on a personal basis, for there were no bookmakers or parimutuel machines at the tracks.[74]

A great deal of high priced betting along with much teasing and fun at the expense of the riders took place during the moments leading up to the start of the contest. During the first heat the Englishman's stirrup broke, causing him to fall off of his horse while making the first turn on the track. Kenner and Wells continued to race at full gallop to the finish line with Wells taking the heat.[75]

Physically used up after the taxing race, both middle-aged gentlemen retired to the weighing room to rest. While stretched out on a bench, Kenner was upbraided by his trainer and close friend, George Graves, for not riding with more skill, and Graves suggested that he ride the next heat. On the other side of the room, Wells' trainer congratulated him for winning the heat and assured him that he had no worry about winning the next heat. Wells, still puffing and blowing from his ride, curtly responded to his trainer, "Don't bother me . . . I wouldn't ride another heat for $10,000." No less fatigued, Kenner, upon overhearing Wells' comments, thought this an excellent opportunity to bluff his opponent. Hoping to get a walkover win, Kenner nimbly sprang to his feet and exclaimed that he was ready to start the next heat. Wells, with his honor on the line, rose and started toward the track. Realizing that a continuation of the contest could have dangerous consequences for the two riders, friends convinced them to postpone the race until a future day. When the race was finally run professional jockeys were used, and Kenner's rider, wearing the "red and red" (cap and jacket of the same shade) colors of his stables and riding his Richard of York, won the contest and collected the winnings.[76]

In addition to his competition with Wells, Kenner also had a long-standing, spirited—though friendly—rivalry with his uncle William Minor, which centered around two of their favorite horses. In the 1840s hundreds of dollars passed between the two racing enthusiasts at the various competitions between Kenner's Verifier and Minor's Voucher. That Kenner took his racing seriously was again demonstrated in the spring of 1853 at the Metairie Course when, after the completion of a two-mile race in which his fine three-year-old Arrow was beaten by Sallie Waters of Mobile, Kenner offered to put up an additional $20,000 for a purse for another race between the two horses. To Kenner's chagrin the offer was declined.[77]

Family and Society 421

Obviously, winning meant much to Kenner. But on at least one occasion, losing was preferred by him or someone else involved with the Kenner stables. Sometime after the Metairie Jockey Club adopted rules to insure honest racing, track stewards expelled Kenner's leading jockey, Abe Hawkins, "for plain, positive, and palpable dishonesty—in plain terms, 'throwing off' a race which he had already won by sawing his horse around."[78]

Among the planter turf enthusiasts of Southeast Louisiana, Kenner maintained one of the largest stables of thoroughbreds. For example, Alexander Porter, the leading turfman of the Teche region, usually maintained around a dozen horses in his stable, and William J. Minor maintained twenty animals; in comparison Kenner kept stabled about thirty thoroughbreds. Included among his horses were such animals as Grey Medoc, who won eighteen of his first twenty-three races; Minnehaha, who held for several years the record for running the mile; Kendall, whom Kenner named for his friend, George W. Kendall, founder of the *New Orleans Picayune*; Louis d'Or, Panic, Luda, Rupee, Grey Fannie, and Pat Golray. To acquire such quality stock Kenner readily paid premium prices. For instance, in 1859 when the average price for a good thoroughbred horse was about $1200, Kenner willingly paid the top price of over $1800 for his new animals.[79]

Kenner's interest in the sport went deeper than just the breeding and racing of his horses. He was among the leading turfmen who actively worked to improve the sport by increasing its acceptance by the public, particularly the social elites of the community. For example, when the racing enthusiast Richard Ten Broeck established a joint-stock company called the Metairie Association and purchased full control of the fashionable Metairie Course in 1851, Kenner was among the fourteen additional stockholders of the association. Only 300 shares of stock were issued at $100 each. Of these, Ten Broeck held 145 shares and Kenner and William J. Minor each owned twenty-five. The association completely renovated the track's facilities by erecting new stables, enlarging and beautifying the grandstand, and by furnishing the ladies' stand with parlors and retiring rooms.[80]

Though the changes brought by the association were successful in upgrading the track, policy differences between Ten Broeck and Kenner, Minor, and Thomas Jefferson Wells led to considerable feuding among the stockholders. The quarreling finally resulted in the reorganization of the Metairie Association in 1857 with the purchase of Ten Broeck's interest in the Metairie Course by Kenner, Minor, and Wells. At that time the new majority stockholders added additional improvements to the racing facility, including the first brick-and-iron grandstand in the United States.[81]

The efforts of Kenner and his cohorts met with great success. Attendance at the local tracks swelled. Largely because of the endeavors of the region's planters, by the eve of the Civil War New Orleans was recognized as the center of thoroughbred racing in America. No track in the country could consistently duplicate the races sponsored by the Metairie Association. Regardless of any shortcomings possessed by the region's planter class, the quality and success of their thoroughbreds were beyond dispute. Their wealth, leisure, and land made it possible for them to develop fully the Southern gentry's commitment to a sport long identified with the aristocratic classes of Europe and America.[82]

Notes for "Family and Society"

[1]Catherine Clinton, *The Plantation Mistress: Woman's World in the Old South* (New York, 1982), 223; J. Carlyle Sitterson, *Sugar Country: The Cane Sugar Industry in the South, 1753-1950* (Lexington, 1953), 70-71.

[2]Sitterson, *Sugar Country*, 71.

[3]Ezra J. Warner and W. Buck Yearns, *Biographical Register of the Confederate Congress* (Baton Rouge, 1975), 144.

[4]Edwin Adams Davis, *Louisiana: A Narrative History*, third ed. (Baton Rouge, 1971), 201; John R. Kemp, *New Orleans* (Woodland Hills, Calif., 1981), 75.

[5]Folders 1, 4, Bringier Notes in Trist Wood Papers; Mary Louise Christovitch et al., *New Orleans Architecture*, Vol. 2, *The American Section (Faubourg St. Mary)* (Gretna, La., 1972), 148; *New Orleans Daily True Delta*, February 21, 1865; Succession of Duncan Farrar Kenner in New Orleans Public Library (hereafter cited as Succession of Duncan Farrar Kenner, NOPL).

[6]Stock Receipt, Southern Pacific Railroad, Duncan Farrar Kenner Papers; Miscellaneous Notes, Bringier Notes in Trist Wood Papers, The Urquhart Collection, Historic New Orleans Collection, New Orleans, Louisiana; Roseland Plantation Account Book, Kenner Family Papers, Louisiana State University.

[7]The term "Creole" is often used by writers to refer variously to all-white, all-French, all-Spanish, all-European, mixed French and Spanish, and upper class individuals who settled the region before the Americans obtained possession of the area. Despite the current wide-spread acceptance of this use of the term "Creole," during the antebellum period the term was most often used simply to designate anyone who was a native of Louisiana, regardless of race, ethnic origin, language, or social position. Hence, in this paper the term *"ancienne population"* shall be used to refer to those individuals who were descendants of the European settlers in Louisiana before the American regime. See Joseph G. Tregle, "Early New Orleans Society: A Reappraisal," *Journal of Southern History,* 18 (1952): 20-36; Joseph G. Tregle, "On That Word 'Creole' Again," *Louisiana History,* 9 (1968): 193-98.

[8]Tregle, "On That Word 'Creole' Again," 198; Sitterson, *Sugar Country*, 69; Raimondo Luraghi, *The Rise and Fall of the Plantation South* (New York, 1978), 52; Davis, *Louisiana*, 229.

[9]Kemp, *New Orleans*, 78-79.

[10]Tregle, "On That Word 'Creole' Again," 198.

[11]Charles L. Dufour, *Ten Flags in the Wind: The Story of Louisiana* (New York, 1967), 157.

[12]Sitterson, *Sugar Country*, 69; Davis, *Louisiana*, 229.

[13]Davis, *Louisiana*, 229.

[14]Harnett T. Kane, *Plantation Parade: The Grand Manner in Louisiana* (New York, 1945), 9-10; Sitterson, *Sugar Country*, 69.

[15]*New Orleans Daily Picayune*, June 27, 1909; Grace King, *Creole Families of New Orleans* (New York, 1921), 413-14.

[16]*Daily Picayune*, June 27, 1909; King, *Creole Families*, 416; Stanley C. Arthur and George C. Huchet de Kernion, *Old Families of Louisiana* (1931; reprint ed., Baton Rouge 1971), 426-29; Mark Mayo Boatner, *The Civil War Dictionary* (New York, 1959), 835.

[17] Arthur and Huchet de Kernion, *Old Families*, 426-29; Allan C. Ashcraft, "Richard 'Dick' Taylor," in David C. Roller and Robert W. Tyman, eds., *The Encyclopedia of Southern History* (Baton Rouge, 1979), 1181-82.

[18] Arthur and Huchet de Kernion, *Old Families*, 426-29; Folders 3, 4, Bringier Notes, in Trist Wood Papers.

[19] Folders 1, 4, 26, Bringier Notes, in Trist Wood Papers; King, *Creole Families*, 414-16.

[20] Clinton, *Plantation Mistress*, 62-63.

[21] Kane, *Plantation Parade*, 190.

[22] Clinton, *Plantation Mistress*, 67.

[23] Folder 3, Bringier Papers in Trist Wood Papers; Certificate of Marriage of Duncan Farrar Kenner and Anne Guillelmine Bringier, June 1, 1839, Department of the Archives, Diocese of Baton Rouge.

[24] Kathleen H. McKee, "Belle Helene Plantation," Research Paper, Architectural Archives, Special Collections Division, Tulane University, 3; Kane, *Plantation Parade*, 193.

[25] Clinton, *Plantation Mistress*, 44; Miscellaneous Notes, Bringier Notes in Trist Wood Papers.

[26] Clinton, *Plantation Mistress*, 45; Folder 4, Bringier Notes in Trist Wood Papers.

[27] Davis, *Louisiana*, 229; Clement Eaton, *Jefferson Davis* (New York, 1977), 27; Folders 3, 409, Bringier Notes in Trist Wood Papers.

[28] Folders 3, 409, Bringier Notes in Trist Wood Papers; Clinton, *Plantation Mistress*, 45.

[29] Clinton, *Plantation Mistress*, 156.

[30] Born in Maryland, Brent served during the war on the staff of Dick Taylor as Chief of Artillery and Ordnance. In 1863 he led the force which captured the Union ironclad *Indianola*. Later he was appointed a Brigadier General of Cavalry. At the time the war ended he was commander of the Southern forces in the front line of the West from Arkansas to the Gulf. After the war he practiced law in Baltimore and later returned to Louisiana, where he and Rosella took over the management of Ashland. See Boatner, *Civil War Dictionary*, 83.

[31] Folders 3, 409, Bringier Notes in the Trist Wood Papers.

[32] Clinton, *Plantation Mistress*, 45-46.

[33] Clement Eaton, *A History of the Old South*, 2nd ed. (New York, 1966), 396-97; Eaton, *Jefferson Davis*, 28-29.

[34] Clinton, *Plantation Mistress*, 18; Eaton, *History of the Old South*, 398.

[35] Clinton, *Plantation Mistress*, 47-48.

[36] Quoted in Eaton, *History of the Old South*, 398-99.

[37] Clinton, *Plantation Mistress*, 160; Sitterson, *Sugar Country*, 86.

[38] Sitterson, *Sugar Country*, 86; Clinton, *Plantation Mistress*, 160; *New Orleans Daily States*, July 4, 1887.

[39] Olive Isabell Arceneaux, "A Brief History of Public Education in Louisiana, 1805-1845" (M.A. thesis, Tulane University, 1938), 77-78; Sitterson, *Sugar Country*, 84; Lester J. Cappon, "The Provincial South," *Journal of Southern History*, 16 (1950): 19-20.

[40] Arceneaux, "Public Education," 49; Lionel C. Durel, "Creole Civilization in Donaldsonville, 1850, According to 'Le Vigilant'," *Louisiana Historical Quarterly*, 31 (1948): 985; T. H. Harris, "The Story of Public Education in Louisiana" (M.A. thesis, Louisiana State University, 1924), 3; Seebold, *Plantation Homes*, I, 142.

[41] Noble, "Schools of New Orleans," 68; Clement Eaton, *The Mind of the Old South*, Revised ed. (Baton Rouge, 1976), 291-92.

[42] Edwin L. Jewell, *Crescent City Illustrated: The Commercial, Social, Political, and General History of New Orleans* (New Orleans, 1873), n.p.; Succession of Duncan Farrar Kenner, NOPL; Davis, *Louisiana*, 224-25.

[43] G. U. Patrick, "Literature in the Louisiana Plantation Home" (Ph.D. dissertation, Louisiana State University, 1935), 153-58; Eaton, *Mind of the Old South*, 246-47, 296-97; Durel, "Creole Civilization," 981.

[44] Sitterson, *Sugar Country*, 78-79.

[45] Sidney A. Marchand, *The Flight of a Century (1800-1900) In Ascension Parish Louisiana* (Donaldsonville, La., 1936), 67; Clinton, *Plantation Mistress*, 176.

[46] Sitterson, *Sugar Country*, 76-77.

[47] Dufour, *Ten Flags in the Wind*, 151; Davis, *Louisiana*, 203.

[48] Marchand, *Flight of a Century*, 67; Durel, "Creole Civilization," 988-89; Davis, *Louisiana*, 203; Sitterson, *Sugar Country*, 110.

[49] Durel, "Creole Civilization," 990-91.

[50] Succession of Duncan Farrar Kenner, NOPL; Sitterson, *Sugar Country*, 80; John Hervey, *Racing in America: 1665-1865*, 2 vols. (New York, 1944), 2:195; Folders 1, 3, 4, Bringier Notes in Trist Wood Papers.

[51] Albert Fossier, *New Orleans: Glamour Period, 1800-1840* (New Orleans, 1947); 452; Herman de Bachellé Seebold, *Old Louisiana Plantation Homes and Family Trees*, 2 vols. (New Orleans, 1941), 1:139.

[52] Fossier, *Glamour Period*, 471-72, 479; Sitterson, *Sugar Country*, 80-81.

[53] Dufour, *Ten Flags in the Wind*, 158; Stuart O. Landry, *History of the Boston Club* (New Orleans, 1953), 265.

[54] Landry, *History of the Boston Club*, 61; Robert Douthat Meade, *Judah P. Benjamin: Confederate Statesman* (New York, 1943), 82; Henry Rightor, *Standard History of New Orleans, Louisiana* (New Orleans, Chicago, 1900), 607.

[55] Landry, *Boston Club*, 203.

[56] Fossier, *Glamour Period*, 464; Sitterson, *Sugar Country*, 81.

[57] Fossier, *Glamour Period*, 461, 485.

[58] Jewell, *Cresent City Illustrated*, n.p.; Kemp, *New Orleans*, 85-86.

[59] Clinton, *Plantation Mistress*, 176, 177-78.

[60] Louise Butler, "The Louisiana Planter and His Home," *Louisiana Historical Quarterly*, 10 (1927): 359-60.

[61] Quoted in Sitterson, *Sugar Country*, 81; Folder 1, Bringier Notes in Trist Wood Papers; Ruth Irene Jones, "Ante-Bellum Watering Places of Louisiana, Mississippi, Alabama, and Arkansas" (M.A. thesis, University of Texas, 1954), 1-2; Butler, "Louisiana Planter," 360.

[62] Dale A. Somers, *The Rise of Sports in New Orleans, 1850-1900* (Baton Rouge, 1972), 9.

Family and Society

[63] Ibid., 24-25.

[64] Ibid., 27-28.

[65] Ibid, 24.

[66] Fossier, *Glamour Period*, 265-66; John Hervey, *Racing in America: 1665-1865*, 2 vols. (New York, 1944), 1:19; 2:182.

[67] Hervey, *Racing in America,* 1:182; Kane, *Plantation Parade*, 192.

[68] Plan of Ashland; Notes on G. W. Graves, Rosella Kenner Brent Papers.

[69] Quoted in Kane, *Plantation Parade*, 192.

[70] Jewell, *Crescent City Illustrated*, n.p.; Hervey, *Racing in America*, 2:195; Notes on Henry Hammond, Rosella Kenner Brent Papers, Louisiana State University Archives, Baton Rouge, Louisiana; Somers, *Sports in New Orleans*, 29-30.

[71] Somers, *Sports in New Orleans*, 30; Hervey, *Racing in America*, 2:194.

[72] Wilbur J. Cash, *The Mind of the South* (New York, 1941), 44; Somers, *Sports in New Orleans*, 30.

[73] Landry, *History of the Boston Club*, 59; Kane, *Plantation Parade*, 193.

[74] Somers, *Sports in New Orleans*, 29.

[75] Landry, *History of the Boston Club*, 59.

[76] Ibid., 59-60; Hervey, *Racing in America*, 2:195; Kane, *Plantation Parade*, 193.

[77] Sitterson, *Sugar Country*, 80.

[78] Somers, *Sports in New Orleans*, 30.

[79] Sitterson, *Sugar Country*, 79; Hervey, *Racing in America*, 2:200, 209, 243, 247, 353; Landry, *History of the Boston Club*, 57-58; Fayette Copeland, *Kendall of the Picayune, Being His Adventures in New Orleans, on the Texan Santa Fe Expedition, in the Mexican War, and in the Colonization of the Texas Frontier* (Norman, Okla., 1943), 314; Notes on G. W. Graves, Rosella Kenner Brent Papers; *Daily States*, July 4, 1887.

[80] Hervey, *Racing in America*, 2:239; Somers, *Sports in New Orleans*, 33.

[81] Somers, *Sports in New Orleans*, 33.

[82] Ibid., 34.

THE WETTEST DRY CITY IN AMERICA*

Louis Vyhnanek

There has been considerable debate about which city was the "wettest" city in America during the 1920s. One survey published during the period was Martha Bruere's *Does Prohibition Work?*, which appeared in 1927. Bruere's survey of social workers found that New Orleans was the "wettest" city in America, with its citizens general disregard for the Prohibition law and evidence of widespread bootlegging activity. This survey was not the final word on the subject, but New Orleans was clearly one of the "wettest" cities in the United States. Prohibition in New Orleans was in the words of one authority the "unlikeliest crusade."[1] It was an effort doomed to failure from the very beginning because of the many ways of satisfying New Orleanians desire for alcoholic beverages.

There were a number of sources of illegal liquor in New Orleans. A major source during the early part of the decade was through smuggling from outside the United States. New Orleans served as a major center for the importation of illegal liquor. If one looks at a map of New Orleans and the coastline of southern Louisiana the reason is readily apparent. There were literally hundreds of ways to smuggle liquor into the city from ships anchored in the Gulf of Mexico. The principal smuggling avenues into New Orleans included Lake Pontchartrain, Lake Borgne, the passes at the mouth of the Mississippi River, and the numerous bayous and inlets of St. Bernard Parish. Bayou Bienvenue, running west from Lake Borgne, and the Navigation Canal were also used by liquor runners to deliver cargoes that quenched the thirst of many New Orleanians.[2] During the first part of the 1920s Lake Pontchartrain served as a haven for liquor smugglers. For example, in 1922 Prohibition agents discovered a major bootleg cache including both liquor and champagne valued at between $50,000 and $75,000 in the area of the lake between West End and Spanish Fort. Later the lake became a problem for smugglers because of the presence of hijackers who lay in wait in swift boats ready to

---

*Excerpt first published in chapter 4 of Louis Vyhnanek, *Unorganized Crime: New Orleans in the 1920s* (Lafayette, La.: Center for Louisiana Studies, 1998), 53-89. Reprinted with the kind permission of the author and the University of Louisiana at Lafayette.

pounce upon slower bootleg vessels as they made their way toward the city. The focus of smuggling then shifted to St. Bernard Parish, which throughout the decade remained a constant refuge for illegal liquor suppliers.[3]

During the early 1920s a Rum Row was set up in the gulf near the Chandeleur and Breton Islands, located about twenty miles off the coast of St. Bernard Parish. Here a fleet of vessels loaded with liquor anchored for a rendezvous with smaller boats that transported the cargo to shore for delivery into the city. This Rum Row continued in operation until the middle part of the decade, when it shifted farther west to a point off Timbalier Light, where liquor runners made use of Bayou Lafourche and Barataria Bay to gain access to the New Orleans market through Algiers, Gretna, and other west bank cities.[4]

A major reason for the early success of Rum Row off the coast of Louisiana was the lack of federal enforcement efforts in the area. As late as 1923 the Customs Department had only two vessels to patrol all the avenues into the port of New Orleans, and the Coast Guard had only one small vessel to cover the vast area of water around the city. Not until 1925, when the Coast Guard began to patrol the gulf with swift vessels armed with guns and searchlights, was Rum Row substantially broken up. After that year part of Rum Row continued to operate west of the Atchafalaya River, but the amount of liquor smuggled in never reached the levels of the mid-1920s.[5]

The liquor smuggled into New Orleans came from three principal sources—Cuba, the Bahamas, and British Honduras. Europe served as the original source of supply for these countries, but not in every case. Dealers in Nassau and in Cuba were not above selling merchandise that was little better than local New Orleans home brew, and passing it off as the finest European brands. Fake bottles, labels, corks, and seals helped disguise the true quality of much of their product. Liquor cargoes from Cuba, the Bahamas, and British Honduras went through several steps on their journey to the Crescent City. First, arrangements were made between liquor dealers in Havana, Nassau, and Belize and syndicates in New Orleans. An amount, price, and time of arrival were agreed upon, and the liquor was then transported to Rum Row. Scores of vessels carried the liquor, including fishing boats, boats with large gasoline-powered engines, and small steamships. Many of these ships were under foreign registry, usually British, although quite a few were locally owned. There were also independent operators, who sold to whoever met their price. Some liquor-bearing vessels carried as many as 4,000 cases in a single trip.[6]

Once a liquor-running vessel arrived in the gulf, it was met by smaller oyster luggers and speedy pleasure craft that transported the cargo to shore. On the shores of the bayous, swamps, and marshes of St. Bernard Parish the liquor was unloaded onto motor trucks or passenger cars. Veteran liquor runners always devised a system to protect their shipments from hijackers. Traveling at night the trucks were camouflaged for maximum concealment. Liquor was disguised as molasses, canned vegetables, and in one case was transported in a funeral coach. Armed gunmen frequently rode with the trucks or followed behind in an automobile with its lights off. The gunmen drove up shooting if a truck was stopped for any reason; they were under orders to do whatever was necessary to protect the liquor shipment. St. Bernard Parish furnished the ideal atmosphere for this type of liquor running. Local residents were generally willing, for fees of $100 to $500, to transfer liquor from the mother ship offshore and then to help transport it to its final destination. Most people in St. Bernard Parish considered bootlegging to be a legitimate way of making a living, and local authorities generally ignored a shipment of liquor passing through the parish.[7]

Much of the liquor entering New Orleans was landed and loaded onto trucks at Shell Beach on the shores of Lake Borgne. The trucks were then driven at high speed west over the St. Bernard Highway toward New Orleans. St. Bernard Highway extended south and east of the city to the town of Pointe-a-la-Hache in Plaquemines Parish, a distance of forty-five miles. South of New Orleans at the little town of Poydras the highway divided, one section continuing south to Pointe-a-la-Hache, the other heading east to Shell Beach. Rumrunners followed this road from Shell Beach west to the town of Violet, where a canal connected Lake Borgne with the Mississippi River. At Violet there was a bridge that all motor traffic from the south had to cross on its way into New Orleans. Beyond Violet the liquor convoys continued west through Chalmette into the outskirts of the Crescent City.[8]

The New Orleans liquor wholesaler often paid for his liquor after it had been delivered to shore. He then hired the trucks that drove the shipment into the city, paying their owner roughly $5 a case to protect the cargo from hijackers. A veteran wholesaler hired several armed guards to ride with the liquor shipment. If it was lost or stolen, he stood to lose everything he had invested. Once safely into New Orleans the liquor was delivered to the wholesaler's warehouse, where it was stored until it was sold to a retail bootlegger who distributed it to his customers.[9] In the case of some major smuggling operations the New Orleans group controlled all phases of the liquor transaction, from buying liquor in Cuba to the final local sale in the city.

The profits involved in liquor smuggling usually far outweighed the risks. In 1923 it was estimated that the profits made in running liquor into New Orleans ran to over $2,000,000 annually. Theodore Jacques, head of Prohibition enforcement in New Orleans, estimated that, if a smuggler equipped two boats a month, each making one round trip carrying 300 cases, he could import 6,000 cases over a ten-month period. For these 6,000 cases the bootlegger paid $35 a case for delivery to New Orleans, which, coupled with payments for storage, spotters, hauling, and miscellaneous services, came to a total of $213,500. The same liquor was then sold for $85 a case, or $510,000, giving the smuggler a substantial profit of $296,500 for ten months' work. Another true case involved a liquor runner who conducted a select trade in Scotch whiskey. The smuggler made regular trips between Belize, British Honduras, and New Orleans, carrying 2,000 cases of Scotch whiskey each time. If he sold the whiskey for a minimum of $65 a case, he doubled the amount of his investment each trip; the profit for each voyage averaged around $65,000.[10]

Ships docking at the port of New Orleans often carried illegal liquor, much of it ingeniously concealed on board the vessel. Bottles of liquor were found everywhere by customs officials: in bunkers, in crow's nests, under steel floors, down in after-peaks and fore-peaks, in forecastles, in washrooms, near portholes, anywhere aboard ship.[11] The caches could be large or small. Some sailors, seeing a quick way to make a profit, attempted to smuggle a few bottles off the ship hidden on their persons. Others were after a larger profit. When a Japanese steamship docked in New Orleans in 1921, a search by customs officials revealed 1,500 quarts of high-grade liquor; the chief steward admitted ownership of the spirits, which he intended to sell for a sizeable return on his investment. Customs officials watched the docks but sometimes smugglers brazenly brought liquor across the wharves in the early morning hours. Prohibition agents suspected that at night tugs operating on the river helped unload liquor shipments from ships entering the port. The amount of liquor seized by customs officials was not insignificant. Records show that as of March 1921, 16,000 bottles had been confiscated since Prohibition had gone into effect, their value conservatively estimated at nearly $300,000.[12]

Much of the imported liquor reaching New Orleans went on to other destinations. Some was shipped to Chicago, St. Louis, Kansas City, and other cities in the Mississippi Valley. Additional amounts were also transported to Texas and other neighboring states. The liquor shipments were made by boat, car, and rail, although the largest cargoes usually went by rail. They were disguised as canned tomatoes or corn, molasses, soda fountain syrup, and large drums of house paint. Sometimes liquor was hidden under other items, like eggs or oyster shell. One ring shipped its liquor in big casks camouflaged as molasses. As a final touch they dripped molasses along the outside of the casks and used a regular brand name to hide the contents.[13]

Several of these inland smuggling ventures operated on a large scale. One large operation made use of Pullman conductors and porters to transport liquor by rail between New Orleans and Chicago. The liquor was first brought into the city by West Indian fishermen and then carried on board the train by the porters in steel, cushion-lined cases, each holding a dozen bottles. During this ring's peak period, before it was discovered and broken up in 1922, 300 cases of liquor were transported north every week, bringing its participants a total of $750,000 to $1,000,000.[14] Another New Orleans ring, aided by connections in St. Louis, supplied that city and other Midwestern metropolises with thousands of cases of imported scotch, bourbon, and rye. Much of it, camouflaged as drums of house paint, was transported north by barges and freight cars. The minimum retail value of the liquor shipped by the New Orleans-St. Louis operation was estimated at nearly $5,000,000. When the operation was discovered in 1925, a New Orleans attorney was implicated and charged with conspiring with several St. Louis bootleggers to bring illegal liquor into that city.[15] Some of the liquor imported into New Orleans was even smuggled to Al Capone's successful bootlegging operation in Chicago. Two carloads of liquor registered to a fruit shipping concern in Kenner, a small town just outside New Orleans, were shipped to Chicago, where they were delivered to the address of a speakeasy run by Al Brown, one of Capone's aliases. Later Prohibition raids on Capone's headquarters linked the shipping of liquor between New Orleans and the Windy City.[16]

New Orleans liquor smuggling produced some colorful and successful figures. Among the most colorful was Mark Boasberg, better known as Jack Sheehan. Sheehan was known as the "Coconut King," a reference to his claim in the local press that a submarine chaser and other vessels he had purchased were to be used strictly for importing coconuts from the Bahamas. Born in Chicago, Sheehan moved to New Orleans in 1917. In that year he began operating the Suburban Gardens, a roadhouse just across the parish line in Jefferson that served as a center for gambling, dancing, and drinking by many New Orleanians. Very few people put much stock in Sheehan's claim that he was involved in the coconut trade; particularly skeptical were New Orleans Prohibition agents. In late December 1921, Prohibition officials learned that Sheehan had received two boatloads of liquor that had been brought up the Mississippi River and unloaded near his residence. On New Year's Eve agents led by Director Hugh Larre and armed with a search warrant raided Sheehan's place. Sheehan, asserting that he had purchased the liquor before Prohibition became law, obtained a temporary injunction blocking its immediate removal. However, customs officials intervened and removed the liquor under a warrant citing smuggling charges. Moving vans carried Sheehan's stock to the Customhouse, where it was stored. Altogether, liquor valued at between $80,000 and $150,000 was seized. While under indictment by a grand jury on smuggling charges, Sheehan filed a motion to quash the indictment, which was granted by federal Judge Rufus Foster in June 1922. Charging that the terms of the search warrant were faulty, the judge ordered Sheehan's liquor returned. As a result, the government was placed in the embarrassing position of having to hire five motor trucks to return 4,000 quarts of liquor and champagne it had seized six months earlier to Jack Sheehan. It was reported that Sheehan gave a party for a number of friends that same evening and "a good time was had by all." What particularly enraged the agents was their belief that Sheehan was still selling liquor; trucks came and went from his residence, apparently delivering liquor to customers in the city.[17]

For the remainder of the 1920s Sheehan continued to evade the efforts of Prohibition agents to catch him in bootlegging activities. In 1925 the government charged him with heading a conspiracy to smuggle thousands of cases of liquor from Havana into New Orleans. The captain of the British power sloop *Panama* told federal officials, following the seizure of his vessel by the Coast Guard, that he had made a number of trips between Havana and New Orleans delivering liquor for Sheehan. In his statement the captain testified that he met Sheehan in Havana several times, that Sheehan was the one who purchased and outfitted the *Panama*, that Sheehan sent boats out from shore to pick up the liquor off the coast near Breton Island, and that Sheehan paid him upon delivery of the shipments. Despite the testimony of the captain and his crew, the government was never able to obtain enough evidence to take the case to court. No evidence of the liquor cargo smuggled into New Orleans was ever produced, and without the physical evidence the government had no case. Sheehan, careful to cover his involvement in the *Panama* episode, managed to escape prosecution. Sheehan never spent a day in jail during the entire decade, although in 1926 he was sentenced to pay substantial fines for gambling violations. In 1929 he pleaded guilty to several liquor law violations, but received only a suspended sentence. Sheehan sold the Suburban Gardens in 1930 and retired to a quieter life until his death at the age of eighty-two in 1956. After Prohibition was repealed, Sheehan's Suburban Gardens, later the Beverly Club, continued to prosper as a gambling establishment well into the 1930s.[18]

Many New Orleans liquor smugglers like Sheehan prospered during the 1920s, but the government did achieve some success in breaking up several large-scale operations. The most spectacular success by Prohibition agents came in August 1925, when federal forces smashed the Patterson-Battistella liquor ring, the largest operation in the city and one of the largest in the United States. Alonzo Patterson, one of the most powerful liquor smugglers in New Orleans, and his partner, Andrew Battistella, attempted to smuggle thousands of cases of liquor from Havana into the Crescent City during the period from May to August 1925. This operation ended when Prohibition agents, beginning on August 11, conducted a series of massive liquor raids in New Orleans, St. Bernard Parish, and all along the Gulf Coast. Involving over 200 agents from every area of the country, the raids were described by the *Item* as the "biggest prohibition drive in the United States." Ten thousand cases of liquor valued at $1,000,000 were seized in the day-long series of raids.[19]

A prime reason for the success of the government operation was that local Prohibition agents had infiltrated the smuggling ring. Patrick Needham, a twenty-seven-year-old member of O. D. Jackson's force, worked undercover to learn the details of the operation. Emphasizing his poor pay as a government agent, Needham met with both Patterson and Battistella, who offered money for information that would guarantee the protection of their liquor shipments. Over the course of the summer a total of $15,560 in bribes was paid to Needham and Joe Thomas, another agent. The largest bribe was for $10,000, to be delivered to O. D. Jackson in return for transferring a Coast Guard vessel so that a liquor schooner could safely unload its cargo.[20]

Patterson and Battistella were arrested during the August raids and charged with bribery. When their trial began in federal court in December 1925, Needham was the star government witness. He told of being present at Patterson's plush North Carrollton Avenue home, where most of the money changed hands. Here he heard Patterson make arrangements to have liquor shipped from Honduras and to send Battistella to Havana to obtain liquor. Needham told of a number of instances where he shifted Prohibition agents off certain roads so that smuggled liquor could reach the city undetected. In addition, Needham testified that he arranged a meeting between Patterson and Walter Cohen, the black Republican Comptroller of Customs in New Orleans. At that meeting, held in Patterson's home, Cohen agreed to consider shifting the movements of the customs boat *Rita* to allow Patterson the opportunity to bring in his liquor shipment. Patterson had instructed Needham to tell Cohen that he would give the comptroller $1,000 to have the *Rita*'s movements changed. The boat was later shifted from its position monitoring the Industrial Canal just before Patterson's shipment passed through. Needham further testified that some of the liquor was brought into New Orleans in small boats via the New Basin Canal. He helped unload several shipments near the Tenth Precinct police station; from there the liquor was moved to Canal Street through a cemetery. Several New Orleans policemen served as lookouts while the shipments were being unloaded. Needham's testimony in the December trial was also aided by the work of the New Orleans police department. The police, led by Captain George Reyer and Detective John Grosch, visited Patterson's home in July and seized over 1,500 quarts of whiskey. Patterson was convicted in New Orleans Criminal Court and the whiskey seized by the police was later used as evidence in federal court.[21]

Needham's testimony led to the conviction of Patterson and Battistella, both of whom received prison terms for their role in heading the conspiracy. However, the indictments did not end there. Altogether, over thirty people were indicted as a result of the August raids. Among those charged were Cohen, Henry Dedeaux, the acting supervisor of customs, Sheriff L. A. Meraux of St. Bernard Parish, three St. Bernard deputies, Lyall Shiel, former enforcement officer under O. D. Jackson, a New Orleans police captain, and two New Orleans policemen. Needham was the key witness at many of the trials. For instance, his testimony showed collusion between Sheriff Meraux, his deputies, and the Patterson-Battistella operation. He provided testimony that Meraux and the others were receiving money for convoying liquor safely through St. Bernard Parish.[22] Not all of those indicted were convicted. Sheriff Meraux was never brought to trial because of insufficient evidence, although one official later described him as being "derelict in his duties" and called his actions "morally reprehensible." Two of his deputies were acquitted by a jury after being tried for their role in the operation. While the resulting prosecutions were less than completely successful, the August raids did break up what Treasury officials described as "one of the largest liquor conspiracies as yet uncovered in this country."[23]

The irony of the breakup of the largest smuggling ring in New Orleans was that it eventually led to the dismissal of the man largely responsible for the success of the raids, Patrick Needham. Purposely kept in the dark about Needham's role by O. D. Jackson until the raids were over, many people in New Orleans initially regarded him as a crooked agent.[24] One newspaper, referring to Needham's testimony in the Cohen case, felt that the agent had overstepped the guidelines of his undercover role. The *States* believed that it would "be a miscarriage of justice for any man, white or negro, to be convicted and forced into felon's stripes on the supported testimony of a witness who acknowledges he enacts the role of a crook, grafter, Judas and double-crosser even if his excuse is that he is serving the government's cause...."[25] On September 20, 1927, Needham was dismissed from the force. In a signed statement at the time of his release he blamed his dismissal on the influence of Walter Cohen, who resented Needham's testimony against him in the liquor conspiracy case. The *Times-Picayune* noted it was the first time "political interference" had been directly brought to bear upon Prohibition enforcement in New Orleans.[26]

If smuggling was a lucrative profession, there was always the danger of violence. There were clashes between the bootleggers themselves as rival groups vied for control of the market. One of the most brutal bootleg murders in New Orleans occurred in April 1922, when Frankie Russell, an ex-pugilist and police character, and Michael Walsh, his partner in crime, were shot dead in what proved to be a conflict between rival bootleggers. Arthur Masson and Philip Gehlbach, who were also involved in liquor running, were tried for the murders. Each group had stolen liquor from the other's shipments, thus precipitating a tense situation that led to the final shootout. Masson and Gehlbach were acquitted in the murder trial, primarily because Russell and Walsh had held them up first and they fired only in self-defense. Masson remained a notorious bootlegger throughout the rest of the 1920s, but he managed to avoid going to prison on any of the numerous charges against him, receiving only fines for Prohibition violations. Several assault charges were not prosecuted and an accessory to murder charge was dismissed. When Prohibition ended Masson turned to another area of crime, drugs, where he was active when he died as he had lived, violently, in November 1934.[27]

The most shocking smuggling murders of the 1920s occurred on April 17, 1923, with the killing of two St. Bernard deputy sheriffs at the Violet bridge. Sheriff Albert Estopinal of St. Bernard Parish, learning that a liquor shipment was to be convoyed through the area, stationed three deputies at the Violet bridge in the hope of intercepting the caravan. At about 5:00 on the morning of April 17 deputies stopped the first truck in the convoy. However, at that instant a Ford touring car swerved from behind the truck, and one of the men in the car fired several shotgun blasts at the deputies. When the firing was over, Deputies Joseph Estopinal, the sheriff's brother, and August Esteves lay dead, their bodies disfigured by buckshot.[28]

Judge Leander Perez immediately convened the St. Bernard Parish grand jury, which indicted a number of suspects. The leading suspect was Gus Tomes, alias Dutch Gardner, an ex-prize fighter with a lengthy police record in New Orleans, who was identified by several witnesses as the one who fired the fatal shots. Tomes was tried and sentenced to life imprisonment when a jury found him guilty. He was spared the death penalty because the jury believed his story that he thought the men who stopped the liquor truck were hijackers. As it turned out, Tomes was the only person convicted of the murders. The next defendant was found innocent, and no other individual was ever brought to trial for the crime. One of the men indicted by the grand jury was J. Claude Meraux, who was implicated as an accessory after the fact. Meraux, former Tulane football star, aviator, prominent lawyer, and secretary of the Lake Borgne Levee Board, was the brother of Dr. L. A. Meraux, leader of one of the two major political factions in the parish. He was accused of helping Tomes escape capture immediately after the killings. Meraux fled the parish shortly before the indictments were handed down, claiming he feared the methods employed by local enforcement officials. He later turned himself in to St. Bernard authorities in July. However, Meraux never did stand trial on the indictment, and it was eventually dropped about one year later.[29]

The lack of convictions in the murder cases must be seen in the light of St. Bernard politics. Sheriff Albert Estopinal headed a political faction that was allied with the Old Regulars in New Orleans. Dr. L. A. Meraux headed another faction that supported the New Regulars. Judge Perez, a member of the Meraux faction, frustrated District Attorney Philip Livaudais' attempts at gaining convictions in the cases. He ordered the trials held so quickly that Livaudais was unable to gather sufficient evidence. As a result the district attorney was forced to drop the remaining indictments. In addition, after the cases were dropped, Perez had Livaudais and Estopinal indicted for using "third degree" methods on suspects arrested for the April murders. Though these indictments were quickly quashed, the political squabbling continued between the two factions and came to a head in 1924. Sheriff Estopinal, who had served two terms, was defeated by Dr. Meraux in the January 1924, election for sheriff.[30] Later that same year J. Claude Meraux ran for district judge against District Attorney Livaudais. Meraux's opponents brought up his role following the murder of the deputies, feeling that if he were elected "they ought to finish the good work by getting Dutch Gardner pardoned and making him chief deputy sheriff and crier of the court in St. Bernard Parish, as the atmosphere would then be more congenial and homelike."[31] Meraux's less than reputable conduct following the killings did not hurt him in the campaign. He won the election by a two-to-one margin, joining his brother in ousting the Estopinal faction from power. The campaign charges against Meraux proved prophetic. In October 1928, Gus Tomes was granted a full pardon by the state parole board. Judge J. Claude Meraux cast the deciding vote recommending Tomes' release. Tomes survived the 1920s but, like Arthur Masson, met his death violently in the following decade. He was killed by his girlfriend, Lou O'Neil, in July 1933.[32]

Smuggled liquor provided one source of illegal alcohol in New Orleans. A second source was moonshine, liquor produced illegally by stills in New Orleans homes, buildings, and in outlying areas of the parish. Moonshine included hard liquor, or "overnight" whiskey, as well as home brew, beer or wine manufactured in a residence, and sometimes sold to local customers. Imported liquor was the major source of supply for the city of New Orleans during the early 1920s, but the quantity of moonshine being produced increased steadily until by the latter part of the decade it was the leading source of liquor in the city.[33] Moonshine could be made using an inexpensive still that produced a few gallons, or in a huge distillery that occupied several floors of a building and produced hundreds of gallons. As was true in virtually all large American cities during the period, many New Orleans families made home brew, both to drink themselves and to sell to supplement their income.[34]

Recipes for making "the finest oldtime beer in your home," as well as ingredients like malt and hops, were readily available. Although Prohibition officials frequently tried to stop the sale of beer-making outfits, use of the equipment was widespread. Shortly after Prohibition went into effect, in May 1920, government officials in New Orleans charged that more than 10,000 persons were technically guilty of violating the Eighteenth Amendment because they had bought beer-making outfits from a local concern, the Tropical Food Products Company, located on St. Charles Avenue. Later in the decade federal agents moved against another such enterprise, the New Orleans Hops, Malt and Extracts Company, which had been operating four stores in the city selling all the ingredients for making home brew. The company filed a complaint against the government in federal district court, which was dismissed by the judge. In the case file there was a recipe for making home brew and testimony from several agents, including Patrick Needham, who had purchased beer-making materials from the company. Prohibition agents concentrated their efforts upon the suppliers; the small still owner producing beer for his own use was generally not bothered.[35] However, even if the agents were successful in cutting off the supply of this apparatus, an enterprising person could still improvise and tap the open market for parts to make their own still.

More important than the small local still was the illicit distillery, designed to produce great quantities of illegal liquor. These larger stills, some of them having a capacity of up to 500 gallons, were located in sheds, basements, and in buildings that looked from the outside like residences. Sometimes the whiskey-producing plant occupied the upper floors of a building in which the ground floor served as the headquarters for a legitimate business, such as a grocery store or other small concern. Periodically during the 1920s Prohibition agents in New Orleans raided liquor operations capable of producing hundreds and even thousands of gallons of liquor per week. In 1921 agents found a complete whiskey distillery on the second floor of a building on Decatur Street. Altogether, they confiscated nine stills, two 500-gallon cisterns filled with mash, a quantity of bottles, labels, corks, and several books containing recipes for making liquor. The operation was elaborately equipped with an electric alarm system and trap doors. Denying any knowledge of the liquor operation, the owner of the grocery on the ground floor claimed that he rented the upper floors of the building to a man involved in the "perfumery" manufacturing business. Another raid on a house on St. Philip Street yielded a complete plant and 3,000 quarts of illegal liquor. The value of the operation was estimated at $50,000.[36]

New Orleans bootleggers were continually devising new ways to elude Prohibition agents and still supply their customers. It is estimated that in the early 1920s there were 200 bootleggers in New Orleans doing an annual business of $5,000,000. Their methods were legion. One competitor operated through a small store in the downtown area. A customer drove his car in front of the store, went inside, purchased his liquor and paid for it. Meanwhile his car was driven away and returned with his liquor in the back seat. Sometimes the bootlegger set up a traveling bar system, in which an automobile cruised the downtown area dispensing drinks at fifty cents a shot.[37] By nature bootleggers were a suspicious lot and took elaborate precautions to make sure they sold to the right people. In one downtown building a person went up to the second floor, where a wall panel slid out revealing a large elevator, operated by hand. The buyer then took the elevator down several flights of stairs, getting off in a large room where part of the floor slid back to disclose a basement full of expensive liquors. Many large retail bootleggers in New Orleans also had their own "fingermen" working at the entrance to their places of business. If these individuals did not already know the Prohibition agents on sight, they frequented the federal building to spot the agents as they entered their offices. Bootleggers even had their own insurance policies. Some were covered through a Bootlegger Underwriting Company to which they paid a premium. The company was financed by a major figure in bootlegging circles. In return for his premium, the bootlegger received the services of a lawyer if he got in trouble, payment of his bond, court costs, half his fine if he was convicted, and money to support his loved ones if he was sentenced to jail.[38]

Retail bootlegging in New Orleans could be extremely lucrative. One retailer who had 200 regular customers, lived in a pleasant, middle-class section of the city, while his office was in a rooming house in another section of town. There on a table he spread out a sampling of his wares—twenty-five different types of liquor. His annual income was $60,000, and he was welcomed into the homes of "bankers, lawyers, brokers, capitalists, manufacturers, in fact the big men of all classes."[39] Not all bootleggers lived in luxury. A few went bankrupt and could not pay their fines when they were convicted. In New Orleans in 1927 the government issued 214 certificates to bankrupt bootleggers. This allowed a bootlegger, if he swore he was without funds, to be released after serving a thirty-day jail sentence.[40] However, bootlegging generally paid off handsomely for the average operator. Light fines and minimal jail sentences failed to dissuade enterprising entrepreneurs from entering the profession.

There were plenty of places in New Orleans that sold the bootlegger's product. Once wartime prohibition began in the city in 1919 the corner saloon disappeared. It was replaced by those creations of the Volstead Act—the soft drink stand and the speakeasy.[41] The name "soft drink stand" was something of a misnomer. Nothing was soft about the contents of the beverages served there. A typical soft drink stand was a simple operation that served mostly home brew and some hard liquor. It was the poor man's speakeasy, and the drinks served there were inferior to those poured at more exclusive establishments. Soft drink stands were sometimes used for gambling and were locations where violence could occur. Several of their owners died violently during the decade. More impressive than the soft drink stand was the speakeasy, which generally catered to a more select clientele and served a better quality of liquor. Numbering conservatively in the hundreds, soft drink stands and speakeasies were located all over the city.[42]

Speakeasies operated on many different levels. There were exclusive speakeasies that catered to a prominent clientele. One such establishment was the Transportation Club, run by an ex-Prohibition agent and located on Common Street in the heart of the business district. To gain admittance to the club, the customer had to have a key that fit the street door. Once inside the potential customer went up a flight of stairs under the watchful eyes of the proprietor who looked through a peephole in the upstairs door to prevent the entrance of any unwanted ex-colleagues. Other less elaborate speakeasies in office buildings downtown catered to ordinary business employees.[43] There were even bootleg establishments directly across from police headquarters. The story was told about a man coming out of the Criminal Courts Building who had a hip flask, a trademark of the Prohibition era. Walking down the steps the man slipped and fell. As the liquid ran down his leg he cried, "God! I hope it's blood!"[44]

Restaurants, cafes, roadhouses, and nightclubs in New Orleans furnished liquor to their customers. At first some exclusive restaurants provided liquor only in their private dining rooms. By the mid-1920s, however, liquor was served in the open. In some restaurants and roadhouses liquor was served in demitasses, the small cups in which New Orleanians took their coffee. Many of the city's most exclusive restaurants and nightclubs were subject to periodic raids by Prohibition agents who had purchased liquor and obtained a search warrant. These included Delmonico's, a refined eating establishment on St. Charles Avenue; the Cadillac Cafe, a famous night spot on Rampart and Conti Streets; and the Hotsy Totsy Club, an elegant dance and supper club on Common and Dryades Streets. In 1924 agents even raided the Boston Club, one of the city's oldest and most exclusive social clubs, which had a membership of about four hundred, among them many of the city's leading business and professional people. One hundred bottles of liquor were seized in the raid.[45]

New Orleans speakeasies went to elaborate lengths to prevent or delay the entrance of Prohibition agents. One speakeasy, the Bat, catered to businessmen in the downtown area and had a 2,000 pound steel door that was activated whenever agents approached. Another speakeasy had three barred doors, one with heavy locks. A lookout was posted to signal the bartenders that a raid was imminent so that by the time agents broke down the doors with their axes, they could only sniff the fumes of liquor already poured down the drain. As Prohibition enforcement became more vigorous many restaurants and speakeasies moved their stocks of liquor to a nearby place for storage, keeping on the premises only a minimal amount, and disposing of it quickly whenever a raid occurred. Restaurants especially used nearby buildings for caching their liquor. In one restaurant when a customer wanted a drink with his meal the waiter went to the storage area and brought him one. Customers at another restaurant were served from a pint flask that an employee carried in his pocket. If the establishment were raided, the employee would run out and destroy the evidence. Another establishment even provided curb service for its customers. A person drove up, honked his horn, and the bartender brought him a mixed drink. Some places decided to put their stocks in safes as a precautionary measure. As a result agents began carrying sledge-hammers to gain access to the liquor cache.[46] However, the prize for ingenuity in storing liquor went to city newspaper reporters. They cooled their beer by placing it at the feet of the corpses at the morgue, where there was always room for a half dozen bottles. The electrical refrigeration system in the morgue kept their beer at the perfect temperature.[47]

If keeping their liquor in a safe place was important to New Orleanians, so too was the cost of their drinks. The price of a drink of liquor ranged from ten to twenty-five cents at some of the sleazier soft drink stands to one dollar at the most exclusive places. Generally, the price of a drink sold over the counter was forty to fifty cents. By the end of the decade a glass of wine sold on average for twenty-five cents and a glass of spirits for twenty-five to fifty cents, which was comparable to the price in other cities around the country. Liquor prices during the 1920s, however, fluctuated with supply and demand. If the supply was plentiful, the price was low. If Prohibition agents succeeded in making good liquor scarce, the price was high. For example, in July 1923, a case of good imported whiskey sold for $45; two months earlier that same whiskey had sold for $65 a case due to a tighter market. Moonshine and home brew were the cheapest beverages in both price and quality; imported liquor and good bonded whiskey were the best and the highest priced. During the mid-1920s moonshine sold for $1.50 to $2 a quart, good bourbon and rye $12 a bottle, quality scotch $9 a quart, and imported champagne $15 a quart. Whiskey issued under a doctor's prescription, which was excellent bonded liquor, sold for $3.50 to $4.00 a pint. By the late 1920s prices had dropped. Bottles of bourbon, scotch, tequila, and whiskey were running $5 a quart and gin, rye, and rum were going for $4.50 to $5 a quart. The prices for bourbon and scotch were well below the national average based on prices in a number of cities, while the prices for gin and rye were about the average. In 1930 the price of domestic beer in New Orleans stood at fifty cents a quart, which was roughly equal to the average in a number of cities. Domestic wine sold for $3 a quart, which was higher than the city average, and domestic spirits sold for from $4 to $8 a quart, while the average for other cities was about $4.[48]

The trend during the 1920s was that as imported liquor grew scarcer owing to the vigilance of the Coast Guard and the Customs Service, the quality of liquor declined, and people depended more and more on the suspect overnight products. Also, bootleggers were not above using a little ingenuity in fooling a gullible public. Fake government stamps and labels were used to disguise ordinary moonshine as choice liquor. Liquor made in the city often bore the label King George or another select imported brand, and was sold at a considerably higher price than the overnight merchandise.[49]

New Orleanians faced real dangers if they drank the overnight liquor. Much of the moonshine was literally hazardous to a person's health and potentially even fatal. Several persons died in New Orleans during the decade as a result of drinking poisonous liquor. The imported brands were prepared according to scientifically correct procedures and posed little health threat. That was not the case with much of the overnight liquor. It was prepared by entrepreneurs interested mainly in making a dishonest dollar and not in maintaining proper distillation procedures. Stills made exclusively of copper were relatively safe for producing liquor. However, stills that contained connections or coils that were made of cheaper metals, like lead or zinc, produced deadly poisons. Poisons such as wood alcohol and sulphuric acid were sometimes added to give liquor tone and taste but then not completely filtered out in the distillation process. Another deadly poison, fusel oil, a substance with a pungent, unpleasant smell, was found in many insufficiently distilled liquors.[50]

A major danger stemmed from the unsanitary conditions under which some liquor was made. Prohibition raids turned up casks of liquor containing dead spiders, roaches, mice, and, in one instance, a cat. A New Orleans policeman during the 1920s remembers raiding a place that produced home brew beer. As the policemen poured out the barrels, they found dead rats that had drowned in the beer.[51] Undoubtedly many New Orleanians drank beer or moonshine that had at one time all sorts of dead animals mixed in with the liquor. Several Prohibition agents, including Patrick Needham, became violently ill after purchasing drinks in New Orleans soft drink stands. Federal chemists warned New Orleanians not to drink the cheap overnight liquor that was readily available. At times the problem of poison liquor became acute. W. T. Day, Prohibition divisional chief for the gulf area, estimated in February 1923, that over 40 percent of the liquor seized by his agents contained some amount of potentially harmful ingredients.[52]

A third source of liquor in New Orleans was industrial alcohol, a product used mainly by businesses and made legitimately during Prohibition under close governmental supervision. New Orleans was the largest center for the manufacture of industrial alcohol in the United States; in 1921 the city produced nearly 30,000,000 gallons annually, one-third of America's total production. Most of the alcohol manufacturing plants were located on the west bank of the Mississippi River in such towns as Gretna, Westwego, and Harvey. Although industrial alcohol was a much smaller source of illegal liquor than smuggled beverages or moonshine, it did present a problem for federal authorities, particularly in the early 1920s. One gallon of industrial alcohol, when watered down, colored and purged of impurities, could yield three gallons of liquor.[53] Thus the plants and warehouses near New Orleans presented a tempting target to bootleg thieves constantly searching for a cheap source of supply.

The most ambitious alcohol theft in the New Orleans area occurred in March 1921. A group of thieves, apparently with advance warning from one of the plant's night watchmen, came across the river on a barge and stole over fifty barrels of high proof alcohol from the Kentucky Distillery in Westwego. A tug transported the alcohol to a farm near Harahan, another west bank town, where it was stored. When watered down, the alcohol had a potential bootleg value of over $100,000. Federal agents tracked the alcohol to the farm and recovered the stolen merchandise. Eleven men involved in the theft were found guilty in federal court of violations of the Volstead Act and received sentences of from one to two years in prison.[54] Other elaborate attempts were made at stealing industrial alcohol. One group of thieves stole several thousand gallons of alcohol from a railroad car, while another group at a distillery in Algiers siphoned off industrial alcohol for sale to buyers in several Southern states and as far north as New Jersey.[55]

Some bootleggers who could not steal their private supplies of alcohol produced their own. In September 1926, Prohibition agents raided what proved to be the largest alcohol distillery discovered in New Orleans. The giant plant, occupying three floors of a four-story building, contained nine large vats of mash feeding several enormous boilers. It was located in the heart of the business district only a block and a half from Prohibition headquarters in the Customhouse, and was estimated to have a capacity of over 2,000 gallons a week, enough alcohol to make over 16,000 quarts of bootleg liquor. An alarm system and artificial ventilation capable of carrying fumes high above the building had made the operation hard to detect.[56]

Illegal beer provided a fourth source of problems for Prohibition agents in New Orleans. This was beer illegally produced in New Orleans' major breweries, not to be confused with the home-brewed beer manufactured by many local residents. Once the Volstead Act became law New Orleans breweries were not allowed to manufacture beer with an alcoholic content of more than one half of one percent. They were allowed to produce and market beer with a lesser alcoholic content known as "near-beer." Although the production of near-beer never reached the pre-Prohibition levels of regular beer, it still created trouble for enforcement officials. The problem arose because it was impossible to produce legal beer without first making the illegal product. It was up to the Prohibition agents to make sure breweries were not marketing illegal beer or supplying alcohol to their customers so that they could "spike" the weaker legal brew.[57]

Discovering that local breweries were selling illegal beer to city soft drink stands and speakeasies, the government retaliated in a dramatic series of raids. In June 1921, thirty Prohibition agents raided six major breweries, confiscating thousands of cases of beer worth $35,000. They took charge of all the buildings, machinery, vats, trucks, and automobiles owned by the companies. Property seized was valued at close to $500,000, and hundreds of employees were temporarily out of work. The Standard, Dixie, American, Columbia, National, and Union breweries were raided. A few days after the raids a settlement was reached between federal officials and attorneys representing the breweries. As a result the breweries agreed to pay a tax penalty to the government in excess of $100,000.[58]

In July 1921, United States District Court Judge Rufus Foster issued an injunction that implemented the terms of the settlement between the federal government and the breweries. Foster's injunction made it clear that the companies were allowed to reopen provided they produced only legal beer. If they failed to comply, they would be cited for contempt. Any future violation of the injunction and the delinquent company would be closed permanently. Judge Foster's ruling was cited as being the first issued in the United States specifically restraining a brewery from violating the Prohibition law. Not all the breweries, however, abided by the injunction. In the massive raid of August 1925, the agents' first objectives were the Standard and Union breweries. The properties of both were temporarily seized by the government, and three Standard officers were indicted for offering over $500 in bribes to Prohibition agents to allow the company to manufacture illegal beer. After deliberating only fifteen minutes a jury found the men guilty and each was sentenced to two years in prison. The president of the Union Brewery was also tried and convicted of bribing enforcement agents.[59] After the 1925 federal crackdown there were few incidents of brewery officials being tried for violations of the Prohibition statute.

The fifth and least important source of illegal liquor in New Orleans was the unauthorized obtaining of liquor reserved for medicinal purposes. With the Prohibition forces constantly undermanned, the opportunity was always there for doctors and druggists to make illegal profits from the sale of prescription liquor. Doctors were allowed legally to prescribe liquor for their patients but the amount was closely monitored by Prohibition officials. Physicians were issued booklets of prescription blanks in amounts of 100 every ninety days, regardless of the size of the doctor's practice. At the end of each quarter the doctor returned his stubs to the Prohibition office. If a doctor prescribed more than a pint of whiskey or a quart of wine to one patient within a ten-day period he was subject to a fine for violating the Volstead Act. For more serious violations the government had the power to revoke a physician's permit to prescribe medicinal liquor. As an example, in April 1925, the local Prohibition office in New Orleans charged a number of doctors with issuing prescriptions in bad faith. According to the government, the doctors had not even made an effort to examine their patients.[60] Druggists also supplied liquor upon prescription. They received their supply from one of the local wholesalers still legally distributing liquor. Sometimes the druggist watered down his product to make his supply go further and to make a greater profit. The customer thus received inferior liquor at a high price. In one instance during the late 1920s government agents for the first time raided a drugstore holding a permit for selling liquor. Agents charged the druggist with selling liquor openly and his place of business with "acting virtually as a speakeasy."[61]

In an attempt to dry up the sources of illegal liquor in New Orleans, Prohibition agents conducted periodic raids against establishments serving beverages in violation of the law. Before a raid was conducted agents working undercover made "buys" of illegal liquor and then obtained a search warrant for the place where it was sold. Establishments where illegal liquor was purchased were added to a list of locations to be raided. Raids occurred at least several times a month, with the number of targets raided depending upon the intensity of the operation. Generally, the raids came in clusters, with at least five to ten establishments being raided in a single night. Peak times of Prohibition raiding activity frequently coincided with the holiday revelry of the Fourth of July, Mardi Gras, and New Year's Eve. Heavy periods of raiding also occurred when a new Prohibition administrator took over in New Orleans or there was a major reorganization at the national level.[62] New administrators, eager to show their zeal in the war to keep America dry, always intensified raiding activity.

The largest series of raids in the city's history occurred in August 1925, with over 200 agents from all areas of the country involved. In these raids the agents formed into squads, which then fanned out to cover every area of the city. Usually, however, the raiding was on a much smaller scale as local agents concentrated on visiting key establishments that repeatedly violated the law. Sometimes national headquarters sent its top agents to New Orleans to help, as was the case in November 1923, when Izzy Einstein, the Prohibition era's master of disguise, arrived in the city. Einstein, variously disguised as a longshoreman, a businessman, and a traveling salesman, visited over fifty different places where he purchased liquor during his short stay in New Orleans.[63] Conducting his own poll of American cities to see in which one he was able to purchase a drink the quickest, Izzy nominated New Orleans for first place. Less than a minute after he arrived in the city Einstein asked a taxi driver where he could obtain a drink. The driver promptly displayed a bottle which he offered to sell.[64]

Upon entering a place, agents attempted to keep a low profile while searching for the establishment's liquor supply. This was not always easy to do because agents were sometimes forced to use axes or other means to gain entry. Many times agents were forced to move quickly to prevent the proprietor or one of his employees from destroying the evidence. Government enforcement officials also faced the hostility of patrons and a lack of cooperation from local police. One incident in July 1924, suggests the problems involved. Mack Overpeck, divisional chief of the New Orleans Prohibition force, and three of his agents were arrested by police when they attempted to raid Felix Tranchina's fashionable Spanish Fort restaurant. There were differing versions as to what actually happened. The press charged that the raiders entered by leaping through windows and crashing down the doors to the crowded establishment. Patrons were reported to have cheered as the agents were taken to jail. According to the official police report, no liquor was found in the restaurant. Overpeck, however, told a different tale. He said that guests were pouring and drinking liquor when his agents broke in. When the agents attempted to conduct an orderly search and to seize liquor as evidence, the patrons rushed his men and took the bottles away from them. New Orleans police then interfered and took the agents to jail. Prohibition officials threatened to press charges against the patrolmen involved for interfering with federal agents. Charges of disturbing the peace filed against the agents were dropped and the men were quickly released.[65] This incident, resolved without further conflict, illustrated the growing tension between federal and local officials.

Any liquor confiscated by Prohibition agents in New Orleans was usually stored in the Customhouse, although most home brew was destroyed on the spot, with just enough seized to be used as evidence in court. When a person was convicted, the liquor seized automatically became the property of the federal government. The government sometimes sold the confiscated property at auction to those businesses, like wholesale and retail drug houses and hospitals, that used and were licensed to buy liquor for medicinal purposes. If the liquor was not of sufficient quality for their needs, it was destroyed. Imported liquor, however, could not be destroyed without an authorization from a federal judge.[66] On occasion, if the government acted illegally, as in the case of Jack Sheehan, the liquor was returned to its original owner.

During the early 1920s liquor seized in federal raids sometimes disappeared from government storerooms owing to lax security procedures. In December 1922, several hundred bottles of imported liquor were taken from a storeroom adjoining the office of the

United States marshal in the Post Office Building. Six guards were suspended following this disappearance, but were later reinstated. The liquor was subsequently found in the attic hidden under some floorboards.[67] A year and a half earlier, a federal grand jury had investigated the problem of liquor theft from the Prohibition storeroom in New Orleans. In its report the grand jury found indications of systematic thefts of liquor by federal agents, but not enough evidence to indict individual members of the force. Calling the thefts "a matter of public scandal," the grand jury criticized the local Prohibition office for being "loosely and inefficiently conducted." Citing an example of liquor ordered returned to a woman whose home had been raided, the jury noted that the original contents of the bottles had been removed and replaced with grape juice and other ingredients. It declared that the amount of the thefts was "disgracefully large" and it called for the implementation of procedures designed to provide security against future losses.[68] Evidently the grand jury report and reaction to the December 1922 theft tightened security methods, for after the early part of the decade the local press reported fewer thefts from federal storage facilities.

The value of the liquor and property seized during federal raids in New Orleans ran into millions of dollars. For the year 1922 agents seized liquor, trucks, automobiles, and smuggling vessels totalling more than $500,000. Statistics for New Orleans in the 1920s are incomplete, but figures for the first year and a half of O. D. Jackson's term as Prohibition administrator, from May 1923 to December 1924, show that the government conducted more than 1,000 raids. In those raids agents confiscated more than 30,000 gallons of distilled liquor and over 50,000 gallons of wine, worth over $700,000. A total of 400 stills were seized and destroyed; twelve boats and 136 automobiles and trucks were taken by federal agents. The amount of liquor and property confiscated surpassed $1,000,000.[69]

Prohibition statistics for the remainder of the 1920s are available for the state of Louisiana but not for the city of New Orleans. However, it can be inferred that a large part of the state statistics came from New Orleans, which was by far the largest city in Louisiana and a hotbed of violations of the Prohibition amendment. Statistics show that statewide the peak enforcement period was the years 1924 to 1928, with the largest state totals in distilleries, stills, automobiles, and value of property seized occurring during this period. The amount of spirits, malt liquor, wine, and mash seized were also greater than during the early 1920s. In Louisiana from 1924 to 1930 Prohibition agents seized 912 distilleries, 1,115 stills, and 736 automobiles. During this same period they seized 211,000 gallons of spirits, 221,000 gallons of wine, 109,000 gallons of malt liquor, and 1,650,000 gallons of mash. Total property seized had a value of more than $1,000,000 and agents arrested 8,956 persons for violations of the Volstead Act.[70]

In addition to liquor raids, by the mid-1920s the most effective weapon in the government's Prohibition enforcement arsenal was its use of the padlock procedure. Applying the padlock provisions of the Volstead Act, the United States attorney in New Orleans obtained injunctions in federal court closing certain places as public nuisances, establishments guilty of multiple violations of the Prohibition law. Basing each case on evidence provided by local Prohibition agents, the government petitioned the court to grant its request for an injunction, which stipulated that if the owner of the establishment did not agree to comply fully with the law, his place of business was ordered closed for a period of one year. The owner could not reopen until the judge was satisfied with his efforts at compliance; the padlock would then be removed and the place was allowed to resume operation.

New Orleans soft drink stands, restaurants, and cafes used all their resources in resisting government efforts to apply the padlock law. In what proved to be a test case, the proprietors of seven prominent establishments, including the Little Club and the Moulin Rouge, fought the government all the way to the court of appeals, which upheld a district court decision closing the places as common nuisances. In February 1925, United States marshals served the first padlock orders in the city closing the offenders, three of which were still doing business.[71] From the mid-1920s on the United States attorney moved vigorously to apply the padlock provision in New Orleans. The campaign was most effective in the years 1925 and 1926. By March 1926, fifty establishments throughout the city bore the sign "Closed by United States Marshal for Violation of the Prohibition Act." Holiday visitors to New Orleans in December 1926, found eighty-six cabarets and nightclubs under federal padlock and forty-four more under bond as a guarantee not to sell liquor. Some of the city's most celebrated institutions— the Old Absinthe House, a landmark in New Orleans for over a hundred years, and the Ace, formerly the Bat, a notorious speakeasy—at one time were under federal padlock. According to government figures for 1927, New Orleans had more cabarets and nightclubs under padlock than any other major city in the country. While the courts generally sided with the government in padlock cases, occasionally it would rule that they had gone too far. In one 1926 case the court of appeals ruled that the district court went too far in ruling that an establishment should be padlocked, even though liquor was purchased by agents on the premises. The court of appeals ruled that the parties in the appeal were not aware of what was occurring in the building and should not be punished by having the building padlocked for a year, They were allowed to post bond and keep possession of the property.[72]

Federal district court in New Orleans handled the bulk of the padlock suits and other Prohibition cases brought by the government. Generally, a first offense resulted in a fine or suspended jail sentence. Multiple offenses resulted in higher fines and prison sentences. Fines reached as high as $500-$1,000 for multiple or serious violations, but this was rare; normally fines ranged from a low of $5 up to $100-$200. Most first offenders who pleaded guilty got off with a fine of $50. Prison sentences were generally limited to from thirty to sixty days, but could reach several years for more serious offenses, such as smuggling or hijacking. Federal judges in New Orleans also imposed harsher sentences upon those who pleaded not guilty and were convicted. Those pleading guilty and throwing themselves upon the mercy of the court received lesser sentences. Judge Rufus Foster of the federal district court during the early 1920s stated that the great majority of Prohibition arrests were for mere possession or transportation of liquor, and for these he usually assessed a $50 fine for a guilty plea. A first offense for selling liquor resulted in a fine of $100, which Foster believed was not a light punishment since most of the persons fined were not wealthy individuals.[73]

Prohibition penalties lacked teeth until Congress passed the Jones Act in 1929, which provided for a maximum penalty of five years in jail and a fine of $10,000 for first offenders. Passage of the Jones Act resulted in tougher Prohibition sentences in federal court. Court statistics for the Eastern District of Louisiana, which included mainly New Orleans cases, illustrate this change. In 1928 (the fiscal year running from July 1, 1927, to June 30, 1928), before passage of the Jones Act, the percentage of those convicted for Prohibition violations receiving jail sentences was only eleven percent. The average jail sentence during this same period was 12.6 days and the average fine was $174. Statistics for 1929 (the fiscal year ending June 30, 1929) and 1930 (the fiscal year ending June 30, 1930) show much tougher jail sentences. In 1929 the percentage of those convicted receiving jail sentences rose dramatically to 85 percent, the highest rate of any judicial district in the country. The average jail sentence also increased significantly to 85.6 days and the average fine to $209. These 1929 statistics seem to be contrary to previous trends and, if they were in error, this would be reflected in a change in the 1930 statistics. However, court statistics for the Eastern District of Louisiana show the trend toward tougher jail sentences continuing. In 1930 the percentage of those convicted receiving jail sentences remained very high at 83 percent, the second-highest rate in the country. The average sentence rose again to 106.8 days, although the average fine dropped to $158. If the statistics are accurate, federal judges in the late 1920s in eastern Louisiana were definitely handing down stiffer jail terms for Prohibition violators.[74]

Those convicted of Prohibition violations in district court had a further recourse; they could appeal those convictions to the Fifth Circuit Court of Appeals. A sampling of cases from New Orleans shows some of those convicted of manufacturing illegal liquor appealed their convictions, questioning in particular whether a search warrant was first necessary to search for liquor at their place of residence. The court of appeals generally ruled that if there was evidence of the manufacturing of liquor in a garage or shed next to the residence, then a search warrant was not necessary, the evidence seized was valid, and the conviction was affirmed. If the agents, however, attempted to search a private residence without a warrant, this search was unconstitutional, any evidence seized was inadmissible, and the conviction was reversed. Also, even if the search warrant was defective, and liquor was found on the premises, this did not necessarily mean the liquor would be returned. In one instance the court of appeals ruled that this liquor did not automatically have to be returned to the plaintiff. On another occasion three men convicted of bribing a Prohibition agent to manufacture intoxicating liquor at their brewery appealed on grounds of entrapment. The court of appeals disagreed and upheld their conviction.[75]

By far the greatest number of convictions under the Prohibition law resulted from guilty pleas. In the four years from 1920 through 1923 there were only seventy trials by jury for Prohibition violations in New Orleans, with fifty-nine of them resulting in acquittals. This trend continued through the rest of the decade. Out of over 3,000 Prohibition cases from 1928 to 1930 in district court, only 181 resulted in a jury trial, and of these over half resulted in acquittals. Of the over 3,000 cases prosecuted during this period, more than 2,600 defendants plead guilty, a total of 86 percent. Most offenders pleaded guilty, realizing that a fine, and probably a small one, would be their only punishment. Jail sentences were in the distinct minority until the late 1920s. Many bootleggers preferred to pay the fine, which they considered a cost of doing business, and return to their normal operation. In a memorandum Louis Burns, the United States attorney in New Orleans, was critical of the federal court. He argued that in many cases, particularly those involving multiple offenders, sentences should have been heavier. Burns noted that often the previous offenses of multiple violators were not taken into account when passing sentence.[76]

The persons convicted or pleading guilty to Prohibition violations in New Orleans were a diverse lot, ranging in age from a fourteen-year-old boy to a ninety-five-year-old man. Many were of foreign birth. Prohibition agents estimated that over half of those involved in bootlegging offenses were illegal aliens, and there were moves to have them deported. In one instance when the judge learned that a man who pleaded guilty to operating a still had been in the country only ten days, he instructed the district attorney to notify the immigration authorities. Some violators became instant celebrities. Gertrude Lythgoe, labeled by the press the so-called "Queen of the Bootleggers," turned state's evidence and testified at a sensational liquor-smuggling trial in New Orleans during the mid-1920s. After her testimony Lythgoe's case was not prosecuted and she later wrote a book about her exploits.[77] Prohibition cases were not without their humor. Facing the federal judge, one man admitted he was guilty of making wine. However, he insisted, his doctor had advised him to drink it because he suffered from tuberculosis. The district attorney pointed out that the accused was found to be in possession of 144 gallons of wine. "Too much medicine," stated the judge, and fined him $100.[78]

In New Orleans, as in the rest of the nation, Prohibition cases clogged the court calendar. As the decade wore on, more and more cases were pending, putting a tremendous burden on the United States attorney and the federal judges. Most of the criminal cases occupying the federal court calendar were Prohibition cases. Figures compiled by the United States attorney's office for the fiscal year ending June 30, 1927, showed that of a total of 1,214 criminal cases decided, 1,088 were the result of Prohibition raids. During the same year, of 1,109 criminal cases begun, 998 involved violations of the Prohibition law.[79] Something obviously had to be done about the growing backlog of cases. The expedient answer for New Orleans and the rest of the nation was court sessions known as "bargain days" that involved whirlwind court sittings in which great numbers of violators pleaded guilty in return for reduced fines. March 1926 marked the beginning of bargain days in New Orleans. In September 1925, there were 1,367 Prohibition cases pending. By the time bargain days ended in the latter part of March there were fewer than 100 cases remaining. From January to April 1926, fines totalling $187,700 were collected from 935 defendants. During the month of March 631 Prohibition cases were disposed of, primarily through guilty pleas. On the day of March 11, 131 offenders were dispensed with by the court; with over $21,000 in fines collected. By the end of May the federal court docket in New Orleans was in the best shape it had been since the Volstead Act went into effect.[80] Bargain days continued to be a feature of the New Orleans court calendar during the remainder of the 1920s.

Federal Prohibition officials were less than satisfied with the prosecution of Volstead Act violators in New Orleans. E. C. Yellowley, chief of General Prohibition Agents, in a report to Robert A. Haynes, the Prohibition commissioner, detailed some of the problems involved. Yellowley criticized the actions of the United States commissioner in New Orleans, who made the final decision if there was sufficient evidence to issue an affidavit against a Prohibition violator. He noted that the commissioner often paroled an offender before he could be questioned fully by federal agents and before an affidavit could be filed against the individual. The commissioner's action made it considerably harder to locate a violator once the government was ready to charge him. Judge Rufus Foster was also singled out by Yellowley. Noting that the general talk among Prohibition suspects was that "the Judge is easy," Yellowley remarked that it was easier to pay the fine imposed by the court than it was to pay for a liquor license before Prohibition went into effect.[81]

In addition, federal officials were sometimes critical of Louis Burns, the United States attorney in New Orleans during the early 1920s. The national office believed that Burns had mishandled a number of Prohibition cases. In a memorandum Mabel Walker Willebrandt, assistant attorney general in charge of Prohibition enforcement, commented upon her displeasure with Burns: "Frankly, either thru incompetence or something every possibly good case is hoodooed when you send it to New Orleans. Burns is a smooth proposition. . . ."[82] Things were further complicated by public clashes over procedure between Burns and O. D. Jackson, head of the local enforcement unit.[83] Relations later improved between the United States attorney and the national Prohibition office, but these periodic conflicts did not make the task of federal enforcement any easier.

While the federal courts handled the major Prohibition cases in New Orleans, arrests made by local police for violation of the Hood Act, the state Prohibition law, were prosecuted in local criminal court. A sampling of the criminal court cases for the 1920s shows that the cases brought for violation of the Hood Act, which prohibited the manufacture, sale, transportation, and possession of intoxicating liquor, generally resulted in lesser fines than those given in federal court. The average fine for a first offense ranged from $15 to $50 and a number of cases were not even prosecuted. Higher fines were the exception, with the highest being for $350-$500. Those found guilty were usually given a choice between paying the fine or serving from 10 to 60 days in Parish Prison. In only a few cases were those found guilty given both fines and jail time. The individuals arrested for state liquor violations in New Orleans were mainly small-time operators who had sometimes as little as one pint of liquor in their possession. With the rare exception of someone like Alonzo Patterson, most of the individuals arrested by New Orleans police only had small quantities of beer, whiskey, or home brew. It was rare that they had more than a hundred bottles of beer or whiskey or more than a few cases of alcoholic beverages.[84] It is clear from examining these cases that the larger operators were arrested by federal Prohibition agents.

Those found guilty of Hood Act violations in New Orleans Criminal Court could appeal their convictions to the Louisiana Supreme Court. Generally, those appealing included major smugglers like Alonzo Patterson or those receiving stiffer fines ($350 or more) and jail terms. Some of the cases appealed to the Louisiana Supreme Court contained the testimony of New Orleans police officers, stating how they had arrested particular individuals and what they found when they made the arrest. This was the case in the appeal of Alonzo Patterson, which included the transcript of testimony by George Reyer and John Grosch. In those Hood Act cases that were appealed to the Louisiana Supreme Court, the court generally sided with the lower court and affirmed the verdict in the original decision.[85]

As was the case with prosecution of Volstead Act violators, federal officials were not satisfied with local enforcement of the state Prohibition act in New Orleans. United States Attorney Burns worried that there appeared to be some tacit understanding between officials in New Orleans so that no real effort was made to enforce the Hood Act: "Spasmodically the police make raids on soft drink stands or illicit manufactories, but few seem to be prosecuted. No examination of the State Court dockets has been made, but it is believed that for all practical purposes the law is disregarded."[86] Relations between local Prohibition officials and city police were also tenuous. Police sometimes cooperated in federal enforcement raids, but generally their efforts at arresting violators of the Hood Act were clearly secondary to gambling or prostitution crusades. In one instance, in April 1922, the strained relations between New Orleans police and local Prohibition agents came to the fore. Three Prohibition agents were arrested by city police and charged with assault with dangerous weapons. They had been watching for liquor smugglers and stopped a car driven by a New Orleans police captain in civilian clothes. Suspecting that the car contained liquor, they covered the occupants with their guns. Once the agents realized their mistake, they apologized to the captain and the other passengers and the vehicle continued on its way.[87]

Superintendent of Police Guy Molony was incensed at the treatment his officer had received and ordered the agents arrested, even threatening to "shoot off the running board" any Prohibition agent attempting to stop his police automobile. There was a conflict between federal and city officials as to whether the agents should be tried in federal or city court. The men were eventually tried in New Orleans Criminal Court, found not guilty, and released, but before the charges were dismissed, the agents were admonished by the court. Criticizing the agents for stopping motorists with weapons drawn, the judge felt that this action was extremely dangerous.[88] It was clear that the agents' actions were not deliberate, but the incident heightened the tension between New Orleans police and Prohibition authorities.

An incident that occurred during Arthur O'Keefe's administration involving Tom Hill, the clerk of the city council, and Thomas Healy, the superintendent of police, showed how the fears of federal officials about lack of enforcement by the police were justified and how the Old Regular machine was sometimes selective in the places it ordered raided by police. Tom Hill was a patron of the Little Club, a place run by Tony Denapolis that sold whiskey and wine. Hill accrued a bill of $400 or $500 but refused to pay it. Without informing Superintendent Healy Hill then got the police captain in that district to raid Denapolis' club. Denapolis went to Healy "raising hell" about the police raid. Healy then telephoned Mayor O'Keefe and made it quite clear that the clerk of the city council was not running the police department. Hill, said Healy, was not using the police department to get free liquor in New Orleans. He told O'Keefe that if this ever happened again, he would put Hill in jail.[89]

Besides its cool relationship with city authorities, there were other reasons for the government's lack of success in enforcing Prohibition in New Orleans. Many problems originated with the agents themselves. They were poorly paid, making between $1,200 and $2,000 a year in 1920, and still only $2,300 by 1930. In comparison in 1924 the Labor Department estimated that a family of five needed a minimal annual income of $1,920 just to make ends meet. The agents' low pay, which was less than that of many garbage collectors, made them susceptible to bribes for looking the other way when a liquor shipment entered the city or when an establishment was raided. Furthermore, poor pay was not likely to attract the highest qualified candidates into Prohibition work. Prohibition agents were also political appointees for most of the decade. They were exempt from the federal civil service until the late 1920s, when competitive examinations finally went into effect. When these tests were first administered in January 1928, 52 percent of the force attached to the New Orleans office failed them.[90]

Largely because of the poor pay and lack of standards, the caliber of agents varied. Some, like Patrick Needham, were dedicated public servants who did their best with the meager resources available. Others just went through the motions, and still others realized the hopeless nature of their task. One FBI agent in New Orleans, when that organization became involved in Prohibition enforcement, resigned because he felt enforcing liquor laws was not the moral thing for the government to do.[91]

Besides being poorly qualified, the New Orleans force was constantly undermanned. Theodore Jacques, federal enforcement officer in New Orleans, resigned in 1921 complaining about "trying to catch 10,000—yes, there are that many—liquor law violators with about ten men."[92] There was also a great deal of turnover in the force, reflecting the national trend. Agents were dismissed for insubordination and incompetence. Nationally it is estimated that by 1926 one of every twelve agents had been dismissed from the force because of some type of corrupt activities.[93] Politics always played a role; Patrick Needham, one of the most capable New Orleans agents, was dismissed because of political pressure. Other agents who quit or were dismissed from the force sometimes turned up on the other side of the law as bootleggers, where the monetary rewards were certainly greater. One agent Lyall Shiel, arrested in the 1925 government raids, had been a former enforcement chief. The most significant thing about the New Orleans Prohibition force was that it was still occasionally effective, given all the obstacles working against it.

New Orleanians had never been in favor of the Prohibition Amendment and, as the decade ended, they began to voice their disapproval much more vigorously. By 1932 organized business groups such as the Cotton Exchange, the Sugar Exchange, and the Board of Trade clamored for repeal. Raids were still made by Prohibition agents and gun battles were still fought by rival bootleggers, but the climate was changing. In 1932 Louisiana voters passed a constitutional amendment repealing state Prohibition laws. Though the amendment was later declared unconstitutional, its overwhelming approval foreshadowed events to come. On March 24, 1933, the Louisiana legislature repealed the Hood Act, and in New Orleans and the rest of the state the sale of beer became legal at noon on April 13. This came after the Volstead Act had been amended following Franklin Roosevelt's inauguration, making beer legal again nationally and ending thirteen years of dry rule. There was a noisy celebration in New Orleans as 300 brewery trucks drove through the crowded streets bringing citizens 1,000,000 gallons of local brew. Eight months later, on December 5, 1933, the Twenty-first Amendment was ratified, repealing Prohibition.[94] New Orleanians could now legally consume their favorite brand of hard liquor.

There were distinct differences concerning the development of Prohibition in New Orleans as compared to that of other large American cities. By the beginning of the 1930s bootlegging in many other cities led to the rise of organized or syndicate crime, where a single individual or group of individuals dominated the illegal liquor market. The main example of this is the rise of Al Capone to dominance of organized criminal activity in Chicago, but this was also true in other large cities such as Boston, Philadelphia, and Cleveland, where syndicate crime was well on its way by the end of the decade. This did not happen in New Orleans. The Crescent City experience was similar to what happened in San Francisco, where no one individual or organized group dominated the illicit liquor trade.[95] There was no sign of any significant organized criminal activity in New Orleans until well after Prohibition was repealed.

New Orleans was also different from a number of other Northern and Midwestern cities in the level of violence associated with Prohibition. The violence level in terms of gangster killings was much more frequent and numerous in cities like Chicago and New York. There were certainly bootleg killings in New Orleans but not on the scale of those occurring in other large cities. New Orleans also experienced political and police corruption associated with Prohibition but it was on a much smaller scale than that in cities like Chicago or Philadelphia.

Unlike the situation in other cities, no one ethnic group or groups dominated the illegal liquor market in New Orleans. Italians such as Al Capone were strong in Chicago and Jewish criminals such as Charles "King" Solomon in Boston and Max "Boo Boo" Hoff in Philadelphia were powerful individuals who were successful in grabbing a large share of the illicit liquor activities in their communities. Various ethnic groups were definitely involved in violating the Prohibition Amendment in New Orleans but no individual or group dominated the market. There were strong groups like the Patterson-Battistella smuggling ring or individuals such as Jack Sheehan, but they did not exercise the kind of control over the market exercised by a Capone in Chicago or by Italians in other cities such as Kansas City, Denver, and Los Angeles.[96]

Without question Prohibition was a failure in New Orleans. During the 1920s the city remained one of the wettest in the country. Anyone who wanted a drink and could pay for it could always find one. Smuggling brought a fine selection of imported liquor into New Orleans, although after 1925 the Coast Guard was effective in slowing down the amount of imported beverages reaching the Crescent City. In the latter part of the decade the quality of liquor declined as New Orleanians were forced to depend more upon the locally brewed product. Large operations dominated the New Orleans smuggling scene, although none of them gained control of a major portion of the bootleg market, as Al Capone did in Chicago. There were violent bootleg killings, but none of them could be traced to any type of organized criminal activity. The bootleg market in New Orleans was shared by both large and small operators.

Prohibition agents attempted to enforce the Volstead Act in New Orleans, but it was clearly a losing battle. Only a small portion of the violators were caught and prosecuted. As late as 1927 Assistant Attorney General Mabel Walker Willebrandt estimated that 90 percent of the Prohibition violators in New Orleans were never caught or prosecuted by enforcement officials.[97] The real reason for the failure of Prohibition in New Orleans was the attitude of its citizens. A great majority disapproved of the government's attempt at legislating morality and were determined to continue their drinking just as they had before the law went into effect. One prominent New Orleanian summed up the attitude of most people:

> Now remember this: if New Orleans had voted dry, the situation would be different. But neither of those things did the State or city do. And then along came these Volstead laws that branded a doctor as a criminal if he prescribed more than so much alcohol for a sick, perhaps dying man or woman, that gave the most law abiding citizen to understand that he was beyond the pale of civilization if he drank a glass of harmless red wine or quenched his thirst with a glass of good beer, or drank the health of a friend in a sparkling tumbler of champagne. I don't believe the majority of our people ever intended that any such puritanical law as that should control in this country. And so New Orleans has just kept on being New Orleans.[98]

Notes for "The Wettest Dry City in America"

[1] Joy Jackson, "Prohibition in New Orleans: The Unlikeliest Crusade," *Louisiana History*, 19 (1978): 261; David E. Kyvig, *Repealing National Prohibition* (Chicago, 1979), 25; Mark Edward Lender and James Kirby Martin, *Drinking in America: A History* (New York, 1982), 139.

[2] Letter to Mr. Ernest Camp, February 8, 1922, File No. 601, in Coast Guard Records, Record Group 26, National Archives; *New Orleans States*, April 22, 1923; *New Orleans Times-Picayune*, April 22, 1923.

[3] *States*, July 6, 1922, April 22, 1923.

[4] *New Orleans Item*, May 18, 1925; Jackson, "Prohibition in New Orleans," 277-78; *States*, May 20, 1925; Malcolm F. Willoughby, *Rum War at Sea* (Washington, D.C., 1964), 121.

[5] *Item*, August 9, 1925; Jackson, "Prohibition in New Orleans," 278; *Times-Picayune*, April 22, 1923.

[6] Jackson, "Prohibition in New Orleans," 277; *States*, April 22, 1923; *Times-Picayune*, April 22, 1923.

[7] *Item*, August 9, 1925; Glen Jeansonne, *Leander Perez: Boss of the Delta* (Baton Rouge, 1977), 22-23; *States*, November 13, 1920, April 22, 1923.

[8] *Item*, January 21, 1923, Magazine Section, August 9, 1925.

[9] *Times-Picayune*, April 22, 1923.

[10] *States*, December 15, 1921, April 22, 1923.

[11] *Item*, March 20, 1920.

[12] Ibid., March 20, 1920, October 31, 1920; Jackson, "Prohibition in New Orleans," 278; *States*, July 22, 1921.

[13] *Item*, October 27, 1922, July 31, 1924, July 25, 1925; *States*, November 12, 1924; *Times-Picayune*, October 28, 1922, December 21, 1924, March 6, 1925, July 25, 1925, March 10, 1926.

[14] *Item*, September 6, 1922, September 8, 1922; *States*, September 7, 1922, September 8, 1922, September 9, 1922, September 10, 1922; *Times-Picayune*, September 6, 1922, September 8, 1922.

[15] *Item*, July 25, 1925, August 9, 1925, November 20, 1925; *Times-Picayune*, July 25, 1925, October 3, 1925, November 21, 1925.

[16] *Item*, April 10, 1925; *Times-Picayune*, December 23, 1924.

[17] Hugh Larre to Prohibition Director, January 19, 1922, File No. 23, in Department of Justice Records, Record Group 60, National Archives; Department of Justice Records cited are all located in the National Archives; *Item*, January 3, 1922, January 20, 1922; Louis H. Burns to Rush L. Holland, January 23, 1923, in Department of Justice Records; Report, E. P. Gueymard to Prohibition Office, undated but probably July or August 1922, File No. 23, in Department of Justice Records; *Times-Picayune*, December 23, 1921, January 1, 1922, January 4, 1922, June 8, 1922, June 9, 1922, June 10, 1922, Obituary for Mark Boasberg, *Times-Picayune*, December 31, 1956.

[18] Case No. 36266, December 3, 1926, No. 36519, December 18, 1926, in Criminal Court Records, City Archives, Louisiana Division, New Orleans Public Library; George W. Healy, Jr., Interview with author, August 10, 1978; A. F. Scharff to Don A. Stone, May 27, 1924, File No. 23 in Department of Justice Records; Louis H. Burns to Assistant Attorney General Mabel Walker Willebrandt, June 16, 1924, File No. 23-74-21, in Department of Justice Records; Louis H. Burns to Attorney General, August 8, 1924, File No. 23, in Department of Justice Records; Statement of Captain Emile Fremont, May 25, 1924, File No. 23-74, in Department of Justice Records; *States*, February 7, 1929; *Times-Picayune*, February 26, 1925, March 27, 1925; Obituary for Mark Boasberg, *Times-Picayune*, December 31, 1956.

[19] *Item*, August 11, 1925; Jackson, "Prohibition in New Orleans," 276; *Times-Picayune*, August 12, 1925, December 11, 1925.

[20] Jackson, "Prohibition in New Orleans," 274-76; *Times-Picayune*, December 10, 1925, December 12, 1925.

[21]Jackson, "Prohibition in New Orleans," 275-76; *State of Louisiana v. Alonzo Patterson*, No. 29906, July 18, 1925, in Criminal Court Records; *State of Louisiana v. Alonzo Patterson, In re Patterson*, No. 27552, November 2, 1925, *State of Louisiana v. Alonzo Patterson*, No. 27569, January 4, 1926, in Supreme Court of Louisiana Records, Clerk's Office, Supreme Court of Louisiana, Supreme Court Building, New Orleans; the Supreme Court of Lousiana records contain the transcript of the trial in New Orleans Criminal Court, including the testimony of Reyer and Grosch; *Times-Picayune*, November 20, 1925, December 10, 1925, December 17, 1925, December 18, 1925.

[22]Jackson, "Prohibition in New Orleans," 277; Report, Patrick Needham to O. D. Jackson, undated but probably August 1925, File No. 23, in Department of Justice Records; *Times-Picayune*, August 28, 1925, August 30, 1925, December 12, 1925, December 20, 1925, March 19, 1926.

[23]Jackson, "Prohibition in New Orleans," 277; *Times-Picayune*, March 4, 1927; Wayne G. Borah to Attorney General, February 25, 1927, File No. 23-32-105, in Department of Justice Records.

[24]Jackson, "Prohibition in New Orleans," 276.

[25]Editorial, *States*, December 21, 1925.

[26]Jackson, "Prohibition in New Orleans," 279; *Times-Picayune*, September 20, 1927.

[27]*Item*, May 21, 1925; Jackson, "Prohibition in New Orleans," 284; New Orleans Police Department, Arthur Masson file, No. 6331, in *Bureau of Identification Files on Deceased Criminals*, City Archives, Louisiana Division, New Orleans Public Library; New Orleans Police Department, *Reports of Homicides, 1922*, in City Archives, Louisiana Division, New Orleans Public Library; *Times-Picayune*, April 21, 1922, November 17, 1922, May 22, 1925.

[28]*Item*, April 17, 1923; Jeansonne, *Leander Perez*, 23; *Times-Picayune*, April 18, 1923.

[29]Jeansonne, *Leander Perez*, 23-24; New Orleans Police Department, Gus Tomes file, No. 5001, in *Bureau of Identification Files on Deceased Criminals*; *Times-Picayune*, April 24, 1923, May 16, 1923, May 17, 1923, June 30, 1923, July 6, 1923, July 24, 1923, July 3, 1924.

[30]*Item*, January 18, 1924; Jeansonne, *Leander Perez*, 24, 30; *Times-Picayune*, July 26, 1923, November 11, 1923, November 18, 1923, November 28, 1923.

[31]*Times-Picayune*, August 29, 1924.

[32]Gus Tomes file, in *Bureau of Identification Files on Deceased Criminals; Item*, September 10, 1924, October 21, 1928.

[33]*Times-Picayune*, December 30, 1928.

[34]Dempsey Interview, June 27, 1978.

[35]*New Orleans Hops, Malt and Extract Co. Inc. v. Mack Overpeck, Divisional Chief, Prohibition Department*, No. 17341, April 21, 1926, United States District Court, Eastern District of Louisiana (Copy in Department of Justice Records); *Times-Picayune*, May 15, 1920, June 11, 1925.

[36]*Times-Picayune*, October 14, 1921, January 6, 1922, January 9, 1925.

[37]*Item*, February 24, 1924; *New York Times*, September 18, 1921; *States*, March 22, 1929.

[38]*Item*, February 19, 1924, February 24, 1924.

[39]*New York Times*, September 18, 1921.

[40]*Item*, April 8, 1928.

[41]*States*, January 13, 1920.

[42]Healy Interview, August 10, 1978; *Reports of Homicides, 1926-1929*; *State of Louisiana v. Peter Valenti*, No. 3370, January 26, 1921, in Criminal Court Records.

[43]*Item*, July 22, 1927; Ogden Interview, July 18, 1978.

[44]Ogden Interview, July 18, 1978.

[45]*Item*, April 25, 1920; Jackson, "Prohibition in New Orleans," 267-68; *States*, July 24, 1921, March 9, 1927; *Times-Picayune*, May 17, 1924.

[46]*Item*, January 15, 1928, July 13, 1928, November 24, 1928, March 31, 1929; *Times-Picayune*, November 25, 1923, February 12, 1927.

[47]Ogden Interview, July 18, 1978.

[48]Healy Interview, August 10, 1978; *Item*, December 20, 1926, November 25, 1929; *States*, July 26, 1923; Clark Warburton, *The Economic Results of Prohibition* (New York, 1932), 152, 155-58.

[49]*States*, October 16, 1921, April 19, 1924.

[50]Ibid., February 1, 1923, February 2, 1923; *Times-Picayune*, March 18, 1922, February 1, 1923.

[51]Hartman Interview, July 6, 1978; *Item*, February 1, 1923; *States*, August 28, 1929.

[52]*States*, February 1, 1923; *Times-Picayune*, February 1, 1923, February 2, 1923.

[53]*Item*, August 28, 1927; Andrew Sinclair, *Era of Excess. A Social History of the Prohibition Movement* (New York, 1962), 200; *States*, January 7, 1920, October 16, 1922.

[54]*Item*, March 5, 1921, April 16, 1921; *Times-Picayune*, March 5, 1921, March 13, 1921, March 14, 1921.

[55]*Times-Picayune*, July 13, 1921, June 8, 1924.

[56]Ibid., September 11, 1926.

[57]Charles Merz, *The Dry Decade* (Garden City, N.Y., 1932), 66-67; Sinclair, *Era of Excess*, 205.

[58]Jackson, "Prohibition in New Orleans," 270-71; *Times-Picayune*, June 26, 1921, June 29, 1921, July 10, 1921.

[59]*Item*, August 13, 1925, August 15, 1925, April 19, 1926, April 21, 1926; Jackson, "Prohibition in New Orleans," 271; *Standard Brewing Company, Inc. v. A. R. Harris, Division Chief, Prohibition Department, et als.*, No. 18104, August 14, 1925, United States District Court, Eastern District of Louisiana (Copy in Department of Justice Records); *Times-Picayune*, July 12, 1921, August 12, 1925, April 20, 1926.

[60]*Item*, April 5, 1925, August 28, 1927.

[61]Herbert Asbury, *The Great Illusion: An Informal History of Prohibition* (Garden City, N.Y., 1950), 218-19; Healy Interview, August 10, 1978; *States*, December 19, 1928.

[62]Jackson, "Prohibition in New Orleans," 268; Examination of issues of the *Item*, *States*, and *Times-Picayune* for the years 1920-1929.

[63]*Item*, November 14, 1923, November 21, 1923; *States*, November 14, 1923, November 18, 1923.

[64]Jackson, "Prohibition in New Orleans," 269.

[65]*Item*, July 14, 1924, July 15, 1924; *Times-Picayune*, July 14, 1924, July 15, 1924.

[66]Jackson, "Prohibition in New Orleans," 272; *Times-Picayune*, June 5, 1922.

[67]*Item*, December 2, 1922, February 3, 1923; Jackson, "Prohibition in New Orleans," 272.

[68]Report, United States Grand Jury for the Eastern District of Louisiana, New Orleans Division, to Henry Mooney, May 12, 1921, File No. 23, in Department of Justice Records.

[69]*States*, December 26, 1924; *Times-Picayune*, January 1, 1923, December 7, 1924.

[70]U. S. Treasury Department, *Annual Report of the Commissioner of Internal Revenue*, 1920, 189; 1921, 174; 1922, 181; 1923, 181, 184; 1924, 186, 188; 1925, 176, 178; 1926, 173, 175, 177, 181; U. S. Treasury Department, *Annual Report of the Commissioner of Prohibition*, 1927, 84, 86; 1928, 88, 90; 1929, 100, 103; 1930, 110, 112. These annual reports cover the fiscal year ending June 30 of the year of the report, for example, 1923 covers the period from July 1, 1922, to June 30, 1923.

[71]*Denapolis et al. v. United States*, 3 F.2d 722 (5th Cir. 1925); *Times-Picayune*, March 13, 1924, March 14, 1924, March 15, 1924, January 14, 1925, February 21, 1925.

[72]*Item*, January 15, 1926, December 10, 1926; *Schlieder et al. v. United States*, 11 F.2d 345, (5th Cir. 1926); *Times-Picayune*, November 6, 1926, October 4, 1927, August 29, 1928.

[73]*Item*, April 12, 1929, June 18, 1929; *States*, March 6, 1923.

[74]*Annual Report of the Commissioner of Prohibition*, 1928, 93, 97; 1929, 107, 111; 1930, 115; Sinclair, *Era of Excess*, 192.

[75]*Gargano et al. v. United States*, 24 F.2d 625 (5th Cir. 1928); *Lindsly v. United States*, 12 F.2d 771 (5th Cir. 1926); *Monaghan v. United States*, 5 F.2d 424 (5th Cir. 1925); *Schulte v. United States*, 11 F.2d 105 (5th Cir. 1926).

[76]*Annual Report of the Commissioner of Prohibition*, 1928, 93; 1929, 107; 1930, 115; Louis H. Burns to Rush L. Holland, May 5, 1924, File 23, in Department of Justice Records.

[77]*Item*, December 7, 1925, March 2, 1926, January 10, 1929; Gertrude "Cleo" Lythgoe, *The Bahama Queen: The Autobiography of Gertrude "Cleo" Lythgoe* (New York, 1964), 155-57, 159; *Times-Picayune*, May 8, 1923, March 25, 1926.

[78]*Item*, March 30, 1926.

[79]Ibid., July 17, 1927.

[80]Ibid., April 4, 1926; *Times-Picayune*, March 12, 1926, March 26, 1926, May 30, 1926.

[81]Report, E. C. Yellowley to Robert A. Haynes, March 5, 1924, File 23, in Department of Justice Records.

[82]Memorandum, B. M. Coon to Assistant Attorney General Mabel Walker Willebrandt, September 21, 1925, in Department of Justice Records; Memorandum by Mabel Walker Willebrandt, August 10, 1924, File No. 23, in Department of Justice Records.

[83]Louis H. Burns to Attorney General, July 16, 1923, File No. 23, in Department of Justice Records.

[84]Criminal Court Records, City Archives, Louisiana Division, New Orleans Public Library. There are over 50,000 Criminal Court cases for the city of New Orleans for the 1920s, all located in the Louisiana Division of the New Orleans Public Library. The author examined about 5 percent of these, or about 2,500 cases, for the years 1921-22, 1925, and 1929, focusing on those associated with Prohibition, gambling, prostitution, and drugs.

[85]*State of Louisiana v. Anthony Maniacol*, No. 25925, June 4, 1923; *State of Louisiana v. Jacob Marcella*, No. 26428, February 18, 1924; *State of Louisiana v. James Melerine*, No. 27112, April 27, 1925; *State of Louisiana v. Alonzo Patterson*, No. 27569, January 4, 1926; *State of Louisiana v. Bennie Russo*, No. 29694, January 28, 1929. The documents and, in some cases, transcripts of these cases are located in the Clerk's Office, Supreme Court of Louisiana, Supreme Court Building, New Orleans.

[86]Louis H. Burns to Attorney General, probably Mabel Walker Willebrandt, April 21, 1924, File No. 23, in Department of Justice Records.

[87]W. T. Day to E. C. Yellowley, April 14, 1922, in Department of Justice Records.

[88]Harry Daugherty to U. S. Attorney, New Orleans, April 26, 1922; in Department of Justice Records; L. P. Bryant, Jr., to Attorney General, April 15, 1922, File No. 23, No. 3041, in Department of Justice Records;

States, April 13, 1922, April 14, 1922; *Times-Picayune*, April 20, 1922, April 21, 1922; W. T. Day to E. C. Yellowley, April 14, 1922, File No. 23, in Department of Justice Records.

[89] Healy Interview, August 10, 1978.

[90] Sean Dennis Cashman, *Prohibition: The Lie of the Land* (New York, 1981), 46; Sinclair, *Era of Excess*, 184.

[91] Healy Interview, August 10, 1978.

[92] *States*, October 16, 1921.

[93] Kyvig, *Repealing National Prohibition*, 31.

[94] Jackson, "Prohibition in New Orleans," 283-84.

[95] Humbert S. Nelli, "American Syndicate Crime: A Legacy of Prohibition," in *Law, Alcohol, and Order: Perspectives on National Prohibition*, ed. David E. Kyvig (Westport, Conn., 1985), 126-27.

[96] Ibid, 126-27. For a perspective on Prohibition in other large cities see Larry Engelmann, *Intemperance: The Lost War Against Liquor* (New York, 1979); Mark H. Haller, "Organized Crime in Urban Society: Chicago in the Twentieth Century," *Journal of Social History*, 5 (1971-1972): 210-34; Mark H. Haller, "Philadelphia Bootlegging and the Report of the Special August Grand Jury," *Pennsylvania Magazine of History and Biography*, 109 (1985): 215-33; James E. Hansen, II, "Moonshine and Murder: Prohibition in Denver," *Colorado Magazine*, 50 (1973): 1-23; Kenneth D. Rose, "Wettest in the West: San Francisco & Prohibition in 1924," *California History*, 65 (1986): 284-95, 314-15.

[97] Jackson, "Prohibition in New Orleans," 281.

[98] *New York Times*, November 12, 1922.

THE HUMAN DIMENSION OF
THE FLOOD OF 1927*

Carl A. Brasseaux

Contemporary journalists identified the 1927 flood as "America's greatest peacetime disaster."[1] This assessment was amply supported by the magnitude of the destruction wrought by the southward advance of a great wall of muddy water. In the spring of 1927, 16,570,627 acres (approximately 26,000 square miles) of prime farmland were submerged in 170 counties across seven states. An estimated 931,159 persons were displaced by floodwaters; 325,554 of these refugees sought shelter in Red Cross "concentration camps," while an additional 311,922 flood victims received Red Cross rations.[2]

The enormity of the resulting relief operation was eclipsed only by the magnitude of the flood's destructive force. The flood caused crop losses of $101,562,395 and farm property losses of $23,086,150.[3] The farm property loss totals reflect the drowning deaths of 165,298 heads of livestock and 1,010,375 poultry animals, but they do not indicate the damage sustained by homes, ancillary buildings, businesses, furnishings, fences, and farm implements. Red Cross reports indicate that 162,017 residences and at least 92,431 businesses were inundated and that more than half of these structures sustained major structural damage.[4] Although contemporary relief authorities did not produce cumulative property damage estimates, the losses sustained by the already economically beleaguered lower Mississippi Valley farmering community was staggering.[5]

The widespread destruction wrought by the surging floodwaters throughout the lower Mississippi Valley in late spring, 1927, tended to divert attention away from the experiences of those individuals forced to contend with the unfolding natural disaster. But, for those individuals who experienced the flood, the cataclysm remained one of the defining moments of their lives.

---

*First published in Glenn R. Conrad and Carl A. Brasseaux, *Crevasse! The 1927 Flood in Acadiana* (Lafayette, La.: Center for Louisiana Studies, 1994), 31-76. Reprinted with the kind permission of the author and the University of Louisiana at Lafayette.

The flood was remembered so vividly in part because it was so unexpected. Although Acadiana[6] newspapers had carried front-page accounts of flooding in Arkansas and Mississippi, many area journalists—the editors of the *Lafayette Daily Advertiser* and the *Opelousas Clarion-Progress* excepted—repeatedly reassured their readers that the flood would not significantly impact the Teche Valley region—even after it had become clear that their readership was in grave danger. The editor of the *New Iberia Enterprise* tacitly provided reassurance by simply ignoring the flood threat. Meanwhile "a group of municipal leaders had posted bills and spread the word that no flood waters would reach the city."[7] The May 14, 1927, issue of the *Enterprise,* the last weekly number released before the flood, contained no flood news whatsoever!

The editor of the *St. Martinville Weekly Messenger* took a different tact, distributing disinformation in the face of the worsening crisis. Attempting to quell rising popular concerns about local safety, the latter journalist insisted that St. Martin Parish residents ignore rumor mongers then frightening their neighbors with tales of impending doom: "Some people in their excitement and their exaggerated reports are creating an unnecessary panic among the people of the flood sections. The people at Isle Labbé and Catahoula are not back of levees and cannot be swamped by the rushing water. . . . The creating of a panic will confuse instead of helping."[8] While conceding—in another article buried in a less conspicuous part of the paper—that "we don't know what our status in the flood is as yet," the editor nevertheless belittled rumors that St. Martinville would be inundated. Noting that St. Martinville was seventeen feet above sea-level, the editor maintained that the natural levees along the Teche were safe from inundation.

Morgan City Chamber of Commerce officers issued equally irresponsible statements regarding their flood-prone community. Responding to a *New Orleans Times-Picayune* article suggesting that the Avoyelles Parish levee breaks should be a source of concern for Morgan City residents, these St. Mary Parish businessmen attacked the Crescent City newspaper for irresponsible journalism, noting in a public statement that "Morgan City is not in danger even of partial inundation from the crevasses along Bayou des Glaises." Conceding that weakening of the Mississippi River levees between New Roads and Donaldsonville was a possible source of concern, the Chamber of Commerce confidently predicted that "even should the main levees along the Mississippi river on the west bank break, not all of the town would be under water, and business would continue."[9]

While Morgan City residents who had experienced the 1912 flooding caused by Torras crevasse had ample cause for scepticism about the Chamber of Commerce's assurances, "old-timers" along Bayou Teche who had been left unscathed by earlier floods gave credence to such disinformation, for, according the St. Martinville newspaper, the Teche's high natural levees had not been inundated since 1796. "No one here," proclaimed the *Weekly Messenger*, "takes this [flood] news seriously."[10] Indeed, local journalists and politicians urged St. Martinville residents to mobilize to help residents of the low-lying areas along the Atchafalaya Basin who were expected to eventually succumb to the rising waters. In the days immediately preceding the inundation, residents of area parish seats consequently channeled much time and energy into the formation and organization of local Red Cross chapters for the anticipated influx of flood victims.

The resulting false sense of security was reinforced by unjustifiably optimistic reports issued by Dr. I. M. Cline, head of the New Orleans weather bureau. Sometime during the third week of May, for example, Cline telegraphed New Iberia authorities that "there was no necessity to evacuate, and that maybe between the 25th and June 1st there might be a rise from six inches to two feet of water in the low spots of New Iberia." This announcement "in a great measure composed many [New Iberia] citizens," leaving them largely unprepared for the onslaught of floodwaters on May 26.[11]

Only the most ardent and perceptive readers took heed of the alarming flood development reports often buried among inconsequential news articles and perceived the state and local governments' growing concern about the levee system's ability to protect the parish as evidenced by the increasing number of levee and emergency services inspections in May 1927 and the growing number of volunteers laboring to reinforce the beleaguered levee system. Articles and oral reports regarding levee work were particularly disconcerting, for local newspapers had reported the collapse of comparable levee systems in equally floodprone areas to the north, despite the valiant efforts of 1,000 men to strengthen the earthen wall.[12] In late April, heavy rains and wind gusts had weakened protection levees in the Cecilia area, prompting an urgent call for assistance. Thirty St. Martin Parish high school boys answered the call, laboring all day and into the night to shore up the earthen dike. In early May, fire sirens sounded sporadically to alert Teche Valley townspeople to levee emergencies. Groups of civic-minded men responded to these calls for help; laboring through the night, often "unloading barges of dirt," these volunteers usually returned home exhausted the following morning.[13] But such repairs were only temporary and highly localized solutions to the growing threat of levee failure all along the protective wall. By the end of the first week of May, many local volunteers were physically and emotionally drained.[14]

As the local populace became progressively less capable of battling the floodwaters, the demand for levee workers increased at an alarming rate. By May 7, 1927, 1,300 men were required to maintain the protection levees against rising floodwaters.[15] Such heavy labor demands greatly exceeded the limited resources of the thinly populated basin fringe, and, in early May, St. Martin officials evidently encountered some difficulty in recruiting levee workers from the parish's more densely populated, but less flood-prone areas. On the first Sunday of May, the Catholic clergy was consequently compelled to press their parishioners at St. Martinville, Parks, and Breaux Bridge to assist with the levee maintenance work.

By May 8, 1927, the situation in the Atchafalaya Basin had become so desperate that hundreds of laborers from throughout southwestern Louisiana were being rushed to the levees running from Port Barre to Henderson. Many of these levee workers were volunteers, including eighty Southwestern Louisiana Institute[16] students organized into a "volunteer labor company" by Coach T. R. Mobley.[17] Some volunteers were either employees of civic-minded companies, municipalities, or parish governmental entities, or war veterans who repeatedly turned out on designated "American Legion days,"[18] but most of the laborers were individuals lured by the promise of financial remuneration. Lafayette Parish's Red Cross chapter, at the urging of the national organization, began soliciting in early May for contributions to a special flood emergency fund.[19] The *Lafayette Daily Advertiser* strongly encouraged this Red Cross effort by stressing the urgent need of levee workers and by publishing lists of contributors. The resulting contributions, supplemented with funds from the national organization, permitted Lafayette's Red Cross chapter to offer volunteers a per diem wage of $2.00. Area farmers, locked in the grips of an ongoing economic depression, rushed to accept the offer. By the second week of May, hundreds of Lafayette Parish residents were transported daily to St. Martin Parish's crumbling levee system.[20] They were joined en route by smaller numbers of workers from western St. Martin Parish. Recruits from isolated rural areas were usually instructed to congregate at specified, centralized sites, where they were picked up by trucks, often provided by large landowners, and transported to stations along the Southern Pacific rail line.[21] At these stations, these workers boarded special trains bound for Nina, the rail stop nearest the flood-threatened areas to the east. Upon arrival, they were greeted by St. Martin Parish civic and governmental leaders[22] and transported to work sites between "Sidney Huval's place and Port Barre."[23] Food and coffee for the workers was donated by Lafayette Parish bakeries and philanthropists.[24]

Similar measures were taken by parochial officials and civic organizations in the Opelousas area. By late April, the Opelousas Chamber of Commerce and Rotary Club had joined with officials of the Missouri Pacific Railroad and Company C, 155th Infantry (the local National Guard unit) to formulate plans "to combat whatever danger might arise from the high water situation," particularly in the Melville area.[25] The resulting proposals were put into motion in early May, as the Missouri Pacific dispatched "a large number of men" to "sand bag" levees and tie-down the company's tracks, while the St. Landry Parish Police Jury stationed guards along the levee "to give the alarm if this becomes necessary."[26]

These well organized efforts to stem the rising floodtide along the western rim of the Atchafalaya Basin rapidly gained momentum. By May 10, 1927, more than 3,500 Lafayette-area men were mobilized in a single day to man the St. Martin Parish levees.[27] Businesses closed in St. Martinville and other Bayou Teche communities to permit the townspeople to join the prairie residents in the last, desperate attempt to stave off the inundation. Even with such massive reinforcements, however, the army of workers laboring to strengthen the western Basin's crumbling earthen walls was unable to prevent the area's inevitable inundation.

The Bayou des Glaises levee in Avoyelles Parish was the first to succumb to the high waters. The first crevasse appeared on Friday, May 13, and, over the next two days, the earthen structure was virtually washed away as the pent-up flood waters rushed southward toward the Teche country. On May 16, flood watches determined that the

Teche country's protective levees could not withstand the watery onslaught. Levee workers consequently suspended work on the earthern wall running from Port Barre to Henderson and withdrew to higher ground. Emergency officials also encouraged residents of low-lying areas throughout upper St. Landry and upper St. Martin parishes to evacuate, but many inhabitants of the upper St. Landry flood plain–particularly property owners along the Atchafalaya River–refused to evacuate because the wall of water unleashed by the Bayou des Glaises crevasses posed no direct threat to them as it rolled toward the western edge of the Teche ridge near Port Barre. They would soon have ample cause to regret their decision.

Around 6:00 a.m., May 17, the St. Landry Parish hamlet of Melville was engulfed by a wall of water. Moments before the inundation, "the fire whistle and the Standard Oil plant, shrieked a warning as levee guards sped through the streets, firing pistols and rifles and shouting 'crevasse, crevasse.'"[28] As rushing floodwaters tore the local hotel from its foundation and smashed it into neighboring residences, "women, aroused from their slumbers, frantically clasped their children in their arms and fled before the water to the levees and the upper floors of buildings."[29] Other Melville residents sought refuge in a special Texas and Pacific train, stationed at Melville for just such a flood emergency, "but the water came so quickly that the whole train was marooned with the refugees before it could put out of town."[30] Aware of their neighbors' plight, hundreds of Melville residents flocked to the Texas and Pacific Railroad's bridge over the Atchafalaya River, the community's only remaining link with dry land, and awaited the relief trains they hoped would come to rescue them.[31] According to the *Baton Rouge Morning Advocate,* "hundreds of men, women, and children crossed the railroad's bridge to the east bank [hamlet of Red Cross], carrying hand luggage, trunks or wheeling their possessions in wheelbarrows."[32] Later that day, two freight trains were dispatched to Red Cross from Baton Rouge "to take aboard the hundreds of people who lined the levee." Only a few score men who stubbornly "planned to remain in the upper stories of their homes" stayed behind.[33]

Evacuations

The Melville refugees were transported by rail to Baton Rouge, where they were joined by hundreds of evacuees from Avoyelles Parish. As the Bayou des Glaises and Bayou Rouge levee systems collapsed on May 13, much of the local population began to make its way along the levee road to Long Bridge, a "high spot" on the main road to the nearest high ground.[34] Upon arrival at Long Bridge, however, the refugees found themselves stranded by floodwater which had inundated both the bridge and the highway. A fleet of Coast Guard surfboats[35]–formerly used to apprehend East Coast rum runners, but redeployed to the Mississippi Valley during the flood–were consequently dispatched to rescue the evacuees. Working through the night, the Coast Guard transported more than 1,800 refugees to Mansura, a neighboring community located on a sixty-foot bluff overlooking the growing expanse of floodwater.[36]

The scope of the Avoyelles Parish evacuation effort expanded with the spreading floodwater. Sometime on May 14, the Coast Guard utilized a ferryboat and evidently some surfboats to evacuate Cottonport residents to Marksville. Women and children in the community were evacuated first, "but before evening the boats were moving the men left marooned on the levee."[37] A second ferry was dispatched to Long Bridge to complete the removal of refugees. Meanwhile surfboats coasted along the main levees rescuing stragglers who now found themselves "marooned" on the rapidly shrinking embankments.[38] In addition, fifteen privately owned skiffs and shallow-draft boats ventured into the floodwater in the Indian Bayou area below Cottonport to rescue "marooned farmers who were firing guns and crying for aid."[39] These myriad relief efforts cut deeply into the Coast Guard's limited resources, and rescuers consequently pressed barges into service as transport vessels for the evacuation of "hundreds of men who stayed behind to try to hold the levees" between Bordelonville and Long Bridge.[40] On May 15, the *Baton Rouge Morning Advocate* estimated that approximately 25,000 Avoyelles Parish residents had been "evacuated safely to high ground."[41]

Rescue operations continued throughout the weekend and into Monday, May 16, 1927, following the pattern established in the early stages of the evacuation. A flotilla of approximately fifty Coast Guard cutters and assorted "river craft" remained in the deep water, ferrying refugees from the crumbling levees to safety at Mansura, Marksville, Torras, Alexandria, and, in the latter stages of the operation, to Baton Rouge.[42] These vessels also evidently participated in the evacuation of Simmesport. Though the local population believed that the town, situated on a high bluff overlooking the Atchafalaya River, was in no imminent danger of flooding, emergency officials ordered the evacuation of the town to prevent large numbers of refugees from trying to reach the community and thereby both endangering themselves and prolonging the evacuation operation.[43] The evacuation of Simmesport proved most fortuitous, for, by May 20, water stood several feet deep in the hamlet's streets. Some of the Simmesport refugees were moved to "tents on the Louisiana Railway and Navigation Company railroad embankments," while others were assigned to houseboats.[44]

Meanwhile, small boats equipped with outboard motors sought out families trapped in their residences by the flood. Many of these families stubbornly refused to leave their homes, obliging the Coast Guard to build "a large fleet of boats, with outboard motors, and skiffs" to distribute food throughout the floodplain. As the shallow-draft boats moved farther and farther into the inundated farmlands, the rescue workers encountered myriad navigational problems produced by swift and often treacherous currents, floating debris, and the presence of submerged navigational hazards. By May 15, relief authorities had begun to issue shears to boat operators "to cut barbed wire when the boats become entangled in [it while] passing over fences."[45]

The flotilla of rescue craft in the spreading inland sea was augmented on the evening of May 16, as "twenty truckloads" of Red Cross volunteers, National Guardsmen, and small boats departed Opelousas for the now inundated communities of Rosa and Palmetto.

After travelling by highway as far as possible, the rescuers boarded small boats and groped their way through the darkness to the stricken communities, only to find that many residents stubbornly refused to leave.[46] The *New Orleans Times-Picayune* reported that "hundreds clung to their home spots until the waters rose about them, driving them to the roofs from which they had to be removed by boats. Many refused to leave even after the waters had left them precariously located on levees or high spots, preferring to remain in the vicinity of their homes rather than take up quarters at refugee camps."[47] Persons who congregated on the remaining bits of levees and high spots soon found themselves besieged by snakes, other predatory animals, and mosquitoes.[48] After brief exposure to these circumstances, the many holdouts left gladly. A survey of the Bayou des Glaises area on May 20 found "only five people . . . marooned in the entire section."[49] Marooned refugees in other areas, however, proved more determined to remain near their inundated homes and farms. As late as May 30, "several hundred refugees were [reportedly] assembled along the levees in the neighborhood of Torras, Krotz Springs and Melville, relying upon boats sent by the Red Cross for sustenance."[50]

Residents of the lower Acadiana parishes directly in the path of the still surging floodwater demonstrated better judgment. Reports of numerous drownings among Avoyelles Parish families who chose to remain in their homes,[51] stories of widespread destruction of livestock in the flood zone,[52] and sensational journalistic accounts of the Atchafalaya crevasse and the inundation of Melville, travelled quickly throughout the neighboring regions and helped prepare the notoriously sedentary and independent Teche Valley residents for their inevitable flight from the encroaching high waters. Throughout late April and early May, evacuations had been largely restricted to livestock in the Atchafalaya Basin's Bayou Chene community and other ribbons of high land in the basin,[53] but large-scale evacuations did not begin until after the Bayou des Glaises crevasse of May 13 and the Melville levee break of May 17 had unleashed separate torrents of floodwater running respectively along the western and eastern edges of the Teche Ridge. Residents of northeastern St. Landry Parish took flight when verbal reports of the Bayou des Glaises break were followed, in rapid succession, by the loud roar of the approaching floodwater.[54] In the Lebeau area, farmers drove their cattle to higher ground, after placing their families and their small barnyard animals[55] aboard shallow-draft flatboats sent into their area by the Red Cross to expedite evacuation of the region's first flood victims.[56] On May 18, a U. S. Weather Bureau evacuation advisory for the Port Barre to Leonville area galvanized the potential flood victims into action. Having endured the ravages of the destructive 1912 flood, which reportedly claimed numerous lives, residents of the most vulnerable areas in the floodplain south of Melville, who had been carefully monitoring the levee situation, wasted no time in evacuating their homes. Gathering their clothing, their children, and most of their livestock, they began to make their way to higher ground. Residents of Catahoula and Isle Labbé in St. Martin Parish joined in the exodus as soon as water levels began to rise in their areas. By May 19, the roads leading from the Atchafalaya Basin to Opelousas and Lafayette were literally choked with caravans including approximately 7,000 refugees and even larger numbers of horses, mules, and cattle. These roads remained congested for some time as perhaps as many as 72,000 persons attempted to escape the surging tide.

TABLE I
Demographic Impact of the Flood[57]

Parish	Total Population	Reported Flood Victims	%	Percentage of Parish Area Inundated
Iberia	26,855	20,000	74	67
Lafayette	31,601	1,000	3	10
St. Landry	53,308	41,000	77	81
St. Martin	21,990	10,000	45	67

Persons who tarried or who stubbornly refused to abandon their property[58] soon had ample cause to regret their decision.[59] Approximately one hundred Palmetto-area residents, for example, were trapped by flood waters rising two feet per hour. After telegraphing an urgent appeal for help[60] and then taking refuge in a boxcar on a rail siding near the Brewer Nienstat Lumber Mill, these individuals nearly drowned before government boats were able to reach them one day later. Other Palmetto residents clung to "the limbs of a large tree that jutted above the water line" after their makeshift raft was destroyed by surging floodwaters. Like their counterparts in the boxcar, they were also rescued by boat in timely fashion.[61] Stragglers at Arnaudville were nearly killed as floodwaters swept a large frame store into the Bayou Fuselier bridge they were crossing.[62] Boats manned by American Legion volunteers from Monroe and Alexandria subsequently plucked from roofs and attics of residences those townspeople trapped in the St. Landry Parish community by the bridge's destruction.[63]

Reports of such harrowing flirtations with death, helped to enlarge the swelling tide of refugees from the floodplain. Indeed, the congestion on the public thoroughfares was such that public authorities along the major escape routes were compelled to wire neighboring communities for assistance.[64] Volunteers from throughout the prairie region responded on May 19, as trucks from Rayne, Ridge, Duson, Crowley, Jennings, Lake Charles, "and other southwestern Louisiana communities" made their way to St. Martin Parish to assist with the evacuation.[65] A trainload of thirty trucks and a crew of volunteer relief workers from Beaumont, Texas, led by Mayor J. Austin Barnes, reached Lafayette the following day.[66] By May 21, "hundreds of trucks and cars" were reportedly assisting in the evacuation of refugees from the Isle Labbé and Catahoula areas.[67] Meanwhile, Company F, 155th Infantry, Breaux Bridge's National Guard unit under the direction of

Lieut. Robert E. Chaplin,[68] assumed responsibility for evacuation of the low-lying Coonville and Anse La Butte areas of western St. Martin Parish.

The presence of these cars, trucks, and volunteers was timely, for by May 21, 1927, three major crevasses[69] had punctured St. Martin Parish's protective levee system, resulting in the rapid inundation of several densely populated agricultural communities along Bayou Teche.[70] According to the *New Iberia Enterprise,* a wall of water crossed the Teche ridge and rushed westward to the edge of the prairie terrace, striking the escarpment with "such force as to make it appear to be running up hill." Rebounding from this collision, the floodwater moved "back across the Teche ridges," eventually smashing into the protection levee at St. Martinville. The floodwater then moved southward, "filling all the low bottoms between St. Martinville on the East and Broussard on the West, rushing into Spanish Lake on one side while the Bayou filled rapidly on the East."[71]

TABLE II
Extent of the Flooding

Parish	Percentage of Parish Area Inundated
Iberia	67
Lafayette	10
St. Landry	81
St. Martin	67

The floodwater moved southward more slowly evidently because of Bayou Teche's meanders below St. Martinville,[72] arriving at New Iberia on the morning of May 26. Two waves of refugees fled before the flood's southward march—the first from Loreauville,[73] the second from New Iberia. Concerns about the increasingly strong current in Bayou Teche and reports about flooding to the north together drove 250 Loreauville residents from their homes sometime before May 22;[74] hundreds followed in their wake. The Loreauville refugees initially sought sanctuary at New Iberia before rising water forced many of them to relocate on the bluff near Burke Station overlooking Spanish Lake. New Iberia's emergency officials provided segregated quarters for the refugees. Approximately 600 blacks were assigned to a "temporary camp" at "the New Iberia school," while an undetermined number of whites were quartered in the upper floor of the city's high school. Local health officials also established an emergency medical facility to deal with possible outbreaks of epidemic diseases among the refugees.[75]

Other Loreauville flood victims made their way to Jeanerette, which was largely spared the flood.[76] They were joined by large numbers of black New Iberia residents, who began evacuating their low-lying residences in large numbers as soon as floodwaters

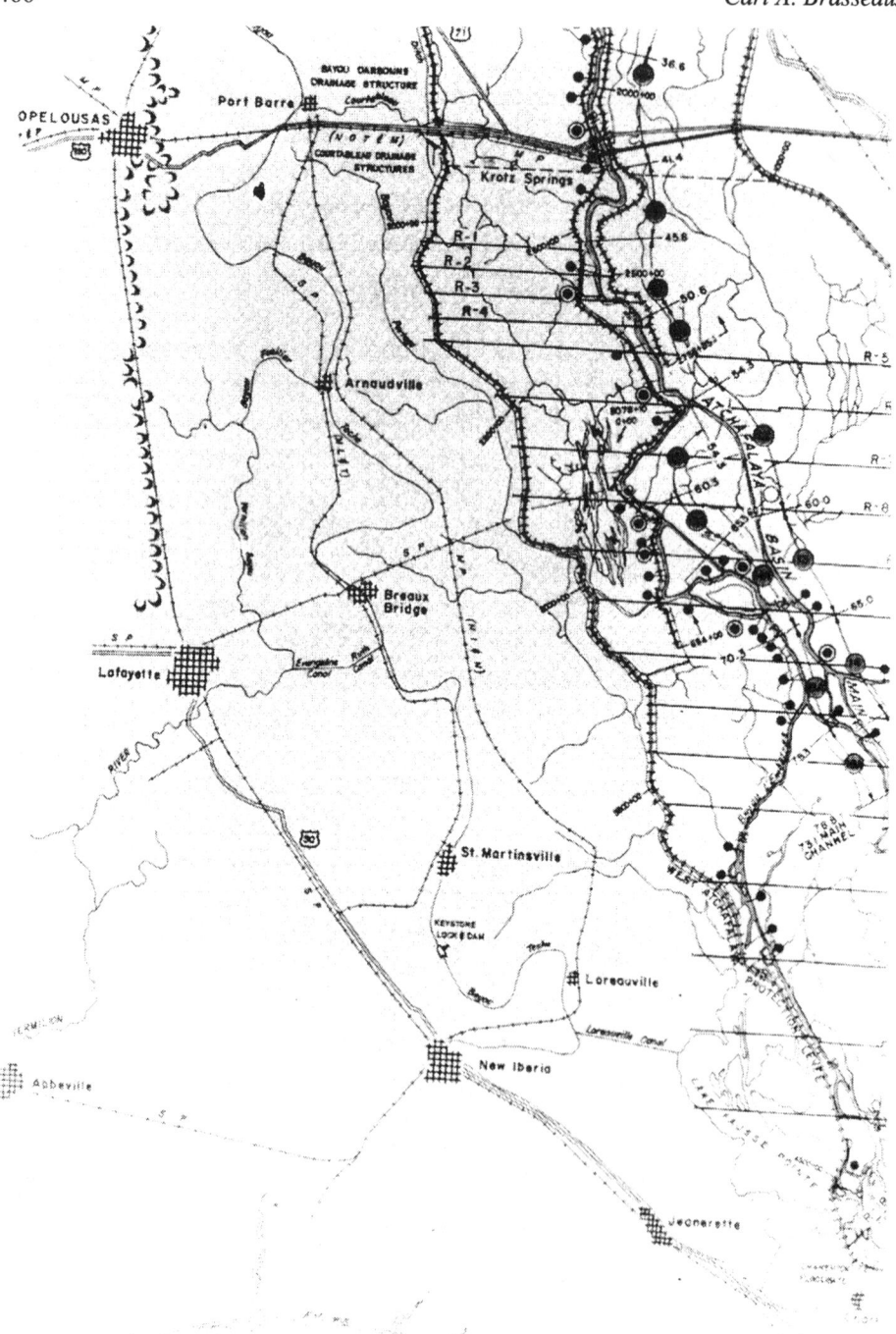

Figure 1. The western rim of the Atchafalaya Basin, ca. 1927.
Note the railroad lines leading into the flood-threatened areas.

The Flood of 1927

began to move toward the city from Spanish Lake. The editor of the *Enterprise* estimated that approximately 1,000 persons—80 of whom were African-Americans—participated in this stage of the exodus from New Iberia.[77] Other residents—including most of the white middle class—initially chose to remain because of misplaced faith in either the Weather Bureau's overly optimistic predictions, or unfounded assurances by municipal officials that no floodwater would reach the city, but "when the Spanish Lake filled up and began to overflow itself, many people became panic stricken and boarded their automobiles and trains, seeking places of safety."[78] Red Cross authorities informed the *Times-Picayune* that between May 24 and May 29, the relief agency provided free transportation to 4,000 persons leaving New Iberia.[79] Approximately 1,500 refugees departed New Iberia on May 28 alone, with "many going to the camp on high ground near Burke, others to Beaumont."[80] Many men, however, placed their wives and children on westbound trains and then prepared to face the flood in their homes. Fortunately for them, New Iberia was spared much of the devastation experienced in neighboring communities upstream.

Fortune smiled less kindly upon rural folk who also evidently attempted to brave the flood at home or who decided to evacuate when traveling conditions were no longer safe. Hundreds of St. Martin Parish refugees were inundated by the floodwaters as, encumbered by their herds, the families slowly made their way to higher ground. Historian Harry Lewis Griffin recalled that "there were many cars on the road between Lafayette and Breaux Bridge which were stalled as the rushing waters engulfed the road. The occupants found safety by clinging to the tops of their cars until rescued by boats" operated by volunteers.[81] Evacuees were later transferred to large trucks operated by the National Guard. Evacuation of such stranded St. Martin Parish refugees, however, was hampered by curious Lafayette residents who congregated in large numbers at the foot of the Teche Ridge, near the present Lafayette diocesan chancery to view the "high waters," thereby creating a "traffic jam" that greatly retarded the movement of the rescuers' trucks.[82]

The many unsung heroes of the rescue effort repeatedly surmounted such unanticipated problems, often working around the clock without rest until the last accessible refugees were out of harm's way. The *St. Martinville Weekly Messenger* recorded the following, second-hand account of one such individual:

> It was reported to us that a Catholic priest of Lake Arthur, La., whose name we could not obtain, was seen here on a truck getting the people from the flooded Catahoula and Isle Labbé, and after working night and day, removing the people, was invited by one of our citizens to come home, have a bite and rest a while before going back to work, replied that he could not accept the invitation because he had too much pressing work to do.[83]

Volunteers undertook similar rescue work in St. Landry Parish—though on a much smaller scale—with the assistance of major local corporations: "The Southern Pacific railroad company, through Assistant Division Superintendent Elmo Hodges, donated a special train early this morning on which boats secured from the Texas Oil Company, were rushed to Opelousas from which point they have been sent out to flooded sections to bring in refugees."[84]

Once the refugees had reached safety, the rescuers turned their attention to the thousands of livestock[85] either abandoned by the refugee families trapped by floodwaters en route to Lafayette or marooned aboard special livestock evacuation trains stranded in the St. Martin Parish lowlands.[86] Prof. W. E. "Daddy" Stokes of Southwestern Louisiana Institute, who barely escaped the flood, arriving atop "the hill at Oakbourne Plantation" aboard a refugee wagon just "before the whole area behind it was covered with the swirling waters," poignantly described the plight of some of those animals stranded in eastern Lafayette Parish: "As he stood safely at the top of the hill, Professor Stokes could hear hundreds of cattle in the adjoining woods struggling and mooing in their fright and efforts to survive."[87]

News of the stranded cattle elicited an immediate, sympathetic response from Louisiana's prairie country, where small-scale ranching was still a way of life. According to the *New Iberia Enterprise,* the cattle herders rescued literally "hundreds of head of livestock" from starvation or drowning. "Trucks and men from nearly every nearby town in the state, Abbeville, Broussard, Crowley, Rayne, Lake Charles, Monroe, Vinton, Eunice, Jeanerette, Youngsville, Franklin, Avery and Jefferson Islands, and others to [sic] mention" from places as distant as Beaumont participated in the rescue effort, but contemporary observers reserved special praise for an undetermined number of East Texas cowboys.

The Texas cowboys travelled to Louisiana in response to a Red Cross appeal to Sol M. White, mayor of Orange, Texas, for assistance with Acadiana's mushrooming livestock problem. The mayor's office in turn contacted the Dr. E. W. Brown estate, which "quickly organized a force of cowboys and horses."[88] Transported to Louisiana aboard a special train, these cowpokes "plunged headlong into the thick of the great rescue work, with their horses, their boats, [and] their trucks."[89] This "great rescue work" entailed great risk to life and limb, as evidenced in the following account of their exploits:

> two cowboys . . . were apparently on the verge of drowning when rescued. It happens that these cowboys were driving cattle through Wyche's field, on the edge of Spanish Lake, which had been unloaded from the trained [sic] marooned there that day. Some of the cattle had strayed into deep and swifter waters than the path chosen. In an attempt to round them two of the cowboys drove their horses into the swift current, and in so doing, were carried too far into the waters to control their horses. Being overcome by the swift current they sighted [a] boat and called for help. The cowboys tied their lassos around their body and threw the other end to the boat and were pulled to safety.[90]

Despite such perilous conditions, the cowboys—aided by hundreds of Louisiana volunteers—succeeded in moving "hundreds of heads of stock" to the present Evangeline-Longfellow Commemorative Area site, which had remained "high and dry" and which afforded the only available local grazing.[91] Other livestock evidently captured near rail stations were placed on special trains of as many as ten cattle cars and transported to designated grazing areas in the prairie region between Crowley and Midland, where cattle driven to safety earlier at Lafayette had already been taken for pasturage.[92] Approximately 1,000 cattle and mules were reportedly saved in the New Iberia area alone. The rescue mission ended around May 27, as the cowboys began returning home after announcing that it was "impossible for them to rescue more live stock on account of the depth of water" which claimed the lives of hundreds of farm animals.[93]

Refugee Camps

Daily reports of the on-going rescue mission's successes notwithstanding, the fate of their abandoned homes and livestock remained a nagging concern of many refugees long after their flight from the flood. For the first refugees, this flight to safety was more circuitous than that of their successors. According to the *St. Martinville Weekly Messenger*, flood victims, in the early stages of the evacuation, refused to leave St. Martin Parish.[94] These refugees were temporarily housed at the parish seat, until advancing floodwater forced their relocation. By May 28, floodwater stood six feet deep in Pinaudville (the portion of St. Martinville east of the Bridge Street crossing) and two feet deep in the stores along Main Street; only a few die-hard property owners remained in the community.[95]

Upon departure from their home parishes, refugees generally faced three choices regarding their temporary disposition: 1) They could rent accommodations in local hostelries, as did the Stockstill family of Bayou Chene.[96] 2) They could join relatives beyond the flood zone. Many refugees–both black and white–joined relatives in Mansura, Marksville, Bunkie, Alexandria, Baton Rouge, Lafayette, Carencro,[97] Opelousas, Jeanerette, and a host of other Louisiana towns. Others travelled by train to meet relatives in the Golden Triangle area of southeastern Texas. Indeed, by May 25, 1927, more than 200 flood victims were reportedly residing with relatives in Orange, Texas, alone;[98] by June 11, there were also 800 St. Martin Parish refugees in Port Arthur, Texas, and "about 1,000 at Beaumont."[99] 3) The refugees could seek assistance from the Red Cross. Without any financial means or local relatives, the overwhelming majority of refugees were compelled to seek out the charitable organization.

Mansura, Marksville, and Alexandria

The first refugee camps established by the Red Cross in Acadiana were–as indicated above–established at Mansura and Marksville.[100] As the influx began, Red Cross volunteers mobilized to provide hot food, temporary shelter, and "innoculations for typhoid and smallpox" to the refugees, most of whom "came away with only the clothes they wore. . . . Many of them . . . had just deserted their task of topping the levees [and] wore only shirts and trousers, not having had time to return to their homes for their other clothing."[101] An unidentified journalist reported that "each woman seemed to want to take away a prized possession, a picture or some valuable lace or dress and in many cases the family Bible, while the tired, mud-covered children clutched a toy or sometimes carried a pet cat or small dog."[102]

Moved with pity for the refugees, the Mansura townspeople took refugee families into their homes while the Red Cross struggled to establish a tent city for the Bayou des Glaises flood victims.[103] When the supply of available homes was exhausted, relief officials housed refugees in the community's theater, bank, and town hall.[104] Most of the refugees, however, were obliged to enter the Red Cross cantonment, and, by the end of May, 3,975 persons had registered at the tent city.

Marksville accorded a similarly cordial reception to the Cottonport-area refugees. Lucien Laborde recalls that his family, like many other Marksville residents, took refugee families into their homes,[105] but, as in Mansura, most refugees were obliged to seek shelter and assistance at the Red Cross cantonment, established in the municipal ballpark.[106]

The Marksville and Mansura camps quickly became overcrowded,[107] forcing local relief agencies to dispatch an undetermined, but small number of refugees and their attendant livestock to Bunkie.[108] Many Bunkie families evidently extended their hospitality to most of the refugees, and local farmers provided pasturage for some–but not all–of the refugees' farm animals. From Bunkie, some of the cattle were transported to St. Landry Parish grasslands.

The modest number of refugees at Bunkie soon outstripped the small community's ability to assist them, and, by May 16, 1927, Red Cross officials reported "about five thousand" refugees "to be moved from the section adjacent to Mansura and Marksville, although the camps in the two places already house about 3000."[109] Louisiana's Red Cross officials were thus compelled to establish a third camp to accommodate the overflow. Secretary of Commerce Herbert Hoover, coordinator of the national relief effort who visited Alexandria in the wake of the Bayou des Glaises crevasse, announced, after consultations with local Red Cross officials, that "preparations will be made in Alexandria to receive between 25,000 and 30,000 refugees from the newly flooded area."[110] A tent city was indeed subsequently established in Alexandria and, at the peak of the influx, the facility accommodated 3,956 refugees.[111]

Baton Rouge

Three refugee camps established at Baton Rouge in May 1927 also helped accommodate the overflow. Several hundred Avoyelles Parish refugees and at least 500 refugee-owned cattle were transported by the Coast Guard to Baton Rouge in the days following May 13.[112] They were joined by refugees from Melville[113] and from Pointe Coupée Parish. Red Cross officials established three Baton Rouge facilities to accommodate the influx. White women and children were assigned to the barracks near the present state capital. White men and teenage boys were taken to the "old agronomy building across the roadway" from the barracks.[114] "Several hundred" blacks were sent to "the camp of tents at the L.S.U. experimental station tract on the Jackson road."[115] Upon arrival at the camps, Red Cross workers provided the refugees with hot food, bedding, and assignment to temporary quarters.

The initially excellent relations between the refugees and the Red Cross workers who ran the camps, and the professional Red Cross staff who had been brought in to run the facilities rapidly deteriorated. Though grateful for the assistance provided by the relief agency, the refugees would not brook the arrogance, brusqueness, and ethnocentrism of the Red Cross personnel, whose intolerance is accurately reflected in the following excerpt from a letter by Red Cross "nutrition nurse" Maude Chambers: "Do I intend to feed them just whay they've been accustomed to? I do not. They would like gumbo with rice and coffee every day. I give them gumbo once a week–not the expensive chicken gumbo a New Yorker gloats over in Antoine's but–weine[r] gumbo. 'Cafe au lait' for the children is a universal custom. That must be stopped."[116] Unabashedly appalled by Chambers' culinary abominations, the refugees–particularly the women–at first attempted discrete recommendations about possible dietary alternatives, such as cornbread and syrup, but these polite suggestions evidently went unheeded. The refugee women then tried a more direct approach, telling Chambers–as best they could with their limited English vocabulary–precisely what they wanted to eat.[117] The monolingual English-speaking Red Cross workers, however, made no real effort to comprehend the refugees' "Cajun jabber with a sprinking of English,"[118] and thus the women's pleas went unheeded.

The seething frustrations of the refugee population abated only when Mrs. Charles Saint, who had served as a translator in World War I, stepped forward as "the official interpreter for the camp," around May 20, 1927.[119] No longer able to disregard cavelierly the refugees' complaints, Chambers was evidently forced to make some concessions, and the "nutrition nurse" grudgingly came to respect her charges, noting that they were "the most courteous but the most individualistic people on the face of the globe."[120]

Lafayette

Relations between refugees and Red Cross officials appears to have been far more harmonious in Lafayette, perhaps because of the larger role played by local relief officials. The American Red Cross and the city of Lafayette had begun to lay the groundwork for assistance to large numbers of Louisiana flood victims in late April and early May. On April 26, 1927, Mayor Robert L. Mouton had issued a proclamation urging area residents to contribute money, food, or clothing to the Red Cross's flood relief operations along the Mississippi River.[121] Responding to this call for assistance, the local citizenry eventually raised more than $1,500 for the Red Cross and for levee repair work—a princely sum during the agricultural depression of the late 1920s. On May 5, 1927, Lieut. Harry J. Stahl of Company M, the 158th Infantry, National Guard (Lafayette's hometown unit)[122] announced that a camp for flood victims would open in Lafayette on May 5, but the documentary record suggests that this refugee shelter was woefully neglected as Red Cross workers channeled their efforts into raising moneys and recruiting workers for emergency levee repairs in St. Martin Parish.[123] Such neglect stemmed in part from regional developments that appeared to obviate the need for such a facility. On May 7, a state conference of parochial Red Cross administrators proposed a secondary network of "concentration camps"[124] to be located at the St. Martin Parish communities of St. Martinville, Parks, Breaux Bridge, and Cecilia. These facilities, to be operated by the Red Cross and the State Department of Health, but administered and policed by Company F of the Breaux Bridge National Guard unit, were to provide "immediate help" to the limited number of refugees expected to result from possible flooding.[125] Although Red Cross volunteers envisioned the creation of an infrastructure necessary to support these projected facilities, deteriorating conditions prevented St. Martin Parish authorities from establishing them. Indeed, Chairman Marcel J. Voorhies of the St. Martin Parish Red Cross Chapter informed leaders of the Lafayette chapter on May 14, 1927, that "camps had been planned at St. Martinville, Breaux Bridge, Cecilia and Parks, but that in view of the new flood outlook, it appeared that these camps might not be possible, in which case the refugees would be concentrated here [Lafayette]."[126] Hence, when confronted by the arrival of thousands of unexpected flood refugees in mid-May, the Hub City found itself unprepared to receive them.

On May 15 1927, the Lafayette Chapter[127] of the American Red Cross rushed into readiness plans formulated the previous day "to take care of the emergency which follows the flooding of the Atchafalaya Basin area behind Cecilia." Having been informed by L. D. MacIntyre and Harold B. Atkinson, Red Cross national representatives with considerable recent experience with the Vicksburg, Mississippi, flood relief effort, that the Hub City could expect "2,000 to 20,000 refugees" within hours, Lafayette's Red Cross and governmental officials raced to prepare for the onslaught. Working with local governmental authorities and business leaders, O. B. Hopkins, general chairman of the parish relief organization, Mrs. F. E. Davis, chairman of the Lafayette Red Cross chapter, and Gertrude McDowell, chapter secretary, scrambled to establish facilities to identify, process, and shelter the anticipated refugees. Lafayette Parish Clerk of Court Felix H. Mouton established and personally supervised registration facilities.[128] Other volunteers rushed to locate and establish "sites for the [camps], storage provisions for food supplies, water and sewer facilities and other matters."[129] One thousand tents were requested from the national Red Cross headquarters to provide shelter for the anticipated flood victims. Meanwhile, the local Red Cross chapter obtained authorization from the Texas Oil Company to use its idle Baldwin Lumber Company property (later site of Trappey's canning plant) in Lafayette's Greenville section as a camp site; no work appears to have been done by relief agencies, however, to prepare the location for occupation by refugees. Evidently believing that the lumber yard grounds could not accommodate the anticipated crush of flood victims, Lafayette authorities took other potential camp sites under consideration, pending inspection by "members of the executive committee of the relief organization." Red Cross officials also secured commitments from local homeowners to host refugee families upon their arrival, while other volunteers coaxed local property owners into renting vacant buildings to displaced families if such a need developed.[130]

Having laid the foundation for refugee housing, Lafayette's municipal government and Red Cross chapter initiated efforts to transport flood victims to safety. Following negotiations between Assistant Division Superintendent Elmo Hodges of the Southern Pacific Railroad, G. R. Tucker of the Texas Oil Company, and Mayor Robert L. Mouton, special trains equipped with boats and other rescue equipment were dispatched into the flood zone each morning for several days after May 15 "to bring in refugees."[131] Meanwhile, R. E. Soulier, chairman of the Lafayette Red Cross Committee on Trucks, mounted a high-profile campaign to recruit every available local truck to the evacuation effort.

Once the rescue operations commenced, local Red Cross officials quickly created the administrative infrastructure necessary for coordination of these myriad relief efforts. By May 15, 1927, leaders of the Lafayette chapter had established a general headquarters in the Heymann Department Store on Jefferson Street in downtown Lafayette and had reserved space on the second floor of the neighboring Lafayette Building and Loan Association. Special telephone lines were installed to provide constant communications between these command posts. The Southwestern Louisiana Institute (present-day University of Southwestern Louisiana) dispatched typewriters from the Commerce Department to the headquarters offices and assigned faculty members and students to assist Red Cross and local governmental officials with the registration of flood victims. Under national Red Cross guidelines, registration was a prerequisite for emergency assistance, for it allowed relief authorities to assess the refugees' material needs. Upon registration, families were assigned to tents or other lodgings and issued cots and blankets. The head of the household was then issued a copy of his registration card, listing his/her name and the names of his/her dependents. This card was required to obtain "rations and supplies" from Red Cross distribution centers in the camps.[132]

The rapid growth of the refugee population and the proportionate increase in records keeping that it entailed caused a corresponding increase in the Red Cross's administrative apparatus. Sometime before May 21, the "executive offices" of the relief effort had taken over the entire second floor of the general headquarters building. The "department[s] of Registration, Information, Medical, Volunteer, Workers, and Food" took up the building's first floor.[133]

Special relief agencies were created to deal with the refugees' material needs; a Red Cross "Production Unit," for example, was established at 524 Jefferson Street[134] specifically to feed and clothe destitute flood victims. Once the facility opened, Mrs. F. E. Davis, chairwoman of the parish Red Cross chapter, began to solicit donations of "clothing, shoes, and hats" through area newspapers, while Mrs. J. W. Harrington recruited volunteers to transport, process, and distribute donated apparel, food, and other supplies.[135] Mrs. Harold Demanade, director of production at the facility, transformed the volunteers into a highly productive workforce. Working six-hour shifts at a battery of sewing machines, Mrs. Demanade's workers "sorted and mended thousands of garments, donated to the refugees."[136] Indeed, within forty-eight hours of its opening, the Production Unit had refurbished 2,845 children's and 1,495 women's garments for distribution at the camps and an additional 2,583 pieces of clothing for use by patients in the emergency hospitals. The volunteer workforce subsequently produced "several hundred sheets."[137]

The Red Cross also established emergency hospitals at N. P. Moss and Lafayette High schools as well as at the black school located at the end of East Vermilion Street."[138] Dr. Marc M. Mouton, president of Lafayette's City Board of Health, became the de facto director of emergency health care services at these facilities.[139]

Meanwhile, Red Cross representatives searched for potential camp sites at the Fair Grounds,[140] Mouton Addition, College Park Addition, Greenville section, Tissington Addition, Holy Rosary property, Barry Addition, and Voorhies Addition sections of Lafayette's rapidly growing northside. In keeping with the segregationist practices of the day, two sites were chosen: the Fair Grounds as the white camp and property in Greenville as the black camp location. Committees under the direction of local Boy Scout official H. F. Cosey and Registrar of Voters George J. Breaux were then named to administer the as yet undeveloped facilities.[141]

The Red Cross's new infrastructure was pressed into service almost immediately. On May 15, 1927, 175 refugees reportedly sought assistance from the Lafayette Red Cross, but, by 11:00 p.m., May 18, 1927, 395 families totaling 4,002 individuals had registered at Red Cross headquarters for admission to the camps. Among this number were "1,235 refugees . . . from Carencro where they [were] being quartered in homes, barns, public buildings, and other places."[142] (At least 413 St. Martin Parish refugees remained in Carencro, often among relatives,[143] along with a large herd of livestock from the inundated areas to the east.)[144]

As a result of this massive influx, the number of refugees far exceeded the resources available for emergency relief in Lafayette, but still the flood victims came–by the thousands. On May 21, the *Times-Picayune* reported that the population of Lafayette's camps was increasing at the rate of 300 persons per hour. The demographic and logistical consequences of this increase for the Red Cross were staggering: There were 10,156 refugees in the Hub City on the morning of May 21,[145] but, by 10:00 a.m., May 24, 1927, Lafayette's refugee population had grown to 16,733 individuals from 3,280 families.[146] There were 17,322 refugees in Lafayette's camps the following morning[147] and 19,426 on the morning of May 31.[148] According to Red Cross records, this surging tide of displaced humanity crested at 21,529, evidently in early June.[149] To put these figures into perspective, one need only note that the number of refugees exceeded Lafayette's established population on the morning of May 21.[150]

The geometric increase in the number of refugees, particularly between May 15 and 24, greatly exceeded the manpower and material resources of the local Red Cross organization. On May 19, Dr. L. A. Butler, speaking on behalf of the local relief organization, issued a plea for "colored men volunteers to help serve the flood refugees in the colored concentration camp here."[151] Additional white workers were also recruited by existing civic and charitable organizations. White and black volunteers were quickly pressed into service providing shelter for the new arrivals. The most fortunate refugees found refuge with relatives in the area.[152] The vast majority of flood victims, however, placed their fate in the hands of the Lafayette relief agencies.

Until May 17, the first refugees were—according to one eyewitness—sent to the Greenville lumber yard. On May 17, however, the number of flood victims exceeded the small number of tents available at the campground.[153] A "large force of men" consequently labored around the clock to erect at the Fair Grounds 275 tents received from Alexandria shortly before midnight; an undetermined number of additional tents were erected at the Fair Grounds following their arrival the following morning.[154]

Despite the commendable efforts of local officials to provide temporary shelter for the refugees during the early days of the influx, the rapidly growing demand for emergency housing consistently outstripped the local supply of tents. By May 18, Red Cross officials were compelled to secure temporary accommodations for flood victims in private homes and at "the Greenville Camp, the Central High School, Elks Home, Masonic Temple, Woodmen Hall, the new filling station building being erected on East Vermilion Street, and other places."[155]

Southwestern Louisiana Institute (present-day University of Southwestern Louisiana) was the most notable of these "other places." On May 21, President Edwin L. Stephens closed the college, designated the physical plant an emergency center, and assigned the faculty and staff to assist in the relief effort.[156] The facility was soon filled to capacity by 1,200 refugees who arrived throughout the evening of May 22. Upon registration at the registration desk in the lobby of Martin Hall, the college's administration building, individual refugees—who usually arrived drenched after a drive in open motor vehicles or wagons through torrential rains—were given a blanket and conducted by faculty members to their quarters. The first women and children were given priority and placed in dormitory rooms until all available beds were occupied. According to local oral tradition, several babies were born to women among the refugees and part of Martin Hall was used as a nursery.[157] Late-arrivals were crammed into any available space, eventually finding their way into the industrial arts workshop in Brown Ayres Hall, where refugees slept among "the work tables, lathes and other machines"[158] until new temporary housing became available at the refugee camps.

Plans for new housing at the camps were formulated on the morning of May 18, as O. B. Hopkins "and other officials of the Red Cross relief organization"—including L. D. MacIntyre[159]—authorized construction of more substantial, temporary quarters for the refugees. These wood-frame structures, measuring twelve by fourteen feet, were to be clustered into elongated sectional buildings containing twelve adjacent rooms. The sectional buildings, in turn, were "grouped in three main buildings, 2,000 feet long."[160] Two of the "main buildings" were designated for use by whites, the third by blacks, but African-Americans would not ultimately be housed at the Fair Grounds because of the larger than expected influx of white refugees. Blacks originally designated for settlement at the Fair Grounds were redirected to the "tent camp" established on the grounds of Holy Rosary Institute.[161] The vast majority of black refugees, however, would be sent to the rapidly burgeoning tent city at Greenville.[162]

The challenge of creating housing quickly enough and in sufficient quantities to meet the demands of the swelling tide of immigration was compounded by the unconventional baggage carried by many refugee families. The *New Iberia Enterprise* reported, on May 21, 1927, that "At Breaux Bridge, hundreds of trucks were coming out of the flooded area, loaded with furniture, hogs, chickens and men, en route to the refugee camps at Lafayette." Another account recalled the "pathetic scenes" presented as cars, trucks, mule-drawn wagons, one after another, arrived in front of the headquarters building loaded with refugees, their household goods and other movable property, including chickens, pigs, dogs, and in many cases, their all."[163] Upon arrival at the camps, these barnyard animals were tagged with identification numbers and then moved to holding pens and barns at the Fair Grounds, "pending further arrangements for their care or sale."[164] Red Cross officials thus had to cope with the demands of accommodating and feeding untold numbers of hogs, chickens, and cows in the midst of an ever more crowded refugee camp.

A solution to the latter dilemma was soon forthcoming as relief officers grappled with the demands of feeding the hungry multitudes. While the residential halls were under construction, H. F. Cosey and George J. Breaux arranged for the construction of large, outdoor kitchens, dining facilities, and food warehouses at the Greenville and Fair Grounds camps. After the onset of construction work at the campsites, Lafayette businessman and philanthropist Maurice Heymann assumed direction of the "food supplies for the refugee camps." Working day and night, Heymann and his subordinates distributed "huge quantities of sandwiches" and coffee to refugees following their registration at Red Cross headquarters. By May 19, Heymann's food distribution system required a daily caravan of trucks laden with at least 3,000 loaves of bread, 1,400 pounds of meat, 400 pounds of rice, 400 pounds of beans, "and other large quantities of provisions," including 150 gallons of milk shipped daily to Lafayette from Crowley. Some of these shipments included vegetables donated by the Jennings Red Cross chapter.[165] To alleviate the heavy logistical demands of the camps, Heymann began to purchase livestock from the refugees in order to secure a local meat supply. This, in turn, diminished the distracting obligations placed upon camp managers by the refugees' large livestock herds.[166] Surplus livestock were shipped by rail to grazing areas on the prairies.

While Heymann moved and processed mountains of supplies for hungry refugees, other relief officials sought to assuage the flood victims' anguish by tending to their spiritual and emotional needs. Catholic priests and Protestant ministers offered regular services for both religious groups. The Catholic church, however, attempted to use its considerable local influence to prevent evangelical Protestant missionaries from approaching the overwhelmingly Catholic refugees. In public letters to the *Lafayette Daily Advertiser*, Bishop Jules B. Jeanmard maintained that he was "grieved and pained to learn" that numerous Catholic families had been approached by preachers "who left their literature in their tents." "A dear old lady," Jeanmard continued, "weepingly told me that their only comfort and consolation in this dark hour was their Catholic faith and, having lost everything else, it did not seem right that attempts should now be made to rob them of this."[167] Jeanmard's efforts appear to have been for naught, for the overwhelmingly Protestant Red Cross personnel then running the local camps were not swayed by the Catholic bishop's appeal, and members of the Protestant clergy continued to visit the camps evidently without restriction.

The Catholic church responded with a pontifical mass for the refugees celebrated by Bishop Jules Jeanmard of the Diocese of Lafayette on June 23, a major religious ceremony intended to reinforce the refugees' Catholic faith. The mass, performed by Jeanmard in the grandstand of a local baseball park, attracted over 15,000 people who covered the playing field. "All the worshippers were from a single parish. . . . It is St. Martin's, which is inundated."[168] Children who had just made their first communion sang French religious hymns, while the Cathedral choir "sang the Mass." "The pastor of the historic church of St. Martinville preached a sermon in which he recalled the heroic story of the Acadians and exhorted his hearers, descendants of the Acadian exiles, to seek consolation and strength in the same old Faith which was so dear to their forebears that they chose exile and poverty to be free to practice it."[169]

Such exhortations were necessary because of the sense of depression and disorientation among flood victims in the camps. Many of the refugees encountered such technological innovations such as electricity, electrical lights, radios, running water, and indoor plumbing for the first time in these host facilities. A member of one host family recalls that his mother told her refugee counterpart to turn out the lights before she and her family fell asleep in the living room. The host awoke during the night and found that the living-room light was still burning. She, therefore, walked to the living room and asked the refugee mother about the light. The refugee, very much chagrined, replied that she "blew and blew, but could never get the light to go out."[170] Though comical from the host's perspective, such encounters with new technology served to heighten the sense of disorientation experienced by many refugees in the Hub City, especially in large public facilities where large numbers of refugees from different geographic areas were forced to congregate under adverse conditions.[171] Because of the flooding in Lafayette, these refugees were forced to relocate at least once, and sometimes several times. The resulting disorientation was compounded by an increasingly pervasive sense of gloom among adult refugees, who were preoccupied with the loss of their homes, possessions, and livelihood. The *St. Martinville Weekly Messenger* reported on June 4, 1927, that "We have received a number of inquiries from our people who have removed to the other towns for the duration of this inundation. These inquiries center around one question, which is, 'how many feet of water are there in my yard or in my house?"

Local officials consequently attempted to restore some basic services—particularly mail deliveries—to restore some semblance of normalcy to the refugees' disrupted lives. Lafayette Postmaster J. R. Domengeaux began to lay the groundwork for mail delivery to the refugees in a meeting with Red Cross officials on May 21. Five days later, postal officials re-established the Breaux Bridge and Arnaudville post offices in Lafayette's tent cities to provide basic mail service to the thousands of former St. Martin Parish residents stranded there.[172]

Other officials sought to divert the victims' attention, as much as possible, from their myriad problems. Through meetings held on May 21 with representatives of the Young Men's Christian Association, Dean James M. Smith of Southwestern Louisiana Institute, chairman of the Committee on Recreation,[173] established a blueprint for recreational services at the camps.[174] The first recreational activities established were those requiring the least preparation. The committee appropriated the Technical Arts Building at the Fair Grounds for use as a recreational center. Reading and writing tables were installed and books, magazines, and Victrola records obtained from Lafayette residents were assembled in the building for use by refugees. The *Lafayette Daily Advertiser* also delivered an unspecified number of newspapers to the camps for use by the refugees.[175]

Once the recreational center had been established at the Fair Grounds, volunteers began to provide various recreational activities for the white refugees: Dr. R. H. Bolyard of the SLI faculty, director of cinematic programming at both camps, arranged for free showings of numerous movies at the Fair Grounds dining center. These showings were quite popular; a double-feature including "God's Country and the Law" and a "Charlie Chaplin comedy," for example, drew more than 1,000 viewers. In addition, local performers presented plays and performed music for the refugees.[176] Other activities were tailored to the interests of specific age groups. Mrs. H. E. Robinson of New Orleans joined Lafayette residents Vesta Richard, Inez Neyland, Annie Carter in providing "story-telling and games for the small girls, volley ball, basket ball, and story-telling for the larger girls." H. E. Robinson of the New Orleans Y.M.C.A. organized "baseball and basketball for the boys."[177] Men were given the opportunity to acquire woodworking skills through SLI. In a program coordinated by Prof. Ashby Woodson of the SLI Engineering Department, local lumber yards contributed wood, Woodson the patterns, SLI and the Hopkins Lumber Company the equipment, and the refugees the manpower to fabricate, assemble, and finish furniture components. In a typical week, this cottage industry produced "thirty benches, twenty tables, three wardrobes, and two cabinets." The finished products were used in the camps.[178]

Black refugees were afforded significantly fewer recreational opportunities, with the apparent exception of movies. The *Lafayette Daily Advertiser* reported on May 25, that "a[t] the negro camp in Greenville an audience of about 500 attended a picture show which was in charge of H. E. Robinson, of the Tulane Y.M.C.A. at New Orleans. Reverend Father Thomas Wrenn, who is in charge of the negro refugee camp, expressed appreciation over the arrangements of the program which he stated was of much assistance in carrying on the work." The "work" to which Fr. Wrenn so cryptically referred was the cleric's effort to combat the sense of gloom and depression pervading the black camp, in part as a result of the lack of diversions for the refugees. This pervading sense of gloom was noted on June 5-6, 1927, by several members of the Colored Advisory Committee[179] appointed by Secretary of Commerce Herbert Hoover to assess the condition of black refugees in the disaster areas of the lower Mississippi Valley. Though publicly expressing themselves to be "highly pleased with the work and the conditions found," committee members privately confided grave concern about the psychological condition of the displaced blacks.[180] According to Claude A. Barnett, director of the Associated Negro Press, and Jesse O. Thomas, Southern field secretary for the National Urban League, the typical black camp resident was overwhelmed by

> The suddenness of the disaster and the fact that on a number of previous occasions they had been told that water was coming and the water did not come. [This] must have created a feeling closely akin to panic, as information came to them that they must move within a few hours in order to save their lives. The shock of fleeing for their lives in many instances when water was already in the houses, has left its imprint upon these people. Few of them have gotten back to a normal frame of mind. There is worry about their crops, and there is worry about their hogs, cattle, chickens, and the condition of their homes. There are rumors of all sorts that filter into the camps about this house being swept away and about that neighbor having lost all of their mules, etc. To talk to them one gets a conglomerate mass of statements that are depressing. Back of it all, however, there is a feeling of deep gratitude to the Red Cross for having saved their lives. They sit in groups and talk and smile, but one hears no singing or loud laughter. The children romp and play; the mothers look tired and weary and there is, undoubtedly, among the men the feeling of uncertainty as to what will become of them when they leave the refugee camps. They appreciate what is being done for them; they appreciate the friendly attitude of the white officials; they appreciate the kind offices of the colored people who are helping in conducting the affairs of the camp, but they want to get back home. They are curious to know what they will find when they return.[181]

Some officials—particularly those associated directly with the Red Cross—sought to prepare the refugees for "what they would find when they return." Many "mothers learned for the first time something about modern health measures from Red Cross nurses, who made daily visits to the sick."[182] At sanitation lectures presented in the camps, speakers discussed, in minute detail, the means by which homes should be cleaned, wells disinfected, drinking water purified, and putrefied animal carcasses interred. These public health evangelists also often used the disaster as an opportunity to preach the gospel of personal hygiene.[183]

While Red Cross officials sought to prepare refugees for the potential health problems awaiting them upon their return, Lafayette's health care professionals confronted the myriad medical problems actually facing the flood victims during their confinement in the increasingly insalubrious tent cities.[184] Dr. Marc M. Mouton of Lafayette and numerous, unidentified volunteer nurses—eventually assisted by physicians, dentists, and nurses from throughout southwestern Louisiana and southeastern Texas[185]—worked "night and day in looking after the health of the refugees." Mouton set up a small emergency clinic in the Red Cross headquarters to deal with the most severe medical problems among the registering refugees. Dr. Mouton also established an emergency "hospital" in Greenville for the black camp. Subsequently demoted to the status of an isolation facility for contagious diseases, this field hospital was soon replaced by a more adequately staffed and maintained clinic at the black public school.[186] A hospital for whites was established near the Fair Grounds, as several rooms at N. P. Moss School were converted for use as an emergency medical facility—with the approbation of Lafayette Parish Superintendent of Schools J. W. Faulk.[187] A maternity hospital was also established, first in the Elks Home Building on Lafayette's northside and later in the Convent of the Most Holy Sacrament, on St. Mary Street, near St. John's Hospital.[188] An ambulance lent by the Orange, Texas, Red Cross chapter to its Lafayette counterpart evidently transported refugees to these medical facilities.[189]

Having secured the establishment of essential emergency facilities, Mouton was relieved of the daily tedium of medical administration, as Dr. R. O. Young of Youngsville began to coordinate medical affairs at the general headquarters in the name of the Board of Health[190] and as Ann C. Munn of the Red Cross's national headquarters assumed responsibility for hospitals, nursing, and vaccinations.[191] Munn moved quickly to inoculate all refugees against typhoid and smallpox, administering more than 1,200 vaccinations per day within a week of assuming the directorship.[192]

Public health and safety remained overriding concerns of Lafayette's public and private relief authorities as the camps settled into an orderly, if mundane existence following the explosive growth of the refugee population in the third and fourth weeks of May. A board of sanitation was established to supervise construction and maintenance of privies at the campsites. In addition, a crew of workers under the direction of Lafayette Trustee of Public Property Wilson J. Peck extended electrical and water lines into the camps.[193] The National Guard and other public authorities established a mechanism for maintenance of public order in and around the camps. Because Lafayette's national guardsmen had already been assigned to active duty in the Baton Rouge area,[194] Company F, Breaux Bridge's displaced national guardsmen who were then heavily involved in the evacuation of the Anse La Butte and "Coonville" areas,[195] were given responsibility for public order at the camps. In addition, Chaplin's men, who were encamped near N. P. Moss school, were required subjected to "traffic duty in the downtown section, near the relief headquarters building, and about the Fair Grounds."[196]

The Breaux Bridge company was reinforced by Troop F, 108th Cavalry—Jennings' National Guard Unit shortly after May 21.[197] Capt. Bruder of Company F, the highest ranking officer, assumed supervision of the unified command. Together these National Guard units not only supervised the rapidly concluding evacuation operations in the flooded portions of St. Martin Parish, but also patrolled the camps,[198] maintaining order and limiting contact between camp residents and townspeople to an absolute minimum. (Use of guardsmen for patrol duty ended around June 8.)[199]

Emergency relief officials deemed restricted access to the camps essential for reasons of security, sanitation, and public health–problems of unprecedented magnitude in the Lafayette area resulting from the unexpectedly large influx of flood victims. Indeed, by the end of May, Lafayette's refugee population was more than twice that of the host community. Patrols were thus necessary both to prevent potential looting and other possible criminal behavior by refugees and to protect the refugees from unscrupulous townspeople. Such fears were not unfounded. Capt. F. B. Putney, national director of disaster relief for the Red Cross who had taken control of the Lafayette headquarters, complained to another Red Cross official in June 1927 that two New Orleans prostitutes had infiltrated the Lafayette camp and, on the day after receiving a tent, had "started business."[200] Putney evidently utilized the National Guard to arrest thirty-five men–some townspeople and some refugees–for "indecency," evidently for fraternizing with the prostitutes. The prostitutes were expelled from the camp and given twenty-four hours to leave town, while the men were put to "work on the rock pile."[201] Other alleged incidents evidently went unpunished in the camps both in Lafayette and in Opelousas, for Dr. Valeria H. Parker, quoting a camp employee, reported that "the boys around here are 'free' (promiscuous) with girls" in "both white and colored camps."[202] Red Cross health officials maintained that National Guardsmen were among this "bad lot,"[203] noting the presence of "acute gonococcus infections" among the troops.[204] The Red Cross attempted to combat such promiscuity through the efforts of Dr. Albert J. Read, a Red Cross "social hygiene" evangelist, who preached against sexual promiscuity and about venereal diseases in the "camps that remained open in early June."[205] Read's effectiveness, however, was sharply limited by the efforts of the local Catholic clergy who attempted to censor any possible discussions of birth control.[206]

This short-lived furor over sexual licentiousness in the camps has tended to produce a distorted picture of the refugees in the historical literature on the 1927 flood.[207] The sexual escapades of some refugees notwithstanding, the large camp populations at Lafayette and elsewhere in Acadiana were remarkably well-behaved. Indeed, no incidents of violence or thefts were reported by journalists in their extensive daily coverage of the unfolding disaster. The refugees' exemplary overall behavior was universally recognized by visiting Red Cross officials and national and state governmental dignitaries (including Secretary of Commerce Herbert Hoover),[208] who often ascribed the camps' good order to the administrative acumen of local relief authorities, who devoted unusual attention to detail.[209] Indeed, the cost of feeding the refugees at the Lafayette camps was the lowest in

Red Cross disaster relief work.[210] Capt. Harold P. Nathan of the National Guard, sent to Lafayette to "liaison work between the Red Cross, National Guard, and civilian" volunteers, commented that he was "very pleased with the situation and concluded that remarkable work had been done in such a short time in taking care of the thousands of refugees."[211]

This astute leadership was nowhere more evident than in the midst of the precipitous deterioration of local conditions at the height of the influx. As in the 1993 Midwestern disaster, the huge body of water created by the 1927 inundation disrupted local weather patterns, producing an inordinate amount of rain. Rain fell almost incessantly from May 22 through May 28. More than six inches of precipitation fell on the Lafayette area on May 28—after nearly four inches of rainfall the previous two days.[212] Such intensive, sustained rainfall quickly created a secondary natural disaster along the eastern fringe of the prairie terrace, to which the vast majority of Acadiana flood victims had fled, believing that the area's modest elevation afforded them a haven from flooding.

In Lafayette, these heavy rains transformed the Fair Grounds into a virtual swamp, and the refugees were forced to deal with several inches of water in their tents. Women and children in the camps were moved to local schools, while the men went to work to refurbish the tents with elevated wooden floors.[213] The situation was more serious in the Greenville camp. Heavy runoff coupled with the diversion of some Mississippi floodwater into the Vermilion River by way of Bayou Fuselier caused the Vermilion to rise beyond its normal flood stage. Some of the Greenville tent city was inundated, forcing the relocation of hundreds of black refugees to higher ground near the black school.[214] On May 25, the force of the current in the swollen Vermilion "swept several houses from the Greenville section . . . against the railroad bridge on the new Lafayette-Broussard highway where motor and other vehicle traffic [was] cut off."[215] The rising water also forced the closure of the Pinhook Bridge. On May 26, 1927, the river gauge at Pinhook Bridge stood at 26'0", that at the Pershing Highway (present-day U.S. Hwy. 90) bridge, 26'3".[216] Such high water levels prevented drainage of rainwater from the surrounding areas into the river, the area's only outlet to the Gulf of Mexico. Much of the region from Lafayette to Crowley was consequently under water, as were the areas to the south and southeast of the Hub City.[217] Unable to accommodate the runoff from "a 14 inch rainfall . . . north of Abbeville" on May 22, the flood-swollen Vermilion River left its banks below Maurice sometime before May 25.[218] By May 27, Lafayette was virtually cut off from the outside world. Only the Southern Pacific rail line remained a dependable communications artery.

Crowley

Fearing that the flow of food into Lafayette would be disrupted, relief officials in Lafayette proposed transfer of at least some refugees from Lafayette camps to Crowley. The Red Cross had notified Crowley officials on May 21 that the rice capital should be prepared to establish a "camp site" in the event that the unexpectedly large number of refugees exhausted Lafayette's limited resources. On the night of May 22, one carload of flood victims from the Lafayette camps was deposited at Crowley. These unfortunate people were sheltered in an empty warehouse until tents could be procured and erected. On May 23, H. G. Keib from the Washington office of the National Red Cross arrived at Crowley to "organize and build a refugee camp of sufficient porportoins [sic] to accommodate 20,000 people."[219] Keib was accompanied by two carloads of tents and equipment, including "stoves for the camp kitchen." Volunteers subsequently established an encampment on vacant lots in the Lawrence Addition. This site was selected because it constituted the highest available property and because of its proximity to existing municipal water and electrical lines.[220]

Apprised of the rapid progress in the establishment of the Crowley encampment, Capt. F. B. Putney, national director of disaster relief for the Red Cross who had taken control of the Lafayette headquarters, announced on May 24 that 6,000 refugees would be transferred from Lafayette to Crowley by train because of overcrowding and flooding in the Lafayette camps. Hundreds of affected refugees, however, refused to be relocated and Southern Pacific Railroad administrators initially balked at the proposal, citing heavy demands already levied upon the carrier by the flood emergency. Putney publicly rescinded the removal order on May 24, only to reverse his position the following day as continued rains caused continued deterioration of the Lafayette situation.[221]

Having settled upon a course of action, Putney mobilized hundreds of Lafayette refugees for relocation.[222] On May 25, 997 black refugees were transported to Crowley aboard a special train. Later that day, a second train carrying 1,200 black and white refugees departed for the Acadia Parish community, while a third special train was reserved for transportation of 600 refugees from Broussard to Crowley.[223] According to Red Cross statistics, approximately 3,900 flood victims would eventually make their way to the Crowley tent city.[224] Refugees would remain in Crowley until late June. Shortly before June 25, Red Cross officials began dismantling the Acadia Parish facility. Eight hospitalized refugees were taken to Lafayette's emergency medical centers, while able-bodied refugees from Lafayette and St. Martin parishes were transported to the Fair Grounds and Greenville encampments in Lafayette. Flood victims from St. Landry Parish were sent by rail to tent cities in Opelousas, and "those from Iberia parish [were] taken to the Segura camp."

New Iberia

The Segura camp was one of two refugee centers established near New Iberia during the flood. At the time of New Iberia's inundation, refugees from the Loreauville area as well as from the low-lying areas of New Iberia were moved to higher ground by local authorities. Approximately 300 white and black refugees as well as 600 head of refugee-owned cattle were sheltered at Avery Island,[225] but most of the refugees were moved to segregated camps between Segura and Burke stations, on the bluffs overlooking nearby Spanish Lake.[226] The white-refugee facility, Camp Roy, named for the local National Guard commander,[227] was located on the Atkinson farm,[228] while black refugees were assembled at the "old Pharr plantation" in a tent city called McGlade Camp in honor of the local Catholic priest[229] who assumed the duties of camp manager.[230] According to Red Cross records, enrollment at both facilities peaked at 4,103, probably in early June.[231]

The Red Cross established a "ration store and warehouse"[232] to feed and clothe the refugees in the cantonments. Using a "generous cash appropriation" from the national Red Cross, the volunteer managers of these facilities purchased shoes, overalls and shirts for men, work dresses and undergarments for women, and miscellaneous clothes for children in local clothing establishments. These purchases were supplemented by "liberal donations" of clothing from the Specialty Store, the Globe store, the A. Ackal store, and numerous individuals.[233] These donations were perhaps made in gratitude for services provided local companies by relief agencies, particularly by the National Guardsmen who "closely guarded" businesses throughout the flood emergency.[234]

The medical needs of the refugees were addressed by local healthcare professionals. Dr. J. W. Sanders, acting medical and evidently administrative director for both camps despite the presence of national Red Cross officials,[235] transformed the Atkinson house, "a large[,] spacious[,] and commodious building," into a field hospital, staffed by local nurses and pharmacists.[236] Sanders gave priority to "sanitation and health conditions of the camps," and, as a consequence, "few persons . . . had to occupy the hospital."[237]

As in Lafayette, lectures on hygiene, venereal diseases, and family values became an integral part of the Red Cross health program in the summer months. In early July, Dr. Albert J. Read of Albany, N.Y., called upon the New Iberia camps "in connection with the Red Cross flood relief Social Hygiene activities"—a program for the "conservation and protection of family life among refugees." Read warned the flood victims that "the changed surroundings expose . . . parents and their children to many dangers of which they have no idea. In some instances deliberate attempts have been made to lead these plain people astray and damage the morals of their children." Read called upon the local government and civic-minded citizens to "do everything possible" to maintain the camps as restricted areas as a means of safeguarding "family welfare." Albert Reed noted that the Red Cross was doing its part by sending sociologists to the refugee camps to "correlat[e] the forces that will safeguard the family life and help return the refugees to their normal life in normal condition."[238]

Reed's lectures on the potential social evils of camp life were presented long after a time when the cantonments' populations were declining precipitously, for the refugees had begun to return home by June 11. Though briefly slowed by the arrival of flood victims from Crowley in late June, the exodus was virtually complete by July 15, when the camps formally closed. The camps' ration store and warehouse were moved to the Lewald Building at the corner of Main and French streets in New Iberia to provide continuing assistance to flood victims, while a "clothing department" consisting of leftover clothing from the camps was established in Loreauville, "nearer the seat of its usefulness."[239]

St. Mary Parish

As the movement of the New Iberia "clothing department" to Loreauville suggests, the flood's impact diminished greatly below New Iberia. Residents of the Grand Marais area near Jeanerette were forced by local flooding to evacuate their homes, and many of these refugees appear to have made their way to the New Iberia camps.[240] Jeanerette itself remained dry, with the exception of waterfront stores. Sometime before May 30, hundreds of reportedly panic-stricken bayou-front property owners also briefly left their homes between Jeanerette and Franklin in anticipation of flooding around Charenton.[241] By May 31, the "low places" in Charenton were indeed flooded to a depth of several feet, with floodwater moving through the town with great force toward Grand Lake.[242] The rising waters in Grand Lake quickly breached the lake's small protection levees, causing the inundation of most of the low-lying area east of Franklin. On May 29, Grand Lake and Bayou Teche were "within a few acres of meeting."[243]

The beleaguered community of Franklin mobilized all of its human resources to combat the encroaching floodwater. On May 28, following closure of the last bayoufront business establishment because of flooding, Mayor Charles Lauve declared a state of emergency, and all business places in town consequently closed to permit the entire male population to erect a levee through the community. Conceding "the business section of the east side of main street" to flooding, the workers built an earthen wall "down the neutral ground into the town" to protect businesses on the west side of main street as well as the community's residential sections. The levee appears to have served its intended purpose, and flood damage was limited largely to the bayouside business places.[244]

From Franklin, the flood crest moved downstream to Morgan City, where it encountered floodwater from the Atchafalaya Basin which together raised the Atchafalaya River to levels well above the normal flood stage. The city's levee system was unable to withstand the rising waters, and, by May 28, "two to three feet of water covered two-thirds of the town and many of the 5,000 population had deserted their homes." Residents of Morgan City's northside and their livestock were the first to be evacuated from the area. They were joined by "hundreds of refugees" from the flood-prone Avoca Island and Berwick Bay areas, where the rising Atchafalaya breeched the levee systems. These refugees were dispatched to refugee camps at Thibodaux. Over 1,000 others, including most of Morgan City's white women and children and a large portion of the African-American population, "left for the hills"–probably Lafayette's Red Cross camps.[245] Some of the lower St. Mary Parish refugees, however, appear to have been housed in local emergency shelters at least on a temporary basis. The official Red Cross report of the 1927 flood indicates that two refugee camps were established in St. Mary Parish. Open only a short period at the height of the flood, the Baldwin camp accommodated 424 refugees, its counterpart at Franklin only 200.[246]

Three thousand Morgan City residents reportedly remained to protect their homes and businesses, boasting to journalists that they knew how "to save themselves from drowning" and thus had no fear of the floodwater.[247] Having received innoculations against waterborne diseases and having elevated their food, drinking water, clothing, and business wares on platforms, these hardy and resourceful folk went about their lives. The *Times-Picayune* reported that "banks and business places are doing business as usual . . ., and even a pool room is accommodating its patrons, despite the flood."[248]

Opelousas

Residents of the uppermost reaches of the Teche Valley were less successful in coping with the flood and the myriad problems it created. The Opelousas area had been the first Acadiana region to feel the full impact of the flood as Melville's refugees made their way to the parish seat. Opelousas had begun to prepare for a flood emergency in early May in response to a Red Cross appeal for "refugee protection." On May 6, 1927, the *Opelousas Clarion-Progress* boasted that "the city [had] whipped its civic resources into shape to prepare for the opening of its gates to a refugee camp in the event that the levees give way on the Atchafalaya River or the Bayou des Glases [*sic*]." Opelousas' three main banks even went so far as to publish a prominently featured advertisement in the *Clarion-Progress* extending to "Mississippi flood sufferers" a "combined personal invitation of welcome."[249] One week later, Mayor A. J. Perrault of Opelousas and Adolphe Jacobs, chariman of the Food and Supplies Committee of the recently organized St. Landry Relief organization, who had just arranged shipment of a truckload of relief supplies to the flood-threatened community of Port Barre, were directed by the Red Cross to "prepare quickly" for an influx of refugees.[250] Perrault "immediately appointed numerous committees, acquired a camp site, and perfected a complete organization, ready at a moment's notice to provide full relief for refugees from near by [*sic*] section[s]."[251] Perrault's "perfected" relief organization consisted of eight committees: health and sanitation, food and supplies, ladies general, housing, finance, transportation, and camp grounds. The last committee's initial responsibilities were effectively restricted to recommendations of potential black camp sites, for E. M. Boagni and already offered the relief organization land across South Railroad Avenue from the Dietlein and Jacobs Wholesale Grocery Company in Opelousas for use as a white refugee center.[252] The committee recommended three locations to Mayor Perrault sometime before May 27, but the location of the black encampment—subsequently named Camp Lamson[253]—is veiled in obscurity. Circumstantial evidence suggests that Camp Lamson was located on, or on property adjacent to, the original white camp site. The camp site selection process appears to have been haphazard at best, for both the white and black[254] refugee facilities were wholly inadequate for the massive flood emergency facing Opelousas.

The Flood of 1927

As in Lafayette, the number of flood victims greatly exceded officials' expectations. Refugees from fifteen Opelousas-area communities congregated in these camp sites "in a steady stream" over the course of the following week, and, by May 20, the number of registered refugees in Opelousas stood at 5,700; Opelousas itself had a population of only 6,000.[255] Though local Red Cross officials maintained publicly that the city's refugee camp was adequate "for an indefinite additional number" of flood victims, it was common knowledge that Opelousas' emergency facilities were incapable of handling the influx. On the night of Tuesday, May 16, "a countless number of negroes were forced to sleep on the cement floor of Bordelon's garage, on the floor and on the benches of the local negro church, and in any other place that they could find."[256] The white camp also experienced overcrowding,[257] as refugees were crammed into "a huge cotton warehouse."[258] Apprised of this situation, the town of Eunice rallied to Opelousas's assistance, accepting approximately 800 St. Landry flood victims destined for the parish seat.[259] On the afternoon of May 18, Mayor S. Wyble notified Red Cross officials that Eunice stood prepared to "provide quarters for at least another 5,000 refugees."[260] By the end of May, the refugee population in Eunice stood at 1,107, according to the national Red Cross.[261]

Eunice's altruism did little to alleviate Opelousas's continuing refugee housing shortage. Approximately 6,000 refugees arrived at Opelousas on the evening of May 18, doubling the number of flood victims in the community, and, on May 20, 1927, the *New Orleans Times-Picayune* reported that a "continuous stream of refugees" poured into Opelousas from the Pecanière, Arnaudville, and Leonville areas of southeastern St. Landry parish.[262] By May 25, 1927, the registered refugees in Opelousas totalled 13,097,[263] while an additional 2,000 unregistered refugees found temporary accommodations in the town, evidently in relatives' residences.[264] Eleven hundred other flood victims were sent to Lafayette's refugee camps.[265] By June 3, the number of registered refugees in Opelousas had grown to 14,210, and an additional 3,849 whites and 4,192 blacks were being fed, clothed, and sheltered by the Red Cross in other St. Landry Parish communities. The official Red Cross report on the flood indicates that 2,075 refugees received assistance in Sunset and 2,700 in Washington.[266] On June 15, the number of registered refugees in St. Landry Parish peaked at 20,635.[267]

The late-May dispersal of refugees in St. Landry Parish evidently resulted from continuing housing shortages in Opelousas. As in Lafayette, Opelousas's relief workers struggled to meet the demand for temporary housing—but with less success than their Hub City counterparts. By May 27, St. Landry Parish volunteers had erected 575 "sanitary army squad tent[s] . . . , measuring 16 by 16 feet, pyramid in shape, and equipped with wooden floors."[268] Yet, only 2,456 of the 5,701 registered white refugees would find lodging in the "old camp" on the Boagni property. "The remainder had been distributed about the city, staying with relatives, friends, and in barns or other quarters that were made available by property owners."[269] Most of these refugees and some newly arrived refugees were eventually resettled at Camp Hamilton, a new white campsite east of the "Opelousas cemetery"[270] established sometime around May 20 on property provided by

E. M. Boagni.[271] They were joined by the residents of the original Boagni camp after Secretary of Commerce Herbert Hoover personally inspected the Opelousas camps and found unacceptable conditions in both white and black facilities. Approximately 7,000 white refugees[272] had been driven by torrential rains to "the spacious wooden sheds of the Opelousas Compress Company," sometime before May 27. Deeming the resulting congestion and declining sanitation intolerable, Hoover ordered removal of the white refugees to the new camp,[273] but the white refugees were forced to remain in the warehouses until the expansion of the Camp Hamilton facility permitted their relocation.[274] Under the direction of camp manager Paul Pavy, electricity, water, drainage, and sanitation facilities were quickly installed in the cantonment.[275] Meanwhile, according to the *Opelousas Clarion-Progress,* no effort was made to alleviate the chronic overcrowding in the original black camp;[276] relief authorities did, however, improve the once deplorable drainage at the facility in an attempt to improve the quality of life at the black cantonment.

In an effort to deal more effectively with the staggering logistical problems created by the explosive growth of the camps, the Opelousas relief organization underwent a second "compete reorganization" within one month. The following committees were established to deal with problems unanticipated by the organization's earlier incarnation: "executive, camps, information, housing, stock, dairying, food supplies, health and sanitation, national guards, transportation, ladies', sewing, layettes and soup, bathing older children, central hotel, general needs, recreation and amusement."[277] As with other refugee operations, however, the committees responsible for health, sanitation, security, and logistical support were the most active segments of the Opelousas organization. Because of the magnitude of these problems, the committees were obliged to delegate as much responsibility as possible. The refugees, for example, were made accountable for their own internal security. According to one observer, "leaders among the refugees, both white and negro, were made policemen of the camps, wearing red brassards as insignia of officers."[278]

External security matters remained the exclusive domain of the National Guard, who, acting in conformity with Red Cross directives, sought to reduce contacts between the refugees and the townspeople to an absolute minimum as a means of preventing outbreaks of epidemic diseases. National Red Cross regulations for refugee centers mandated typoid and smallpox vaccinations for all refugees, particularly after numerous flood victims contracted those diseases at Harrisonburg, Louisiana, earlier in May.[279] These health concerns were underscored when, during his tour of the Opelousas cantonments, Herbert Hoover "warned the [local] medical authorities to be on guard for any outbreaks" of epidemic diseases.[280] Opelousas relief officials consequently accorded health care top priority. On May 19, Dr. B. A. Littell, municipal health officer for Opelousas, urged all permanent residents of the community to "take immediate steps to procure both vaccinations against small pox and an injection of typhoid virus" as a means of protection against refugee-transmitted infections.[281] Littell also implemented "drastic measures" at the camps "to obliterate any possible chances of disease contagion."[282] The white and black refugee encampments were quarantined. Refugees were banned from leaving camp without a pass, and Opelousas residents were not admitted to the cantonments without proof of official business. The movement of pedestrians and supplies was closely monitored by Company D, 155th Infantry[283]—a New Orleans National Guard unit assigned to Opelousas around May 20—who manned the gateways to each cantonment and patrolled all roadways near the camps.[284]

Inside the camps, teams of local physicians innoculated every refugee against smallpox and typhoid; the doctors then isolated the vaccinated refugees from their unvaccinated counterparts. Physicians also ministered to a small number of refugees sent to isolation camps with infantile paralysis (polio), typhoid, malaria, or mumps, and supervised camp sanitation.[285] The physical toll upon the attending physicians was high, as doctors vaccinated 6,000 refugees in eight days while also attending to their regular medical duties. Two prominent local doctors, sapped by chronic exhaustion, were injured in auto accidents shortly after leaving the Opelousas camps. Around May 27, Dr. Octavus Pavy of Leonville, "after five days of steady work in [sic] behalf of refugee families," left Opelousas on an emergency call. He fell asleep at the wheel "for only a brief second or two. Suddenly he awakened, opened the door of the car and stepped out into the road. The car was still in motion. . . . The momentum of the moving machine threw him headlong to the road when he stepped off the running board. His collar bone was dislocated."[286]

Opelousas-area religious leaders also zealously ministered to the spiritual needs of the refugees. The *Opelousas Clarion-Progress* reported on June 3, 1927, that "the pastors of the various churches of this community have held regular services at the several campus, mass being said every morning at the camps by the Catholic priests located here, and at night or in the evening the pastors of several Protestant churches have held services at these camps."[287] Methodist minister Rev. D. B. Beadle of Opelousas, perhaps the most indefatigable of these clerics, conducted vesper services daily at sundown.[288]

Local lay people also did their part to comfort the refugees by addressing their material and emotional needs. Relief officials, for example, appointed a committee consisting of Aaron Jacobs, Dr. A. J. Boudreaux, and Allen Desauche to procure and distribute the tobacco products demanded by the refugees. The Red Cross also secured and maintained ample supplies of food and clothing for the flood victims.[289] Volunteers also distributed significant amounts of food and clothing donated by business and civic or religious groups in other Gulf Coast communities. David F. Hollier, grand knight of the Opelousas Knights of Columbus, for example, distributed to children in the camps candy donated by the Purity Candy Company of Beaumont, Texas.[290] Still other volunteers organized "many entertainments" for the refugees, including performances by the "brass band from the Catholic colored school" at both the white and black camps.[291] Photographs preserved by the Red Cross indicate that the Cajun refugees also organized many impromptu dances to entertain themselves.[292]

Care providers in Opelousas—like their counterparts at Lafayette, Carencro, and New Iberia—were compelled to satisfy the needs not of the refugees themselves, but also of the farm animals that accompanied them to high ground. By mid-June, the Red Cross was reportedly caring for 10,000 head of livestock, 2,975 head of work stock, 2,015 milk cows, and 5,388 hogs transported to St. Landry Parish by refugees. As elsewhere, these animals were tagged and—in the few instances when sufficient labor was available—vaccinated. After processing, the cattle, horses, and mules were widely dispersed among areas in Evangeline and St. Landry parishes where pasturage was available.[293] According to one eyewitness, some of these animals displayed the marked physical effects of prolonged exposure to floodwater.[294] The demands of maintaining tens of thousands of farm animals, however, paled in comparison to the difficulties of returning them to their owners at the end of the flood emergency.

Refugees at Opelousas—like their counterparts in other camps—anxiously awaited permission to return home. One journalist, covering the situation in the Opelousas cantonments, observed that "they are showing a determined spirit to get settled again, as soon as possible and to build up their homes and farms again following the damage caused by the high waters."[295] Health officials, however, attempted to prevent the departure of refugees returning to "places where the receding water will leave deposits that will aggravate and create disease germs of every kind."[296] Only when the camp physicians were convinced that the health risks had fallen to acceptable levels were flood victims authorized to leave.[297] Residents of the Prairie Laurent and Ross areas of St. Landry parish were among the first to return home, departing Opelousas sometime before June 4.[298]

The vacancies in the camps by their departure were filled by 13 white and 110 black families—constituting 473 individuals—transferred to Opelousas from the Crowley refugee camps.[299] An additional 1,100 refugees were transferred from Lafayette to Opelousas around June 24.[300] Most of these new arrivals, like most of their fellow refugees in the St. Landry cantonments, were residents of the Palmetto, Big Cane, and Arnaudville sections, who were forced by lingering high water to remain in Opelousas until mid-July. By July 21, however, the Opelousas cantonments were virtually empty, with only 100 refugees remaining at Camp Lamson; Camp Hamilton had already been vacated. Both Opelousas camp sites were closed and dismantled by July 28. The few refugees remaining in Opelousas were transferred to private residences.[301]

Closure of the Lafayette Camp

Refugees from the Lafayette camps joined their northern counterparts in the post-flood exodus. As in Opelousas, medical authorities attempted to discourage refugees to remain in camp until conditions improved in their home areas. Shortly before June 4, Dr. Marc M. Mouton, medical director of the Lafayette cantonments, warned "refugees not to ask to return home until they had opportunity to learn definitely the condition of their lands and homes, and particularly not to do so until they [had] been vaccinated against typhoid fever and smallpox."[302] Camp physicians, however, found it increasingly difficult to keep refugees in camp as reports of thefts at abandoned homes began to circulate among flood victims.[303]

Bowing to this pressure in late May and early June,[304] Capt. F. B. Putney, national Red Cross coordinator in Lafayette, permitted refugees to petition the local relief headquarters for permission to either inspect the flood damage at their homes or to care for their remaining livestock at Red Cross facilities. Citing healthcare concerns, Red Cross officials discouraged, but evenidently could not prevent, many inspection trips. By June 4, Putney had established a daily quota of refugee departures to the Breaux Bridge area, provided that the flood victims' homes were again habitable.[305] Noli Champagne and Alexandre Patin were the first refugees in Lafayette given authorization to return home permanently.[306] Departing St. Martin Parish refugees were replaced by refugees from other communities. Eighty flood victims who "had been at Youngsville" were transported to the Lafayette camps around June 11[307] and an undetermined number of refugees from Crowley who arrived in the Hub City shortly thereafter.[308]

St. Martin officials supported Putney's decision to permit only a few daily departures. Sheriff Wade O. Martin of St. Martin Parish, who had reestablished his headquarters in Lafayette during the flood emergency, established a committee consisting of St. Martin Parish physicians[309] to "inspect lands and homes owned by refugees making application to return and . . . to report . . . whether it is considered safe, especially from a health standpoint[,] for the applicants to return home."[310] As a consequence, the return of the Lafayette refugees to their homes proceeded much more slowly than in other Acadiana refugee centers. The last refugees departed the Hub City on August 25.[311]

Rehabilitation

While awaiting permission to depart, refugees often received advice and material assistance from the Lafayette and St. Martin "rehabilitation committees" established to monitor and coordinate repatriation of the refugees. Rehabilitation committees for Lafayette and St. Martin parishes were established on May 31. These committees—like comparable institutions in other area camps—surveyed conditions in the flooded areas of the two parishes reported to the Red Cross the projected needs of the refugees following their resettlement. The St. Martin Parish committee, for instance, urged the following expenditures: $75,000 for soy bean, rice, sweet potato, sorghum, cow pea, Irish potato, and winter truck crop seeds to feed the refugees through the winter, $225,000 for replacement of work stock; $25,000 for replacement of lost farm implements, $200,000 for short-term rations, $168,000 for livestock feed, and $100,000 in discretionary funds for the committee.[312] The Red Cross, of course, was able to fund only a portion of the requested assistance. St. Landry Parish, which sustained more extensive flood damage than St. Martin, received rehabilitation funds totalling $150,682.54, including

$37,940.79 for food; $9,571,54 for clothing; $414,656.17 for household furnishings; $42,914.93 for medical care; $42,100.88 for seed; and $3,921.68 for replacement of livestock and poultry.[313] Even at the reduced funding levels, however, Red Cross funds permitted thousands of Acadiana refugees to make a new start.

These reports were accompanied by requests for financial assistance from individuals. The Red Cross, for example, had received a total of 1,169 requests for aid from individual refugees by June 11; 1,021 had been approved, 109 were pending, and only 39 were rejected. Approximately $12,000 in farm credit was distributed among refugees in Lafayette Parish to permit them to resume agricultural operations.[314] Far more refugees received Red Cross assistance in the form of seeds, tools, and rations[315] necessary to clean the farm, survive the winter and begin farming operations the following spring.[316] The national Red Cross also provided workers to repair damaged buildings,[317] and committed itself to erect 600 pre-fabricated cabins to replace those lost in St. Martin Parish during the flood.[318]

Thanks to the Red Cross assistance, even the most destitute former refugees were able to eke out an existance until the next growing season. The most fortunate farmers— those whose farmlands drained most rapidly—were able to plant a small corn crop and a small amount of winter forage for their work animals.[319] These crops, however, were decimated by insect infestations that followed in the flood's wake. The *St. Martinville Weekly Messenger* of July 16, 1927, lamented that "the young corn and beans which have been planted since the high water is being eaten up by worms. The corn is so badly eaten that replanting will be necessary." Discouraged from replanting by county agents, the victims of the army worm invasion and farmers in low-lying areas whose lands had drained most slowly were obliged by the advanced season to concentrate on production of fall and winter vegetables.[320]

Aftermath

The restoration of farming operations, however, was merely the culmination of a long and arduous rehabilitative process that began with a dangerous trip home. Upon departing the camps, refugees had to locate livestock placed earlier under the care of the Red Cross;[321] the problems of locating farm animals was sometimes compounded by the initial dispersal of cows, horses, mules, and hogs among specialized foraging areas and the subsequent movement of these animals to centralized reclamation areas in St. Martin Parish after the flood waters receded.[322] Having accomplished this task, refugees soon discovered that many area highways were still under water.[323] In addition, most bridges below the prairie terrace had been destroyed by floodwater, and crossing swift-flowing, flood-swollen streams in small boats was both difficult and dangerous.[324] Upon arrival at their destination, many found that outbuildings (and farm implements) and fences had been entirely washed away.[325] Indeed, so many fences had been destroyed in St. Martin Parish that area residents seriously debated the merits of even attempting to plant crops.[326]

The Flood of 1927

Many homes had also been destroyed; surviving homes were filled with mud. Yards and fields were covered with debris[327] and, in some cases, mouldering carcasses of dead animals.[328] Wells were contaminated; and potable water was difficult, if not impossible, to find.[329] Many former refugees consequently contracted typhoid fever from unsanitary water shortly after returning home.[330]

The travails of the former refugees collectively constitute perhaps the most poignant chapter in the flood's largely undocumented denouement. In August 1927, as the last refugees were making their way home, an anonymous Associated Press writer penned perhaps the best account of the devastation confronted by the returning refugees in a nationally syndicated article paradoxically entitled "Evangeline's Country Is Now Back to Normal":

> . . . the land has suffered. The trees have not been hurt, and new foliage is springing up to cover the earth where a few weeks ago it was desolate mud, void of vegetation in the wake of the flood. But there are many farms, only recently out of the water, which are to the passing motorist merely fields of barron [sic] brown sod.
>
> Little farmhouses, bearing brown watermarks at various heights according to the depth the water reached, are once more occupied, and some of the farmers are plowing in preparation for new plantings. A few have new crops already growing, and cane and corn are making a brave attempt to put forth fruit despite the late start given them.
>
> But there are many houses still vacant. Some are no longer fit for habitation, and the former dwellers have gone elsewhere to start life again. In some parts of the country the current was strong, and in these sections cottages lean awry, warped and broken—the wrecks of once cozy homes. One such dwelling by the side of the road has a grimly humorous sign attached to its porch posts by an owner gone to other parts: 'For Sale!—Cheap!'

And yet the vast majority endured and ultimately flourished, displaying the same resilience as the floodprone land that had given them birth.

Notes for "The Human Dimension of the Flood of 1927"

[1] *New Orleans Times-Picayune*, May 15, 1927.

[2] Red Cross, *The Mississippi Valley Flood of 1927: Official Report of the Relief Operations* (Washington, D.C., 1929), 5-6.

[3] Ibid.

[4] Ibid., 5-7.

[5] Red Cross, *The Mississippi Valley Flood of 1927*, 1-10. See also Pete Daniel, *Deep'n As It Come: The 1927 Mississippi River Flood* (New York, 1977), 4-11.

[6] Acadiana is a twenty-two parish area of southern Louisiana consisting of Calcasieu, Cameron, Allen, Jefferson Davis, Evangeline, Acadia, Vermilion, St. Landry, Avoyelles, Pointe Coupée, West Baton Rouge, Iberville, St. Martin, Lafayette, Iberia, St. Mary, Terrebonne, Lafourche, Assumption, Ascension, St. James, St. John, St. Charles, and Jefferson parishes.

[7]*Morning Advocate*, May 28, 1927.

[8]*St. Martinville Weekly Messenger,* May 21, 1927.

[9]*Times-Picayune*, May 15, 1927.

[10]*St. Martinville Weekly Messenger*, May 21, 1927.

[11]*New Iberia Enterprise,* May 28, 1927.

[12]*Lafayette Advertiser*, May 9, 1927. Two hundred of the 1,000 levee workers in the Hamburg area were Mexican laborers "brought in by the railroad." *Baton Rouge Morning Advocate*, May 13, 1927.

[13]In one such episode, the St. Martinville fire siren sounded at 4:00 p.m. One hundred volunteers answered the call and were pressed into service at "a danger spot . . . at Cypremort on [the] protection levee." At 10:00 p.m., J. J. Burdin, Devince Bienvenu, and Charley Willis distributed sandwiches, chewing gum, and coffee among the workers. Using their own garden implements, the volunteers worked through the night, returning home around 5:00 a.m. *Weekly Messenger,* May 7, 1927.

[14]Ibid., May 7, 1927.

[15]Ibid.

[16]Present-day University of Southwestern Louisiana.

[17]*Daily Advertiser,* May 4,1 927.

[18]*Weekly Messenger,* May 14, 1927.

[19]*Daily Advertiser,* May 6, 13, 1927.

[20]Ibid., May 13, 1927.

[21]Waltoy Switch, Landry Switch, Broussard, Cade, Duchamp, St. Martinville, and Breaux Bridge. Ibid., May 13, 1927.

[22]Including Dr. Eugene E. Soulier, a leader of the St. Martin Red Cross chapter, and state Representative Pierre Landry. Ibid.

[23]Ibid.

[24]Ben Hur, Castille, Huval, Purity, Hinckley, and Sunrise bakeries of Lafayette donated the bread for sandwiches. Charles Billeaud of Broussard, Louisiana, contributed the meat, while John Reaux, also of Broussard, provided the coffee. Ibid.

[25]*Opelousas Clarion-Progress,* April 22, 1927.

[26]*Daily Advertiser,* May 9, 1927.

[27]Ibid., May 10, 1927.

[28]*Daily Advertiser,* May 17, 1927.

[29]Ibid.

[30]Ibid.

[31]Trains dispatched from places as far away as Crowley converged on the bridge later that day. Equipped with boats and rescue workers, these relief missions carried most of the flood victims—including those trapped in the attics or on the roofs of their homes—to safety. Ibid.

[32]*Morning Advocate*, May 18, 1927.

[33] Ibid.

[34] *Times-Picayune*, May 16, 1927.

[35] Ibid., June 7, 1927. In early June, after the evacuation of refugees from lower Louisiana had been completed, these twenty-six-foot-long vessels were sailed to Plaquemine, Louisiana, from whence they were towed to New Orleans. In New Orleans, the boats were placed on trains and transported to their East Coast bases. Ibid.

[36] *Morning Advocate*, May 14, 1927.

[37] *Times-Picayune*, May 14, 1927.

[38] Ibid.

[39] Ibid.

[40] Ibid.

[41] *Morning Advocate*, May 15, 1927.

[42] Ibid.

[43] Ibid.

[44] *Times-Picayune*, May 20, 1927.

[45] Ibid.

[46] Ibid., May 16, 1927.

[47] Ibid., May 20, 1927.

[48] Daniel, *Deep'n as It Come*, 75; Lyle Saxon, *Father Mississippi* (New York, 1927), 361; Red Cross, *The Mississippi Valley Flood of 1927*, 6-7.

[49] *Times-Picayune*, May 20, 1927.

[50] Ibid., May 30, 1927.

[51] Ibid., May 20, 1927.

[52] The *Morning Advocate* reported on May 18, 1927, that 400 cattle and "several hundreds of mules, horses, hogs and poultry" were believed to have been drowned shortly after the Melville levee break.

[53] *Weekly Messenger*, April 30, 1927.

[54] For a vivid description of the roaring sound generated by the surging waters, see Henry Blanc's account in "Refugee Camp Shows Comic, Tragic Sides," *Morning Advocate*, May 18, 1927. One area resident recalled that the water struck the area with such force that it literally washed away the local railroad bed. Interview with Mrs. Mary Stelly, Opelousas, March 10, 1994.

[55] According to one eyewitness, Lebeau-area farmers loaded chicken coups and hogs onto the barges. Interview with Eli Stelly, Opelousas, March 10, 1994.

[56] Ibid. According to Eli Stelly, who untilized one of these barges, they were equipped with small, three-horsepower outboard engines. Ibid.

[57] Statistics from the Louisiana State Board of Health, published in the *Weekly Messenger*, July 9, 1927.

[58] *Daily Advertiser*, May 21, 1927.

[59]Ibid., May 19, 1927.

[60]The telegram read: "The water has risen 4 feet since one o'clock. For God's sake do something." *Clarion-Progress,* May 20, 1927.

[61]Ibid.

[62]*Daily Advertiser,* May 20, 1927.

[63]Ibid., May 21, 1927.

[64]Ibid., May 19, 1927.

[65]Ibid.

[66]Ibid., May 20, 1927.

[67]*Weekly Messenger,* May 21, 1927.

[68]Lieut. Chaplin, then principal at Breaux Bridge High School, would be appointed principal of Lafayette High School shortly after the end of the flood emergency.

[69]A 200-foot-wide crevasse near Huval Landing, a break "on Lake Doremus about four miles above the break near Cecelia," and at Huron Plantation. *Weekly Messenger,* May 21, 1927.

[70]Ibid.

[71]*Enterprise,* May 28, 1927.

[72]Ibid.

[73]Ibid.

[74]*Morning Advocate*, May 22, 1927.

[75]*Times-Picayune*, May 27, 29, 1927.

[76]According to the *New Iberia Enterprise,* only those buildings along the bayou were damaged by floodwaters at Jeanerette. Ibid., June 4, 1927.

[77]Ibid.; *Morning Advocate,* May 28, 1927.

[78]*Enterprise*, June 4, 1927.

[79]*Times-Picayune*, May 29, 1927.

[80]Ibid., May 28, 1927.

[81]Griffin, *Attakapas Country,* 162.

[82]*Daily Advertiser,* May 24, 1927.

[83]*Weekly Messenger*, June 11, 1927.

[84]*Daily Advertisser,* May 16, 1927.

[85]Ibid., May 25, 1927.

[86]*Enterprise,* May 28, 1927.

[87]Griffin, *Attakapas Country,* 163.

[88] *Daily Advertiser,* May 25, 1927.

[89] *Enterprise,* May 28, 1927.

[90] *Weekly Messenger,* June 4, 1927.

[91] Ibid., June 11, 1927.

[92] Ibid.; *Daily Advertiser,* May 28, 1927; *Enterprise,* May 28, 1927.

[93] *Times-Picayune,* May 27, 1927.

[94] *Weekly Messenger,* May 21, 1927.

[95] Ibid., May 28, 1927.

[96] Ibid., June 18, 1927.

[97] Interview with Eli Stelly, March 10, 1994.

[98] *Daily Advertiser,* May 25, 1927.

[99] Ibid., June 11, 1927.

[100] *Morning Advocate,* May 14, 1927.

[101] Ibid.

[102] Ibid.

[103] *Times-Picayune,* May 16, 1927.

[104] *Morning Advocate,* May 14, 1927.

[105] Interview with Lucien Laborde, Hamburg, Louisiana, April 6, 1994.

[106] Ibid.

[107] *Morning Advocate,* May 20, 1927.

[108] *Times-Picayune,* May 25, 1927.

[109] Ibid., May 16, 1927.

[110] *Morning Advocate,* May 15, 1927.

[111] Red Cross, *The Mississippi Valley Flood of 1927,* 129.

[112] *Times-Picayune,* May 15, 1927.

[113] *Morning Advocate,* May 18, 1927.

[114] Ibid.

[115] Ibid.

[116] Quoted in Daniel, *Deep'n as It Come,* 118.

[117] Ibid.

[118] Ibid.

[119] *Morning Advocate*, May 20, 1927.

[120] Denial, *Deep'n as It Come*, 118.

[121] Griffin, *Attakapas Country*, 159.

[122] The Lafayette unit.

[123] Ibid., May 5, 1927.

[124] This term was universally applied to the refugee camps by contemporary observers.

[125] *Weekly Messenger*, May 7, 1927.

[126] *Daily Advertiser*, May 15, 1927.

[127] Ibid.

[128] Ibid., May 21, 1927.

[129] Ibid., May 15, 1927.

[130] Ibid.

[131] Ibid.

[132] Red Cross, *The Mississippi Valley Flood of 1927*, 41.

[133] *Daily Advertiser*, May 21, 1927.

[134] Adjacent to the Hopkins Drug Store. *Daily Advertiser*, May 15, 1927. This facility opened daily at 3:00 p.m. "to gather and arrange clothing for flood victims." Ibid., May 7, 1927.

[135] Ibid., May 15, 1927.

[136] Griffin, *Attakapas Country*, 163.

[137] The Red Cross provided $245,000 in late May and early June to underwrite the cost of operating the Production Unit. Ibid., 164.

[138] *Daily Advertiser*, May 19, 1927.

[139] Ibid., May 15, 18, 1927.

[140] Acquired by the Lafayette Parish Fair Association in late summer 1910; *Daily Advertiser*, August 16, 1910; September 6, 30, 1910.

[141] Ibid., May 18, 1927.

[142] Ibid., May 26, 1927.

[143] Interview with Eli Stelly, March 10, 1994.

[144] These refugees were under the care of Father Grace, of Grand Coteau, and Dr. Ben Guilbeau of Carencro. Ibid., June 11, 1927.

[145] Ibid., May 21, 1927. The following analysis of the refugees arriving between 10:00 a.m., May 19, and 10:00 a.m., May 21 appeared in ibid.: 3,104 whites from 629 families; and 1,906 blacks from 395 families.

[146] Ibid., May 24, 1927.

[147] Ibid., May 25, 1927.

The Flood of 1927

[148] Ibid., May 31, 1927.

[149] American National Red Cross, *The Mississippi Valley Flood Disaster of 1927: Official Report of the Relief Operations* (Washington, D. C., 1929), 129.

[150] *Morning Advocate*, May 22, 1927.

[151] Volunteers answering the call were asked to report to "the colored public school at the end of East Vermilion Street, or at the Red Cross relief headquarters in the old Heymann building." *Daily Advertiser*, May 19, 1927.

[152] Interview with Rebecca Batiste, Lafayette, Louisiana, November 20, 1993.

[153] Griffin, *Attakapas Country*, 159.

[154] *Daily Advertiser*, May 18, 1927.

[155] *Daily Advertiser*, May 21, 1927.

[156] Ibid.

[157] Interview with John Stephan, Lafayette, Louisiana, May 9, 1994.

[158] Griffin, *Attakapas Country*, 162.

[159] Ibid., 159.

[160] *Daily Advertiser*, May 21, 1927.

[161] Ibid.

[162] Ibid., May 25, 1927.

[163] Griffin, *Attakapas Country*, p. 159.

[164] Ibid.

[165] Ibid., May 19, 1927.

[166] Ibid., May 18, 1927.

[167] *Daily Advertiser*, May 27, 1927.

[168] *Weekly Messenger*, July 2, 1927.

[169] Ibid.

[170] Interview with John Stephan, Lafayette, Louisiana, December 17, 1993.

[171] See Griffin, *Attakapas Country*, 161-62.

[172] *Daily Advertiser*, May 26, 1927.

[173] This committee included R. H. Bolyard, H. E. Robinson, and Frank J. Kennedy. Griffin, *Attakapas Country*, 164.

[174] *Daily Advertiser*, May 21, 1927. W. E. Robinson of the Tulane University organization and one Hoppen of the Bogalusa organization were among the Y.M.C.A. representatives.

[175] *Daily Advertiser*, May 25, 1927.

[176] The stage and musical performers included Mrs. Eloi Girard, Mrs. Robert S. Barnett, Mrs. P. R. Dupleix, Mary Louise Dugas, Ida Katherine Hopkins, Pansy Glover, Rosabelle Whitfield, Spencer Barnett, Lloyd Whitfield, Leslie Norton, Hugh Billeaud, C. J. McNaspy, Jr., and Henry Voorhies, Jr. Griffin, *Attakapas Country*, 164.

[177] *Daily Advertiser*, May 25, 1927.

[178] Griffin, *Attakapas Country*, 164.

[179] R. R. Taylor, Bishop R. E. Jones, A. L. Holsey, Claude A. Barnett, and Jesse O. Thomas were among the committee members present in Lafayette. Ibid.; Daniel, *Deep'n As It Come*, 109-11.

[180] *Daily Advertiser*, June 6, 1927.

[181] Daniel, *Deepn' As It Come*, 109-11.

[182] Red Cross, *The Mississippi Valley Flood of 1927*, 40.

[183] Ibid., 40-41.

[184] See below the discussion of flooding in the campsites.

[185] Ibid., May 21, 24, 1927; Griffin, *Attakapas Country*, 158. The May 19, 1927, issue of the *Daily Advertiser* reported that Dr. Mouton was assisted by a "large corps of physicians and nurses on duty."

[186] *Daily Advertiser*, May 21, 1927. Longtime educator Paul Breaux was principal of this facility.

[187] Ibid., May 18, 1927.

[188] Ibid., May 21, 1927. The staff of St. John's Hospital helped to operate the maternity facility.

[189] Griffin, *Attakapas Country*, 158.

[190] Ibid., May 19, 1927.

[191] Ibid., May 19, 21, 1927.

[192] Ibid., May 18, 1927.

[193] Griffin, *Attakapas Country*, 158.

[194] *Daily Advertiser*, May 26, 1927. Part of the company was demobilized in late May.

[195] *Daily Advertiser*, May 24, 1927.

[196] Ibid., May 18, 1927.

[197] Ibid., May 21, 1927.

[198] Ibid., May 18, June 8, 1927.

[199] Ibid., June 8, 1927.

[200] Daniel, *Deep'n as It Come*, 120. This information has been independently verified with two Lafayette residents who were young men at the time of the flood.

[201] Ibid.

[202] Quoted in ibid., 119-20.

[203] Ibid.

The Flood of 1927

[204] Ibid., 119.

[205] Ibid.

[206] Ibid., 120.

[207] See, for example, ibid., 116-19.

[208] Ibid., May 20, 1927. Hoover called for the assignment of additional National Guard troops to Lafayette as well as the shipment of emergency supplies to the camps.

[209] Ibid., May 19, 1927.

[210] Ibid., June 3, 1927.

[211] Ibid., May 19, 1927.

[212] Griffin, *Attakapas Country*, 162.

[213] *Daily Advertiser*, May 19, 1927.

[214] Ibid., May 26, 1927.

[215] Ibid., May 25, 1927.

[216] Ibid., May 26, 1927.

[217] Rayne and Broussard were also surrounded by water. Ibid., May 24, 27, 1927.

[218] D. L. McPherson to E. A. McIlhenny, May 25, 1927, E. A. McIlhenny Papers, McIlhenny Company Archives, Avery Island, Louisiana; hereafter cited as McIlhenny Papers.

[219] *Enterprise*, May 28, 1927.

[220] Ibid.

[221] Ibid.

[222] Ibid.

[223] *Daily Advertiser*, May 26, 1927.

[224] Red Cross, *The Mississippi Valley Flood of 1927*, 129.

[225] E. A. McIlhenny to J. S. Clark, May 28, 1927, McIlhenny Papers; E. A. McIlhenny to Ernest B. Tracy, May 30, 1927, Ibid.

[226] *Enterprise*, May 28, 1927.

[227] Lieut.-Col. E. P. Roy, "commanding National Guardsmen" at New Iberia. *Times-Picayune*, May 27, 29, 1927.

[228] At the time of the 1927 flood, this property was also known as the "Doremus farm." *Enterprise*, June 11, 1927.

[229] John McGlade.

[230] Ibid.

[231] Red Cross, *The Mississippi Valley Flood of 1927*, 129.

[232] Mrs. John R. Taylor and Mrs. D. D. Avery administered the clothing warehouse. *Enterprise*, July 23, 1927.

[233] Ibid.

[234] National guardsmen in New Iberia were authorized to shoot looters on sight. *Times-Picayune*, May 29, 1927.

[235] See Maurine Bergerie, *They Tasted Bayou Water: A Brief History of Iberia Parish* (New Orleans, 1962), 39.

[236] *Enterprise,* June 11, 1927.

[237] Ibid.

[238] *Enterprise,* July 2, 1927.

[239] Ibid., July 23, 1927.

[240] *Times-Picayune*, May 28, 1927.

[241] Ibid., May 30, 1927.

[242] Ibid., May 31, 1927.

[243] Ibid., May 29, 1927.

[244] Ibid.

[245] Ibid., May 30-31, 1927.

[246] Red Cross, *The Mississippi Valley Flood of 1927,* 129.

[247] *Times-Picayune*, May 30, 1927.

[248] Ibid., May 31, 1927.

[249] *Clarion-Progress*, May 6, 1927.

[250] Ibid., May 13, 1927.

[251] Ibid.

[252] Ibid.

[253] Ibid., June 17, 1927.

[254] The location of the black refugee camp has not been recorded.

[255] *Morning Advocate*, May 28, 1927.

[256] *Clarion-Progress,* May 20, 1927.

[257] *Times-Picayune*, May 20, 1927.

[258] *Morning Advocate*, May 28 ,1927.

[259] Ibid., May 20, 1927.

[260] *Clarion-Progress*, May 20, 1927.

[261] Red Cross, *The Mississippi Valley Flood of 1927,* 129.

[262] *Times-Picayune*, May 20, 1927.

The Flood of 1927

[263] Ibid., May 27, 1927.

[264] *Daily Advertiser,* May 28, 1927.

[265] *Clarion-Progress,* June 24, 1927.

[266] Red Cross, *The Mississippi Valley Flood of 1927,* 129.

[267] *Clarion-Progress,* June 17, 1927.

[268] Ibid., May 27, 1927..

[269] Ibid.

[270] Camp Hamiltion was located near the present intersection of Interstate 49 and Highway 190. Interview with Keith P. Fontenot, Opelousas, February 9, 1994.

[271] Ibid., June 3, 1927.

[272] *Morning Advocate*, May 28, 1927.

[273] Ibid.

[274] *Clarion-Progress*, May 27, 1927.

[275] Ibid.; *Daily Advertiser,* May 28, 1927.

[276] *Clarion-Progress*, May 27, 1927; June 3, 1927.

[277] Ibid., May 27, 1927.

[278] *Morning Advocate*, May 28, 1927.

[279] Ibid., May 12, 1927.

[280] Ibid., May 28, 1927.

[281] *Clarion-Progress*, May 20, 1927.

[282] Ibid.

[283] These troops were quartered in tents "on the Elementary School campus." Ibid., June 3, 1927.

[284] Ibid., May 20, 1927.

[285] Ibid.

[286] Ibid., May 27, 1927.

[287] Ibid., June 3, 1927.

[288] Ibid., May 20, 1927.

[289] Ibid., May 27, 1927. There was a temporary shortage of clothing around May 27, after two boxcar loads of clothing had been distributed among the refugees. The donation of ten boxes of "good clothing" by the Lake Charles branches of the Knights of Columbus and Catholic Daughters of America, however, helped meet the demand for apparel in the camps until additional clothing could be procured by the national Red Cross. Ibid.

[290] Ibid.

[291] Ibid., June 3, 1927.

[292] Daniel, *Deep'n as It Come*, 117.

[293] Ibid., June 17, 1927.

[294] According to Keith P. Fontenot, whose father saw the cattle transported to the Petit Anse settlement of Evangeline Parish, the hide on the lower legs of many animals from flooded sections had literally fallen off. Fontenot interview, February 9, 1994.

[295] *Daily Advertiser*, June 4, 1927.

[296] *Clarion-Progress*, June 3, 1927.

[297] Ibid.

[298] *Daily Advertiser*, June 4, 1927.

[299] *Clarion-Progress*, June 17, 1927.

[300] Ibid., June 24, 1927.

[301] *Opelousas News*, July 21, 2927.

[302] *Daily Advertiser*, June 4, 1927.

[303] Ibid., June 10, 1927.

[304] Ibid., May 30, 1927.

[305] Ibid., June 4, 1927.

[306] Ibid., May 30, 1927.

[307] Ibid., June 11, 1927.

[308] Ibid., June 25, 1927.

[309] Drs. G. W. Martin, M. Boudreaux, T. J. Labbé, and P. H. Fleming. Ibid., May 30, 1927.

[310] Ibid.

[311] Griffin, *Attakapas Country*, 166.

[312] Ibid., 165. See also *Weekly Messenger*, June 11, 1927.

[313] *Weekly Messenger*, August 27, 1927.

[314] *Daily Advertiser*, June 6, 1927.

[315] *Weekly Messenger*, June 4, 1927.

[316] Red Cross, *The Mississippi Valley Flood of 1917*, 48.

[317] Ibid., August 20, 1927.

[318] *Daily Advertiser*, June 4, 1927; *Weekly Messenger*, June 11, 1927; *Clarion-Progress*, June 17, 1927.

[319] Interview with Eli Stelly, March 10, 1994.

[320] *Enterprise*, August 13, 1927; Weekly Messenger, July 16, 1927.

[321] Red Cross, *The Mississippi Valley Flood of 1927*, 44.

The Flood of 1927

[322] *Daily Advertiser,* June 11, 1927; *Weekly Messenger,* June 11, 1927; July 30, 1927; August 13, 1927.

[323] *Weekly Messenger,* June 11, 1927; July 9, 1927, August 6, 1927.

[324] Ibid., June 11, 18, 1927; *Enterprise,* June 18, 1927.

[325] *Weekly Messenger*, July 23, 1927; August 20, 1927.

[326] Ibid., August 6, 13, 1927.

[327] Ibid., June 11, 1927.

[328] Ibid., June 25, 1927.

[329] Ibid., June 4, 1927.

[330] Interview with Eli Stelly, March 10, 1994.

CULTURAL CONFLICT AND THE 1928 PRESIDENTIAL CAMPAIGN IN LOUISIANA*

Steven D. Zink

The emotional issues raised by the 1928 presidential campaign stimulated basic political-cultural divisions with the Louisiana electorate. During the 1920s rural-urban tensions, 100 percent Americanism and prohibition were frequent salient issues in state elections; Louisiana's prominent Protestant-Catholic diversity was of subliminal importance. Emerging as a critical factor in 1928, the religion issue joined with contingent cultural issues, Louisiana political tradition, and the tragic example offered by the national campaign to shape the outcome of the presidential election in the state.[1]

A contender for the nomination in 1924, Gov. Alfred E. Smith of New York easily captured the 1928 Democratic nomination at Houston on 28 June.[2] Smith was well known and as well qualified as any candidate the Democrats could have run. Yet Smith had great liabilities for the party as the head of the ticket. The Democratic Party was still the only truly intersectional party in the nation, and as such its ranks were much more diverse than those of its Republican counterpart. Basically, the party's two chief components were the fundamentalist Protestant, Anglo-Saxon, white South and the urban, industrial East with its concentration of first and second generation Americans. Never had a candidate so completely epitomized all of one component of the party and none of the other. Al Smith was a native of New York City, a member of a poor, Irish-Catholic immigrant family, and had entered politics via Tammany Hall. To many voters his background was a composite of the problems plaguing America, and throughout the campaign he served as a focus for the xenophobic, Protestant-Catholic, rural-urban rivalries and tensions so manifest in the 1920s. The Democrats sought to balance the nomination of Smith by choosing as his running-mate Joseph T. Robinson. The antithesis of Smith, Robinson was a Protestant senator from rural Arkansas who loathed the consumption of alcohol, a position that Smith could not complement. The effort to balance the ticket proved futile.

*First published in *Southern Studies*, 17 (1978): 175-97. Reprinted with the kind permission of the author.

Earlier in June, in Kansas City, the Republicans had nominated Secretary of Commerce Herbert Hoover. Born of Quaker parents in a rural Iowa town, Hoover, in the words of historian John Hicks, ". . . possessed most of the qualifications for the Presidency that tradition-bound Americans had come to expect."[3] Through ability and hard work, Hoover had risen from a humble background to become, by 1914, a successful engineer and world businessman. During World War I President Woodrow Wilson first appointed him to direct the Committee for the Relief of Belgium and later to head the domestic Food Administration. Hoover's enlightened management of these programs still dominated the public's image of him in 1928 despite his active eight years as Secretary of Commerce under Presidents Harding and Coolidge. The only noticeable objections to Hoover's nomination came from certain farming interests, but the naming of Senator Charles Curtis of Kansas, a former member of the farm bloc, as Hoover's running mate quashed most demurrers. General prosperity and the power of the incumbency gave the Republicans unity and confidence as they entered the campaign.

With the aid of hindsight, historians quibble little over the unlikeliness of a Smith victory.[4] What they do disagree over is what occurred between the nominating conventions in June and the election in November to make the 1928 election one of the most controversial in American political annals. An anti-Smith movement within the Democratic party gained strength throughout July and August, all the while receiving the added encouragement and enthusiasm of the Republicans. By the time both campaigns were in high gear in September, a discussion of the two parties' similar platforms had given way to the only glaring differences in the campaign: the candidates' personal backgrounds and characteristics.

For the most part what historians have written about the campaign of 1928 has been intended to apply to the nation at large. There has never been a full-length regional study of the South in the election, but historians generally have alleged that the nomination of the "wet" and Catholic Al Smith by the Democratic party alienated the fundamentalist Protestant, white, Democratic South for the first time since the days of Reconstruction. Indeed, the "solid South" was broken. The Republicans captured the border states and won enough votes in the Deep South to force a significant decline in the Democratic totals.[5] In his seminal study of Southern politics, V. O. Key explained that the Southern bolt to Hoover revealed the "fundamental basis" of Southern solidarity. Key found an inverse relationship between a state's Hoover vote and the percentage of its population of African descent: all the Southern states that Hoover carried had a relatively small black population. Key further inspected the voting patterns on the county level and found that, "Within each state the counties with high percentages of Negro population generally cast Democratic majorities. . . ."[6] He explained this fact by noting that "The whites of the blackbelt counties were bound in loyalty to the Democracy by a common tradition and anxiety about the Negro. Whites elsewhere could afford the luxury of voting their convictions on the religious and prohibition issues."[7] Subsequent studies have incorporated Key's findings.[8]

Despite the interest which historians have shown in the 1928 election, no one has extensively analyzed the presidential contest in Louisiana.[9] Perhaps the election has been historically obscured by Huey Long's winning the governorship in the same year. Or perhaps the election has been ignored because it did not square with historians' view of Louisiana in the late twenties as a hotbed of class consciousness that somehow spawned the hero of the downtrodden. Whatever the reasons for its neglect, the election in Louisiana demonstrates in abundance all the factors that historians have found determining the outcome of the contest: Louisiana contained a wide variety of economic areas, it was the home of one of the most active chapters of the Ku Klux Klan, it had a large Negro population, and it was culturally diverse.

Louisiana in 1928 could be roughly divided into three cultural sections. The northern section of the state comprised a largely rural, Anglo-Saxon Protestant population, many of whom had emigrated from other Southern states. For the most part, that section fervently supported the hottest cultural issue of the decade, prohibition. The second section, located in the southern portion of the state, consisted chiefly of settlers of French stock. They were predominantly Catholic in faith and were less disposed to favor the total abstinence demanded by their northern neighbors. The third section of the state, distinguished by its uniqueness, was New Orleans, which was the only truly urban area in Louisiana. As such it felt the antipathy of much of the rest of the state, not only for its lurid national reputation, but also for its influence in state political affairs, its boss-controlled municipal government, and its relatively high immigrant population.[10]

The single most striking aspect of the electoral totals for Louisiana in 1928 was the predominance of the traditional Democratic vote. Louisiana gave the Democratic ticket 76.3 percent of the votes cast in the state, the third highest percentage in the nation behind only South Carolina and Mississippi.[11] No doubt many of those Democratic votes were cast out of habit or tradition. In some sections of the state Democratic predominance was so great that a pre-election Republican newspaper advertisement, in all seriousness, noted that it was not illegal to vote Republican.[12] Democratic newspapers countered that one should continue ". . . being a Democrat because you live in the South."[13] Often no other reason seemed necessary to newspaper editors, or indeed to the electorate. If not stated, the implicit vested interest in a voter's allegiance to the Democracy rested upon the legacy of Reconstruction or race hatred. During the campaign of 1928 the alleged horrors of the aftermath of the Civil War were frequently revived in newspaper editorials. Many newspapers recalled the ruthlessness of Republican rule.[14] One editorial, not at all uncommon, lamented:

> It is hard for us to conclude that any such thing [as voting Republican], is true of Southerners whose fathers and grandfathers were baptized in blood in the campaigns of the Civil War and in fire and persecution at the vile hands of Republican scalawags,

carpetbaggers, thieves and plunderers for fifteen years after the War in the dark Reconstruction period.[15]

It was impossible for editors to recount the "horrors" of post-Civil War Louisiana without reminding the readers that blacks often played a prominent role in Reconstruction. Newspapers published the names of Reconstruction Negro officeholders, and the *Shreveport Times* even printed a photograph of the predominantly Negro 1868 Louisiana legislature.[16] The Democratic party was revered as the savior in the crusade against the misrule of Reconstruction. Voters were asked not to forget that fact. Lest they did, most local newspapers provided enough material to remind them. At some point in the campaign almost every pro-Smith newspaper sought to activate the race-Republican fears of the electorate.[17] Some unabashedly used the tactic from the outset. Others resorted to the practice only after it appeared that Smith might lose the Deep South, and they did so almost apologetically.[18]

Both Smith and Hoover supporters sought to gain votes by race-baiting. Hoover supporters ran newspaper advertisements which stressed that racial segregation had broken down in New York and that even racial intermarriage was not uncommon. A photograph of a black New York officeholder dictating a letter to a young white secretary garnished the advertisement.[19] Other advertisements maintained that Smith would receive the black vote in the North.[20] Smith supporters made the more orthodox race-baiting appeal. They noted that Hoover, as secretary of commerce, had issued an order desegregating his department.[21] This one order was repeatedly mentioned, but other, less subtle, charges were also made. The editor of the *Farmerville Gazette* related a "rumor" to his readers that Hoover planned to appoint two Southerners to his cabinet, Ben Davis of Georgia and Perry Howard of Mississippi, both of whom were black.[22] Hoover, himself, later recalled that in the South various innuendoes were spread about his relationship to black women during his Mississippi Valley flood work of the previous year.[23]

As prominent as race-baiting was in the campaign, it appeared less often and in a less virulent form in Louisiana than it did in other Southern states.[24] While one could scarcely say, as one historian has, that "The Louisiana Negro, unlike the Negro of other southern states, was not used as a political issue,"[25] there is a certain validity in the statement. Perhaps this was so because the Negro held such a subservient status in the state that he was perceived to pose no threat; more likely other issues undercut the usefulness of the practice.

Contrary to V. O. Key's findings, the whites of the predominantly black parishes did not remain the "most steadfast in their loyalty to the Democratic Party. . . ."[26] Of the sixteen parishes with a majority of their population black, twelve showed a decrease from their Democratic vote of 1924 by an average of 11.3 percent.[27] Of the remaining four parishes, three increased their Democratic vote by an average of 16.6 percent over their 1924 totals.[28] The most striking aspect of this variance of support for Smith among "black" parishes was not the percentage of blacks, as Key maintained, but the religious composition. All but one of the twelve "black" parishes which registered a decline in their Democratic percentage were overwhelmingly populated by Protestants (averaged 92.6 percent).[29] The other parish which showed only a small decrease, was nearly evenly split in religious composition between Catholics and Protestants.[30] The three parishes which dramatically increased their Democratic percentage over 1924 were all over 50 percent Catholic in population.[31]

If the Key thesis that the whites of the "black" parishes remained "most steadfast" to the Democracy has been shown false, what might be said about the second half of his argument, namely, that the heaviest Democratic losses occurred in predominantly white parishes, because these voters (free from immediate race fear) "could afford the luxury of voting their convictions on the religious and prohibition issues."?[32] Key's argument here is right, but only in a diametrical sense. He clearly meant that these voters were free to vote for Hoover, a Republican, and against Smith, a Democrat, a Catholic, and a "wet". Quite the opposite occurred. Of the twenty-one parishes with 70 percent or more of their population white, twelve registered an average decline of nearly 11 percent from their Democratic vote of 1924.[33] Nine of these twelve parishes, however, boasted an average Protestant population of 79.7 percent.[34] Another nine of the twenty-one "white" parishes increased their average Democratic percentage 13.7 percent.[35] Out of these nine, eight parishes were comprised of an average Catholic population of 85.4 percent.[36] At least in Louisiana, Key's thesis regarding the role of race-baiting in the 1928 election appears to have been supplanted by a Protestant-Catholic division unique to Louisiana among the states of the South.

The Catholic-Protestant voting cleavage apparent in the "black" parishes of the state demonstrates the necessity to consider the possibility that such a division existed statewide. An analysis of the electoral behavior of the fifty parishes whose populations were either at least 75 percent Protestant or 75 percent Catholic netted significant results (see table at end of article).

In 1924 the Democratic party ran John W. Davis for the presidency. A former member of Congress from West Virginia and solicitor-general under Woodrow Wilson, Davis was a Protestant of Anglo-Saxon descent. Louisiana gave the Democratic ticket 76.4 percent of all votes cast. In 1928 Louisiana gave Al Smith only .1 percent less than it had given Davis in 1924.[37] On the surface it appears that the Democratic vote was relatively constant and its voting groups stable. This, however, was not the case. Individual parish voting changed dramatically. For example, predominantly Catholic Assumption Parish gave Davis only 33.7 percent of its vote in 1924. In 1928 the voters gave Smith 75.5 percent of all votes cast. The shift also operated in an inverse manner. In predominantly Protestant Madison Parish, voters in 1924 cast 95.5 percent of all votes cast for John Davis. In 1928 the same parish cast only 67.8 percent of its vote for Al Smith (see table). Granted these are extreme examples, but they indicate the change in Democratic allegiance that took place in the two elections. This change is most clearly observable along Protestant-Catholic lines. In the twenty parishes in the state with 75 percent or more of their inhabitants Catholic, Al Smith registered an 18.1 percent gain over the average 1924 Democratic vote for Davis. In the thirty parishes in the state with 75 percent or more of their inhabitants Protestant, Al Smith suffered an 11.5 percent decrease from the average Democratic vote for Davis in 1924 (see table).

Clearly the 1928 presidential election appears to have divided the Catholic and Protestant vote in Louisiana. This phenomenon was not an aberration, but merely a projection into a national election of recent state electoral behavior. Catholic-Protestant tensions had existed throughout Louisiana's history, but the decade of the twenties had presented an unusually high number of public forums for confrontation. Bitter encounters over such issues as prohibition, state funding of parochial schools, and the flowering of such exclusive organizations as the Knights of Columbus and the Ku Klux Klan combined with mutual long-term Protestant-Catholic suspicions to influence the outcome of at least three statewide political contests.

In 1924 United States Senator Joseph E. Ransdell of Louisiana ran for reelection. Ransdell was a Catholic from East Carroll Parish in northern Louisiana. His opponent was Lee E. Thomas, the Protestant mayor of Shreveport. Then at the peak of its power, the Ku Klux Klan opposed Ransdell and actively campaigned against him. The backing of the Choctaw Club in New Orleans, however, more than offset the opposition of the Klan. The Club and its members, the "Old Regulars," under the leadership of Mayor Martin Behrman had dominated the politics of the city for almost a quarter of a century before 1920. Over the years the machine had also come to influence, with varying degrees of strength, many aspects of state government and politics. Despite its defeat in 1920, the Club was still a political power with which to be reckoned.[38] Ransdell won the election with 54.9 percent of the vote. The election reflected a marked cleavage in voting along Protestant-Catholic lines. The thirty parishes in the state with 75 percent or more of their population Protestant gave an average of only 36.6 percent of their vote to the Catholic candidate. Only two of the "Protestant" parishes gave Ransdell support above the state average. One was his home parish, the other was Tensas Parish, just downstream. On the other hand, the twenty parishes in the state with populations of over 75 percent Catholic all voted for Ransdell at an average vote of 73.5 percent (see table).

The other senatorial contest two years later resulted in another marked split along religious lines. The prohibition issue undoubtedly exacerbated the cleavage as it played a significant part in this election.[39] The election pitted the Catholic, "wet" United States Senator Edwin Broussard from southwest Louisiana against the Protestant ex-Governor J. Y. Sanders from the Florida parishes. Sanders received the backing of the "Old Regular" machine in New Orleans which was once again in power, but this failed to prevent his defeat. Broussard won the election with 51.1 percent of the statewide vote. Despite Huey Long's feverish campaigning for Broussard in the northern parishes, only two of the thirty parishes in the state over 75 percent Protestant voted for Broussard.[40] To Long's credit, both were in the extreme northern section of the state. The average vote for Broussard in the predominantly Protestant parishes was only 37.8 percent. On the other hand,

Broussard did quite well in the twenty parishes with 75 percent or more of their population Catholic. Sixteen of these parishes gave an average vote to Broussard of 66.9 percent. The remaining four parishes gave Broussard significantly less support (see table). All were in close proximity to New Orleans and may have been under the political influence of the "Old Regular" machine. As divisive as the senatorial campaigns of the mid-twenties were, the gubernatorial race of 1924 far surpassed both in intensity.

The 1924 gubernatorial race was a complex affair. It revolved chiefly around the Klan issue, which only served further to delineate Protestant-Catholic voting. The primary found three candidates vying for the Democratic nomination: (1) Hewitt Bouanchaud, a French Catholic from Pointe Coupee Parish who was serving as lieutenant governor under Gov. John Parker; (2) Henry Fuqua, a Protestant Baton Rouge businessman who was serving as general manager of the state penitentiary in the Parker administration; and (3) Public Service Commissioner Huey P. Long, a Protestant from Winn Parish in northern Louisiana. No candidate received a majority in the election. Long received the lowest vote of the three, his name was dropped, and a run-off election was held. After the hotly contested first election in which Bouanchaud had whipped up Catholic enthusiasm against the Klan, the vote in the run-off followed fairly strict religious lines. Fuqua won the run-off with 59 percent of the vote. Bouanchaud received only 41 percent. Eighteen of the twenty parishes in the state with 75 percent or more of their population Catholic voted an average of 69.1 percent for Bouanchaud. Of the two Catholic parishes which failed to give Bouanchaud a majority one, Jefferson Parish, gave him 47.5 percent of its vote, a full 6.5 percent above the state average; the other, Orleans, gave him only 39.3 percent. This small vote undoubtedly reflected the "Old Regulars'" support for Fuqua and also goes a long way to explain the low vote of the contiguous Jefferson Parish. All thirty predominantly Protestant parishes rallied to Fuqua's support with an average of a 78.1 percent vote (see table).

No one single force directly determined these three state elections. The elections turned on such culturally divisive issues as prohibition, the status of parochial schools, and the influence of the Klan and the New Orleans machine on state politics. Religion, in itself, was not an issue, perhaps because the religion issue in Louisiana had been an influential but accepted factor in voting behavior for so long that it simply had become subliminal in state politics. Despite the voting patterns which statistically emerged, religion served only as the most easily observable manifestation of the strength of the other cultural factors.

The 1928 presidential election gave new impetus to the culturally divisive issues that had plagued Louisiana politics, but, unlike past episodes, the religion controversy so apparent in the national campaign brought into the open in a very explicit manner the subliminal Catholic-Protestant split in the state. The forces which nurtured this open division came primarily from outside Louisiana. Ostensibly the impetus came from a growing national reaction to Al Smith's stand on prohibition. The support of the Women's Christian Temperance Union and the major Protestant denominations of the country, along with their well-known spokesmen, gave unusual strength to the dissension that followed Smith's nomination.[41] With all sincerity, this opposition fought against what it viewed as a threat to one of the soundest and most basic social reforms of all time. The attacks, however, took on a broader scope as the campaign moved into the autumnal months. Although still focusing upon prohibition, those opposing Smith also showed a distrust of his association with Tammany Hall and the urban way of life, in general.[42] The nationally known Reverend Dr. John Roach Straton of New York referred to Smith as "the deadliest foe in America today of the forces of moral progress and true political wisdom."[43] Influential evangelists contributed to this aura of a total condemnation of Smith beyond the issue of prohibition. Billy Sunday maintained that as the "Ambassador of God" it was his duty to "defy the forces of hell—Al Smith and the rest of them."[44] These broad condemnations are noteworthy for the fact that the Protestant ministers who led the fight against Smith created an aura of religious conflict, regardless of whether such a conflict existed. They not only indicated the ministry's opposition to Smith's stand on prohibition, but demonstrated how intricately bound together both prohibition and Protestantism were and also how antithetical the Protestant ministry believed prohibition and Catholicism to be. Obviously Smith's questionable position on prohibition, combined with his Catholicism was more serious to many than a mere weakness on the prohibition issue alone. For example, in 1919 President Woodrow Wilson, a Protestant, refused to sign the Volstead Act which provided for the national enforcement of prohibition. A year later, at the very height of the initial public enthusiasm for prohibition, the Protestant Democratic presidential nominee, James M. Cox, advocated 2.75 beer.[45] Neither, however, had received any national disapproval of their actions similar to that directed against Al Smith for his stand on prohibition.[46]

Thus, just as many historians have argued that Smith's religion and the prohibition issue were indistinguishable to the voter, the same may be said to be true of the ministry's view of the evils of Al Smith. Throughout the course of the campaign, ministers could not present a clear condemnation of Al Smith on the prohibition issue alone because prohibition to them was more than a social reform, it was a Protestant article of faith. Even when distinctions were made, they were too fine to be fully perceived by many voters.

Vague charges that Smith was a drunkard who favored legalizing gambling and prostitution bolstered many voters' predilections against him. Even according to Smith, himself, the explicit anti-Catholicism of the "whispering campaign" played the largest role in his defeat. On various occasions it was rumored that if Smith were elected, the Pope might move to the United States to influence his decisions, that all Protestant marriages would be nullified, and that all fourth-degree members of the Knights of Columbus would fulfill their alleged oath and conduct a war of extermination and mutilation against all heretics.[47] The Ku Klux Klan conducted its own campaign of vilification that followed similar or even more preposterous lines. National Republican campaign workers below the upper echelons also trafficked in anti-Catholicism, mostly playing upon those fears that already existed. For example, Virginia National Committeewoman Mrs. Willie W. Caldwell, in a widely publicized letter, wrote:

> Mr. Hoover himself and the National Committee are depending on the women to save our country in this hour of very vital moral religious crisis. We must save the United States from being Romanized and rum-ridden, and the call is to the women to do something.[48]

The anti-Smith national uproar brought to Louisianians a new awareness of their most prominent and basic state political division.

On October 21, a mere two weeks before the election, the *New York Times* noted the extent of anti-Catholic bigotry against Smith in the South.[49] The South appeared to be forming its ranks against Smith on the basis of his Catholicism. This perception of the campaign was not uncommon. The same view was echoed in many loyal Democratic organs throughout Louisiana. There, just as on the national level, many of the issues of the contest seemed to blend imperceptibly together to give the campaign an anti-Catholic tint. This view of the presidential race in the South grew in part out of the region's history of Catholic intolerance, but even more, it was based firmly upon the nature of the campaign in the region.[50] In the South, and even more particularly in Louisiana, there existed no strong Republican party machinery. The most vocal opposition to Smith came from defecting Democrats. Often the entire campaign in Louisiana seemed to revolve around an internecine party war. Loyal Democrats called for Smith defectors to resign their public offices, while the Hooverites made outlandish charges against Smith in their claim that he had betrayed the party.[51] The recriminations that grew out of this struggle knew no limit, and many anti-Smith diatribes contributed to the image of anti-Catholicism in the campaign.

Another reason for the appearance of anti-Catholicism in the campaign was the important role the ministry played in the ranks of the Hoover supporters, and the critical part the Protestant churches of the state played in the election. As on the national level, both the ministry and church organizations did not limit themselves to the prohibition question in the heat of the campaign. The past president of the state Baptist Convention, Reverend Leon Sloan of Shreveport, was the most conspicuous anti-Smith minister in the state. As a member of the executive committee of the national anti-Smith Democrats, he, with the aid of Mrs. W. N. Collins, vice president of the Louisiana Women's Christian Temperance Union, opened an anti-Smith state headquarters early in September.[52] Sloan remained active throughout the campaign, often serving as principal speaker at Hoover rallies. At one such rally in Livingston Parish, Sloan denounced Smith for his religion.[53] Other ministers also attacked Smith and threw their support behind Hoover through the use of their pulpits and by joining Hoover Clubs.[54] The ministers did not act without local and state sanction. For the most part, Protestant church organizations wholeheartedly supported their efforts.[55] Most stressed what they believed to be the benefits of prohibition. The Amite River Baptist Association (St.

Helena Parish) proclaimed that, as a result of prohibition, labor was enriched, business had prospered, public savings and capital resources had increased, public health had benefited, and home conditions, food, clothing, and personal comfort had improved.[56] The attack, of course, did not stop with just a condemnation of Smith's stand on prohibition, for Smith was the "archenemy of righteousness."[57] Frequently the Women's Christian Temperance Union issued a broad condemnation of Smith. In an article in defense of its anti-Smith position, the Union claimed it was not attacking Smith's religion, because in its eyes he had none.[58]

The most noteworthy attack upon Al Smith by organized religion in Louisiana took place in October. In that month the chief foe of Al Smith in the nation's ministry, Reverend John Roach Straton, toured the Protestant northern section of the state in a well-publicized anti-Smith campaign. In all his fury, Straton addressed large crowds in both Monroe and Shreveport. In the latter city thirty-five ministers from throughout the state flanked Straton on the speaker's platform.[59]

Although most religious spokesmen and organizations were sincere in their condemnation of Smith on the prohibition issue, it was easy for the voter to perceive an aura of anti-Catholicism in the Smith critique. If this perception needed any reinforcement, it was readily available close at hand. The "whispering campaign" conducted across the nation was also widespread throughout Protestant northern Louisiana. In 1928 the Louisiana Ku Klux Klan enjoyed a brief revival of its former strength. Even though the Klan had never been able to deliver a vote in the state as a whole, it was still able to spread more than its share of vicious propaganda.[60] Perhaps of more importance than the Klan's physical existence was the continued vitality of the organization's tenets, for its revival gauged the broader religious prejudice that had given strength to the Klan in the north of the state from its outset.[61]

No source attests to the strength of anti-Catholicism in the 1928 campaign as well as do Louisiana newspapers. Of course, nearly all of the state's newspapers were Democratic in political orientation, and most remained loyal to the Democratic party in the election. Therefore the editors were interested throughout the campaign in determining and combating the voters' chief antipathies toward Smith. Beyond making the flat claim that the Democratic party represented what was best for the South, the editors fought strongest against what they perceived to be the growing anti-Catholic reaction to Smith.

A few of the state's newspapers preferred to combat the growing anti-Catholicism during the campaign by following a positive approach. They maintained that their readers were not accepting the Republican party's campaign of "bigotry and intolerance" against Smith.[62] The *New Orleans Times-Picayune* asserted that Republican hopes to trade upon "ignorance, passion and prejudice in the South" had failed.[63] Other editors were not so sure. One in Union Parish maintained that the Republicans shrewdly issued literature about Smith's Catholicism, alleged drunkenness, and the imminent threat of Papal rule to "feed the minds of prejudice[d] Southern people," and that "some redblooded Southerners, seem to relish this specially prepared morsel from up in Yankeedom" and swallow all of it. In a final plea the editor attempted to convince his readers that Smith's "hated religion" was his own business and that the voter should only be concerned with his qualifications for office.[64]

Most of the state's newspapers took a more direct route in combating religious bigotry in the campaign. On September 26, the *Baton Rouge State Times,* claimed that "in Louisiana 90 percent of the opposition to Governor Smith, among former life-long Democrats, is because he is a Catholic."[65] Although this arbitrary figure was undoubtedly an exaggeration calculated for effect, it does serve to demonstrate the degree of anti-Catholicism the state newspaper editors sensed as they denounced such excesses of the "whispering campaign" as the revived use of the alleged membership oath of the Knights of Columbus, the idea that Catholics voted as a bloc under the strict orders of the Pope, and the charge that Smith as governor of New York had a record of partisan Catholic appointments to offices of trust.[66] In one effort to stem the tide of anti-Catholicism against Smith the *Shreveport Times* and *Alexandria Town-Talk,* throughout the month of October, ran Article VI, Section 2, and the First Amendment to the United States Constitution in every issue of their papers to try to emphasize the fundamental illegality of the Catholic issue as a test for selecting a president.[67]

In their effort to take the offensive in the campaign from the Republicans, editors also printed such disparate articles as those on Hoover's pacific Quaker religion and the number of Catholic officers who served in the Confederate Army.[68] They also sought to offset Tammany Hall's shoddy reputation by extolling its charitable activities and its aid to the South after the Civil War.[69] Still other newspapers sought to battle the prohibition issue head-on by championing Smith's "states' rights" stand that the individual states could more effectively manage their own prohibition programs.[70] Editors also asked voters to weigh other factors favorable to the Democrats in the election. The *Shreveport Journal,* for example, noted that a vote for Smith was a vote for "Joe" Robinson, the first Southerner on the ticket in over half a century. It also emphasized that success in November might result in a Democratic Congress with key committee posts to be held by Southerners. The editor urged his readers not to turn down the ticket because of "prejudice and fanaticism."[71] In the last issue of the *Farmerville Gazette* before the election, the editor pleaded with his readers to "approach the polls . . . seriously, sacredly and with an open, unbiased, unprejudiced mind."[72]

Democratic politicians in the state who campaigned for Smith and the Democratic ticket agreed with the newspapers that anti-Catholic prejudice was a major factor in the Smith campaign in Louisiana. Mississippi governor Theodore G. Bilbo spoke at Baton Rouge just a few days before the election. In his speech, Bilbo maintained that voters had defected from Smith only because of his religion.[73] Louisiana governor Huey P. Long concurred. While campaigning statewide for the Democratic candidate, Long became disgusted by the religious bigotry he encountered. Furthermore, he felt that the chief source of the bigotry was the state's ministry, and at one point in the campaign Long proclaimed, "I have no patience with two-bit ministers who are injecting religion into

Cultural Conflict

this campaign."[74] Thus Governors Bilbo and Long, along with many of the state's newspapers, perceived that the attack upon Smith was one with religious overtones, exclusive of other issues. Yet, just as in the nation as a whole, other issues played a part in the presidential campaign in Louisiana. The difference was that they were clearly subordinate to, or only further aggravated, the Protestant-Catholic division among the Louisiana electorate.

Apart from the religion and prohibition issues, but not necessarily unrelated to either one, was the rural-urban confrontation which historians have often noted in the 1928 election. Within Louisiana the potentiality of a political confrontation between New Orleans and the rural areas of the state had been alleviated somewhat by 1928. Not only had the New Orleans "Old Regular" machine been weakened by its poor political fortunes of the decade, but its long-time power merchant, Martin Behrman, had died in 1926.

Although undoubtedly still an issue, the urban-rural confrontation by itself played a small part in the 1928 presidential election in comparison to the Catholic-Protestant division in the state. The parishes classified as over 40 percent for Smith compared to a total state average of 76.3 percent.[75] Of these parishes Orleans gave Smith the highest percentage, 79.5. It was also the only "urban" parish with a majority of its population Catholic. Together, all the "rural" parishes of the state (or the remaining parishes) averaged a 78.9 percent vote for Smith. Those "rural" parishes with a majority of their population Protestant averaged only 74.2 percent for Smith; those with Catholic majorities, 84.1 percent; and those parishes with a more than 75 percent Catholic population averaged an 87 percent Smith vote.[76]

Although it is possible that the north-south, Protestant-Catholic division may have, by itself, accounted for the difference in Smith's support, it is unlikely that the long-term northern, rural Protestant antipathy toward New Orleans had really abated. It was still a factor, but the Catholic-Protestant division in the state shrouded its identity. Beyond Al Smith's Catholicism, the most obvious personal fact about him was his New York City background. It may well be that Smith's being from New York City and the "East" in itself distressed many Protestant voters.[77] Yet, in the voters' perception of Smith his urban background was not necessarily distinct from his Catholicism. Smith's Catholic-Irish immigrant background, his stand on prohibition, and his rise to political office via the notorious Irish-Catholic dominated Tammany Hall all could be viewed as hinging upon his Catholicism. Indeed, if one makes allowances for historian Paul Carter's assertion that to the rural mind there was little distinction between one large city and another, Al Smith may have garnered not only the antipathy directed towards New York City but also that traditionally directed towards New Orleans.[78] Certainly a case could be made for a transference of this antipathy in 1928. The rural northern Protestants disliked New Orleans for many of the same reasons that they detested Smith's New York background. Aside from the fact that the politics of the city of New Orleans and downstate Louisiana had long been in Catholic hands (Choctaw Club), as was the Tammany organization in New York City, both cities had significant numbers of foreign-born inhabitants.[79] Both cities also held lurid national reputations in the twenties for gambling, prostitution, and flagrantly violating prohibition. It remained only that these issues (aliens, vice, and prohibition) be hitched in tandem and preached as gospel by a Protestant ministry in a broad denunciation of Smith to enhance the anti-Catholic aura. This was done as early as the Asheville, North Carolina, convention of anti-Smith Democrats in July 1928. There it was proclaimed that "The danger to American civilization today is the big cities with their alien population, their lack of moral principles, and their ignorance of American history and traditions."[80] It almost goes without saying that most of this immigrant population was Catholic in religion. Their "lack of moral principles" could easily signify an indifference to the virtues of prohibition, and their "ignorance of American history and tradition" might easily explain their tolerance toward such political organizations as Tammany Hall and the "Old Regular" machine.

As an issue by itself, the prosperity of the decade was infrequently mentioned in the Louisiana campaign. It still, however, may have had some effect upon drawing into the Republican fold some urban voters such as the bankers and real estate managers who spoke at Hoover gatherings.[81] More than likely, however, this was offset by the poor agricultural prices received in the river parishes. Both parties pledged tariff relief for the sugar and rice districts, but their stands were similarly vague and the issue never captured the interest of most Louisiana voters.[82]

Yet, in another sense, the issue of prosperity had a supporting appeal for the Protestant Democrats' defection from Smith. It was widely proclaimed that the decade of prosperity had not accidentally coincided with the decade of prohibition. Like other factors, the effects of this contributing issue would be impossible to measure in isolation, but must be viewed as a part of the successful argument against Smith: his wavering prohibition stand in the anti-Catholic aura that surrounded the election in Louisiana.

This inquiry poses a negative question in asking why "Protestant" parishes of the state reacted adversely towards Al Smith. It should not necessarily be construed from such an approach that Smith's appeal to Catholic voters was due entirely to his religion. On the surface this often appears to have been the case, but some of the electorate may have voted for Smith on the basis of his stand on prohibition, or for any number of other more local or subtle reasons. In a similar vein, there were Catholics utterly opposed to Smith for the same reasons as Protestants. His urban, Eastern origins, or even his stand on prohibition may have raised their ire.

Individuals' perceptions of issues differed widely. There can be little doubt that issues, personalities, or patronage on a parish or even a precinct level influenced votes one way or the other, and the widely varying precinct voting returns within some parishes tend to confirm this. For example, one of the most interesting regional issues within the state that had an unknown effect upon the number of defections from Smith occurred in the Mississippi River parishes. During the spring and summer of 1927, the Mississippi spilled over its banks in one of the worst floods in its history. President Calvin Coolidge

Cultural Conflict

responded to the disaster by organizing a Special Mississippi Flood Committee. At its head he placed Secretary of Commerce Herbert Hoover. Hoover lived and worked in the Mississippi Valley flood area as he directed various local relief operations and the construction and maintenance of over 150 refugee camps. After the flooding had abated, Hoover focused his efforts on reestablishing credit in the devastated areas.[83] What effect Hoover's presence and assistance in the flooded parishes had in the 1928 campaign is incalculable, but that there existed some sympathy towards Hoover for his efforts can be gleaned from occasional newspaper mention. The *Baton Rouge State Times* of September 14, 1928, noted that the political interest in the state was greatest in the areas along the rivers, especially in those homes safely in the shadow of the levees. The Fifth District Democratic Campaign Chairman felt the pressure sufficiently to publish a disparaging article on Hoover's weak flood control policy for northern Louisiana.[84]

Louisiana's long-term political division between Protestant and Catholic sections of the state had by the late 1920s become such a political fact of life that overt mention of its existence, except by the most extreme groups, was infrequent. Elections turned on issues that reflected the religious divisions, but not on religion itself. The 1928 presidential election broke the calm. Vibrant issues of the decade came to the fore and were associated with a new phenomenon in American history—a Catholic presidential nominee. A campaign against Smith gained strength first outside the state, then within. Perhaps unwittingly, though by no means alone, Protestant ministers gave strength to an anti-Catholic sentiment in the election and aroused an old, but still powerful and fundamental, division within the state in a new and virulent form. It even succeeded in undercutting the alleged "fundamental basis" of Southern solidarity (race) in one of the strongest Democratic areas of the state, the predominantly black Mississippi River parishes. Yet even after all this is said, one cannot easily draw larger national or, in particular, regional conclusions from the Louisiana election. Louisiana's politics, even those on the national level, remain her own.

PROTESTANT PARISHES
(75 percent or more of the population)

	Change in Dem. Pres. Vote 1924-1928	% of vote for Ransdell	% of vote for Fuqua	% of vote for Broussard
Beauregard	— 7.1	29.6	69.5	34.1
Bienville	—13.7	37.1	84.1	39.6
Bossier	—7.3	32.2	85.6	47.9
Caldwell	—10.9	34.1	65.7	41.8
Catahoula	—6	28.5	71.5	24
Claiborne	—9.7	46.8	93	51.5
Concordia	+5.8	49	80.5	40.5
DeSoto	—16.3	32.4	85	27.5
East Carroll	—2.6	55.7	83.6	33.6
East Feliciana	—15.8	27.3	82.5	39.6
Franklin	—12.9	36.4	90	28.5
Grant	—11.1	30.4	71.5	39.5
Jackson	+11.4	38.1	75.1	41.6
LaSalle	—13.9	38	76.5	33.6
Lincoln	—25.4	30.8	90	29.4
Madison	—27.7	37.4	96	11.4
Morehouse	—9.3	44.8	77.7	57.2
Ouachita	—6.6	41.7	65	49.5
Red River	—16.4	37.8	82	47.4
Richland	—3.7	36.3	80	34.2
Sabine	—18	40.3	62.8	48.7
St. Helena	—10.3	24	55	46
Tensas	—15.7	61	87.5	13.6
Union	—27.2	24.7	79	48.2
Vernon	—7.3	35.2	68.5	39.3
Washington	—20.7	19.8	86.4	31.8
Webster	—9.8	47	85.6	38.3
West Carroll	—5.7	30	79	29.1
West Feliciana	—13.5	42	69	45.5
Winn	—18.4	30.2	64.2	39.8

CATHOLIC PARISHES
(75 percent or more of the population)

	Change in Dem. Pres. Vote 1924-1928	% of vote for Ransdell	% of vote for Fuqua	% of vote for Broussard
Acadia	+12.5	63.6	42	60.8
Assumption	+41.8	94.9	22.7	80.2
Avoyelles	+11.1	62.5	34	50.3
Cameron	—4.1	80.3	28	71.3
Evangeline	+6.5	66.7	29.4	77.2
Iberia	+34	73.4	26.3	76.6
Jefferson	+11.3	47	52.5	42.5
Lafayette	+31	67.2	26.9	70.8
Lafourche	+36.5	82.7	25.3	85
Orleans	+.4	67	60.7	52.5
Plaquemines	+15.8	51.7	46.7	29
Pointe Coupée	+23	85.5	16	60.5
St. Bernard	—.8	81	30.8	12.1
St. Charles	+12.5	70.5	27.5	54.5
St. James	+23.5	94.4	18.8	35.5
St. John	+25.8	78.5	38.3	62
St. Landry	+3.4	71.6	36	57.6
St. Martin	+18.4	87.6	25.8	76.5
Terrebonne	+32.3	80.5	35	80.9
Vermilion	+26.1	63.4	46.4	54

Notes for "Cultural Conflict and the 1928 Presidential Campaign in Louisiana"

[1] The following statistical sources were used throughout the paper: Richard M. Scammon, comp., *America at the Polls, A Handbook of American Presidential Election Statistics, 1920-1964* (Pittsburgh, 1965), 189-92. State primary election returns for the 1924 United States Senate contest were taken from: Louisiana, *Report of the Secretary of State to his Excellency the Governor of Louisiana, January 1, 1925*, appendix, 49-50. State primary election returns for the 1924 gubernatorial contest were taken from *Report of the Secretary of State, 1925*, 347-48. State primary election returns for the 1926 United States Senate contest were taken from: Louisiana, *Report of the Secretary of State to his Excellency the Governor of Louisiana, January 1, 1927*, appendix, 67-8. The religious composition of the Louisiana parishes may be found in: U.S. Department of Commerce, Bureau of the Census, *Religious Bodies: 1926*, 1:620-22. The racial compositioin of the Louisiana parishes may be found in: U. S. Department of Commerce, Bureau of the Census, *Fifteenth Census of the United States, 1930: Population*, vol. 3, part 1:980-84. The rural-urban breakdown for the parishes may be found in the same place.

[2] *Official Report of the Proceedings of the Democratic National Convention Held at Houston, Texas, June 26, 27, 28 and 29, 1928...* (Indianapolis, n.d.), 211.

[3] John D. Hicks, *Republican Ascendancy, 1921-1933* (New York, 1960), 208.

[4] Richard Hofstadter, "Could a Protestant Have Beaten Hoover in 1928?." *The Reporter*, 22 (March 17, 1960): 31-33. Although there is general agreement among histodrians on this point, there is considerable controversy over the proper hierarchy of the diverse factors which played a part in Smith's defeat. Almost without exception historians have noted the many factors involved and their interrelated nature. Still, analysts at one time or another have maintained that the election turned on the issue of anti-Catholicism: [David Burner, *The Politics of Provincialism, The Democratic Party in Transition, 1918-1932* (New York, 1968), 220-22; Oscar Handlin, *Al; Smith and His Reality of America* (Boston, 1958), 129-31; Allan J. Lichtman, "Critical Election Theory and the Reality of American presidential Politics, 1916-40," *American Historical Review*, 81 (1976): 327; Edmund A. Moore, *A Catholic Runs for President, The Campaign of 1928* (New York, 1956)] prohibition: [William F. Ogburn and Neil S. taslbot, "A Measurement of the Factors in the Presidential Election of 1928," *Social Forces*, 8 (1929): 178-85] Smith's "total urban complexion": [Paul A. Carter, "The Campaign of 1928 Reexamined: A Study in Political Folklore," *The Wisconsin Magazine of History*, 465 (1963): 263-72] the predominant Republican prosperity of the times: [Frederick Lewis Allen, *Only Yesterday, An Informal History of the Nineteen-Twenties* (New York, 1931): 215; Roy V. Peel and Thomas C Donnelly, *The 1928 Campaign, An Analysis* (New Yoirk, 1931): 52] or the fact that Smith was simply the candidate of a minority party: [Ruth C. Silva, *Rum, Religion, and Votes: 1928 Reexamined* (University Park, Penn., 1962)]

[5] In 1928, Tennessee, Florida, North Carolina, Texas, and Virginia voted Republican. Alabama came within three percentage points of voting Republican.

[6] V. O. Key, Jr., *Southern Politics in State and Nation* (New York, 1949), 318.

[7] Ibid., 319.

[8] Burner, *Politics of Provincialism*, 224; Wendell Holmes Stephenson and E. Merton Coulter, gen. eds., *A History of the South*, 10 vols. (Baton Rouge, 1951), vol. 10, *The Emergence of the New South, 1913-1945*, by George B. Tindall, 250; Dewey Granthan, Jr., *The Democratic South* [Eugenia Dorothy Lamar Memorial lectures] (Athens, 1963): 67; Hugh D. Reagan, "The Presidential Campaign in Alabama" (Ph. D. dissertation, University of Texas, Austin, 1961): 486; Donald B. Kelley, "Deep South Dilemma: The mississippi Press in the Presidential Election of 1928," *The Journal of Mississippi History*, 25 (1963): 63-92.

[9] Perry Howard, *Political Tendencies in Louisiana*, rev. ed. (Baton Rouge, 1971), 298-99. Howard devoted only two paragraphs, albeit incisive ones, to the 1928 presidential election in Louisiana. He noted that the parish returns indicatee that the cultural issues in Louisiana undercut the racial issue, but he neither elaborated upon it nor placed it in historiographical perspective.

[10] Marie S. Dunn, "A Comparative Study: Louisiana's French and Anglo-Saxon Cultures," *Louisiana Studies*, 10 (1971): 131-69; T. Lynn Smith and Homer L. Hitt, *The People of Louisiana* (Baton Rouge, 1952). Both works provide valuable information about the demographic characteristics of Louisiana.

[11] Scammon, *Presidential Election statistics*, 192, 246, 394. Louisiana voted 76.3 percent for the Democratic candidate. Mississippi and South Carolina gave the Democratic candidate 82.8 percent and 91.5 percent, respectively.

[12] *Alexandria Town Talk*, November 5, 1928.

[13]*Richland Beacon-News* (Rayville), November 15, 1928.

[14]Ibid.

[15]*Farmerville Gazette,* October 17, 1928.

[16]*Shreveport Times,* November 1, 1928.

[17]*Farmerville Gazette,* September 19, 1928.

[18]*Madison Journal* (Tallulah), September 22, 1928.

[19]*Shreveport Journal,* October 30, 1928.

[20]Ibid., November 3, 1928.

[21]*Baton Rouge State Times,* September 24, 1928.

[22]*Farmerville Gazette,* September 19, 1928.

[23]Herbert Hoover, *The Memoirs of Herbert Hoover,* vol. 2: *The Cabinet and the Presidency, 1920-1933* (New York, 1952), 129.

[24]For example, see Hugh D. Reagan, "Race as a Factor in the Presidential Election of 1928 in Alabama," *The Alabama Review, A Quarterly Journal of Alabama History,* 19 (1966): 5-19; Kelley "Dee South Dilemma," 63-92.

[25]Edwin Adams Davis, *Louisiana: A Narrative History,* 3rd ed. (Baton Rouge, 1971), 34.

[26]Key, *Southern Policits,* 318.

[27]Bossier, -7.3; Claiborne, -9.7; DeSoto, -16.3; East Carroll, -2.6; East Feliciana, -15.8; Madison, -27.7; Morehouse, -9.3; Richland, -3.7; Saint Helena, -10.3; Tensas, -15.7; West Feliciana, -13.5; Natchitoches, -4.1. The vote for the third party candidate, Robert M. La Follette, counted very little as a consideration in comparing the 1924 and 1928 election totals. La Follette received only 3.5 percent of the vote, statewide. Orleans Parish supplied half of his vote. La Follette averaged only 1.75 percent of the total vote in the remaining parishes of the state.

[28]Iberville, +27.1; West Baton Rouge, +29.6; Pointe Coupee, +23.

[29]Bossier, Claiborne, DeSoto, East Carroll, East Feliciana, Madison, Morehouse, Richland, St. Helena, Tensas, West Feliciana.

[30]Natchitoches.

[31]Iberville, Pointe Coupee, West Baton Rouge. Concordia was the only deviant parish. This parish was 90 percent Protestant in population but had a increase of 5.8 percent in its Democratic vote in 1928.

[32]Key, *Southern Politics,* 319.

[33]Over 70 percent of the population in the following parishes was white (those parishes followed by an asterisk suffered a decline in their parish Democratic vote from 1924 to 1928): Acadia, Allen*, Avoyelles, Beauregard*, Calcasieu*, Cameron*, Evangeline, Jackson, Jefferson, Jefferson Davis, Lafourche, LaSalle*, Livingston*, Orleans, Sabine*, St. Bernard*, Tangipahoa*, Vermilion, Vernon*, West Carroll*, Winn*.

[34]Allen, Beauregard, LaSalle, Livingston, Sabine, Tangipahoa, Vernon, West Carroll, Winn.

[35]Acadia, Avoyelles, Evangeline, Jackson, Jefferson, Jefferson Davis, Lafourche, Orleans, Vermilion.

[36]Acadia, Avoyelles, Evangeline, Jefferson, Jefferson Davis, lafourche, Orleans, Vermilion.

[37]Scammon, *Presidential Election Statistics,* 190, 192.

[38] Faculty of the Political Science Department of Columbia University, ed., *Columbia University Studies in the Social Sciences* (New York, 1936), Number 421: *Machine Politics in New Orleans, 1897-1926,* by George M. Reynolds.

[39] T. Harry Williams, *Huey Long* (New York, 1969), 248.

[40] Ibid., 249.

[41] *Methodist Review,* 3 (September-October, 1928): 755; Moore, *Catholic Runs for President,* 170.

[42] Hillyer H. Straton and Ferenc M. Szasz, "The Reverend John Roach Straton and the Presidential Campaign of 1928," *New York History,* 49 (1968): 213, 217.

[43] Moore, *Catholic Runs for President,* 137.

[44] Richard O'Connor, *The First Hurrah, A Biograpohy of Alfred E. Smith* (New York, 1970), 206.

[45] Wesley M. Bagby, *The Road to Normalcy: The Presidential Campaign and Election of 1920* (Baltimore, 1962), 151.

[46] *Baton Rouge State Times,* September 26, November 5, 1928.

[47] Al Smith, *Up to Now, An Autobiography* (New York, 1929), 406-18; Moore, *Catholic Runs for President,* 134, 153.

[48] Moore, *Catholic Runs for President,* 146.

[49] *New York Times,* October 21, 1928.

[50] W. J. Cash, *The Mind of the South* (New York, 1941), 342-43.

[51] *New Orleans Item,* September 26, 1928; *Richland Beacon News* (Rayville), September 22, 29, 1928; *Baton Rouge State Times,* September 14, 1928.

[52] *Baton Rouge State Times,* September 18, 1928.

[53] *Denham Springs News,* October 4, 1928.

[54] *Baton Rouge State Times,* September 5, 1928; *Franklin Sun* (Winnsboro), October 12, 1928.

[55] See, for example, *Minutes of the Fifth Annual Session of the Bossier Parish Missionary Baptist Association held with Salem Baptist Church—Red Land, Louisiana—September 18-19, 1928,* 12; *Minutes of the Nineteenth Annual Session Held with the Red Bluff Baptist Church, October 6, 7, 8, 1928* (St. Helena Parish), 12.

[56] *Minutes of the Red Bluff Baptist Churcy, 1928,* 7.

[57] *Minutes of the Thirty-Sixth Session of the Carey Baptist Association held with the Trinity Baptist Church, Lake Charles, Louisiana—August 7th, 8th, 9th, 1928,* 32.

[58] *Madison Journal* (Tallulah), September 11, 1928

[59] *Alexandria Town-Talk,* October 3, 1928; *Franklin Sun* (Winnsboro), October 12, 1928.

[60] Charles C. Alexander, *The Ku Klux Klan in the Southwest* (Lexington, 1965), 118.

[61] Kenneth Earl Harrell, "The Ku Klux Klan in Louisiana" (Ph.D. dissertation, Louisiana State University, Baton Rouge, 1966), v.

[62] *Concordia Sentinel* (Ferriday), November 3, 1928.

[63] *New Orleans Times-Picayune,* September 8, 1928.

[64] *Farmerville Gazette,* October 17, 1928.

[65] *Baton Rouge State Times,* September 26, 1928.

[66] *Shreveport Times,* September 6, 1928; *Farmerville Gazette,* September 12, 1928; *Lafourche Comet* (Thibodaux), September 20, 1928; *Tensas Gazette* (St. Joseph), October 5, 1928; *St. Francisville Democrat,* November 3, 1928.

[67] *Shreveport Times* and *Alexandria Town-Talk.* dContinuous throughout the month of October 1928.

[68] *Concordia Sentinel* (Ferriday), September 14, October 13, 1928; *New Orleans Item,* October 15, 1928.

[69] *Shreveport Times,* September 9, 1928; *Baton Rouge State Times,* November 5, 1928.

[70] *Farmerville Gazette,* August 29, September 19, 1928; *Tensas Gazette* (St. Joseph), October 5, 1928.

[71] *Shreveport Journal,* September 4, 1928.

[72] *Farmerville Gazette,* October 31, 1928.

[73] *Baton Rouge State Times,* November 5, 1928.

[74] *Farmerville Gazette,* September 19, 1928.

[75] An urban community was classified by the United States Bureau of the Census as any community over 2,500 in population. According to this criterion, the following parishes and their percent of "urban" population were: Beauregard, 43.7; Caddo, 61.5; Calcasieu, 46.2; East Baton Rouge, 45.1; Orleans, 100; Ouachita, 60; Rapides, 40.7; Washington, 46.9.

[76] The following were the rural parishes (under 40 percent urban) with a majority of their population Protestant: Allen, Bienville, Bossier, Caldwell, Catahoula, Claiborne, Concordia, DeSoto, East Carroll, East Feliciana, Franklin, Grant, Jackson, LaSalle, Lincoln, Livingston, Madison, Morehouse, Red River, Richland, Sabine, St. Helena, Tangipahoa, Tensas, Union, Vernon, Webster, West Feliciana, Winn. The following were the rural parishes (under 40 percent urban) with a majority of their population Catholic: (those more than 75 percent Catholic are followed by an asterisk) Acadia*, Ascension, Assumption*, Avoyelles*, Cameron*, Evangeline*, Iberia*, Iberville, Jefferson*, Jefferson Davis, Lafayette*, Lafourche*, Natchitoches, Orleans*, Plaquemines*, Pointe Coupee*, St. Bernard*, St. Chalres*, St. James*, St. John*, St. Landry*, St. Martin*, St. Mary, St. Tammany, Terrebonne*, Vermilion*, West Baton Rouge.

[77] Carter, "Campaign of 1928 Reexamined," 269-70.

[78] Ibid., 270.

[79] *Denhan Springs News,* October 4, 1928. The Hoover Club expressed a not uncommon fear that if Smith became president he would reopen the floodgates of immigration; Reynolds, *Machine Politics in New Orleans,* 13. New Orleans had a far larger immigrant population than any other city in the South at this time.

[80] *New York Times,* July 19, 1928.

[81] *Baton Rouge State Times,* September 5, 1928; *Denham Springs News,* October 4, 1928.

[82] *New Orleans Item,* October 15, 1928; *Baton Rouge State Times,* October 30, 1928.

[83] Bruce A. Lohof, "Herbert Hoover, Spokesman of Humane Efficiency: The Mississippi Flood of 1927," *American Quarterly,* 22 (1970): 690-700.

[84] *Baton Rouge State Times,* September 5, 14, 1928; *Tensas Gazette* (St. Joseph), October 26, 1928.

PART IV

LOUISIANIANS AT WORK

THE BUSINESS COMMUNITY 1803-1815*

John D. Clark

Beverly Chew and Richard Relf, partners in the New Orleans firm of Chew and Relf, were two of the more prominent members of a business elite which controlled the economic and political development of New Orleans during the decade following the Louisiana Purchase. The men established a business in 1801 which weathered successfuly the tumultuous years prior to the War of 1812, rode the war years out without damage, survived the postwar boom, bust, and recession, and was still operating in the 1830s. Both men were intimately involved in the organization and operation of the new forms of capitalistic enterprise which were chartered after 1803.[1]

Few men played a more significant role in the initiation of the insurance business in New Orleans. Relf was one of the founders of the New Orleans Insurance Company, chartered in 1805; Chew and Relf were among the original subscribers to company stock; and the partners served at different times on the company's board of directors. While this insurance company was organizing, the two announced their appointment as the exclusive agents of the Phoenix Fire Assurance Company of London, holding this agency until at least 1818. There was no conflict here since the London firm insured only real property while the New Orleans firm insured vessels, cargoes, and money in port and in transit. After the war, the New Orleans firm was reorganized as the Louisiana Insurance Company, with Relf serving as one of the directors.

Banking also opened up new opportunities for the two men. The firm subscribed to stock in the Bank of Louisiana and Relf sat on the board from 1807 to 1813. From 1818 to 1847 Relf was the cashier of the Louisiana State Bank. Chew was appointed to the board of directors of the New Orleans branch of the first Bank of the United States in 1805, serving until the charter expired in 1811, and again as a director for the local branch of the second Bank of the United States between 1817 and the time of his resignation as

---

*First published as chapter 16 in John D. Clark, *New Orleans, 1718-1812: An Economic History* (Baton Rouge: Louisiana State University, © 1970), 330-53. Reprinted with the kind permission of the author and publisher.

president in 1831. In 1831 Chew was appointed cashier of the Canal and Banking Company and was elected president in 1832. Among the other positions held by the partners, Relf was a director of the New Orleans Navigation Company from 1806 to 1810 and Chew received the appointment as Collector of Customs at New Orleans in 1816, serving until his dismissal in 1829.

This brief resume of the careers of Chew and Relf reflects a deep and durable involvement in the economic life of New Orleans. They were neither average—typical— businessmen nor completely atypical. Rather, they belonged to the business "establishment" of the community, having achieved this position by the rapid success of their mercantile house and their leadership in other areas of the community's economic life. Their acquired reputations paid immediate dividends. In 1804 Collector H. B. Trist suggested fifteen individuals to Secretary of the Treasury Gallatin as possible directors of the branch Bank of the United States. Chew's name was on the list. His partner, one of the half-dozen founders of the local Chamber of Commerce in 1806, was elected to the city council in 1810. A few years later, Relf contributed to the organization of the Thespian Benevolent Society. In 1810 Chew was a founding father and among the first elected as vestrymen of the new Episcopal Church. The other vestrymen, the men recommended by Trist, the chamber organizers and the Thespians, were with few exceptions as much a part of the business elite of the town as Chew and Relf.

It is easy enough to say that a business elite functioned in New Orleans prior to the Peace of Ghent, but it is quite another matter to define its functions and characteristics or to catalog its members. In terms of American urban development, New Orleans was a unique city as of 1803, combining as it did the attributes of many American cities both new and old. Like New York, Philadelphia, or Baltimore, New Orleans was a seaport located on a river. Unlike those towns, New Orleans' river system penetrated almost every crop region in the United States, making the city an entrepot for virtually every staple, northern or southern. New Orleans was as much a river city as a coastal city and new as well as old. It was newer to the United States than Cincinnati, Louisville, or other western river cities, but it was older than Savannah in chronological age. To the casual observer, society in New Orleans appeared as fluid as in other western communities, yet operating beneath the flux was a solidly entrenched establishment. This inner core of individuals ran the town politically, set the social tone, and controlled its economic development through a virtual monopoly of corporate enterprise in the city.

As might be expected in a preindustrial and commercial city, merchants contributed an overwhelming majority of members to the elite group. Entry to the commercial class in the city was open at all levels to those caring to take the risk. Men with a few dollars could easily buy goods and commence a career of hawking and peddling. Many obviously did, for the city council, at the insistence of the solid burghers of the town, passed ordinances regulating and taxing street peddlers. But entry on a shoestring did not guarantee the wherewithal to purchase the shoes. Nor were the new merchants, arriving with capital or credit and goods, who initiated more solid ventures, likely to advance into the ranks of the elite before 1815. This was especially true of those arriving after 1808 and to a certain extent even after 1803.

At least some information is available relative to the careers of 149 businessmen operating in New Orleans between 1803 and 1815.[2] Although many more than 149 pursued trade and commerce during those years, this group provides as satisfactory a cross-section of the business community as extant data allow. This group will later be divided and subdivided according to certain objective criteria in an effort to identify with some precision the most prominent members of the business elite in New Orleans. At this point, however, some basic facts concerning the entire group will be discussed; these then can be contrasted with data relative to the subgroups.

The general period in which these individuals established their businesses is known. Of the 149, 19 percent were operating prior to 1800; 22 percent opened their establishments between 1800 and 1803; and the remaining 59 percent thereafter. Sixty-two, or 41 percent, owned going concerns before the Louisiana Purchase. Of the total, at least 31 percent continued their businesses into the postwar decades while no fewer than six of the group outlived John C. Calhoun and at least two, William W. Montgomery and Rezin D. Shepherd, witnessed secession and civil war. Both of the latter retired to plantations with large fortunes. Montgomery was said to own a large portion of northwestern Louisiana. Within the group, 20 men owned plantations prior to 1815, while after 1815, 34 pursued planting and business simultaneously or retired to plantations. The lure of the plantation continued to attract many of the most prominent businessmen in later years, making it difficult to generalize concerning the urban commitment of the community's leadership.

Again from the total group, 36 held either elective or appointive positions in the city or state government prior to 1815 while 56 held one or more directorships in one or more of the corporations established after 1804. After the war, at least 46, including Chew and Relf, continued to serve on the board of directors of an increasing number of corporate enterprises. James Freret served in the 1830s as a director of the New Orleans and Carrollton Railroad and the Union Bank of Louisiana. Samuel Packwood and Maunsel White were among the organizers of the Plaquemines Railroad Company in 1835; John McDonogh and Martin Gordon served as directors of the New Orleans and Nashville Railroad Company in 1836 and 1837. Benjamin Levy, who began his career as a stationer in 1811, was a founder of the Orleans Insurance Company in 1835 and invested heavily in land, railroads, and banks. Of these entrepreneurs, all but McDonogh belong more properly to the postwar elite of New Orleans.

For purposes of analysis, the original list of 149 individuals was divided into two groups. Active participation as a member of either the city council or the board of directors of one of the corporations was assumed to reflect a capacity for leadership; proven influence with the voting public of the city or the stockholders of the corporation; and, as only stockholders could be directors, the possession of and the willingness to invest funds in institutions that served as vehicles for economic growth in the city as well as potential sources of profit. Group one, therefore, was composed of all those serving as directors or city councilmen, totaling 64 individuals. Group two originally included 69 firms or 84 men, but so little information was available regarding a number of them that the list was reduced to 40 firms, or 56 merchants. A comparison between the two groups uncovered differences additional to and perhaps explanatory of the initial distinction utilized in constructing the lists.

The merchants in group one established their businesses in New Orleans considerably earlier than those in group two.[3] The average EBR for group one was 2.25; for group two, 3.25. More specifically, 55 percent, or 33 merchants, in group one were operating in New Orleans before 1803 compared with 25 percent, or 10 merchants from group two. Twenty-five percent of the individuals in group two arrived in New Orleans after 1809, compared to 3 percent of group one. Merchants in group one were more likely to be in on the organization of the corporations as original investors and to retain their positions of leadership at least through 1815. Moreover, the merchants in group one seem to include the largest business establishments in the city.

There is no way of knowing the annual dollar volume of any of the firms involved here. Instead, it was tentatively assumed that size could be determined by focusing attention on the number of business services rendered and the kinds of venture engaged in.[4] The SBR for the firms included in group one was 3.75; for group two, 2.50. None of the firms in the latter group engaged in all of the functions rated, only two engaged in five functions, and only one in four. Fourteen of the firms were exclusively commission houses according to their circulars and advertisements. One of these houses was established by John James Audubon, who came from Lexington, Kentucky, shortly after his encounter with Vincent Nolte. The business failed shortly after its inception. Related to the large proportion of strictly commission merchants in group two is the fact that 43 percent of them operated as agents for overseas firms compared to 33 percent in group one. Some merchants in group two, such as William McCormick, Cochran and Rhea, and Francis Wells apparently served no other purpose than to purchase staples for and sell the goods of various merchants along the East Coast of the United States. Of the firms in group one, Chew and Relf, Kenner and Henderson, Shepherd, Brown, and Company, T. & D. Urquhart, and Samuel Winter engaged in all six functions while 11 other firms engaged in at least four. Forty-five percent of those in group one were shipowners compared to 25 percent in group two. This explains at least partially the much larger proportion of group one—76 percent—than group two—53 percent—engaged in the export-import business on their own account. Merchants in group one were less specialized in their functions than those in group two.

Operating as they did across a wider spectrum of business activities, the houses represented in group one were in touch with more areas for potentially profitable enterprise than the more specialized and smaller businessmen in group two. Profits derived from such enterprise enabled the older and larger merchants to invest heavily in corporations as well as land and slaves. For instance, the merchants in group one subscribed 58 percent of the original stock issue of the New Orleans Insurance Company in 1805 and still controlled 44 percent of the stock in 1816. Less than 20 percent of the shares were in the hands of the merchants in group two during this period. Nicholas Girod, the largest stockholder, owned 30 shares in 1809 with $30,000 at par value and 16 shares in 1816. Thomas Callendar owned 12 shares in 1816; Benjamin Morgan, 10; Paul Lanusse, 17. All of the above group one merchants owned stock in one or more of the other corporations, as did all other individuals in the group some of whom also invested heavily in other enterprises. Morgan in partnership with William Kenner (group one) purchased a sugar plantation several miles above New Orleans for $90,000. In 1806 Chew and Relf in association with George St. Phillips engaged in townsite speculation and promotion three miles above Baton Rouge; John McDonogh and William W. Montgomery advertised in 1818 the subdivision of Shepherd Brown's estate directly across the river from New Orleans. Within the city Kenner and Henderson and Maunsel White purchased a number of lots at the corner of Chartres and Royal Streets. Of the 20 merchants known to have owned and operated plantations—frequently through overseers—before 1815, 75 percent were included in group one. These men were concurrently members of both an urban and country elite.

Table X offers a composite view of the merchants in the two groups and provides a reasonable cross-section of the mercantile community of New Orleans in terms of establishment and function. Four of every ten merchants were in business prior to the Louisiana Purchase. Most of those established prior to 1800 were French, such as Antoine Cavalier, Jr., Francis Duplessis, Michel Fortier, Nicholas Girod, Paul Lanusse, and James Pitot. There were, however, some Americans, notably Daniel Clark, Jr., Evan Jones, Joseph McNeil, James Mather, and George and Oliver Pollock. Only two Spaniards, Fernando Alzar and Gerome Lechiapella, were uncovered. The influx between 1801 and 1803 was largely American. Thomas and David Urquhart, Scots, were exceptions. Beverly Chew had a prior career in New York and Philadelphia and in 1810 married the daughter of the late William Duer of New York; John McDonogh arrived with backing in Baltimore, as did John Palfrey; and Maunsel White came down from Louisville. The preponderance of Americans increased in later years, leavened however by a number of Europeans such as Vincent Nolte, born in Leghorn; A. and J. Denistoun from Glasgow; and Manuel J. de Lizardi, representing Lizardi and Company, a prominent house in Paris and London.

One of every three merchants managed a store, generally combining retail and wholsale services, or owned a ship. One of every five owned both a store and shipping. This combination made it likely that the merchant would engage in all the other functions listed, except perhaps the negotiation of money. The latter service was, of course, a concern of all merchants, but only 15 percent seem to have made a business of buying and selling exchange on various parts of the world. Most merchants probably utilized the discounting and exchange services offered by local banks.

Table X
Date Established in Business and Functions Engaged in by 104 Merchants in New Orleans before 1812, in Percentages[a]

Date Established in Business	%	Functions Engaged in	%
Before 1800	25	Storeowner	34
1801-03	16	Shipowner	36
1804-08	38	Export-Import on Commission	69
1804-12[b]	10	Export-Import on Own Account	67
1809-12	11	Negotiate notes, etc.	15
		Agent	37

[a] Excluded from the calculations relative to function were four auctioneers and two newspaper owners whose functions were somewhat different from those of the typical merchant.
[b] More precise information was lacking relative to the date of establishment for these ten. Rather than exclude them, a catchall category was utilized.

Available data indicate that between 30 and 40 percent of the combined groups traded with the United States, Europe, and an area including Central and South America and the Caribbean. As far as can be determined, there was no direct trade from New Orleans with North or West Africa, the British North American colonies, the Pacific Coast of North America, or Asia. Trade with South America was largely confined to Atlantic ports from Laguna, Brazil, to the north. Trade in southern waters was pursued by both American and French firms. The latter enjoyed superior contacts in the French and Spanish possessions which were more significant to New Orleans than the English islands. Michel Fortier and Company developed out of Reaud and Fortier, a firm engaged in the Indian and West Indian trade in the early 1780s. The Duplantier, Duplessis, and Olivier firms followed similar business traditions. Armand Duplantier, Jr., succeeded to a business established in 1783 by his father, who retired in Baton Rouge before 1803. The Olivier firm probably antedated the American Revolution.

French firms, as might be anticipated, controlled most of the French trade but there was no absolute division whereby the French traded exclusively with France while the Anglo-Saxons dealt entirely with England. Fortier traded in the three areas noted above and Gerome Lechiapella served as an agent of Low and Wallace of New York in the 1780s. Anglo-Saxon merchants controlled most of the English trade and a growing proportion of the upriver trade with the Old Northwest, as well as the coasting trade to the eastern United States. Distinctions in geographic focus, however, were as much a factor of the time of establishment as ethnic group. Merchants in group one, older, larger, and more intimately involved in the economic life of the community, were more likely to trade in all three areas than merchants in group two. At least 16, or 25 percent, of the former are known to have done so, compared to three or four—less than 10 percent—of the latter. The trade in southern waters attracted the active attention of at least 25 merchants in group one, or 40 percent, compared to less than 15 percent of group two. Merchants in group two were the most specialized in geographic focus as well as business functions. They arrived later, took fewer risks, probably made less money, and were less involved in extracurricular economic and political activities. The nucleus of an elite does not exist in group two. It does in group one.

More than half of the merchants in group one were established prior to 1803 while slightly less than half of the firms represented engaged in four or more of the business functions listed in Table X. Thirteen of the merchants served only on the city council for at least one year, while 51 served at some time as a director. Sixteen served in both positions. Seven men served in all three capacities. For the purpose of defining an elite, membership on a board of directors was regarded as the most critical area of service, with a high frequency of service assumed to reflect an equivalent degree of wealth and prominence.[5]

Four corporations were established in 1805 and two more in 1811. The following discussion is confined to the period 1805-11 because the membership of each board of directors is known for each year and because 1811 represents the first year in which new administrative and investment opportunities were available to men who reached New Orleans after 1805. While each corporation was guided by ten directors, deaths and resignations meant that more than 40 positions were filled annually. Taking the average for the six years, positions for as many as 282 individuals were available if each corporation in each year chose different men; in other words, with no person serving more than once or on the board of more than one company. In fact, 52 men filled the positions for an average of 5.2 directorships per man.[6] In 1811 two new banks were chartered, creating positions for 24 new directors. Seventeen men who had no previous board experience plus seven previous directors were elected to those positions. Sixty-nine men, then, filled 351 positions during the seven years 1805-1811 for an average of five positions per man.[7] . . . The business elite of New Orleans derived from this group if, indeed, it was not this group.

Table XI, represents an effort further to refine the membership of the elite by identifying those individuals who by available criteria were among the most prestigious in the city. Inclusion in the table was confined to those men holding six or more directorships during the seven years 1805-11. The list, while not presuming to identify *the* elite, is an objective and representative selection of men who incontestably belonged *to* the elite. Several men come to mind who, holding fewer than the required number of directorships, belonged to the establishment as surely as those listed. Edward Livingston and Abner Duncan, both attorneys; John McDonogh and Julien Poydras, two of the wealthiest men in Louisiana; James Mather, appointed to the legislative council in 1804 and mayor of New Orleans from 1807 to 1811; and Thomas L. Harmon and Daniel Clark, Jr., two of the must successful merchants in town, are a few examples of the elite group not included in Table XI.

The individuals included in Table XI composed 30 percent of all those serving as directors from 1805 to 1811. They filled 68 percent of the positions, averaging over ten per man. The EBR for this list is 1.82, compared with 2.25 for group one and 3.25 for group two. Of those in the table, 76 percent were established prior to the Louisiana Purchase and of those, half antedated 1800. While the SBR for group one was 3.75 compared to a rating of 3.25 for group two, the rating for those in the table is 4.16. Those individuals engaged in the six activities utilized in Table X are all included in Table XI. Many of those in the table were planters and all but five are known to have pursued active careers after 1815.

TABLE XI

Directors Holding Six or More Directorships, 1805–11, and Other Data

	No. of Director-ships	No. of Yrs. as Director	Director-ships after 1815[a]	No. of Yrs. on City Council	E.B.R.	S.B.R.	Planters[b]
Thomas Urquhart	20	7	B	0	2	6	—
Benjamin Morgan	19	7	B	6	2	2	BA
James Pitot	17	7	?	2	1	4	—
Paul Lanusse	16	7	B	0[c]	1	2	—
Richard Relf	14	6	B,I	2	2	6	—
William Kenner	13	7	B	0	2	6	BA
J. B. Labutat	13	7	B,I,O	0	3	4	—
Joseph McNeil	13	7	B	2	1	3	—
William Nott	12	7	B,I	0	3	3	A
Rezin D. Shepherd	12	7	B,I	0	3	6	A
Thomas Callendar	10	7	?	0	3	3	BA
Samuel Winter	10	6	d.1813	5	2	6	—
John Soulé	9	7	B,I,O	2	2	?	—
Joseph Tricou	9	6	?	0	3	?	—
Nicholas Girod	9	5	B	3	1	2	A
Beverly Chew	8	7	B	0	2	6	—
P. F. DuBourg	8	7	?	1	2	3	—
A. Cavalier, Jr.	7	7	?	0	1	?	—
Francis Duplessis	7	6	B	5	1	2	BA
Michel Fortier	7	7	B	0	1	5	BA
J. F. Livaudais	6	6	?	2	1	?	BA

[a] B = bank; I = insurance; O = other
[b] B = before 1815; A = after 1815
[c] Councilman, 1814-15
[d] Auctioneer

By taking certain partnerships into account, the degree to which corporate enterprise in New Orleans was controlled by relatively few individuals is accentuated. Chew and Relf, for example, filled 6 percent of all available corporate positions, as did William Nott and Thomas Callendar of Amory, Callendar and Company. Benjamin Morgan, an inactive partner of Kenner and Henderson, and William Kenner, of the same firm, controlled 32 positions between them, to which might be added the directorship held by Stephen Henderson in 1811. Shepherd, Brown, and Company filled 12 positions through Rezin D. Shepherd, four through John McDonogh, and one through Shepherd Brown. The firm [Sanuel] Winter and [Thomas L.] Harmon controlled 15 positions. These five houses held 31 percent of the directorships available. If the positions held by Thomas Urquhart, James Pitot, Paul Lanusse, J. B.Labatut, and Joseph McNeil are added, partners in or owners of ten firms occupied 54 percent of all the directorships between 1805 and 1811.

The degree of involvement of the ten firms in the new corporation is shown in Table XII. In 1809 those houses filled 61 percent of all the directorships available, averaging 58 percent for the six years 1805-10. This proportion declined in 1811 as none of the individuals associated with those firms was involved in the Louisiana Planter's Bank. Chew and Relf was represented on the boards of all four corporations in 1808, 1809, and 1810, while Kenner and Henderson held two positions on two corporations in five of the seven years, the firms controlled a majority of each board 79 percent of the time. The Bank of Orleans, chartered in 1811, appears to be a replacement for the liquidating branch Bank of the United States. Five directors of the branch bank from the ten firms shifted to the nine-man board of the new bank in 1811. This led to accusations that the Bank of Orleans was the "American" bank *vis-a-vis* the Bank of Louisiana and the new Louisiana Planter's Bank which were supposedly the "Creole" institutions. With regard to the Bank of Louisiana, such a distinction is untenable. Three of the firms in Table XII—Amory, Callendar and Company, Chew and Relf, and Shepherd, Brown, and Company—had representatives after 1811 on both the Bank of Orleans and the Bank of Louisiana concurrently. The position of the Louisiana Planter's Bank is less clear.

There were more planters on the board of the Louisiana Planter's Bank than on the boards of the other corporations but merchants composed the majority. The merchants sitting on the board, while not included in Table XI (with the exception of Francis Duplessis), were from solidly established firms. Solomon Hillen, Jr., was the partner of an ex-director of the branch bank, as was Nathaniel Coxe. Two of the directors in 1811, Richard Butler and William W. Montgomery, were appointed directors of the branch of the Second Bank of the United States in 1816 while Samuel Packwood moved to the board of the Bank of Orleans in 1817. Francis Duplessis, Jr., took over his father's position on the board of the Bank of Louisiana in 1812 so that the senior Duplessis could serve on the board of the Planter's bank. The banks were in competition, of course, but there is no overt evidence pointing to any kind of political tension between the Bank of Orleans and the Louisiana Planter's Bank.

There was nothing in the charter of the Louisiana Planter's Bank which discriminated against other groups in favor of planters or compelled the bank to serve planters in any special way. However, the act of incorporation of the Louisiana State Bank in 1818 established branches at Donaldsonville, Baton Rouge, St. Francisville, Alexandria, and St. Martinville.[8] A proportion of the total capital stock was reserved for those branches in an effort to augment sources of credit for the planters. The charters of the Bank of Orleans, the Louisiana Planter's Bank, and the Louisiana State Bank reflected an awareness by the legislators of the degree of control which a few men exercised over the corporations organized prior to 1811. All three charters prohibited election as a director of more than one partner from any commercial firm or any director of another bank. The charter of the Bank of Orleans, in addition, denied election to the partner of any person serving as a director of any other bank. When Kenner and Henderson, in 1811, divided their operations between two firms, William Kenner and Company and Stephen Henderson and Company, Benjamin Morgan retained an interest in the latter firm, thus circumventing the intent of the charter of the Bank of Orleans and allowing both Kenner and Morgan to serve on the board.

TABLE XII

Directorships Held by Ten Mercantile Houses in Six
Corporations in New Orleans for the Seven Years, 1805-11

	1805 1 2 3 4	1806 1 2 3 4	1807 1 2 3 4	1808 1 2 3 4	1809 1 2 3 4	1810 1 2 3 4	1811 1 2 3 4 5 6
Amory, Callendar and Co.	2 1	2 1	1 1	1 2	1 1 2	1 1 2	1 1 1
Chew and Relf	1	1 1 1,	1 1 1	1 1 1 1	1 1 1 1	1 1 2 1	1 1
Kenner and Henderson	1 2	2 1 2	2 1 2	2 1 2	2 1 2	1 1 2	1 2 2
Shepherd, Brown and Co.	1 1 1 1 1	1 1	1 1	1 1 1	1 1	1 1	1 1 1
Winter and Harmon	1 2	1 1 1	1 1 1	1 1	1	1 1 1	
J. B. Labutat	1 1	1 1	1 1	1 1	1 1	1 1	1 1
Paul Lanusse	1 1	1 1 1	1 1 1	1 1	1 1	1 1	1 1
Joseph McNeil	1	1 1	1 1	1 1	1 1	1 1	1 1
James Pitot	1 1	1 1	1 1	1 1 1	1 1 1	1 1 1	1 1
Thomas Urquhart	1 1	1 1 1	1 1 1	1 1 1	1 1 1	1 1 1	1 1 1
Total	5 1 9 6	6 8 8 5	6 8 8 5	7 8 7 7	7 7 7 7	7 7 9 7	5 6 3 6 5 0

Key: 1...Bank of Louisiana
2...New Orleans Navigation Co.
3...New Orleans Insurance Co.
4...Branch Bank of the United States
5...Bank of Orleans
6...Louisiana Planter's Bank

The investment commitment of the individuals and firms included in Tables XI and XII is known only in the case of the New Orleans Insurance Company. Individuals associated with the firms cited in Tables XI and XII owned 55 percent of the stock in 1809. Nicholas Girod, with 30 shares, Benjamin Morgan, with 16, and Thomas Callendar, with 10, controlled 28 percent of the total issue, representing an investment of $56,000. Those businessmen included in Table XI invested a total of $109,000 in the company. A very tentative and minimal investment projection for the 21 merchants in Table XI can be made, as it is known that directors of the Bank of Louisiana, Louisiana Planter's Bank, and the Bank of Orleans were required to own at least ten shares of stock. Assuming this to be the case for the New Orleans Navigation Company and with the stockholders of the insurance company known, the 21 merchants owned at least $210,000 worth of stock in five corporations.

Even the minimal figure is impressive—the more so since the Bank of the United States was excluded because of ignorance of stock requirements for directors—for it represents exactly 10 percent of the nominal capitalization of the five local corporations. Moreover, because the actual capitalization represented by paid-up shares was lower than the nominal figure, the investment commitment of the 21 merchants was undoubtedly much higher than 10 percent. The Bank of Louisiana did not market the full $600,000 in stock authorized by its charter, which was amended to allow the bank to operate when subscriptions for $300,000 in shares were received. Advertising extensively, the bank's promoters pointed out the advantages of a "home-owned" institution to both merchants and planters. An editorial in the *Louisiana Gazette* conjured up a view of the Bank of the United States, about to open a branch in New Orleans, reminiscent of later Jacksonian criticism of the second bank. According to the editor: "The Bank of the United States is owned chiefly by Europeans . . . all the profits arising from that Bank . . . will be drawn away from us . . . and it must in the end leave us poorer than it found us—whereas the Louisiana Bank, being owned altogether by the inhabitants of the country, all the profits which it may make will be divided among them & remain in the country."[9] After the war, when the second bank sought subscriptions, investment from New Orleans at $315,000 ranked below thirteen other cities including such smaller places as Wilmington, Delaware; Lexington, Kentucky; and Cincinnati, Ohio. Richmond, Virginia, subscribed to about five times more stock and Charleston, South Carolina, almost eight times more than New Orleans. But in 1811 stock for the Bank of Orleans and Louisiana Planter's Bank was taken up rapidly.

The record of political participation reflected in column 4 of Table XI does less than full justice to several of the merchants. Some, like Fortier, Cavalier, Tricou, Callendar, Shepherd, Nott, and Labatut, were apparently politically inactive, at least prior to 1815. Others who did not serve on the city council held other positions. Thomas Urquhart, a member of the territorial House of Representatives, was elected speaker in 1808-10, elected to the territorial constitutional convention in 1812, and to the United States Senate from which he resigned in 1815. His brother David sat on the municipal council from 1806 to 1808. Benjamin Morgan and William Kenner received appointments to the legislative council from Governor Claiborne in 1804. James Pitot and Nicholas Girod were mayors of New Orleans, the former serving in 1804-05, the latter from 1812 to 1814. Pitot was appointed parish judge in 1812. Peter Dubourg was Collector of Customs between 1813 and 1815.[10] Francis Duplessis was a member of the Spanish Cabildo and treasurer of the city in 1800. Beverly Chew held down several positions: Justice of the territorial Court of Common Pleas, territorial postmaster, and Collector of Customs from 1816 to 1829.

There were few men in New Orleans possessed of greater economic power or political influence than those appearing in Table XI. Most were established prior to the assumption of control by the United States and were either sufficiently eminent at that time or enjoyed such influential backing in the United States to attract the attention of the new sovereigns. Among the fifteen men recommended as possible directors of the branch bank by Collector Trist were Chew, Kenner, Callendar, Morgan, Fortier, Lanusse, and Dubourg. Several of the remaining eight have been encountered previously: John McDonogh, William Donaldson, Gerome Lachiapella, J. F. Merricult, and Charles Patton of Meeker, Williamson & Patton. William Taylor of Baltimore worked diligently for the appointment of a member of Shepherd, Brown to the board of the branch bank. John McDonogh was disqualified because of his connection with the Bank of Louisiana. Chandler Price, a director of the parent bank, at the suggestion of Benjamin Morgan and Taylor, saw to the selection of Shepherd Brown in 1805. Morgan, Kenner, Callendar, Chew, McNeil, and Cavalier (all in Table XI) were also chosen along with John Palfrey—associated at that time with Rezin D. Shepherd, who was appointed to the board in 1808—George St. Phillips, Nathaniel Evans, and three others.

The political organization imposed on Louisiana by the United States proved unsatisfactory to some and gave rise to a degree of political factionalism between the so-called "French" and "American" parties. The elite furnished leadership to the factions, both of which maintained a certain liveliness during the territorial and war years, feeding on unsettling events such as the Burr conspiracy, the embargo, and finally the war and subsequent British invasion. Claiborne and other federal officials at the center of the strife were opposed by such men as Edward Livingston, Daniel Clark, Jr., and Evan Jones. Factionalism was serious and substantive during the earlier years but degenerated into a matter of personal antagonism and pique during the latter years of the period. In 1804 Claiborne's offers of appointments to the Legislative Council were refused on principle by Evan Jones, Daniel Clark, Etienne Boré, Colonel Bellechasse, and others. Morgan, Kenner, Dr. John Watkins, James Mather, Julien Poydras, William Wikoff, and Gaspar Dubuys (Dubourg and Dubuys) were among those willing to accept appointments.

How far the political division carried over into economic affairs and with what impact is not a matter of record. Only one of the known opponents of territorial policy, Pierre Sauvé, was considered for appointment to the board of the branch bank. However, Sauvé, Edward Livingston, and Evan Jones, along with John McDonogh, Nicholas Girod, Paul Lanusse, Benjamin Morgan, and Michel Fortier were among the original promoters of the Bank of Louisiana in 1804-05. Sauvé was apparently sufficiently acceptable to the regime by 1805 to prompt his appointment to the Legislative Council, serving as its president in 1806, succeeding J. Noel Destrehan and succeeded by Colonel Bellechasse, both dissidents in 1804. Evan Jones served as the first president of the Bank of Louisiana and in 1810 as president of the branch Bank of the United States. So tenuous were the political allegiances that the defeat of Jones, erstwhile leader of the "French" faction in 1804, and the election of Benjamin Morgan as president of the branch bank in 1811 was considered a victory for the "French" faction.

Men associated with both factions served concurrently as the directors of several corporations. There is no evidence that such divisions penetrated the board. As directors, the men guiding the companies were capitalists rather than politicians, entrepreneurs not factionalists, intent on maximizing profits and exploiting the services offered by the companies. The local banks were not established to provide a profitable source of investment for surplus capital nor did men invest in anticipation of large dividends. Their purpose was to deepen the well of credit available to the investors, thus augmenting the capital of each investor in proportion to his credit (reputation) and means. Merchants with access to bank credit were no longer limited in their ventures by their actual capital resources. Through the issue of bank notes and acceptance paper, banks multiplied the operating capital of the community and somewhat relieved merchants of the inconvenience of making and receiving payments in bullion. Given the crucial services dispensed by the banks, it was an obvious advantage to a merchant to participate in the policy making of these institutions. The houses in Table XII controlled numerical majorities in three of the four banks before 1812.

Of the two nonbanking corporations, the insurance company promised the greatest immediate returns from dividends. In view of the fact that the navigation company had first to sow before it could reap, motivation for investment in it is elusive. Any improvement in the transportation and port facilities of the city would benefit merchants and advance both public and private interests. Property [values] along the line of the improvement would also rise. Kenner and Henderson owned property fronting Bayou St. John. Kenner served as a director of the improvement company and it is likely that other stockholders and directors had similar property interests between Lake Pontchartrain and the river. Both the insurance and improvement ventures were capital pools, the former for protec-tion and the latter for construction. The insurance company contributed to the capital resources of the community by keeping insurance premiums at home. This was the import of the patriotic cry: "Citizens of American, insure yourselves."[11] It could just as easily have read "Citizens of New Orleans." Such reasoning mixed with a pinch of Anglophobia partially explains the annual tax of $1,000 levied in 1818 by Louisiana on the New Orleans branch of the Phoenix Insurance Company of London. Such sentiments also resulted in the adoption of a resolution in 1819 by the state House of Representatives to investigate the expediency and constitutionality of taxing the New Orleans branch Bank of the United States.

Except for the Bank of the United States, the corporations in New Orleans, were home-owned and home- and investor-controlled. With few exceptions, their affairs were managed by merchants—by relatively few merchants at that. Merchants established in New Orleans prior to 1803 occupied some 65 percent of all directorships in four corporations to 1810. While there is no evidence to support the contention that the directors sought their positions for the purpose of self-aggrandizement, it can be assumed that they managed the institutions in a manner reconcilable with both institutional policy and self-interest. Bank directors, among other functions, decided whether notes would be accepted for discount and negotiated with those seeking credit. Directors of the insurance company made decisions regarding the insurability of an applicant's ship and cargo and established premium rates. Each separate decision was of supreme importance to the applicant and at the same time the balance and accuracy of each corporate decision determined the degree of success experienced by the corporation. There were few positions in the city of a more sensitive nature than that of director.

The Business Community, 1803-1815

The function of an elite depends upon the fostering society, its customs and traditions—or its historical value structure—and evolving needs, which may or may not clash with historic patterns. Great hunters and warriors filled the council halls of the Chickawsaw planning forays against the less aggressive Choctaw. But the convergence of the paths of England, Spain, and France in the land of the Chickasaw, Choctaw, and other tribes disrupted hoary patterns of conflict, giving rise to the politician-Indian who played one European nation against the other in an effort to achieve some security for his tribe or tribal faction. The French elite consisted of administrator-soldiers, appointed by the crown to defend and advance the territorial dominions of the king. Ranking below the governors and intendents were the members of the Superior Council, largely colonists but restricted in their role to an advisory capacity and certain judicial functions. Local power and some wealth accrued to members of the council and caused fierce competition for a place on that body. Below the council, a handful of merchants and planters or planter-merchants achieved some prosperity. Du Breuil, Pradel, Father Beaubois, Paul Rasteau, Pictet, Caminada, and a few others gained local notoriety for their wealth but served in no leadership capacity except perhaps as members of the local militia. Outlets for leadership ability were few and restricted to those with influence rather than capacity.

Spanish institutions, particularly the Cabildo, the large influx of Anglo-Saxons into the city, and the pragmatic application of Spanish commercial law by local officials vastly extended the potential field of endeavor for ambitious individuals. Members of the Cabildo assumed tasks previously executed with small results by French governors and intendants. The responsibilities of the Cabildo were monumental compared with those of the Superior Council, and the Spanish properly filled this body with the most prominent residents of the city and surrounding countryside. The city existed for the first time as a corporate entity; the Cabildo existed as a potential reward for prominence. Cabildo members were preeminently merchants and the mercantile community, availing itself of legitimate and illicit trading opportunities, advanced rapidly in wealth. Many newcomers, especially British and Americans, took up residence, a movement that was accelerated with the winning of independence by the American colonies, the dependence of New Orleans upon the United States for foodstuffs and the outbreak of the French Revolutionary wars.

By the 1790s the solid nucleus of an American elite operated in New Orleans. Evan Jones drifted into New Orleans from Mobile in 1765, selling his vessel, making contact with local merchants, and establishing a business in New Orleans by 1790. Oliver Pollock gained General O'Reilly's favor, establishing the firm of Pollock and Wraught by the early 1770s and bringing his brother George to the city in the 1780s. [James] Mather and [George] Pollock set up shop in 1776. Mather was heavily involved in the Indian trade by the mid-1780s, about the time Daniel Clark, Jr., arrived from Philadlephia. Clark and William E. Hulings, merchant, served as unofficial consular agents for the United States in New Orleans in the late 1790s. By this time, Joseph McNeil and Shepherd Brown were both solidly established in business. These merchants—officially unrecognized and regarded with suspicion by the Spanish government—joined with such French merchants as Francis Duplessis, Michel Fortier, Nicholas Girod, and Paul Lanusse to provide the basis for a ruling commercial class by the turn of the century.

Immigrants arriving between 1800 and 1803 provided additional personnel for the elite which assumed control of the most strategic sectors of economic life in New Orleans subsequent to the Louisiana Purchase. Beverly Chew and Richard Relf, William Kenner and Thomas Callendar were among the arrivals of those years. The elite group evidenced no dramatic growth from 1805 through the conclusion of the War of 1812. Membership in the group was a factor of economic success and stability. Vincent Nolte, in a barbed statement descriptive of prewar years, maintained that none of the American merchants possessed any capital worth mentioning. Singling out Amory and Callendar as exceptions to the generality of American trade, Nolte described that firm as possessed of integrity and "a certain distrust of all undertaking which involved the least risk . . . two qualities which are rather rare in American business circles. . . . "[12]

Compared with New York, Philadelphia, or Boston, Nolte's judgment regarding the capital resources of the city was incontroverible. Still, merchants in the city invested about two million dollars in five corporations and certainly more than that sum if subscriptions to the water works and the steamboat company are included. Nicholas Girod purchased $30,000 in insurance company stock while Thomas Callendar subscribed to $10,000 worth of stock in the same firm. Benjamin Morgan owned, at a bare minimum, $22,000 worth of stock in three corporations. Obviously, the wealth of these merchants is unimpressive if contrasted with Stephen Girard or Alexander Brown but, unlike Philadelphia and Baltimore, New Orleans was just beginning to experience sustained economic growth.

Nolte was less than charitable in his judgment of the integrity and stability of merchants in New Orleans. One can assume that there were firms with less than the proper measure of both ingredients, but there is no evidence to support the contention that most or even many of the merchants in the city lacked integrity. Nolte's judgments reflect the application of European standards of behavior to business life in New Orleans. American merchants were more venturesome than French merchants. More Americans than French were involved, at least as directors, in the new forms of corporate enterprise introduced into New Orleans. The corporate form of business was less common in France than in England or the United States where the economy was less fettered by the encumbrances of arbitrary government, class distinctions, and internal barriers. French merchants were less attracted by high potential profits if the risk factor was abnormally high. To engage in traditional patterns of trade, American merchants, as colonists and after independence, were forced to accept risk as the norm. If they had not done so, there would have been no trade with the foreign West Indies or Spanish Main. They would not have come to New Orleans while it was a Spanish city.

The stability of a business can be judged in part by its capacity for survival; the character and reputation of a merchant by his ability to rebound after a serious business

The Business Community, 1803-1815

reverse. The elite merchants in New Orleans measure up well in both instances. Of the original 149 merchants, 15 failed between 1803 and 1815. Four of the failures were included in group one and represent three firms: H. and A. Amelung, George St. Phillips, and Palfrey and Shepherd. St. Phillips died; the Amelungs were operating again within two years; Palfrey turned to planting; and Shepherd became a senior partner in Shepherd, Brown, and Company. The individuals in Table XI and the firms they represent survived the fall of Napoleon. They survived a period of time when America's neutrality was ignored, the port of New Orleans closed to foreign trade for two years, and the United States engaged in a war against the premier naval power in the world.

These firms entered the postwar world with confidence as did the nation in general. Times had never looked better. The world was at peace. Demand for cotton was great and prices high. The Mississippi River Valley was the destination for thousands and thousands of settlers whose only route to market passed New Orleans. Steamboat service spread rapidly throughout the valley. New banks and insurance companies were organized in the city. New adventurers, braving the fever, invaded the town. It was the beginning of a new era and the eleventh hour for the old. The demise of the old was sped along by the Panic of 1819 and the subsequent years of depression.

The old guard, the original elite, lost their rather complete control of economic affairs while the nation and the city worked itself out of depression. Paul Lanusse failed in 1823 and died in Mexico in 1825 trying to recoup his fortune. William Kenner and Company collapsed in 1825. T. and D. Urquhart barely survived a series of severe blows. Benjamin Morgan died in 1826. The survivors shared their positions of influence and power with new men. John Palfrey placed two of his five sons, Henry and William, with merchants in New Orleans. Henry learned business from Chew and Relf and in 1819 joined with William Taylor as Palfrey and Taylor.[13] As the hinterlands of New Orleans became more productive and business expanded in the city, the numbers of the elite were augmented and economic power somewhat diffused. More men possessed more capital to invest in a greater variety of enterprises. Mobility and fluidity engendered by extraordinary growth displaced the relative stability enjoyed by the business community during the first American years. Lists of vestrymen and managers of dramatic groups serve less well in identifying this new elite.

Notes for "The Business Community, 1803-1815"

[1] Many of the individuals encountered in chapter 14 as members of the city council will be discussed in this chapter as part of the business elite. Instead of referring the reader to the earlier chapter for essential information relative to these men, certain facts pertinent to their careers will be repeated. Unless otherwise indicated, the corporations dealt with include the Bank of Louisiana, New Orleans branch of the First Bank of the United States, Bank of Orleans, Louisiana Planter's Bank, New Orleans Navigation Company, and New Orleans Insurance

[2] The number of firms involved is less than the number of individuals. Both are fluctuating numbers because of deaths, changes in partnership, failures, retirement, and the like. More data are available regarding some men than others. It is hoped that those who are ultimately identified as "elite" will not be done so merely because they left behind a full business record.

[3] A simple Establishment in Business Rating (EBR) was constructed according to the following scale: merchants established before 1800 were rated as 1; between 1800-1803, as 2; 1804-1808, as 3; sometime between 1804 and 1812 as 4; and 1809-12, as 5.

[4] A Size of Business Rating (SBR) was constructed, based upon the performance of the following six functions: storeowner, shipowner, export-import on commission, export-import on own account, negotiation of notes and letters of exchange, and agent for one or more overseas firms. This rating is more tentative than the EBR because it is likely that some merchants of both groups engaged in activities included above that I am unaware of. Hopefully, the factor of ignorance is equally relevant to both groups.

[5] References are now exclusively to those firms and men included in group one. Twelve other individuals also served in both capacities but they are not included in group one. A few were nonmerchants, such as Colonel Bellechasse, a planter; John Watkins, M.D.; and L. S. Fontaine, editor of the *Moniteur de la Louisiane*. For others, such as Louis Blanc and J. Blanque, no information was discovered other than their terms as directors or councilmen. Their vocations are unknown.

[6] This could mean one directorship in each of five different years or some other combination.

[7] Not all of the directors were included in group one. Some of the directors, notably Julien Poydras, William Donaldson, and Richard Butler, were planters maintaining residences in New Orleans. At least one director, Abner L. Duncan, was an attorney, and information was lacking regarding a few others, particularly those elected as directors in 1811.

[8] The governor appointed six of the eighteen directors of the Louisiana State Bank.

[9] New Orleans *Louisiana Gazette*, December 28, 1804.

[10] Dubourg launched the New Orleans *General Weekly Price Current* in 1816.

[11] Charleston *Gazette*, n.d., quoted in New Orleans *Louisiana Gazette*, September 29, 1809.

[12] Vincent Nolte, *Fifty years in Both Hemispheres, or Reminiscences of the Life of a Former Merchant* (New York, 1854), 90. Nolte failed in 1823-26.

[13] Henry Palfrey, Maunsel White, and Rezin D. Shepherd were among the delegates from New Orleans to the railroad convention held in New Orleans in January 1852. Two others in attendance antedated the War of 1812, E. J. Forstall and James W. Zacherie.

WORKHOUSES AND VAGRANCY IN NINETEENTH CENTURY NEW ORLEANS*

Nathaniel P. Weston

Workhouses, along with almshouses and poorhouses, originated as an institutional and administrative response to the urban "problem" of the vagrant in many cities in the eighteenth and nineteenth century United States and Europe.[1] The figure of the vagrant was a symbol of vice, corruption, and immorality—a drunkard, homeless, or unemployed person who resided outside of the social order of the city.[2] Reformers, in various locations, believed such persons could and should be rehabilitated apart from more serious criminals, and thus the workhouse was built as a means of effecting change within these "offenders" and across the urban landscape as a whole.[3] This article will demonstrate the attempt made by the New Orleans penal system to control the social problem of vagrancy through the establishment of workhouses—institutions of both incarceration and moral improvement.

The history of workhouses and vagrancy in New Orleans are subjects so far largely ignored.[4] Indeed, the lack of documentary evidence is problematic, but few historians have approached the interconnection of these topics in the United States,[5] let alone the state of Louisiana.[6] As the twentieth century quickly ends, welfare institutions of the nineteenth century still have not been adequately explored, nor given their proper historical place. Although fragmented, an array of primary sources exist untouched on the New Orleans Workhouses, making a cohesive historical narrative not only possible, but necessary for an institutional perspective on nineteenth century urban New Orleans society.

By approaching its structural environment, vagrancy is shown as a legal definition that encompasses various people at different times from the antebellum to the postbellum period. No attempt will be made to describe the "experience" of vagrancy since these people left no known personal records of their own. Instead, vagrancy will be depicted as

---

*First published in *Clio's Quill*, 1 (1998): 3-16. Reprinted with the kind permission of the author and the University of Southwestern Louisiana.

a social problem, one which led to an institutional response in the form of the workhouses, and one that appeared in contemporary newspapers on a regular basis. This may not present a complete portrait of the vagrants themselves, but should expand the idea of the public sphere of nineteenth century New Orleans.

As early as 1806, Louisiana territorial law defined "vagrants" and designated their place of commitment as the New Orleans (later, Orleans Parish) Prison—a remnant of the Spanish colonial period, owned by the city of New Orleans and subsequently leased to Orleans Parish.[7] During his term in office, Gov. W. C. C. Claiborne urged the construction of a penitentiary, in order to separate the various classes of criminals, although it was not until 1835 that the prisoners were moved out of New Orleans to a new penitentiary in Baton Rouge.[8] Edward Livingston had proposed a separation of carceral institutions in his penal code of 1822 which was distributed to several members of the Louisiana legislature. He suggested a penitentiary, school of reform, house of detention, and house of refuge and industry (workhouse), but his code was never directly adopted in part or in whole, by the state of Louisiana.[9]

Documentary evidence of the legislative effort to found the workhouses in New Orleans began on January 29, 1841, when a Senator Burke introduced the bill entitled "An Act to establish Work Houses and Houses of Refuge by the several municipal councils of the City of New Orleans, and for other purposes." After its customary second reading, an amendment was proposed by one Senator Hoa, who suggested that the second section of the bill be struck out. The second section granted authority to the Municipal Councils over the workhouses in their respective municipalities, and thereby diminished the power and jurisdiction of the police juries. Senator Hoa claimed the bill "in its present form, would create a confusion in the public business of the city." Senator Burke replied that the second section intended to remove the police jury from "all matters which properly belong to municipal councils." By February 1, the House had insisted on adopting the second section, which the Senate had sought to reject, and subsequently a bi-cameral committee was formed to resolve the impasse.[10]

A report from the Grand Jury conveniently appeared in paraphrase in the *New Orleans Daily Picayune* of the next day, and discussed the inadequacies of the New Orleans prison system. The Second Municipality prison was "filthy and wretched, and object to the system which prevails of putting vagrants and persons imprisoned for disorderly conduct in the same apartments with persons charged with larceny and capital offenses." As for the Parish Prison, the "vagrants' apartment" was "exceedingly filthy, owing to the construction of the prison." Ten to twelve inmates were located in one cell, ten by eighteen feet, and at night "they sleep on the damp floor and have no other covering than what the rags they wear by day afford them!" The Jury concluded in favor of "the workhouse system, the establishment of which the bill brought before the Legislature by Mr. Burke has in view."[11] The legislative committee concluded that the second section would remain in the bill on February 8, and the act was signed into law on March 5, 1841.[12]

The act that established the workhouses also defined the legal limits of vagrancy as follows:

> all persons being able to work, and having neither profession, nor trade, nor any dwelling place, nor any visible property wherewith to maintain themselves, shall live idle, those who habitually frequent grog shops or gaming houses, or other disorderly places, or found wandering about at an unseasonable hour of the night, who are unable to show what resources they possess, or unable to produce creditable testimony of their good conduct and morals: or those who lodge in out-houses, market places, sheds or barns, or in the open air, and . . . all persons apprehended with any picklock or other instrument with probable intention feloniously to break and enter any dwelling house or other house, or with any offensive weapon with probable intent feloniously to assault any person, or who shall be found in any dwelling house, out-house, store, yard or garden, with probable intent to steal, or who shall give a false account of themselves after warning of the consequences, shall be deemed vagrants.[13]

With its boundaries codified in law, the term "vagrant" assumed multiple meanings that included persons unemployed, homeless, loitering, alcoholic, disturbing the peace, propertyless, of "questionable" moral chracter, or petty offenders. As the foundations of the workhouses were put into place, a flexible definition of vagrancy contributed to the variety of offenses a person could commit to be sent to the workhouse instead of prison. On the one hand, this measure was a reform in that petty offenders would not be incarcerated with more serious or violent criminals; on the other hand, this law more specifically defined illegal behavior and therefore contributed to more stringent social control in nineteenth-century New Orleans.[14]

The First Municipality Council ordered construction of a workhouse in 1842, after the criminal court sheriff had informed the council he would no longer accept vagrants or other violators of municipal ordinances at the Parish Prison. In response, the Police Committee of the Council proposed that the workhouse be located in the portion of the police jail appended to the parish prison. The governance of the workhouse fell under a board of inspectors that included the mayor, recorder, and police committee members. The goaler of the police jail also served as the warden to the workhouse who would secure custody of the inmates, supervise their labor, keep a list of their tools and record this activity in a register.[15] The First Municipality Workhouse opened its doors April 1, 1842.[16]

The *Daily Picayune* reported with optimism, in the same year, the opening of the Second Municipality Workhouse:

> This new establishment is now in operation, and swiftly rising into important usefulness. Poor vagrants, who used to be confined in mischievous and destructive idleness, are now furnished with wholesome occupation. The institution, we are convinced, will prove one of the most decisive improvements ever made in our section, and it will have an effect which should be the proper aim of all judicious

engines—that of *reforming* instead of *degrading*. Many of the individuals placed under confinement in this asylum have little to answer for more than drunken excess, and the idleness consequent to such indulgence. These persons are restored to a more healthful state of existence by salutary rule and employment, so as, when released, to fuel incentive to more useful and honorable conduct. This is a vast stride in advance of the old system of imprisonment.

Half a dozen mechanical arts are already under cultivation in the establishment, and a very substantial building has been erected by the labor of the prisoners. The women are employed in tailoring, making up clothes, both for themselves and the men, and the most extensive arrangements—some completed, some still in progress—have been projected to secure comfort for the unfortunate people who fall thus under municipal charge.

We are told that prisoners evincing a gentle disposition and worthy conduct under confinement, have the advantage of being allowed certain working wages, at the discretion of the directors, for some term of their service, enabling them to leave the work-house with a trifle to assist them in commencing a better career. There are some now within the walls whose allotted time of confinement has expired, and who have found the place so salutary upon their moral well-being, that they voluntarily remain and cheerfully go through the daily employment of the house. This fact tells loudly in favor of the organization of the work-house, and we have no doubt, as so conducted, but a very few years will clear the whole expense of the building, and leave it one of the most useful institutions of the kind in the South.[17]

The Second Municipality Workhouse opened its doors on February 28, 1842.[18]

In 1844, on the same day they elected the keeper for the workhouse, the Third Municipality Council ordered estimates on a reformatory, asylum, and jail by an inspection bureau headed by the recorder.[19] The Third Municipality Workhouse opened well after the other two—on October 12, 1844.[20] The *Daily Picayune* reported optimistically in 1845 regarding the operations of the Third Municipality Workhouse and its "victims of intemperance": "Too much praise cannot be awarded the projectors of this receptacle for vice and drunkenness, where a strict discipline and no rum are the order of the day."[21] The administrative functions of the workhouses had been outlined and carried out, and early in their existence the administrators of these institutions still hoped for their inmates' rehabilitation.

In 1846, however, a report from the grand jury on the condition of the workhouses began with a censuring of the procedures of committing people there: "Far be it from our wish to desire to screen from the punishment due to offenses those who work iniquity, but we do most emphatically condemn the practice of committing men without a trial, for months, to a loathsome prison, for an occasional aberration from sobriety, when the jovial and bedizened [*sic*] blackleg, and tinselled courtesan, stalk abroad with the brazen consciousness of impunity stamped upon every feature."

As for the institutions themselves, both the Second and Third Municipality Workhouses appeared "neat and orderly"; while in the Third Municipality Workhouse the inmates seemed "cheerful and contented" and its "committing magistrate" had an "absence of complaints." The Second Municipality, though, had undergone "a manifest change for the better" through "the abandonment of the disgusting punishment of the 'cat'"—a form of correction "barely reconcilable with even naval usages." The author assured his audience, however, that "the naked backs of white men and women shall no more be excorciated by the officers of that house of correction, nor by their negro assistants, clothed with their authority."[22]

As labor was the root of "rehabilitation" for the inmates, its availability determined whether the workhouses would rehabilitate, or merely incarcerate, their residents.[23] A scarcity of work most likely contributed to the overall number of vagrant persons in the city of New Orleans, at the same time it led the keepers of the workhouses to resort to other means of discipline for their inmates. Despite the apparent transgression from moral improvement, the grand jury report pointed out that reform and new ideas were always sought.

Evidence that the vagrant "problem" was perhaps beyond the capacity of the workhouses appeared in the 1848 Report of the Board of Administrators of the New Orleans Charity Hospital. Governor Isaac Johnson, also ex-officio president of the board of administrators of the hospital, reported of "the evident necessity of the creation of an *Alms House*, wherein a proper system of labor could be organized, for the reception, employment, and instruction in various branch[es] of mechanical pursuits, of the indigent and vagrants who accumulate yearly in great numbers in this metropolis." Governor Johnson continued:

> A large proportion of these incumber [sic] the wards of the Charity Hospital under the plea of disordered health, and whose diseased condition is exclusively owing to their being completely destitute of all the necessaries of life. An institution of this kind would, after a lapse of time left for experiment, with proper managers or contractors, and a wise direction given to the labor of its inmates, become a source of profit to the State, in the same manner as the Penitentiaries of this and other States. It might usefully employ a host of paupers, whose only recourse is mendicity or vice—whose very sight and importunities in all the public thoroughfares, are annoying and offensive.[24]

The idea that labor served as moral improvement was disappearing, to be replaced by the desire for economic self-sufficiency. If not eventually self-supporting, at least the workhouses would help remove the supposed "stain" of vagrancy from public view.

The rehabilitative impetus behind the workhouses was clearly evaporating, only to regress to the administrative function of incarceration. This was due in large part to the fact that it seemed rehabilitation was not occurring at the workhouses: inmates were being committed and recommitted as many as nine separate times, and the number of vagrants seemed to be increasing instead of abating.[25] Evidence that the workhouses served as mere administrative apparatuses is shown in the fact that orphans as well as mentally insane persons were committed to them—persons supposedly in need of their own forms of rehabilitation.[26] A slave was also held in the Second Municipality Workhouse, placed there by his owner "under wages."[27]

Although the New Orleans municipalities unified into the Common Council in 1852, thereby consolidating the municipal workhouses into a single city workhouse, this institution continued to operate as one of incarceration—now accepting vagrants from Jefferson Parish for twenty-five cents per day.[28] Three years later, the council decided to lease the labor of the workhouse to a private party.[29] Evidently, the public cost had become the main concern for the overseers of the workhouse, and the registers became stringent economic records which hoped to insure this institution's financial efficiency.[30] Such efforts at cost-saving would continue until the Civil War radically and permanently altered both the social context of New Orleans society, and the complexion of the inmates in the workhouse. The scarcity of labor, however, would ultimately lead to the end of the workhouse altogether as an alternative to the regular imprisonment of vagrant persons.

The outcome of the Civil War changed the legal status of a large percentage of the United States' population, and subsequently displaced numbers of them and other persons directly and indirectly affected by the conditions of the war.[31] One historian claimed that before New Orleans was occupied by Federal forces, the inmates of the workhouse were released to join the Confederate Army.[32] Whether or not this assertion is true, during the Federal occupation, the workhouse fell under the jurisdiction of the military provost court, and in addition to its regular duty of "solving" the problem of vagrancy, this institution functioned as a place of incarceration for wartime exigencies. For example, in 1863, a woman was committed for thirty days for "rescuing a soldier from the police," and then "making a fierce assault upon the arresting officer." In a different vein, three soldiers were committed for three months each for "visiting the houses of colored people for felonious purposes."[33] The results of the Civil War would not only affect New Orleans society, but also the public will and ability to cope with urban problems.

Although free persons of color had been committed during the antebellum period, many more persons of African descent would be found behind the walls of the workhouse in the postbellum period.[34] By the end of the Civil War, black persons outnumbered whites within the workhouse, and the grand jury reported that these institutions were failing in their original purposes, finding that out of 277 current inmates with 108 whites, and 169 blacks, "there were only five employed in any kind of labor" while the rest "were all left to idleness and their own thoughts." After costing the city treasury a total of $27,629.79 for 1864, the grand jury still hoped that the workhouse would be able to carry out its "original design" of becoming "self-sustaining and promotive of habits of industry and improved morals of the prisoners."[35]

A law passed in 1865 used the pretext of vagrancy to keep freed people on plantations, while reinforcing the power of the planters. The law read: "if the accused be a person who has abandoned his employer, before his contract expired, the preference shall be given to such employer of hiring the accused." The only piece of this law which protected the employee to any extent was "that the person hiring such vagrant shall be compelled to furnish clothing, food and medical attention as they furnish their other laborers."[36] This law, however, did not appear to directly affect the New Orleans

Workhouse, but may have further contributed to competion for cheap labor in the Reconstruction economy of postbellum Louisiana.

The volume of inmates only increased during Reconstruction, with the added element of foreign inmates. On February 4, 1867, the *Picayune* reported the commitment of some fifteen to twenty persons "from among whom could be selected an indifferent type of many of the nationalities of the world."[37] An act of the same year "authorized" and "empowered" the City Council of New Orleans to "compel" inmates of the workhouse "to do any public work within the corporate limits of the city."[38]

Statistics from the workhouse from January 1868 showed 439 inmates, 81 white male natives, 121 white male foreigners, 138 colored male natives, 28 colored female natives, 32 white female natives, and 39 white female foreigners.[39] In the next year, Governor H. C. Warmoth urged the legislature to enact measures against vagrancy, instead of freed people, because "a man who eats but does not work is a bad citizen, and should be forced into honest employment. The streets of the capital are filled with idlers, who are too lazy or proud to work, and constitute a fungus on society, which needs legislative surgery."[40] The legislature subsequently passed an act almost word for word the same as the initial vagrancy act of 1841.[41]

It is not clear precisely when the New Orleans Workhouse ceased functioning. Despite the 1869 act on vagrancy, the *Picayune* no longer reported commitments to the workhouse after 1868, if there were any, and by 1876, vagrants were being locked up in city precinct jails.[42]

The workhouse failed in its purpose because it neither rehabilitated the inmates, nor economically supported itself, and in effect acted as a prison, the very structure it was founded to reform. The connection between vagrancy and the availability of labor was never made by the reformers who saw vagrants as morally flawed individuals. It was, in fact, the lack of labor that most contributed to the abandoning of the workhouses as institutions of moral improvement and later economic self-sufficiency. The results of the Civil War not only uprooted a major portion of the American population, but also contributed to the use of the New Orleans Workhouse as a mere institution of incarceration.

The "problem" of vagrancy would not disappear, although the workhouse ultimately did, and various attempts would be made in the future to promote a public policy on poverty.[43] The workhouse is a short chapter in the history of poverty, vagrancy, and legal institutions in New Orleans, but one worth noticing because of its relation to other nineteenth-century welfare institutions, such as the public mental asylum, hospital, and orphanage.

Notes for "Workhouses and Vagrancy in Nineteenth Century New Orleans"

[1] Workhouses existed throughout Europe, but the most comprehensive studies have been done on England. See, for example, Felix Driver, *Power and Pauperism: The Workhouse System, 1834-1884* (Cambridge, England, 1993); and Margaret Anne Crowther, *The Workhouse System, 1834-1929* (London, 1981).

For perspectives on the United States and individual states, see James Leiby, *A History of Social Welfare and Social Work in the United States* (New York, 1978); David M. Schneider, *The History of Public Welfare in New York State, 1609-1866* (Chicago, 1938); Schneider and Albert Deutsch, *The History of Public Welfare in New York State, 1867-1940* (Chicago, 1941); Mary Roberts Smith, *Almshouse Women: A Study of Two Hundred and Twenty-eight Women in the City and County Almshouses of San Francisco* (Palo Alto, Ca., 1896); John F. Alexander, *Render Them Submissive: Responses to Poverty in Philadelphia, 1760-1800* (Amherst, Mass., 1980); Leiby, *Charity and Correction in New Jersey: A History of State Welfare Institutions* (New Brunswick, N.J., 1967); Roy Melton Brown, *Public Poor Relief in North Carolina* (Chapel Hill, 1928); and Poverty, USA, Historical Record Series, *The Almshouse Experience: Collected Reports, 1821-1827* (New York, 1971).

[2] Paul Boyer, *Urban Masses and Moral Order in America, 1820-1920* (Cambridge, Mass., 1978), vii-viii, and passim.

[3] David J. Rothman, *The Discovery of the Asylum: Social Order and Disorder in the New Republic* (Boston, 1971), "The Almshouse Experience," 184. Rothman describes the development of workhouses in New York, Boston, the East Coast, and Midwest, but fails to mention the workhouses of New Orleans. Michel Foucault, *Discipline and Punishment: The Birth of the Prison*, trans. Alan Sheridan (New York, 1995), 24, states in regard to the changing terms of punishment that "the industrial system requires a free market in labour and, in the nineteenth century, the role of forced labor in the mechanisms of punishment diminishes accordingly and 'corrective' detention takes its place."

[4] Professor Gilles Vandal of the University of Sherbrooke, Quebec, Canada, told this author at the 1998 annual meeting of the Louisiana Historical Association, New Iberia, La., that his forthcoming book on New Orleans' institutions of the nineteenth century will include a chapter on its workhouses.

[5] One exceptional example is Michael B. Katz, *Poverty and Policy in American History* (New York, 1983), which focuses on the issue of poverty, connecting it with a case study of workhouses in nineteenth-century New York state. Gary B. Nash, "Urban Wealth and Poverty in Pre-Revolutionary America," *Journal of Interdisciplinary History*, 6 (1976): 555, uses statistics from the workhouses of Boston, New York, and Philadelphia to help determine the level of poverty in (British) colonial America.

[6] The standard source on welfare institutions in the state historiography, Elizabeth Wisner, *Public Welfare Administration in Louisiana* (Chicago, 1930), 100, is the only secondary reference to the New Orleans workhouses, albeit *en passant*—Wisner cites the legislature's act establishing the workhouses of New Orleans, but nothing further in regard to their subsequent development and administration.

Julianna Liles Boudreaux, "A History of Philanthropy in New Orleans 1835-1862" (Ph.D. dissertation, Tulane University, 1961); Mark T. Carleton, *Politics and Punishment: The History of the Louisiana State Penal System* (Baton Rouge, 1971); Joy J. Jackson, *The Gilded Age in New Orleans 1880-1896* ([Baton Rouge,] 1969); and Robert Moran, *The History of Child Welfare in Louisiana* (Lafayette, 1980) are all silent on the subject of the New Orleans workhouses.

Other sources deal with the punishment of nonviolent crime in the French and Spanish colonial periods in Louisiana: Henry Plauché Dart, "Imprisonment for Debt in French Louisiana," *Louisiana Historical Quarterly*, 8 (1925): 549-56; Dart, "Courts and Law in Colonial Louisiana," ibid., 4 (1921): 255-89; and Derek Kerr, "Petty Felony, Slave Defiance, and Frontier Villany: Crime and Criminal Justice in Spanish Louisiana, 1770-1803" (Ph.D. dissertation, Tulane University, 1983).

[7] Wisner, *Welfare in Louisiana*, 138-40.

[8] Ibid., 142-43. For another contemporary account which urged reform of the Orleans Parish Prison, see Gustav de Beaumont and Alexis de Tocqueville, *On the Penitentiary System in the United States*, trans. Francis Lieber (Philadelphia, 1833).

[9] Joseph Clarence Mouledous, "Sociological Perspectives on a Prison Social System" (M.A. thesis, Louisiana State University, 1962), 39-44. This author compares the later Louisiana convict lease system with the Nazi concentration camps. Ibid., 81. Other sources on the history of prisons in Louisiana include James Wayne Allgood, "A Sociological Analysis of the Transition of the Louisiana Penal System" (M.A. thesis, Louisiana State University, 1956); and Charlotte Mae Richardson, "Women in Prison" (M.A. thesis, Louisiana State University, 1959).

[10] *Journal of the Senate* (1841), 1st session, 48, 54; and *New Orleans Daily Picayune*, January 30, 1841. The House had "adopted" the bill on January 27. *Daily Picayune*, January 28, 1841.

[11] *Daily Picayune*, January 31, 1841.

[12] *Journal of the Senate* (1841), 1st session, 56, 60; and "An Act to establish Work Houses and Houses of Refuge by the several Municipalities of the City of New Orleans, and for other purposes," Louisiana *Acts* (1841), 1st session, 48. It is this author's understanding that houses of refuge were orphanages funded by the municipalities instead of the state, and usually appended to the jail or prison. The purpose of the houses of refuge was largely the same as the Workhouses. The board of commissioners of the House of Refuge reported in 1867, that 103 boys and 29 girls remained. During the month, the girls had made 96 shirts for the Boys' House of Refuge, and 22 other articles of clothing; in addition, they had also mended 150 articles, and washed 1675 articles. For the same month, the Boys' House of Refuge had earned $1748.12 through their indentured labor. *Daily Picayune*, February 17, 1867. A grand jury report from two years prior, however, had described the institutions for young persons as "revolting prisons, from which juvenile minds turn with horror." Ibid., July 7, 1865. The only work solely devoted to children's institutions in Louisiana does not mention the houses of refuge of the nineteenth century. Moran, *Child Welfare in Louisiana*.

[13] "An Act to establish Work Houses," 46-47.

[14] For further discussion of the idea of institutionalization as social control, see Stephen Spitzer, "Towards a Marxist Theory of Deviance," *Social Problems*, 22 (1975): 638-51; Lois W. Banner, "Religious Benevolence as Social Control: A Critique of an Interpretation," *Journal of American History*, 60 (1973): 23-48; William A. Muraskin, "The Social Control Theory in American History: A Critique," *Journal of Social History*, 9 (1976): 566, passim; and Constance McGovern, "The Myths of Social Control and Custodial Oppression: Patterns of Psychiatric Medicine in Late Nineteenth-Century Institutions," ibid., 20 (1986): 3-23.

[15] Proceedings of the First Municipality Council, March 14, 1842, New Orleans Public Library; Workhouse Inventories, 1844-1850, 1851-1856, ibid. On February 20, 1846, the *New Orleans Daily Picayune* described a recorder's court:

> A few half-naked wretches were presented to his honor as usual, for indulging in too frequent libations of cheap whiskey and kicking up general rows in the street—while some were up for having no home and being unable to obtain one. The latter class were provided with a temporary residence in the work-house, and the former fined. Three little ragged, vicious-looking boys, with their heads almost as destitute of hair as a barber's block or the head of a patient suffering with the brain fever, were ensconced in one corner of the box. One was engaged in the pleasing occupation of picking the bare foot of another of the trio, while he amused himself by pinching his neighbor, receiving in return several severe blows in the face. These precious sprigs were found sleeping in a shed the preceding night, and actually shed tears when they were dragged out by the ears and taken to the watch-house. They were sent to play in the "juvenile yard," and will probably before long be chanting, "The Poor Vork'us [sic] Boy."

[16] *New Orleans Daily Delta*, October 23, 1845.

[17] *Daily Picayune*, March 27, 1842.

[18] *Daily Delta*, October 23, 1845.

[19] Proceedings of the Third Municipality Council, June 13, 1844, New Orleans Public Library.

[20] *Daily Delta*, October 23, 1845.

[21] *Daily Picayune*, February 18, 1845.

[22] Ibid., February 8, 1846. The cat the quote refers to is a cat-o'-nine tails. This report is in stark contrast to the cheerful description present in the *Picayune* less than four years prior.

[23] See, for example, Workhouse Work Records, 1852-1856, New Orleans Public Library.

[24] Report of the Board of Administrators of the Charity Hospital, 1848, reprinted in part in the *Daily Picayune*, February 12, 1848.

[25] Register of Persons Committed to the Third Municipality Workhouse, 1844-1851, New Orleans Public Library. Evidence that the population of vagrant persons was increasing is shown in the *Daily Picayune*, February 19, 1850, which reported: "Some forty vagrants, drunkards, & c., were brought up yesterday before acting Recorder Bonneval and discharged, after being lectured on the wickedness of their ways." Although he did not commit them, the recorder still took the opportunity to attempt moral improvement. The recorder may have been granted such leniency by his office, or perhaps the workhouse was at full capacity.

The Second Municipality Recorder responded to the "problem" by refusing to commit persons to the workhouse since he personally felt the workhouse act was unconstitutional. All of those left in the institution under his jurisdiction were "two women, one of whom is blind, and the other remaining as her companion. They have been in for four months, and are not disposed to leave." Ibid., March 29, 1851.

[26] Persons Committed to the Third Municipality Workhouse; *Daily Picayune*, February 13, 1850; and Richard Lawrence Gordon, "The Development of Louisiana's Public Mental Institutions, 1769-1943" (Ph.D. dissertation, Louisiana State University, 1978), passim. The Charity Hospital founded its own mental asylum in 1841. See Louisiana *Acts* (1840), 2nd session, 125-26. The State of Louisiana founded its first independent state mental institution in 1848. See Louisiana *Acts* (1847), 2nd session, "An Act to establish an Insane Asylum in the State of Louisiana," 56. Various other state-funded institutions for the "dependent" operated during the antebellum period, including the Charity Hospital, orphanages, women's asylums, and a school for the deaf and mute. See Louisiana *House Journal* (1854), appendix, "Report of the Joint Committee on Charitable Institutions," 5.

The city of New Orleans also founded its own mental asylum during the antebellum period, because there was not enough room at the state asylum. See Stanford Chaillé, "A Memoir of the Insane Asylum of the State of Louisiana, at Jackson," *New Orleans Medical and Surgical Journal*, 15 (1848): 23, passim; New Orleans Insane Asylum, Record of Entries and Releases, 1858-1882, New Orleans Public Library; and Joy J. Jackson, *The Gilded Age in New Orleans 1880-1896* (Baton Rouge, 1969). Inmates from the workhouses served as assistants at the New Orleans City Asylum. See Workhouse Inventories, 1851-1856.

[27] *Daily Picayune*, February 6, 1850. For an excellent legal discussion of slavery in Louisiana, see Judith Kelleher Schafer, *Slavery, the Civil Law, and the Supreme Court of Louisiana* (Baton Rouge, 1994). The Third Municipality contained Christine Jones, "a mulatto woman, from Baton Rouge," who "avers that she is free, and has been detained three months and a half, because of her inability to prove her freedom." *New Orleans Daily Picayune*, March 29, 1851.

[28] Common Council Proceedings, November 5, 1852, New Orleans Public Library.

[29] Ibid., July 7, 1855.

[30] See Workhouse Inventories of Stock on Hand, 1851-1856, New Orleans Public Library; and Workhouse Account Book, 1852-1857, ibid.

[31] For a discussion of the effects of the Civil War on state welfare institutions in the South and North, see Robert H. Bremner, "The Impact of the Civil War on Philanthropy and Social Welfare," *Civil War History*, 12 (1966): 293-303. For the changing legal status of blacks in Louisiana, see Paul A. Kunkel, "Modifications of Louisiana Negro Legal Status Under Louisiana's Constitutions, 1812-1957," in *An Uncommon Experience: Law and Judicial Institutions in Louisiana, 1803-2003*, eds. Judith Kelleher Schafer and Warren M. Billings (Lafayette, La., 1997), 545-65.

[32] Roger C. Shugg, *Origins of Class Struggle in Louisiana: A Social History of White Farmers and Laborers During Slavery and After, 1840-1875* (University, La., 1939), 171-72. Shugg, however, cited no source for this claim. For a critical assessment of Shugg's methodology, see Joseph G. Tregle, Jr., "Another Look at Shugg's Louisiana," *Louisiana Histiory*, 17 (1976): 245-81. Tregle concludes: "The moral should be clear: it is time for Louisiana historians to set Shugg aside and to approach research into antebellum Louisiana with open and receptive minds." Ibid., 275.

[33] *New Orleans Daily Picayune*, February 28, 1863; and ibid., February 12, 1863.

[34] See, for example, ibid., February 28, 1850, February 21, 1859; and Richard Tansey, "Out-of-State Free Blacks in Late Antebellum New Orleans," *Louisiana History*, 22 (1981): 369-86, passim. People of all types apparently found themselves at the mercy of the recorder's court. The *Daily Picayune* of February 20, 1859 described one such scene: "The motley crowd of petty offenders formed a solid phalanx behind the wooden grating in the court room this morning. Niggers black, women white and red, men with blueish looks, stood up together, offering to the gaze of the curious the faded variegated colors of a beggar's tattered cloak." On the same day, a "colored gent" was sentenced for six months for "having cohabited with a white woman"; a white

woman also received six months because she "cohabits with a negro man." It was unclear, however, if the two had been involved with one another. Ibid.

[35] *Daily Picayune*, July 7, 1865.

[36] Louisiana *Acts* (1865), extra session, "An Act to amend and re-enact the one hundred and twenty-first section of an act entitled 'An Act relative to crimes and offenses,' approved March 14, 1855," 18-19.

[37] *Daily Picayune*, February 4, 1867. Many women at this time were committed for being "lewd and abandoned," demonstrating the use of the workhouses as an institution for social (and moral) control. Ibid., February 9, 11, 16, and 20, 1867.

[38] Louisiana *Acts* (1867), 2nd session, "An Act relative to vagrants committed to workhouse in the city of New Orleans," 205.

[39] *Daily Picayune*, February 8, 1868.

[40] Louisiana *House Journal* (1869), 2nd session, "Message From the Governor," 7.

[41] Louisiana *Acts* (1869), 2nd session, "An Act Relative to Vagrants in the Metropolitan Police District," 87. Section 1 defined vagrancy in similar terms as the 1841 law (see above). This law was more detailed and intricate than the 1841 law, however. Section 2, for example, outlined the examination and trial; Section 4 discussed trial by jury; Section 7 described the conditions of release—if requested, from home parish or state, if repatriated, to the country of origin, if "repentant," claimed by two responsible property holding citizens who will supply permanent employment; and Section 8 defined the penalty for harboring vagrants. Ibid., 87-88.

[42] *Daily Picayune*, February 14, 16, 17, 1876. The New Orleans German-language newspaper, *Deutschen Zeitung*, reported that the workhouse had been set afire by the prisoners, May 22, 1870.

[43] See, for example, James T. Patterson, *America's Struggle Against Poverty 1900-1980* (Cambridge, Mass., 1981).

FREE MEN OF COLOR AS TOMB BUILDERS IN THE NINETEENTH CENTURY*

Patricia Brady

The cities of the dead—New Orleans cemeteries, their streets and alleys lined with tombs—have stood as symbols of the foreignness of the city in relation to the rest of the United States since the early nineteenth century. In the city's first century (the eighteenth), however, the dead, if distinguished, were buried in the parish church of St. Louis and its adjacent grounds, otherwise belowground in the St. Peter Street cemetery outside the original municipal boundaries.

The practical reasons for a growing preference for tomb burial are obvious: graves dug in the swampy ground of New Orleans rapidly filled with water to the disgust of the survivors; land in the city was scarce, as was burial space in the church. The first of the classic St. Louis cemeteries was created because of the fire, flood, and pestilence of 1788: more space was needed to bury the dead. St. Louis Cemetery I was opened officially in 1789. Belowground burials continued there, but tombs rapidly became common. Those early tombs were simple and functional. They were built of local soft red brick, plastered and whitewashed; marble—expensive because it was imported—was used mainly for enclosure tablets.[1]

Memorial style and order developed as more impressive tombs were built in St. Louis I, and successive cemeteries—St. Louis II in 1823 and St. Louis III in 1854—were laid out in neat grids (the aisles of St. Louis I were uneven). There were still below-ground burials in St. Louis I and II well into the nineteenth century, especially in times of epidemics, but tomb burial became the norm.

Sophisticated tomb design came with the arrival of Jacques Nicolas Bussière de Pouilly, a French architect who came to New Orleans in 1833. With French academic training, De Pouilly brought to his many commissions for tomb design the influences of classical monuments and of the great Parisian cemetery, Père Lachaise. His designs, as

---

*First published in Glenn R. Conrad, ed., *Cross, Crozier and Crucible: A Volume Celebrating the Bicentennial of a Catholic Diocese in Louisiana* (New Orleans, La.: Archdiocese of New Orleans in Cooperation with the Center for Louisiana Studies, 1993), 478-88. Reprinted with the kind permission of the author and the publisher.

Free Men of Color as Tomb Builders 555

executed by local marble cutters, beautified New Orleans cemeteries and encouraged others to design grander and more aesthetically ambitious tombs.[2] Marble cutters *cum* sculptors began to set standards of stylistic excellence in the execution of tombs. Besides utilitarian tombs, cutters also turned their tools to funerary sculpture—plaques, bas-reliefs, and carved decorative elements.

In the early nineteenth century, the craft was dominated by French marble cutters who had been trained in Europe. Few blacks were marble cutters or sculptors, though they often worked at tasks associated with cemeteries—masonry, foundation and tomb erection, and marble setting. Three remarkable free men of color—Florville Foy and Eugène and Daniel Warburg—however, did begin distinguished careers as marble cutters in the antebellum period and influenced the look of New Orleans cemeteries.[3]

Foy and the Warburg brothers all had artistic talent, but artistic talent can languish in neglect, as was particularly true for African-Americans in the slave-owning South. Besides talent and ambition, the men shared family and financial advantages. The sons of white men and women of color, they were reared in supportive households. Though their parents were unmarried—interracial marriages were illegal—they nevertheless had enduring relationships. Their fathers, both Europeans by birth, made themselves responsible for their mulatto children, providing educations for their sons and setting them up in business. They also used their friendships with other influential whites for the benefit of those sons.

Florville Foy (1820-1903), like many nineteenth-century craftsmen, learned his trade from his father. A native of Orléans, Prosper Foy (1787-1854) had been one of Bonaparte's soldiers in the ill-fated expedition against Saint-Domingue. Immigrating to New Orleans, in 1807 Foy first advertised his services as a marble cutter and sculptor who sculpted in the "European style"; he produced tombstones with inscriptions, as well as mantels and tables. Sociable and popular, he associated largely with the foreign French in the city, especially the Bonapartists. As early as 1810, he began a lifelong relationship with a free woman of color, Azelie Aubry (c.1795-1870); though they were unmarried, after Foy's death she listed herself in city directories as the widow of Prosper Foy and was so styled in her obituary and on her tombstone. They had several children, of whom four daughters and a son, Florville, lived to adulthood. The elder Foy joined the American forces in the Battle of New Orleans, later added engraving and instruction in architecture to his trade of marble cutting, and wrote articles for local newspapers. He eventually acquired a plantation in St. James Parish, where he spent a great deal of his time, though he continued to share a house on Love (now Rampart) Street in the Third Municipality with Aubry.[4]

For convenience in moving large, heavy slabs of marble, marble yards clustered near cemeteries. In the 1830s, Prosper Foy's atelier was on Basin Street near St. Louis I. There he was joined by Florville, who had been sent to France to study, and had returned ready to learn a lucrative and respected trade. The adolescent Florville Foy showed an aptitude and application that made him one of the leading marble cutters in New Orleans for the next fifty years. Marble cutting in the nineteenth century was still as much a skilled craft as it had been in the Middle Ages. Cutting was learned through apprenticeship, and competent marble cutters set up workshops with relatively small capital requirements, whether on their own or employing one or two workmen. It would appear that Prosper Foy stayed in the trade only long enough to train his son adequately. By 1838, he had permanently retired from marble cutting. Eighteen-year-old Florville opened his own marble yard, no doubt bankrolled by the elder Foy; as a marble cutter and sculptor, he would far surpass his father.[5]

The Warburg brothers, Eugène (c. 1825/26-1859) and Daniel (1836-1911), like Florville Foy, had a concerned father who saw to their education. They were the sons of Daniel Samuel Warburg (1789-1860), a member of a distinguished German Jewish family, who came to New Orleans in 1821 as a commission merchant. Financially successful, he, like Prosper Foy, found his friends mainly among the contingent of foreigners in the city—more politically radical, more racially tolerant, and generally better educated than native New Orleanians. One of his friends was Pierre Soulé, a French antimonarchist who had worked with Alexandre Dumas, a mulatto, on a republican publication in Paris. Soulé arrived in the city in 1825 and set up a law practice, later marrying into a very cultured Creole family, the Merciers. Soulé represented Warburg in at least one legal case and was involved with him in property transactions.

During his early years in the city, Warburg acquired a Cuban mulatto slave, Marie Rose Blondeau (c. 1804-1837), who became his mistress. In 1825 or early 1826, she gave birth to a son, Eugène, who was born into slavery. In the early 1830s their next child was born free, indicating that Warburg had freed Blondeau between the births of the two children. Warburg's emancipation of his four-year-old son Eugène in February 1830, however, is well documented.

He and his friend Soulé posted a $500 bond, obliging themselves to provide for Eugène until he came of age, to teach him to read and write, and to educate him in a trade so that he could support himself. Soulé was in effect the boy's godfather.

Warburg and Blondeau had five children, four of them born free; Daniel, the youngest, was born in 1836. Although they were unmarried, Blondeau gave her name as Warburg in a business transaction, and the name on her tomb in St. Louis Cemetery I is Marie Rose Warburg alias Blondeau. When she died in 1837, Warburg continued to maintain a household for the family.

During the 1830s Daniel Warburg grew wealthy through land speculation. The records of the notarial archives for the decade are filled with his transactions as he bought and sold large amounts of property—city buildings and lots, as well as plantations. The latter he subdivided and resold as lots; one of the largest such transactions was the purchase of the De La Ronde plantation for $127,000. He served as a director of New Levee Steam Cotton Press and on the board of the Citizens' Bank of Louisiana. Well educated but eccentric, he also devised peculiar scientific and mathematical theories which he published and attempted, unsuccessfully, to market. Warburg's intricate financial network fell apart in the aftermath of the disastrous Panic of 1837; with payments unmet, mortgages were called and properties sold in a losing game of financial dominoes. Like many speculators, he lost most of his money between 1839 and 1841; he did retain enough city property to support himself and the children modestly.

After the financial collapse, the family moved to a less prestigious area, out of the French Quarter into the Foys' neighborhood in the Third Municipality. Whatever plans Warburg may have made for his sons' educations and futures clearly had to be modified by financial realities: the brothers would have to support themselves in the future. Where they studied as boys is unknown, but their father obviously saw to their education. Eugène, for example, wrote fluent, grammatical French with the flowing, well-formed hand of the educated man.[6]

In the 1840s Eugène studied with the best sculptor in New Orleans, Philippe Garbeille. Garbeille, a Frenchman who had studied in Marseilles and Paris and with the noted sculptor Bertel Thorvaldsen, arrived in the city in 1841. His specialty was portrait busts of the well known: politicians, businessmen, actors, musicians, prominent visitors to the city. One of his earliest sitters was Pierre Soulé, who doubtless helped arrange for Eugène's studies, sometime between 1841 and 1847. Eugène may have worked with his teacher on two important marble statues—*St. Francis* and the *Virgin and Child*—commissioned by St. Louis Cathedral in 1846. After Garbeille's departure from the city in 1848, for about a year Eugène neither advertised nor listed himself in the city directory as a sculptor. Perhaps he spent that time working with an experienced artisan in the trade of cutting tombs—a practical skill for a sculptor without private means in a city with a growing market for fine tombs.[7]

In 1849 young Warburg, who lived with his father and brother Daniel, listed himself as a marble cutter. By the next year he had opened an atelier on St. Louis Street between Basin and Franklin across the street from St. Louis Cemetery I in an area thick with marble workshops. This shop was his headquarters throughout his New Orleans career; Daniel became his helper, learning the trade as an apprentice in his teens.[8] Eugène Warburg's small, independent workshop was not at all unusual in the antebellum period; marble cutting was still very much a craftsman's operation. The owners of even the large yards were generally cutters themselves, and the Warburgs lacked the capital to finance a large marble yard on the scale of Florville Foy.

Although Eugène Warburg was the more talented sculptor, Florville Foy became one of the most successful marble cutters in New Orleans. Certainly in his early years, Foy shared some of Warburg's artistic ambitions and hoped to be recognized as a sculptor of works apart from tombs. One of his early sculptures was a marble figure on a base entitled *Child with Drum*, acquired by the Louisiana State Museum in the early twentieth century. When Achille Perelli, Italian-born sculptor, came to New Orleans in 1850, Foy became one of his intimate friends. Perelli, who replaced Garbeille as the city's leading sculptor, sculpted Foy's bust, one of his cherished possessions. Foy was also a friend of the painter Paul Poincy.[9]

But for most sculptors in New Orleans, including Foy, cemetery work paid the bills. Foy early specialized in tablets, headstones, and tombs. Not particularly lucrative, but a steady source of work was building tombs and vaults for the churchwardens of St. Louis Cathedral. The wardens regularly had wall vaults and simple tombs, as well as a few large tombs, built in the St. Louis cemeteries, which they controlled. These were then sold as the need arose. Early in his career, from September 1836 through May 1837, Foy was employed by the wardens. During that time he built eighty-four wall vaults in St. Louis I and II, at $35 per vault. In June 1837 he was replaced by builders Gurlie and Guillot; they were shortly succeeded by the guardian of the two cemeteries, who maintained the cemeteries, oversaw workers, such as slaves spreading earth over the belowground graves, and built the vaults and tombs commissioned by the wardens.[10]

More important for his artistic development, Foy built tombs designed by J. N. B. de Pouilly, acquiring elegance and precision of execution. The French architect's influence can be seen in the grander tombs that Foy himself designed and built later in his career. Many elegant tombs and fine sculptures in the St. Louis cemeteries were executed by Foy.

In the 1850s Foy acquired the property next door to the mortuary chapel of St. Anthony—a suitable site for a marble yard specializing in tombs. He lived in a large apartment over his workshop with an adjoining lot filled with both rough and fine marble. By 1850 a white woman from Mississippi, Louisa Whittaker, lived with him; they eventually married in 1885. Foy owned at least two slave house servants and lived with considerable style. On a farm at the intersection of Broad and Dumaine, he experimented with the breeding of imported horses, cows, and hogs, which fetched top prizes throughout the state.[11]

In New Orleans, he generally signed tombs with only his first name, Florville. Among the many signed tombs from this period are the classical marble Reseq, Adam, and Cavelier tombs. Privately commissioned tombs of high quality cost in the range of $800 to $2,250. Foy also purchased cemetery lots and built brick tombs on speculation, such as the Aleix tomb in St. Louis Cemetery I (1861). He also expanded his business to neighboring states in the 1850s, providing signed tombs for St. Michael Cemetery, Pensacola, and the Old Biloxi Cemetery.[12]

Foy's younger compatriot Eugène Warburg concentrated his energies on a career as a serious sculptor. By December 1850 he had created at least one major piece, a marble statue of Ganymede, kneeling and presenting a cup of nectar. In a creative marketing attempt, Warburg arranged to display the statue—with the considerable value of $500—at a Canal Street gilding establishment, where chances on it were sold in a raffle. The outcome of the raffle scheme and the fate of the sculpture are unknown, but it is unlikely that Warburg realized anything like his estimate of Ganymede's worth. The *Bee* headlined its review 'A Creole Sculptor,' and declared that "the design is beautiful, and the execution reflects infinite credit upon the taste and talent of our townsmen."[13]

In a more prosaic vein, Warburg executed the familiar funerary objects, including signed enclosure tablets in St. Louis I and II. Although he reportedly executed more ambitious statuary and fine tombs, no grand pieces signed with his name have been discovered.[14]

In mid-century, the cathedral was undergoing extensive reconstruction, offering opportunities to many craftsmen and artists. Though he was young, Warburg's work had gained enough respect that the church wardens invited him to submit a bid for marble flooring in the cathedral. In February 1851 he responded with a detailed proposal, including a sketch of the black-and-white checkerboard marble pattern. The existing central aisle of the cathedral is probably Warburg's work.[15]

But his heart was not in the commonplace work that provided a living for other marble cutters. Warburg continued to carve allegorical pieces and portrait busts, though none is known to survive today. Making a living as an artist in nineteenth-century America was difficult. And in New Orleans competition with the very talented and experienced—and white—Achille Perelli probably made the career of the young mulatto sculptor especially difficult. The city could hardly support two major sculptors. Discouraged by his lack of commissions, Warburg decided to go to Europe to study and work.

The money to support this undertaking was not readily to be found. His own savings, probably augmented by assistance from his father, could pay for the journey, but an extended stay abroad while he attracted commissions for his sculpture would be expensive. Eugène and his father went through the legal steps necessary to sell three slaves remaining from his mother's estate, the joint inheritance of the Warburg children. Eugène gave his father power of attorney and sailed for France sometime around the end of November 1852, leaving his workshop in the hands of his sixteen-year-old brother Daniel. The following year he realized his share of the slave sale—one-fifth of $1400.[16]

With the departure of Eugène Warburg, New Orleans lost her best native sculptor. He never returned to the city, but his career in Europe and the notice given him by New Orleans newspapers should be briefly followed.

From 1852 through 1856, Warburg studied and worked largely in France. Seeking a recommendation from an influential figure, he naturally approached his family friend, Pierre Soulé, now United States minister to Spain, who was in Paris during the autumns of 1853 and 1854. Soulé's friendship for the young man was an ironic counterpoint to his pro-slavery views and fears of the "Africanization" of Cuba. He provided Warburg with the desired letter of recommendation and almost certainly brought his work to the attention of the United States minister to France, John Young Mason.

Warburg was commissioned by Mason to sculpt a portrait bust. The artist completed a classically chaste bust of Mason in 1855; now at the Virginia Historical Society, it is his only known extant sculpture. Warburg was reportedly in Belgium during this time; he probably modeled Mason's bust and visited with Soulé in 1854 while the diplomats met in Ostend on the question of American acquisition of Cuba, hammering out the imperialistic Ostend Manifesto.[17]

Traveling to London, Warburg became a protégé of the philanthropic, abolitionist Harriet Leveson-Gower, Duchess of Sutherland. The duchess, a friend and admirer of Harriet Beecher Stowe, commissioned him to do a series of bas-reliefs from *Uncle Tom's Cabin*. Warburg probably met Stowe at Dunrobin Castle in the late summer of 1856 while working on this commission. Both Stowe and the duchess provided the sculptor with letters of recommendation as he set out for Italy.[18]

When Warburg arrived in Florence in 1857, his presence and the three recommendations were reported by a Northern newspaper; the story was picked up by New Orleans newspapers. The notoriously race-baiting *Crescent*, fearful of free people of color, waxed sarcastic and criticized Soulé for his support of Warburg, apparently ignorant of their connection.[19] Race relations in New Orleans had changed since the early part of the century when Soulé stood sponsor to Daniel Warburg's mulatto son and Henry B. Latrobe, godfather to Prosper Foy's mulatto daughter.

Warburg soon left Florence for Rome, where he died on January 12, 1859. The *Bee*, less racist than the *Crescent*, praised Warburg as one of the most promising of Louisiana's native sons: he was among the galaxy of American artists adding luster to their country; his death was a great loss to America and to New Orleans.[20]

After Eugène's departure, the adolescent Daniel Warburg continued in the marble cutting trade in the workshop near St. Louis I. The skills and standards he learned from his professionally trained brother stood him in good stead. For nearly twenty years, he maintained an independent atelier, doing marble cutting of excellent quality. Less ambitious than his brother, Daniel Warburg's life was one of steady work and care for his family. He and his father continued to live together even after Daniel's marriage in 1859. They were not wealthy, but lived comfortably, employing a live-in Irish maidservant. Daniel and his wife, Josephine Rosario (1842-1901), had at least four children, including Joseph Daniel, Jr. (1867-1921) who also became a marble cutter—Warburg's full name, never used, was Joseph Daniel. The elder Daniel Warburg died in late 1860.[21]

The identifiable works from the first twenty years of Daniel Warburg's life are marble enclosure tablets for wall vaults in St. Louis Cemeteries I and II. During the 1850s and 1860s he signed a number of these well-cut marble pieces, decorated with crosses—alone or enclosed in decorative borders or wreaths—such as those of Anne Emilie Mioton (1852), Marie Lucrecia (1853), Daniel Rivoil (1853), Catherine Barry, 185[?], Charles Mony (1860), Rose Marceline LeMarois (1861), A. Sainville Casbergue (1863), and Famille M. A. Levasseur (undated).[22]

By the 1870s, the tomb business had changed under the influence of burgeoning post-Civil War capitalism. Large monument companies could provide better service at lower prices—employing large numbers of workers with different specialties, purchasing costly steam equipment, and controlling large supplies of marble and granite, as the latter stone became increasingly more fashionable for tombs and markers. It became much more difficult for an independent artisan to support himself. Warburg finally gave up his own studio in 1871. He at first worked for Florville Foy for a year, moving on to Joseph Llula, and then to a major marble yard, Kursheedt and Bienvenu, where he worked for many years. He continued to sign enclosure tablets in the St. Louis cemeteries, such as those of Joseph Masaneillo Dias (1872), Famille Esnard (1872), and E. Lavenere (1884), and also in the new Cypress Grove Cemetery, that of Ann McGuire (1889).

He ended his career with Albert Weiblen where he worked into the twentieth century. Weiblen, a German immigrant, personified the new marble trade, purchasing a large plant, employing numerous designers and cutters, and leasing a granite quarry at Stone Mountain, Georgia. The Weiblen firm was responsible for most of the tombs in Metairie Cemetery. There Warburg's carving, beautifully cut with well-finished edges, was much admired. He was unusual in that he was able to carve both marble and granite; other cutters were expert in only one medium. Many of his well-cut tombs, such as those of James L. McLean (1891) and Godfrey Lob (undated), were adorned with morning glory vines, which seems to have been a recurring motif. His best-known work is the Holcombe-Aiken column, designed by Albert Weiblen—a tall unfluted shaft entwined with morning glory vines and blossoms. Quiet and reserved, Daniel Warburg continued working until shortly before his death in 1911. He was buried in a modest wall vault in St. Louis II. [23]

While Daniel Warburg was forced to give up his independent workshop in the 1870s and go to work for larger firms, Florville Foy also struggled financially to maintain his marble yard against large competitors, but succeeded in staying in business until his death. He owned a considerable amount of property throughout the city, most of it apparently rental property, which was his buffer against business reverses. For twenty years, into the 1890s, he frequently mortgaged property or traded it back and forth with Louisa Whittaker before their marriage or with James F. Johnson, the manager of the marble yard. The frequency with which these sales occurred and their equally frequent resales to Foy indicates that they were financial ploys to keep his business running. By 1880, annual transactions of the yard reached $20,000, and Foy employed eight artisans.

As Foy grew old—he was childless and with no natural successor— the business wound down. He died, a widower, in 1903, tended by a servant who had been his slave. He was buried in St. Louis III in a tomb much simpler than those he created for clients at the height of his powers. [24]

The lives of Florville Foy and Eugène and Daniel Warburg illustrate much about the free community of color and about the cemetery business in New Orleans. Typical of free men of color, they earned their livings in skilled trades. They grew up in intact families: their European fathers were influential in their lives, seeing to their education and training and helping to set them up in business. They were aided in their careers by white compatriots of their fathers and had frequent business dealings with whites. However, their particular trade—marble cutting—was an unusual choice for free men of color, who clustered in the building and cigar- making trades.

Foy and the Warburg brothers share historical obscurity with even the most prolific white marble cutters, such as the Frenchman Paul H. Monsseaux. Their careers provide valuable insights into nineteenth-century cemetery work. But more information is needed about the trade of marble cutting in general–where the men trained, how their businesses were financed, how much money they made, the nature of their business and social relationships with one another. Understanding marble cutting is an avenue to a fuller understanding of the history of the cemeteries of New Orleans.

Notes for "Free Men of Color as Tomb Builders in the Nineteenth Century"

[1] Leonard V. Huber, Peggy McDowell, and Mary Louise Christovich, *The Cemeteries*, vol. 3 of Friends of the Cabildo, *New Orleans Architecture*, 6 vols. (Gretna, 1971-1980): 3-6.

[2] Peggy McDowell, "J. N. B. de Pouilly and French Sources of Revival Style Design in New Orleans Cemetery Architecture," in Richard E. Meyer, ed., *Cemeteries and Gravemakers: Voices of American Culture* (Ann Arbor, 1989), 139-40.

[3] A fourth black marble cutter, Alexander Nelder of Saint-Domingue (c. 1823-c. 1867), also worked in the city as early as 1845. One signed work is the imposing tomb of Gabriel Toutant Beauregard in St. Bernard Cemetery (1854). Nelder, however, never enjoyed the recognition or financial success of Foy or the Warburgs. New Orleans city directories (hereafter cited as NOCD), 1846-1869; "Alexander Nelder" in John A. Mahé II et al., eds., *Encyclopaedia of New Orleans Artists, 1718-1918* (New Orleans, 1987) (hereafter cited as *Encyclopaedia*); U.S. Census, Louisiana (1850), roll 238, (1860), roll 419.

[4] "René Prosper Foy" in *Encyclopaedia;* Prosper Foy Papers, Howard-Tilton Memorial Library, Tulane University; *Moniteur de la Louisiane*, August 11, 1807; Simone de la Souchère Deléry, *Napoleon's Soldiers in America* (Gretna, 1972), 109, 163; NOCD 1811-1855; *New Orleans Bee*, January 25, 1870; Charles Testut, *Portraits Litteraires de la Nouvelle-Orléans* (New Orleans, 1850), 177-78; New Orleans Notarial Archives, M. V. Dejan, July 29, 1892; *New Orleans Bee*, February 8, 1854.

[5] "Prosper Florville Foy" in *Encyclopaedia;* NOCD 1834-1841.

[6] Bertram Wallace Korn, *The Early Jews of New Orleans* (Waltham, Mass., 1969), 179-81, 321; *Dictionary of American Biography;* First Judicial District Court (1827), 7640; New Orleans Notarial Archives, Charles Janin, February 9, 1830; Samuel Wilson, Jr., *Plantation Houses on the Battlefield of New Orleans* (New Orleans, 1965), 70-72; Daniel Warburg, *Buy a Lottery Ticket; or A Chance to Get Rid of Money . . .* (New Orleans, 1839); Daniel Warburg, *"The Goddess Eve." Two Tables, Constructed to Demonstrate by Numbers the True Mode for Extracting the Square Root Out of All Entire Numbers Above 100 . . .* (New Orleans, 1839); Eugène Warburg to Messieurs les membres du Comité de Construction de l'Eglise St. Louis, February 12, 1851, Historic New Orleans Collection.

[7] NOCD 1822-1846; "Philippe Garbeille" in *Encyclopaedia*.

[8] NOCD 1850-1853.

[9] Robert Glenk, *Handbook and Guide to the Louisiana State Museum* (New Orleans, 1934), 96; *New Orleans Daily Picayune*, March 17, 1903.

[10] Financial Reports of St. Louis Cathedral (1836-1849), October 20, November 5, November 10, 1836, January 5, February 3, March 4, April 3, May 2, June 6, 1837, May 15, June 10, 1839, March 25, 1840, Archives of the Archdiocese of New Orleans.

[11] *Daily Picayune*, March 17, 1903; U.S. Census, Louisiana (1850), roll 235, (1870), roll 521; New Orleans Notarial Archives, James Fahey, March 5, 1885; Register of Marriages, New Orleans Health Department, 1885-1886, 11:107, New Orleans Public Library.

[12] New Orleans Notarial Archives, Paul Bertus, July 15, 1835, Theodore Guyol, March 9, 1847, Laurence R. Kenny, October 20, 1849, Joseph Cohn, October 24, 1855, Selim Magner, November 18, 1861; Survey of Historic New Orleans Cemeteries, Historic New Orleans Collection; Sharyn Thompson, "Stone Carvers and Monument Dealers Whose Work Appears in St. Michael Cemetery, Pensacola, Florida," 1988; Sharyn Thompson, "Stone Carvers and Monument Dealers Whose Work Appears in Old Biloxi Cemetery, Biloxi, Mississippi," 1988.

[13] *New Orleans Bee*, December 13, 1850.

[14] Rodolphe Lucien Desdunes, *Our People and Our History*, trans. Dorothea Olga McCants (Baton Rouge, 1973), 69-70; Survey of Historic New Orleans Cemeteries.

[15] Eugène Warburg to Messieurs les membres du Comité de Construction de l'Eglise St. Louis, February 12, 1851.

[16] Desdunes, *Our People,* 69-70; New Orleans Notarial Archives, Antoine Doriocourt, November 18, 1852, January 5, 6, 1853; Charles Edwards O'Neill, "Fine Arts and Literature: Nineteenth-Century Louisiana Black Artists and Authors," in Robert R. Macdonald et al., eds., *Louisiana's Black Heritage* (New Orleans, 1979), 75; NOCD 1853.

[17] Desdunes, *Our People,* 70; *Dictionary of American Biography;* Amos A. Ettinger, *The Mission to Spain of Pierre Soulé, 1853-1855: A Study in the Cuban Diplomacy of the United States* (New Haven, Conn., 1932), 177-79, 190, 344; Regenia A. Perry, *Selections of 19th-Century Afro-American Art* (New York, 1976), n.p.

[18] Desdunes, *Our People,* 70; *Dictionary of National Biography; Dictionary of American Biography;* Noel B. Gerson, *Harriet Beecher Stowe: A Biography* (New York, 1976), 109.

[19] *Daily Picayune*, December 26, 1857; *New Orleans Daily Crescent*, December 26, 1857.

[20] O'Neill, "Fine Arts and Literature," 76-77; *New Orleans Bee*, March 9, 1859.

[21] U.S. Census, Louisiana (1850), roll 235, (1860), roll 418, index (1880, 1900, 1910); NOCD 1854-1911; O'Neill, "Fine Arts and Literature," 78; Survey of Historic Cemeteries.

[22] Survey of Historic New Orleans Cemeteries.

[23] New Orleans Death Certificate (1911), 153:109, New Orleans Public Library; Henri A. Gandolfo, interview April 10, 1989; Henri A. Gandolfo, *Metairie Cemetery: An Historical Memoir* (New Orleans, 1981), 99; Huber et al., *The Cemeteries*, 92.

[24] New Orleans Death Certificate (1903), 129:582, New Orleans Public Library; *New Orleans Daily Picayune*, March 17, 1903.

LOUISIANA LABOR IN THE FIRST HALF OF THE TWENTIETH CENTURY*

Thomas A. Becnel

Labor relations in Louisiana in the early twentieth century differed little from those in the rest of the South, where few significant innovations occurred. In industrial sectors of the United States organized labor experienced lean years prior to 1933 and enjoyed only limited successes during the New Deal period. The rural South, with strong provincial ties to its agricultural tradition and few contracts with industrial unions, presented formidable obstacles to the labor movement. Wilbur Cash concluded that intense individualism, unfortunate labor experiences, fear of communism, and a strong conviction that prosperity was imminent was factors in "a curious, widespread, and active antagonism" by Southerners toward unionism. Unions tended to be even weaker in rural and agricultural states that restricted suffrage.[1]

During the first four decades of the twentieth century, agricultural unions failed to achieve the organizational levels of the cane-field unions affiliated with the Knights of Labor in the 1880s. Increasingly, tenant farming and sharecropping became the *modus operandi* for Southern agriculture while industrial growth swept the rest of the United States. In Louisiana the Populists briefly posed a political threat to Bourbon Democrats, many of whom were cotton or sugar planters. However, when Southern Populists attempted to unify a biracial agrarian proletariat in the 1890s, Democrats took steps that had disfranchised black voters throughout the South by about 1911. Sugar growers complained of railroads "unfairly" hiring away their natural labor supply in 1907 and 1908. Planters also called for stringent enforcement of New Orleans vagrancy laws, hoping to make idle men available for farm labor. In the 1920s, when even industrial unions were weakened, many agricultural unions disappeared completely, victims of economic setbacks and political policies.[2]

---

*First published as chapter 1 in Thomas A. Becnel, *Labor, Church, and the Sugar Establishment: Louisiana, 1887-1976* (Baton Rouge: Louisiana State University Press, © 1980), 13-29. Reprinted with the kind permission of the author and publisher.

For many reasons, when organized labor set agricultural rather than general goals, its chances for success declined considerably. With the exception of the Bankhead-Jones Farm Tenancy Act of 1937, every major farm and labor bill excluded agricultural workers from its definition of labor. The Agricultural Adjustment Act did not specifically grant them benefit payments; Section 7 (a) of the National Recovery Administration did not guarantee them collective bargaining rights; Social Security did not cover them at first; the Wagner Act's National Labor Relations Board did not assure them arbitration; the Fair Labor Standards Act of 1938 specifically exempted them from its minimum wage provisions; and Section 14 (b) of the Taft-Hartley Act allowed states to pass right-to-work laws that operated to the detriment of farm workers.[3]

Unions representing timber workers, who are usually more radical and vociferous than craftsmen, failed to improve the legal standing or the economic lot of their constituents in Louisiana before World War I, but noisy campaigns alarmed antiunion forces and often encouraged retaliatory countermeasures. In 1906 John H. Kirby, a wealthy Texan, rallied lumbermen to form the Southern Lumber Operators' Association (SLOA) to counter union threats in the pine forests of Louisiana. Nevertheless, in 1910 unionized timber workers organized the Brotherhood of Timber Workers in Louisiana, and two years later it merged with the Industrial Workers of the World at a meeting in Alexandria. In Southwest Louisiana, at Graybow and Merryville, timber workers walked off their jobs in 1911 and 1912 over wages and working conditions. Authorities arrested union leaders in Graybow, charging them with conspiracy, but most workers were acquitted or never brought to trial. After this incident, harassment inspired by the SLOA diminished union activity in Louisiana lumber camps.[4]

Public policy in the South favored the most prosperous rural landowners, but few politicians could ignore Southern labor. Vocal labor minorities asserted their demands while the Southern business community helped to perpetuate the myth that labor unions were large, wealthy, and influential. This misconception of union strength was applied especially to the Congress of Industrial Organizations, whose Political Action Committee encouraged voter registration by paying poll taxes for prospective voters. In some cases, endorsement of a candidate for public office by the PAC meant sure defeat.[5]

Southern politicians, generally inexperienced in dealing with organized labor, reacted in a variety of ways to labor demands. Gov. Cole Blease of South Carolina, although he was one of the first demagogues to appeal to cotton mill workers, developed no programs for them. In a successful reelection campaign in 1946, Senator Harry Byrd of Virginia accused his rival of receiving support from the powerful CIO, but Sen. Claude Pepper used union support to win in Florida, where union members were numerous. Florida Attorney Gen. J. Tom Watson worked to undermine the influence of organized labor, and Georgia's Gov. Eugene Talmadge generally opposed the labor movement. Talmadge's campaigns dramatized the support he received from small farmers, but he pleased business leaders, who financed the campaigns, with his low tax policy and his assault on textile unions in 1934. Textile union leaders were employing caravans of strikers in "flying squadrons" who traveled about persuading or forcing workers to shut down mills. Talmadge declared martial law and placed the leaders behind barbed wire enclosures at Fort McPherson in Atlanta. But because the Talmadges—Eugene and later his son, Herman—enjoyed long tenure in office, organized labor did not antagonize them unduly. E. H. "Boss" Crump of Tennessee, who chased off CIO poll watchers in 1946, blamed organized labor for his defeat in the 1948 gubernatorial campaign, and Estes Kefauver, a liberal on civil rights and labor matters, moderated his views to appease conservative constituents and win his 1948 race for a U. S. Senate seat. He denied receiving campaign funds from the CIO Political Action Committee in Tennessee. In Virginia the CIO intervened in 1946 to secure the Democratic nomination of Willis Robertson who defeated Howard Smith, an ultraconservative, in the gubernatorial election. In Texas, Governor W. Lee O'Daniel supported legislation requiring union members to carry identification cards and submit detailed reports regarding their activities, and the legislation passed, although it was later struck down in the courts.[6]

Obviously, the strength of organized labor in the South varied from state to state. In the years after World War II, Tennessee had the highest percentage of unionized workers in the South (20.6 percent) and North Carolina the lowest (7.8 percent). Few Southern steel and textile workers joined unions. Florida had a regressive tax system and right-to-work policy that William Havard associated with the conservatism supported by the Farm Bureau, chain stores, and the liquor industry. Labor in Mississippi had little influence partly because potential white supporters were alienated by the civil rights activities of blacks. Only 12.5 percent of Louisiana's labor force joined unions in the years after World War II, compared to 28 percent nationwide.[7]

Louisiana experienced the same labor disabilities that stymied other Southern states during the 1930s, and, in addition, the state had unique problems brought on by local politicians and labor leaders. Allan Sindler blamed self-serving labor leaders for Louisiana's failure to enact child-labor, minimum wage, or workmen's compensation legislation. All too often the AFL leaders in the state resorted to personal bargaining that won them high posts in government but gained workingmen nothing. A Huey Long associate remembered that Long often said organized labor in Louisiana never defeated or elected a candidate in a statewide race.[8]

Huey Long failed to alter labor's plight directly, but labor consistently supported him. "Huey's sorry labor record," Allan Sindler wrote, "typed him, at best, a rural liberal." Long put in no strong labor legislation, Sindler noted, not even a workmen's compensation bill. Yet even though Long produced no important labor legislation—despite his nearly complete control over the legislature—his biographer, T. Harry Williams, thinks he helped workingmen in other ways. Williams attributes Long's failure to help labor to the agricultural power structure of Louisiana, where the organized labor movement was too small to realize legislative success. Yet Long's road and bridge construction, free hospital service, free textbook, and homestead exemption law benefited the masses directly and seemed a logical outgrowth of his early struggles to increase workmen's compensation benefits. Furthermore, his vocal opposition to big business won him labor support while alienating mercantile, banking, shipping, timbering, and cane- and cotton-growing interests.[9]

The Long faction continued to receive labor's endorsement after Huey's death. Governor Richard Leche made overtures to the State Federation of Labor and sounded like a labor supporter at Labor Day rallies. But one observer considered Leche "favorable to business" with his tax exemptions for business and his termination of the Huey Long-Standard Oil feud. Although he did not attempt to suppress labor organizations, Leche encouraged an anti-sit-down strike bill, vetoed a bill limiting the work week for women in 1936, and usually allowed the business-oriented State Board of Commerce and Industry a free hand.[10]

New Deal legislation changed the economic life of Louisiana and the South. For example, the National Labor Relations Board, created by the Wagner Act in 1935, helped to settle countless labor disputes. In the 1930s Charles Logan, who was hired and trained by William Leiserson, the NLRB director, became director of NLRB Region 15, which included Louisiana. He followed Leiserson's precedent of refusing to recognize company unions as bargaining agents. In 1940 he recognized the Oil Workers' International Union (CIO) as bargaining agent rather than the Solvay Employers' Council, a company union that Solvay had helped to set up in Baton Rouge. Short and red-faced, he had worked for eight years with Monsignor Peter Wynhoven at Hope Haven, a home for wayward boys in the Archdiocese of New Orleans.[11]

Organized labor especially concerned itself with two aspects of the Louisiana seafood industry. One dealt with child labor in seafood processing plants and, therefore, fell under the jurisdiction of the Children's Bureau of the Department of Labor. The other involved strikes in processing plants, which, ironically, did not always concern the Department of Labor since seasonal workers were not covered by the Wagner Act and therefore did not qualify for the protection provided by the National Labor Relations Board. Although denied basic New Deal labor law benefits, seafood industry workers were, at times, amazingly militant, considering their isolation from urban life, their high illiteracy rate, and, for many, their inability to communicate except in French.

Managers of seafood-processing plants employed child labor, in defiance of compulsory school attendance and child-labor laws, until the 1940s. In 1919 the findings of a Children's Bureau study of shrimp and oyster plants were bleak: many child workers in seafood plants endured sore hands and infection from shrimp spines embedded beneath the skin. Work also curtailed school attendance. The illiteracy rate in shrimp and oyster areas for working children ten to fifteen years of age was 25 percent compared to about 4 percent elsewhere in the nation. The rate of pay at Louisiana's twenty-eight large shrimp canneries in 1930 for young boys and girls was $.01 per pound of peeled, or about $2.50 per day. Federal authorities indicted shrimp-processing firms in Arabi, Houma, and

Lafitte for child-labor violations of the Fair Labor Standards Act in 1940, and dealers who sold shrimp in interstate commerce within thirty days of using child labor in their plants because subject to Interstate Commerce Commission regulations which forbade child labor.[12] But even in the late 1940s, children regularly left school to catch or process shrimp when the May season opened in South Louisiana.

In 1938 shrimpers' unions in several Gulf Coast ports decided to withhold shrimp from canneries unless fishermen received more than the $7.00 per barrel the canneries offered. Some unions held out for the $8.50 price set by members representing the Gulf Coast Fishermen's and Oystermen's Association of Biloxi and the Fishermen's Oystermen's, and Fur Trappers' Producers' Cooperative Association of Louisiana both of which had applied to the American Federation of Labor for charters. When the shrimp season opened on August 10, plants in Houma, Morgan City, Golden Meadow, Buras, Westwego, Harvey, Grand Isle, and New Orleans remained closed. Violence broke out when nonunion fishermen attempted to sell shrimp to factories at the cannery-set price of $7.00 per barrel. Union men, armed with shotguns, roamed the shrimping area. They poured kerosene on shrimp en route to market and dumped two hundred barrels of shrimp into Bayou Lafourche at the Lafourche Ice and Shrimp Company dock in Golden Meadow. Authorities arrested twelve fishermen for destroying several truckloads of shrimp in the Barataria-Lafitte area. Nonunion shrimpers finally rallied behind several rebel unions and worked for a compromise settlement. Jesty Collins of Golden Meadow revived the Louisiana Shrimp Fishermen's Cooperative Association with a fiery speech—in French—in Golden Meadow. He charged large canneries with intentionally causing the strike so they could unload surplus holdings from the 1937 season while prices remained high. His efforts increased support for the rebel unions and hastened the settlement that came on August 27 when a large cannery agreed to a compromise of $8.00 per barrel and the strike ended.[13]

A year later, a picketer was killed when the Violet Seafood Workers' Association struck the Dunbar-Dukate Company in Violet. The union was seeking wages of twenty-five cents per hour for its members. Mrs. Angelina Treadaway was standing in the picket line when she was struck by shots fired from a speeding car. She died three days later, and although the case was brought before the St. Bernard Parish Grand Jury and, later, a federal grand jury, in neither case was an indictment returned. Mrs. Treadaway's death did not prove to be a rallying point for seafood workers, however. Fishermen did not see her as a symbol of their struggle. District Attorney Leander Perez, with vested political and economic interests in the labor dispute, helped break the strike and the union. His critics accused him not only of intimidating union workers, but of failing to prosecute Mrs. Treadaway's murderer.[14]

From time to time the problems of national labor groups caused disputes in Louisiana. Since antebellum days New Orleans longshoremen had tended to join unions and to fight for their economic well-being, but during the lean years of the 1920s a business-sponsored open shop movement decimated both black and white locals of the International Longshoremen's Association (AFL). There were clashes, sometimes, between black and white longshoremen over meager job pickings. When the New Deal created the National Recovery Administration in 1933 and allowed workers to join organizations of their own choosing, steamship associations formed company unions. In 1936 Governor O. K. Allen closed the port at Lake Charles, Louisiana, after three men died in the fighting between ILA members and their company union rivals. After 1935, CIO waterfront unions, such as the International Longshoremen and Warehousemen's Union (ILWU) locals, began to compete with ILA locals affiliated with the AFL. The CIO sent Harry Bridges to New Orleans to organize for the ILWU. City police harassed CIO organizers, and the Louisiana Legislature adopted a resolution that called the ILWU communistic and considered the unionization of blacks a threat to white supremacy. In 1937 the ILA in New Orleans defeated the ILWU in a bargaining election.[15]

Labor was occasionally an issue in state politics also. Most disputes in the Louisiana strawberry industry centered around various marketing agreements for selling the early ripening Louisiana berries. Jimmy Morrison of Hammond, who sounded like a Populist, advocating Huey Long-like reforms to aid the little man, was nearly always in the midst of these controversies. Morrison, a Tulane University Law School graduate, was the leader of a strawberry farmers union. He ran for governor in 1940, advocating removal of the tax on gasoline used in fishing boats and a free college education for indigent students. Morrison criticized Governor Leche, a member of the Long faction, for not opposing a sales tax whose burden fell heavily on poor families. He also accused Leche of reneging on a promise to obtain a subsidy from the Louisiana Legislature of one dollar per crate to strawberry growers, and during the 1940 gubernatorial campaign, he accused Leche for trying to starve berry farmers. Nonetheless, Leche at least tried to get federal aid for Morrison's constituents, as his many letters to Senator Allen J. Ellender and the Agriculture Department attest. Locally, the best Leche could do was pledge to maintain law and order when violence flared in the strawberry belt.[16]

Morrison did not win the 1940 Louisiana gubernatorial election, nor did the Long faction. The campaign was replete with rhetoric in support of organized labor, perhaps because the Long faction considered labor the issue to detract attention from the scandals that wrecked the Leche administration. However, in courting labor, candidates overplayed the importance of the labor movement and of their own labor records. Candidate Earl Long told labor leaders he favored a tax on laborsaving devices that replaced workers. In the campaign, Sam Jones led the anti-Long forces, a faction dedicated to preventing the remnants of Huey's organization from returning to power. Jones considered the recent scandals a main campaign issue, but he did not overlook the labor vote. He told labor leaders that he was willing to be judged on his Lake Charles labor record. Speaking before a state labor convention that had endorsed Earl Long, Jones cautioned the group: "Keep your organization out of politics." Jimmy Morrison criticized both Long and

Jones during the campaign. He suggested that Earl Long had not helped strawberry farmers as much as he could have but Earl replied: "Why that man stole from the strawberry farmers." Senator Ellender and the State Federation of Labor endorsed Earl Long, but other union groups sensing an end to Longism, endorsed Jones the eventual winner.[17]

During the war, antiunion forces aggressively tried to undermine organized labor and offset rapid union growth. The American Farm Bureau Federation and the Southern States Industrial Council joined the antiunion Christian American Program, consisting mainly of conservative Protestant ministers. Founded in 1936, the Christian American Program was active in Alabama, Arkansas, Florida, Louisiana, and Texas. In 1942 the Christian American Program was circulating antilabor material. E. H. "Lige" Williams of the State Federation of Labor believed Senator W. Lee O'Daniel of Texas to be the sponsor of this antilabor campaign. Williams sent the mimeographed flyer to Senator Ellender, who had denounced any attempt to use the war as an excuse to suppress labor. The flyer outlined the organization's plans to introduce antilabor measures when the Louisiana Legislature convened on May 11, 1942. Other objectives included right-to-work legislation, antiviolence statutes, legal restrictions against farm-labor groups, and measures for controlling communists and radical labor groups In 1944 Christian American leaders tried to push through the Louisiana Legislature a right-to-work bill which would have outlawed the union shop and the closed shop. The also backed a bill that would have imposed sweeping controls over organized labor. Father Jerome Drolet, a controversial, outspoken labor priest, who had clashed with Harry Bridges over Communist influence on the New Orleans waterfront, called the Christian American Program a "sweatshop front" and testified against the bill at hearings.[18] It did not pass.

In the summer of 1946, however, the Louisiana Legislature did pass a right-to-work bill. Jimmie H. Davis vetoed the measure, and "Lige" Williams expressed his gratitude by calling Davis "the best governor Louisiana labor ever had." That same year the legislature repealed the Goff Act of 1946 that had outlawed certain strikes and labor practices. In addition, it enacted a law that prohibited transporting strikebreakers into the state and one that raised workmen's compensation benefits.[19]

World War II brought to the United States full industrial productivity, an end to the Great Depression, and an expanding bureaucracy to deal with an acute labor shortage. Union membership increased rapidly as a result of economic recovery and a favorable government attitude toward labor. Determined to prevent strikes and to ease demands for higher wages, Roosevelt established the National Defense Mediation Board in 1941. The board, consisting of representatives from labor, management, and public life, failed in November when CIO members resigned over its refusal to recommend a union shop arrangement. To replace it Roosevelt created a stronger unit in January, 1942, the National War Labor Board, which could determine wages, hours, and working conditions and could even seize plants under certain circumstances. The NWLB encouraged union membership and exacted no-strike, no lock-out pledges from unions and management, using regional boards throughout the country to settle wage disputes and stabilize wages. Unlike the National Labor Relations Board, the NWLB's functions extended beyond conducting elections to choose bargaining representatives; they now included negotiating contracts between labor and management. In the union shop controversy the board compromised with "maintenance of membership" clauses that required senior workers to remain in the union, but did not require new members to join. In the Fourth Regional War Labor Board, whose jurisdiction included the South, unions organized such war plants as Ingalls Shipbuilding Company, Andrew Higgins Company, and Aluminum Company of America.[20]

Congress created the War Food Administration in March, 1943, to establish national priority needs for food. The WFA was also involved with labor relations since it made county agents responsible for mobilizing farm labor and provided funds for state agricultural extension service systems. The United States Employment Service and the Agricultural Extension Service were trying to prevent an exodus of farm workers from Southern fields to higher-paying factory jobs. Regulation No. 7 of the War Manpower Commission, created in the fall of 1943, required a specific job reference from the United States Employment Service before a farm worker could transfer to nonfarm employment. Congress had already passed the Tydings Amendment to the Selective Service Act in November, 1942, to allow local boards to defer men classified as essential to local agriculture. After June, 1943, the War Food Administration's Office of Labor imported workers from foreign countries. The WFA also established Farm-Labor Supply Centers that used old Civilian Conservation Corps camps and buildings formerly occupied by the National Youth Administration and the Farm Security Administration. Louisiana Senator Allen J. Ellender, who otherwise generally supported the Farm Security Administration, objected to its wartime policy of transporting Louisiana laborers to other sections of the country.[21]

Senator Allen Ellender arrived in Washington in 1937 when organized labor was expanding dramatically and sugarcane producers were demanding a permanent comprehensive program to regulate the production and importation of sugar. As a member of Senate committees on agriculture and labor, he helped draft legislation affecting both farmers and industrial workers. A product of the Long organization and heir to political support from organized labor in Louisiana, he came to detest CIO president John L. Lewis, whom he considered irresponsible and unpatriotic. In time, his animosity toward Lewis led to his estrangement from the entire labor movement. Within a decade Ellender underwent a metamorphosis that changed him from a supporter of the prolabor Wagner Act to cosponsor of the antiunion Taft-Hartley Act of 1947.

In the power struggle after Long's assassination in September, 1935, Ellender had emerged as the Long faction's choice for Long's seat in the U. S. Senate. Ellender won the election after a heated fight. He found the Washington legislative format different from Louisiana's. "When Huey was living he took matters in his own hands and appeared in person before his committees," Ellender wrote in 1937. "Up here the wishes of the President are put through by various department heads who act as his agents." Ellender adjusted quickly, however, and became a New Deal supporter. In a 1940 speech he cited FDR's recognition of labor's right to organize as one reason he backed Roosevelt. He often expressed his belief that the president's program improved chances for maximum wartime production. He opposed Senator Harry Byrd's antistrike legislation and suspected antiunion forces of encouraging persistent calls for new labor laws. During his early years in Washington, he won the respect of liberal reformers and labor leaders alike for these antiestablishment, pro-little man views. Paternalistically, he advised "Lige" Williams to run his union honestly, without corruption or unreasonable fees, and said most antiunion legislation would die a natural death.[22]

Ellender's labor support was somewhat underminded when Sam Jones was elected governor. He confronted "Lige" Williams directly about the State Federation of Labor's drift from the Long organization into Jones's. "As you know," he wrote a labor leader, in disbelief at being mistrusted, "I have a 100% labor record in Washington which shows that I have been doing all in my power to help organized labor." Nevertheless, State Federation leaders, no doubt thinking that the Long era in Louisiana had come to an end, heeded Jones's warning against maintaining political ties to Longism. "The labor situation is awful," a political supporter of Ellender reported, "Jones and Noe and their representatives are in control." Jimmy Morrison, the voice for strawberry farmers, who acted as spokesman for Ellender, asked W. Horace Williams, the prime contractor at a military base in the state, Camp Polk, to place someone friendly to Senator Ellender in the camp's personnel office. Later, obviously pleased, Morrison informed Ellender that Williams had fired Speedy Rhodes, a personnel office who backed Jones and discriminated against workers who supported the Long faction.[23]

John L. Lewis, the dynamic and forceful leader of the CIO, was a catalyst in Allen Ellender's change of attitude toward organized labor. As early as the 1937 sit-down strikes, Ellender called Lewis a "Mussolini of the mines," and during World War II, while he denounced antilabor forces with vigor, he criticized John L. Lewis even more. In May, 1943, Lewis' United Mine Workers demanded wage increases in excess of the 15 percent provided in the Roosevelt administration's "Little Steel Formula." Congress reacted the following month by overriding President Roosevelt's veto to pass the Smith-Connally (War Labor Disputes) Act. The law authorized presidential seizure of war plants on strike. Ellender criticized the UMW action and supported passage of the act. He asked for legislation to set a new national labor policy "that will curb the power of would-be labor dictators like Lewis." No longer reluctant to support antilabor bills, he wrote: "I am actively supporting the [Harry] Byrd Amendment to prevent labor unions from exacting tribute from management."[24]

By the end of World War II, AFL President William Green, after examining congressional voting records, considered both Ellender and Louisiana's senior senator,

John Overton, opponents of labor. Overton was a Longite, like Ellender, who spoke eloquently about the plight of the masses but never endeared himself to workers or became popular with them. Senator Ellender still believed himself to be prolabor; it was the corrupt labor leaders he opposed. "I have always done everything I could for the laboring man," he observed in 1948, "and I am in favor of labor unions, if they are administered properly, but many labor unions have been victimized by these racketeers." Indeed, during congressional debate on the Taft-Hartley Bill in 1947, he opposed punitive amendments to the bill, emphasizing that 30 percent of all industries operated under a closed shop arrangement and adding: "Industry as a whole has made huge profits since the war." Nonetheless, the Louisiana Federation of Labor placed him on its "enemies" list and planned to campaign against him at the polls.[25]

Ellender believed that the Wagner Act gave labor an unfair edge over management, and through the years, he supported a number of schemes designed to correct the imbalance. He wanted to modify the act to give independent unions more autonomy and to convince NLRB officials that company unions were indeed real unions. It was Ellender who helped guide the Taft-Hartley Bill through Congress and over President Truman's veto, in 1947, but the Taft-Hartley Act hurt organized labor in several significant ways. It removed antiunion citizens' committees from NLRB jurisdiction by changing the definition of *employer*. It outlawed secondary boycotts and prevented strong unions from helping weak ones. It permitted charges of unfair labor practices against unions to drag on for long periods before being settled. It denied men on strike the right to vote in representation elections. It permitted states to pass right-to-work laws and outlawed the closed shop. It required unions to submit financial reports that made their weaknesses known to industry. And, generally, the Taft-Hartley Act, by guaranteeing the rights of nonunion workers, helped create the impression that workers did not need unions.[26]

Most of the Louisiana congressional delegation joined Ellender and Overton in supporting the Taft-Hartley Act; the two exceptions were not surprising. Hale Boggs, the liberal New Orleans-born Democrat and Tulane Law School graduate, voted against final passage of the Taft Hartley Bill. Jimmy Morrison, formerly a close political ally of Ellender and a supporter of strawberry farm unions, did not vote on the bill. The six other congressmen—F. Edward Hebert, Otto Passman, Overton Brooks, A. Leonard Allen, James Domengeaux, and Harry Larcade, Jr.—voted for the measure.[27]

At a strategy meeting of the Long faction in New Orleans in September, 1943, Earl Long announced his intention to seek the governorship. Ellender, who was willing to run only if all Longites declined in deference to him, blamed labor racketeers for encouraging Earl Long to run. He said that labor criticized members of Congress who voted for the Smith-Connally Act, which curtailed arbitrary actions by labor leaders. Even so, Ellender, refusing to concede the labor vote, wrote in 1943: "I cannot make up my mind that the bulk of labor is against me." But one of the senator's strong supporters, viewing his position more realistically, cautioned him: "Your position with labor is not nearly so strong as it was." Another political ally indicated other kinds of political support for the senator: "In your case it was the members of the Chamber of Commerce, AAA Committeemen who were counted on for you." Neither Ellender nor Earl Long received the nomination in 1944, but the man who did, Lewis Morgan, chose E. J. Bourg, treasurer of the Louisiana Federation of Labor, as the Long faction's candidate for auditor.[28] Jimmie H. Davis, an anti-Long Democrat, won the election.

In the 1948 gubernatorial election the State Federation of Labor again endorsed Earl Long for governor, and when he won, labor realized several minor legislative gains. (By 1949, though, Long was not on speaking terms with Federation president "Lige" Williams.)[29] Labor leaders failed to oust several members of the congressional delegation who had voted for the antilabor Taft-Hartley Act the previous year. They opposed Ellender in his reelection campaign, but the veteran lawmaker won again.

The Dixiecrat revolt of 1948 had direct repercussions for organized labor in Louisiana. Louisiana Dixiecrat leaders supported Strom Thurmond of South Carolina against the incumbent Democratic nominee Harry S Truman, who had vetoed the Taft-Hartley Bill. John U. Barr and Leander Perez, leaders of the Louisiana Dixiecrats, both expressed strong antilabor sentiments. Barr was a major supporter of right-to-work legislation and had been a leader of the Louisiana Citizens' Committee. Perez, who had asked voters to repudiate labor leaders Dave Dubinsky and Walter Reuther, had instructed the sheriff of Plaquemines Parish to arrest labor leaders who came into his bailiwick. When Dixiecrats gave the rooster, the traditional Democratic party symbol in Louisiana, to the Dixiecrat faction rather than to the Democrats, organized labor protested.[30]

DeLesseps S. Morrison, mayor of New Orleans, had an indifferent labor attitude. Both he and his predecessor, Robert Maestri, learned to make concessions to organized labor, but Morrison never gained the confidence of most legitimate labor leaders. His friendship with Clarence "Chink" Henry, black president of General Longshore Workers' Local 1419, was a gesture of racial-political accommodation rather than a genuine prolabor proclivity. The political arm of Henry's local, The Crescent City Independent Voters League, supported Morrison in exchange for political funds with no strings attached from the Morrison-dominated Crescent City Democratic Organization. When sanitation workers struck in 1946 during his first year in office, Morrison's response to their demands for higher wages and shorter hours alerted union leaders to the new mayor's position. Morrison considered the strike illegal, an attack against city government, and called on volunteers to collect garbage. Regular sanitation workers returned after city engineers redrew garbage routes and replaced mule-drawn wagons with modern sanitation equipment. In 1948, however, when sanitation workers threatened to strike again, Morrison, who had relented somewhat, agreed to a new contract and found $30,000 for salary increases. That same year the mayor asserted the right of National Airlines workers to picket peacefully. Because Morrison's attitude toward labor had improved and because his political opponents had labor records worse than his own, Morrison received labor support in his 1949 mayoral campaign and his 1960 campaign for governor. But important labor leaders such as Fred Cassibry, a popular CIO lawyer later active in city government, continued to oppose the man whose efforts reflected only an image of reform.[31]

During the first half of the twentieth century, organized labor in Louisiana posed no serious threat to the economic and political status quo. By mid-century Louisiana laborers, like workingmen throughout the United States, had gained a legal status by virtue of New Deal labor legislation. Agricultural and rural Louisiana still had large numbers of seasonal and casual workers, however, who did not qualify for the protections enjoyed by industrial laborers. Furthermore, the labor movement in the state lacked a unified voice and a steady political ally, especially after the 1939 scandals decimated the Long ranks. But even Huey Long had never attempted a frontal attack against the bulwark of antiunion forces; instead, he had tried to help workingmen by pushing programs designed to bring free textbooks, better roads and bridges, state-operated hospitals, and other needed reforms to the masses. Jimmy Morrison came closest to being a prolabor politician, openly vying for labor support, but he was primarily identified with strawberry farmers, agrarians who had problems with complicated marketing agreements. In his early years in Washington, Senator Ellender supported organized labor, but he later became antagonistic toward organized labor. DeLesseps Morrison at least responded to worker needs when political expediency demanded it. Earl Long, like his brother Huey, received support from organized labor because he sponsored legislative programs beneficial to the masses, not because he introduced labor laws per se.

Notes for "Louisiana Labor in the First Half of the Twentieth Century"

[1]Wilbur Cash, *The Mind of the South* (New York, 1941), 304.

[2]U. S. Department of Agriculture, *The Yearbook of Agriculture, 1940: Farmers in a Changing World* (Washington, 1949), 888-93; Stuart Jamieson, *Labor Unionism in American Agriculture* (Washington, 1945), 12-13.

[3]H. L. Mitchell, interview, June 23, 1970.

[4]James Fickle, "The Louisiana-Texas Lumber War of 1911-1912," *Louisiana History*, 16 (1975): 59-85; F. Ray Marshall, *Labor in the South* (Cambridge, 1967), 94-98; Merl Reed, "The IWW and Individual Freedom in Western Louisiana, 1913," *Louisiana History*, 10 (1969): 61-69.

[5]V. O. Key, Jr., *Southern Politics in Senate and Nation* (New York, 1949), 528, 57, 673-74, 480, 32.

[6]Cash, *Mind of the South*, 250; Marshall, *Labor in the South*, 214-45; William Anderson, *The Wild Man from Sugar Creek: The Political Career of Eugene Talmadge* (Baton Rouge, 1975), 110-11, 237; George Tindall, *The Emergence of the New South, 1913-1945* (Baton Rouge, 1967), 511; Key, *Southern Politics*, 413, 125-26, 64, 73, 24-25; Joseph B. Gorman, *Kefauver: A Political Biography* (New York, 1971), 56.

[7]Charles Roland, *The Improbable Era: The South Since World War II* (Lexington, 1975), 17; William Havard, ed., *The Changing Politics of the South* (Baton Rouge, 1972), 152, 161, 505, 517, 537-38, 587.

[8]Allan P. Sindler, *Huey Long's Louisiana: State Politics, 1920-1952* (Baltimore, 1956), 254; Fred Benton to Allen Ellender, October 2, 1943, in "Gubernatorial Campaign—1944" folder, Box 408, Allen J. Ellender Papers, Division of Archives, Nicholls State University, Thibodaux, La., hereinafter cited as AEP.

[9]Sindler, *Huey Long's Louisiana*, 105, 254; T. Harry Williams, *Huey Long, A Biography* (New York, 1969), 857-58, 109-11.

[10]Sindler, *Huey Long's Louisiana*, 131.

[11]Charles Logan, interview, September 26, 1974; Logan to Ellender, May 11, 1949, in "Federal Trade Commission, 1949," folder, Box 9, AEP.

[12]Viola I. Paradise, *Child Labor and the Work of Mothers in Oyster and Shrimp Canning Communities on the Gulf Coast* (Washington, 1922), 5-6.

[13]Thomas Becnel, "A History of the Louisiana Shrimp Industry, 1867-1961" (M.A. thesis, Louisiana State University, 1962), 34-37.

[14]Glen Jeansonne, *Leander Perez: Boss of the Delta* (Baton Rouge, 1977), 88-91.

[15]Marshall, *Labor in the South*, 202-10.

[16]*New Orleans Times-Picayune*, March 10, October 3, November 16, December 4, 1939; Ellender to Jimmy Morrison, December 21, 1937, in "Strawberry Marketing Agreement" folder, Box 321, AEP.

[17]Sindler, *Huey Long's Louisiana*, 255; *New Orleans Times-Picayune*, March 15, 1939-January 14, 1940; H. J. Marmande to Ellender, March 14, 1940, in "Agriculture, Sugar Prices" folder, Box 280, AEP.

[18]Marshall, *Labor in the South*, 241-42; E. H. Williams to Ellender, April 21, 1942, with *Christian American Program for 1942*, in "Labor, General, 1942" folder, Box 333, AEP.

[19]Quoted in Sindler, *Huey Long's Louisiana*, 194-95; Key, *Southern Politics*, 165.

[20]U. S. Department of Labor, *Brief History of the American Labor Movement* (Washington, 1976), 27-33; Marshall, *Labor in the South*, 225-27.

[21]War Food Administration, *Food Program for 1944* (Washington, 1943), 52-54, in "War Food Administration #2" folder, Box 445, *Final Report of the War Food Administration 1945* (Washington, 1943), 28-29, in "Agriculture, General, 1945" folder, Box 27, Ellender to R. W. Collier, April 21, 1943, in "Pace Bill" folder, Box 77, all in AEP.

[22]Ellender to Harry Wilson, January 15, 1937, in "FSA, Farm Tenancy" folder, Box 321, "Why Elect Roosevelt," in "Miscellaneous Presidential Campaign—1940" folder, Box 50, Sam Sibley to Ellender, March 23, 1942, E. H. Williams to Ellender, April 24, 1942, Ellender to Williams, May 4, 1942, all in "Labor, General, 1942" folder, Box 333, all in AEP.

[23]Ellender to Paul Fink, October 16, 1941, Ellender to E. H. Williams, March 27, 1942, in "War National Defense, General #2" folder, Box 50, Robert McGehee to Ellender, February 22, 1941, Jimmy Morrison to Ellender, February 11, 1941, Ellender to W. Horace Williams, February 10, 1941, Morrison to Ellender, February 14, 1941, in "General Somervell Investigation" folder, Box 198, all in AEP.

[24]Unidentified clipping, in "Labor Situation (July 1, 1937)" folder, Box 92, Ellender speeches, May 4, 1946, in "Education and Labor Committee, Case Bill" folder, Ellender to Dallas A. Picou, November 2, 1945, in "Education and Labor, Minimum Wage Bill, #1" folder, Ellender to O. J. Hood, May 15, 1946, Ellender to W. Scott Heywood, May 18, 1946, both in "Education and Labor Committee, Case Bill" folder, Box 211, all in AEP.

[25]William Green to John Overton, April 15, 1946, in "Education and Labor, Minimum Wage Bill" folder, Box 211, Ellender to C. C. Sheppard, April 23, 1948, in "S. 2386, Minimum Wage Legislation" folder, Ellender to Harvey Peltier, March 22, 1947, in "Labor, 1947" folder, Box 463, *New Orleans Times-Picayune*, August 25, 1947, in "Miscellaneous 'B' " folder, Box 408, all in AEP; Williams, *Huey Long*, 269.

[26]Ellender to George Hutchins, March 20, 1940, in "National Labor Relations Act, To Amend, S. 2123" folder, Box 92, AEP; Marshall, *Labor in the South*, 324-25.

[27]*Congressional Record*, 80th Cong., 1st Sess., 1947, Vol. 93, Part 3, pp. 3670-71.

[28]"Gubernatorial Campaign—1944" folder, *passim*, Ellender to Fred Benton, October 5, 1943, J. L. McInnis to Ellender, October 4, 1943, L. Austin Fontenot to Ellender, September 7, 1944, all in "Senator John H. Overton" folder, Box 408, all in AEP.

[29]I. Lee Parker to H. L. Mitchell, October 4, 1949, Box 63, Folder 1214 of the Southern Tenant Farmers Union Papers, housed in the Southern Collection (an photoduplicated by the Microfilm Corporation of America in 60 rolls), University of North Carolina, Chapel Hill cited as STFU, with box and folder number or roll number.

[30]Sindler, *Huey Long's Louisiana*, 220-22; Robert Sherrill, *Gothic Politics in the Deep South: Stars of the New Confederacy* (New York, 1968), 25, 19.

[31]Edward Haas, *DeLesseps S. Morrison and the Image of Reform: New Orleans Politics, 1946-1961* (Baton Rouge, 1974), 252, 23-24, 56-57, 94-95, 247, 176.

GETTING PLACES IN A HURRY: THE DEVELOPMENT OF AVIATION IN LONG-ERA SOUTH LOUISIANA*

John A. Heitmann

During the past fifty years a massive body of scholarship has been generated related to the life and times of Louisiana's most famous native son—Huey Pierce Long. Notwithstanding the fine studies of T. Harry Williams and Alan Brinkley, however, an important gap curiously remains.[1] Namely, while scholars have exhaustively examined the "Kingfish's" political environment, the modern industrial world that emerged in the Louisiana of Long's day awaits exploration and analysis. Although Brinkley maintained in *Voices of Protest* that Long's ideology was a response to industrialism, his work did little to characterize these complex influences. Yet Long was a product of his times, and the rise of new technologies and their powerful impact upon society most certainly helped to shape his ideas and perceptions.[2]

Long's understanding of Depression Era science and technology is best seen in his posthumously published *My First Days in the White House,* a fictitious account of Huey's initial decisions after a victorious presidential campaign in 1936.[3] Long clearly recognized that modern technology was a two-edged sword. At one point in the book he remarks that "we never know what problems these new contrivances and inventions bring to us."[4] To eradicate the dust bowl he proposed a massive public works project in the West, costing some 10 billion dollars and involving some 1,600 individual projects, including navigation improvements, the construction of dams and extensive irrigation. Work would be costly, but Long asserted that technology would create wealth, wealth that would ultimately be shared within his organic society. He claimed that

> by the time you have completed your project the wealth of America will have been increased by not less than some 50 to 100 billions of dollars, and the people

---

*First published in *Louisiana History*, 29 (1988): 325-42. Reprinted with the kind permission of the author and the Louisiana Historical Association.

employed in the meantime. Besides that, we can pay for it either by general taxation or from our Share Our Wealth Program. You need not worry about the cost. The American people will be far more eager to spend the billion dollars on this wealth-giving and farsighted program than it was to squander billions on the hit or miss programs of the last administration.[5]

Long's followers also embraced similar technocratic ideas, as evidenced in the magazine *Transmission,* the official journal of the police juries of Louisiana during the late 1920s, and in the campaign newspaper *Louisiana* (later *American*) *Progress.*[6] On the cover of *Transmission* man was depicted at the center of a massive power wheel, and within its pages authors celebrated the triumph of technology in modernizing a once-backward state. And the *Louisiana Progress,* despite its political thrust, was filled with references mentioning recent exploits on the part of Lindbergh and other aviators, the flights of German zeppelins, and the profitability of air service in shipping passengers, cargo, and mail.

While lack of adequate manuscript and printed material limits the analysis of Long's views concerning modern technology, the external environment at the source of these ideas awaits exploration. This article will focus on the development during the Long era of perhaps the most dynamic technology of the day—aviation.[7] Clearly, the potential of aviation did not escape the "Kingfish." By looking through this window into Huey Long's world I shall trace the significance of boosters, entrepreneurs, and local institutions in promoting and stimulating regional technological change.[8] Between 1928 and 1935 a new industrial order—including the aviation business—gradually emerged, and Huey Long stood squarely in the gap between the traditional agricultural-based economy of his forefathers and a new Louisiana increasingly dependent upon science-based technology. Despite a favorable beginning, however, Louisiana aviation during the pre-World War II era possessed inherent weaknesses that ultimately contributed to the loss of local control and the failure to sustain technological momentum. A most fundamental shortcoming can be traced to Louisiana's educational and research institutions. Both Louisiana State University and Tulane University were unable or unwilling to respond to the new technological challenges of the 1930s by either training the large number of experts necessary for industrial leadership or creating the new knowledge that lay at the heart of dynamic, science-based industry. Further, the inconsistent policies of the federal government, particularly the U. S. Post Office, served to quench the hopes of native entrepreneurs during a most crucial state of development.

By the time of Long's successful gubernatorial bid in 1928 a vibrant interest in commercial aviation had already developed in Louisiana. Indeed, the state had been the scene of numerous pioneering efforts, including a 1910 "Aviation Tournament" in New Orleans and an early airmail flight by French aviator George Mestach from New Orleans to Baton Rouge in 1912.[9] One of the first post-World War I commercial airmail ventures in the United States was undertaken in 1923 when a specialized mail route between New Orleans and Pilottown, located at the mouth of the Mississippi River, was inaugurated.[10]

For each trip pilot-entrepreneur Merrill K. Riddick received ninety dollars to transport mail destined for South America to steamers that had departed from the port of New Orleans the day before.

The New Orleans-Pilottown venture proved profitable for more than a decade, and the service demonstrated the value, particularly to the banking community, of an air route in connecting New Orleans to Central and South America. During the 1920s American business interests were aggressively opening new markets abroad, and New Orleans boosters quickly recognized Crescent City's inherent geographic advantages for developing commerce south of the border.

In 1924 the New Orleans Chamber of Commerce began a campaign for federal government support of an airmail service to Central and South America. Walter Parker, representing the Chamber of Commerce, prepared a well-documented proposal to postal authorities citing the advantages and benefits of such an air link. Parker argued that New Orleans was already at the hub of an extensive trade network linking the mid-North American continent to Central America. Further, he claimed that the presence of an excellent weather bureau directed by I. M. Cline, author of *Tropical Cyclones,* the importance of Tulane University's Middle American Research Center and Medical College, and the existence of a large number of foreign consuls in New Orleans were all important reasons why an air connection should be established in the Crescent City. In related correspondence Parker stated

> The entire region now must have markets abroad, and Latin America offers the markets of greatest and most immediate as well as most permanent promise. Communications is the key. Quick mail service will bring freight transportation because it will foster commercial exchange.[11]

Despite Parker's rather convincing plea, the federal government was unwilling in 1924 to subsidize the route. And during this early stage of development the economic feasibility of commercial aviation was linked to this indirect form of government assistance. While initially stymied, local business groups continued to work towards the goal of federal government support during the next four years.

Perhaps the most effective local organization between 1924 and 1928 was the Young Men's Business Club (YMBC) of New Orleans. Among its members were several ex-World War I aviators who spearheaded a campaign for the promotion of local aviation.[12] In 1925 the YMBC secured a 215-acre tract eight-and-one-half miles from New Orleans's business district and named the landing field constructed on that site after Alvin Callender, the only New Orleanian flyer killed during the recent war. Additionally, the YMBC was instrumental not only in establishing in 1925 an Airport Commission to oversee the operation of Callender Field but also in raising funds for the erection of a hanger and other facilities there. The Club's leadership next shifted its strategy towards gaining an airmail contract for the city. In 1927 YMBC President Zatarain presided at a meeting in which prominent barge line executive Lewis I. Bourgeois was given authority to mount a concerted effort to bring airmail to New Orleans. Bourgeois petitioned senators, congressmen, and postal authorities while concurrently cultivating public opinion by means of extensive newspaper publicity. During this time other local groups joined in this aviation boosterism.

One organization that drew from the membership of the YMBC was the Aero Club of Louisiana. Its leaders were former World War I pilots who not only recognized the potential of aviation technology but also in many cases wanted to profit from the coming of commercial aviation to New Orleans. Other groups caught in the aviation boosterism spirit of the day included the New Orleans Association of Commerce and the Louisiana Chamber of Commerce. Committees were formed, and speeches were made; the argument always seemed to be that Louisiana had to embrace aviation technology or fall hopelessly behind.[13] As one down-home writer expressed it in the magazine *Louisiana*:

> Aviation is comin' along so fast, if we get a couple hoe-handle lengths behind we'll never catch up with the rest of the country.... There ain't no reason in the world New Orleans, say, shouldn't be the Second Airport, same as it is Second Seaport, except that about ninety percent of the people of New Orleans would have to be hog tied to git 'em into a plane. But once they got used to flying, you'd have to tie 'em to keep 'em on the ground.[14]

On a different level, New Orleanian and Assistant Secretary of the Navy Ernst Lee Jahncke echoed similar thoughts.

> The American cities that recognize this fact and build airports to meet it, will tap new sources of wealth so great that the most optimistic are more likely to under-estimate it than to over-estimate it.
> The American cities that ignore the airplane or think it a minor factor in their development, before long will find themselves in the same position as the cities that two or three generations ago ignored the railroad.[15]

Spokesmen, politicians, and industrial entrepreneurs all proclaimed basically the same message. However, Harry Williams, a shrewd entrepreneur just embarking in the aviation business, asserted that without government assistance, regional aviation progress would be stunted. Williams remarked

> Primarily, New Orleans is going to lag far behind the rest of the country within the next few years, because of a lack of landing facilities.... And Mark! As the ships of the future become larger and larger it will become necessary to provide constantly growing landing fields. Private enterprise and private capital cannot be relied upon to keep up with this demand. Only public enterprise and public financing will be equal to it.[16]

This general enthusiasm for aviation and the recognition of its enormous commercial potential intensified markedly in Louisiana after Lindbergh's successful May 1927 non-stop Atlantic flight and the "lone eagle's" subsequent tour of Central America, Venezuela, and Cuba. In the fall of 1927 Bourgeois and the YMBC's campaign for a federally subsidized airmail route finally bore fruit, and as a result a flurry of commercial activity followed.

The contract for the federally subsidized route was awarded to the St. Tammany Gulf Coast Airways, which had agreed to provide airmail service to Atlanta with intermediate stops in Mobile and Birmingham. While operatons did not begin until May 1928, St. Tammany Gulf Coast's energetic manager, William de Wald, worked hard to expand his company's airways to include a connection with Mexico City. In January 1928 he made an aerial survey of the route between New Orleans and Brownsville, Texas, and returned claiming that "New Orleans is the shortest and best all-year route between New York and Mexico City, as well as the most feasible path for airmail to follow from coast to coast when winter makes the northern transcontinental route dangerous."[17]

De Wald's firm was not the only airline in New Orleans during this time of optimism and promise for commercial aviation.[18] The pioneering airmail service to Pilottown, called the New Orleans Air Line, was purchased in 1928 by Arthur E. Cambas, who subsequently expanded operations to include the building of seaplanes. Another firm, Louisiana Airways, headed by Morris P. Le Compte, had grown rapidly during 1927 as it provided aerial surveys of areas inundated by the Mississippi River flooding of that year. Le Compte established a flying school and had elaborate plans to run passenger lines from New Orleans to Shreveport, Shreveport to Memphis, and Shreveport to Monroe, Louisiana.

In addition to these entrepreneurial ventures, J. C. Menefee, a New Orleans businessman and Chevrolet dealer, formed Menefee Airways during the spring of 1928. Menefee leased forty acres on the Jefferson Highway for a landing strip, purchased two Lincoln-Page planes, and planned to bid on an airmail route from New Orleans to Laredo, Texas, an important link on a proposed route to Mexico City. Menefee's lead pilot, general manager, and plane builder was James Wedell, a colorful individual who soon played a crucial role in the development of aviation in South Louisiana during the late 1920s and early 1930s.

James Robert Wedell had a background typical of many of the pilots of his day. Born in 1900, he was the son of Texas City, Texas, saloon keeper. Wedell began his career as an auto mechanic, and at age fourteen using his manual skills rebuilt two Thomas-Morse planes from scrap parts. He then received rudimentary flight instruction from barnstormer Francis Rust. Demonstrating entrepreneurial ability at an early age, young Wedell took his fixed up plane to a local cattleman's barbecue where he sold 200 rides at $5 per ride.[19] Rejected by the military because he had lost sight in one eye in a motorcycle accident, Wedell was for a time involved in shady border activities, including perhaps the running of guns and liquor back and forth between Texas and Mexico. During the spring of 1928 Wedell toured South Louisiana as chief pilot for an "Aircade" or promotional barnstorming show sponsored by a New Orleans newspaper. At Patterson,

Louisiana, he met Harry P. Williams, then mayor of the small town, and soon thereafter Wedell would dissolve his partnership with Menefee and join with Williams in establishing a new firm.

Williams, born in 1889, was the son of a successful Patterson lumber manufacturer.[20] After attending a Lawrenceville, New Jersey, school and the University of the South at Sewanee he returned home in 1906, where he learned his father's business and rose to a position of prominence within the local community. He became director and treasurer of the Williams Lumber Co., F. B. Williams Cypress Co., and the St. Bernard Cypress Co., Ltd., as well as president of Louisiana Moss Products and Patterson State Bank. In addition, Williams was quick to realize the changing nature of Louisiana's fortunes in extractive industry, amassing vast oil fields while actively engaged in the sugar business as the owner of Maryland and Calumet plantations.

Within a month after meeting Wedell, Williams cleared one of his sugar plantations and directed the construction of Patterson Airport. Shortly thereafter he and Wedell formed a partnership, Wedell-Williams Air Service, a company that for a brief period would have a major impact in commercial aviation and in aeronautical technology. The purpose of this newly formed company was "to engage in a general aviation business, covering a flying school, short sight-seeing trips, long passenger trips and aerial photography."[21] In July of 1929 Wedell-Williams inaugurated two lines of service starting from New Orleans; one route north to St. Louis via Jackson, Mississippi, and Memphis and another to Shreveport via Baton Rouge and Alexandria.[22] In addition to these transport operations the partners opened an aviation school at Menefee Airport with branch schools in Alexandria, Baton Rouge, Patterson and Gulfport, Mississippi. The school's brochure encouraged prospective students to "learn and earn":

> Where are the pilots and mechanics to fly and maintain all the new planes coming from? In 1929 more than 10,000 planes will be built in the United States, and there are not enough skilled men in the industry to fill places open for pilots, instructors and expert mechanics.
> No field offers the opportunities to young men that Aviation does. In what other business can young men expect to earn from $100 to $200 weekly, the remuneration of good Transport Pilots? Some pilots earn as much as $1000 monthly, and opportunities to the right men to fill executive positions are numerous.[23]

Various course offerings were extended to students, from ten hours of dual flying at a cost of $250 to two hundred hours of dual and solo flying that qualified the student for a transport pilot's license. The company also served as an agent for various aircraft companies, including Ryan and Lincoln Page. Salesman E. F. Newman contacted various potential clients in the Deep South, including Bogalusa Paper Company, Celotex Co., First State Bank of New Orleans, Great Southern Lumber Co., Louisiana Power and Light and the Texas Oil Company in Shreveport.[24]

At the onset of the Great Depression Wedell-Williams continued to expand, as service was established to Houston via Patterson and Beaumont in 1930. By the fall of that year the firm employed twelve pilots, owned forty planes, and began manufacturing operations at Patterson.[25] Yet this promising start was short-lived for two reasons, namely the lack of federal government support in terms of airmail contracts and vigorous competition from companies with much greater resources.[26]

Despite Williams' influence with both Assistant Secretary of the Navy Jahncke and Congressman Numa Montet of Thibodaux, Postmaster General Walter Brown was determined in 1930 to award contracts to the "big four" of the aviation business rather than cultivate smaller, regional companies like Wedell-Williams. And American Airlines soon gained a foothold in South Louisiana when it purchased in 1931 Gulf Coast Airlines, an organization that had earlier absorbed de Wald's pioneering St. Tammany Gulf Coast Airline.

American was forging a national network, and New Orleans was considered by its executives as an important hub. Soon a team of pilots, mechanics and helpers were sent to New Orleans, along with three tri-motor Fokker transport planes.[27] On June 15, 1931, passenger and airmail service was inaugurated from New Orleans to Memphis via Jackson, Mississippi, and a month later the service was extended to Chicago. Before long New Orleans was linked to Nashville, Louisville, Cincinnati, Columbus, Cleveland and New York City. Because of the presence of American Airways intermediate landing fields were improved, the latest design of lights were installed at Menefee Field and a two-way radio telephone system was set up between the airport and all American Airways ships in the field. In June of 1932 passenger service was inaugurated between New Orleans and Atlanta and New Orleans and Houston, with intermediate stops at Mobile and Montgomery, Baton Rouge and Beaumont. With the implementation of night service from Dallas to Los Angeles in July of 1932 it was possible to leave New Orleans at noon on one day and have breakfast the next morning on the West Coast.

Unable to compete with the likes of American Airlines, and faced with apparently insurmountable institutional obstacles, Wedell-Williams ceased all transport operations in late 1931. Partners Wedell and Williams had been involved in the design and construction of air racers beginning in 1929; apparently the firm responded to external threats by finding a niche that was seemingly beyond the control of large corporations and the inconsistencies of federal government decision-making.

Success in air-racing competition for Wedell-Williams was almost immediate. At the prestigious Chicago National Air Races of 1930 two Wedell-Williams placed among the leaders. And despite a crash on take-off in Los Angeles Wedell finished eighth in the 5,541 mile 1930 All-American Flying Derby sponsored by American Cirrus Engines, Inc. Wedell's #17 had demonstrated its capabilities, as Wedell was among the leaders on several legs of the race.[28] Fortunes would improve in 1931, perhaps because of the enormous sums of money invested by partner Williams. In the much publicized

Thompson Race held in Cleveland that year Wedell placed second averaging more than 227 mph and collected $4500 for his efforts.

From 1932 to 1934 the Wedell-Williams planes, along with the Gee Bees designed by the Granville brothers of Springfield, Massachusetts, dominated the airracing circuit and shattered speed records. Early in 1932 work in Patterson was started on three low wing monoplanes, each identical except for markings.[29] One would be flown by Wedell, while the other two would be piloted by veteran racers Roscoe Turner and Jimmy Haizlip. Weighing 1500 pounds empty, with a wingspan of twenty-six feet, two inches and twenty-one feet, three inches long, the structure of these aircraft was conventional. Constructed of welded steel tubing covered with fabric and aluminum, the Wedell-Williams planes initially were powered with 550 HP Pratt and Whitney (P & W) Jr. Wasp engines, later changed to 800 HP P & W Wasp radial powerplants. In the 1932 Thompson Race Wedell-Williams planes finished 2, 3, and 4 behind Jimmy Dolittle in a Gee Bee and a year later swept the field in the same race. Also in 1933 the company built *Miss Patterson,* a low wing monoplane that would establish a new land speed record of 305.33 mph at Chicago.[30] Indeed, because of the exploits of Wedell and the financial backing of Williams, Louisiana technology was in the national limelight.

Wedell's ability to design these fast aircraft can be traced to his intuitive feel for proper proportion and streamlining. Apparently he never relied upon technical knowledge, mathematical calculations or scientific principles. As Jimmie's shop foreman, Eddie Roberton, once stated, Wedell was a genius who took steel tubing, plywood, glue and linen and came up with the world's fastest plane.[31] But Wedell also recognized that the aviation business was changing, and that his practices would not work in the future. In giving advice to the younger generation in 1929, Wedell remarked, "Flying is no longer merely a matter of learning how to operate the stick and rudder bar. You must have some idea of why, for example, the wing surfaces of an airplane are curved just the way they are and how such curves are figured out."[32]

Concurrent with and as a consequence of the spectacular rise of Wedell-Williams, increased activity in Southern aviation and the rise of civic boosterism the need for modern airport facilities in New Orleans became increasingly acute.[33] While in 1929 Wedell-Williams began construction of an airport near the present-day site of the Huey Long bridge and J. C. Menefee established a commercial landing strip in Chalmette, a large public facility remained lacking, in large part because of local government inaction and legal obstacles. Finally in 1928 an amendment to the Louisiana constitution gave the board of levee commissioners of the Orleans Levee District authority to construct aviation fields as a part of a general project to improve the area of the New Orleans lakefront.[34]

Lakefront development had its origins in legislation dating back to 1916, but little work was actually accomplished until the mid-1920s when the first fill was pumped into an area that was five-and-one-half miles in length, one half mile in width and containing some 2200 acres. Intense litigation hindered this project for some time, as critics asserted that the work was not primarily one of flood control but rather a vast real estate enterprise, since the cost of the project was to be defrayed by the sale of residential and commercial property. The proposed airport was to be located in the fifth zone of the lakefront development tract, and work on the airport was stifled by lawsuits asserting that work could not begin until the development of the first four zones was completed. This suit was ultimately upheld and it was only in November 1930 that a new amendment was adopted permitting the immediate resumption of airport construction in zone 5. During the campaign for the passage of this amendment Long supporters argued in the *Louisiana Progress* that

> The finest airport in the United States through the passage of this amendment—and it will be created out of waste marshlands, without an additional cent of taxation for anyone.
> The airport will have a U. S. government rating of A-1A, and its fine facilities will make New Orleans the Air Capital of two continents.
> New Orleans needs such an airport as this NOW, to secure its place as the air capital of two continents.[35]

A sketch of the proposed airport featured a Zeppelin docked at its center, and above planes and Zeppelins hovered with the captions "From California," "From New York," "From Cuba," "From Mexico," "From Europe," "From Central America."

Construction resumed, but with the impact of the Depression the board of levee commissioners found it impossible to carry on the work due to lack of finances and a poor bond market. However, in August 1932, the newly created Reconstruction Finance Corporation approved a loan which would be repaid from airport revenues. Airport construction under the direction of Abe Shushan and John Klorer, staunch Long supporters, then entered high gear. It was constructed by erecting a concrete sea-wall around a triangular area of lakebottom and filling the enclosed area with sand from the lake bottom through the use of hydraulic dredges.[36] The area formed a triangle jutting out about one mile into Lake Pontchartrain, encompassing some 315 acres and containing four runways, two outside about a mile in length and two diagonal about 3000 yards long. The terminal's ostentatious decoration was perhaps typical of buildings erected during the Long era. Marble walls in tones of red, cream and buff, terrazzo floors, an ornamental plaster ceiling and Xavier Gonzolez murals depicting the various sections of the world invaded by the airplane all contributed to this showcase of power.[37]

Two months after the airport's completion the airport was inaugurated with the Pan-American Air Races of February 9-13, 1934, the weekend that preceded Mardi Gras. The purpose of the event was

> to dramatically portray the progress of aeronautical achievement and indicates the trend of the future. Happily it serves the dual mission of constructively informing America and all the world of the aggressive civic, industrial and commercial tempo possessed by the City of New Orleans and the State of Louisiana.[38]

While it was to be an event showcasing the achievements of the Long regime, big business sponsorship was extremely visible to those attending the airshow. The Shell Company sponsored an event and Standard Oil made possible the appearance of Michael de Troyat, European Champion Aerobatic Flyer, and the Texas Company brought to New Orleans the Texaco Fire Chiefs Hollywood Duo-Aerobatic Smoke Screen.[39]

Controversy and tragedy surrounded the planned spectacle well before the first parachute opened and the first race began. During the week before the festivities were to begin, the "Ladybirds"—women airracers—were banned from all competitive events, a move that made nationwide headlines and reflected the deep-rooted tensions in the sport and society of the day. This controversy, however, was soon overshadowed by a mounting series of mishaps and tragedies.

The Pan-American Race was to be a showcase for new technology, and the Boeing Company, in an attempt to capitalize on it, sent a new, sleek twin engine 247A filled with press corps from New York. Intending to set a new record of six hours and thirty minutes to New Orleans the plane encountered terrible weather on route—snow in Washington, D. C., haze over Atlanta and then finally a severe storm as it neared New Orleans—forcing the 247A to land in Hammond, Louisiana. Everyone was safe, however, and the next day the aircraft continued to New Orleans. Boeing flight's passengers were lucky compared to Z. D. Granville, also bound to New Orleans from New York. Granville, one of the team of brothers who had designed the Gee Bee Racers fatally crashed as he tried to land on a runway that was being worked on by laborers who were slow to move as Granville's stubby little plane circled overhead.

Those who arrived safely in New Orleans for the dedication ceremonies were soon to be disappointed. On Friday, February 9, opening ceremonies included LSU's marching band, and the celebration began as scheduled. Perhaps because the weather was threatening all morning only 3,000 spectators sat in grandstands built for 35,000. Before the first parachute jump of the day a driving storm hit the airport, forcing the crowd in the stands to run for shelter and resulting in the postponement of all events until the Wednesday after Mardi Gras.

Once resumed, the misfortunes of the event seemingly continued from one event to the next. The first parachutist, Jack Monahan, was injured on a spot jump as he struck the edge of the seawall, dislocating his shoulder. Monahan's accident was trivial, however, to what took place that night. Captain Merle Nelson, a California stunt pilot, had planned to dazzle the crowd by flying overhead in his "Comet" airplane, an aircraft with nine giant rockets strapped to the lower wing surfaces. Once in the air Nelson thought that he would perform a series of inside loops as the rockets spewed flame away from the aircraft, thus creating a giant aerial pin-wheel in the sky.

Apparently Nelson wasn't totally confident about this stunt, as he left a note with a race official containing a premonition of his death: "in case of accident . . . please follow instructions. Have American Legion cooperate and body cremated and have pilots scatter ashes over the field." Nelson's plane roared off, and with all lights extinguished below he reached altitude. He then ignited the rockets, and after completing a loop something happened. Whether he was too close to the field or one of the rockets ignited his rudder is now a matter of conjecture, but he crashed at the edge of the field, the crowd hearing Nelson's piercing screams as he burned inside the shattered plane.

Three days later another fatal accident plagued the Lakefront Airport dedication activities. Before a sparse audience experienced parachute jumper Ben Grew boarded a plane piloted by Charles A. Kenily. Grew was to jump at an altitude of 2000 feet, and as he did, for some reason, he pulled his rip-cord too soon, entangling his chute in the tail of the plane. The plane and its grisly bundle bobbing after it spun into Lake Pontchartrain, killing both Grew and Kenily.

With tragedy came heroics at the meet, including Jimmy Wedell's setting a new speed record for a 100 kilometer course of 266 mph. But Wedell's fame would prove to be short-lived. He had raced with death for almost two decades, and in June of 1934 would be killed in a crash at Patterson while instructing a student flier.[40]

Wedell-Williams Air Service continued for a time after Wedell's untimely death, however. In 1934 the firm sold a design contract to the U. S. Army for a pursuit plane based on the racing plane Wedell had flown in New Orleans. The XP-34 had supporters within the military, including Captain Claire Chennault, but its limited visibility, lack of maneuverability and high landing speed eventually led to its abandonment by the Army before it entered into production.[41] And in the same year the Louisiana aviation company also acquired an airmail contract for route 20 linking New Orleans to Houston; a year later San Antonio would also be served by Wedell-Williams.[42]

The firm was now solely in the hands of Harry Williams, who met a fate similar to that of Wedell, dying in an air crash at Baton Rouge in May of 1936.[43] Subsequently Williams' widow donated the airport to Patterson and sold the air service to Eastern Airlines, thus ending one chapter in the development of aviation in South Louisiana.

While the lack of consistent federal government support proved to contribute to the failure of native Louisianians to break the shackles of a colonial economy, the inability of local educational institutions to respond decisively to the opportunities of a new technology was perhaps also a factor. The untimely deaths of Wedell and Williams illustrated the frailty of "home" industries in part because of the short supply of inventor-entrepreneurs.

One major thrust of the Aero Club of Louisiana during the 1920s was in campaigning for an aeronautical engineering program at Tulane University that would have trained a generation of aeronautics experts in Louisiana.[44] In January 1927, the Aero Club petitioned Tulane to establish such a department, and one of the club's members, Albert E. Holleman, had an inside track. As director of student activities at Tulane, Holleman took the lead in establishing the Tulane Aero Club on campus. However, university administrators and faculty in general did not share the group's enthusiasm. President Dinwiddie expressed concern over the school's possible liability if an accident were to occur. And one faculty member wrote Herbert C. Sadler at the University of

Michigan that "I am of the opinion that they [the Aero Club] have a very inadequate idea of what constitutes a school of aeronautics, thinking perhaps that it means a field and a few planes for the teaching of the practice of flying." While courses in theoretical aerodynamics and airplane design were taught to mechanical and electrical engineers as electives during 1928 and 1929, Tulane administrators were reluctant to establish a program until external funding from the Guggenheim Foundation or other sources could be secured—which ultimately never materialized.

Thus, aeronautical studies at Tulane never took root, but at Louisiana State University an aeronautical department was finally established in the academic year 1933-34, during a time of marked expansion at that institution. In the promotional brochure for the new program aeronautical engineering was defined

> as that branch of engineering which consists of the application of fundamental scientific principles to the particular problems of aeronautics. The curriculum . . . is therefore devoted first to imparting a thorough understanding of basic scientific principles, and then to training the student in the methods of applying this knowledge usefully in the field.[45]

In reality, however, LSU administrators were reluctant to make a firm commitment to the discipline. The entire program centered on the efforts of one person, J. P. Fraim, a former army pilot with no scientific training. At LSU, then, aeronautics was basically flight training. The native scientific and technical expertise necessary to nurture an infant industry based upon dynamic technology was thus absent from the Pelican State during the 1930s. Therefore, a colonial economy was in this case perpetuated rather than transformed by local educational institutions. Indeed, the only school that embraced aeronautics during the 1930s was the Isaac Delgado Trade School located in New Orleans, where student mechanics worked on some of Jimmy Wedell's air racers and later designed and constructed their own aircraft for national competition.[46] But theoretical knowledge was not a focal point of the curriculum, and while Delgado produced many good mechanics, it did not train the engineer-entrepreneurs necessary for economic growth.

By the end of the 1930s the exploits of Jimmy Wedell and the legacy of Huey Long were subsumed by the new concerns of American military involvement overseas. With increased defense preparations LSU's flight training program boomed and South Louisiana began a revolutionary phase of development marked by the rise of science-based technology, as evidenced in the manufacture of PBY flying boats and C-46 cargo planes near New Orleans.[47] During the years 1941-1945 important steps were taken that ultimately resulted in the emergence of a new South Louisiana, one far removed from its tradition-bound past. But these changes were in large part externally induced rather than internally driven, a situation that continues to influence and shape today's Louisiana economy.

Notes for "Getting Places in a Hurry: The Development of Aviation in Long-Era South Louisiana"

[1] T. Harry Williams, *Huey Long* (New York, 1969); Alan Brinkley, *Voices of Protest: Huey Long, Father Coughlin, and the Great Depression* (New York, 1982).

[2] On the dramatic changes taking place in early twentieth century Louisiana, see Henry C. Dethloff, "The Longs: Revolution or Populist Retrenchment?," *Louisiana History*, 19 (1978): 409. See also J. F. Coleman Engineering Company, *A Statement of Facts Concerning New Orleans, La. as a Suitable Location for Textile Industries* (New Orleans, 1929); *The Book of New Orleans and the Industrial South* (New Orleans, 1919).

[3] Huey Pierce Long, *My First Days in the White House* (Harrisburg, Penn., 1935); Williams, *Huey Long*, 845-47.

[4] Ibid., 28.

[5] Ibid., 31-32.

[6] *Louisiana Progress*, November 6, 1930; March 1931; May 1931; July 15, 1931; *American Progress*, September 21, 1931; October 13, 1933; December 14, 1933. On matters related to aviation, *Transmission* began a regular column beginning in 1930. See *Transmission*, 3 (1930): 27-28.

[7] The development of aviation and its impact upon Louisiana are to my knowledge totally ignored subjects. On Louisiana's neighbor state, see Roger E. Bilstein and Jay Miller, *Aviation in Texas* (Austin, Tex., 1985). Other local histories include Arlene Elliot, "The Rise of Aeronautics in California, 1849-1940," *Southern California Quarterly*, 52 (1970): 1-32; Preston R. Bassett, "Aeronautics in New York State," *New York History*, 43 (1962): 115-48.

[8] For a description of aviation's impact upon local business communities, see Roger E. Bilstein, *Flight Patterns: Trends of Aeronautical Development in the United States, 1918-1929* (Athens, Ga., 1983), 68-73.

[9] *Official Program: International Aviation Tournament, City Park Race Track, New Orleans, December 24, 1910, to January 2, 1911* (n.p., n.d.); "Fast Flight to Capital," *New Orleans Times-Democrat*, April 11, 1912.

[10] "Airmail Service Will Begin Today," *New Orleans Times-Picayune*, April 9, 1923; "Ten Year Aviation Gains to Be Feted," *New Orleans Times-Picayune*, April 9, 1933. On early airmail efforts, see William M. Leary, *Aerial Pioneers: The U. S. Air Mail Service, 1918-1927* (Washington, D. C., 1985).

[11] Walter Parker, "New Orleans Chamber of Commerce Report for the Extension of Airmail Service to Latin America," December 9, 1924; Walter Parker to James Magee, October 28, 1924, all in Louisiana Collection, Tulane University, Vertical File "Air-Air Rights."

[12] "Orleans Is Linked with Nation by Air," *New Orleans Item*, May 1, 1928; "Inauguration of Air Mail Service Marks Victory for Y.M.B.C. Drive," *New Orleans Item*, May 1, 1928; clippings in Louisiana Collection, Tulane University, Vertical File, "Airports." Membership lists of the YMBC can be found in the organization's *Blue Book*, 1926-1944.

[13] New Orleans Association of Commerce, *What the New Orleans Association of Commerce Is, How It Functions, and What Its Activities Are for 1933* (n.p., 1933).

[14] W. I. Smith, "Seein' Louisiana With Uncle Jim," *Louisiana*, 1 (1929): 11-12.

[15] Ernest Lee Jahncke, "Present and Prospective Field for Aviation," *Louisiana*, 1 (1929): 9-10.

[16] Harry P. Williams, "New Orleans Begins to Take Its Rightful Place in the Air," *The Whitney Observer*, 4 (1929): 5.

[17] *Times-Picayune*, January 20, 1928, January 22, 1928.

[18] Ibid., April 29, 1928.

Development of Aviation in Long-Era South Louisiana

[19]Louisiana Board of Commissioners of the Orleans Levee District, *Official Directory Pan-American Air Races and Formal Dedication of Shushan Airport* (New Orleans, 1934), 14; S. H. Schmid and Truman Weaver, *The Golden Age of Air Racing,* 2 vols. (Oshkosh, Wis., 1983), 1:84-94.

[20]"Williams, Harry Palmerston," *National Cyclopedia of American Biography,* 27 (1939): 61.

[21]"Wedell-Williams Air Service, Inc." (typescript in Newman Collection, University of New Orleans, n.d.); hereafter cited as Newman Collection.

[22]"Wedell-Williams Air Service, Inc., Schedules," ibid.

[23]*Wedell-Williams Flying School* (New Orleans, n.d.), 6.

[24]"Salesman's Record for Detroit Aircraft" (manuscript in Newman Collection).

[25]Personal communication with Truman Weaver, June 1987.

[26]Henry Ladd Smith, *Airways: The History of Commercial Aviation in the United States* (New York, 1944), 239-41. See also *Hearings Before the Special Committee Investigating the Air Mail and Ocean Mail Contracts,* United States Senate, 73rd Congress, 2d Session (Washington, D. C., 1934), 1443-57; Elsbeth E. Freudenthal, *The Aviation Business: From Kitty Hawk to Wall Street* (New York, 1940), 108-17.

[27]On American Airlines and its expansion during the 1930s, see P. P. Willis, *Your Future Is in the Air* (New York, 1940).

[28]"Timer's Report" (manuscript in Research Office, United States Air Force Museum, Dayton, Ohio, File Q4 1930).

[29]Fred W. Buehl and Harry S. Gann, *The National Air-Race Sketchbook, 1930 to 1949* (Los Angeles, 1949), 11-16; see also "Wedell-Williams Racer" (clipping in Racing Airplanes Scrapbook, U. S. Air Force Museum, Dayton, Ohio).

[30]*National Charity Air Pageant, Roosevelt Field, N.Y., October 7-8, 1933* (n.p., [1933?]), 46; Donald J. Seiler, "The 1932 Thompson Race," *Air Classics,* 8 (1972): 54-57, 64.

[31]"Speed Was the Air He Breathed," *Dixie-Roto Magazine,* November 1, 1953.

[32]Jimmy Wedell, "A Message to Pilots of the Future," *New Orleans Home Journal,* (Fall, 1929), (clipping in "Aeronautics" Vertical File, Department of Archives and Manuscripts, Louisiana State University).

[33]"History of Air Transportation in New Orleans" (typescript in Tulane University Vertical File, "Airports," n.d.); R. Paul Greene, "Louisiana's Progress in Aviation," *Louisiana,* 1 (1929): 21-24.

[34]*Official Directory, Pan-American Air Races,* 6.

[35]*Louisiana Progress,* October 30, 1930.

[36]For a description, see Louisiana, Board of Commissioners of the Orleans Levee District, *Commemorating the Formal Opening of Shushan Airport* (New Orleans, n.d.); "New Orleans: City Gets One of the World's Finest Airports," *Newsweek,* 3 (February 24, 1934): 36; "New Orleans Builds for Trade," *Review of Reviews and World's Work,* 88 (1933): 44-45; *Louisiana Progress,* December 7, 1933.

[37]"Shushan Airport, New Orleans, La.," *The Architectural Forum,* 41 (1934): 240.

[38]*Official Directory, Pan-American Air Races,* 9.

[39]Ibid., 14. William Faulkner used this event as the setting for *Pylon* (New York, 1962). On the airshow, see "Banning of Women Pilots in New Orleans Races Revives Equal Rights Controversy," *New York Herald Tribune,* February 4, 1934; "May Protest Ban on Ladybirds at Air Races," *Sharon, Pa., Herald,* February 8, 1934; "Storm Halts Speeding Plane," *New York Sun,* February 9, 1934; "Flying Man's Week," *Boston Transcript,* February 12, 1934; "Z. D. Granville, Air Head, Killed," *Hartford Times,* February 13, 1934; *New York Herald Tribune,* February 10, 1934; *Philadelphia Inquirer,* February 12, 1934; "Crash at Orleans Races Kills Flier," *Memphis Commercial Appeal,* February 15, 1934; "Stunt Pilot Dies in Fire at Night Flying Exhibition," *New York American,* February 15, 1934; "Two Near Death in Plane Meet," *New York Times,*

February 17, 1934; "Parachute Snarls Plane and Sends 2 Fliers to Death," ibid., February 18, 1934; "Flyer's Body Found After Three Weeks," *Washington Star,* March 12, 1934. All in Shushan Scrapbook, January 22-March 12, 1934, University of New Orleans; "New Orleans: Tragedy and Heroics Mark Airport Show," *Newsweek,* 3 (February 24, 1934): 20.

[40]"Wedell Is Killed Teaching a Flier," *New York Times,* June 25, 1934.

[41]H. P. Williams to Major C. W. Howard, December 19, 1933; Claire L. Chennault to Chief of the Air Corps, February 14, 1934; A. J. Lyon to Chief Material Liaison Section, March 31, 1934. All in File A1(X)P-34/his, U. S. Air Force Museum, Dayton.

[42]*Aircraft Year Book, 1935,* 151; *Aircraft Year Book, 1936,* 191.

[43]"Crash Kills H. Williams" *New York Times,* May 20, 1936.

[44]"Foundation of Chair in Aeronautics," January 25, 1927; Douglas Anderson to Herbert C. Sadler, February 15, 1927; "Facilities of the College of Engineering of Tulane University with Reference to the Establishment of a School of Aeronautics," n.d. All in Tulane University Archives, "Aeronautics" folder. "Tulane Students Taken Aloft as First Collegiate Flying Club Is Organized at Local School," clipping from the *New Orleans Times-Democrat,* March 4, 1928, in "Tulane Scraps," Volume 15, Tulane University Archives. "A of C Seeking Air Engineering School for City," *Times-Democrat,* December 24, 1929; *The Final Report of the Daniel Guggenheim Fund for the Promotion of Aeronautics, 1929* (n.p., 1930), 1-2.

[45]"Aeronautical Department," Louisiana State University, *University Bulletin,* 25 (1933): 17.

[46]Truman C. Weaver, "The Delgado Racers," in Schmid and Weaver, *The Golden Age of Air Racing,* 2:442-46.

[47]"Large Contingent Rushes to Enroll in L.S.U. Pilot Training Course," *Baton Rouge State-Times,* October 2, 1939, clipping in "Aeronautics School" Vertical File, Louisiana State University.

LATE PLANTATION DAYS, 1930-1959*

Michael G. Wade

The three decades after 1930 were years of gradual but significant change for M. A. Patout and Son, Ltd. Willie Patout was the last manager born in the nineteenth century; he directed the company's slow recovery during the perilous Depression years when many other sugar families decided that the struggle was no longer worth it. Changes in the industry and a spate of federal government regulations forced the family to make hard decisions about modernization of all phases of their business. While the personal element remained crucial to the organization, its records displayed an increasingly corporate tone. In the community, continuity and cohesion were provided by family ties, the store, St. Nicholas Church, and other community institutions. These would prove especially important in hard times.

Bub Patout left an estate with a net value of almost $483,000. This included his stock in M. A. Patout and his own holdings, which included Lydia Plantation. Most of this was community property, half to go to his widow, Clelie Romero Patout, and the remainder to be divided equally among his five children. However, fifty-year-old Ory Patout died slightly more than a month after his father, so his portion was divided among his six children. Clelie Patout died intestate on February 26, 1931, leading to the same division of the remainder of the couple's estate. That August, three of their children–Oswell, Sebastian and Annie–bought out the interests of their sister, Bessie, and Ory's children to create H. Patout, Incorporated, to run Lydia Plantation. Oswell and Sebastian each owned 40 percent of the new entity, and Annie the remainder.[1]

At M. A. Patout, the transition from Hippolyte to Willie Patout was a smooth one. "Mr. Willie" had been handling the financial side of the business for years and had an intimate knowledge of the plantation and its workings. He received his early education in Iberia Parish schools and graduated from Jefferson College in Convent, Louisiana, in 1893. Thereafter, he returned to Patoutville where he learned the sugar business firsthand,

---

*First published as chapter 9 in *Sugar Dynasty: M. A. Patout and Son, Ltd., 1791-1993* (Lafayette, La.: Center for Louisiana Studies, 1995), 280-321. Reprinted with the kind permission of the author and the University of Louisiana at Lafayette.

working with his mother and older brother. In a family noted for its diligence, his work habits remained legendary long after his passing.[2]

In the off-season, he was in the fields at 6 a.m. to talk to the overseer. He worked until nightfall when the last man was in. During the grinding season, he put in eighteen-hour days. He had little tolerance for those who did not share his dedication. Workers who incurred his displeasure had little hope of restoring their credit with him. Willie had an aversion to debt and, like the board of directors, did not mind doing without if the alternative was borrowing money. In the late 1930s, when his office manager told him what was needed to improve the mill's operation, Willie's answer was, "Well, Mr. Smith, you can spend anything that you can make." In tough times, this was perhaps only prudent, but the result was that major repairs were made only in good years, which were irregular.[3]

Sugar planters had barely begun to recover from the mosaic crisis of the 1920s when the Great Depression dealt them yet another setback. The financial crisis depleted the investment capital necessary for full recovery. Sugar prices fell from just under five cents a pound in 1926 to less than three cents in 1932. The Smoot-Hawley Tariff increased the duty on Cuban raw sugar to two cents per pound, but the world price quickly fell more than the tariff increase. To make matters worse, the lowest prices came during years of low production. One result was a great increase in idled cane land. In 1934, an estimated 260,000 acres in thirteen parishes, or approximately 35 percent of total cultivable land, lay fallow. Farmers could not maintain their equipment, their mills and workers' housing fell into disrepair, and they offered lower pay and less work.[4]

M. A. Patout's board of directors met in August 1931 to authorize Willie to borrow $85,125 to meet the season's operating expenses and to liquidate existing mortgage indebtedness. The loan was secured by mortgaging Enterprise Plantation and other properties. Forty-five thousand dollars of the balance was due on August 26, 1932, with the remainder payable in installments at 6 percent interest. Unfortunately, the 1931 season did little to help the company's cash flow. An extended drought meant that the mill produced only 126 pounds of sugar per ton on a crop of 35,600 tons. Production probably would have been even lower had it not been for Hippolyte's installation of Ramsay cane-cutting knives in 1929.[5]

After the grinding season, William S. Patout, Jr., was married. On January 22, 1932, he wed Hester Catherine Bernadas in New Orleans. She was the daughter of long-time friends of the Patout family, Hester Kinberger Bernadas and Dr. Hector Emile Bernadas, Chief of Surgery at Hotel Dieu Hospital and a Professor at Tulane Medical School. Following their honeymoon, the couple moved into their newly built house on Main Street in New Iberia.

The 1932 crop was larger, and richer in sugar. The firm made 6,842,000 pounds of 96-test sugar from a crop of 42,240 tons of cane, or 151 pounds of sugar per ton. They realized an additional eleven pounds per ton from summer drying of string goods and approximately five gallons of blackstrap molasses per ton. Approximately one-third of the total crop was raised on Patout-owned lands. The family continued to avoid commercial fertilizers, holding to a traditional three-year rotation with corn and soybeans grown in a field the third year. In the 1920s, the experiment station had found soybeans to be superior to cowpeas and they were in standard use by the 1930s. Three-fourths of the soybeans were turned under to replenish the soil and the remainder was saved for hay. The method was tried and true, and meant that the company did not have to expend scarce cash.[6]

The Depression helped to bring change to the town of Patoutville. The town continued to center around the church and the store, remaining for most of the year a sleepy hamlet until it awoke for the fall grinding season. The old Delahoussaye and Patout store closed a year or so after Hippolyte and August Delahoussaye died, but Willie later built one across the street, possibly in 1936, enclosing a smaller store formerly operated by Marcel Moron. William Jr., now finished with college, ran the store, keeping the family in a business which had originated with Simeon Patout. Just in front of the store, Pascal Marento operated a small shop from which he sold fruit and homemade pralines. Marento also had oysters for fifteen cents a dozen, accompanied by pickled hot peppers which he canned himself. Gustave LeBeau also had a tiny grocery store, which boasted the town's first public telephone. He also operated a blacksmith shop.[7]

To the north of the store and church was a wooden, four-room schoolhouse for the neighborhood's white children. Kids going beyond the seventh grade went by buggy or other conveyance, and later by bus, to Jeanerette. Dr. Ursin S. Perret's office and drugstore was on a side street between the store and the school. Just beyond was the post office, operated at one time by Daisy Gary Domingue. To the south, between the store and the mill road, was a barbershop. Across the street was the late Ory Patout's plantation, complete with residence quarters and a saloon and community hall opposite each other. The hall was rented for dances and was the site of the church fair when it rained. Felix D'Albor fried fish there on Saturday evenings. Those with good credit could transfer the price of their drinks from the saloon to their store accounts. A white horse in front proclaimed the presence of Alcide Goulas. Gin was his poison and cheese his antidote.[8]

Although the store and the saloon served as recreation centers for local people, there were drawbacks. Unpaid credit accounts were a continual problem, especially in years when crops were short or prices low. Eunice Threadgill said that the store was "rather off limits for me as there were always men and blacks around the steps and porch. I would go in sometimes with Mother when she wanted to talk to Ory."[9] The store sold package liquor and some residents practiced the art of moonshining. There was gambling in the small building next to the store. Drunkenness, particularly on Saturday nights, led to fights outside and sometimes worse. Once, a white man with a reputation as a troublemaker killed a black resident with a fourteen-inch butcher knife. He successfully pled self-defense. While certainly disturbing to more respectable residents, it should be noted that weekend excesses of this nature were common to many Southern rural communities.[10]

Though the community remained vibrant in many ways, it was engaged in a losing battle with modernity. The New Iberia-Jeanerette trolley had a roundhouse at nearby Olivier, making it relatively easy for Isle Piquant residents without cars to shop in one of the larger towns. The long trend toward school consolidation had already begun and small communities like Patoutville became victims of the movement. R. P. Bonin was principal at Patoutville White School in 1929-30 and 1930-31. Leona Deslatte was the only other teacher at the school. In 1932-33, Mr. Bonin left and she became the principal at a salary of $80 a month. Her counterpart at the Patoutville Colored School, Letha Pearl Mitchell, made $36 a month. There is no record of the white school's operation in 1933. On August 2, 1934, the Iberia Parish School Board recommended that the Patoutville building be dismantled and re-erected at the New Iberia Training School. Patoutville Colored School seems to have operated through the 1947-48 school year, after which it too was closed.[11]

Actually, schooling for the town's black children took place at several locations over the years. Originally, what long-time resident Lucille Bernard called "our school" was housed in two small "souvenir houses," i.e., two slave shacks in the northeast corner of the Quarters that had survived into the twentieth century. A Methodist minister named Johnson walked in from Olivier each day to teach the children their letters and numbers. Students then attended grammar school at nearby Mt. Carmel Baptist Church until it was destroyed by a storm. Until the church could be rebuilt, they walked to Bayard, where classes were held in a boarding house. Any student wishing to go beyond the fifth grade had to go to the Connell school in Jeanerette until Willie Patout finally convinced the school board to provide teachers in Patoutville.[12]

If one judges solely by the pastoral reports, it would appear that St. Nicholas went into a steep membership decline in the early 1930s. Father Catherin reported 1100 communicants in 1929 and receipts of over $2300. His replacement, an older priest who had been at Rayne the previous ten years, reported half that number for 1930 and receipts of only $585. Father B. W. Neyboer complained that when he arrived the rectory was filthy, leaky, and empty. There were no candles, no linens, no kitchenware, not a drop of wine, and no automobile: "This is the fourth time I find an empty house and no automobile."[13]

Reporting on his dual ministry at Patoutville and Lydia after two weeks, Neyboer said "it looks like an uphill pull all around," apparently referring to the total of $4.35 garnered at the Offertories. No more income could be anticipated until the January sale of pews five months hence and that would produce only $300 from both places. Furthermore, he reported, "I was also requested indirectly not to hold the annual fair this year on account of the recent deaths in the Patout family."[14]

Despite this shaky beginning and the onset of the Depression, Father Catherin tripled receipts and made repairs to the church and rectory. Income dipped a bit in 1932 as the economy worsened, but Father Neyboer managed to put in a new cistern, paint the chapel and repair its roof and gutters. In his final report in early 1933, he praised the spirituality of the congregation. However, he said that financially the situation was nearly hopeless. Pew rents had decreased each year: "the people do not or cannot support this parish . . . the only way to keep this place going is a fair, although this form of amusement to raise money for the church is practically out of date; the young people of today have too many other attractions."[15]

By the time of the New Deal's Agricultural Adjustment Act in 1933, the sugar industry was plagued by abundant stocks and low prices. In 1932, the world price of sugar had declined to about a penny a pound. An effort to establish a marketing agreement had failed. Franklin Roosevelt recommended a quota system which would retain the American sugar industry but not encourage its expansion. The Jones-Costigan Act, which amended the Agricultural Adjustment Act, established such quotas, along with a benefit payment to producers funded by a processing tax on sugar. A cane quota of 260,000 tons, based on depressed 1929-1933 production figures, was established. Each grower was given a tonnage allotment which he could not exceed if he wanted the benefit payment.[16]

The Patout's 1933 crop was 40,233 tons of cane, from which they made 6,236,115 pounds of raw sugar, 36,000 pounds of summer sugar, and 201,165 gallons of blackstrap molasses. The company improved its boiler operation, primarily by using higher quality water, thus reducing its fuel oil consumption to slightly over one gallon per ton of cane ground. Agricultural costs aside, they spent $55,840 on the production and shipping of sugar in 1933. Although their summer sugar constituted only a tiny percentage of their total production, it accounted for 20 percent of wages paid for sugarmaking. In 1934, for the first time, M. A. Patout began to use a commercial fertilizer, Cynamid, on its stubble cane while still rotating corn and soybeans with cane. No sugar production figures were available for the 1934 grinding of 53,252 tons of cane but, using a yield of 150 pounds of sugar per ton, the factory probably finished with slightly over 7.5 million pounds of raw sugar. In 1935, the company improved its steam plant, replacing three old bagasse-fired 60" x 18' horizontal return tube boilers with three 84" x 20' units with shaker grates. This further reduced their fuel oil consumption. That fall, the mill produced just over eleven million pounds of 96-test sugar and 721,000 of low-grade summer sugar from a record 74,630 tons of cane, 22,000 of which was grown in Patout fields.[17]

Given these production figures, M. A. Patout may not have participated in the processing tax and benefit payment sections of the Sugar Act of 1934. Growers and raw sugar producers correctly concluded that the system favored the refiners, who wanted cheap foreign sugar. The American Sugar Cane League was formed to protect producers. M. A. Patout joined immediately. In 1936, the Supreme Court struck down these provisions. The Sugar Act of 1937 restored the quota system, levied a one-half cent per pound excise tax on sugar, and specified a benefit payment of sixty cents per one hundred pounds of sugar. Louisiana and Florida were allowed 5.35 percent and .94 percent of the domestic market respectively, assuring them of a minimum allowable production of 420,000 tons.[18]

M. A. Patout's production figures for 1936 were quite similar to those of the previous year. The factory made 11,040,000 of first sugars, 770,000 pounds of thirds, and some 425,000 gallons of molasses from a crop of 73,804 tons of cane. The succession of decent years gave the Patout's conservative board much-needed capital for modernization. In 1937, anticipating a record crop, they made major improvements throughout the mill, increasing their grinding capacity, on paper, from 1200 to 1800 tons of cane per day.[19]

Under the direction of Chief Engineer E. P. Lorio, employees installed a nine-roll Reading tandem back of the existing eight-roll Birmingham tandem to create a seventeen-roll mill train consisting of a crusher and five mills, preceded by a set of revolving knives which could cut cane to within one-half inch of the newly-installed steel cane carrier. The Reading equipment had originally been part of a Brownsville, Texas, mill which had gone bankrupt. The steam plant received another pair of 84" x 20' 250-horsepower boilers. To improve clarification, two new 1000-square foot Murphy pressure juice heaters joined the existing three 500-square foot heaters. Lorio created a triple-effect evaporation system with the addition of a 10' Goslin-Birmingham evaporator to the original 14' unit and the dual 9' evaporators (which acted as one).[20] As the expansion progressed, other workers erected a new steel building over the mill and boiler room to complete the $203,000 expansion. The work was completed in time for the mill to handle a record crop of 85,396 tons of cane from which it produced 12,479,871 pounds of first-grade raw sugar, about 900,000 pounds of seconds, and approximately 425,000 gallons of molasses. While theoretically capable of 1800 tons per day, in reality the mill was able to grind about 1400 tons of cane, and occasionally 1500. The evaporation and filtration systems remained inadequate, more juice heaters and sugar storage space were needed, and the fifteen old thirty-inch centrifugals needed replacement.[21]

Late in the 1937 grinding season, M. A. Patout hired a new employee who would prove to be enormously important to the company's development over the next five decades. Willie Patout, in need of an office man to finish the grinding season, asked one of his New Orleans suppliers where he might find a suitable person. They recommended George Smith, a young man from East Texas with a sawmill background and general store experience in Mississippi. Smith first walked down the mill road at about a quarter to five on Sunday, November 28, carrying only a paper bag containing a pair of shoes and a change of clothes. By five o'clock, Willie had hired him as office manager at a salary of $150 a month for the remaining six weeks of the grinding season. Smith's first task was to create a more systematic bookkeeping system, beginning with two washtubs full of papers which Willie transferred to him. With only a break for a chicken spaghetti supper at Lucille Bernard's house in the quarters, Smith worked until midnight that first day and then bedded down on a moss mattress in an unheated room. Three weeks later his wife arrived and, as Smith put it, "the six weeks never did come to an end."[22]

Having arrived during the harvest, Smith quickly found that there was little time to think about anything else. E. P. Lorio, Chemist A. G. Lucas, and Mr. Hebert, the sugarmaker, saw to the mill while Field Superintendent Alphonse Broussard and his overseers ensured a steady supply of cane. The logistics of providing for the enormous harvest-time work force quickly became the responsibility of George Smith. In addition to year-round workers, the company brought in several hundred workers from the cotton country around Opelousas and Ville Platte. Perhaps seventy-five to one hundred worked in the mill and the rest cut cane for ninety-five cents a day.[23]

In the 1937 season, growers faced pressure to raise the wages of cane cutters. Donald Henderson, president of the Congress of Industrial Organizations (CIO)-affiliated United Cannery, Agricultural, Packing and Allied Workers of America, Gordon McIntire of the Louisiana chapter of the Farmers' Union, and concerned ministers demanded that the Agricultural Adjustment Administration conduct hearings which could be attended by field laborers, about nine-tenths of whom were black. McIntire reported that some growers paid as little as seventy-five cents for a workday that ran from dawn until dark. He noted that piece workers were frequently cheated at the weigh station, and that many workers were "paid in script, and have to take all or part of their wages at company stores, where exorbitant prices are charged." The Farmers' Union wanted higher wages, in cash, and provision of garden spaces and woodlots. For year-round hands, it asked the right to raise cows, pigs, and chickens. Most of all, it wanted planters to allow organizing and collective bargaining.[24]

However, an October 8 attempt in LaPlace to organize the workers of St. John the Baptist Parish was broken up by sheriff's deputies, who told workers that they were not allowed on the public roads after 7 p.m. They shot at one worker, apparently without result, because he and a companion were placed in "sweatboxes" in nearby Reserve until such time as they could post $500 bond. J. O. Montegut, large planter and parish school superintendent, reportedly barred McIntire from returning to St. John Parish. Nonetheless, the AAA heard the workers early in 1938 and increased wages to $1.20 a day for skilled males and $1.00 for unskilled females.[25]

At Enterprise, seasonal workers were housed in one-room company shacks about 10' x 14' and in a boardinghouse. Eight workers slept in each room. They ate in two and sometimes three shifts. Breakfast began at four a.m. to enable workers to be in the fields by about 6:30. Lunch was delivered to the fields in big wagons equipped with racks. Supper began at five p.m. and lasted until around seven. Mill hands changed shifts every six hours, so that a worker who went in at six a.m. was off at noon and back on at six p.m. had to be at the boardinghouse at five in order to eat and get to work on time.

Few people worked harder than the boardinghouse cooks, who started work at 3 a.m. and did not finish until ten p.m. seven days a week. Lucille Bernard and four ladies from New Iberia labored over a gigantic cookstove, starting the workers off with biscuits, grits, and potatoes. Then they began preparing the meat, rice, and gravy that were staple items in harvest cuisine. Willie thought that there should also be plenty of soup each day, fifty gallons of it in fact, made from available vegetables, mostly potatoes and turnips, canned tomatoes, and beef trimmings.

Boarders consumed enough meat to keep Mr. Joubert, also from Opelousas, almost constantly busy with the butcher knife when he wasn't firing the stove with twenty-inch pieces of wood. The company bought its beef, and wood, from Sebastian Patout's Lydia Plantation. Dried beans were also a regular menu item, as was cornbread and mustard greens. One year, there was even shrimp stew, made from dried shrimp that the company bought at a bargain price. For millworkers, there was Creole Belle coffee, at least after Willie's unpopular experiment with some sort of coffee substitute.

At lunchtime, the cooks filled little two-compartment metal lunch pails for the field hands. These were then delivered to the field in a big long spring wagon with folding sides which could be used as tables. At suppertime, the boardinghouse could accommodate maybe one hundred diners at a time. Alphonse Broussard stood by the door to ensure against overcrowding. The food was plentiful and wholesome, if a bit monotonous. For the workers, there was no charge. George Smith recalled that in the late thirties, the cost of feeding a worker, including labor, fuel, and food, was thirty-nine and one-half cents a day.[26]

The duration of the rolling season varied from year to year, but sugar manufacturers usually started in mid-October and fervently hoped to be done in time for Christmas. The out-of-town workers wanted to bring their kids Christmas presents with their hard-earned money. Management and labor alike dreaded years when there were early hard freezes. That meant non-stop work until the harvest was complete because the cane deteriorated daily as it stood in the fields. When this happened, planters could expect to lose part of their labor force, despite threats of non-payment. When there was no danger of losing the cane, the Patouts tried to shut the mill down for twenty-four or thirty-six hours in order to allow harvest workers to get home for Christmas day. Even then, about half failed to return, making it very difficult to finish the season's work.

The burden of the season fell on all, however. George Smith admitted that

> They went through some hard times. I think that I did too. Probably not as bitter hard . . . but my first child, I didn't see him until he was five weeks old. My wife, we hadn't been down here but a couple of years, wanted to go to her family doctor back home and I sent her to her mother's and he was born on November 27, and I couldn't get off to get up there. We finished grinding, fortunately, on December 21 and I got up there on the 22nd of December. That's the first I saw of him. But it was a hard life for everybody. The plantation came first. You had to give up everything for that.

In the mill, the labor situation was a bit different. There, M. A. Patout was overstaffed, especially after wage increases mandated by the Wagner Act (National Labor Relations Act) of 1935 made investments in labor-saving mill equipment cost-effective. Arthur Keller, formerly the head of Louisiana State University's Audubon Experimental Sugar Factory, said that the industry was more interested in cutting labor costs than in increasing efficiency when it rapidly converted to continuous clarifiers, rotary vacuum filters, and larger boilers.[27]

When Smith arrived, there were 170 people employed in the mill, many merely "making watch." This ingrained habit stemmed from the belief that watchmen were necessary in the event of a major malfunction in the machinery. They could shut down quickly, thus minimizing damage and repair time. This practice continued partly out of fears about the reliability of the new equipment. Even Smith, who favored cutting labor expenses, admitted that there were some areas where he was reluctant to run the risk of doing without vigilant people on hand. When the minimum wages and hours requirements of the Fair Labor Standards Act of 1938 took effect, Willie said, "Mr. Smith, we're never going to make it, we're going to have to close down." Soon enough, however, they cut the mill force to 128, now making twenty-five cents an hour for twelve-hour shifts. This initial mill labor reduction became a trend that was not reversed until mill capacity was considerably expanded several decades later.[28]

Reductions in the fields also began shortly after Smith came to Patoutville, largely because of the growing mechanization of the agricultural sector of the raw sugar industry. In part, these technical advances were the fruit of decades of effort to modernize field work. Planters were all the more interested in labor-saving equipment because the higher wages mandated for mill workers created pressures for increased field wages. Ultimately, new labor shortages created by World War II provided the greatest impetus to rapid changes in the sugar fields. George Smith's experiences in his first few years in Patoutville coincided with the passing of an era in plantation labor patterns.

During the remainder of the year, as many as eighty families lived in Enterprise Plantation's "Quarters." Before the war, the Quarters consisted of four rows of small, uninsulated wood-frame houses with unscreened windows, open fireplaces, and front porches. Later, heat would be provided by woodstoves, then wood heaters, then kerosene stoves, and finally gas space heaters. The houses seem to have been insulated and the windows screened possibly in the late thirties, more probably in the early forties. Outhouses and clotheslines were in the back yards. Residents got their drinking water from wells and lighted their houses with kerosene lamps and lanterns.

In some ways, the Depression was not as hard on Quarter occupants as on some others in American society. Its occupants, black and white alike, shared a common poverty. Most residents, children especially, had the same as others, which was little enough. But, they were neither jobless nor homeless. There was enough to eat. There was not much money. For some this was not all-important. As Lucille Bernard, an uncommonly wise resident, said: "If you don't have it in your head, you don't have it."[29]

With few exceptions, Quarter residents did hard manual labor in the fields or around the mill. Ditching and hoeing were still mostly done by hand. Lucille Bernard hoed cane, broke corn, and, early in her tenure at Enterprise, even cut cane for fifty cents a day. Victoria "Vic" Freeman cooked for Willie Patout's family, much as Bama had for Bub Patout's. Between sugar harvests, the work day started early to enable a break from the oppressive heat. During grinding season, work days necessarily began at sunrise. Alphonse Broussard was there at daybreak to unceremoniously rouse anyone who was not ready and waiting. One morning, one unfortunate and temporarily anonymous soul made the mistake of replying to his brusque entreaties with: "Go away, you old son of a bitch!" Broussard, not noted for his sense of humor, identified the culprit after some hours, confronted him in the fields, and gave him until five o'clock to vacate the premises. After that time, the enraged Broussard promised to shoot him. Assured by others that this was not an idle threat, the shaken man hurriedly left.

Since there was so little money, gardening was important to the Quarter. The older men gardened in fields prepared for plantation residents, tending potatoes, turnips, corn, mustard greens, yams, tomatoes, okra and probably other vegetables as well. Not all families were interested in gardening. However, nearly every family raised a hog for fall butchering. The men hunted rabbits and racoons and went seining for fish in the marsh back of the old Bayard Plantation. Turtles went into stews and soup and *choupique* (bowfin) and garfish were transformed into fishballs for spaghetti. Despite this seeming diversity in foodstuffs, inadequate diets were in fact a problem. George Smith noted that diabetes was prevalent at Enterprise and attributed it to diet, especially to avoidance of vegetables, and to excessive drinking among the men.[30]

Hunting and fishing served as a form of recreation for the men and older boys. A baseball team from Enterprise played those from the Cherry Grove, Bayard, and Lewis plantations. There was a dance hall in a back pasture for the use of plantation workers. Guitarist Eugene LeBlanc was a particular favorite at these affairs. There were also "house dances," held in an empty Quarters house when someone moved. There was music in the front and gambling in the back. At one of these parties a man remembered only as Slim was killed when he cheated an older man who lived across the street. He was sentenced to three years in prison, but Willie Patout's efforts got him released after a year and a half. In general, the social dynamics of the Quarters, both good and bad, appear to have been similar to those of poor people who had only modest prospects and few outlets for their inevitable frustrations.[31]

Relations between white and black residents appear to have been largely cordial but reserved. At any given time, the black population of the Quarters was probably more than twice that of the whites. There was a white section of the quarters on the northeast side, but sometimes blacks and whites were neighbors. Black residents said that the whites were generally friendly as long as they had only black neighbors. They became much more distant when white neighbors were nearby. Like the non-Quarter whites, they feared being characterized as "nigger lovers," a curious but fearsome phrase for describing what later generations might consider basic neighborliness. In general, how the Enterprise Quarters rated in comparison to other such plantation accomodations is not known, but Albania Plantation had the reputation of being a bad place to live because the residents did not get along. Patoutville was certainly not without its problems. For instance, some people objected to blacks attending mass with whites at St. Nicholas. When it was suggested that black citizens should attend services in Jeanerette, Father Neyboer delivered a sermon on the issue and integrated services, with separate seating, remaining.[32]

In March 1933, Neyboer was reassigned to Youngsville and Father Oscar Joseph Chauvin came to Patoutville. This energetic, outspoken young priest remained at St. Nicholas until 1952. He immediately undertook a census of the faithful and concluded that there had been a substantial undercounting in recent parish censuses. For 1934, he reported 1200 white and 400 black parishioners. Hard times had caused a decline in attendance at both religious society meetings and public schools. Two years later, Chauvin reported that he had begun conducting Masses on Sunday at St. Joseph's Chapel in Lydia, alternating the time of services with St. Nicholas.[33]

Finances remained a problem. Chauvin received an Extension Subsidy from the diocese during his first two years at St. Nicholas. Upon learning that it would cease, he whimsically warned the bishop, "Please do not be surprised if you hear before long that I've turned beggar!" He did not, of course, but he did lose his organist in a dispute over payment for her services. Like his predecessor, Chauvin thought the church fair an outdated means of raising money and, in 1937, tried to secure contributions sufficient to do without the annual event. This must have failed, because the next fall he was reporting that the church fair netted $1177, much of which went to paint the church and repair the fence and roof. Father Chauvin seems to have made some effort to attract black Catholics because, by 1939, minority membership was up by 30 percent to 520 parishioners. By 1941, the number had risen to 600 while white membership had dropped to 900, a 25 percent decline in five years.[34]

The black church fair clearly benefited from the growth in minority membership. According to Chauvin, it did not make as much as the white fair, "but it's a grand occasion. . . . Their friends and relatives come from far to be here for the fair. I am sure that many a good marriage among these Colored folk was started at the annual fair."[35] Whether or not this decline in white members was related to increased black membership is unclear. Church records contain no evidence of white dissatisfaction, church revenues increased, and Willie Patout remained a trustee of the church and a regular financial contributor. In addition, the annual reports lump attendance at Patoutville and Lydia together, making it impossible to reach any conclusions about relative numbers at each place. All that is certain is that the Lydia congregation was growing and that Mass was said on Sundays and on Wednesdays. The Wednesday Mass was said from the second Wednesday of Lent to the start of grinding season, after which "no one would come on a weekday then." Even the Church made concessions to the rhythms of the sugar season.[36]

Despite their conservative reputation, M. A. Patout's board of directors continued to invest in mill improvements in the late 1930s. Willie, the president and manager, enjoyed the support of his sister, Ida Burns, the vice-president, and his Texas-based brother, Rivers, the secretary of the company. Also important to the program was Oswell Patout, the company's on-site assistant secretary. Another record crop of 87,941 tons which produced 14,935,794 pounds of sugar provided capital for an additional smokestack in 1938 and a new steel warehouse (60' x 120' x 20') with a capacity for an additional 20,000 bags of sugar. In 1939, with sugar prices much higher because of

Germany's invasion of Poland, production was 13,056,000 pounds and 506,552 gallons of molasses, a return sufficient to enable the 1940 replacement of four older boilers with two 300 horsepower Union water tube boilers and the installation of a sprinkler system which greatly reduced their insurance rates.[37] Even with these changes, the mill still lacked the crystallizers which would enable it to abandon the manufacture of summer sugars. Used in combination with "seed" grain storage tanks, they made possible a larger, more uniform size of sugar crystal. Virtually unknown in 1930, they were in general use a decade later. The industry had also moved toward forty-inch (diameter) centrifugals, which operated at higher speeds, made for a better separation of sugar crystals from molasses, and did the work of two thirty-inch machines. Despite its improved milling efficiency, M. A. Patout was still granulating sugar with fifteen old thirty-inch machines.[38]

Other aspects of the business also continued unchanged. Like his late brother, Willie liked plantation-processed products. Whereas Hippolyte's passion had been wine, Willie's was canned goods. Apparently, his dream was to develop a full-fledged commercial canning plant. In the early thirties, he purchased the equipment and canned everything from fruit to sausages. His specialty was pears with a slice of pineapple added to impart additional flavor. Each fall, he put up fresh pork sausages preserved in lard in 70-gallon cans. These he shipped to family members all over the country. Made from ham shoulders, they were fondly remembered by older family members forty years later. Less appreciated was Willie's early spring sauerkraut which he made for the workers in three or four large cisterns each year. Despite his persistence, most recipients steadfastly refused to eat it.[39]

More popular were his entertainments. In a business where most of a mill's cane came from outside suppliers, it was vital to cultivate farmers as well as cane. It was also important that political figures be informed of the needs of the industry and social occasions were a favored means of doing this. Bub Patout had been been a master at this kind of socializing, wining and dining farmers and politicians at the camp on the bay and elsewhere. A friend of his, the manager of a nearby plantation owned by rival Sterling Sugars, one day complained jokingly that he was going to have to stop hauling cane from the area because he could not offer the farmers a week at the camp. Bub Patout reportedly handed the man the camp keys and promised to keep him supplied with drink while he was down there!

Willie continued the tradition in good order. There was of course the annual sugar party, which remained a much anticipated event. Following the grinding season, he took the smaller farmers out to Weeks Island, where they fished, dredged for oysters, and played cards. He hosted local politicians at the Bayard camp, where they fried fresh-caught fish. Like his brother, Willie owned a boat but never took quite the same interest in it. Even more popular were his parties at the boardinghouse, which attracted area officials and sometimes state senators and representatives for roast pigs stuffed with oyster dressing, fine wines and whisky. George Smith described these affairs as "real wingdingers" and allowed that "about half of them that drove home couldn't."[40]

Probably in 1939, the company extended its use of Cyanamid fertilizers from rattoons to plant cane, at a rate of 200 pounds per acre. The annual reports make no further mention of soybeans or cowpeas in the rotation. Other, more revolutionary changes, were in the offing in the fields. The 1940 season was a bad one. Bad weather, capped off by a fall storm, reduced the size of the cane crop and the Patouts ground only 51,200 tons, producing just 8,334,990 pounds of raws and 307,200 gallons of blackstrap. The next season was much improved and, since sugar prices remained high because of the war, the company was able to buy improved cane handling and sugar packaging equipment for the 1942 season.[41]

Higher prices, as well as family tradition, were a factor in William S. Patout, Jr.,'s decision to go into the syrup business in 1941. Early in the year, he suggested that George Smith join him and Cornelius Voorhies for dinner to talk about a partnership in a syrup mill. The younger Patout leased them the land and, by working nearly every Sunday, Smith and Voorhies had a fairly crude little mill ready to go by harvesttime. Willie, who had at one time made syrup himself, stopped by regularly to see how the venture was doing. They made seven or eight thousand gallons of syrup, which they managed to sell. Thus encouraged, they invested in modern labor-saving equipment for the 1942 season. Unfortunately, the mill burned down before they were able to ship the first freight car load of syrup that fall.[42]

Shortly before the 1941 harvest, M. A. Patout's stockholders amended their corporation charter. They increased the membership of the board of directors from three to five to reflect the growing number of shareholders. As time claimed the original shareholders, their children inherited the stock, reducing the number of individual shares but increasing the numbers who held voting stock. In addition, they changed the time of the annual meeting from January to October, i. e., from just after the rolling season to just before it. The president was now required to present a yearly report "in such detail and showing such particulars as the board of directors from time to time may require." The board was vested with full power to borrow funds. The president could also borrow money, provided that he used only unsold sugar as security. He or she could also borrow on the promissory notes of the corporation, in amounts not to exceed $50,000. If there were any reservations about these actions, they were not reflected in the vote, which was 3110 to zero.[43]

Research-based agricultural practices, improved transportation, and the modernization of sugar factories had been key ingredients in the revival of the Louisiana sugar industry in the 1930s. As factories modernized, their numbers declined. By 1940, there were only sixty or so raw sugar factories, most of them fairly well-equipped. Even so, the mechanization of field work was perhaps the most important advance in this period. By the end of the decade, many growers were using high-wheeled, general purpose cane tractors which actually required less capital than mules and equipment and reduced costs of cultivation by an estimated 47 percent. Hoeing machines, cane pilers, and field loaders were also coming into general use by 1940, their adoption further encouraged by the prospect of a war-induced labor shortage.[44]

With the industry more robust than at any time since World War I, large plantations continued to dominate cane production. But there were over 10,000 cane farmers and more than 200,000 people whose living was derived directly or indirectly from the sugar industry. In 1935, fewer than 10 percent of these farmers had more than twenty acres, but they accounted for more than three-quarters of total cane acreage. Only 2 percent had more than eighty acres, but they had 60 percent of the state's total acreage. It was in this group that the machine revolution focused.[45]

The most significant development at M. A. Patout in this period was the firm's purchase of a Thompson single-row cane harvester to assist with the taking off of the 1941 crop. They bought another for the 1942 season. They had already had tractors for some years. In 1940, finding it increasingly difficult to get enough cutters because other better-paying jobs were plentiful, the company had begun to experiment with burning cane in the fields to remove the leaves. Although the cane was easier to cut if it was burned while still standing, they quickly concluded that the danger of wildfire made it preferable to burn it after cutting. George Smith estimated that eliminating the necessity of stripping the cane tripled the capacity of a cutter from three to ten tons a day.[46]

Even then, however, they could not get enough cutters, so they went to the new harvesters. Efforts to develop such equipment had been ongoing since before World War I, but early machines were generally too bulky and heavy. In Terrebonne Parish, the South Coast Corporation used sixteen of them in cutting the 1939 crop. Some estimated that it reduced the cost of cutting cane from ninety cents to forty cents a ton. By the 1941 harvest, approximately forty of the one-row machines were in use, capable of cutting nearly one acre an hour and reducing cane cutting costs by an estimated two-thirds. There were many problems with the new equipment, but the growing labor shortage left little alternative, especially for large growers.[47]

Willie Patout died suddenly, just before the start of the 1942 grinding season, on September 28, 1942. He suffered a heart attack while he was driving into town one day, took to his bed at home, and on Monday morning signed six checks for George Smith. He died later that day just after noon. Willie Patout had been a long-time supporter of the church and an active member of the Knights of Columbus. Five priests officiated at his funeral the next day, with Father Neyboer returning to deliver the sermon in French.[48]

The board of directors met on September 30 to elect a new president and appoint a new manager. Ida Patout Burns was named president, Sebastian Patout became the new vice-president, and Rivers Patout Wall was the newest member of the board of directors. William Schwing Patout, Jr., became the new manager at $1500 a year and George Smith was promoted to assistant manager. Ida was to negotiate for a new sugar warehouseman to fill the vacancy created by William Jr.'s promotion. The corporation opened two accounts at the First National Bank of Jeanerette, one a "Cane Account," out of which they would buy cane, and the other a general account for the remainder of the corporation's business. Finally, the company drew up a note for $15,000 owed to Willie Patout. At the regularly scheduled meeting a month later, the president and manager were authorized to negotiate loans not to exceed $300,000 within the next five months. This meeting marked the beginning of what was to become a sustained program of modernizing the company's financial affairs.[49]

That fall, the mill at Enterprise ground 82,612 tons of cane, making 13,848,003 pounds of raw sugar and 520,000 gallons of molasses. The company kept its two nine-foot vacuum pans for boiling sugar, but retained Jeffrey and Sons to convert the eleven-foot pan into a forty-two inch calandria pan. There had been only eight of these in Louisiana in 1930, but there were fifty-one by 1940. The newer pans speeded up sugar boiling considerably and reduced fuel requirements since they operated on low-pressure steam. With this improvement, the crystallizers and centrifugal stations remained the only factory areas in need of significant upgrading.[50]

Judging by the grinding figures, their first cane cutters probably performed reasonably well despite frequent stops for repairs, especially on lighter stands of cane. Alphonse Broussard had grave doubts about the newfangled devices. He was not mechanically inclined to begin with and his fearsome presence, so inspiring to slow workers, had no effect at all on the harvesters. Toward the end of the 1941 season, Broussard told Willie that if he persisted in his use of harvesters, they were going to have to cut down on fertilizer and quit growing such good cane. "Every time I get into cane over eight feet high the harvester quits. It won't cut more than 18-ton [per acre] cane."[51]

Conditioned his whole life to traditional labor-intensive cane culture, it did not occur to this otherwise intelligent octogenarian that something should be done to alter the machine rather than the cane stand. Like Willie, he put in eighteen-hour days during the milling season, standing watches in the sugar mill after the day's field work was done. Those who had occasion to hear him when he woke the quarters in the morning swore that he could be heard half a mile away. He rode his horse through the fields, directing the men and to the women cutters, screaming, "Gals, cut 'em high and cut'em low." Broussard was a memorable curser. Lucille Bernard recalled that, on one occasion when Broussard thought her work was too slow, he bellowed: "Oh, Lucille. Oh, Lucille. You didn't come out here on your goddamned good looks, you know." Broussard also swore at Lucille's brother Johnny with regularity.[52]

The old-timers, particularly the women, remembered his profanity but they also spoke fondly of him and recalled many kindnesses from this gruff old Frenchman. After he was grown, Johnny Bernard always made a point of stopping in to see Broussard when he was in Patoutville, suggesting that there was much more to the man than just his volume and vocabulary. He was apparently as meek as a lamb around his wife, a formidable person in her own right. It was well known that Broussard had no use for the Long political machine. If his nighttime visits to the office during grinding season caused the staff to get behind in their work, the timekeeper would buddy up to him and say, "Mr. Alphonse, do you know Huey Long, that's the greatest man that ever lived." Without fail, Broussard would say "Oh goddam," and be on his way. He worked one more season after Mr. Willie's death and, unwilling to adapt to the new ways at Enterprise, he retired. Not counting four years when he worked elsewhere, Alphonse Broussard devoted fifty years of his life to Enterprise Plantation.[53]

War-created scarcities of food commodities not only produced a Victory Garden movement, but also led to new pressures for self-sufficiency and housing improvements on sugar plantations. After interviewing large growers, *Gilmore's Louisiana Sugar Manual* reported that rationing and planter pressure were causing resident laborers to alter their diet to include more vegetables. Furthermore, planters found themselves in the position of having to make their housing more attractive if they wanted to retain their workers.

Speaking for M. A. Patout, George Smith said that more residents were tending gardens and that a housing improvement program was underway:

> As is the case on many plantations, our housing facilities in the past have not been all that we would have liked to provide. However, we have a crew of carpenters who will repair and patch cabins practically all this year. Our housing plans cover a three-year period due to labor shortages and scarcity of materials. This year we expect to put a staunch foundation, a good floor, good outside walls, good roof, and glass window[s] in place of shutters on every house. Next year, we expect to be ceiling [sic] the houses on the inside and exterior painting is due to follow.[54]

Other plantations gave pretty much the same reports about what the industry termed its "Labor Care" program.

Early in 1943, the company's board met to prepare for the year's work. Ida Burns was reelected president and Rivers Patout, Sr., became the new vice-president, replacing Sebastian Patout, who had died the previous June. J. Patout Burns was named secretary-treasurer. William Patout, Jr., continued as manager with a raise in salary to $5000 annually. The trend toward a more businesslike, less personal managerial style continued as the board compiled a lengthy list of the manager's duties. George Smith remained as assistant manager at $3300 a year plus an additional $300 for the same duties at Little Valley.

In other business, the company granted a right of way to Texas Pipeline Company and authorized an engineering study of the mill which would produce detailed plans for improvements. The board also resolved to donate $200 annually for the personal support of the priest at St. Nicholas. Noting that the heirs of Hippolyte and Clelie Patout had used the main residence "for storage purposes and for the keeping therein for their convenience of various articles of furniture, clothing, household goods, and other movable effects, all without charge to this date," and that the house badly needed repairs, the board authorized repairs and directed that the heirs either remove their goods or begin paying a $40 a month storage charge.[55]

The 1943 season brought both a record crop and looming financial crisis to Enterprise Plantation. That fall, the mill ground a then-record 91,754 tons of cane, which yielded 13,898,644 pounds of sugar, all sold to neighboring Sterling Sugars for refining, and 637,490 gallons of blackstrap molasses. For the 1943 grinding, the company had 460 acres of plant cane and 480 acres of first-year ratoons. The remaining cane came from others farming an estimated 3000 acres. Much of the cane was still delivered in 220 four-ton cars pulled by four Porter locomotives along a 12-mile tramroad whose most distant station was ten miles from the factory. Patout, Smith, and Voorhies had borrowed money to rebuild their syrup mill for the season, only to discover that the syrup market was so soft that they lost even more money. Undaunted, they resolved to try again in 1944. More serious was the disarray in the company's financial records. The confusion in the books, combined with a large debt load, wartime regulations, and excess profits taxes, had produced a cash flow crisis for the company by 1942.[56]

On November 23, 1943, Ida Burns reported to the stockholders on the dearth of dividends. The loans from Hippolyte and Willie Patout, totaling $85,125.00, were still outstanding. An additional $46,798.28 was due various company officers and stockholders on notes, making a total fixed debt of $131,923.28. During the years of slow recovery in the late twenties and early thirties, a critical shortage of funds had led to the deferment of ordinary repairs and improvements. The eventual result of that was larger repair expenses in the late thirties and early forties. Changing sugar technology had necessitated certain expenditures in order to keep the company competitive. Finally, World War II had produced, of necessity, the fastest rate of mechanization in industry history.[57]

A more recent consideration was that "increasing federal income taxes which continue to take a growing percentage of profits have contributed to the continuation of the shortage of working funds." Mrs. Burns said that whereas in 1935, M. A. Patout's taxes were 16 percent of reported income, in 1942, they had been 50 percent, and that they were 69 percent for 1943. For the fiscal year ending March 31, 1943, the company's profit was $110,053.05. Their net profit after deducting $80,637.30 in income taxes was $29,415.75, most of which was used for improvements. These figures were not wholly unexpected. According to Mrs. Burns, "It became alarmingly evident last year that our accounting procedures were outmoded by developments and that our tax burden was assuming alarming proportions."[58]

It was this financial hemorrhaging that led the board, at its February meeting, to authorize William Patout to retain the accounting firm of Barton, Pilie, Sere, and Wermuth to report on the financial operations and the tax structure of the business. This proved to be such a challenge that accountant David Hearne moved his family from New Orleans because the job was going to take so long. He encountered a system of bookkeeping practices that were holdovers from the nineteenth century plantation era. For example, he found $2513.51 in undeposited cash being held for contingencies. Since the related expenses entered in a journal were not verifiably "paid or incurred," they were not properly deductible from income taxes. The general ledger indicated that, between

April 11, 1942, and March 31, 1943, slightly over $54,000 had been withdrawn from the company bank account in the form of checks made out to "Bearer Payroll" or similar designations. This had been a long-standing practice. Hearne was unable to verify all of the items due to inadequately integrated records.[59]

Payroll procedures were also confusing. The store (Patout & Patout) made advances to M. A. Patout employees on the authority of the overseers. The corporation then paid them in cash withdrawn from the company account, but there was no reconciliation made between cash advances reported by the store and payroll deductions which presumably offset the advances. Frequently there was no endorsement on the checks to indicate who withdrew the cash from the bank and, for the fiscal year ending March 31, 1943, $4250 in checks had been endorsed by unbonded employees. Final settlements of the difference between wages and cash advances were made only at the close of grinding when the office prepared payrolls. A satisfactory test of the authenticity of the payments was impossible due to the lack of records control, particularly in the handling of cash through Patout and Patout.[60]

Hearne found that M. A. Patout's investment in the store was substantial, but had difficulty measuring it to his satisfaction because he had only single-entry and memorandum records to work with. They were deficient in both accuracy and scope. No record of cash on hand had been maintained and many items of income and expense had gone unrecorded. Bank deposits had been made intermittently in round sums whenever the amount on hand seemed to warrant reduction. Records of store transactions by M. A. Patout were informal, kept in a day book with no indication of the buyer or the purpose of the purchase. These procedures had also been passed down from generation to generation.

After discussions with William Patout and George Smith about the store, Hearne provided Smith with detailed instructions for a minimum system of double-entry accounts with daily recording of charge account transactions and cash on hand. With regard to the sugar business, Smith felt, and Hearne agreed, that the existing system of accounts classification did not provide the information and protection necessary for an operation as large and diversified as M. A. Patout. However, because of the company's limited staff, it was impractical to establish the kind of internal control wherein duties were so arranged that one employee automatically checked the actions of another. Hearne recommended revisions in the accounting records, outlined procedures for positive control of cash and payroll transactions, and designed an account classification which met the company's needs without any appreciable expenditure of time or money.

Although the tangle and confusion of the records must have been unnerving and even appalling to a big city accountant, William Patout, George Smith, and David Hearne worked well together in the months-long process. In the end, Hearne placed the episode in perspective, reporting that

> many of the practices were handed down as an accumulation of expedients which were adopted piecemeal when corporation taxation and regulations were comparatively

simple and practically all details could be handled and/or supervised by one person. Many actions which seemed proper at the time have now been placed in a different aspect by the trend of events and taxation legislation.

In the final analysis, all three understood that the company could save a great deal of money by modernizing its accounting procedures.[61] Prior to Hearne's audit, the Internal Revenue Service claimed that M. A. Patout owed a considerable sum above and beyond what it had already paid for 1940 and 1941. Hearne determined their liability to be about $4900, and further negotiations with the government led to an agreement on $3,621.45. More importantly, the firm was able to file claims for federal and state refunds totaling over $39,000 for extra taxes paid in 1942 and 1943. Furthermore, its excess profits credits were substantially increased as a result of the audit. For the 1943-44 season, this resulted in an increased net profit ($33,087.84) despite a decreased operating profit. A net loss for the fiscal year ending March 31, 1945 (the 1944-45 crop), enabled them to file additional claims for refunds of taxes paid in fiscal 1943 and 1944 since the tax law permitted losses to be used to reduce the tax liability of the two previous years.[62]

The additional claims brought the total federal and state overassessments to $118,626.41. That year, the company also had an unused excess profits credit of $27,000 which could be applied to any excess profits made in fiscal 1946 and 1947. Despite the good news, Ida Burns cautioned the stockholders that, while the tax refunds would do much to relieve the shortage of working funds, she did not foresee an early resumption of dividends. The double drain of excess profits taxes and the necessity of repairing the plant had "deprived us of the benefits which might otherwise have been enjoyed."[63]

With its cash flow problems resolved, the company was able to devote full attention to the sugar business once more. The scarcity of labor continued to be a problem. This was partially resolved in several ways. Early in the war, following inquiries about Mexican labor that did not develop, M. A. Patout began to hire workers from the Caribbean, particularly Cuba, on a seasonal basis. This temporary expedient proved so satisfactory that the arrangement lasted for two decades. To retain existing employees and because repair expenses were chargeable against income otherwise subject to the 95 percent excess profits tax, the company devoted more money to reconditioning its properties, reasoning that it would promote employee morale as well as operating efficiency and safety.[64]

The 1944 season provided ample evidence of the impact the war had wrought in the labor force. First, there were far fewer workers in the fields, probably not more than one hundred. Howard Hebert apparently transferred from his position as sugarmaker to field superintendent, replacing Alphonse Broussard. The new sugarmaker was Paul Hebert. Assisting him was a crew of skilled Cuban sugar factory operatives, who took up residence in the boardinghouse. They were headed by Chemist J. G. Rodriguez, who succeeded John Fuchs. Prior to the Cubans, the company had used Filipinos from New Orleans in the sugarhouse, but they subsequently found higher-paying jobs.

T. L. Mitchell was the new chief engineer, replacing George H. Gibbens. This massive turnover in skilled personnel appears not to have affected production very much, but the rapid depletion of the field force probably affected the traditional delivery system. The mill ground 85,548 tons of cane, over 68,000 tons of it provided by about 150 outside shippers. M. A. Patout experienced growing problems with its narrow-gauge railroad deliveries in 1944, largely because of frequent breakdowns of rolling stock and deteriorating roadbeds. Delayed shipments, escalating maintenance costs, and the labor shortage were making the use of trucks, which already supplied the cane for daytime grinding, more cost effective.[65]

Sixteen German prisoners of war from a nearby POW camp also provided some skilled labor. The Patouts initially tried these members of Erwin Rommel's Afrika Korps in the fields, but they balked at having an overseer on a horse barking orders at them. When it was discovered that many of them had mechanical and construction skills, some were put to work in the mill and others were assigned to new house construction in the quarters. There they built brick cottages which are still in use today. Despite the military's worries that the company did not assign the requisite number of guards to watch the prisoners, there were no escape attempts and only minor trouble. When the POWs found out that Hippolyte had maintained a wine cellar, they found it and consumed a considerable percentage of the remaining stock. On another occasion, one or two of them borrowed young William Patout III's .22 calibre rifle and honed their shooting skills on the local chickens. They also borrowed shotguns and took him hunting in their off hours. Many of them retained fond memories of their time at Enterprise and a few kept in touch with William Patout, Jr., over the years.[66]

With this patchwork labor force, M. A. Patout made 12,895,584 pounds of raw sugar and 557,000 gallons of molasses in 1944. As soon as the season concluded, the mill workers began extensive improvements to the cane feeding system, relocating and raising both derricks and adding two 20' x 28' steel cane feeding tables equipped with Link-Belt chain. The company also purchased four 40" belt-driven Hepworth centrifugals to replace ten of its older 30" machines. Because of the improvements, high labor costs, and price controls on sugar, the company finished the year with an operating loss of $8673.[67]

The syrup mill also did well. The demand for syrup was so great that they did not have to ship their product. Buyers sent trucks to pick it up. Much of the syrup was processed in gallon buckets for a Mr. Dowl from Meridian, Mississippi, who was taking it to Georgia. When George Smith ran out of buckets and gallon cans, he suggested that they use fifty-gallon steel drums. Dowl replied, " Just how in the hell you think a man is going to carry a drum of that stuff over them mountains in Georgia?" The syrup, closely watched by treasury agents, went from Patoutville to the farmers' market in Atlanta, where it was sold in smaller quantities. Sales of under five cases did not have to be accounted for. Apparently, the syrup was bought by whiskey bootleggers who could not get sugar for their operation. The Patoutville syrup-makers were suspicious, but were sure of their legal ground. They were merely doing a contract processing job for $1.25 a case, well within the ceiling price of $6.32 a case. In any event, they made enough money to pay off all of their debts and had another good year the following season.[68]

Barton, Pilie, Sere, and Wermuth's 1945 report to the company indicated that old habits died hard. Noting that the degree of internal control of funds had improved, the accounting firm said that further improvements were needed. It was still unable to verify considerable petty cash expenditures to workers during grinding season. The monthly balancing of bank accounts and the reconciling of company and store accounts apparently was neglected during the busy fall months. Trial balances of the general ledger and accounts receivable and payable ledgers were also needed. None had been done since mid-1943. Because illiteracy among the workers was a problem, Barton recommended that metal employees' tags, whose number could be traced on to the checks, be used to verify whose "X" was on the transaction.[69]

While there were obviously still problems in the company's financial methods, the clear advancement in cost information contained in the report indicated how much improvement had been made. A subsequent report contained detailed statistics on comparative production costs for 1943, 1944, and 1945, complete with a breakdown of all expenses for both the agricultural and manufacturing operations. Also included was a complete analysis of M. A. Patout's fire, liability, and accident insurance in force as of March 31, 1945, and an outline of its debts, which amounted to $137,625.00. Reducing this debt and continuing the improvements programs remained the board's top priorities.

Debt reduction was difficult to accomplish because the costs of cultivating cane and manufacturing sugar rose sharply between 1941 and 1946. Larger growers like M. A. Patout raised cane for about ninety dollars an acre in the late thirties. By 1946, their cost was more like $165 an acre and profit margins were smaller because total receipts had also risen. Rigid price controls between 1942 and 1948 prevented M. A. Patout and other sugar millers from making the kinds of profits that might have enabled them to modernize their plants more fully in this period. According to J. Carlyle Sitterson, large farms with an average capital investment of $150,000 averaged a 1.9 percent return between 1937 and 1945. In 1944, M. A. Patout showed total assets of slightly over one million dollars.[70]

In 1945, Enterprise ground a new record 95,712 tons of cane, most of it bought from 160 outside growers. Much of the field loading of the cane was done by four power loaders and an increasing percentage of the cane was delivered in trucks or tractor-hauled carts. The home fields at Enterprise and Cherry Grove continued to account for slightly more than one-fifth of the tonnage. The Patouts traditional three-year rotation of cane and soybeans continued. To till and harvest its fields, the company now had twelve tractors, twenty-six carts, and a Woolery ditch-bank burner for weed control. It used the herbicide 2, 4-D on alligator grass.[71]

The mill's 1945 production totals were 14,308,944 pounds of raws and 622,128 gallons of molasses. The new Hepworth centrifugals, for which the company had paid $15,000, $10,000 of it borrowed, worked beautifully and the company ended fiscal 1945 with an after-tax profit of $40,700. The succeeding year was not so impressive. The syrup enterprise of Patout, Smith, and Voorhies shut down after a seventeen-day run because they had no orders for the syrup already made. It took them three years to liquidate that modest stock. At Enterprise, production declined to 9,258,784 pounds of sugar and 566,500 gallons of molasses from 72,260 tons of cane. Some 63 percent of the cane was delivered to the factory by truck. Another 22 percent arrived in tractor-hauled carts. Only 15 percent came via the tramway. One reason for the production decline may have been lost time at the mill, which amounted to 21.1 percent of the sixty-one day grinding run. Improving the mill's performance was a primary reason for the 1946 hiring of Chief Engineer Guy A. Porche, one of the top sugar engineers in Louisiana. B. J. Martin was fabrication superintendent.[72]

Despite the short crop, and aided by the termination of the excess profits taxes and the capital stock tax, the company's after-tax profit for the fiscal year ending July 31, 1947, was $38,961.55. The firm applied $8400 of that sum to auditing expenses and used the remainder, plus almost $55,000 from the general fund, to pay off the $85,125 due the heirs of Hippolyte and Willie, on the books since 1926, when it again came due on September 1, 1946. An imminent federal tax rebate of $35,000 in mid-1946 and an anticipated $96,000 refund later enabled the board of directors to declare a 5 percent dividend. The board decided that the first use of additional tax refunds would be to retire any demand notes held by persons or businessess outside the family, with the balance to be carried in the general fund. The second consecutive dividend was good news to stockholders, some of whom had questioned the company's policy of continually investing in improvements.[73]

The tax windfall meant that the board of directors could fund a modernization program:

> As you know, our mill is old and was in very bad repair up to a few years ago. Some equipment is still old and inefficient, which means that other replacements must be made in the next few years. We have followed the plan, dictated at times by dire necessity, of replacing the old and most inefficient equipment first, always of course subject to having funds available.

For the 1947 season, the company spent $14,000 on a second set of cane knives and a 430-horsepower Moore turbine with Worthington reduction gear to drive them. It installed an Oliver-Campbell rotary vacuum filter to handle clarifier muds, replacing its old mud presses at a cost of $26,000. To eliminate lost time caused by clogging in the mill's ten old Dutch-oven furnaces, the company replaced them with Dennis horseshoe furnaces for $23,000. For about $9,600, it put in two Pomona deep well, turbine-driven pumps. The conversion of another of the vacuum pans to a calandria pan was probably also part of the program. Another $10,500 was invested in three clarifier mud tanks, five syrup tanks, and an overseer's house at Cherry Grove. It was also necessary to install new Crown wheels and crusher shells on two of Enterprise's aging mills. In all, the firm invested $127,400 in improvements in fiscal 1946-47. Despite this impressive investment, more would be needed.[74]

Acting on David Hearne's report, the board of directors informed the stockholders that, since the entire net worth of the company was represented by fixed assets:

> This requires us to borrow and to carry heavy accounts payable in order to finance current transactions. This chronic shortage of working capital has hampered operations and will continue to do so. . . . [Hearne] recommended to the Board that they consider some plan of making more capital available, possibly through long-term financing, to be retired according to an arranged schedule over a period of years. The Company's charter will have to be renewed in 1960, at which time it may be expedient to increase the capital stock of the Company. In the meantime, financing to be liquidated by 1960 will have to be considered. In recent years several new mills have been erected in our vicinity and we cannot allow our mill to be placed at so great an operating disadvantage as to be unprofitable.

The 1947 crop offered little help since it was suffering from drought and was expected to yield less than the 1946 crop. But, barring some unforeseen circum-stance, the company predicted a small profit.[75]

M. A. Patout was one of the few companies still making summer sugar by the 1930s. Lacking crystallizers, they started the mill up in June, boiled left-over massecuite, and put it in large tanks to cool. As it cooled, it formed granules, slowly building them over the summer. It was an expensive, time-consuming process which produced a low grade sugar the Patouts sold to chewing tobacco manufacturers. At the outset of the 1946 harvest, William Patout recommended that crystallizers be installed just as soon as it was financially feasible. These were prophetic words, because in 1947 the company was unable to market its summer sugar. Unfortunately, the other repair and modernization needs were more pressing and the crystallizers had to wait.[76]

On April 20, 1947, the board hired David Hearne, who had gone into business for himself with a branch office in New Iberia, as its auditor at a figure not to exceed $1800 a year. It appreciated the work done by his previous firm but hoped to save money on auditing expenses. Aided by a loan from William Patout and Ida Burns, the company began to pay its insurance premiums on a five-year basis to save money. The board decided not to sell bagasse to a wall board plant because natural gas lines near the mill were insufficient to supply its needs and it would be necessary to add a facility for drying, baling, and storing bagasse. They were already using fuel oil and the new horseshoe burners promised to burn the bagasse more efficiently, so it was more profitable not to make any changes.[77]

William Patout reported that a five-year program to develop more cane land at Bacque Pastures was proceeding as planned and added that there was a possibility that 500 acres there could be incorporated into a farming unit. By October, Hearne was able to report that all approved tax refunds had been paid, received, and used in paying debts and repairing the sugar factory. The feeling was that the labor supply would be somewhat better that fall. The effects of mechanization could be seen in a report that the corporation had only thirty mules and horses remaining, instead of seventy mules and six to eight horses as in years past. The major portion of the crop was now mechanically harvested and the leaves burned rather than stripped.[78]

Sebastian Patout suggested that the board consider buying more land to make the corporation less dependent on outside cane. Such a move, combined with the continuing need for factory improvements, would necessitate a large line of credit. Board Member Rivers Patout, who had recently resigned as vice-president because his residence in Texas kept him too far from company business, suggested negotiating a loan through the Reconstruction Finance Corporation. David Hearne recommended refinancing existing notes so as to have them mature at different dates, rather than having them all appear as demand notes. The matter of financing was deferred until after the grinding season, when the board would be in a better position to know the company's needs.[79]

As predicted, the drought-afflicted 1947 crop was smaller than the previous one. The improved mill, now able to grind 2200 tons of cane every twenty-four hours, ground only 63,931 tons, but it proved to be quite rich in sucrose, yielding 9,924,009 pounds of raws and 430,395 gallons of molasses. Most of the cane was delivered by truck and tractor carts. Like most Louisiana mills, Enterprise sold its 1947 sugar at the season's average price, which was the method by which regulations forced them to purchase cane. That price held for most of the trading period, until the Waterford Sugar Cooperative sold 3000 bags of sugar at a 65-cent a bag discount, breaking the market and costing M. A. Patout an estimated eleven thousand dollars. George Smith was furious, reporting to the board that "It is estimated that the stupidity of the Waterford Sugar Co-op cost the industry better than 8 1/2 million dollars."[80]

Smith estimated that the weather-related crop shortage had reduced net profit at Enterprise by $26,800 and at Cherry Grove by $10,500. At both places crops were about two-thirds of normal, largely because only 14.96 inches of rain had fallen between June 1 and September 30, 1947. The same period in 1946 produced 36.42 inches of rain. The two plantations actually showed a small profit totaling just over $19,061.93 while the mill showed a net after-depreciation loss of $19,295.57. The result was a worsening shortage of working capital which threatened the company's competitiveness.[81]

Smith noted that some were saying that the production gains achieved did not justify the expenditures of the past few years. He disagreed:

> I personally believe this theory to be misused when applied to Enterprise or any other sugar factory in its category. It must be remembered that for every pound of sugar sold, part of the factory is sold with it. Naturally the machinery eventually wears out and must be replaced. Much of the improvements made here have been for worn out machinery. In each instance these new installations have been larger than the old ones, as we are working constantly for greater production; however, it is not [necessarily] reasonable to expect such improvements to increase production.

Smith concluded that, regardless of opinions, the money was spent, a bad crop followed, no money was made, and the company had no operating capital.[82]

With this problem still unresolved, the company felt that it was an "absolute necessity" to install a 602-horsepower Stirling water tube boiler fired by three Detrick-arch horseshoe furnaces which could run on either bagasse or fuel oil. A new Thornton harvester replaced the oldest Thompson single-row machine. Enterprise also moved away from bagged sugar, purchasing bulk sugar loading equipment to transfer its product directly to standard gauge railroad cars. The management improved its cash position somewhat by selling $7400 worth of scrap iron. It also got $1200 for its "Black Cat" engine, $2400 from the sale of old filter presses, and was trying to market another lot of scrap steel and $1500 worth of corn. There was not the usual expense of making summer sugar because the company had sold all molasses from the 1947 crop. These measures, and a $40,000 loan for agricultural operations served to delay the need for special financing for the remainder of the crop year.[83]

Even with the best efforts of Guy Porche, lost time had been unacceptably high and it got worse in 1948. Despite milling a record 14,638,408 pounds of sugar from a record 101,087 tons of cane in a seventy-four day run, lost time amounted to 32.56 percent of total time. Molasses production amounted to 765,228 gallons. Although most of the problem was in the mill, some of it may have been related to cane deliveries. After the '48 season, the company discontinued the use of the increasingly unreliable and costly plantation railroad, idling 200 cars and four locomotives.[84]

In 1949, George Smith spent a week in New Orleans knocking on doors, trying to get time extensions on bills due until the family could raise enough money to save the business. Finally, M. A. Patout borrowed $80,000 from Prudential Life Insurance Company and another $120,000 from the Reconstruction Finance Corporation (RFC). To do so, it mortgaged all land, buildings, improvements, machinery, and equipment owned by the corporation. The RFC's mortgage on Enterprise, Cherry Grove, and Bacque plantations was subject to a first lien held by Prudential, which would not accept a mortgage on the sugar factory. Twenty-six thousand dollars of the Prudential loan went to pay off existing indebtedness to family members and the New Iberia National Bank. To get the Prudential loan, the firm had to agree not to incur additional debt in excess of $10,000 in any one year without prior written consent. The Prudential loan was for a minimum of five years and a maximum of twenty, while the RFC money had to be repaid over a seven-year period.[85]

Most of the monies went for a major overhaul of the factory, including the reshelling of two more mills, the construction of a cane washer, and the installation of seven much-needed U-type, 1000-cubic foot capacity crystallizers. The loans also paid for four more 40" Hepworth centrifugals, the conversion of the third vacuum pan to calandria configuration, and a fifty-foot crane and dragline to be use for both cane handling and maintenance of the plantation's drainage system. The loan agreement specified spending limits for each purchase and dictated that the balance of the money was to be used solely for operating expenses. While the improvements were vital to the company's survival, it negotiated these loans with the greatest reluctance because it limited their traditional independence and put the family lands at risk.

George Smith and William Patout were particularly uncomfortable with the RFC loan because of all of the limitations placed on the company. Stockholders could not freely buy and sell shares even as the company was trying to end the practice of allowing fractional shares of stock. The government's repayment provisions were much stricter than Prudential's. As Smith remembered it, the company was bound to pay the RFC whatever it made before depreciation and after income tax. In later years, Smith, hearing that the RFC actually lost money on loans, wondered how it had happened because they were so hard to do business with.[86]

For the 1949 grinding, the company had 485 acres in plant cane, 627 acres in first-year ratoon, and no second-year ratoon. The remaining cane was provided by 160 growers who had an estimated 4000 acres under cultivation. Probably in 1948, when they switched to anhydrous ammonia fertilizer, Enterprise dropped its plantings of soybeans and allowed the land to lie fallow every third year. On 150 acres of its worst land, it augmented soybean plantings with spreadings of bagasse ashes, filter muds, and stable manure.[87]

Despite their misgivings, the loans worked out well for M. A. Patout. The improvements were sufficient to keep the company competitive for a few more years. And the 1949 crop of 84,221 tons was respectable if not spectacular. The refurbished mill made 13,419,660 pounds of raws and 547,769 gallons of molasses. Most important, the new equipment greatly reduced mill operating costs, enabling Enterprise Factory to earn a gross profit of $123,168.27, less $42,000 in depreciation. Enterprise Plantation made $9,655.84 after depreciation and Cherry Grove recorded a net loss of $5,234.82. In comparison with the three other area sugar mills, Enterprise did "good average work" in 1949.

At its January meeting, the board of directors authorized William Patout to return the unused portion of the RFC loan, amounting to $27,771.85, and to pay $44,228.15 on the principal, leaving an unpaid balance of $50,000. It decided to repair the older smokestack and the braces on the tower tank for the coming season and instructed management to have a competent water well expert investigate the inadequate flow rate on the company's water wells. It authorized application for a $40,000 loan from an agricultural lending agency to finance upcoming crop operations and discussed the feasibility of substituting natural gas for fuel oil at the factory.[88]

In April, the board learned that gas use would save at least $6,000 a year. The cost of installation of a United Gas Company connection, including gas burners, would be between $14,500 and $16,000. Upon learning that there was nothing mortgageable in the installation, they decided to shelve the project until the project could be paid for from surplus funds. The well expert's report indicated that a new well was probably the best course of action, so the board authorized a new 350-foot deep well for an estimated $9250. It was completed by mid-summer at an actual cost of about $9700. There was some discussion of developing the firm's marshlands for trapping purposes but, after Rivers Wall talked with the McIlhenny Company at Avery Island, the idea was dropped.[89]

News on the cane crop was good. Management projected that the yield would be 15-18 percent above normal. Furthermore, the Cuban crop had been a short one, causing the molasses market to be very strong. All recommended repairs had been done and the factory was in much better shape than last year. The soil on some acreage had deteriorated to a point where it might require the discontinuance of cane planting there, but it was judged uneconomic to do so immediately because the factory needed the cane. As had become customary, the Cuban mill crew was scheduled to arrive in late September to prepare for a mid-October start. The company may have paid off more of the Reconstruction Finance Corporation loan that summer, because when stockholder Bessie Patout Faison asked what payments had been made on corporate indebtedness in the past year, George Smith's reply was $119,000. More likely, part of this money went to repay loans made by family members, particularly part of the $45,400 which had apparently been reborrowed from Willie's widow, Louise Decuir Patout, in the late forties.[90]

Nineteen fifty was a banner year for M. A. Patout. On its own lands, the company had 576 acres of plant cane, 578 acres of first-year ratoons, and 120 acres in second-year ratoon. For the remaining cane supply, it drew on an additional 5,000 acres. It also planted forty-five acres of cotton, thirty acres of shallots, and twenty acres of bell peppers. For cultivating the crops, it had a Dixie cotton chopper equipped with Pitre hoes to scrape plant cane, four tractor-mounted Hebert hoes, spraying equipment for fertilizing and weed control, and seventeen tractors. Also on hand for field maintenance was a dragline for breaking high ditch banks and a Caterpillar D-4 bulldozer with an eight-foot blade. In a sixty-four day season which began on October 18 and ended five days before Christmas, the mill crushed a record 128,910 tons of cane, producing all-time bests of 21,662,580 pounds of sugar and 897,268 gallons of molasses with only 8.81 percent lost time. The short Cuban crop produced a big scare in the sugar market, sending prices soaring and giving the Patouts, and other sugar producers, one of the best years in industry history.[91]

Early in 1951, the company granted United Gas Pipeline Company permission to survey M. A. Patout property in connection with the proposed laying of a natural gas pipeline from Weeks Island to United's main line. This would place a line only 1500 feet from the mill and management hoped that a gas supply for the factory would result. With the RFC loan scheduled to be paid in full on August 1, the board of directors decided to cancel the extended insurance coverage that the RFC had required at a cost of $2600 per year. Encouraged by the previous season, the company planted seventy-five acres of cotton. Cold weather had retarded cane growth. The crop was expected to be late and to have a relatively low sucrose content because of a mid-year drought. Sugar prices continued their return to normal as the Cuban crop recovered. Cane tonnage was down only 6 percent that fall, to 113,583 tons, but it was poor in quality. Much of the purchased cane was classified as "salvage cane." The late crop was hit by a severe freeze on November 3, two days before grinding began. Consequently sugar production, as predicted, declined 38 percent to 13,485,417 pounds. Lost time in the factory was up, to 15.40 percent. Actually, the small farmers in the area probably suffered most. Shortly before Christmas, Father Chauvin reported that parishioners were "extremely discouraged" because they had lost 25-40 percent of their crop.[92]

The company's projected net profit for the season was $93,140.33, sufficient for the board to ratify bonuses of $1500 for Guy Porche and $1000 for Head Overseer Howard Hebert. George Smith recommended the purchase of a 1000-horsepower Casey Hedges Water Tube Boiler and a ten-foot coil vacuum pan, both used, from the Shadyside Planting Company of Centerville for $7500. With refurbishing, this equipment represented "a long step in the right direction" toward the company's goal of a 3000-ton grinding capacity. The Casey Hedges equipment replaced the 350-horsepower Heine boiler. In addition, a third smokestack, 10' x 150', joined the two 9' x 125' stacks. The natural gas hookup was completed and the company began to discuss other uses for its bagasse as it worried about the lack of rain. At harvest time, William Patout was able to report that the firm had reduced its indebtedness by $257,781.89 over the previous three years. Its current debt was still almost $165,000.[93]

The quality of the 1952 harvest was disappointing, largely because of drought, cane borers, and poor cane varieties. Some 60 percent of the tonnage handled by M. A. Patout was raised in other parts of the state. It appeared to have had a late maturation date and did not produce much sugar except under ideal conditions. Enterprise produced 15,448,150 pounds of sugar and more than 729,000 gallons of molasses from 105,053 tons of cane. The price of sugar was up and manufacturing costs were much cheaper than in several years, but lost time was still too high at 12.55 percent. The mill averaged about 105 tons per hour for actual operating time and the company finished with a net profit of $24,711.09. As usual, M. A. Patout sold its sugar on the season's average price, eliminating any gamble between the price paid farmers and the price it got from refiners.[94]

Drought problems continued in 1953. A severe early season dry spell was accompanied by an insect infestation, leading the company to try dusting 400 acres of Enterprise and 30 percent of Cherry Grove with an insecticide for the first time. What the murky sugar quota situation would mean for sugar prices was still unclear and, to make matters worse, there was the threat of a strike by sugar workers that fall. Labor unrest in Terrebonne and Lafourche parishes was sufficiently serious for each mill to pledge a penny per ton to a fund to "handle all labor troubles." This may have included intimidation of National Agricultural Workers' Union representatives who held an organizing meeting in Franklin on September 25, 1953. Attendance was disappointing and the organizers were followed when they hastily departed. While there were labor problems that fall, there were apparently none to speak of at Enterprise.[95]

In addition to 1420 acres of cane, the company had planted 100 acres of corn, only fifteen of cotton, and just four of peppers. Most of the fallowed land was planted in soybeans. Cane was fertilized with eighty pounds of nitrogen per acre. The firm continued to use anhydrous ammonia for which it had purchased a 30,000 gallon storage

Late Plantation Days, 1930-1959 621

tank, two 1000-gallon field tanks, and five complete tractor units for application. For the harvest, it had added seven trucks with cane trailers to haul cane from field derricks to the mill. To drive the mill's centrifugals, it replaced the old Corliss engine with a 325-horsepower Elliot turbine with Farrel gears.[96]

In a sixty-three day campaign that began on October 15, Enterprise processed 114,504 tons of cane into 18,680,574 pounds of sugar and 777,598 gallons of blackstrap. While that result seemed respectable, the cane had too much fiber and too little moisture. To handle such cane, the mill needed more evaporating capacity so that it could add water to the cane and heavier mills to exert more pressure on the cane to maximize juice extraction. While the board of directors considered this, it also continued to investigate ways of disposing of its bagasse at a profit. Even though the mill required no major repairs, profit margins were still so slim that the board looked for every opportunity to cut costs. It balked when company lawyer Jacob Landry suggested that his annual retainer be increased and expressed displeasure at David Hearne's inability to keep his yearly fee at $1500 or less.[97]

Hearne pointed out that his charges of $1905 for auditing the books of the company and the store were down $75 from the previous year. If he billed them at standard rates, his fee would have been $2140. He had been giving the firm the benefit of rates established five or six years ago despite rising costs. Although this reply generated "favorable discussion" and the retention of Hearne, the board voted to retain Lawrence Simon as the corporation's attorney. Having done that, they approved the purchase of a cane cutter for Cherry Grove, enabling them to complete the 1954 harvest there with five fewer men than the year before.[98]

Low sugar extraction continued to be a problem in 1954 as Enterprise produced almost 17 million pounds of sugar from 105,530 tons of cane with 14.41 percent lost time in fifty-four days of operation. Worried that the mills might not be performing well, William Patout had cane samples sent to the LSU Sugar Experiment Station for evaluation. Their verdict was that it was overly fibrous. The factory reported a $60,000 gross profit while Enterprise and Cherry Grove registered small losses. Encouraged by the performance of the Cherry Grove cane cutter, the board recommended that one be purchased for Enterprise. In the off-season, the factory crew replaced the cast-iron number five mill with a new steel mill that exerted double the pressure of the old one. The old mill had a cracked roller shaft and needed reshelling.[99]

This expense, and a government-mandated 9 percent reduction in cane acreage, effectively ended any chance of a dividend in 1955. William Patout explained that the money had to be spent on factory modernization "since the continuing high cost of material and labor made maximum efficiency necessary in order to remain in business." Fifteen years before, plant capacity had been about 60,000 tons per season. In 1955, it was 125,000 tons, just enough to keep pace with other area factories. High maintenance costs on worn-out tractors were contributing to agricultural losses at Enterprise and Cherry Grove. Some were more than twenty years old. Five or six new ones were needed.

In addition, a portion of the corporation's land was very run down. A long-range soil-building program was required to restore normal production. The mill ground only 94,000 tons that fall, producing 15,251,500 pounds of sugar and 630,740 gallons of molasses.[100] There were other problems in Patoutville. The rapidly growing town of Lydia, which had developed around Hippolyte Patout's plantation, wanted St. Nicholas Parish to be headquartered at a new church in their town. Father Chauvin had worked hard to build the parish in the 1940s, with good results if attendance figures and receipts are any indication. He managed to finance and pay for a new rectory by 1950. However, by then he had grown disenchanted.

> A new pastor could do well here. Many whites here seem to hate Negroes and go to Sunday Mass in Jeanerette. They do not support their pastor and parish church. A spirit of spiritual outlawry prevails among them, just as among an alarming percentage of parishioners of St. Peter's, New Iberia, attending Mass at the new parish and not supporting their own parish and pastor.

However, most of his ire was directed at some of his more enthusiastic colleagues.[101]

In 1951, he complained to Bishop Jeanmard that the priest in Jeanerette had taken some St. Nicholas parishioners for his catechism, First Communion, and Confirmation classes. He had solicited Chauvin's people for subscriptions to *Lafayette Catholic Action* and had sought donations for his seminary and orphanage funds. Even worse

> He has accepted some of my outlaws and bad Catholics as Knights of Columbus and Catholic Daughters and even as officers in those organizations; and now he is . . . giving out regular Sunday church support envelopes to some of my parishioners. . . . Most of the same passe-droits are being practiced by the three pastors in New Iberia. The pastor of the Colored Church in Jeanerette is also courting some of my parishioners in various and devious ways.

Chauvin wanted to know if he was supposed to take all of this lying down. There is no record of the bishop's answer, but in 1952, Father Joseph Vaillancourt replaced Chauvin at St. Nicholas.[102]

Father Vaillancourt proved to be quite interested in the independent development of St. Joseph's Chapel in Lydia. In 1954, he reported that he had separated the funds of the two chapels and asked if St. Joseph's could have its own trustees. "These people will feel more at ease if they know that they don't have to do with what Patoutville thinks best for them . . . for they don't see what interest Patoutville might have in the development of the chapel." Perhaps aware of the growing challenge to its primacy, Patoutville completed the construction of the long-sought parish hall in 1954.[103]

Father T. James Hebert replaced Vaillancourt some time in 1954 as the drive to transfer the church to Lydia gained momentum. Hebert's annual report for 1954 showed, for the first time, comparative white membership at the two locations. According to

Father Hebert, there were 388 parishioners in Patoutville, 403 at St. Joseph's in Lydia, and 544 black Catholics in St. Nicholas Parish. Hebert's primary concern seems to have been to get a new church built. St. Nicholas Chapel was old and in poor condition. St. Joseph's Chapel was inadequate to serve the needs of a growing congregation. Initially, Hebert wanted to build a new church in Patoutville, to be financed by a fundraising drive to raise $50,000.[104]

However, he changed his mind a couple of weeks later and decided, apparently because he was offered an attractive site on rapidly developing Weeks Island Road, to propose that the rear part of St. Nicholas and St. Joseph Chapel both be moved to the new location, where they would be joined to create a larger St. Nicholas Church. Currently, the offering averaged $80-85 a week with $25-30 of it coming from Lydia. With such a limited financial base, neither church could develop. Quoting St. Augustine, Hebert wrote: "There is no standstill, one either goes forward or backwards."

His argument was that this action would bring the church to the center of the parish, where it would be closer to the majority of the membership. The new location was at a junction of roads to Jeanerette, Weeks Island, New Iberia, and U. S. Highway 90. Two were already paved, a third was being blacktopped, and the fourth was scheduled for improvement. Thirty lots had already been sold in the area. This action would relieve the expense of maintaining two churches and would put St. Nicholas in a "budding little community and thus, as one of them, [it] will be in a better position to guide the development along Catholic lines."

As to the argument that the new church would be remote from parishioners in the eastern and western ends of the parish, Hebert said that the distance was no more than five miles, with most within three miles, and that some traveled more than that under the present arrangement. Regarding the charge that these members would go to church in Jeanerette or elsewhere, Hebert responded that St. Nicholas had been losing parishioners to adjoining parishes for some time and that it had been disastrous financially.

Concerning the assertion that much money was invested in recent improvements (the rectory, parish hall, graveyard statuary) at the Patoutville chapel, he said that the parish hall would continue to be used and that the cemetery would of course remain where it was. Furthermore, the financial investment in the hall was the result of five years hard labor with assistance from Lydia, the mission, and considerable financial backing from New Iberia and Jeanerette. The majority of parishioners were clearly in favor of the move. Only a handful, including William Patout and Howard Hebert and others, would not attend the new church and delaying the move would only harm the parish.[105]

Opponents countered that such a move would be against the "outspoken opposition of eighty-five to ninety per cent of all of our parishioners. . . . St. Nicholas Parish is one of the oldest Parishes in the whole diocese, having been established nearly a century ago." They argued that there had been no migration from Patoutville and no change in the center of population:

> The farmers and artisans are not selling their valuable farms, homes, and heritages to move away; on the contrary, more people are coming into the immediate area, and now we have new homes, improved homes, economic conveniences, [such] as make Patoutville more desirable now than at any other time in the past. . . . The enthusiasm of the promoters [of the move] is natural as the human element is so strong a factor in a thing of this nature.[106]

The enthusiasm of Patoutville residents for their historic community was equally understandable.

Stung by the charge that opponents of the move were the one who had "caused hardship among the colored people in the past," they pointed out, correctly, that about half St. Nicholas's congregation was black and that many of them were home owners. They perhaps overstated their case when they claimed that "the congregation gets along . . . without the slightest friction," since that could hardly be said of any congregation, regardless of makeup. It was probably true that almost all of the black parishioners in Patoutville wanted the church to remain since they would have the greatest transportation difficulties. In this matter, the white community definitely wanted their black brethren to be heard: "Should not such numbers have a voice in the matter?"[107]

The Patoutville contingent said that the parish had no financial problems which could not be swiftly resolved, that there was no land monopoly in Patoutville, and that there was no guarantee that the new area would develop. "As to the statement that one man or family owns all the land in the Patoutville area and would not sell any to deliberately discourage investment is unsound, as a two minute look at any reliable ownership map of property in the area will prove that there are many hundreds of acres owned by others." The proposed new location was so low that drainage would be difficult. As to it being in a potentially vibrant business area, the nearest businesses were two night clubs![108]

Caught in the middle of a contest between two groups who sincerely believed that they were acting in the best interests of the parish, Bishop Jeanmard directed Father Hebert to come up with a compromise proposal. Hebert's suggestion was that only the Lydia mission church be moved to the Weeks Island Road site. Otherwise, according to the terms of sale, if a church was not put on the site that property would revert to its owner. Apparently, this was not done, because in 1956 Father Hebert was authorized to buy back the former site of the Lydia Chapel because a condition of the previous sale could not be fulfilled.

By mid-decade then, both St. Nicholas Chapel and Enterprise Mill had been saved by concerted action and the commitment of the residents to their community. However, Lydia continued to grow and the pressure for a full-fledged church of its own continued to build. In Patoutville, despite the enormous commitment of resources, the mill's future remained uncertain. Government quotas had reduced production even as the mill expanded its capacity to meet competition from other, newer mills. Lost time remained a problem as the installation of new equipment in some areas seemed only to reveal the inadequacy of the aging machinery in others. The improvements were crucial, but they were temporary solutions at best. As George Smith put it, "each year we would continue to add some little something or other" to raise the grinding capacity sufficiently to convince their farmers that Enterprise would be able to grind their cane.[109]

Considering the fluctuations of the sugar market, the vagaries of the weather, and problems with cane quality, it was apparent even in the fifties that the decade did not provide enough financial return to resolve M. A. Patout's working capital shortage sufficiently to completely modernize the mill. According to Smith,

> Even under the best conditions, the sugar markets were more wishy-washy through those years. About every five years you'd get a fantastic price and make money and everybody would get encouraged, and of course they'd spend it when they made it, and that would help a little bit. Then the first thing you knew, it would be down again. . . . It was always rags to riches and then back to rags. That's the way the industry has been. It's a romantic industry and I think people just sort of fell in love with it and couldn't turn it loose. I often wondered what made them stay there all those years. Work like a damned dog for nothing. But, I did too, and I loved every minute of it.

As Smith suggested, the strength of the company remained its people, with their expertise, dedication, and deep commitment to the land and the business in an era when other families with long ties to sugar were finally giving it up.[110]

M. A. Patout's crop and sugar production statistics for the late 1950s indicate a continuation of the above trends and problems. Production was up in 1956, to 17,803,164 pounds of raws on an increased crop of 103,614 tons. The mill averaged a record 2,115 tons a day for the forty-nine day season with only 11.7 percent lost time. Company President Ida Burns died midway through this successful season. Her son, J. Patout Burns, was elected to the board of directors and named President. This was a tribute to his ability and also an indication that financial concerns continued to be paramount. William Patout continued as manager and assumed Patout Burns' post of secretary-treasurer.[111]

Next year's crop was about the same, 105,437 tons, but production was only 15,446,175 pounds and the grinding rate was down to only 1,074 tons, largely because of stoppages that consumed 23.2 percent of total grinding time. Rivers Aristide Patout, Sr., who had devoted many years to the company, died just before the harvest. His place on the board was taken by his son, Rivers, Jr. Despite years of mineral leases and hopes that oil and gas might be found on company land, nothing tangible had developed by the late fifties. A test well and core samples revealed only water-bearing sands to a depth of over 13,000 feet, with 3,000 feet of shale below that. Rivers Wall reported that there seemed to be little merit in further testing for petroleum.[112]

The factory had a much-improved year in 1958. Enterprise ground 139,145 tons of cane in fifty-seven days, averaging 2441 tons per day and producing 23,874,302 pounds of sucrose and 876,134 gallons of molasses, all new records. Buoyed by its success, the board declared a 3 percent dividend, payable on March 5, 1959, and authorized management to locate and buy one or two second-hand boilers. Due to a lack of funds, the matter of a new derrick was deferred until February of 1960. As it happened, the dividend would also have to be deferred because, early on the morning of March 3, 1959, Enterprise Mill was destroyed by fire. The board met in emergency session the following day to consider the company's future.

Notes for "Late Plantation Days, 1930-1959"

[1] Estate of Hippolyte Patout to Oswell Patout, et als., November 25, 1930, ICR No. 45048, Book 115, 397; Estate of Clelie Romero to Bessie Patout Faison, et als., July 20, 1931, ICR No. 45634, Book 117, 367; Oswell, Sebastian, and Annie Patout to H. Patout, Incorporated, August 24, 1931, ICR NO. 45722, Book 117, 462.

[2] Edwin A. Davis, *The Historical Encyclopedia of Louisiana*, 513; Interview with George Smith, December 21, 1983.

[3] Interviews with George Smith, December 21, 28, 1983

[4] Joseph Carlyle Sitterson, *Sugar Country: The Cane Sugar Industry in the South, 1753-1950* (Lexington, 1950), 380-81.

[5] Board of Director's Minutes, August 28 and September 1, 1931; *Gilmore's Louisiana Sugar Manual*, 1933-34, 28.

[6] *Gilmore's Louisiana Sugar Manual*, 1933-34, 28; Sitterson, *Sugar Country*, 386.

[7] Interview with William S. Patout, Jr., December 21, 1983, Patoutville, La.; Interview with George Smith, December 21, 1983, Patoutville, La.; Interview with Mrs. Forrest Roy, December 29, 1983, Patoutville, La.; Clara Delahoussaye, et als. to William S. Patout, Sr., July 27, 1932, ICR No. 46779, Book 118, 242; Partition of Delahoussaye and Patout, July 27, 1932, ICR No. 46780, Book 118, 243. See also, *William S. Patout v. Clara Delahoussaye*, Iberia Civil Suit No. 9797, wherein Patout sought liquidation of the firm, and M. A. Patout's Board of Directors' Minutes, March 4, 1936, which indicate that the company was to buy a two-thirds interest in the Patoutville lot owned by Interstate Wholesale Grocers, Inc. of New Orleans.

[8] Interview with William S. Patout, Jr., November 24, 1987; Interview with Son Slaughter, November 24, 1987; Interview with Forrest Roy, December 29, 1983, Patoutville, La.

[9] Eunice Threadgill to Peter Patout, January 25, 1993, copy in author's possession.

[10] Interview with William S. Patout, Jr., December 21, 1983.

[11] Minutes, 1929-1947, Iberia Parish School Board, New Iberia, La.; Interview with Son Slaughter, November 4, 1987.

[12] Interview with Lucille Bernard, November 6, 1987.

[13] Annual Report, 1929; Neyboer to Vigliero, July 29, 1930, Diocese of Lafayette Archives, Lafayette, La.

[14] Neyboer to Vigliero, July 29, 1930.

[15] Annual Reports, 1930-32; Neyboer to Vigliero, July 29, 1930; Neyboer to Vigliero, January 25, 1933.

Late Plantation Days, 1930-1959 627

[16]Sitterson, *Sugar Country*, 383-84.

[17]*Gilmore's Louisiana Sugar Manual*, 1934-35, 82; 1936-37, 56; Notes on 1933 Season, Burns Papers.

[18]Sitterson, *Sugar Country*, 384-85; Notes on the 1933 Season, Burns Papers, lists the League as one of the costs of marketing sugar.

[19]*Gilmore's Louisiana Sugar Manual*, 1937-38, 99.

[20]Ibid., 99; M. A. Patout Balance Sheet, September 30, 1940, Burns Papers. By this date, the company had paid off all but $15,000 of this expenditure.

[21]Interview with George Smith, December 21, 1983.

[22]Ibid., December 20, 1983; Interview with Forrest Roy, January 29, 1983; Inteview with Lucille Bernard, November 6, 1987.

[23]Interview with George Smith, December 21, 1983. Smith said that the firm brought in 450-500 workers; Interview with Lucille Bernard, November 6, 1987. Mrs. Bernard cooked in the boarding house for twenty years and recalls feeding about 200 people a day; Thomas Becnel, *Labor, Church, and the Sugar Establishment* (Baton Rouge, 1980), 36-37, indicates that the efforts of Gordon McIntire, leader of the Louisiana Farmers' Union, led to a prevailing wage of $1.50 a day by the following season. Whether M. A. Patout paid this new wage or not is unknown.

[24]"Cane Cutters and Small Planters Need Help," *New Orleans Louisiana Weekly*, October 16, 1937; "AAA Fights for Higher Wages for Sugar Cane Cutters in Louisiana," *Louisiana Weekly*, October 23, 1937.

[25]Ibid., October 23, 1937; "AAA Hears Startling Facts About Plantation Laborers' Problems," *Louisiana Weekly*, March 5, 1938; "AAA Sets New Wage Scale for State," *Louisiana Weekly*, July 30, 1938.

[26]Interview with William S. Patout, Jr., December 21, 1983; Interview with George Smith, December 28, 1983.

[27]Arthur G. Keller, "Review of a 10-Year Program of Changes and Improvements in Louisiana Sugar Factories," *Gilmore's Louisiana Sugar Manual*, 1940-41, iv-vi.

[28]Interviews with George Smith, December 21 and 22, 1983; Becnel, *Labor, Church, and the Sugar Establishment*, 70. Raw sugar producers were exempted from seasonal overtime pay and farm workers were excluded from the minimum wage provisions of the Act.

[29]Interview with Lucille Bernard, November 6, 1987.

[30]Ibid.; Interview with George Smith, December 21, 1983.

[31]Interview with Lucille Bernard, November 6, 1987.

[32]Ibid.

[33]St. Nicholas Annual Reports, 1934-36.

[34]St. Nicholas Annual Reports, 1936-41; O. J. Chauvin to Mrs. Forrest Roy, November 15, 1934; Mrs. Forrest Roy to Bishop Jeanmard, December 16, 1934 and January 17, 1935; Chauvin to Jeanmard, February 7, 1935;

Jeanmard to Chauvin, September 1, 1937; Chauvin to Jeanmard, October 5, 1938 and April 25, 1940, all Diocese of Lafayette Archives.

[35] St. Nicholas Annual Report, 1941; Chauvin to Jeanmard, September 15, 1941.

[36] St. Nicholas Annual Report, 1936.

[37] *Gilmore's Louisiana Sugar Manual*, 1940-41, 89-90.

[38] Arthur Keller, "Changes and Improvements in Louisiana Sugar Factories," *Gilmore's Louisiana Sugar Manual,* 1940-41, vi-vii.

[39] Interview with George Smith, December 21, 1983.

[40] Ibid.; Interview with Lucille Bernard, November 6, 1987.

[41] *Gilmore's Louisiana Sugar Manual*, 1940-41, 92; Father Chauvin to Bishop Jeanmard, April 25, 1940.

[42] Interview with George Smith, December 22, 1983.

[43] Board of Directors' Minutes, October 3, 1941.

[44] Sitterson, *Sugar Country*, 386-88.

[45] Ibid., 388.

[46] *Gilmore's Louisiana Sugar Manual*, 1942-43, 92. In 1941, the factory ground 67,306 tons. It made 11,312,488 pounds of 96-test sugar and 396,000 gallons of blackstrap; Interviews with George Smith, December 20 and 21, 1983. Even smaller farmers acquired tractors in the 1930s. Forrest Roy, who farmed 120 acres and sold cane to the Patouts, bought his first tractor in 1936.

[47] Interview with George Smith, December 21, 1983; Sitterson, *Sugar Country*, 387; F. A. Vought, "Windrowing and Harvesting Machines," *Gilmore's Louisiana Sugar Manual*, 1940-41, viii-xii. Vought was the chief engineer for the South Coast Corporation. For a more general summary of other changes in the industry in the 1930s and 1940s, see Gilbert J. Durbin, "Changes in the Louisiana Sugar Industry in the Nineteen Thirties, Forties, and Fifties," in *Green Fields: Two Hundred Years of Louisiana Sugar* (Lafayette, La., 1980), 83-98.

[48] "Willie S. Patout Dies Monday at Patoutville," news clipping, Burns Papers; Interview with George Smith, December 21, 1983.

[49] Board of Directors' Minutes, September 30 and October 24, 1942.

[50] *Gilmore's Louisiana Sugar Manual*, 1940-41, vi.

[51] Interview with George Smith, December 28, 1983; *Gilmore's Louisiana Sugar Manual*, 1940-41, 92.

[52] Interview with Lucille Bernard, November 6, 1987; Interview with George Smith, December 21, 1983.

[53] Ibid.

[54] *Gilmore's Louisiana Sugar Manual*, 1942-43, xv.

[55] Board of Directors' Minutes, February 21, 1943.

[56] *Gilmore's Louisiana Sugar Manual*, 1942-43, 92; 1944-45, 108; Interview with George Smith, December 22, 1983; Board of Directors' Minutes, October 31, 1943.

[57] M. A. Patout Financial Report, November 23, 1943, Burns Papers; Sitterson, *Sugar Country*, 393.

[58] M. A. Patout Financial Report, November 23, 1943.

[59] Barton, Pilie, Sere & Wermuth to M. A. Patout Board of Directors, August 30, 1943 (hereinafter Barton to Board), Burns Papers; Mrs. Theo (J. Patout) Burns, Interview with Michael G. Wade, November 6, 1987, New Iberia, La.

[60] Barton to Board.

[61] Ibid.

[62] Ibid., July 28, 1945.

[63] Ibid.; President's Report to M. A. Patout Stockholders, September, 1944, Burns Papers.

[64] President's Report to Stockholders, September 15, 1944; M. A. Patout Financial Reports, Burns Papers.

[65] Interview with George Smith, December 20, 1983. Smith recalled an engineer from Mississippi, last name Thomas, who had the locomotive which ran on the main line. "Old Man Thomas" invariably called in about 8 p. m.: "Mr. Smith, I'm off the track." "Where at, Mr. Thomas?" "Out here at the L'Bitch." This last was Thomas's verbal approximation of a field derrick location known as Labiche.

[66] Interview with George Smith, William S. Patout, Jr., and William S. Patout III, December 21, 1983; Interview with George Smith, December 28, 1983; "Germans in Sugar Cane Fields," New Iberia *Daily Iberian*, May 17, 1984; Otto Gmeindl to William S. Patout, Jr., September 13, 1946; Leo to William S. Patout, Jr., August 8, 1982, Patout Family Papers; William S. Patout III to Michael G. Wade, August 27, 1993.

[67] *Gilmore's Louisiana Sugar Manual*, 1944-45, 108-9; Barton to Board, July 28, 1945, Burns Papers; Interview with George Smith, December 22, 1983.

[68] Interview with George Smith, December 22, 1983.

[69] Barton to Board, July 28, 1945; Sitterson, *Sugar Country*, 390, reported an "astonishingly low" educational level among resident laborers of both races on sugarcane plantations.

[70] Sitterson, *Sugar Country*, 393, 395; Report to Stockholders, September 15, 1944, Burns Papers.

[71] *Gilmore's Louisiana Sugar Manual*, 1946-47, 117-18.

[72] Interview with George Smith, December 22, 1983; *Gilmore's Louisiana Sugar Manual*, 1946-47, 117-18; Board of Directors' Minutes, March 25, 1945 and January 19, 1947.

[73] Board of Directors' Minutes, July 21, 1946 and January 19, 1947; Board of Directors to Stockholders, January 31, 1947; Barton Annual Audit Report, November 1, 1947, Burns Papers.

[74]Manager's Report of Improvements, October 13, 1947; Board to Stockholders, November 1, 1947, Burns Papers.

[75]Board to Stockholders, November 1, 1947, Burns Papers.

[76]Interview with George Smith, December 21, 1983; Minutes, Stockholders Meeting, October 14, 1946.

[77]Board of Directors' Minutes, April 20 and July 20, 1947.

[78]Ibid., April 20, July 20, and October 13, 1947.

[79]Board of Directors' Minutes, October 13, 1947.

[80]*Gilmore's Louisiana Sugar Manual*, 1948-49, 84; Report on Operations, Board of Directors' Minutes, January 18, 1948.

[81]Report on Operations, Board of Directors' Minutes, January 18, 1948.

[82]Ibid.

[83]*Gilmore's Louisiana Sugar Manual*, 1948-49, 84-85; Board of Directors' Minutes, June 8 and July 18, 1948.

[84]Ibid. Three of the locomotives were Porters. The other was a five-ton Plymouth gasoline locomotive.

[85]Reconstruction Finance Corporation Resolution, June 9, 1949, Burns Papers; Interview with George Smith, December 21, 1983.

[86]Interview with George Smith, December 21, 1983.

[87]*Gilmore's Louisiana Sugar Manual*, 1948-49, 84; Board of Directors' Minutes, January 18, 1948.

[88]Board of Directors' Minutes, January 15, 1950.

[89]Ibid., April 16 and July 15, 1950.

[90]Minutes of Stockholders Meeting, October 9, 1950; Board of Directors' Minutes, October 9, 1950; List of Expenditures (Travel Expenses for September 27, 1950, for six Cubans from Havana to Patoutville), Burns Papers; Interview with George Smith, December 21, 1983.

[91]*The Gilmore Louisiana-Florida Sugar Manual*, 1951, 95-96; for illustrations of early sugarcane field machinery, see Durbin, "Changes in the Louisiana Sugar Industry," in *Green Fields*, 83-98.

[92]Board of Directors' Minutes, April 14, July 8, and October 8, 1951, January 13, 1952; Report to Stockholders, October 13, 1952; *Gilmore Louisiana-Florida Sugar Manual*, 1953, 99; Father Chauvin to Bishop Jeanmard, December 21, 1951, Diocese of Lafayette Archives.

[93]Report to Stockholders, October 13, 1952.

[94]*Gilmore Louisiana-Florida Sugar Manual*, 1953, 98-99; Board of Directors' Minutes, October 13, 1952, and January 25, 1953.

[95] Board of Directors' Minutes, April 12, 1953; Becnel, *Labor, Church, and the Sugar Establishment*, 127; Interview with Lucille Bernard, November 6, 1987.

[96] *Gilmore Louisiana-Florida Sugar Manual*, 1953, 97-98.

[97] Ibid., 98; Board of Directors' Minutes, January 17, April 11, and October 11, 1954.

[98] Board of Directors' Minutes, October 11, 1954.

[99] *Gilmore Louisiana-Florida Sugar Manual*, 1955, 96-98; Board of Directors' Minutes, January 23 and April 17, 1955.

[100] Report to the Stockholders, October 8, 1955.

[101] St. Nicholas Annual Report, 1950.

[102] Father Chauvin to Bishop Jeanmard, December 21, 1951; St. Nicholas Annual Report, 1952.

[103] Father Joseph Vaillancourt to Bishop Jeanmard, February 16, 1954. Vaillancourt recommended William Brady, Allen Patout, and Howard Hebert as trustees.

[104] Lawrence Goula, et als. to Bishop Jeanmard, August 2, 1955.

[105] Father Hebert to Bishop Jeanmard, July 5, 1955.

[106] Lawrence Goula, et als. to Bishop Jeanmard, August 2, 1955.

[107] Father Hebert to Bishop Jeanmard, July 5, 1955; Lawrence Goula, et als. to Bishop Jeanmard, August 2, 1955.

[108] Lawrence Goula, et als. to Bishop Jeanmard, August 2, 1955.

[109] Interview with George Smith, December 21, 1983.

[110] Ibid.

[111] Board of Directors' Minutes, January 26, 1957; *Gilmore Louisiana-Florida Sugar Manual*, 1959, 87; Enterprise Factory Production Statistics, 1950-1984, M. A. Patout and Son, Ltd. Offices, Patoutville, La.

[112] Board of Directors' Minutes, October 14, 1957; Enterprise Factory Production Statistics, 1950-1984.

PART V

LOUISIANIANS AT LEISURE

A WINDOW ON SLAVE CULTURE: DANCES AT CONGO SQUARE IN NEW ORLEANS, 1800-1862*

Gary A. Donaldson

Many of the cultural characteristics brought to America by African slaves were forgotten, suppressed, or changed by the third generation in America. Slaveowners, in an attempt to suppress paganism and to Christianize the pagan, often forbade African-originated activities on the plantation. Even though music, dance, and religion were probably among the most enduring of the cultural characteristics brought from Africa, they, too suffered at the hands of the culture-suppressing slaveowner, and at the hands of time which took an equally great toll on all things African. Those remnants of African culture that continued to exist in the American slave South prior to the Civil War usually emerged in private, clandestine meetings, away from the eye of the white man. Consequently, little information exists on the cultural traits of African slaves, even of their music, dance, and religion despite the enduring qualities of those customs.

An exception is the early nineteenth-century slave dances held at Congo Square in New Orleans. There, slaves recently from Africa were allowed to spend Sunday afternoons dancing and singing, and remembering their African heritage. This spectacular site of hundreds and even thousands of slaves engaged in what seemed to be wild and frantic dances often drew white observers, some of whom took the time to write intelligibly on what they saw. The result is a glance at the music, dance, and other cultural traits of African slaves in that period as they attempted in vain to keep alive their African heritage.

Few of the white writers realized the cultural expression that was being exhibited at Congo Square, but it is obvious from many of the accounts that the slaves were engaged in important social activities beyond the obvious dancing and singing. For instance, a religion, Voodoo, was in common practice there, and even a crude economic system developed among those attending the activities. These and other factors place Congo

---

*First published in the *Journal of Negro History*, 69 (1984): 63-72. Reprinted with the kind permission of the author and the publisher.

A Window on Slave Culture

Square at the focal point of a distinct subculture of New Orleans slave life, one that existed within the framework of the dominant white culture. The situation in New Orleans was unique. Although subcultures of slaves certainly existed throughout the South (even among the smallest groups on plantations), only at Congo Square did slaves gather for social, cultural, economic, and religious interaction in such large numbers and with such great intensity.

New Orleans in the early nineteenth century was a wide open town, with a Spanish-French cultural influence that dictated an attitude toward slavery that was less stringent than the English way of slaveholding in that period. One of the prerogatives of New Orleans slaves was to attend the Sunday afternoon festivities at Congo Square, a parade ground outside the original city walls. Today the area is bounded by St. Ann, Rampart, and St. Claude streets. The dances at Congo Square began sometime around the beginning of the nineteenth century and ended in 1862, with the height of the festivities occurring in the first two decades of the century.

The area that became Congo Square was originally the site of a fort built by the French in 1758 as part of a walled fortification to protect New Orleans from the English; it was rebuilt by the Spanish in 1792 to protect them from the English. Fort San Fernando, as it was named by the Spanish was ordered removed by the Americans following the Louisiana Purchase in 1803.[1] Two years later the New Orleans City Council issued a decree insisting that the promise be fulfilled to demolish the fort, and in August, 1805, the fort was finally removed and the earthen walls shoveled into the moat.[2] However, as late as 1810 the site was still referred to as Fort San Fernando in local publications, suggesting that sessions of the fort still existed as late as that date.[3] It was not until 1812 that the old site of Fort San Fernando received the name "Place Publique" on local maps. It was also obviously outside the realm of a military installation by then.[4] The square has remained a public common since that time.

Congo Square was never its official name. It was first Place Publique, but it was also known as Circus Square because of the big top circuses that often used the grounds. It became Place d'Armes in 1851 after the original Place d'Armes on the riverfront was renamed Jackson Square. In 1893 it became Beauregard Square, named after the civil War General from Louisiana. In 1975 the name was changed again to Armstrong Park, commemorating jazz trumpeter Louis Armstrong. But to most, at least during the antebellum period when New Orleans' slaves danced and sang there on Sundays, the square was known as Congo Square.[5]

The area surrounding Congo Square was known as Congo Plains, probably because earlier military use had produced a flat treeless space. As New Orleans began to overflow into this area, and as new homes were built there, the residents complained to the city council about noise and other problems resulting from the weekly festivities. The complaints produced an ordinance, passed sometime in 1817, that restricted dancing to Sunday afternoons and only at such places designated by the mayor. The mayor apparently responded by choosing Congo Square as the place for such activities because it was after this date that the Congo Square dances reached their heyday. The Sunday afternoon dances at Congo Square had become institutionalized—albeit for only a shot time.[6]

Before Congo Square became the common meeting place for such dances, New Orleans slaves apparently congregated for dancing and singing in other parts of the city. As early as 1786, when New Orleans was a Spanish colony with a population of just over 3,000, dancing had become widespread enough (an enough of a problem) that the Spanish army outlawed the "nightly congregation," and the "dances of colored people" throughout the city.[7]

In 1799, a visitor to the city wrote of "vast numbers of negro slaves, [sic] men, women, and children assembled together on the levee, drumming, fifing and dancing in large rings.[8] These rings, as other observers would later report, represented various African tribes and nationalities as they danced, sang, and played the instruments of their homeland while acting out whatever African-originated customs and religious rituals that accompanied such activities. In 1808 another traveler visiting New Orleans reported seeing groups of slaves dancing and singing somewhere in the city. Although the traveler did not mention Congo Square, the activities he described may have occurred there. His descriptions of the instruments are particularly interesting. These, he wrote, "consist[ed] for the most part of a long narrow drum of various sizes, from two to eight feet in length, three or four of which make up a band."[9] Similar descriptions of drums used at Congo Square were echoed by later observers of the activities there.

Shortly after the New Orleans' mayor restricted dancing to Congo Square, and probably at the height of activity there, Benjamin Latrobe stumbled upon the square one Sunday after church. Latrobe, early America's great architect and engineer, had come to New Orleans to build the city's first waterworks system. Born in England and living most of his adult life in New York, Latrobe's impressions of slavery in the Deep South were rudimentary at best. But as an outsider, he was intrigued by the South and its peculiar institution and took great care to meticulously observe and record her life and culture of the South and slavery. His account is probably the best, most thorough observation available from the heyday at Congo Square. While walking among St. Peter Street, Latrobe recorded hearing "a most extraordinary noise which . . . proceeded from a crowd of five or six hundred persons, assembled in an open space or public square." Latrobe followed the noise, finding blacks ("I did not observe a dozen yellow faces") "formed into circular groups in the midst of [which] was a ring . . . ten feet in diameter." He observed in one ring two women dancing, "They held each a coarse handkerchief, extended by the corners, in their hands. . . ."[10] Again, later observers pointed out that these circles represented different African nationalities and cultural groups. "The music," Latrobe continued, "consisted of two drums and a stringed instrument." He described an old man who played a large cylindrical drum, "and beat it with incredible quickness with the edge of his hand and fingers." Together with a second, smaller, drum, "they made an incredible noise." However, it is Latrobe's description of the stringed instrument that is the most interesting. He described it as a "most curious instrument . . . which no doubt was imported from Africa." The carving on top of the finger board was "the rude figure of a man in a sitting posture." "The body," he added, "was a calabash. It was played upon by a very little old man, apparently eighty or ninety years old."[11]

Latrobe described another instrument that "consisted of a block cut into something of the form of a cricket bat, with a long and deep mortice down the center. . . ." He also observed an instrument in the shape of "a calabash with a round hole in it, the hole studded with brass nails. . . ." This instrument was beaten by a woman with two short sticks. "A man sung an uncouth song to the dancing which I suppose was in some African language, for it was not French," Latrobe added.[12]

One additional aspect of Latrobe's comments seems to defy both common and historical beliefs about the Congo Square dances. The events there were often described as raucous, wild affairs that spilled over into the streets around the square, causing problems that led to a final halting of the dances sometime in the 1830s. But according to Latrobe: "There was not the least disorder among the crowd, nor do I learn on inquiry, that these weekly meetings of the negroes [sic] have ever produced any mischief."[13]

In 1879, several decades after the dances at Congo Square had come to an end, a reporter in a New Orleans newspaper wrote a personal recollection of the Congo Square dances that is remarkably descriptive and supplementary to Latrobe's accounts. "[O]n a Sunday afternoon," he wrote, "not less than two or three thousand people would congregate there to see the dusky dancers. About three o'clock the negroes [sic] began to gather, each nation taking their places in different parts of the square. The Minahs would not dance near the Congos, nor the Mandringos near the Gangas." The representatives of each nationality, the writer continued, "could be seen on the square, teeth filed and their cheeks still bearing the tattoo marks."[14]

The reporter also described instruments similar to those related by Latrobe. "Each had its own orchestra," he wrote. "The instruments were a peculiar kind of banjo, made of a Louisiana gourd, several drums made of a gum stump dug out, with a sheepskin head, and beaten with the fingers, and two jawbones of a horse, which when shaken would rattle the loose teeth, keeping time with the drums."

"It took some little time," he added, "before the tapping of the drums would arouse the dull and sluggish dancers, but when the point of excitement came, nothing can faithfully portray the wild and frenzied motions they would go through." When the day ended, the writer continued, "a stream of people poured out of the turnstiles, and the gensdarmes walking through the square would order the dispersion of the negroes [sic], and by gun-fire; at 9 o'clock, the place was well-nigh deserted." The writer concluded that "these dances kept up until about 1819, but not later."[15]

However, by the early 1820s at least one observer was annoyed by the Sunday activities at Congo Square. John A. Paxton, the compiler of New Orleans' first city directory, wrote in 1822 that Congo Square was not aiding the development of New Orleans' image. The square, he wrote, "is very noted on account of its being the place where the Congo and other Negroes dance, carouse and debauch on the Sabbath, to the great injury of the morals of the rising generation: it is a foolish custom that elicits the ridicule of most respectable persons who visit the city. . . ." Paxton supported putting a stop to the dances, but, he added, "if it is not considered good policy to abolish the practice entirely, surely they could be ordered to assemble at some place more distant from the houses, by which means the evil would be measureably remedied."[16] Despite Paxton's observations, there is evidence that Congo Square was something of a tourist attraction. A New Orleans historian wrote in 1900: "White people, from motives of curiosity or fun, invariably attended these innocent pastimes."[17] In the same year, a writer for the *Picayune's Guide* remembered: "The scene, so picturesque and animated, was very interesting, and hundreds of the best class of whites used to promenade in the vicinity of the square to see the Negroes dance 'Congo.' "[18]

But Congo Square was more than just music and dance. One writer described an inner-cultural economy, where goods produced by slaves were brought and sold on or near the grounds: "On the sidewalks around the square the old negresses [sic] with their spruce beer and pralines of peanuts, coconuts and popcorn, did a thriving trade, and now and then beneath petticoats bottles of tafia, a kind of Louisiana rum, peeped out. . . ."[19] Another writer observed that slaves came to Congo Square not only to dance, sing, and socialize but to "spend whatever surplus picayunes and dimes they may have acquired from their honest labors. . . ." It was apparently a vibrant economy. "Around the square," the writer continued, "were distributed small booths or stands for the sale of cakes, pies and pop beer, all of which . . . were well patronized."[20]

Also, Voodoo was practiced at Congo Square although it is difficult to determine to what extent; sources dealing with the subject are often sensationalist in their method, dealing mostly with crude, bloody and sexually related themes. Voodoo had its origins in African religions and was practiced by African slaves throughout the West Indies and in some parts of the Deep South, but particularly in Cuba, Haiti and New Orleans.[21] To more than one writer, the mayor's designation in 1817 of Congo Square as the only place for slave gatherings was an attempt to thwart a much-feared slave revolt being spawned (so it was thought) through Voodoo rituals conducted by Haitian slaves. The *Bamboula* and *Calinda*, popular songs at Congo Square, may have had Voodoo at the base of some of their lyrics. One observer stated that the "Voodoo Queen" was always present at the Congo Square activities.[22]

Sometimes in the late 1830s or early 1840s the activities at Congo Square ended, undoubtedly outlawed as a result of a general reaction throughout the South to an intensification of Northern abolitionist activities in the 1830s, and to the Nat Turner slave insurrection in Virginia. These two occurrences (the first fostering the second in the minds of many Southerners) struck fear throughout the South, and one result was the elimination of all slave gatherings, meetings, or organized assemblies. Sundays at Congo Square apparently fell victim to that fear.

So, for nearly a decade Congo Square became a memory. In 1845, *Norman's Directory* listed Congo Square as "the place where the negroes [*sic*], in olden times, were accustomed to meet.... Though the loud laugh, and the unsophisticated break-down and double-shuffle of these primitive days have ceased, the spot yet remains, with all its reminiscences."[23] However, in that year, a group of citizens petitioned the New Orleans City Council to allow slaves, again, to congregate at Congo Square, but only on summer Sundays between four and six-thirty in the afternoon, and only with written permission from their owners. Police were to be present and the activities were not to be "offensive to public decency...."[24] A few weeks later, a reporter from the *Daily Picayune* challenged that "any one who says that the thousands of negroes [*sic*] congregated in and about Congo Square on Sunday afternoon last were unhappy we put down as no judge of human physiognomy." The newspaper described the playing of "rude instruments of their own contrivance, the likes of which we have never seen before...."[25] With only occasional interruption, Sunday dancing continued unabated at Congo Square until the practice was finally ended by Federal troops in 1862.[26]

By 1845 it had become apparent that for those attending the activities at Congo Square the maintenance of a cultural heritage was less important than it had been to the earlier generation of revelers. One observer, writing after the war, told of a comparatively uninspired group of dancers in the period after 1845: "Subsequently, however, the descendants of the original Africans got up an imitation, but it could not compare to the weird orgie [of] their progenitors."[27] Another observer, also writing of this period, told of hearing tunes that were obviously not of African origin, such as "Hey, Jim Along," and "Get Along Home You Yallow Gals."[28] Another visitor observed tamborines, violins, and banjos instead of the African-style instruments used in the period prior to 1820.[29] Also, just after the dances were allowed to begin again a New Orleans newspaper reported that the area around the square had become dangerous on Sunday nights, with slaves roaming the streets carrying weapons, even guns, and that "several dangerous incidents" had already occurred.[30] This is in contrast to the Congo Square that Latrobe observed in 1819 where "there was not the least disorder among the crowd, nor do I learn on inquiry, that these weekly meetings of negroes [*sic*] have ever produced any mischief." By 1845, the effects of time together with the white suppression of African-originated cultural characteristics had taken their toll on the activities at Congo Square.

In the years after the dances at Congo Square ended, several New Orleans reporters and writers took time to remember the activities there. These reminiscences were written in the same vain as a multitude of other post-war writings, with a longing for the happier days of the antebellum past. However, through these reminiscences have been handed down many of the best descriptions of Congo Square from both periods of activity there. They also show clearly that Congo Square was more than just a place to dance and sing on Sunday afternoons. One reporter wrote remorsefully in 1864 of how things used to be "prior to the period of change": "They assembled here by hundreds ... to renew old loves, and to gather new friendships; to talk over affairs of the past week, and lay new plans for enjoyment in the coming ones. . . ." They dressed their best on this important day. Many came "arrayed in the accumulated cast off finery of their patronizing superiors; the women usually sporting the stylish bandanas snugly tied about the back part of the head . . . whilst the more independent men . . . made the best show they could in what they inherited of their masters' toilette. . . ." When a sufficient number had assembled, the reporter continued, the usual circles were formed, and the music and dancing began. Often couples entered into the circle, usually at a challenge. However, "the first to lead off would be aspiring professionals who had obtained a knowledge of the art at one of the down town assemblies . . . but these generally gave way . . . to the less artistic." All of this was spurred on by the musicians, the observer concluded. They "held a prominent place in the drama. There is nothing . . . that has a more controlling influence over the negro [sic] than music."[31]

In the 1880s George Washington Cable wrote an elaborate description of the events at Congo Square in two articles for *Century Magazine*.[32] Cable described in detail the dances, songs, and social events that took place at the square. Cable probably drew on his own knowledge of the place as he observed it as an adolescent in the years just before the Civil War and from the reminiscences of those who recalled the square's most active, earlier period.[33]

Cable was the first to truly understand that the slaves at the Congo Square dances were doing more than simply carousing, venting frustrations, or previewing sexual acts. To Cable, the Sunday activities were a direct reflection of black African heritage, black slaves trying to maintain a grasp on their culture in a hostile cultural environment. Cable's articles are filled with songs, explanations of specific dances, descriptions of instruments, accounts of social activities, drawings of dancers, artists' renditions of various African physical types, and even sheet music. Not since Benjamin Latrobe stumbled on Congo Square in 1819 has such a valuable description of New Orleans' slave life been recorded. According to Cable, the day began with a call from the "booming of African drums and blasts of huge wooden horns," calling the slaves to the gathering at the square. The drums, Cable wrote, "were very long, hollowed, often from a single piece of wood, open at one end and having a sheep or goat skin stretched across the other." One drum was large, the other small. The drummers "beat them on the head madly with fingers, fists, and feet,—with slow vehemence on the great drum, and fiercely and rapidly on the small one." The smaller drum, according to Cable, was made from a large piece of bamboo and was known as a bamboula. Other instruments described by Cable included "a gourd partly filled with pebbles or grains of corn, flourished violently at the end of a stout staff with one hand and beaten upon the palm with the other." Cable wrote that some performers rang triangles, while others twanged from jew's-harps. The result was an astonishing amount of sound. Another instrument was composed of the jaw bone of a large animal; a key was rattled rhythmically along the weather-beaten teeth. A stringed instrument was composed of a "single strand of wire [that] ran lengthwise of a bit of wooden board . . . some eight inches long by four or five in width, across which, under

A Window on Slave Culture 639

the wire, were several joints of reed about a quarter of an inch in diameter and of graduated lengths. The performer, sitting cross-legged, held the board in both hands and plucked the ends of the reeds with his thumbnails. This was called—music." Cable goes on to describe the banjo as the "grand instrument" and "the first violin" of the music makers."[34]

The *Bamboula*, according to Cable, was not only a type of drum but the name of the most popular dance at Congo Square. It was, he wrote, "constant, exhilarating novelty—endless invention—in the turning, bowing, arm-swinging, posturing and leaping of the dancers. Now for the fantastic leaps! Now for frenzy! The ecstacy rises to madness; one—two—three of the dancers fall . . . with foam on their lips and are dragged out by the arms and legs from under the tumultuous feet of crowding new-comers. The musicians know no fatigue; still the dance rages on. . . ." But according to Cable, the *Bamboula* was stopped by the police in Congo Square because "it grew everywhere more and more gross." Another popular song was the *Calinda*, "a dance of multitude, a sort of vehement cotillion. The contortions of the encircling crowd were strange and terrible, the din was hideous."[35] It was the *Calinda* that Cable believed held the secrets of Voodoo. The *Bamboula* and the *Calinda* are reproduced in sheet music in Cable's *Century Magazine* article.[36]

The origin of jazz has been linked to Congo Square ever since attempts were first made to trace the origins of the music.[37] The reasoning seems obvious: jazz, a musical heritage with a strong sound and strong rhythms based in African music, emerged just fifty or sixty years after the primitive music at Congo Square ended. In addition, some of the first jazzmen, such as Buddy Bolden, witnessed the music and dancing at Congo Square; and many early jazz halls sprung up around the square, including the Caledonia and Perseverance Hall. Even today Armstrong Park is the starting point for many jazz funerals, and for Zulu, the black Mardi Gras parade.[38]

Certainly, New Orleans jazz and the music at Congo Square both had similar origins in black rhythms and in the black musical heritage that originated in Africa. And it cannot be denied that the music at Congo Square perpetuated that musical style. However, it takes a great deal of imagination to find Congo Square at the foundation of New Orleans jazz. Jazz brought together many types of music. In addition, the black African influence on jazz came directly from Latin America, not from New Orleans.[39]

The importance of Congo Square cannot be underestimated as an attempt by African slaves to hold on to what they could of their heritage. Throughout the first half of the nineteenth century Congo Square was the focal point of a subculture of New Orleans black slaves who carried on a lifestyle as close as possible to what they had remembered from their earlier lives in Africa (or what they had been told Africa was like). Congo Square was not only music and dance, those activities obvious to white observers, but an entire gambit of social activities which included a religion and a working economy. Congo Square was a place where a slave could hear the music and language of Africa, and even practice tribal differentiation.

If it is true that music and dance are the last characteristics of a culture to be suppressed then the activities at Congo Square are witness to the death of those cultural traits. What Latrobe saw in 1819 was not what observers saw in the years just prior to the Civil War. By then what had been African music had been replaced by "Hey, Jim Along," and filed teeth and tattooed faces had become just a memory. It seems that when activities ended at Congo Square a recollection of the past also ended.

Notes for "A Window on Slave Culture: Dances at Congo Square in New Orleans, 1800-1862"

[1] See Jerome A. Greene, "The Defense of New Orleans, 1718-1900" (unpublished manuscript completed under the auspices of the National Park Service, United States Department of Interior, Denver, 1982), 22, 41, 59. Maps of Fort San Fernando (St. Ferdinand) are reproduced here on pages 354, 35, and 358.

[2] New Orleans City Council, *Proceedings of Council Meetings* (Session of July 20, 1805), 69. Ibid. (Session of August 14, 1805), 85-86.

[3] *Louisiana Gazette*, April 10, 1810.

[4] J. Richard Shenkel, Robert Sauder, and Edward R. Chatelain, "Archaelogy of the Jazz Complex and Beauregard (Congo) Square, Louis Armstrong Park, New Orleans, Louisiana," Archaeology and Cultural Research Program, Research Report No. 2, (unpublished manuscript, University of New Orleans Library, n.d., 1980?), 18-20. Hereafter, cited as "Archaeology Report." The map cited is by Jacques Tanesse, drawn in 1803. Ibid., 22. See also Greene, "Defense of New Orleans," 22-23, 41.

[5] Roulhac Toledano and Mary Louise Christovich, *New Orleans Architecture: Faubourg Tremé and the Bayou Road: North Rampart Street to North Broad Street, Canal Street to St. Bernard Avenue* (Gretna, Louisiana, 1980), 65; Shenkel, "Archaeology Report," 26. The square has also been called Place d'Congo, Place des Negres, and Negro Square. See *Picayune's Guide to New Orleans*, 4th ed. (New Orleans, 1900), 62; and John Smith Kendall, *History of New Orleans*, 2 vols. (Chicago, 1922), 2:679.

[6] At least two sources have stated that a city ordinance was enacted on October 15, 1817, regulating slaves in New Orleans and activities at Congo Square. See Henry Kmen, "The Roots of Jazz and the Dance in Place Congo: A Reappraisal," *Yearbook* (Austin, 1972), 9; and Toledano and Christovich, *New Orleans Architecture*, 65. See also Henry Kmen, *Music in New Orleans, The Formative Years, 1791-1841* (Baton Rouge), 227. However, New Orleans city records do not concur; no law regarding slavery in the city was passed or considered on that date. However, on October 8, 1817, a law was passed regulating the activities of slaves in the city, although nothing is specifically mentioned in the proceedings concerning Congo Square, dancing, or the mayor's obligation to choose a gathering place for slaves. See, Conseil de Ville, *Council Proceedings*, Vol. 2, Book 1 (June 7, 1817, to December 29, 1818), 62-63; and Conseil de Ville, *Resolutions and Ordinances* (January 4, 1817, to December 27, 1817). Kmen cites Reuben Gold Thwaites, ed., *Early Western Travels, 1748-1846* (Cleveland, 1904), 4:363, 388; and Henry Bradshaw Fearon, *Sketches of America: A Narrative of a Journey of Five Thousand Miles through the Eastern and Western States of America*, 3rd ed. (London, 1819), 277-78. Probably the ordinance of October 8 regulated slave activities in New Orleans and Congo Square but was not specified as such in the council proceedings, as was often the case for ordinances passed by the council.

[7] *Records and Deliberations of the Cabildo*, 1 (July 13, 1784 to December 14, 1787), 108.

[8] Thwaites, ed., *Early Western Travels*, 4:363, 366.

[9] Christian Schultz, *Travels On An Inland Voyage . . . In the Years 1807 and 1808*, 2 vols. (New York, 1810), 2:197-98.

[10] Benjamin Henry Latrobe, *The Journal of Latrobe; Being the Notes and Sketches of an Architect, Naturalist and Traveler in the United States from 1796 to 1820* (New York, 1905), 180-81. A more recent review of

Latrobe's journals is Benjamin Henry Bonveal Latrobe, *The Journals of Benjamin Henry Latrobe, 1799-1820; From Philadelphia to New Orleans*, Edward C. Carter, II, John C. Van Horne, and Lee W. Formwalt, eds. (New Haven, 1980), 204. See also, Benjamin Henry Bonveal Latrobe, *Impressions Respecting New Orleans: Diary and Sketches, 1818-1820*, Samuel Wilson, Jr., ed. (New York, 1951), 49-50. Each of these sources quotes Latrobe's account of the activities at Congo Square. The sources vary only in the editors' interpretations of Latrobe's syntax and spelling.

[11]Latrobe, *Journal*, 180-81.

[12]Ibid., 181. For a look at musical instruments used in Africa, see Basil Davidson, *African Genius* (Boston, 1969), 167. A drawing on page 167 is remarkably similar to Latrobe's description of the "stringed instrument which no doubt was imported from Africa." For an account of modern and historical African dances and dancing, including the dancing by different tribes in different circles, see Kariamu Welsh Asante, "Commonalities In African Dance; An Aesthetic Foundation," in Molefi Kete Asante and Kariamu Welsh Asante, ed., *African Culture; The Rhythms of Unitey* (Westport, Conn., 1985), 75. For other descriptions of African dancing and musical instruments, see Geoffrey Gorer, *African Dances; A Book About West African Negroes* (New York, 1962, first published, 1935), see particularly, 213-28. Gorer was an English explorer and writer who toured Africa in the 1930s. His description of African dance for that period is strikingly similar to observations made by whites of slave dancing in New Orleans a century earlier.

[13]Latrobe, *Journal*, 182.

[14]*Daily Picayune*, October 12, 1879. Portions of this article were later published as "The Congo Dance," in *Kunkel's Music Review* (September, 1884), also reprinted in Faruk von Turk, ed., *The Dance in Place Congo and Creole Slave Songs by George W. Cable; Containing Also the Congo Dance* (New Orleans, 1976), 37-39.

[15]*Daily Picayune*, October 12, 1879.

[16]John A. Paxton, *Paxton's Directory of New Orleans* (New Orleans, 1822), 40.

[17]Henry C. Castellanos, *New Orleans As It Was* (New Orleans, 1895), 158-59.

[18]*Picayune's Guide to New Orleans* (New Orleans, 1900), 63.

[19]*Daily Picayune*, October 12, 1879.

[20]Ibid., December 11, 1864.

[21]The best source on Voodoo in New Orleans is Blake Touchstone, "Voodoo in New Orleans," *Louisiana History*, 13 (1972): 371-86. However, Touchstone does not discuss Voodoo at Congo Square. For that, see Robert Tallant, *Voodoo in New Orleans* (New York, 1946), 28-43. Touchstone dismisses Tallant as sensationalist, but Tallant makes important points and considers the importance of Congo Square in the development of Voodoo in New Orleans. See also, George Washington Cable, "Creole Slave Songs," *Century Illustrated Monthly Magazine* (1886), 807-28. Reprinted in Turk, ed., *The Dance in Place Congo*, 2-16; and Castellanos, *New Orleans As It Was*, 90-101.

[22]*The Picayune's Guide to New Orleans*, 62-67; Cable, "Creole Slave Songs," 807-28; Tallant, *Voodoo in New Orleans*, 28-29.

[23]Benjamin M. Norman, *Norman's New Orleans and Environs* (New Orleans, 1845), 182.

[24]*Journal of the Deliberations of the First Municipality, 1841-1845* (April 28, 1845), 37-38.

[25]*Daily Picayune*, June 24, 1845.

[26]There is some evidence that activities at Congo Square were at best an on again-off again affair between 1845 and 1862. See particularly, Kmen, "The Roots of Jazz," 5-16. However, if dancing was occasionally suspended, there is evidence that Congo Square was generally active until 1862. See *Daily Picayune*, December 11, 1864, which states that activities continued until 1862. Activities were observed in the late 1840s. See A. Oakey Hall, *The Manhattener in New Orleans; Or, Phases of "Crescent City" Life*, Louisiana Bicentenial Series (1851; reprint ed., Baton Rouge, 1976), 108. One source even states that activities at Congo Square continued until 1885, "when authorities terminated them because they were 'disruptive.'"

However, no source is given for this information. Jack V. Buerkle and Danny Baker, *Bourbon Street Black: New Orleans Jazzman* (New York, 1973), 13.

[27]*Daily Picayune*, October 12, 1879.

[28]Ibid., June 24, 1845.

[29]Ibid., December 11, 1864.

[30]Ibid., July 15, 1845.

[31]Ibid., December 11, 1864.

[32]George Washington Cable, "Dance in Place Congo," *Century Illustrated Monthly Magazine* (November 27, 1883), 423-516. Reprinted in Turk, ed., *The Dance in Place Congo*, 2-29.

[33]Cable writes that information for at least one song came from "a manuscript copy of the words, probably a hundred years old, that fell into my hands through the courtesy of a Creole lady some two years ago." Cable, "Dance in Place Congo," 526.

[34]Ibid., 519.

[35]Ibid., 523, 525, 527.

[36]Cable, "Creole Slave Songs," 807-28. Prior to Cable's publications, the pianist and classical composer Louis Gottschalk put both the *Calinda* and *Bamboula* to popular tunes that took the popular music world by storm in the 1840s and 1850s. For a serious discussion of Gottschalk and how he was influenced by Congo Square music, see Martin Williams, *Jazz Masters of New Orleans* (New York, 1967), 7-9.

[37]See particularly, Frank Ramsey, Jr., and Charles Edwin Smith, eds., *Jazzmen* (New York, 1939); Rudi Blesh, *Shinning Trumpets: A History of Jazz*, 2nd ed., rev. (New York, 1958); Robert Goffin, *Jazz: From the Congo to the Metropolitan* (New York, 1944). For more on the relationship of Congo Square to the birth of jazz, see Kmen, "The Roots of Jazz," 5-16. Kmen is emphatic in his conclusion that the music at Congo Square had a negligible effect on the birth of New Orleans jazz.

[38]Ramsey and Smith, *Jazzmen*, 5, 8, 9. The writers state: "in New Orleans you could still hear the *Bamboula* on Congo Square when Buddy Bolden cut his first chorus on the coronet." See also, Herbert Asbury, *The French Quarter* (New York, 1936), 252-53. However, Donald M. Marquis, in his exhaustive biography of Bolden, states that Bolden may have played music at nearby Perseverance Hall and even occasionally at Congo Square, but several decades after slave music and dancing ended there. Donald M. Marquis, *In Search of Buddy Bolden; First Man of Jazz* (Baton Rouge, 1978), 70. Bolden lived between 1877 and 1931.

[39]Kmen, "The Roots of Jazz," 5-16.

A COMMUNITY AND ITS TEAM: THE EVANGELINE LEAGUE'S LAFAYETTE WHITE SOX, 1934-1942*

Doug Taylor

"You wouldn't believe it by what you see around here now, but at one time this used to be one helluva baseball town. Why, back in the days of the old Evangeline League people would pack this place by the thousands; boy those were the days."[1] Such reminiscences from old-timers among the sparse groups of spectators attending high school and summer league games in several towns throughout Southwest Louisiana today lend insight into Lafayette's participation in the Evangeline League. As a popular institution forced to adapt to survive, this league reflected changes which occurred in its surrounding society.

The Evangeline League, formed in Southwest Louisiana in 1934 and commonly identified as the "Pepper Sauce League," "Hot Sauce League" or "Tabasco Circuit," began as a Class D league, the lowest of all minor league classifications, which emphasized the development of young talent for parent organizations.[2] The Evangeline League operated, with the exception of the World War II years, from 1934 until 1957. Participation in these leagues provided not only entertainment for communities such as Lafayette, but the team's ballpark became a focal point of social contact for local citizens, and their franchises became a conduit for dialogue between the town and other baseball communities. The success of their team and the sophistication of their playing facilities provided Lafayette and cities like it a yardstick to measure their progress as a community with the outside world.

The formation, success, expansion, interruption, and decline of the Evangeline League coincided with similar national trends in baseball. By 1932 the Great Depression had reduced operating minor league circuits in the United States to thirteen, only two of which were class D.[3] However, by 1950, that number had swollen to fifty-eight leagues

---

*First published in *Louisiana History*, 36 (1995): 149-70. Reprinted with the kind permission of the author and the Louisiana Historical Association.

operating in 446 cities.[4] Although the Evangeline League had moved to class C by then, twenty-six of the circuits, representing approximately 200 small communities, remained at the class D level.[5] Today only seventeen leagues exist with franchises in about 170 predominantly large communities.[6]

The disappearance of professional baseball in so many small towns makes one question the level of involvement necessary to make a community a thriving baseball town. During the 1930s, ballparks became objects of intense civic pride in Lafayette and hundreds of cities like it, and the competition between local communities helped create a love affair between the town, the team, and the new local hero—the successful ballplayer.

This intense relationship between town, team, and ballplayer developed in Lafayette during the 1930s. Before 1933 some semi-pro teams operated in Lafayette, but the sport remained uncultivated on a professional level. As early as the 1890s, teams such as the Pilette Sluggers, the Lafayette Independents, and the Iron Men of Baseball, who possessed little more than a few gloves, a few bats, and a mask, competed locally, traveling by horse and wagon to nearby fields.[7] These teams generally played for fun, and their schedules were irregular. Local railroad workers organized a team which claimed area baseball supremacy for much of the 1920s.[8] By the early 1930s, a handful of semi-pro teams such as the Lafayette Cubs, Giants, Greys, Browns, and Mouton Switch Braves competed against each other and other semi-pro teams from such nearby towns as Youngsville, Milton, Rayne, Parks, and Arnaudville. However, no organized league existed, and team managers simply scheduled games a week or two in advance. Clubs played twenty to thirty games a summer, and toward the end of each year, the more successful teams would issue challenges to rival clubs through the local newspaper to settle claims to the city championship.[9] These teams drew crowds to Browns Diamond, Lafayette High School, Cathedral High School, or Martin School, fields having little more than a backstop and some bases. These parks lacked outfield fences, and spectators stood or sat on the grass behind the backstop or along the baselines. A grandstand which seated a few hundred spectators and a partially fenced field made Lincoln Park Lafayette's best baseball facility before 1933.[10] This field's location on the north end of St. John Street made it the home of Lafayette's black teams, but a white club could follow the black games on a Saturday or Sunday afternoon and play to small crowds.[11]

Some old-timers remember baseball greats such as Mel Ott and "Oyster Joe" Martina barnstorming through early Depression-era Lafayette and attempting to pick up some money in contests against local clubs.[12] Lafayette's semi-pro teams, however, charged modest admission fees and thus made little money. "Pee-wee" Girouard, a local star during the 1930s, claimed, "We weren't making anything; we just wanted to play. Every once in a while you'd charge a little, but it was to pay an official or buy equipment or get gas." Only local players, such as pitcher Johnny Johns, blessed with unusually advanced skills, could expect real remuneration, particularly outside of Lafayette.

> We'd put together a team and play towns in the area with the winner taking 60 percent, but that only amounted to a few dollars for each player if you got anything at

all. Sometimes collecting from an out-of-town loser on their field could be hard. But they were drawing great crowds for games in Berwick, and even bigger ones in Franklin. Berwick gave me 35 dollars a game. When I was pitching for Berwick, I beat Franklin, so Franklin gave me 50 dollars plus board to pitch for them. . . . That's where Johnny Nee, a scout for the Yankees, found me. . . . You just couldn't make that kind of money in Lafayette.[13]

Like Berwick and Franklin, other cities in Southwest Louisiana, including Opelousas, Patterson, and Rayne, experienced increased interest in baseball. The growing popularity of semi-pro baseball in these towns evidently made an impression on some local enthusiasts because in the spring of 1933, three energetic investors established the Lafayette White Sox.

In February, 1933, Lafayette businessman Frem Boustany joined forces with local athletes Morgan Rodemacher and Herbert Schilling to form the Lafayette Baseball Association, Inc. The group secured the use of a baseball field site across the street from the municipal swimming pool along the Breaux Bridge highway from prominent Lafayette sports enthusiast Dr. E. F. Girard.[14] Through February and March the three investors canvassed local businesses and visited individuals, selling advertisements on the outfield fence and soliciting contributions for the new field. On February 28, Boustany prophetically announced that "with the park arranged for and a good team being lined up, the move will meet with the support of the fans."[15] Toward the end of March, construction began on the grandstand in preparation for the April 16 Easter Sunday opening date.[16]

In a promotional contest carried out through the *Daily Advertiser*, J. J. Maitre won a pair of tickets for his recommendation of the White Sox for the team's name, and Dr. E. F. Girard received a pair for naming the Sox new home Parkdale Park.[17] By the opening date, workers completed a grandstand which could seat 600 spectators as well as bleachers which could hold a few hundred on each side. A wooden twenty-foot-high, double-decked fence placed 273 feet down the right field line, 300 feet down the left field line, and 373 feet from home plate at center field enclosed the new park.[18]

With Boustany serving as team president and Rodemacher and Schilling functioning as player-managers, the club arranged several contests per week against South Louisiana's best semi-pro teams. Price of admission varied from 35 cents for an adult male grandstand seat to 25 cents for women or for a bleacher seat. A child's ticket cost 10 cents, and African American bleacher seats located behind first base went for 15 cents. Boys who returned a foul ball earned free admittance.[19] The White Sox home opener drew over 1,000 spectators, and crowds grew even larger for weekend games, especially on Sundays. Games on the Sabbath became so popular that the White Sox management began to arrange both Sunday morning and afternoon contests. On a good Sunday, around 1,200 fans attended the 10 a.m. contest, and approximately 1,800 in the afternoon. These crowds often exceeded grandstand and bleacher capacities, forcing latecomers to stand along the foul lines. In May, just one month into the season, workers extended the grandstand an additional fifty feet down the third base line to accommodate the swelling crowds.[20] In 1934 seating capacity expanded to 1,500 when the grandstand was again enlarged. By the end of 1934, Lafayette fans claimed to have the best park in Southwest Louisiana.

The large crowds allowed the White Sox to pay their players higher wagers than other area teams—as much as $35 a game to star pitchers, sums sufficient to attract the best local talent. The White Sox played approximately seventy games in 1933, most of them at Parkdale, and won over fifty. Intense rivalries soon developed between Lafayette and the semi-pro teams in towns such as Rayne, Abbeville, Opelousas, Lake Arthur, and Franklin.

For much of the season, "Pete" Castex and "Lefty" LeBlanc successfully carried most of the pitching load, but in July the White Sox acquired T. Paul LeBlanc, a twenty-five-year-old pitcher from Kaplan.[21] This move had a profound impact on the team's fortunes, and LeBlanc's acquisition gave the Lafayete area its first real baseball hero.

LeBlanc quickly became the keystone of the White Sox pitching staff. When LeBlanc pitched, people packed the stands, and the Sox usually won. One fan exclaimed, "T. Paul just love to pitch. . . . Why, he'd pitch every day if you'd let him . . . and he was quite a showman, too. . . . The people here just loved him."[22] In mid-September the Baton Rouge Senators, recent winners of the Cotton States' League and "little" Dixie championships, went to Parkdale. T. Paul shut out Baton Rouge 4-0. Ten days later the White Sox played Franklin at Parkdale to settle a claim for semi-pro superiority in Louisiana. "Half the town of Franklin took the train to Lafayette" that Sunday as T. Paul mastered the Franklin lineup 4-2 before an overflow crowd.[23]

The pinnacle of this amazing season, however, occurred the following Saturday, September 30, when the White Sox management arranged a game with the New Orleans Pelicans. The Pelicans operated in the prestigious Class A Southern Association as a top farm club for the Cleveland Indians. The Pelicans had just garnered the Southern Association pennant as well as the Dixie championship against San Antonio, the Texas League winner. In the absence of a Southern major league franchise, people recognized the winner of the Dixie series as the South's best team. Although the Pels played without Dennis Galehouse and Andy Messenger, two of their star players, the rest of Larry Gilbert's lineup remained intact. Sensing the huge regional interest in the game, Boustany nearly doubled ticket prices to 50 cents and accepted no passes; yet the park could barely accommodate the overflow crowd. The grandstand and bleachers filled quickly and ropes extending the length of each foul line kept spectators off the playing field.[24]

T. Paul treated the huge crowd to one of his greatest performances. LeBlanc's superb control and cool disposition resulted in a four-hit shutout of the Pels as the Sox won a tension-packed pitchers' duel 1-0.[25] New Orleans manager Larry Gilbert had high praise for LeBlanc, claiming that LeBlanc had caught his Pels "by surprise" and offering T. Paul a try-out contract for the following spring.[26] This unprecedented contest did more than anything else to establish the Lafayette team's credibility, and it won for the team's management the affection of local fans. "This game," according to the *Lafayette Daily Advertiser* reporter Kaliste Saloom, "is what got professional baseball in Lafayette started."

In 1934, following several organizational meetings, a March 4 New Iberia gathering resulted in an official announcement of the formation of the Evangeline League.[27] On behalf of the White Sox, Schilling and Boustany met with twenty men representing the other five Louisiana franchises constituting the new circuit. Clayton Guilbeau and Mayor Dave Hollier of Opelousas, "Hooky" Irwin and Lozen Leger of Rayne, Cecil Coombs and Art Pehlan of Alexandria; Louis Jenaro of New Iberia, and Charles Schilling of Lake Charles represented the other league cities.[28] J. Walter Morris, promotional director of the Professional Association of Baseball Leagues, also attended as a delegate of the sport's governing body. In a series of meetings that spring, owners agreed upon a 120-game split-season schedule, thirteen-man rosters, and a $780 per month salary limit.[29] Over the next few years, owners increased the number of games, roster sizes, and salaries until they stabilized at approximately 140 games played by fifteen-man squads with a $1,200 salary cap. After the 1934 season, a Shaughnessy playoff system determined league champions.[30]

The White Sox management spent March and early April assembling personnel and making preparations for the league's opening day. Retaining the best players from the 1933 club as a nucleus for 1934, the White Sox bosses added several New Orleans-area stars and a few out-of-state prospects sent by professional scouts to complete the Lafayette roster. Throughout the Evangeline League, mayors of host cities urged businesses to close for the afternoon on each town's big opening day. In Lafayette, the Young Men's Business Club band led a car parade transporting White Sox players, their management, and various local officials from the courthouse to Jefferson Street and down Jefferson Street to the ballpark.[31] Once at Parkdale, Mayor R. L. Mouton threw out the first pitch to trustee Wilson J. Peck, catcher for the ceremony, while fellow trustee Edgar G. Mouton stood at the plate. Twelve hundred fans assembled to watch this inaugural event in an unsuccessful attempt to help Lafayette "kop the kup" for attendance.[32] Around every Easter, events similar to this one took place in Lafayette and in cities throughout the league to usher in the new season.

The White Sox enjoyed success in 1934 and for seven years afterwards. Success for a minor league franchise can be measured by achievements in three related areas: winning percentage, acquisition and development of young talent for the parent organization, and sustaining a high level of local support. The White Sox competed in the Evangeline League from 1934 until the organization's 1942 mid-season collapse. But, during the league's first eight years, this franchise kept pace with the circuit's most stable and successful operations.

In 1934 the White Sox benefitted from the leadership of player-manager Clarence Tregre who utilized the pitching of T. Paul LeBlanc and "Red" Dowie, combined with the baseball skills of such stars as catcher Walter Stephenson and infielders "Meatball"

Folger, Don Motlow, Stanley Sonnier, and Lenny Mock to capture the league's first league pennant. Player-manager Bobby Goff's 1937 White Sox placed first in the year's final standings, but fell short of a championship when Lake Charles eliminated them in the playoffs. The 1939 club, under the astute direction of player-manager Rod Whitney, utilized the talents of first baseman Jerry Witte, center fielder Allen Zarilla, and pitcher Tommy Finger among others, made Lafayette the first league franchise to win two titles. With the exception of 1936, 1938, and the ill-fated 1942 season, the Sox finished "in the money" by qualifying for the playoffs the remaining six years. Excluding the Alexandria Aces, no team won more pre-war Evangeline League games than the Lafayette White Sox.

Another measure of success involves a team's proficiency in the development of talent for a parent organization. The 1934 Lafayette team possessed a working agreement with the Chicago White Sox. In 1935 the Lafayette management terminated that association and in 1936 gave their allegiance to the St. Louis Browns.[33] This relationship with the Browns lasted for the remainder of the White Sox's existence. Working agreements with major league clubs usually meant that the minor league team relied heavily upon the parent organization's scouting system to supply a stream of young talent. A player who enjoyed an outstanding year in Lafayette hoped for a promotion to a more prestigious franchise in the Brown's farm system, such as Texas League affiliate San Antonio. At least six White Sox players—Marshal Mauldin, Walter Stephenson, Clyde McCullough, Jack Kramer, Jerry Witte, and Allen Zarilla—eventually spent time in the major leagues.[34] Countless other White Sox players moved up to Class C, B and A clubs.

Lafayette's small population base made promotional efforts for Parkdale events fundamental to the franchise's economic survival. Grandstand seats for White Sox Evangeline League contests went for 40 cents, while segregated bleachers sold for 25 cents. Paid attendance of over 1,000 during a weekday game or twice that number for a weekend encounter constituted a good crowd. On evenings when good weather combined with a key matchup or a promotional gimmick, attendance easily surpassed these figures. Playoff games and all-star contests generally drew two to four thousand spectators. Although records of attendance are sketchy, approximately 40,000 fans paid to see White Sox games in 1934, and in 1937 paid attendance surpassed 60,000.[35] To put these figures into perspective, one must consider that Lafayette possessed only 14,635 residents in 1930, 19,210 in 1940.[36] Crowds of a few thousand indicated exceptional fan loyalty. The White Sox enjoyed healthy community support until 1941, when Lafayette residents' preoccupation with the unfolding events of World War II began to shrink the gate.

A lack of alternative entertainment in the area, improvements in transportation and communication, and the spread of new technologies such as electrical lighting combined with the promotional techniques of team owners to create a situation conducive to baseball prosperity. The team's resulting success helped forge a love affair between the city and its team, especially the exceptional player.

Historian Joseph Altobello explored one of these factors in his 1976 thesis "The Evangeline League, 1934-1948: The History of a Class D Circuit." Altobello asserted that high sustained fan interest, created by a demand for entertainment, was responsible for the league's formation and long-term success. Like most other urban inhabitants of South Louisiana, Lafayette residents lived in a small, fairly homogeneous town with limited leisure-time options. Needless to say, television did not exist in 1934, but until 1936 Lafayette did not even have a local radio station.[37] The end of prohibition resulted in the establishment of a handful of area nightclubs; however, few Depression-era residents could afford to frequent such establishments. The Jefferson and Royal theaters supplied the town's only movie houses. Here, for 10-25 cents one could attend movies, radio shows, or occasional live performances. Despite the events at the Jefferson Theater, many people came to the ballpark because of so little else to do. One Lafayette resident who claimed to have almost lived at the park commented that back then, "Every once in a while a circus might come through town. You could go to the movies or the live shows at the Jefferson, shoot pool at Antlers, get some ice cream at the Forum, a sandwich at Stansbury's, or talk to the old men at the post office . . . that was about it."[38]

Improvements in Louisiana roads and vehicles also aided the White Sox fortunes. In the spring of 1934, St. Louis Cardinal boss Branch Rickey correctly predicted that "when the times get better, we'll have more minor leagues working then ever. The reason is obvious as transportation has developed to such a degree that operating expenses for minor league clubs has [sic] been reduced considerably."[39] Before 1930, Lafayette Parish, as well as the rest of Southwest Louisiana, lacked paved highways. Improvements made to these roads during the 1930s enabled teams and their fans to travel greater distances less expensively and in more enjoyable fashion. The gravel roads which made up Louisiana's early highway system certainly required motorists to travel at slower speeds but "weren't all that bad." Said one Lafayette resident, "Now, you'd slide a little bit when the rocks were fresh, but when packed down the roads were ok . . . you just went a little slower, had more blowouts, and got covered with dust. Now there was about a half-mile stretch right on the parish line going to Rayne which no one kept up. We called it 'no man's land' . . . you didn't want to get caught there on a rainy day."[40] A Lafayette semi-pro star had this to say about the dirt and gravel roads of the early 1930s: "We'd jump in the back of truck back then. . . . I'm surprised no one got hurt. When got to an out-of-town park, everyone was full of dust and sore from being bounced around so much."[41] Because of the gravel roads and small number of good bridges, many Lafayette residents preferred to travel by train for trips beyond nearby communities. For $1.50, a passenger could take a round-trip on a Southern Pacific excursion train to New Orleans, or for a bit more, to Houston or Dallas.

The Louisiana Highway Department, created in 1911, spent only $19,000 in its initial year. Throughout the 1920s the department received on average about $10 million per year and spent that money mainly to lay gravel on major state highways.[42] In 1929 Governor Huey P. Long's New Good Roads Act went into effect. The legislation resulted in Louisiana's first and most extensive highway paving program. Over the next three years Long spent over $120 million and paved over a thousand miles of 18-foot-wide two-lane highways.[43] During 1931 work crews completed the paving of the Old Spanish Trail. Officially designated U. S. Highway 90, this road ran from the Louisiana-Mississippi border westward through New Orleans to Houma and across Southwest Louisiana to Beaumont, Texas. This concrete highway connected Lafayette with the future Evangeline League towns of New Iberia, Jeanerette, Rayne, and Lake Charles. However, in 1934 the Louisiana Highway Department cut spending, and the paving of new roads decreased. Therefore, portions of Highway 43 to Abbeville, Highway 5 to Opelousas, and the series of highways required to reach Alexandria went unpaved until 1938.[44]

Although the paved, partially paved, and gravel roads of the 1930s produced a vastly improved transportation system, the traveling conditions of the 1930s were still far from ideal. Teams at first used automobiles or rented school buses to get from town to town. Within a couple of years the White Sox, like most other teams, purchased their own team bus. Painted white, the Lafayette bus held 21 passengers, including the players, their managers, and occasionally an umpire or a sportswriter.[45] Richard Taylor, an ex-White Sox catcher, commented on the less than comfortable rides, "You sure didn't get any sleep on the way home . . . and you did not want to chew tobacco if you were sitting near the rear either. . . . You'd bounce so much that the tobacco would end up in your stomach. But those were great times . . . we had a lot of fun."[46]

The proximity of the Evangeline League's franchises gave them an advantage over most other circuits. With the exception of Alexandria and Lake Charles, less than 35 miles of road separated the White Sox from the other five league clubs. Because of the geographic compactness of the league, hundreds of fans loyally followed their teams to other towns throughout the circuit. Key games, playoffs, and all-star contests often drew many more. The circuit's geographic density also allowed league owners to approve schedules which provided for contests between different opponents each day rather than a two- or three-game series between teams. In the league's early years, on occasions such as the Fourth of July or on Sundays when rain outs had to be made up, teams would play two games in one day—in different cities!

Effectively publicizing game results to a large audience also assisted the White Sox in their success. Throughout their existence, telegraph-fed newspaper stories constituted the primary medium the White Sox used to disseminate team news and promote upcoming contests. While the mode of communication remained the same, the team's use of it expanded tremendously as South Louisiana residents and many people outside the region received league results. Before the Evangeline League's formation, Lafayette's primary newspaper, the *Daily Advertiser*, relied mainly on state and national stories from the Associated Press wire, supplemented by brief accounts of local sporting events, to fill the paper's sports page. After 1933, White Sox results became the paper's featured sports story. In 1934, the *Daily Advertiser,* unable to pay a sports reporter, occasionally used accounts from Kaliste Saloom, who claimed he covered the White Sox as a sixteen-year-old boy in exchange for free admission to the games.[47] Saloom also sent "shorts" or abbreviated versions of the game by postal telegraph to the *Beaumont Enterprise*, the *New Orleans Times-Picayune*, and the visiting team's hometown paper.[48] Before long most Louisiana papers, including the *Times-Picayune* and the *Baton Rouge Morning Advocate*, as well as several Texas papers and the nationally circulated *Sporting News*, carried league results.

During the mid- and late 1930s, the local newspaper expanded and improved its league coverage by giving reporter Francis Guchereau space for two daily columns, one for the White Sox games and another devoted to events of interest around the league. Papers across the U. S. occasionally pulled and printed interesting Evangeline League stories from the AP wire. On at least one occasion, the nation took notice of an unusual Parkdale incident. In May 1937, White Sox pitcher Truett Richardson married his hometown sweetheart in an on-the-field ceremony and threw a no-hitter the following night.[49] Over 400 U. S. newspapers printed a picture and account of this appealing human-interest story.[50] In 1938 Sox management remodeled the Parkdale press box and installed telegraph hook-ups so that stories could be sent directly from the field.

The use of radio for game broadcasts and promotions came later for the White Sox than for many clubs and played only a peripheral part in the the club's pre-war prosperity. In the late 1920s Jack Halliday began announcing Pelican road games by reading play-by-play accounts off the telegraph wire over a New Orleans station.[51] During the 1930s most Texas and East Texas League clubs began broadcasting game coverage, and in 1937 Alexandria's KALB made the first Evangeline League transmission.[52] Although no accounts appear in the *Daily Advertiser*, a few informants recalled broadcasts of some of the White Sox's more important contests by Lafayette's KVOL radio station. By 1941, however, the Hub City newspaper mentions that manager Bobby Goff occasionally visited the KVOL studio for short pre-game interviews.[53]

Although the White Sox endured a miserable season on the field in 1936, the team benefitted tremendously from the introduction of night baseball that year. Night contests made their appearance in professional baseball in 1930, when the Des Moines, Iowa, franchise of the Western League played Wichita, Kansas, under artificial lights.[54] The Des Moines team enjoyed a tremendous increase in attendance, and other minor league teams consequently adopted the innovation. Southwest Louisiana's first night game occurred when the nomadic House of David team played at Opelousas in 1932, using their own set of lights![55] Perhaps this event made an impression on Opelousas fans because in April 1935 their ballpark became the first in the league to install lights. Fans in Opelousas warmly embraced the innovation, and owners throughout the league took notice of the Indians' increased attendance. In May 1936, Lafayette's Parkdale Park became the league's second lighted field. Anticipating increased fan support, Boustany and Schilling had 1,000 additional seats constructed to boost Parkdale's seating capacity to 2,500.[56] The team planned an elaborate ceremony for the inauguration of the lights. A parade preceding the event, followed by speeches by several local political figures, the introduction of fourteen maids, and finally the crowning of a queen, Mayor Maxime T. Roy's daughter. As 2,600 spectators looked on, Lafayette Bishop Jules B. Jeanmard blessed the field and proclaimed, "Next to the church and family life, I would rather see our people in this grandstand, watching this interesting sport, than anywhere else."[57]

Not everyone loved the concept of night baseball. Some players, coaches, and baseball traditionalists insisted that the game was meant to be played during the daylight hours. In 1935 Boston manager Joe Cronin stated that "owl ball" or night baseball "was a big joke and just a fad."[58] At least one player, Chicago White Sox pitcher Johnny Salveson, blamed his failing vision on the years of night ball he played while in the minors.[59] Some players complained of dimness and claimed, "If you could see your shadow, the lights were no good."[60] Pete Taylor, who played briefly for Thibodaux in 1947, contended that while most parks were suitably lighted, electrical lights of that period were not very bright, and some parks were downright dark. Taylor commented, "Back then when the inning ended, players would take off their gloves, turn around, throw their gloves on the ground behind them, then run off the field . . . I forget which part it was in, but I've seen it when an out-fielder had to get help from the dugout to find his glove the next inning."[61]

From all accounts, players easily found their gloves at Parkdale; no one saw shadows, and the park possessed first-class equipment. Most of all, the fans loved the evening games. "It was the heat," claimed Herbert Schilling's wife Olga. "Back then a lady dressed for an afternoon game like you were going to church . . . no shorts like today. . . . Why during July and August, day games were just unbearable."[62] For this reason, games before night baseball were mostly men's affairs. After teams installed lights, fans had time to follow the team "down the road" for night contests after work, and luring women to the park became a mission of front offices. Although ladies' days never succeeded in drawing large numbers of female fans, ladies' nights turned into such popular attractions they became weekly events. Free admission to women brought crowds in excess of 2,000 on most ladies' nights, and the White Sox won with amazing frequency when large numbers of female fans were in attendance. During the entire 1938 season, the White Sox lost only one of the weekly ladies' night events.[63] Because of the success of such evening events, all league fields were lighted by the middle of the 1939 season.

Sometimes, however, it took more than lights to attract fans to the ballpark. Boustany, Schilling, and the owners of every other club in the circuit worked tirelessly on promotions designed to boost attendance. Lafayette management occasionally featured traveling baseball comic Al Schacht, sponsored high school nights, Southwest Louisiana Institute nights, American Legion nights, and appliance raffles among various other promotions to lure spectators. Truett Richardson's 1937 wedding served as one feature attraction, and it drew a capacity crowd.[64] On another occasion, the White Sox played for a few innings of a night game with a gimmick—a high-visibility "yellow ball." And on a 1936 police uniform benefit night, assistant police chief Trahan lined up a program which included the raffling of a $109 radio and two boxing matches, along with the added attraction of a boxing battle royal involving "six of the blackest, scrappiest boys we can round up" who will be permitted to "go in there and throw the works."[65]

Without a doubt, Boustany and Schilling's most successful promotional event was an evening simply named Big Night. Starting in 1935 and for one night per season every year afterwards, the White Sox management gave away, following the game, a new automobile to someone in attendance. This ploy attracted fans like no other Lafayette event. Lafayette native Lucy B. Schilling claimed, "I just loved baseball, why I'd spend my last nickle on a game back then . . . but no, you couldn't drag me to that car night . . why it was just a complete madhouse!"[66] Although additions eventually brought seating at Parkdale to 3,500, crowds usually in excess of 5,000 and occasionally around 6,000 showed up for Big Night. Placing this many people in the small park while still allowing room for a game required creativity in the arrangement of spectators. To accommodate the huge crowd, Sox management placed additional chairs in the box seat area; borrowed the Mardi Gras queen's platform, joined it to the side of the grandstand, and filled it with chairs; erected temporary bleachers down both foul lines; and placed 1,000 individual chairs along the outfield fence.[67] In effect, no foul territory existed down either foul line, and a rope kept fans within about twenty feet of the outfield fence. Special rules for the evening declared any ball going into the outfield seating area a ground-rule double.[68] Because of the addition of lights and successful attractions such as Big Night, Lafayette's yearly attendance for 1937 set a new club record by attracting over 60,000 paying customers for the year. By 1941, however, war concerns diminished fan interest in baseball. War bond nights and aluminum collection nights replaced traditional promotions, and even crowds for Big Night diminished.[69]

Participation by the White Sox in the Evangeline League helped create a strong bond of loyalty between hometown fans and their heroes. In April of 1934, just 12 games into the season, an incident during a Parkdale matchup between Lafayette and first place Rayne displayed the emotional attachment of White Sox fans for their team. In the seventh inning an argument developed between hot-tempered White Sox catcher Walter "Tarzan" Stephenson and umpire Mabry. As the argument intensified, "Mabry took off his mask, and . . . Stephenson just decked him."[70] Stephenson found himself not only ejected from the game but fined $100 and suspended indefinitely. Fans and teammates swarmed onto the field, gathering around the unfortunate umpire. This activity led to a short delay of the game and required the police to restore order.[71] The police were also obliged to escort Mabry safely from Parkdale. To calm the crowd, team president Frem Boustany announced via the public address system that the Sox would file an appeal with the league office and insisted that the team would withdraw from the circuit if Mabry continued to umpire.[72] Stephenson served a two-week suspension for his part in the melee, and within days loyal fans collected enough money for the player's fine.[73] By May, umpire Mabry no longer appeared as a league arbiter. Over the next eight seasons, dozens of situations warranted police assistance to extricate unfortunate umpires from the wrath of the aggressively vindictive and partisan Parkdale crowds.

The attachment of local fans to players often went beyond emotional support to material displays of gratitude. Minor league players often tell stories of the extraordinary generosity fans displayed toward them during this period. Perhaps the lack of the strong national media which exists today kept small-town residents out of touch with national figures and made young ballplayers local celebrities. Richard Taylor, a veteran of several different minor league circuits during the 1930s, commented, "Lafayette; Monroe, Louisiana; Fort Worth, Texas; Andalusia, Alabama—it did not matter. People everywhere treated you well. My favorite was Monroe . . . although my salary wasn't much, you never had to buy a meal, and if a merchant saw you looking at a shirt in his window, it was yours. In five or six years of minor league ball I never had to buy clothes." The most successful players, of course, received the greatest demonstrations of gratitude. During the semi-pro days, fans showed appreciation for outstanding fielding plays, pitching performances, or climactic home runs by "passing the hat" around the stands for their hero. South Louisiana residents were known for betting on these contests, and the ecstasy a better felt when his local player delivered a heroic performance to "make good" the bet certainly heightened a gambler's appreciation for that player.[74] But, non-gamblers, including respectable local merchants, often contributed to "the hat."

In the depths of the early Depression, players considered ten or twenty dollars to be a pretty good "hat."[75] In 1933, following T. Paul LeBlanc's amazing defeat of the Pelicans, fans passed the hat and showed appreciation for their hero with a $200 collection.[76] Following pitcher "Red" Dowie's four 1935 playoff victories in just eight days against Alexandria, Lafayette's mayor declared August 12 "Red Terror" day to honor the hurler. Local merchants presented "Red" with gifts. Fans and players collected additional cash and gifts, and the White Sox management donated $50 to "Red's" fund.[77]

In White Sox league games, fans sent gifts or written pledges for gifts to the press box in lieu of "passing the hat." During one intense Parkdale game against first-place rival Abbeville in July 1938, first baseman Jerry Witte broke the game open by slugging two home runs in a single inning. *Lafayette Daily Advertiser* sportswriter Francis Guchereau penned the following inventory of Jerry Witte's gifts in his "Fanning with Francis" column.

> Witte enjoys an occasional bottle beer, today he has something like 192 bottles on hand . . . some of the other gifts were headed off by the $29.75 watch . . . a 1930s 32 radio . . . and a $12.50 radio table. Announcer Lacour was occupied until the end of the game (the homers came in the sixth stanza) announcing the various gifts from the fans. Other noteworthy gifts included a case of beer and four rounds of golf 'on the house' at the Municipal Golf Course . . . a caddy with a high sense of humor (believed to be Peter Landry) said, 'I'll caddy for Witte . . . all four rounds . . . for nuttin' . . . Witte has no car, but now he has 20 gallons of gas . . . several Abbeville fans got together and sent 50 cents up to the press box to give Witte 'to buy ice for

his beer' . . . and a young miss (name unknown) sent a note to the press box stating that she'd give Witte a bottle opener.[78]

While incidents such as this may seem unusual and extreme, former White Sox player and local baseball enthusiast "Pee-wee" Girouard claimed "that sort of thing happened all of the time at Parkdale."

In late January 1942 at a city hall meeting, Frem Boustany announced that he and partner Sheldon Blue were unable to continue operation of the White Sox, and Lafayette's continued participation in the league would require another local source of funding.[79] Businessman Louis Mann purchased Boustany's shares and attempted to save the struggling franchise. The league opened in 1942 as a six-team circuit, but dwindling gate receipts forced New Iberia to fold on May 21. Two days later, just 31 games into the season, Lafayette followed suit.[80] The remaining teams drew up new schedules and attempted to complete the year as a four-team circuit, but on Sunday, May 31, after an unsuccessful effort to move the failing Natchez franchise to Orange, Texas, the league played its final games and disbanded for the duration of the war.[81]

The league re-formed in 1946 without a Lafayette franchise. The following year, Alcide Dominique, a prosperous area cattleman, purchased a league team and named it the Brahman Bulls. About a mile north of Lafayette on the Carencro highway, Dominique built a new stadium for his team. (A deteriorating, abandoned movie theater called the Nona stands today at the site of Parkdale Park.)

Around the mid-1950s, people began to lose interest in the Evangeline League, and in 1957 the circuit folded. Further improvements in transportation, communication, and other technologies—the forces which helped give rise to the league—assisted in its demise. Some local fans blamed television, others considered air conditioning the culprit, and still others mentioned the growth of organized youth baseball for the league's failure. Surely all of these factors, combined with increased entertainment opportunities and the rising cost of operating a franchise, played a part. During the last four decades, interstate highways, improved air travel, cable television, fax machines, and other technologies have increasingly linked small communities to larger cities and centralized sources of information. This shift has given people unprecedented exposure to national sports figures and helped fans identify more closely with these personalities. Therefore, the popularity of the local hero suffered. During the 1950s and 1960s, over thirty leagues comprising hundreds of teams throughout the United States collapsed, and the allegiance of fans shifted to major league franchises. The decline of minor league baseball during these years left Lafayette, and communities like it with one less point of contact for its citizens, fewer local heroes, a diminished interest in surrounding communities, one less rallying point of civic pride, and one less institution defining community identity.

Notes for "A Community and Its Team: The Evangeline League's Lafayette White Sox, 1934-1942"

[1] Paraphrased comment often made at Acadian area ballparks, derived from the author's personal experiences as a high school coach, 1979-91.

[2] See Brian Joseph Altobello, "The Evangeline League, 1934-1948: The History of a Class D Circuit" (M.A. thesis, Louisiana State University, 1976).

[3] W. G. Brahnam, "Minor Leagues Face Bright Outlook During New Season" (A. P. story Durham, N.C.) *Lafayette Daily Advertiser* (hereafter referred to as *LDA*) January 9, 1935.

[4] *The Baseball Blue Book* (Fort Wayne, Ind., 1940), 15.

[5] Ibid.

[6] David Lamb, "A Season in the Minors," *National Geographic Magazine,* 179 (1991): 51.

[7] "Baseball Through the Years in Lafayette and Vicinity," *LDA*, July 25-27, 1939.

[8] Henry Girouard, interview, Lafayette, Louisiana, March 8, 1993.

[9] "Greys, Browns Play for City Title," *LDA*, October 14, 1931.

[10] "Legion Games Expect to Attract Many," *LDA*, July 2, 1932.

[11] Johnny Johns, interview, Bunkie, Louisiana, March 23, 1993.

[12] John Young, interview, Lafayette, Louisiana, March 15, 1993.

[13] Johnny Johns, interview.

[14] "New Park Here Is Arranged For," *LDA*, February 28, 1933.

[15] Ibid.

[16] "Lafayette's New Baseball Club Plans To Open Season April 16," *LDA*, March 29, 1933.

[17] "Lafayette White Sox Offer Strong Club For Next Season," *LDA*, March 23, 1934.

[18] "Figures About Local Park Are Told," *LDA*, March 23, 1934.

[19] Wallace Mouton, interview, Lafayette, Louisiana, March 9, 1993.

[20] "White Sox to Battle Rayne Next Sunday," *LDA*, May 11, 1933.

[21] Lillie Leger, interview, Indian Bayou, Louisiana, April 15, 1993.

[22] John Young, interview.

[23] Johnny Johns, interview.

[24] Kaliste Saloom, interview, Lafayette, Louisiana, April 2, 1993.

[25] "T. Paul LeBlanc Leads Lafayette to Victory Over Pelicans," *LDA*, October 2, 1933.

[26] William McG. Keefe, "Viewing the News," *New Orleans Times-Picayune*, October 5, 1933.

[27] "Evangeline League Formed," *LDA*, March 5, 1934.

[28] Ibid.

[29] Teams were allowed to carry 15 men for the first and last two weeks of the season. Roster requirements also determined the number of rookies and class men (those with two years or more of professional experience) who could be carried. Also Brian Joseph Altobelo in "The Evangeline League, 1934-1948: The History of a Class D Circuit" points out that salary limits were illusionary.

[30] Split season playoff systems matched the winner of the first half of the season against the winner of the second half. The Shaughnessy playoff system included the top four finishers of a full season in best-of-seven series to determine league champions.

[31] "Big Crowd Sees New Iberia Defeat White Sox in Opener Here," *LDA*, April 13, 1934.

[32] Ibid. Most years the league office offered a cash incentive and a trophy to the city with the highest opening-day attendance.

[33] "Lafayette Club Has Working Pact with St. Louis Browns," *LDA*, March 7, 1936.

[34] Sam Tarleton, "Evangeline League Graduates Would Form Own Major League All-Star Club," *The Beaumont Enterprise*, June 22, 1947. Also see Hy Turkin and S. C. Thompson, *The Official Encyclopedia of Baseball* (New York, 1951).

[35] Francis Guchereau, "Evangeline Chatter Box," *LDA*, September 11, 1937. As a semi-pro team in 1933, the Sox charged less, but prices for Evangeline League games stayed around 40 cents grandstand and 25 cents bleachers throughout the pre-war era.

[36] Milburn Calhoun, ed., *Louisiana Almanac 1992-1993* (Gretna, La., 1992), 144-53.

[37] Harry Lewis Griffin, *The Attakapas Country: A History of Lafayette Parish, Louisiana* (New Orleans, 1959), 120-21.

[38] Henry Girouard, interview.

[39] "Sees Better Outlook for Minor Loops" (St. Louis AP story), *LDA*, January 26, 1934.

[40] John Young, interview.

[41] Johnny Johns, interview.

[42] Stuart O. Landry, ed., *Louisiana Almanac and Fact Book* (New Orleans, 1949), 338.

[43] Ibid.

[44] Griffin, *Attakapas Country*, 90.

[45] "White Sox President Back from Camp with Bright Outlook," *LDA*, March 23, 1937.

[46] Richard Taylor, interview, New Orleans, April 12, 1993.

[47] Kaliste Saloom, interview.

[48] Ibid.

[49] Francis Guchereau, "Evangeline Chatter Box," *LDA*, May 12, 1937.

[50] Ibid., May 21, 1937.

[51] Arthur Schott, interview, New Orleans, April 12, 1993.

[52] Francis Guchereau, "Evangeline Chatter Box," *LDA*, May 21, 1937. Also see Altobello, "The Evangeline League, 1934-1948."

[53] "Sox Hold Lengthy Workout under Lights at Parkdale," *LDA*, April 12, 1941.

[54] "100 Years of Baseball," *LDA*, November 24, 1935.

[55]"Win for House of David," *LDA*, May 10, 1932.

[56]"Big Program for Night Opener Here Thursday," *LDA*, May 5, 1936.

[57]Donald C. Dailey, "2,600 Fans Watch Night Baseball Game Staged Here," *LDA*, May 8, 1936.

[58]"Cronin Considers Night Baseball Is Only 'Big Joke,'" *LDA*, February 11, 1935.

[59]Untitled paragraph, *LDA*, May 9, 1936.

[60]Henry Girouard, interview.

[61]C. J. "Pete" Taylor, interview, Hattiesburg, Mississippi, April 11, 1993.

[62]Olga Schilling, interview, Lafayette, Louisiana, March 27, 1993.

[63]"Cardinals Defeat White Sox by Score of 10-5," *LDA*, August 5, 1938.

[64]Francis Guchereau, "Evangeline Chatter Box," *LDA*, May 12, 1937.

[65]"Big Parkdale Program Tonight for Police Department Uniform Fund," *LDA*, August 11, 1936.

[66]Lucy B. Schilling, interview, Lafayette, Louisiana, March 25, 1993.

[67]Francis Guchereau, "Fanning with Francis," *LDA*, July 13, 1938.

[68]Ibid.

[69]"Tonight Will Be Aluminum Night at Parkdale," *LDA*, July 23, 1941. Also "Baseball Defense Bond Night at Parkdale Here Tonight," *LDA*, August 28, 1941.

[70]Henry Girouard, interview.

[71]"Castex Hurls Three-Hit Game as White Sox Defeat Rayne," *LDA*, April 27, 1934.

[72]Ibid.

[73]Henry Girouard, interview. Girouard also claimed that Stephenson's temper resulted in continued fights which shortened his major-league career.

[74]C. J. "Pete" Taylor, interview.

[75]Ibid.

[76]See Brian Joseph Altobella, "The Evangeline League, 1934-1948: The History of a Class D Circuit."

[77]Leonard Montabalo, "White Sox Even Up Series in 8-4 Game with Blues," *LDA*, September 14, 1935.

[78]Francis Guchereau, "Fanning with Francis," *LDA*, July 15, 1938.

[79]"Franchise of Lafayette Club Discussed," *LDA*, January 27, 1942. Also note: In 1935, M. Rodemacher sold his shares of the team to Boustany. Schilling, in 1940, sold his team shares to Sheldon Blue and started the Port Arthur franchise with his brother Charles. See "Lafayette White Sox Prepare for Opening," *LDA*, March 9, 1940.

[80]"Sox Defeat Aces in Final Tilt for Local Club," *LDA*, May 23, 1942.

[81]"Evangeline League Ends for Duration of War," *LDA*, May 30, 1942. In 1940, the Abbeville franchise moved to Houma. Later that season, the franchise failed and moved to Natchez.

THE PRESENCE OF THE PAST
IN THE CAJUN COUNTRY MARDI GRAS*

Carl Lindahl

Until recently, nearly all folkloric accounts of Mardi Gras and related festival sprang from two opposed approaches. *Ancients* have seen in such festivities the shadows of prehistoric rites of fertility, death, and resurrection and have sought to peel away the skin of the present to lay bare the aged core of the game: in knowing the nature of the first Mardi Gras we would know all that we needed to know about the present celebration. A second group, the *moderns,* viewed the celebration only as it is currently enacted. In exclusively synchronic fashion, they have plotted carnival's outer shape, internal structures, and place in a larger social world. All that a folklorist could see on a Mardi Gras day was all that mattered.

Ancient and modern perspectives differ irreconcilably in their choices of the "right" time for viewing Mardi Gras. For the ancients, origins define purpose: the earliest enactments are far more significant than anything that now remains for us to witness.[1] For the moderns, however, the event immediately under scrutiny is far more important than any unseen predecessor.

For all their obvious surface opposition, the two views remain remarkably alike in two respects. First, both characterize carnival as an agon. While ancients define it as a symbolic battle between winter and spring, moderns stress a social rather than a natural battleground upon which public order and disorder, high and low strata go to war. In the moderns' view, carnival rests on a series of "balanced oppositions[2] through the symbolic means of the festival, oppositional values like order and disorder, . . . public and private space, and respect and aggression are played out."[3]

A second similarity linking ancients and moderns is lack of historical depth. Scholarly accounts of Mardi Gras have tended to depict the celebration as timeless in two senses. Trapped between two paradigms—the first a search for ancient origins and the

---

*First published in the *Journal of Folklore Research*, 33 (1996): 125-32, 144-48. Reprinted with the kind permission of the author and publisher.

second a synchronic account of what happens on any given Mardi Gras day—we have created our own agon, pitting prehistory against a-history without paying sufficient heed to the vast stretches of recoverable past between these poles. As a characteristic example, Harry Oster and Revon Reed meticulously described the Mamou Mardi Gras as they observed it and then derived it from ancient Celtic fertility rituals.[4] We have shifted back and forth between prehistoric origins and present-day performances as if the first Mardi Gras could really explain the most recent, as if simply by watching people we could determine their thoughts and feelings better than they themselves could express them.[5]

Lately, however, a dual motion has opened up the space between the two synchronic poles of "first" and "now." An academic interest in historical change and its interplay with developing festive traditions has inspired a creative partnership between folklorists and historians. Susan G. Davis's *Parades and Power,* Samuel Kinser's *Carnival, American Style,* and Roger D. Abrahams's *Singing the Master* all fuse historical and folkloric methods to add chronological depth and dynamism to festival studies.[6]

Yet like the ancients and the moderns, even the best recent historical-folkloric studies have tended to ignore the role of verbalized memory. Even more important than our recent interdisciplinary partnerships is what we have gained from listening, from attempting to share the experience of the festive actors themselves. Arguably the most effective aspect of the past, the *remembered past* informs the actions and emotions of the players. Henry Glassie has brought such a past most fully to bear upon festival studies. Employing oral memory to reconstruct folk festival, Glassie's *All Silver and No Brass* provides the informing premise of this essay: "Events in the past, held in the memory, can be as influential upon people's actions as events in their immediate contexts. Memory is a behavioral reality."[7] Unfortunately, the County Fermanagh community described in Glassie's work had discontinued its mumming practices before Glassie began his fieldwork, leaving him no opportunity to trace the influence of older members' memories on younger performers and their performances. In contrast to the Fermanagh mummings, Cajun country Mardi Gras possesses both a vividly remembered past and a vitally enacted present. As folklorists begin to call upon the speech of past players to illuminate present Mardi Gras actions, powerful new readings are emerging.[8]

Here I take Mardi Gras' verbalized past in two relatively unexplored directions—emotional interpretation and narrated memories, two of the most common types of discourse that accompany the celebration. Attempts to explain how Mardi Gras feels and stories of Mardi Gras past act palpably upon the revelers. In emotional interpretation, participants respond most directly to the festival. In narrated memories, older celebrants actively transform past acts into scripts for action as young people compete to play the roles modeled in their elders' stories.[9]

To add the dimensions of the emotionally experienced and narrated past to the folkloric record, this essay examines one Mardi Gras community: Basile, Louisiana. In this town of approximately 1,700 people, the festival known as the Cajun country Mardi Gras, or *courir de Mardi Gras* ('Mardi Gras run'), is yearly enacted. During the past sixty years, the Basile Mardi Gras has engaged as few as a dozen riders and never more than 110. Such a small procession of masked men (and women, since the 1960s) bears little resemblance to the far larger and better known urban Mardi Gras of New Orleans, Mobile, and Galveston.[10] Yet Cajun country Mardi Gras has attracted a significant literature, most of it informed by the ancient and modern approaches I have outlined.

To help fill the gap between "first" and "now," I begin by juxtaposing two synchronic accounts of Mardi Gras viewed in two different frames: the horseback processions of past generations, reconstructed from the memories of former riders; and today's celebration as seen by outsiders. After outlining the most obvious changes in the festival, I hope to illumine the Mardi Gras community's own sense of the past as well as its sense of change by examining the Mardi Gras stories of a few of the most respected older participants and by noting the effect of these stories on the community. This insider's history reveals that the people of Basile are concerned with both the first Mardi Gras and the most recent. Yet the most important festive time for them may well be neither the ancient past nor the present, but the remembered past. The agons—the wars between order and disorder pitting whip-carrying *capitaines* against outlaw *sauvages*—perceived as so important by outsiders are often relatively unimportant to insiders for whom the festival is far more orderly and unifying than to the unmasked. In short, the people of Basile combine ancient, modern, *and* local historical perspectives to see beneath the surface of their Mardi Gras. To begin to understand their festive vision, we must do the same.

The Form of Mardi Gras:
As it is to Outsiders; As it was, from Within

At first sight, there is only misrule and disorder. Swarms of masked men, so thoroughly disguised that their mothers would not know them, break the boundaries of an ordered environment. They spill into the farmer's yard, charge his house, intimidate his family, grab his wife, and force her to dance. They run off with bicycles, wheelbarrows, food, and anything else they can find, including children. Their breath, voices, and lurching motions feed suspicion—sometimes founded—that they have been drinking for days.

Viewed from a distance (as it nearly always has been, by tourists and even by folklorists) and then rendered even more distant when treated in print or on film, Mardi Gras appears to be pure riot, mad play. Outsiders see Cajun Mardi Gras as a rustic, only slightly less licentious cousin of the most lurid enactments of the more familiar new Orleans Mardi Gras in which barebreasted women walk the streets (only the men have tops on their dresses), screaming adults wrestle plastic coins from the hands of sobbing children, and mobs start fights resulting in injuries and even deaths as they clamor over strings of beads. Outside interpretations of Cajun Mardi Gras,[11] like those of New Orleans's, have emphasized the mindless drunkenness, but as Cajun insider Barry J. Ancelet has said, Cajun Mardi Gras offers "mindless drunkenness with a history," a history that ultimately makes festive action anything but mindless.[12] The authoritative history of Cajun Mardi Gras can be provided only with the help of its most ardent practitioners.

To what lengths would a young man pursue this "mindlessness"? After visiting thirty houses, dancing two dances and singing a song at each, chasing one or more chickens at many, and committing continual acts of slapstick trickery all along the way, the Mardi Gras returns to the center of town, where the members dance, parade, beg and dodge the strokes of whips for another hour. Then they file to the Woodman Hall in Basile to eat a gumbo cooked from the chickens, rice, and other food that they have gathered.[13]

After the 1993 Basile Mardi Gras, I stood outside the Woodman Hall and listened to the Mardi Gras review their day. I listened as five young men talked about losing their jobs for participating in the festival. Their employers had told them that if they did not come to work on Tuesday morning, they would not be coming back. And that is exactly what happened. One of the riders at the same Mardi Gras had just been released from the hospital with a serious knee injury. After a day of chicken chasing, begging, and trickery, his pants were red with the blood of his injured leg. Another man, nearly fifty years old, also had a leg injury and was unable to walk at the end of the day. A third man, who had been scheduled for neck surgery, instead chased chickens, climbed trees, ran through fields for eight hours, and was chosen best all around Mardi Gras at the *bal* that night. Some of these men sacrificed their livelihoods, other arguably risked their lives, for one day of calculated madness.

What is it that these Mardi Gras risk their jobs and health to do? Once the physical and emotional costs of this game are weighed in with the riot, a dual image emerges. At the same time that the festival unleashes disorder on the outside, it also subjects itself to an often punishing discipline from within. At the root of this perceived tension is a particular order embedded in the day, an order whose form is easily charted. The pattern explained here is a conservative one. It is the Mardi Gras as performed one or two generations ago, the one that is most often described when one asks the older men of Basile what Mardi Gras is.[14]

A visitor in the 1940s or '60s would see the festival unfold as follows. Masked men and boys assemble in the early morning under the leadership of the *capitaine,* a temporary despot who will play the "most important single role"[15] in the festive drama by standing in full command of the day's proceedings. He and his *co-capitaines* are the only unmasked riders. The group leaves from a central location in the town, moving to its rural outskirts. When they reach a farmhouse, the riders begin a cycle that will be repeated perhaps thirty times before the day is out. The *capitaine* stops the masked horsemen on the road, then rides forward alone to ask the owner's permission to enter the yard. When consent is granted, the leader waves a flag signaling his masked followers into the farmyard. Dismounting, the men begin to sing and dance in a ritual of supplication:

C'est les Mardi Gras, c'est tout des bons jeunes gens,
Des bons jeunes gens, ça devient de toutes des bonnes familles...
C'est pas des malfaicteurs, c'est juste des quémandeurs.

The Mardi Gras, they are all good people,
Good people who all come from good families....
They are not evil-doers, they are just beggars.[16]

When the troupe has groveled to the farmer's satisfaction, he presents a chicken or two to the *capitaine* who summons the masked men behind an imaginary line where they await the chase. The *capitaine* throws the chicken into the air and the men pursue. The one who catches it is hailed as a victor, and the entire troupe celebrates his victory with various acts of play—climbing trees, running off with children, daring the host to guess their identities—until the *capitaine* blows a horn calling them back to the road. This pattern of action is repeated at various farmhouses until the Mardi Gras has circled the town, at which time the *capitaine* leads the group back to its center. The whole town then shares a gumbo cooked from captured chickens and ends the evening with a *bal masqué*. Next morning is Ash Wednesday, day of atonement, beginning of Lent, and as more than one rider has told me, "If you do Mardi Gras right, you'll have enough to pray about when you get up early and go to church."

It does not take long to trace the shape of Cajun Mardi Gras, but describing its meanings and purposes would take much longer. The following brief sketch of the festival's signal functions reflects the views of older people from Basile and neighboring Cajun prairie communities.

First, Mardi Gras maps shared territory. The riders leave from and return to the *moyeu*, the hub, the center of their community.[17] On their ride, they circle their town, marking with horses' hooves the boundaries of their common interests. Within the palpably precise physical circle marked by the ride, there is also a series of selections and negotiations, a sifting process that separates insiders from outsiders. The Basile Mardi Gras, for example, generally skips the houses of Protestants, African Americans, and new arrivals in town to affirm its long-standing ties to older, Catholic Cajuns.

Mardi Gras marks manhood. Older riders remember it as an all-male affair, a rite of passage incorporating boys into the adult community and accentuating the skills most prized by male Cajun adults: horsemanship, resourceful farming, prowess at racing and dancing, hard work, hard play—all combined. The boy who plays well is accepted as a peer, and when he catches his first chicken he becomes a provider in a very real sense for the first time by adding his own chicken to the gumbo that will feed the group that night.

Mardi Gras presents a moving image of interdependence: anonymous masked men, symbolic of anyone who may be hungry, beg for food and receive chickens, rice, and other foodstuffs given impartially by the farmers. Theoretically at least, this is a feast in which everyone gives and everyone gets. The hosts sacrifice the chickens they have worked to raise (but only after a fight), and the riders beg, sing, and struggle with each other to win those chickens. At the *bal* that night, all share the food thus earned, lost, and earned again. In the early modern France that the Cajuns abandoned for the new world, sharing was a strategy of survival. Droughts and crop failures created widespread famine ensuring that half the time, more than half the people had less than enough to eat.[18]

Finally, Mardi Gras defines the vitality and promotes the continuity of the group. At the end of the day-long ride, the boys who have become men through their adventures join the older men at the *bal*. Here, for the first time, the "new" men participate in accepted social interaction with females. They dance with, court, and ultimately marry the girls and women who have witnessed and admired their holiday feats.

Yet an enormous gulf divides the Mardi Gras just described from the Basile of the 1990s. The celebratory circle just described can only be forced with difficulty upon the contemporary Cajun cultural landscape. For example, although much of Cajun country experiences economic trouble, winter starvation is no longer a fear. And while the oldest Mardi Gras runners remember when all courtship took place during chaperoned dances, today's Cajun teenagers enjoy much the same range of dating options and sexual freedoms available to most other American teenagers.

These and other changes in Cajun lifestyle have made their marks on Mardi Gras, because this festival, like any other living tradition, has changed with—and in ways reflective of—its community. Though Cajun Mardi Gras clearly follows a rural paradigm that celebrates the interdependence of village and farm, the Basile ride is now restricted almost exclusively to town because the countryside has largely been abandoned. After visiting more than two dozen homes and businesses inside Basile, the Mardi Gras takes a long loop into the countryside to invade one lone farmhouse. In terms of time spent both in travel and at the house, the visit to the farmhouse is the longest of the Mardi Gras visits. As if in compensation for all the food that the countryside once provided the Mardi Gras, the owner of this house annually provides lunch for the entire troupe.

Older riders remember a time when they could see a dozen other farmhouses, visible in all directions, from their own front porches. Today's landscape reveals miles of fields between farmhouses. The subsistence farm has largely disappeared, replaced by giant (often corporate) fields of specialty crops such as rice and crawfish. Boys whose fathers worked their own farms now live in town and travel to these fields to work long hours for little pay on other people's land.

Though the old Mardi Gras were almost exclusively horseback processions, the lack of farms, the dearth of horses, the now longer distances between rural dwellings, and the fact that riding is a vanishing art have caused many Mardi Gras to exchange horses for horsepower. The celebrants now travel from house to house on truck drawn wagons.

Though older celebrations reflected a male-dominated world from which unmarried women were strictly excluded, several contemporary Mardi Gras now have female runners. In some towns these girls and women rival the men in rowdiness, drunkenness, and sexual play, performing feats of exhibitionism unthinkable to their mothers. At Basile, the tradition of women running Mardi Gras is older than in most places. In fact, women are credited with reviving the entire Basile Mardi Gras in the 1960s after the men's run had been discontinued. Since the 1970s, Basile's women and men have run Mardi Gras together—that is, riding separate trucks to visit the same house at the same time and to perform nearly identical antics.[19]

As the demonstrably ancient form of Mardi Gras absorbs the newest cultural developments and changes shape to accommodate them, the clash between the archaic and the contemporary is visible everywhere within the celebration. The innovations appear so striking and sometimes so discordant that one must question why the older forms continued to exist at all. Why would the celebrants want to keep alive a form of play that bears only a passing—if not thoroughly past—resemblance to their current lifestyle?

The extraordinary disjunction between the festival's "archaic" form and the current shape of the community it celebrates is primarily an outsider's problem. The people of Basile do not limit themselves to such choices. They are both ancients and moderns. Many of Basile's core Mardi Gras do in fact nurture theories about Mardi Gras's origins, theories that are very important to them. Furthermore, even the oldest of the corps tend to find themselves so excited by the Mardi Gras immediately at hand that they have trouble getting to sleep or staying asleep on Mardi Grave eve. With a fabric of narrated memories, these same Mardi Gras participants bind together the first and the most recent Mardi Gras, thus investing the festival with three temporal dimensions. Scholarly speculation about ancient origins or contemporary structures receded, as did all that I had witnessed over their Mardi Gras, as past and present players shared with me the memories and emotions they don along with their masks as they enter the celebration. . . .

Among the countless surface changes that Cajun Mardi Gras has undergone in the past fifty years, one fundamental structural change stands out. In Basile, as in some other communities, the maskers visit one site where they do not beg for food: the local nursing home. There they ask for nothing but come to please, to entertain. The Basile nursing home is filled with women and men who once lived on the farms that the Mardi Gras invaded yearly. With this one visit, the revelers have institutionalized the memory and importance of their rural past and marked Mardi Gras as a two-way giving process. "We go to the old folks' home to give Mardi Gras back to the people who gave it to us," Mardi Gras Tony Johnson has said. As surely as today's young people capture chickens to give a gumbo to the town, the older people have given Mardi Gras to the young. Quite self-consciously, the ritual participants affirm the ties binding young and old.

Kim Moreau, Vories's son and a *grand Mardi Gras* in his own right, also says, "When we go to the old folks' home, we're taking the Mardi Gras back to where it came from." When Kim enters the home, he embodies quite literally an image of the past. Wearing a mask made by his father in 1950, a mask even older than he is, his Mardi Gras face stirs memories far older still. One old woman laughs even as she shudders involuntarily because, like most of her companions, she was frightened when, as a child, she first saw the Mardi Gras. Like many in the room, she is re-experiencing that early childhood moment. As she begins to shudder, Kim turns his face down and kisses her hand through the screening of the mask.

Perhaps everything else about Mardi Gras and Cajun culture has changed, but the need to mend transgenerational rifts has not. The young boys who become men in today's Mardi Gras have played so many video games and watched so many futuristic movies that the wild men in costume who descend on farm houses seem quaint rather than alien and frightening, as they seemed to their fathers. Paradoxically, what seems most outrageous to the young riders today is the *order* of the festival: the begging, the groveling, the chicken chasing, the control of the *capitaine*—those things which seemed the most realistic extensions of community life in their parents' days. Mardi Gras can hardly provide license for a group of teenagers who stretch the moral limits of their community daily. In a period when childhood crime and extramarital pregnancy are becoming relatively widespread for the first time, there is not too much a boy can do to shock his community on Mardi Gras day.

But the bonding continues. In awe, kids watch their parents and grandparents dance, cross-dress, act like fools, and play roles that test their endurance and that may otherwise seem senselessly old-fashioned. Some kids drink too much and fall down as their fathers run past them to capture the chickens that the young men are supposed to win. Others grow up in the process of that one day, inspired by the stories they have heard in the past month and by those whose actions that day most clearly embody the promise of the stories. In 1994 a young reveler told me that he could not run Mardi Gras *just for himself* anymore because the younger Mardi Gras did not know what they were doing; he had to show them. In 1996 that same young man was chosen Best All-Around Mardi Gras by the *capitaines* who lauded him for the way he taught the young. By the end of the night, after dancing without stop for hours, he was telling his Mardi Gras stories about his uncle and his Mardi Gras father, Potic Rider.

That night at the *bal*, exhausted young men speak with animation knowing either that tomorrow at six a.m. they will be back working in the rice fields or that at seven they will be starting back to school. Even their exhaustion cannot mask their exhilaration. They will tell you how many chickens they caught, how much money they begged, who they fooled, who they scared. They will also tell you that the fathers did it all better. Finally, they will tell you that they—and their parents—have fed the town. . . .

Tomorrow is Ash Wednesday, Day of Atonement, but today, Mardi Gras, brings its own atonement as community divisions are ultimately, if temporarily, mended. Order and disorder, past and present, old and young melt together as kids without futures suddenly find them, tricksters feed their parents' dreams, and outlaws feed the town. We do not even have to ask—all we have to do is listen—to hear our own opposed ancient and modern notions of Mardi Gras dissolve into a stream of continuities that includes and transcends them all.

Notes for "The Presence of the Past in the Cajun Country Mardi Gras"

[1] Sir James George Frazer, *The Golden Bough: A Study in Magric and Religion* (London, 1922), 347-66, 679; Harry Oster and Revon Reed, "Country Mardi Gras in Louisiana," *Louisiana Folklore Miscellany*, 1 (1960): 1-17.

[2] Roger D. Abrahams, "Folklore in Culture: Notes Toward an Analytic Method," *Texas Studies in Literature and Language;* reprinted in *Readings in American Folklore*, ed. Jan Harold Brunvand (New York, 1979), 390-403; cf. Abrahams, *The Man of Words in the West Indies: Performance and the Emergence of Creole Culture* (Baltimore, 1983), 108.

[3] Carolyn Ware, "Reading the Rules Backward: Women and the Rural Cajun Mardi Gras" (Ph.D. dissertation, University of Pennsylvania), 138. Although Ware's essay cites earlier festival scholarship that characterizes carnival as primarily an agon between order and disorder, her own perspective, like mine, minimizes the opposition. Ware contends that the Cajun women's Mardi Gras of Tee Mamou and Basile do not "deny the normative order. . . . Although chaos is often foregrounded, the female Mardi Gras' clowning includes a range of behaviors encompassing both disorder and order, both conformity and nonconformity to cultural expectations . . . [that] coexist within the women's performance." Ware, "'I Read the Rules Backward': Women, Symbolic Inversion and the Cajun Mardi Gras Run," *Southern Folklore*, 52 (1995): 137-60.

[4] Oster and Reed, "Country Mardi Gras."

[5] I consider the following list representative of the works on Cajun Mardi Gras that have imparted substantial information about the festival, but which have limited themselves to ancient or modern interpretations, or to a combination of the two: Wendy Adair, "Mardi Gras in the Country," *Houston Chronicle, Texas Magazine,* February 13, 1983, 1, 9-10; Barry Jean Ancelet, "Courir du Mardi Gras," *Louisiane,* 54 (1982): 193-208; Ancelet, *"Capitaine, voyage ton flag": The Traditional Cajun Country Mardi Gras* (Lafayette, La., 1989); Ancelet, "Mardi Gras and the Media: Who's Fooling Whom?" *Southern Folklore,* 46 (1989): 211-19; Ancelet, Jay Edwards, and Glen Pitre, *Cajun Country* (Jackson, Miss., 1991); Ancelet and Elemore Morgan, Jr., *Cajun Country Mardi Gras.* Booklet and slide presentation (Lafayette, La., 1979); Philip Gould and Nicholas Spitzer, *Louisiana: A Land Apart* (Lafayette, La., 1985); Carl Lindahl, "Unraveling the Mysteries of Cajun Mardi Gras," *Houston Metropolitan* (1992): 23-26; Lindahl, "Bakhtin's Carnival Laughter and the Cajun Country Mardi Gras," *Folklore,* 107 (1996): 49-62; Pat Mire, "Dance for a Chicken," *Cultural Vistas: Louisiana Endowment for the Humanities,* 32 (1992): 16-19, 37-43; Harry Oster, "Country Mardi Gras," in *Buying the Wind: Region Folklore in the United States,* ed. Richard Dorson (Chicago, 1964), 274-81; Oster and Reed "Country Mardi Gras"; Lauren C. Post, "Country Mardi Gras," in *Cajun Sketches from the Prairies of Southwest Louisiana* (Baton Rouge, 1974), 163-68; Nicholas Spitzer, "Zydeco and Mardi Gras: Creole Identity and Performance Genres in Rural French Louisiana" (Ph.D. dissertation, University of Texas, 1986).

[6] Susan G. Davis, *Parades and Power: Street Theatre in Nineteenth-Century Philadelphia* (Philadelphia, 1986); Samuel Kinser, *Carnival, American Style: Mardi Gras at New Orleans and Mobile* (Chicago, 1990); Roger D. Abrahams, *Singing the Master: The Emergence of African-American Culture in the Plantation South* (New York, 1992).

[7] Henry Glassie, *All Silver and No Brass: An Irish Christmas Mumming* (Bloomington, Ind., 1975), 57.

[8] Pat Mire, *Dance for a Chicken: The Cajun Mardi Gras,* Color VHS, 57 min. (Eunice, La., 1993); Spitzer, "Zydeco and Mardi Gras"; Ware, "Reading the Rules Backward"; Ware, "I Read the Rules Backward."

[9] Folklorists are not unique in ignoring the emic effects of verbalized memory. Although there have been many recent and exciting attempts to add historical dimension to anthropological studies, the role of narrative in mirroring and informing actions and in adapting to and creating change has not been examined. See, for example, the many essays in Emiko Ohnuki-Tierney, *Culture through Time: Anthropological Approaches* (Stanford, 1990) as well as the work of James Fentress and Chris Wickham, *Social Memory* (Oxford and Cambridge, Mass., 1992); William Roseberry, *Anthropologies and Histories: Essays in Culture, History, and Political Economy* (New Brunswick, N. J., 1989); and David C. Rubin, *Memory in Oral Traditions: The Cognitive Psychology of Epic, Ballads, and Counting-out Rhymes* (New York, 1995), For further discussion of these points, see Lindahl, "Three Mardi Gras in *Dance for a Chicken.*" Unpublished essay based on a paper delivered at the annual meeting of the American Folklore Society, Eugene, Oregon, 1993; and Lindahl,

Review essay of *Carnival, American Style: Mardi Gras at New Orleans and Mobile* and *Rabelais's Carnival: Text, Context, Metatext,* by Samuel Kinser, *Journal of American Folklore,* 108 (1995): 102-5.

[10] Kinser, *Carnival, American Style.*

[11] For example, "In Louisiana: A Mad, Mad Mardi Gras," *Time* (March 4, 1985): 14.

[12] Barry J. Ancelet and Carl Lindahl, Observations on some twenty Mardi Gras enactments in which we participated and some sixty which we observed in Mamou, Church Point, Ossun, Basile, Elton, Evangeline, Grand Marais, Lacassine, Le Bleu Settlement, Oberlin, Soilou, Tee Mamou, Topsy, and Ville Platte, among other locales. See also Mire, *Dance for a Chicken: The Cajun Marti Gras.*

[13] In Basile, as in most present-day Cajun Mardi Gras communities, the Mardi Gras adopts the fiction that the chickens caught that day will be added to the gumbo. The chickens captured that day will indeed eventually end up in a gumbo that will feed the people of Basile. However, all the chickens actually served on Mardi Gras day are purchased in advance with money raised by Mardi Gras beggars.

[14] This construction of the form and functions of Mardi Gras was gathered not only from the older people of Basile but also from former and current Mardi Gras in the surrounding area, particularly people from Church Point, Eunice, Mamou, and Ossun. My brief description is largely modeled on a lengthier piece: Carl Lindahl, "Bakhtin's Carnival Laughter and the Cajun Country Mardi Gras," *Folklore,* 107:49-62.

[15] Spitzer, "Zydeco and Mardi Gras," 455.

[16] Helena Putnam and Barry Jean Ancelet, "Chanson de Mardi Gras (Basile)." Transcription and translation of the traditional song in "Cajun Country Mardi Gras: Variety within a Culture." Program for a performance presented at the Liberty Theater, Eunice, La., February 18, 1996. Eunice, Liberty Cultural Association.

[17] Several communities' traditional Mardi Gras songs contain the phrase, "Les Mardi Gras devient de tout partout; Mais tout à l'entour du moyeu" ("The Mardi Gras comes from all around; all around the hub.). Oster, "Country Mardi Gras," 279. The Basile Mardi Gras sings, "Tout le tour du moyeu" ('All around the hub.). Putnam and Ancelet, "Chanson de Mardi Gras." Many interpretations see the "hub" as the center of the community from which the Mardi Gras leaves that morning, and which it circles in the progress of the day. Many leaders, however, interpret the "hub" simply as the hub of a wagon wheel, and they do not see the phrase as symbolic of the communal center of their circular route.

[18] Fernand Braudel, *The Structures of Everyday Life.* Vol. 1 of *Civilization and Capitalism,* trans. Sian Reynolds (New York, 1981), 74.

[19] Ware, "Reading the Rules Backward," and "I Read the Rules Backward."

PART VI

JUSTICE AND INJUSTICE IN THE LOUISIANA EXPERIENCE

TWO UTOPIAN SOCIALIST PLANS FOR EMANCIPATION IN ANTEBELLUM LOUISIANA*

Carl J. Guarneri

In August 1847, in a long letter to a fellow disciple of the French utopian Charles Fourier, Osborne Macdaniel unveiled a plan for gradual emancipation which had been drawn up after an extended visit to Louisiana and approved by Albert Brisbane, the leading American Fourierist. One month later another emancipation proposal appeared in *The Harbinger*, the utopian socialists' official paper; it was suggested by Marx E. Lazarus in response to a Louisiana planter's inquiry as to how he might apply Fourierist "science" to his plantation.[1] Though neither became the basis of an actual experiment, these plans—by far the most detailed proposals to emerge from the Fourierist movement—are fascinating additions to the brief catalogue of attempts to apply cooperative principles to the problem of emancipation before the Civil War.[2] The story of their origin reveals an intriguing collaboration between national utopian-socialist leaders and an important but little-known circle of Louisiana reformers who dared to adopt one of the most dreaded of Northern "isms." At the same time, as the products of Southern-born utopians, these plans reflect, at least in part, the relatively conservative attitudes which Carl Degler found prevalent among antislavery dissenters of "the other South."[3] Most importantly, Macdaniel's and Lazarus's proposals present the most concrete opportunity available to assess the nature and limitations of the utopian-socialist approach to slavery. By examining these blueprints and their outcome, we can test the Fourierists' claim that their strategy of peaceful social reconstruction was an enlightened and workable alternative to the more aggressive antislavery tactics of moral suasion and political coercion.

According to Charles Fourier's sweeping indictment of human history, slavery was only one of many "servitudes" inflicted upon humanity by corrupt and immoral social arrangements. Deriving from the age of "Barbarism," human bondage had been succeeded

---

*First printed in *Louisiana History*, 24 (1983): 5-24. Reprinted with the kind permission of the author and the Louisiana Historical Association.

by the more sophisticated exploitation of "Civilization," Fourier's pejorative term for the nineteenth-century environment of selfish competition and isolated enterprise. In the world of Civilization employers hired laborers for subsistence wages, doctors and lawyers profited from others' woes, and husbands exercised financial and sexual tyranny over wives—practices less obviously coercive than slavery but no less unjust. What was needed was a total reconstruction of society, "civilized" as well as "barbarous," according to the dictates of justice and brotherly love. Fourier proposed that model communities called "phalanxes" gather 1,600 persons of all types and classes into cooperative harmony. Inside these phalanxes, joint-stock ownership, communal living, and an equitable distribution of profits would remove the evils of competition while also guaranteeing personal freedom and property rights. Once a few exemplary phalanxes prospered, those currently caught in the dehumanizing relations of slavery or competitive capitalism would gladly join the peaceful transition to the era of "Association."[4]

Preaching this program in the early 1840s, Fourierists like Macdaniel, Brisbane, Lazarus, and Horace Greeley convinced thousands of reform-minded Northerners to join nearly three dozen miniature phalanxes outside major Northern cities, to gather together in twenty-five local Fourierist clubs called "unions," or to subscribe to *The Harbinger*, which the "American Union of Associationists" published weekly from its New York headquarters. It was a remarkable achievement for men who had first heard of Fourier only a few years before.[5] By 1847, however, the Fourierist movement was in trouble. All but three of the phalanxes had disbanded, most the victims of internal discord or inefficient production. Many of the Fourierist "unions" were languishing, and the editors of *The Harbinger* were issuing desperate appeals to keep the paper alive. If these problems were not enough, the antislavery agitation, which Fourierist leaders had successfully kept at bay, was threatening to carry off many of the most active and vocal socialists.

The initial Fourierist response to abolitionism had been cool. Abolitionists were being hypocritical, utopians charged, when they attacked distant evils and ignored local ones. As Charles Dana remarked, "it does not become those who daily live by civilized slavery, who have it in their kitchens, their work-shops, and their manufactories [*sic*], to use loud words of denunciation against those who live by barbarous slavery, which is only the elder sister of the same monstrous family." Horace Greeley explained to antislaveryites that he was "less troubled concerning the Slavery prevalent in Charleston or New Orleans . . . because I see so much Slavery in New York," and urged abolitionists to "be at least as ardent in opposing the near as the distant forms of Oppression." Not only would the abolitionists' "partial" reform leave the ills of "Civilization" intact, but their aggressive tactics would inflame slaveholders to secession and bring on civil war. General social reconstruction along Fourier's guidelines promised a more peaceful and thorough remedy.[6]

But when war broke out with Mexico in 1846 and raised the spectre of territorial slavery, many Fourierists were drawn toward antislavery activism. At public meetings in

Massachusetts and Rhode Island, William Henry Channing and other New England Fourierists joined with abolitionists in condemning the Mexican War and even repudiating the Constitution. When, under Channing's influence, the Boston Associationists adopted a resolution pledging resistance to the war, the national socialist headquarters publicly disclaimed it as personal opinion rather than Fourierist doctrine.[7] While Fourierists from the Midatlantic and Midwestern states tended to deplore abolitionist "extremism" they were themselves attracted to the free-soil movement. Had not Fourier listed land monopoly as one of the vicious tendencies of Civilization? And if the slave system were adopted in the new territories, what would become of Associationist hopes for the West? As the territorial controversy grew more intense, Greeley, Parke Godwin, H. H. Van Amringe, and other important utopians began to shift their energies to political antislavery. Whether by the defection of the Free Soilers or the more disruptive tactics of the abolitionist, Fourierism was losing prominent and badly needed advocates.

It was against this background that Macdaniel and Lazarus attempted to apply Fourier's constructive and "scientific" reform directly to emancipation. As faithful utopians they continued to believe that cooperative principles could end slavery peacefully, and as reformers from the upper South their natural preference for sectional conciliation reinforced this faith. Macdaniel, who was raised in Georgetown, D. C., had moved to New York around 1840, where he co-edited *The Phalanx* with Albert Brisbane while his mother and two sisters lived at the Brook Farm Phalanx outside Boston.[8] With his experience in the land of slavery he had quickly become the movement's "expert" on the issue. His early articles were cautious, warning that abolitionism was a "dangerous" reform, recommending Fourierism as a means of emancipating the slaves "in a peaceful and satisfactory manner to all parties," yet carefully avoiding any specific plan.[9] But when the Mexican War fueled antislavery passions Macdaniel acted more decisively. First, in a public letter he contended that despite the war's apparent "knavery" it represented, in the long run, the triumph of civilized over barbarous nations and hence a step toward socialism; he advised Fourierists to remain silent while history ran its course.[10] Second, and more positively, Macdaniel personally decided to work out a practical proposal that would solve the vexing problem of slavery once and for all—and in the process give a boost to the sagging Fourierist movement. To develop it he journeyed to Louisiana in April 1847.

Why Louisiana? Of all the slave states Macdaniel chose Louisiana because there he could draw upon a remarkable, indeed unique, connection between Northern Fourierists and a group of Southern sympathizers. John D. Wilkins, whose sugar plantation Macdaniel visited, was an elderly Virginian settled in St. Mary Parish, the owner of over seventy slaves, and an eccentric philanthropist who had contributed thousands of dollars to the Associationist movement. For two years Wilkins's money had sent *The Phalanx* and *The Harbinger* to every college in the country, as well as Fourierist lecturers to cities and towns in the Northeast. At one point Wilkins even had to be talked out of mortgaging his plantation for the cause.[11] Robert Wilson, whose weekly *Planters' Banner* of Franklin reported Macdaniel's doings in Louisiana, endorsed Fourierism in his paper as early as 1844, corresponded with and sent gifts to the New York headquarters, and once expressed interest in joining a Fourierist phalanx in Ohio.[12] There were others in the sugar growing region sympathetic to Fourierism—Thomas May of St. John the Baptist Parish pledged over a thousand dollars to the movement, while another planter sent his son to the school at Brook Farm.[13] In addition, a circle of important Fourierists in New Orleans included Thomas J. Durant, then a federal attorney and later Louisiana's attorney general during wartime Reconstruction, and T. Wharton Collens, an attorney and city judge active after the Civil War as a Christian Socialist author.[14] It was Durant, Macdaniel's contact in New Orleans, who organized the Louisiana group and channeled their money and suggestions to the national Fourierist leaders.

Quite naturally these Southern socialists, well aware of their isolation in an area Durant called "peculiarly unsusceptible to the influences of associative doctrines," kept a low profile. They corresponded and gathered privately, concentrating on collecting weekly contributions for the New York headquarters.[15] While Durant and Wilkins expressed the hope that Fourierist lectures could come to Louisiana they had no illusions about leading a full-fledged utopian movement there. It was probably with their advice that Macdaniel gave only one lecture on Association in Louisiana—in Franklin on May 8—and that it elaborated Fourier's abstruse theory of human nature, apparently never even mentioning the phalanx.[16]

For his part, Macdaniel came not to bring more local converts to Fourierism but rather to assess, with the help of Louisiana colleagues, the prospects for a model experiment in the region he had heard so much about from Wilson and the *Planters' Banner*. We know that he was in New Orleans in the first half of April and returned on June 4; in the interim, by his own account, he "ranged all over the country . . . and in all sorts of localities, on foot and horseback," consulting with Wilson, Wilkins and other residents and scrupulously recording his observations.[17] What he found pleased him immensely. Southern Louisiana blacks were indeed degraded by slavery, but with cultivation they could become "intelligent and noble being[s]." The experiment of John McDonogh, the stern but philanthropic local planter who gave his slaves a chance to earn their freedom by working extra hours for wages, proved that the promise of emancipation would be a great stimulant to hard work and self-improvement.[18]

Most promising of all was the land itself. Macdaniel, as his letters reveal, was overwhelmed by the Attakapas region of southwestern Louisiana, it was "the garden spot of the U. S.," a sort of tropical paradise where fruits and vegetables were "lavishly abundant" and where they grew to enormous sizes "almost spontaneously."[19] "There is not a foot of poor land," he told the Ohio Fourierist E. P. Grant, and the soil is "inexhaustible." Fresh and salt water fish "of the most delicious kind" were easily caught in the bays and bayous, while the cool Gulf breeze assured "a delightful climate the year round" and helped to prevent tropical diseases. There was also easy access to markets:

"Steam Boats penetrate in every direction, visiting the doors of almost every planter; and sea vessels come up to many places, allowing of direct shipment to New York and other eastern cities, or even Europe itself." The only problem Macdaniel found was the mosquitos, but these, he told his correspondent in his one deliberate fantasy, were "rascals [who] belong to civilization and other subversive societies as emblems of *lawyers* and other kinds of social suckers, and as soon as we get a Phalanstery erected they will not dare to show their *Bills* any more than their prototypes." In short, there was "not a spot in the Union, and perhaps none out of it, so admirably prepared and adopted by nature for a practical trial of Association" as the Attakapas region. He had even selected "the grandest site" ten or fifteen miles from Vermilion Bay, and was urging its owner to sell. All this breathless hyperbole culminated in an attempt to prove that Southwest Louisiana, being "nearly central in its location with reference to the Domain of the U. S. (present and prospective)," was a "pivotal" district—a term pregnant with meaning in Fourierist science—and would doubtless contain the future "great Capital of this continent and sub-pivot of the world."

With such boundless optimism Macdaniel returned to the North to deliberate with Albert Brisbane at the latter's family homestead in Batavia, New York. Brisbane, meanwhile, had written to Thomas Durant for advice on the slavery issue: "Should we or should we not attack slavery openly and strongly as one of the giant evils of Civilization," he asked the New Orleanian, "or had we better try and conciliate the South?" Durant's response—that Fourierists should rely upon reason rather than emotion and should present cooperative Association as a plausible substitute for the plantation—must have confirmed Brisbane and Macdaniel's faith in the idea of a model experiment.[20] After a few days' discussion Macdaniel drew up a plan which Brisbane approved, and was ready to introduce it to trusted Fourierist colleagues.

At the outset Macdaniel stipulated four conditions his plan would meet:

1. Satisfy the property claim of the Master, by paying him the value set upon the slave.
2. Secure the prosecution of Industry without interruption.
3. Educate the Negro and prepare him for self-government.
4. Provide for the continued welfare of the Negroes after they are liberated.[21]

The mechanism to achieve these goals was a kind of Fourierist colony where blacks would work their way to freedom. The colony's founders, Macdaniel and other Fourierists, would procure slaves on the understanding that the owners would be paid the slaves' market price from the products of their labor. Macdaniel was confident that philanthropic slaveholders, possibly from Louisiana but more probably from Virginia and Kentucky, would "gladly get rid of their negroes, and . . . put them in the way of freedom if they could do so without pecuniary loss." In the process of constructing the colony's buildings, tilling its fields, and manning its workshops, the blacks would be earning their own freedom. Once this inducement replaced the coercion of slavery, wrote Macdaniel, "the most wonderful results" would ensure. The slaves would not only become more efficient laborers, but would grasp at all new opportunities for self-improvement, while the domain itself would be transformed rapidly into a productive phalanx. When specifically Fourierist institutions like the "serial" organization of work in rival teams and periodic community festivals were added, the colony would exhibit all the benefits of what Fourier called "attractive labor."

Thus far Macdaniel's proposal was essentially a Fourierist variation on the theme common to other emancipation plans aired in the antebellum era that slaves "earn" their own freedom.[22] But Macdaniel introduced a novel feature: as they worked for their freedom the blacks would be providing the labor to build up a model Fourierist phalanx for whites to inhabit and enjoy thereafter. Macdaniel's goal was not simply to emancipate slaves but to "establish Association with the Whites, and [thereby] . . . lead the way to Universal Association." Indeed, he left no doubt as to which aim was more important:

> The abolition of slavery is a great thing, but for itself alone, disconnected with general progress, I am not much concerned. I propose to avail myself of the slaves as agents to accomplish higher purposes than effecting their freedom only, which is incidental, and furnishes the opportunity I desire . . . for a successful practical trial of Association.

The word "successful" is a key term here, for Macdaniel, like Albert Brisbane, was appalled by the tiny, "unscientific" Fourierist communities struggling to stay alive in the North, and desperately sought a prosperous model phalanx which would display Fourier's principles in their best light. To create it Brisbane had been proposing that Fourierists accumulate as much as $500,000 and hire laborers to prepare the domain before the inhabitants moved in.[23] Macdaniel believed he could accomplish the same end without having to pay for labor—by using borrowed slaves. As the phalanx neared completion whites would gradually be substituted for the blacks, and the slaves would be moved to build up another site. The process would be continued indefinitely as fresh slaves replaced those earning their freedom and more whites were attracted to the new communities. Thus, "gradually the whole southern country may pass into Association through the intervention of the negroes."

What would become of the freed slaves? After the colony had educated blacks and fit them for "an independent career," Macdaniel thought they probably would be colonized somewhere outside the United States. On the other hand, he wrote, "it may possibly be advisable to retain the Negroes in this country for ages to come, as subordinate to the whites, though not as slaves, for their own good in the career of improvement and training, and as powerful agents to conquer the vast tracts of country which need reclaiming from the swamp and wilderness." Even if we leave aside the self-serving racial paternalism expressed here, the absence of specific provisions for the freedmen meant that

Macdaniel failed to satisfy one of his own stated conditions for a sound emancipation plan.

Apart from this omission the whole plan was an ingenious and plausible way to slay the twin monsters of slavery and capitalism with the same stroke—given Macdaniel's racial and ideological assumptions. Before analyzing these crucial assumptions, however, let us turn to Lazarus's emancipation plan, which shared several important features with Macdaniel's.

The rebellious offspring of a wealthy, slaveholding Jewish family in North Carolina, "Edgeworth" Lazarus passionately embraced several "isms" of the antebellum North. For much of the Fourierist vogue Lazarus lived at the North American Phalanx in New Jersey where he wrote a series of now-obscure treatises illustrating his peculiar blend of Fourierism, free love, and homeopathy.[24] Such enthusiasms distressed his ultra-respectable Carolina relatives, but in at least one attitude Lazarus remained true to this Southern roots: his opposition to antislavery agitation. Lazarus's writing frequently portrayed the abolitionists as arrogant fanatics leading the nation into civil war and killing any prospect for voluntary reform in the South; the duty of utopian socialists was to head off such extremism with more conciliatory overtures and practical suggestions for slaveholders.[25] Thus, when John Wilkins wrote to *The Harbinger* for advice on applying Fourierist "science" to his plantation, Lazarus saw his chance to propose an emancipation plan that would take the wind out of abolitionist sails.

The Louisiana planter inquired specifically about the yield of various types of corn and sugar cane, but Lazarus, after dabbling in some pseudo-scientific generalizations, felt compelled to go further. The best way to increase productivity, he wrote, would be to substitute "attractive" for coercive labor by introducing Fourierist arrangements on the plantation. As in a phalanx, music would send the workers out to the fields in the morning and greet them when they returned. The most productive would be honored with badges and titles, and on Saturday evenings great feasts would celebrate the week's devoted labor. Most importantly, individual slaves would rotate jobs every three or four hours wherever possible, each time joining a new work group competing with others in the same task; the gains in health, morale, and productivity would be immense.[26] Taken by themselves these changes could be the work of an enlightened despot intent upon maximizing profits and assuring a loyal work force. (The *Anti-Slavery Standard* once predicted that "slaveholders may resort to social re-organization for their own benefit," and in fact Jefferson Davis's older brother did just this on his plantation at Davis Bend.[27]) But Lazarus intended them to be implemented simultaneously with his emancipation plan.

According to this plan, a planter's slaves could work extra hours for wages, using the money to "buy" more time and eventually their freedom. Frankly borrowing his formula from John McDonogh's experiment, Lazarus proposed that when a slave had worked enough to pay off one twelfth of his market price, he was free for a half day, and so on until he earned full freedom. Purchasing free time would become easier and easier because "the opportunity of gaining money increases in the same proportion as the sum remaining to be paid diminishes." If the requirement to work off the entire cost sounded harsh, the slaveowner's property right had to be respected. Moreover, "the process by which they will have gained their freedom," Lazarus explained, "will be a guarantee to themselves and to society of their energy, fitness for freedom, and ability to sustain themselves in the social medium."[28] Thus Lazarus, like Macdaniel, viewed emancipation as a way of inculcating attitudes and habits that would prepare slaves for the competitive work of Civilization.

Unlike Macdaniel, however, Lazarus believed that the freedmen's future lay in the United States. The motives of colonizationists were humane but their scheme was impossible to carry out. Instead, Lazarus hoped most freedmen would remain in the South as laborers, but with "ties of good will and reciprocal service" somehow replacing coercive relations with their masters. Also unlike Macdaniel, Lazarus did not envision his model farms as the building blocks of full Association. Plantations adopting his plan would not become phalanxes, nor would their black slaves be replaced by white socialists. Though a partial demonstration of Fourierist principles would benefit the cause if successful, emancipationist leaders were not required to be card-carrying socialists. Indeed, Lazarus suggested that the abolitionists themselves, instead of protesting self-righteously against slavery, invest their funds in purchasing slaves and adopting his system, thus setting an example of peaceful emancipation for Southerners to follow.[29]

While Macdaniel's and Lazarus's plans differed in some details, and while both were drawn up independently of the official Fourierist movement, their key provisions clearly reflected the utopian socialist approach to slavery. First and most basic of their assumptions was the idea that slavery was not at bottom an issue of elementary freedom being denied or a system of racial domination, but a question of labor being controlled or appropriated. As has been seen, from the socialist standpoint slavery, like many contemporary evils, traced its origins to a corrupt social environment where all labor was based on coercion and competition, and where few workers received a fair return. If the South had its chattel slavery, and an increasing number of Northern workers were experiencing the "wage slavery" of competitive Civilization, "free" only to compete for wages approaching subsistence and lacking "guarantees" in case of unemployment, sickness and old age. The difference between sectional "servitudes of labor" was one of degree rather than kind; both would have to be eliminated for the nineteenth century ever to witness full Association.[30]

The implications of this analysis were clear to utopians. First, since slavery was primarily a labor system it had to be addressed in economic terms. Appeals to slaveholders' consciences would have little effect, while on the other hand attempts to abolish it through legislation could be blocked by powerful interests. The best way to put slavery on the road to extinction was to out compete it: to establish alternative work arrangements which were at once more equitable and more efficient.[31] When Macdaniel and Lazarus proposed to make labor truly "attractive" and to return its fruits to the slaves as increments of freedom, they meant to build this kind of alternative. While doing full justice to the slaves, the combined incentives of freedom and cooperation would at the same time increase the colonies' productivity far beyond that of even superior plantations. Second, since the ultimate goal was the abolition of all servitudes, those of competitive capitalism as well as slavery, an emancipation plan should point the way to total social reconstruction. Macdaniel's colonies were expressly designed as engines of utopian reform, cleverly (and coldly) using the slaves to build model phalanxes through which the "feudal" South could leap directly to socialism without passing through a capitalist phase. Lazarus was less explicit about his ultimate aim, but in planning a peaceful end to slavery and silencing the abolitionists he was clearly trying to remove major obstacles to utopian socialism both North and South.

One particularly positive result of this insistence upon the evils of both contemporary labor systems was the emphasis Fourierists put upon preparing slaves for the harsh freedom of "Civilization." Prior to the Civil War, abolitionists tended either to reject as obstructionist the question of what happens to the slaves when freed, or to gloss it over with paeans to self-help and the tradition Protestant virtues. But Fourierists pointed out that immediate emancipation would leave the slaves adrift with few skills and no education, ripe to become dependent "hirelings of Capital."[32] Thus, Macdaniel and Lazarus designed their plans to instill the industriousness and frugality the slaves needed to survive in the outside world. Yet they also went beyond simply adjusting the slaves to competitive capitalism. In their colonies the slaves would be acquainted with Fourierist mechanisms, such as the "serial" organization of work in teams, task rotation, and mutual insurance, which might lay the groundwork for future cooperative efforts.

A second Fourierist principle governing these plans was voluntarism, or, as Fourierists called it, "attraction." Like Fourier's own method of replacing Civilization with Association's phalanxes, Macdaniel's and Lazarus's proposals are peaceful and gradual, resting upon the power of example rather than the coercion of politics. Both recognized the planters' property rights and took care not to disrupt farm and workshop production. Instead, change was to come through "attraction" as slaveowners realized that they had nothing to lose through emancipation and perhaps much to gain. As Thomas Durant advised Brisbane:

> Slaveholders do not hold slaves for the mere love of the system itself, but because they have not or they are not yet convinced that they have a better mode of making labor effective. Convince them that there is another and better mode, and you may be sure that they will adopt it.[33]

In Macdaniel's plan, owners were promised fair market value for their slaves, plus the chance to enjoy full Association in the future. Lazarus went further, guaranteeing huge profits for owners if they channelled enough slaves through his system or combined resources with other planters on one large joint-stock domain. "When you have convinced the interest of the slaveholder," he wrote in a passage the shrewd Fourier would have approved, "you will have convinced his conscience, too, and when he sees you thrive, [he] will not be long in following your example."[34]

This pragmatic appeal to slaveholder self-interest suited the cautious path which Southern-born antislaveryites like Macdaniel and Lazarus, caught as they were between their criticism of slavery and their distrust of the mounting Northern crusade against it, tended to follow. In fact, when taken along with Fourier's prescription for peaceful, gradual emancipation it suggests a striking convergence between utopian socialism and the kind of conservative opposition to slavery that animated the small minority of Southerners who voiced their dissent in the antebellum years. While men like Daniel Goodloe, Robert Breckinridge, or even John McDonogh hardly shared the Fourierist dream of transforming planters' mansions into phalansteries, they would have approved the utopians' gradualist strategy, their economic "realism," and their hostility to Garrisonian impatience.[35]

A third feature of Macdaniel and Lazarus's proposals also reflects this conservative pattern: their not-so-subtle indifference, despite professed emancipationist intentions, to the brutal oppression of slavery and to the human needs of the slaves themselves. Macdaniel's plan to "avail" himself of slaves to build communities for whites frankly viewed emancipation as a secondary aim about which he was "not much concerned." Just as explicitly, Lazarus's "mechanisms" to increase productivity treated slaves as passive objects to be manipulated by enlightened overseers. Neither utopian devoted space to condemning slavery on purely moral grounds, nor did they offer a detailed post-emancipation scenario to ensure that ex-slaves would not be exploited as much as their predecessors had been.

How much of this insensitivity can be attributed to Fourierism? To neglect post-emancipation arrangements was to violate Fourierist principles rather than express them, and the entire Fourierist endeavor was premised on the immorality of involuntary "servitudes." Still, it can be argued that utopian socialism did encourage a certain tolerance of slavery in these men. When Macdaniel and Lazarus contended that the "wage slavery" of the North was comparable to the South's chattel slavery they were, after all, using a standard Fourierist argument. And when the two proposed to replace slavery with colonies where slaves would be manipulated through utopian social engineering, they were only following Fourier's environmentalist assumptions. By concentrating upon reconstructing the "Civilization" of the North and by considering slavery a derivative, secondary social evil Fourierism did little to encourage sympathy for the slave among its adherents and may sometimes, as the abolitionists charged, have palliated the evils of human bondage.[36]

Nevertheless, Macdaniel and Lazarus went far beyond Fourierist policy by basing their attitudes toward blacks on the ground of racial superiority rather than the fact of slavery itself. Like most white Americans of the mid-nineteenth century—Northern or Southern—Macdaniel and Lazarus believed that blacks were inherently inferior beings destined to occupy a separate, subordinate position in society, and their plans were obviously riddled with such prejudice. Not only did Macdaniel foresee deporting blacks after freedom, but in his emancipation colonies the slaves would merely serve as the tools of white socialists' ambitions, constructing Fourierist utopias for Southern whites—perhaps their former masters!—to enjoy thereafter. Blacks were particularly suited for this undertaking, he explained, because they are "children; . . . grown infants with the muscular power of men . . . [whom] we can lead and wield . . . as we choose." Macdaniel at least saw the potential for "a high degree of elevation" among the free blacks; to Lazarus blacks were fundamentally sensual, sentimental beings whose intellectual capacities were extremely limited. He advised planters who adopted his plan not to teach slaves to read and write, for it would tax their brains unnecessarily. At one point he recommended that Fourierist reforms could make slavery more palatable to blacks and thus render his emancipation plan even more gradual. And while Lazarus rejected colonization he evidently believed that the Negro race was doomed to extinction in the New World.[37] These racial attitudes were in no sense derived from Fourierism, but they demonstrate how easily race prejudice could influence opponents of slavery, especially those furthering the interests of free labor, whether Northern Free Soilers, Southern dissenters like Hinton Helper, or utopian socialists like Macdaniel and Lazarus.[38]

An increasing number of Northern Fourierists, however, believed that expressing such attitudes or downplaying the horror of slavery tainted the socialist cause and merely gave comfort to slaveowners. The editors of *The Harbinger*, while not commenting upon Lazarus's emancipation plan, were careful to disclaim responsibility for his views of slavery and blacks, which expressed "the point of view prevailing at the South."[39] The hostile reaction to Macdaniel's Louisiana mission gave a far more direct indication of antislavery gains among the Fourierists. First, while Macdaniel was in Louisiana William Henry Channing introduced a motion at the Fourierists' national convention which would require the movement to refuse any funds connected with slavery. Aimed directly at Wilkins and the Louisiana planters, the motion was defeated only after a "very animated discussion" during which Brisbane and Lazarus defended a socialist alliance with slaveholders.[40] Then when reports reached the North that Macdaniel, in introductory remarks to his Franklin lecture, had criticized the abolitionists as "rash" and informed planters that the North's "white slavery" was in some respects worse than black bondage, a storm of protests erupted. Angry letters from antislavery Associationists poured into *The Harbinger* office, claiming that Macdaniel had misrepresented the Fourierist position and that his remarks would serve to "quiet the conscience of the slaveholders . . . and . . . confirm their prejudices against the Abolitionists." Macdaniel replied that his statements were "in accordance with the doctrines of our School," but his critics were not satisfied. According to these Fourierists the "wage slavery" argument was no longer viable because it carried the sinister implication that chattel slavery was actually *preferable* to free labor (an implication proslavery ideologues like George Fitzhugh would soon develop). Moreover, slave ownership was so monstrously unjust that the old socialist idea of compensated emancipation now seemed "absurd."[41] Gradually the controversy died down, but the episode demonstrated that the antislavery crusade had made powerful inroads among Northern utopians, just as Macdaniel and Lazarus had feared, and was helping to discredit the independent, conciliatory stance which Fourierism had advocated and these Southern-born utopians still stood for.

What then became of the two plans? Macdaniel's evidently won his correspondent's approval as well as Albert Brisbane's, but the three lacked the means to carry it out.[42] Macdaniel was counting upon his own investments to provide the initial $30,000 required; these apparently failed him. Without financial backing and with only a few Northern Fourierists willing to join him, Macdaniel never published his proposal, though it was "constantly" on his mind for the next three years.[43] In 1849 Lazarus's plan was publicly endorsed by a Northern Fourierist who had moved to Georgia. Perhaps encouraged by this, Lazarus reprinted it in articles and books published in the early 1850s, adding a few details and suggesting Attakapas, the Texas prairie, and upcountry Carolina as possible sites.[44] By then, however, the Fourierist movement was virtually defunct, abandoned in part because so many members had been absorbed by the sectional dispute over slavery. Northern utopians stirred by the uncompromising moralism of the abolitionists now rejected gradual and compensated emancipation out of hand; others drawn to the militant defense of free soil and free labor against slavery concentrated upon containing the institution within the South rather than freeing its victims.

Southerners as well kept their distance from such plans. Macdaniel and Lazarus had hoped that the Fourierists' cautious, conservative strategy would attract liberal planters and other Southern opponents of slavery. But utopian socialism, however, diluted by gradualism, was too advanced a reform for fledgling liberals to swallow. In their fondest dreams most Southern dissenters envisioned nothing more than "the labor system of the South's . . . made over in the image of the North's," a capitalist not a cooperative utopia. As Macdaniel discovered in an exchange with Cassius M. Clay of Kentucky, it was one thing to oppose slavery in the name of the "dignity of labor"; it was quite another to endorse Fourierism for the same reason.[45]

Yet the characteristic Southern aversion to radicalism only partly explains the silence that met these proposals, for even the Fourierists' best friends in the South apparently were unwilling to follow Macdaniel and Lazarus's lead. While they gave advice to Macdaniel and they may have approved Lazarus's plan in principle, neither Durant, Wilkins, or any of the Louisiana Fourierists committed themselves to an emancipation project. In fact, when Wilkins announced plans in the early 1850s to form an "Agricultural and Industrial Association" in Texas he intended to people it with Northern emigrants rather than Southern slaves; his own slaves were left to his heirs.[46] There were intense political, economic, and social pressures upon slaveholders not to free their slaves, but the utopian socialists were simply not equipped to dispel these pressures or even to fully appreciate them. Macdaniel and Lazarus may have shown more sophistication than abolitionists when they argued that immediate emancipation would leave the unskilled and uneducated slaves totally dependent upon their former masters.

But they were far more naïve than abolitionists in understanding the nature of slavery and the slaveholder mentality. Partly because slavery was very profitable to men like John Wilkins and Thomas May, but also because it was a system of race control as well as a system of labor, appeals to philanthropy, the "attractions" of a Fourierist experiment, and promises of excellent compensation were not enough to induce planters to abandon it. Slaveowners found it nearly impossible to imagine a satisfactory way either to sustain production without slaves or to keep blacks under complete control as freedmen. Their course after 1847 demonstrated how deeply they and other Southern whites were attached to their peculiar institution, and by implication how inadequate "solutions" like Macdaniel's and Lazarus's had been.

Notes for "Two Utopian Socialist Plans for Emancipation in Antebellum Louisiana"

[1] Macdaniel to E. P. Grant, Batavia, New York, August 13, 1847, Elijah P. Grant Papers, Department of Special Collections, University of Chicago Library; *The Harbinger*, 5 (1847): 247-50.

[2] A survey of several such attempts, actual and projected, is William H. Pease and Jane H. Pease, *Black Utopias: Negro Communal Experiments in America* (Madison, Wis., 1963). Articles dealing specifically with Frances Wright's Owenite experiment at Nashoba include O. B. Emerson, "Frances Wright and Her Nashoba Experiment," *Tennessee Historical Quarterly*, 6 (1947): 291-314; and Helen Elliott, "Frances Wright's Experiment with Negro Emancipation," *Indiana Magazine of History*, 34 (1939): 141-57. For a Fourierist proposal similar to Macdaniel's and Lazarus's but less detailed, see Parke Godwin, "The Slavery Question," *The Pathfinder*, 10 (1843): 145-46.

[3] Carl N. Degler, *The Other South: Southern Dissenters in the Nineteenth Century* (New York, 1974).

[4] The best guide to Fourier's ideas is Nicholas V. Riasnovsky, *The Teaching of Charles Fourier* (Berkeley & Los Angeles, 1969). for the American adaptation of Fourierism, see, among many titles, Albert Brisbane's two treatises: *Social Destiny of Man* (Philadelphia, 1840); and *Association; or A Concise Exposition of the Practical Part of Fourier's Social Science* (New York, 1843). The Fourierist position on slavery was first outlined in Charles Dain, *De l'abolition de l'esclavage* (Paris, 1836); see especially Fourier, "Remède aux Divers Esclavages," reprinted on pp. 43-54.

[5] On the early diffusion of Fourierism, see Arthur E. Bestor, Jr., "Albert Brisbane—Propagandist for Socialism in the 1840s," *New York History*, 28 (1947): 128-58. For a list of the phalanxes see Bestor, "Checklist of Communitarian Experiments," in *Backwoods Utopias: The Sectarian Origins and the Owenite Phase of Communitarian Socialism, 163-1829*, 2nd ed. (Philadelphia, 1970), 280-82; for "unions" affiliated to the A. U. A. see *The Harbinger*, 7 (1848): 56.

[6] Dana, "Cassius M. Clay—Slavery," *The Harbinger*, 1 (1845): 205; Greeley, "Slavery at Home," *New York Tribune*, June 20, 1845; Brisbane, *Social Destiny*, 93-114.

[7] "Fourth of July at Dedham," *The Harbinger*, 3 (1846): 84-85; "Convention in Boston—Organization of The American Union of Associationists,'" *The Harbinger*, 2 (1846).

[8] Information on Macdaniel's background is scarce. Brook Farm records indicate that his sisters were born in Georgetown in 1815 and 1824, and Brook Farmers referred to his family as "Southern." See Constitutions and Minutes, Brook Farm Papers, Massachusetts Historical Society; and Marianne Dwight, *Letters from Brook Farm 1844-1847*, ed., Amy L. Reed (Poughkeepsie, 1928), 125-28, and passim. As early as June 1841 Macdaniel was a member of the "Fourier Association of the City of New York." See *The Future*, 1 (1841).

[9] Macdaniel (with Brisbane), "Dangers Which Threaten the Future," *The Phalanx*, 1 (1843): 17-19; Macdaniel, "The Daily Delta," *The Harbinger*, 1 (1845): 352.

[10] Ibid., 3 (1846): 17.

[11] *The Phalanx*, 1 (1844): 45, 80, 164; *The Harbinger*, 2 (1846): 300, 366; George Ripley, "Another Good Movement," *The Harbinger*, 4 (1847): 142. Thomas J. Durant to Wilkins, New Orleans, March 22, 1845, Thomas J. Durant Papers, New York Historical Society. For a memoir of Wilkins see A. Duperier, "A Narrative of Events Connected with the Early Settlement of New Iberia [1899]," reprinted in *Attakapas Gazette*, 7 (1972): 120.

[12] *The Harbinger*, 6 (1848): 85; E. P. Grant to Wilson, Canton, Ohio, March 28, 1844, Grant Papers. For Wilson's reports of Macdaniel's visit, see *Planters' Banner*, May 6, 13, 20, 1847.

[13] Thomas J. Durant to Albert Brisbane, New Orleans, March 24, 1847, Durant Papers; Georgiana Bruce Kirby, *Years of Experience: An Autobiographical Narrative* (New York, 1887), 178.

[14] On Durant, see Joseph G. Tregle, Jr., "Thomas J. Durant, Utopian Socialism, and the Failure of Presidential Reconstruction in Louisiana," *Journal of Southern History*, 45 (1979): 485-512, along with many letters in the Durant Papers, New York Historical Society, and the Albert Brisbane Papers, Illinois Historical Survey, University of Illinois, Urbana. For Collens's career see Robert C. Reinders, "T. Wharton Collens: Catholic and Christian Socialist," *Catholic Historical Review*, 52 (1966): 212-33; on his specifically Fourierist affiliation, see Collens, "The Era of Guarantism," *The Harbinger*, 7 (1848): 114. On general interest in Fourier in New Orleans, see "New Orleans," ibid., 2 (1846): 271.

[15] Durant to John D. Wilkins, New Orleans, April 1, 1847, Durant papers.

[16] "Lecture on Association," *Planters' Banner*, May 20, 1847.

[17] Macdaniel to E. P. Grant, August 13, 1847, Grant Papers.

[18] On McDonogh, see Degler, *The Other South*, 41-46, and the biographies cited therein.

[19] Macdaniel to E. P. Grant, Cleveland, July 8, 1847; and Batavia, New York, August 13, 1847, Grant Papers. The quotations that follow are from Macdaniel's letter of August 13.

[20] Durant to Brisbane, New Orleans, June 6, 1847, Durant Papers.

[21] This and the following quotations are from Macdaniel to E. P. Grant, August 13, 1847, Grant Papers.

[22] See for example, Frances Wright's Nashoba experiment (cited in note 2 above) and John McDonogh's system at McDonoghville (note 18 above).

[23] "Letter from Mr. Brisbane," *The Harbinger*, 4 (1847): 375-76.

[24] See Lazarus, *Comparative Psychology and Universal Analogy* (New York, 1851); *Homeopathy, A Theoretic Demonstration, with Social Applications* (New York, 1851); *Love vs. Marriage* (New York, 1852); *Passional Hygiene and Natural Medicine* (New York, 1852). Biographical information can be found in Clement Eaton, *The Freedom-of-Thought Struggle in the Old South*, rev. ed. (New York, 1964), 252, 340, 342, and in Lazarus's sketch of his own religious history in the Record book of the Religious Union of Associationist, Massachusetts Historical Society.

[25] See, for example, "Edgeworth," "Abolition of Slavery, By a Carolinian," *Spirit of the Age*, 1 (1849): 291-93; *Comparative Psychology and University Analogy*, 49.

[26] *The Harbinger*, 5 (1847): 248-49.

[27] "The Associationists and the Abolitionists," *National Anti-Slavery Standard* (October 14, 1847), 78; Janet Sharp Hermann, *Pursuit of a Dream* (New York, 1981), 3-34.

[28] *The Harbinger*, 5 (1847): 249-50.

[29] Ibid., 250.

[30] Brisbane, *Social Destiny*, 93-114.

[31] Lazarus called these alternative arrangements "counter institutions." See "Edgeworth," "Abolition of Slavery," 293.

[32] Albert Brisbane, "The Organization of Labor—No. III," *The Harbinger*, 3 (1846): 108, note. William and Jane Pease deplore "the almost total failure of the antislavery movement as a whole to provide any direct, organized, sustained, and practical assistance in training the Negro for freedom in white society." *Black Utopias*, 14. Abolitionist support of self-help and competitive capitalism is analyzed by Eric Foner, "Abolitionism and the Labor Movement in Ante-bellum America," in *Politics and Ideology in the Age of the Civil War* (New York, 1980), 57-76; Aileen S. Kraditor, *Means and Ends in American Abolitionism: Garrison and His Critics on Strategy and Tactics, 1834-1850* (New York, 1969), 244-55; and Jonathan A. Glickstein, "'Poverty Is Not Slavery': American Abolitionists and the Competitive Labor Market," in Lewis Perry and Michael Fellman, eds., *Antislavery Reconsidered: New Perspectives on the Abolitionists* (Baton Rouge, 1979), 195-218.

[33] Durant to Brisbane, New Orleans, June 6, 1847, Durant Papers.

[34] *The Harbinger*, 5 (1847): 250.

[35] See Degler, *The Other South*, 41-46, 49-53, 90-91.

[36] "Edgeworth," "Comparative Anatomy of Labor for Wages and Slavery," *Spirit of the Age*, 2 (1850): 91-92. Foner, "Abolitionists and the Labor Movement," 60-61, argues that labor reformers were more hostile to abolitionists than indifferent to the evil of chattel slavery, but he does acknowledge that they "tended to see . . . slavery as simply one example of more pervasive problems in American." (67)

[37] Macdaniel to E. P. Grant, August 13, 1847, Grant Papers; *The Harbinger*, 5 (1847): 248-49; Lazarus, *Passional Hygiene and Natural Medicine*, 436.

[38] Eugene Berwanger, *The Frontier Against Slavery* (Urbana, 1967); and Charles B. Going, *David Wilmot Free-Soiler* (New York, 1924), 174 document racism among Northern Free Soilers. For Helper, see Hugh C. Bailey, *Hinton Rowan Helper, Abolitionist-Racist* (University, Ala., 1965).

[39] *The Harbinger*, 5 (1847): 256.

[40] "Annual Meeting of the American Union of Associationists," *The Harbinger*, 4 (1847): 389.

[41] J. L. Clarke, "Mr. Macdaniel's Lecture," *The Harbinger*, 5 (1847): 19; "Our Policy—Slavery—Letter from Mr. Macdaniel," *The Harbinger*, 5 (1847): 82-83; "Slavery," *The Harbinger*, 5 (1847): 150-51. Macdaniel's speech was reported in *Planters' Banner*, May 20, 1847, and excerpted in "Lecture on Association," *The Harbinger*, 4 (1847): 407-8.

[42] F. L. Macdaniel to E. P. Grant, Boston, December 12, 1847, Grant Papers.

[43] Osborne Macdaniel to E. P. Grant, New York, July 26, 1848, Grant Papers. In 1850 Macdaniel intended to contribute "an essay on abolition by scientific means" to a proposed Fourierist monthly, but the magazine never appeared. See Albert Brisbane to John S. Dwight, New York, April 26 [1850], Brisbane Papers, Illinois Historical Survey.

[44] For the endorsement by "J." see "Abolition of Slavery. No. 2," *Boston Weekly Chronotype*, December 22, 1849. Lazarus reiterated his plan in "Abolition of Slavery, By a Carolinian. Number Two," *Spirit of the Age*, 1 (1849): 308-9; *Comparative Psychology and Universal Analogy*, 49; and *Passional Hygiene and Natural Medicine*, 369-70. In 1852 he projected a book entitled *Slavery: A Clear method of annulling its evils, and rendering the relations of the white and black races mutually beneficial*, but it was not published; see the announcement in *Passional Hygiene*, 439.

[45] Degler, *The Other South*, 96; Macdaniel, "Cassius M. Clay, His Notions of Association," *The Harbinger*, 1 (1845): 415-16; Macdaniel, "Cassius M. Clay and the Harbinger," *The Harbinger*, 2 (1846): 95.

[46] "Association at the South," *New York Tribune*, November 2, 1850.

KEEPING LAW AND ORDER IN NEW ORLEANS UNDER GENERAL BUTLER, 1862*

Joy J. Jackson

In the spring of 1862, the fabric of everyday life seemed to be coming apart in New Orleans. As a result of the war, the blockade, and martial law in the city, many could not even find or afford to buy the necessities of life. Unemployment was high, and spirits were low. During the first year of the Civil War, local troops, arms, and munitions had been sent to distant battlefields, leaving New Orleans with forces totally inadequate for its defense. Commercial stagnation and declining river trade had resulted from the Federal naval blockade which kept ships from entering the Mississippi River's passes. Cotton came into the city, but then waited in vain for ship passage out of port. A serious shortage of flour and meat was beginning to plague grocers, butchers, and housewives.[1]

Money to conduct business and pay household bills was also scarce. Banks had been encouraged by the Confederate government to send their specie out of the city and use Confederate paper money or bank notes instead. Small change was nowhere to be found. Streetcar and omnibus tickets took its place as a medium of exchange. Various businesses and banks also issued such paper "shinplasters," and counterfeiting of the most common ones became a local curse.[2]

The number of indigent poor also increased as the wives and children of men sent to fight in Virginia or Tennessee found that their income had fallen below what they needed to buy food or pay rent. A group of local merchants and professional men operated a Free Market to hand out donated foodstuffs to such families.[3] The ranks of the city's young men thinned markedly. Many either joined a Confederate regiment or were in the process of doing so. Older men, thick around the waistline, were in the militia. Even the city's large foreign population, which made up about 38 percent of the residents, organized military brigades to aid in keeping order if an attempt was made to attack the city.[4] The

---

*First published in *Louisiana History*, 34 (1993): 51-68. Reprinted with the kind permission of the Louisiana Historical Association.

possibility of this seemed remote to many who went on with their business, attended plays, operas, and the races if they could afford such entertainment, and even enjoyed a subdued Mardi Gras day on which masking was prohibited by order of Mayor John T. Monroe, who feared Union spies and subversives.[5]

Martial law was declared in mid-March. A curfew of 8 p.m. was placed on saloons and restaurants. This was difficult for the police to enforce, but violators appeared frequently on the police arrest logs.[6] As flour became scarce, bakers tried to sell smaller loaves for the same or higher prices. Special regulations were enacted into law by the city aldermen setting the size and price of bread. Like the curfew violators, a baker or two would be arrested by the police.[7] Both of these were entirely new types of lawbreakers for the police and the courts to handle.

In April an emotionally moving event for New Orleanians was Gen. Albert Sidney Johnston's funeral cortege marching slowly up St. Charles Avenue to the sound of muffled drums.[8] April was to be an especially cruel month for the blockaded city. Its defenses were breached on the lower river at the forts—Jackson and St. Philip, and their garrisons surrendered by April 29.

Two days later on the night of May 1, Gen. Benjamin F. Butler arrived in the city and took up temporary quarters the next day in the St. Charles Hotel. The riverfront was blackened with the debris of the cotton which had been burned there earlier in the week. The riots and looting of April 24, 25, and 26 had been contained by the Foreign Brigade and the French Brigade under Gen. Paul Juge, Jr. These foreign-born militia had been called out by the mayor to aid the police in trying to restore order.[9] But angry sullen crowds' had greeted Butler upon his arrival and gathered in front of the St. Charles Hotel on May 2 as he met with the mayor.[10] Two meetings took place between Butler and Mayor Monroe on that day.[11] At the second meeting, Butler explained that he would try to work with the city government allowing them to continue to control most municipal activities.[12] Butler had issued his first proclamation declaring martial law in the city the day before, May 1.[13] It had been printed in handbills and posted in public places.[14] There was little about its martial law directives that differed from martial law under Confederate rule with the big exception that now citizens would be prosecuted for seditious behavior against the United States government. The bitter taste of conquest which this document set before New Orleanians was hard to swallow—both for the city officials sitting in the St. Charles Hotel talking with Butler and the angry masses who discussed and cursed their situation in city streets, markets, on the levee, and in their homes.[15] By the next day, however, Butler's terms were accepted by the mayor.[16] An uneasy partnership in keeping law and order in the stricken city was thus formed between the United States Army and the city government. But this rapprochement was not to last. Butler also requested that the foreign brigades continue to patrol the city. General Juge refused this invitation.[17]

During the next two weeks there were innumerable incidents in which the scorn and contempt that local citizens felt for Union soldiers were exhibited. The soldiers and their officers had been told to resist the urge to answer back in word or action. One soldier standing in front of the Customhouse on May 7 was suddenly set upon by an indignant woman who dropped her market basket and began screaming and hitting him. The wife of a Confederate soldier, she had just come from the Free Market where its operators had informed the hungry line of applicants that the rioting and capture of the city had wiped out their supplies. There was no food to give away. Other women joined her attack. They chased the hapless soldier all the way to the levee.[18] To show their hostility, many New Orleans women wore Confederate flags on their bonnets or their bosoms, sang secession songs, and snubbed or sneered at Union soldiers in public places.[19] In response to these abuses, Butler issued his famous Woman Order No. 28 on May 15 ordering that when any female by word, gesture, or movement insulted or showed contempt for any officer or soldier of the United States, "she shall be regarded and held liable to be treated as a woman of the town plying her avocation."[20] The publication of this order marked the break between the mayor and General Butler. Within several days of its issuance, Mayor Monroe was arrested along with Chief of Police John McClelland and sent to Fort Jackson for neglect of duty, insubordination, and obstruction of Federal authorities.[21] Butler's action was taken because he felt Monroe was an intransigent rebel who had also collaborated with six paroled Confederate prisoners in their plan to violate parole and slip out of town.[22]

With the removal of the mayor and chief of police by May 21, General Butler appointed Gen. George F. Shepley as acting mayor. Shepley served as acting mayor until he was appointed military governor of Louisiana by President Abraham Lincoln in July 1862.[23] In addition to Shepley, four other military men were to serve as acting mayors of New Orleans during Butler's eight months' command of the Department of the Gulf. They were Lieut. Godfrey Weitzel, Acting Lieut. Col. Jonas H. French, Capt. Henry C. Deming, and Capt. J. F. Miller. The city's board of aldermen continued in office until late June when they too were replaced by two committees, the Bureau of Finance, and the Bureau of Streets and Landings. Their membership, chosen by the military establishment.were citizens with Union sympathies. By midsummer, the entire municipal government was under military control.[24]

Taking over on May 21 one of the most difficult jobs in the city, the post of chief of police, was Col. Jonas H. French who had earlier been named provost marshal on Butler's staff. In August 1862, French served briefly as acting mayor when Weitzel was called away to Baton Rouge. In October 1862, French was named provost marshal for Louisiana. He was to carry out both jobs of provost marshal and chief of police throughout Butler's command in New Orleans and until May 1863 under Gen. Nathaniel P. Banks.[25]

A native of Boston, Massachusetts, French had worked in the grocery and distillery business before the war, as a Democrat was three times elected to the Boston Common Council, and had served on the Massachusetts governor's staff at one time.[26] A capable man, he understood the workings of municipal government. But in the early days of the occupation, French faced a difficult task in assuming command of the police. They were naturally insecure and demoralized at the prospect of working under a military man whom they considered "the enemy." The arrest and imprisonment of their chief on the charge that he supported the mayor was also a sore point. Most did not wish to take the oath of allegiance to the United States and wondered if this would mean mere dismissal or possibly imprisonment.[27]

On May 22, Colonel French spoke to the police forces at the stations of the First, Second, and Third districts. In each case the men gathered in the police yards, and French explained to them that they must take the oath. This did not guarantee that they would keep their jobs. They would have to prove good character and acceptable work records as well. But if they did not take the oath, they would be dismissed from the force. At each station when he asked those to step forward who would take the oath, he got only a few old men. The overwhelming majority resigned.[28] Several days later he visited the Fourth District with the same results. To police the city until he could hire a new force, French had to station soldiers temporarily in the four police districts.[29]

Between May 27 and 31, Colonel French hired a large number of men for the new police force.[30] He advertised for five hundred men and probably reached that number by the middle of the summer. Only a few were holdovers. The majority seem to have been Union men who kept quiet about their feelings during the first year of the war or men who desperately needed a job and swallowed their pride about the oath. Some men of questionable character who slipped by without revealing their shady records were also hired. This was not an ideal combination to keep law and order in the city. The public resented the new police force whom they viewed as collaborators. The Union soldiers in the city were also hostile, as a rule, to the municipal police who they believed had no right to question their behavior or arrest them. The new police were caught between these two antagonistic elements. It was difficult for them to build up a feeling of confidence, or to perform their jobs without the cooperation of the public. Colonel French had to work with these disadvantages and make the most of a bad situation. Throughout his tenure as chief of police, he tried to instill a dedication to duty in the police corps and moved swiftly to punish misconduct.[31]

The most common complaints against police were sleeping on the job or being absent from their posts, drunkenness, fighting with other policemen, brutality toward prisoners, and the most serious, bribery and securing money under false pretenses. Some police took bribes to let prisoners go. One took five dollars from a man who wanted his alcoholic wife arrested. Another policeman collected money as "license fees" from two women who ran businesses, although he was not empowered to do such collecting. But there were officers who did outstanding jobs in law enforcement. One detective solved in one week the biggest robbery of the year, the theft of a safe with over one hundred thousand dollars worth of bonds and other valuables. Another was tender-hearted in rescuing poor mothers and children who were evicted. He found them temporary shelter and even bought them breakfast before seeing that they got reinstated in their lodgings.[32]

Duties of the police in wartime New Orleans were broad and could be unpleasant to carry out when they involved unpopular actions against average citizens. They had to continue to enforce regular municipal criminal laws against theft, assault and battery, public drunkenness, vandalism, violence, public nuisances, and vice. Police arrests made during the occupation years averaged about 1,500 a month.[33] This was slightly lower than arrests in the antebellum period, but may be accounted for in several ways. Thousands of young Orleanians were serving in the Confederate army, thousands of other citizens had fled at the outset of the occupation, and the military authorities arrested many of the Federal soldiers who got drunk or disturbed the peace.

Police were also charged with searching the houses of citizens reported to be hiding concealed weapons, picking up the increasing number of homeless and mentally ill people wandering the streets, destroying stray dogs, recovering army overcoats which soldiers had sold to civilians, and arresting bakers who continued to sell bread not up to weight standards. Two of the most chronic violations of law they were constantly encountering were selling liquor to soldiers and passing or printing counterfeit streetcar tickets which were used as small change.[34]

After Congress passed the second Confiscation Act in July 1862, which gave Federal authorities in conquered territory the right to seize property of individuals who did not take the oath of allegiance within a specified time, local residents finally rushed to take the dreaded oath. Approximately 68,000 persons did so in New Orleans.[35] General Butler then issued an order requiring anyone who had not taken the oath to register as "enemies" of the United States, giving details of their property and the members of their families. The police were charged with seeing that such individuals in their districts registered on penalty of losing their positions if they missed anyone.[36]

A Mrs. Clealand was arrested for tearing up the registry form and throwing it in the face of the neighborhood policeman while telling him what she thought of Lincoln and his government. She was arrested and later sentenced to six months on Ship Island. One policeman in order to trap recalcitrant men who had not registered, rode his horse into several saloons. He would demand that all bar patrons who had not taken the oath sign registration papers. While they did so, he ordered beer for himself and his horse. After about three such forays, his horse became visibly intoxicated. His behavior was made public, and discipline against him was probably taken swiftly.[37]

Although several historians claim that only about 12 to 14 percent of the arrests in New Orleans during the Civil War were Union soldiers, some who were arrested were involved in violent crimes and often resisted arrest. Out of 131 cases disposed of on November 25, 1862, in Provost Court, one fourth dealt with soldiers from the New York Zouaves whom the police reporter said "had been knocking around in a rather loose way." Three days later another New York Zouave was arrested for robbing a man at gunpoint on the shell road leading to Lake Pontchartrain. Several others involved in this crime were picked up later by police officer Rufus Long. In retaliation against Long, another soldier tried to search Long's house by posing as a policeman. He hoped to discredit Long by uncovering hidden weapons, but he was discovered. In another case in which the servant of a Union officer was picked up for beating a child, soldiers in the officer's company snatched the servant from the police and ran away with him. Such incidents created a tension between the two groups which did not lessen during Butler's tenure.[38]

During 1862 it was sometimes difficult for the population to tell which men really were police. They did not wear regulation uniforms, only a round silver badge, which one newspaper reporter referred to as a "moon," on their coats or jackets. Special police, who did undercover work and sometimes went out of town on what might be called spying assignments, did not even wear a badge. The result was frequent impersonation of police by unscrupulous underworld characters who wished to gain entrance to houses and confiscate property.[39]

Criminal cases of persons arrested by the police had been handled prior to the city's occupation by four recorders courts—one for each city district. But these courts and their recorders or judges were suspended at the time the mayor and chief of police were dismissed. All complaints of minor violations of the peace or of martial law were to be heard before a provost court during Butler's regime. It was presided over by Maj. Joseph M. Bell, provost judge. To aid indigent persons who appeared before this court, General Butler in Order 209 set up a legal bureau. It was placed under the direction of the assistant provost marshal, Col. S. H. Stafford.[40]

Judge Bell was a native of Massachusetts who had a thriving law practice in Boston before the war. A handsome man, he was equally pleasing in his personality. He was polite, courteous, and had a keen sense of humor. Presiding over the Provost Court during turbulent times when Butler's various orders caused tempers to fly and tongues to wag all over the city, Bell had to be stern in many cases. Fines and prison sentences were imposed for any show of seditious behavior. But he always tried to be fair and show mercy to persons maliciously accused, the homeless, the chronic alcoholics, or juvenile offenders.[41]

Dealing with military as well as civilian cases in a state whose law reflected both French and Spanish precedents, Bell had a formidable task to perform as provost judge. He had to pore over law books and briefs to familiarize himself with French and Spanish laws, municipal, state, and admiralty laws, the slave codes, and the military orders of General Butler who issued over two hundred between May 1 and December 1, 1862. When he admitted a black person as a witness for the first time, the defense attorney objected stating that a black man could not testify against a white man in Louisiana courts. Bell asked him, "Has Louisiana gone out of the Union?" When he answered, "Yes," the judge retorted, "then she took her laws with her." The black witness was sworn in.[42]

Sometimes, Bell interested himself in legal situations which did not come before his court. Noticing an elderly black woman hanging around outside his office, he asked her what she wanted. She explained that her landlord had seized property of hers to reimburse himself for rent owed by another boarder in her tenement who had left without paying.

She had paid her rent and had a receipt. When the judge called in the landlord to explain this unfair behavior, the landlord pointed out that under local law he had the right to seize property in a house if a tenant had not paid rent. The law did not stipulate that the seized property had to belong to the delinquent tenant. Checking the law, Judge Bell had to admit with amazement that this was so. Then he got an idea. He asked the woman if she were free or a slave. She replied that she was a slave. Many slaves were abandoned in New Orleans during the hard times of the Civil War and left to support themselves while their masters fled the city. She was working as a washerwoman. Judge Bell then informed the landlord that according to another local law, he had to have a written permit from her master to rent her a room. If he did not have it, he would have to pay a fine—or give the woman back her property. The landlord returned the property. In July 1862, Deputy Provost Marshal S. H. Stafford was put in charge of hearing all disputes between landlords and tenants. No tenants were to be evicted without Stafford's consent.[43]

The status of slaves who began to show up at the Customhouse or at U. S. Army camps in or near the city was complicated and tragic. General Butler and Judge Bell as provost judge found they had a difficult task to determine what to do with these "contrabands" as Butler had named them. Some were runaway city slaves or slaves from plantations outside the city who straggled into New Orleans to find freedom and sustenance. Others were abandoned slaves like the washerwoman whose master had left town. They were trying to survive on their own without anyone's help. A third group had been told by their masters or mistresses in the city "to go to the Yankees." Some white) urban slave owners who may have lost their jobs or businesses and now found that they could hardly feed their families were beginning to send their slaves to U. S. Army camps or Federal offices in the city. It was understood that they should stay there and get food and shelter from the Union army until the master got a steady income. This callous treatment resulted in crowded squatter camps near army quarters and a shortage of army rations for the regular troops as some of it was used to feed up to ten thousand slave refugees.[44]

Judge Bell handled several cases involving plantation runaways who fought their way into the city.[45] But just as aggravating a problem was that of the city runaways and the abandoned slaves who had been told "to go to the Yankees." To curb the latter group, Butler issued an order which freed any slave whose master or mistress had told him or her before a witness "to go to the Yankees." Since this was a difficult case to prove, none of the few slaves who applied to the Provost Court for emancipation was successful in the last half of 1862. Butler had meant this order as a ploy to deter slave owners from sending their slaves to the U. S. Army for upkeep. But since the national government at this time was trying to woo Southern slave owners back to the Union, he knew he could not take action to free slaves on a large scale.[46]

Some slaves did win freedom through the Provost Court, however. Two of them, Parthena and Fanny, were freed for informing on their owners who were concealing weapons in their homes.[47] Butler had ordered all arms of residents who had not taken the oath to be handed over to Federal officials in August, following the Battle of Baton Rouge.[48] Sentences for disobeying this order were severe, since the Federal authorities were worried about the possibility of armed insurrection. This was an order which was never completely obeyed. There is no way to estimate how many persons kept guns, swords, or keepsake knifes.

The authorized soldiers and police who had the right to search private residences and businesses for hidden arms were strictly forbidden to keep any of the articles they seized. When soldiers violated this order, the ones who were discovered were usually turned over to the Military Commission, a select court which in collaboration with General Butler dealt with serious crimes within the military and with civilian crimes of murder or serious sedition.[49]

A rare pardon for hiding weapons was granted to Marcellin Secard, who had fought in the Battle of New Orleans. General Butler issued it himself, citing Secard's service to the United States and saying that he could understand how an old soldier would wish to keep his weapons.[50] One of the most interesting cases of this sort was that of Mrs. Henry Guild, accused of hiding in her home a rifle, a revolver, a sword, and a Bowie knife. After she had been sentenced to a prison term, she asked to speak against her accuser, a lawyer who had represented her husband when he was arrested for purchasing stolen gas gauges. He had requested $200 from her to get her husband out of jail. When she refused, her husband, out of spite, had told the lawyer about the hidden weapons, and the lawyer turned her in. Judge J. Burnham Kinsman, substituting for Bell revoked the woman's sentence and gave the lawyer one month in jail for his act of malice.[51]

Another serious infraction of martial law which brought violators almost daily into Judge Bell's court was founded on charges of seditious language or actions against the United States. Like keeping concealed weapons on one's premises, this carried a stern penalty, usually a stiff fine or a prison term. The *Picayune* police reporter who covered the Provost Court used the phrase "hurrahing for Jeff Davis" to describe this charge. Usually, it was brought against men who had gotten drunk and loudly condemned General Butler or the United States government, sang secession songs, or got into a fight with a Union man. One man was arrested and fined $100 for letting the Bonnie Blue Flag remain flying in his backyard after his children put it up.[52] Serious sedition cases such as that of William Mumford, condemned and later hanged for pulling down the United States flag from the Mint, and that of Mrs. Eugenia Phillips, who was accused of laughing at a Union officer's funeral passing her home, were heard by the Military Commission and General Butler.[53] But the majority of minor cases of this category went before the Provost Court.

In one case, a policeman, Barney Williams, brought charges against his landlady for singing seditious songs and insulting him as a policeman. The landlady explained that Williams owed her over $100 in rent, and she was trying to sue him for it in civil court. That was his motive for accusing her of seditious behavior. The charges against her were dismissed, and Williams was fined $50.[54]

Two other serious types of wartime cases which came into the Provost Court were attempting to leave the city without a pass and smuggling letters, contraband, or medicines out of the city. One schooner captain who sailed between the New Basin Canal in New Orleans and Mobile had his schooner confiscated and was sentenced to six months at hard labor at Fort Jackson for smuggling out letters and other papers and allowing persons without passes to travel on his boat. Another man who had a pass, but tried to smuggle out a small amount of quinine in his horse's harness, had his horse and wagon seized and was sentenced to three months on Ship Island. A third man was caught with numerous pairs of shoes and 6,000 percussion caps he was smuggling out of New Orleans. He received six months in prison.[55]

The cases and sentences of the unlucky blockade-runners and smugglers who were caught must have been read in local newspapers with irony by businessmen and Federal officials in the city who knew about the cotton and sugar buying escapades of General Butler's brother, Andrew Jackson Butler. He was allowed to use Union boats to trade for cotton and other staples.[56] General Butler had also allowed trade in contraband, especially salt, on the north shore of Lake Pontchartrain.[57]

Butler earned only criticism and hostility from all elements of the city population for his harsh and controversial actions. Few citizens gave him credit for his remarkable levee repairs, the clean-up of the streets and canals which probably saved the city from yellow fever, and his sponsorship of the United States Relief Commission which replaced the Free Market and was feeding over 34,000 persons weekly by November 1862.[58]

In September rumors were circulating, even in the local newspapers, that President Lincoln was considering replacing Butler. On December 12, 1862, Gen. Nathaniel P. Banks arrived in New Orleans and revealed what Butler already suspected—that Banks was the new commander of the Department of the Gulf. Banks took over from Butler on December 16.[59]

Both provost judge Joseph Bell and his assistant judge, Lieut. J. Burnham Kinsman, were to return East with Butler. Colonel French was asked to remain for awhile to train someone else in the formidable task of directing the police department and handling the duties of the provost marshal. On December 20, the officers of the Provost Court surprised Judge Bell "by presenting him a large silver goblet and salver . . . as a testimonial of their high respect and esteem."[60]

The lawyers who had practiced before the Provost Court also gave him a walking cane and put a notice in the newspapers in which they praised him for his uniform courtesy, humanity, and high sense of justice. "Coming among us as a judge in times of extraordinary trouble," they noted, "he has, by his impartial administration of the duties of his difficult position endeared himself to all classes of citizens, both those who have come before him as litigants and the public generally."[61]

Lieutenant Kinsman, Bell's assistant, did not, unfortunately, get a silver salver or a cane. He got a challenge to a duel from a native of St. Bernard Parish who claimed that Kinsman had gravely insulted him. He wanted a chance to meet him on the field of

Keeping Law and Order in New Orleans 693

honor. What the gentleman got instead was a summons to Provost Court where he was slapped with a fine by Judge Bell's successor.[62]

On December 24 when Butler and his staff departed, there was only one sentence in the *Daily Picayune* about this leave-taking. It read,"We learn that General Butler and staff will leave the city at 10 o'clock this morning for the North."[63] Butler's departure brought a great wave of hope to many who viewed Banks's arrival as a new beginning. It would not prove to be as satisfactory as they believed. The struggle for order in the conquered city continued to plague Federal officials as well as citizens. But the first difficult year of occupation was over.

The burden of law enforcement had been heavy in 1862 for Colonel French, Major Bell, their staffs, and the police, whose honest, conscientious members never made headlines, but did make up the majority of the force. Together they had handled ordinary criminal cases, as well as the stressful violations of marshal law in an overall fair and equitable manner. In a city torn apart with hatred and hostility, that was quite a laudable accomplishment, although only the staff and lawyers of the Provost Court seemed to have realized it at the time. In no other era of the city's history has the burden of law enforcement been as urgent or as challenging.

Notes for "Keeping Law and Order in New Orleans Under General Butler, 1862"

[1] George Washington Cable, "New Orleans Before the Capture," in Cable, *The Cable Story Book*, eds., Mary E. Burt and Lucy Leffingwell Cable (New York, 1902), 106-14; Howard Palmer Johnson, "New Orleans Under General Butler," *Louisiana Historical Quarterly,* 24 (1941): 447-48.

[2] Johnson, "New Orleans Under General Butler," 447-48; Thomas Ewing Dabney, "The Butler Regime in Louisiana," *Louisiana Historical Quarterly,* 27 (1944): 492-93; Cable, "New Orleans Before the Capture," 113; *New Orleans Daily True Delta*, May 2, 1862.

[3] Dabney, "The Butler Regime in Louisiana," 492-93; Mary Elizabeth Massey, "The Free Market of New Orleans, 1861-1862," *Louisiana History*, 3 (1962): 202-20.

[4] On the percentage of foreign born in New Orleans, see Gerald M. Capers, *Occupied City: New Orleans Under the Federals, 1862-1865* (Lexington, 1965): 5-7; on the purpose for forming the foreign brigades, see Cable, "New Orleans Before the Capture," 109.

[5] Johnson, "New Orleans Under General Butler," 447.

[6] Ibid., New Orleans Second District Police Log Book of Arrests, March 21, 1862, to June 30, 1864, in City Archives, New Orleans Public Library, Main Branch, New Orleans, Louisiana, 13, 15, 18, 19, 22, 33, 42, 50. These citations refer to curfew violation arrests made between March 31 and April 23-24, 1862.

[7] New Orleans Second District Police Log Book of Arrests, 10, March 28, 1862, for arrest of baker who sold "light" bread.

[8] Cable, "New Orleans Before the Capture," 116-17; Johnson, "New Orleans Under General Butler," 448.

[9] On Butler's arrival, see John Smith Kendall, *History of New Orleans*, 3 vols. (New York, 1922), 1:274; and Howard P. Nash, *Stormy Petrel: The Life and Times of General Benjamin F. Butler, 1818-1893* (Cranbury, N.

J., 1969), 147-48; on the riots, looting, and burning of the cotton, see Cable, "New Orleans Before the Capture," 119-21, and Bvt. Lieut. Col. Robert N. Scott, comp., *The War of the Rebellion: A Compilation of the Official Records of the Union and Confederate Armies* (1882; reprint ed., Ann Arbor, 1985), Ser. I, Vol. 6:568, 576-77; hereinafter cited as *O. R.*; on the foreign brigades, see *New Orleans Daily Picayune*, March 15, April 29, 30, May 1, 2, 4, 1862; and *Daily True Delta*, May 3, 1862.

[10] Benjamin F. Butler, *Autobiography and Personal Reminiscences of Major-General Benjamin F. Butler: Butler's Book* (Boston, 1892), 374-77; Hans L. Trefousse, *Ben Butler: The South Called Him Beast* (New York, 1957), 110; Robert S. Holzman, *Stormy Ben Butler* (New York, 1954), 67-68.

[11] Kendall, *History of New Orleans*, I:275; James Parton, *General Butler in New Orleans*, 10th ed. (New York, 1864), 290-91; *Daily Picayune*, May 3, 1862.

[12] Capers, *Occupied City*, 62-65; Trefousse, *Ben Butler*, 108-9; Parton, *General Butler in New Orleans*, 291-97.

[13] Butler, *Butler's Book*, 379-82; Capers, *Occupied City*, 63-64. This proclamation also appeared in the daily newspapers a few days after it was issued. See *Daily True Delta*, May 4, 1862, and *Daily Picayune*, May 4, 1862, for the full text.

[14] Nash, *Stormy Petrel*, 147.

[15] "Crowds," a short piece on the mood of the city which appears in the column "The City," *Daily Picayune*, May 13, 1862.

[16] Capers, *Occupied City*, 65; Parton, *General Butler in New Orleans*, 298.

[17] Parton, *General Butler in New Orleans*, 298; *Daily True Delta*, May 3, 1862, for General Juge's farewell to the men who served under him.

[18] *Daily True Delta*, May 8, 1862.

[19] Trefousse, *Ben Butler: The South Called Him Beast*, 110; Nash, *Stormy Petrel*, 161; Holzman, *Stormy Ben Butler*, 84; Robert Werlich, *"Beast Butler:" The Incredible Career of Major General Benjamin Franklin Butler* (Washington, D.C., 1962): 38-39.

[20] Butler, *Butler's Book*, 418; Nash, *Stormy Petrel*, 162.

[21] Parton, *General Butler in New Orleans*, 325-26; Nash, *Stormy Petrel*, 161; Holzman, *Stormy Ben Butler*, 84.

[22] Kendall, *History of New Orleans*, I:278-80; Parton, *General Butler in New Orleans*, 331-35; *O.R.*, Ser. I, Vol. 53 (Supplement): 526-27.

[23] Works Progress Administration, *Biographies of the Mayors of New Orleans* (New Orleans, 1939), 69, 70-72; Melvin G. Holli and Peter d'A. Jones, *Biographical Dictionary of American Mayors, 1820-1880: Big City Mayors* (Westport, 1981), 329.

[24] *Biographies of the Mayors of New Orleans*, 69, 74, 76, 78; *Biographical Dictionary of American Mayors*, 99, 124, 384.

[25] French was a captain in the Eastern Bay State Regiment (later Thirteenth Massachusetts): but was never commissioned by the governor. When his regiment joined Butler's Department of the Gulf, he was made an aide-de-camp and assistant inspector general with the rank of acting lieutenant colonel. *Biographical*

Dictionary of American Mayors, 124; Kendall, *History of New Orleans,* 1:124, for French's appointment as provost marshal on Butler's staff; Parton, *General Butler in New Orleans,* 336, for French taking over office of chief of police; *Daily Picayune,* May 22, 1862; for appointment as chief of police and October 14, 1862, for French's appointment as provost marshal of Louisiana.

[26] *Biographical Dictionary of American Mayors,* 124.

[27] *Daily True Delta,* May 22, 1862.

[28] *Daily Picayune,* May 24, 1862.

[29] Ibid.

[30] Personnel Records for the Department of Police for First, Second, Third, and Fourth Districts, kept in the Mayor's office for years 1862-1863, in City Archives, New Orleans Public Library, Main Branch, New Orleans, Louisiana.

[31] Examples of police discipline are in *Daily Picayune,* July 19, August 28, September 19, 28, October 3, 10, 11, 14, November 20, 30, 1862.

[32] *Daily Picayune,* June 29, July 10, 19, 31, August 1, 7, September 10, 19, 27, 28, October 10, 11, 12, 14, 17, 23, November 6, 20, 22, 30, December 5, 6, 7, 1862; *Daily True Delta,* June 19, 20, September 10, 28, October 10, 1862.

[33] Elizabeth Joan Doyle, "Civilian Life in Occupied New Orleans, 1862-65" (Ph.D. dissertation, Louisiana State University, 1955), 130.

[34] For persons selling liquor to soldiers see *Daily Picayune*, May 31, July 26, September 7, 18, 24, 26, October 2, 9, 11, 24, November 14, 1862, and *Daily True Delta,* August 30, 1862; for stories on shinplasters and counterfeiting, see *Daily Picayune,* May 24, July 10, 11, 13, 30, September 23, 30, October 19, November 22, 30, December 9, 12, 13, 16, 1862.

[35] Capers, *Occupied City,* 86-87, 93-94.

[36] *Daily Picayune,* September 26, 1862; John Winters, *The Civil War in Louisiana* (Baton Rouge, 1963), 140; Parton, *New Orleans Under General Butler,* 467-74.

[37] See *Daily Picayune*, October 2, 1862, for case of Mrs. Clealand and ibid., October 12, 1862, for story on policeman who rode his horse into saloons.

[38] *Daily Picayune*, October 14, November 25, 28, 30, 1862.

[39] Ibid., June 7, 28, September 26, October 2, 18, November 22, 28, 30, 1862; Doyle, "Civilian Life in Occupied New Orleans," 127-28.

[40] *Daily Picayune,* May 22, and July 24, 1862; Butler, *Butler's Book,* 526; Parton, *New Orleans Under General Butler,* 336.

[41] Butler, *Butler's Book,* 893, 897; an example of Judge Bell's humane touch in his court is found in counseling he gave to several juveniles brought before him for stealing from a blind woman, see *Daily Picayune,* November 27, 1862.

[42] Parton, *New Orleans Under General Butler,* 432-34; Werlich, *"Beast" Butler,* 34.

[43] Parton, *General Butler in New Orleans*, 433-34; *Daily Picayune*, July 23, 26, 1862.

[44] *Daily Picayune*, July 15, 22, 23, 26, December 7, 1862.

[45] *Daily True Delta*, July 22, 1862; *Daily Picayune*, July 23, August 22, 1862.

[46] *Daily Picayune*, July 25, 26, August 2, 29, 1862.

[47] Ibid., September 7, October 26, 1862.

[48] Capers, *Occupied City*, 93.

[49] Capers, *Occupied City*, 71; *Daily Picayune*, September 23, 1862; Johnson, "New Orleans Under General Butler," 487; the Military Commission is discussed in *Daily Picayune*, November 8, December 20, 1862.

[50] Ibid., August 28, 29, 1862.

[51] Ibid., October 8, 1862.

[52] Ibid., July 16, 1862.

[53] Johnson, "New Orleans Under General Butler," 488-89; Trefousse, *Ben Butler*, 117-18; *Daily True Delta*, July 2, 1862; *Daily Picayune*, July 2, 1862; Parton, *General Butler in New Orleans*, 438-42.

[54] *Daily Picayune*, October 31, 1862.

[55] Ibid., August 10, 15, October 3, 1862.

[56] Trefousse, *Ben Butler*, 122-23; Winters, *The Civil War in Louisiana*, 138.

[57] George S. Denison, "Letters from Denison to Chase," *Annual Report of the American Historical Association for the Year 1902* (Washington, D.C., 1903), 320-25; Holzman, *Stormy Ben Butler*, 92-94.

[58] *Daily Picayune*, November 22, 1862.

[59] Ibid., September 4, 5, 1862; Butler, *Butler's Book*, 526-30.

[60] *Daily Picayune*, December 21, 1862.

[61] Ibid.

[62] Ibid., December 21, 27, 1862.

[63] Ibid., December 24, 1862.

BLACK POLICEMEN IN NEW ORLEANS DURING RECONSTRUCTION*

Dennis C. Rousey

For Southerners, both black and white, Reconstruction brought about many changes, raising sublime hopes for some and evoking nightmarish fears for others. Some of the changes became permanent fixtures in the firmament of Southern society—others were mere ephemera. One of the new (though transitory) experiences for black men in some parts of the South was the opportunity to join the forces of "law and order," when some municipal governments, for the first time, hired black policemen. Of course, not all cities opened their police forces to black recruits, and some of those departments which hired blacks practiced a policy of internal segregation, confining black policemen to official activities within the black community.

New Orleans came as close to equalitarianism in policing as any other Southern city, and probably closer. Though the conservative restoration of the late 1870s destroyed any prospect of permanent reform, during Reconstruction black officers in the Crescent City arrested whites, held important administrative and command posts, carried firearms, wore uniforms, and at times held a percentage of police jobs roughly equal to the black proportion of the city's total population. Such progress was possible during Reconstruction because New Orleans carried over a tradition of unusual race relations from the antebellum period, when the barriers of race were formidable but not impermeable. Admittedly not a utopia of color blindness, New Orleans entered the post-slavery period with an extraordinary heritage promising exceptional potential for building up black institutions and extending black participation in urban public life.

The Crescent City's antebellum tradition in race relations was probably unique—certainly, at least, it was a rarity in the United States.[1] Although the formal law imposed a considerable "web of restraints" (in Richard Wade's phrase) on both slaves and free blacks, in practice both groups found numerous ways to circumvent such laws. Many whites—including employers, policemen, grogshop keepers and professional criminals—

---

*First published in *The Historian*, 49 (1987): 223-43. Reprinted with the kind permission of the author.

had a vested interest in helping blacks flout the law.[2] The large number of Northerners in the city may have contributed to white toleration of black freedoms, as most evidently were not much concerned about the institution of slavery.[3]

Free blacks probably made the most important contribution to the special racial mixture of New Orleans. Of all Deep South cities, New Orleans had been home to the largest prewar population of free people of color, second only to Baltimore. The free black community of the Crescent City had a rich and dynamic tradition, especially distinctive because of the large number of mulattoes and the influence of French culture. Though separated from slaves by law (and often by culture), free blacks forged links with the slave community by many means. They played a major role in manumitting slaves,[4] and became increasingly conscious of a racial bond with the enslaved, thus experiencing an "awakening of liberal conscience" as a result of the Civil War.[5] Those blacks who had been free during the antebellum period expected to lead the black community after abolition,[6] and in fact most of the city's black leaders of the postwar period had been free before the war.[7]

And so the nouveau regime proved more genuinely reformist in New Orleans than in most of the South. During Reconstruction New Orleans became a center—perhaps *the* center—of black progress. More Afro-Americans lived there than in any other city in the country: 50,456 according to the 1870 census (followed by Baltimore with 39,558 and Washington, D.C., with 35,455). After the Civil War New Orleans made remarkable advances in city rights for blacks. Racial integration afforded blacks access to the city's streetcars, the New Orleans Opera House, the Boys' House of Refuge, the City Insane Asylum, and some of the city's social clubs, churches, saloons, steamboats, theaters and public schools. Three colleges offered educational opportunities to blacks, including the academically esteemed and racially integrated Straight University. As the site of the state capitol, New Orleans served as headquarters for a state legislature with a substantial percentage of blacks, and for three black lieutenant governors. Despite widespread and persistent white resistance, black New Orleanians were pushing across the color line into a new frontier.[8]

*

New Orleans, in 1867, appears to have been the first Southern city to integrate its police force during Reconstruction. By 1870, racially integrated forces policed at least twelve Southern cities. In the entire South, there were probably about 350 black city policemen in 1870, or perhaps somewhat less. New Orleans had by far the largest contingent of black officers, some 182 men (in a total force of 647). Thus, though the experiences of black policemen in New Orleans may not have been typical for all Southern cities, this case study encompasses a majority of the black Southern urban policemen. Moreover, if black policemen were ever to achieve equal status with their white counterparts, it would most likely happen first in the Crescent City.[9]

It was appropriate that New Orleans should have witnessed the debut of black policemen in the postwar South. Their appearance there revived an earlier practice, hearkening back to the first decades of the nineteenth century when New Orleans had inaugurated racially mixed civil policing. As early as 1804, the new urban center of the American Southwest displayed a willingness to consider the employment of black policemen. Mayor Etienne Boré suggested in that year the formation of a mounted patrol service, and called for a company of white men, "or in lieu thereof, of free mulattoes whose officers will be white men." When the following year the city government established a municipal police force known as the Gendarmerie, modeled along the contours of Mayor Boré's proposal of the previous year, there may have been a substantial number of free black men on that early force.[10]

Although the racial composition of the Gendarmerie is conjectural, black men certainly served on subsequent police forces in New Orleans. The city authorities abolished the Gendarmerie in 1806, but by 1809 a permanent municipal force called the city guard was operational. In a ten-man sample of that force in 1814, at least two city guardsmen (Charles Allegre and Constant Michel) were free men of color. Of a sample of 17 city guardsmen in 1820, at least one (Pierre Aubry) was black. Samples for 1828 and 1830 both show at least one black policeman on the city guard muster roll (August Bolen).[11]

Black participation in policing also involved the militia. Most students of Louisiana history are familiar with the role played by free black troops in the Battle of New Orleans in 1815. Although state law deactivated the black militia in 1834, the black veterans of 1815 participated in public commemorations of the victory over the British until the outbreak of the Civil War. On many occasions in the first quarter century of American hegemony over New Orleans, state and city authorities deployed the militia as an auxiliary police force. In 1817, the city council explicitly ordered that both whites and free blacks render service in these militia patrols. In addition to the Gendarmerie, and its successor the city guard, several other officers of civil government exercised police functions, among them the rural/suburban syndic. At least one of the syndics in 1803 was a free quadroon (Delille Dupard).[12]

Black men thus played the roles of gendarme, city guardsman, militia man and syndic during the first third of the century. But those early black policemen found themselves in a tense and ambivalent relationship with the white establishment. If any part of the United States ever transcended the rigid dichotomy of black and white—with blackness understood by whites as a designation of slave status—it was Franco-Hispanic Louisiana. Free people of color stood apart in New Orleans, constituting a third category between free whites and enslaved blacks to a greater extent than anywhere else in the United States. Yet that peculiar and precarious status relegated its occupants to an ambiguous, marginal niche in society that racism eroded over time—reducing many of them, as Ira Berlin has suggested, to become virtual "slaves without masters."[13] Still, blacks in New Orleans enjoyed more freedom than in most other cities in the slave states.

The tension produced by this growing marginality affected the black role in policing. As early as 1804, Mayor Boré's proposal for a mounted police force showed a distinct preference for white men to serve as rank and file, and stipulated that its commanders be white. When in 1816, the city council sought to prevent looting in a flooded portion of the city by deploying a patrol boat, it insisted that all rowers be white. The double standard of the city council led to occasional ironies: it allowed free black militiamen to bear arms when they participated in police patrols, but prevented blacks from giving or receiving instruction in fencing.[14]

From 1830 to Reconstruction, no evidence exists of black policemen in New Orleans. The hardening of white Southern attitudes on race and slavery evidently led to their exclusion from the police force, although this policy was never embodied in law or ordinance. Even though the 1860 census shows two Afro-Americans (one "black," one "mulatto") who gave their occupation as police officer, neither man's name appears in the personnel books of the police department. If there were Negro policemen, at that late date they must have been light-skinned mulattoes, probably Franco-Americans, passing for white. It would be difficult to imagine white toleration of revolver-carrying black policemen in the 1850s, given the intensity of white racial anxieties and antipathies in the late antebellum period.[15]

Not until 1867 did the Crescent City once again hire black men as police officers. In early May, the federal military commander in New Orleans, General Sheridan, ordered Mayor Edward Heath to "adjust the present police force so that at least one half of said force shall be composed of ex-Union soldiers." The black community immediately pressed for the inclusion of Negroes on the force. The editor of the black-managed *New Orleans Tribune* pointed out that a large proportion of the population of New Orleans had African ancestry. His appeal for black policemen emphasized not only the justice of appointing black officers, but also the capacity for such service demonstrated by the many black men who had fought in the Civil War.[16]

Under pressure from the black community, the Republican party and the military government, Mayor Heath proceeded to integrate the force. On May 30, 1867, he appointed Dusseau Picou and Emile Farrar as policemen in the second district. They were the first black men—"newly enfranchised citizens," as the editor of the *New Orleans Tribune* called them—to serve as police officers in New Orleans in more than a generation. In the next week, the city appointed more than a dozen black officers, with additional appointments following later. Governor Wells also initiated the appointment of black men to the board of police commissioners with the selection of Charles J. Courcelle.[17]

Despite the appointment of white Unionists and black men to the police force, the department did not immediately become a preserve of racial equality and harmony. White resistance to black policemen was remarkably moderate at the outset, but in their position at the vanguard of social change, black officers held a precarious beachhead. Their position was especially vulnerable because they depended on unreliable local leadership and the federal government. When President Andrew Johnson ordered the enforcement of a state law excluding blacks from jury service, the *New Orleans Tribune* asserted that his example had triggered an open avowal of hostility to both the Republican party and racial equality by white members of the police. The result for blacks and for white Republicans on the force was, the *Tribune* said, "every means is resorted to [to] make them abandon their position." The inconsistency of local leadership also placed black policemen in an anomalous situation. Mayor Heath, who had appointed the first black officers, also proclaimed the right of white businessmen to refuse service to Negroes.[18]

After reorganization of the police force in 1868 black police officers received more consistent long-term support. In that year the legislature abolished the old municipal police force and replaced it with a state-controlled, Republican-dominated Metropolitan organization. This force was headed by a board of commissioners, fifty percent black, and police ranks were sixty-five percent black in October of 1868 when they went on duty for the first time. Their jurisdiction extended well beyond the bounds of the city, embracing the neighboring parishes of Jefferson and St. Bernard, and Metropolitan officers were authorized to execute warrants throughout the state. In 1873, the police force was incorporated as a state militia brigade, subject to the governor's call for military service anywhere in Louisiana.[19]

The new organization faced serious opposition. From their institutional beginnings to their extinction as a police agency, the Metropolitans were engaged in a virtual war for individual and collective survival. Many whites refused to accept the legitimacy of this force and opposed it with physical violence, litigation, and economic sanctions.

Even before the Civil War and Reconstruction brought so much bloodshed to the South, the job of policing had been filled with danger. New Orleans had long been a hotbed of violence. Its people fairly bristled with lethal weaponry: revolvers, pepperbox pistols, dirks, bowie knives and slungshots—a private arsenal concealed in the pockets and waistbands of respectable gentlemen and proletarian thugs alike. The murder rate in New Orleans was evidently the worst of any major city in America, far higher than in other large port cities like Philadelphia and Boston. At least eight New Orleans policemen were killed in the line of duty between 1854 and 1860—surely a per capita record for American cities of the period—and many officers received non-fatal wounds.[20]

Policing grew even more dangerous during Reconstruction. The first appearance of the Metropolitans on the job led to antipolice riots, and during their tenure of less than nine years, they fought several battles and quelled a number of riotous disorders. In May 1869, the Metropolitans had to fight the Jefferson City police to secure jurisdiction over Jefferson Parish; in the struggle they suffered one fatality and eleven wounded. In November 1872 the Metropolitans massed for an attack against a detachment of the state militia at the Carondelet Street armory, but the timely intervention of federal authorities brought about a peaceful resolution. The following year, in March, the police confronted several hundred armed opponents at Jackson Square by firing blank cartridges from a cannon. The confrontation ended with the accidental death of an unfortunate bystander. In the next two months, the Metropolitans were called out of the district on militia service, arriving at an interracial battle in Colfax after the fighting had ceased. In May, the police found themselves trapped and besieged at St. Martinville. Two Metropolitans suffered wounds there, but the arrival of federal troops spared them further casualties. But the most serious of all armed struggles for the Metropolitans, the battle of Liberty Place, occurred in September 1874, when paramilitary units of the conservative White League drove the police from the streets, killing eleven and wounding sixty. Federal intervention once again saved the Metropolitans, restoring the police to their duties until January 1877 when Reconstruction ended in Louisiana.[21]

Unable to win acceptance from most whites, the police had to adapt and endure. For safety, they often patrolled in pairs, which had not been the usual practice of the antebellum police when one man per beat had been the prewar norm. Opposition to their legal authority also drove them into adopting a military mode of organization. Uniformed in the style of Union soldiers and drilled in infantry formation, with a detachment of mounted men, they armed themselves with revolvers, repeating rifles, cannon, and Gatling guns. They looked and sometimes acted like a small army. They paid a high price: from 1868 through 1874 the Metropolitan Police suffered an average of twenty-two gunshot wounds (not to mention other types of wounds).[22]

Conservative whites also endeavored to strangle the Metropolitan force, choking off needed revenue by a strategy of massive tax delinquencies, aimed at subverting the entire Republican state government. Financial constraints compelled a reduction by more than 50 percent in the size of the force between 1870 and 1876; policemen meanwhile were usually paid in warrants whose real value rarely exceeded 60 percent of face value.[23]

White Democrats predictably castigated the Metropolitans, likening them to a brutal and repressive army of occupation. The Metropolitan Police were caught in a severe bind, compelled to present as formidable a police presence as possible to defeat overtly illegal resistance from conservatives, yet damned for their every effort to exercise any authority at all.

As a racially integrated body, the Metropolitans found the criticism from racist whites vitriolic. The racial composition of the force registered high among the explicit complaints. When the Metropolitan force first went on duty in 1868 and encountered violent protest, the superintendent (a Union army officer) felt obliged to suspend all of the black policemen. In a city whose population was approximately 26 percent black, a police force 65 percent black—as it was at the outset—certainly overrepresented black people, just as the earlier all-white force had underrepresented them. But by 1870 the black percentage of the force had dropped to 28.1 percent, roughly proportional to their 26.4 percent of the whole population.[24]

Despite such avid opposition, the Metropolitan Police had a fair claim to distinction as the best force the city had fielded at any time during the nineteenth century. The Metropolitan force was less abusive of civil liberties than either its predecessors or successors and its officers were held to a strict accountability. Police delinquencies dropped from the 1850s, with about 2.0 complaints per officer annually, compared with 2.5 in the years 1854-56. A complaint against a Metropolitan officer was also more likely to result in punishment (77.1 percent led to some form of punishment, in contrast to only 45.6 for the period 1854-56). The Metropolitan police sharply reduced arrests on the vague and antilibertarian charges of vagrancy and suspicion, down from 17.8 percent of total arrests in the mid-fifties to 4.8 percent in the years 1868-74. Police commanders even sought to decriminalize prostitution, which had long been a lucrative source of graft for the police.[25]

The Metropolitans were more productive in nearly every measurable and presumably desirable sense in which a police force may display activity. By 1874, the number of arrests per officer averaged sixty-two per year, compared with an annual rate of forty-seven during the 1850s. Their involvement in public health increased with the creation of a company of sanitary police in 1868. The social welfare function of the police also expanded, as they provided stationhouse lodging for nearly 15,000 people each year, an increase of fifteen times from the immediate antebellum era. Police absenteeism dropped with the establishment of stricter medical discipline, from the prewar range of 13 to 28 percent per year to just 1.7 percent annually. Opportunities for modest pensions, never before widely available, also gave stability to the Metropolitan police.[26]

Of fundamental importance to any evaluation of their record was the hiring of black officers in numbers approximating the proportion of black people in the city's population. Although the police department in New Orleans formed the largest integrated force in the urban South, it was not the only one to include black officers. In 1870, at least twelve Southern cities employed black policemen, most of them in proportions close to the percentage of blacks in the local population (see Table 1).

Local political consideration rather than any national or regional policy determined the employment of black policemen. A tradition of decentralization in the American criminal justice system thus persisted during Reconstruction. Savannah and Charleston, for example, were similar cities in roughly the same class in terms of population size (49,000 in Charleston in 1870 and 28,000 in Savannah). Both had a large proportion of blacks (54 percent in Charleston, 47 percent in Savannah), and almost the same proportion of immigrants (42 percent of the white adult male population in Charleston, 43 percent in Savannah). Situated near one another, they shared the same geography and climate, and each served as a commercial outlet for an agricultural hinterland. Yet Charleston had a racially integrated force, while Savannah had an all-white corps, dressed in Confederate gray and under the command of a former Confederate officer.[27]

Savannah and Charleston were separated by a state boundary, but even within the jurisdiction of a single state there could be great variation in the racial composition of urban police forces. In Virginia, the Petersburg force was integrated, while Richmond had no black policemen at all. Norfolk had only token integration on its force, yet the twin city of Portsmouth was almost fully integrated. The struggle for integration was thus largely localized. In some places, conditions and forces within the individual city determined the outcome; in other cases such as Tennessee and Louisiana, the involvement of the state government in municipal politics shaped the course of change.[28]

Winning jobs on the force did not end the struggle for black policemen. One historian, Howard Rabinowitz, has suggested that in some cities black officers were restricted from official interaction with whites by law, administrative order, or custom. Rabinowitz observes an exception in Montgomery, where black policemen gained the authority to arrest whites but only after a struggle between the leading black and white Republicans in the city.[29]

TABLE 1
Black Police in Southern Cities, 1870 and 1880

	1870		1880	
	Police Depts.	Total Pop.	Police Depts.	Total Pop.
New Orleans	28%	26%	7%	27%
Charleston	42%	54%	19%	55%
Mobile	37%	44%	0%	42%
Montgomery	50%	49%	0%	59%
Vicksburg	50%	55%	14%	49%
Petersburg	37%	54%	0%	54%
Portsmouth	29%	35%	0%	54%
Norfolk	3%	46%	0%	46%
Augusta	2%	42%	0%	46%
San Antonio	13%	16%	12%	15%
Galveston	8%	22%	13%	24%
Washington, D.C.	4%	33%	5%	33%
Savannah	0%	46%	0%	51%
Nashville	0%	38%	0%	38%
Richmond	0%	45%	0%	44%
Atlanta	0%	46%	0%	44%
Memphis	0%	39%	23%	44%
Louisville	0%	15%	0%	17%
St. Louis	0%	7%	--	--
Baltimore	0%	15%	--	--

Sources: Ninth Census (1870) and Tenth Census (1880), Population Schedules, U. S. Census Office, *Ninth Census—Volume 1. The Statistics of the Population of the United States* (Washington, 1872). U. S. Census Office, *Statistics of the Population of the United States at the Tenth Census* (Washington, 1883).

Although the Rabinowitz hypothesis may apply to many Southern towns during Reconstruction, New Orleans, with nearly half of all black policemen in the South, operated in a more equalitarian fashion. Evidence suggests that there were no invidious distinctions between black and white police officers in the Crescent City. Black men held positions on the board of police commissioners and commanded precincts. As ordinary cops on the beat, they wore uniforms, carried guns, and otherwise fully embodied the authority of police officers. No formal rules restrained black policemen from arresting whites, nor is there evidence to indicate any informal or covert efforts within the police force to apply any segregationist policy. Indeed, in a city only partially desegregated, the police were among the pioneers of integration. In one case, for example, a black policeman found himself assigned to duty at a ballroom catering to whites only— doubtless a considerable shock to the white patrons who found themselves under a black officer's scrutiny.[30]

Black officers did in fact have the power to arrest whites, and they exercised that power. Whether or not they arrested proportionately more blacks than whites must remain unknown, because for most arrests it is not possible to ascertain the race of both the policeman and the arrestee. However, at least some interracial arrests did occur. For example, during the months of June, July, and August 1870, black policemen arrested whites on at least sixteen occasions, and possibly on many more.[31]

The fact that blacks held important police leadership positions also indicates that black men were full-fledged police officers serving on an integrated force. The board of police commissioners which served as the governing body of the force included several black men. At the outset blacks held three of the six seats. Among the black commissioners were Charles J. Courcelle, J. B. Gaudette, James Lewis, J. W. Quinn, C. C. Antoine, Oscar J. Dunn, and Thomas Isabelle.[32]

Although a black man never held the post of police superintendent, blacks did serve at the next level of command, as precinct commander. At least seven blacks commanded either a precinct or a precinct substation. Four of these men held the rank of captain: Octave Rey, James Lewis, Eugene Rapp and Peter Joseph. Three other precinct or substation commanders were sergeants: H. E. deFuentes, J. B. Gaudette and Ernest Chaumette. Black officers headed at least two precincts during most years. In 1873, blacks commanded three of the ten precincts in the city plus an additional substation, while in the previous year, three of nine precincts were under black leadership.[33]

Black policemen participated fully in their work and this meant that they carried firearms on duty. During one of the early battles of the Metropolitan Police, the *New Orleans Times* mentioned the carrying of Enfield rifles—as well as the usual revolver—by black policemen. In more peaceful times, a traveler to New Orleans visited the state legislature and observed that at "the doors stand negro policemen, armed with clubs and revolvers."[34]

Integration of the policy brought with it internal racial frictions. In December 1867, some white members of the force evidently expressed open hostility toward the Republicans, as "they prefer to be 'damned' rather than give their votes to a party which recognized *negro equality*." In 1872, a white police captain argued with his white sergeant, and in the heat of the moment, called the sergeant a "nigger." The sergeant then shot the captain. The use of that racial epithet by a police captain, and the sergeant's reaction, suggests that prejudice must have persisted among many white policemen. Some black policemen evidenced prejudice, too. In 1869, a black secretary of the board of commissioners called a civilian, P. V. J. Kennedy, a "d- -d Irish- - - -," and stated that Kennedy had been "transported to this country, and every foreigner like him."[35]

Despite some continuing prejudice, the police force as a whole seems to have exercised the power of arrest without any pattern of racial discrimination. Arrest data classified by race are available only for one year, October 1, 1868, to September 30, 1869. In that year, 27.2 percent of persons arrested by the police were black, roughly equal to the black share of the population (26.4 percent). The absence of a discriminatory arrest policy can only be inferred. If the actual crime rate among blacks was higher or lower than for whites, then the rate of arrests should have reflected the difference. Unless blacks committed proportionately fewer crimes than whites, however, it is reasonable to assume that the police did not arrest black people more readily than others.[36]

Although almost all policemen lived with people of their own race, a few police officers maintained racially mixed households. Such cases constituted no more than one percent of all police households, but it is noteworthy that members of the Metropolitan Police could participate in interracial cohabitation without jeopardizing their position on the force. New Orleans had a tradition of interracial sexual relationships that was much stronger than elsewhere in the South, although the antebellum quadroon balls and the open resort to black women by white men had been an embarrassment to many of the city's residents.[37] The interracial police households of 1870 all involved men of French descent or immigrants from Europe. In three households, white officers—a German, an Italian, and a Spaniard—lived with black or mulatto women. Two of these households included children, although the 1870 census does not indicate the familial relationship of the head of household to its other members. Perhaps more startling, the census revealed four households where mulatto policemen lived with white women. Three of these men were Louisianans with French surnames, and the fourth was a native of Spain. The white women were natives of Ireland, England, New York and Louisiana. Despite the long-standing toleration of relationships between white men and Negro women, white women who wanted respectability among whites would certainly have had to avoid open cohabitation with male Negroes.

The absolute number of interracial unions involving policemen in 1870 was not striking, but their relative number was. Historian John Blassingame has found a total of 205 interracial unions in New Orleans in the 1870 census, twenty-nine of them involving white women and Afro-American men. Policemen constituted only 1.3 percent of all employed males over the age of sixteen, yet 3.4 percent of all interracial couples included policemen. Although only .4 percent of the male work force was comprised of Negro policemen, 13.8 percent of all interracial unions with white women involved Afro-American police officers. Thus, in a rare form of interracial relationship, policemen could be regarded as leaders. It is likely officials of the Metropolitan Police knew of these unions, for policemen were public figures and usually got their jobs because they had some standing in their ward or neighborhood. This suggests that toleration of interracial cohabitation must have been the practice among police commissioners and supervisory officers.[38]

The census reveals still more about black policemen. Most were fairly young men. In fact, 77 percent of white officers were forty years or younger. But black policemen were younger still, with 92 percent no older than forty, and with a mean age three years below that of their white counterparts (32.4 compared with 35.5).[39]

Black officers were also more likely to have been native-born than their white counterparts. A large percentage of white policemen in New Orleans were immigrants, notably Irish; black policemen were mostly Louisianans. Of the 182 Afro-American policemen in the 1870 census, only three (1.6 percent) were foreign-born. Of the native Americans, 130 (71.4 percent) came from Louisiana, while forty-two (23.1 percent) were from former slave states. Only seven (3.8 percent) immigrated to Louisiana from the Northern states.[40]

Though more often native than their white fellow officers, most of the black police shared the same socioeconomic niche with the white officers. Most policemen of both races owned less than $100 of personal property and no real estate at all. About one-sixth of each racial group transcended the $100 barrier in personalty, and about one-tenth for realty. However, black policemen were considerably likelier to own $100 or more of property, either real or personal than the general black adult male population of New Orleans. Thus, black policemen did not represent only the bottom of the black class structure; instead they were spread over the middle and lower class.[41]

In one sense, black policemen fared better economically than white cops. Black police came from a relative range higher in the black class structure than the range in the white economic structure from which white officers were drawn. White policemen in 1870 were less likely to own either personal or real property than the white public. Yet black policemen were *more* likely than the black public to own both kinds of property.[42]

Though most policemen came from fairly humble economic circumstances, a minority of them occupied a middling position in the class structure. For the black policemen of 1870, it is possible to trace about one-tenth back to earlier years through the city directories and determine their prior occupations. Of seventeen men, two had low white collar jobs, seven worked in skilled blue collar trades, six were semiskilled or service workers, and two were employed as unskilled laborers.[43]

The city directories provide another link to black officers' pasts, for about one-tenth of the 1870 black policemen can be traced backward to determine their status as free men before the Civil War. That would not, however, be an accurate measure of how many black policemen of the Reconstruction Era had been free or slave before the war. City directories would have included only a few free black laborers, thus underrepresenting free men of color. Moreover, blacks who migrated to New Orleans during and after the war cannot be traced through New Orleans city directories for the antebellum period.

It seems likely that the black policemen of 1870 came disproportionately from the ranks of antebellum free men of color rather than from the prewar slave population. A suggestive indication of this comes from the relative number of Negro policemen designated as "mulatto" by the census takers, as opposed to "black." Of the 1870 Afro-American policemen in New Orleans, the census marshals described 75.8 percent as mulatto, but in the adult Negro male population of the city, only 34.5 percent appear on the returns as mulatto. The antebellum free black community had been heavily mulatto (77.3 percent), but the slave population was distinctively black (75.2 percent). Thus, a majority of the Afro-American policemen in New Orleans probably had been free before the war.[44]

Some of the 1870 black policemen had served in the Civil War. Approximately one-tenth (eighteen men) of the 1870 black police contingent can be identified as Union soldiers from Louisiana units. Others may have served under different names or in units from other states. The Louisiana black veterans all served with one of two regiments, the Sixth and Seventh Louisiana Colored Infantry.

Perhaps the most distinguished of the black policemen to have Civil War service was Jordan B. Noble. Noble gained fame in antebellum New Orleans as a veteran of three wars. A free black from Georgia, Noble joined the Seventh U. S. Infantry in 1813 at the age of thirteen. He served as a drummer in the Battle of New Orleans in January 1815, and later in the same capacity during the Seminole War in Florida in the 1830s and the Mexican War of the 1840s. In a parade in 1860 commemorating the victory over the British, Noble delivered a short speech to the crowd and received a special medal at the order of General Winfield Scott. During the Civil War, the former drummer held the rank of captain, commanding C Company, Seventh Louisiana Colored Infantry. The 1870 census described Noble as "mulatto" and noted that he held real estate valued at $1500. He had achieved a higher rank in the Union Army than any of the other black police veterans.[45]

The next highest ranking black veteran on the police force was Octave Rey. Born in New Orleans in 1837, Rey was the youngest of three brothers and the son of Barthelemy Rey, a member of the first school board of an institution for indigent orphans. Octave Rey married Louise Belleme in 1859 at St. Augustine Catholic Church and the couple had at least six children. A cooper by profession, Rey joined the Union Army during the Civil War, serving as a lieutenant in E Co., Sixth Louisiana Colored Infantry, and sustaining a leg injury while on an extended march. Encountering racial prejudice, Rey resigned his commission in 1863 because "concord does not exist among the officers of the army and . . ." the difference of race [was] the cause of it.[46]

Rey joined the Metropolitan Police and became a captain commanding the fourth precinct. After losing his position as a result of "Redemption." Rey remained a respected member of the community and property owner (he held $500 worth of personal and $500 of realty in 1870). He served as chief of special election of 1882. When he was involved in a shooting incident in 1886, the *Daily Picayune* referred to his service on the force during Reconstruction and described him as a "tall, fine looking man." At 6/2 1/2", Rey was described by a fellow black New Orleanian as a "tall man of herculean proportions—energetic, powerful, and dynamic in his thinking." Although not highly educated, Rey was reputed to have a "prodigious memory for names and people," a trait that must have served him well as a policeman. He received a federal pension for his military service, and died in 1908.[47]

The restoration of conservative white government in Louisiana severely undercut the position of black policemen like Octave Rey. The size of the police force was reduced, and the percentage of black officers dropped precipitously. Only twenty-two of the 333 policemen in the 1880 census were black (6.6 percent), considerably less than the black population proportion of 26.7 percent. Of the 182 black men on the force in 1870, only four remained in 1880. Police forces throughout the South were "bleached" by Redemption, as Table 1 indicates. The result of Redemption was not only the underrepresentation of black people on the police force, but also the reemergence of racially intolerant and discriminatory policing.[48]

Yet blacks continued to hang on to some police positions in New Orleans. In 1900, fifteen of 293 policemen (5.1 percent) in the census were black. These black officers were "solid citizens" even more so than their white counterparts: 93 percent were married (compared to 78 percent of whites); 93 percent were heads of family (79 percent for whites); and 36 percent of heads of family owned their homes (in contrast to 19 percent of white police heads of family). Moreover, the median age of black policemen was four years older than that of white officers, reversing the age relationship of the Reconstruction period. This suggests constricted opportunities for black policemen, and a lower accession rate of black men onto the force. One black cop, fifty-five-year-old Joseph Johnson, had been in service at least since 1870. Married 33 years, Johnson owned a mortgaged home, and had served in the army during the Civil War. Another black officer, George Doyle, subsequently became a deputy U. S. marshal during Taft's presidency. Doyle was active in the plasterers' union, and headed an organization dedicated to commemorating the Battle of New Orleans of 1815.[49]

*

The Reconstruction Era offered far more opportunities for black policemen than could be found in turn-of-the-century New Orleans. During Reconstruction blacks had enjoyed a remarkable degree of success in gaining access to police positions. The absolute size of the black community—the largest in America in 1870—probably helped make this possible. Certainly the strength of the antebellum free black community was important, too. Free black militiamen from New Orleans had played an important role in the American victory over the British in 1815, and these black veterans participated in commemorative parades even as late as 1860, a major source of pride for free people of color. Even slaves had been able to win greater de facto control over their own lives in the relatively loose urban fabric of New Orleans, as Richard Wade has suggested. A tradition among Afro-Americans in the Crescent City of comparative prosperity, high self-esteem and leadership—nurtured by the fluidity of racial attitudes and relationships in the Caribbean and by the pervasive and often egalitarian effects of Catholicism—proved a relatively strong foundation for postbellum black achievement.[50]

Few black men found employment as police officers in late nineteenth-century America. Even where black policemen were employed, they usually found themselves restricted to patrolling black neighborhoods and arresting people of their own color. New Orleans had been a national leader, the first city to hire black policemen in the early 1800s and again during Reconstruction, and the first to allow black officers to operate on a basis of equality with white officers, something that most American communities would not attempt until the 1960s.

Even though the Metropolitan Police experiment in New Orleans can be classified a failure, the fault did not lie with the police. Though imperfect, the police during Reconstruction performed the normal police functions as well or better than any previous or subsequent police force in nineteenth-century New Orleans. The relationships between the police and the white community, and between the state and federal governments were responsible for the failure. White conservatives did, at times, admit the competence of the Metropolitan Police, but would not accept the legitimacy of the Republican, racially integrated government that created the Metropolitan organization. Thus, federal involvement was critical to the creation and survival of the Metropolitan Police. When the federal government withdrew that support in 1877, the Metropolitans were adrift in a sea of implacable white hostility.[51]

Police officers have a highly public role, one especially sensitive in a society with democratic values and institutions. After all, the police can be dangerous to life and destructive of civil liberties. Americans have long been critical of their police, even as they have depended upon them to enforce the law. One consequence of this mixture of dependence and fear has been a persistent desire to see police forces manned by trustworthy friends and allies. During much of the nineteenth century (and even the twentieth) American urban policing was heavily politicized with police personnel usually recruited from the ranks of the party in power. Police forces operated in a very personal, rather than formal style (as historian Wilbur Miller has argued), often responsive to pressures and incentives from the political system.[52]

Yet, the abuses of the politicized and personalized American police led not so much to public sentiment for formal, impartial policing as to bids by each self-conscious ethnic or racial group to be allowed to share in the system of responsive favoritism. In such a pluralistic society it became important for the police force to become a microcosm of the whole society—or at least the whole community. Irish Americans thus found it easy to accept the legitimacy of police forces in whose ranks members of their own ethnic group were well represented. Black Americans have been just as reluctant to accept police forces with few or no black officers. The bar against blacks in policing meant the denial of job opportunities, role models, connections to political power, and aspirations to dignity and first-class citizenship.

Representation on the police force was thus important to many ethnic and racial groups. Of course, a police force was not a legislature, but the vital public role played by the police made representation symbolically as well as substantively important to excluded groups. This sense of sharing helped legitimize authority in a heterogeneous and democratic society. For most black New Orleanians, black policemen were a source of pride and dignity, a further proof of black manhood and courage, and testimony to the legitimacy of democratic government. As pioneers in a new frontier of race relationships, black policemen provided role models for their contemporaries and for future generations.

Notes for "Black Policemen in New Orleans During Reconstruction"

[1] For a realistic assessment of the city's distinctive qualities, see Joseph G. Tregle, "Early New Orleans Society: A Reappraisal," *Journal of Southern History*, 28 (1952): 20-36.

[2] Richard Wade, *Slavery in the Cities: The South, 1820-1860* (New York, 1964), 83-89, 92, 145-46, 150-52, 164-66, 178, 219-20, 223-25. Other evidence of the relative freedom of blacks in New Orleans can be found in Richard Tansey, "Out-of-State Free Blacks in Late Antebellum New Orleans," *Louisiana History*, 22 (1981): 369-86; and in the experiences of James Thomas recounted in Loren Schweninger, "A Negro Sojourner in Antebellum New Orleans," *Louisiana History*, 20 (1979): 305-14. See also Ira Berlin, *Slaves Without Masters: The Free Negro in the Antebellum South* (New York, 1974), 108-32, 172, 174, 262, 278.

[3] William W. Chenault and Robert C. Reinders have suggested that Northerners in New Orleans were "largely indifferent to the question of slavery." See their article, "The Northern-born Community of New Orleans in the 1850s," *Journal of American History*, 51 (1964): 232-47.

[4] Laurence J. Kotlikoff and Anton J. Rupert, "The Manumission of Slaves in New Orleans, 1827-1846," *Southern Studies*, 19 (1980): 172-81.

[5] Ted Tunnell, "Free Negroes and the Freedmen: Black Politics in New Orleans During the Civil War," *Southern Studies*, 19 (1980): 28.

[6] Ibid., 24-25.

[7] David C. Rankin, "The Origins of Black Leadership in New Orleans During Reconstruction," *Journal of Southern History*, 40 (1974): 417-40. Rankin has also argued that demographic and economic conditions, more than "Latin heritage" created a unique version of slavery and race relations in New Orleans, see his "The Tannenbaum Thesis Reconsidered: Slavery and Race Relations in Antebellum Louisiana," *Southern Studies*, 18 (1979): 5-31.

[8] The best study of the black community in New Orleans is John W. Blassingame, *Black New Orleans, 1860-1880* (Chicago and London, 1973). His chapter on "Race Relations" (173-210) is particularly valuable. Although there is no substantial account of Reconstruction-Era police in New Orleans, some useful material can be found in Joe Gray Taylor, *Louisiana Reconstructed, 1863-1877* (Baton Rouge, 1974), which is also good for context. See also Roger A. Fischer, *The Segregation Struggle in Louisiana, 1862-1877* (Urbana, 1974). The population data are derived from U. S. Census Office, *Ninth Census—Volume 1. The Statistics of the Population of the United States* (Washington, 1872), 77-295, and U. S. Census Office, *Population of the United States in 1860* (Washington, 1864), lvii-lviii.

[9] The numerical strengths are based on a count of policemen from the population schedules of the 1870 census.

[10] Proceedings of City Council Meetings, March 17, 1804; documents and letters of Laussat, colonial prefect and commissioner of the French government, and of the commissioners of His Catholic Majesty, November

30, 1803, New Orleans Public Library [NOPL]. Herbery Asbury, *The French Quarter: An Informal History of the New Orleans Underworld* (1936; reprint ed., St. Simons Island, Ga., 1964), 70.

[11] Allegre and Michel are identifiable from the city guard payrolls (January, March, April, June, July and August 1814 in Historic New Orleans Collection and May 1814 in Louisiana Collection, Howard-Tilton Memorial Library, Tulane University); death records of the city of New Orleans (Allegre was identified as black, Michel had no designation of race—microfilm, NOPL); the census of 1820, in which Michel was listed as a free men of color (there were no other heads of family of the same name in the 1820 census, and the only Allegre family was composed of free persons of color); and military service records for the War of 1812 (Allegre served in Fortier's Battalion of free men of color). See M. J. B. Pierson, *Louisiana Soldiers in the War of 1812* (Baton Rouge, 1963).

For Pierre Aubry, see death records of New Orleans, 10:141. He served in Fortier's Battalion of free men of color in the War of 1812; see Pierson, *Louisiana Soldiers*. In the 1820 census, the household headed by Pierre Aubry included only one adult male, a free man of color between 26 and 45 years of age. See also Payroll of City Guard, December 1820, Louisiana Collection. For Augustus Bolen, see death records of New Orleans, 32:525.

[12] Berlin, *Slaves Without Masters*, 118-28. Ordinances and Resolutions of the City Council of New Orleans, December 18, 1817, Documents of Laussat, December 9, 16, 1803, NOPL.

[13] Berlin, *Slaves Without Masters*.

[14] Ordinances and Resolutions of the City Council of New Orleans, May 21, 1816; Proceedings of City Council Meetings, July 9, 1804, and April 30, 1808; Documents of Laussat, November 30, 1803, NOPL.

[15] Eighth U. S. Census (1860), Population Schedules, New Orleans, M653, Reel 418, p. 113 shows black police officer Marie Ursin, and Reel 419, p. 309 shows mulatto police officer R. Palio. Reel 419, p. 15 shows L. Badey, a black man whose occupation, nearly illegible, might be watchman. Ursin, Palio and Badey do not appear anywhere in the personnel books of the police department for the years 1859-1861.

[16] *New Orleans Times*, May 3, 10, 11 and June 4, 1867. *New Orleans Tribune*, May 10, 1867.

[17] *Tribune*, May 28, 31 and June 1, 2, 4, 6, 1867.

[18] *Tribune*, June 18 and December 18, 1867.

[19] *Times*, December 4, 1868; *Acts of Louisiana* (1868), 85-98; (1873), 76.

[20] The homicide rate for New Orleans in the years 1857-1859 was 30 per 100,000 population annually; for Philadelphia in the years 1853-1859, 3.6 per 100,000 annually; and although no exact figure exists for Boston in this period, it was undoubtedly quite low. New Orleans rate: *Annual Report of the Attorney General to the Legislature of the State of Louisiana* (New Orleans, 1860), 7. Boston rate: Roger lane, *Policing the City: Boston, 1822-1885* (Cambridge, 1967), 149. Philadelphia rate: Lane, *Violent Death in the City: Suicide, Accident, and Murder in Nineteenth-Century Philadelphia* (Cambridge, 1979), 71.

The figure for the New Orleans policemen killed represents homicides only—accidental deaths are excluded. *Daily True Delta*, March 28, 1855; *Commercial Bulletin*, March 26 and 27, 1856; *Louisiana Courier*, March 20, 1856. Messages of Mayors, December 26, 1860, NOPL. *Daily Picayune*, March 29, 1854, June 13, 1855, December 24, 1859; *New Orleans Bee*, March 19, 1856, December 24, 1860, and January 10 and March 4, 25, 1861.

A slungshot was a small lead or iron ball attached to a short wooden handle by a cable or cord—a sort of unspiked pocketsized version of the medieval morning star.

[21] *New Orleans Times*, October 27-31 and November 5, 1868, May 18-20, 1869, March 6-8, April 7, 13, 16, 23, 27 and 30, May 1, 6-11, 1873; *Daily Picayune*, March 6-8, 1873, and September 9-13, 1874; *New Orleans Republican*, March 6 and 7, April 22 and 26, 1873. Stuart Omer Landry, *The Battle of Liberty Place: The Overthrow of Carpetbag Rule in New Orleans—September 14, 1874* (New Orleans, 1955), 123, 129.

[22] Calculated from data reported in *Annual Report of the Board of Metropolitan Police*, 1868-1869, 1873-1874.

[23] *Metropolitan Police Annual Report*, (1868-1869), 7-9, 44-48; (1869-1870), 10-16; (1870-1871), 7-8; (1872-1873), 8; (1873-1874), 11-12. *Acts of Louisiana* (1867), 171-173; (1869), 42, 65; (1870 Extra Session), 213-14; (1874), 68-72; (1875), 35-39. *Report of the Attorney General* (1869), 7. *Daily Picayune*, June 16, 1869; *New Orleans Republican*, June 15, 1869; *Times*, September 16-18, 1868 and May 28, 1870.

[24]*Times*, December 4, 1868. Ninth Census (1870), Population Schedules, New Orleans. Blacks did not fare so well in securing jobs in other forms of law enforcement or security: three of twenty-three constables, (13.0 percent); two of fifteen marshals and deputy marshals, (13.3 percent); eight of 161 private watchmen (5.0 percent); and none of thirty-eight sheriff's officers.

[25]*Metropolitan Police Annual Report*, 1868-1869, 1873-1874; Police Board Records, 1854-1856, NOPL.

[26]*Metropolitan Police Annual Report* (1868-1868, 1873-1874); Police Board Records, 1854-1856; Reports of the Third District Police, 1852-1863, NOPL.

[27]Ninth Census (1870), Population Schedules, Charleston and Savannah. U. S. Census Office, *Ninth Census*. Edward King, *The Great South* (Hartford, 1875), 369.

[28]Ninth Census (1870), Population Schedules, Norfolk, Petersburg, Portsmouth and Richmond. Robert Thompson Mowrey, "The Evolution of the Nashville Police From Early Times to 1880" (Bachelor's thesis, Princeton University, 1974), 35, 47-48 (copy in Tennessee State Library).

[29]Howard N. Rabinowitz, *Race Relations in the Urban South, 1865-1890* (New York, 1978), 41-43.

[30]*Tribune*, June 19, 1867.

[31]No official arrest books from the period survive. The only useful records are the newspaper reports of the period, but these do not indicate the race of police and arrestees. Many of the published arrests did not even report the names of the persons involved. When the newspaper did report names, the police officer were often cited only by last name, and while the arrestees' full names were usually given, they were not often accompanied by a designation of race. No police rosters for the period are available, but one can be reconstructed for the summer of 1870 from the population schedules of the federal census, and this list includes the officers' racial identities. Some of the arrestees can be found in the city directories for 1870 and 1871, which showed blacks as "colored," but most of the arrestees did not appear in the directories (probably due to their transience or social marginality). One further complication was the sharing of surnames by some white and black officers.

Thus, while some positive identifications of black-on-white arrests can be made, an accurate estimate of frequency or proportionality by race is impossible.

For arrest reports, see the *Daily Picayune*, June 2 to August 31, 1870. City directories: *Graham's Crescent City Directory* (New Orleans, 1870), and *Edward's Annual Directory* (New Orleans, 1871-1873). For the police roster see the Ninth Census (1870), Population Schedules, New Orleans.

[32]Courcelle: *Tribune*, May 28, 1867. Gaudette and Lewis: Ninth Census (1870), Population Schedules, New Orleans. Quinn: *Times*, May 9, 1872. Isabelle: Blassingame, *Black New Orleans*, 157. C. C. Antoine and Oscar J. Dunn both served as lieutenant governor of Louisiana, and were ex-officio members of the board.

[33]Ninth Census (1870), Population Schedules, New Orleans. *Gardner's New Orleans Directory* (New Orleans, 186, 1868, 1869); *Graham's Crescent City Directory* (New Orleans, 1867, 1870); *Edward's Annual Directory* (New Orleans, 1871-1873); *Soards' Directory* (New Orleans, 1874-1877).

[34]*Times*, October 20, 1868; King, *The Great South*, 95.

[35]*Tribune*, December 18, 1867. *Daily Picayune*, October 3, and November 28, 1872; *Times*, May 13, 1869.

[36]*Metropolitan Police Annual Report* (1868-1869), 33. Blassingame suggests that blacks had a relatively high crime rate, citing their percentage of all arrestees in October and November 1867 (38 and 35 percent). He also observes that 30 percent of the inmates in the parish prison in the 1870 census were Negroes, and 43 percent in September 1874. Although he acknowledges the problem of inferring crime rates from arrest reports, he does not comment on the difficulty in inferring crime rates, or even arrest rates, it was quite possible that few black arrestees would have been able to make bail, secure release on their own recognizance, or win their case in court because of economic inequality or discrimination by judges or juries. Blassingame, *Black New Orleans*, 162.

[37]Edward Sullivan, *Rambles and Scrambles in North and South America* (London, 1852), 223-25.

[38]Blassingame, *Black New Orleans*, 206-207.

[39]Calculations based on Ninth Census (1870), Population Schedules, New Orleans.

[40]Ibid.

[41]The property values for white and black male populations of the city are based on systematic random samples consisting of 2,378 whites and 856 blacks. Calculations for police property values are based on complete enumerations of 465 white officers and 182 black officers.

Roughly the same fraction of white and black policemen owned over $100 personalty: 17.9 percent of black policemen, 16.3 percent of whites. But among the one-sixth of blacks and whites who exceeded $100 of personal property, whites held substantially more. The mean value of personalty for that 16.3 percent of white policemen was approximately $428, while for the 17.9 percent of blacks, only $255. Few policemen owned real estate: 8.7 percent of blacks, 10.3 percent of whites. For this minority of police real property owners, the mean value was higher for whites than blacks: $1203 in contrast to $972 for blacks.

Only 5.7 percent of the black population owned personal property worth more than $100, while the figure for black policemen was 17.9 percent. The mean value for policemen who had such property was less, however, than for the black population: $255 (police), $487 (population). The same was true for real estate. More black policemen owned real estate than was true for the general population of black males (8.7 percent versus 6.8 percent), but their mean value was less ($972 for black policemen, $1879 for the black population).

Of the white adult male population, 31.9 percent owned $100 or more of personalty, and 17.6 percent held realty. Among white policemen, only 16.3 percent possessed $100 or more of personal property and just 10.3 percent owned real estate.

[42]For information on real and personal property, see note 41.

[43]The occupations are classified in this manner: low white collar—clerk, barkeeper; skilled blue collar—bricklayer (2), carpenter (2), cigar maker, painter, shoemaker; semiskilled and service workers—butcher, drayman, cook, barber (3); unskilled—laborer (2). The butcher may have owned his shop, in which case he ought to be reclassified as low white collar (proprietor).

[44]Ninth Census (1870), Population Schedules, New Orleans. *Population of the United States in 1860*, 194.

[45]Ninth Census (1870), Population Schedules, New Orleans. Roland C. McConnell, *Negro Troops of Antebellum Louisiana: A History of the Battalion of Free Men of Color* (Baton Rouge, 1968), 74, 85, 114-15.

[46]Rodolphe Lucien Desdunes, *Our People and Our History* (Baton Rouge, 1973), 114-20. Military service and pension file of Octave Rey, Records of the Veterans Bureau, Record Group 15, National Archives.

[47]Tenth census (1880), Population Schedules, New Orleans. Desdunes, *Our People*, 114-20. *Daily Picayune*, November 7, 1882, April 21, 1886.

[48]Tenth Census (1880), Population Schedules, New Orleans. Dennis C. Rousey, "The New Orleans Police, 1805-1889: A Social History" (Ph.D. dissertation, Cornell University, 1978), 269-90. Only Memphis was an exception to this trend. A series of yellow fever epidemics there in the 1870s encouraged the hiring of black police officers, because they were less vulnerable to the disease than the Irish immigrants who dominated the police force. See Dennis C. Rousey, "Yellow Fever and Black Policemen in Memphis: A Post-Reconstruction Anomaly," *Journal of Southern History*, 51 (1985): 357-74.

[49]Twelfth Census (1900), Population Schedules, New Orleans. *Times-Picayune*, November 23, 1937.

[50]Wade, *Slavery in the Cities*.

[51]*Times*, April 7, 1873, provides an example of conservative acknowledgement of Metropolitan Police competence.

[52]Wilbur R. Miller, *Cops and Bobbies: Police Authority in New York and London, 1830-1870* (Chicago and London, 1977).

JUSTICE DELAYED:
APPOLINE PATOUT V. THE UNITED STATES,
1864-1918*

Michael G. Wade

Historians and other writers have written extensively about the Civil War and Reconstruction era in Louisiana. Immediately following the war, reporters filed reams of copy about the prostrated South.[1] Military campaigns, the politics of the postwar era, and race relations have received considerable attention. Researchers have also investigated the slow recovery of the cotton and sugar economies in the post-bellum era.[2] And scholars have even focused on the positions of most non-combatants, including those residing in Louisiana, who described war-related losses.[3]

But relatively little attention has been paid to the damage claims of 726 residents of the United States who were not heard by the Southern Claims Commission.[4] For the most part, the claimants were French-born residents of the Bayou Teche region of South Louisiana. The war, particularly the Great Texas Overland Expedition of 1863-1864, had resulted in heavy damage to their sugarcane plantations. Consequently, owners sought compensation for their losses at the hands of the Union army, which invaded the region in the spring of 1863 and then lived off the countryside of St. Martin and St. Mary parishes for some two months in late 1863 and early 1864.[5] American neutrals were able to file their petitions as early as 1870, but French subjects had to await the establishment of the French and American Claims Commission a decade later. By that time, a number of the original claimants had died and their heirs had to prosecute the suits.

Appoline Patout, for example, had died in March of 1879 after trying for sixteen years to collect what she felt was just recompense for her losses. Born Pauline Napoléone Fournier in Lizy-sur-Ourc, France, in 1805, she had come to South Louisiana in 1829 with her husband, Siméon, who established a plantation near New Iberia and made two sugar crops before his death in 1847.[6] Left with ten children and an imminent

---

*First published in *Louisiana History*, 31 (1990): 141-59. Reprinted with the kind permission of the author and the Louisiana Historical Association.

cane harvest, Madame Patout built her plantation into one of the largest ones in St. Mary Parish. On the eve of the Civil War, she owned 2,100 acres and 107 slaves.[7] In 1861, her mill produced 507 hogsheads of sugar.[8]

Most sugar producers had already begun to feel the effects of the war even as they harvested the record 1861-1862 cane crop. Their industry operated largely on credit, which began to tighten in 1860. As a result, land values declined, but the routine on plantations continued. The outbreak of war drained manpower from sugar plantations, producing a critical shortage of overseers and growing apprehension about the loyalty of the captive black population. In June of 1861, the Union effectively blockaded the Mississippi and engendered a vigorous search for alternative markets for sugar. New Orleans fell the next April and in the spring of 1863, Gen. Nathaniel Banks carried the war into the Teche and Red River regions, marching through New Iberia and forcing large numbers of Teche planters to flee to Texas with their slaves.[9]

In mid-April, the Patouts and their neighbors got a foretaste of what was to come when Union commanders confiscated supplies for the remainder of their campaign and troopers exercised individual initiative in securing their share of the spoils of war.[10] On April 18, Mrs. Patout was forced to relinquish seven wagons, sixteen American mules, eight head of cattle, and six American horses in return for a receipt. About two weeks later, troops seized 150 head of cattle and eighteen mules from the Patouts and drove them to Berwick Bay. A week later, an agent of the local provost marshal seized a bale of cotton from her plantation.[11] His supplies replenished, Banks captured Alexandria before turning his attention to the siege of Port Hudson.[12]

Meanwhile, the French invasion of Mexico had made Washington fearful of a possible French-Confederate rapprochement. Accordingly, Gen. Henry Halleck instructed Banks to invade Texas in order to demonstrate American resolve regarding French violations of the Monroe Doctrine. Following an embarrassing defeat at Sabine Pass in early September, Banks launched an overland invasion across southwestern Louisiana. His forces, commanded by Maj. Gen. William Buel Franklin, began moving out of Algiers by rail on September 13, 1863, bound for Brashear City. Banks' detractors derisively dubbed the undertaking The Great Texas Overland Expedition.[13] The Nineteenth Army Corps and the First and Third Divisions of the Thirteenth Army Crops reached the Jeanerette-New Iberia area on October 4 and 5. These troops apparently paid little attention to the reminders from their commanding officers that straggling for purposes of pillage and plunder was a capital offense. Respecting neither orders nor "protection papers" provided loyal citizens, the troops sacked stores and warehouses as well as sugar plantations.[14] Pausing briefly, they then moved on to Vermilionville (present-day Lafayette) and points north and west.

As early as May 31, 1864, Appoline Patout began pressing her damage claim against the United States government on the grounds that she was a neutral foreign national. Her claims and extensive relative correspondence provide a detailed and occasionally graphic account of how the war affected her plantation.[15] Mrs. Patout's narrative of events is consistent with published accounts and with the descriptions provided by her neighbors in their own claims against the federal government.

After the end of the Union army's campaign through the Teche region, Mrs. Patout went to New Orleans and had Justice of the Peace Edmond Meunier draft a petition on her behalf. She swore that she was a French citizen, not naturalized, that she had taken the oath of neutrality required by General Order Number 41,[16] and that she resided alone with her daughters on her plantation. She assessed her claims on the original cost of the property and on its value in gold or silver to account for the "circulation and depreciation of paper money which constituted the unit of account."[17]

According to this beleaguered widow, the war reached her property on April 18, 1863, when units of Gen. Nathaniel Banks' Nineteenth Army Corps appropriated the aforementioned livestock, carts, and harness. Mrs. Patout was issued a receipt for these goods but apparently not for the herd of cattle which Banks' troops seized from the nearby Grand Marais for transport to Berwick Bay. Fifteen of these were prime milk cows. Shortly thereafter, she was visited on several occasions by squads of seven or eight soldiers who took whatever horses and mules they could catch. She lost eighteen more mules in this fashion and was unable to obtain receipts. At this juncture, she claimed losses of almost $10,500.[18] Little did she know that worst was yet to come.

After a campaign to the west and north of St. Mary Parish, General Franklin's forces, including the Nineteenth Army Corps, retreated from Vermilionville and began arriving in New Iberia, about ten miles west of the Patout plantation, on the morning of November 17. A significant portion of this force made camp on the Charles Olivier plantation, only three miles from the Patouts.[19] Bands of infantry entered their plantation on the eighteenth and stayed for three days, ransacking the place. In the words of Appoline Patout, "alone with her daughters, the petitioner was forced to let everything be done, to endure all outrage, to open her apartments, her wardrobes, her drawers from the smallest to the largest, since the soldiers were intent on seeing everything and appropriating all that they fancied . . . having tried to complain the petitioner was rudely addressed and, that since she does not understand the English language, she cannot repeat the soldiers' answers, but that these answers must have been insulting, considering the animation of the soldiers and the refusal of the petitioner's daughters to translate what they were saying."[20]

When she confronted a soldier who appeared to be leading one of the bands of marauders, he told her that he did not care to prevent the looting and that she should not be surprised at what was occurring since the soldiers with him were prison escapees. This may or may not have been the case, but Mrs. Patout, "with a broken heart . . . bowed to letting her properties be destroyed, resolving to demand compensation." Among other household items, the troopers took linens, undergarments, cooking utensils, and three zinc bath tubs. They also helped themselves to eight hogsheads of sugar, forty barrels of potatoes, twelve hogs, fifteen milk cows, six beehives, and 550 chickens, ducks, and geese.[21] She estimated her losses for the three-day period at $1,648. On November 21, bands of blacks attached to the Nineteenth Army Corps and armed with cane knives entered the premises and rifled the place for three hours, carrying off an additional $490 worth of goods.[22]

Less traumatic but more damaging were the recurring visits of elements of the Thirteenth and Nineteenth Army corps between late November 1863 and mid-January 1864. Soldiers appropriated large quantities of corn, dismantled storage barns, and carried off the fences. Mrs. Patout was issued receipts for the corn, but she claimed that they were for amounts much smaller than those actually taken, and that the troops destroyed some 3,000 bushels by removing the storage facilities. She maintained that daily crossings of her plantation by federal troops and the general destruction of enclosures and fences produced a complete loss of the 1863 cane, corn, and cotton crops. She also lost fifty-six barrels of raw syrup, and 41,850 pounds of sugar (thirty-one hogsheads), fifty more hogs, forty sheep, and forty-five oxen and cows.[23]

Taking an English-speaking relative with her, Appoline Patout went to General Franklin's headquarters in New Iberia, "intending to submit a complaint to him for all the thefts and violence . . . and to ask him for protection as a citizen of the French Empire." An intermediary refused her an interview with Franklin, telling her that it was preferable for the Union army to use whatever was on the plantation as opposed to leaving it for the Confederates. She was granted an authorization to keep very modest quantities of corn and molasses and some livestock. While Franklin did not speak with Mrs. Patout, he was well aware of the complaints of local residents regarding the seizures of movable property.[24]

On December 14, 1863, Franklin issued General Order No. 45, which noted that more than fifty men had been captured by the enemy while on unauthorized foraging and robbing expeditions. Franklin announced that he would exchange such prisoners only after all others had been exchanged. He also informed the commanding general of the Confederate forces that he wanted any soldier of his command found robbing to be treated as such. Franklin instructed that the order be read to every company and closed by saying that "the commanding general believes there is yet self respect enough among the officers of this command to force them to put a stop to these daily outrages."[25]

By the time these orders were issued, the Patouts had suffered additional losses. A few days after Madame Patout returned to her estate, federal troops took 150 hogs, 180 barrels of sweet potatoes, still more corn, and about 5,300 pounds of "middling" cotton. They helped themselves to 245 cords of various types of wood, including willow for fireplaces, oak for wheel-making and oak, cypress, and tupelo gum for the sugar house. To protect themselves from the unusually severe winter of 1863-1864, they dismantled three storehouses, two corn cribs, an old store, and much of the plantation's fencing. They also comandeered the plantation's carts and oxen to haul away the plunder. Finally, on or around January 24, 1864, some five to six hundred cavalry drove off another 175 head of livestock.[26]

George Hepworth, who was with the Union forces in the Teche region, observed that "there is not a single planter in this department who has not personally suffered through this war. Their crops of sugar-cane, yielding from five hundred to a thousand hogsheads of sugar, are still standing in February. . . . I have ridden through miles of plantations, from which only a few hogsheads of sugar had been made. Cane is standing now in March, thousands and thousands of acres of it. Thus the crop of the past year is nothing, and that of the coming year will be the same. . . ."[27]

Regarding the acquisitive capacities of the boys in blue, Hepworth said that "never did an army make cleaner work than ours. . . . Our boys drove to the rear every pony and mule, every ox and cow and sheep. They did not leave, on an average, two chickens to a plantation. Wherever they encamped, the fences served as beds and firewood."[28] Private Augustus George Sinks of the Forty-sixth Indiana wrote that, "we had made it a practice during the past year to never lie on the ground. After taking all the loose boards and board fences, we went for a number of unoccupied houses and appropriated them for making bunks. . . . The men would go several miles up the bayou and tear down sugarhouses, corn cribs, etc., and make a raft of the lumber, float it downstream to camp and build their huts."[29] This thoroughness is perhaps explained in part by General Banks' chief of staff, who reported to him on October 31, 1863, that the forage on hand was very limited while the army's animal population was increasing rapidly. He also reported fuel shortages, adding that supplies were sufficient for perhaps fifteen days.[30]

On November 17, the Nineteenth Army Corps was back in the New Iberia area after six weeks' absence. The Union camp stretched east from New Iberia for more than six miles.[31] The troops were ordered to prepare to remain stationary for at least thirty days. Foraging expeditions were to focus on the area to the immediate south and east to minimize the possibility of contact with the enemy. There was to be no excessive destruction or looting and receipts were to be furnished for seized goods.[32]

Historian Peter Ripley noted that St. Mary Parish, because it was controlled alternately by Union and Confederate troops, suffered wartime destruction that other parishes had not.[33] Patoutville was one of the focal points of the devastation and the plantation of Appoline Patout was a favorite target, especially on November 18, 19, and 20.[34] A neighbor of the Patouts, Emilien Landry, testifying years later on an unrelated matter, was asked to describe the Patout plantation in April 1865. He replied that "immediately after the war the Patout Plantation was almost naked. The residence and a portion of the sugar house were standing and there was no fencing on it. There were a few cabins. It had during the war been very much devastated."[35]

Though crop, livestock, and equipment losses constituted the major portion of her claim, Mrs. Patout also listed damages to plantation buildings and fixtures. She noted that the destruction of fences had allowed the intrusion of some 800 head of her neighbor's livestock into her fields. In addition to the fencing and the aforementioned grain barns, she also specified damage to the sugarhouse and to St. Nicholas Church (built with a donation from Appoline Patout). Madame Patout asked for $46,234.34 in specific damages and, after her attorney consulted with the French consul, added $10,000 in punitive damages and accrued interest.[36] The claim was submitted some time in the spring of 1864 after she failed to get satisfaction from local authorities. Exactly who she submitted it to is unclear, but there was a claims board in New Orleans throughout the four years of military rule.

Gen. Benjamin F. Butler had established a commission of three army officers to determine the allegiance of property owners and to condemn captured rebel property. His successor, Nathaniel Banks, continued the commission, using members of his personal staff. This body did order some payments for sugar, and Gen. Samuel B. Holabird, custodian of the funds, did make some payments for sugar. However, he experienced difficulty in settling these accounts with the Quartermaster's Department. When Gen. E. R. S. Canby arrived in 1864, his powers were limited to auditing claims and to recording an opinion as to the "justice and propriety of the evidence" for future reference.[37]

War's end found Mrs. Patout still doggedly pursuing her claim. Her lawyer, Auguste Barq, informed her that the War Department had indicated that her claim for lost livestock had been presented to the "Minister of Finance" for payment. His knowledge of the Washington power structure may have been deficient, but he did indicate that he would await actual payment before announcing the good news.[38] This was wise, because no payment materialized, and by mid-1866 the determined widow was seeking restitution from the quartermaster general of the United States. She instructed Barq to find out what the French government intended to do on behalf of the Louisiana French who had suffered losses during the late war.[39]

Though only one or two receipts appear in the official records, it is apparent from her references that she had a number of them and that she had even been reimbursed before the war ended for some relatively small seizures. This is interesting because army orders specified that only loyal citizens were "to be given receipts redeemable after the war, for quartermaster and commissary goods furnished to authorized officers of the Union army as it moved south."[40] And there is no evidence that Appoline Patout's loyalty was ever questioned.

In June 1866, Auguste Barq notified Mrs. Patout that her testimony had been forwarded to Washington. Regarding the French government, he included a letter which noted the exchange of "very urgent" diplomatic notes. Barq concluded that they would probably have to await "the meeting of the Commission on claims which will convene and decide on the French claims and . . . neither influence nor other measures can make them pass judgment on [some] claims before others."[41]

In retrospect, Mrs. Patout's claim appears to have been reasonable enough. She asked only restitution for direct damages suffered in 1863 and early 1864. Little seed cane was planted in 1863 and most of that year's crop was grown from rattoons. Many planters, Mrs. Patout included, were unable to manufacture their crop into sugar. Whereas 1,291 sugarhouses produced the 1861 crop, the 1864 crop was only 10,000 hogsheads produced by only 175 sugarhouses. Much of the 1865 crop had to be reserved for seed as 188 factories produced 18,000 hogsheads.[42] In 1860, Mrs. Patout's net worth was listed as $140,000.[43] The 1870 figure was $20,000.[44] Measured against these factors, her claim of $56,000 seems relatively modest.

Fidelity and reasonableness, however, would prove insufficient. The government placed every conceivable obstacle in the way of both native and foreign-born claimants. It required not only the formal receipts, but scrupulous detail about the quantity and value of each item claimed. These standards were quite difficult to meet in the face of haphazard accounting by Union officers, unrestrained marauding, and the hostility of Congress and the claims boards. Even allowing for exaggeration and for completely spurious claims, the small percentage of successful appeals and the meagerness of the awards is striking. The Southern Claims Commission's Driver Board in Nashville awarded only $140,747.46 on approximately $4 million in claims.[45]

The reluctant pace at which the government moved to consider the cases worked against all claims, regardless of their particular merit. American petitioners found that, with the passage of five years, witnesses had died or moved away. This problem was compounded for foreign claimants, who had to wait much longer to be heard. Appoline Patout's lawyer died sometime after informing her in mid-1868 that the fate of war claims was being debated in the Senate.[46] Available records show no activity on the case for the next seven years.

Fortunately, Mrs. Patout had no illusions about her prospects for an early or even a successful resolution of her suit. She and her husband were from the Seine and Marne district near Paris. Both of their families had weathered the vicissitudes of the French Revolution and the Napoleonic Wars. Indeed, the Patouts had invested 10,000 *francs* in Napoleon's government and had to wait almost four decades until the accession of Napoleon III to recover it."[47]

Armed with this perspective, this pious and practical lady set about rebuilding her plantation with the help of her sons in a place and time fraught with problems and uncertainties. Unlike cotton farming, sugar production required a large investment in the mill and in an elaborate system of ditches, levees, bridges, and pumps.[48] These had to be restored by a labor force, consisting mostly of freedmen, that was, by planter standards, expensive and unreliable.[49] The banks, preferring to make short-term loans, wanted 10-15% interest for the long-term loans planters required. Thus, rehabilitation proceeded slowly, and largely on a cash basis.[50]

Also retarding recovery was the political situation in St. Mary Parish and newly created Iberia Parish. Planters charged that corrupt local officials did not provide required services and that they did not enforce the laws. Even if one allows for a full measure of unreconstructed white bitterness, it is clear that arson, burglary, armed robbery, and murder were all clear and present dangers to area residents of both races.[51] And to compound these difficulties, local planters had to cope with floods, impassable roads, and short crops.[52]

The recovery of the local sugar economy was slow, but certainly no slower than the progress of the war claims of area planters. Following Auguste Barq's death, his widow placed his clients' papers with the New Orleans firm of De Loffre and Cambray, who informed Mrs. Patout's eldest son, Hippolyte, that the Southern Claims Commission only had jurisdiction over the appeals of American citizens. De Loffre said that the Patout case was being handled like all other French claims, i.e., through the mediation of the French consul. He thought that it would be necessary to draft a treaty establishing a commission to consider the numerous French claims.[53]

Following that communique, the firm somehow lost touch with Mrs. Patout for better than three years. Meanwhile, one Paul Cornen contacted Mrs. Patout in September 1876 wanting to know if someone was working on the case and informing her that Mrs. Barq was once again in possession of her deceased husband's records. Then the widow Barq and a somewhat mysterious character listed only as Guillaume Dupuy sent Appoline a letter promising that they could put her claim in order within one year. However, they said that it would be very expensive and that their fee would be 50 percent of the award. They indicated that unless they received a reply by the end of the month, they would assume that Mrs. Patout agreed to their conditions and that she authorized them to act on her behalf in Washington.[54] It appears that the Patouts did not reply, because fifteen days later the aggressive Mr. Dupuy warned Mrs. Patout not to ignore the fact that he and Madame Barq had "all the documents relative to and concerning your claim against the government of the United States." He then claimed status as her sole representative and asked for prompt payment of an unstipulated fee before they pursued her claim any further."[55]

When he learned of Dupuy's actions in early 1877, attorney De Loffre contacted Hippolyte Patout.[56] Regarding exactly who was in possession of the Patout legal file, he said: "I had and have at this moment in my possession all the papers left by Mr. B at his death. . . ."[57] He described Dupuy as a small-time dealer who was "ignorant of all that concerns the claims affair against the government. . . ."[58] De Loffre suggested that Patout contact the firm of Beraud & Gilbert, lawyers that Hippolyte Patout knew, for verification of his estimate of Dupuy.

Shortly after Hippolyte Patout received this letter, a Monsieur Destes, representing himself to be Mrs. Barq's agent, wrote Appoline Patout regarding her agreement of June 4, 1864, with Auguste Barq, in which she agreed to pay him a fee amounting to 10 percent of her claim when it was settled, or $5,234. Mrs. Barq, he said, was asking for a $500 advance on the sum owed Mr. Barq. Hoping to improve his chances of getting this advance, Destes said that "you must know that everyone thinks the claims will be settled within a few months."[59] This after De Loffre had informed the Patouts that there was no agency available to even consider the claim, much less pay it.

Mrs. Patout died in March 1879, leaving behind a plantation that had survived the hazardous Reconstruction era more or less intact.[60] Hippolyte Patout, in his capacity as the administrator of his mother's estate, took up the claim and, in 1881, filed it with the recently formed French and American Claims Commission. This body was established in 1880 to consider the claims of French nationals against the United States and to hear the pleas of American citizens that the French republic pay them for the damages incurred during the Franco-Prussian War.[61] On March 24, 1881, Patout filed a revised petition which asked $57,945.35 and damages of $10,000 plus 6 percent interest. He alleged that except for $1,617.20 paid for corn taken in November 1863, no restitution had ever been made. The increase in damages asked derived mainly from larger amounts requested for personal and household items for which Appoline Patout had made only the most minimal claims.[62]

Hippolyte Patout had no more success with legal counsel and claims boards than had his mother. Working through George D'Autry of New Orleans, he employed the Washington, D. C., firm of Taylor and Laberie to represent him.[63] George Taylor and Pierre Laberie were handling a large number of the French claims and did not have the time and resources to pay sufficient attention to each case. Much like their predecessors, they seem to have been hoping for a more or less receptive commission which would produce a windfall for the claimants and their attorneys. The firm had Nathaniel Wilson registered as their attorney of record to assist with the case in New Iberia. While less venal and more business-like than the Widow Barq and her shadowy cohort, they were no more effective.[64]

They did revise the Patout petition in order to provide information required by the Commission and they prepared to take the testimony of witnesses in New Iberia. They were also honest about the progress of the case, informing Hippolyte on one occasion that "it is unnecessary to tell you that the grind is slow, [and] as a result, detrimental to you."[65] On June 23, 1882, the Commission held a hearing in New Iberia to take the testimony of Felix Patout, with E. Cullom North rather than Nathaniel Wilson present on behalf of the claimants. North questioned the younger Patout about the nationality of his parents and siblings and about his activities during the late unpleasantries. Taylor Beattie, the government's counsel, then requested that the claimants provide birth and marriage records to substantiate the testimony, whereupon North abruptly entered a formal abandonment of the case on the grounds that the surviving Patouts were American citizens. He reserved only the right to prosecute the claim before some future body which might be constituted to hear additional claims.[66]

Six months later, the counsel for the United States, George Boutwell, asked the Commission to order the case dismissed on the grounds of abandonment.[67] The counsel for the French Republic asked that the Patouts be granted more time to complete their testimony.[68] George Taylor's affidavit averred that North had been engaged only to examine the witnesses, that he did not fully understand the nationality issue, and that, in any event, he had no authority to move for abandonment. Taylor asked for an additional sixty days to take testimony and to introduce an amendment regarding the nationality of the claimants.[69] The requests for extensions were denied and the case was dismissed on

February 23, 1883. In April, the government refused to accept notice of a meeting convening in New Iberia to take testimony, citing the earlier dismissal.[70]

Following a series of appeals, a hearing on the merits of the case was held in early 1884. The government's contention was that the documents offered were of no value as evidence because they were *ex-parte* in nature and that the signatures were not shown to be genuine. Therefore, the heirs and their nationality were beside the point. The claimants were not properly before the Commission. The Commission agreed, finally dismissing the case "for want of jurisdiction" on January 19, 1884. By this time, Hippolyte Patout had been dead for more than a year.

Felix Patout and Hippolyte's wife, Mary Ann, operated the plantation in partnership as they sought alternative courses of action regarding the claim. None was immediately forthcoming. Felix sold his interest to Mary Ann after a year or so and moved into New Iberia. He bought Hope Plantation and developed interests in banking, real estate, and the hotel business while Hippolyte's widow concentrated her efforts on modernizing what had come to be called Enterprise Plantation.[71] Under her management, Enterprise in the 1890s became one of the more competitive central factories which were beginning to dominate the raw-sugar industry.[72]

There is no evidence of further action on the Patout claim until March 16, 1900, when Colonel Gilbert Moyers, a Washington attorney retained by the Patouts, filed a petition and depositions with the House Committee on War Claims.[73] Congressman Robert F. Broussard then introduced House Resolution 7911 "for the relief of the Succession of Appoline Fournier" on December 16, 1903.[74] The bill died in committee, but its introduction made it possible to refer the case to the Court of Claims under the provisions of the Tucker Act. Moyers and Consaul then contacted New Iberia attorney Edwin Sidney Broussard to do the local work necessary to revive the claim. Their expectation was that they would be fortunate to collect one-quarter of the $56,000 sought and they emphasized the need to move quickly.[75] "Witnesses are dying very fast now," they said, "and it is a question of but a short time when no witnesses can be found."[76]

In fact, the dearth of witnesses proved to be a problem in all fifteen Civil War claims cases being handled by Moyers and Consaul. By late 1908, Felix Patout was the only witness from whom Consaul had taken testimony and the firm noted that there was "practically no evidence ever submitted which would tend to substantiate the allegations of the petition." He explained that the supporting evidence was missing from the petition because the treaty establishing the French and American Claims Commission provided that claims could be presented only "by persons who were at that date [January 15, 1880] citizens of France and who were citizens of France when their claim arose. . . . Mrs. Patout departed this life before said Commission was established and . . . all of her heirs were citizens of the United States, the heirs being therefore barred from prosecuting the claim."[77] Moyers and Consaul wanted to interview witnesses in New Iberia very quickly because persons who could corroborate information in all of their claims were "now becoming very scarce."[78]

There is no evidence to indicate that additional witnesses were located, but Congressman Broussard got the necessary reference of the case to the Court of Claims early in 1910.[79] This approach ran into problems when the court indicated that, since Congress had not paid any of the allowed claims for over six years, it did not wish to try any more cases until those claims already allowed were honored.[80] While they awaited the resolution of this issue, Edwin Broussard worked to establish that Appoline Patout, whose affirmative loyalty need not be proved, was indeed the sole owner of the property and that her children, whose loyalty could not be legally established, were not part owners. Emphasizing the necessity for this clarification, Moyers and Consaul said that "the whole record in this case is about as mixed as any we have ever seen, but if we can establish that the property belonged to Mrs. Patout, and not to her children, and can show by the birth record her French citizenship, we will prepare the brief and make the best showing of which we are capable."[81]

This matter was cleared up, but shortly before it adjourned in early 1911, Congress passed a law relieving the Court of Claims of all jurisdiction in pending Civil War claims from the South.[82] Responsibility for clearing up all remaining cases passed to the Department of Justice, which quickly began to interview witnesses. This produced a new concern for the Patouts, because some Justice Department attorneys were more open-minded about the cases than others. Moyers and Consaul were prepared to have Felix Patout give testimony in the fall of 1911, but advised that they should

> keep quiet about this just at present. A certain attorney of the Department of Justice is expected to leave some time this month for a trip through the South, handling cases with various local counsel. Without meaning to say anything derogatory to this attorney as a man, we may say that the writer has taken considerable testimony with him and found that almost continual controversy was necessary in order to secure fair treatment of witnesses.[83]

They counseled delay, emphasizing that nothing could really be lost because business in the Court of Claims continued at a standstill.

In mid-1912, Moyers and Consaul were ready for Felix Patout to testify once again. To their credit, they took great care to prepare him so that there would be no questions raised about the validity or relevance of his testimony. Nonetheless, the reality was that this gentle, unassuming 78-year-old man was being asked about events that had occurred almost a half-century before. Actually, he was quite effective. And testifying about his mother, he summed up quite poignantly the difficulties the Patouts had experienced:

> Mother made out this claim about 1864, I believe, and we tried to make the claim right after the war and there was no place to file it. Then when the French and American Commission came, we filed it there, but mother had died and when they found out that the heirs were American citizens, the case was dropped. . . . As soon as we found out that we could make the claim to Congress, we did that. If there had been any place where we could prove the claims, years ago, we could have proved

everything, I supposed by twenty witnesses, but it is too late now to prove anything more. The witnesses are all dead.[84]

And, for all practical purposes, so was the case. The record of correspondence between Broussard and Consaul does not go beyond 1912 and the prosecution of *Patout* v. *the United States* ended about as inconclusively as it began. Congress considered an Omnibus Claims Bill, but another war was about to occupy center stage and its claims were more immediate. Felix Patout, the last witness to the events of that trying spring and fall of 1863, died on December 8, 1918, shortly after the end of that terrible new war. And with him died the feeble remaining chances of *Patout* v. *the United States*.

The Constitution guarantees equal justice under the law and the right to a fair, impartial, and speedy trial. The Patouts, and hundreds like them, asked that their government measure up to that standard. For many, the government's failure to do so meant ruin, for they had no means to recoup their losses. For others, including the Patouts, federal intransigence meant material hardship, the attentions of unsavory and incompetent lawyers, and the vexation of being even unable to find the source of justice, much less obtain it. In any event, no consideration was given to the psychological costs of having to watch the work of a lifetime ruined in the space of a few months. The Patout family would recover, and even prosper, but there are indications that Appoline Patout was so emotionally shaken by the experience that she was never again able to resume full control of the plantation.[85] The events themselves, and their immediate effects, may perhaps be dismissed as the unfortunate but unavoidable result of civil war. But the aftermath, the failure of the federal government to provide a reasonably prompt and impartial hearing to neutrals who had suffered obvious losses, can only remind one of the old adage that justice delayed is justice denied.

Notes for "Justice Delayed: *Appoline Patout* v. *the United States*, 1864-1918"

[1] See, for example, John Richard Dennett, *The South As It Is, 1865-1866* (New York, 1965).

[2] Paul W. Gates, *Agriculture and the Civil War* (New York, 1965); Ralph Andreano, ed., *The Economic Impact of the American Civil War* (rev. ed., Cambridge, Mass., 1967); J. Carlyle Sitterson, *Sugar Country: The Cane Sugar Industry in the South, 1753-1950* (Lexington, Ky., 1950).

[3] Frank W. Klingberg, *The Southern Claims Commission* (Berkeley, Calif., 1955).

[4] A notable exception is David C. Edmonds, *Yankee Autumn in Acadiana: A Narrative of the Great Texas Overland Expedition Through Southwestern Lousiana, October-December 1863* (Lafayette, La., 1979). Edmonds uses some of the French claims to illustrate the damage caused by Union forces in the Teche region.

[5] United States War Department, *War of the Rebellion, Official Records of the Union and Confederate Armies*, 70 vols. (Washington, D.C., 1880-1901), Series I, vol. 26, Pt. I; hereafter cited as *War of the Rebellion*, with series, volume, and part numbers; Charles P. Roland, *Louisiana Sugar Planters During the American Civil War* (Leiden, The Netherlands, 1957).

[6] "Passenger Lists of Vessels Arriving at New Orleans, October 3, 1827-March 31, 1829," Record Group 259, Reel 7, National Archives, Washington, D.C.; "Comparative Statement of Sugar Produced in the Parish of St.

Mary in 1843, '44, '45, '46 and '47," *Franklin Planters' Banner,* February 10, 1848; Probate No. 629, Clerk of Court's Office, St. Mary Parish Courthouse, Franklin, Louisiana.

[7] Eighth census of the United States, 1860, St. Mary Parish, Schedules of Free Inhabitants, of Slaves, and of Agriculture.

[8] P. A. Champomier, *Statement of the Sugar Crop Made in Louisiana in 1861-62* (New Orleans, 1862).

[9] Eunice Faison, "The Last of the Patout Slaves" (1925), copy in the author's possession. At this time, Hippolyte Patout may have taken some of the family's slaves to Texas. Henry Waggoner, an ex-slave of the Patout's, recalled in 1925 that he ran away to Texas as Union troops approached. Once there, he wandered around for a while and then walked miles to rejoin Hippolyte Patout when he learned that he too was in Texas. Shortly thereafter, they returned to the plantation; J. Carlyle Sitterson, *Sugar Country,* 215, says that there was almost a mass exodus of planters and their hands to Texas in the fall of 1862 and the spring of 1863. There planters hired their slaves out. Some used their hands, teams and wagons to haul Confederate supplies to North Louisiana at the rate of $10.00 per day for driver and cart.

[10] Richard Bache Irwin, *History of the Nineteenth Army Corps* (New York, 1892), 132. Irwin says that there was not adequate enforcement of the anti-plundering orders, that the region was sparsely populated, and that most of the residents had fled their homes at the news of approaching Union troops. Men on short rations availed themselves of opportunity in what they considered enemy territory.

[11] *Hippolyte Patout v. the United States,* Claim No. 239, French and American Claims Commission, Record Group 76, National Archives; hereafter cited as *Hippolyte Patout v. the United States.*

[12] Roland, *Louisiana Sugar Planters,* 27-47.

[13] Edmonds, *Yankee Autumn,* 6.

[14] Ibid., 23.

[15] "Reclamation de Madame Veuve Patout contre les Etats-Unis, $56,234," George P. Broussard Papers, Southwestern Archives, University of Southwestern Louisiana, Lafayette, La.; hereafter cited as "Madame Veuve Patout."

[16] Actually what was required was an oath of allegiance, to which Mrs. Patout apparently agreed. Her use of the word "neutrality" probably reflects her understanding of what she was agreeing to. See David C. Edmonds, ed., *The Conduct of Federal Troops in Louisiana During the Invasions of 1863 and 1864* (Lafayette, La., 1988), 93-94. This is the official report on the Teche campaign and the capture of Alexandria, compiled from sworn testimony under the direction of Confederate Governor Henry Watkins Allen.

[17] Ibid., n.p.

[18] Ibid.

[19] Edmonds, *Yankee Autumn,* 12-13. Franklin graduated first in the West Point Class of 1843 in which Ulysses S. Grant finished twenty-first. Ambrose Burnside blamed Franklin for the disaster at the Battle of Fredericksburg and had the cautious engineer assigned to the low priority Department of the Gulf.

[20] "Madame Veuve Patout," n.p.; Mrs. Patout's account, while obviously designed to reinforce her claims, is consistent with that given by Irwin in his *History of the Nineteenth Army Corps.* Writing about the above unit's activities in the Teche region, he spoke of "the twin evils of straggling and marauding."

[21] *Hippolyte Patout v. the United States,* Pt. IV.

[22] Ibid.; "Madame Veuve Patout."

[23] Ibid.

[24] Ibid.

[25] *War of the Rebellion,* Ser. I, 26, Pt. I, 854.

[26] "Madame Veuve Patout;" *Hippolyte Patout v. the United States.*

[27] George H. Hepworth, *Whip, Hoe, and Sword: Or, the Gulf Department in '63* (Boston, 1864), 92.

[28] Ibid., 272.

[29] Quoted in Edmonds, *Yankee Autumn in Acadiana*, 355.

[30] *War of the Rebellion*, Ser. I, 26, Pt. 1:782.

[31] Edmonds, *Yankee Autumn in Acadiana*, 353-54.

[32] Ibid., 354.

[33] Peter Ripley, *Slaves and Freedmen in Civil War in Louisiana* (Baton Rouge, 1976), 59.

[34] Edmonds, *Yankee Autumn in Acadiana*, 356.

[35] Succession of Appoline Patout, Clerk of Court's Office, Iberia Parish Courthouse, New Iberia, La., Probates, Vol. 5, no. 287:325.

[36] "Madame Veuve Patout."

[37] Klingberg, *The Southern Claims Commission*, 23.

[38] Auguste Barq to Appoline Patout, July 11, 1865, Broussard Family Papers.

[39] Ibid., June 5, 1866.

[40] Klingberg, *The Southern Claims Commission*, 16.

[41] Barq to Patout, June 5, 1866, Broussard Family Papers.

[42] Walter Prichard, "The Effects of the Civil War on the Louisiana Sugar Industry," *Journal of Southern History*, 5 (1939): 318-21.

[43] Eighth census of the United States, 1860, St. Mary Parish, Schedule 1, Free Inhabitants.

[44] Ninth census of the United States, 1870, Iberia Parish; this is consistent with Henry Latham's 1867 estimate (*Black and White: A Journal of a Three Month's Tour in the United States*) that the postwar value of sugar properties was about 1/8 of their pre-war worth. Latham's calculations are cited in *Louisiana Sugar Planters*, 10.

[45] Klingberg, *The Southern Claims Commission*, 21-22.

[46] Barq to Patout, July 14, 1866, Broussard Family Papers.

[47] Patout Family Papers, M. A. Patout and Son, Ltd., Patoutville, La.

[48] Paul Wallace Gates, *Agriculture and the Civil War* (New York, 1965), 371.

[49] Sitterson, *Sugar Country*, 233. This lack of "reliability" was partly due to the quite natural exuberance produced by emancipation. James L. Roark, *Masters Without Slaves: Southern Planters in the Civil War and Reconstruction* (New York, 1977), 119, says that it was due not so much to black reluctance to work as to planters' attempts to continue work conditions that were only slavery in another guise.

[50] Prichard, "Effects of the Civil War," 324.

[51] "A Negro Killed," *Planters' Banner*, June 16, 1869. Daniel Dennett, the Maine-born, anti-Radical editor, said that the killer would not be prosecuted because he was black and the Radicals could derive no political benefit from his conviction; other issues of the *Banner* for June, July, and August (and succeeding months) contain accounts of criminals at large, of domestic violence, and even of the Radical sheriff engaging in a

street fight with his ex-deputy; the New Iberia *Louisiana Sugar Bowl* issues in 1870 and 1871 cover burnings of saw mills, stores, and sugar houses as well as shooting incidents and street fights..

[52] *Planters' Banner,* June 1869-July 1870; Sitterson, *Sugar Country,* 231-233.

[53] A. De Loffre to Hippolyte Patout, August 14, 1873, Broussard Family Papers.

[54] Paul Cornen to Appoline Patout, September 10, 1876, Broussard Family Papers.

[55] Guillaume Dupuy to Appoline Patout, September 26, 1876, Broussard Family Papers. My investigation of attorneys listed in New Orleans directories for the period showed no listing for Mr. Dupuy.

[56] De Loffre may have also learned from Beraud and Gilbert, from whom he secured the Patout's address, that Mrs. Patout had named Hippolyte her agent regarding the claim after January 27, 1877. See Hippolyte Patout to George d'Autry, October 11, 1877, Broussard Family Papers.

[57] A. De Loffre to Hippolyte Patout, February 8, 1877, Broussard Family Papers.

[58] Ibid.

[59] Destes to Appoline Patout, February 16, 1877, Broussard Family Papers.

[60] Sitterson, *Sugar Country,* 250. Sitterson indicates that recovery in the sugar district was virtually complete by 1880.

[61] *United States Statutes at Large,* Volume 21, No. 673.

[62] *Hippolyte Patout v. the United States.*

[63] George d'Autry to Hippolyte Patout, July 11, 1877, Broussard Family Papers.

[64] There was certainly no shortage of persons willing to handle the Patout's suit. See, for example, Emile Brung(?) to Hippolyte Patout, July 27, 1877, and B. P. Alat to Hippolyte Patout, n.d., Broussard Family Papers.

[65] O. J. Morel to Hippolyte Patout, March 22, 1881, Broussard Family Papers.

[66] Testimony of Felix Patout, *Hippolyte Patout v. the United States,* No. 239.

[67] Motion to Dismiss, *Hippolyte Patout v. the United States.*

[68] Motion by Charles H. Sechaunbrun, counsel for the French Republic, *Hippolyte Patout v. the United States.*

[69] Affidavit, George Taylor, January 20, 1883, *Hippolyte Patout v. the United States.*

[70] Petition to T. Edwards, assistant counsel for the United States, *Hippolyte Patout v. the United States.*

[71] "Felix Patout," Glenn R. Conrad, ed., *Dictionary of Louisiana Biography,* 2 vols. (New Orleans, 1988), 2:633.

[72] "Mary Ann Schwing Patout," in ibid., 2:633.

[73] Moyers and Consaul to Robert F. Broussard, September 24, 1904, Robert F. Broussard and Edwin S. Broussard Papers, Southwestern Archives, University of Southwestern Louisiana.

[74] *Congressional Record,* 58th Cong., 2 Sess., Vol. 38, Pt. I; Conrad, ed., *Dictionary,* 1:116. Broussard served in the United States House of Representatives from 1897-1915 and in the United States Senate from 1915-1918.

[75] Moyers and Consaul to Camack and Broussard, attorneys, October 4, 1906, Edwin S. Broussard Papers. The Washington lawyers listed property in the amount of $12,478.00 as the only items of the claim which were still worth mentioning.

[76] Moyers and Consaul to Edwin S. Broussard, August 4, 1906, Edwin S. Broussard Papers. Broussard was Felix Patout's son-in-law and served in the United States Senate from 1920-1933.

[77] Moyers and Consaul to Edwin S. Broussard, October 24, 1908, Edwin S. Broussard Papers.

[78] Ibid.

[79] Moyers and Consaul to Edwin S. Broussard, February 28, 1910, ibid.

[80] Ibid., March 24, 1911.

[81] Ibid.

[82] Moyers and Consaul to Edwin S. Broussard, n.d., ibid.

[83] Ibid., October 3, 1911.

[84] Testimony of Felix Patout, n.d., Broussard Family Papers.

[85] Succession of Appoline Patout.

LOUISIANA AND THE CHILD OFFENDER*

Robert E. Moran

When Edward Livingston codified Louisiana's criminal laws in 1825, he called for the establishment of a reform school to complete his penal system. He assumed that convicts were men who were motivated in much the same way as other men and that it was the duty of the penal system "to turn them into a course that will promote the true happiness of the individual, by making them cease to injure that of society...."[1]

In order to achieve this objective for juveniles, Livingston suggested a special institution of confinement for those above six and below eighteen years of age. The school would contain separate divisions for the sexes and separate rooms for each prisoner. Inmates would be employed in open courts or in shops, and there was to be a schoolroom with a competent teacher and an infirmary for each division. Every inmate was to be taught mechanical arts, and their work was to be interrupted only by intermissions for meals, instruction, relaxation, and sleep. Discipline was to be persuasive whenever that method was serviceable. No male under twenty-one or female under nineteen was to be released, except by apprenticeship, regardless of the term of service prescribed in the sentence. Discharge for apprenticeship was to be made only after the inmate had completed two years of residence in the institution and had achieved a certain proficiency in elementary education. Before the inmate could be freed, he was required to have a written recommendation signed and approved by the inspectors.[2] As has been pointed out, Louisiana did not accept Livingston's penal code and prison reforms, but the code's influence was felt throughout the United States and the rest of the world. Commenting on the importance of the code, historian George Bancroft wrote:

> The code which he [Livingston] prepared at the insistence of the State of Louisiana is in its simplicity, completeness, and humanity at once an impersonation of the man and a exposition of American constitutions. If it has never yet been

---

*First published as chapter seven in Robert E. Moran, *One Hundred Years of Child Welfare in Louisiana, 1860-1960* (Lafayette, La.: Center for Louisiana Studies, 1980), 63-79. Reprinted with the kind permission of the author and the University of Louisiana at Lafayette.

adopted as a whole, it has probed an unfailing fountain of reforms suggested by its principles. . . . The great doctrines which it develops will, as time advances, be more and more nearly reduced to practice; for they are but the expression of true philanthropy.[3]

The long evolution toward adequate penal institutions for juveniles in Louisiana has borne out the prophecy which Bancroft made in 1860.

The history of institutions for child offenders in Louisiana parallels that of the rest of the nation. As a result of the reform movement against confinement of adult and juvenile offenders in the same institution, houses of refuge were founded in New York in 1825, Boston in 1826, and Philadelphia in 1828. The movement finally moved South when in 1847, the state legislature empowered New Orleans to establish houses of refuge for its juvenile delinquents and vagrants who were fifteen years of age or younger.

The New Orleans House of Refuge opened in 1848 with about 16 boys. Four years later, however, the institution was said to be in a disgraceful condition and a "positive stain upon the character of the city, the building being more suitable for cattle than humans."[4] As a result, the male inmates were indentured to landholders in nearby parishes whenever possible.

A similar institution, the Girls' House of Refuge, was established in New Orleans in 1852. It housed about 100 inmates from ages two to seventeen. The girls were subjected to rigid discipline, given manual training, and, on Sunday, given moral lectures by a Presbyterian elder and a prominent businessman. In 1859, the Catholic church established the House of the Good Shepherd "to reclaim the erring daughters of dissipation and licentiousness and afford them due opportunity to reform their habits and retrieve, as far as possible, their ruined character."[5] Fourteen years later, the Girls' House of Refuge was abolished by the city and the inmates were transferred to the House of the Good Shepherd. for many years this private institution was subsidized by the City of New Orleans as its sole detention home and the house of correction for girls.

In the early 1880s, however, George Washington Cable, the noted New Orleans writer and reformer, drew the public's attention to the need for adequate, municipal, juvenile detention facilities. In May 1881, Cable tendered his services to Mayor Joseph A. Shakspeare of New Orleans, offering to visit, at his own expense, a number of model institutions in northern and eastern cities. In July 1881, the reformer issued a report to the grand jury and proposed that the mayor appoint a board of prison and asylum commissioners to supervise municipal welfare institutions. Cable also recommended formation of a large voluntary Prison and Charities Aid Association to help improve construction, discipline, and management of prisons and poor houses and to lobby for legislation providing for efficient management of the city's houses of detention and correction.[6]

Cable also advocated municipal prison reform in an article published by the *New Orleans Times-Democrat*:

> One glance at our Parish Prison, our Insane Asylum, or our House of Refuge ought to be to any informed and observing, a dreadful revelation. And it is. . . . Concerning every house of detention or charity, purely and entirely under the control of our city government, there is but one conviction—that it is disgrace to the community.[7]

Speaking of the parish jail he said:

> All ages sometimes even down to childhood and all degrees of viciousness and depravity and brutality—from a lad who has stolen $5 out of a carelessly kept till, to a man who has killed his wife with an ax—swarm and companion together.[8]

Mayor Shakspeare did appoint a Board of Prisons and Asylums with Hugh Miller Thompson, pastor of Trinity Episcopal Church as chairman. On March 7, 1882, a group of interested citizens organized the Prison Reform and Asylums Aid Association with Cable as its secretary, to conduct further investigations and to campaign for prison reform in the Crescent City. In 1886, the Prison Reform Association was organized to do similar work for the entire state, for the same conditions then existing in New Orleans Parish Jail prevailed in all other parishes of the Pelican State. Cable was particularly interested in eradicating Louisiana's system of leasing convicts to private contractors for work. The Prison Reform Association was instrumental in getting laws passed which not only abolished the convict lease system but contained numerous additional reforms which were implemented in the early twentieth century.

Before this legislation, however, the Prison Reform Association had compelled New Orleans to improve conditions within its jails. The New Orleans House of Refuge, for example, was built in 1868 on the edge of a swamp from which the inmates contracted chills and fever. During 1881, after Cable visited the facility, the city entered into an agreement with two men to instruct 112 boys, ages 5 to 19 years, in the art of shoemaking. For two hours in the morning and afternoon on weekdays, the boys were instructed in spelling and reading, and the rest of the day was spent in learning a trade, such as shoemaking or broom manufacturing. On Sunday religious services were held. When the City Insane Asylum abandoned the old U. S. Marine Hospital, the city obtained permission from the federal government to move the House of Refuge to this location. The former hospital was not ideally suited for a boys' detention home, but it was an improvement over the initial site.[9]

The New Orleans Board of Commissioners reported on December 31, 1890, that there were twenty-one white and sixty-seven black boys in the House of Refuge. Rabbi Leucht, commenting upon the provisions for delinquent boys in the city said: "We have also a house of refuge for refractory boys, boys convicted of vagrancy and minor offenses. It is a refuge, but not a reformatory and here is not the place to pass any criticism, even were I inclined to do so."[10]

The void in the child detention system depicted by Leucht was filled in 1893, when the Louisiana Society for the Prevention of Cruelty to Children established a Waifs'

Home for the temporary shelter and protection of both white and black youths. With the establishment of the institution, the Prison Reform Association called for the abolition of the ill-managed boys' reformatory and the transfer of its inmates to the Waif's Home. The Association also called for the establishment of a juvenile court and a state reformatory.

A state reformatory was sorely needed by Louisiana which had traditionally incarcerated child offenders outside of New Orleans in parish jails, where they mingled with adult offenders. In 1904, however, a state reform school, the Louisiana Training Institute, was founded at Monroe as a correctional school for delinquent, neglected, and dependent boys, aged eight to twenty-one.[11] Although the legislation creating the institution did not bar black admittance, the board of trustees was given the authority to restrict admission to white boys. Therefore Negro boys and girls outside of New Orleans continued to be confined in parish jails because, until 1940, there was no state institution for their detention.

After the opening of the state reformatory, New Orleans closed its House of Refuge and used only the Waifs' Home as a house of detention for boys and the House of the Good Shepherd for girls. Slingerland reported in 1916 that the Louisiana Training Institute had a capacity of eighty boys, but that its average occupancy was sixty. The white Waifs' Home averaged about seventy-five inmates, while its black counterpart usually housed about eighty-five child offenders; each institution, however, had a capacity of one hundred. Moreover, the House of Good Shepherd had a daily average of 185 inmates and a capacity of 200.

The New Orleans institutions, however, were hardly model reformatories. A private agency, the Bureau of Municipal Research, reported after its investigation of the welfare institutions of New Orleans in 1921, that there was need for a complete reorganization of the city's correctional institutions. The report suggested a need for a change in policy from one of punishment for prisoners to one of training in self-help. The investigators also discovered the Waifs' Home administrators were too inclined to treat the boys as criminals who had to be guarded and driven. The immediate needs at the Home were additional facilities, especially cottages; more recreation for the inmates; and extensive parole system; and a trained staff. The report concluded that, because of these conditions, it was far better to release the boys than to maintain them in the existing facilities.[12]

Much the same could have been said about the Institute at Monroe. Very little prisoner rehabilitation was accomplished at the state school because the institution stressed custodial care. The Institute had guard towers like a prison and whipping and confinement in small cells were the usual methods of discipline.[13] Moreover, upon completion of sentence, prisoners were returned to their home environment with no probationary supervision. The result was a high rate of recidivism.

In order to provide temporary public care for delinquent or neglected children, the 1920 legislature authorized police juries to enter into contracts with children's foundling societies for proper care. The legislature thus not only legalized what New Orleans had already been doing, but made it possible for other parishes to emulate the Crescent City.

Louisiana and the Child Offender

The above-mentioned child offender programs were devoted exclusively to young males. Not until 1926 did Louisiana establish a similar program for young women—the State Industrial School for Girls. The school was located eight miles north of Alexandria on forty acres of "cut-over" piney woodland. The school received its first inmate in 1928. It, like its male counterpart, also housed delinquent, dependent, and neglected juveniles. The school was built to accommodate sixty-nine girls, but, during its first years of operation, its population ranged from forty-two to seventy-six. By 1935, however, the Institute could accommodate only one-third of the girls who needed its care and protection.

Upon admission to the Institute, girls received physical, psychometric, and psychiatric examinations and a large number of girls were treated for venereal disease. Nearly 20 percent were found to be feebleminded and thus should have been transferred to another institution. Another very small percentage of admissions included girls who were either neglected or dependent and who thus should not have been in a correctional institution. Inmates were allowed to remain in the school only seven years, and following their release, they were given no probationary supervision.[14]

The inmates engaged in no agriculture or dairy operations like their male counterparts, but they operated their own laundry and made their own clothes. Until 1943, slapping and paddling were used as a means of punishment. After 1943, punishment consisted primarily of confinement to the punishment room for periods of two to six weeks. The governor's committee to investigate the state's institutions condemned this type of punishment because the room became a breeding ground for recidivism, encouraged lesbian relations, and was detrimental to the girls' health and welfare.

The expansion of the state reform school system prompted the New Orleans government to streamline its municipal reformatory system. In 1932, the old Waifs' Home was closed and replaced by the Milne Municipal Boys' Home for white and black boys. The Milne Home became a catch-all for boys ages eight to twenty-one, housing the feebleminded, the neglected, the maladjusted, the destitute, runaways, the incorrigibles, truants; the little boy of eight, frightened and homesick; and the juvenile of eighteen, approaching manhood either maladjusted or incorrigible, but in the main rebellious and thwarted. Some of the boys were sent to the Louisiana Training Institute, but the feebleminded, white and black alike, and black incorrigibles remained to bog down the Home's program.[15]

In 1946, the New Orleans Department of Public Welfare assumed responsibility for administration of the Home. The department made strides in eliminating deficiencies and inadequacies in administration by hiring trained personnel and planning recreational and educational programs. The problem of the feebleminded and older Negro delinquents, however, continued to fester because of the absence of proper facilities.

As early as 1900, concerned Louisianians, such as J. B. Lafargue, president of the Louisiana Colored Teachers Association, and J. S. Clark, president of Southern University, had called for the establishment of a special institution for black juvenile delinquents. In 1928, Dr. Clark served as the spokesman for the committee of citizens who prevailed upon the state legislature to approve legislation creating and maintaining the Industrial School for Colored Male Youths. The legislature not only adopted the measure, but it authorized the district prison farms to maintain special departments where black juveniles might be held. Juvenile court judges subsequently sentenced Negro delinquents to the prison farm, for a statewide, black reformatory was not built until 1948.

During the twenty-year lapse between the enabling act's passage and the black reformatory's construction, police juries were authorized to create parish industrial schools for black youths. East Carroll Parish, with the cooperation of Madison and Tensas parishes provided for the placement of juveniles in one section of the parish penal farm.[16] Other police juries, however, were reluctant to provide information for their black delinquents because they felt that the state institution would adequately serve their purposes.

In order to ensure that a state institution would indeed provide adequate services, J. S. Clark, before his death in 1944 secured assurances that the black reform school would be controlled and operated by blacks. When the school opened in 1948, its superintendent, Dallas B. Matthews and his staff were black and the chairman of the three-man Board of Commissioners was an outstanding East Baton Rouge Parish Negro, John G. Lewis, Jr. In 1942, the black school was placed under the Louisiana Board of Institutions which had no black members but it was nevertheless staffed by Negro personnel. The physical plant, covering 417 acres of which 315 were used for crop land, consisted of two dormitories, a commissary, a classroom building, and the superintendent's home. Less than a year after the institution opened the dormitories, originally designed for thirty boys, housed sixty.[17] The institution was not only overcrowded, but it also lacked necessary personnel in rehabilitation work.

In 1952 the juvenile and district courts were authorized to commit both males and females to the institution. The first two female trainees were admitted in 1956. During 1962, nearly 800 boys and 150 girls received care at the school in fifteen dormitories: ten for male and five for female trainees.

The Board of Institutions reported in 1956 that more than 800 youths were detained n the state's three correctional schools and the number kept mounting each year. The resulting overcrowding and understaffing made rehabilitation almost impossible in any of the training schools.[18]

On September 22, 1958, the state opened the Louisiana Correctional Institute for Males near DeQuincy. The institute relieved both city and state correctional schools and detention homes of all incorrigible juvenile males at least twenty years of age. Although their behavior rendered them unfit for the correctional schools at Monroe or Baton Rouge, these juveniles were too young to be placed in the Louisiana State Penitentiary at Angola. While at DeQuincy, juvenile and adult inmates were maintained in separate facilities.

Modern state care for juvenile delinquents stems from an 1870 state law regarding the detention of minors. This law, as amended in 1892, stated that any child found begging of alms or soliciting charity from door to door or in the street should be deemed a vagrant and committed to the New Orleans House of Refuge, to the Society for the Prevention of Cruelty to Children (LSPCC), or to similar institutions provided by parochial authorities.[19] While the law was placing responsibility for the care of juvenile delinquents in the hands of LSPCC, the Society along with other groups and individuals was working for the establishment of juvenile courts throughout the state.[20]

In 1898 the Committee of Children of the National Conference of Charities and Corrections not only recommended the creation of a special children's court in which there would be no semblance of formal criminal procedure, but proposed the creation of a commission whose responsibility would begin with the complaint against the child and end with the juvenile's release from state supervision.[21] The juvenile court's advocates also believed that if children were separated from adult offenders and if the judge dealt with the problems of "erring children" as a "wise and kind father," then the problem child's wayward tendencies could be checked and delinquency and crime prevented or reduced. Under such a court, the child offender was to be regarded not as a criminal, but as a delinquent, as a misdirected and misguided child needing aid, encouragement, help, and assistance. As Grace Abbot has said, "The challenging and seminal idea which was back of the juvenile court was that its function was to cure, rather than punish delinquency—a very much more difficult task."[22]

The first juvenile court in Louisiana opened in 1908 with Andrew H. Wilson on the bench. The state legislature subsequently provided for a statewide juvenile court system consisting of the Orleans Parish Juvenile Court and district courts throughout Louisiana sitting as juvenile courts. The New Orleans Juvenile Court enjoyed separate facilities and maintained separate trial periods for juveniles and adults, as well as black and white children. The court had complete jurisdiction over delinquent and neglected children seventeen years of age or under, except in cases involving murder, manslaughter, and rape.[23] Statistics regarding the number, character and disposition of cases brought before the court were compiled annually by the Board of Charities and Corrections. The Orleans Parish Juvenile Court remained Louisiana's sole child offender tribunal until 1924, when a state court was established.

The legislation establishing Louisiana's juvenile court system also provided that children arrested by police officers, sheriffs, or probation officers would not be incarcerated at police stations or jails. Pending trial, the child offenders would remain in the custody of their parents or guardians, or responsible citizens or institutions. These regulations, however, were largely disregarded by both law enforcement and judicial officials; many juveniles were sentenced as criminals by district and city courts to imprisonment in parish jails, and, in some cases, the state penitentiary at Angola. For example, in 1920, three Negro boys, aged ten, thirteen, and fourteen years were sentenced to the state farm at Angola for ten, thirteen, and fourteen years respectively. The district judge who sentenced the children to hard labor, attempted to justify his actions by citing their extensive criminal records. He further stated that he was unable to tell a Negro's age by looking at him, and no proof was offered that they were juveniles.

When Gov. John M. Parker, whose attention had been called to the matter, requested an opinion from Atty. Gen. A. V. Coco, the state prosecutor indicated that the children should never have been tried and convicted as criminals by the East Baton Rouge District Court, because the court lacked jurisdiction over the defendants. Moreover, the children should have been tried as juveniles and, upon conviction, they should have been confined in a reformatory. He thus concluded that their conviction was illegal.[24]

Coco's admonition that black child offenders be sentenced to reformatories was pointless, for the state lacked such an institution for Negroes. In 1938, to point up the need for an institution for black delinquents, the Board of Charities cited the case of the Tom Mix gang, which terrorized Baton Rouge for several years. Members of the gang were arrested and detained in the parish jail from five to ten days, then returned to the streets. This routine was repeated until the leader entered his eighteenth year and was sentenced to the state penitentiary. The Mix gang then dissolved.[25]

From 1938 to 1940 the Council of Social Agencies of New Orleans and other civic groups were vigorously trying to secure better physical conditions for the juvenile court. None of their efforts however, brought concrete results. Mrs. Judith Douglas, president of the Child Conservation League, a statewide, child-placing agency, sponsored a bill in the state legislature calling for a committee to study the problem of juvenile delinquency on a statewide basis. The bill lacked significant backing, but it also lacked opposition. As a result of widespread insistence on the part of many citizens to do something about the problem of increasing juvenile crime, Gov. Jimmie Davis appointed the Juvenile Court Commission in November 1946. The Commission consisted of Judge Chris Barnett of Shreveport, chairman; Mrs. Roger P. Sharp of New Orleans; W. S. Terry, Jr. of Baton Rouge; Dr. Elizabeth Wisner of New Orleans; Judge Frank Voelker of Lake Providence; and Lawrence E. Higgins, who was appointed in July 1948 to replace Terry.

The Commission held open hearings in several Louisiana cities during 1947 and thereby secured suggestions and comments from members of the legal, social-work, teaching, medical, psychiatric and ministerial professions. The Commission also called on experts on juvenile crime for advice and sponsored research in cooperation with courts, state departments, and private institutions. After compiling all of its research, the Commission issued a report recommending that judges of city courts be attorneys; that the Department of Public Welfare provide properly equipped and managed detention homes; that individual cases of juvenile delinquency not be publicized; that better training be given members of law enforcement agencies; and that the state establish a permanent Youth Commission to study and make recommendations on al problems pertaining to youth.[26]

The Juvenile Court Commission's findings were reinforced by a study undertaken by the National Probation Association in New Orleans. This study disclosed that New

Orleans had one of the most poorly equipped, urban juvenile courts in the country. Its major faults were inadequate quarters, poor organization, lack of trained probation personnel, and ineffective procedural policies.[27] The effects of both of these studies were to be felt in New Orleans in 1951, when the juvenile court quarters were renovated and enlarged, its social worker staff was increased from three to eight, and the court's budget for 1951 was increased from $90,940 to $102,406.[28]

Another result of the Juvenile Court Commission's study was legislation giving the Department of Public Welfare the authority to construct and operate detention facilities and to contract with individuals to provide foster home care to children with special needs.[29] Following the passage of this act in 1948, the Department made contracts for foster home care for special children, but made little headway in building and operating detention homes.

How the acts setting up juvenile courts worked in other parts of the state, excluding New Orleans and Shreveport, is best exemplified by the experience of Baton Rouge before 1954. In 1952, the East Baton Rouge Parish Council authorized representatives of the National Probation and Parole Association to make a survey in the parish of the treatment of neglected and dependent children. Representatives of the national association found that the juvenile court in East Baton Rouge Parish was not a special court with exclusive jurisdiction in children's cases. Instead the court was presided over by four district court judges who rotated by agreement every five months, each judge serving as *ex-officio* judge of the juvenile court. The criminal court docket was similarly rotated to include the proper balance of juvenile and adult cases.

In the district court, two days were set aside for juvenile cases and three days for criminal cases. Cases of neglect and delinquency might be heard at any time, sandwiched between other cases or heard before the court convened for adult suits. Cases involving children were heard in the judge's chambers, while cases of non-support were heard in the courtroom. During the 1952 session, the court heard 1,560 cases of non-support, 82 adoption hearings, 140 cases of delinquency, 92 cases of neglect, 31 cases of contributing to the neglect, and 2 cases of contributing to the delinquency of a minor.

The sole probation officer of East Baton Rouge Parish failed to furnish the judge with a written report regarding the charges brought against the child defendants. As a consequence, 13 percent of the delinquency cases were dismissed by the judge with either the issuance of a warning, or by placing the child in the custody of his parents, a usually ineffective disciplinary measure; 11 percent were committed to institutions; and an additional 10.2 percent were officially placed on probation. Twice as many black children as whites were sentenced to parish jails; three times as many Negroes were committed to institutions; and only one-third as many were placed on probation. Investigators, therefore, concluded that a less perfunctory, milder treatment policy operated in favor of white juveniles. Judges gave little consideration to the fact that there were fewer parochial resources for blacks and that fewer black delinquents obtained probation officers' services.

Investigators also described the East Baton Rouge detention facilities in great detail. The jail had a wide central hallway off which were "tanks" for prisoners segregated according to sex and race. One of the "tanks" was reserved for Negro women and girls. Here young girls were often locked up with prostitutes. At the far end of the central hallway was a small shower room which contained mops, cleaning material and a medical examining table. This room was used for Negro boys who slept on mattresses on the concrete floor. When so many boys were detained that the mattresses occupied the entire floor, additional mattresses were placed in the central hallway.

Near the jail's entrance were five small cells. The first, about ten feet square, was reserved for white boys. It contained one bunk bed and a toilet, but no wash basin. When more than two boys were detained in a cell, mattresses were placed on the floor. In the adjoining two cells were drunks and mentally disturbed prisoners. The fourth cell was used for white women and girls. When girls were jailed, every effort was made to move the women to other cells. In 1951, 243 juveniles between the ages of eight and sixteen were held in the East Baton Rouge Parish jail from one to seventy-eight days; 118 black boys, 90 white boys, 27 black girls, and 8 white girls.

The survey concluded that in Baton Rouge the poor facilities provided in the jail, the lack of probation services in the district court and the lack of a state institution for delinquent Negro girls tended to encourage the very delinquency decried by the community. The report also recommended that the city judge refer all juvenile cases to the district juvenile court, that the parish commissioners appoint an advisory committee to the juvenile court and develop an adequate probation department.[30]

Following the 1952 East Baton Rouge Parish survey, no action was taken for several months on its recommendations. Several groups, including the Ministerial Alliance, the Inter-Civil Club, the League of Women Voters, Parent-Teachers Association Council, Kiwanis Club, and the Amvets discussed the report in 1953. The Amvets were the first group to take action, passing a resolution favoring the establishment of a detention home in Baton Rouge.[31] The parish PTA subsequently coordinated efforts by various groups to improve the parish's probation and detention programs. Through the PTA's public relations committee, public awareness was aroused. In the meantime the Kiwanis Club renovated, at a cost of $8,500, an old army administration building at Harding Field as a detention home. The PTA then appealed to the city-parish council which after deliberation, appropriated sustaining funds for the home. On February 15, 1954, Baton Rouge's first detention home opened with an appropriate staff, both white and black, and new probation personnel.[32]

In conjunction with the founding of the detention home the legislature submitted to Louisiana's voters a state constitutional ammendment establishing a family court in East Baton Rouge Parish. Established on November 2, 1954, the Family Court had exclusive jurisdiction over all juvenile cases, except those involving capital crimes by minors under seventeen years of age; all cases of desertion, non-support or criminal neglect; adoption;

and cases of divorce or annulment of marriage. The Family Court began operation on December 10, 1954, with Judge Joe W. Sanders presiding.

During the court's first year, 280 children, including runaways from other states, were cared for at the Juvenile Detention Home. The sum of $83,924.55 was collected for the support of dependents under probation plans imposed by court sentence in criminal neglect of family cases. The court also heard 658 cases involving 570 children, as well as 105 adoption cases.

The Family Court also made arrangements with the East Baton Rouge Parish Department of Public Welfare for the establishment of receiving homes for temporary emergency care of neglected, dependent or homeless children. Receiving homes were made available to white children by December 17, 1954, and during the year, forty-nine children received care in such facilities.

The city-parish council created the Family Court Advisory Committee of twenty-one citizens for the purpose of lending guidance, assistance, and support to the improvement of court services and facilities. At its first meeting on January 7, 1955, the Family Court judge referred to the Committee for study the creation of a family counseling service and the establishment of receiving homes for black children. Receiving homes for Negro children were made available on September 23, 1955, and by the Family Court's first anniversary, twelve Negro children had been cared for in receiving homes.[33] In 1956 a private agency affiliated with the Family Service Association of America made family counseling services available to the people of Baton Rouge. Mrs. Inez Land and other interested citizens were instrumental in establishing the East Baton Rouge Parish Family Counseling Service. Between 1956 and 1967 the agency's budget had grown from $2,000 to $65,229 and its staff from one to three full-time caseworkers, an office staff, and several part-time workers. The agency, like its counterparts in New Orleans and throughout the United States, provided counseling in all phases of family problems on a pay-as-you-can-basis. Most of its operational funds, however, were derived from the United Givers' Fund.[34]

The juvenile delinquency problem, however, was not confined to East Baton Rouge Parish. In 1968, nearly 14,000 Louisiana youngsters were referred by the courts. One effort to solve Louisiana's juvenile delinquency problem began with the establishment of the Louisiana Youth Commission by Gov. Earl K. Long in November 1950. The nine-member commission was composed of Judge Chris Barnett, who, as chairman of the now defunct Juvenile Court Commission, remained for two more years as chairman of the new committee; Senator G. J. D'Antonio of New Orleans; Mrs. G. W. Pomeroy of Ruston; Rabbi M. M. Thurman of Alexandria; Mrs. A. Dent Tisdale of Monroe; Judge Frank Voelker of Lake Providence; and Dr. C. H. Webb of Shreveport. In September 1951, Rabbi Thurman resigned and was replaced in November 1952 by Herbert Heymann of Lafayette.

The commission was charged with the responsibility of collecting facts and statistics, making special studies of conditions affecting children and youth in the state, keeping abreast of the developments in this field throughout the nation, interpreting its findings to the public, providing for mutual exchange of ideas and information on national, state and local levels, conducting hearings, making recommendations for improvements in the field of child care, serving as an advisory body in regard to new legislation in the field, and coordinating the services of all agencies in the state serving children."[35] The commission was to be advisory, investigatory; consultative but not administrative; and its work was subsidized by a $20,000 state appropriation. The commissioners received no monetary compensation for their services, except travel expenses.

In 1959, the commission reviewed its accomplishments during the preceding nine years. Several of its recommendations had been translated into vibrant programs by the legislature, including a juvenile probation system with the Department of Public Welfare in 1952, the development of facilities for delinquent Negro girls at the Industrial School for Colored Youths in 1956, centralized administration of juvenile correctional schools under the Department of Institutions in 1956, a larger staff and improved facilities at the Industrial School, and the opening of an intermediate institution at DeQuincy for juveniles aged eighteen to twenty-five years.[36]

In its surveys and studies, the Youth Commission found that although the law forbade the jailing of children under fifteen years of age, 11.7 percent of all children brought before the courts spent some time in jail. The commission also found that in 75 percent of the cases, the police decided the child criminal's fate, with only 25 percent of all cases being referred to the juvenile court or to another social agency. For example, police departments placed juveniles on informal probation, ordered restitution, or revoked the driver's permit. The lack of uniformity in the manner in which the juvenile cases were handled and the resulting confusion were the results of dual jurisdiction between district and city courts. The Youth Commission therefore attempted to remedy this situation by developing a series of judicial reforms designed to begin a semblance of uniform treatment of children in Louisiana's judicial system.

The Youth Commission also encouraged the development of juvenile courts and attempted to educate the public concerning the problems of delinquent and handicapped children by its publications, by holding institutes, and by working with statewide citizen groups, such as the PTA, the League of Women Voters, the Business and Professional Women's Club, and other religious and civic groups on problems of children and youth.

Throughout its existence, the commission was directed by Lawrence E. Higgins, a former member of the Juvenile Court Commission as well as the former head of the Department of Public Welfare. While serving as Commission Director, Higgins, an alumnus of Tulane University and the L.S.U. School of Social Work, was invited to appear before congressional committees considering bills affecting American youth. He also served on international councils on public welfare and youth.[37]

Through the efforts of reformers, such as Higgins, the rights afforded juvenile criminals were gradually expanded. Under common law a child under seven years of age was incapable of committing a crime. Between the ages of seven and fourteen, however, he might be judged guilty of committing a crime if he was cognizant that his actions were wrong and if he was aware of the legal penalties for the commission of the crime. In a test case, *State* vs. *Nickelson* of 1893, a child between the ages of 10 and 12 was charged with setting fire to, and burning, a barn and was later indicated because he had acted "feloniously, unlawfully, and maliciously." He was found guilty on the basis of his confession that he was fully aware of what he was doing and that he was aware that what he did was wrong.[38] Nickelson's conviction was debated for many years and was not settled until the Louisiana legislature approved legislation in 1942 stating that children less than ten years of age were exempt from full criminal responsibility. Their crimes therefore fell within the jurisdiction of the juvenile courts.[39]

The Louisiana law also established two classes of illegitimate children: children whose parents were not legally married at the time of conception, and bastards produced by incestuous or adulterous unions.[40] Before 1948 neither the child of adulterous nor incestuous unions could be legitimated by subsequent marriage of the parents, nor could the child attain through acknowledgment the status of a "natural child." The Civil Code of 1950, however, deleted the words "adulterous and incestuous" thereby permitting a child's natural parents to legitimate him by notarial act, provided no other legal impediments to the marriage, such as color, existed at the time of conception.[41] Fathers and mothers owed support to their illegitimate children when they were in need and the children had a right to claim such assistance. Nevertheless, in order to claim such support the child had to be acknowledged by either the father or mother.[42] Therefore, if the father refused to support his child, criminal proceedings could not be brought against him, unless he had previously acknowledged paternity of the child by notarial act, or if his paternity had been established by the district court.[43] The juvenile court was never given jurisdiction in cases establishing the paternity of an illegitimate child and therefore could only force support from fathers who acknowledged their illegitimate children.

The abandoned child, whether legitimate or illegitimate, was legally judged to be a vagrant and a foundling. As previously stated, the deserted child was to be placed in the House of Refuge or turned over to the Louisiana Society for the Prevention of Cruelty to Children. A child was considered to be abandoned when his parents had failed to support him for two years.[44] In 1938, the period of abandonment was reduced to one year and then later reduced to four months. Once a child was declared abandoned, he could be placed for adoption by the agency charged with his custody.

While the status of abandoned children improved in Louisiana during the 1930s and 1940s, the legal position of illegitimate offspring remained poor. For example, Louisiana law failed to provide damages for the wrongful death of illegitimate children. As a consequence, a district court dismissed a suit by a woman for the drowning death of her two illegitimate children in a Baton Rouge drainage canal. In a 6 to 3 decision on May 20, 1968, the United States Supreme Court barred Louisiana from blocking damage suits involving illegitimate children. The ruling involved two cases. In the first suit, Louise Levy's five illegitimate children had been barred by state courts from suing a physician and a hospital for their mother's death. The damage suit claimed that Miss Levy did as a result of negligent medical treatment. In the second case, Mrs. Glona Brady Glona of Giddings, Texas, was barred from suing a motorist and an insurance company for the death of her illegitimate son in a New Orleans automobile accident.

Former Louisiana Atty. Gen. Jack P. F. Gremillion, supporting the state law, said Louisiana's purpose was "the encouragement of marriage as one of the most important institutions known to the law, the preservation of the legitimate family as the preferred environment for socializing the child and the preservation of the security and certainty of property rights linked with the family."[45] On the other hand, Justice William O. Douglas stated in the majority opinion: "Illegitimate children are not non-persons, they are human beings, live and have their being. They are clearly persons within the meaning of the equal protection clause of the Fourteenth Amendment."[46]

Despite the state's opposition to damages for the wrongful death of illegitimate children, Louisiana's policy was to place the children's welfare above any right of parental custody when such welfare became endangered morally or physically by the parents' misconduct or neglect of the child.[47] For example, the earliest legislation regarding child neglect or abuse, adopted in 1892, authorized the Louisiana Society for the Prevention of Cruelty to Children to enforce all laws concerning child abuse. Legislation approved in 1894 stated that district court judges could remove children from parental custody whenever the child's physical well being or moral welfare were endangered by neglect or abuse. The law further stated, as previously mentioned, that, pending a hearing, no child should be held in the parish jail or police station in the company of adult convicts. Such a child should be placed in a foster home having the same religious beliefs as the child's parents and no child under twelve years should be placed in a correctional institution.

By the 1950s, the words "district judge," in the 1894 law proved to be ambiguous. Was the judge to sit as a district judge or a juvenile court judge? In order to preclude further questions of concurrent jurisdiction in child neglect cases, the 1894 act was repealed in 1956. Juvenile courts then assumed complete jurisdiction over suits involving child neglect and abuse.[48]

Before 1944, rudimentary child-abuse services had been provided by the Louisiana Society for the Prevention of Cruelty to Children, also known as the New Orleans Children's Bureau. When these services were assumed by the Department of Public Welfare in 1944, and later shared by the Department, the New Orleans District Court, and the municipal police department's Juvenile Bureau, the Children's Bureau modified its program to provide foster care, as well as other services, to abused children, transferring its protective services to the above-mentioned agencies. For the remainder of the state, the Office of Family Services was charged with the protection of neglected and abused children. In child-abuse cases the office was empowered to take legal action against responsible adults and remove children from their homes through their courts.[49]

With the proliferation of child welfare services in the early 1940s, the state was confronted with the need to centralize the administrative machinery for the institutions upon which the programs were based. Before 1940 each of Louisiana's public institutions was administered by its own board of supervisors as well as the Board of Charities and Corrections. By 1940, nineteen boards or individuals administered the state's hospitals and industrial schools. In 1940, however, Gov. Sam Jones restructured Louisiana's administrative framework, placing all state institutions, except schools and colleges, under an umbrella agency, christened the Department of Institutions. The Department, which consisted of a director, assistant director, and a nine-member board of institutions,[50] endured until Earl Long occupied the governor's mansion in 1948.

In 1948, Long secured the repeal of the legislation creating the Department of Institutions. The act of repeal met with little opposition in the legislature, and the various hospitals and schools reverted to local control.

State institutional administration, however, emerged as a fiery issue in the 1952 gubernatorial campaign. Gubernatorial candidate Robert F. Kennon proposed a reorganizational program advocating not only the reestablishment of the defunct Board of Institutions, but also insulating such high cost agencies as the departments of Welfare, Education, Highways, and Institutions from "power politics." According to the Public Affairs Research Council, which studied Kennon's proposal, boards governing the state's welfare programs and institutions were to be staffed by former members of the Louisiana Boards Panels. The Panels would, in turn, be staffed by persons nominated by non-profit organizations and other concerned citizens. Whenever vacancies would occur on the supervisory boards, the remaining board members would select seven names from the panel and send them to the governor within thirty days; the chief executive would then appoint one of the seven nominees to the supervisory board.

Following Kennon's election and the program's implementation, no names were ever submitted for the panel, and Kennon therefore made appointments without the above-mentioned restrictions.[51] Thus, the new machinery failed. As a consequence, the Board of Institutions was re-created in 1952 and Gov. Robert F. Kennon imported Dr. Edward D. Grant of Richmond, Virginia, to assume the arduous task of administering Louisiana's far-flung institutional system.[52]

When Earl Long, who had decentralized supervision of state institution in 1948, was reelected governor in 1956, he suggested a change in the Department of Institutions' organization. For example, he advocated separate administrative units for Louisiana's penal and correctional institutions and hospitals. A Baton Rouge newspaper approved of Long's proposal.[53] PAR, on the other hand, opposed the changes, for they would "in many instances extend further the complexities, duplications, and inconsistencies of the existing structure."[54] In 1956, the legislation establishing the Department of Institutions was repealed, and a new supervisory department and board were created for mental, penal, and correctional institutions. Dr. Grant, who was appointed director of the Board of Institutions in 1952, remained as director of the new department until 1958. After the Louisiana Colony and Training School was placed under the Department of Hospitals in

1960 the Board of Institutions became the Department of Institutions with jurisdiction over penal and correctional institutions.

The political observer and newscaster, Ed Clinton, astutely summarized the history of the administration of state institutions when he said: "Long a political football, to be passed, kicked, and punted during campaigns, the state's institutional set-up used to wind up at the end of the legislative session as an undernourished stepchild, fed enough to keep it alive, but by a badly balanced diet that forstalled a healthy life."[55]

Notes for "Louisiana and the Child Offender"

[1] Edward Livingston, *A System of Penal Law* (Philadelphia, 1833), 338.

[2] Ibid., 714-22.

[3] Charles Haven Hunt, *Life of Edward Livingston* (New York, 1864), xvii.

[4] Robert C. Reinders, *End of an Era, New Orleans, 1850-1860* (New Orleans, 1964), 71.

[5] *Report of the Joint Committee on Charitable Institutions*. Documents of the Louisiana Legislature (Baton Rouge, 1860).

[6] *New Orleans Times-Democrat*, December 24, 1881.

[7] George W. Cable, "Our Vice Mills and Jails for the Aged and Insane," *New Orleans Times-Democrat*, December 25, 1881.

[8] George W. Cable, "A Rogue's Congress," *New Orleans Times-Democrat*, January 22, 1882.

[9] *New Orleans Daily Picayune*, March 10, May 8, August 14, 1881; November 17, December 12, 1882.

[10] Ibid., March 7, 1897.

[11] F. S. Sheilds, *Prison Reform: Its Principles and Purposes, What It Has Accomplished, The Work Yet to Be Done* (New Orleans, 1905), 20.

[12] "Report on Welfare in New Orleans," *New Orleans Times-Picayune*, December 20, 1921.

[13] *Annual Report of the Department of Institutions, 1955*, 29.

[14] *Annual Report of the Department of Institutions, 1941*, non-paginated.

[15] "Report of the Advisory Committee to the Department of Institutions" (New Orleans, 1944), 60.

[16] Robert G. Pugh, *Juvenile Laws of Louisiana: History and Development* (Baton Rouge, 1957).

[17] *Annual Report of the Board of Commissioners of the State Industrial School for Colored Youths* (Baton Rouge, 1949-1950).

[18] Throughout the 1960s, overcrowding, understaffing, and lack of funds continued to plague all of the state institutions, especially the coeducational black reform school at Scotlandville. On June 20, 1969, Dallas Matthews stated that the Institution was operating with a budget for 450 inmates, while 486 were on the rolls. "We can't clothe, supervise or feed them properly," he said, adding that the institution is a "powder keg" requiring immediate attention and improvement. Family Court Judge Thomas Pugh, commenting on the school's deplorable conditions, stated that at the Pineville institution $13 was spent per day for approximately 133 inmates, at Monroe the figure was $7 for 350, while at Scotlandville the figure dropped to about $5 per day for 750 juveniles.

On September 22, 1969, the problems of Scotlandville finally received some attention, for the institution was ordered by the federal courts to desegregate its facilities. In fact, soon after the issuance of this order an additional $100,000 was obtained by the Louisiana Department of Corrections for the Scotlandville institution, bringing its budgetary funding in line with those of the formerly white institutions. Not only was more money found for the reform school, but once the all-black Industrial School for Colored Youths was integrated, the institution's enrollment decreased from over 700 to approximately 450 boys and 50 girls, including 70 white males and 13 white females. Juvenile judges in South Louisiana began assigning all boys and girls to the Scotlandville training school, whose name had been changed to the Louisiana Training Institute at Baton Rouge.

The institutions at Monroe and Pineville were also desegregated. Once they had accepted blacks and their South Louisiana inmates had been transferred to Baton Rouge their enrollments became predominantly black. For example, of the 106 girls at Pineville, 60 were black, while only 46 were white. Moreover, 72 percent of the total male population at the Monroe institute were black.

According to the various institute superintendents—Fred Lindsay at Monroe, Jack Pearce at Pineville, and Dallas Matthews at Baton Rouge (Scotlandville)—the integration of the Louisiana training institutes produced few, if any problems. The smooth transition resulted largely from the superintendent's efforts to prepare their respective staffs through meetings and consultation. *Baton Rouge Morning Advocate*, June 20, 1969; October 6, 1970.

In the late 1970s, the state, through the Department of Corrections, operated four juvenile correctional facilities: the Louisiana Training Institute at Baton rouge with 220 students, LTI at New Orleans with 142, LTI at Monroe with 220, and LTI at Pineville with 96 students.

[19]*Louisiana Courts of 1892*, no. 28.

[20]Ibid.

[21]Frank J. Bruno, *Trends in Social Work, 1874-1956* (New York, 1957), 67.

[22]Grace Abbott, *The Child and the State*, 2 vols. (Chicago, 1938), 2:331.

[23]*Louisiana Acts of 1908*, Act No. 83.

[24]*Report of the Attorney General of Louisiana* (New Orleans, 1922), 472.

[25]*Annual Report of the Board of Charities, 1938*. This report is in the form of a letter addressed to Governor Leche.

[26]*Report of the Juvenile Court Commission for the State of Louisiana* (Baton Rouge, 1946), 1.

[27]*Times-Picayune*, November 21, 1947.

[28]Ibid., February 26, 1951.

[29]*Louisiana Acts of 1948*, No. 54.

[30]*Baton Rouge State-Times*, July 9, 10, 1952.

[31]Margaret G. Beste, "Operation Detention Home," *Louisiana Welfare*, 15 (1954): 6-19.

[32]*Annual Report of the Family Court for the Parish of East Baton Rouge for 1955* (Baton Rouge, 1955), 3, 4.

[33]In 1972 the facilities of the Family Court and the detention home annex were renovated and enlarged. For example, the Family Court Center presently houses a Detention Center, a Probation Department, and a courtroom where juvenile matters are heard. Presently serving on the Family Court bench are Thomas B. Pugh, the second judge to hold that position, and E. Donald Moseley who was first elected in 1972. Demographers predict that violent crime will decrease during the 1980s because the age-group responsible for most violent crimes—persons between the ages of fourteen and twenty-nine—will gradually decline. For the moment, however, the state's juvenile delinquency problem is growing in severity. For example, the 2,890 referrals of 1977 compare unfavorably with the 2,538 of 1976, while the number of convictions has grown from 1,686 in 1976 to 1,932 in 1977.

[34]Many of the juveniles appearing before the city court were traffic offenders. These juveniles, however, were tried in the Family Court following its establishment. In 1962, a juvenile traffic court with a panel of

five-to-six high school jurors was chosen by the Baton Rouge Youth Council. Jurors were licensed drivers who served for six weeks. The growing problem of juvenile traffic violations was demonstrated by the fact that in 1965 only 562 violators appeared before the court while in 1966 there were 1,293 juvenile traffic violations.

By the 1970s, all traffic offenses committed by young adults under seventeen years of age in East Baton Rouge Parish fell within the jurisdiction of the Juvenile Traffic Court. The district attorney's office was represented in all contested traffic hearings, and defendants were given the benefit of legal counsel. In 1977, there were 2,768 juvenile traffic citations. Since these violations reflected lack of driver training or experience rather than personality flaws, the court consistently mandated additional training for traffic violators at the traffic school operated by the Baton Rouge City Police Department and the Greater Baton Rouge Safety Council.

[35]*Louisiana Acts of 1950*, special session, no. 25.

[36]*Biennial Report of the Louisiana Youth Commission, 1957-1959*, 7.

[37]In 1963 Higgins received the meritorious service award of the National Council of Juvenile Court Judges. That citation said in part:

> Lawrence E. Higgins has not only made significant contributions to the development and improvements of juvenile courts in Louisiana, but on the national level has made many contributions in the area of legislation affecting children and youth, development of programs for rehabilitation of youth, juvenile correctional institutions, programs for handicapped children and the propagation of the concept of the juvenile court.

Baton Rouge Morning Advocate, July 18, 1973.

[38]*State* vs. *Nickelson* (45 La. Ann. 1172).

[39]*Louisiana Revised Statutes of 1959*, Title 14:13.

[40]*Louisiana Acts of 1948*, no. 482.

[41]*Revised Statutes of 1950*, Title 9:91.

[42]Harriet S. Daggett, *A Compilation of Louisiana Statutes Affecting Child Welfare and Report of the Louisiana Children's Code Committee* (Baton Rouge, 1933), 275.

[43]Robert C. Pugh, *Juvenile Laws of Louisiana, History and Development*, 1962 supplement, 96.

[44]*Louisiana Acts of 1910*, no. 173.

[45]*Morning Advocate*, January 16, May 21, 1968.

[46]Ibid.

[47]Pugh, *Juvenile Laws of Louisiana*, 297.

[48]Ibid., 310.

[49]Each year throughout the nation, tens of thousands of children are willfully beaten, burned, smothered, and starved. Such battered children have constituted an alarmingly high percentage of the patients in New Orleans Charity Hospital as well as other hospitals throughout the state. Dr. H. C. Tolmas has stated that most patients who come to the hospital as abused children are under the age of three. He further indicated that the culpable parents leave the hospital quickly and seldom subsequently visit the child.

Because child abusers usually go from doctor to doctor and hospital to hospital to avoid detection, and because child abuse usually occurs in the absence of witnesses, convictions are difficult to obtain. Therefore, in 1964, the state legislature adopted the Battered Child Act, requiring physicians and hospitals to report bodily injuries inflicted upon children by their parents. According to Dr. Tolmas, reporting incidents is not enough. Once a report is issued, a multi-disciplinary network of protection, including pediatricians, psychiatrists, lawyers, and social workers, should act for the benefit of the child and his parents. *New Orleans Times-Picayune*, October 19, 1967.

[50] *Louisiana Acts of 1940*, no. 47.

[51] *State-Times*, July 13, 1953.

[52] Ibid., April 23, 1956.

[53] *Morning Advocate*, July 24, 1953.

[54] *State-Times*, July 24, 1953.

[55] *Sunday Advocate*, January 21, 1968.
   More recently Margaret Dixon, managing editor of the *Baton Rouge Morning Advocate*, reported that the shocking conditions of the state's penal and correctional institutions pointed up the lack of planning provided the above-mentioned agencies as well as the intolerable conditions spawned by so-called economy measures. She further indicated that most of the state's correctional institutions which receive an incredible amount of wear and tear have simply not received maintenance funds for years and hardly a cent has gone into repairing the greatly overcrowded schools and prisons. One building at the Louisiana Training Institute was reportedly so damaged by termites that "only the fact that termites have joined hands and formed a chain is holding it up." Dixon concluded that at the very least it was bad management, at worst it was neglect of the worst sort, and it was high time that something to done to improve the situation.

ORGANIZED CRIME IN LOUISIANA HISTORY: MYTH AND REALITY*

Michael L. Kurtz**

On January 3, 1855, the body of Francisco Domingo, a Sicilian truck farmer, was discovered on an embankment near the Mississippi River in New Orleans. He had been stabbed over a dozen times, and his throat was slit from ear to ear. Domingo's widow gave investigating officers a note her husband had received a few days before the murder. The note demanded that Domingo pay its anonymous author $500 in return for his life. Near the bottom o the note, stamped in black ink, lay the imprint of a black hand.[1] In the ensuing five years, six similar murders occurred in New Orleans, each involving a victim of Sicilian or Italian origin who had received a threatening note containing the black hand symbol.[2] Shortly after the outbreak of the Civil War, the *New Orleans True Delta* insisted that the authorities take action against an "organized gang of Spanish and Sicilian thieves and burglars."[3] In that same year, 1861, the newspaper reported the arrest of a gang of Sicilian immigrants on counterfeiting charges.[4]

These incidents have led some writers to allege the existence of an organized criminal syndicate in Louisiana, its origins dating to the antebellum era.[5] Other writers have traced the beginnings of organized crime in Louisiana to the postbellum period.[6] United States government agencies investigating organized crime have expressed similar views. In 1972, for example, the Federal Bureau of Investigation (FBI), reported that "the first 'family' of what has now, become known as La Cosa Nostra (LCN) came from Sicily and settled in New Orleans after the Civil War." The FBI obtained this information from a highly "reliable source," who went on to note that "inasmuch as this 'family' was the predecessor of all subsequent 'families,' it has been afforded the highest respect and esteem, and because of its exalted position, the New Orleans 'family' could make decisions on its own without going to the 'Commission'."[7] In 1979, the Select Committee on Assassinations of the United States House of Representatives echoed the FBI report:

---

*First published in *Louisiana History*, 24 (1983): 355-76. Reprinted with the kind permission of the author and the Louisiana Historical Association.

" ... [T]he New Orleans Mafia had been the first branch of the Mafia in America (the Sicilian La Cosa Nostra had entered the United States through the port of New Orleans during the 1880s). ..."[8]

Although differing on details, these accounts generally agree that in nineteenth century New Orleans there existed an organized criminal syndicate operated and staffed by Italian and Sicilian immigrants. Moreover, this syndicate was the earliest of those criminal brotherhoods commonly called the American Mafia. Finally, this nineteenth century syndicate perpetuated itself in power, and a continuous succession of underworld associations has dominated organized criminal activity in Louisiana.

In fact, this widely believed account is a myth, given popular currency by nineteenth century newspaper reporters and politicians, and by contemporary journalists and writers, and even by such organizations as the FBI and the Metropolitan Crime Commission of Greater New Orleans. One reason for the myth is the dearth of scholarly research on the topic, most of the works written about it combining unsubstantiated speculation with irresponsible sensationalism.[9] Some studies do present the appearance of serious scholarly inquiries, but in reality, offer little more than a rehashing of press accounts and political news releases. For example, the studies by John E. Coxe and John S. Kendall of the murder of New Orleans police chief David C. Hennessy and the subsequent mob lynching of eleven Italians acquitted of the crime agree with the official and popular versions that Hennessy's murder resulted from a Mafia vendetta.[10] Two recent studies of the Hennessy case, by Richard Gambino and Humbert Nelli, have convincingly demonstrated the lack of reliable documentation for the Coxe-Kendall Mafia thesis.[11] In like manner, none of the numerous accounts of a New Orleans based organized criminal syndicate can be supported by the available evidence.

THE STRUCTURE OF ORGANIZED CRIME

Another reason for the myth lies in the confusion surrounding the term "organized crime." Like other generalizations, "organized crime" lacks precise definition and is often employed to characterize a host of illegal enterprises ranging from betting on football games to homicide. None of the myriad studies of organized crime give the term a concrete definition. However, most authorities concur in the general definition of "organized crime" as describing the underworld organizations in the United States which engage in such illegal activities as prostitution, narcotics, gambling, blackmail, extortion, and bribery. Centered in large metropolitan areas, these organizations are part of a national criminal syndicate generally referred to as the Mafia, La Cosa Nostra, the Mob, and similar terminology. Each of these criminal organizations is a "family," headed by a "boss," or, to employ a popular term, a "godfather." Each family boss is a member of the national syndicate hierarchy called the "commission," which dictates national underworld policy.[12]

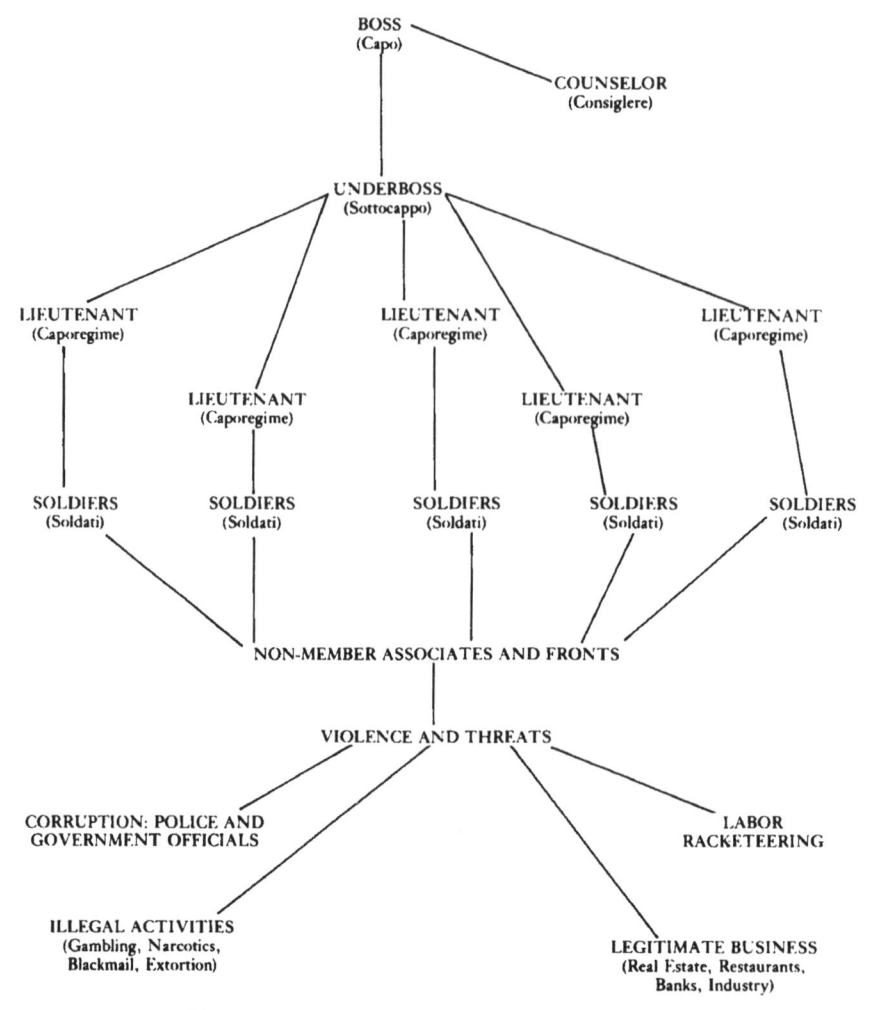

```
                    BOSS
                   (Capo)
                     |
                     |————————COUNSELOR
                     |        (Consigliere)
                     |
                 UNDERBOSS
                 (Sottocappo)
```

Figure 1. A Typical Organized Crime Family

Source: FBI Report, 1963

Most of the syndicate "families" in the United States originated in the 1920s and 1930s when they gained domination of the organized illegal enterprises in many large cities. Through bribery, intimidation, and murder, the "families" of such well-known underworld "bosses" as Charles "Lucky" Luciano, Frank Costello, Vito Genovese, and Al Capone won control of the local underworlds in which they operated.[13] A characteristic of organized criminal syndicates in the United States is their domination by individuals of Italian and Sicilian nationality.[14] Another characteristic of organized crime is the use of violence to eliminate competition, e.g., the St. Valentine's Day Massacre of 1929, in which members of the Capone gang executed seven members of the rival "Bugs" Moran gang. In addition, organized crime wins the connivance of local public officials and law enforcement agencies through bribery and of the local citizenry through intimidation.[15]

The term most frequently used to describe organized crime, "Mafia," is a misnomer. It derives from the word used to describe late nineteenth century peasant organizations in western Sicily. Established to defend themselves against attacks by roving bandits and against unscrupulous landlords, these peasant organizations fell under the control of certain leaders called *mafioso*. Similar organizations developed in Calabria (*fibbia*) and Naples (*camorra*). Because these organizations operated outside the law, they employed secretive passwords, distinctive rituals and uniforms, and an elaborate code of behavior, the most rigidly enforced aspect of which was *Omerta*, the responsibility of each member to maintain strict silence about everything related to the organization. Strongly supported by most of the Sicilian peasantry because it opposed the entrenched landlords, the Mafia by 1900 came to dominate the island politically, socially, and economically.[16]

THE MYTH OF THE MAFIA IN NINETEENTH CENTURY LOUISIANA

While some writers have alleged the existence of the Mafia in antebellum Louisiana, none of the evidence supports their thesis. In 1860, only 1,019 persons of Italian or Sicilian origin lived in New Orleans, virtually all of them produce wholesalers and distributors.[17] Although some of these people undoubtedly committed crimes, the crimes do not appear the result of syndicate activity. For example, the gangs of thieves, burglars, and counterfeiters reported by the New Orleans press clearly referred to groups of petty criminals of which antebellum New Orleans abounded.[18] The six "black hand" murders went unsolved and thus could not be attributed to the Mafia or any other organization. In addition, the "black hand" was not, as some writers have claimed, the exclusive symbol of the Mafia. On the contrary, it was widely employed as a terrorist symbol in many parts of Europe in the nineteenth and early twentieth centuries. For example, the Narodna Odbrana, the Serbian nationalist organization responsible for the assassination of Archduke Franz Ferdinand in 1914, used the "black hand" as a trademark. The symbol also enjoyed widespread currency in such diverse areas as Russia, Sicily, France, and Prussia.[19] Some studies assert that the Mafia employed the "black hand" symbol as a means of intimidation of its victims, while other studies deny the assertion.[20] In any event, none of the evidence supports the thesis that the antebellum "black hand" murders in New Orleans resulted from the vengeance wreaked by an organized criminal syndicate against Italian and Sicilian victims who refused to pay "protection" money.

Italian and Sicilian immigration into Louisiana accelerated during the postbellum era. According to a recent study, in 1900, some 17,000 native Italians and Sicilians had emigrated to Louisiana, the majority coming from Sicily rather than Italy.[21] Most Sicilians chose New Orleans as their port of entry into the United States. In 1889, 456 of the 459 Sicilian immigrants into America arrived through the port of New Orleans; in 1891,

2,868 of 3,351, and in 1892, 2,714 of 2,938.[22] The vast majority of these people lived in New Orleans, although some did move to the Florida Parishes and the sugar-growing areas. The New Orleans area offered a favorable climate, a strong Roman Catholic religious tradition, and a cosmopolitan society into which foreigners were easily assimilated. Congregated in the French Quarter, especially in the vicinity of St. Louis Cathedral and the French Market, these Sicilian immigrants worked on the waterfront, operated grocery stores, and sold fruits and vegetables.[23]

Various theories concerning the origins of organized crime in postbellum Louisiana have been proposed. One concerns the Sicilian organization founded by Joseph Macheca in New Orleans. The son of Sicilian immigrants, Macheca was born in New Orleans in 1834. As a young man, he worked with his father in fruit vending and in the food wholesaling business. During the Civil War, Macheca moved to Texas, where he accumulated a large fortune, most probably through blockade running. After the war, Macheca returned to New Orleans, where he acquired real estate and founded a steamship company handling trade between the Crescent City and Central America (this company became the famous United Fruit Company).[24] In 1868, Joseph Macheca became actively involved in Democratic party politics. Because of his wealth and influence, he joined the party's hierarchy in New Orleans. In the rough-and-tumble world of Reconstruction politics in Louisiana, violence, rioting, and even murder often accompanied the balloting process. "Black" Republicans and "White" Democrats formed a number of political clubs to protect themselves against attacks by their enemies.[25] One such club was the Innocents, a organization of Sicilian immigrants founded by Macheca in 1868. The earliest recorded action of the Innocents came on October 24 1868, when the group joined with other Democratic clubs in assaulting blacks campaigning for the election of the Republican candidate, Ulysses S. Grant, to the presidency.[26] For three days the Innocents led the Democratic dubs in violent attacks upon blacks in New Orleans, leaving several persons dead, scores injured, and a large amount of property damage.[27]

The Innocents wore white, sometimes red, caped uniforms embossed with the Maltese Cross, and they carried pistols, knives, and clubs. Its membership was overwhelmingly Sicilian, although the club did include several Irish and German members.[28] Disbanded after the 1868 election, the Innocents were reorganized by, Joseph Macheca the following year into a club whose primary purpose lay in protecting Sicilian commercial interests against acts of violence by their competitors.[29] By 1870, the Sicilian community in New Orleans dominated the city's fruit, vegetable, and seafood trade and it had established control over the lucrative Central America trade. In the absence of any effective enforcement of the law by the authorities, many businessmen in New Orleans hired bodyguards and watchmen to protect their establishments. As the wealthiest Sicilian in New Orleans, Joseph Macheca had an enormous vested interest in his commercial holdings. He employed the Innocents to safeguard those holdings against potential rivals both within and without the Sicilian community.[30]

According to David Chandler, the arrival in New Orleans in late 1868 or early 1869 of members of the Sicilian Mafia threatened Macheca's previously undisputed leadership of the city's Italian and Sicilian community, and he responded by attacking them with the Innocents. The resulting internecine warfare among rival Sicilian gangs ended with Macheca victorious and the unchallenged "boss" of a full-fledged Mafia organization.[31] There is no verification for Chandler's thesis. It is true that in March 1869, the *New Orleans True Delta* published a news story about a "band of about twelve well-known and notorious Sicilian murderers, counterfeiters, and burglars, who in the last month, have formed a sort of general co-partnership or stock company for the plunder and disturbance of the City."[32] This news account hardly confirms the existence of a Mafia organization in New Orleans, especially since no other contemporary account confirms it.

Chandler's assertion that members of the Sicilian Mafia arrived in New Orleans in 1868 or 1869 also lacks substantiation. Most of the Sicilian immigrants who arrived in New Orleans during the postbellum era were illiterate peasants and laborers. Not only were they not members of the Sicilian Mafia, many were themselves refugees from it. Many of these immigrants had been harassed by the Mafia in Sicily, a major factor in their decision to emigrate to America. In Sicily, some of these people had organized militia groups to clash with the Mafia, and some of these groups did emigrate to the United States, but they hardly constituted criminal syndicates.[33]

Although formally organized and quick to resort to violence to protect their interests, the Innocents had little in common with modern underworld brotherhoods. Joseph Macheca ruled the Innocents with an iron hand, but he never formed the "family" that constitutes the most visible element of underworld organization in America today. Nor did the Innocents engage in such illegal activities as gambling, prostitution, and narcotics. On the contrary, Macheca's various commercial enterprises were legal and highly profitable, and he remained a leading member of New Orleans commercial activity for several decades. Macheca did contribute funds and organization to the New Orleans Democratic political machine, the "Ring," and he strongly supported the Louisiana State Lottery. In so doing, he merely reflected the views of his Sicilian constituents who were among the "Ring's" and the Lottery's most steadfast supporters.[34]

A second theory involving postbellum organized crime in Louisiana centers on Giuseppe Esposito, a refugee from Sicilian justice who arrived in New Orleans in 1879. John S. Kendall claimed that Esposito founded the Mafia in Louisiana.[35] There is no serious evidence to support the allegation. Never a member of the Sicilian Mafia, Giuseppe Esposito fled his native land to escape prosecution on a variety of petty criminal charges. Although he achieved much notoriety through some of his more daring escapades, Esposito did not engage in organized criminal activity. Instead, he committed most of his crimes alone.[36] Once in New Orleans, Esposito found himself in great difficulty with the city's Sicilian community because of his propensity to violate the law. A fellow Sicilian betrayed him to the authorities, who extradited him to New York. Had

Esposito actually been a Mafioso, such a betrayal would have violated the most sacrosanct of all the Mafia's codes, that of Omerta, or strict silence.[37]

In 1890 and 1891, the sensational Hennessy case gave rise to further allegations of the existence of a formal Mafia organization in New Orleans. John Coxe, John Kendall, and Herbert Asbury are among the many writers who connect the Hennessy murders with the New Orleans underworld.[38] The details of the case have been covered by many writers and need not concern us here.[39] Mayor Joseph A. Shakspeare and New Orleans Police Superintendent D. G. Gaster announced publicly that Hennessy's death resulted from a Mafia vendetta because of Hennessy's investigation of Italian criminal ventures in New Orleans.[40] To substantiate their charge, Shakespeare and Gaster produced records of a series of murders reputedly committed by Sicilians during the quarter century preceding the slaying.[41] Another reason for the charge was that Hennessy allegedly told an associate that "the Dagoes" had shot him.[42] In his study of organized crime, Humbert Nelli demonstrated conclusively that the allegations about the Mafia's responsibility for Hennessy's death were false. The so-called "Mafia executions" did not, in fact, result from Mafia vendettas. Most of them involved victims who were not Italian or Sicilian; a few were due to family disputes; and the perpetrators and motives for the rest could not be ascertained.[43]

The Hennessy murder and subsequent lynchings generated much publicity about the Mafia in Louisiana.[44] With the exception of the local Italian language newspapers, all New Orleans papers repeated the official line that the slaying was the work of the Mafia, and some papers even condoned the lynching of the eleven Italians acquitted of the crime.[45] The *New Orleans Picayune,* for example, argued that "the work done was a marvel of moderation when we consider the terrible nature of the forces at work," an incredible justification of the cold-blooded murder of eleven citizens.[46]

From the available evidence, it appears that the political faction headed by Mayor Shakspeare used the Hennessy slaying to stir up anti-Italian sentiment in New Orleans because the Italians strongly supported the opposing faction, the "Ring." The Committee of Fifty, a body appointed by the mayor to bring the Hennessy culprits to justice, led the mob that lynched the eleven Italians acquitted of the murder. This Committee of Fifty comprised mainly members of the Anti-Lottery League, a bogus "reform" group ostensibly organized to eliminate vice and political corruption from New Orleans, but actually formed to help elect the Shakspeare faction.[47]

A final theory of organized crime in New Orleans during the nineteenth century concerned the lengthy and violent dispute between two prominent Sicilian families, the Matrangas and the Provenzanos, over the loading and unloading of ships engaged in the Latin American fruit trade. On May 5, 1890, the dispute erupted into violence when five members of the Matranga faction were ambushed, and three were seriously wounded.[48] Police Chic Hennessy arrested live members of the Provenzano faction, and they were found guilty of the crime. Because of certain irregularities, a new trial was held, and this time the five men were acquitted.[49] Several writers have depicted the Matranga-

Provenzano feud as a conflict between the Sicilian Mafia and the Neapolitan Camorra.[50] Humbert Nelli, however, has shown that the feud contained none of the elements of an underworld rivalry between competing gangs. On the contrary, the feud resulted from commercial competition for the lucrative waterfront business.[51]

These findings support the proposition that no reliable evidence exists to substantiate the commonly repeated assertion that in nineteenth century New Orleans the nation's first organized criminal syndicate was established. A careful perusal of the major New Orleans newspapers between 1860 and 1890 reveals only a few scattered references to the "Mafia." The context of these press accounts makes it clear that the references were based on rumor and speculation rather than concrete fact.[52] After the 1890-1891 Hennessy case, the press loaded its columns with references to the "Mafia," and even went so fir as to attribute virtually every crime involving Italians to the mob.[53] None of these accounts, however substantiated the allegations made. The New Orleans press apparently repeated the anti-Italian sentiments voiced by Mayor Shakespeare and gave editorial expression to the wave of the anti-foreign xenophobia that swept the nation during the 1890s.[54]

ORGANIZED CRIME IN TWENTIETH-CENTURY LOUISIANA

Substantially more evidence is available about the structure of organized crime in twentieth century Louisiana. In the first three decades of the twentieth century, no formal organized criminal syndicate existed in the state. Scattered press references to the "Mafia" proved as lacking in documentation as their nineteenth century precursors. For example, when six Italians were convicted and hanged in 1926 for the 1921 murder of an Independence grocer, many newspaper stories accused the defendants of membership in the Mafia, accusations that were completely unfounded.[55]

The most complete description of twentieth century organized crime in Louisiana comes from the pen of David Chandler. According to Chandler, Charles Matranga emerged victorious from his dispute with the Provenzanos and in 1891 became "Mafia boss of New Orleans," a position he held unchallenged until 1922. Investing in shipping and fishing, Matranga acquired immense wealth, and his Mafia empire spread from New Orleans to the surrounding areas. "Almost every community within a two-hundred-mile radius of New Orleans had its resident Mafioso," Chandler asserted, and these communities had strawberry Mafias, orange Mafias, and vegetable Mafias.[56] Under the control of Charles Matranga, these rural Mafias dominated their local communities until Tangipahoa Parish District Attorney Matt Allen arrested and had convicted six Italians on murder charges. The executions of the six ended the reign of the country Mafia, but the New Orleans organization continued its illegal ways.[57]

In 1923, Chandler contends that Matranga turned over control of his Mafia empire to Sylvestro "Silver Dollar Sam" Carolla, a young Sicilian immigrant who had become Matranga's most capable and, reliable lieutenant. Carolla built an empire based on bootlegging during the Prohibition era. In 1935, Carolla and the New York mobster, Frank

Costello, made an arrangement with Huey Long to establish a gambling domain in Louisiana. Carolla was deported in 1947, and his place as Louisiana's Mafia boss was taken by Leoluca T_____, who remained relatively unknown, while his lieutenant Carlos Marcello, operated the empire.[58]

In Chandler's version, Carlos Marcello took over as the leader the Louisiana underworld in the summer of 1963, and since that time has vastly expanded its illegal operations. In 1966, undercover FBI agent Pat Collins infiltrated the Marcello organization and crippled its gambling operations "with devastating effect."[59] Collins's intelligence breakthrough led to a series of FBI raids on Mafia gambling activities throughout the South. In September 1966, the national Mafia "commission" summoned Marcello to New York to explain his failure to protect his empire against government infiltration. After that, Marcello extended his illegal enterprises to Texas where he joined forces with the resident mafioso, Joe Civello. Under Marcello's control, the Louisiana Mafia engaged in illegal operations that included gambling, narcotics, automobile theft, loan-sharking, and extortion. That, as Chandler concluded the story, "was the state of affairs as the Louisiana family closed out its first century of operations."[60]

Chandler's story of organized crime in twentieth-century Louisiana blends careless research, sensationalism, and a flagrant disregard for accuracy. The available evidence supports few of Chandler's undocumented assertions. For example, the claim W. Charles Matranga reigned as Louisiana's Mafia boss for three decades cannot be substantiated. Matranga was one of the persons tried and acquitted for the Hennessy murder, and escaped the lynching meted out to his companions by hiding from the mob.[61] After that, he worked on the New Orleans waterfront for the United Fruit and Standard Fruit Companies and, according to the available evidence, never engaged in illegal activities.[62]

Chandler's description of strawberry and orange Mafias, presumably flourishing in Tangipahoa and Plaquemines Parishes, also remains open to question. His methodology must be challenged because his account of the Amite trial and execution of six Italians contains numerous errors of fact. For example, Chandler asserts that the men were arrested for the 1923 robbery of an Amite bank and murder of a bank guard.[63] In reality, the crime occurred in 1921, and it entailed the fatal shooting of a grocer in Independence.[64] Chandler's chronicle of the organized criminal empire of Sylvestro "Silver Dollar Sam" Carolla, whom he incorrectly nicknames "Silver," is loaded with unsupported generalizations and gross inaccuracies. Chandler describes the reputed clash between Carolla and his underworld rival in New Orleans, William Bailey, as a series of gunfights, ambushes, and executions that made "New Orleans look like movies of Chicago."[65] In fact, the police records and press accounts of the era do not reveal any unusual rise in crimes of violence.[66] Furthermore, "Silver Dollar Sam" Carolla was never more than a minor bootlegger and narcotics trafficker. The documentary records for the entire Prohibition period show that Carolla did not engage in organized bootlegging activities to a greater extent than persons of Irish, Jewish, Anglo-Saxon, or Creole background, and that Carolla's organization consisted of little more than a group of individuals paid to smuggle booze and drugs from the numerous inlets along the southern Louisiana coast and to transport them to New Orleans.[67]

The first concrete evidence of the establishment of an organized criminal syndicate in Louisiana is that of the development of a slot machine empire in New Orleans by Frank Costello, a well-known New York underworld figure. There are two conflicting versions of the origin of Costello's gambling operations in Louisiana. One is that United States Senator Huey P. Long invited him to place slot machines in selected areas of South Louisiana in return for a share of the profits.[68] The other version is that New Orleans politicians headed by Mayor T. Semmes Walmsley invited Costello to set up his operations in the Crescent City.[69] Huey Long's biographer, T. Harry Williams, denies that a Long-Costello deal was made because the "Kingfish's" political enemy, Mayor Walmsley, controlled the New Orleans police and would not have enforced such an arrangement and because Costello revealed the details of the deal in his testimony before a congressional committee in 1940, telling the Huey Long story in order to conceal the real identities of those with whom he made the deal.[70] Although inconclusive, the evidence does support the Long-Costello theory. In the byzantine world of Louisiana politics, deals between political enemies are not uncommon, and it does not appear unreasonable that Walmsley, who was not known for a puritanical attitude toward vice, would not have allowed the machines in New Orleans for a share of the "take." Williams also does not mention the fact that the Long dominated state legislature passed a series of bills in 1934 and 1935 that crippled the independence of the city government and placed control of such local functions as the city police under state control.[71] Therefore, Long, not Walmsley, exercised ultimate control over the New Orleans police. Williams also ignores the installation of slot machines in other parts of Louisiana. For example, the devices were common in Jefferson Parish, at that time under the political domination of State Senator Jules Fisher, a close political ally of Huey Long. Finally, two of Long's closest political associates, Robert S. Maestri and Seymour Weiss, told the author that Long did indeed make the arrangement with Costello, an arrangement which was continued after the "Kingfish's" death in September 1935.[72]

By the beginning of 1936, an extensive slot machine empire had been established in the New Orleans metropolitan area. Under the supervision of Costello lieutenant "Dandy Phil" Kastel, this empire, "was broadened into one of the nation's largest illegal gambling operations. With the connivance of the administration of New Orleans Mayor Robert Maestri, Costello built a gambling domain that included slot machines, pinball machines, lotteries, and handbook operations. Using such legitimate businesses as novelty and amusement companies as "fronts," the Costello organization opened establishments throughout the area.[73] The large influx of military and naval personnel into New Orleans during the war provided the market for the expansion of these activities into such areas as prostitution and narcotics.[74] So flagrantly did the vice flourish in wartime New Orleans that lotteries and illegal handbook practices openly operated next to the Third Precinct Police Station and the Second Ward headquarters of Maestri's Old Regular political machine.[75]

In 1946, the anti-Long reformer, deLesseps S. "Chep" Morrison was elected mayor of New Orleans. In his campaign, Morrison promised to "sweep the city clean" of organized crime and vice. Consequently, the center of the illegal gambling operations moved to the neighboring parish of Jefferson. A partnership consisting primarily of Frank Costello, Meyer Lansky, the Miami-based underworld figure, and a Jefferson Parish amusement company operator and produce wholesaler named Carlos Marcello opened the Beverly Club just across the boundary separating Orleans and Jefferson Parishes. Operating under the permissive eye of Jefferson Parish Sheriff Frank Clancy, the club quickly became one of America's favorite casinos. In 1948, the syndicate opened another casino, the Southport Club, also in Jefferson Parish.[76]

By 1950, the New Orleans metropolitan area had become one of the largest centers of illegal vice in the United States. In February of that year, Mayor Morrison addressed the Conference on Organized Crime sponsored by Attorney General J. Howard McGrath "We have seen . . . this national scene of organized crime . . . several highly organized syndicates whose wealth, power, scope of operations, and influence have recently grown to alarming proportions."[77] The organized criminal syndicate to which Morrison referred had, by 1950, allegedly come under the total domination of a man whose career and reputation have been associated with the Mafia for over thirty years, Carlos Marcello.[78]

Born in Tunis, North Africa, in 1910, with the name of Calogero Minacore or Minacori, Marcello was brought to the United States that year by his parents. A few years later, they changed the family surname to Marcello, and although they were Sicilian, they gave him the Spanish first name, Carlos. Carlos went to school for a few years but quit at the age of fourteen and went to work on a vegetable farm leased by his father.[79] His first brush with the law came in 1930 when he was arrested and convicted of assault, robbery, and grand larceny. Sentenced to nine years in the state penitentiary Marcello was pardoned in 1934 by Gov. Oscar K. Allen. Upon his release from prison, he bought a bar in Gretna. In 1938, Marcello pleaded guilty to narcotics charges and served ten months in the federal penitentiary in Atlanta.[80] After his release, the thirty-year-old Marcello went to work for the family-owned Jefferson Music Company, which allegedly served as a distributor for Costello's slot machines, pinball machines, and juke boxes. During the Second World War, Marcello supposedly entered into an arrangement with Gretna Police Chief Beauregard Miller, whereby Marcello operated the Southern News Service and Publishing Company, the largest racing wire service in New Orleans, and Miller received a share of the profits.[81] So successful was Carlos in these endeavors that when "Silver Dollar Sam" Carolla was deported to Sicily in 1947, Frank Costello gave his "blessing" to Marcello as Louisiana's new "godfather."[82]

According to Aaron M. Kohn, the head of the Metropolitan Crime Commission of Greater New Orleans, by 1951, the Marcello empire was functioning at high gear.[83] Kohn's contention was based on the famous United States Senate committee investigating the status of organized crime in America. Chaired by Sen. Estes Kefauver, the committee held hearings in New Orleans and concluded that Louisiana was one of the centers of organized crime in the United States. The committee stated that Carlos Marcello dominated organized crime in Louisiana and maintained his operations though the bribery of "sheriffs, marshalls, and other law enforcement officials" who received payoffs for "their failure to enforce gambling laws and other statutes relating to vice."[84] In testimony in 1970 before a United States House of Representatives subcommittee, Aaron Kohn provided a more detailed description of Marcello's activities:

> Marcello and his growing organization developed their capital or bankroll through extensive gambling, including casinos, slot machines, pinball, handbooks, layoff, football pools, dice, card games, roulette and bingo; also narcotics, prostitution, extortion, clip-joint operations, B-drinking, marketing stolen goods, robberies, burglaries, and thefts. Their criminal enterprise required, and had, the corrupt collusion of public officials at every critical level including police, sheriffs, justices of the peace, prosecutors, mayors, governors, judges, councilmen, licensing authorities, State legislators, and at least one member of Congress.[85]

By the mid-1960s, Carlos Marcello was widely reputed to be one of the most powerful Mafia bosses in America. Federal investigative agencies attempted to connect him with various criminal undertakings, but they failed to secure the evidence necessary for arrest and conviction. In 1961, federal agents seized Marcello and deported him to Guatemala, but he managed to return to the United States two months later.[86] Since that time, Carlos Marcello has remained in the public spotlight. Several national magazine articles portrayed him as one of the small group of Mafia bosses controlling the vast multibillion dollar underworld in the United States. In 1964, an article in the *Saturday Evening Post* called the Marcello empire in Louisiana the "Wall Street of Cosa Nostra."[87] In 1967, two articles in *Life* magazine depicted Marcello as one of America's leading figures in organized crime.[88] On several occasions, Marcello testified before congressional committees investigating organized crime and racketeering. His testimony consisted primarily of invoking the Fifth Amendment's protection against self-incrimination.[89]

According to the Metropolitan Crime Commission, the Marcello empire today generates an annual income of $500 million from a combination of legal and illegal enterprises. In addition to the gambling, narcotics, and other illegal operations, the Marcello organization derives some $100 million annually from legitimate business investments, most of them in real estate.[90] In 1979, the House Select Committee on Assassinations went so far as to accuse Marcello of being one of the prime suspects in the conspiracy to assassinate President Kennedy.[91] Marcello's criminal convictions since 1940 include a one year sentence in 1967 for assaulting a federal officer—he punched an FBI agent—and two convictions in 1981 of attempting to bribe a federal judge and of conspiracy to influence federal officials.[92]

The question of Carlos Marcello's position as a leading Mafia boss is clouded by the vast amount of sensationalism surrounding him and by the scarcity of the documentary evidence concerning his activities. On the one hand, Marcello's partnership with Costello and Lansky in the operation of the Jefferson Parish casinos, his attendance at a September 1966 meeting in New York with mobsters Joseph Columbo, Carlo Gambino, Anthony Carolla, and other leading members of the national "commission," and his acknowledged friendship with Florida Mafia boss Santos Trafficante, Jr., provide some support for the accusations about him.[93] The bulk of the evidence, however, does not lend support to the charges. Despite a massive investigation into Marcello's enterprises, the FBI never developed serious evidence of his involvement in organized criminal activities. In 1961, the Bureau reported that "continued investigation of Carlos Marcello since December 1957 has failed to develop vulnerable area wherein Marcello may be in violation of statutes within the FBI's jurisdiction."[94] In 1978, the senior FBI official in charge of the FBI's New Orleans office, which had Marcello under continual surveillance, testified that he did not believe that Marcello was a significant figure in organized crime.[95] The numerous allegations leveled by Aaron Kohn and the Metropolitan Crime Commission about Marcello's criminal empire have never been substantiated by concrete evidence.

For the historian researching a past event, the most obvious responsibility is to accuracy of information. With little difficulty, the historian can discover innumerable statements about Carlos Marcello as a mobster, a "godfather," etc. While it is not possible to disprove these claims, the absence of proof leaves the historian with no alternative than to question their reliability. For example, the Louisiana "Mafia family," of which Carlos Marcello is the "boss," appears to exist only in fantasy. The FBI managed to infiltrate and expose virtually all other organized criminal syndicates in the United States, but it failed to do so with the Marcello organization. In a 1961 report on Marcello, for example, the FBI admitted that it knew nothing whatsoever about the structure of the Marcello empire, nor did it possess any knowledge of the identity of the individual members of that empire.[96] None of the characteristics of the Mafia have ever been reliably attributed to Marcello, and the state of Louisiana has escaped the turmoil of the gangland-style executions associated with organized crime in such places as Chicago, Miami, and New York.

This brief summary of organized crime in Louisiana history clearly establishes the necessity for thorough and reliable scholarly research into the topic. Contrary to the repeated assertions of many writers, the existence of organized crime in nineteenth century Louisiana is not established by the available evidence. In the twentieth century, the slot machine empire of Frank Costello conducted widespread operations in South Louisiana. The rise of Carlos Marcello and the publicity about him does not corroborate the allegations of his Mafia connections, and the existence of his organized criminal empire remains the subject of speculation rather than fact.

Notes for "Organized Crime in Louisiana History: Myth and Reality"

**The author does not presume to judge the legal guilt or innocence of the persons mentioned in this article; that is a matter for courts of law to determine.

[1] *New Orleans True Delta,* June 18, 1861.

[2] David Chandler, *Brothers in Blood: The Rise of the Criminal Brotherhoods* (New York, 1975),

[3] *New Orleans True Delta,* January 4, 1855.

[4] Ibid., August 15, 1861.

[5] Thomas Monroe Pitkin and Francesco Cordasco, *The Black Hand: A Chapter in Ethnic Crime* (Totowa, N. J., 1977), 23.

[6] Chandler, *Brothers in Blood,* 77.

[7] Federal Bureau of Investigation, "Report on Organized Crime," October 24, 1972, FBI File # 92-6054-3 176.

[8] U.S. Congress, House, *Investigation of the Assassination of President John F. Kennedy: Appendix to Hearings Before the Select Committee on Assassinations of the U.S. House of Representatives* 95th Cong., 2nd Sess., 12 vols. (Washington, D.C., 1978-1979) 9:65; hereafter cited as Howe *Select Committee on Assassinations,* with volume and page numbers.

[9] Virtually every study of organized crime lacks documentation. For examples, see Chandier, *Brothers in Blood;* Ed Reid, *Mafia,* 2nd ed. (New York, 1964); Fred J. Cook, "Gambling, Inc.: Treasure Chest of the Underworld," *The Nation,* CIXC (1960), 291-97. Two documented studies include the Nelli book cited below and Annelise Graebner Anderson, *The Business of Organized Crime: A Cosa Nostra Family* (Stanford, Cal., 1979).

[10] John E. Coxe, "The New Orleans Mafia Incident," *Louisiana Historical Quarterly,* 20 (1937): 1067-1110; John S. Kendall, "Who Killa de Chief?," *Louisiana Historical Quarterly,* 22 (1939): 492-530; "Blood on the Banquette," *Louisiana Historical Quarterly,* 22 (1939): 819-56.

[11] Richard Gambino, *Vendetta: A True Story of the Worst Lynching in America, the Mass Murder of Italian-Americans in 1891, the Vicious Motivations Behind It, and Tragic Repercussions That Linger to This Day* (New York, 1977); 1; Humbert S. Nelli, *The Business of Crime: Italians and Syndicate Crime in the United States* (New York, 1976); see also Barbara Botein, "The Hennessy Case: An Episode in Anti-Italian Nativism," *Louisiana History,* 20 (1979): 261-79. The surname of the murdered New Orleans police chief is often given as "Hennessey." However, the two most authoritative sources on the caw, Nelli and Botein me "Hennessy," and that version will he used 154 article.

[12] See Figure 1.

[13] Nelli, *The Business of Crime,* 144-218.

[14] Many writers do not distinguish between Italian and Sicilian. This article will differentiate between the two.

[15] "Report of Ralph Salerno, Consultant to the Select Committee on Assassins," *House Select Committee on Assassinations,* 9:5, 27-31.

[16] Nelli, *The Business of Crime,* 7-20; Anton Blok, *The Mafia of a Sicilian Village, 1860-1960: A Study of Violent Peasant Entrepreneurs* (New York, 1974), 173.

[17] Robert C. Reinders, *End of an Era: New Orleans, 1850-1860* (Gretna, La., 1964), 19

[18] See Herbert Asbury, *The French Quarter; An Informal History of the New Orleans Underworld* (New York, 1936).

[19] Pitkin and Cordasco, *The Black Hand,* 17-18.

[20]Arthur Woods, "The Problem of the Black Land," *McClure's Magazine* (May, 1909), 40-41; Gaetano D'Amato, "The Black Hand Myth," *North America Review,* 187 (1908): 543-49; Luciano J. Iorizzo and Salvatore Mondello, *The Italian-Americans* (New York, 1971), 163.

[21]A. V. Margavio and Jerome J. Salomone, "The Passage, Settlement, and Occupational Characteristics of Louisiana's Italian Immigrants," *Sociological Spectrum,* 1 (1981): 345-59.

[22]Coxe, "The New Orleans Mafia Incident," 1105.

[23]Margavio and Salomone, "Louisiana's Italian Immigrants," 353.

[24]*New Orleans Daily Picayune,* March 13-15, 1891.

[25]Melinda Meek Hennessey, "Race and Violence in Reconstruction New Orleans: The 1868 Riot," *Louisiana History,* 20 (1979): 78-80; Joe Gray Taylor, *Louisiana Reconstructed, 1863-1877* (Baton Rouge, 1974), 163, 167, 169.

[26]Hennessey, "Race and Violence," 77-91.

[27]Ibid., 81-91.

[28]Ibid., 80.

[29]Ibid.; Robert F. Foerster, "Coming of the Italians," in Fransesco Cordasco and Eugene Bucchioni, eds., *The Italians: Social Background of an American Group* (Clifton, N. J., 1974), 48.

[30]*New Orleans Picayune,* March 14, 1891.

[31]Chandler, *Brothers in Blood,* 77-79.

[32]*New Orleans True Delta,* March 19, 1869.

[33]Denis Mack-Smith, *Italy: A Modern History* (Ann Arbor, 1959), 51; John V. Baiamonte, Jr., "New Immigrants in the South: A Study of the Italians of Tangipahoa Parish Louisiana" (M. A. Thesis, Southeastern Louisiana University, 1969), 8.

[34]*Daily Picayune,* March 13-14, 1891.

[35]Kendall, "Who Killa de Chief?" 507.

[36]Nelli, *The Business of Crime,* 28-29.

[37]Ibid., 29-31.

[38]Coxe, "The New Orleans Mafia Incident," 1083; Kendall, "Who Killa de Chief?" 519-28; Asbury, *The French Quarter,* 415-16. The titles of Coxe's and Kendall's articles clearly reveal their bias. It should be noted that although published in a scholarly journal, Kendall's article contains no documentation.

[39]The articles by Coxe, Kendall, and Botein, and the books by Nelli and Gambino, provide full coverage of the case. See also Joy J. Jackson, *New Orleans in the Gilded Age: Politics and Urban Progress, 1880-1896* (Baton Rouge, 1969), 244-53.

[40]*Daily Picayune,* October 19, 1890; *New Orleans Times-Democrat,* October 19, 1890.

[41]Nelli, *The Business of Crime,* 32.

[42]*New Orleans States,* October 16, 1890; *Daily Picayune,* October 17, 1890.

[43]Nelli, *The Business of Crime,* 32-36.

[44]See John C. Wickliffe, "The Mafia in New Orleans," *Truth,* 10 (March 26, 1891), 9; Robert H. Marr, "The New Orleans Mafia Case," *American Law Review,* 25 (1891): 414-31; Botein, "The Hennessy Case," 273-79.

[45] See *Daily Picayune, Times-Democrat,* and *New Orleans States,* October 16, 1890-April 1, 1891.

[46] *New Orleans Picayune,* March 17, 1891.

[47] Ibid., March 14, 1891; Nelli, *The Business of Crime,* 65.

[48] *Times-Democrat,* May 6, 1890.

[49] *Daily Picayune,* January 24, 1891.

[50] See Reid, *Mafia,* 110.

[51] Nelli, *The Business of Crime,* 37-46.

[52] *Daily Picayune,* January 19, 1889; *Times-Democrat,* July 20, 1890.

[53] *New Orleans Times-Democrat,* December 9, 1892.

[54] Botein, "The Hennessy Case," 273-79; J. Alexander Karlin, "New Orleans Lynching of 1891 and the American Press," *Louisiana Historical Quarterly,* 24 (1941): 187-204. In discussing the Hennessy case, the *New York Times* referred to "thieves and cutthroats." New York Times, March 25, 1891; for another example of anti-Italian sentiment of the era, see Appleton Morgan, "What Shall We Do With the Dago?" *Popular Science Monthly,* 38 (December 1890): 172-79.

[55] John V. Baiamonte, Jr., "Spirit of Vengance: The Case of *State of Louisiana vs. Rini* et al." (unpublished manuscript), chapters 1-3.

[56] Chandler, *Brothers in Blood,* 174-75.

[57] Ibid., 175.

[58] Ibid., 175-85.

[59] Ibid., 192-93.

[60] Ibid., 193-94.

[61] Nelli, *The Business of Crime,* 64.

[62] Ibid.

[63] Chandler, *Brothers in Blood,* 175.

[64] Ibid., 177.

[65] Baiamonte, "Spirit of Vengance," chapters 3-5.

[66] The New Orleans newspapers for 1929-1931 do not disclose any unusual increase in crimes of violence and certainly no Chicago-style gang wars. Joy J. Jackson, "Prohibition in New Orleans: The Unlikeliest Crusade," *Louisiana History,* 19 (1978): 281, records several instances of "shoots-outs" among rival bootleggers, but again, no large-scale underworld warfare.

[67] Baiamonte, "Spirit of Vengance," chapter 26.

[68] Edward F. Haas, "New Orleans on the Half Shell: The Maestri Era, 1936-1946," *Louisiana History,* 13 (1972): 197; Courtney Vaughn, "The Legacy of Huey Long," *Louisiana History,* 20 (1979): 95.

[69] T. Harry Williams, *Huey Long* (New York, 1969), 824-25.

[70] Ibid., 825.

[71] Ibid., 851-52.

[72] Author's interviews with Robert S. Maestri (1969) and Seymour Weiss (1968).

[73] Nelli, *The Business of Crime*, 188-89; August Bequi, *Organized Crime: The Fifth Estate* (Lexington, Mass., 1979), 41.

[74] Haas, "New Orleans on the Half Shell," 306.

[75] Ibid., 307.

[76] Jim Amoss and Dean Briquet, "Carlos Marcello," Part One, *Dixie* (February 14, 1982), 11.

[77] deLesseps S. Morrison, "National Crime Syndicates: Coordination of Local, State, and Federal Law Enforcement Imperative, *Vital Speeches of the Day,* 16 (1950): 380.

[78] Amoss and Baquet, "Carlos Marcello," 6.

[79] Nelli, *The Business of Crime,* 189.

[80] *New Orleans Item,* March 28, 1938.

[81] "Carlos Marcello," *House Select Committee on Assassinations,* 9:63.

[82] Amoss and Baquet, "Carlos Marcello," 16.

[83] Aaron M. Kohn, testimony before the U. S. Senate, Permanent investigations Subcommittee No. 5 of the U. S. House August 30, 1961. No page numbers in the subcommittee's unpublished report.

[84] U.S. Congress, Senate, *Report of the Select Committee to Investigate Organized Crime in Interstate Commerce,* 82nd Cong., 2nd Sess. (Washington, 1951), 90.

[85] Aaron M. Kohn, testimony before Subcommittee No. 5 of the U.S. House judiciary Committee, June 11, 1950. No page numbers cited in the subcommittee transcript.

[86] "Carlos Marcello," *House Select Committee on Assassinations,* 9:66.

[87] Bill Davidson, "New Orleans: Cosa Nostra's Wall Street," *The Saturday Evening Post* (February 19, 1964), 15-21.

[88] Sandy Smith, "The Crime Cartel," *Life* (September 1, 1967), 20-21; (September 8, 1961), 91, 94-97.

[89] "Carlos Marcello," testimony before the U.S. Senate Select Committee to Investigate Organized Crime in Interstate Commerce, January 25, 1961.

[90] "Carlos Marcello," *House Select Committee on Assassinations,* 9:65.

[91] U.S. Congress, House, *Report of the Select Committee on Assassinations* (Washington, 1979), 165.

[92] Jim Amoss and Dean Baquet, "Carlos Marcello," *Dixie* (Sunday supplement, *New Orleans Times-Picayune*), February 21, 1982, and February 28, 1982. Full coverage of the Marcello "Brilab" trial may he found in *New Orleans Times-Picayune/States-Item,* April 22, 1981-August 4, 1981. The account of Marcello's conviction on charges of attempted bribery may be found in *New Orleans Times-Picayune/States-Item,* December 12, 1981.

[93] "Carlos Marcello," *House Select Committee on Assassinations,* 9:66-67.

[94] FBI Report on Organized Crime, Carlos Marcello File, March 3, 1961.

[95] "Carlos Marcello," *House Select Committee on Assassinations,* 9:70.

[96] FBI Report on Organized Crime, Carlos Marcello File, March 3, 1972.

LYNCHING AND CRIMINAL JUSTICE IN SOUTH LOUISIANA, 1878-1930*

Michael J. Pfeifer

In June 1896, Walter T. Starks, an African American, allegedly robbed and attempted to murder the wife of a section boss on the Vacherie Plantation in St. Mary Parish. A recent emigrant from Atlanta, Starks died in a volley of bullets from the pistols, rifles, and shotguns of white lynchers as he hanged from an oak tree. Undoubtedly white St. Mary residents sought in this mob killing to amplify for black sugar workers the price to be paid for harming a white woman. African Americans in the locale of the Vacherie plantation came in large numbers to see Starks's displayed corpse. Starks's killing was an especially brutal manifestation of the system of racial hierarchy that underlay South Louisiana's sugar economy.[1] Yet, in broad context, lynching formed a relatively minor component in the series of practices that sustained racial control in the region. Instead, sugar and cotton planters in South Louisiana manipulated plantation arrangements and the criminal justice system to ensure the maintenance of white supremacy.

South Louisiana lynchings claimed well under half of the more than four hundred lives lost to Pelican State lynch mobs between 1878 and 1930.[2] Mob violence in the southern portion of the state was most prevalent in the late nineteenth century, and lynchings in southern parishes became quite rare after 1900.[3] In the northwestern and north-central cotton parishes, white planters supplanted the formal criminal justice system by assuming informal police powers and orchestrating mob executions, while working class whites used lynchings to perpetuate a racial hierarchy in the midst of change wrought by urbanization and industrialization in the early twentieth century.[4] By contrast, in the Sugar Bowl, an ethnically and racially diverse region of sugar plantations which formed the heart of South Louisiana, ruling elites most commonly enforced racial dominance over an African American labor force through frequent use of the gallows instead of extralegal violence. Moreover, the heavily Cajun southwestern parishes were marginal cotton areas, where poor white farmers sometimes targeted their African

---

*First published in *Louisiana History*, 40 (1999): 155-77. Reprinted with the kind permission of the author and the Louisiana Historical Association.

American competitors in the rural economy. In Acadiana, a highly informal style of criminal justice may have mitigated any impulses towards group murder.[5]

I.

Louisiana's Sugar Bowl comprised twelve parishes in the south-central portion of the state. In the late nineteenth century, a new sugar planter class composed of elite Creole, Anglo-American, and Northern elements sought to control a large African American labor force. A complementary mercantile class of white Creoles and Anglo-Americans greased the wheels of the sugar plantation economy. Cajuns occupied the lowest rung in the Sugar Bowl's native white social order. The racial and ethnic mix of the Sugar Bowl was further complicated by descendants of French-speaking *gens de couleur libre* (free persons of color), who maintained increasingly precarious autonomous communities of propertyholders. By the early twentieth century, Creoles of Color lost much of their former status as an intermediate, propertied caste and increasingly melded into a larger population of descendants of French-speaking slaves, black Creoles, who labored on sugar plantations with the descendants of English-speaking slaves. Further, by the 1880s, planters dissatisfied with their inability to control African American laborers and maintain a steady labor supply throughout the cultivation process encouraged Sicilians to immigrate to the sugar parishes. Perhaps 60,000 Sicilians worked in the sugar fields during an average season in the late 1880s and early 1890s, adding yet another strand to the region's intricate racial and ethnic fabric.[6]

Racial repression and intimidation underlay the sugar labor system, which differed substantially from that of the cotton regime prevalent in northern parishes. Many postbellum South Louisiana sugar plantations utilized gang labor on a wage basis. This system was far less prone to the disruptions caused by confrontations between white employers and African American tenants over individual compensation for labor that characterized sharecropping in northwestern Louisiana.[7] Gang labor, on the other hand, contributed to "labor riots," periodic large-scale work stoppages, and demonstrations for higher wages. Frightened sugar planters suppressed wage strikes in St. John, St. Charles, and neighboring parishes in the early 1880s with the assistance of militia dispatched by the governor.[8] By comparison, the decentralized nature of cotton plantations elsewhere in the state discouraged unified protests. Recent scholarship emphasizes the importance of labor control in a coercive cotton economy as the impetus for high rates of lynching.[9] Although lynching did not constitute a regular aspect of sugar planters' efforts to control their work force, they resorted to vigilantism in desperate circumstances. For example, in 1887, after the Knights of Labor achieved considerable success in organizing African American sugar workers, planters from St. Mary and neighboring parishes orchestrated the murder of at least thirty African Americans.[10]

The political dynamics of the Sugar Bowl parishes also varied significantly from those in north Louisiana, largely because of the sugar planters' support of the Republican party's pro-tariff policies necessary to keep foreign sugar out of the domestic market.[11]

As a result, white and black Republicans held local political positions into the late nineteenth century. In addition, Republican "fusion" tickets with independent Democratic and Populist candidates for statewide offices were sometimes quite competitive with the regular Democratic slate in the sugar parishes. The political process became enmeshed in pervasive violence from the Reconstruction period through the mid-1880s, as Democrats employed terrorist tactics in some parts of the Sugar Bowl to regain power through intimidation of African Americans.[12] Yet, Sugar Bowl Democrats failed to consolidate one-party dominance and white supremacy in electoral politics to the extent that they did by the end of Reconstruction in the rest of Louisiana. Until the late 1890s, African American males in the sugar parishes retained many of the perquisites of citizenship they had gained during Reconstruction, including largely unencumbered voting rights, officeholding, and jury duty.[13] By 1900, however, a new voter registration law and state constitution effectively disfranchised blacks statewide.[14]

Forty-six documented lynchings occurred in the Sugar Bowl between 1878 and 1946, far fewer than occurred in the state's northwestern cotton belt. Respective racial compositions explain little, for African Americans constituted between 50 and 80 percent of all residents of both the Sugar Bowl parishes and the northwestern cotton parishes in the postbellum era.[15] Exploitative sugar labor arrangements that inadvertently preserved a greater degree of black solidarity may account for some of the disparity in extralegal violence. A more flexible political system and the survival of African American participation in governmental institutions through the late nineteenth century also may have mitigated naked displays of white power. It is also most significant that Sugar Bowl residents generally held the formal legal system, which had become a well-honed instrument for racial control, in higher regard.[16]

The Sugar Bowl's complicated ethnic and cultural environment also mitigated against the violence that plagued North Louisiana. The Sugar Bowl's reconstituted postbellum planter class included Northerners and white Creoles who maintained less acrimonious race relations than their counterparts in the Anglo-Protestant northern portion of the state. Furthermore, because of the special intermediate social status formerly enjoyed by the *gens de couleur libre,* South Louisiana's antebellum racial caste system had a greater degree of elasticity than elsewhere in the Deep South.[17] It is also possible that the Catholicism of the Sugar Bowl, while certainly susceptible to white supremacist arguments and praxis, proved less amenable to intractable racism and blunt social control mechanisms than the evangelical Protestantism so well adapted to the harsher racial codes of the state's northern parishes.[18]

While lynching occurred relatively infrequently in the Sugar Bowl, its incidence nonetheless reflected the social, cultural, and legal realities of the sugar economy. Eighty percent of mob killings in the sugar parishes preceded 1900. The sugar region escaped the entrenched racial violence that accompanied urbanization and industrialization in North Louisiana after the turn of the twentieth century. Lynchings in South Louisiana were instead occasional, punctuating white sugar planters' and merchants' efforts to subdue the local black labor force and ensure white dominance in the two decades that followed Reconstruction.[19]

Sugar labor arrangements were apparently less prone than those in the cotton belt to erupt into violent disputes between white planters and black employees that eventually resulted in lynching. Despite this, nearly a fourth of mob killings in the sugar parishes can be traced to tensions between white sugar planters or overseers and the African American laborers they employed. For example, in April 1878, members of a lynch mob in rural South Louisiana murdered "a man . . . for attempting to set fire to a sugar house.[20]" In October 1892, a posse of "prominent" whites shot and killed Thomas Courtney, an African American who had allegedly shot and wounded one Moreau, an overseer on the Hundred Mile Plantation in Iberville Parish.[21] In lynchings such as these, Sugar Bowl whites responded to challenges to the sugar labor system and, beyond punishing individual African Americans who violated the plantation racial order, sought to cow the collective black labor force into compliance. This aim succeeded all too well in West Baton Rouge Parish in 1900, as black laborers "failed to return to work" on sugar plantations near where whites lynched Ned Cobb on June 12.[22] In addition, five Sugar Bowl killings by mob action resulted from allegations that African Americans had murdered white clerks while in the act of robbing general stores, possibly a product of the friction generated by low wages and exorbitant prices charged by the sugar plantation stores.[23]

Sugar parish lynch mobs responded far more frequently to charges of homicide than accusations of rape—48 percent to 22 percent. The alleged murder of a white man by a black man sometimes signaled for Sugar Bowl whites a temporary crisis in the maintenance of social boundaries. The murder of a sugar planter represented perhaps the most direct assault on the sugar labor system. The killing of James Norman, "a popular sugar planter" in West Baton Rouge Parish consequently motivated a small masked mob to hang Norm Cadore in December 1912, in view of the state capitol across the Mississippi River.[24]

Challenges to white authority could also take other forms. In the same parish in October 1900, a mob of about seventy-five persons hanged Melby Dotson near the railroad junction where he had supposedly shot and killed white train conductor Will Jordan.[25]

However, the massive reprisal of South Louisiana whites against an African American who flouted the prerogatives of white power can be seen most vividly in a posse's slaying of John Thomas in St. Charles Parish in January 1903. Thomas worked on sugar plantations and as a railroad laborer in the area surrounding Luling, a town populated by freedmen and a center for black economic and political autonomy from Reconstruction through the late nineteenth century. White officials targeted Thomas as a "bad negro" involved in gambling and thefts. After white parish officials seized guns from his home, Thomas swore out an affidavit at the parish courthouse charging them with robbery. When law officers subsequently tried to arrest him on an assault charge,

Thomas exchanged gunfire with and killed Sheriff Lewis Oury. After a prolonged chase and fight, members of a posse managed to shoot and instantly kill Thomas, who had taken refuge in a drainage ditch. The crowd then dragged Thomas's corpse back to his house and, after making a funeral pyre of his "household effects," burned his body. "Cooler heads" reportedly prevented some of the crowd, who "suggested teaching some of the other bad negroes a lesson they would remember," from driving out the "undesirable" black population at Luling by torching their homes.

A closer examination of the Thomas killing provides insight into the nature of the struggle for political and racial control in the sugar parishes after the Civil War. Lewis Oury had served as St. Charles Parish's public recorder during the twilight years of Reconstruction, and he became the first Democratic sheriff in a "Redeemed" St. Charles Parish in 1884. Thomas's refusal to submit to white officials, the officials' characterization of him as a "bad negro," and the burning of Thomas's body and possessions drew significance from the white establishment's long struggle with the autonomous black settlement of Luling.[26]

Racial and sexual phobias elicited responses from South Louisiana whites, but the fear of African American rapists generated few episodes of group violence, perhaps in part because of the region's intricate ethnic and racial mix. Of the ten Sugar Bowl mobs that lynched alleged rapists, several were small bands of vigilantes that failed to elicit the participation or the overt support of large numbers of local whites. For instance, in 1878 a small group of relatives and acquaintances of the St. Mary Parish sheriff hanged one Moustand, a black man, from a belfry and then threw his body into the Bayou Teche in Franklin. These vigilantes responded to an allegation that Moustand had made "indecent advances" to a female member of the sheriff's family. Although the Moustand lynching had failed to galvanize the local white community in post-Reconstruction St. Mary, the event prompted some Franklin whites to petition local authorities for formation of a volunteer police force "for the suppression of all [nocturnal] lawlessness."[27]

Other accusations of rape provoked a large-scale white backlash, resulting in the participation of significant numbers of whites in lynchings. In Ascension Parish in November 1888, for example, an African American man allegedly raped a white girl "in the [sugar] cane." Several hours after the alleged assailant had been placed in jail, a mob reportedly consisting of "[one] hundred or two hundred men" seized the alleged rapist and hanged him. The victim's corpse remained suspended outside the jail building until the next day.[28]

Sugar Bowl whites nevertheless generally failed to evince strong support for lynching. Small groups of vigilantes who were often disguised and whose acts of collective vengeance were carefully orchestrated were most frequently responsible for South Louisiana lynchings.[29]

Killings by such bands were sometimes condemned by other elements of white Sugar Bowl society. A group of "thirty-five masked men overpowered Constable Walter Marrionneaux," subsequently seizing and hanging William Carr, an African American accused of stealing a calf in Iberville Parish in March 1906. A newspaper reporter wrote that "great indignation is felt at this crime," and a district judge quickly convened a grand jury to investigate the murder. This public expression of disapproval may have reflected the conflicting interests of planter and mercantile class whites, who held parish and district offices, and lower class whites who competed with African Americans for their livelihood.[30]

Furthermore, some areas of South Louisiana were plagued by intense political factionalism that occasionally spilled into mob violence throughout the postbellum era. Rooted in unresolved questions of political and communal leadership from the Reconstruction era, these conflicts pitted conservative whites, who wished to impose a strict racial order, against moderate whites who were more flexible on issues of black rights. Moderate Sugar Bowl whites sometimes allied with Creoles of Color, who composed a black political and social elite in several locales. This problem was perhaps most acute in Iberia Parish. White Democrats reclaimed political power in the parish in 1884 by killing more than twenty African Americans and arresting prominent white Republicans.[31] Tensions remained high in the wake of this confrontation. In January 1889, a posse killed Samuel Wakefield, an African American accused of shooting his white supervisor at a "door and blinds factory" in New Iberia. Wakefield's relatives were black Republicans who had held political offices. Not content with the lynch mob's assertion of white dominance in the parish, "Regulators" attacked business establishments owned by Creoles of Color, hanged another African American accused of theft, and flogged several other blacks in the days that followed.[32]

Divisions within the white community regarding lynching in Iberia Parish and elsewhere in the Sugar Bowl region are indicative of the underlying reason why extralegal violence remained a minor component in the region's legal environment. South Louisiana whites of diverse ethnic, political, and economic orientations opposed mob violence as a means of enforcing white supremacy. Instead, Sugar Bowl whites entrusted the criminal justice system with that critical responsibility. Expressions of frustration with legal mechanisms were quite rare in Sugar Bowl lynchings.[33]

It is indeed noteworthy that criminal courts in South Louisiana apparently enjoyed greater jurisdiction over serious offenses against persons and property, prosecuted such cases more diligently, and received greater popular respect than their counterparts in North Louisiana. The criminal justice system's role in the social control of crime was much more comprehensive in the Sugar Bowl area than in the north-central and northwestern parishes, where informal white authority often coopted the formal justice system by severely punishing African Americans accused of the murder or rape of whites. In the late nineteenth century, criminal courts in sugar parishes frequently applied the death penalty against African Americans convicted of serious crimes; judges in the northern cotton parishes, on the other hand, ordered executions only rarely—with the notable exception of jurists in the parishes along the Mississippi River with large black majorities.[34]

Intrastate variations in the application of capital punishment in the late nineteenth century are quite revealing. Sugar Bowl parishes that experienced few lynchings legally executed large numbers of African Americans; cotton-belt parishes with pronounced proclivities for lynchings sent few blacks to the gallows. Between 1878 and 1910, West Baton Rouge Parish legally executed eight blacks, while two individuals were lynched; St. Mary Parish tallied eight executions of blacks, and four lynch victims; and Ascension Parish, which legally hanged ten blacks, had only one lynching victim. By comparison, in Louisiana's northwestern region, Bossier Parish had two legal executions of blacks, but twenty-seven African American lynching victims. Caddo Parish officials hanged seven blacks, but eleven African Americans were killed by lynching. In the northern bluff land region, Ouachita Parish officials performed one legal execution of an African American, and thirteen persons were lynched.[35]

The mixture of Creole, Northern, and Anglo-Americans in the Sugar Bowl's ruling class, and the influence of continental European legal traditions may have encouraged a greater emphasis on and respect for formal law in the Sugar Bowl.[36] In the sugar parishes, the criminal justice system became an extremely effective tool for the punishment of African American offenders. The overwhelming majority (88 percent) of persons legally hanged in the Sugar Bowl region were African American.[37]

Although criminal courts observed due process procedures, justice eluded African Americans prosecuted for serious crimes, especially those against white persons. The qualitative gap between procedural safeguards and a fair trial for a black defendant can be discerned in a case originating in St. Mary Parish. The state supreme court upheld African American Monroe Underwood's 1897 conviction for "burglary in the night with intent to rape" despite testimony that one juror had expressed support for lynching Underwood and that another advocated the defendant's castration.[38]

South Louisiana parish officials also executed a number of African Americans convicted of the murder or rape of blacks.[39] By contrast, an examination of criminal court proceedings in St. Mary and St. Landry parishes indicates that whites accused of murder and rape were either tried on lesser charges, given more lenient sentences, or simply not prosecuted. Whites also were acquitted more frequently than blacks.[40]

By dispensing harsh punishments to black criminals, the Sugar Bowl's legal system sought to perpetuate the subordinate position of African Americans in the region's intricate social order. Despite the ethnic and racial complexity of the sugar parishes, the color line represented the clearest demarcation of social status in the region, as black Creoles, Creoles of Color, and English-speaking blacks who met their end on the gallows could attest.[41] An analysis of the postbellum rite of execution in the Sugar Bowl indicates its significance as a means for parish officials to convey the consequences of black deviancy and the prerogatives of white power.

In the late nineteenth century, large crowds composed predominantly of African Americans typically gathered to view legal hangings in sugar parishes. Crowds reportedly including more than 2,000 persons assembled in Iberville Parish in 1879, West Baton

Rouge and St. James parishes in 1880, and Ascension Parish in 1882.[42] After a dramatic procession of the prisoner and officials to the gallows, the condemned often made a statement, either repenting for crimes and wayward lives or professing innocence. Following final prayers offered by a priest or minister, the hangman "adjusted the noose and cowl, tied the feet of the victim, and cut with one blow of his hatchet the rope supporting the trap."[43] It is difficult to interpret the meaning of the rite of execution for black witnesses. Drawn perhaps by curiosity, a sense of racial solidarity, or the compulsion exerted by whites, African Americans could not fail to miss the intent of white authorities to impress a message of racial control upon them. The presence of battalions of armed guards, sometimes numbering more than fifty, supposedly for preserving "order," suggested the fear of white officials that a restive black crowd might interrupt the proceedings. The participation of so many armed guards was a pointed reminder of the superior firepower advantage that whites enjoyed in parishes with large black majorities. Sugar Bowl executions remained highly public events even after the state legislature reformed the death penalty statute in 1884 by stipulating that executions must be performed in an enclosed area with only fifteen witnesses. In 1896, Iberia Parish officials defied the statute by hanging William Patterson, an African American convicted of murdering a black woman, "in full sight of some 2000 people, negro men and women from all parts of the parish thronging the courthouse yard.[44]"

II.

A very different set of socio-economic circumstances existed in the northern and western portions of the Louisiana Sugar Bowl. In postbellum St. Landry, Lafayette, and Avoyelles parishes,[45] the complicated ethnic, class, and race relations of a marginal cotton economy produced a unique but relatively minor pattern of racial violence. Following Reconstruction, the region's lower class French (Cajun) and black Creole populations lost their previous subsistence agricultural orientation and were drawn into the vortex of staple crop cotton production on inferior lands. Formerly autonomous Creole of Color propertyholders, who constituted a black leadership class during Reconstruction, slowly merged into the larger population of black Creoles and worked as the employees of white cotton planters. African Americans and Anglo-Americans also participated as laborers and landowners in the economy of what was a peripheral area of the cotton South.[46] Lacking the full coercive cotton regime of the northwest and northcentral cotton belts, the South Central Prairies failed to tally a single lynching deriving from the tensions of cotton labor relations.[47] To the west, rice cultivation, the raising of livestock, lumber camps, and trapping and fishing in extensive wetlands filled out the economy of predominantly white Calcasieu Parish, where five lynchings of African Americans occurred, four of them after the turn of the century.[48] Neither of the two lightly populated coastal parishes, Vermilion and Cameron, experienced a lynching in the late nineteenth or early twentieth centuries.[49]

Lynch mobs claimed twenty-five victims, twenty-two of them African American, in the South Central Prairies and Southwest parishes between 1878 and 1930.[50] Several characteristics distinguished mob killings in these regions. Mobs seldom cited the punishment of serious crime such as homicide or rape as their motivation, asserting instead that the individuals they killed had assaulted or shot at whites, or had committed some other miscellaneous "crime," such as making "threats to kill," using "incendiary language," or "aiding" or "defending" a murderer or rapist. At least fourteen lynching victims were black Creoles, and the circumstances of their deaths at the hands of mobs suggest that they had challenged attempts by lower-class whites to assert racial dominance in a region where racial, ethnic, and class identities were especially intricate and bitterly contested. Secretive, well organized, and carefully orchestrated terrorist mobs killed more than 60 percent of victims, a substantial deviation from the Sugar Bowl, where private mobs and mass mobs performed most lynchings.[51] Law officers arrested persons implicated in the mob killings in one-fourth of the cases, a strong indication that whites in Acadiana divided over the propriety of mob violence. Half of the lynchings in this marginal cotton area occurred after 1900, suggesting that the racial and class friction that underlay the collective violence persisted into the early twentieth century. Interestingly, though, Cajun whites did not lynch Cajun whites, contradicting what we might expect from a largely rural community with high rates of interpersonal violence. Indeed, extensive vigilante movements in Acadian parishes in the late antebellum years also might have predisposed postbellum Cajuns to lynch mobs. Yet there is little record of intragroup vigilantism among Cajuns after 1880.[52]

The postbellum socioeconomic order generated hostilities between lower class whites, especially Cajuns, and the black Creole population. Creoles of Color lost much of their former status in the late nineteenth century, but even as they melded into the larger population of black Creoles, they retained a distinct communal identity, a desire for freedom from white prerogatives, and a commitment to civil rights.[53] Meanwhile, blacks and lower-class whites in the south-central prairies, who had previously relied on diversified crops grown mostly for home consumption, became increasingly dependent on the cotton economy after 1880. Lower-class, French-speaking whites saw their social status plummet, as the cotton economy transformed the region's social order into a hierarchy consisting of a planter elite, a few struggling yeoman farmers and urban professionals, and a large mass of landless white and black sharecroppers. Anglo-Americans and assimilated upper-class white Creoles sought to eradicate the French language and culture and stigmatized lower-class Cajuns and black Creoles who retained traditional customs.[54]

At least one-third of the lynchings recorded in southwestern Louisiana were part of a sporadic, but systematic effort by lower-class whites—especially Cajuns—to intimidate the black Creoles with whom they competed in the local cotton economy. The resistance of black Creoles to the claims of white supremacy asserted by lower-class whites resulted in a whitecapping episode in Avoyelles Parish during the fall of 1892. According to a newspaper report, an African American teacher allegedly "made insulting remarks about some white ladies." When a white mob visited the teacher's home and attempted to flog him, the African American fired into the crowd and killed a man. After Ed Laurent, a black Creole politician, reportedly helped the teacher escape and then threatened to kill four whites, the mob hanged Laurent and filled "his body with bullets." Gabriel Magliore, a black Creole preacher, was also hanged by white vigilantes after he allegedly urged his flock at a church meeting to avenge the Laurent lynching.[55]

White residents of Avoyelles Parish were sharply divided over the regulators' actions. The sheriff arrested five whites involved in the lynchings, and these prisoners were taken to Natchitoches Parish for safekeeping. Night-riders nevertheless continued a campaign of intimidation against African Americans in the weeks that followed in an apparent attempt to drive blacks from the parish. Meanwhile, white planters fretted over the loss of their labor supply, prompting parish authorities to suppress the "white cap" organization by arresting forty-seven participants.[56] The press, sympathetic to the planters' position, derided the "Regulators." The parish newspaper, the *Bunkie Blade*, argued that "Every White Cap should have the noose adjusted and be strung up."[57] A Baton Rouge editor was equally scathing in his castigation of the Avoyelles whitecappers, whose avowed intention of social leveling among whites by expelling local blacks was purportedly evidence of incipient "Socialism" which "must be rooted out at any cost.[58]"

As with extralegal violence, southwestern Louisiana's criminal justice system reflected the complexity of the region's social and cultural milieux. When compared with other regions of the state, the south-central parish governments legally executed few persons. Calcasieu Parish, however, was a conspicuous exception to this rule, for its judicial system executed nineteen persons (fourteen of them black) between 1878 and 1930. This is put into perspective when one considers that parish officials throughout southwestern Louisiana executed thirty-nine persons, twenty-seven (69 percent) of whom were African Americans. Eighty percent of the persons executed had been convicted of homicide or "robbery and murder" charges.[59]

Criminal justice in St. Landry Parish also displayed distinctive local characteristics, which were heavily influenced by lower-class French values. The local judicial system consequently afforded leniency for white offenders, but harsh punishments for blacks.[60] The informality of local legal institutions may also have dampened any impulse for vigilante activities. Although the case of Helaire Carriere, executed in 1917 for murdering St. Landry Parish sheriff Marion Swords, is hardly typical, it suggests some interesting things about courtroom procedure and the way in which legal safeguards could be subordinated to public opinion. Carriere, a Cajun, escaped from the jail at Jennings where he was imprisoned for killing an African American. In statements providing insight into Cajun racial ideology, Carriere argued that he shot the sheriff because his posse included "negroes." During the oral examination of potential jurors for the Carriere case, the judge consistently overruled defense objections that local men could not serve impartially because they had already formed strong opinions concerning the defendant's guilt. The judge argued in at least three instances that he knew that men of Cajun descent would make "impartial jurors" because he had known them personally for twenty years.

The judge rejected a motion for a change of venue, heard in the presence of the impanelled jury, despite the murdered sheriff's prominence and the threats made to lynch Carriere after commission of the crime. A close reading of the trial transcript reveals the ascendancy of form over substance in the local justice system. This is seen most clearly in the significance of personal relationships in the Cajun community in the administration of the courtroom, and the direct linkage between community opinion and a trial's result. While none of these characteristics were unique to St. Landry, the peculiar ethnic relations there appear to have accentuated them.[61]

A comparison of the records of criminal district courts in South Louisiana parishes with those in the northern part of the state also reveals tremendous differences in the way legal authorities prosecuted particular kinds of crimes.

An examination of Ouachita Parish's district court minute book is especially striking. Through the minute book, one can follow all local prosecutions from indictment or bill of information through the final disposition of a case. It is remarkable that Ouachita Parish authorities failed to charge a single person with rape or sexual assault between 1890 and 1900. Yet mobs cited rape as justification for lynchings of blacks in Ouachita in 1889, 1896, and 1897.[62] By contrast, St. Landry Parish authorities charged three persons with rape in 1890-91, but none of the charges resulted in a conviction.[63] In St. Mary Parish, the criminal court prosecuted a number of rape cases in the late 1890s. Sam Watson, who was convicted and executed in 1896, was among those charged with rape.[64] On the basis of the evidence from southern Louisiana parishes, it appears that the absence of rape prosecutions in Ouachita surely does not reflect an absence of rapes in that parish. Rather, legal authorities may have failed to prosecute sexual assault because they expected an extralegal response when whites accused African Americans of that crime. The diverse white groups in the Sugar Bowl region opted for legal responses to allegations of serious crimes like rape and murder more frequently than did whites in northern parishes, where informal and extralegal social control measures prevailed against African Americans.[65]

In conclusion, lynching and the criminal justice system upheld racial prerogatives in southern Louisiana, but white elites in southern parishes seemed less overtly concerned with using extralegal means to regiment black labor forces than their North Louisiana counterparts. Differences in the frequency and nature of mob violence, in the rates of legal execution, and possibly in the style of criminal court proceedings illustrate the contrasts in regional systems of authority.

Notes for "Lynching and Criminal Justice in South Louisiana, 1878-1930"

[1] *New Orleans Daily Picayune* (hereafter referred to as NOP), June 10, 1896.

[2] There were 157 lynching victims out of a total of approximately 409 deaths (38.4 percent) by lynching in Louisiana. An examination of newspapers, court records, and personal correspondence reveals that lynchers in South Louisiana killed 157 persons between 1878 and 1930, 129 of them African Americans, nineteen of them whites; race could not be determined for nine victims. This is probably a slight undercount, as it includes only cases that could be documented. I thank Professor E. M. Beck for sharing the Georgia Lynching Project's data with me. The Georgia Lynching Project's lists of mob victims and citations for Louisiana proved invaluable for the compilation of my database. Lynching lists, Georgia Lynching Project, Department of Sociology, University of Georgia.

[3] 114 of 157 lynchings in South Louisiana occurred before 1900 (72 percent).

[4] Michael J. Pfeifer, "Lynching and Criminal Justice in Regional Context: Iowa, Wyoming, and Louisiana, 1878-1946" (Ph. D. dissertation, University of Iowa, 1998), Chapter 5.

[5] My conceptualization of the regions of southern Louisiana is informed by Gilles Vandal, "Black Violence in Post-Civil War Louisiana," *Journal of Interdisciplinary History,* 25 (1994): 45-64. Two areas in the southern half of the state saw anomalous patterns of racial violence. The eastern Florida Parishes, a piney woods subregion north of New Orleans that experienced rapid industrialization and in-migration after Reconstruction, witnessed elevated rates of lynching comparable to those in northern Louisiana. In the eastern Florida Parishes, a period of drastic socieoconomic transformation catalyzed political factionalism that fractured legal authority, permitting plainfolk whites unfamiliar with cotton belt and sugar belt systems of racial control to exercise their wrath on African Americans. Jefferson Parish, immediately south and west of the Crescent City, also acquired a virulently racist white subculture that endorsed the profligate mob murder of African Americans in the 1890s. Pfeifer, "Lynching and Criminal Justice in Regional Context," Chapter 4; and Samuel C. Hyde, Jr., *Pistols and Politics: The Dilemma of Democracy in Louisiana's Florida Parishes, 1810-1899* (Baton Rouge, 1996).

[6] For the reconstitution of the social arrangements in the Sugar Bowl in the postbellum era, see William Ivy Hair, *Bourbonism and Agrarian Protest, Louisiana Politics, 1877-1900* (Baton Rouge, 1969), 37-39. For Creoles of Color and Black Creoles, consult Carl A. Brasseaux, Keith P. Fontenot, and Claude F. Oubre, *Creoles of Color in the Bayou Country* (Jackson, Miss., 1994). Carl A. Brasseaux, *Acadian to Cajun: Transformation of a People, 1803-1877* (Jackson, Miss., 1992) examines the creation of Cajun social and cultural identity from lower class white Creole and Acadian sources in the late nineteenth century. Scarpaci, "Italian Immigrants In Louisiana's Sugar Parishes" (Ph. D. Dissertation, Rutgers University, 1972), discusses Sicilian immigration to the Sugar Bowl. Lynchers killed three Italians in St. Charles Parish in 1896. This incident involved a dispute stemming from economic competition between Italian plantation laborers and merchants, and white Creole and Anglo-American laborers and merchants. Ethnic prejudice also played an important role in the mob killing. The lynchers in St. Charles Parish reportedly cited the popular association of Sicilians with criminal organizations and sought to teach "lawless Italians a salutary lesson." Scarpaci, 248-50; NOP, August 9, 1896. I use the confusing but essential term 'Creole' to refer to the amalgam of French-speaking peoples in southern Louisiana.

[7] Terrence Finnegan highlights the tension between white landlords and African American tenants, and lynching as retaliation after violent disputes in Mississippi and South Carolina, in "'At the Hands of Parties Unknown': Lynching in Mississippi and South Carolina, 1881-1940" (Ph. D. dissertation, University of Illinois, 1993), 189-90, 199-202. Experienced sugar laborers also possessed the lucrative skill that enabled them to properly harvest the sucrose-rich bottom inch of cane, and were thus comparatively more difficult to replace than cotton workers.

[8] NOP, March 20, 29, April 1, 2, 1880; Hair, *Bourbonism and Agrarian Protest,* 171-75.

[9] For lynching as labor control in the Cotton Belt, see W. Fitzhugh Brundage, *Lynching in the New South: Georgia and Virginia, 1880-1930* (Urbana, Ill., 1993), especially 108-11. Stewart E. Tolnay and E. M. Beck also argue for a strong association between the social relations of cotton culture and lynching, in *Festival of Violence: An Analysis of Southern Lynchings, 1882-1930* (Urbana, Ill., 1995), 119-60.

[10] For a concise account of the 1887 Sugar Laborer's Strike, see Hair, *Bourbonism and Agrarian Protest,* 176-85.

[11] Ibid., 88.

[12] For the complex postbellum political experience in the sugar parish of Iberia, and Democrats' successful use of violence to thwart white Republican leaders and to keep African Americans from voting Republican in

1884, see Gilles Vandal, "Politics and Violence in Bourbon Louisiana: The Loreauville Riot of 1884 as a Case Study," *Louisiana History*, 30 (1989): 23-42.

[13] See, for example, references to a black constable in St. James Parish in 1896 in NOP, March 1, 1896, and a racially balanced jury of blacks and whites in the trial of a black man charged with murdering an African American boy in St. Mary Parish in 1882 in NOP, June 23, 1882.

[14] Hair, *Bourbonism and Agrarian Protest*, 268-79. The disfranchisement measures were at least partially in response to the near victory of a Republican-Populist fusion gubernatorial Candidate, John N. Pharr, a sugar planter from St. Mary Parish, in 1896. Pharr carried four black majority parishes in South Louisiana and twenty-five of thirty-two parishes throughout the state that had majorities of white voters. Massive fraud by white Democrats in black-majority parishes, especially those along the Mississippi River, deprived Pharr of victory. In addition to white sugar planters, Pharr's strength lay with African American voters and upcountry white farmers, suggesting the potential for a biracial working class alliance contesting power with the cotton planters and New Orleans business interests that controlled the Democratic Party.

[15] See maps in Hair, *Bourbonism and Agrarian Protest*.

[16] Attempting to explain southwide lynching trends, Edward L. Ayers argues in *The Promise of the New South: Life After Reconstruction* (New York, 1992), 156: "The only state whose Gulf Plain area had a relatively low lynching rate, close to that of the region as a whole, was Louisiana's, which did not see great black population change." While I do not dismiss the importance of demographic shifts, my analysis emphasizes the interaction of labor, ethnic, legal, and political cultures in understanding the relatively low incidence of lynching in the Sugar Bowl.

[17] Joseph Logsdon and Caryn Cossé Bell, "The Americanization of Black New Orleans, 1850-1900," in Arnold R. Hirsch and Joseph Logsdon, eds., *Creole New Orleans: Race and Americanization* (Baton Rouge, 1992), 201-9.

[18] Ibid., 233-34. The historical relationship between race and the Catholic church in South Louisiana is a complex one. Even in the antebellum period, the church segregated its educational institutions, refused to ordain black priests, and prohibited racial intermarriage. Yet the church also refused to fully segregate its congregations until the early twentieth century. Additionally, Jim Crow crumbled much more quickly (in the early 1950s) in predominantly Catholic areas of South Louisiana than it did in Protestant North Louisiana (the 1960s). In his study of the civil rights movement in Lousiana, Adam Fairclough found an impressive correlation "between high black [voter] registration and south Louisana Catholicism" in the 1950s. Adam Fairclough, *Race and Democracy: The Civil Rights Struggle In Louisiana* (Athens, Ga., 1995), 132. Similarly, political historian Perry H. Howard discovered a tendency in the 1960s and 1970s towards racial and political moderation among South Louisiana Catholics that contrasted with the pronounced conservatism of Protestant North Louisiana. Howard asserted that "in South Louisiana Catholic faith and practice provide a more congenial setting for the exercise of citizenship by blacks." Perry H. Howard, "The Politics of the Acadian Parishes," in Glenn R. Conrad, ed., *The Cajuns: Essays on Their History and Culture* (Lafayette, La., 1978), 237.

[19] For a lynching in Ascension Parish, see NOP, November 15, 1888. For Assumption Parish, see NOP, May 15, 1890. For mob killings in Iberia Parish, see NOP, October 8, 20, 1881; *New Iberia Enterprise* (hereafter referred to as NIE), March 25, 1885; NOP, January 26, 27, 1889; NOP, January 31, 1889; NOP, April 18, 1889; *Weekly Iberian*, July 28, August 4, 1894, NOP, July 24, 1894; NOP, May 10, 1902. For Iberville Parish, see NOP, October 23, 1892; NOP, January 18, 1897; NOP, December 14, 1897; NOP, March 19, 1906. For St. Charles Parish, see NOP, September 27, 1878; NOP, December 30, 1892; NOP, August 9, 1896; NOP, July 16, 1899; NOP, October 12, 1899; NOP, January 27, 1903. For St. James Parish, see NOP, January 22, 1893; NOP, March 1, 1896; NOP, May 9, 1914. For St. John Parish, see NOP, November 7, 1898; *New Orleans Times-Democrat* (hereafter cited as NOTD), June 15, 1899; NOP, February 18, 1901. For St. Martin Parish, see NOP, May 14, 23, June 16, 1882, NOTD, May 17, 1882; *Opelousas Courier* (hereafter cited as OC), September 17, 22, 1888. For St. Mary Parish, see NOP, December 4, 12, 1878; NOP, August 12, 1887; NOP, June 10, 1896; NOP, July 22, 1897. For West Baton Rouge Parish, see NOP, June 13, 1900; NOP, October 20, 1900; NOP, December 24, 1912.

[20] NOP, April 28, 1878.

[21] NOP, October 23, 1892.

[22] NOP, June 13, 1900.

[23] NOP, December 30, 1892; January 22, 1893. Some wage-earning sugar workers bristled at wages that were payable only in script at the plantation store. See Hair, *Bourbonism and Agrarian Protest*, 87-88.

[24] NOP, December 24, 1912.

[25] NOP, October 20, 1900.

[26] NOP, January 27, 1903.

[27] NOP, December 4, 1878.

[28] NOP, November 15, 1888.

[29] This analysis uses W. Fitzhugh Brundage's four categories of lynch mobs, which he describes in *Lynching in the New South*, 17-48. In the Sugar Bowl, private mobs killed 37.5 percent of total victims; mass mobs 25 percent; posses 17.5 percent; terrorist mobs 3 percent. The orientation of 19 percent of the mobs could not be determined.

[30] OP, March 19, 1906.

[31] Vandal, "Politics and Violence in Bourbon Louisiana," 23-42.

[32] NOP, January 26, 27, 31, 1889.

[33] I have identified only three mob killings that involved explicit responses to the criminal justice system, in St. James Parish in February 1896, in Iberville Parish in December 1897, and in West Baton Rouge Parish in December 1912.

[34] M. Watt Espy and John Ortiz Smykla, *Executions in The United States, 1608-1991: The Espy File*, bcomputerfilec, 3rd ICPSR ed. (Ann Arbor, Mich., 1994); State of Louisiana, Executive Department, Death Warrants, 1892-1930, Louisiana State Archives, Baton Rouge. The Espy File may understate the number of legal executions in late nineteenth and early twentieth century Louisiana. My analysis of state death warrants and newspapers indicates that at least a few more legal executions occurred than enumerated by M. Watt Espy, but these additional numbers of legal hangings do not seem to affect the pattern of instrastate variation in the frequency of state-sponsored executions and lynchings.

[35] Espy and Smykla, *Executions in The United States, 1608-1991: The Espy File*; State of Louisiana, Executive Department, Death Warrants, 1892-1930, Louisiana State Archives, Baton Rouge.

[36] Gallic legal traditions, especially the Napoleonic Code, profoundly influenced civil law in Louisiana. However, English common law and American criminal procedure were the primary influences on Lousiana's criminal law, which the state legislature codified in the late antebellum period. Warren M. Billings, "Origins of Criminal Law in Louisiana," *Louisiana History*, 32 (1991): 63-76.

[37] 45 of the 51 persons reported legally executed in the 12 sugar parishes between 1878 and 1910 were African American (88 percent); four were white (8 percent); race could not determined for two of those hanged. 46 of those executed (90 percent) had been convicted on a murder charge (half of these exclusively on a homicide charge; the rest on combined charges of robbery/murder, rape/murder, or kidnap/murder). Six of those legally hanged (12 percent) had been convicted on a rape charge (rape, rape/murder, or attempted rape); all of these were African American. Espy and Smykla, *Executions in The United States, 1608-1991: The Espy File*.

[38] Criminal Suit, *State of Louisiana v. J. Monroe Underwood*, Clerk of Court's Office, St. Mary Parish, Franklin.

[39] It is difficult to devise a precise breakdown of the race of the alleged victims of those receiving death sentences and executed in Louisiana. However, on the execution of blacks accused of murdering blacks in South Louisiana, see NOP, April 13, 1878, March 26, 1880, December 9, 1882, for reports of legal hangings in St. Mary, St. Landry, and Ascension Parishes. For the commutation of the death sentence of a black man convicted of murdering an African American in Lafayette Parish, see NOP, May 23, 1882. The district judge and parish district attorney petitioned Governor McEnery for clemency, arguing that Joseph Padillo's murder of his wife was not premeditated, that Padillo was ignorant and in a "lowly condition," and that matters should be left to the "Chief Magistrate" [God]. Similarly, the judge and district attorney petitioned and received a commutation to a life sentence for James Andrew, an African American convicted of murdering a black man in Tensas Parish, a black majority parish along the Mississippi River. NOP, January 18, 1882. The clemency bestowed upon blacks convicted of capital crimes against blacks may have been a product of white Louisianans' opinion that the lives of African Americans meant less than the lives of whites, or the result of pressure from blacks in areas where African Americans constituted a majority of the population.

[40] Criminal Suits and District Court Minute Book, Clerk of Court's Office, St. Mary Parish, Franklin; District Court Minute Book, Clerk of Court's Office, St. Landry Parish, Opelousas. For references to the disposition of homicide cases in St. Mary Parish, see NOP, January 15, November 23, 1880; July 29, November 15, 20, 28, 1881; January 1, 17, 20, June 23, 24, 1882; January 21, 27, 1883. An account of sentencing proceedings in

the postbellum Sugar Bowl suggests the authoritative role of the criminal court in exercising social control over African American offenders. On January 26, 1883, near the conclusion of a St. Mary Parish Criminal District Court session, Judge Goode sentenced two African Americans to death and a white man convicted of manslaughter to a five-year prison term. A correspondent reported: "The court-house was crowded, and the Judge delivered a very solemn and impressive address to the criminals and the audience, dwelling forcibly upon the causes to which so frequent crime is attributable, especially among the colored population." The judge linked pervasive crime to whiskey consumption, reprimanding "the proprietors of plantation stores in selling whiskey to the laborers. . . ." NOP, January 27, 1883.

[41] Six out of 45 African Americans executed in the Sugar Bowl had identifiably Creole names; a number of others had names that could not easily be distinguished as either Anglo or Creole. Espy and Smykla, *Executions in The United States, 1608-1991: The Espy File.*

[42] NOP, May 17, 1879, April 3, 1880, September 4, 1880, December 9, 1882.

[43] NOP, December 9, 1882.

[44] NOP, January 11, 1896.

[45] In 1888, Acadia Parish was carved out of the southwestern portion of St. Landry Parish. In the early twentieth century, lawmakers created Evangeline Parish from what was formerly the northwestern portion of St. Landry.

[46] See Hair, *Bourbonism and Agrarian Protest*, 40, 43-44, and Carl A. Brasseaux, *Acadian to Cajun*, 150-51. For Creoles of Color in the South Central Prairies, see Brasseaux, Fontenot, and Oubre, *Creoles of Color in the Bayou Country*. De-emphasizing race, Hair attributes the volatile political situation in late nineteenth century St. Landry Parish to its diverse "topography and soil" and the combustible mixture of "hill and bottomland whites," 42-43. St. Landry Parish was the scene of one of the worst incidents of Reconstruction political violence in Louisiana. In September 1868, members of the Seymour Knights, a paramilitary club of conservative whites, attacked a white Republican school teacher in Opelousas. African Americans in the parish, a number of them armed, responded by flooding into the town. The Knights of the White Camelia, another paramilitary organization of conservative whites that was extremely strong in the region, interpreted this as a "Negro Revolt," took command of Opelousas, and ordered the blacks to surrender their weapons. A massacre ensued, eventually extending into the countryside. Whites murdered at least 150 black Republicans. For succinct accounts of these events, see Ted Tunnell, *Crucible of Reconstruction: War, Radicalism, and Race in Louisiana 1862-1877* (Baton Rouge, 1984), 153, 156, and Brasseaux, Fontenot, and Oubre, *Creoles of Color in the Bayou Country*, 99-103.

[47] Not surprisingly, violence and coercion did accompany the cotton labor arrangement in the South Central Prairies, even if it did not provoke lynching. For an example of a fatal dispute between a white farmer and an African American employee in which a jury acquitted the white farmer on murder charges, see Coroner's Inquest, July 10, 1890, and District Court Minute Book, Clerk of Court's Office, St. Landry Parish, Opelousas. OC, October 6, 1906, details another instance where a white planter killed a black laborer in a scrape over work authority. Furthermore, in the summer of 1901, an African American shot an overseer in Acadia Parish and "a lynching nearly resulted then." NOP, July 20, 1901.

[48] Lawmakers created Jefferson Davis, Allen, and Beauregard Parishes from the northern and eastern parts of Calcasieu Parish in the early twentieth century. Significant numbers of Cajuns and black Creoles lived in portions of postbellum Calcasieu Parish.

[49] Hair, *Bourbonism and Agrarian Protest*, 42. Blacks represented about half of the population in St. Landry and Avoyelles Parishes in the postbellum era, with the proportion of whites in Avoyelles increasing to about 60 percent in 1900. Whites made up 58 percent of Lafayette Parish residents in 1880 and 1900. White majorities exceeded 75 percent in Calcasieu, Cameron, and Vermilion Parishes throughout the period. *Twelfth Census of the United States* (Washington, 1902).

[50] For a lynching in Acadia Parish, see NOP, July 20, 1901. For a mob murder in Evangeline Parish, see NOP, January 23, 1911. For mob killings in Avoyelles Parish, see NOP, September 9, 1892; *Alexandria Town-Talk*, August 3, 1896; NOP, April 17, 1907; NOP, July 16, 1915. For Lafayette Parish, see NOP, July 12, 1889; NOTD, July 21, 1895; NOTD, March 25, 1896; NOP, November 26, 1906. For St. Landry Parish, see NIE, March 7, 1885; NOP, September 18, 1888, OC, September 15, October 6, 13, 20, December 22, 1888, Coroner's Inquest, September 18, 1888, Clerk of Court's Office, St. Landry Parish, Opelousas; OC, August 14, 1909, Coroner's Inquest, July 30, 1909, Clerk of Court's Office, St. Landry Parish, Opelousas; NOP, November 16, 1916. For a lynching in Jefferson Davis Parish, see NOP, August 28, October 22, 1913. For mob killings in Calcasieu Parish, see NOTD, October 13, 1883; NOP, February 22, 1901; NOP, December 9, 1901; NOP, October 14, 1902.

[51] In the south-central prairies and Southwest Louisiana, mobs fell into the following categories as percentages of total victims: Private 32 percent (8 victims), Terrorist 28 percent (7 victims), Posse 8 percent (2 victims), Mass 4 percent (1 victim), Unknown 28 percent (7 victims).

[52] A typical incident of interpersonal violence among Cajuns, involving insults, a fight, and a fatal stabbing at a whiskey-sodden "ball," is detailed in Coroner's Inquest, July 21, 1890, Clerk of Court's Office, St. Landry Parish, Opelousas. In an exception to the later pattern, Cajun whites lynched Cajun whites in St. Martin Parish during Reconstruction. The South Central Prairies had a history of extralegal violence, but the postbellum lynchings marked a shift in direction. An extensive vigilante movement in 1859 led by Acadian landholders targeted lower-class white deviants and sparked "antivigilante campaigns" by landless and yeomen whites and an ensuing bloodbath in 1859-60. Eventually local vigilantes also directed their efforts against free persons of color, leading historian Carl Brasseaux to write: "the vigilante-antivigilante struggle had evolved from a crusade for law and order into a class struggle with strong racial overtones (*Acadian to Cajun*, 131)." During the Civil War, the region saw prolonged guerilla violence between 'Jayhawkers', who supported the Union and allied with Creoles of Color and ex-slaves, and Confederate supporters. Brasseaux, Fontenot, and Oubre, *Creoles of Color in the Bayou Country*, 85. During the war and after, vigilante bands also turned their attention to freed people, seeking to reassert the racial control altered by emancipation.

[53] Brasseaux, Fontenot, and Oubre, *Creoles of Color in the Bayou Country*.

[54] Brasseaux, *Acadian to Cajun*, 12-15, 112-36, 150-53.

[55] NOP, September 6, 1892, November 2, 1892, BRWA, December 17, 1892. Cajun 'regulators' lynched two black Creoles, may have killed another black man, and effectively terrified the black Creole community in St. Landry Parish in the fall of 1888. Coroner's Inquest, September 16, 1888, Clerk of Court's Office, St. Landry Parish, Opelousas; NOP, September 18, 1888; OC, September 22, 29, October 6, 13, 20, 27, November 17, December 1, December 22, 1888.

[56] NOP, September 6, 1892, November 2, 1892, BRWA, December 17, 1892.

[57] Quoted in NOP, November 2, 1892.

[58] BRWA, December 17, 1892. An additional incident where lower class white 'Regulators' lynched a black Creole who challenged their attempt to intimidate the black Creole population by "holding up negroes who visited town at night" occurred in Lafayette Parish in November 1906. NOP, November 26, 1906. For whitecapping in Georgia, see Brundage, *Lynching in the New South*, 24-25.

[59] Espy and Smykla, *Executions in The United States, 1608-1991: The Espy File*.

[60] District Court Minute Book, Clerk of Court's Office, St. Landry Parish, Opelousas. A lawyer in St. Landry admitted in a 1905 letter to a friend that Cajun whites had railroaded a black defendant accused of shooting into a white man's house. The lawyer believed the charge was manufactured to consolidate political alliances. Letters from Edward P. Veazie of July 16, 22, 1905, in Ozeme Fontenot Papers, Special Collections, Hill Memorial Library, Louisiana State University, Baton Rouge.

[61] NOP, October 20, 1917; Criminal Suit, *State of Louisiana* v. *Eli Carrier*, Clerk of Court's Office, St. Landry Parish, Opelousas. Carl Brasseaux notes that mid-nineteenth century Acadians went to court more often than Anglo American southerners, displaying a preference for litigious solutions of disputes. Brasseaux, *Acadian to Cajun*, 113.

[62] District Court Minute Book, Clerk of Court's Office, Ouachita Parish, Monroe; lynching lists, Georgia Lynching Project.

[63] District Court Minute Book, Clerk of Court's Office, St. Landry Parish, Opelousas.

[64] Criminal Suits, Clerk of Court's Office, St. Mary Parish, Franklin.

[65] Michael Hindus similarly argues that nineteenth-century South Carolinians were ambivalent towards formal authority and that extralegal manifestations of coercive power offset limited legal institutions in preserving order and social cohesion, in *Prison and Plantation: Crime, Justice, and Authority in Massachusetts and South Carolina, 1767-1868* (Chapel Hill, N.C., 1980).

Index

Abbot, Grace, 737
Abell, Edmund, 68, 69
Abrahams, Roger D., 660
Acadians, 380; bougeoisie, development of, 33; cattle production by, 38, 39-40; classes emerge among, 28-44; day laborers among, 36; interpretations of life style of the, 373-74; planters among, emulate Creole and Anglo-Saxon planters, 32; prairie, 39; rice and sugarcane production by, 37-38; slaves acquired by, 29-30; sugarcane growers among, 30-32; westward migration, causes for, 38-39; yeomen farmers among, 35
Ace Club, 444
Adelle v. Bullard, 237
Aero Club of Louisiana, 581, 588
African Americans, as agricultural workers, discussed, 72; black policemen in New Orleans during Reconstruction, 697-713; black workers in the New Orleans building trades, 91; European immigrant workers and 91-92; government jobs, 104-5; racial passing in segregated New Orleans, 125; racial repression of, in New Iberia, 142-58; streetcar employees, 103-4; workers in New Orleans, 1880-1890, 90-124
African Methodist Episcopal Church, 20-21
Agricultural Adjustment Act, 565, 597
Agricultural Adjustment Administration, 599
Agricultural Extension Service, 571
Alabama Dry Dock Co., 145-46
Alethian Club (Lafayette, La.), 286
All Silver and No Brass, 660
Allain, Mathé, 1, 4, 189
Allegre, Charles, 699
Allen, A. Leonard, 573
Allen, Matt, 757
Allen, Oscar K., 569, 760
Almonaster, Andre de, 48
Altobello, Joseph, 649
Aluminum Company of America, 571
Alzar, Fernando, 530
Amelung, A., 541
Amelung, H., 541
American Airlines, 584
American Cirrus Engines, Inc., 584
American Farm Bureau Federation, 566, 570
American Railway Union, 102
American Red Cross, 303
American Sugar Cane League, 597
American Theater, 53, 58
Amite River Baptist Association, 514-15
Amory, Callendar & Co., 533, 534, 535, 540
Ampère, J. J., 54
Ancelet, Barry J., 385 n33, 661
Anders, Quintilla Morgan, 288

Andersen, Hans Christian, 267
Anderson, Tom, 280, 283
Andrew Higgins Co., 571
Anthony, Arthé A., 3, 125
Anti-Lottery League, 756
Anti-Tuberculosis League, 304
Antoine, C. C., 705
Arceneaux, Pamela D., 5, 279
Arlington, Josie, 280
Armstrong, Louis, 633
Armstrong Park, previous names for, 633
Arnaudville, La., flood water in, 464
artisans, in early New Orleans, 349-51
Asbury, Herbert, 756
Association of Southern Women Against Lynching, 155
Atchafalaya Railroad & Bank, 252, 257
Atkinson, Harold B., 472
Attakapas District of Louisiana, actions taken against free people of color, 22; foodstuffs available in early nineteenth-century, 378-79; home furnishings in the, 376-77; house construction in, 375-76; kitchens, pantries, dining areas of home in the, 377-78; material culture of Louisiana's, 373-86; textiles, wearing apparel, and footware in early nineteenth-century, 380-83
Atter, Daniel, 214
Aubry, Azelie, 555
Aubry, Charles Philippe, 337
Aubry, Pierre, 699
Audubon, John James, 529
Audubon Experimental Sugar Factory, 600
Aufrère, Mathurine, 181
Avart, Erasmus R., 13
Avent, Samuel, 388
Avery, Daniel, 205
Avery, Mrs. D. D., 501 n232
Avery, Sarah Marsh, 205, 207
Aviation, in Long-era South Louisiana, 578-92
Avoyelles Parish, La., evacuation of flood refugees from, 461-62
Aycock, Joan Marie, 4, 175
Aymard, Judith Wolf, 133-34

Bailey, Willliam, 758
Baker, Vaughan B., 4, 160, 189
Baldwin Lumber Co., 472
Bancroft, George, 411, 731-32
Bangs, Capt., 206
Bank of Louisiana, 526, 534, 535, 536, 537
Bank of Orleans, 534, 535, 536
Bank of the United States, 526, 527, 534, 536, 538
Bankhead-Jones Farm Tenancy Act, 565
Banks, Nathaniel P., 65, 66, 69, 71, 405, 686, 692, 716, 717, 720
Banville, Mme., 181

783

Barlow, Ailsy, 201
Barlow, Peter, 201
Barnes, J. Austin, 464
Barnett, Chris, 738, 741
Barnett, Claude A., 479
Barnett, Mrs. Robert S., 500 n176
Barnett, Spencer, 500 n176
Baron, Pierre, 332-33, 365
Baronne, Gus, 156
Barot, Catherine, 172 n15
Barq, Auguste, 720, 722
Barq, Mrs. Auguste, 722
Barr, John U., 574
Barr, Robert R., 212
Barry, Catherine, 560
Barton, Pilie, Sere, & Wermuth accounting firm, 609, 613
Basile, La., Cajun country Mardi Gras in, 660
Batista, 10
Baton Rouge, La., becomes capital of Louisiana, 50
Battistella, Andrew, 431-32
Baudier, Roger, 181
Baudin, Mme, 315
Bauer, Craig A., 6, 400
Baym, Nina, 270
Beadle, A. J., 489
Beattie, Taylor, 723
Beaubois, Nicolas-Ignace de, 176, 177, 180, 359, 539
Beaulieu, Widow, 165
Beaumont, Ste-Thérèse de Jésus, 179
Beauregard, Gabriel Toutant, 562 n3
Beaurepos, Luis, 338
Becnel, Thomas A., 7, 564
Behrman, Martin, 511, 517
Bell, Alonzo, 341
Bell, Caryn Cossé, 2, 9
Bell, Joseph M., 689, 690, 691, 692
Bellechasse, Joseph Deville de Goutin, 537, 542 n5
Belleme, Louise, 708
Belmonti, Louis, 227, 231, 233, 234, 236
Belsaguy, Widow, 166
Benjamin, Judah P., 401, 414
Bennetts, David Paul, 3, 90
Bequet, Jean Batiste, 172 n15
Béranger, Jean, 350
Beraud & Gilbert, 722
Berlin, Ira., 699
Bernadas, Hector Emile, 594
Bernadas, Hester Catherine, 594
Bernadas, Hester Kinberger, 594
Bernard, Johnny, 607
Bernard, Lucille, 596, 598, 599, 601, 607
Bernard, St-Pierre, 179
Bertier, Marianne de, 163
Bertrand, Mme, 234
Beverly Club, 431, 760
Bienvenu, Alix, 339, 340

Bienvenu, Antoine, 340
Bienville, Jean-Baptiste Le Moyne, sieur de, 161, 167, 313, 317, 324, 325, 327, 331, 334, 335, 361, 365
Bigeaud de Belair, Elizabeth, 179
Bigeaud de Belair, Marguerite, 179
Bilbo, Theodore G., 516, 517
Billeaud, Charles, 494 n24
Billeaud, Hugh, 500 n176
Billings, Warren, 1
Bimont, Mr., 165
Bingaman, Adam L., 419
Binns, Elizabeth, 386
Bisotton de Saint Martin, 359
Black Code, some provisions of, regarding women, 168
Blair, Karen, 289
Blanc, Louis, 542 n5
Blanchard, Newton C., 300
Blanque, J., 542 n5
Blassingame, John, 706
Blease, Cole, 565
Blondeau, Marie Rose, 556
Blue, Sheldon, 655
"Blue Books," Storyville, 279-84
Boagni, E. M., 486, 488
Board of Prisons and Asylums, 733
Boasberg, Mark, 430
Bodin de Sainte-Marie, Denis, 366
Boeing Co., 587
Bogalusa Paper Co., 583
Boggs, Hale, 573
Boisbriant, Pierre Dugué de, 364, 365
Boisdoré, François, 20
Boisrenaud, Françoise de, 175
Boissy, Joseph, 365
Bolden. Buddy, 639
Bolen, August, 699
Bolyard, R. H., 478, 499 n173
Bonaparte, Napoleon, 12, 56, 555
Bonin, R. P., 596
Boré, Etienne, 48, 537, 699, 700
Boston Club, 437
Bouanchaud, Hewitt, 512
Bouchon, C. N., 339, 440
Boudreaux, A. J., 489
Boudreaux, M., 504 n309
Boulanger, Angélique, 177, 179
Bouligny, Mr., 50
Bourbon, Mme, 181
Bourg, E. J., 574
Bourgeois, Lewis I., 580-81, 582
Boustany, Frem, 645, 646, 647, 652, 653, 654, 655
Boutwell, George, 723
Boutwell, Mr., 73
Boze, Jean, 255
Bradbury, Charles William, 247, 248, 249, 250-51, 252-53, 254, 255-56, 257-58, 259, 260, 261, 262, 264, 265, 266, 267, 268, 270, 271, 272

Index 785

Bradbury, Cornelius, 252, 253-54
Bradbury, James, 250, 252, 255, 256
Bradbury, Marcus, 253
Bradbury, Mary Ann Taylor, 259, 261
Bradbury, Sarah, 254
Brady, Patricia, 1, 554
Brantan, Marie Anne, 181
Brashear, Margaret Barr, 209, 210, 211, 212
Brashear, Rebecca, 209
Brashear, Walter, 208, 209, 210, 212, 213
Brashear, Walter, Jr., 209
Brasseaux, Carl A., 2, 5, 6, 28, 311, 457
Breaux, George J., 474, 476
Breaux, Paul, 500 n186
Breckinridge, Robert, 678
Breedlove, James Waller, 252, 256, 257-58
Breedlove, Maria Ellen Winchester, 257
Bremer, Frederika, 267
Brent, Joseph Lancaster, 408
Breusle, Honnorée Jean, 335
Brewer Nienstat Lumber Mill, 464
brewery, 357
Bridges, Harry, 568, 570
Brien, Mary, 214
Brient, Henry, 211
Bringier, Anne Guillelmine (Nanine), 405, 406, 407, 408, 409, 410, 411, 413, 418
Bringier, Anne Octavie, 404
Bringier, Emmanuel Marius Pons, 404
Bringier, Louise Françoise, 404
Bringier, Louise Marie Myrthe, 404
Bringier, Marie Elizabeth Aglaé, 404
Bringier, Martin, 407
Bringier, Michel Doradou, 404
Bringier, Rosella, 404
Brinkley, Alan, 578
Brisbane, Albert, 669, 670, 671, 673, 674, 677, 679, 680
British Eugenics Association, 304
Briton, John, 201
Briton, Mima, 201
Bromley, J. B., 64
Brooks, Overton, 573
Brotherhood of Boilermakers, Iron Shipbuilders and Helpers of America, 145
Brotherhood of Timber Workers, 565
Brothers of Charity, 176
Broul, Marie Joseph, 179
Broussard, Alphonse, 599, 600, 601, 602, 607-8, 611
Broussard, Amand, 375, 385 n36
Broussard, Augustin, 376
Broussard, Edwin, 511-12, 725, 726
Broussard, Nicolas, 389
Broussard, Robert F., 291, 724, 725
Brousse, Jean Philippe, 172 n15
Broutin, Ignace François, 328, 331, 332, 365
Brown, Alexander, 540
Brown, Angelica Eugenia, 256
Brown, Billy, 210

Brown, E. W., 468
Brown, John M., 21
Brown, Linus, 341
Brown, Shepherd, 530, 533, 537, 539
Brown, Thomas, 264
Brown, Walter, 584
Bruere, Martha, 426
Bruslé, Antoine, 360
Bruslé, Louise Elisabeth, 366
Buchanan, A. M., 233, 236
Buckingham, J. S., 52, 58
Budington, Henry J., 250, 252, 254, 255, 256, 265
Budington, Margaret, 252
Bulkley, William L., 127, 134
Bullard, Henry Adams, 234-35, 237
Bunyan, John, 411
Bureau of Municipal Research, 734
Burel, Geneviève, 360
Burgand, Pierre, 338
Burnley, Hardin, 392
Burnley, Mary Wilkins, 393
Burns, Ida Patout, 603, 606, 608, 609, 611, 615, 625
Burns, J. Patout, 608, 625
Burns, Louis, 446, 447, 448
Butler, Andrew Jackson, 692
Butler, Benjamin F., 8, 684-96, 720
Butler, L. A., 475
Butler, Louise, 415
Butler, Richard, 534, 542 n7
Butler, William, 205
Byrd, Harry, 565, 572
Byron, Lord, 267, 268, 411

Cable, George Washington, 227, 232, 638, 732, 733
Cadillac, Antoine de La Mothe, 161, 162, 314, 317
Cadillac, Mme Antoine de La Mothe, 313
Cadillac Club, 437
Cadore, Norm, 770
Caffery, C. D., 289
Cage, Albert, 245, 246
Cage, Eliza, 245
Cage, Fanny, 245
Cage, Lofton, 245, 246
Cage, Naomi Gillespie, 245
Cage, Selima Madaline, 245, 269
Cage, William, 245
Cage, William, Jr., 245
Caldwell, James Henry, 53
Caldwell, Mrs. Willie W., 513
Calhoun, John C., 528
Callendar, Thomas, 530, 533, 535, 536, 537, 540
Callender, Alvin, 580
Cambas, Arthur E., 582
Caminada, 539
Camorra, Neapolitan, 757
Canby, E. R. S., 720
Canby, Sarah, 230, 234

Canonge, J. F., 12
Capone, Al, 429-30, 450, 451, 752
Capuchin order, 9, 10, 12
Carnival, American Style, 660
Carolla, Anthony, 762
Carolla, Sylvestro "Silver Dollar Sam," 757, 758, 760
Caron, Anne, 181
Carondelet, Luis Hector, Baron de, 11
Carr, William, 771
Carrasco, Rebecca, 5, 299
Carriere, Helaire, 776, 777
Carriere, Widow, 181
Carrière brothers, 360
Carroll, John, 15, 56
Carter, Annie, 478
Carter, Mr., 76
Carter, Paul, 517
Casa Calvo, Marques de, 11, 56
Casbergue, A. Sainville, 560
Caselar, Pierre, 255
Casey, Mr., 76
Cash, W. J., 419
Cash, Wilbur, 564
casket girls, 163
Cassibry, Fred, 575
Castanedo, Mr., 56
Castex, "Pete," 646
Castillon, 56
Catherin, Father, 596
Catholic Messenger, 59
cattle, rescue of, during 1927 flood, 468-69
Caue, Ste-Angele, 179
Cavalier, Antoine, Jr., 530, 533, 537
Cavalier, St-Joseph, 177, 179
Cawthorn, Joseph, 143
Celotex Co., 583
Century Magazine, 638
Cervantes, Miguel de, 411
Chambellan Graton, 360
Chambers, Maude, 471
Champagne, Noli, 491
Chandler, David, 755, 757, 758
Channing, William Henry, 670, 679
Chaplin, Robert E., 465, 480
Charity Hospital (New Orleans), 222
Charity Organization Society, 299
Chase, Salmon P., 71
Chaumette, Ernest, 705
Chaumont, Antoine, 162
Chaumont, Catherine Barré, Madame de, 162-63
Chauvin, Oscar Joseph, 603, 620, 622
Chauvin brothers, 360
Chauvin de Léry, Joseph, 361
Chavan, Mme., 181
Chavannes, Jean-Baptiste de, 359
Chavoy, Pierre Benoît Payen de, 361
Chennault, Claire, 588
Chevalier, Alice Simon, 129-30, 131, 132, 136

Chevalier, Everette, 129-30, 132, 135, 136
Chew, Beverly, 526-27, 528, 530, 533, 536, 537, 540
Chew & Relf, 526, 529, 530, 533, 534, 535, 541
Child Conservation League, 738
Child Labor Bill, Jean Gordon, 300
child welfare and public relief, in antebellum Louisiana, 221-26
children, the child offender and Louisiana penal institutions, 731-49
Choctaw Club, 511, 517
Christenberry, Herbert W., 149
Christian American Program, 570
church wardens, see *marguilliers*
Cidar, Jacques, 172 n15
Cirilo, Bishop, 10
Citizen's Bank of Louisiana, 20, 556
Civello, Joe, 758
Civic League of Lafayette (La.), 286
Civil Code of 1950, 743
Civil Constitution of the Clergy, 11
Civil Rights Section, Department of Justice, 150
Claiborne, John G., 388
Claiborne, Maria Cole, 387, 388, 393
Claiborne, William C. C., 13, 51, 52, 56, 57, 376, 536, 537, 544
Clancy, Frank, 760
Clapp, Theodore, 58, 253, 261, 262-63, 264, 265, 267
Clark, Clinton, 155
Clark, Daniel, Jr., 411, 530, 532, 537, 539
Clark, J. S., 735, 736
Clark, John D., 7, 526
Clark, Tom, 148, 149
Clay, Cassius M., 680
Clay, Henry, 265, 389
Clay, Laura, 305
Cline, I. M., 459, 580
Clinton, Catherine, 408
Clinton, Ed, 746
Cobb, Ned, 770
Cochran & Rhea, 529
Cocke, John W., 386
Coco, A. V., 738
Cohen, Walter, 431-32
Coleman, Eliza Cage, 248
Collens, T. Wharton, 672
Collidge, Calvin, 507
Collins, Jesty, 568
Collins, Mrs. W. N., 514
Collins, Pat, 758
Colomb, A. Christopher, 406
Columbo, Joseph, 762
Combe, George, 264, 266, 267
Commercial Bulletin, 52
Commission on Interracial Cooperation, 155
Comonfort, Ignacio, 23
Company of St. Ursula, 176
Company of the Indies, 161, 166, 167, 168, 175, 177, 179, 350-52, 356, 357, 358, 359, 360,

Index

361, 362, 363, 364, 366; plantation of the, 324-48; recruits craftsmen in France for Louisiana, 350-51
Company of the West, 162, 163
concubinage, 16
Conference on Organized Crime, 760
Conflans de Brienne, Chevalier de, 351
Congo Square, 7, slave dances at, 632-42; various names for, 633
Congregational church, 58
Congress of Industrial Organizations, 565, 566
Conkling, Mr., 73
Conrad, Glenn R., 6, 373, 386
Conservative party, 65
Constitution of 1864, discussed, 67; education in the, 69; wage and hour laws in the, 70
Constitution of 1868, black enfranchisement in the, 76; public education in the, 76; social equality in the, 76; governor's role under the, 77
Constitutional Convention of 1844-45, 46-50; composition of, 46-47
Constitutional Convention of 1864, 66-69
Coolidge, Calvin, 518-19
Coombs, Cecil, 647
Cooper, James Fenimore, 411
Corbin, Bachemin, 361
Cormoray, St-Gabriel, 179
Cornen, Paul, 722
Corrales, Barbara Smith, 5, 285
Cosey, H. F., 474, 476
Costello, Frank, 752, 758, 759, 760, 762
Council of Social Agencies of New Orleans, 738
Courcelle, Charles J., 700, 705
Courtney, Thomas, 770
Coutume de Paris, 189, 192, 194; some provisions of, regarding women, 165-66
Couvent, Mme. Bernard, 225
Cox, Eliza, 214
Cox, Henry, 214
Cox, James M., 513
Coxe, John E., 751, 756
Coxe, Nathaniel, 534
Craig, John, 255
Creole society, beginnings of, 360-61
Crescent City Butcher's Association, 66
Crescent City Democratic Organization, 574
Crescent City Independent Voters League, 574
Crescent, 53
Cresnay, Henry de Poilvilain de, 362-63
crime, organized, in Louisiana, 750-66
criminal justice, in South Louisiana, 767-82
Cronin, Joe, 652
Crozat, Antoine, 164, 189, 313
Crump, E. H. "Boss," 566
Cullo de Crémont, Charles François, 359
Curren, Peter, 234
Curtis, Charles, 507
Cutler, R. King, 64
Cyrille de Rochefort, 176

D'Abbadie, Jean-Jacques-Blaise, 320
Daily Advertiser, reports on Lafayette White Sox team, 650
Dain, Ste-Marthe, 177, 178
D'Albor, Felix, 595
Dalcourt, Etienne, 361
Damaron, François, 361
Dana, Charles, 670
D'Antonio, G. J., 741
Darby, François Optat, 394
Darby family, 375
D'Arensbourg, Charles, 315
D'Arensbourg, Frédéric, 361
D'Arensbourg, Louise, 361
Dartaguiette Diron, 167, 326, 362
D'Autry, George, 723
Daumois, Marthe, 163
Davis, A. L., 143
Davis, Ben, 509
Davis, Ed, 211, 214, 215
Davis, James H., 152
Davis, Jenny, 214, 215
Davis, Jimmie H., 570, 574, 738
Davis, John W., 510, 511
Davis, Mrs. F. E., 287, 288, 472, 473
Davis, Ramus, 383 n9
Davis, Susan G., 660
Day, W. T., 439
De Blanc, César, 364
DeBatz, Alexandre, 330, 332, 333, 337
Debs, Eugene, 102
Dedeaux, Henry, 432
deFuentes, H. E., 705
Degler, Carl, 669
DeHart, Capt., 200
DeHart, John, 200
DeHart, Louisa, 200
DeHart, Sarah, 200
DeHart heirs, 199, 200
Deiler, J. Hanno, 227
Delahoussaye, August, 595
Delatre, Marthe, 179
Delmonico's Restaurant, 437
De Loffre & Cambray, 722
Delta Shipyard, 145, 146
Demanade, Mrs. Harold, 291-92, 474
Deming, Henry C., 686
DeMouy, Mr., 165
Demouÿ, Charles, 366
De Mouy, Charlotte, 179
Denapolis, Tony, 449
Denbo, Anna Margaret, 288
Denisart, Jean Baptiste, 193
Denison, Mr., 70-71
Denistoun, A., 530
Denistoun, J., 530
Derbigny, Pierre, 48, 51
Desauche, Allen, 489
Desdunes, Emile, 23

Deslatte, Leona, 596
Destrehan, J. Noel, 537
Des Tuilettes de Vauparis, 366
Deutsch, Isabel, 171
Devalcourt, John, 389
Deverges, Bernard, 335
de Wald, William, 582, 584
D'Hauterive, Renaul, 362, 363
Dias, Joseph Masaneillo, 561
Dick, Thomas, 264, 267
Dill, Special Agent, 148, 149, 151
Dinwiddie, President, 588
Diocese of Louisiana, placed under jurisidiction of bishop of Baltimore, 11
Dix, Gertrude, 280
Dixie Laundry, 130, 131
Dixon, Margaret, 749 n55
Dolittle, Jimmy, 585
Domengeaux, J. R., 292, 293, 478
Domengeaux, James, 573
Domingo, Francisco, 750
Domingue, Daisy Gary, 595
Dominique, Alcide, 655
Donaldson, Gary A., 7, 632
Donaldson, William, 536, 542 n7
Dorsey, E. L., 148, 151
Dostie, A. P., 73
Dotson, Melby, 770
Douglas, Judith, 738
Douglas, Stephen, 65
Douglas, William O., 744
Dowie, "Red," 647, 654
Downs, Mr., 47
Doyle, George, 709
Dreux brothers, brewery of the, 357
Dreyfous, Jules, 297 n51
Drolet, Jerome, 570
Duag, Paulin, 152
Dubinsky, Dave, 574
DuBois, W. E. B., 74, 78, 96, 98
Dubourg & Dubuys, 537
DuBourg, Elizabeth Aglae, 404
DuBourg, Louis, 13
Dubourg, Louis Guillaume, 56-57, 405
Dubourg, Peter, 536
Du Breuil, 539
Dubreuil, Joseph, 335, 336
Dubuys, Gaspar, 537
Duchesne, Philippine, 12
Du Coderc, Laurent, 366
Duer, William, 530
Dugas, Mary Louise, 500 n176
Dumartrait, Adrien, 384 n19
Dumas, Alexandre, 411, 556
Dunbar-Dukate Co., 568
Duncan, Abner L., 532, 542 n7
Dunn, J., 705
Dunn, Oscar, 75
Dupard, Delille, 699

Duperier, Alfred, 387, 388, 389, 391, 392
Duplantier, Armand, Jr., 531
Dupleix, Mrs. P. R., 500 n176
Duplessis, Francis, 530, 533, 534, 536, 540
Duplessis, Francis, Jr., 534
Dupuy, Guillaume, 722
Duralde, Martin, 375, 376, 384 n19
Durant, Thomas J., 75, 672, 673, 677, 680
du Ru, Paul, 312
Duverje, Barthélemy, 338, 339
Dysart, J. P., 301

East Baton Rouge Parish, Amvets, 740; Department of Welfare, 741; Family Counseling Service, 741; Family Court, 740-41; Family Court Advisory Committee, 741; Inter-Civil Club, 740, Juvenile Detention Home, 741; Kiwanis Club, 740; League of Women Voters, 740; Ministerial Alliance, 740; Parent-Teachers Association Council, 740
Eastern Airlines, 588
Eccles, William J., 311
Edme, Henry, 350, 352
education, in the Constitution of 1864, 69; public, 51-52
Edwards, Madaline Selima Cage Elliot, 5; 243-78
Einstein, Izzy, 442
El Trelles cigar factory, 128, 131
Ellender, Allen J., 143, 569, 570, 571, 572-73, 574, 575
Elliot, Dempsey, 246, 247, 265, 272
Elliot, Isabella, 247
Elliot, Mary Jane, 246
Elliot, William, 246
Elliott, Charlotte, 302
Ellis, Mrs., 253
Ellis, Sarah Stickney, 267
emancipation, of slaves, two utopian socialist plans for, 669-83
Episcopal church, first in New Orleans, 57
Equal Rights Association, 299
Esnard family, 561
Esposito, Giuseppe, 755-56
Esteves, August, 433
Estopinal, Albert, 433, 434
Estopinal, Joseph, 433
Eustis, George, 48, 49
Eustis, George, Jr., 50
Evangeline League, formation of, 647; Lafayette's White Sox [team] in, 643-58; other names for the, 643
Evans, Francis, 199, 200, 201
Evans, John N., 199, 201
Evans, Nathaniel, 198, 199, 537
Evans, Sarah, 199, 201

F. B. Williams Cypress Co., 583
Fabre, Mme., 181

Index

Fair Employment Practices Committee, 144, 145, 146, 147
Fair Labor Standards Act, 565, 568, 601
Fairclough, Adam, 3, 142
Faison, Bessie Patout, 619
Family Service Association of America, 741
Family Service Bureau, 299
Farges, François-Marie, 162
Farm Bureau, 566, 570
Farm Security Administration, 144, 571
Farrar, Emile, 700
Faucon-Dumanoir, Jean Baptiste, 361
Faulk, Herman Joseph, 147, 151, 153
Faulk, J. W., 480
Favrot, Charles Joseph, 366
Favrot, Pierre Joseph, 366
Fayet, Pierre de, 350
Fazende, Jacques, 327, 360
Federal Bureau of Investigation, 143, 148, 149, 150, 151, 152, 153, 154, 750, 751, 758, 762
Female Orphan Asylum, 247, 249
Ferguson, John, 388
Ficklen, J. R., 66, 67
Finger, Tommy, 648
First State Bank of New Orleans, 583
Fisher, Jules, 759
Fishermen's, Oystermen's, and Fur Trappers' Producers' Cooperative Association, 568
Fitzhugh, George, 679
Fleming, P. H., 504, n309
Fleuriau, François, 316, 358, 360, 365
Fleurtel, Pierre, 176
Flint, Timothy, 58, 403
flood of 1927, cattle, rescue of, 468-69; Coast Guard aid in evacuation of flood victims during, 461-62; evacuations during, 461-69; flood waters inundate Melville, La., during, 461; in south-central Louisiana, 457-505; newspaper comments about flood threat to south-central Louisiana, 458; regional damage and destruction statistics for, 457; volunteers work on levees in south-central Louisiana as a prelude to, 459-60
Folger, "Meatball," 648
Fonder, Widow, 181
Fontaine, L. S., 542 n5
Fontenot, Keith P., 504 n294
Forstall, E. J., 542 n13
Fort San Fernando, 633
Fortier, Michel (see also Michel Fortier & Co), 530, 533, 536, 537, 540
Foster, Rufus, 430, 440, 444-45, 447
Foucault, Denis Nicolas, 337, 342
Fouché, Louis Nelson, 22-23
Fourier, Charles, 8, 392, 669, 670, 674
Fournier, Pauline Napoléone (Appoline), (see also Patout, Appoline), 715
Fox-Genovese, Elizabeth, 249
Foy, Florville, 555, 556, 557-58, 561
Foy, Prosper, 555, 556-57, 560
Fraim, J. P., 589
Frances, Anne, 177, 178
Franklin, John Hope, 225
Franklin, William Buel, 716, 717, 718
Free State party, 65, 66, 70, 71
free people of color, 698, 768; black militia abolished, 18; established in Mexican colony, 22-23; from Attakapas District, in Haiti, 23; legislative enactments to restrict activities of, 18-19; property owners among, 19-20; in the Attakapas District, 22; policemen in antebellum New Orleans, 699, population of, in New Orleans, 16; residency law enacted for, 15-16; use of "f.p.c." required by Civil Code, 16; free persons of color, as tomb builders in New Orleans, 554-63
Freeman, Victoria "Vic," 601
French, Jonas H., 686-87, 692, 693
French and American Claims Commission, 715, 723, 724
Freret, James, 528
Fuchs, John, 611
Fuqua, Henry, 512
Fuselier, Agricole, 375

Galehouse, Dennis, 646
Galiece, Margaret, 299
Gallatin, Albert, 527
Gambino, Carlo, 762
Gambino, Richard, 751
Gamble, Harry, 292
Garbeille, Philippe, 557
Gardner, Dutch (alias for Gus Tomes), 433
Garnier, Mme, 317
Garrigou & Abat, 377, 380, 381, 383
Gaster, D. G., 756
Gaudette, J. B., 705
Gauvry, Joachim de, 362, 363, 364, 365, 366
Gayarré, Charles, 50
Gee Bee Racers, 585, 587
Geffrard, Fabre, 23
Gehlbach, Philip, 433
General Longshore Workers Local 1419, 574
Genovese, Vito, 752
German Union, 66
Gibbens, George H., 612
Gibbon, Edward, 411
Gift House, dedication of, 304
Gilbert, Larry, 646
Gilmore's Louisiana Sugar Manual, 608
Girard, E. F., 645
Girard, Mrs. Crow, 287, 290
Girard, Mrs. Eloi, 500 n176
Girard, Stephen, 540
Giraud, Marcel, 6, 349
Girls House of Refuge, 732
Girod, Nicholas, 48, 530, 530, 533, 535, 536, 537, 540

Girouard, "Pee-Wee," 644, 655
Glassie, Henry, 660
Glona, Brandy, 744
Glover, Pansy, 500 n176
Godwin, Parke, 671
Goff, Bobby, 648, 651
Goff Act, repeal of, 570
Golden, Bertha, 282
Goldsmith, Oliver, 411
Gompers, Samuel, 112
Gonzague, St-Louis de, 179
Gonzolez, Xavier, 586
Goodloe, Daniel, 678
Gordon, George Hume, 299
Gordon, Jean M., 5, 286, 287, 299-310
Gordon, Kate, 5, 288, 299, 300, 304, 305, 306
Gordon, Martin, Jr., 404, 416
Gordon, Martin, Sr., 404, 528
Goubert, Pierre, 315
Goulas, Alcide, 595
Goulé, John, 20
Gramont, Comte de, 362
Grandsteever, Capt., 231
Grant, E. P., 672
Grant, Edward D., 745
Grant, Ulysses S., 77, 80, 754
Granville, Z. D., 587
Granville brothers, 585
Graveline, Madame de, 167
Graves, George Washington, 418, 420
Grayson, Thomas, 236
Great Southern Lumber Co., 583
Great Texas Overland Expedition, 715, 716
Greeley, Horace, 670
Green, William, 572
Grégoire, Henri Baptiste, 15
Gremillion, Jack P. F., 744
Grew, Ben, 588
Grey Nuns, 176
Griffin, Harry Lewis, 467
Grimké, Angelina, 409
Grimké, Sarah, 409
Grosch, John, 432, 448
Grymes, John R., 48, 231, 414
Guarneri, Carl J., 8, 669
Guchereau, Francis, 651
Guggenheim Foundation, 589
Guidry, Alexandre, 38
Guilbeau, Ben, 498 n144
Guilbeau, Clayton, 647
Guild, Mrs. Henry, 691
Guillaume's commercial school, 133
Guion, G. S., 46
Gulf Coast Airlines, 584
Gulf Coast Fishermen's and Oystermen's Association, 568
Gulf Public Service Co., 146
Gutman, Herbert, 208

H. Patout, Inc., 593

Hachard, Marie Madeleine, 175, 177, 178, 179, 349, 354
Hahn, Michael, 65-66, 69
Haizlip, Jimmy, 585
Haliday, Jack, 651
Hall, Dominick, 48
Hall, Gwendolyn Midlo, 2
Halleck, Henry, 716
Hamilton, Mary Ann Taylor, 253
Hamilton, Thomas, 14
Hammond, Henry, 419
Hanger, Kimberly, 2
Harbinger, The, 669, 670, 671, 679
Harding, Warren, 507
Hardy, J. Leo, 145, 146-47, 149, 150, 151, 152, 153, 155, 156
Harmon, Thomas L., 532
Harrington, Mrs. J. W., 473
Hart, Hastings, 300, 302
Hart, Helen, 253
Havard, William, 566
Hawkins, Abe, 419, 421
Hayes, David, 390
Haynes, J. K., 144
Haynes, Robert A., 447
Hays, John Coffee, 265, 269
Healy, Thomas, 449
Heaney, Jane Frances, 185
Hearne, David, 609-10, 615, 616, 621
Heath, Edward, 700, 701
Hébert, F. Edward, 143, 573
Hebert, Howard, 611, 620, 623
Hebert, Paul, 611
Hebert, T. James, 622-23, 624
Hébert, François Xavier, 179
Hébert, Paul O., 51
Heitmann, John A., 7, 578
Helper, Hinton, 679
Hemans, Felicia, 267
Henderson, Donald, 599
Henderson, Fanny, 210
Henderson, Isaac, 210
Henderson, James H., 156
Henderson, Stephen, 533
Hennefin, Ann, 256
Hennessy, David C., 751, 756
Henry, Clarence "Chink," 574
Henshaw, John Marsh, 206
Henshaw, Margaret Marsh, 204, 207
Hepworth, George, 718
Hernsheim's Tobacco Manufactory, 107
Heymann, Herbert, 741
Heymann, Maurice, 476
Heymann Department Store, 473
Hicks, John, 507
Higgins, Lawrence E., 738, 742, 748 n 37
Hill, A. S., 302
Hill, Henry H., 106
Hill, Tom, 449
Hillen, Solomon, Jr., 534

Index

Hilliard, Sam B., 387
Hodges, Elmo, 467, 473
Hodson, Mrs. C. B. S., 304
Hoff, Max "Boo Boo," 451
Holabird, Samuel B., 720
Holcombe-Aiken column, 561
Holdship, G. G., 340
Holleman, Albert E., 588
Hollier, Dave, 647
Hollier, David F., 489
Holy Rosary Institute, 476
Honeycutt, Edward, 156
Hood Act, Louisiana prohibition act, 447-48
Hoover, Herbert, 470, 479, 481, 488, 507, 509, 516, 519
Hoover, J. Edgar, 148, 149
Hoover Clubs, 514
Hopkins, Ida Katherine, 500 n176
Hopkins, O. B., 472, 475
Hopkins Lumber Co., 478
Hospital Sisters, 176
Hotsy Totsy Club, 437
House of Refuge, 734, 737, 743
House of the Good Shepherd, 732, 734
Houston, John, 202, 203, 205, 206, 207
Houston, Maria, 202, 203, 204, 206-7
Houston, Tom, 203
Houston, William, 207
Howard, Perry, 509
Howard Association, 224
Hudson, William, 206
Hughes, Langston, 125
Hulings, William E., 539
Hull, Mr., 57
Hunt, Randall, 414
Huot de Vaubercy, 360
Hutcheson, Francis, 264
Hyacinthe, Father, 316

Iberville, Pierre Le Moyne, Sieur d', 161, 162, 168, 312
Industrial School for Colored Male Youths, 735
Industrial School for Colored Youths, 742
Industrial Workers of the World, 565
Ingalls Shipbuilding Co., 571
Ingersoll, Thomas N., 127
Ingraham, Joseph Holt, 58
Innocents Club, 754, 755
Institution for the Deaf, Dumb, and Blind, 222
International Longshoremen and Warehousemen's Union, 569
International Longshoremen's Association, 569
International Typographical Union, 103
Irving, Washington, 267
Irwin, "Hooky," 647
Isaac Delgado Trade School, 589
Isabelle, Thomas, 705

Jackson, Andrew, 56, 256, 404
Jackson, O. D., 431, 432, 447

Jacobs, Aaron, 489
Jacobs, Adolphe, 486
Jacques, Theodore, 449
Jahncke, Ernst Lee, 581, 584
Jansenism, 12
Jean Gordon Child Labor Bill, 300
Jeanmard, Jules B., 476, 622, 624, 652
Jefferson, Thomas, 51, 404
Jefferson College, 593
Jefferson Music Co., 760
Jeffrey & Sons, 607
Jenaro, Louis, 647
Jewish Orphans' Home, 225
John D. Wilkins & Co., 388, 390
Johns, Emile, 232
Johns, Johnny, 644
Johnson, Alexander, 302, 303
Johnson, Andrew, 71, 73, 74, 701
Johnson, Enid, 303
Johnson, Isaac, 51, 547
Johnson, James F., 561
Johnson, James Weldon, 135
Johnson, Joseph, 709
Johnson, Tony, 665
Johnston, Albert Sidney, 685
Jones, Alvin, 156
Jones, Elizabeth (Betsy), 386
Jones, Evan, 530, 537, 539
Jones, Hannah, 210, 212
Jones, John, 386
Jones, Patrick, 212
Jones, Sam, 143, 569, 570, 745
Jones-Costigan Act, 597
Jordan, Will, 770
Joseph, Peter, 705
Josephus, Flavius, 267
Jouaneaulx, Louis, 165
Judde, St-Jean l'Evangéliste, 177, 178
Juen, Andres, 16
Juen, Gaton, 16
Juen, Juan Luis, 16
Juen, Roseta, 16
Juge, Paul, Jr., 685
juvenile court, 737
Juvenile Court Commission, 738, 739, 741, 742

Kastel, "Dandy Phil," 759
Kefauver, Estes, 566, 761
Keib, H. G., 483
Keith, John, 295 n14
Keith, Marie, 286, 287
Keller, Arthur, 600
Keller, Ben, 207
Keller, Georgianna, 207
Kelley, Mary, 269
Kellogg, William P., 76, 77, 80
Kendall, George W., 421
Kendall, John S., 751, 755, 756
Kenily, Charles A., 588
Kennedy, Frank J., 499 n173

Kennedy, John F., 761
Kennedy, P. V. J., 706
Kenner, Duncan F., 6, 400-425; real estate activity of, 401-2
Kenner, Duncan, Jr., 408
Kenner, Frances Rosella, 408
Kenner, George Currie Duncan, 408
Kenner, George, 418
Kenner, Martha Blanche, 408
Kenner, Minor, 406, 417
Kenner, Rodham, 417
Kenner, William, 401, 402, 404, 405, 417, 530, 533, 536, 537, 537, 538, 540
Kenner & Henderson, 529, 530, 533, 534, 535
Kennon, Robert F., 745
Kerlérec, Louis Billouart de, 318, 337
Kessler-Harris, Alice, 130
Key, Jerry, 214, 215
Key, Maria, 214
Key, V. O., 507-8, 509-10
Kingsley House, 299
Kinser, Samuel, 660
Kinsman, J. Burnham, 691, 692, 693
Kirby, John H., 565
Kitchin, A. P., 148, 149
Klorer, John, 586
Knights of Columbus, 511, 513
Knights of Labor, 564, 768
Kohn, Aaron M., 760, 761, 762
Kohn, Joachim, 232
Kramer, Jack, 648
Ku Klux Klan, 508, 511, 513, 515
Kursheedt & Bienvenu, 561
Kurtz, Michael L., 8, 750

Labarre, Rosalie, 232
Labatut, J. B., 533, 534, 535
Labbé, T. J., 504 n309
Laberie, Pierre, 723
Laborde, Lucien, 470
La Boulay, Guérin de, 361, 365, 362
Labranche, Alcée, 50
Lacarra, Eugenia, 128, 129, 131, 136
La Chaise, Félicité de, 360
La Chaise, Jacques de, 329, 330, 331, 353, 354, 358, 359, 363, 364, 365
La Chaise, Jacques de, *fils*, 359
Lachiapella, Gerome, 536
La Cosa Nostra, 750, 751
Ladd, C. F., 106
Lafargue, J. B., 735
Lafayette, Marie Joseph Paul Yves Roch Gilbert Motier, Marquis de, 233
Lafayette, La., clubwomen and the failure of woman suffrage in, 285-98; White Sox [baseball] team of, 643-58
Lafayette Baseball Association, Inc., 645
Lafayette Building and Loan Association, 473
Lafon, Thomy, 106
Lakefront Airport, 587-88

La Loire, Louise Jousset, 166
L'Ami des Lois, 52
La Motte, St-Joseph de, 179
Land, Inez, 741
Landelle, St-Jacques, 179
Landry, Aristide, 50
Landry, Emilien, 719
Landry, Jacob, 621
Landry, P. A., 291
Landry, Peter, 654
Landry, Pierre, 494 n22
Lansky, Meyer, 760, 762
Lanusse, Armand, 225
Lanusse, Paul, 530, 533, 534, 535, 536, 537, 540, 541
Larcade, Harry, Jr., 573
Larme, Madame de, 164
Larned, Sylvester, 262
Larre, Hugh, 430
La Salle, Nicolas de, 162, 313
La Salle, Rene-Robert Cavelier de, 161
LaSère, Emile, 50
Laserna, Evelina, 133, 135
Lassus, Jean-Pierre, 330, 331, 337
Lassus de Marcilly, Joseph, 330, 360, 363
Latrobe, Benjamin Henry, 57, 634-35, 638, 640
Latrobe, Henry B., 402, 560
Laurent, Ed, 776
Laussat, Pierre Clément de, 339, 346
Lauve, Charles, 485
Lavenere, E., 561
La Vallée, Etienne, 350
La Vente, Henry de, 313, 317
La Vergne, Cadet, 365
Lavergne, Hughes, 339
law, community of acquets and gains, 192-93; separation of husband and wife, 193-94; the *douaire*, 194-95
Law, John, 162, 349
Lawrence, Frances Brashear, 210, 211, 212, 213
Lawrence, Henry, 213
Lazarus, Marx E., 669, 670, 671, 674-81
Le Blond de La Tour, Pierre, 324
Le Compte, Morris P., 582
Le Page du Pratz, Jean-Baptiste Michel, 327-29, 330, 332, 334, 335
Le Petit, Mathurin, 180
League of Women Voters (Lafayette, La.), 293
Learned, Mr., 57
LeBeau, Gustave, 595
Lebeuf, Martial, 338
LeBlanc, Dudley J., 28
LeBlanc, Eugene, 602
LeBlanc, Henry, 368
LeBlanc, "Lefty," 646
LeBlanc, Ste-Monique, 179
LeBlanc, T. Paul, 646, 647, 654
Lebsock, Suzanne, 265, 266
Leche, Richard, 567, 569
Lechiapella, Gerome, 530, 531

Index

Legac, Charles, 163
Leger, Lozen, 647
Leiserson, William, 567
Lemaire, Madeleine, 365
LeMarois, Rose Marceline, 560
Lescot, Jean, 351
Lestang, Ste-Reine, 179
Leucht, Rabbi, 733
Levasseur, M. A., 560
Leveson-Gower, Harriet, 560
Lévi-Strauss, Claude, 160, 161
Levis, James, 116
Levy, Benjamin, 528
Levy, Louise, 743-44
Lewis, James, 705
Lewis, John G., Jr., 736
Lewis, John L., 571, 572
Lewis, John Lawson, 235, 238
Liepure, St-Ignace du, 179
Lilly, Octave, 151, 153
Lilly, Octave, Jr., 148
Lincoln, Abraham, 65, 66, 69, 70, 145, 686, 692
Lind, Jenny, 54
Lindahl, Carl, 8, 659
Lindbergh, 579, 581
Lindig, Carmen, 289
Lindsay, Fred, 747 n18
Lines, Como, 282
Lingois, Louis, 381
Littell, B. A., 488
Little Club, 444, 449
Livaudais, J. F., 533
Livaudais, Philip, 434
Livingston, Edward, 14, 221, 231, 532, 537, 544, 731
Lizardi, Manuel J. de, 530
Lizardi & Co., 530
Llula, Joseph, 561
Lob, Godfrey, 561
Logan, Charles, 567
Loire, list of women embarked on the, 170
Long, Earl K., 143, 569, 570, 573, 574, 575, 741, 745
Long, Huey P., 7, 508, 511, 512, 516, 517, 566-67, 571, 575, 578-79, 589, 608, 649-50, 758, 759
Long, Rufus, 688
Longuory, Dagobert de, 25 n2
Loreauville, La., flood activities in, 465
Lorio, E. P., 598
Louboey, Chevalier de, 315, 317
Louboey, Henry de, 362, 365
Louis XIV, 189
Louisiana, 581
Louisiana, Americanization of, 45-63; Attakapas District of, 22; aviation in Long-era South, 578-92; Baton Rouge becomes capital of, 50; Board of Charities and Corrections, 745; Board of Institutions, 736, 745, 746; carpetbag rule, discussed, 78-79; child welfare and public relief in antebellum, 221-26; class and race strife, 1840-1875, 64-89; Colony and Training School, 745; constitutional convention of 1844-45, 46-47; Correctional Institute for Males, 736; cultural conflict in the 1928 presidential campaign, 506-25; Department of Education, 146; Department of Hospitals, 745; Department of Institutions, 742, 744, 745, 746; Department of Public Welfare, 738, 742, 744; first juvenile court in, 737, flood of 1927 in south central, 457-505; free black males prohibited entry into, 15; labor in, 1900-1950, 564; Louisiana Boards Panels, 745; marital laws governing women in French, 189-97; material culture of Attakapas District of, 373-86; moral climate of French, 311-23; Office of Family Services, 744, organized crime in, 750-66; poverty in early colonial, 353, Protestant-Catholic clevage in voting patterns in, 506-25; rivalry between *ancienne population* and American newcomers, discussed, 402-3; shortage of food in early colonial, 354-55; shortage of goods in early colonial, 353-54; South, lynching and criminal justice in, 767-82; taxation in Reconstruction, 79; the child offender and, 731-49; two utopian socialist plans for emancipation in antebellum, 669-83; women in early eighteenth century, 160-74
Louisiana Advertiser, 52, 53
Louisiana Airways, 582
Louisiana Anti-Tuberculosis League, 288
Louisiana Association for the Progress of Negro Citizens, 143
Louisiana Chamber of Commerce, 581
Louisiana Citizens' Committee, 574
Louisiana Colored Teachers Association, 144, 735
Louisiana Courier, 52, 53
Louisiana Farmers Union, 144, 155
Louisiana Federation of Labor, 574
Louisiana Gazette, 52
Louisiana Insurance Co., 134, 526
Louisiana Lottery, 81, 755
Louisiana Moss Products, 583
Louisiana Planters' Bank, 534, 535, 536
Louisiana Power and Light Co., 583
Louisiana Progress, 579, 586
Louisiana Shrimp Fishermen's Cooperative Association, 568
Louisiana Society for the Prevention of Cruelty to Children, 733, 743, 744
Louisiana State Bank, 526, 534
Louisiana State Penitentiary, 735
Louisiana State University, 579, 589; School of Social Work, 742
Louisiana Training Institute, 734, 735

Louisiana Training Institute at Baton Rouge, 747 n18
Louisiana Women's Christian Temperance Union, 514
Louisiana Women's Federated Clubs, 290
Louisiana Youth Commission, 741-42
Low & Wallace, 531
Loyola, Jean Joseph de, 337
Lucas, A. G., 598
Luciano, Charles "Lucky," 752
Lucrecia, Marie, 560
Luxembourg, Raphaël de, 316, 354, 357, 358, 361
Lyell, Charles, 54
lynching, in South Louisiana, 767-82
Lythgoe, Gertrude, 446

M. A. Patout & Son, Ltd., 7, 593-631
McCall, Betsy Ann, 203
McCall, Fanny, 203
McCall, Jesse, 203, 378
McCall, Sarah, 203
McCall, Sawney, 203
Macarty, Barthélemy, 255
Macheca, Joseph, 754, 755
MacIntyre, L. D., 472, 475
McClelland, John, 686
Maclin, William, 387
McCormick, William, 529
McCullough, Clyde, 648
Macdaniel, Osborne, 669, 670, 671, 672-81
McDonogh, John, 224, 528, 530, 532, 536, 537, 672, 675, 678
McDowell, Gertrude, 472
McEnery, 80
McGrath, J. Howard, 760
McGuire, Ann, 561
McIlhenny Co., 619
McIntire, Gordon, 599
McLean, James L., 561
McMain, Eleanor, 299
McNally, John, 341
McNaspy, C. J., Jr., 500 n176
McNeil, Joseph, 530, 533, 534, 535, 537, 539
Madison, James, 56
Maestri, Robert S., 759, 574
Mafia, American, 751; Louisiana, 753, 755, 756, 757, 758, 760, 762; Sicilian, 755, 757
Magliore, Gabriel, 776
Mahieu, St-François Xavier, 177, 178
Maitre, J. J., 645
Malone, Ann Patton, 198
Manadé, Pierre de, 166
Mandeville, François de Marigny de, 362
Mandeville, Madame de, 167
Mangnon de La Tour, Marie Magdelaine, 166
Mann, Louis, 655
Mansion, Lucien, 22
Maquillé, William, 380, 381
Marcard, Justine Frank, 131

Marcello, Carlos, 758, 760, 761-62
Marcilly, Mr., 165
Mardi Gras, Cajun Country, 659-68
Marento, Pascal, 595
Maret, Jean, 362
marguilliers, 11-12
Mariette, Marie-Louise, 352
Marigny, Bernard, 46, 47, 48, 49
Marine, Wallace, 126, 128, 131
Marion, St-Michel, 177, 178
Marrionneaux, Walter, 771
Marsh, George, 204, 207
Marsh, John, 201, 203, 204, 205, 206, 207
Marshall, Thurgood, 148, 149
Marshall School, 249
Martin, A. M., 291
Martin, B. J., 614
Martin, G. W., 504 n309
Martin, Wade O., 491
Martina, "Oyster Joe," 644
Martineau, Harriet, 14
Mason, John Young, 559
Masons, 12
Massachusetts Missionary Society, 57
Masson, Arthur, 433, 434
Massy, Claude, 177, 178
material culture, in Louisiana's Attakapas District, 1804-1818, 373-86
Mather, James, 530, 532, 537, 539
Matranga, Charles, 757, 758
Matranga family, 756
Matthews, Dallas B., 736, 747 n18
Mauldin, Marshal, 648
May, Thomas, 672, 681
Maybin, Joseph A., 258, 262
Mazarin, Duchesse de, 366
Mazureau, Etienne, 48
Mechanics' Association, 66
Medical College of Louisiana, 252
Meeham, Laura Lake, 286
Meeker, Williamson, & Patton, 537
Melançon, Joseph, 381
Melotte, St-André, 179
Melville, La., flood waters inundate, 461
Men's Anti-Woman Suffrage League, 292
Menefee, J. C., 582, 583, 585
Menefee Airport, 583
Menefee Airways, 582
Menn, Karl Joseph, 31
Meraux, J. Claude, 433-34
Meraux, L. A., 432, 433, 434
Mercier, Armand, 232
Mercier family, 556
Merici, Angela, 176, 177
Merricult, J. F., 536
Messenger, Andy, 646
Mestach, George, 579
Metairie Association, 421
Metairie Jockey Club, 421
Metoyer, Marie Thérèse, 171 n3

Index

Metropolitan Police, 701-3, 705, 706, 708, 710
Meunier, Edmond, 717
Michel, Constant, 699
Michel, Françoise, 165
Michel, J. J., 22
Michel de Rouvillère, Honoré, 335
Michel Fortier & Co., 531
Miller, Beauregard, 760
Miller, J. F., 686
Miller, John Fitz, 230, 231, 232, 233, 234, 236, 238, 239
Miller, Margaret, 282
Miller, Wilbur, 710
Millet, Donald J., 230
Mills, Samuel J., 57
Milne, Alexander, 223, 301, 302
Milne Asylum, 225
Milne Board for Destitute Boys, 302
Milne Home, Jean Gordon and the making of the, 299-310
Milne Municipal Boys' Home, 735
Milton, John, 411
Minacore, Calogero, see Marcello, Carlos
Minor, William J., 410, 419, 420, 421
Mioton, Anne Emilie, 560
Mioton, S. F., 303
Miró, Esteban, 10, 11
Missionary Society of Connecticut, 57
Mississippi River, flood of 1927 in south-central Louisiana, 457-505
Mitchell, Letha Pearl, 596
Mitchell, T. L., 612
Mitcheltree, John, 389
Mobley, T. R., 459
Mock, Lenny, 648
Molony, Guy, 448
Monahan, Jack, 587
Moniteur de la Louisiane, 52
Monroe, John T., Mayor, 685, 686
Monsseaux, Paul, 562
Montegut, J. O., 599
Montegut, Joseph, 340
Montet, Numa, 584
Montgomery, William W., 528, 530, 534
Montoya, James M., Sr., 129, 132, 133, 136
Mony, Charles, 560
Moore, Thomas, 411
morality, in French Louisiana, 311-23
Moran, "Bugs," 753
Moran, Robert E., 4, 8, 221, 731
Moreau, Kim, 665, 666
Moreau, Vories, 665
Moresi, L. A., 291
Morgan, Benjamin, 530, 533, 535, 536, 536, 537, 540, 541
Morgan, Lewis, 574
Moron, Marcel, 595
Morris, J. Walter, 647
Morrison, DeLesseps S., 574, 575, 760
Morrison, Jimmy, 569, 570, 572, 573, 575

Moseley, E. Donald, 747 n33
Mossy, Toussaint, 338, 340-41
Mother of Perpetual Help Church, 129
Motlow, Don, 648
Moulin Rouge Club, 444
Mouton, Alexandre, 37, 50
Mouton, Charles O., 289
Mouton, Edgar G., 647
Mouton, F. V., 295 n18
Mouton, Felix H., 472
Mouton, Marc M., 474, 479, 489
Mouton, Robert L., 471, 473, 647
Moyers, Gilbert, 724
Moyers & Consaul, 724, 725, 726
Muller, Daniel, 228, 230, 231
Muller, Daniel, Jr., 229
Muller, Dorothea, 227, 229, 236
Muller, Henry, 228
Muller, Jacob, 229, 230
Muller, Sally, 5; the white slave, 227-42
Muller, Salome, 227
Mumford, William, 691
Munn, Ann C., 480
Murphy, Peter, 201
Murphy, Susan, 201
My First Days in the White House, 578-79

Narodna Odbrana, 753
Natchez massacre, 164; orphans of the, 180-81
Nathan, Harold P., 481
National Agricultural Workers' Union, 620
National American Woman Suffrage Association, 288
National Association for the Advancement of Colored People, 142, 143, 144, 145, 146, 148, 149, 152, 153, 154, 156
National Conference of Charities and Correction, 302, 737
National Council of Juvenile Court Judges, 748 n37
National Defense Mediation Board, 570
National Federation of Woman's Clubs, 287
National Labor Relations Act, 600
National Labor Relations Board, 565, 567, 571
National Negro Conference, 127
National Probation and Parole Association, 739
National Probation Association, 738, 739
National Recovery Administration, 565
National War Labor Board, 570
National Women's Party, 290, 293
National Youth Administration, 571
Neboul, Mr., 327
Nee, Johnny, 645
Needham, Patrick, 431-32, 435, 439, 449, 450
Nelder, Alexander, 562 n3
Nelli, Humbert, 751, 756, 757
Nelson, Merle, 587-88
New Good Roads Act, 649-50
New Iberia, La., branch of NAACP organized, 144-45; evacuees from, during 1927 flood,

466-67; flood activities in, 465; racial repression in, 142-58
New Iberia National Bank, 617
New Levee Steam Cotton Press, 556
New Orleans, African American workers in, 1880-1890, 90-124; black policemen in, during Reconstruction, 697-713; brewery in, 357; business community, 1803-15, 526-42; Chamber of Commerce and air mail service, 580; churches of, 58; Committee of Fifty, 756, District Court, 744; early newspapers of, 52, early Protestant sects in, 57; early society of, 349-71; First Municipality Workhouse in, 545; first food market in, 356; free men of color as tomb builders in, 554-63; freemasonry in, 12; horse racing in antebellum, 417; Jean Gordon and the making of the Milne Home, 299-310; keeping law and order, 1862, 684-96; love and survival in antebellum, 243-78; Metropolitan Crime Commission of Greater, 760, 761, 762; Metropolitan Police of, 701-3, 705, 706, 708, 710; Milne Asylum for Destitute Orphan Girls, 300; opening of St. Louis Cemetery I in, 554; police department's Juvenile Bureau, 744; population of, 1769-1860, 18; prohibition in, 426-56; prostitution in early colonial, 358; racial passing in segregated, 125-41; riot of 1866, discussed, 73-74; Second Municipality Workhouse in, 545-46; segregation in, 17; slave dances at Congo Square in, 632-42; Storyville in, 279-84, theater in, 53-54; Third Municipality Workhouse in, 546; three-tiered caste system of, 9; Ursuline school in, 1727-1771, 175-88; Woman Order No. 28; workhouses and vagrancy in nineteenth-century, 543-53; Young Men's Business Club of, 580
New Orleans Airline, 582
New Orleans and Carrollton Railroad, 528
New Orleans and Nashville Railroad Co., 528
New Orleans Association of Commerce, 581
New Orleans Chamber of Commerce, Richard Relf a co-founder of, 527
New Orleans Childrens Bureau, see Louisiana Society for the Prevention of Cruelty to Children
New Orleans Female Orphan Asylum, 247, 249
New Orleans Hops, Malt and Extracts Co., 435
New Orleans House of Refuge, 732, 733
New Orleans Insurance Co., 529-30, 535, 538; organized by Chew & Relf, 526
New Orleans Jockey Club, 418
New Orleans Milne Asylum for Destitute Orphan Girls, 300
New Orleans Navigation Co., 527, 535
New Orleans Temperance Society, 257
New Orleans Tribune, 73

Newman, E. F., 583
newspapers, French-English, 52-53; New Orleans, 52
Newton, Lewis William, 2-3, 45
Neyboer, B. W., 596, 602, 603, 606
Neyland, Inez, 478
Nicholls, Francis T., 80
Nicholls, P. W., 406
Nichols, Thomas L., 15
Noble, Jordan B., 708
Nolan, Maria, 393, 394
Nolte, Vincent, 529, 530, 540
Nordhoff, Charles, 78, 80, 81
Norman, James, 770
North, E. Cullom, 723
Norton, Leslie, 500 n176
Nott, William, 533
Noyan, Gilles-Augustin Payen de, 331, 361
Nussbaum, Felicity, 272

Oakland Plantation, slave family and kinship development on, 198-201
O'Connor, James, 302
O'Daniel, W. Lee, 566, 570
Ogden, 80
Oil Workers; International Union, 567
O'Keefe, Arthur, 449
Old Absinthe House, 444
Olivier, Charles, 717
Olivier, John, 56
Olivier, Jules G., 393
Olmsted, Frederick Law, 91, 221, 222
O'Neil, Lou, 434
Olson, Harry, 305
Opelousas, La., early Baptist church at, 57
Orange Grove Plantation, 199-201
O'Reilly, Alejandro, 16, 337, 338, 539
Orleans Gazette, 52
Orleans Insurance Co., 528
Orleans Parish Juvenile Court, 737
Orleans Theater, 53
Orr, Benjamin, 70
Oster, Harry, 660
Ott, Mel, 644
Oury, Lewis, 771
Overpeck, Mack, 442
Overton, John, 572
Overton, Sarah, 386
Ozenne, Gilbert, 145, 146, 147, 148, 149, 150, 152, 153, 154, 155

Packard, Stephen B., 76
Packwood, Samuel, 528, 534
Paillet, Jean, 16
Pailloux de Barbezan (Jacques), 324, 328
Palfrey, Henry, 541, 542 n13
Palfrey, John, 530, 537, 541
Palfrey, William, 541
Palfrey & Shepherd, 541
Palfrey & Taylor, 541

Index

Palmer, Roy, 148
Palmetto, La., flood victims of, 464
Panic of 1837, 557
Parades and Power, 660
Parkdale ballpark, outfitted with lights, 651-52
Parker, John M., 738, 290, 292, 512
Parker, Valeria H., 481
Parker, Walter, 580
Passman, Otto, 573
Patin, Alexandre, 491
Patout, Annie, 593
Patout, Appoline, 8, 715, 716, 717, 718, 719-21, 725, 726; versus the United States, 715-30
Patout, Bessie, 593
Patout, Clelie Romero, 593, 608
Patout, Felix, 723, 724, 725, 726
Patout, Hippolyte "Bub", 593, 595, 601, 604, 608, 609, 612, 614, 622, 722, 723, 724
Patout, Louise Decuir, 619
Patout, M. A., & Son, Ltd., see M. A. Patout & Son, Ltd.
Patout, Mary Ann, 724
Patout, Ory, 593, 595
Patout, Oswell, 593, 603
Patout, Rivers Aristide, Jr., 625
Patout, Rivers Aristide, Sr., 603, 608, 616, 625
Patout, Sebastian, 593, 600, 606, 608, 616
Patout, Simeon, 595, 715
Patout, William S. "Willie," 593, 594, 595, 596, 597, 599, 600, 601, 602, 603, 606, 607, 608, 609, 614, 619
Patout, William S., Jr., 594, 595, 605, 606, 608, 609, 610, 612, 614, 615, 618, 620, 621, 623, 625
Patout, William, III, 612
Patout & Patout general store, 610
Patterson, Alonzo, 431-32, 448
Patterson, William, 774
Patterson State Bank, 583
Patton, Charles, 536
Pauger, Adrien de, 324, 325, 326
Paule, St-Francis de, 179
Pavy, Octavus, 489
Pavy, Paul, 488
Paxton, John A., 635-36
Pearce, Jack, 747 n18
Peck, Wilson J., 480, 647
Pecot, Charles, 384 n10, 384 n14
Peebles, Henry Wyche, 388, 389, 394
Peebles, Sterling, 386
Pehlan, Art, 647
Peilleau, Louise, 166
Pelican, list of women and families on the, 169
Peñalver y Cardenas, 55
People's Defense League, 143
Pepper, Claude, 565
Pérault, Jean, 365
Percha, Guillemette, 172 n15
Père Lachaise Cemetery, 554
Perelli, Achille, 557, 559

Perez, Leander, 138 n18, 433, 434, 568, 574
Périer, Etienne de, 162, 315, 317, 325, 327, 329, 330, 331, 334, 353, 355, 356, 358, 359, 360, 361, 365, 366
Perrault, A. J., 486
Perret, Ursin S., 595
Perry, Leslie, 149
Petit, Bernard, 166
Petit de Livilliers, 362, 365
Petite Anse Plantation, slave family and kinship development on, 201-8
Pfeifer, Michael J., 767
Phalanx, The, 392, 671
Phillips, Eugenia, 691
Phillips, Henry, 206
Phoenix Fire Assurance Co., 526
Phoenix Insurance Co., 538
Picou, Dusseau, 700
Pictet, 539
Pierson, Ima A., 147, 148, 151
Pigeau, Eustache Nicolas, 190, 195 n3
Pilié, Joseph, 340, 341
Pinchback, P. B. S., 75, 76
Pinta, Casimere, 204
Piper, Adrian, 125, 129, 134, 239
Pitot, James, 48, 530, 533, 534, 535, 536
Planters' Oil Works, 111
Plaquemines Railroad Co., 528
Pleasant, Ruffin G., 291
Plessy v. *Ferguson*, 127
Poigneau, Mme, 232
Poincy, Paul, 557
Pollock, George, 530, 539
Pollock, Oliver, 530, 539
Pollock & Wraught, 539
Pomeroy, Mrs. G. W., 741
Pontchartrain, Jérôme de, 161
Pope, Alexander, 267
Populus de Saint-Protais, 366
Porche, Guy A., 613, 617, 620
Porter, Alexander, 48, 421
Porter, Lloyd G., 146, 147, 149, 150, 152, 153
Portillo, Joaquin de, 10, 11
Pothier, Robert Joseph, 190, 191, 192
Pouilly, Jacques Nicolas Bussière de, 554, 558
Powderly, Terrence, 115
Power, Tyrone, 53
Poydras, Julien, 48, 223, 532, 537, 542 n7
Poydras Asylum, 223
Poydras Male Orphan Asylum, 223
Pradel, Jean de, 325, 352, 359, 362, 363, 364, 365, 539
Prat, Louis, 259
Presbyterian church, 58; incorporated, 57
Prescott, W. H., 411
Preston, Isaac T., 47
Prévost, Dominique, 381, 384 n29
Prince Hall Masons, 20-21
Prison Reform and Asylums Aid Association, 733

Prison Reform Association, 733, 734
Prohibition, "bargain days" and guilty pleas during, 446-47; convictions of violating law of, 446; illegal beer during, 440-41; illicit distilleries during, 435; in New Orleans, 426-56; Jones Act, 445; liquor prices during, 438; medicinal liquor during, 441; "near-beer" legally allowed during, 440, poisonous liquor during, 438-39; Rum Row during, 427; smuggling in St. Bernard Parish during, 426-27; "soft drink stands" during, 436, speakeasies during, 436-37; value of liquor and property seized during, 443
Prosser, Gabriel, 15
prostitution, in early colonial New Orleans, 357-58
Protestant Orphan Home (Baton Rouge), 225
Protestant Orphans' Home, 224
Protestant Society for the Relief of Destitute Orphan Boys, 224
Protestants, in New Orleans, 57
Provenzano family, 756, 757
Prudential Life Insurance Co., 617
Public Affairs Research Council, 745
public education, 51-52
public relief and child welfare, in antebellum Louisiana, 221-26
Pugh, Thomas, 747 n33
Purnell, William, 386
Puryear, Marguerite "Mag," 128, 136
Putney, F. B., 481, 483, 491

Quemenor, Marie des Anges, 179
Quinn, J. W., 705

Rabinowitz, Howard, 704
Raguet, Gilles, 180
Raguet, Jean-Baptiste, 361
Randolph, A. Philip, 144
Ransdell, Joseph E., 292, 511
Raphaël de Luxembourg, 175-76
Rapp, Eugene, 705
Rasteau, Paul, 539
Ratio Studiorum, 181
Ratliff, Mr. 50
Read, Albert J., 481, 484
Reaux, John, 494 n24
Reconstruction, black policemen in New Orleans during, 697-713; military, 74-78
Reconstruction Finance Corp., 586, 616, 617, 618, 619
Red Cross, in flood of 1927 in south-central Louisiana, 457-505
Reed, Merl, 146
Reed, Revon, 660
refugee camps, during 1927 flood, Alexandria, 470; Baton Rouge, 470-71; Bunkie, 470; Crowley, 482-83; Lafayette, 471-82; Mansura, 469-70; Marksville, 470; New Iberia, 483-85; Saint Landry Parish, 486-90; Saint Mary Parish, 485-86
Reggio, Francisco Maria de, 10
Regis, St-François, 179
Reglemens des Religieuses Ursulines de la Congrégation de Paris, 181-85
Reid, Thomas, 264
Relf, Richard, 526-27, 528, 533, 540
Renaud & Fortier, 531
Republican Loyal League, 75
Reuther, Walter, 574
Rey, Barthelemy, 708
Rey, Octave, 705, 708-9
Reyer, George, 432, 448
Rhodes, Speedy, 572
rice, grown by Acadians, 38
Richard, Vesta, 478
Richardson, Truett, 651, 652
Richaume, Widow, 165
Richebourg, Louis Poncereau de, 362
Rickey, Branch, 649
Riddel, John Leonard, 252, 256, 272
Riddell, John William, 256
Riddick, Merrill K., 580
Rider, Potic, 666
riot, Robert Charles, 127
Ripley, Eliza, 263
Ripley, Peter, 719
Ritchie, James, 265
Rivard, Antoine, 361
Rivard, Jeanne Antoinette, 181
Rivard, Widow Marie, 181
Rivoil, Daniel, 560
Rixner, Jacques, 338
Robertson, Eddie, 585
Robertson, Eliza Marsh, 205
Robertson, William, 205
Robertson, Willis, 566
Robin, C. C., 12, 380, 381, 385 n33
Robinson, H. E., 400 n173, 478, 479
Robinson, Mrs. H. E., 478
Robinson, Joe, 516
Robinson, Joseph T., 506
Rochemore, Vincent de, 336, 337
Rodemacher, Morgan, 645
Rodriguez, J. G., 611
Roman Catholic Church, campaign for humane treatment and spiritual well-being of slaves, 9-11
Rommel, Erwin, 612
Roosevelt, Franklin D., 144, 570, 597
Rosario, Josephine, 560
Rose, Al, 280
Roselius, Christian, 47, 67, 231
Ross, Malcolm, 148
Rost, Pierre, 236
Rotnem, Victor, 148, 149, 150
Roudanez, J. T., 85 n108
Rouff, Mrs. Karl, 227, 230
Rouquette, D., 411

Index

Rousey, Dennis C., 697
Roy, Jim, 211, 214
Roy, Maxime T., 652
Royal Insurance Co., 252
Russell, William, 412
Russell Sage Foundation, 300
Rust, Francis, 582

Sadler, Herbert C., 588
Sahlins, Marshall, 244
Saint, Mrs. Charles, 471
Saint Auge, Joseph, 106
Saint Bernard Cypress Co., Ltd, 583
Saint Charles Theater, 54
Saint James AME Church, 21, 22
Saint-Julien, Brother, 176
Saint Landry Progress, 73
Saint Louis Cathedral, 11, 13, 14, 129; races mix in, 14-15
Saint Louis Cemetery I, opening of, 554
Saint Louis Drug Co., 130
Saint Marc, Ste-Radegonde de, 179
Saint Martin, Louis, 50
Saint Martin Parish, La., flood activities in, 464-65
Saint Mary's Orphan Boys' Asylum, 224
Saint Nicholas [ecclesiastical] Parish, 622-24
Saint Paul's Methodist Episcopal Church, 21
Saint Paul, H. M., 17
Saint Phillips, George, 530, 537, 541
Saint Romes, Joseph Charles, 52
Saint Tammany Gulf Coast Airways, 582
Saint Valentine's Day Massacre, 752
Salaon, Ste-Térèse, 177, 178
Salmon, Edme, 317, 334, 335, 356, 357, 358
Saloom, Kaliste, 647, 651
Salveson, Johnny, 652
San Malo (runaway slave), 10
Sanders, J. W., 484, 511
Saucier, Jean-Baptiste, 360
Saussier, François, 360
Sautier, Marie, 181
Sauvé, Pierre, 537
Sauvinet, Mr., 255
Savary, Gabrielle, 360
Saxe-Weimar, Duke of, 403
Sayre, Mr., 250, 251, 254, 260
Schacht, Al, 652
Schafer, Judith, 1, 238
Schermerhorn, John F., 57
Schilling, Charles, 647
Schilling, Herbert, 645, 647, 652, 653
Schilling, Lucy B., 653
Schilling, Olga, 652
Schuber, Eve, 227, 231, 234
Schuber, Francis, 227, 231
Schurz, Carl, 72
Schweninger, Loren, 127
Scoggins, Howard, 147, 148, 151, 153
Scott, Anne Firor, 289

Scott, Mr., 250
Scott, Walter, 411
Scott, Winfield, 708
Scourion de La Houssaye, Charles, 163
Scourion de Vienne, Hector, 163
Secard, Marcelin, 691
Second Bank of the United States, 534
Sedella, Antonio de, 10-15; 55, 56, 57
Segui, Mr., 10, 11
Seringue, Michel, 356
Shadyside Planting Co., 620
Shakespeare, William, 411
Shakspeare, Joseph A., 732, 733, 756
Sharp, Mrs. Roger P., 738
Sheehan, Jack, 430-31, 442, 451
Shell Co., 587
Shepherd, Rezin D., 528, 533, 537, 542 n13
Shepherd, Brown & Co., 529, 533, 534, 535, 537, 541
Shepley, George F., 686
Sheridan, General, 700
Shiel, Lyall, 432, 450
Shugg, Roger W., 2-3, 64
Shushan, Abe, 586
Sibourd, Reverend, 56
Siete Partidas, Las, 16
Sigourney, Lydia, 267
Simms, William Gilmore, 411
Simon, A. B., 153
Simon, Anecia Paltron, 130
Simon, Lawrence, 621
Simon, Richard, 130
Simonet, Lillian Gelbart, 126, 130
Simpson, Amos, 4, 189
Simpson, Grace, 282
Sindler, Allan, 566
Sing the Master, 660
Sinks, Augustus George, 719
Sitterson, J. Carlyle, 613
slaves, Acadians acquire, 29-30; Catholic Church campaign for humane treatment and spiritual well-being of, 9-11; dancing at Congo Square, New Orleans, 632-42; family and kinship development, 198-220; two utopian socialist plans for emancipation of, 669-83
Slidell, John, 50, 414, 418
Sloan, Leon, 514
Smead, Howard, 155
Smith, Aaron, 213
Smith, Adam, 264
Smith, Alfred E., 506, 507, 511, 512, 513, 514, 515, 516, 517, 518
Smith, George, 598, 599, 600, 601, 602, 605, 606, 608, 609, 610, 612, 614, 616-17, 618, 619, 620, 625
Smith, Howard, 566
Smith, James M., 478
Smith, Roger, 17
Smith-Connally Act, 573

Smoot-Hawley Tariff, 594
Société Catholique pour l'Instruction des Orphelins dans l'Indigence, 225
society, in early colonial New Orleans, 349-71
Solomon, Charles "King," 451
Solvay Employers' Council, 567
Sonnier, Stanley, 648
Soulé, John, 533
Soulé, Pierre, 46, 48, 49, 50, 414, 556, 557, 559
Soulier, Eugene E., 494 n22
Soulier, R. E., 473
Soulouque, Faustian, 23
South Coast Corporation, 606
Southern Association, 646
Southern Claims Commission, 715, 721, 722
Southern Lumber Operators' Association, 565
Southern Negro Youth Congress, 143
Southern News Service and Publishing Co., 760
Southern Sociological Congress, 302
Southern Standard, 59
Southern States Industrial Council, 570
Southern States Woman Suffrage Conference, 292
Southern University, 735
Southport Club, 760
Southwest Louisiana Industrial Institute (University of Louisiana at Lafayette), 287, 289
Southwestern Louisiana Institute, 473, 475
Stafford, S. H., 690
Stahl, Harry J., 471
Stampp, Kenneth, 222
Standard Fruit Co., 758
Standard Oil Co., 587
Stanley, Eugene, 155
Stanley, Joseph, 255
Starks, Walter T., 767
State Federation of Labor, 570, 572
State Federation of Woman's Clubs, 287
State Industrial School for Girls, 735
Stelly, Eli, 495 n55, n56
Stelly, Mary, 495 n54
Stephen Henderson & Co., 535
Stephens, E. A., 143
Stephens, Edwin L., 292-93, 475
Stephens, Lucy McCall, 203
Stephens, Milly, 207
Stephens, Peter, 207
Stephenson, Walter "Tarzan," 647, 648, 653
Sterling Sugars, 609
Stevens, Thaddeus, 73, 74
Stewart, Dugald, 264
Stocker, W. T., 64
Stoddard, Amos, 51
Stokes, W. E. "Daddy," 468
Stone, William, 201, 203, 232
Story, Sidney, 279
Storyville, 279-84
Stowe, Harriet Beecher, 560

Straight University, 116, 698
Straton, John Roach, 513, 515
Streeter, Thomas Winthrop, 283
Struve, Billy, 280
Stuart, James, 52, 53, 58
Suburban Gardens, 430, 431
suffrage, woman, in Lafayette, La., 1897-1922, 285-98
Sumner, Charles, 71, 74
Sunday, Billy, 513
Swords, Marion, 776

T. & D. Urquhart, 529, 541
Taft-Hartley Act, 565, 571, 573
Talmadge, Eugene, 565, 566
Talmadge, Herman, 566
Tanesse, Jacques, 339
Tanner, H. S., 58
Tatoulimataha, Chief, 318
Taylor, Doug, 7, 643
Taylor, George, 723
Taylor, Jane, 386
Taylor, John, of Caroline, 392
Taylor, Mrs. John R., 501 n232
Taylor, Pete, 652
Taylor, Richard, 404, 650, 654
Taylor, William, 537, 541
Taylor, Zachary, 405
Taylor & Laberie, 723
Teche country, Virginia settlers in Louisiana's, 386-99
Telegraph, 52
Ten Broeck, Richard, 421
Tentler, Leslie Woodcock, 130
Terry, W. S., Jr., 738
Texas Oil Co., 467, 472, 473, 583, 587
Texas Pipeline Co., 608
Texas Rangers, 265
Thespian Benevolent Society, Richard Relf an organizer of the, 527
Thibodaux, B. G., 50
Thierry, J. B. S., 52
Thomas, Allen, 404
Thomas, Jesse O., 479
Thomas, Joe, 431
Thomas, John, 770-71
Thomas, Lee E., 511
Thomelain, Mme., 181
Thompson, Hugh Miller, 733
Thorvaldsen, Bertel, 557
Thuet, Lize, 255
Thurman, M. M., 741
Thurmond, Strom, 574
Tiger Island Plantation, slave family and kinship development on, 208-15
Times-Picayune Loving Cup, 304
Tisdale, Mrs. A. Dent, 741
Todd, David, 209, 210
Todd, Emily Barr, 209
Todd, Esther, 211

Index   801

Todd, Henry, 211, 213
Tolmas, H. C., 748 n 49
tombs, free men of color as builders of, 554-63
Tomes, Gus, 433, 434
Touro, Judah, 223, 262
Tower, Luther, 262
Trafficante, Santos, Jr., 762
Tranchepain de St. Augustin, Marie, 177, 178, 180, 223, 316
Tranchina, Felix, 442
Transmissions, 579
Transportation Club, 436
Treadaway, Angelina, 568
Treadgill, Eunice, 595
Tregre, Clarence, 647
Tremant, Jeanne, 172 n15
Trépagnier, Claude, 360
Trépagnier, Widow, 165
Trevigne, Paul, 85 n108
Tricou, Joseph, 533
Trist, Hore Browse, 404, 527, 536
Trist, Nicholas P., 404
Tropical Cyclones, 580
Tropical Food Products Co., 435
Troyat, Michael de, 587
Trudeau, François, 360
Truman, Harry S, 156, 574
Tucker, G. R., 473
Tucker Act, 724
Tulane University, 227, 579, 588-89, 742; Aero Club, 588; Medical School, 594; Middle American Research Center and Medical College, 580
Tureaud, Alexander P., 148, 151, 153
Tureaud, Benjamin, 404, 416
Turner, Nat, 18, 636
Turner, Roscoe, 585
Turner, William, 236
Turpin, Marie, 179
Tyler, John, 252

Ulloa, Antonio de, 16, 337
Underwood, Monroe, 773
Union Bank of Louisiana, 528
Union Oil Mills, 110
Unitarian church, 58
United Cannery, Agricultural, Packing and Allied Workers of America, 599
United Fruit Co., 754, 758
United Gas Co., 618
United Gas Pipeline Co., 619
United Mine Workers, 572
United States, Coast Guard, aids in evacuation of flood victims, 461-62; Department of Justice, Civil Right Section, 150; House of Representatives, Select Committee on Assassinations, 750-51, 761; Supreme Court of, 743
United States Employment Service, 571
United States versus Appoline Patout, 715-30

University of Michigan, 588-89
University of the South, 583
Upton, Dell, 5, 243
Upton, Wheelock S., 233, 235
Urquhart, David, 530, 536
Urquhart, Thomas, 530, 533, 534, 535, 536
Ursuline Convent, 332-33, 338
Ursuline nuns, 55, 166, 168, 176, 177, 223, 357-58
Ursuline school, 175-88

vagrancy, in nineteenth-century New Orleans, 543-53
Vaillancourt, Joseph, 622
Van Amringe, H. H., 671
Vaudreuil, Pierre Rigaud de, 335
Vellard, Philippe François, 335
Vendôme, Mme., 181
Verret, J. Emile, 152
Vesey, Denmark, 21
Vidal, Nicholas, 16
Vielle, Alexandre, 360
vigilante committees, 22
Villars Dubreuil, Joseph, 360
Villemont, Henry Martin de Mirbaise, sieur de, 361
Villeray, Caticyhe, 16
Viltz, Lawrence, 146
Vinache, Joseph, 346
Vincent, Charles, 1
Violet Seafood Workers' Association, 568
Virginia Historical Society, 559
Voelker, Frank, 738, 741
Voices of Protest, 578
Volney, Constantin-François, 264
Volter, Franzella, 148, 156
Vonvergne, Voltaire, 20
voodoo, 636
Voorhies, Cornelius, 605, 609, 614
Voorhies, Henry, Jr., 500 n176
Voorhies, Marcel J., 472
Voorhies, Mrs. R. C., 295 n11
Vyhnanek, Louis, 6, 426

Wade, Michael G., 1, 7, 8, 593
Wade, Richard, 697, 710
Wadsworth, Mr., 48
Waggoner, Henry, 727 n9
Wagner Act, 567
Waifs' Home, 734, 735
Wakefield, Samuel, 772
Walker, Alexander, 260
Walker, David, 17
Walker, Gus, 147, 149, 150, 152
Walker, James, 46
Walker, Norman, 301
Walker, Robert J., 265, 266
Wall, Rivers Patout, 606, 619
Wallin, J. E. Wallace, 305
Walmsley, T. Semmes, 759

Walsh, Michael, 433
Walsh, Patrick, 55
Walsh, Simon, 389
Walton, Ruffin E., 388
War Food Administration, 571
War Manpower Commission, 571
Warburg, Daniel, 555, 556, 557, 559, 560, 561
Warburg, Daniel Samuel, 556
Warburg, Eugène, 555, 556, 557, 558-60, 561
Warburg, Joseph Daniel, Jr., 560
Warmoth, Henry Clay, 75, 76, 77, 80, 549
Washington, Booker T., 98, 116
Waterford Sugar Co-op., 616
Watkins, John, 537, 542 n5
Watson, J. Tom, 565
Watson, Sam, 777
Webb, C. H., 741
Wedell, James Robert, 582-83, 588, 589
Wedell-Williams Air Service, 583-84, 588
Weekly Picayune, 53
Weeks, Mrs. David, 393
Weiblen, Albert, 561
Weinberger, Charles, 304
Weiss, Seymour, 759
Weitzel, Godfrey, 686
Wells, Francis, 529
Wells, J. Madison, 71, 419, 700
Wells, Thomas Jefferson, 419, 420, 421
Wesley Methodist Episcopal Church, 91
West, Jane, 201
West, Jim, 201
Weston, Nathaniel P., 7, 543
Wheaton, Robert, 215
Wheeler, N. W., 234
White, Lulu, 280, 283
White, Maunsel, 528, 530, 542 n13
White, Simon, 390
White, Sol M., 468
White League, 80
Whitfield, Lloyd, 500 n176
Whitfield, Rosabelle, 500 n176
Whitney, Rod, 648
Whittaker, Louisa, 558, 561
Wickliffe, Robert, 22
Wikoff, William, 537
Wilkins, Benjamin, 386, 387, 390
Wilkins, Douglass, 386, 387
Wilkins, Elizabeth, 386
Wilkins, Imogene, 387
Wilkins, John D., 386-99, 671, 672, 675, 680, 681
Wilkins, John Henry, 387, 390
Wilkins, Joseph, 386, 387, 388
Wilkins, Mary Ann, 387, 392-93
Wilkins, Patsy, 386
Wilkins, Richard, 387, 390
Wilkins, Tabitha Ann, 386
Willebrandt, Mabel Walker, 447, 451
William Kenner & Co., 535, 541
Williams, Anthony, 230, 232, 235, 238
Williams, Barney, 691

Williams, E. H. "Lige," 570
Williams, Harry P., 581, 583, 588
Williams, "Lige," 572
Williams, Luins H., 147, 148, 149, 151, 153
Williams, T. Harry, 566, 578, 759
Williams, Virgil, 146
Williams, W. Horace, 572
Williams Lumber Co., 583
Willis, Bob, 214
Wilson, Andrew H., 737
Wilson, Carol, 5, 227
Wilson, Nathaniel, 723
Wilson, Robert, 672
Wilson, Samuel, Jr., 5-6, 324
Wilson, Woodrow, 507, 510, 513
Winchester, James, 245
Winter, Samuel, 529, 533
Winter & Harmon, 535
Wisconsin Society for the Placing Out of Dependent Children, 301
Wisner, Elizabeth, 738
Witte, Jerry, 648, 648, 654
Wolff, Solomon, 303
Woman Order No. 28, Gen. Butler's, 686
Woman's Club (Lafayette, La.), 286, 287, 288, 289
Woman's Suffrage Club (Lafayette, La.), 286
women, African, in early colonial Louisiana, 168; and the suffrage movement in Lafayette, La., 285-98; in early eighteenth-century Louisiana, 160-74; list of women and families on the *Pelican*, 169; list of, embarked on the *Loire*, 170; marital laws governing, in French Louisiana, 189-97; recruited by Company of Indies to go to Louisiana, 352-53; religious, 168, some provision of the *Coutume de Paris* regarding, 165-66
Women's Christian Temperance Union, 512
Woodson, Ashby, 478
Woodward, C. Vann, 117
workhouses, in nineteenth-century New Orleans, 543-53
Working Men's Union League, 65
Workingmen of Louisiana, 66
Workingmen's Association, 66
Wrenn, Thomas, 479
Wright, Ernest J., 143, 144, 145, 150
Wyble, S., 487
Wyche, Tabitha Ann, 386, 387
Wynhoven, Peter, 567

Yellowley, E. C., 447
Young Men's Business Club, 580
Young, R. O., 480
Yviquel, Ste-Marie, 177, 179

Zacherie, James W., 542 n13
Zarilla, Allen, 648
Zimple, Charles, F., 340
Zink, Steven D., 6, 506

DATE DUE

ISSCW 976
.3
V831

VISIONS AND REVIS-
IONS : PERSPECTIVES ON
LOUISIANA SOCIETY AND

ISSCW 976
.3
V831

HOUSTON PUBLIC LIBRARY
CENTRAL LIBRARY